Black **W**riters

THIRD EDITION

Black Writers

A Selection of Sketches from *Contemporary Authors*

THIRD EDITION

Contains entries on a wide-range of twentieth-century black writers, all updated or originally written for this volume.

GALE GROUP

Detroit
San Francisco
London
Boston
Woodbridge, CT

STAFF

Scot Peacock, *Senior Editor and Project Manager*

Jerry Moore, *Project Editor*

Simone Sobel, *Assistant Project Editor*

Amy Francis, John Jorgenson, *Senior Content Editors*

Regie A. Carlton, Dwayne D. Hayes, *Content Editors*

Anja Barnard, Elizabeth A. Cranston, Thomas Wiloch,
Associate Content Editors

Kristen A. Dorsch, *Assistant Content Editor*

Susan M. Trosky, *Managing Editor*

Victoria B. Cariappa, *Research Manager*

Andrew Guy Malonis, Barbara McNeil, Gary J. Oudersluys, Maureen Richards,
Cheryl L. Warnock, *Research Specialists*

Tamara C. Nott, Tracie A. Richardson, Corrine A. Stocker, *Research Associates*

Phyllis J. Blackman, Tim Lehnerer, Patricia L. Love,
Research Assistants

Library of Congress Catalog Card Number 62-52046
ISBN 0-8103-8838-3

Printed in the United States of America

10 9 8 7 6 5 4 3 2 1

Contents

Preface

The first, second, and third editions of *Black Writers* cumulatively provide extensive and accurate biographical, bibliographical, and critical information on nearly 800 black authors active during the twentieth century. This third edition does not replace the previous editions but complements them by:

- Providing completely updated information on approximately 150 authors selected from the first two editions of *Black Writers*, based upon the need for significant revision (e.g., bibliographical additions, changes in address or career, major awards, or personal information such as changes in name, or the addition of a death date). These revised entries have been extensively rewritten, and many include informative new sidelights.

- Presenting nearly 150 new entries, which includes selections that have appeared in Gale's acclaimed *Contemporary Authors* series since 1993 and have been completely updated for the publication of *Black Writers*, as well as entries that will appear in future volumes of *Contemporary Authors*.

Scope

Before preparing the first edition of *Black Writers*, the editors of *Contemporary Authors* conducted a telephone survey of librarians, mailed a print survey to more than four thousand libraries, and met with an advisory board composed of librarians from university, high school, and public libraries throughout the country.

The librarian advisors expressed a need for an information source that specifically covered black writers of the twentieth century, one that would contain the type of in-depth, primary information not found in other works on black writers as well as critical material and sources when available. These librarians also indicated that the inclusion criteria for this volume should be broad, rather than narrow, in terms of types of writers and the predominant periods of activity featured.

Following their advice, the editors of the first edition not only included entries for contemporary pre-eminent black novelists, poets, short story writers, dramatists, and journalists, but also sketched those individuals active in the earlier portion of the century, particularly writers prominent during the Harlem Renaissance. The editors also included individuals who had written books but were better known for their work in the political or social arena. For the second edition of *Black Writers*, we secured the assistance of an advisory board that reviewed the list of revisions from the first edition of *Black Writers* and ranked more than 450 additional names of black authors, and made suggestions of other names, from which nearly 250 new entries were selected. The advisory board consisted of Emily Belcher, General and Humanities Reference Librarian at Princeton Universities Libraries, Doris H. Clack, Professor of Library and Information Studies at Florida State University, Henry Louis Gates, Jr., W. E. B. DuBois Professor of the Humanities at Harvard University, Will Gibson, President of the American Black Book Writers Association, and Alton Hormsby, Jr., Fuller E. Callaway Professor of History at Morehouse College. The editors of the third edition of *Black Writers* expanded upon the work of the second edition's advisory board to select approximately 150 additional new entries and to revise and fully update approximately 150 entries from the first two editions, while adhering to the criteria established through the surveys conducted for the first edition.

Because our advisors thought the volume should reflect an international scope, we have included important African and Caribbean black writers of interest to an American audience (and who have written in English or have had their works translated into English).

Format

Entries in *Black Writers* provide in-depth information that is unavailable in any other single reference source. The format of each entry is designed for ease of use, for students, teachers, scholars, and librarians. Individual paragraphs, labelled with descriptive rubrics, ensure that a reader seeking specific information can quickly focus on the pertinent portion of an entry.

Sketches in *Black Writers* contain the following biographical and bibliographical information:

- **Entry heading:** the most complete form of author's name, plus any pseudonyms or name variations used for writing

- **Personal information:** author's date and place of birth, family data, ethnicity, educational background, political and religious affiliations, and hobbies and leisure interests

- **Addresses:** author's home, office, or agent's addresses, plus e-mail and fax numbers, as available

- **Career summary:** name of employer, position, and dates held for each career post; resume of other vocational achievements; military service

- **Membership information:** professional, civic, and other association memberships and any official posts held

- **Awards and honors:** military and civic citations, major prizes and nominations, fellowships, grants, and honorary degrees

- **Writings:** a comprehensive, chronological list of titles, publishers, dates of original publication and revised editions, and production information for plays, television scripts, and screenplays

- **Adaptations:** a list of films, plays, and other media which have been adapted from the author's work

- **Work in progress:** current or planned projects, with dates of completion and/or publication, and expected publisher, when known

- **Sidelights:** a biographical portrait of the author's development; information about the critical reception of the author's works; revealing comments, often by the author, on personal interests, aspirations, motivations, and thoughts on writing

- **Biographical and critical sources:** a list of books and periodicals in which additional information on an author's life and/or writings appears

Other Features

This edition of *Black Writers* provides indexing to the entries in both the first, second, and third editions and directs the reader to the most current entry.

- **Cumulative Index:** Lists the names, name variations, and pseudonyms of authors featured in the first, second, and third editions of *Black Writers*.

- **Nationality Index:** Lists alphabetically the authors featured in both the first, second, and third editions of *Black Writers* according to country of origin and/or country of citizenship.

The editors hope that you find *Black Writers* a useful reference tool and welcome comments and suggestions on any aspect of this work. Please send comments to : The Editors, *Black Writers*, Gale Group, 27500 Drake Rd., Farmington Hills, MI 48331-3535; or call at 1-248-699-4253; or fax at 1-248-699-8054.

Acknowledgments

Cover photos: **Gwendolyn Brooks:** AP Wide World Photos. Reproduced by permission. **Ernest J. Gaines:** photograph by Alex Brandon. AP Wide World Photos. Reproduced by permission. **Nikki Giovanni:** AP Wide World Photos. Reproduced by permission. **Spike Lee:** AP Wide World Photos. Reproduced by permission.

A

ACHEBE, (Albert) Chinua(lumogu) 1930-

PERSONAL: Born November 16, 1930, Ogidi, Nigeria; son of Isaiah Okafo (a Christian churchman) and Janet N. (Iloegbunam) Achebe; married Christie Chinwe Okoli, September 10, 1961; children: Chinelo (daughter), Ikechukwu (son), Chidi (son), Nwando (daughter). *Education:* Attended University College, Ibadan, 1948-53; London University, B.A., 1953; studied broadcasting at the British Broadcasting Corporation, London, 1956. *Avocational interests:* Music.

ADDRESSES: Home—P.O. Box 53 Nsukka, Anambra State, Nigeria. *Office*—Institute of African Studies, University of Nigeria, Nsukka, Anambra State, Nigeria; and c/o Bard College, P.O. Box 41, Annandale on Hudson, NY, 12504.

CAREER: Writer. Nigerian Broadcasting Corporation, Lagos, Nigeria, talks producer, 1954-57, controller of Eastern Region in Enugu, Nigeria, 1958-61, founder and director of Voice of Nigeria, 1961-66; University of Nigeria, Nsukka, senior research fellow, 1967-72, professor of English, 1976-81, professor emeritus, 1985-; Anambra State University of Technology, Enugu, pro-chancellor and chair of council, 1986-88; University of Massachusetts-Amherst, professor, 1987-88. Served on diplomatic missions for Biafra during the Nigerian Civil War, 1967-69. Visiting professor of English at University of Massachusetts-Amherst, 1972-75, and University of Connecticut, Afro-American Studies department, 1975-76. University of California, Los Angeles, Regents' lecturer, 1984; Cambridge University, Clare Hall, visiting fellow and Ashby lecturer, 1993; lecturer at universities in Nigeria and the United States; speaker at events in numerous countries throughout the world. Chair, Citadel Books Ltd., Enugu, Nigeria, 1967; director, Heinemann Educational Books Ltd., Ibadan, Nigeria, 1970-; director, Nwamife Publishers Ltd., Enugu, Nigeria, 1970-. Founder and publisher, *Uwa Ndi Igbo: A Bilingual Journal of Igbo Life and Arts,* 1984—. Governor, Newsconcern International Foundation, 1983. Member, University of Lagos Council, 1966, East Central State Library Board, 1971-72, Anambra State Arts Council, 1977-79, and National Festival Committee, 1983; director, Okike Arts Centre, Nsukka, 1984—. Deputy national president of People's Redemption Party, 1983; president of town union, Ogidi, Nigeria, 1986-.

MEMBER: International Social Prospects Academy (Geneva), Writers and Scholars International (London), Writers and Scholars Educational Trust (London), Commonwealth Arts Organization (member of executive committee, 1981—), Association of Nigerian Authors (founder; president, 1981-86), Ghana Association of Writers (fellow), Royal Society of Literature (London), Modern Language Association of America (honorary fellow), American Academy and Institute of Arts and Letters (honorary member).

AWARDS, HONORS: Margaret Wrong Memorial Prize, 1959, for *Things Fall Apart;* Rockefeller travel fellowship to East and Central Africa, 1960-1961; Nigerian National Trophy, 1961, for *No Longer at Ease;* UNESCO fellowship for creative artists for travel to United States and Brazil, 1963; Jock Campbell/ *New Statesman* Award, 1965, for *Arrow of God;* Commonwealth Poetry Prize, 1972, for *Beware, Soul-Brother, and Other Poems;* Neil Gunn international fellow, Scottish Arts Council, 1975; Lotus

Award for Afro-Asian Writers, 1975; Nigerian National Merit Award, 1979; named to the Order of the Federal Republic of Nigeria, 1979; Commonwealth Foundation senior visiting practitioner award, 1984; *A Man of the People* was cited in Anthony Burgess's 1984 book *Ninety-nine Novels: The Best in England since 1939;* Booker Prize nomination, 1987, for *Anthills of the Savannah,* Champion Award, 1996. D.Litt., Dartmouth College, 1972, University of Southampton, 1975, University of Ife, 1978, University of Nigeria, Nsukka, 1981, University of Kent, 1982, Mount Allison University, 1984, University of Guelph, 1984, and Franklin Pierce College, 1985, Ibadan University, 1989, Skidmore College, 1991, City College of New York, 1992, Fichburg State College, 1994, Harvard University, 1996, Binghamton University, 1996, Bates College, 1996; D.Univ., University of Stirling, 1975, Open University, 1989; LL.D., University of Prince Edward Island, 1976, Georgetown University, 1990, Port Harcourt University, 1991; D.H.L., University of Massachusetts-Amherst, 1977, Westfield College, 1989, New School for Social Research, 1991, Hobart and William Smith College, 1991, Marymount Manhattan College, 1991, Colgate University, 1993.

WRITINGS:

NOVELS

Things Fall Apart, Heinemann (London), 1958, Obolensky, 1959.

No Longer at Ease, Heinemann, 1960, Obolensky, 1961, second edition, Fawcett, 1988.

Arrow of God, Heinemann, 1964, John Day (New York City), 1967.

A Man of the People, John Day, 1966, published with an introduction by K. W. J. Post, Doubleday (New York City), 1967.

Anthills of the Savannah, Anchor Books (New York City), 1988.

JUVENILE

Chike and the River, Cambridge University Press, 1966.

(With John Iroaganachi) *How the Leopard Got His Claws,* Nwankwo-Ifejika (Enugu, Nigeria), 1972, bound with *Lament of the Deer,* by Christopher Okigbo, Third Press, 1973.

The Flute, Fourth Dimension Publishers (Enugu, Nigeria), 1978.

The Drum, Fourth Dimension Publishers, 1978.

POETRY

Beware, Soul-Brother, and Other Poems, Nwankwo-Ifejika, 1971, Doubleday, 1972, revised edition, Heinemann, 1972.

Christmas in Biafra, and Other Poems, Doubleday, 1973.

(Editor with Dubem Okafor) *Don't Let Him Die: An Anthology of Memorial Poems for Christopher Okigbo,* Fourth Dimension Publishers, 1978.

(Coeditor) *Aka Weta: An Anthology of Igbo Poetry,* Okike (Nsukka, Nigeria), 1982.

OTHER

The Sacrificial Egg, and Other Stories, Etudo (Onitsha, Nigeria), 1962.

Girls at War (short stories), Heinemann, 1972, Fawcett, 1988.

Morning Yet on Creation Day (essays), Doubleday, 1975.

The Trouble with Nigeria (essays), Fourth Dimension Publishers, 1983, Heinemann, 1984.

(Editor with C. L. Innes) *African Short Stories,* Heinemann, 1984.

Hopes and Impediments: Selected Essays 1965-1987, Heinemann, 1988.

(Editor with Innes and contributor) *The Heinemann Book of Contemporary African Short Stories,* Heinemann, 1992.

Another Africa (poems and essays), Anchor Books (New York City), 1997.

Conversations with Chinua Achebe, University Press of Mississippi (Jackson), 1997.

Also author of essay collection *Nigerian Topics,* 1988. Contributor to books, including *Modern African Stories,* edited by Ellis Ayitey Komey and Ezekiel Mphahlele, Faber (London), 1964; and *Africa Speaks: A Prose Anthology with Comprehension and Summary Passages,* Evans, 1970. Author of foreword, *African Rhapsody: Short Stories of the Contemporary African Experience,* 1994. Founding editor, "African Writers Series," Heinemann, 1962-72; editor, *Okike: A Nigerian Journal of New Writing,* 1971—; editor, *Nsukkascope,* a campus magazine.

ADAPTATIONS: Things Fall Apart was adapted for the stage and produced by Eldred Fiberesima in Lagos, Nigeria; it was also adapted for radio and produced by the British Broadcasting Corporation in 1983, and for television in English and Igbo and produced by the Nigerian Television Authority in 1985.

SIDELIGHTS: Since the 1950s, Nigeria has witnessed "the flourishing of a new literature which has drawn sustenance both from traditional oral literature and from the present and rapidly changing society," writes Margaret Laurence in her book *Long Drums and Cannons: Nigerian Dramatists and Novelists.* Thirty years ago, Chinua Achebe was among the founders of this new literature and over the years many critics have come to consider him the finest of the Nigerian novelists. His achievement has not been limited to his native country or continent, however. As Laurence maintains in her 1968 study of his novels, "Chinua Achebe's careful and confident craftsmanship, his firm grasp of his material and his ability to create memorable and living characters place him among the best novelists now writing in any country in the English language."

On the level of ideas, Achebe's "prose writing reflects three essential and related concerns," observes G. D. Killam in his book *The Novels of Chinua Achebe,* "first, with the legacy of colonialism at both the individual and societal level; secondly, with the *fact* of English as a language of national and international exchange; thirdly, with the obligations and responsibilities of the writer both to the society in which he lives and to his art." Over the past century, Africa has been caught in a war for its identity between the forces of tradition, colonialism, and independence. This war has prevented many nations from raising themselves above political and social chaos to achieve true independence. "Most of the problems we see in our politics derive from the moment when we lost our initiative to other people, to colonizers," Achebe observes in his book of essays. He goes on to explain: "What I think is the basic problem of a new African country like Nigeria is really what you might call a 'crisis in the soul.' We have been subjected-we have subjected ourselves too-to this period during which we have accepted everything alien as good and practically everything local or native as inferior."

In order to reestablish the virtues of precolonial Nigeria, chronicle the impact of colonialism on native cultures, and expose present-day corruption, Achebe needed to clearly communicate these concerns to his fellow countrymen and to those outside his country. The best channel for these messages was writing in English, the language of colonialism. It is the way in which Achebe transforms language to achieve his particular ends, however, that many feel distinguishes his writing from the writing of other English-language novelists. To convey the flavor of traditional Nigeria, Achebe translates Ibo proverbs into English and weaves them into his stories. "Among the Ibo the art of conversation is regarded very highly," he writes in his novel *Things Fall Apart,* "and proverbs are the palm-oil with which words are eaten." "Proverbs are cherished by Achebe's people as tribal heirlooms, the treasure boxes of their cultural heritage," explains Adrian A. Roscoe in his book *Mother Is Gold: A Study of West African Literature.* "Through them traditions are received and handed on; and when they disappear or fall into disuse . . . it is a sign that a particular tradition, or indeed a whole way of life, is passing away." Achebe's use of proverbs also has an artistic aim, as Bernth Lindfors suggests in *Folklore in Nigerian Literature.* "Achebe's proverbs can serve as keys to an understanding of his novels," comments the critic, "because he uses them not merely to add touches of local color but to sound and reiterate themes, to sharpen characterization, to clarify conflict, and to focus on the values of the society he is portraying."

Although he has also written poetry, short stories, and essays-both literary and political-Achebe is best known for his novels: *Things Fall Apart, No Longer at Ease, Arrow of God, A Man of the People,* and *Anthills of the Savannah.* Considering Achebe's novels, Anthony Daniels writes in the *Spectator,* "In spare prose of great elegance, without any technical distraction, he has been able to illuminate two emotionally irreconcilable facets of modern African life: the humiliations visited on Africans by colonialism, and the utter moral worthlessness of what replaced colonial rule." Set in this historical context, Achebe's novels develop the theme of "tradition versus change," and offer, as Eustace Palmer observes, "a powerful presentation of the beauty, strength and validity of traditional life and values and the disruptiveness of change." Even so, the author does not appeal for a return to the ways of the past. Palmer notes that "while deploring the imperialists' brutality and condescension, [Achebe] seems to suggest that change is inevitable and wise men . . . reconcile themselves to accommodating change. It is the diehards . . . who resist and are destroyed in the process."

Two of Achebe's novels—*Things Fall Apart* and *Arrow of God*—focus on Nigeria's early experience with colonialism, from first contact with the British to widespread British administration. "With remarkable unity of the word with the deed, the character, the time and the place, Chinua Achebe creates in these two novels a coherent picture of coherence being lost, of the tragic consequences of the African-European collision," offers Robert McDowell in a special issue of *Studies in Black Literature* dedicated to Achebe's work. "There is an artistic unity of all things in these books which is rare anywhere in modern English fiction."

Things Fall Apart, Achebe's first novel, was published in 1958 in the midst of the Nigerian renaissance. Achebe explained his motivation to begin writing at this time in an interview with Lewis Nkosi published in *African Writers Talking: A Collection of Radio Interviews:* "One of the things that set me thinking [about writing] was Joyce Cary's novel set in Nigeria, *Mr. Johnson,* which was praised so much, and it was clear to me that this was a most superficial picture . . . not only of the country, but even of the Nigerian character. . . . I thought if this was famous, then perhaps someone ought to try and look at this from the inside." Charles R. Larson, in his book *The Emergence of African Fiction,* details the success of Achebe's effort, both in investing his novel of Africa with an African sensibility and in making this view available to African readers. "In 1964, . . . *Things Fall Apart* became the first novel by an African writer to be included in the required syllabus for African secondary school students throughout the English-speaking portions of the continent." Later in that decade, it "became recognized by African and non-African literary critics as the first 'classic' in English from tropical Africa," adds Larson.

The novel tells the story of an Ibo village of the late 1800s and one of its great men, Okonkwo. Although the son of a ne'er-do-well, Okonkwo has achieved much in his life. He is a champion wrestler, a wealthy farmer, a husband to three wives, a title-holder among his people, and a member of the select *egwugwu* whose members impersonate ancestral spirits at tribal rituals. "The most impressive achievement of *Things Fall Apart*" maintains David Carroll in his book *Chinua Achebe,* "is the vivid picture it provides of Ibo society at the end of the nineteenth century." He explains: "Here is a clan in the full vigor of its traditional way of life, unperplexed by the present and without nostalgia for the past. Through its rituals the life of the community and the life of the individual are merged into significance and order."

This order is disrupted, however, with the appearance of the white man in Africa and with the introduction of his religion. "The conflict in the novel, vested in Okonkwo, derives from the series of crushing blows which are levelled at traditional values by an alien and more powerful culture causing, in the end, the

traditional society to fall apart," observes Killam. Okonkwo is unable to adapt to the changes that accompany colonialism. In the end, in frustration, he kills an African employed by the British, and then commits suicide, a sin against the tradition to which he had long clung. The novel thus presents "two main, closely intertwined tragedies," writes Arthur Ravenscroft in his study *Chinua Achebe,* "the personal tragedy of Okonkwo . . . and the public tragedy of the eclipse of one culture by another."

Although the author emphasizes the message in his novels, he still receives praise for his artistic achievement. As Palmer comments, "Chinua Achebe's *Things Fall Apart* . . . demonstrates a mastery of plot and structure, strength of characterization, competence in the manipulation of language and consistency and depth of thematic exploration which is rarely found in a first novel." Achebe also achieves balance in recreating the tragic consequences of the clash of two cultures. Killam notes that "in showing Ibo society before and after the coming of the white man he avoids the temptation to present the past as idealized and the present as ugly and unsatisfactory." And, as Killam concludes, Achebe's "success proceeds from his ability to create a sense of real life and real issues in the book and to see his subject from the point of view which is neither idealistic nor dishonest."

Arrow of God, the second of Achebe's novels of colonialism, takes place in the 1920s after the British have established a presence in Nigeria. The "arrow of god" mentioned in the title is Ezeulu, the chief priest of the god Ulu who is the patron deity of an Ibo village. As chief priest, Ezeulu is responsible for initiating the rituals that structure village life, a position vested with a great deal of power. In fact, the central theme of this novel, as Laurence points out, is power: "Ezeulu's testing of his own power and the power of his god, and his effort to maintain his own and his god's authority in the face of village factions and of the [Christian] mission and the British administration." "This, then, is a political novel in which different systems of power are examined and their dependence upon myth and ritual compared," writes Carroll. "Of necessity it is also a study in the psychology of power."

In Ezeulu, Achebe presents a study of the loss of power. After his village rejects his advice to avoid war with a neighboring village, Ezeulu finds himself at odds with his own people and praised by the British administrators. The British, seeking a candidate to install as village chieftain, make him an offer, which he refuses. Caught in the middle with no allies, Ezeulu slowly loses his grip on reality and slips into senility. "As in Achebe's other novels," observes Gerald Moore in *Seven African Writers,* "it is the strong-willed man of tradition who cannot adapt, and who is crushed by his virtues in the war between the new, more worldly order, and the old, conservative values of an isolated society."

The artistry displayed in *Arrow of God,* Achebe's second portrait of cultures in collision, has drawn a great deal of attention, adding to the esteem in which the writer is held. Charles Miller comments in a *Saturday Review* article that Achebe's "approach to the written word is completely unencumbered with verbiage. He never strives for the exalted phrase, he never once raises his voice; even in the most emotion-charged passages the tone is absolutely unruffled, the control impeccable." Concludes Miller, "It is a measure of Achebe's creative gift that he has no need whatever for prose fireworks to light the flame of his intense drama."

Achebe's three other novels—*No Longer at Ease, A Man of the People,* and *Anthills of the Savannah*—examine Africa in the era of independence. This is an Africa less and less under direct European administration, yet still deeply affected by it, an Africa struggling to regain its footing in order to stand on its own two feet. Standing in the way of realizing its goal of true independence is the corruption pervasive in modern Africa, an obstacle Achebe scrutinizes in each of these novels.

In *No Longer at Ease,* set in Nigeria just prior to independence, Achebe extends his history of the Okonkwo family. Here the central character is Obi Okonkwo, grandson of the tragic hero of *Things Fall Apart.* This Okonkwo has been raised a Christian and educated at the university in England. Like many of his peers, he has left the bush behind for a position as a civil servant in Lagos, Nigeria's largest city. "*No Longer at Ease* deals with the plight of [this] new generation of Nigerians," observes Palmer, "who, having been exposed to education in the western world and therefore largely cut off from their roots in traditional society, discover, on their return, that the demands of tradition are still strong, and are hopelessly caught in the clash between the old and the new."

Many faced with this internal conflict succumb to corruption. Obi is no exception. "The novel opens with Obi on trial for accepting bribes," notes Killam, "and the book takes the form of a long flashback." "In a world which is the result of the intermingling of Europe and Africa . . . Achebe traces the decline of his hero from brilliant student to civil servant convicted of bribery and corruption," writes Carroll. "It reads like a postscript to the earlier novel [*Things Fall Apart*] because the same forces are at work but in a confused, diluted, and blurred form." In *This Africa: Novels by West Africans in English and French,* Judith Illsley Gleason points out how the imagery of each book depicts the changes in the Okonkwo family and the Nigeria they represent. As she points out, "The career of the grandson Okonkwo ends not with a machete's swing but with a gavel's tap." *A Man of the People* is "the story of the yokel who visits the sinful city and emerges from it scathed but victorious," writes Martin Tucker in *Africa in Modern Literature,* "while the so-called 'sophisticates' and 'sinners' suffer their just desserts." In this novel, Achebe casts his eye on African politics, taking on, as Moore notes, "the corruption of Nigerians in high places in the central government." The author's eyepiece is the book's narrator Odili, a schoolteacher; the object of his scrutiny is the Honorable M. A. Nanga, Member of Parliament, Odili's former teacher and a popular bush politician who has risen to the post of Minister of Culture in his West African homeland.

At first, Odili is charmed by the politician; but eventually he recognizes the extent of Nanga's abuses and decides to oppose the minister in an election. Odili is beaten, both physically and politically, his appeal to the people heard but ignored. The novel demonstrates, according to Gakwandi, that "the society has been invaded by a wide range of values which have destroyed the traditional balance between the material and the spiritual spheres of life, which has led inevitably to the hypocrisy of double standards." Odili is a victim of these double standards.

Despite his political victory, Nanga, along with the rest of the government, is ousted by a coup. "The novel is a carefully plotted and unified piece of writing," writes Killam. "Achebe achieves balance and proportion in the treatment of his theme of political corruption by evoking both the absurdity of the behavior of the principal characters while at the same time suggesting the serious and destructive consequences of their behavior to the commonwealth." The seriousness of the fictional situation portrayed in *A Man of the People* became real very soon after the novel was first published in 1966 when Nigeria itself was racked by a coup.

Two decades passed between the publications of *A Man of the People* and Achebe's 1988 novel, *Anthills of the Savannah*. During this period, the novelist wrote poetry, short stories, and essays. He also became involved in Nigeria's political struggle, a struggle marked by five coups, a civil war, elections marred by violence, and a number of attempts to return to civilian rule. *Anthills of the Savannah* represents Achebe's return to the novel, and as Nadine Gordimer comments in the *New York Times Book Review,* "it is a work in which 22 years of harsh experience, intellectual growth, self-criticism, deepening understanding and mustered discipline of skill open wide a subject to which Mr. Achebe is now magnificently equal." It also represents a return to the themes informing Achebe's earlier novels of independent Africa. "This is a study of how power corrupts itself and by doing so begins to die," writes *Observer* contributor and fellow Nigerian Ben Okri. "It is also about dissent, and love."

Three former schoolmates have risen to positions of power in an imaginary West African nation, Kangan. Ikem is editor of the state-owned newspaper; Chris is the country's minister of information; Sam is a military man who has become head of state. Sam's quest to have himself voted president for life sends the lives of these three and the lives of all Kangan citizens into turmoil. "In this new novel . . . Chinua Achebe says, with implacable honesty, that Africa itself is to blame," notes Neal Ascherson in the *New York Review of Books,* "and that there is no safety in excuses that place the fault in the colonial past or in the commercial and political manipulations of the First World." Ascherson continues that the novel becomes "a tale about responsibility, and the ways in which men who should know better betray and evade that responsibility."

The turmoil comes to a head in the novel's final pages. All three of the central characters are dead. Ikem, who spoke out against the abuses of the government, is murdered by Sam's secret police. Chris, who flees into the bush to begin a journey of transformation among the people, is shot attempting to stop a rape. Sam is kidnapped and murdered in a coup. "The three murders, senseless as they are, represent the departure of a generation that compromised its own enlightenment for the sake of power," writes Ascherson. And, as Okri observes, "The novel closes with the suggestion that power should reside not within an elite but within the awakened spirit of the people." Here is the hope offered in the novel, hope that is also suggested in its title, as Charles Trueheart

relates in the *Washington Post:* "When the brush fires sweep across the savanna, scorching the earth, they leave behind only anthills, and inside the anthills, the surviving memories of the fires and all that came before."

Anthills of the Savannah was well-received and earned Achebe a nomination for the Booker Prize. In Larson's estimation, printed in the *Tribune Books,* "No other novel in many years has bitten to the core, swallowed and regurgitated contemporary Africa's miseries and expectations as profoundly as *Anthills of the Savannah*." It has also enhanced Achebe's reputation as an artist; as *New Statesman* contributor Margaret Busby writes, "Reading [this novel] is like watching a master carver skillfully chiselling away from every angle at a solid block of wood: at first there is simply fascination at the sureness with which he works, according to a plan apparent to himself. But the point of all this activity gradually begins to emerge-until at last it is possible to step back and admire the image created."

Despite the fact that Achebe's next book, *Hopes and Impediments: Selected Essays 1965-1987,* is a collection of essays and speeches written over a period of twenty-three years, it was perceived in many ways to be a logical extension of the ideas he examined in *Anthills of the Savannah*. In this collection, however, he is not addressing the way in which Africans view themselves but rather the manner in which Africa is viewed by the outside world. The central theme of the essays is the corrosive impact of the racism that pervades the traditional Western appraisal of Africa. The collection opens with an examination of Joseph Conrad's 1902 novella *Heart of Darkness;* Achebe criticizes Conrad for projecting an image of Africa as "the other world"—meaning non-European and, therefore, uncivilized. Achebe argues that to this day, the Condradian myth persists that Africa is a dark and bestial land. The time has come, Achebe states, to sweep away the old prejudices in favor of new myths and socially "beneficent fiction" which will enable Africans and non-Africans alike to redefine the way they look at the continent.

In his writings—particularly his novels—Achebe has created a significant body of work in which he offers a close and balanced examination of contemporary Africa and the historical forces that have shaped it. "His distinction is to have [looked back] without any trace either of chauvinistic idealism or of neurotic rejection, those twin poles of so much African mythologizing," maintains Moore. "Instead, he has recreated for us a way of life which has almost disappeared, and has done so with understanding, with justice and with realism." And Busby commends the author's achievement in "charting the socio-political development of contemporary Nigeria." However, Achebe's writing reverberates beyond the borders of Nigeria and beyond the arenas of anthropology, sociology, and political science. As literature, it deals with universal qualities. And, as Killam writes in his study: "Achebe's novels offer a vision of life which is essentially tragic, compounded of success and failure, informed by knowledge and understanding, relieved by humour and tempered by sympathy, embued with an awareness of human suffering and the human capacity to endure." Concludes the critic, "Sometimes his characters meet with success, more often with defeat and despair. Through it all the spirit of man and the belief in the possibility of triumph endures."

Angelou returns to the genre of the autobiographical essay in *Even the Stars Look Lonesome.* "Like a modern-day Kahlil Gibran," explains a *Publishers Weekly* reviewer, "Angelou offers insights on a wide range of topics—Africa, aging, self-reflection, independence and the importance of understanding both the historical truths of the African American experience and the art that truth inspired." She draws on elements from her own life, including her relationship with Oprah Winfrey, her 1950s career as a nightclub singer, her experience of solitude. "Angelou reflects on how difficult it is to accept both the rewards and demands of fame with grace," writes Donna Seaman in a *Booklist* review of the volume, "but now—regal, smart, eloquent, and witty—she has mastered that skill."

In 1998 Angelou's first experience at directing a feature film, *Down in the Delta,* was released by Miramax. As in *Even the Stars Look Lonesome,* Angelou draws on her own life for inspiration: two characters she directed are depicted as mute, a condition Angelou underwent herself for several years in childhood. "'I'm attracted to projects that have a magnet that reaches inside to my soul and spirit,'" she tells Daisann McLane, writing for *Harper's Bazaar,* "by way of explaining why a woman in her 70s with a full plate and a heap of awards to her credit would want to add director to her list of accomplishments." Major actors and actresses, including Alfre Woodard, Esther Rolle, Wesley Snipes, and Al Freeman, Jr., were attracted to the project because of Angelou's association with it, and "came to work for peanut shells," Angelou tells Grace Lim of *People*

Weekly. Down in the Delta received muted praise from reviewers. Angelou "handles actors and scenes capably," states a *People* reviewer writing about the film, "but one doesn't come out of *Delta* convinced Angelou should forever abandon her pen for a camera." Joe Leydon writes in *Variety* that "Poet Maya Angelou's debut feature directing effort is a solid and affecting piece of work that will need careful marketing and strong critical support to attract ticket buyers."

BIOGRAPHICAL/CRITICAL SOURCES:

BOOKS

Awoonor, Kofi, *The Breast of the Earth,* Doubleday, 1975.

Baldwin, Claudia, *Nigerian Literature: A Bibliography of Criticism,* G. K. Hall (Boston, MA), 1980.

Carroll, David, *Chinua Achebe,* Macmillan (New York City), 1990.

Champion, Ernest A., *Mr. Baldwin, I Presume: James Baldwin-Chinua Achebe, a Meeting of the Minds,* University Press of America (Lanham, MD), 1995.

Contemporary Literary Criticism, Gale (Detroit), Volume 1, 1973; Volume 3, 1975; Volume 5, 1976; Volume 7, 1977; Volume 11, 1979; Volume 26, 1983; Volume 51, 1988; Volume 75, 1993.

Ezenwa-Ohaeto, *Chinua Achebe: A Biography,* Indiana University Press, 1997.

Gakwandi, Shatto Arthur, *The Novel and Contemporary Experience in Africa,* Africana Publishing, 1977.

Gikandi, Simon, *Reading Chinua Achebe: Language and Ideology in Fiction,* Heinemann, 1991.

Indrasena Reddy, K., *The Novels of Achebe and Ngugi: a Study in the Dialectics of Commitment,* Prestige Books (New Delhi), 1994.

Kambaji, Christopher Tshikala, *Chinua Achebe: A Novelist and a Portraitist of His Society,* Vantage Press (New York City), 1994.

Killam, G. D., *The Novels of Chinua Achebe,* Africana Publishing, 1969.

Kim, Soonsik, *Colonial and Post-Colonial Discourse in the Novels of Yaeom Sang-Saeop, Chinua Achebe, and Salman Rushdie,* P. Lang (New York City), 1996.

King, Bruce, *Introduction to Nigerian Literature,* Africana Publishing, 1972.

King, *The New English Literatures: Cultural Nationalism in a Changing World,* Macmillan, 1980.

Laurence, Margaret, *Long Drums and Cannons: Nige-*

rian Dramatists and Novelists, Praeger (New York City), 1968.

Lindfors, Bernth, *Folklore in Nigerian Literature,* Africana Publishing, 1973.

Lindfors, Bernth, *Conversations with Chinua Achebe,* University Press of Mississippi, 1997.

McEwan, Neil, *Africa and the Novel,* Humanities Press (Atlantic Highlands, NJ), 1983.

Moore, Gerald, *Seven African Writers,* Oxford University Press, 1962.

Moses, Michael Valdez, *The Novel and the Globalization of Culture,* Oxford University Press (New York City), 1995.

Muoneke, Romanus Okey, *Art, Rebellion and Redemption: A Reading of the Novels of Chinua Achebe,* Peter Lang (New York City), 1994.

Njoku, Benedict Chiaka, *The Four Novels of Chinua Achebe: A Critical Study,* Peter Lang (New York City), 1984.

Omotoso, Kole, *Achebe or Soyinka?: A Reinterpretation and a Study in Contrasts,* Hans Zell Publishers, 1992.

Palmer, Eustace, *The Growth of the African Novel,* Heinemann, 1979.

Parker, Michael, *Postcolonial Literatures: Achebe, Ngugi, Desai, Wolcott,* St. Martin's Press (New York City), 1995.

Petersen, K. H., *Chinua Achebe: A Celebration,* Heinemann, Dangeroo Press, 1991.

Simola, Raisa, *World Views in Chinua Achebe's Works,* P. Lang (New York City), 1995.

Wren, Robert M., *Achebe's World: The Historical and Cultural Context of the Novels,* Three Continents (Washington, DC), 1980.

PERIODICALS

America, June 22-29, 1991; July 20, 1996.

Booklist, March 1, 1997, p. 1168; August, 1997, p. 1842; January 1, 1998, p. 835.

Boston Globe, March 9, 1988.

Commonweal, December 1, 1967.

Commonwealth Essays and Studies, fall, 1990.

Ebony, February, 1999, p. 96.

Economist, October 24, 1987.

Entertainment Weekly, September 26, 1997, p. 74.

Guardian, April 4, 1998, p. TW5.

Harper's Bazaar, January, 1999, p. 66.

Library Journal, September 15, 1997, p. 74; May 15, 1998, p. 135.

Listener, October 15, 1987.

London Review of Books, October 15, 1981; August 7, 1986; June 22, 1989, p. 16-17.

Los Angeles Times Book Review, February 28, 1988.

Modern Fiction Studies, fall, 1991.

Nation, October 11, 1965; April 16, 1988.

New Statesman, January 4, 1985; September 25, 1987.

New Statesman and Society, July 22, 1988, pp. 41-2; February 9, 1990, p. 30.

New York Review of Books, March 3, 1988.

New York Times, August 10, 1966; February 16, 1988.

New York Times Book Review, December 17, 1967; May 13, 1973; August 11, 1985; February 21, 1988; November 12, 1989, p. 55.

Observer (London), September 20, 1987.

People, January 11, 1999, p. 35; January 25, 1999, p. 33.

Publishers Weekly, February 21, 1994, p. 249; August 4, 1997, p. 54.

Saturday Review, January 6, 1968.

School Library Journal, December, 1992, p. 146.

Spectator, October 21, 1960; September 26, 1987.

Studies in Black Literature: Special Issue; Chinua Achebe, spring, 1971.

Times Educational Supplement, January 25, 1985.

Times Literary Supplement, February 3, 1966; March 3, 1972; May 4, 1973; February 26, 1982; October 12, 1984; October 9, 1987.

Tribune Books (Chicago), February 21, 1988.

Variety, September 21, 1998, p. 110.

Village Voice, March 15, 1988.

Wall Street Journal, February 23, 1988.

Washington Post, February 16, 1988.

Washington Post Book World, February 7, 1988.

World Literature Today, summer, 1985.

World Literature Written in English, November, 1978.*

*   *   *

ADELL, Sandra 1946-

PERSONAL: Born July 19, 1946, in Detroit, MI; daughter of James (a laborer) and Edna Eugenia (a store clerk; maiden name, Hardy) Qualls; children: Sylvia Wasson, Robert Qualls, Crystal Adell. *Education:* Wayne State University, B.A., M.A., Ph.D.

ADDRESSES: Office—Department of Afro-American Studies, University of Wisconsin—Madison, 455 North Park, No. 4217, Madison, WI 53706.

CAREER: University of Wisconsin—Madison, associate professor of Afro-American studies, 1989—.

WRITINGS:

Double-Consciousness/Double Bind: Theoretical Issues in Twentieth-Century Black Literature, University of Illinois Press (Champaign, IL), 1994.
(Editor) *African American Culture,* Gale (Detroit, MI), 1996.

WORK IN PROGRESS: Dictionary of Twentieth-Century Culture; The Contested Site of Blackness; research on Arthur de Gobineau.

SIDELIGHTS: Sandra Adell told *CA:* "What motivates me to write is my curiosity about literature and the arts in general. Also, I love to read and study and cannot think of a better way to spend my life. I think it is somewhat of a luxury to be able to spend time researching and writing about things that interest me, particularly in the arts: music, dance, the visual arts, and, of course, literature. I speak French and Spanish and only wish I had time to learn more languages. That would enable me to study more deeply the literature of other countries. Knowledge is inexhaustible, and I intend to spend the rest of my life reveling in it."

*   *   *

ADISA, Opal Palmer 1954-

PERSONAL: Born November 6, 1954, in Kingston, Jamaica; immigrated to United States, 1970; naturalized U.S. citizen, 1980; daughter of Orlando and Catherine (James) Palmer; children: Shola, Jawara, Teju. *Ethnicity:* "African-Caribbean." *Education:* Hunter College of the City University of New York, B.A., 1975; San Francisco State University, M.A. (English), 1981, M.A. (drama), 1986; University of California, Berkeley, Ph.D., 1992. *Politics:* Democrat. *Religion:* "Humanist." *Avocational interests:* Biking, nature walks.

ADDRESSES: Home—1427 Linden St., Oakland, CA 94607; and P.O. Box 10625, Oakland, CA 94610. *Office*—Ethnic Studies/Cultural Diversity Program, California College of Arts and Crafts, Oakland, CA 94618. *E-mail*—Opalpro@aol.com.

CAREER: Artist and writer. San Francisco State University, San Francisco, CA, lecturer, 1981-87; California College of Arts and Crafts, Oakland, CA, associate professor, 1993-98, chair of ethnic studies/cultural diversity program, 1993—; professor of literature, 1998—. Visiting professor at various institutions, including University of California, Berkeley, 1994-96; lecturer at various institutions, including St. Mary's College, 1993, and Holy Name's College, 1994. Writer in residence at Headlands Center for the Arts, Sausaulito, CA, 1996-97. Developer and consulting writer for reader programs and projects. Member of various museum boards and consortiums.

Art works represented in shows, including *(in)Forming the Visual: (re)Presenting Women of African Descent,* Montgomery Gallery, 1995; and *Art for the Holidays,* Bedford Gallery, 1997-98. Performer on *Fierce Love* (collaborative poetry/jazz recording), Irresistible/Revolution (San Francisco), 1992. Performer the poetry videos "Despair Series," 1994, and "Tamarind and Mango Women," Quilombo Enterprises ICM, 1995.

MEMBER: Women's International League for Peace and Freedom, Society for the Study of Multi-Ethnic Literature of the United States, National Association for Ethnic Studies, National Writers Union, Northern Association of African American Storytellers, Association of Caribbean Women Writers and Scholars, Caribbean Association for Feminist Research and Action, California Poets in the Schools.

AWARDS, HONORS: Third place, American Poetry Association contest, 1982; merit certificate, Jamaica Festival Literature Competition, 1982; Bronze Medal, Jamaica Festival Literature Competition, 1984; Pushcart Prize, 1987, for the short story "Duppy Get Her"; grants, University of California, Berkeley, 1987, 1987-88, and 1988-90; Distinguished Bay Area Woman Writer Award and California Legislative Assembly Certificate, both 1991; PEN Oakland/Josephine Miles Literary Award, 1992, for *Tamarind and Mango Women;* honor, Literary Women, 1994; grants, California College of Arts and Crafts, 1994 and 1995; Daily News Prize, University of the Virgin Islands, 1995, for poems in *The Caribbean Writer;* grant, University of California, Berkeley, 1996; Canute A. Brodhurst Prize, University of the Virgin Islands, 1996, for the story "The Brethren"; named distinguished writer, Middle Atlantic Writers Association, 1998; Creative Work Fund grant, 1998-99, for "West Oakland (CA) Senior Citizen Oral History Project."

WRITINGS:

Pina, the Many-Eyed Fruit (children's book), Julian Richardson (San Francisco, CA), 1985.

Bake-Face, and Other Guava Stories, Kelsey Street Press (Berkeley, CA), 1986.

(With Devorah Major) *Traveling Women* (poetry), Jukebox Press (Oakland, CA), 1989.

Tamarind and Mango Women (poetry), Sister Vision Press (Toronto, Canada), 1992.

It Begins with Tears (novel), Heinemann, 1997.

Poems and short stories represented in anthologies, including *A Bite to Eat,* edited by Andrea Adolph and others, Redwood Press, 1995; *The Garden Thrives: Twentieth-Century African American Poetry,* edited by Clarence Major, HarperPerennial, 1996; *Father Songs,* edited by Gloria Wade-Gayles, Beacon Press, 1997; *An Intricate Weave: Women Writing about Girls and Girlhood,* edited by Margaret Miller, Iris Editions, 1997; and *Bittersweet: Contemporary Black Women's Poetry,* edited by Karen McCarthy, Women's Press, 1998. Member of advisory board, *Caribbean Writer,* 1998— .

CONTRIBUTOR

Evelyn C. White, editor, *The Black Women's Health Book,* Seal Press, 1990.

Ron Padgett, editor, *Old Faithful: Eighteen Writers Present Their Favorite Writing Assignments,* Teachers and Writers Cooperative, 1995.

Carole Boyce Davies and Molara Ogundipe-Leslie, editors, *Moving beyond Boundaries: International Dimensions of Black Women's Writing,* Pluto Press, 1995.

Wesley Brown, editor, *Teachers and Writers Guide to Frederick Douglass,* Teachers and Writers Cooperative, 1996.

Lorenzo Thomas, editor, *Sing the Sun Up: Creative Writing Ideas from African American Literature,* Teachers and Writers Cooperative, 1998.

Adele S. Newson and Linda Strong-Leek, editors, *Winds of Change,* Peter Lang, 1998.

Helen Pyne-Timothy, editor, *The Woman, the Writer, and Caribbean Society,* Center for Afro-American Studies Publications, 1998.

Contributor to reference books, including *Reference Guide to American Literature,* edited by Jim Kamp, St. James Press, 1994; and *The Oxford Companion to African American Literature,* edited by William Andrews and others, Oxford University Press, 1997. Contributor of poetry, short stories, essays, articles and book reviews to periodicals, including *African American Review, Black Elegance, Black Quarterly Review of Books, Caribbean Writer, Chimera, Crab Orchard Review, Garden Design, Journal of Multicultural Heartspeak, Konceptualizations, Papyrus, Scarp, Third Force,* and *Zyzzyva.*

ADAPTATIONS: "Tamarind and Mango Women" (video), Quilombo Enterprises ICM, 1995.

WORK IN PROGRESS: Queen Mother of Verse: Louise Bennett, Jamaica's Folk Poet, interview with Louise Bennett; with photographer Kathy Sloane, *Caribbean Women: Big and Little; Until Judgment Comes,* short stories.

SIDELIGHTS: Opal Palmer Adisa is an artist, storyteller, educator, and author who has established herself as a notable figure in Caribbean culture. As an author, Adisa has published fiction for children and adults, as well as poetry and essays. Her debut novel, *It Begins with Tears,* appeared in 1997. This work, according to a critic in *Kirkus Reviews,* "offers a vibrant slice of Jamaican life shaped by old legends and timeless passions." The novel features two narratives, one of which relates the interactions among various mythical deities, notably an argumentative couple referred to as Devil and She-Devil, who are planning their son's wedding in the timeless village of Kristoff. The novel's other narrative involves villagers of the actual town of Kristoff in Jamaica. Among these villagers is Monica, who had fled home as a young teen and found work as a prostitute, but who has decided to abandon her sordid trade and return to Kristoff. Once home, Monica conducts herself recklessly with several married men. Their jealous wives, in turn, conceive what an *Americas* reviewer described as "a cruel and painful punishment for Monica." The novel's two narratives converge when Monica, having been brutally punished by the vindictive wives, finds herself before the She-Devil. Then, as the *Americas* reviewer noted, "The high priestess of Eternal Valley sends [Monica] back to earth, where she will have a chance to amend her life." The novel culminates in ceremonies in both the eternal village, where the gods celebrate the marriage of their son, and on Earth, where the Kristoff women enact a cleansing ritual and the men renew their bonds of friendship with each other.

It Begins with Tears has been praised as an impressive literary work. The *Americas* reviewer declared that "Adisa's beautiful first novel will bring tears to your eyes and joy to your heart." The same critic noted that the work "contains a number of breathtaking and unforgettable scenes" and summarized it as "a remarkable book." Likewise, *World Literature Today* critic Adele S. Newson proclaimed *It Begins with*

Tears "a splendid book" and affirmed that it is "artfully written and compelling." Newson added that Adisa "masterfully explores the issues, concerns, and motifs central to diaspora writers today: African cosmology, mother-daughter relationships . . . ways of seeing and knowing, as well as the community in flux." The *Kirkus Reviews* critic similarly lauded Adisa's novel for its "rich textures and an exuberant vitality."

Aside from *It Begins with Tears,* Adisa has published the children's book *Pina, the Many-Eyed Fruit,* the short story collections *Bake-Face, and Other Guava Stories,* and the verse volumes *Traveling Women,* written with Devorah Major, and *Tamarind and Mango Women,* for which she received the PEN Oakland/Josephine Miles Literary Award in 1992. In addition, she has exhibited her art work in various shows. She also performed on the 1992 recording *Fierce Love,* a collaborative work involving poetry and jazz. Since the early 1990s Adisa has served as a professor at the California College of Arts and Crafts, where she has also chaired the school's Ethnic Studies/Cultural Diversity Program.

Adisa told *CA:* "The stories I write come from a deep place. I want my writingto help people heal and move from the places where they are stuck. I particularly want my writing to help African people on the continent and throughout the diaspora to revocer from the impact of slavery, to heal their wound, to remember their past glory, to rejoice in the sun and to keep dancing and blessing the world with their spirit and resilience. My writing is a prayer, is a chant, is a hymn. My writing is a gift, a bridge where all people can find a commonality and come together to celebrate life's joys. I write about friendship and people connecting because I know I am blessed, I have had and will continue to have a wonderful life, and despite the obstacles and challenges, everyone can find those places and those moments to just look at the sun, or feel the wind and say, I'm sure glad to be alive. I'm sure glad someone loved me. I'm sure glad someone greeted me today, but the blessing begins with me, meeting someone half way. That's what I am trying to say through my writing."

BIOGRAPHICAL/CRITICAL SOURCES:

BOOKS

Mavor, Anne, *Strong Hearts, Inspired Minds: Twenty Two Interviews with Artists Who Are Mothers,* Rowanberry Books, 1996.

PERIODICALS

Americas, March-April, 1998, p. 61.
Crab Orchard Review, fall/winter, 1998, pp. 1-13.
Kirkus Reviews, April 15, 1997.
Voices, winter, 1997, pp. 4-5.
World Literature Today, winter, 1998, p. 188.

*   *   *

AFTON, Effie
  See HARPER, Frances Ellen Watkins

*   *   *

ALAGOA, Ebiegberi Joe   1933-

PERSONAL: Born March 14, 1933, in Okpoma, Rivers State, Nigeria; son of Joseph Ayibatonye (a chieftan) and Jane Furombogha (Obasi) Alagoa; married Mercy Gboribusuote Nyananyo, September 26, 1961; children: David Ayibatonye. *Education:* University College, Ibadan, Nigeria, B.A. (with honors); University of Wisconsin, Ph.D. (history), 1966.

ADDRESSES: Office—School of Humanities, University of Port Harcourt, Port Harcourt, Rivers State, Nigeria, PMB 5234.

CAREER: National Archives Nigeria, archivist, 1959-62; University of Lagos, Lagos, Nigeria, lecturer in African history, 1965-67, director of Centre of Cultural Studies, 1972-77; Institute of African Studies, University of Ibadan, senior research fellow, 1967-72; School of Humanities, University of Port Harcourt, Port Harcourt, Rivers State, Nigeria, dean, beginning 1977. Chair, Rivers State Council of Arts and Culture, 1973-75.

MEMBER: American Anthropology Association, Historical Society of Nigeria.

WRITINGS:

(Compiler) *Special List of Records Related to Historical, Anthropological, and Social Studies among Provincial Administration Record Groups at National Archives, Kaduna,* National Archives (Kaduna, Nigeria), 1962.

The Small Brave City-State: A History of Nembe-Brass in Niger Delta. University of Wisconsin Press (Madison), 1964.

Kien abibi onde fa pugu. Nembe numerals, Nembe Cultural Association, Lagos (Lagos, Nigeria), 1967.

Jaja of Opobo: The Slave Who Became a King (juvenile nonfiction), Longman (London), 1970.

(With Adadonye Fombo) *A Chronicle of Grand Bonny,* Ibadan University Press (Ibadan, Nigeria), 1972.

A History of the Niger Delta: An Historical Interpretation of Ijo Oral Tradition, Ibadan University Press (Ibadan, Nigeria), 1972.

War Canoe Drums and Topical Songs from Nembe, Rivers State, Rivers State Council for Arts and Culture (Nigeria), 1974.

King Boy of Brass (juvenile nonfiction), Heinemann Educational (London), 1975.

(Editor, with T. N. Tamuno) *Eminent Nigerians of the Rivers State,* Heinemann Educational (Ibadan), 1980.

(Editor) *More Days, More Wisdom: Nembe Proverbs,* University of Harcourt Press (Harcourt, Nigeria), 1983.

(Editor) *Oral Tradition and Oral History in Africa and the Diaspora: Theory and Practice,* Centre for Black and African Arts and Civilization (Lagos, Nigeria), 1990.

SIDELIGHTS: Nigerian historian and educator Ebiegberi Joe Alagoa has written numerous works about his homeland, the Rivers State region of Nigeria. Many of these works deal with history and folklore as incorporated into the oral tradition of Africa. In his 1964 work, *The Small Brave City-State: A History of Nembe-Brass in Niger Delta,* Alagoa chronicles the history of the Nembe people who have lived near the Brass River estuary of the Niger Delta since the fifteenth century. Drawing on oral sources preserved in the national archives, as well as other published sources, Alagoa describes the social and political organizations, commerce, and politics of the Nembe Brass. He also describes the Akassa War between the Nembe and the British colonial trading company.

Several commentators have praised Alagoa's contribution to the recorded history of Nigeria. Judging Alagoa to be "well equipped to fuse the oral traditions of the Nembe people with the more standard sources," Robert O. Collins, writing in the *American Historical Review,* called the work "first a most useful contribution to the local history of the delta region and second

a scholarly addition to the history of Nigeria as a whole." "The chapter on the Akassa War is particularly useful to the African historian," Collins added. In addition, a critic for *Choice* called the work "well written," praising Alagoa's "excellent analysis" of the region's institutions, noting that it supplements other works on Nigeria.

"Alagoa has written a historical study rather than an ethnography, thus omitting many cultural features which would interest anthropologists," noted Donald C. Simmons in a review for *American Anthropologist.* "However, anyone interested in the area can glean much background ethnological information from this interesting, well-documented study, whose minor faults are due not to the author but to the paucity of data available for reconstructing Nembe history." The "principal weakness" of *The Small Brave City-State* is Alagoa's "failure to carry the history of Nembe-Brass well into the twentieth century," according to Collins.

For young readers, Alagoa has contributed several volumes to London publisher Heinemann's "African Historical Biographies" series. The goal of this series is to present African history from a native point of view, rather than from the colonial perspective so frequently employed. Thus, *King Boy of Brass* tells the story of a nineteenth-century boy-king of the Niger Delta, who is at first a disappointment to his father but redeems himself as a ruler and trader. Abiola Odejide, writing in *Reading Teacher,* contended that Alagoa's book turned the reader into a "detached observer, an auditor rather than a vicarious participant of a past experience." "The authors in all the Heinemann series are strongly aware of the historical perspective, leading to an overwhelming factual tone and the relegation of literary quality to the background," stated Odejide. On the other hand, the critic judged Alagoa's 1970 biography, *Jaja of Opobo: The Slave Who Became a King,* to be the more successful of the historian's two juvenile biographies. Because the author fictionalizes the early life of Jaja of Opobo, maintained Odejide, young readers are more likely to become engaged in the work.

BIOGRAPHICAL/CRITICAL SOURCES:

PERIODICALS

American Anthropologist, June, 1965, pp. 793-794.
American Historical Review, April, 1965, pp. 880-881.
Choice, February, 1965, p. 584.
Reading Teacher, March, 1987, pp. 642-643.*

AL-AMIN, Jamil Abdullah 1943-

PERSONAL: Name originally Hubert Gerold Brown; became known as H. Rap Brown; assumed present name during 1970s; born October 4, 1943, in Baton Rouge, LA; son of Eddie C. Brown (a worker for an oil company) and Thelma (Warren) Brown; married Lynne Doswell (a schoolteacher), May 3, 1968 (marriage ended); married Karima; children: C. Ali, Kairi. *Education:* Attended Southern University, 1960-64.

ADDRESSES: Office—The Community Store, 1128 Oak St. SW, Atlanta, GA 30310.

CAREER: U.S. Department of Agriculture, Washington, D.C., librarian, 1964- 65; Nonviolent Action Group, Washington, DC, chairman, beginning in 1964; neighborhood worker in government poverty program in Washington, DC, beginning in 1965; Student Nonviolent Coordinating Committee (SNCC; renamed Student National Coordinating Committee, 1969), organizer in Greene County, AL, beginning in 1966, Alabama state project director, beginning in 1966, chairman, beginning in 1967; imprisoned for robbery in state of New York, 1971-76; Dial Press, writer, lecturer; The Community Store, Atlanta, GA, proprietor, c. 1976—; The Community Mosque, Atlanta, GA, Imam (leader).

WRITINGS:

(Under name H. Rap Brown) *Die Nigger Die!* (autobiography), Dial, 1969.
Revolution by the Book: (The Rap Is Live), Writers' Inc.-International (Beltsville, MD), 1993.

SIDELIGHTS: Jamil Abdullah Al-Amin is an outspoken young African American leader who came to prominence in the late 1960s, when he was widely known as H. Rap Brown. In the aftermath of the struggle by Martin Luther King, Jr., to win black civil rights through nonviolent protest, some in Al-Amin's generation believed that a more direct confrontation with white racism was necessary. Al-Amin became known for his belief that black people should be prepared to use guns to assert their rights, and many charged that he was an advocate of violence. Al-Amin countered that his views were necessitated by the virulence of racism. "I preach a response to violence," he wrote in his 1969 autobiography, *Die Nigger Die!—*"Meet violence with violence." If someone deprives you of your human rights, Al-Amin contended, he is being violent. "It's your responsibil-

ity to jump back" at your oppressor, because "if you don't, he knows that you're scared and that he can control you." The reactions to Al-Amin varied widely. *Newsweek* magazine accused him of "hate-mongering," for instance, while Kiarri Cheatwood in *Black World* called him "a young man of deep sensibilities."

In his autobiography Al-Amin recounted some of the experiences that led him to such controversial views. During the early 1960s he studied sociology at Southern University, a black college in his hometown of Baton Rouge, Louisiana. He concluded, however, that the school's administration was unwilling to stand up to racial injustice. He worked briefly in a government antipoverty program in Washington, D.C., but sensed that blacks were being co-opted there. "The poverty program," he wrote, "was designed to take those people whom the government considered threatening to the structure and buy them off. It didn't address itself to the causes of poverty but to the effects of poverty."

Al-Amin increasingly looked outside of traditional American institutions to change society. While chairman of the Washington, D.C., Nonviolent Action Group in 1965, he joined several black leaders at a meeting with U.S. President Lyndon Johnson. He gained notoriety for berating the strong-willed president. "I'm not happy to be here," he remembered telling Johnson, "and I think it's unnecessary that we have to be here protesting against the brutality that Black people are subjected to." The next year Al-Amin went to Greene County, Alabama, as an organizer for the Student Nonviolent Coordinating Committee (SNCC), facing the hostility of white citizens and police as he encouraged local black people to exercise their rights to vote and to hold public office. He became the SNCC's Alabama project director a few months later and in 1967 was elected chairman of the entire organization.

Al-Amin's post brought him national attention. He made repeated statements about the need for a violent confrontation with racism, becoming widely known for such remarks as "violence is as American as cherry pie." He suggested that the riots sweeping America's poor black neighborhoods heralded a political insurrection, and riots broke out in the cities of Dayton, Ohio, East St. Louis, Illinois, and Cambridge, Maryland, shortly after he spoke there. Authorities in Maryland indicted Al-Amin for inciting the Cambridge riot and engaging in arson, and for the next few years he was mired in a succession of highly publicized legal battles involving such charges as illegally possessing a gun and violating the terms of his bail. Supporters of Al-Amin argued that he was being harassed for his political beliefs.

At the height of his fame Al-Amin wrote *Die Nigger Die!*, and the book garnered mixed reactions, as had its author. John Leonard of the *New York Times* found the work unsatisfactory both as autobiography and as political commentary, charging that Al-Amin was "so busy proving his *machismo* that his material never comes into focus." But in the *New York Times Book Review*, Shane Stevens asserted that *Die Nigger Die!* expressed the author's "essential humanism. . . , cloaked though it may be in fear and hate." Citing Al-Amin's ability to combine his outrage with an irreverent sense of humor, Stevens wrote that "the cutting edge of deep pain is there. But so is the raucous, sometimes slightly hysterical, laughter of life." Cheatwood stressed Al-Amin's political analyses, lauding his "depth," "historically-shaped consciousness," and "mature through." As an example, Cheatwood observed that "perhaps better than anyone before him," the author outlined "the responsibilities of Black student to their people."

In 1970 Al-Amin went into hiding, delaying the start of his riot trial in Maryland. The Federal Bureau of Investigation (FBI) promptly placed him on its list of most-wanted criminals. The next year New York City police took him into custody near the scene of a barroom robbery. He remained imprisoned while he was tried and convicted of taking part in the holdup and was sentenced to further time in jail. When he pleaded guilty to eluding his Maryland trial, authorities in that state dropped their riot and arson charges.

During his incarceration Al-Amin converted to Islam and adopted his current name. Paroled in 1976, he moved to Atlanta, Georgia, where he operates a small grocery. Though no longer in the national headlines, he has given occasional interviews to journalists. In 1985 he met with *Washington Post* columnist George F. Will, who found him "enveloped in a strange serenity." Al-Amin's life, Will suggested, was now centered on his Muslim faith, and the onetime political activist was working with neighbors on plans for a religious school. "Many people reckon time from the '60s," Al-Amin observed, because "time stopped for them then." He added, "I don't miss the '60s."

BIOGRAPHICAL/CRITICAL SOURCES:

BOOKS

Brown, H. Rap, *Die Nigger Die!*, Dial, 1969.

PERIODICALS

Black World, October, 1975.
Chicago Tribune Book World, May 11, 1969.
New Republic, June 14, 1969.
Newsweek, August 7, 1967; June 3, 1968; February 12, 1973.
New York Times, August 13, 1967; April 30, 1969; November 7, 1973; September 25, 1976.
New York Times Book Review, June 15, 1969.
Saturday Review, May 3, 1969.
Village Voice, November 2, 1967.
Washington Post, June 15, 1978; September 19, 1985.

* * *

ALERS, Rochelle 1943-

PERSONAL: Born August 7, 1943, in New York, NY; daughter of James A. and Minnie L. Ford; divorced; children: Noemi V. *Education:* John Jay College of Criminal Justice of the City University of New York, B.A., 1974.

ADDRESSES: Office—Wind Watch Production, P.O. Box 690, Freeport, NY 11520- 0690. *E-mail*—Roclers @aol.com.

CAREER: Empire State Medical Equipment Dealers Association, executive assistant, 1987-91; Nassau County Department of Drugs and Alcohol Addiction Services, community liaison specialist, 1991—. Wind Watch Production, owner.

MEMBER: Women Writers of Color (cofounder; president, 1990-94), Romance Reading Ring, Long Island Quilters Society, Freeport Exchange Club.

AWARDS, HONORS: Pope Pius X Award, Archdiocese of Rockville Centre, NY, 1997.

WRITINGS:

Careless Whispers, Doubleday (New York City), 1988.
My Love's Keeper, 1991.
Happily Ever After, Kensington, 1994.
Hideaway, Kensington, 1995.
Home Sweet Home, Kensington, 1996.
Vows, Kensington, 1997.
Hidden Agenda, Pinnacle Books (New York City), 1997.

Reckless Surrender, Genesis Press (Columbus, MS), 1997.
Heaven Sent, Kensington, 1998.
Gentle Yearning, Genesis Press, 1998.
Summer Magic, Doubleday, 1999.
Harvest Moon, Bet Books, 1999.
(With others) *Rosie's Curl and Weave,* St. Martin's Press, 1999.

Work represented in anthologies, including *Holiday Cheer,* 1995; and *Love Letters,* Pinnacle Books, 1997.

BIOGRAPHICAL/CRITICAL SOURCES:

PERIODICALS

Library Journal, February 15, 1997, p. 125.
Publishers Weekly, April 5, 1999, p. 238.

OTHER

Infokart, http://www.infokart.com/rochellealers/rochelle.html (April 9, 1999).
Rochelle Alers page, wysiwyg://69/http://www.geocities.com/Paris/Rue/4626/rochelle.html (April 9, 1999).*

*   *   *

ALLEN, Sarah A.
  See HOPKINS, Pauline Elizabeth

*   *   *

ALLSOPP, (Stanley Reginald) Richard 1923-

PERSONAL: Born January 23, 1923, in British Guiana (now Guyana); son of Stanley Reginald Richardson (a bookkeeper) and Eloise Rebecca Sophia (Archer) Allsopp; married Dorothy Yolande Bell, November 1, 1971 (divorced); married Jeannette Eileen Mercurius, July 2, 1983; children: Disa, Sophia, John, Marie. *Education:* University of London, B.A. (with honors), 1948, M.A., 1958, Ph.D., 1962. *Politics:* "Disillusioned socialist." *Religion:* Anglican. *Avocational interests:* Caribbean language and culture, public affairs, woodwork.

ADDRESSES: Home—1 Poinsettia Way, Cave Hill, St. Michael, Barbados. *Office*—Caribbean Lexicography Project, University of the West Indies, Cave Hill, Barbados; fax 246-424-3380. *E-mail*—janall@carib surf.com.

CAREER: Senior French teacher at secondary school in Georgetown, Guyana, 1949-60, became deputy headmaster, then headmaster, 1961-63; University of the West Indies, Cave Hill, Barbados, lecturer, 1963-70, senior lecturer, 1970-79, reader, 1979-90. Language consultant for new *Book of Common Prayer,* Anglican Church of the West Indies Province.

MEMBER: Society for Caribbean Linguistics (founding member; honorary life member).

AWARDS, HONORS: Crane Gold medal, most significant contribution to education in British Guiana, 1958.

WRITINGS:

(Coeditor) *Dictionary of Caribbean English Usage,* Oxford University Press (Oxford, England), 1996.
Language and National Unity, Government of Guyana, 1998.

Member of editorial board, *New Oxford English Dictionary,* Oxford University Press, 1984—.

WORK IN PROGRESS: Poems and short stories; research on Caribbean/English language; research on Caribbean proverbs.

SIDELIGHTS: Richard Allsopp told *CA:* "I consider myself a Caribbean person and am fired by the meaning that underpins this belief, especially the integrating nature of our Caribbean history and culture, both with a strong component of African heritage. The peoples of the African diaspora, for whom I have resurrected the term 'Afric' to cover all skin-shades, nationalities, and conditions, tend to despise, or allow to be despised, the truths of our Afric heritage, hardly even understanding its vital contribution to our music, dancing, cricket, athletics, et cetera—these being all in the physical domain—and, worse still, rejecting its contribution to our language, literary oratory, and life-view—the intellectual domain. My comprehensive coverage of the Anglophone Caribbean in the lexicographical domain attempts to demonstrate this integrating heritage. It is ongoing and is now supplemented by new work on Caribbean proverbs.

"I consider such work, especially in view of my age and the realization of the dangers of regional ignorance in the context, to be vital and urgent, because for one thing ignorant misunderstanding means confusion and international puppetry for our peoples; and for another, an increasingly strong East Indian (or Indo-Asiatic, if you like) commercial and political assertion from Trinidad, Guyana, and Suriname threatens the despised Afric heritage (already significantly in Guyana but) ultimately in the whole Caribbean—give two or three decades—bringing with it the ruin of Caribbean harmony."

* * *

ANGELOU, Maya 1928-

PERSONAL: Name originally Marguerite (some sources say Marguerita) Johnson; surname is pronounced "*An*-ge-lo"; born April 4, 1928, in St. Louis, MO; daughter of Bailey (a doorkeeper and naval dietician) and Vivian (a nurse and realtor; maiden name, Baxter) Johnson; married Tosh Angelou (divorced c. 1952); married Paul Du Feu, December, 1973 (divorced); children: Guy Johnson. *Education:* Attended public schools in Arkansas and California; studied music privately; studied dance with Martha Graham, Pearl Primus, and Ann Halprin; studied drama with Frank Silvera and Gene Frankel. *Politics:* Left.

ADDRESSES: Office—c/o Random House, 201 East 50th St., New York, NY, 10017. *Agent*—Gerald W. Purcell Associates Ltd., 133 Fifth Ave., New York, N.Y. 10003.

CAREER: Author, poet, playwright, professional stage and screen producer, director, and performer, and singer. Taught modern dance at Habima Theatre, Tel Aviv, Israel, and the Rome Opera House, Rome, Italy. Appeared in *Porgy and Bess* on twenty-two-nation tour sponsored by the U.S. Department of State, 1954-55; appeared in Off-Broadway plays *Calypso Heatwave,* 1957, and *The Blacks,* 1960; produced and performed in *Cabaret for Freedom,* with Godfrey Cambridge, Off-Broadway, 1960; University of Ghana, Institute of African Studies, Legon-Accra, Ghana, assistant administrator of School of Music and Drama, 1963-66; appeared in *Mother Courage* at University of Ghana, 1964, and in *Meda* in Hollywood, 1966; made Broadway debut in *Look Away,* 1973; directed film *All Day Long,* 1974, and *Down in the Delta,* Miramax, 1998; directed her play *And Still I Rise* in California, 1976; directed Errol John's *Moon on a Rainbow Shawl* in London, England, 1988;

appeared in film *Roots,* 1977. Television narrator, interviewer, and host for Afro-American specials and theatre series, 1972. Lecturer at University of California, Los Angeles, 1966; writer in residence at University of Kansas, 1970; distinguished visiting professor at Wake Forest University, 1974, Wichita State University, 1974, and California State University, Sacramento, 1974; professor at Wake Forest University, 1981—. Northern coordinator of Southern Christian Leadership Conference, 1959-60; appointed member of American Revolution Bicentennial Council by President Gerald R. Ford, 1975-76; member of National Commission on the Observance of International Women's Year.

MEMBER: American Federation of Television and Radio Artists, American Film Institute (member of board of trustees, 1975—), Directors Guild, Equity, Harlem Writers Guild, Women's Prison Association (member of advisory board).

AWARDS, HONORS: Nominated for National Book Award, 1970, for *I Know Why the Caged Bird Sings;* Yale University fellowship, 1970; Pulitzer Prize nomination, 1972, for *Just Give Me a Cool Drink of Water 'Fore I Diiie;* Antoinette Perry ("Tony") Award nomination from League of New York Theatres and Producers, 1973, for performance in *Look Away;* Rockefeller Foundation scholar in Italy, 1975; honorary degrees from Smith College, 1975, Mills College, 1975, Lawrence University, 1976, and Wake Forest University, 1977; named Woman of the Year in Communications by *Ladies' Home Journal,* 1976; Tony Award nomination for best supporting actress, 1977, for *Roots;* named one of the top one hundred most influential women by *Ladies Home Journal,* 1983; North Carolina Award in Literature, 1987; named Woman of the Year by *Essence* magazine, 1992; named Distinguished Woman of North Carolina, 1992; recipient, Horatio Alger Award, 1992; Grammy Award for Best Spoken Word or Non-Traditional Album, 1994, for recording of "On The Pulse of the Morning."

WRITINGS:

I Know Why the Caged Bird Sings (autobiography; also see below), Random House, 1970.
Just Give Me a Cool Drink of Water 'fore I Diiie (poetry), Random House, 1971.
Gather Together in My Name (autobiography), Random House, 1974.
Oh Pray My Wings Are Gonna Fit Me Well (poetry), Random House, 1975.

Singin' and Swingin' and Gettin' Merry Like Christmas (autobiography), Random House, 1976.

And Still I Rise (poetry; includes "One More Round" and "Still I Rise"; also see below), Random House, 1978.

The Heart of a Woman (autobiography; also see below), Random House, 1981.

Shaker, Why Don't You Sing? (poetry), Random House, 1983.

All God's Children Need Traveling Shoes (autobiography), Random House, 1986.

Mrs. Flowers: A Moment of Friendship (fiction), illustrations by Etienne Delessert, Redpath Press, 1986.

Poems: Maya Angelou, four volumes, Bantam, 1986.

Now Sheba Sings the Song, illustrations by Tom Feelings, Dial Books, 1987.

Selections from I Know Why the Caged Bird Sings and The Heart of A Woman, Literacy Volunteers of New York City, 1989.

I Shall Not Be Moved, Random House, 1990.

(Author of introduction) Rosamund Grant, *Caribbean and African Cookery,* Seven Hills, 1990.

(Author of forward) Margaret Courtney-Clarke, *African Canvas: The Art of West African Women,* Rizzoli International, 1991.

(Author of forward) Zora Neale Thurston, *Dust Tracks on the Road: An Autobiography,* HarperCollins, 1991.

(Author of forward) *Double Stitch: Black Women Write about Mothers and Daughters,* edited by Patricia Bell-Scott, Beacon Press, 1991.

Life Doesn't Frighten Me (poetry), Stewart, Tabori, and Chang, 1993.

On the Pulse of the Morning (poem), Random House, 1993.

Lessons in Living, Rnadom House, 1993.

Wouldn't Take Nothing for my Journey Now, Wheeler Publishers (Hingham, MA), 1993.

Soul Looks Back in Wonder (children's poetry), Doubleday, 1994.

The Complete Collected Poems of Maya Angelou (poetry), Random House, 1994.

My Painted House, My Friendly Chicken, and Me, Crown Publishing, 1994.

Phenomenal Woman: Four Poems Celebrating Women, Random House (New York City), 1994.

A Brave and Startling Truth, Random House (New York City), 1995.

Kofi and His Magic, with photographs by Margaret Courtney-Clarke, Clarkson N. Potter (New York City), 1996.

Even the Stars Look Lonesome (essays), Random House, 1997.

Also author of *The True Believers,* with Abbey Lincoln. Contributor of articles, short stories, and poems to periodicals, including *Harper's, Ebony, Ghanaian Times, Mademoiselle, Redbook,* and *Black Scholar.* Associate editor, *Arab Observer* (English-language news weekly in Cairo, Egypt), 1961-62; feature editor, *African Review* (Accra, Ghana), 1964-66. Contributor to Ghanaian Broadcasting Corp., 1963-65.

PLAYS

(With Godfrey Cambridge) *Cabaret for Freedom* (musical revue), first produced in New York at Village Gate Theatre, 1960.

The Least of These (two-act drama), first produced in Los Angeles, 1966.

The Clawing Within, 1966.

Adjoa Amissah (two-act musical), 1967.

Encounters, first produced by Center Theater Group at Mark Taper Forum, 1973.

(Adaptor) Sophocles, *Ajax* (two-act drama), first produced in Los Angeles at Mark Taper Forum, 1974.

And Still I Rise (one-act musical), first produced in Oakland, CA, at Ensemble Theatre, 1976.

SCREENPLAYS

Georgia, Georgia, Independent-Cinerama, 1972.

All Day Long, American Film Institute, 1974.

TELEVISION PLAYS

Blacks, Blues, Black (ten one-hour programs), National Educational Television (NET-TV), 1968.

(With Leona Thuna and Ralph B. Woolsey) *I Know Why the Caged Bird Sings* (adaption of Angelou's autobiography), CBS, 1979.

Sister, Sister (drama), NBC, 1982.

Brewster Place (series premiere), ABC, 1990.

Also author of *Assignment America* series, 1975, and two African-American specials "The Legacy" and "The Inheritors," 1976.

RECORDINGS

Miss Calypso (songs), Liberty Records, 1957.

The Poetry of Maya Angelou, GWP Records, 1969, remastered and rereleased as *Black Pearls: The Poetry of Maya Angelou,* Rhino Wordbeat, 1998.

Women in Business, University of Wisconsin, 1981.

The Heart of a Woman, 1998.

FILM MUSIC

(With Quincy Jones) "You Put It on Me" [and] "For Love of Ivy," Cinerama, 1968.
"I Can Call Down Rain" [and] "Georgia, Georgia," Cinerama, 1972.

Composer of musical scores for her screenplays.

SIDELIGHTS: By the time she was in her early twenties, Maya Angelou had been a Creole cook, a streetcar conductor, a cocktail waitress, a dancer, a madam, and an unwed mother. The following decades saw her emerge as a successful singer, actress, and playwright, an editor for an English-language magazine in Egypt, a lecturer and civil rights activist, and a popular author of five collections of poetry and five autobiographies. In 1993 Angelou gave a moving reading of her poem "On the Pulse of Morning" at Bill Clinton's presidential inauguration, an occasion that gave her wide recognition.

Angelou is hailed as one of the great voices of contemporary black literature and as a remarkable Renaissance woman. She began producing books after some notable friends, including author James Baldwin, heard Angelou's stories of her childhood spent shuttling between rural, segregated Stamps, Arkansas, where her devout grandmother ran a general store, and St. Louis, Missouri, where her worldly, glamorous mother lived. *I Know Why the Caged Bird Sings,* a chronicle of her life up to age sixteen (and ending with the birth of her son, Guy) was published in 1970 with great critical and commercial success. Although many of the stories in the book are grim, as in the author's revelation that she was raped at age eight by her mother's boyfriend, the volume also recounts the self-awakening of the young Angelou. "Her genius as a writer is her ability to recapture the texture of the way of life in the texture of its idioms, its idiosyncratic vocabulary and especially in its process of image-making," reports Sidonie Ann Smith in *Southern Humanities Review.* "The imagery holds the reality, giving it immediacy. That [the author] chooses to recreate the past in its own sounds suggests to the reader that she accepts the past and recognizes its beauty and its ugliness, its assets and its liabilities, its strengths and its weaknesses. Here we witness a return to the final acceptance of the past in the return to and full acceptance of its language, the language a symbolic construct of a way of life. Ultimately Maya Angelou's style testifies to her reaffirmation of self-acceptance, [which] she achieves within the pattern of the autobiography."

Her next two volumes of autobiography, *Gather Together in My Name* and *Singin' and Swingin' and Gettin' Merry Like Christmas,* take Angelou from her late adolescence, when she flirted briefly with prostitution and drug addiction, to her early adulthood as she established a reputation as a performer among the avant-garde of the early 1950s. Not as commercially successful as *I Know Why the Caged Bird Sings,* the two books were guardedly praised by some critics. Lynn Sukenick, for example, remarks in *Village Voice* that *Gather Together in My Name* is "sculpted, concise, rich with flavor and surprises, exuding a natural confidence and command." Sukenick adds, however, that one fault lies "in the tone of the book. . . . [The author's] refusal to let her earlier self get off easy, and the self-mockery which is her means to honesty, finally becomes in itself a glossing over; although her laughter at herself is witty, intelligent, and a good preventative against maudlin confession, . . . it eventually becomes a tic and a substitute for a deeper look." Annie Gottlieb has another view of *Gather Together in My Name.* In her *New York Times Book Review* article, Gottlieb states that Angelou "writes like a song, and like the truth. The wisdom, rue and humor of her storytelling are borne on a lilting rhythm completely her own, the product of a born writer's senses nourished on black church singing and preaching, soft mother talk and salty street talk, and on literature."

The year 1981 brought the publication of *The Heart of a Woman,* a book that "covers one of the most exciting periods in recent African and Afro-American history," according to Adam David Miller in *Black Scholar.* Miller refers to the era of civil rights marches, the emergence of Dr. Martin Luther King, Jr., and Malcolm X, and the upheaval in Africa following the assassination of the Congolese statesman Patrice Lumumba. The 1960s see Angelou active in civil rights both in America and abroad; at the same time she enters into a romance with African activist Vusumzi Make, which dissolves when he cannot accept her independence or even promise fidelity. In a *Dictionary of Literary Biography* piece on Angelou, Lynn Z. Bloom considers *The Heart of a Woman* the author's best work since *I Know Why the Caged Bird Sings:* "Her enlarged focus and clear vision transcend the particulars and give this book a fascinating universality of perspective and psychological depth that almost matches the quality of [Angelou's first volume]. . . . Its motifs are commitment and betrayal."

Washington Post Book World critic David Levering Lewis also sees a universal message in *The Heart of a Woman*. "Angelou has rearranged, edited, and pointed up her coming of age and going abroad in the world with such just-rightness of timing and inner truthfulness that each of her books is a continuing autobiography of Afro-America. Her ability to shatter the opaque prisms of race and class between reader and subject is her special gift," he says. To Bloom, "it is clear from [this series of autobiographies] that Angelou is in the process of becoming a self-created Everywoman. In a literature and a culture where there are many fewer exemplary lives of women than of men, black or white, Angelou's autobiographical self, as it matures through successive volumes, is gradually assuming that exemplary stature."

In her fifth autobiographical work, *All God's Children Need Traveling Shoes,* Angelou describes her four-year stay in Ghana, "just as that African country had won its independence from European colonials," according to Barbara T. Christian in the *Chicago Tribune Book World.* Christian indicates that Angelou's "sojourn in Africa strengthens her bonds to her ancestral home even as she concretely experiences her distinctiveness as an Afro-American."

This book has also received praise from reviewers. Wanda Coleman in the *Los Angeles Times Book Review* calls it "a thoroughly enjoyable segment from the life of a celebrity," while Christian describes it as "a thoughtful yet spirited account of one Afro-American woman's journey into the land of her ancestors." In Coleman's opinion, *All God's Children Need Traveling Shoes* is "an important document drawing more much needed attention to the hidden history of a people both African and American."

Angelou draws on her faith, spirituality, and experiences in her volume of autobiographical essays entitled *Wouldn't Take Nothing for My Journey Now.* Robert Fulghum remarks in *Washington Post Book World* that "everything about Maya Angelou is transcendental in its outreach. From the resources of a specific life, specific gender, color, social place, landscape and vocation, she writes of elemental human experiences, concerns and values."

Angelou's poetry consists mainly of short lyrics with musical rhythms and conventional vocabulary that treat social issues pertaining to African Americans, qualities that make them popular with young readers but open to criticism by some commentators. Her five previously published volumes of poetry were republished in a single volume in 1994 as *The Complete Collected Poems of Maya Angelou.* Sandra Cookson

writes in *World Literature Today:* "Angelou's poems . . . bear witness to the trials of black people in this country. . . . [T]he poems are generous in their directness, in the humor Angelou finds alongside her outrage and pain, in their robust embrace of life. They are truly 'celebratory.'"

Among Angelou's children's books are works that marry words with illustrations. Thandi is the eight-year-old narrator of *My Painted House, My Friendly Chicken, and Me.* The Ndebele girl tells the reader about things special to her in her South Africa village, which are illustrated with photographs and drawings. *Life Doesn't Frighten Me* is a book strong in aural and visual symbolism. The poems, illustrated by Jean-Michel Basquiat paintings, express courage to face one's fears. In *School Library Journal,* Jane Marino calls the book "a powerful exploration of emotion and its expression through the careful blend of words and arts." Paul B. Janeczko says in *Washington Post Book World* that "it is the juxtaposition of the [harsh] paintings with Angelou's comforting, affirming poem that makes this powerful book a success."

BIOGRAPHICAL/CRITICAL SOURCES:

BOOKS

Angelou, Maya, *I Know Why the Caged Bird Sings,* Random House, 1970.

Angelou, *Gather Together in My Name,* Random House, 1974.

Angelou, *Singin' and Swingin' and Gettin' Merry Like Christmas,* Random House, 1976.

Angelou, *The Heart of a Woman,* Random House, 1981.

Angelou, *All God's Children Need Traveling Shoes,* Random House, 1986.

Black Literature Criticism, Gale (Detroit), 1991.

Bloom, Harold, *Maya Angelou's "I Know Why the Caged Bird Sings,"* Chelsea House (New York City), 1995.

Contemporary Literary Criticism, Gale, Volume 12, 1980, Volume 35, 1985, Volume 64, 1991, Volume 77, 1993.

Contemporary Theatre, Film, and Television, Gale, Volume 10, 1992.

Dictionary of Literary Biography, Volume 38: *Afro-American Writers after 1955: Dramatists and Prose Writers,* Gale, 1985.

Elliot, Jeffrey M., editor, *Conversations with Maya Angelou,* University of Mississippi Press, 1989.

Jelinek, Estelle C., editor, *Women's Autobiography: Essays in Criticism,* Indiana University Press, 1980, pp. 180-205.

King, Sarah E., *Maya Angelou: Greeting the Morning,* Millbrook Press (Brookfield, CT), 1994.

Lisandrelli, Elaine Slivinski, *Maya Angelou: More than a Poet,* Enslow Publishers (Springfield, NJ), 1996.

Pettit, Jayne, *Maya Angelou: Journey of the Heart,* Lodestar Books (New York City), 1996.

Shapiro, Miles, *Maya Angelou,* Chelsea House (New York City), 1994.

Spain, Valerie, *Meet Maya Angelou,* Random House (New York City), 1994.

PERIODICALS

Architectural Digest, May, 1994, p. 32.

Black American Literature Forum, Summer, 1990, pp. 221-35, 257-76.

Black Scholar, January-February, 1977, pp. 44-53; summer, 1982.

Black World, July, 1975.

Booklist, September 1, 1993, p. 2.

Chicago Tribune, November 1, 1981.

Chicago Tribune Book World, March 23, 1986.

Christian Century, November 23, 1988, pp. 1031-2.

College Literature, October, 1991, pp. 64-79.

Current Biography, February, 1994, p. 7.

Detroit Free Press, May 9, 1986.

Entertainment Weekly, October 21, 1994, p. 83.

Harper's, November, 1972; March, 1994, p. 28.

Harvard Educational Review, November, 1970.

Ladies' Home Journal, May, 1976.

Library Journal, November 1, 1994, p. 88; October 1, 1995, p. 102; November 1, 1995, p. 82.

Los Angeles Times, May 29, 1983.

Los Angeles Times Book Review, April 13, 1986; August 9, 1987; October 3, 1993.

Ms., January, 1977.

National Review, November 29, 1993, p. 76.

New Republic, July 6, 1974; October 3, 1994, p. 10.

Newsweek, March 2, 1970.

New York Times, February 25, 1970; December 5, 1992, p. L8.

New York Times Book Review, June 16, 1974; December 19, 1993, p. 18.

Observer (London), April 1, 1984; November 28, 1993; December 17, 1995.

Publishers Weekly, September 20, 1993, p. 71; September 12, 1994, p. 91.

School Library Journal, March, 1994, p. 224; May, 1994, p. 144; October, 1994, p. 107.

Southern Living, January, 1994, p. 66.

Time, March 31, 1986.

Times (London), September 29, 1986.

Times Literary Supplement, February 17, 1974, June 14, 1985, January 24, 1986.

Tribune Books, September 11, 1994, p. 8.

Village Voice, July 11, 1974, October 28, 1981.

Washington Post, October 13, 1981.

Washington Post Book World, October 4, 1981; June 26, 1983; May 11, 1986; September 15, 1993, p 4; December 5, 1993, p. 25.

World Literature Today, August, 1995, p. 800.*

*   *   *

ANSTEY, F.
   See GUTHRIE, Thomas Anstey

*   *   *

ANYIDOHO, Kofi   1947-

PERSONAL: Born July 25, 1947, in Wheta, Ghana; son of Abla (a poet; maiden name, Adidi) Anyidoho; married Akosua Anyidoho; children: Akua, Akofa. *Education:* Attended Accra Teacher Training College; Advanced Teacher Training College, diploma; University of Ghana, B.A., 1977; Indiana University, M.A., 1980; University of Texas, Austin, Ph.D., 1983.

ADDRESSES: Office—Department of English, University of Ghana, P.O. Box 25, Legon, Near Accra, Ghana.

CAREER: Poet, critic and educator, 1978—. Worked as elementary school teacher in Nkoranza, Ghana; teacher at Achimota School and E. P. Secondary School, Itohoe; University of Ghana, Legon, began as lecturer in English, became associate professor of English literature, and director of School of Performing Arts. Visiting scholar at Cornell University, 1990-91, and Indiana University; external examiner for University of Botswana and University of Sierra Leone. Member of board of directors of W. E. B. Du Bois Memorial Center for Pan African Culture in Accra, Ghana.

AWARDS, HONORS: Valco Fund Literary Award for Poetry, 1976, for *Brain Surgery;* BBC "Arts and Africa" Poetry Award, 1981; named Poet of the Year in Ghana, 1984; Davidson Nicol Prize; Langston Hughes Prize; Fania Kruger fellowship.

WRITINGS:

POETRY

Elegy for the Revolution, Greenfield Review Press (New York City), 1978.

A Harvest of Our Dreams, with Elegy for the Revolution, Heinemann (London), 1984.

Earthchild, with Brain Surgery, Woeli (Accra, Ghana), 1985.

Kofi Anyidoho, Ghana, W. Pieterse in Poezie (Rotterdam, Netherlands), 1991.

Ancestral Logic and Caribbean Blues, Africa World Press (Trenton, NJ), 1993.

EDITOR

(With Kojo Yankah) *Our Soul's Harvest: An Anthology of Ghanian Poetry,* Bagdala (Yugoslavia), 1978.

(With others, and contributor) *Cross Rhythms: Occasional Papers in African Folklore,* Volume 1, Trickster Press (Bloomington, IN), 1983.

(With Abioseh Porter, Daniel Racine, and Janice Spleth) *Interdisciplinary Dimensions of African Literature: Annual Selected Papers, African Literature Association,* Three Continents Press (Washington, DC), 1985.

(With Peter Porter and Musaemura Zimunya) *The Fate of Vultures: New Poetry of Africa,* Heinemann (Oxford), 1989.

The Word behind Bars and the Paradox of Exile, foreword by Jane I. Guyer, Northwestern University Press (Evanston, IL), 1997.

OTHER

The Pan-African Ideal in Literatures of the Black World, Ghana Universities Press (Accra), 1989.

Contributor of essays to anthologies, including *New West African Literature,* edited by Kolawole Ogungbesan, Heinemann, 1979; *Toward Defining the African Aesthetic,* edited by Lemuel Johnson and others, Three Continents Press, 1982; *Peuples du Golfe du Benin,* edited by Francois de Medeiros, Karthala (Paris), 1984; *African Literary Studies: The Present State/L'Etat present,* edited by Stephen Arnold, Three Continents Press, 1985; *African Literature in Its Social and Political Dimensions,* edited by Eileen Julien and others, Three Continents Press, 1986; *Black Culture and Black Consciousness in Literature,* edited by Ernest N. Emenyonu, Heinemann (Ibadan), 1987; *Literature and National Consciousness,* edited by

Emenyonu, Heinemann (Ibadan), 1989; *Dictionary of Literary Biography,* Volume 117: *Twentieth- Century Caribbean and Black African Writers, First Series,* edited by Bernth Lindfors and Reinhard Sander, Gale (Detroit), 1992; and *West African Association for Commonwealth Literature and Language Studies Lecture Series 1,* edited by Emenyonu, New Generation Books (Owerri), 1992. Also author of introduction, *Music for a Dream Dance,* by Kobina Eyi Acquah, Asempa (Accra), 1989.

Contributor to periodicals, including *Asemka, Black Orpheus, Crosscurrent, French Review, Greenfield Review, Legacy, Legon Journal of the Humanities, Research in African Literatures,* and *Ufahamu.* Editor of *Legacy;* served as guest editor of *Matato.*

ADAPTATIONS: A dramatization of a selection of Anyidoho's poems, *Earthchild and Other Poems,* was produced by Abibigromma, School of Performing Arts, University of Ghana, 1986.

SIDELIGHTS: Kofi Anyidoho is among the most notable African poets writing in English. A. N. Mensah, writing in the *Dictionary of Literary Biography,* affirmed that since the appearance of Anyidoho's first volume of verse in 1978, "with each subsequent published collection, he has strengthened his claim to preeminence among African poets of English expression." Mensah added, "As a poet he belongs to that select group of verbal craftsmen and craftswomen who have successfully fashioned a distinctively African voice out of that ambivalent legacy of colonialism, the English language."

Anyidoho was born in 1947 in Ghana. He trained in education and eventually taught at elementary and secondary schools. He also attended the University of Ghana, earning an undergraduate degree in 1977, and then traveled to the United States, continuing his education at Indiana University, where he received a master's degree in 1980, and the University of Texas, Austin, from which he secured a doctorate in 1983. He has since become an associate professor at the University of Ghana and served as director of its School of Performing Arts.

Anyidoho began publishing poems while he was still training as a teacher. In 1976 he obtained a poetry award from the Valco Fund for the unpublished collection that became *Brain Surgery.* Mensah reported that the significance of this volume "is in what it reveals of the poet's first real attempts to find his voice as an African poet writing in English." Among the poems in this collection, which was eventually published in 1985 as *Earthchild, with Brain Surgery,* are "A Dirge for Christmas," in which he describes his homeland as a barren, despairing place devoid of hope; "Go Tell Jesus," wherein he protests what he sees as the annihilation of African values through Christian colonialism; and "The Rise of the New Poet," in which he advocates social change and a renewal of African culture. Mensah called *Brain Surgery* "a precocious collection that promises the coming harvest."

In 1978 Anyidoho realized his first publication, *Elegy for the Revolution,* a somber work that reflects the instability of Ghana's political climate. The collection includes such poems as "Oath of Destiny," wherein he decries what he perceives to be the destructively hypocritical nature of Christians; and the title work, where he considers the death of a student who was shot during a worker's strike at the University of Ghana. Another key poem in the volume is "Dance of the Hunchback," in which Anyidoho depicts a pitiful cripple who struggles to maintain his dignity despite his physical disadvantage and the consequent scorn from others. Mensah, writing in the *Dictionary of Literary Biography,* lauded "Dance of the Hunchback" as "an excellent illustration of Anyidoho's ability to express in English the mood of the traditional dirge."

In his next poetry book, *A Harvest of Our Dreams, with Elegy for the Revolution,* published in 1984, Anyidoho produced a dynamic series of poems relating the turbulent times in Ghana, where the military had assumed control in 1979. Derek Wright commented in *Contemporary Poets* on the volume's "raw vigor and imagistic power," while Mensah reported in the *Dictionary of Literary Biography* that the poems are well served by being read aloud. The collection includes "Mythmaker," wherein Anyidoho laments Ghana's violent times and writes "our scholars, deployed from campuses / into ghost communal farms, / walked the streets at dawn like zombies / peddling posters proclaiming final obsequies / for the revolution that went astray." Mensah stated that "Mythmaker" is intended "to be heard rather than merely read silently to oneself."

In his ensuing poetry collection, *Earthchild, with Brain Surgery,* Anyidoho collects several poems written during his time in the United States. Derek Wright, in his *Contemporary Poets* profile of Anyidoho, noted that a "vague, earth-mysticism . . . becomes more pronounced" in this volume, and he affirmed that the "energetic particularity of his earlier work . . . gives

way to the stately abstractions of time, space, eternity, and the soul." Wright found this mysticism exemplified in "Sunbird," where Anyidoho writes, "Here we stand naked in fields of snow / drinking pollen from breasts of shooting stars."

Ancestral Logic and Caribbean Blues, which followed *Earthchild, with Brain Surgery,* shows Anyidoho in a more self-reflective vein. Mensah declared that the volume's recurrent theme is "the assessment of the black man's place in history and contemporary world affairs; his bonds with other races . . . and his need to refuse to cooperate in his own marginalization." Mensah was especially impressed with "The Taino in 1992," which relates the genocide of the Taino-Arawaks tribe, an indigenous people of the Americas, and "Domingo Blues," which reflects on tourists who are oblivious to the abuses endured by the surrounding natives of the Caribbean. Mensah asserted that these works "are among Anyidoho's finest and most mature poems."

BIOGRAPHICAL/CRITICAL SOURCES:

BOOKS

Contemporary Poets, St. James Press (Detroit), 1996.

Dictionary of Literary Biography, Volume 157: *Twentieth-Century Caribbean and Black African Writers, Third Series,* Gale (Detroit, MI), 1995.

Talking with African Writers: Interviews with African Poets, Playwrights and Novelists, edited by Wilkinson, Currey (London), 1992.

Wilkinson, Jane, *Orpheus in Africa: Fragmentation and Renewal in the Work of Four African Writers,* Bulzoni Editore (Rome), 1990.

PERIODICALS

Africa (Rome), December 1988, pp. 543-73.

African Concord, April 2, 1990, p. 40.

African Literature Association Bulletin, vol. 17, no. 3, 1991, pp. 7-8.

Legon Journal of the Humanities, no. 3, 1987, pp. 67-78.*

*   *   *

ATKINS, Russell 1926-

PERSONAL: Born February 25, 1926, in Cleveland, OH; son of Perry Kelly and Mamie Atkins. *Educa-*

tion: Attended Cleveland School of Art (now Cleveland Institute of Art), 1943-44, and Cleveland Institute of Music, 1944-45; private music study, 1950-54. *Politics:* "Nothing particular." *Religion:* None.

ADDRESSES: Home—1005 Grand Ave., Cleveland, OH 44104.

CAREER: Editor, writer and composer; cofounder and editor of *Free Lance* magazine, 1950-79. Publicity manager and assistant to director, Sutphen School of Music (of National Guild of Community Music Schools), Cleveland, OH, 1957-60; lecturer, Poets and Lecturers Alliance, 1963-65; writing instructor, Karamu House, 1972-86; writer in residence, Cuyahoga Community College, summer, 1973; instructor, Ohio Program in the Humanities, 1978. Affiliated with Iowa Workshop, University of Iowa, 1953-54. Member, Artists-in-Schools Program of Ohio Arts Council and National Endowment for the Arts, 1973—. Participant, Bread Loaf Writers' Conference, 1956; member of literary advisory panel, Ohio Arts Council, 1973-76; member, Cleveland State University Poetry Forum; member, Coordinating Council of Literary Magazines of National Endowment for the Arts. Consultant to Karamu Writers Conference, 1971, and to other writers' conferences and workshops; consultant to WVIZ-TV, 1969-72, and to Cleveland Board of Education, 1972-73.

MEMBER: Committee of Small Magazine Editors and Publishers, Poets League of Greater Cleveland (member of board of trustees).

AWARDS, HONORS: Honorary Ph.D., Cleveland State University, 1976; individual artist grant, Ohio Arts Council, 1978.

WRITINGS:

POETRY

A Podium Presentation, Poetry Seminar Press, 1960.
Phenomena, Free Lance Poets and Prose Workshop, Wilberforce University, 1961.
Objects, Hearse Press, 1963.
Objects 2, Renegade Press, 1963.
Heretofore, Paul Breman (London), 1968.
Presentations, Podium Press, 1969.
Sounds and Silences: Poetry for Now, edited by Richard E. Peck, Delacorte (New York City), 1969.
Here in The, Cleveland State University Poetry Center (Cleveland, OH), 1976.
Celebrations, edited by Arnold Adoff, Follett, 1977.

Whichever, Free Lance Press, 1978.
Juxtapositions: A Manifesto, privately printed, 1991.

MUSICAL COMPOSITIONS

(With Langston Hughes and Hale Smith) *Elegy* (poetry set to music), Highgate Press, 1968.
Objects (for piano), Free Lance Press, 1969.

Also composer of unpublished musical works.

OTHER

Psychovisual Perspective for 'Musical' Composition (chapbook; musical theory), Free Lance Press, 1958.
Two by Atkins: The Abortionist and The Corpse: Two Poetic Dramas to Be Set to Music, Free Lance Press, 1963.
The Nail, to Be Set to Music (poetic libretto), Free Lance Press, 1970.
Maleficium (short stories), Free Lance Press, 1971.
Poetry: An Introduction through Writing, edited by Lewis Turco, Reston Prentice-Hall (Reston, VA), 1972.
"By Yearning and by Beautiful" (poem set to music by Hale Smith), first performed at Lincoln Center for the Performing Arts, New York City, 1986.
Letters to America, edited by Jim Daniels, Wayne State University Press (Detroit), 1995.

Contributor to anthologies, including *Silver Cesspool,* edited by Adelaide Simon, Renegade Press, 1964; *Penguin Book of Verse,* edited by Willemien Vroom, Penguin (England), 1973; *Poems, 1978-1983,* edited by Robert Fox, Ohio Arts Council, 1983; *80 on the 80s: A Decade's History in Verse,* edited by Robert McGovern and Joan Baranow, Ashland Poetry Press (Ashland, OH), 1990; *An Ear to the Ground: An Anthology of Contemporary American Poetry,* edited by Marie Harris and Kathleen Aguero, University of Georgia Press (Athens), 1991; *Beyond the Reef* (children's reader), Houghton (Boston), 1991; *Anthology of Western Reserve Literature,* edited by David R. Anderson and Gladys Haddad, Kent State University Press (Kent, OH), 1992; *Scarecrow Poetry: The Muse in Post-Middle Age,* edited by Robert McGovern and Stephen Haven, Ashland Poetry Press, 1994.

Contributor of poems and articles to *New York Times Book Review, Beloit Poetry Journal, Western Review, Minnesota Quarterly, Hearse, Poetry Now, The Gamut,* and numerous other journals.

WORK IN PROGRESS: Revising and adding to "Spyrytuals," for piano; a volume of poetry delineating stylistic development in technique as "meaning."

SIDELIGHTS: Russell Atkins' writing, says Ronald Henry High in the *Dictionary of Literary Biography,* distinguishes him as "one of the leading experimental figures of the past three decades." His works in music and poetic drama, according to High, place him firmly in the avant-garde. An early exponent of concrete poetry—in which the arrangement or design of the words takes precedence over the words themselves—Atkins' "starkly dramatic handling of such subjects in poetry as dope addiction, sexual aberration, necrophilia, and abortion went beyond the academic reserve of the early 1950s," High continues. His theory of psychovisualism, the critic states, is based on Gestalt hypotheses which study the formation of patterns, and "explains how we perceive the nonverbal 'high and low' in music," by recognizing the function of the brain in understanding music.

Atkins's education in the arts—from his parents' and teachers' encouragement in music, painting, drawing, poetry, and play writing in elementary school through his own extracurricular study of literary classics and poetry in high school—led to the publication of his early work in the late 1940s and early 1950s in journals including *Experiment, View,* and the *Beloit Poetry Journal.* At age twenty-six he co-founded *Free Lance,* which High describes as "probably the oldest black-owned literary magazine, although white writers were included in its pages." Contributors included Langston Hughes, Rose Greene, Beatrice Augustus, Helen Collins, and Vera Steckler, and the journal found audiences in the United States, England, Scotland, Ireland, France, Denmark, Sweden, and Australia. High notes that *Free Lance* "was established as Cleveland's avant-garde periodical" and was "significant in that it played a major part in the development of ideas and techniques of the New American poetry."

Atkins published two plays in 1963: *The Abortionist* and *The Corpse. The Abortionist* concerns a doctor who seeks revenge against a colleague by performing a violent abortion on the colleague's daughter; in *The Corpse* a widow visits her husband's tomb each year to watch his body decay. High comments: "Until the 'theatre of the absurd,' which was imported from Europe, established itself in the 1960s, Atkins' little poem-plays were avant-garde and unique on the American scene. A nude woman being given an abortion on the stage was not commonplace in the 1950s;

neither was a widow kneeling in a mausoleum fondling her husband's bones and skull ordinary American playfare."

Atkins' poetry collection *Phenomena* was published in 1961. "The works had all been written in the middle '50s," Atkins wrote in an essay for *Contemporary Authors Autobiography Series* (*CAAS*). "When the book was published. . ., it went (as expected) unnoticed by the establishment." "*Phenomena* and especially [the poem] 'Of Angela' struck some readers as 'explicitly crude,'" High observes. "The entire book has an unsettling mood which overtakes the reader, even when the meaning escapes one. Strangely enough, the book was a remarkable forecast of the 1960s' themes: nudity, four-letter words, police brutality, and sexual aberration."

Atkins published several more collections of poetry in the 1960s, and began the next decade with *The Nail* and *Maleficium,* both published in *Free Lance* in 1970 and 1971 respectively. *The Nail,* a poetic libretto adapted from the short story by Pedro Antonio de Alarcon, tells of a judge who is unaware that the fugitive murderess he is hunting is his lover. *Maleficium,* according to High, "is a series of twenty short stories, many of which portray their characters as having an underlying viciousness." An example is "Story No. 2," in which a young man writes to his mother to tell her of his crimes, including murder and rape. Two more poetry collections appeared in the 1970s: *Here in The* in 1976 and *Whichever* in 1978. High comments, "Unfortunately, there has been no critical review of [*Here in The*]; however, the poems are written in a refined, mellower style, yet within the experimental framework which so characteristically flavors Atkins's writing." Of *Whichever,* High observes, "The poems in this volume are on a wide range of subjects . . . but seem to be less complex than poems in previous collections; however, there is no doubt that the works flow from Atkins's pen. There is freshness and excitement in each one of them."

"Unfortunately, there has been little critical comment on Atkins's works, which could be due in part to their daring nature," High concludes. "Also, his works are disparate and perhaps need to be collected in order for readers to recognize him as one of the most innovative forces in poetry of the past thirty years. . . . As more people get familiar with Atkins, his approach to literary expression will be better appreciated and more fully understood. As his work is more performed and more read, as it garners more critical attention and documentation, his genius will come to be recognized in the United States as it is in Europe."

BIOGRAPHICAL/CRITICAL SOURCES:

BOOKS

Contemporary Authors Autobiography Series, Volume 16, Gale, 1992.
Dictionary of Literary Biography, Volume 41: *Afro-American Poets Since 1955,* Gale, 1985.

PERIODICALS

Free Lance (special Russell Atkins issue), number 14, 1970-71.*

*   *   *

ATTAWAY, William (Alexander)   1911-1986

PERSONAL: Born November 19, 1911, in Greenville, MS; died of heart failure, June 17, 1986, in Los Angeles, CA; son of William S. (a physician) and Florence Parry (a schoolteacher) Attaway; married Frances Settele, December 28, 1962; children: a son and a daughter. *Education:* University of Illinois, B.A., 1936.

CAREER: Novelist, playwright, screenwriter, and songwriter. Worked briefly as a seaman, salesman, labor organizer, and actor, touring in *You Can't Take It With You.* Writer and consultant for the film industry.

WRITINGS:

Carnival (play), produced at University of Illinois, Urbana, 1935.
Let Me Breathe Thunder (novel), Doubleday, 1939.
Blood on the Forge (novel), Doubleday, 1941, reprinted, 1993.
Hear America Singing, Lion, 1967.
One Hundred Years of Laughter (television script), American Broadcasting Company (ABC-TV), 1967.

Contributing editor, *Calypso Song Book,* McGraw-Hill, 1957. Contributor to periodicals, including *Challenge* and *Tiger's Eye.* Arranger of songs for Harry Belafonte.

SIDELIGHTS: Despite the versatility which he demonstrated during his career, William Attaway is remembered primarily as a chronicler of the great migration of black Americans from the South to the industrial North during the 1920s and 1930s. He displayed his knowledge of this topic in his second and last novel, *Blood on the Forge,* published in 1941. Attaway's abandonment of this promising genre at age thirty led to a distinguished career as a composer and arranger and as a television and film writer.

Attaway moved with his parents from Greenville, Mississippi, to Chicago, Illinois, when he was about ten years old and attended public schools in that city. His father and mother, a physician and schoolteacher respectively, wanted him to enter a profession. Instead he decided to become an auto mechanic and attended a vocational high school. But his plans changed when a teacher introduced him to the work of Langston Hughes. Influenced by both Hughes's poetry and his sister, Broadway actress Ruth Attaway, he began to write plays and short stories while still in secondary school.

Attaway's parents persuaded him to enroll at the University of Illinois in Urbana, but he dropped out after the death of his father and traveled as a hobo for two years. He worked at a series of jobs—seaman, salesman and labor organizer—before returning to the university where his play *Carnival* was produced in 1935, a year before his graduation in 1936. During this time Attaway befriended Richard Wright, whose popular success with the book *Native Son* would later eclipse that of Attaway's novels.

After receiving his B.A. degree Attaway moved to New York City, where he wrote his first novel, *Let Me Breathe Thunder,* at age twenty-five. He worked at a string of odd jobs while writing and was touring in George S. Kaufman and Moss Hart's *You Can't Take It With You* when he received word that the novel would be published. Attaway abandoned acting and began his second novel with the help of a grant from the Julius Rosenwald Fund.

Let Me Breathe Thunder is the story of two white hoboes, Ed and Step, who take under their wing an innocent Mexican boy who joins the men in their wanderings. Stanley Young in the *New York Times* wrote: "All the emotions of the book are direct and primitive, and the bareness of the speech cuts the action to lean and powerful lines." Young compared the story and characters to those featured in American novelist John Steinbeck's *Of Mice and Men;* other reviewers compared Attaway's style to that of American author Ernest Hemingway.

The central event of *Let Me Breathe Thunder* is the tragic corruption of the young waif, Hi-Boy, by the two jaded older men. Although the men have a tender love for the boy, the starkness of the world they all inhabit is played out in the relationships among the trio. Step takes Hi-Boy to a prostitute and during this visit—to prove his courage to the older man—Hi-Boy stabs himself in the hand. The wound ultimately kills him, but not before his moral downfall at a ranch where he shoots animals and lies to cover up Step's seduction of a young woman. The novel is replete with Biblical metaphor, as in Hi-Boy's hand wound and the setting of apple orchards at the ranch.

Attaway's second novel, like his first, is based on personal experience. *Blood on the Forge* is the story of three black brothers, Big Mat, Chinatown, and Melody Moss, who are sharecroppers in Kentucky until Big Mat badly beats a white overseer for insulting his mother. The three men are then forced to accept an offer to travel in a sealed boxcar to a Pennsylvania steel mill, where their attempts to build new lives fail tragically. Attaway addressed not only obstacles faced by blacks in the South and North, but a tapestry of dilemmas created by the ripening industrial age: early struggles to organize labor, the uneasy mixture of Irish, Italian and Eastern European immigrants, and the spiritual damage done to men made to work like machines.

The sharply drawn characters of the brothers illustrate three aspects of the human soul, three ways of responding to the uprooting and loss of family which were common in the 1930s. Melody symbolizes the artist, with his love of blues guitar. Chinatown loves pleasure; his greatest pride is his own gold tooth. Big Mat is a man torn from the outset—he is deeply religious, an assiduous student of the Bible who hopes to become a preacher someday, but his wife Hattie's six miscarriages together with the destruction wreaked by this new, rootless life gnaw at him.

The noise of the steel mill renders mute the strings of Melody's guitar, and he falls in love with a young Mexican-American prostitute named Anna. But she is drawn instead to Mat, whose strength at a dog fight brawl saved her from harm. Mat, having learned from afar that Hattie lost her seventh baby, gives up on his dream of sending for her to join him, and he moves in with Anna. He begins to erupt in random anger, beating Anna severely, and he is arrested for the at-tempted murder of a man. Melody badly damages his hand in an accident, and an explosion which kills several other workers blinds Chinatown.

The town is troubled by mounting racial tensions. White union workers are threatening to strike. Steel bosses pit one man against another by preparing to bring in more southern black men, who will work for cheaper wages. In this milieu, the final tragedies of the three brothers unfold.

Attaway's second novel was even more lauded than his first. Wrote critic Milton Rugoff in the *New York Herald Tribune Books:* "[Attaway] writes of the frustration and suffering of his people and does so with crude power and naked intensity." Drake de Kay of the *New York Times Book Review* similarly praised the work of this twenty-nine-year-old author: "[*Blood on the Forge*] is a starkly realistic story involving social criticism as searching as any to be found in contemporary literature."

Literary commentators speculated on why Attaway never wrote another novel. Despite the acclaim of reviewers and their anticipation of his next book, *Blood on the Forge* did not sell many copies. In a twist of irony, Attaway's success may have been eclipsed by that of his friend Wright. Wright's novel, *Native Son*—published just one year before *Blood on the Forge*—met with both critical and popular success. Some critics suggested that mainstream America may have been prepared at that time for only one black novelist to burst on the scene.

When *Blood on the Forge* was reprinted in 1969, the country, now widely examining its own racist past, was perhaps more prepared to receive it. In 1987 Cynthia Hamilton wrote in *Black American Literature Forum:* "*Blood on the Forge* is a masterpiece of social analysis." The complexity of Attaway's characters and their story have stood up well to the passage of half a century since its initial publication.

Attaway's two later books were both about music. *Calypso Song Book* was a collection of songs and *Hear America Singing* describes for young readers the history of American popular music. In addition, Attaway composed songs and arranged tunes for his friend, Harry Belafonte.

Attaway took time out from his writing career to march for African American voting rights in Selma, Alabama, in 1965. Among other projects, he subsequently completed *One Hundred Years of Laughter,* a special on the comedy of blacks which aired on ABC-TV in 1967. Attaway was engaged by the producers of *The Man,* the film based on Irving Wallace's novel about a senator who becomes the first black president of the United States. The script, however, was deemed too rough and Attaway was released from the project; Rod Serling later received credit on the final screenplay.

After living for a decade with his family in Barbados, Attaway returned to California where he continued to write scripts for film, radio, and television. He was writing *The Atlanta Child Murders* script when he suffered a heart attack which resulted in his death in Los Angeles, California, on June 17, 1986.

BIOGRAPHICAL/CRITICAL SOURCES:

BOOKS

Black Literature Criticism, Volume 1, Gale, 1992.
Dictionary of Literary Biography, Volume 76: *Afro-American Writers, 1940-1955,* Gale, 1988.
Margolies, Edward, *Native Sons: A Critical Study of Twentieth-Century Negro American Authors,* Lippincott, 1968.
Young, James O., *Black Writers of the Thirties,* Louisiana State University Press, 1973.

PERIODICALS

Black American Literature Forum, spring-summer, 1987, pp. 147-63.
CLA Journal, June, 1972, pp. 459-64.
Library Journal, March 1, 1993.
New York Herald Tribune Books, August 24, 1941, p. 8.
New York Times Book Review, June 25, 1939, p. 7; August 24, 1941, pp. 18, 20.
Publishers Weekly, March 30, 1970, p. 66.
Saturday Review of Literature, July, 1939, p. 20.
Studies in Black Literature, spring, 1973, pp. 1-3.*

*   *   *

AUBERT, Alvin (Bernard) 1930-

PERSONAL: Born March 12, 1930, in Lutcher, LA; son of Albert (a laborer) and Lucille (Roussel) Aubert; married second wife, Bernadine Tenant (a teacher and librarian), October 29, 1960; children: (first marriage) Stephenie; (second marriage) Miriam,

Deborah. *Education:* Southern University, B.A., 1959; University of Michigan, A.M., 1960; further graduate study at University of Illinois, 1963-64, 1966-67.

ADDRESSES: Home—18234 Parkside Ave., Detroit, MI 48221. *Office*—Department of English, Wayne State University, Detroit, MI 48202.

CAREER: Southern University, Baton Rouge, LA, instructor, 1960-62, assistant professor, 1962-65, associate professor of English, 1965-70; State University of New York College at Fredonia, associate professor, 1970-74, professor of English, 1974-79; Wayne State University, Detroit, MI, professor of English, 1980-92, professor emeritus, 1992—. Visiting professor at University of Oregon, summer, 1970. Member of board of directors, Coordinating Council of Literary Magazines, 1982-86. Has given readings of his poems at educational institutions.

MEMBER: Modern Language Association of America, National Council of Teachers of English, African Heritage Studies Association, National Council for Black Studies.

AWARDS, HONORS: Woodrow Wilson fellow, 1959; National Endowment for the Arts grants, 1973, 1981; Bread Loaf Writers' Conference scholarship, 1978; Coordinating Council of Literary Magazines Editors fellow, 1979; Annual Callaloo award, 1989.

WRITINGS:

Against the Blues (poems), Broadside Press (Detroit), 1972.
Feeling Through (poems), Greenfield Review Press (Greenfield Center, NY), 1976.
A Noisesome Music (poems), Blackenergy South Press, 1979.
South Louisiana: New and Selected Poems, Lunchroom Press (Grosse Pointe Farms, MI), 1985.
Home from Harlem (play; adapted from *The Sport of the Gods* by Paul Laurence Dunbar; produced in Detroit, 1986), Obsidian Press (Detroit), 1986.
If Winter Come: Collected Poems, 1967-1992, Carnegie Mellon University Press (Pittsburgh), 1994.
Harlem Wrestler, and Other Poems, Michigan State University Press (East Lansing), 1995.

CONTRIBUTOR TO ANTHOLOGIES

J. W. Corrington and Miller Williams, editors, *Southern Writing in the Sixties: Poetry,* Volumes I and

II, Louisiana State University Press (Baton Rouge), 1966.

M. Williams, editor, *Contemporary Poetry in America,* Random House (Garden City, NY), 1973.

Arnold Adoff, editor, *Celebrations: An Anthology of Black Poetry,* Follett, 1979.

Edward Field, editor, *A Geography of Poets: An Anthology of the New Poetry,* Bantam (New York City), 1979.

Guy Owen and Mary C. Williams, editors, *Contemporary Southern Poetry,* Louisiana State University Press, 1979.

Williams, editor, *Patterns of Poetry: An Encyclopedia of Forms,* Louisiana State University Press, 1986.

Leon Stokesburg, editor, *The Made Thing: An Anthology of Contemporary Southern Poetry,* University of Arkansas Press, 1987.

Also author, with Von Washington, of one-act play *Decision at Detroit.* Contributor to *Contemporary Novelists,* 1972, and *Writers of the English Language,* 1979. Contributor of poems, articles, and reviews to literary journals, including *Nimrod, Black American Literature Forum, American Poetry Review, Black World, Prairie Schooner, Black Scholar, Iowa Review, Journal of Black Poetry, American Book Review,* and *Epoch.* Book reviewer, *Library Journal,* 1972-74. Advisory editor of *Drama and Theatre,* 1973-75, *Black Box,* 1974—, *Gumbo,* 1976-78, and *Callaloo,* 1977—; founding editor of *Obsidian: Black Literature in Review,* 1975-85; senior editorial consultant, *Obsidian II,* 1985—.

SIDELIGHTS: Alvin Aubert has distinguished himself both as a skilled poet and as the founder of *Obsidian,* a literary journal for African-American literature. During the 1960s and early 1970s, Aubert's relatively unpolitical poetic voice diverged from prevailing literary trends in the African-American community. While most black writers of the time were producing highly charged social commentary and polemical verse, Aubert tended toward objective description and dispassionate personal reflection in his work.

A native of Louisiana, Aubert recalls the people and setting of his upbringing in the Deep South within his verse. The youngest of seven children, Aubert dropped out of high school at age fourteen, worked for several years in a local general store, then enlisted in the Army during the Korean War. In 1955, after obtaining a general equivalency diploma, he enrolled at Southern University in Baton Rouge, Louisiana, where he earned a bachelor's degree in English with a minor in French. While at Southern, Aubert also

cultivated his interest in poetry and began to publish his work in major African-American periodicals such as *Black World, Black Scholar, Black American Literature Forum,* and the *Journal of Black Poetry.*

Aubert went on to complete a master's degree at the University of Michigan and, in 1960, returned to Southern University as an instructor where he remained for the next decade. During this time, he also attended graduate classes in sixteenth- and seventeenth- century English literature at the University of Illinois in Urbana. In 1970 he moved to the State University of New York at Fredonia where, five years later, he launched the publication of *Obsidian.* With a distinguished editorial board including Kofi Awooner, Ernest Gaines, Blyden Jackson, Saunders Redding, and Darwin Turner, *Obsidian* was well received and became an important outlet for African-American literature and criticism.

Aubert's first volume of poetry, *Against the Blues,* appeared in 1972. As Norman Harris notes in *Dictionary of Literary Biography,* "the kind of poetry that Aubert wrote was not especially in vogue with many younger black poets who still adhered to the black aesthetic that emerged from the black arts movement of the 1960s." Even the most political poem in the volume, "Nat Turner in the Clearing," evinces quiet patience and optimism regarding social change. Most of the brief, direct poems describe isolated moments of personal experience through anecdote and the idiom of black speech and expression, similar to blues lyrics. Here, as John M. Reilly writes in *Contemporary Poets,* "the typicality provided by linguistic patterns acknowledged by poet and reader serves as subject for creative imagination." Commenting on "Whispers in a Country Church," another poem from *Against the Blues,* Harris writes, "This poem, like several others in the volume, achieves universality through its personalized portrayal of a relatively local incident of random gossip."

In 1975 Aubert produced a second volume of poetry, *Feeling Through.* In this collection, as Harris observes, "Aubert broadens the personal dimension to include more cultural heroes and heroines as themes for poems." For example, "Dayton Dateline" is a paean to black poet Paul Laurence Dunbar and "Notes for a Future Memory" reflects on the death of Malcolm X. In *Feeling Through* Aubert attempts to address some of the contemporary social issues that received little attention in his earlier work. In "Black Aesthetic," he reverses the imagery of Marcel Duchamp's Cubist painting "Nude Descending a

Staircase" to illustrate the ascent of the black man. Aubert also experiments with syntax and punctuation in this poem, using all lowercase letters and inserting periods mid-sentence to create a staccato effect. According to Reilly, Aubert's "characteristic syntactic economy" is "almost elliptical."

Commenting on his own writing, Aubert wrote: "I grew up in a small Mississippi River town about midway between New Orleans and Baton Rouge, and this locale—particularly the river—and the people, but especially the people, continue to motivate me; not to the extent of my finding out exactly who and what they were (if that were possible), but of initiating and maintaining a spiritual connection. Most representative of this influence are poems of mine such as 'Baptism,' 'Remembrance,' 'Feeling Through,' 'Spring 1937,' 'Father, There,' 'South Louisiana,' 'The Housemovers,' 'All Singing in a Pie,' and 'Fall of '43.' I like to think that all of my writings explore various aspects of the human situation and celebrate human existence at a particular and consequently universal level."

Despite Aubert's generally undidactic approach, as Reilly notes, "The texts of his poems maintain a continuity with Afro-American tradition by simulation and innovation that become a commentary on the richness of his sources and evidence of authentic re-creation." Aubert produced additional volumes of poetry during the 1980s and 1990s. His work has also appeared in numerous literary journals and several anthologies. As Harris concludes, "Alvin Aubert's work as a poet, editor, and publisher places him at the center of creative activity among African-Americans during the last three decades."

BIOGRAPHICAL/CRITICAL SOURCES:

BOOKS

Contemporary Authors Autobiography Series, Volume 20, Gale (Detroit), 1994.
Contemporary Poets, sixth edition, St. James Press (Detroit), 1996.
Dictionary of Literary Biography, Volume 41: *Afro-American Poets since 1955,* Gale, 1985.

PERIODICALS

American Book Review, March, 1987.
Black American Literature Forum, fall, 1987.
Buffalo Courier Express, June 8, 1973.
Callaloo, fall, 1990, p. 915.

Kliatt, November, 1972.
Virginia Quarterly Review, summer, 1994, p. 98.*

*   *   *

AWOONOR, Kofi (Nyidevu) 1935-
(George Awoonor-Williams)

PERSONAL: Name originally George Awoonor-Williams; born March 13, 1935, in Wheta, Ghana; son of Atsu E. (a tailor) and Kosiwo (Nyidevu) Awoonor; married; children: three sons, one daughter, including Sika, Dunyo, Kalepe. *Education:* University College of Ghana, B.A., 1960; University College, London, M.A., 1970; State University of New York at Stony Brook, Ph.D., 1972. *Religion:* Ancestralist. *Avocational interests:* Politics, jazz, tennis, herbal medicine (African).

ADDRESSES: Home—P.O. Box C 536, Accra, Ghana. *Agent*—Harold Ober Associates, Inc., 40 East 49th St., New York, NY 10017.

CAREER: University of Ghana, Accra, lecturer and research fellow, 1960-64; Ghana Ministry of Information, Accra, director of films, 1964-67; State University of New York at Stony Brook, assistant professor of English, 1968-75; University of Texas, Austin, visiting professor, 1972-73; arrested for suspected subversion, charged with harboring a subversionist, served one year in prison in Ghana, 1975-76; University of Cape Coast, Cape Coast, Ghana, professor of English, beginning 1976; Ghana ambassador to Brazil in Brasilia, with accreditation to Argentina, Uruguay, Venezuela, Surinam, and Guyana, 1983-88; Ghana ambassador to Cuba, 1988-90; Ghana ambassador to the United States, 1990-94.

MEMBER: African Studies Association of America.

AWARDS, HONORS: Longmans fellow, University of London, 1967-68; Fairfield fellow; Gurrey Prize and National Book Council award, both 1979, for poetry.

WRITINGS:

(Under name George Awoonor-Williams) *Rediscovery, and Other Poems,* Northwestern University Press, 1964.
(Editor, with G. Adali-Mortty) *Messages: Poems from Ghana,* Heinemann (London), 1970, Humanities, 1971.

Ancestral Power [and] *Lament* (plays), Heinemann, 1970.

This Earth, My Brother: An Allegorical Tale of Africa, Doubleday, 1971.

Night of My Blood (poetry), Doubleday, 1971.

Ride Me, Memory (poetry), Greenfield Review Press, 1973.

(Translator) *Guardians of the Sacred Word: Ewe Poetry,* Nok Publishers, 1974.

The Breast of the Earth: A Survey of the History, Culture, and Literature of Africa South of the Sahara, Doubleday, 1975.

The House by the Sea (poetry), Greenfield Review Press, 1978.

(Translator) *When Sorrow-Song Descends on You* (chapbook), edited by Stanley H. Barkan, Cross-Cultural Communications, 1981.

Fire in the Valley: Ewe Folktales, Nok Publishers, 1983.

The Ghana Revolution: Background Account from a Personal Perspective (essays), Oasis Publishers, 1984.

Until the Morning After: Selected Poems, 1963-1985, Greenfield Review Press, 1987.

Alien Corn (novel), Oasis Publishers, 1988.

Ghana: A Political History from Pre-European to Modern Times, Sedco Publishing, 1990.

Comes the Voyager at Last: A Tale of Return to Africa, Africa World Press, 1992.

Latin American and Caribbean Notebook, Africa World Press (Trenton, NJ),1992.

Africa: The Marginalized Continent, Woeli Publishers' Services (Accra), 1994.

Contributor to *Africa Report* and *Books Abroad.* Associate editor of *Transition,* 1967-68, *World View,* and *Okike.*

SIDELIGHTS: Noted African poet Kofi Awoonor is also an accomplished novelist, critic, and playwright, as well as Ghana's ambassador to Brazil. Interested in the language of his people, he incorporates the vernacular into much of his poetry. His first book, *Rediscovery,* was "very much an effort to move the oral poetry from which I learnt so much into perhaps a higher literary plane, even if it lost much in the process," explains Awoonor in *Contemporary Authors Autobiography Series (CAAS).* Jon M. Warner, writing in the *Library Journal,* notes that "his themes are soul-deep in African identity: his voice is gentle and painfully honest; and he perceives things we perhaps know but have never heard said so concisely."

Awoonor was born in the anteroom of his grandfather's hut in Wheta, Ghana, in 1935. "Childhood, as it must have been for many Africans of my generation and peasant background, was for me a time of general poverty and deprivation, even though it was relieved by the warmth of a doting extended family," writes Awoonor in an essay in *CAAS.* Raised with his mother's family, he remembers his maternal grandparents "most lovingly," and his grandmother appears in several pieces of poetry as a focus of childhood memories. As a baby, Awoonor was baptized a Presbyterian due to his father's beliefs, but was raised in traditional African towns with shrines to the thunder gods Yeve and So. He grew up hearing the native stories, war songs, and funeral dirges of his people in their own language, which later influenced his poetry. At the age of nine, Awoonor was sent away to school and boarded with a wealthy family for whom he worked as a domestic servant. The rest of his education followed a similar pattern, always boarding and learning away from home. Eventually, Awoonor's studies took him to England and the United States. "But it is Wheta, my natal village, which remains my spiritual hometown," declares Awoonor in *CAAS.*

In *This Earth, My Brother: An Allegorical Tale of Africa,* Awoonor explores the journey of one man from his native African roots into the contemporary Western world. "It is a journey not only across distances, but also across several hundred years," describes *New York Times Book Review* contributor Jan Carew. From school inspections and the King's Birthday parade to ritual circumcision and home-made gin, Awoonor's protagonist, a lawyer called Amamu, remembers growing up in West Africa. As an adult, Amamu returns to the continent and becomes disillusioned with what he sees around him. "The novel is part visionary, part realistic . . . [with] a strongly biographical element," comments a reviewer in *Choice.* The "sketches add up to a mysterious but not wholly opaque portrait of Amamu and an account of his disintegration," judges a critic in the *Times Literary Supplement.* Carew, however, writes: "The author seems intoxicated not only with life but with language. His words assault the senses and the intellect simultaneously. Images leap from the pages . . . and yet the book is serious and its message of new and positive forces emerging from the African chaos, unmistakable."

Night of My Blood contains most of the poems in *Rediscovery,* along with new compositions that reveal Awoonor's assimilation of his poetic forebears and increasing mastery of his own style and voice. While maintaining the tone of the traditional dirge, Awoonor evinces hope for redemption in life, rather than in death, with growing urgency. Incorporating the rhythmic patterns of drums and dance, as well as the technique of collage, the poetry of *Night of My Blood* aspires to reunite fragmentary elements of human experience in images and songs that allude to the colonial history of modern Ghana and the African continent as a whole. Commenting on the poem "Hymn to My Dumb Earth" from *Night of My Blood,* Kofi Anyidoho writes in *Dictionary of Literary Biography,* "The various contradictions built into the independence experience are effectively captured in the various voices, tunes, and rhythms. The Christian, biblical voice blends into an uneasy harmony with the rhythms of jazz, dirge, and political demagoguery."

With *Ride Me, Memory* Awoonor continued many of his earlier themes, drawing attention to the suffering of African people throughout the world and in the United States through the notable incorporation of elements of African-American music and literature. In this volume Awoonor also experimented with insult poems, or *halo,* derived from traditional contests of public humiliation in which opposing groups or tribes organized to taunt each other in musical performances and verse. In these pieces Awoonor directly confronts and challenges the object of his scorn with humorous derision directed at his adversary's physical appearance and morality. Though returning to the dirge mode at the end of the collection, *Ride Me, Memory,* reveals a further broadening of Awoonor's artistic concerns and stylistic devices. As Anyidoho notes, "*Ride Me, Memory,* as a whole, moves away from the lament into other areas of the oral-poetry tradition and into artistic traditions outside Awoonor's immediate ancestral heritage."

Awoonor takes a closer look at his African heritage in *The Breast of the Earth: A Survey of the History, Culture, and Literature of Africa South of the Sahara.* A collection of essays based on his lectures, *The Breast of the Earth* covers precolonial and colonial history as well as oral tradition and literature, and includes commentary on contemporary African writing. Several critics noted that Awoonor concentrates on literature—"a term which he interprets broadly and constantly relates to other concepts"—using history and culture as "backdrops," as R. Kent Rasmussen notes in the *Library Journal.* As a survey, *The Breast of the Earth* is "necessarily selective and subject to broad generalization," remarks a reviewer in *Choice,* noting that the critical commentary will please readers because of its "perceptive intelligence and wit." Writing in *Publishers Weekly,* Albert H. Johnson judges *The Breast of the Earth* to be "wide-ranging

and sensitive," and Rasmussen comments that the book's "significance lies in [Awoonor's] broad, integrative approach."

Until the Morning After: Selected Poems, 1963-85, is a collection of Awoonor's poetry from his earliest published work, *Rediscovery,* through *The House by the Sea* and contains nine previously unpublished poems. He also includes a brief autobiographical appendix explaining his relationship with language and writing. *Until the Morning After* traces Awoonor's development as a poet, from his early lyrics about nature and heritage, through his "transitional" period formed by his experiences in a Ghanaian prison, to his more politically oriented, contemporary verse. The title of the volume is based on Awoonor's belief in the basic human need for freedom, and two of his later poems explain that freedom is so important that death will be postponed "until the morning after" it is finally achieved. "The selection is judicious," comments M. Tucker in *Choice,* judging that "this volume is a fine tribute to a significant . . . African poet." *World Literature Today* contributor Richard F. Bauerle concludes: "*Until the Morning After* should increase Awoonor's already large audience and further enhance his international stature."

Awoonor once wrote: "The written word came almost as if it had no forebears. So my poetry assays to restate the oral beginnings, to articulate the mysterious relation between the WORD and the magical dimensions of our cognitive world. I work with forces that are beyond me, ancestral and ritualized entities who dictate and determine all my literary endeavors. Simply put, my work takes off from the world of all our aboriginal instincts. It is for this reason that I have translated poetry from my own society, the Ewes, and sat at the feet of ancient poets whose medium is the voice and whose forum is the village square and the market place."

BIOGRAPHICAL/CRITICAL SOURCES:

BOOKS

Awoonor, Kofi, *Ghana: A Political History from Pre-European to Modern Times,* Sedco Publishing, 1990.

Contemporary Authors Autobiography Series, Volume 13, Gale (Detroit), 1991.

Dictionary of Literary Biography, Volume 117: Twentieth-Century Caribbean and Black African Writers, Gale, 1992.

PERIODICALS

Ariel, January, 1975.
Choice, July, 1971, p. 682; July/August, 1975, p. 690; April, 1988, p. 1253.
Library Journal, June 1, 1971, p. 1984; April 15, 1975, p. 763.
New York Times Book Review, April 2, 1972, p. 7.
Publishers Weekly, February 24, 1975, p. 110.
Times Literary Supplement, March 24, 1972, p. 325.
World Literature Today, autumn 1988, p. 715.*

*   *   *

AWOONOR-WILLIAMS, George
  See AWOONOR, Kofi (Nyidevu)

*   *   *

AYITTEY, George B. N. 1945-

PERSONAL: Born in 1945, in Ghana. *Education:* University of Manitoba, Ph.D.

ADDRESSES: Agent—c/o St. Martin's Press, 175 Fifth Ave., Rm. 1715, New York, NY 10010. *E-mail*—ayittey@american.edu.

CAREER: Economist, writer. American University, Washington, DC, visiting associate professor.

MEMBER: The Free African Foundation (president).

WRITINGS:

Indigenous African Institutions, Transnational Publishers (Ardsley-on-Hudson, NY), 1991.
Africa Betrayed, St. Martin's Press (New York City), 1992.
Africa in Chaos, St. Martin's Press (New York City), 1998.

Contributor to other works concerning African social and economic policy, including *The Collapse of Development Planning,* edited by Peter J. Boettke, 1994; *Perpetuating Poverty: The World Bank, the IMF and the Developing World,* the Cato Institute, 1994; *The Somali Crisis: Time for an African Solution,* the Cato Institute, 1994; *Economic Reform Today,* 1995; *Structural Adjustment,* edited by Danil Schydlowsky, 1995; *Africana Printing,* 1997; and *Issues and Trends in Contemporary African Politics,* 1997. Contributor to magazines, including *Newsweek,* the *Los Angeles Times, The World & I,* and *Newsday.*

SIDELIGHTS: George B. N. Ayittey, professor of economics at American University, has written several books about African economic, political, and social issues. His first book, *Indigenous African Institutions,* offers a critical examination of African institutions—government, legal, economic, and community-based—with discussion on how these institutions evolved under colonial rule and their prospects for becoming more effective institutions for the African people. Ayittey stresses the need for Africans to work through these institutions in problem solving, drawing on their own cultural roots rather than relying on Western countries to determine their policies. R. A. Corby reviewing the book for *Choice,* while faulting "inaccuracies" in the "inadequate" maps, did find the research "solid and impressive in its scope."

Ayyitey's second book, *Africa Betrayed,* focuses on post-colonial African leaders, their unscrupulous behavior, and the lack of effective administration of African political institutions. In reviewing *Africa Betrayed* for the *Christian Science Monitor,* David C. Walters wrote that "Ayittey scolds the world press for being soft on black African tyrants. South Africa's racist regime is the target of countless articles and television reports . . . Yet the press rarely reports that in Sudan, Mauritania, and other African states, several million black Africans are still held as slaves." Ayittey wrote that tyranny is condoned "as long as the tyrants are black." He relates how many African leaders have "pillaged" billions of dollars from their countries and hidden the funds in foreign bank accounts. The sums he describes in some cases are equal to the national debts of the countries. A reviewer for *Publishers Weekly* said that Ayittey lays the blame on "African elites, foreign powers and even black Americans for aiding and abetting black dictators."

Africa in Chaos examines African political and economic institutions and discusses their corruption by poor leadership. *Washington Times* reviewer Michael Maren wrote that "the book provides a thousand ways to say 'fiasco.' Debt. War. Starvation. Corruption. Especially corruption. It sounds depressing, and it is. But, at its core, this is an optimistic book . . . because of its relentless message that Africans can solve Africa's problems. The failure of Western aid programs in Africa indicates only that the programs were misguided, not that the continent is hopeless." Ayittey's position is that external agencies favor external solutions, ensuring a flow of money through charities such as CARE or World Vision, creating jobs and prestige for these groups. Maren wrote that "to admit that Africa's problems are internal would be an admission of their own powerless position to do anything about it. Their interests are just the opposite. . . . And once again, Africans suffer." *New York Times* reviewer Jeremy Harding called Ayittey "a writer who takes no prisoners—especially when it comes to Africa's postcolonial leaders." According to Harding, externalists "see Africa's difficulties arising from 'Western imperialism, the slave trade, an unjust international economic system and exploitation' by multinational corporations. Internalists, including Ayittey, believe the heart of the matter is incompetent leadership and the establishment of defective political and economic systems in postcolonial Africa. Ayittey believes that the huge debts not approved by the people should be forgiven and that the African people should not be burdened with the result of 'extravagant lending policies.'"

BIOGRAPHICAL/CRITICAL SOURCES:

PERIODICALS

Choice, May, 1992, p. 1447-1448; October, 1995, pp. 245-257.

Christian Science Monitor, March 15, 1993, p. 11.

Library Journal, January, 1998, pp. 119-120.

Los Angeles Times, June 14, 1998, p. M-2.

Newsday, March 31, 1998, p. A37.

New York Times, March 8, 1998.

Publishers Weekly, November 23, 1992, p.46.

Reference & Research Book News, April, 1992, p. 13; September, 1993, p. 30.

Village Voice, September 14, 1993, p. 97.

Wall Street Journal, March 17, 1993, p. A12.

Washington Times, March 15, 1995, p.25.*

B

BAKER, Calvin 1972-

PERSONAL: Born in 1972. *Education:* Graduate of Amherst College.

ADDRESSES: Office—c/o *People Weekly,* Time & Life Bldg., Rockefeller Center, New York, NY 10020. *Agent*—St. Martin's Press, Inc., 175 Fifth Ave., New York, NY 10010.

CAREER: Writer. *People* magazine, New York City, staff writer.

WRITINGS:

Naming the New World (novel), St. Martin's/Wyatt (New York City), 1997.

Contributor of articles to periodicals, including *People;* contributor of book reviews to periodicals, including *Library Journal, Publishers Weekly,* and *Time.*

SIDELIGHTS: Calvin Baker's debut novel, *Naming the New World,* is a slim volume that takes its reader on a generational journey spanning four hundred years and winding from Africa to the United States and back again. The book opens with a young man's search for his name, which he finds is River. Like a river, the man's own life story flows throughout the novel, appearing periodically as the author gives voices to other characters, including Ampofo, a slave newly arrived in the Americas, Tom, a plantation owner's biracial son who feels displaced in a segregated world, and others. Baker eventually advances his story to contemporary times, as Richard, a government agent, returns to Africa after the death of his brother in Vietnam to connect with himself and his past. Similarly, another character, Robert, searches within to make sense of his feelings of intense love coupled with disgust for his brother, a drug addict who murdered a young man to punish him for a petty offense. "The haunting tales [are] often intertwined and the stories conveyed in heart-wrenching prose," commented *Booklist* reviewer Kathleen Hughes.

Baker's novel met with mixed reviews. Lise Funderberg, writing in the *New York Times Book Review* for example, described *Naming the New World* as "too lean," but found that "when Mr. Baker spends time with a character . . . , his writing can be taut and evocative." A *Publishers Weekly* critic issued only praise for Baker's effort, proclaiming: "Through his virtuostic creation of myriad ancestral voices, Baker proves himself a powerful new male voice in African American literature." Acknowledging that the shifts of time, place and character might make the novel somewhat inaccessible to some readers, Mosi Reeves of the *Quarterly Black Review of Books* nonetheless added, "After each of the narrators has spoken, they clearly emerge as varied faces of the African in America. . . . [it] is an elegantly written novel that encourages contemplation of the Middle Passage and its effects."

Baker, a graduate of Amherst College, grew up in Chicago. He said in an interview for the online source, *The Book Report,* that inspiration for his novel came from a year he spent living in Kenya alongside the nomadic Samburu tribe. There he witnessed a coming of age ritual for the boys of the tribe in which they journey to lands that their ancestors had inhabited, imbuing a sense of history in their lives. "This made me wonder: what would happen if someone made that arduous journey alone? To go back to the place you came from—to discover your past," commented Baker. "My book is about grappling with the relationship between Africa and America, history and modernity. . . . I see it as one continuous line—the exploration of the machinations of history which go into the making of America—the things that are carried and the things that are lost."

BIOGRAPHICAL/CRITICAL SOURCES:

PERIODICALS

Booklist, January 1 & 15, 1997, p. 815.
Library Journal, January, 1997, p. 141.
New York Times Book Review, March 23, 1997.
Publishers Weekly, November 25, 1996, p. 56.
Time, March 3, 1997, p. 78.

OTHER

The Book Report, http://www.bookwire.com/TBR/First-Look/read.Review$4826, 1997.
Quarterly Black Review of Books, http://www.bookwire.com/QBR/Fiction/read.Review$4085, 1995.*

*   *   *

BAMBARA, Toni Cade   1939-1995
   (Toni Cade)

PERSONAL: Surname originally Cade, name legally changed in 1970; born March 25, 1939, in New York, NY; died of colon cancer, December 9, 1995; daughter of Helen Brent Henderson Cade; children: Karma (daughter). *Education:* Queens College (now Queens College of the City University of New York), B.A., 1959; University of Florence, studied at Commedia dell'Arte, 1961; student at Ecole de Mime Etienne Decroux in Paris, 1961, New York, 1963; City College of the City University of New York, M.A., 1964; additional study in linguistics at New York University and New School for Social Research. Also attended Katherine Dunham Dance Studio, Syvilla Fort School of Dance, Clark Center of Performing Arts, 1958-69, and Studio Museum of Harlem Film Institute, 1970.

CAREER: Free-lance writer and lecturer. Social investigator, New York State Department of Welfare, 1959-61; director of recreation in psychiatry depart-ment, Metropolitan Hospital, New York City, 1961-62; program director, Colony House Community Center, New York City, 1962-65; English instructor in Seek Program, City College of the City University of New York, New York City, 1965-69, and in New Careers Program of Newark, NJ, 1969; assistant professor, Livingston College, Rutgers University, New Brunswick, NJ, 1969-74; visiting professor of African-American studies, Stephens College, Columbia, MO, 1975; Atlanta University, visiting professor, 1977, research mentor and instructor, School of Social Work, 1977, 1979. Founder and director of Pamoja Writers Collective, 1976-85. Production artist-in-residence for Neighborhood Arts Center, 1975-79, Stephens College, 1976, and Spelman College, 1978-79. Production consultant, WHYY-TV, Philadelphia, PA. Conducted numerous workshops on writing, self-publishing, and community organizing for community centers, museums, prisons, libraries, and universities. Lectured and conducted literary readings at many institutions, including the Library of Congress, Smithsonian Institute, Afro-American Museum of History and Culture, and for numerous other organizations and universities. Humanities consultant to New Jersey Department of Corrections, 1974, Institute of Language Arts, New York Institute for Human Services Training, 1978, and Emory University, 1980. Art consultant to New York State Arts Council, 1974, Georgia State Arts Council, 1976, 1981, National Endowment for the Arts, 1980, and the Black Arts South Conference, 1981.

MEMBER: National Association of Third World Writers, Screen Writers Guild of America, African-American Film Society, Sisters in Support of South African Sisterhood.

AWARDS, HONORS: Peter Pauper Press Award, 1958; John Golden Award for Fiction from Queens College (now Queens College of the City University of New York), 1959; Theatre of Black Experience award, 1969; Rutgers University research fellowship, 1972; Black Child Development Institute service award, 1973; Black Rose Award from Encore, 1973; Black Community Award from Livingston College, Rutgers University, 1974; award from the National Association of Negro Business and Professional Women's Club League; George Washington Carver Distinguished African-American Lecturer Award from Simpson College; *Ebony's* Achievement in the Arts Award; Black Arts Award from University of Missouri; American Book Award, 1981, for *The Salt Eaters;* Best Documentary of 1986 Award from Pennsylvania Association of Broadcasters and Documentary Award from National Black Programming Consortium, both 1986, for *The Bombing of Osage;* nominated for Black Caucus of the American Library Association Literary Award, 1997, for *Deep Sightings and Rescue Missions: Fiction, Essays, and Conversations.*

WRITINGS:

Gorilla, My Love (short stories), Random House (New York City), 1972, reprinted, Vintage (New York City), 1992.

The Sea Birds Are Still Alive (short stories), Random House, 1977.

The Salt Eaters (novel), Random House, 1980, reprinted, Vintage, 1992.

(Author of preface) Cecelia Smith, *Cracks,* Select Press, 1980.

(Author of foreword) Cherrie Moraga and Gloria Anzaldua, editors, *This Bridge Called My Back: Radical Women of Color,* Persephone Press (Watertown, MA), 1981.

(Author of foreword) *The Sanctified Church: Collected Essays by Zora Neale Hurston,* Turtle Island (Berkeley, CA), 1982.

If Blessing Comes (novel), Random House, 1987.

Raymond's Run (juvenile; also see below), Creative Education (Mankato, MN), 1990.

Deep Sightings and Rescue Missions: Fiction, Essays, and Conversations, edited by Toni Morrison, Pantheon, 1996.

SCREENPLAYS

Zora, produced by WGBH-TV, 1971.

The Johnson Girls, produced by National Educational Television, 1972.

Transactions, produced by School of Social Work, Atlanta University, 1979.

The Long Night, produced by American Broadcasting Co., 1981.

Epitaph for Willie, produced by K. Heran Productions, Inc., 1982.

Tar Baby (based on Toni Morrison's novel), produced by Sanger/Brooks Film Productions, 1984.

Raymond's Run, produced by Public Broadcasting System, 1985.

The Bombing of Osage, produced by WHYY-TV, 1986.

Cecil B. Moore: Master Tactician of Direct Action, produced by WHYY-TV, 1987.

(With others) *W. E. B. Du Bois: A Biography in Four Voices,* produced by Public Broadcasting System, 1997.

EDITOR

(And contributor, under name Toni Cade) *The Black Woman: An Anthology,* New American Library (New York City), 1970.

(And contributor) *Tales and Stories for Black Folks,* Doubleday (New York City), 1971.

(With Leah Wise) *Southern Black Utterances Today,* Institute for Southern Studies (Durham, NC), 1975.

CONTRIBUTOR

Addison Gayle, Jr., editor, *Black Expression: Essays by and about Black Americans in the Creative Arts,* Weybright, 1969.

Jules Chametsky, editor, *Black and White in American Culture,* University of Massachusetts Press, 1970.

Ruth Miller, *Backgrounds to Blackamerican Literature,* Chandler Publishing, 1971.

Janet Sternburg, editor, *The Writer on Her Work,* Norton (New York City), 1980.

Paul H. Connolly, editor, *On Essays: A Reader for Writers,* Harper (New York City), 1981.

Florence Howe, editor, *Women Working,* Feminist Press (Old Westbury, NY), 1982.

Mari Evans, editor, *Black Women Writers (1950-1980): A Critical Evaluation,* Doubleday, 1984.

Baraka and Baraka, editors, *Confirmations,* Morrow (New York City), 1984.

Claudia Tate, editor, *The Black Writer at Work,* Howard University Press (Washington, DC), 1984.

Contributor to *What's Happnin, Somethin Else,* and *Another Eye,* all readers published by Scott, Foresman, 1969-70. Contributor of articles and book and film reviews to *Massachusetts Review, Negro Digest, Liberator, Prairie Schooner, Redbook, Audience, Black Works, Umbra, Onyx,* and other periodicals. Guest editor of special issue of *Southern Exposure,* summer, 1976, devoted to new southern black writers and visual artists.

ADAPTATIONS: Three of Bambara's short stories, "Gorilla, My Love," "Medley," and "Witchbird," have been adapted for film.

SIDELIGHTS: Toni Cade Bambara was a well-known and respected civil rights activist, professor of English and of African-American studies, editor of anthologies of black literature, and author of short stories and novels. Throughout her career, Bambara used her art to convey social and political messages about the welfare of the African-American community and of African-American women especially. According to Alice A. Deck in the *Dictionary of Literary Biography,* the author was "one of the best representatives of the group of Afro-American writers who, during the 1960s, became directly involved in the cultural and sociopolitical activities in urban communities across the country." However, Deck pointed out that "Bambara is one of the few who continued to work within the black urban communities (filming, lecturing, organizing, and reading from her works at rallies and conferences), producing imaginative reenactments of these experiences in her fiction. In addition, Bambara established herself over the years as an educator, teaching in colleges and independent community schools in various cities on the East Coast." For Bambara, the duties of writer, social activist, teacher, and even student combined to influence her perspective. "It's a tremendous responsibility—responsibility and honor—to be a writer, an artist, a cultural worker . . . whatever you call this vocation," she explained in an interview in *Black Women Writers at Work.* "One's got to see what the factory worker sees, what the prisoner sees, what the welfare children see, what the scholar sees, got to see what the ruling-class mythmakers see as well, in order to tell the truth and not get trapped." Bambara made it her objective to describe the urban black community without resorting to stereotype or simplification. A deep understanding of the complexities of African-American life informs all of her work.

Born Toni Cade in New York City in 1939, Bambara credited her mother with providing a nurturing environment for her budding creativity. Growing up in Harlem, Bedford-Stuyvesant, and Queens, and in Jersey City, New Jersey, she was encouraged to explore her imagination, to daydream, and to follow her inner motives. She published her first short story at the age of 20, a piece called "Sweet Town." The name "Bambara," which she later appended to her own, was discovered as part of a signature on a sketchbook she found in her great-grandmother's trunk. Bambara received a bachelor's degree in theater arts and English from Queens College in 1959. In the following decade she served as a social worker and director of neighborhood programs in Harlem and Brooklyn, published short stories in periodicals, earned a master's degree and spent a year at the Commedia dell'Arte in Milan, Italy, and directed a theater program and various publications funded by the City College Seek program. This wide variety of experience inevitably

found its way into her fiction and influenced her political sensibility as well.

Bambara's first book-length publication was *The Black Woman: An Anthology,* a collection of essays that was envisioned as a response to the so-called "experts" who had been conducting studies on the status of black American women. One of the first of its kind, the anthology provided an arena for black women's opinions not only on racism and sexism but also on a wealth of other equally important issues. She followed this work with *Tales and Stories for Black Folks,* a sourcebook intended to stimulate an interest in storytelling among young African-American students. The two anthologies and her first volume of fiction, *Gorilla, My Love,* were all published while she held a professorship at Livingston College, a division of Rutgers University. Bambara's first two books of fiction, *Gorilla, My Love* and *The Sea Birds Are Still Alive,* are collections of her short stories. Susan Lardner remarked in the *New Yorker* that the stories in these two works, "describing the lives of black people in the North and the South, could be more exactly typed as vignettes and significant anecdotes, although a few of them are fairly long. . . . All are notable for their purposefulness, a more or less explicit inspirational angle, and a distinctive motion of the prose, which swings from colloquial narrative to precarious metaphorical heights and over to street talk, at which Bambara is unbeatable." In a review of *Gorilla, My Love,* for example, a writer remarked in the *Saturday Review* that the stories "are among the best portraits of black life to have appeared in some time. They are written in a breezy, engaging style that owes a good deal to street dialect."

A critic writing in *Newsweek* made a similar observation, describing Bambara's second collection of short stories, *The Sea Birds Are Still Alive,* in this manner: "Bambara directs her vigorous sense and sensibility to black neighborhoods in big cities, with occasional trips to small Southern towns. . . . The stories start and stop like rapid-fire conversations conducted in a rhythmic, black-inflected, sweet-and-sour language." In fact, according to Anne Tyler in the *Washington Post Book World,* Bambara's particular style of narration is one of the most distinctive qualities of her writing. "What pulls us along is the language of her characters, which is startlingly beautiful without once striking a false note," declared Tyler. "Everything these people say, you feel, ordinary, real-life people are saying right now on any street corner. It's only that the rest of us didn't realize it was sheer poetry they were speaking."

In terms of plot, Bambara tended to avoid linear development in favor of presenting "situations that build like improvisations of a melody," according to a *Newsweek* reviewer. Commenting on *Gorilla, My Love,* Bell Gale Chevigny observed in the *Village Voice* that despite the "often sketchy" plots, the stories were always "lavish in their strokes—there are elaborate illustrations, soaring asides, aggressive subplots. They are never didactic, but they abound in far-out common sense, exotic home truths." Numerous reviewers also remarked on Bambara's sensitive portrayals of her characters and the handling of their situations, portrayals marked by an affectionate warmth and pride. Laura Marcus wrote in the *Times Literary Supplement* that Bambara "presents black culture as embattled but unbowed. . . . Bambara depicts black communities in which ties of blood and friendship are fiercely defended." Deck expanded on this idea, remarking that "the basic implication of all of Toni Cade Bambara's stories is that there is an undercurrent of caring for one's neighbors that sustains black Americans. In her view the presence of those individuals who intend to do harm to people is counterbalanced by as many if not more persons who have a genuine concern for other people." C. D. B. Bryan admired this expression of the author's concern for other people, declaring in the *New York Times Book Review* that "Bambara tells me more about being black through her quiet, proud, silly, tender, hip, acute, loving stories than any amount of literary polemicizing could hope to do. She writes about love: a love for one's family, one's friends, one's race, one's neighborhood and it is the sort of love that comes with maturity and inner peace." According to Bryan, "all of Bambara's stories share the affection that their narrator feels for the subject, an affection that is sometimes terribly painful, at other times fiercely proud. But at all times it is an affection that is so genuinely genus *homo sapiens* that her stories are not only black stories." In 1980, Bambara published her first novel, a generally well-received work entitled *The Salt Eaters.* Written in an almost dream-like style, *The Salt Eaters* explores the relationship between two women with totally different backgrounds and lifestyles brought together by a suicide attempt by one of the women. John Leonard, who describes the book as "extraordinary," wrote in the *New York Times* that *The Salt Eaters* "is almost an incantation, poem-drunk, myth-happy, mud- caked, jazz-ridden, prodigal in meanings, a kite and a mask. It astonishes because Toni Cade Bambara is so adept at switching from politics to legend, from particularities of character to prehistorical song, from LaSalle Street to voodoo. It is as if she jived the very stones to groan." In a *Times Literary Supplement* review, Carol Rumens stated that *The Salt Eaters* "is a hymn to individual courage, a sombre message of hope that has confronted the late twentieth-century pathology of racist violence and is still able to articulate its faith in 'the dream'." And John Wideman noted in the *New York Times Book Review:* "In her highly acclaimed fiction and in lectures, Bambara emphasizes the necessity for black people to maintain their best traditions, to remain healthy and whole as they struggle for political power. *The Salt Eaters,* her first novel, eloquently summarizes and extends the abiding concerns of her previous work." After serving as writer-in-residence at Spelman College during the 1970s, Bambara relocated to Philadelphia, where she continued to write both fiction and film scripts. One of her best-known projects for film, *The Bombing of Osage,* explored a notorious incident in which the administration of Philadelphia Mayor Wilson Goode, himself an African American, used lethal force against a group of militant black citizens. The author's later books included another adult novel, *If Blessing Comes,* and a juvenile work, *Raymond's Run,* about a pair of siblings who like to run foot races. While never completely relinquishing her fiction work, however, Bambara became more and more involved with film. As she commented in *Black Women Writers at Work,* "I've always considered myself a film person. . . . There's not too much more I want to experiment with in terms of writing. It gives me pleasure, insight, keeps me centered, sane. But, oh, to get my hands on some movie equipment."

BIOGRAPHICAL/CRITICAL SOURCES:

BOOKS

Black Literature Criticism, Gale (Detroit), 1990.

Butler-Evans, Elliott, *Race, Gender, and Desire: Narrative Strategies in the Fiction of Toni Cade Bambara, Toni Morrison, and Alice Walker,* Temple University Press (Philadelphia), 1989.

Contemporary Literary Criticism, Volume 29, Gale, 1984.

Dictionary of Literary Biography, Volume 38: *Afro-American Writers after 1955: Dramatists and Prose Writers,* Gale, 1985.

Notable Black American Women, Gale, 1992.

Parker, Bell, and Beverly Guy-Sheftall, *Sturdy Black Bridges: Visions of Black Women in Literature,* Doubleday, 1979.

Prenshaw, Peggy Whitman, editor, *Women Writers of the Contemporary South,* University Press of Mississippi, 1984.

Tate, Claudia, editor, *Black Women Writers at Work,* Continuum (New York City), 1983.

PERIODICALS

Black World, July, 1973.
Books of the Times, June, 1980.
Chicago Tribune Book World, March 23, 1980.
Drum, spring, 1982.
First World, Volume 2, number 4, 1980.
Los Angeles Times, December 15, 1995, p. A51.
Los Angeles Times Book Review, May 4, 1980.
Ms., July, 1977; July, 1980.
National Observer, May 9, 1977.
Newsweek, May 2, 1977.
New Yorker, May 5, 1980.
New York Times, October 11, 1972; October 15, 1972; April 4, 1980.
New York Times Book Review, February 21, 1971; May 2, 1971; November 7, 1971; October 15, 1972; December 3, 1972; March 27, 1977; June 1, 1980; November 1, 1981.
Saturday Review, November 18, 1972; December 2, 1972; April 12, 1980.
Sewanee Review, November 18, 1972; December 2, 1972.
Times Literary Supplement, September 27, 1985.
Village Voice, April 12, 1973.
Washington Post, December 13, 1995, P. D5.
Washington Post Book World, November 18, 1973; March 30, 1980.*

*   *   *

BANDELE, Biyi 1967-
    (Biyi Bandele-Thomas)

PERSONAL: Born October 13, 1967 in Kafanchan, Nigeria. *Education:* Obafemi Awolowo University, Ile-Ife (dramatic arts), 1990.

ADDRESSES: Agent—Leah Schmidt, The Agency, 24 Pottery Ln., Holland Park, London W11 4LZ.

CAREER: Playwright and novelist. Royal Court Theatre, London, associate writer, 1992—; Talawa Theatre Company, writer-in-residence, 1994-95; Royal National Theatre Studio, resident dramatist, 1996.

MEMBER: Society of Authors, Writers Guild, PEN.

AWARDS, HONORS: International Student Playscript Competition award; Arts Council Writers Bursary; London New Play Festival award, 1994, for *Two Horsemen.*

WRITINGS:

The Man Who Came in from the Back of Beyond, Bellew (London), 1991.
The Sympathetic Undertaker and Other Dreams, Bellew (London), 1991.

PLAYS

Rain, produced in London at Taa Abantewaa, 1991.
Marching for Fausa, produced in London at Royal Court Theatre, 1993.
Two Horsemen, produced in London at Gate Theatre, 1994.
Resurrections, produced in London at Cochrane Theatre, 1994.
Death Catches the Hunter, produced in London at the BAC, 1995.
Things Fall Apart (adaptation of the novel by Chinua Achebe), produced in London at Royal Court Theatre, 1997.
Thieves Like Us, produced in London at Southwark Playhouse, 1998.

SCREENPLAYS

Not Even God Is Wise Enough, BBC, 1993.
Bad Boy Blues, BBC, 1996.

Some writings appear under the name Biyi Bandele-Thomas.

WORK IN PROGRESS: SW2, for Picador, expected in 1999; *Oroonoko,* a commission for the Royal Shakespeare Company.

SIDELIGHTS: Biyi Bandele was an award-winning playwright before the publication of his first novel, *The Man Who Came in from the Back of Beyond.* Called a "natural storyteller" by a writer for the *Independent,* he began writing while a university student in Nigeria. His plays have been performed on stage, radio, and television in the United Kingdom, and his play *Two Horseman* won several awards at the 1994 London New Play Festival.

The Man Who Came in from the Back of Beyond is, according to Richard Burns of the *Observer,* "very much a story of Africa: exotic, sprawling, overcrowded, and bizarre." It has a "complex narrative structure with framing devices and stories within stories," wrote Peter Lewis of the *Stand.* Although the novel is composed of "layers of illusions," Lewis noted that it still manages to "mediate the realities of contemporary Nigeria."

Critics praised Bandele for his intricate use of language. Richard Burns, in his *Observer* review, declared that the most striking feature of the novel to be its "lush language." He noted that Bandele uses an "erudite vocabulary throughout" so that the "writing sometimes even achieves a kind of formal perfection."

In his second novel, *The Sympathetic Undertaker and Other Dreams,* one of the dreams tells the story of the president of a fictitious African country, a figure who parallels a real Nigerian leader. The president is offered a multimillion dollar bribe to dispose of some of Europe's industrial waste, and the dream traces the president's reaction to the bribe against the backdrop of his country's political landscape. As in his first novel, critics commented that Bandele' use of language illustrated his talents as a storyteller.

BIOGRAPHICAL/CRITICAL SOURCES:

PERIODICALS

Canadian Literature, spring, 1996, p. 204.
Independent, September 28, 1994, p. 21.
Observer (London), April 14, 1991, p. 62; November 10, 1991, p. 58.
Stand (London), summer 1992, p. 74.
World Literature Today, spring, 1994, p. 204.

*   *   *

BANDELE-THOMAS, Biyi
  See BANDELE, Biyi

*   *   *

BARAKA, Amiri 1934-
  (LeRoi Jones)

PERSONAL: Born October 7, 1934, in Newark, NJ; original name Everett LeRoi Jones; name changed to Imamu ("spiritual leader") Ameer ("blessed") Baraka ("prince"); later modified to Amiri Baraka; son of Coyette Leroy (a postal worker and elevator operator) and Anna Lois (Russ) Jones; married Hettie Roberta Cohen, October 13, 1958 (divorced, August, 1965); married Sylvia Robinson (Bibi Amina Baraka), 1966; children: (first marriage) Kellie Elisabeth, Lisa Victoria Chapman; (second marriage) Obalaji Malik Ali, Ras Jua Al Aziz, Shani Isis, Amiri Seku, Ahi Mwenge. *Education:* Attended Rutgers University, 1951-52; Howard University, B.A., 1954; Columbia University, M.A. in philosophy; New School for Social Research, M.A. in German literature.

ADDRESSES: Office—Department of Africana Studies, State University of New York, Long Island, NY 11794-4340.   *Agent*—Joan Brandt, Sterling Lord Agency, 660 Madison Ave., New York, NY 10021.

CAREER: State University of New York at Stony Brook, assistant professor, 1980-83, associate professor, 1983-85, professor of African Studies, 1985—. Instructor, New School for Social Research, New York City, 1962-64; visiting professor, University of Buffalo, summer, 1964, Columbia University, fall, 1964, and 1966-67, San Francisco State University, 1967, Yale University, 1977-78, George Washington University, 1978-79, and Rutgers University, 1988. Founded *Yugen* magazine and Totem Press, 1958; co-editor and founder of *Floating Bar* magazine, 1961-63; editor of *Black Nation.* Founder and director, 1964-66, of Black Arts Repertory Theatre (disbanded, 1966); director of Spirit House (a black community theater; also known as Heckalu Community Center), 1965-75, and head of advisory group at Treat Elementary School, both in Newark. Founder, Congress of African People, 1970-76. Member, Political Prisoners Relief Fund, and African Liberation Day Commission. Candidate, Newark community council, 1968. *Military service:* U.S. Air Force, 1954-57; weather-gunner; stationed for two and a half years in Puerto Rico with intervening trips to Europe, Africa, and the Middle East.

MEMBER: All African Games, Pan African Federation, Black Academy of Arts and Letters, National Black Political Assembly (secretary general; co-governor), National Black United Front, Congress of African People (co-founder, chairperson), Black Writers' Union, League of Revolutionary Struggle, United Brothers (Newark), Newark Writers Collective.

AWARDS, HONORS: Longview Best Essay of the Year award, 1961, for "Cuba Libre"; John Whitney Foundation fellowship for poetry and fiction, 1962;

Obie Award, Best American Off-Broadway Play, 1964, for *Dutchman;* Guggenheim fellowship, 1965-66; Yoruba Academy fellow, 1965; second prize, International Art Festival, Dakar, 1966, for *The Slave;* National Endowment for the Arts grant, 1966; Doctorate of Humane Letters, Malcolm X College, Chicago, IL, 1972; Rockefeller Foundation fellow (drama), 1981; Poetry Award, National Endowment for the Arts, 1981; New Jersey Council for the Arts award, 1982; American Book Award, Before Columbus Foundation, 1984, for *Confirmation: An Anthology of African-American Women;* Drama Award, 1985; PEN-Faulkner Award, 1989; Langston Hughes Medal, 1989, for outstanding contribution to literature; Ferroni Award, Italy, and Foreign Poet Award, 1993; Playwright's Award, Black Drama Festival, Winston-Salem, NC, 1997.

WRITINGS:

UNDER NAME LEROI JONES UNTIL 1967; PLAYS

A Good Girl Is Hard to Find, produced in Montclair, NJ, at Sterington House, 1958.

Dante (one act; an excerpt from the novel *The System of Dante's Hell;* also see below), produced in New York at Off-Bowery Theatre, 1961; produced again as *The Eighth Ditch,* at the New Bowery Theatre, 1964.

Dutchman, (also see below; produced Off-Broadway at Village South Theatre, 1964; produced Off-Broadway at Cherry Lane Theater, 1964; produced in London, 1967), Faber & Faber, 1967.

The Baptism: A Comedy in One Act (also see below; produced Off-Broadway at Writers' Stage Theatre, 1964, produced in London, 1970-71), Sterling Lord, 1966.

The Toilet (also see below; produced with *The Slave: A Fable* Off-Broadway at St. Mark's Playhouse, 1964; produced at International Festival of Negro Arts at Dakar, Senegal, 1966), Sterling Lord, 1964.

J-E-L-L-O (one act comedy; also see below; produced in New York by Black Arts Repertory Theatre, 1965), Third World Press, 1970.

Experimental Death Unit #1 (one act; also see below), produced Off-Broadway at St. Mark's Playhouse, 1965.

The Death of Malcolm X (one act), produced in Newark at Spirit House, 1965, published in *New Plays from the Black Theatre,* edited by Ed Bullins, Bantam, 1969.

A Black Mass (also see below), produced in Newark at Proctor's Theatre, 1966.

Slave Ship (also see below; produced as *Slave Ship: A Historical Pageant* at Spirit House, 1967; produced in New York City, 1969), Jihad, 1967.

Madheart: Morality Drama (one act; also see below), produced at San Francisco State College, May, 1967.

Arm Yourself, or Harm Yourself, A One-Act Play (also see below; produced at Spirit House, 1967), Jihad, 1967.

Great Goodness of Life (A Coon Show) (one act; also see below), produced at Spirit House, 1967; produced Off-Broadway at Tambellini's Gate Theater, 1969.

Home on the Range (one act comedy; also see below), first produced at Spirit House, 1968; produced in New York City at a Town Hall rally, 1968.

Junkies Are Full of SHHH . . . , produced at Spirit House, 1968; produced with *Bloodrites* (also see below) Off-Broadway at Henry Street Playhouse, 1970.

Board of Education (children's play), produced at Spirit House, 1968.·

Resurrection in Life (one act pantomime) produced under the title Insurrection in Harlem, NY, 1969.

Black Dada Nihilism (one act), produced Off-Broadway at Afro-American Studio, 1971.

A Recent Killing (three acts), produced Off-Broadway at the New Federal Theatre, 1973.

Columbia the Gem of the Ocean, produced in Washington, DC, by Howard University Spirit House Movers, 1973.

The New Ark's A-Moverin, produced in Newark, February, 1974.

The Sidnee Poet Heroical, in Twenty-Nine Scenes, (one act comedy; also see below; produced Off-Broadway at the New Federal Theatre, 1975), Reed & Cannon, 1979.

S-1: A Play with Music in 26 Scenes (also see below), produced in New York at Washington Square Methodist Church, 1976, produced at Afro-American Studio, August, 1976.

(With Frank Chin and Leslie Siko) *America More or Less* (musical), produced in San Francisco at Marine's Memorial Theater, 1976.

The Motion of History (four acts; also see below), produced at New York City Theatre Ensemble, 1977.

What Was the Relationship of the Lone Ranger to the Means of Production?: A Play in One Act, (also see below; produced in New York at Ladies Fort, 1979), Anti-Imperialist Cultural Union, 1978.

Dim Cracker Party Convention, produced in New York at Columbia University, 1980.

Boy and Tarzan Appear in a Clearing, produced Off-Broadway at New Federal Theatre, 1981.
Money: Jazz Opera, produced Off-Broadway at La Mama Experimental Theatre Club, 1982.
Song: A One Act Play about the Relationship of Art to Real Life, produced in Jamaica, NY, 1983.

Also author of the play *Police,* published in *Drama Review,* summer, 1968; *Rockgroup,* published in *Cricket,* December, 1969; *Black Power Chant,* published in *Drama Review,* December, 1972; *The Coronation of the Black Queen,* published in *Black Scholar,* June, 1970; *Vomit and the Jungle Bunnies,* unpublished; *Revolt of the Moonflowers,* 1969, lost in manuscript; *Primitive World,* 1991; *Jackpot Melting,* 1996; *Election Machine Warehouse,* 1996; *Meeting Lillie,* 1997; *Biko,* 1997; and *Black Renaissance in Harlem,* 1998.

PLAY COLLECTIONS

Dutchman [and] The Slave: A Fable, Morrow, 1964.
The Baptism [and] The Toilet, Grove, 1967.
Four Black Revolutionary Plays: All Praises to the Black Man (contains *Experimental Death Unit #1, A Black Mass, Great Goodness of Life (A Coon Show),* and *Madheart*), Bobbs-Merrill, 1969.
(Contributor) Woodie King and Ron Milner, editors, *Black Drama Anthology* (includes *Bloodrites* and *Junkies Are Full of SHHH . . .*), New American Library, 1971.
(Contributor) Rochelle Owens, editor, *Spontaneous Combustion: Eight New American Plays* (includes *Ba-Ra- Ka*), Winter House, 1972.
The Motion of History and Other Plays (contains *Slave Ship* and *S-1: A Play with Music in 26 Scenes*), Morrow, 1978.
Selected Plays and Prose of Amiri Baraka/LeRoi Jones, Morrow, 1979.

SCREENPLAYS

Dutchman, Gene Persson Enterprises, Ltd., 1967.
Black Spring, Jihad Productions, 1968.
A Fable (based on *The Slave: A Fable*), MFR Productions, 1971.
Supercoon, Gene Persson Enterprises, Ltd., 1971.

POETRY

April 13 (broadside Number 133), Penny Poems (New Haven), 1959.
Spring & So Forth (broadside Number 141), Penny Poems, 1960.

Preface to a Twenty Volume Suicide Note, Totem/Corinth, 1961.
The Disguise (broadside), [New Haven], 1961.
The Dead Lecturer (also see below), Grove, 1964.
Black Art (also see below), Jihad, 1966.
Black Magic (also see below), Morrow, 1967.
A Poem for Black Hearts, Broadside Press, 1967.
Black Magic: Sabotage; Target Study; Black Art; Collected Poetry, 1961-1967, Bobbs-Merrill, 1969.
It's Nation Time, Third World Press, 1970.
Spirit Reach, Jihad, 1972.
Afrikan Revolution: A Poem, Jihad, 1973.
Hard Facts: Excerpts, People's War, 1975, 2nd edition, Revolutionary Communist League, 1975.
Spring Song, Baraka, 1979.
AM/TRAK, Phoenix Bookship, 1979.
Selected Poetry of Amiri Baraka/Leroi Jones (includes Poetry for the Advanced), Morrow, 1979.
In the Tradition: For Black Arthur Blythe, Jihad, 1980.
Reggae or Not! Poems, Contact Two, 1982.
LeRoi Jones—Amiri, Thunder's Mouth Press, 1991.
Transbluency: The Selected Poems of Amiri Baraka/LeRoi Jones (1961-1995), Marsilio, 1995.
Funk Lore: New Poems, 1984-1995, Sun & Moon Press, 1996.

ESSAYS

Cuba Libre, Fair Play for Cuba Committee (New York City), 1961.
Blues People: Negro Music in White America, Morrow, 1963, reprinted, Greenwood Press, 1980, published in England as *Negro Music in White America,* MacGibbon & Kee, 1965.
Home: Social Essays (contains "Cuba Libre," "The Myth of a 'Negro Literature,'" "Expressive Language," "the legacy of malcolm x, and the coming of the black nation," and "state/meant"), Morrow, 1966, Ecco Press (Hopewell, NJ), 1998.
Black Music, Morrow, 1968, reprinted, Greenwood Press, 1980.
Raise, Race, Rays, Raze: Essays since 1965, Random House, 1971.
Strategy and Tactics of a Pan-African Nationalist Party, Jihad, 1971.
Kawaida Studies: The New Nationalism, Third World Press, 1972.
Crisis in Boston!, Vita Wa Watu People's War, 1974.
Daggers and Javelins: Essays, 1974-1979, Morrow, 1984.
(With wife, Amina Baraka) *The Music: Reflections on Jazz and Blues,* Morrow, 1987.

Also contributor of essays to *Lorraine Hansberry, A Raisin in the Sun;* and *The Sign in Sidney Brustein's Window,* Vintage Books (New York City), 1995.

EDITOR

January 1st 1959: Fidel Castro, Totem, 1959.

Four Young Lady Poets, Corinth, 1962.

(And author of introduction) *The Moderns: An Anthology of New Writing in America,* 1963, published as *The Moderns: New Fiction in America,* 1964.

(And co-author) *In-formation,* Totem, 1965.

Gilbert Sorrentino, Black & White, Corinth, 1965.

Edward Dorn, Hands Up!, Corinth, 1965.

(And contributor) *Afro-American Festival of the Arts Magazine,* Jihad, 1966, published as *Anthology of Our Black Selves,* 1969.

(With Larry Neal and A. B. Spellman) *The Cricket: Black Music in Evolution,* Jihad, 1968, published as *Trippin': A Need for Change,* New Ark, 1969.

(And contributor, with Larry Neal) *Black Fire: An Anthology of Afro-American Writing,* Morrow, 1968.

A Black Value System, Jihad, 1970.

(With Billy Abernathy under pseudonym Fundi) *In Our Terribleness (Some Elements of Meaning in Black Style),* Bobbs-Merrill, 1970.

(And author of introduction) *African Congress: A Documentary of the First Modern Pan-African Congress,* Morrow, 1972.

(With Diane Di Prima) *The Floating Bear, A Newsletter, No.1-37, 1961-1969,* McGilvery, 1974.

(With Amina Baraka) *Confirmation: An Anthology of African-American Women,* Morrow, 1983.

OTHER

(Contributor) Herbert Hill, editor, *Soon, One Morning,* Knopf, 1963.

The System of Dante's Hell (novel; includes the play *Dante*), Grove, 1965.

(Author of introduction) David Henderson, *Felix of the Silent Forest,* Poets Press, 1967.

Striptease, Parallax, 1967.

Tales (short stories), Grove, 1967.

(Author of preface) *Black Boogaloo (Notes on Black Liberation),* Journal of Black Poetry Press, 1969.

Focus on Amiri Baraka: Playwright LeRoi Jones Analyzes the 1st National Black Political Convention (sound recording), Center for Cassette Studies, 1973.

Three Books by Imamu Amiri Baraka (LeRoi Jones), (contains *The System of Dante's Hell, Tales,* and *The Dead Lecturer*), Grove, 1975.

The Autobiography of LeRoi Jones/Amiri Baraka, Freundlich, 1984, Lawrence Hill Books (Chicago), 1997.

(Author of introduction) Martin Espada, *Rebellion is the Circle of a Lover's Hand,* Curbstone Press, 1990.

(Author of introduction) *Eliot Katz, Space, and Other Poems,* Northern Lights, 1990.

LeRoi Jones/Amiri Baraka Reader, Thunder's Mouth Press, 1991.

Thornton Dial: Images of the Tiger, Harry N. Abrams, 1993.

Jesse Jackson and Black People, Third World Press, 1994.

Shy's Wise, Y's: The Griot's Tale, Third World Press, 1994.

(With Charlie Reilly) *Conversations with Amiri Baraka* (also see below), University Press of Mississippi (Jackson), 1994.

Eulogies, Marsilio Publishers (New York City), 1996.

Works represented in more than seventy-five anthologies, including *A Broadside Treasury, For Malcolm, The New Black Poetry, Nommo,* and *The Trembling Lamb.* Contributor to *Evergreen Review, Poetry, Downbeat, Metronome, Nation, Negro Digest, Saturday Review,* and other periodicals. Editor with Diane Di Prima, *The Floating Bear,* 1961-63.

Baraka's works have been translated into Japanese, Norwegian, Italian, German, French, and Spanish.

SIDELIGHTS: Amiri Baraka (known as LeRoi Jones until 1967) is a major author whose strident social criticism and incendiary style have made it difficult for audiences and critics to respond with objectivity to his works. His art stems from his African-American heritage. His method in poetry, drama, fiction and essays is confrontational, calculated to shock and awaken audiences to the political concerns of black Americans. Baraka's own political stance has changed several times, each time finding expression in his plays, poems, and essays so that his works can be divided into periods; a member of the avant garde during the 1950s, Baraka became a black nationalist, and later a Marxist with socialist ideals. Critical opinion has been sharply divided between those who feel, with *Dissent* contributor Stanley Kaufman, that Baraka's race and political moment account for his fame, and those who feel that Baraka stands among the most important writers of the age. In *American Book Review,* Arnold Rampersad counts Baraka with Phyllis Wheatley, Frederick Douglass, Paul Laurence Dunbar, Langston Hughes, Zora Neale Hurston, Richard Wright, and Ralph Ellison "as one of the eight figures . . . who have significantly affected the course of African-American literary culture."

Baraka did not always identify with radical politics, nor did he always train his writing to be their tool. He was born in Newark, New Jersey, and enjoyed a middle-class education. During the 1950s he attended Rutgers University and Howard University. Then he spent two years in the Air Force, stationed for most of that time in Puerto Rico. When he returned to New York City, he attended Columbia University and the New School of Social Research. He lived in Greenwich Village's lower east side where his friends were the Beat poets Allen Ginsberg, Frank O'Hara, and Gilbert Sorrentino. The white avant garde—primarily Ginsberg, O'Hara, and leader of the Black Mountain poets Charles Olson—and Baraka believed that writing poetry is a process of discovery rather than an exercise in fulfilling traditional expectations of what poems should be. Baraka, like the projectivist poets, believed that a poem's form should follow the shape determined by the poet's own breath and intensity of feeling. In 1958 Baraka founded *Yugen* magazine and Totem Press, important forums for new verse. His first play, *A Good Girl Is Hard to Find,* was produced at Sterington House in Montclair, New Jersey, that same year.

Preface to a Twenty Volume Suicide Note, Baraka's first published collection of poems, appeared in 1961. M. L. Rosenthal writes in *The New Poets: American and British Poetry* that these poems show Baraka's "natural gift for quick, vivid imagery and spontaneous humor." The reviewer also praised the "sardonic or sensuous or slangily knowledgeable passages" that fill the early poems. While the cadence of blues and many allusions to black culture are found in the poems, the subject of blackness does not predominate. Throughout, rather, the poet shows his integrated, Bohemian social roots. For example, the poem "Notes for a Speech" states, "African blues / does not know me . . . Does / not feel / what I am," and the book's last line is "You are / as any other sad man here / american."

With the rise of the civil rights movement, however, Baraka's works took on a more militant tone, and he began a reluctant separation from his Bohemian beginnings. His trip to Castro's Cuba in July of 1959 marked an important turning point in his life. His view of his role as a writer, the purpose of art, and the degree to which ethnic awareness deserved to be his subject changed dramatically. In Cuba he met

writers and artists from Third World countries whose political concerns included the fight against poverty, famine, and oppressive governments. They felt he was merely being self-indulgent, "cultivating his soul" in poetry while there were social problems to solve in America. In *Home: Social Essays,* Baraka explains how he tried to defend himself against these accusations, and was further challenged by Jaime Shelley, a Mexican poet, who had said, "'In that ugliness you live in, you want to cultivate your soul? Well, we've got millions of starving people to feed, and that moves me enough to make poems out of.'" Soon Baraka began to identify with Third World writers and to write poems and plays that had strong ethnic and political messages.

Dutchman, a play of entrapment in which a white woman and a middle-class black man both express their murderous hatred on a subway, was first performed Off-Broadway in New York City in 1964. The one-act play makes many references to sex and violence and ends in the black man's murder. While other dramatists of the time were using the techniques of naturalism, Baraka used symbolism and other experimental techniques to enhance the play's emotional impact. Lula, the white woman, represents the white state, and Clay, the black man in the play, represents ethnic identity and non- white manhood. Lula kills Clay after taunting him with sexual invitations and insults such as "You ain't no nigger, you're just a dirty white man. Get up, Clay. Dance with me, Clay." The play established Baraka's reputation as a playwright and has been often anthologized and performed. Considered by many to be the best play of the year, it won the Village Voice Obie Award in 1964. Later, Anthony Harvey adapted it for a film made in Britain, and in the 1990s it was revived for several productions in New York City. Darryl Pinckney comments in the *New York Times Book Review* that *Dutchman* has survived the test of time better than other protest plays of the 1960s due to its economic use of vivid language, its surprise ending, and its quick pacing.

The plays and poems following *Dutchman* expressed Baraka's increasing disappointment with white America and his growing need to separate from it. Baraka wrote in *Cuba Libre* that the Beat generation had become a counterculture of drop-outs, which did not amount to very meaningful politics. Baraka felt there had to be a more effective alternative to disengagement from the political, legal, and moral morass that the country had become. In *The Dead Lecturer,* Baraka explored the alternatives, finding that there is no room for compromise: if he identifies with an ethnic cause, he can find hope of meaningful action and change; but if he remains in his comfortable assimilated position, writing "quiet" poems, he will remain "a dead lecturer." The voice in these poems is more sure of itself, led by a "moral earnestness" that is wedded to action, Baraka wrote in a 1961 letter to Edward Dorn. Critics observed that as the poems became more politically intense, they left behind some of the flawless technique of the earlier poems. *Nation* review contributor Richard Howard comments, "These are the agonized poems of a man writing to save his skin, or at least to settle in it, and so urgent is their purpose that not one of them can trouble to be perfect."

To make a clean break with the Beat influence, Baraka turned to writing fiction in the mid-1960s. He wrote *The System of Dante's Hell,* a novel, and *Tales,* a collection of short stories. The novel echoes the themes and structures found in earlier poems and plays. The stories, like the poems in *Black Magic,* also published in 1967, are "'fugitive narratives' that describe the harried flight of an intensely self-conscious Afro-American artist / intellectual from neo-slavery of blinding, neutralizing whiteness, where the area of struggle is basically within the mind," Robert Eliot Fox writes in *Conscientious Sorcerers: The Black Post-Modernist Fiction of LeRoi Jones/Baraka, Ishmael Reed, and Samuel R. Delany.* The role of violent action in achieving political change is more prominent in these stories. Unlike Shakespeare's Hamlet, who deliberates at length before taking violent action, during this period Baraka sought to stand with "the straight ahead people, who think when that's called for, who don't when they don't have to," he wrote in *Tales.* The role of music in black life is seen more often in these books, also. In the story "Screamers," the screams from a jazz saxophone galvanize the people into a powerful uprising.

Baraka's classic history *Blues People: Negro Music in White America,* published in 1963, traces black music from slavery to contemporary jazz. The blues, a staple of black American music, grew out of the encounter between African and American cultures in the South to become an art form uniquely connected to both the African past and the American soil. Finding indigenous black art forms was important to Baraka at this time, for he was searching for a more authentic ethnic voice for his own poetry. In this important study, Baraka became known as an articulate jazz critic and a perceptive observer of social change. As Clyde Taylor states in *Amiri Baraka: The Kaleido-scopic Torch* edited by James B. Gwynne, "The connection he nailed down between the many faces of black music, the sociological sets that nurtured them, and their symbolic evolutions through socio-economic changes, in *Blues People,* is his most durable conception, as well as probably the one most indispensable thing said about black music."

Baraka will also be long remembered for his other important studies, *Black Music,* which expresses black nationalist ideals, and *The Music: Reflections on Jazz and Blues,* which expresses his Marxist views. In *Black Music,* John Coltrane emerges as the patron saint of the black arts movement, for replacing "weak Western forms" of music with more fluid forms learned from a global vision of black culture. Though some critics feel that Baraka's essay writing is not all of the same quality, Lloyd W. Brown comments in *Amiri Baraka* that his essays on music are flawless: "As historian, musicological analyst, or as a journalist covering a particular performance Baraka always commands attention because of his obvious knowledge of the subject and because of a style that is engaging and persuasive even when the sentiments are questionable and controversial."

After Black Muslim leader Malcolm X was killed in 1965, Baraka moved to Harlem and became a black nationalist. He founded the Black Arts Repertory Theatre/School in Harlem and published the collection *Black Magic.* Poems in *Black Magic* chronicle Baraka's divorce from white culture and values and display his mastery of poetic techniques. In *Amiri Baraka: The Kaleidoscopic Torch,* Taylor observes, "There are enough brilliant poems of such variety in *Black Magic* and *In Our Terribleness* to establish the unique identity and claim for respect of several poets. But it is beside the point that Baraka is probably the finest poet, black or white, writing in this country these days." There was no doubt that Baraka's political concerns superseded his just claims to literary excellence, and the challenge to critics was to respond to the political content of the works. Some critics who felt the best art must be apolitical, dismissed his new work as "a loss to literature." Kenneth Rexroth writes in *With Eye and Ear,* "In recent years [Baraka] has succumbed to the temptation to become a professional Race Man of the most irresponsible sort. . . . His loss to literature is more serious than any literary casualty of the Second War." In 1966 he moved back to Newark, New Jersey, and a year later changed his name to the Bantuized Muslim appellation Imamu ("spiritual leader," later dropped) Ameer (later Amiri, "blessed") Baraka ("prince").

A new aesthetic for black art was being developed in Harlem and Baraka was its primary theorist. Black American artists should follow "black," not "white" standards of beauty and value, he maintained, and should stop looking to white culture for validation. The black artist's role, he wrote in *Home: Social Essays,* was to "aid in the destruction of America as he knows it." Foremost in this endeavor was the imperative to portray society and its ills faithfully so that the portrayal would move people to take necessary corrective action.

By the early 1970s Baraka was recognized as "a teacher of great talent" by Broadside Press publisher Dudley Randall and many others. Randall notes in *Black World* that younger black poets Nikki Giovanni and Don. L. Lee (now Haki R. Madhubuti) were "learning from LeRoi Jones, a man versed in German philosophy, conscious of literary tradition . . . who uses the structure of Dante's *Divine Comedy* in his *System of Dante's Hell* and the punctuation, spelling and line divisions of sophisticated contemporary poets." More importantly, Rampersad writes in the *American Book Review,* "More than any other black poet, however, he taught younger black poets of the generation past how to respond poetically to their lived experience, rather than to depend as artists on embalmed reputations and outmoded rhetorical strategies derived from a culture often substantially different from their own."

After coming to see black nationalism as a destructive form of racism, Baraka denounced it in 1974 and became a Third World Socialist. Hatred of non-whites, he declared in the *New York Times,* "is sickness or criminality, in fact, a form of fascism." Since 1974 he has produced a number of Marxist poetry collections and plays. His new political goal is the formation of socialist communities and a socialist state. *Daggers and Javelins* and the other books produced during this period lack the emotional power of the works from the black nationalist period, say the American critics. However, critics who agree with his new politics such as exiled Filipino leftist intellectual E. San Juan praise his work of the late 1970s. San Juan writes in *Amiri Baraka: The Kaleidoscopic Torch* that Baraka's 1978 play *Lone Ranger* was "the most significant theatrical achievement of 1978 in the Western hemisphere." Joe Weixlmann responds in the same source to the tendency to categorize the radical Baraka instead of analyze him: "At the very least, dismissing someone with a label does not make for very satisfactory scholarship. Initially, Baraka's reputation as a writer and thinker derived from a recog-

nition of the talents with which he is so obviously endowed. The assaults on that reputation have, too frequently, derived from concerns which should be extrinsic to informed criticism."

In recent years, recognition of Baraka's impact on contemporary American culture has taken the form of two anthologies of his literary oeuvre. In 1991 *The LeRoi Jones/Amiri Baraka Reader* presented a thorough overview of the writer's development, covering the period from 1957 to 1983. The volume presents Baraka's work from four different periods and emphasizes lesser-known works rather than the author's most-famous writings. Although criticizing the anthology for offering little in the way of original poetry, *Sulfur* reviewer Andrew Schelling terms the collection "a sweeping account of Baraka's development." A *Choice* contributor also praises the volume, calling it "a landmark volume in African American literature." *Transbluency: The Selected Poems of Amiri Baraka/ LeRoi Jones (1961-1995),* published in 1995, is hailed by Daniel L. Guillory in *Library Journal* as "critically important." And Donna Seaman, writing in *Booklist,* commends the "lyric boldness of this passionate collection."

Baraka's standing as a major poet is matched by his importance as a cultural and political leader. His influence on younger writers has been so significant and widespread that it would be difficult to discuss American literary history without mentioning his name. As leader of the Black Arts movement of the 1960s, Baraka did much to define and support black literature's mission into the twenty-first century. His experimental fiction of the 1960s is yet considered some of the most significant contribution to black fiction since that of Jean Toomer, who wrote during the Harlem Renaissance of the 1920s. Writers from other ethnic groups credit Baraka with opening "tightly guarded doors" in the white publishing establishment, notes Native American author Maurice Kenney in *Amiri Baraka: The Kaleidoscopic Torch.* Kenny adds, "We'd all still be waiting the invitation from the New Yorker without him. He taught us how to claim it and take it."

BIOGRAPHICAL/CRITICAL SOURCES:

BOOKS

Allen, Donald M., and Warren Tallman, editors, *Poetics of the New American Poetry,* Grove, 1973.

Anadolu-Okur, Nilgun, *Contemporary African American Theater: Afrocentricity in the Works of Larry Neal, Amiri Baraka, and Charles Fuller,* Garland, 1997.

Baraka, Amiri, *Tales,* Grove, 1967.

Baraka, and Larry Neal, editors, *Black Fire: An Anthology of Afro-American Writing,* Morrow, 1968.

Baraka, *Black Magic: Sabotage; Target Study; Black Art; Collected Poetry, 1961-1967,* Bobbs-Merrill, 1969.

Baraka, *The Autobiography of LeRoi Jones/Amiri Baraka,* Freundlich Books, 1984.

Baraka and Charlie Reilly, *Conversations with Amiri Baraka,* University Press of Mississippi (Jackson), 1994.

Benston, Kimberly A., editor, *Baraka: The Renegade and the Mask,* Yale University Press, 1976.

Benston, *Imamu Amiri Baraka (LeRoi Jones): A Collection of Critical Essays,* Prentice-Hall, 1978.

Bigsby, C. W. E., *Confrontation and Commitment: A Study of Contemporary American Drama, 1959-1966,* University of Missouri Press, 1968.

Bigsby, editor, *The Black American Writer, Volume II: Poetry and Drama,* Everett/Edwards, 1970, Penguin, 1971.

Bigsby, *The Second Black Renaissance: Essays in Black Literature,* Greenwood Press, 1980.

Birnebaum, William M., *Something for Everybody Is Not Enough,* Random House, 1972.

Black Literature Criticism, Gale, 1991.

Brown, Lloyd W., *Amiri Baraka,* Twayne, 1980.

Concise Dictionary of American Literary Biography, Volume 1: The New Consciousness, Gale, 1987.

Contemporary Literary Criticism, Gale, Volume 1, 1973, Volume 2, 1974, Volume 3, 1975, Volume 5, 1976, Volume 10, 1979, Volume 14, 1980, Volume 33, 1985.

Cook, Bruce, *The Beat Generation,* Scribner, 1971.

Dace, Letitia, *LeRoi Jones (Imamu Amiri Baraka): A Checklist of Works by and about Him,* Nether Press, 1971.

Dace, and Wallace Dace, *The Theatre Student: Modern Theatre and Drama,* Richards Rosen Press, 1973.

Debusscher, Gilbert, and Henry I. Schvey, editors, *New Essays on American Drama,* Rodopi, 1989.

Dictionary of Literary Biography, Gale, Volume 5: *American Poets since World War II,* 1980, Volume 7: *Twentieth Century American Dramatists,* 1981, Volume 16: *The Beats; Literary Bohemians in Postwar America,* 1983, Volume 38: *Afro-American Writers after 1955: Dramatists and Prose Writers,* 1985.

Dukore, Bernard F., *Drama and Revolution,* Holt, 1971.

Elam, Harry Justin, *Taking It to the Streets: The Social Protest Theater of Luis Valdez and Amiri Baraka,* University of Michigan Press (Ann Arbor), 1997.

Ellison, Ralph, *Shadow and Act,* New American Library, 1966.

Emanuel, James A., and Theodore L. Gross, editors, *Dark Symphony: Negro Literature in America,* Free Press, 1968.

Fox, Robert Elliot, *Conscientious Sorcerers: The Black Post-modernist Fiction of LeRoi Jones/ Baraka, Ishmael Reed and Samuel R. Delany,* Greenwood Press, 1987.

Frost, David, *The Americans,* Stein & Day, 1970.

Gayle, Addison, editor, *Black Expression: Essays by and about Black Americans in the Creative Arts,* Weybright & Talley, 1969.

Gayle, *The Way of the New World: The Black Novel in America,* Anchor/Doubleday, 1975.

Gwynne, James B., editor, *Amiri Baraka: The Kaleidoscopic Torch,* Steppingstones Press, 1985.

Hall, Veronica, *Chicorel Theater Index to Plays in Anthologies, Periodicals, Discs and Tapes,* Chicorel Library Publishing, 1970.

Harris, William J., *The Poetry and Poetics of Amiri Baraka: The Jazz Aesthetic,* University of Missouri Press, 1985.

Haskins, James, *Black Theater in America,* Crowell, 1982.

Hatch, James V., *Black Image on the American Stage: A Bibliography of Plays and Musicals, 1770-1970,* Drama Book Specialists, 1970.

Hatch, editor, *Black Theatre, U.S.A.,* Free Press, 1974.

Henderson, Stephen E., *Understanding the New Black Poetry: Black Speech and Black Music as Poetic References,* Morrow, 1973.

Hill, Herbert, *Soon, One Morning,* Knopf, 1963.

Hill, editor, *Anger, and Beyond: The Negro Writer in the United States,* Harper, 1966.

Hudson, Theodore, *From LeRoi Jones to Amiri Baraka: The Literary Works,* Duke University Press, 1973.

Inge, M. Thomas, Maurice Duke, and Jackson R. Bryer, editors, *Black American Writers: Bibliographic Essays; Richard Wright, Ralph Ellison, James Baldwin, and Amiri Baraka,* St. Martin's, 1978.

International Authors and Writers Who's Who, 1991-1992, International Biographical Centre, 1991.

Jones, LeRoi, *Preface to a Twenty Volume Suicide Note,* Totem Press/Corinth Books, 1961.

Jones, *Blues People: Negro Music in White America,* Morrow, 1963.

Jones, *The Dead Lecturer,* Grove, 1964.

Jones, *Home: Social Essays,* Morrow, 1966.

Keil, Charles, *Urban Blues,* University of Chicago Press, 1966.

King, Woodie, and Ron Milner, editors, *Black Drama Anthology,* New American Library, 1971.

Knight, Arthur and Kit Knight, editors, *The Beat Vision,* Paragon House, 1987.

Kofsky, Frank, *Black Nationalism and the Revolution in Music,* Pathfinder, 1970.

Lacey, Henry C., *To Raise, Destroy, and Create: The Poetry, Drama, and Fiction of Imamu Amiri Baraka (LeRoi Jones),* The Whitson Publishing Company, 1981.

Lewis, Allan, *American Plays and Playwrights,* Crown, 1965.

Littlejohn, David, *Black on White: A Critical Survey of Writing by American Negroes,* Viking, 1966.

O'Brien, John, *Interviews with Black Writers,* Liveright, 1973.

Olaniyan, Tejumola, *Scars of Conquest/Masks of Resistance: The Invention of Cultural Identities in African, African-American, and Caribbean Drama,* Oxford University Press (New York City), 1995.

Ossman, David, *The Sullen Art: Interviews with Modern American Poets,* Corinth, 1963.

Rexroth, Kenneth, *With Eye and Ear,* Herder and Herder, 1970.

Rosenthal, M. L., *The New Poets: American and British Poetry since World War II,* Oxford University Press, 1967.

Sollors, Werner, *Amiri Baraka/LeRoi Jones: The Quest for a "Populist Modernism,"* Columbia University Press, 1978.

Stepanchev, Stephen, *American Poetry since 1945,* Harper, 1965.

Weales, Gerald, *The Jumping-Off Place: American Drama in the 1960s,* Macmillan, 1969.

Whitlow, Roger, *Black American Literature: A Critical History,* Nelson Hall, 1973.

Who's Who in America, 1992, Marquis, 1992.

Williams, Martin, *The Jazz Tradition,* New American Library, 1971.

Williams, Sherley Anne, *Give Birth to Brightness: A Thematic Study in Neo-Black Literature,* Dial, 1972.

PERIODICALS

American Book Review, February, 1980; May-June, 1985.

Atlantic, January, 1966; May, 1966.

Avant Garde, September, 1968.

Black American Literature Forum, spring, 1980; spring, 1981; fall, 1982; spring, 1983; winter, 1985.

Black World, Volume 29, number 6, April, 1971; December, 1971; November, 1974; July, 1975.

Booklist, January 1, 1994, p. 799; February 15, 1994, p. 1052; October 15, 1995, p. 380.

Book Week, December 24, 1967.

Book World, October 28, 1979.

Boundary 2, number 6, 1978.

Chicago Defender, January 11, 1965.

Chicago Tribune, October 4, 1968.

Commentary, February, 1965.

Contemporary Literature, Volume 12, 1971.

Detroit Free Press, January 31, 1965.

Detroit News, January 15, 1984; August 12, 1984.

Dissent, spring, 1965.

Ebony, August, 1967; August, 1969; February, 1971.

Educational Theatre Journal, March, 1968; March, 1970; March, 1976.

Esquire, June, 1966.

Essence, September, 1970; May, 1984; September, 1984; May, 1985.

Jazz Review, June, 1959.

Journal of Black Poetry, fall, 1968; spring, 1969; summer, 1969; fall, 1969.

Library Journal, January, 1994, p. 112; November, 1995, pp. 78-9.

Los Angeles Free Press, Volume 5, number 18, May 3, 1968.

Los Angeles Times, April 20, 1990.

Los Angeles Times Book Review, May 15, 1983; March 29, 1987.

Nation, October 14, 1961; November 14, 1961; March 13, 1964; April 13, 1964; January 4, 1965; March 15, 1965; January 22, 1968; February 2, 1970.

Negro American Literature Forum, March, 1966; winter, 1973.

Negro Digest, December, 1963; February, 1964; Volume 13, number 19, August, 1964; March, 1965; April, 1965; March, 1966; April, 1966; June, 1966; April, 1967; April, 1968; January, 1969; April, 1969.

Newsweek, March 13, 1964; April 13, 1964; November 22, 1965; May 2, 1966; March 6, 1967; December 4, 1967; December 1, 1969; February 19, 1973.

New York, November 5, 1979.

New Yorker, April 4, 1964; December 26, 1964; March 4, 1967; December 30, 1972.

New York Herald Tribune, March 25, 1964; April 2, 1964; December 13, 1964; October 27, 1965.

New York Post, March 16, 1964; March 24, 1964; January 15, 1965; March 18, 1965.

New York Review of Books, January 20, 1966; May
    22, 1964; July 2, 1970; October 17, 1974; June
    11, 1984; June 14, 1984.
New York Times, April 28, 1966; May 8, 1966; Au-
    gust 10, 1966; September 14, 1966; October 5,
    1966; January 20, 1967; February 28, 1967; July
    15, 1967; January 5, 1968; January 6, 1968;
    January 9, 1968; January 10, 1968; February 7,
    1968; April 14, 1968; August 16, 1968; Novem-
    ber 27, 1968; December 24, 1968; August 26,
    1969; November 23, 1969; February 6, 1970;
    May 11, 1972; June 11, 1972; November 11,
    1972; November 14, 1972; November 23, 1972;
    December 5, 1972; December 27, 1974; Decem-
    ber 29, 1974; November 19, 1979; October 15,
    1981; January 23, 1984; February 9, 1991.
New York Times Book Review, January 31, 1965;
    November 28, 1965; May 8, 1966; February 4,
    1968; March 17, 1968; February 14, 1971; June
    6, 1971; June 27, 1971; December 5, 1971;
    March 12, 1972; December 16, 1979; March 11,
    1984; July 5, 1987; December 20, 1987.
New York Times Magazine, February 5, 1984.
Salmagundi, spring-summer, 1973.
Saturday Review, April 20, 1963; January 11, 1964;
    January 9, 1965; December 11, 1965; December
    9, 1967; October 2, 1971; July 12, 1975.
Studies in Black Literature, spring, 1970; volume 1,
    number 2, 1970; volume 3, number 2, 1972; vol-
    ume 3, number 3, 1972; volume 4, number 1, 1973.
Sulfur, spring, 1992.
Sunday News (New York), January 21, 1973.
Time, December 25, 1964; November 19, 1965; May
    6, 1966; January 12, 1968; April 26, 1968; June
    28, 1968; June 28, 1971.
Times Literary Supplement, November 25, 1965; Sep-
    tember 1, 1966; September 11, 1969; October 9,
    1969; August 2, 1991.
Tribune Books, March 29, 1987.
Village Voice, December 17, 1964; May 6, 1965;
    May 19, 1965; August 30, 1976; August 1, 1977;
    December 17-23, 1980; October 2, 1984.
Washington Post, August 15, 1968; September 12,
    1968; November 27, 1968; December 5, 1980;
    January 23, 1981; June 29, 1987.
Washington Post Book World, December 24, 1967;
    May 22, 1983.

*   *   *

BASS, Kingsley B., Jr.
  See BULLINS, Ed

BENNETT, Louise (Simone) 1919-
  (Miss Lou)

PERSONAL: Also known professionally as Louise
Bennett-Coverley; born September 7, 1919, in
Kingston, Jamaica; daughter of Cornelius A. (a
baker) and Kerene (a seamstress; maiden name,
Robinson) Bennett; married Eric Coverley (a drafts-
man and impresario), May 30, 1954; children: Fabian
(stepson), Christine. *Education:* Studied journalism,
late 1930s; attended Friends' College, Highgate, St.
Mary, beginning c. 1943, and Royal Academy of
Dramatic Art (RADA), 1945-47. *Religion:* Presbyterian.

ADDRESSES: Home and office—Enfield House, P.O.
Box 11, Gordon Town, St. Andrew, Jamaica.

CAREER: Writer, poet, folklorist, and performer.
British Broadcasting Corporation (BBC), West Indies
Section, London, England, resident artist on "Caribbean Carnival" (variety show), 1945-46, and "West
Indian Guest Night," 1950-53; high school drama
teacher, Jamaica, 1947-49; actor in repertory companies in Coventry, England, Huddersfield, England,
and Amersham, England; folk singer and performer
in New York City, New Jersey, and Connecticut,
1953-55; Jamaica Social Welfare Commission, drama
specialist and head of recreation department, c. 1955-
59, director, c. 1959-63; University of the West
Indies, Kingston, Jamaica, lecturer and extra-mural
drama officer, c. 1955-69. Director, with Eric
Coverley, of *Day in Jamaica* (folk musical), c. 1953;
Miss Lou's Views, radio commentator, c. 1965-82;
Ring Ding (children's television Commonwealth Arts
Festival, Britain, 1965. Member of Little Theatre
Movement pantomime management committee,
1961—; member of board of directors of Radio Ja-
maica and Rediffusion; patron of National Dance
Theatre Company, 1962—; director of Jamaica Sugar
Welfare Board, 1972-76, and National Savings Com-
mittee.

MEMBER: Writers Union of Jamaica.

AWARDS, HONORS: Member of Order of the British
Empire, 1960; Silver Musgrave Medal of the Institute
of Jamaica, 1965; Norman Manley Award for Excellence in the Arts, 1972; Unity Award from United
Manchester Association, 1972; Order of Jamaica,
1974; Gold Musgrave Medal, 1978; Institute of Jamaica Centenary Medal, 1979; D. Litt, University of
West Indies, 1983.

WRITINGS:

Dialect Verses, Gleaner, 1940.

Jamaica Dialect Verses, compiled by George R. Bowen, Herald, 1942, enlarged edition, Pioneer Press, 1951.

Jamaican Humour in Dialect, Gleaner, 1943.

Miss Lulu Sez: A Collection of Dialect Poems, Gleaner, 1948.

(With others) *Anancy Stories and Dialect Verse,* introduced by P. M. Sherlock, Pioneer Press, 1950, new series, 1957.

Folk Stories and Verses, Pioneer Press, 1952.

Laugh with Louise: A Potpourri of Jamaican Folklore, Stories, Songs, Verses, foreword by Robert Verity, City Printery, 1961.

Jamaica Labrish, introduced and edited by Rex Nettleford, Sangster's Book Stores, 1966.

(As Miss Lou) *Anancy and Miss Lou,* Sangster's Book Stores, 1979.

(Editor) *Mother Goose/Jamaica Maddah Goose,* Friends of the Jamaica School of Art Association, 1981.

Selected Poems, edited by Mervyn Morris, Sangster's Book Stores, 1982, revised edition, 1983.

Aunt Roachy Seh, Sangster, 1993.

Also author of *Lulu Sey: Dialect Verse,* 1943. Work presented in anthologies, including *Independence Anthology of Jamaica, Jamaican Ministry of Development; Brightlight: An Anthology of Caribbean Poetry,* Hamish Hamilton; *Bite In: A Three-Year Secondary Course on Reading Poems,* Thomas Nelson. Contributor to *Jamaica Talk* and *Dictionary of Jamaican English.* Contributor to Jamaican periodicals; author of a column in *Sunday Gleaner.*

RECORDINGS

Jamaican Folk Songs, Folkways, 1954.

Jamaican Singing Games, Folkways, 1954.

Children's Jamaican Songs and Games, Folkways, 1957.

West Indies Festival of Arts, Cook, 1958.

Miss Lou's Views, Federal Records, 1967.

Listen to Louise, Federal Records, 1968.

The Honourable Miss Lou, Premiere Productions, 1981.

"Yes, M'Dear": Miss Lou Live, Imani Music, 1983.

Aunty Roachy seh, edited by Mervyn Morris, Sangster's, 1993.

Also recorded *Anancy Stories,* Federal Records, and *Carifesta Ring Ding,* Record Specialists.

SIDELIGHTS: Louise Bennett is a prominent poet, writer, and performer, internationally known for capturing the language and folklore of Jamaican culture both in print and in her oral presentations. Since the late 1930s, Bennett has been writing and reading her poems and stories in Jamaica, England, and the United States, and has earned a loyal popular following. She draws her material from Jamaica's traditional folk stories, proverbs, myths, and songs, which were preserved primarily through oral retellings, and Bennett may have saved many of these works from possible oblivion. Believing that Jamaican folklore is best expressed within the language of the people, Bennett performs and writes in the native Jamaican English dialect, which is known variously as Creole, "Jamaica talk," West Indian English, Jamaican dialect, or Patois. "One reason I persisted writing in dialect," explained Bennett, as cited by Carolyn Cooper in *World Literature Written in English,* "was because . . . there was such rich material in the dialect that I wanted to put on paper some of the wonderful things that people say in dialect. You could never say 'look here' as vividly as 'kuyah'."

Bennett, an only child, was born in Kingston, Jamaica. Her father, Cornelius, owned a bakery but died when Bennett was only seven years old, leaving her mother, Kerene, to provide for the family through her work as a dressmaker. From her mother, Bennett learned early to respect people, and she became acquainted with a cross-section of social and economic classes by observing the women for whom her mother sewed. As Bennett explained in an interview with Don Buckner in 1976, as quoted by Mervyn Morris in *Fifty Caribbean Writers: A Bio-Bibliographical Critical Sourcebook,* "Everybody was a lady—the fish lady, the yam lady, the store lady, the teacher lady." Later, her poetry would focus on those everyday people of Jamaica. As Bennett matured, her interest in people grew along with her love of Jamaican folklore. Like many children, Bennett loved the folktales she had heard in her youth; unlike other children, however, her interest stayed with her into her teenage years when she traveled, on her own, to the interior of the island looking for folklore. As quoted in *Black Literature Criticism,* Bennett explained: "There I was, still a teenager, living in a society that expected respectable girls to stay home with their mother, traveling on donkeyback into the remote towns of the Maroons, the ex-slaves who had escaped and established their own free territory." This experience exposed her to a sampling of the variety of folklore in her heritage—and whetted her appetite for travel and research.

From 1936 to 1938 Bennett attended Excelsior High School, where she began writing poems in standard English, but she switched to Jamaican Creole after overhearing a vivid conversation in dialect on a Kingston tramcar. Bennett's use of dialect was long considered by many critics as a limiting factor in her art. In a 1968 *Caribbean Quarterly* interview, Bennett told Dennis Scott: "For too long, it was considered not respectable to use the dialect. Because there was a social stigma attached to the kind of person who used dialect habitually. Many people still do not accept the fact that for us there are many things which are best said in the language of the 'common man.'" It was during her high school years that Bennett began to perform, presenting renditions of her poems to audiences. Her success brought her to the attention of Eric Coverley, the organizer of a popular Christmas concert on the island. Bennett made her professional debut at that concert in 1938, and by 1940 she had published a book of poetry titled *Dialect Verses*.

Because of her evident talent as a performer, Bennett was awarded by the renowned Royal Academy of Dramatic Art in London. Within a short time after her arrival in England, Bennett also found a job at the British Broadcasting Corporation (BBC), performing in a program of her own, the "Caribbean Carnival." She was invited to remain after her schooling to pursue a career as a professional actor; however, Bennett was homesick for Jamaica and returned to her homeland in 1947. Continuing to write poetry, she taught school for a short time but returned to England two years later to continue her work with the BBC as a resident artist on the "West Indian Guest Night" program. In 1953 Bennett moved to the United States, where, for two years, she pursued a career in radio as well as drama, performing at St. Martin's Little Theater in Harlem, New York, singing folk songs at the Village Vanguard in Greenwich Village, and then directing, with Eric Coverley, a folk musical. On May 30, 1954, Bennett married Coverley in New York, and the couple returned to Jamaica the same year. Back home once more—she has not lived abroad since—Bennett resumed her travels throughout the island, gathering Jamaican folklore and oral history and giving international radio, stage, and television performances.

Characteristically, Bennett's poems focus on typical Jamaicans—their individual responses to experiences, events, topical issues, and even politics—bringing humor and insight into everyday life. Rex Nettleford, in the introduction to Bennett's 1966 publication, *Jamaica Labrish*, marvelled that in her poems Bennett captures "all the spontaneity of the ordinary Jamaican's joys and even sorrows, his ready poignant and even wicked wit, his religion and his philosophy of life." The form that most closely describes Bennett's style is the ballad, a story typically told in song. She also uses the dramatic monologue, a poem that is delivered as a speech to the audience and often reveals the speaker's character. The persona in "Uriah Preach" from *Selected Poems* for example, is a mother who boasts about how her son reproaches relatives through a Sunday sermon: "Him tell dem off, dem know is dem, / Dem heart full to de brim; / But as Uriah eena pulpit / Dem cyaan back-answer him." The reaction of the audience (or reader) to the son's behavior is the perception of both a subtle irony at work (through the mother's wicked approval of her son's conduct) and a recognition of the humor in the situation—distinctive trademarks of Bennett's poetry. It has been claimed by many critics that her poems are at their best in performance. A *Times Literary Supplement* reviewer asserted that without an oral presentation of the work, "not merely something, but too much, is lost." The poems lend themselves to voice, the rhythms of speaking, movement, and a punch-line delivery technique which Bennett often employs.

Believing it important to pass on the folklore and culture of ordinary people to the children of the island, Bennett has often targeted young people through her work. For twelve years, from 1970 to 1982, she hosted a weekly television show, *Ring Ding,* in which children were invited to share their pride in Jamaican culture through folk stories and songs. Bennett recorded many of the songs, games, and stories featured on the program, including the well-loved "Brer Anancy" narratives. The adventures of Anancy, the African spider hero-rascal of Jamaican folk tales, is the protagonist in several of Bennett's books, including *Anancy Stories* and *Dialect Verse,* first published in 1950, and 1979's *Anancy and Miss Lou.*

Though long hailed as a performer and an entertainer, Bennett has only recently gained critical recognition for her written work. In her *Caribbean Quarterly* interview with Scott in 1968, Bennett commented that, although people at that time primarily thought of her as an entertainer, "I did start to write before I started to perform." Among her most popular books are *Jamaica Labrish* and *Selected Poems,* published in 1982. Because of the language and the light, often comic tone of her poetry, Bennett's work, though enormously popular, had been largely dismissed for decades by literary critics, several of whom considered her work as humorous entertainment, not as serious art. Critical recognition of Bennett's art increased beginning in the mid-1960s, influenced in part by Jamaica's political independence, achieved in 1962, which created a renewed appreciation for the Jamaican heritage. In addition, linguistic specialists have recently begun to recognize Creole not as substandard English but as a language in itself, with formal rules of grammar and syntax. "That the earlier criticisms are far less applicable today is to the credit of Louise Bennett," insisted Nettleford in his foreword. "[She] has never doubted the power of the language she uses to express the essential passions of her protagonists hearts." Bennett's loyal stand on the traditional Jamaican dialect began to be seen more as an asset than as a limitation, and her work was analyzed by many more critics as serious literature. "Her claim that dialect be taken seriously is not only valid," wrote Louis James in the introduction to *The Islands in Between: Essays on West Indian Literature,* "it is borne out by many of her own successful pieces. Through dialect she catches conversational tones that illuminate both individual and national character."

Morris's opinion of Bennett's writing is typical of other later reviews of her work: "Some of the art involved [in Bennett's poems] is unavailable to even the most alert of listeners; it is when we can linger over the page that the tightness of the organization becomes more fully apparent." By "lingering," the reader may identify puns, repeated rhyme schemes, plays on words, and literary allusions to English literature, proverbs, hymns, and the Bible. Other reviewers, such as Cooper in 1978's *World Literature Written in English,* pointed to the "comedy of manners in which those recurring rascals of Caribbean societies . . . come decidedly to grief." Cooper concluded that "the strength of Bennett's poetry then is the accuracy with which it depicts and attempts to correct through laughter the absurdities of Jamaican society. Its comic vision affirms a norm of common sense and good-natured decorum." In reviewing Bennett's *Selected Poems,* Loreto Todd in *World Literature Written in English* reflected that "every poem, almost every line is worth a comment for its humour, satire, pathos, irony, insight, its love of people and life. . . . [Bennett's] firm opinions and keen insights are like maypoles around which the language dances."

BIOGRAPHICAL/CRITICAL SOURCES:

BOOKS

Contemporary Poets, sixth edition, St. James Press, 1996.

Dictionary of Literary Biography, Vol. 117: Twentieth-Century Caribbean and Black African Writers, First Series, Gale, 1992.

PERIODICALS

Caribbean Quarterly, March-June, 1968, pp. 97-101.
Times Literary Supplement, December 15, 1966, p. 1173.
World Literature Written in English, April, 1978, pp. 317-27; spring, 1984, pp. 414-16.*

*   *   *

BENSON, Angela

PERSONAL: Female. *Education:* Spelman College, B.S.; Georgia Institute of Technology, M.S.

ADDRESSES: Home—P.O. Box 360571, Decatur, GA 30036. *E-mail*—abenson@atl.mindspring.com; reader @BensonInk.com.

CAREER: Writer, c. 1994—. Worked as a professional engineer until 1995.

WRITINGS:

Bands of Gold, Pinnacle Books (New York City), 1994.
For All Time, Pinnacle Books, 1995.
Between the Lines, Pinnacle Books, 1996.
A Family Wedding, Silhouette, 1997.
The Way Home, Pinnacle Books, 1997.
The Nicest Guy in America, Pinnacle Books, 1997.

Also author of *Second Chance Dad,* Silhouette. Work represented in anthologies, including *Holiday Cheer,* Pinnacle Books, 1995.

BIOGRAPHICAL/CRITICAL SOURCES:

PERIODICALS

Library Journal, May 15, 1996, p. 50; February 15, 1997, p. 125.
Publishers Weekly, February 17, 1997, p. 21; September 8, 1997, p. 73.

OTHER

Amazon.com, http://www.amazon.com/exec/obidos... b-a-ensonngela/002-8537756-9257209 (April 14, 1999).

Angela Benson site, wysiwyg://183/http://www.geo
cities.com/Paris/Rue/4626/interangela.html, April
9, 1999.

The World According to Angela, http://www.atl.
mindspring.com/~abenson/index.htm (August 6,
1999).

Write Page, http://www.writepage.com/authors/benso
na.htm, April 9, 1999.*

*   *   *

BETI, Mongo
  See BIYIDI, Alexandre

*   *   *

BIYIDI, Alexandre 1932-
  (Mongo Beti, Eza Boto)

PERSONAL: Professionally known as Mongo Beti;
born June 30, 1932, in M'Balmayo (one source says
Akometam), Cameroon; married; children: three.
Education: Attended University of Aix-Marseille; received B.A. (with honors) from Sorbonne, University
of Paris, M.A., 1966. *Politics:* Marxist.

ADDRESSES: Agent—Helena Strassova, Paris, France.

CAREER: Educator in Lamballe, France; secondary
education instructor in classical Greek, Latin, and
French literature in Rouen, France. Writer, 1953—.

AWARDS, HONORS: Sainte-Beuve Prize, 1948, for
Mission Accomplished, and 1957, for *King Lazarus.*

WRITINGS:

*NOVELS; UNDER PSEUDONYM MONGO BETI, EXCEPT AS
  NOTED*

(Under pseudonym Eza Boto) *Ville cruelle* (title
  means "Cruel City"), Editions Africaines, 1954.

Le Pauvre Christ de Bomba, Laffont, 1956, translation by Gerald Moore published as *The Poor
  Christ of Bomba,* Heinemann Educational (London), African Writers Series, 1971.

Mission terminee, Buchet Chastel/Correa, 1957,
  translation by Peter Green published as *Mission
  Accomplished,* Macmillan, 1958 (published in
  England as *Mission to Kala,* Muller, 1958), re-

written by John Davey and published as *Mission
to Kala,* Heinemann Educational, African Writers
Series, 1964.

Le Roi miracule: Chronique des Essazam, Buchet
Chastel/Correa, 1958, English translation published as *King Lazarus,* Muller, 1960, published
as *King Lazarus: A Novel,* introduction by O. R.
Dathorne, Macmillan/Collier, 1971.

Main basse sur le Cameroun (political essay; title
means "The Plundering of Cameroon"), F.
Maspero, 1972.

Remember Ruben (title in pidgin English), Buchet
Chastel, 1973, translation by Moore published
under the same title, Three Continents Press,
1980.

Perpetue et l'habitude du malheur, Buchet Chastel,
1974, translation by John Reed and Clive Wake
published as *Perpetua and the Habit of Unhappiness,* Heinemann Educational, African Writers
Series, 1978.

*La Ruine presque cocasse d'un polichinelle: Remem-
ber Ruben deux,* Harmattan, 1979, translation by
Richard Bjornson published as *Lament for an
African Pol,* Three Continents Press, 1985.

*Les Deux Meres de Guillaume Ismael Dzewatama:
Futur Camionneur,* Buchet Chastel, 1982.

La Revanche de Guillaume Ismael Dzewatama, Buchet
Chastel, 1984.

Founder in 1978 and editor of *Peuples noirs Peuples
africains* (tribune of French-speaking black radicals).
Contributor during the early 1960s to the anti-colonial
journals *Tumultueux Cameroun* and *Revue camerou-
naise.*

*ADAPTATIONS: Perpetua and the Habit of Unhappi-
ness* was adapted by Michael Etherton as a play of the
same title; it was first produced in Zaria, Nigeria, in
1981.

SIDELIGHTS: Born in the Cameroon town of M'Balmayo
and educated in French missionary schools and universities, Mongo Beti, as he prefers to be known,
centers his novels on the encroachment of Western
ideals, education, and religion upon African civilization. In particular, he laments the inability of European administrators and missionaries during the early
twentieth century colonial rule to recognize the inherent value of existing African religions and beliefs, as
well as the Africans' own inability to withstand European influence. Calling Beti "one of the most elegant
and sophisticated of African writers," Eustace Palmer
reflected in his book *The Growth of the African Novel*
that "taken as a whole [Beti's work] probably gives

the most thoroughgoing exposure to the stupidity of the imperialist attempt to devalue traditional education and religion and replace them by an inadequate western educational system and a hypocritical Christian religion."

In his first four novels, written from 1954 to 1958, Beti couches his disdain for European imperialist advances and his own countrymen's gullibility in episodic tales combining comic farce and bitter satire. Thomas Cassirer pointed out in a *L'Esprit Createur* review that each of Beti's anti-imperialist novels features an "African village . . . situated at the meeting point between traditional communal life and a new awareness of imminent change." When European administrators and missionaries—sometimes well-meaning and sometimes corrupt, but always ignorant—arrive in an untouched African village, misunderstanding and chaos inevitably ensue. Beti emphasizes the absurdity of the misunderstandings, suggesting through satire the harm that befalls both the modern and traditional societies when their people attempt to impose conflicting values on one another.

While a student at Aix, Beti penned his first novel, *Ville cruelle*—which means "Cruel City"—under the pseudonym Eza Boto. He has since repudiated both the name and the novel, which is generally considered weak and melodramatic. Critics have noted, however, that this early effort displays much of the perceptive wit found in his later writings. Set in Tanga, the site of lumber mills and rail yards, the novel details the bewilderment and anger of African workers and their families at this unsolicited imposition of Western industrialization.

In *The Poor Christ of Bomba,* set in the colonial 1930s, comic irony arises when the well-meaning Reverend Father Superior Drumont sets out to convert the inhabitants of a bush village and save them from the greed and temptation that had corrupted Europeans, later to discover that the Africans had only embraced his religion hoping to learn the Europeans' secrets of material success. He also learns that the "sixa," a missionary house where African girls live for several months to learn the duties of a Christian wife, has become an agent not of Christian piety but of venereal disease. "Faced with this horrendous proof that he has unknowingly [perpetrated] the very corruption from which he tried to protect the Africans," Cassirer related, "Father Drumont returns to Europe in despair."

Father Drumont represents the type of missionary Beti treats sympathetically in his novels, according to

Cassirer. "They are . . . the only ones who explicitly believe in a universal humanity that transcends barriers of race and culture," he explained. "Yet the missionaries' faith in universal humanity remains purely abstract because their primitivist view of the African leads them to treat him as a pure child of nature with no cultural identity of his own." A. C. Brench further described Beti's missionaries in *The Novelists' Inheritance in French Africa* as "the kind who want to do good for the Africans but, unfortunately for them, start from the premise that all Africans are unable to organize their lives unless helped by Europeans." This well-meaning denial of an inherent African culture and intellect is not only insulting to Africans, Brench suggested, but is harmful to both cultures, as the character Father Drumont learns. "The change that takes place in the Father is one of the most interesting features of the novel," Palmer found. Although not all missionaries are so enlightened during the course of their work, Palmer explained, with each discovery of a failed good intention "the Father seems to be gradually groping his way towards a realization of the validity of traditional life and culture."

The missionary in *King Lazarus,* Father Le Guen, is somewhat more zealous and uncompromising than Father Drumont of *The Poor Christ of Bomba.* Palmer noted, "Thematically, [*King Lazarus*] is similar to the earlier novels ce it is also concerned with the exposure of the pretentiousness of an alien cultural and imperialist system which shows little respect for the traditional life and dignity of the people." In the novel, Father Le Guen persuades the polygamous tribal chief of the Essazam to convert to Christianity and give up all but one of his wives. The twenty-two former wives and their families, outraged at the breach of tribal custom as well as at the rudeness of turning the women out of their home, protest to the French colonial authorities. In the confrontation between the civil administration, the missionary, and the tribal chief, Beti exposes the vices of each party. The authorities, attempting to stop Father Le Guen from converting the chief, do not do so out of any respect for the tribal culture but for reasons of political expediency, Palmer pointed out. Father Le Guen believes his firm stand on Christianity and monogamy are for the best, but he ignores such thoughtful and practical considerations as where the now-homeless ex-wives will live. "His zeal might have been partly excused if the conversion to Christianity had made the chief a better man," Palmer maintained. "On the contrary, it seems to liberate the most repulsive impulses in him." Irony and comedy pervade in *King Lazarus* as in Beti's other works, but, according to Palmer, "its prevailing cynicism suggests the bitterness of a man who is probably fed up with most things."

Like *The Poor Christ of Bomba* and *King Lazarus,* Beti's *Mission Accomplished* "is a farce but, at the same time, there is bitterness and sorrow," judged Brench. Set in the 1950s—the last decade of colonial rule in Cameroon—the novel details the shortcomings of the colonial educational system. No whites appear in the novel, but European influence is introduced by the protagonist, Jean-Marie Medza, who returns to his village home after failing his exams at a French secondary school. He is immediately sent to Kala, a bush village, to retrieve the runaway wife of a distant relative. "Initially, he looks upon this mission as a means of parading his superior knowledge," Brench related, and the villagers reward him with food, animals, and the chief's daughter in marriage for the wisdom they believe he is teaching them. "Only later does he realize how inadequate his education and understanding of life really are," Brench remarked. "Jean-Marie appreciates more and more, as his stay lengthens, the positive qualities they have and which he has never been able to acquire." Summarizing Beti's thesis in the novel, Palmer explained that "the formal classical education to which young francophones were exposed was ultimately valueless, since it alienated them from their roots in traditional society, taught them to consider the values of that society inferior to French ones and gave them little preparation for the life they were to lead."

An opponent of the French government in control of his country and, later, of the Yaounde regime in power, Beti left Cameroon before it achieved its independence in 1960. After settling in France, Beti became a teacher and for more than a decade gave up writing. In 1972, however, he composed a lengthy essay entitled *Main basse sur le Cameroun: Autopsie d'une decolonisation* (the title means "The Plundering of Cameroon"), criticizing the Yaounde regime for remaining under the control of the French after the country's formal liberation.

A series of novels soon followed, focusing more on the problems of modern, decolonized Cameroon than on the country during its colonization. Still containing elements of satire, the books assume a documentary-style narrative and approach cynicism more closely than Beti's previous works. In *Remember Ruben, Perpetua and the Habit of Unhappiness,* and *Lament for an African Pol,* Beti depicts the harsh aspects of life under the rule of Baba Toura, a tyrannical president of the United Republic of Cameroon after the country's independence. Wrote Robert P. Smith, Jr.,

in *World Literature Today,* "Toura's administration, which fosters famine, misery, persecution and corruption in the wake of African independence, is perpetuated by evil characters in the novels against whom heroic protagonists struggle constantly." Heroic inspiration arises from the memory of patriot Ruben Urn Nyobe, leader of political opposition in Cameroon before its independence. Although Ruben himself never appears in the novels, tales of his valiant deeds and lofty ideals motivate oppressed villagers into revolutionary action.

Remember Ruben follows the life of a solitary, young boy renamed Mor-Zamba by the villagers who take him in, and a friend he makes, Abena. When Mor-Zamba is older his neighbors send him to a labor camp to prevent his marriage to the daughter of a prominent villager, and Abena goes after him. The men reunite eighteen years later, Abena having become a revolutionary and a hero, and Mor-Zamba having learned his true origin. Ben Okri of *New Statesman* praised the author's handling of "the relationship between individuals and a complex, clouded situation of emerging national politics," adding that "Beti's depiction of a colony's traumas, confusions and corruptions is vivid and masterly."

Again emphasizing the corruption of national politics through glimpses of the harshness of individual lives, Beti laments the slave-like conditions of the modern woman in contemporary Africa in his *Perpetua and the Habit of Unhappiness.* The novel focuses on the miserable marriage of the main character, Perpetua, to her husband, Edouard; the tender but doomed affair between Perpetua and her lover, Zeyang; and the true friendship between Perpetua and her companion, Anna-Marie. Smith, writing in the *College Language Association Journal,* called the novel "a dramatic indictment of the ill-fated independence in [Beti's] native land dominated by corrupt dictatorial power, as well as a forceful denunciation of the disgraceful status of African women in such regimes." Smith praised Beti's treatment of modern-day Africa, saying the author wrote *Perpetua* "not to criticize the colonial past as was his custom, but to accuse the present period of independence and self-government, and to pave the way to a better future for Africa and Africans."

A novel that "no serious reader of African literature can afford to neglect," according to *Choice* contributor N. F. Lazarus, Beti's *Lament for an African Pol* chronicles the activities of Mor-Zamba, who reappears from the novel *Remember Ruben* with two revolutionary friends to organize a resistance "against the despotic rule of a colonially sanctioned chief." According to Smith in *World Literature Today,* "the novel takes on a 'Robin Hood' atmosphere when the three resolute Rubenists set out on their long journey, robbing the rich and giving to the poor, outwitting the oppressors and conveying courage to the oppressed." Affirming that Beti's "storytelling technique remains vibrant and captivating," Smith noted that, as in *Perpetua,* "of particular interest is the author's sympathetic treatment of African women."

Again "studying marriage patterns and the evolving roles of women," Beti's 1982 novel, *Les Deux Meres de Guillaume Ismael Dzewatama: Futur Camionneur,* recounts "a curious love story, full of drama, harmonizing the political and literary," assessed Hal Wylie in a review of the book in *World Literature Today.* Wylie explained that, similar to Beti's other writings, *Les Deux Meres* "focuses on a unique family which nevertheless dramatizes the sad plight of a corrupt, dictatorial country like Beti's own Cameroon." The family in the novel consists of young Guillaume Ismael, his father, and Guillaume's two mothers—the father's first wife and his French mistress, whom he married to resolve a difficult situation. The double marriage solves nothing; instead, it prompts more confusion. Reflected Wylie, "Seeing the tensions from the point of view of the African boy and his good-hearted, idealistic but naive white mother throws into relief the melodrama and pathos of modern Africa and all its ironies."

Commenting on Beti's range of political and social statements and his episodic, satirical method of conveying them, Brench remarked: "Nothing is sacred: prejudices, passions, ideals, purity are all corrupted by Beti's unrelenting laughter and insistence on the physical nature of things. . . . Yet, behind all this there is this inexpressible sadness, as if a great deception had made life bitter and cynical humour was the only relief." Several critics have pointed to a statement about Cameroon made by the character Jean-Marie at the end of *Mission Accomplished,* calling it Beti's lament for the plight of the African people: "The tragedy which our nation is suffering today is that of a man left to his own devices in a world which does not belong to him, which he has not made and does not understand."

BIOGRAPHICAL/CRITICAL SOURCES:

BOOKS

Arnold, Stephen H., editor, *Critical Perspectives on Mongo Beti,* Lynne Rienner (Boulder, CO), 1997.

Brench, A. C., *The Novelists' Inheritance in French Africa: Writers from Senegal to Cameroon,* Oxford University Press, 1967.
Contemporary Literary Criticism, Volume 27, Gale, 1984.
Moore, Gerald, *Seven African Writers,* Oxford University Press, 1962.
Palmer, Eustace, *The Growth of the African Novel,* Heinemann Educational, 1979.
The Penguin Companion to Classical, Oriental, and African Literature, McGraw, 1969.
Study of the Novels of Mongo Beti and Ngugi wa Thiong, Maxwell School of Citizenship and Public Affairs, Syracuse University (Syracuse, NY), 1990.

PERIODICALS

Choice, October, 1975, January, 1986.
College Language Association Journal, March, 1976.
Journal of Black Studies, December, 1976.
L'Esprit Createur, autumn, 1970.
Nation, October 11, 1965.
New Statesman, January 30, 1981.
Times Literary Supplement, May 15, 1969, October 29, 1971.
World Literature Today, winter, 1982, winter, 1984.

*   *   *

BLACKWELL, David (Harold) 1919-

PERSONAL: Born April 24, 1919, in Centralia, IL; son of Grover (a hostler for the Illinois Central Railroad) and Mabel (a homemaker; maiden name, Johnson) Blackwell; married Ann Madison, December 27, 1944; children: three sons, five daughters. *Education:* University of Illinois, A.B., 1938, A.M., 1939, Ph.D., 1941.

ADDRESSES: Office—Department of Statistics, University of California, Berkeley, CA 94720.

CAREER: Institute for Advanced Study (IAS), Rosenwald fellow, 1941-42; Southern Agricultural and Mechanical College (later Southern University), Baton Rouge, LA, instructor of mathematics and physics, 1942-43; Clark College, Atlanta, GA, instructor of mathematics, 1943-44; Howard University, professor, 1944-54; University of California, Berkeley, professor of statistics, 1954-73, chair of department of statistics, 1956-61, director of Study Center, United

Kingdom and Ireland, 1973-75, professor, 1973-89, emeritus professor of statistics and mathematics, 1989—. Brown University, research fellow, 1943; Rand Corporation, mathematician, 1948-50; Stanford University, visiting professor, 1950-51; University of California, Berkeley, visiting professor, 1954-55.

MEMBER: International Association for Statistics in the Physical Sciences, National Academy of Sciences, American Association for the Advancement of Science, American Mathematical Society (vice president, 1968-71), American Academy of Arts and Sciences, American Statistical Association (vice president, 1978—), Institute of Mathematical Statistics (fellow; president, 1955).

AWARDS, HONORS: W. W. Rouse Ball lecturer, University of Cambridge, 1974; Wald lecturer, Institute of Mathematical Statistics, 1977; John Von Neumann Theory Prize, 1979; R. A. Fisher Award, Committee of Presidents of Statistical Societies, 1986; awarded honorary degrees by twelve institutions, including Carnegie-Mellon University, Yale University, Howard University, Harvard University, and the National University of Lesotho.

WRITINGS:

Some Properties of Markoff Chains, [Urbana, IL], 1941.
(With Richard Bellman) *On Games Involving Bluffing,* Rand Corporation (Santa Monica, CA), 1950.
(With M. A. Girshick) *Theory of Games and Statistical Decisions,* Wiley, 1954, Dover (New York City), 1979.
Basic Statistics, McGraw-Hill, 1969.
(With Leon Henkin) *Mathematics: Report of the Project 2061 Phase I Mathematics Panel,* American Association for the Advancement of Science (Washington, DC), 1989.
Statistics, Probability, and Game Theory: Papers in Honor of David Blackwell, edited by Thomas Shelburne Ferguson, Lloyd S. Shapely, and James B. MacQueen, Institute of Mathematical Statistics (Hayward, CA), 1996.

Contributor of articles to journals, including *Annual of Mathematical Statistics, Econometrica, Naval Research Logistics Quarterly, Pacific Journal of Mathematics,* and *Proceedings of the National Academy of Science.*

SIDELIGHTS: David Blackwell is a theoretical statistician noted for the rigor and clarity of his work. Most of his career has been dedicated to teaching and

to exploring topics in Bayesian statistics, probability theory, game theory, set theory, dynamic programming, and information theory. Blackwell is a member of the National Academy of Sciences and the National Academy of Arts and Sciences and holds honorary doctorates from twelve universities, including Carnegie-Mellon, Yale, Harvard, Howard, and the National University of Lesotho. In 1986, Blackwell received the R. A. Fisher Award from the Committee of Presidents of Statistical Societies, in recognition of his career accomplishments.

Blackwell grew up in Centralia, Illinois, where he was born on April 24, 1919, to Grover and Mabel Johnson Blackwell. His brothers, J. W. and Joseph, and his sister, Elizabeth, were younger than he. His mother was a full-time homemaker, and his father was a hostler for the Illinois Central Railroad. Although two of the city's elementary schools were racially segregated, the one Blackwell attended was integrated.

Blackwell was intrigued with games like checkers, and wondered about such questions as whether the first player could always win. His interest in mathematical topics increased in high school. The mathematics club advisor would challenge members with problems from the *School Science and Mathematics* journal and submit their solutions; Blackwell was identified three times in the magazine as having solved a problem, and one of his solutions was published.

After graduating from high school at the age of sixteen, Blackwell entered the University of Illinois in 1935. After his freshman year, Blackwell became concerned that his father was borrowing money to send him to college, and he decided to support himself. His jobs included washing dishes, waiting tables, and cleaning the equipment in the entomology lab. By taking summer courses and proficiency exams, Blackwell graduated in three years, and continued on at the university to earn a master's degree and a doctorate. His dissertation on Markov chains led to his first publications in 1942 and 1945. After receiving his Ph.D. in mathematics in 1941, Blackwell spent a year as a Rosenwald Fellow at the Institute for Advanced Study (IAS) in Princeton, where he became acquainted with John von Neumann.

Blackwell then launched a job search by writing to each of the 105 African-American colleges in the country. Although he was not aware of any overt racial discrimination directed at him, he simply assumed that his role would be teaching at an African-

American school. In later years, he would learn of some behind-the-scenes difficulties related to his race, including opposition to his appointment as an honorary faculty member at Princeton (which was customary for members of the Institute for Advanced Study). In 1942, Jerzy Neyman interviewed Blackwell for a possible position at the University of California at Berkeley; Neyman's support apparently did not prevail over others' prejudices, and no offer was made.

One of the first of three schools to offer Blackwell a position was Southern University in Baton Rouge, and he taught there for the 1942-1943 academic year. In the following year, Blackwell was an instructor at Clark College in Atlanta. In 1944, he joined the faculty of Howard University, which was the most prestigious employer of black scholars in the country. He was promoted to full professor in 1947 and served as head of the Mathematics Department until 1954. Two days after Christmas in 1944, Blackwell married Ann Madison, with whom he had three sons and five daughters.

The focus of Blackwell's mathematical interests shifted to statistics in 1945, when he heard Abe Girshick lecture on sequential analysis. He was intrigued by the presentation, and later contacted Girshick with what he thought was a counterexample to a theorem presented in the lecture. That contact resulted in an enduring friendship and fruitful collaboration. The two co-authored *Theory of Games and Statistical Decisions,* which was first published in 1954 and revised in 1980. Blackwell's first statistical paper, published in 1946, contained what he saw as his first original contribution to mathematics. He produced an elegant proof that extended an important equation to a weaker set of constraints.

During the summers of 1948-1950, Blackwell worked at the Rand Corporation. He and a few colleagues, including Girshick, became interested in the theory of duels. The initial condition concerned two people advancing toward each other, each holding a gun with one bullet; if one fires and misses, he is required to continue walking toward his opponent. The problem was how a dueler should decide the optimal time to shoot. After developing the theory of that situation, Blackwell proposed and investigated the more challenging case where each gun was silent, so a dueler does not know whether his opponent has fired unless he has been hit. Pursuing such topics earned Blackwell a reputation as a pioneer in the theory of duels.

In 1954, Blackwell accepted a professorship at the University of California at Berkeley. From 1956 to 1961, he served as chairman of the Department of Statistics. During the 1973-1975 academic years, Blackwell was director of the University of California Study Center for the United Kingdom and Ireland. While in England, he was invited to give the Rouse Ball Lecture at the University of Cambridge. In 1989, Blackwell retired from the University of California, Berkeley, where he remains a professor emeritus.

Blackwell told Donald Albers in an interview for *Mathematical People* that he had never been interested in doing research. "I'm interested in *understanding,* which is quite a different thing." He explored topics that intrigued him in many mathematical areas. He told Morris DeGroot in an interview for *Statistical Science,* "Don't worry about the overall importance of the problem; work on it if it looks interesting. I think there's probably a sufficient correlation between interest and importance." Indeed, results of his work have found application in a variety of fields, including economics and accounting. In 1979, he was awarded the John von Neumann Theory Prize for his work in dynamic programming.

One of Blackwell's most satisfying accomplishments was finding a game theory proof for the Kuratowski Reduction Theorem in topology. Some fifteen years after it was published, he told Albers, "That gave me real joy, connecting these two fields that had not been previously connected."

BIOGRAPHICAL/CRITICAL SOURCES:

BOOKS

Albers, Donald J., and G. L. Alexanderson, editors, *Mathematical People,* Birkhauser (Boston), 1985, pp. 18-32.
Duren, Peter, editor, *A Century of Mathematics in America,* Part III, American Mathematical Society (Providence, RI), 1989, pp. 589-615.

PERIODICALS

Statistical Science, February, 1986, pp. 40-53.*

*   *   *

BOLES, Robert (E.)   1943-

PERSONAL: Born in 1943.

ADDRESSES: Home—7 Union Park, Boston, MA 02118.

CAREER: Writer.

WRITINGS:

The People One Knows: A Novel, Houghton, 1964.
Curling: A Novel, Houghton, 1968.

Short stories published in anthologies, including *The Best Short Stories by Negro Writers: An Anthology from 1899 to the Present,* edited by Langston Hughes, Little, Brown, 1967; and *An Introduction to Black Literature in America.* Contributor to periodicals, including *Tri-Quarterly.*

BIOGRAPHICAL/CRITICAL SOURCES:

PERIODICALS

Negro Digest, May, 1965, p. 52; January, 1968, p. 38; August, 1968, p. 86.
Saturday Review, February 17, 1968, p. 38.

*   *   *

BOTO, Eza
   See BIYIDI, Alexandre

*   *   *

BOUCOLON, Maryse 1937-
   (Maryse Conde)

PERSONAL: Born February 11, 1937, in Guadeloupe, West Indies; daughter of Auguste and Jeanne (Quidal) Boucolon; married Mamadou Conde, 1958 (divorced, 1981); married Richard Philcox (a translator), 1982; children: (first marriage) Leila, Sylvie, Aicha. *Education:* Sorbonne, University of Paris, Ph.D., 1976.

ADDRESSES: Home—Montebello, 97170 Petit Bourg, Guadeloupe, French West Indies. *Agent*—Rosalie Siegel, Act III Productions, 711 Fifth St., New York, NY 10022.

CAREER: Ecole Normale Superieure, Conakry, Guinea, instructor, 1960-64; Ghana Institute of Languages, Accra, Ghana, 1964-66; Lycee Charles de Gaulle,

Saint Louis, Senegal, instructor, 1966-68; French Services of the BBC, London, program producer, 1968-70; University of Paris, Paris, France, assistant at Jussieu, 1970-72, lecturer at Nanterre, 1973-80, charge de cours at Sorbonne, 1980-85; program producer, Radio France Internationale, France Culture, 1980—. Bellagio Writer in Residence, Rockefeller Foundation, 1986; visiting professor, University of Virginia and University of Maryland, 1992—; lecturer in the United States, Africa, and the West Indies. Presenter of a literary program for Africa on Radio-France.

AWARDS, HONORS: Fulbright Scholar, 1985-86; Prix litteraire de la Femme, Prix Alain Boucheron, 1986, for *Moi, Tituba, Sorciere Noire de Salem;* Guggenheim fellow, 1987-88; Puterbaugh fellow, University of Oklahoma, Norman, 1993.

WRITINGS:

(Editor) *Anthologie de la litterature africaine d'expression francaise,* Ghana Institute of Languages, 1966.
Dieu nous l'a donne (four-act play; title means "God Given"; first produced in Martinique, West Indies, at Fort de France, 1973), Oswald, 1972.
Mort d'Oluwemi d'Ajumako (four-act play; title means "Death of a King"; first produced in Haiti at Theatre d'Alliance Francaise, 1975), Oswald, 1973.
Heremakhonon (novel), Union Generale d'Editions, 1976, translation by husband, Richard Philcox, published under same title, Three Continents Press, 1982.
(Translator into French with Philcox) Eric Williams, *From Columbus to Castro: The History of the Caribbean,* Presence Africaine, 1977.
(Editor) *La Poesie antillaise* (also see below), Nathan (Paris), 1977.
(Editor) *Le Roman antillais* (also see below), Nathan, 1977.
La Civilisation du bossale (criticism), Harmattan (Paris), 1978.
Le profil d'une oeuvre: Cahier d'un retour au pays natal (criticism), Hatier (Paris), 1978.
La Parole des femmes (criticism), Harmattan, 1979.
Tim tim? Bois sec! Bloemlezing uit de Franstalige Caribsche Literatuur (contains revised and translated editions of *Le Roman antillais* and *La Poesie antillaise*), edited by Andries van der Wal, In de Knipscheer, 1980.
Une Saison a Rihata (novel), Robert Laffont (Paris), 1981, translation by Philcox published as *A Season in Rihata,* Heinemann, 1988.

Segou: Les murailles de terre (novel), Robert Laffont,
    1984, translation by Barbara Bray published as
    Segu, Viking, 1987.

Segou II: La terre en miettes (novel), Robert Laffont,
    1985, translation by Linda Coverdale published as
    The Children of Segu, Viking, 1989.

Pays Mele (short stories), Hatier, 1985.

Moi, Tituba, sorciere noire de Salem (novel),
    Mercure de France (Paris), 1986, translation by
    Philcox published as *I, Tituba, Black Witch of
    Salem,* University Press of Virginia, 1992.

La Vie scelerate (novel), Seghers, 1987, translation
    by Victoria Reiter published as *Tree of Life,*
    Ballantine, 1992.

Haiti Cherie (juvenile), Bayard Presse, 1987.

Pension les Alizes (play), Mercure de France, 1988.

The Children of Nya, Viking, 1989.

Victor et les barricades (juvenile), Bayard Presse,
    1989.

Traversee de la mangrove (novel), Mercure de
    France, 1990, translation by Richard Philcox pub-
    lished as *Crossing the Mangrove,* Doubleday,
    1995.

Les derniers rois mages (novel), Mercure de France,
    1992.

Tree of Life: A Novel of the Caribbean, Ballantine,
    1992.

La colonie du nouveau monde (novel), Robert Laffont,
    1993.

The Tropical Breeze Hotel (play), Ubu Repertory
    Theater Publications, 1994.

The Last of the African Kings, translated by Richard
    Philcox, University of Nebraska Press, 1997.

Windward Heights, translated by Richard Philcox,
    Soho Press, 1999.

OTHER

(With Francoise Pfaff) *Conversations with Maryse
    Conde,* University of Nebraska Press, 1996.

Also author of recordings for Record CLEF and Radio France Internationale. Contributor to anthologies;
contributor to journals, including *Presence Africaine*
and *Recherche Pedagogique.*

SIDELIGHTS: West Indian author Maryse Boucolon,
published as Maryse Conde, "deals with characters in
domestic situations and employs fictitious narratives
as a means of elaborating large-scale activities," assert *World Literature Today* writers Charlotte and
David Bruner. Drawing on her experiences in Paris,
West Africa, and her native Guadeloupe, Conde has
created several novels which "attempt to make cred-

ible on an increasingly larger scale the personal human complexities involved in holy wars, national ri-
valries, and migrations of peoples," the Bruners state.
Heremakhonon, for example, relates the journey of
Veronica, an Antillean student searching for her roots
in a newly liberated West African country. During
her stay Veronica becomes involved with both a powerful government official and a young school director
opposed to the new regime; "to her dismay," David
Bruner summarizes, "she is unable to stay out of the
political struggle, and yet she is aware that she does
not know enough to understand what is happening."

The result of Veronica's exploration, which is told
with an "insinuating prose [that] has a surreal, airless
quality," as Carole Bovoso relates in the *Voice Literary Supplement,* is that "there were times I longed to
rush in and break the spell, to shout at this black
woman and shake her. But no one can rescue
Veronica," the critic continues, "least of all herself;
Conde conveys the seriousness of her plight by means
of a tone of relentless irony and reproach." "Justly or
not," write the Bruners, "one gains a comprehension
of what a revolution is like, what new African nations
are like, yet one is aware that this comprehension is
nothing more than a feeling. The wise reader will go
home as Veronica does," the critics conclude, "to
continue more calmly to reflect, and to observe."

Conde expands her scope in *Segu,* "a wondrous novel
about a period of African history few other writers
have addressed," notes *New York Times Book Review*
contributor Charles R. Larson. In tracing three generations of a West African family during the early and
mid-1800s, "Conde has chosen for her subject . . . [a]
chaotic stage, when the animism (which she calls
fetishism) native to the region began to yield to Islam," the critic describes. "The result is the most
significant historical novel about black Africa published in many a year." Beginning with Dousika, a
Bambara nobleman caught up in court intrigue, *Segu*
trails the exploits of his family, from one son's conversion to Islam to another's enslavement to a third's
successful career in commerce, connected with stories
of their wives and concubines and servants. In addition, Conde's "knowledge of African history is prodigious, and she is equally versed in the continent's
folklore," remarks Larson. "The unseen world haunts
her characters and vibrates with the spirits of the
dead."

Some critics, however, fault the author for an excess
of detail; *Washington Post* contributor Harold
Courlander, for example, comments that "the plethora

of happenings in the book does not always make for easy reading." The critic explains that "the reader is sometimes uncertain whether history and culture are being used to illuminate the fiction or the novel exists to tell us about the culture and its history." While Howard Kaplan concurs with this assessment, he adds in the *Los Angeles Times Book Review* that *Segu* "glitters with nuggets of cultural fascination. . . . For those willing to make their way through this dense saga, genuine rewards will be reaped." "With such an overwhelming mass of data and with so extensive a literary objective, the risks of . . . producing a heavy, didactic treatise are, of course, great," the Bruners maintain. "The main reason that Conde has done neither is, perhaps, because she has written here essentially as she did in her two earlier novels: she has followed the lives of the fictional characters as individuals dominated by interests and concerns which are very personal and often selfish and petty, even when those characters are perceived by other characters as powerful leaders in significant national or religious movements." Because of this, the critics conclude, *Segu* is "a truly remarkable book. . . . To know [the subjects of her work] better, as well as to know Maryse Conde even better, would be a good thing."

BIOGRAPHICAL/CRITICAL SOURCES:

PERIODICALS

Library Journal, March 15, 1995, p. 96.
Los Angeles Times Book Review, March 8, 1987.
New York Times, February 22, 1995, p. C15.
New York Times Book Review, May 31, 1987; October 25, 1992, p. 11.
Washington Post, March 3, 1987.
World Literature Today, winter, 1982; winter, 1985, pp. 9-13; spring, 1985; summer, 1986; spring, 1987; summer, 1988; autumn 1993, pp. 1-768.*

*   *   *

BOUTROS-GHALI, Boutros 1922-

PERSONAL: Born November 14, 1922, in Cairo, Egypt; married to Leah Nadler. *Education:* Cairo University, LL.D (law), 1946; Sorbonne, Ph.D. (international law), 1949; Columbia University, Fulbright Research Scholar, 1954-55. *Religion:* Coptic-Christian. *Avocational interests:* Swimming, collecting Greek antiquities.

ADDRESSES: Home—2 Avenue El-Nil Giza, Cairo, Egypt.

CAREER: University of Cairo, professor of international law and international relations, 1949-77; *Al-Ahram Al-Iktisadi,* editor, 1960-75; *Al-Siyasa Al-Dawlyya* (a foreign affairs journal), editor; Egyptian diplomat; acting Egyptian Minister of State for Foreign Affairs under Anwar Sadat, 1977-91; Foreign Minister of State of Egypt; Vice President of the Socialist International; Secretary General of the United Nations, 1992-96; author.

MEMBER: Academie des sciences morales et politiques (Academie francaise); Egyptian Society of International Law (vice president); International Legal Center (trustee); International Commission of Jurists; Council and Executive Committee of the International Institute of Human Rights; African Society of Political Studies (president, 1980).

WRITINGS:

An Agenda For Peace 1995, United Nations (New York City), 1995.
An Agenda for Development 1995, United Nations (New York City), 1995.
An Agenda for Democratization, United Nations (New York City), 1996.
Egypt's Road to Jerusalem: A Diplomat's Story of the Struggle for Peace in the Middle East, Random House (New York City), 1997.
Unvanquished: A U.S.-U.N. Saga, Random House, 1999.

SIDELIGHTS: Boutros Boutros-Ghali, who achieved international fame as United Nations Secretary General, was born into a wealthy family in Cairo, Egypt. Boutros-Ghali's family added the surname "Boutros" after his grandfather, Boutros Ghali, a Coptic Christian and the prime minister of Egypt, was assassinated in 1910 by a Muslim man.

After studying in Paris and receiving a Ph.D. in international law from the Sorbonne in 1949, Boutros-Ghali returned to Egypt and became a professor of international law and international relations at the University of Cairo. Boutros-Ghali's strong background in international politics eventually earned him a place in an influential circle of persons who wrote in the 1950's and 1960's for *Al-Ahram* (title means *The Pyramids*), an Egyptian foreign policy journal. Egyptian President Anwar Sadat made Boutros-Ghali his acting foreign minister during Sadat's 1977 visit to

Jerusalem, and in 1979 Boutros-Ghali assisted Sadat during Egypt's negotiations with Israel for the Camp David Accords.

After the Camp David achievements, Boutros-Ghali continued to rise in rank within Egyptian government. By 1991, he had gained enough respect in the sphere of international politics to be considered for the United Nations' top office. In November of 1991, Boutros-Ghali ran for the position of United Nations Secretary General and won easily. During his tenure as head of the United Nations, Boutros-Ghali walked a tightrope between competing international powers.

In 1995, the United Nations published two documents written by Boutros-Ghali, *An Agenda For Peace 1995* and *An Agenda for Development 1995,* and a third, *An Agenda for Democratization,* in 1996. In all three publications, the title topic is discussed with analyses and arguments formed by Boutros-Ghali and his advisers. The publications also contain related United Nations documents.

The year 1997 saw the release of Boutros-Ghali's first foray into non-academic literature, *Egypt's Road to Jerusalem: A Diplomat's Story of the Struggle for Peace in the Middle East.* Based on journals he kept from 1979 through 1981, the book is Boutros-Ghali's account of political events in Egypt during those years. Beginning with Sadat's historic trip to Jerusalem and ending with Sadat's assassination, the book contains many details about the behind-the-scenes maneuvering of the peace process and the personalities of Sadat, United States President Jimmy Carter, and Israeli Prime Minister Menachem Begin. Boutros-Ghali, a major player in the negotiations for Egypt, also discusses interesting negotiations he conducted with less-developed countries, countries whose support was crucial to Egypt when Egypt lost the support of Arab states. A *Kirkus Reviews* critic commented "Boutros-Ghali . . . gives a convincing view of . . . [the] exhausting process of international diplomacy." Nader Entessar, writing for *Library Journal,* recommended the book for its "easy narrative [which] makes the book especially accessible to nonspecialists."

BIOGRAPHICAL/CRITICAL SOURCES:

PERIODICALS

Academic Library Book Review, October, 1995, p. 33.
American Political Science Review, June, 1997, pp. 494-496.

Book World, May 25, 1997, p. 11.
Economist, July 19, 1997, p. 9.
Foreign Affairs, July, 1997, p. 163.
Guardian (Manchester), May 31, 1992, p. 8.
Journal of Economic Literature, September, 1995, p. 1501.
Journal of Government Information, September, 1996, p. 676.
Kirkus Reviews, April 1, 1997, p. 542.
Library Journal, May 1, 1997, p.124.
New Republic, June 18, 1993, pp. 16-20; May 19, 1997, p. 28.
New York Review of Books, June 26, 1997, p. 19.
New York Times, November 22, 1991, p. 12; December 30, 1991, p. 1.
New York Times Book Review, July 20, 1997, p. 7.
Observer (London), November 24, 1991, p. 23.
Publisher's Weekly, April 14, 1997, p. 66.
Social Education, November, 1994, p. 454.*

*   *   *

BOYD, Candy Dawson 1946-

PERSONAL: Full name is Marguerite Dawson Boyd; born August 8, 1946, in Chicago, IL; daughter of Julian Dawson and Mary Ruth Ridley. *Education:* Northeastern Illinois State University, B.A., 1967; University of California, Berkeley, M.A., 1978, Ph.D., 1982.

ADDRESSES: Home—1416 Madrone Way, San Pablo, CA 94806. *Office*—St. Mary's College of California, School of Education, Box 4350, Morgana, CA 94575.

CAREER: Overton Elementary School, Chicago, IL, teacher, 1968-71; Longfellow School, Berkeley, CA, teacher, 1971-73; University of California, Berkeley, extension instructor in the language arts, 1972-79; Berkeley Unified School District, Berkeley, district teacher trainer in reading and communication skills, 1973-76; St. Mary's College of California, Morgana, extension instructor in language arts, 1972-79, lecturer, 1975, assistant professor and director of reading leadership and teacher effectiveness programs, 1976-87, director of elementary education, 1983-88, associate professor, 1983-91, professor of education, 1991—; writer.

MEMBER: International Reading Association, American Educational Research Association, California Reading Association.

AWARDS, HONORS: Circle of Gold was named a notable children's trade book in the field of social studies by the National Council for the Social Studies and the Children's Book Council in 1984, and a Coretta Scott King Award Honor Book by the American Library Association in 1985; *Breadsticks and Blessing Places* was selected for the Children's Books of the Year List by the Child Study Children's Book Committee at Bank Street College; *Charlie Pippin* was nominated for the Mark Twain Award and the Dorothy Canfield Fisher Children's Book Award, 1988, and was selected by the International Reading Association and Children's Book Council for the Children's Choices for 1988 List, and by the Oklahoma Library Association for the Oklahoma Sequoyah Children's Book Award Master List, 1989. Boyd received the Outstanding Bay Area Woman Award, 1986; Outstanding Person in Mount Diablo Unified School District, Black Educators Association, 1988; The Author's Hall of Fame Certificate of Appreciation for literary and artistic contributions to the field of literature for children and adults, San Francisco Reading Association and Santa Clara Reading Association, 1989; Celebrate Literacy Award for exemplary service in the promotion of literacy, International Reading Association and the San Francisco Reading Association, 1991; Distinguished Achievement Award, National Women's Political Caucus, San Francisco Chapter, 1991; and she was the first recipient of the St. Mary's College of California Professor of the Year Award, 1992.

WRITINGS:

Circle of Gold, Scholastic (New York City), 1984.
Breadsticks and Blessing Places, Macmillan (New York City), 1985, published as *Forever Friends,* Puffin (New York City), 1986.
Charlie Pippin, Macmillan, 1987.
Chevrolet Saturday, Macmillan, 1992.
Fall Secrets, Puffin, 1994.
Daddy, Daddy Be There, Philomel (New York City), 1995.
A Different Beat, Puffin, 1996.

Contributor of articles and essays to professional journals. Reviewer of children's literature for the *Los Angeles Times* and *San Francisco Chronicle.*

SIDELIGHTS: Candy Dawson Boyd is a professor of education and an award-winning children's writer. A former teacher of children of many ethnic and cultural backgrounds, Boyd strives to provide children with the kind of rich cultural knowledge she derived from her own childhood in an African-American family. In an interview with *CA,* Boyd remarked that throughout her life she has been strengthened by the stories she heard as a child about the determination and fortitude of her family and ancestors. "Chicago schools were segregated," the author told *CA,* "so I got stories at school about Africa and its kingdoms. But the stories I got at home were the ones that were more powerful because they were about the things that happened to family members and how we had survived and prevailed." As a writer for children and young adults she provides the positive message she once took from those stories, the message "that you make it. It's going to be hard and tough and it's not fair," she told *CA,* "but you make it."

Among many interests, including jazz singing and acting, Boyd grew up with a deep commitment to social change. She told *CA* that a pivotal moment in her childhood came while she read *The Moved Outers,* a book by Florence Crandall Means. This book tells the story of a Japanese-American girl who lived in California during World War II, when the U.S. government placed many Americans of Japanese descent in internment camps. Boyd remembered: "One day the girl and her family were just moved out and put into a camp. Everything was taken away from them because they were Japanese. I was just hysterical. How could they do this to her? How could they come, these soldiers, and just take a family away and take all their stuff? I remember running to my mother screaming, 'They didn't do this—it didn't happen, did it?' I remember my mother telling me 'yes.' And after that I was different. That was when I became a political child. Of course, I was aware of what it meant to be black; racism was always a part of life. With that, plus what happened in this book, something totally changed inside. I lost my innocence and trust about how protected you were as a citizen of this country."

In college, she was active in the civil rights movement, and her increasing involvement in the cause eventually superseded her schoolwork. She quit school and went to work as a field staff organizer with Martin Luther King, Jr.'s, Southern Christian Leadership Conference. After working for over a year in both the North and the South, the violent deaths of movement leaders such as Medgar Evers, the Kennedys, and Martin Luther King, Jr., left Boyd emotionally devastated. She returned to college, this time to pursue a degree in education, continuing to participate in the civil rights movement with activist

Jessie Jackson in the teacher's division of Operation PUSH (People United to Save Humanity).

After college, Boyd worked for several years as an elementary school teacher in her own predominantly black Chicago neighborhood. Although external circumstances had forced her out of the civil rights movement and into teaching, she found that she was able to pursue her social ideals in the classroom. "I was a militant teacher," Boyd told *CA*. "I knew that being black and poor meant life was going to be a lot harder for my students, and I wanted them to have as much opportunity as possible." Boyd demanded that the black national anthem be played in school and organized marches for beautifying the neighborhood. In her way, she "adopted" her students. "Some of my children had never seen Lake Michigan," she told *CA*. "So we would meet by the liquor store on Saturdays and we would go downtown to the Goodman Theater and we took a Greyhound bus tour of Chicago. They became my children, and I wanted them."

Boyd moved to Berkeley, California, in 1971, where, she told *CA*, "I ended up teaching children who weren't black: Asian children and Latino children and Caucasian children and children from India and all over the world." Seeking reading material for her students, Boyd found a disturbing lack of children's books from the diverse cultural backgrounds that comprised her classroom. "I got absolutely enraged when I went out and I looked at the atrocity of the books out there. I couldn't even find decent books for some of the white ethnic groups that I had. I wanted material, good books, strong books, books that had very interesting characters and ordinary stories. But I never saw children of color in realistic fiction depicted as children whose culture—a culture embedded within them as a part of who they are—comes out in ways that are ordinary and regular. That enraged me and I decided to become a writer."

After making the decision to become a writer, Boyd went to work. "I spent the first two years reading all the books written for children in the Berkeley Public Library—from A to Z, fiction and nonfiction—because I wanted to see what was out there and what wasn't there. I also did research and took two courses at the University of California, Berkeley, on writing for children. I wrote manuscripts that my teachers thought were good, but for nine years I was rejected by publishing companies." One of the manuscripts Boyd sent to many publishers was *Breadsticks and Blessing Places,* a book that, Boyd told *CA,* was "very, very important" to her.

Breadsticks and Blessing Places is the story of Toni, a twelve-year-old girl whose parents want to send her to a prestigious prep school. Toni, who has difficulties with math in her present school, fears disappointing her parents. She also struggles with two friends who are very different from one another and don't always get along. When one of them, the carefree Susan, is killed by a drunk driver, Toni is inconsolable. The novel follows her slow and painful route toward recovery from this trauma. A reviewer of *Breadsticks and Blessing Places* for the *Bulletin of the Center for Children's Books* commented: "Boyd deals fully and candidly with a child's reaction to the death of a close friend as well as to other aspects of the maturation process that are universal." The critic added that the story is presented "with insight and compassion."

Boyd told *CA* that publishers who rejected *Breadsticks and Blessing Places* said it was "relentless" on the subject of death. Boyd wrote the novel in a personal effort to work out her feelings about the death of her best friend in childhood. She also created *Breadsticks and Blessing Places* to help children who have experienced loss to work out their own emotions. To write the book, Boyd conducted two years of research on grief as experienced by children. "In that period of research," she told *CA,* "I learned that children grieve deeply over a long period of time and that the rituals that adults use at wakes and funerals don't work for children." Boyd wanted her book to respect children's emotions and give them a safe forum. "I call my books a safe place. Children are complex. They have very strong, meaningful ideas and questions about the world that they live in. They have deep emotions that persist, and I think that there should be a genre of books that they read that respect that."

Boyd's first published novel was the award-winning *Circle of Gold,* the story of Mattie Benson, a young girl on a quest to buy a gold pin for her mother. Mattie's father has died prior to the opening of the story, leaving her mother to support Mattie and her twin brother by working long hours at a factory and managing the apartment building in which they live. Mattie works hard to help out at home, but her mother is tired and unhappy and shows more irritation than love for her daughter. Mattie, already suffering the loss of her father, feels she is losing her mother as well. In school, a mean-spirited girl named Angel accuses Mattie of stealing her bracelet and, although Mattie is not punished, she is treated like a thief by her teacher and her peers. Against these harsh and daunting odds, Mattie's quest to buy the expensive pin—the circle of gold—for her mother vividly symbolizes her love of her family and her determination to make things right again.

Boyd's 1987 book, *Charlie Pippin,* again explores family relationships that have become troubled due to outside circumstances. Charlie is an energetic and curious eleven-year-old girl with unusual entrepreneurial skills. Despite her very good intentions, Charlie has difficulty following her school's disciplinary code. At home, she has difficulty with her father, a Vietnam War veteran who is embittered, isolated, and unwilling to discuss his experience except by defending the war. Charlie, trying to better understand her father, undertakes a report on the Vietnam War for her social studies class. In her research she finds a newspaper clipping about her father and two of his friends who were killed in action during the war. Asking her grandparents and her mother about the article, Charlie learns that her father was a war hero and, before his experience in Vietnam, a man of dreams and joy.

Charlie's father is not pleased with her choice of report topics, or the trouble that her extracurricular business dealings have caused at school, but Charlie's spirit is invincible. She deceives her parents and convinces a favorite uncle to take her to Washington, D.C., to see the Vietnam Veteran's War Memorial. There she acquires rubbings from the wall of the names of her father's dead friends. On her return, Charlie provokes her father to honestly confront the anguish of his past—an anguish that has broken down some of the family's lines of communication. Sybil Steinberg wrote in her *Publishers Weekly* review of *Charlie Pippin:* "A strong black protagonist makes this a rare YA book; the finesse with which Boyd ties its many themes into a very moving, unified whole turns this into a stellar offering."

Boyd commented to *CA* about her strong feelings that books about blacks need to be written by those who understand the black experience in America. "That's something I have fought other writers about," she said. "You don't have the right to write about my people when you don't know anything about them. You don't have the right to portray neighborhoods as full of gangs, with no fathers. The statistics show that is not true. Although more neighborhoods are like that now because of crack [cocaine], at the same time there are lots of families that go to work and kids that go to work and try to make it every day." Boyd has received letters from readers confirming her view that not enough literature has depicted normal African-American life. "I've had white kids write to me and

say, 'I didn't know that black kids had feelings like me.' My attitude was, How could you know? You don't live in a country that lets that happen. And if a book could reach you in that kind of way, then . . . wow!"

In Boyd's novels, families, although loving, are besieged with real problems. Parents often inadvertently impose a cynicism—brought about by the injustice and grief they have encountered—upon children who are better able to maintain dreams and an idealistic approach to life. The young protagonists of Boyd's novels strive for a place in the world of their family as well as the world at large, despite the harshness they witness. Through youthful endeavors to set things right, the stories conclude optimistically. Boyd told *CA:* "I refuse to have losers as characters. I hate the words 'coping' and 'adjusting.' In my families there is always a possibility of renewal."

Boyd recognizes that the family is only one aspect in children's lives. "School is a major part of what happens to the child," she told *CA.* "School is one of the places where children can have an opportunity to grow outside of the family—to find parts of themselves that they may not be able to find inside the family." Boyd's interest in what school systems have to offer children surfaces both in her novels and in her career. After completing her doctorate in education, she taught at St. Mary's College of California, where she was named the first Professor of the Year in 1992. She has become renowned for her devotion to training teachers and developing systems that help young people become enthusiastic readers.

Both her books and her teaching have won Boyd many distinguished awards. "My dreams of being famous were satisfied when I was still a child," Boyd told *CA.* "Yes, I'm honored when I receive an award, but often the decision [to grant her an award] is political, and I don't know how these decisions are made. Not knowing, I take it all with less ego." The idealism that Boyd has exhibited since her own childhood now hinges on her profound belief in children. "I still have hope," she told *CA.* "I have a lot invested in the children. Not much of my hope lies with adults. If books help children, or give them a safe place to go, then that's the biggest reward for writing."

BIOGRAPHICAL/CRITICAL SOURCES:

PERIODICALS

Bulletin of the Center for Children's Books, July-August, 1985; May, 1987.

Publishers Weekly, June 7, 1985, p. 81; April 10, 1987, p. 96.
School Library Journal, September, 1985, p. 142; April, 1987, p. 92; November, 1988, p. 53.
Voice of Youth Advocates, February, 1986, p. 382; October, 1987.

*　　*　　*

BRADLEY, David (Henry), Jr. 1950-

PERSONAL: Born September 7, 1950, in Bedford, PA; son of David Henry (a minister and historian) and Harriette Marie (maiden name, Jackson) Bradley. *Education:* University of Pennsylvania, B.A. (summa cum laude), 1972; attended Institute for United States Studies, London; King's College, London, M.A., 1974.

ADDRESSES: Home—433270 Viamarin, La Jolla, CA 92024. *Agent*—c/o Wendy Weil Agency, 232 Madison Ave., New York, NY 10016.

MEMBER: Authors Guild (Author's Guild Council member, 1988—), Authors League of America, PEN, National Book Critics Circle, Screen Writers Guild.

AWARDS, HONORS: Presidential Scholarship, U. S. Office of Education, 1968; PEN/Faulkner Award, American Academy and Institute of Arts and Letters award for literature, and *New York Times Book Review* "Editors' Choice" citation, all 1982, all for *The Chaneysville Incident;* Guggenheim fellowship, 1989; National Endowment for the Arts fellowship, 1991.

WRITINGS:

South Street (novel), Viking, 1975, reprinted, Scribner's, 1986.
The Chaneysville Incident (novel; Book-of-the-Month Club alternate selection), Harper, 1981.
(Editor with Shelley Fisher Fishkin) *The Encyclopedia of Civil Rights in America,* M. E. Sharpe Reference, 1998.

Contributor of articles, stories, and reviews to magazines and newspapers, including *Signature, Savvy, Tracks, Quest, New York Arts Journal, Esquire, New York Times Magazine, Philadelphia Magazine, Southern Review, New York Times Book Review, Los Angeles Times Book Review, Washington Post Book World,* and *Philadelphia Inquirer Magazine.*

WORK IN PROGRESS: A nonfiction book on race in America.

SIDELIGHTS: David Bradley has reaped considerable critical acclaim for his novels *South Street* and *The Chaneysville Incident,* both published before he turned thirty-five. *Dictionary of Literary Biography* contributor Valerie Smith ranks Bradley "among the most sophisticated literary stylists of his generation," a fiction writer whose works "present subtle and original perspectives on issues that traditionally have concerned significant Afro-American writers: the meaning of community, the effects of racism, the shape and substance of history." Indeed, *The Chaneysville Incident,* winner of the 1982 PEN/Faulkner Award, blends historical fact and fiction in its representation of a rural Pennsylvania community through which the Underground Railroad once ran. Acclaimed "by fiction writers and by popular and scholarly writers alike," the work has "placed Bradley in the vanguard of contemporary novelists," according to Smith. A professor of English at Philadelphia's Temple University, Bradley is a self-styled perfectionist who can work many years crafting a novel. He also writes nonfiction articles for magazines and newspapers, including *Esquire* and the *New York Times Book Review,* and is a member of the National Book Critics Circle.

Geographically, the city of Philadelphia is less than three hundred miles from Bradley's home town of Bedford, Pennsylvania. As Bradley notes in a *New York Times Book Review* profile, however, the region that formed his authorial sensibility was starkly different from the urban area in which he now lives. "The town of Bedford is perilously close to the Mason-Dixon line," he said. ". . . It was not that hospitable for blacks-or that comfortable." Bradley grew up among a community of about one hundred blacks in a county that imbued him with skepticism toward the Black Power movement that was gaining momentum as he entered college. "I had grown up in a rural white society," he said, "and I knew damn well we [blacks] had no power." Although an honors student at the University of Pennsylvania, Bradley felt alienated from his peers because of his rural background. As an undergraduate he discovered a group of compatriots in an unlikely setting-a bar on Philadelphia's South Street. "I really enjoyed that place," he recollected. ". . . My experiences there confirmed my impression that the things I saw in the blacks at the university, my contemporaries, were as artificial as everything else. The people on South Street were totally without power. Their lives were terrible-they just lived with the situation and made the best of it."

Bradley's first novel-written while he was still an undergraduate-was inspired by his visits to the South Street bar. "Without blunting the pathos of this tale, Mr. Bradley has infused what could have been a standard story and stock characters with new vigor. Probing beneath the sociological stereotypes, he portrays his characters with a fullness that amplifies much of the lusty irony of ghetto life. . . . It is Bradley's unerring depiction of the vitality that rears itself even within this despairing setting that distinguishes this novel," notes Mel Watkins in the *New York Times*. The work centers on Adlai Stevenson Brown, a young poet who begins to frequent Lightnin' Ed's Bar. There he talks to patrons and listens to their stories; this plot structure provides for vignettes recounted by other characters. "The novel is really about the street itself, as Bradley's energetic and shifting narrative makes clear," Smith writes. ". . . These frequent changes in perspective illustrate various to life. Furthermore, the shifts imitate the vibrancy and the multifariousness of the world the author explores."

Bradley began to conceive *The Chaneysville Incident* while he was in college, too, but he spent nearly a decade reworking four different drafts of the story before arriving at the final manuscript. The author had grown up hearing stories about the Underground Railroad in Bedford County. But in 1969, Bradley's mother told him a story he had not heard before, about thirteen runaway slaves who, upon the point of recapture in Bedford County, had chosen death over a return to slavery. The slaves were buried in thirteen unmarked graves in a family burial plot on a nearby farm. Bradley told the *New York Times Book Review:* "I knew my second novel would be about those 13 runaway slaves. And in writing about them I wanted to use material that had been glossed over, material that had been mined for descriptions of the horror of slavery without bringing along any understanding of how the system came about."

The Chaneysville Incident is the story of a young man's confrontation with his personal past, his family history, and the living legacies of racism and slavery. The protagonist, a history professor, returns to his hometown in western Pennsylvania to visit the deathbed of a man who helped to raise him. With the aid of his dying mentor, the professor begins to explore his father's mysterious death in the mountains outside Bedford-and this exploration leads, in time, to a reconstruction of one telling moment in the history of American blacks. Smith contends that the novel "is somewhat reminiscent of a musical composition in which the different movements represent variations on a common theme." Smith also notes that the varieties of narrative—the protagonist's pedantic lectures and ncreasingly emotional flashbacks, his old friend's tales of bootlegging and lynchings—"all exemplify the kinds of physical and emotional cruelty that are commonplace within a racist culture."

In addition to the prestigious PEN/Faulkner Award, *The Chaneysville Incident* won an American Academy and Institute of Arts and Letters grant for literature, and it was cited by the editors of the *New York Times Book Review* as one of the best novels of 1981. *Los Angeles Times* book editor Art Seidenbaum calls the book "the most significant work by a new male black author since James Baldwin," and *Christian Science Monitor* contributor Bruce Allen finds it "the best novel about the black experience in America since Ellison's *Invisible Man* nearly 30 years ago." Vance Bourjaily offers similar praise in the *New York Times Book Review*. "Whatever else may be said," Bourjaily claims, ". . . [Bradley's] a writer. What he can do, at a pretty high level of a complicated plot, manage a good- sized cast of characters, convey a lot of information, handle an intricate time scheme, pull off a couple of final tricks that dramatize provocative ideas, and generally keep things going for 200,000 words." The critic concludes that *The Chaneysville Incident* "deserves what it seems pretty sure to get: a lot of interested and challenged readers."

Bradley told *CA:* "I think of myself as an 'old-fashioned' writer, primarily because my fictional models are 'old-fashioned.' Like the Victorians, I am interested in the basics of plot and character, less concerned with abstract ideas. It is my belief that writers of novels should have no belief, that the idea of what is true is something that emerges from the writing, rather than being placed into it. Ultimately, I believe that if I cannot create a character who holds an idea, write a conversation (as opposed to a speech) that expresses it, or work out a plot that exemplifies it, idea or with the idea itself. In either case it has no place in my writing.

"I must frankly say that I do not love many 'contemporary' novels. For the most part they seem to me self-absorbed, self-indulgent, derivative, and basically lacking truth. Our technique has become an end rather than a means, primarily, I think, because we writers have been led to believe that truth does not sell. If we would write well, we are told, we will be obscure.

Obscurity, then, becomes the measure of writing well. I do not believe this. I have faith in the ability of people to respond to a story that treats them with kindness, honesty, dignity, and understanding. I put my faith not in publishers, and certainly not in reviewers and/or critics, but in those who read."

BIOGRAPHICAL/CRITICAL SOURCES:

BOOKS

Contemporary Literary Criticism, Volume 23, Gale, 1983.
Gliserman, Martin J., *Psychoanalysis, Language, and the Body of the Text,* University Press of Florida (Gainesville), 1996.

PERIODICALS

America, May 30, 1981.
Atlantic, May, 1981.
Christian Science Monitor, May 20, 1981.
Los Angeles Times, April 8, 1981.
New York Times, October 4, 1975, May 12, 1981.
New York Times Book Review, September 28, 1975, April 19, 1981.
Publishers Weekly, April 10, 1981.
Saturday Review, July, 1981.
Times Literary Supplement, January 16, 1987.
Washington Post, April 12, 1982.
Washington Post Book World, April 12, 1981.*

*   *   *

BRATHWAITE, Edward (Kamau)   1930-

PERSONAL: Born Lawson Edward Brathwaite May 11, 1930, in Bridgetown, Barbados West Indies; son of Hilton Edward and Beryl (Gill) Brathwaite; married Doris Monica Welcome (a teacher and librarian), March 26, 1960; children: Michael. *Education:* Attended Harrison College, Barbados; Pembroke College, Cambridge, England, B.A. (honors in history), 1953, Diploma of Education, 1954; University of Sussex, D. Phil., 1968.

ADDRESSES: Office—Department of History, University of the West Indies, Mona, Kingston 7, Jamaica.

CAREER: Writer, poet, playwright, and editor. Ministry of Education of Ghana, Education Officer, 1955-62; University of the West Indies, Kingston, Jamaica,

Department of Extra Mural Studies, tutor, assigned to island of Saint Lucia, 1962-63, university lecturer, 1963-72, senior lecturer in history, 1972-76, reader, 1976-83, professor of social and cultural history, 1982—. Plebiscite Office for the United Nations in the Trans-Volta Togoland, 1956-57.

MEMBER: Caribbean Artists Movement (founding secretary, 1966—).

AWARDS, HONORS: Arts Council of Great Britain bursary, 1967; Camden Arts Festival prize, 1967; Cholmondeley Award, 1970, for *Islands;* Guggenheim fellowship, 1972; City of Nairobi fellowship, 1972; Bussa Award, 1973; Casa de las Americas Prize for Poetry, 1976; Fulbright fellowship, 1982; Institute of Jamaica Musgrave Medal, 1983.

WRITINGS:

The People Who Came, three volumes, Longman, 1968- 72.
Folk Culture of the Slaves in Jamaica, New Beacon, 1970, revised edition, 1981.
The Development of Creole Society in Jamaica, 1770-1820, Clarendon Press, 1971.
Caribbean Man in Space and Time, Savacou Publications, 1974.
Contradictory Omens: Cultural Diversity and Integration in the Caribbean, Savacou Publications, 1974.
Our Ancestral Heritage: A Bibliography of the Roots of Culture, Carifesta, 1976.
Wars of Respect: Nanny, Sam Sharpe, and the Struggle for People's Liberation, API, 1977.
The Colonial Encounter: Language, University of Mysore, 1984.
History of the Voice: The Development of Nation Language in Anglophone Caribbean Poetry, New Beacon, 1984.

POETRY

Rights of Passage (also see below), Oxford University Press, 1967.
Masks (also see below), Oxford University Press, 1969.
Panda No. 349, Roy Institute for the Blind, 1969.
The Arrivants: A New World Trilogy (contains *Rights of Passage, Masks,* and *Islands*), Oxford University Press, 1973.
Day and Nights, Caldwell Press, 1975.
Other Exiles, Oxford University Press, 1975.
Black and Blues, Casa de las Americas, 1976.

Mother Poem, Oxford University Press, 1977.
Word Making Man: A Poem for Nicolas Guillen, Savacou Publications, 1979.
Sun Poem, Oxford University Press, 1982.
Third World Poems, Longman, 1983.
X/Self, Oxford University Press, 1987.

PLAYS

Odale's Choice (first produced in Saltpond, Ghana, 1962), Evans Brothers, 1967.

EDITOR

Iouanaloa: Recent Writing from St. Lucia, Department of Extra Mural Studies, University of West Indies, 1963.
Barbados Poetry, 1661-1979, Savacou Publications, 1979.
New Poets from Jamaica (anthology), Savacou Publications, 1979.

RECORDINGS

The Poet Speaks 10, Argo, 1968.
Rights of Passage, Argo, 1969.
Masks, Argo, 1972.
Islands, Argo, 1973.
The Poetry of Edward Kamau Brathwaite, Casa de las Americas, 1976.
Poemas, Casa de las Americas, 1976.

Contributor to *Bim* and other periodicals. Editor, *Savacou* (magazine), 1970—.

SIDELIGHTS: Edward Brathwaite is generally regarded as one of the West Indies' most prolific and talented writers. More well known for his poetry, most of Brathwaite's writings seek to explore his past and present self while examining his identity as a black person living in the Caribbean. Andrew Motion writes in the *Times Literary Supplement* that "throughout his career Brathwaite has been concerned to define his identity as a West Indian."

It was the publication of *Rights of Passage* in 1967, *Masks* in 1968, and *Islands* in 1969, that brought Brathwaite to the attention of a larger group of critics and readers. These three books of poetry constitute an autobiographical trilogy collectively entitled *The Arrivants: A New World Trilogy* that examines a Caribbean man's search for identity. The volumes trace Brathwaite's initial encounter with white culture, his journey to Africa in search of a racial self-image, and

his eventual return to his Caribbean homeland. Laurence Lieberman writes in *Poetry:* "[Brathwaite] has been able to invent a hybrid prosody which, combining jazz/folk rhythms with English-speaking meters, captures the authenticity of primitive African rituals." "In general," writes Hayden Carruth in the *Hudson Review,* "[Brathwaite] has been remarkably successful in reproducing black speech patterns, both African and Caribbean, in English syntax, using the standard techniques of contemporary poetry, and he has been equally successful in suggesting to an international audience the cultural identities and attitudes of his own people."

In 1977 Brathwaite released *Mother Poem,* the first book in a proposed second trilogy. The second book of the trilogy, *Sun Poem,* was published in 1982. As in Brathwaite's first trilogy, *Mother Poem* and *Sun Poem* continue Brathwaite's exploration of his selfhood. As Andrew Motion explains in the *Times Literary Supplement:* "In *Mother Poem,* [Brathwaite] provides another detailed account of his home [in the West Indies]. But in addition to exploring his complex relationship with the place, he also recounts its own efforts to find an independent and homogeneous character." David Dorsey remarks in *World Literature Today:* "Brathwaite is particularly ingenious in achieving semantic complexity through his use of assonance, enjambment, word divisions, grammatical and lexical ambiguity, puns and neologisms. This joie d'esprit occurs within a rhythm always obedient to the emphases and feelings intended. The style paradoxically reveals the author's sober, passionate and lucid perception on the beauty and pain black Barbadians are heir to."

In a *World Literature Today* review of *Sun Poem* Andrew Salkey comments that "Brathwaite writes 'performance,' 'rituals' and 'illuminations' which result in conflated portraits of persons, places and events recalled through a filter of sequential evocative poems—no ordinary creative accomplishment."

BIOGRAPHICAL/CRITICAL SOURCES:

BOOKS

Authors and Areas of the West Indies, Steck-Vaughn, 1970.
Caribbean Writers, Three Continents, 1979.
Contemporary Literary Criticism, Volume 11, Gale, 1979.
West Indian Literature, Archon Books, 1979.

PERIODICALS

Books, January, 1970.
Books and Bookmen, May, 1967.
Book World, November 3, 1968.
Caribbean Quarterly, June, 1973.
Caribbean Studies, January, 1971. 1976.
Critical Quarterly, summer, 1970.
Hudson Review, summer, 1974.
Library Journal, March 15, 1970.
Nation, April 9, 1988.
New Statesman, April 7, 1967.
Poetry, April, 1969, May, 1971.
Saturday Review, October 14, 1967.
Times Literary Supplement, February 16, 1967, August 15, 1968, January 28, 1972, June 30, 1972, November 14, 1975, January 20, 1978, February 18, 1983.
Virginia Quarterly Review, autumn, 1963, autumn, 1968, spring, 1970.
World Literature Today, winter, 1977, summer, 1978, summer, 1983.

*   *   *

BRAY, Rosemary L. 1955-

PERSONAL: Born in 1955 in Chicago, IL; daughter of Nehemiah and Mary (Love) Bray; married; children: two. *Education:* Yale University, B.A., 1976.

ADDRESSES: Agent—c/o Greenwillow Books, 1350 Avenue of the Americas, New York, NY 10019.

CAREER: Journalist, editor, and writer. Has held editorial positions at *Essence,* the *Wall Street Journal, Ms.,* and the *New York Times Book Review.*

WRITINGS:

Martin Luther King (juvenile biography), illustrated by Malcah Zeldis, Greenwillow (New York), 1995.
Unafraid of the Dark: A Memoir, Random House (New York), 1998.
Nelson Mandela (juvenile biography), illustrated by Malcah Zeldis, Greenwillow, 1998.

SIDELIGHTS: "Had I been born a few years earlier, or a decade later," journalist Rosemary Bray wrote in a 1992 *New York Times* essay, "I might now be living on welfare . . . or working as a hospital nurse's aide

for $6.67 an hour." Yet the girl who grew up on welfare earned an Ivy League degree and became a successful editor and writer—largely, she believes, because of the government's financial support of her family during its years of desperate poverty. When the issue of welfare reform came to a head in the United States in the 1990s, Bray felt compelled to tell her story to challenge misleading stereotypes about the system. "In spite of a wealth of evidence about the true nature of welfare and poverty in America," she wrote in the *New York Times,* "the debate has turned ugly, vicious and racist. The 'welfare question' has become the race question and the woman question in disguise." In her account of her childhood, Bray described the difficulty and pain of living poor, but argues that the very modest funding her family received from Aid to Families with Dependent Children (AFDC) enabled her mother to keep the family together, obtain crucial medical care for her children, and nurture them toward successful, independent, and productive futures that might not have been possible had welfare payments been restricted.

Bray grew up in Chicago, the oldest of four children born to Nehemiah Bray and his wife, Mary Love Bray. Both of Bray's parents had moved to Chicago from the rural south; both had attained only minimal formal education. Nehemiah Bray worked at odd jobs—hauling junk, working as a butcher, or peddling food from a lunch wagon—and her mother initially worked in a laundry and then in a restaurant. What began as an apparently happy marriage, however, deteriorated when Mary Bray became pregnant with her first child, and her husband forbade her to go on working outside the home. Though he continued to earn wages, his serious gambling habit threatened the family's support. During Bray's first years of life, the family barely got by; when Bray was about four years old, her mother decided to apply for welfare. Though this decision infuriated Nehemiah and, in his daughter's words "closed a door between my parents that never reopened," he reluctantly accepted Mary Bray's action and arranged not to be at home when welfare officials visited, since payments were available only to families without a male head of household. "'There were times when we hardly had a loaf of bread in here,'" Mary Bray later told her daughter as the author recounted in the *New York Times.* "'It was close. I wasn't going to let you all go hungry.'"

Bray's 1992 account of her childhood was expanded into a book-length memoir, *Unafraid of the Dark* in 1998. Her story, reviewers noted, is an inspiring one. Bray recounts her mother's hard work to make ends meet on AFDC payments that barely covered the necessities and the family's day-long trips on public transportation to medical clinics. She credits her parents for their resolve to educate their children; Mary Bray found a way to send all her offspring to Catholic schools, which she felt were a better option than public schools, and served as a solid role model. Bray recalled in the *New York Times* essay: "She volunteered as a chaperone for every class trip, sat with us as we did homework she did not understand herself. She and my father reminded us again and again and again that every book, every test, every page of homework was in fact a ticket out and away from the life we lived." Bray earned her first ticket in grade six, when a perceptive teacher recognized the young girl's intellectual talent and recommended her for a scholarship to the more challenging Francis W. Parker School, an almost all-white private school. Bray overcame her initial sense of alienation and resentment there and went on to attend Yale University, from which she graduated in 1976. Her life on welfare, she notes, ended two weeks later. Bray began a journalism career with a small newspaper in Connecticut, going on to editorial positions at such national publications as *Essence,* the *Wall Street Journal, Ms.,* and the *New York Times Book Review.*

Bray's story, as detailed in *Unafraid of the Dark,* was well-received by critics. Martha Nichols, in the *Women's Review of Books,* noted that the book reflects the author's "clear political agenda." Nichols pointed out that Bray analyzes complex issues of race, class, and gender in an affecting and intellectually stimulating way and observed that the material dealing with Bray's difficult relationship with her father is powerfully written. Yet Nichols also found a reticence in Bray's book that she felt stopped the author from a more revealing and honest confrontation of her feelings. "Too often her most complex observations have . . . pat endings," the reviewer wrote. Nichols further commented that some of the writing "veers perilously close to the inspiration glosses of women's magazines like *Essence.* . . . Perhaps because Bray is reporting on her own life for a larger purpose, the lyricism and edginess that invigorate are missing."

Detroit Free Press book editor Linnea Lannon expressed similar opinions about *Unafraid of the Dark.* Lannon wrote that the memoir is "inspiring if a trifle bland," and added that, given the difficulties Bray recounts, the book is "surprisingly mild." Furthermore, Lannon remained unconvinced by Bray's political message. She disagreed with the author's claim that, had her mother been forced to accept low-paying

work instead of receiving welfare benefits, she would not have been able to nurture her children effectively. "Though Bray intends her life story as a testament to welfare," Lannon wrote, "her memoir ironically makes it clear that AFDC might not have mattered." What pushed Bray and her siblings to succeed, in Lannon's view, was their intelligence, their strength of character, and their parents' insistence that they do their best. "Welfare made a tough life marginally better," Lannon acknowledged. "But one finishes *Unafraid of the Dark* knowing that welfare didn't make [the Brays] who they are."

In a 1998 *Essence* interview with columnist E. R. Shipp, Bray defended her views on welfare. She emphasized that, by 1998 welfare rules, her mother would have been required to be away from the home, working. "I think [welfare reform] would have completely destabilized our family," she told Shipp. "My mother would have been away. And my mother was the buffer that protected us, not only from the outside world but also from my father." Bray also pointed out that the culture of poverty has changed dramatically since the 1960s. "I cried all day" when President Clinton signed the 1998 welfare reform bill, she said. "I cried because we are so much more a consumerist culture than we were . . . and the drug culture as we understand it now didn't exist. So there were not these vast disparities that could lead you to believe that the only way you could get these things was to start selling stuff that would destroy other people's lives. None of that happened when I was a child." Bray went on to say that it is incorrect to believe that most welfare recipients are African-American women, and that welfare creates or perpetuates poverty. "If you don't want people to be poor anymore," she concluded, "then give them the tools [education, child care, health care] not to be poor. . . . Because welfare is not the problem. Poverty is the problem. Not working is the problem. The nature of work in America is the problem. That needs to be the focus."

In addition to her memoir, Bray has also written two juvenile biographies in picture-book format, intended for readers from grades two to five. *Martin Luther King* (1995), a biography of civil rights leader Dr. Martin Luther King, Jr., received favorable reviews. A contributor to *Publishers Weekly* considered it an "able biography," enhanced by the impressive folk-style illustrations of Malcah Zeldis. In *Horn Book,* Mary M. Burns found Bray's writing to be "focused and sharp" and "filled with detail." Burns especially admired Bray's ability to depict Dr. King as "both a hero and as a human being." Bray and Zeldis worked together again on *Nelson Mandela* (1998), a biography about the South African anti-apartheid leader and 1993 Nobel peace prize winner.

BIOGRAPHICAL/CRITICAL SOURCES:

BOOKS

Bray, Rosemary L., *Unafraid of the Dark: A Memoir,* Random House (New York), 1998.

PERIODICALS

Booklist, January 1, 1998, p. 768.
Detroit Free Press, February 22, 1998, p. 7E.
Essence, May, 1998, pp. 102, 206, 208.
Horn Book, May-June, 1995, p. 340.
Kirkus Reviews, February 15, 1995, p. 221.
New York Times, November 8, 1992.
New York Times Book Review, February 12, 1995, p. 18; March 8, 1998, p. 8.
Publishers Weekly, November 28, 1994, p. 61; January 19, 1998, p. 361.
School Library Journal, February, 1995, p. 89.
Women's Review of Books, September, 1998, pp. 16-18.*

*   *   *

BROOKS, Gwendolyn 1917-

PERSONAL: Born June 7, 1917, in Topeka, KS; daughter of David Anderson and Keziah Corinne (Wims) Brooks; married Henry Lowington Blakely II, September 17, 1939; children: Henry Lowington III, Nora. *Education:* Graduate of Wilson Junior College, 1936.

ADDRESSES: Home—7428 South Evans Ave., Chicago, IL 60619.

CAREER: Poet and novelist. Publicity director, National Association for the Advancement of Colored People (NAACP) Youth Council, Chicago, IL, 1937-38. Taught poetry at numerous colleges and universities, including Columbia College, Elmhurst College, Northeastern Illinois State College (now Northwestern Illinois University), and University of Wisconsin-Madison, 1969; Distinguished Professor of the Arts, City College of the City University of New York, 1971; currently professor at Chicago State University. Member, Illinois Arts Council.

MEMBER: National Institute of Arts and Letters, American Academy of Arts and Letters, Society of Midland Authors (Chicago), Cliff Dwellers Club, Tavern Club (honorary member), Caxton Club (honorary member).

AWARDS, HONORS: Named one of ten women of the year, *Mademoiselle* magazine, 1945; National Institute of Arts and Letters grant in literature, 1946; American Academy of Arts and Letters Award for creative writing, 1946; Guggenheim fellowships, 1946 and 1947; Eunice Tietjens Memorial Prize, *Poetry* magazine, 1949; Pulitzer prize in poetry, 1950, for *Annie Allen;* Robert F. Ferguson Memorial Award, Friends of Literature, 1964, for *Selected Poems;* Thormod Monsen Literature Award, 1964; Anisfield-Wolf Award, 1968, for *In the Mecca;* named Poet Laureate of Illinois, 1968; National Book Award nomination, for *In the Mecca;* Black Academy of Arts and Letters Award, 1971, for outstanding achievement in letters; Shelley Memorial Award, 1976; Poetry Consultant to the Library of Congress, 1985-86; inducted into National Women's Hall of Fame, 1988; Essence Award, 1988; Frost Medal, Poetry Society of America, 1989; Lifetime Achievement Award, National Endowment for the Arts, 1989; Society for Literature Award, University of Thessoloniki (Athens, Greece), 1990; Kuumba Liberation Award; Aiken-Taylor award, 1992; Jefferson Lecturer award, 1994; National Book Foundation medal for Lifetime Achievement, 1994; Gwendolyn Brooks Elementary School named in her honor, Aurora, IL, 1995; approximately fifty honorary degrees from universities and colleges, including Columbia College, 1964, Lake Forest College, 1965, and Brown University, 1974.

WRITINGS:

POETRY

A Street in Bronzeville (also see below), Harper (New York City), 1945.
Annie Allen (also see below), Harper, 1949.
The Bean Eaters (also see below), Harper, 1960.
In the Time of Detachment, In the Time of Cold, Civil War Centennial Commission of Illinois, 1965.
In the Mecca (also see below), Harper, 1968.
For Illinois 1968: A Sesquicentennial Poem, Harper, 1968.
Riot (also see below), Broadside Press (Highland Park, MI), 1969.
Family Pictures (also see below), Broadside Press, 1970.

Aloneness, Broadside Press, 1971.

Aurora, Broadside Press, 1972.

Beckonings, Broadside Press, 1975.

Primer for Blacks, Black Position Press, 1980.

To Disembark, Third World Press (Chicago, IL), 1981.

Black Love, Brooks Press, 1982.

Mayor Harold Washington [and] *Chicago, The I Will City,* Brooks Press, 1983.

The Near-Johannesburg Boy, and Other Poems, David Co., 1987.

Gottschalk and the Grande Tarantelle, David Co., 1988.

Winnie, Third World Press, 1988.

Children Coming Home, David Co., 1991.

Also author of *A Catch of Shy Fish* (also see below), 1963.

JUVENILE

Bronzeville Boys and Girls (poems), Harper, 1956.

The Tiger Who Wore White Gloves: Or You Are What You Are, Third World Press, 1974, reissued, 1987.

FICTION

Maud Martha (novel; also see below), Harper, 1953.

Stories included in books, including *Soon One Morning: New Writing by American Negroes, 1940-1962* (includes "The Life of Lincoln West"), edited by Herbert Hill, Knopf (New York City), 1963, published in England as *Black Voices,* Elek, 1964; and *The Best Short Stories by Negro Writers; An Anthology from 1899 to the Present,* edited by Langston Hughes, Little, Brown (Boston), 1967.

COLLECTED WORKS

Selected Poems, Harper, 1963.

(With others) *A Portion of That Field: The Centennial of the Burial of Lincoln,* University of Illinois Press (Champaign), 1967.

The World of Gwendolyn Brooks (contains *A Street in Bronzeville, Annie Allen, Maud Martha, The Bean Eaters,* and *In the Mecca;* also see below), Harper, 1971.

(Editor) *A Broadside Treasury* (poems), Broadside Press, 1971.

(Editor) *Jump Bad: A New Chicago Anthology,* Broadside Press, 1971.

Report from Part One: An Autobiography, Broadside Press, 1972.

(With Keorapetse Kgositsile, Haki R. Madhubuti, and Dudley Randall) *A Capsule Course in Black Poetry Writing,* Broadside Press, 1975.

Young Poet's Primer (writing manual), Brooks Press, 1981.

Very Young Poets (writing manual), Brooks Press, 1983.

The Day of the Gwendolyn: A Lecture (sound recording), Library of Congress (Washington, DC), 1986.

Blacks (includes *A Street in Bronzeville, Annie Allen, The Bean Eaters, Maud Martha, A Catch of Shy Fish, Riot, In the Mecca,* and most of *Family Pictures*), David Co., 1987.

The Gwendolyn Brooks Library, Moonbeam Publications, 1991.

Also author of broadsides *The Wall* and *We Real Cool,* for Broadside Press, and *I See Chicago,* 1964. Contributor to books, including *New Negro Poets USA,* edited by Langston Hughes, Indiana University Press, 1964; *The Poetry of Black America: Anthology of the Twentieth Century,* edited by Arnold Doff, Harper, 1973; and *Celebrate the Midwest! Poems and Stories for David D. Anderson,* edited by Marcia Noe, Lake Shore, 1991. Contributor of poems and articles to *Ebony, McCall's, Nation, Poetry,* and other periodicals. Contributor of reviews to Chicago *Sun-Times,* *Chicago Daily News,* *New York Herald Tribune,* and *New York Times Book Review.*

SIDELIGHTS: In 1950 Gwendolyn Brooks, a highly regarded poet, became the first black author to win the Pulitzer prize. Her poems from this period, specifically *A Street in Bronzeville* and *Annie Allen,* were "devoted to small, carefully cerebrated, terse portraits of the Black urban poor," Richard K. Barksdale comments in *Modern Black Poets: A Collection of Critical Essays.* Jeanne-Marie A. Miller calls this "city-folk poetry" and describes Brooks's characters as "unheroic black people who fled the land for the city only to discover that there is little difference between the world of the North and the world of the South."

Though best known for her poetry, in the 1950s Brooks published her first novel. *Maud Martha* presents vignettes from a ghetto woman's life in short chapters, says Harry B. Shaw in *Gwendolyn Brooks.* It is "a story of a woman with doubts about herself and where and how she fits into the world. Maud's concern is not so much that she is inferior but that she is perceived as being ugly." Eventually, she takes a stand for her own dignity by turning her back on a patronizing, racist store clerk. "The book is . . . about the triumph of the lowly," comments Shaw.

"[Brooks] shows what they go through and exposes the shallowness of the popular, beautiful white people with 'good' hair. One way of looking at the book, then, is as a war with . . . people's concepts of beauty." Its other themes include "the importance of spiritual and physical death," disillusionment with a marriage that amounts to "a step down" in living conditions, and the discovery "that even through disillusionment and spiritual death life will prevail," Shaw maintains.

Other reviewers feel that Brooks is more effective when treating the same themes in her poetry, but David Littlejohn, writing in *Black on White: A Critical Survey of Writing by American Negroes,* feels the novel "is a striking human experiment, as exquisitely written . . . as any of Gwendolyn Brook's poetry in verse. . . . It is a powerful, beautiful dagger of a book, as generous as it can possibly be. It teaches more, more quickly, more lastingly, than a thousand pages of protest." In a *Black World* review, Annette Oliver Shands appreciates the way in which *Maud Martha* differs from the works of other early black writers: "Miss Brooks does not specify traits, niceties or assets for members of the Black community to acquire in order to attain their just rights. . . . So, this is not a novel to inspire social advancement on the part of fellow Blacks. Nor does it say *be poor, Black and happy.* The message is to accept the challenge of being human and to assert humanness with urgency."

However, Brooks's later poems show a marked change in tone and content. Just as her first poems reflected the mood of their era, her later works mirror their age by displaying what *National Observer* contributor Bruce Cook calls "an intense awareness of the problems of color and justice." Toni Cade Bambara comments in the *New York Times Book Review* that at the age of fifty "something happened [to Brooks], a something most certainly in evidence in 'In the Mecca' (1968) and subsequent works-a new movement and energy, intensity, richness, power of statement and a new stripped lean, compressed style. A change of style prompted by a change of mind."

"Though some of her work in the early 1960s had a terse abbreviated style, her conversion to direct political expression happened rapidly after a gathering of black writers at Fisk University in 1967," Jacqueline Trescott reports in the *Washington Post.* Brooks told Tate, "They seemed proud and so committed to their own people. . . . The poets among them felt that black poets should write as blacks, about blacks, and address themselves *to* blacks." If many of her earlier poems had fulfilled this aim, it was not due to conscious intent, she said; but from this time forward, Brooks has thought of herself as an African who has determined not to compromise social comment for the sake of technical proficiency.

Although *In the Mecca* and later works are characterized as tougher and possess what a reviewer for the *Virginia Quarterly Review* describes as "raw power and roughness," critics are quick to indicate that these poems are neither bitter nor vengeful. Instead, according to Cook, they are more "about bitterness" than bitter in themselves. *Dictionary of Literary Biography* essayist Charles Israel suggests that *In the Mecca*'s title poem, for example, shows "a deepening of Brooks's concern with social problems." A mother has lost a small daughter in the block-long ghetto tenement, the Mecca; the long poem traces her steps through the building, revealing her neighbors to be indifferent or insulated by their own personal obsessions. The mother finds her little girl, who "never learned that black is not beloved," who "was royalty when poised, / sly, at the A and P's fly-open door," under a Jamaican resident's cot, murdered. A *Virginia Quarterly Review* contributor compares the poem's impact to that of Richard Wright's fiction. R. Baxter Miller, writing in *Black American Poets between Worlds, 1940-1960,* comments, "*In the Mecca* is a most complex and intriguing book; it seeks to balance the sordid realities of urban life with an imaginative process of reconciliation and redemption." Other poems in the book, occasioned by the death of Malcolm X or the dedication of a mural of black heroes painted on a Chicago slum building, express the poet's commitment to her people's awareness of themselves as a political as well as a cultural entity.

Her interest in encouraging young blacks to assist and appreciate fledgling black publishing companies led her to leave Harper & Row. In the seventies, she chose Dudley Randall's Broadside Press to publish her poetry (*Riot, Family Pictures, Aloneness, Aurora,* and *Beckonings*) and *Report from Part One,* the first volume of her autobiography. She edited two collections of poetry-*A Broadside Treasury* and *Jump Bad: A New Chicago Anthology*-for the Detroit-based press. The Chicago-based Third World Press, run by Haki

R. Madhubuti (formerly Don L. Lee, one of the young poets she had met during the sixties), has also brought two Brooks titles into print. She does not regret having given her support to small publishers who dedicated themselves to the needs of the black community. Brooks was the first writer to read in Broadside's Poet's Theatre Series when it began and was also the first poet to read in the second opening of the series when the press revived under new ownership in 1988.

Riot, Family Pictures, Beckonings, and other books brought out by black publishers were given brief notice by critics of the literary establishment who "did not wish to encourage Black publishers," said Brooks. Some were disturbed by the political content of these poems. *Riot,* in particular, in which Brooks is the spokesman for the "HEALTHY REBELLION" going on then, as she calls it, was accused of "celebrating violence" by L. L. Shapiro in a *School Library Journal* review. Key poems from these books, later collected in *To Disembark,* call blacks to "work together toward their own REAL emancipation," Brooks indicated. Even so, "the strength here is not in declamation but in [the poet's] genius for psychological insight," claims J. A. Lipari in the *Library Journal.* Addison Gayle points out that the softer poems of this period-the ones asking for stronger interpersonal bonds among black Americans-are no less political: "To espouse and exult in a Black identity, outside the psychic boundaries of white Americans, was to threaten. . . . To advocate and demand love between one Black and another was to begin a new chapter in American history. Taken together, the acknowledgment of a common racial identity among Blacks throughout the world and the suggestion of a love based upon the brotherhood and sisterhood of the oppressed were meant to transform Blacks in America from a minority to a majority, from world victims to, to use Madhubuti's phrase, 'world makers'."

When *Report from Part One* came out in 1972, some reviewers complained that it did not provide the level of personal detail or the insight into black literature that they had expected. "They wanted a list of domestic spats," remarked Brooks. Bambara notes that it "is not a sustained dramatic narrative for the nosey, being neither the confessions of a private woman poet or the usual sort of mahogany-desk memoir public personages inflict upon the populace at the first sign of a cardiac. . . . It documents the growth of Gwen Brooks." Other reviewers value it for explaining the poet's new orientation toward her racial heritage and her role as a poet. In a passage she has presented

again in later books as a definitive statement, she writes: "I—who have 'gone the gamut' from an almost angry rejection of my dark skin by some of my brainwashed brothers and sisters to a surprised queenhood in the new Black sun—am qualified to enter at least the kindergarten of new consciousness now. New consciousness and trudge-toward-progress. I have hopes for myself. . . . I know now that I am essentially an essential African, in occupancy here because of an indeed 'peculiar' institution. . . . I know that Black fellow-feeling must be the Black man's encyclopedic Primer. I know that the Black-and-white integration concept, which in the mind of some beaming early saint was a dainty spinning dream, has wound down to farce. . . . I know that the Black emphasis must be not *against white* but *FOR Black.* . . . In the Conference-That-Counts, whose date may be 1980 or 2080 (woe betide the Fabric of Man if it is 2080), there will be no looking up nor looking down." In the future, she envisions "the profound and frequent shaking of hands, which in Africa is so important. The shaking of hands in warmth and strength and union."

Brooks put some of the finishing touches on the second volume of her autobiography while serving as Poetry Consultant to the Library of Congress. Brooks was sixty-eight when she became the first black woman to be appointed to the post. Of her many duties there, the most important, in her view, were visits to local schools. Similar visits to colleges, universities, prisons, hospitals, and drug rehabilitation centers characterize her tenure as Poet Laureate of Illinois. In that role, she has sponsored and hosted annual literary awards ceremonies at which she presents prizes paid for "out of [her] own pocket, which, despite her modest means, is of legendary depth," Reginald Gibbons relates in Chicago *Tribune Books.* She has honored and encouraged many poets in her state through the Illinois Poets Laureate Awards and Significant Illinois Poets Awards programs.

Brook's objectivity is considered by some reviewers as one of the most widely acclaimed features of her poetry. Janet Overmeyer notes in the *Christian Science Monitor* that Brooks's "particular, outstanding, genius is her unsentimental regard and respect for all human beings. . . . She neither foolishly pities nor condemns-she creates." Overmeyer continues, "From her poet's craft bursts a whole gallery of wholly alive persons, preening, squabbling, loving, weeping; many a novelist cannot do so well in ten times the space." Brooks achieves this effect through a high "degree of artistic control," claims Littlejohn. "The words, lines, and arrangements," he states, "have been worked and worked and worked again into poised exactness: the unexpected apt metaphor, the mock-colloquial asides amid jewelled phrases, the half-ironic repetitions-she knows it all." More importantly, Brooks's objective treatment of issues such as poverty and racism "produces genuine emotional tension," he writes.

Proving the breadth of Brooks's appeal, poets representing a wide variety of "races and . . . poetic camps" gathered at the University of Chicago to celebrate the poet's seventieth birthday in 1987, reports Gibbons. Brooks brought them together, he says, "in . . . a moment of good will and cheer." In recognition of her service and achievements, a junior high school in Harvey, IL, has been named for her. She is also honored at Western Illinois University's Gwendolyn Brooks Center for African-American Literature.

BIOGRAPHICAL/CRITICAL SOURCES:

BOOKS

Berry, S. L., *Gwendolyn Brooks,* Creative Education, 1993.
Bigsby, C. W. E., *The Second Black Renaissance: Essays in Black Literature,* Greenwood Press, 1980.
Black Literature Criticism, Gale, 1992.
Children's Literature Review, Volume 27, Gale, 1992.
Concise Dictionary of American Literary Biography: The New Consciousness, 1941-1968, Gale, 1985.
Contemporary Literary Criticism, Gale, Detroit, Volume 1, 1973; Volume 2, 1974; Volume 4, 1975; Volume 5, 1976; Volume 15, 1980; Volume 49, 1988.
Dictionary of Literary Biography, Gale, Volume 5: *American Poets since World War II,* 1980; Volume 75: *Afro-American Writers, 1940-1955,* 1988.
Evans, Mari, editor, *Black Women Writers (1950-1980): A Critical Evaluation,* Anchor/Doubleday, 1984.
Gates, Henry Louis, Jr., editor, *Black Literature and Literary Theory,* Methuen, 1984.
Gibson, Donald B., editor, *Modern Black Poets: A Collection of Critical Essays,* Prentice-Hall, 1973.
Gould, Jean, *Modern American Women Poets,* Dodd, Mead, 1985.
Kent, George, *Gwendolyn Brooks: A Life,* University Press of Kentucky, 1988.
Kufrin, Joan, *Uncommon Women,* New Century Publications, 1981.

Madhubuti, Haki R., *Say that the River Turns: The Impact of Gwendolyn Brooks,* Third World Press, 1987.
Melhem, D. H., *Gwendolyn Brooks: Poetry and the Heroic Voice,* University Press of Kentucky, 1987.
Miller, R. Baxter, *Black American Poets between Worlds, 1940-1960,* University of Tennessee Press, 1986.
Mootry, Maria K., and Gary Smith, editors, *A Life Distilled: Gwendolyn Brooks, Her Poetry and Fiction,* University of Illinois Press, 1987.
Poetry Criticism, Gale, Detroit, Volume 7, 1994.
Shaw, Harry F., *Gwendolyn Brooks,* Twayne, 1980.
World Literature Criticism, Gale, 1992.
Wright, Stephen Caldwell, editor, *On Gwendolyn Brooks: Reliant Contemplation,* University of Michigan Press, 1996.

PERIODICALS

African American Review, summer, 1992, pp. 197-211.
American Literature, December, 1990, pp. 606-16.
Atlantic Monthly, September, 1960.
Best Sellers, April 1, 1973.
Black American Literature Forum, spring, 1977; winter, 1984; fall, 1990, p. 567.
Black Enterprise, June, 1985.
Black Scholar, March, 1981; November, 1984.
Black World, August, 1970; January, 1971; July, 1971; September, 1971; October, 1971; January, 1972; March, 1973; June, 1973; December, 1975.
Book Week, October 27, 1963.
Book World, November 3, 1968.
Chicago Tribune, January 14, 1986; June 7, 1987; June 12, 1989.
Christian Science Monitor, September 19, 1968.
CLA Journal, December, 1962; December, 1963; December, 1969; September, 1972; September, 1973; September, 1977; December, 1982.
Contemporary Literature, March 28, 1969; winter, 1970.
Critique, summer. 1984.
Discourse, spring, 1967.
Ebony, July, 1968; June, 1987, p. 154.
English Journal, November, 1990, pp. 84-8.
Essence, April, 1971; September, 1984.
Explicator, April, 1976; Volume 36, number 4, 1978.
Houston Post, February 11, 1974.
Jet, May 30, 1994, p. 37.
Kenyon Review, winter, 1995, p. 136.
Journal of Negro Education, winter, 1970.

Library Journal, September 15, 1970.

Los Angeles Times, November 6, 1987; September 14, 1993, p. F3; April 21, 1997.

Los Angeles Times Book Review, September 2, 1984.

Modern Fiction Studies, winter, 1985.

Nation, September, 1962; July 7, 1969; September 26, 1987, p. 308.

National Observer, November 9, 1968.

Negro American Literature Forum, fall, 1967; summer, 1974.

Negro Digest, December, 1961; January, 1962; August, 1962; July, 1963; June, 1964; January, 1968.

New Statesman, May 3, 1985.

New Yorker, September 22, 1945; December 17, 1949; October 10, 1953; December 3, 1979.

New York Times, November 4, 1945; October 5, 1953; December 9, 1956; October 6, 1963; March 2, 1969; April 30, 1990, p. C11.

New York Times Book Review, October 23, 1960; October 6, 1963; March 2, 1969; January 2, 1972; June 4, 1972; December 3, 1972; January 7, 1973; June 10, 1973; December 2, 1973; September 23, 1984; July 5, 1987; March 18, 1990, p. 21.

Phylon, summer, 1961; March, 1976.

Poetry, December, 1945; volume 126, 1950; March, 1964.

Publishers Weekly, June 6, 1970.

Ramparts, December, 1968.

Saturday Review, February 1, 1964.

Saturday Review of Literature, January 19, 1946; September 17, 1949; May 20, 1950.

Southern Review, spring, 1965.

Southwest Review, winter, 1989, pp. 25-35.

Studies in Black Literature, autumn, 1973; spring, 1974; summer, 1974; spring, 1977.

Tribune Books (Chicago), July 12, 1987.

Virginia Quarterly Review, winter, 1969; winter, 1971.

Washington Post, May 19, 1971; April 19, 1973; March 31, 1987.

Washington Post Book World, November 11, 1973; May 4, 1994, p. C1.

Women's Review of Books, December, 1984.

World Literature Today, winter, 1985.*

*   *   *

BROWN, Claude 1937-

PERSONAL: Born February 23, 1937, in New York, NY; son of Henry Lee (a railroad worker) and Ossie (a domestic; maiden name, Brock) Brown; married Helen Jones (a telephone operator), September 9, 1961. *Education:* Howard University, B.A., 1965; further study at Stanford University and Rutgers University.

ADDRESSES: Home—2736 8th Ave., New York, NY 10039.

CAREER: Member of Harlem Buccaneers Gang's "Forty Thieves" division and served three terms at Warwick School, New York City, during 1940s; worked confidence games and dealt in drugs, New York City, 1953-54; worked as a busboy, watch crystal fitter, shipping clerk and jazz pianist in Greenich Village, 1954-57; writer and lecturer.

MEMBER: Harlem Improvement Group.

AWARDS, HONORS: Metropolitan Community Methodist Church grant, 1959; *Saturday Review* Ansfield-Wolf Award, for furthering intergroup relations.

WRITINGS:

Manchild in the Promised Land, Macmillan, 1965.
The Children of Ham, Stein & Day, 1976.

Contributor of articles to *Dissent, Esquire,* and other periodicals.

SIDELIGHTS: "There is no doubt that Negroes have much to be angry about," William Mathes wrote in 1965, "and I'm all for anger, righteous or otherwise. Not hate, but anger. There is room for dialogue in that emotion. It gets things moving; someone answers with shock; someone applauds; something happens." Tired of the "high-pitched" anger of James Baldwin and the "too fraught-with-love" anger of Roy Wilkins and James Farmer, Mathes called for "words that convey hurt and deprivation themselves, words that can permit many people—especially white people—to identify with the Negro. So far we have lacked words that impart the feelings of what it is to be a Negro in this country at this time." The words, Mathes and other social commentators agreed, came with *Manchild in the Promised Land.* Its publication caused Tom Wolfe to write: "Claude Brown makes James Baldwin and all that old Rock of Ages rhetoric sound like some kind of Moral Rearmament tourist from Toronto come to visit the poor."

Brown, a survivor of Harlem's "Bebopping gang," the Bucaneers, received his primary education from two reformatories and years of "roaming the streets with junkies, whores, pimps, hustlers, the 'mean cats' and the numbers runners." By the time he was thirteen he had been struck by a bus, chain-whipped, tossed into a river, and shot in the stomach. Four years later he decided to resume his formal education and moved from his home, a move, he wrote, "away from fear, toward challenges, towards the positive anger that I think every young man should have."

Encouraged by Ernest Papanek, his former mentor at Wiltwyck School, Brown wrote an article on Harlem for *Dissent*. After its publication, Macmillan offered Brown an expense account to write a book about his life in Harlem. By 1963 he completed a 1,537-page manuscript of *Manchild in the Promised Land*.

Praised by critics for its deft realism and remarkable clarity, Brown's book became a harbinger of hope to the civil rights movement as it drew increasing interest and concern to the plight of urban blacks. "I want to talk about the experiences of a misplaced generation," Brown began, "of a misplaced people in an extremely complex, confused society. This is a story of their searching, their dreams, their sorrows, their small and futile rebellions, and their endless battle to establish their own place in America's greatest metropolis—and in America itself." Romulus Linney wrote that *Manchild in the Promised Land* "is written with brutal and unvarnished honesty in the plain talk of the people, in language that is fierce, uproarious, obscene and tender, but always sensible and direct. And to its enormous credit, this youthful autobiography gives us its devastating portrait of life without one cry of self-pity, outrage or malice, with no caustic sermons or searing rhetoric [. . .] the effect is both shattering and deeply satisfying." More than a decade later, George Davis in *New York Times Book Review* claimed that *Manchild in the Promised Land* "remains one of the great personal, nonideological view, of life in the rawest parts of Harlem."

Brown's second book, *The Children of Ham*, is an account of a group of Harlem teenagers who banded together and transformed abandoned apartments into "spots" where they could "interact free of the 'monster' heroin that dominated their homes and the narrow Harlem side street out front," related Davis. The group maintained little connection to anything except themselves, their religion was survival and they "encouraged each other to stay clean and stay in school, or to develop whatever latent talents each might have." Although some critics found the book less moving than Brown's first, *New Republic* contributor

Arnold Rampersad wrote that "it is alike in its power, if not in its art, to Stephen Crane's first novel, *Maggie, A Girl of the Streets;* as a book about those young people whose primary gift is a determination to live, it reminds one of the diary of another tenement prisoner struggling for the right of survival, Anne Frank."

"As a child," Brown wrote in *Manchild in the Promised Land*, "I remember being morbidly afraid. It was a fear that was like a fever that never lets up. Sometimes it became so intense that it would just swallow you. At other times, it just kept you shaking. But it was always there. I suppose, in Harlem, even now, the fear is still here." *The Children of Ham* reportrays Harlem, and finds it to be a neighborhood "that ten years of neglect has rubbed even more raw."

BIOGRAPHICAL/CRITICAL SOURCES:

PERIODICALS

Antioch Review, fall, 1965, pp. 456-62.
Bestsellers, September, 1976, p. 207.
Commonweal, September 24, 1965, pp. 700-02.
Detroit Free Press, March 12, 1967.
New Republic, September 25, 1965; May 8, 1976.
New Statesman, August 5, 1966.
New York Times, August 14, 1965; April 16, 1976.
New York Times Book Review, August 22, 1965, pp. 1, 14; August 15, 1976.
Washington Post Book World, April 11, 1976.

*   *   *

BROWN, Sterling Allen   1901-1989

PERSONAL: Born May 1, 1901, in Washington, DC; died of leukemia, January 13, 1989, Takoma Park, MD; son of Sterling Nelson (a writer and professor of religion at Howard University) and Adelaide Allen Brown; married Daisy Turnbull, September, 1927; children: John L. Dennis. *Education:* Williams College, A.B., 1922; Harvard University, A.M., 1923, graduate study, 1930-31.

CAREER: Virginia Seminary and College, Lynchburg, VA, English teacher, 1923-26; also worked as a teacher at Lincoln University in Jefferson City, Mo., 1926-28, and at Fisk University, 1928-29; Howard University, Washington, DC, professor of English, 1929-69. Visiting professor at University of Illinois, University of Minnesota, New York University, New

School for Social Research, Sarah Lawrence College, and Vassar College. Editor on Negro Affairs, Federal Writers' Project, 1936-39, and staff member of Carnegie-Myrdal Study of the Negro, 1939.

MEMBER: Phi Beta Kappa.

AWARDS, HONORS: Guggenheim fellowship for creative writing, 1937; honorary doctorates from Howard University, 1971, University of Massachusetts, 1971, Northwestern University, 1973, Williams College and Boston University, both 1974, Brown University and Lewis and Clark College, both 1975, Harvard University, Yale University, University of Maryland, Baltimore County, Lincoln University (Pennsylvania), and University of Pennsylvania; Lenore Marshall Poetry Prize, 1982, for *The Collected Poems of Sterling A. Brown;* poet laureate of District of Columbia, 1984.

WRITINGS:

POETRY

Southern Road, Harcourt, 1932, revised edition, Beacon Press, 1974.
The Last Ride of Wild Bill, and Eleven Narrative Poems, Broadside Press, 1975.
The Collected Poems of Sterling A. Brown, selected by Michael S. Harper, Harper, 1980.

NONFICTION

The Negro in American Fiction (also see below), Associates in Negro Folk Education, 1937, Argosy-Antiquarian, 1969.
Negro Poetry and Drama (also see below), Associates in Negro Folk Education, 1937, revised edition, Atheneum, 1969.
(Editor with Arthur P. Davis and Ulysses Lee, and contributor) *The Negro Caravan,* Dryden, 1941, revised edition, Arno, 1970.
Negro Poetry and Drama [and] *The Negro in American Fiction,* Ayer, 1969.
(With George E. Haynes) *The Negro Newcomers in Detroit* [and] *The Negro in Washington,* Arno, 1970.
A Son's Return: Selected Essays of Sterling A. Brown, edited by Mark A. Sanders, Northeastern University Press (Boston), 1996.

CONTRIBUTOR

Benjamin A. Botkin, editor, *Folk-Say,* University of Oklahoma Press, 1930.

American Stuff: An Anthology of Prose and Verse by Members of the Federal Writers' Project, with Sixteen Prints by the Federal Arts Project, U.S. Government Printing Office, 1937.
Washington City and Capital, U.S. Government Printing Office, 1937.
The Integration of the Negro into American Society, Howard University Press, 1951.
Lillian D. Hornstein, G. D. Percy, and others, editors, *The Reader's Companion to World Literature,* New American Library, 1956.
Langston Hughes and Arna Bontemps, editors, *The Book of Negro Folklore,* Dodd, Mead, 1958.
John Henrik Clarke, editor, *American Negro Short Stories,* Hill & Wang, 1966.

OTHER

Sixteen Poems by Sterling Brown (sound recording), Folkway Records, 1973.

Also author of *Outline for the Study of the Poetry of American Negroes,* 1930, and contributor to *What the Negro Wants,* 1948. Contributor of poetry and articles to anthologies and journals, including *Crisis, Contempo, Nation, New Republic,* and *Journal of Negro Education.* Contributor of column, "The Literary Scene: Chronicle and Comment" to *Opportunity,* beginning 1931.

SIDELIGHTS: Sterling Allen Brown has devoted his life to the development of an authentic black folk literature. A poet, critic, and teacher at Howard University for 40 years, Brown was one of the first people to identify folklore as a vital component of the black aesthetic and to recognize its validity as a form of artistic expression. He has worked to legitimatize this genre in several ways. As a critic, he has exposed the shortcomings of white literature that stereotypes blacks and demonstrated why black authors are best suited to describe the negro experience. As a poet, he has mined the rich vein of black Southern culture, replacing primitive or sentimental caricatures with authentic folk heroes drawn from Afro-American sources. As a teacher, Brown has encouraged self-confidence among his students, urging them to find their own literary voices and to educate themselves to be an audience worthy of receiving the special gifts of black literature. Overall, Brown's influence in the field of Afro-American literature has been so great that scholar Darwin T. Turner told *Ebony* magazine: "I discovered that all trails led, at some point, to Sterling Brown. His *Negro Caravan* was *the* anthology of Afro-American literature. His unpublished study of Afro-American theater was *the* major work in the field. His study of images of Afro-Americans in American literature was a pioneer work. His essays on folk literature and folklore were preeminent. He was not always the best critic . . . but Brown was and is the literary historian who wrote the Bible for the study of Afro-American literature."

Brown's dedication to his field has been unflinching, but it was not until he was in his late sixties that the author received widespread public acclaim. Before then, he labored in obscurity on the campus of Howard University. His fortune improved in 1968 when the Black Consciousness movement revived an interest in his work. In 1969, two of his most important books of criticism, *Negro Poetry and Drama* and *The Negro in American Fiction,* were reprinted by Argosy; five years later, in 1974, Beacon Press reissued *Southern Road,* his first book of poems. These reprintings stimulated a reconsideration of the author, which culminated in the publication of *The Collected Poems of Sterling A. Brown* in 1980. More than any other single publication, it is this title, which won the 1982 Lenore Marshall Poetry prize, that has brought Brown the widespread recognition that he deserves.

Because he had largely stopped writing poetry by the end of the 1940s, most of *Collected Poems* is comprised of Brown's early verse. Yet the collection is not the work of an apprentice, but rather "reveals Brown as a master and presence indeed," in the view of a *Virginia Quarterly Review* critic. While acknowledging that "his effective range is narrow," the critic calls Brown "a first-rate narrative poet, an eloquent prophet of the folk, and certainly our finest author of Afro-American dialect." *New York Times Book Review* contributor Henry Louis Gates appreciates that in *Collected Poems* "Brown never lapses into bathos or sentimentality. His characters confront catastrophe with all of the irony and stoicism of the blues and of black folklore. What's more, he is able to realize such splendid results in a variety of forms, including the classic and standard blues, the ballad, the sonnet and free verse." Despite Brown's relatively small poetic output, *Washington Post* critic Joseph McClellen believes this collection "is enough to establish the poet as one of our best."

After high school, Brown won a scholarship to the predominantly white, ivy league institution, Williams College. There he first began writing poetry. While other young poets his age were imitating T. S. Eliot, Ezra Pound, and other high modernists, Brown was not impressed with their "puzzle poetry." Instead, he turned for his models to the narrative versifiers, poets such as Edward Arlington Robinson, who captured the tragic drama of ordinary lives, and Robert Frost, who used terse vernacular that sounded like real people talking. At Williams, Brown studied literature with George Dutton, a critical realist who would exert a lasting influence. "Dutton was teaching Joseph Conrad," Brown recalled, as reported in the *New Republic.* "He said Joseph Conrad was being lionized in England . . . [but] Conrad was sitting over in the corner, quiet, not participating. Dutton said he was brooding and probably thinking about his native Poland and the plight of his people. He looked straight at me. I don't know what he meant, but I think he meant, and this is symbolic to me, I think he meant don't get fooled by any lionizing, don't get fooled by being here at Williams with a selective clientele. There is business out there that you have to take care of. Your people, too, are in a plight. I've never forgotten it."

Brown came to believe that one way to help his people was through his writing. "When Carl Sandburg said 'yes' to the American people, I wanted to say 'yes' to my people," Brown recalled in *New Directions: The Howard University Magazine.* In 1923, after receiving his Masters degree from Harvard, Brown embarked on a series of teaching jobs that would help him determine what form that "yes" should assume. He moved south and began to teach among the common people. As an instructor, he gained a reputation as a "red ink man," because he covered his students' papers with corrections. But as a poet, he was learning important lessons from students about black Southern life. Attracted by his openness and easygoing manner, they invited him into their homes to hear worksongs, ballads, and the colorful tales of local lore. He met ex-coal-miner Calvin "Big Boy" Davis, who became the inspiration for Brown's "Odyssey of Big Boy" and "Long Gone," as well as singer Luke Johnson, whom he paid a quarter for each song Luke wrote down. As Brown began to amass his own folklore collection, "he realized that worksongs, ballads, blues, and spirituals were, at their best, poetical expressions of Afro-American life," writes Robert O'Meally in the *New Republic.* "And he became increasingly aware of black language as often ironic, understated and double-edged."

In 1929, the same year his father died, Brown returned to Howard University, where he would remain for the rest of his career. Three years later, Harcourt, Brace published *Southern Road,* a first book of poems, drawn primarily from material he had gathered during his travels south. The book was heralded as a breakthrough for black poetry. Alain Locke, one of the chief proponents of what was then called the New Negro Movement, acknowledged the importance of the work in an essay collected in *Negro Anthology*. After explaining that the primary objective of Negro poetry should be "the poetic portrayal of Negro folk-life . . . true in both letter and spirit to the idiom of the folk's own way of feeling and thinking," he declared that with the appearance of *Southern Road,* it could be said "that here for the first time is that much-desired and long-awaited acme attained or brought within actual reach."

The success of *Southern Road* did not insure Brown's future as a publishing poet. Not only did Harcourt, Brace reject *No Hiding Place* when Brown submitted the manuscript a few years later, they also declined to issue a second printing of *Southern Road,* because they did not think it would be profitable. These decisions had a devastating impact upon Brown's poetic reputation. Because no new poems appeared, many of his admirers assumed he had stopped writing. "That assumption," writes Sterling Stuckey in his introduction to *Collected Poems,* "together with sadly deficient criticism from some quarters, helped to fix his place in time-as a not very important poet of the past."

Discouraged over the reception of his poems, Brown shifted his energies to other arenas; he continued teaching, but also produced a steady stream of book reviews, essays, and sketches about black life. He argued critically for many of the same goals he had pursued in verse: recognition of a black aesthetic, accurate depiction of the black experience, and the development of a literature worthy of his people's past. One of his most influential forums for dissemination of his ideas was a regular column he wrote for *Opportunity* magazine. There "Brown argued for realism as a mode in literature and against such romantic interpretations of the South as the ones presented in *I'll Take My Stand* (1930), the manifesto of Southern agrarianism produced by contributors to the *Fugitive,* including John Crowe Ransom, Allen Tate, and Robert Penn Warren," writes R. V. Burnette in the *Dictionary of Literary Biography*. "Although he praised the efforts of white writers like Howard Odum ('he is a poetic craftsman as well as a social observer'), he was relentless in his criticism of popular works that distorted black life and character."

Brown did not limit his writing to periodicals, but also produced several major books on Afro-American

studies. His 1938 works, *Negro Poetry and Drama* and *The Negro in American Fiction,* are seminal studies of black literary history. The former shows the growth of black artists within the context of American literature and delineates a black aesthetic; the latter examines what has been written about the black man in American fiction since his first appearance in obscure novels of the 1700s. A pioneering work that depicts how the prejudice facing blacks in real life is duplicated in their stereotyped treatment in literature, *The Negro in American Fiction* differs "from the usual academic survey by giving a penetrating analysis of the social factors and attitudes behind the various schools and periods considered," Alain Locke believes, as quoted in Volume 63 of the *Dictionary of Literary Biography*.

In 1941, Brown and two colleagues Arthur P. Davis and Ulysses S. Lee edited *The Negro Caravan,* a book that "defined the field of Afro-American literature as a scholarly and academic discipline," according to *Ebony*. In this anthology, Brown demonstrates how black writers have been influenced by the same literary currents that have shaped the consciousness of all American writers—"puritan didacticism, sentimental humanitarianism, local color, regionalism, realism, naturalism, and experimentalism"—and thus are not exclusively bound by strictures of race. The work has timeless merit, according to Julius Lester, who writes in the introduction to the 1970 revised edition that "it comes as close today as it did in 1941 to being the most important single volume of black writing ever published."

BIOGRAPHICAL/CRITICAL SOURCES:

BOOKS

Contemporary Literary Criticism, Gale, Volume 1, 1973; Volume 23, 1983; Volume 59, 1990.
Cunard, Nancy, editor, *Negro Anthology,* Wishart Co., 1934.
Davis, Arthur P., *From the Dark Tower: Afro-American Writers, 1900-1960,* Howard University Press, 1974.
Dictionary of Literary Biography, Gale, Volume 48: *American Poets, 1880-1945,* Second Series, 1986; Volume 51: *Afro-American Writers from the Harlem Renaissance to 1940,* 1987; Volume 63: *Modern American Critics, 1920-1955,* 1988.
Gabbin, Joanne V., *Sterling A. Brown: Building the Black Aesthetic Tradition,* University Press of Virginia (Charlottesville), 1994.

Gayle, Addison, Jr., editor, *Black Expression: Essays by and About Black Americans in the Creative Arts,* Weybright & Talley, 1969.

Mangione, Jerre, *The Dream and the Deal: The Federal Writers' Project, 1935-1943,* Little, Brown, 1972.

Wagner, Jean, *Black Poets of the United States: From Paul Laurence Dunbar to Langston Hughes,* translated by Kenneth Douglas, University of Illinois Press, 1973.

PERIODICALS

Black American Literature Forum, spring, 1980.
Callaloo: A Black South Journal of Arts and Letters, February-May, 1982.
Ebony, October, 1976.
Los Angeles Times Book Review, August 3, 1980.
New Directions: The Howard University Magazine, winter, 1974.
New Republic, February 11, 1978; December 20, 1982.
New York Times, May 15, 1932.
New York Times Book Review, November 30, 1969; January 11, 1981.
Studies in the Literary Imagination, fall, 1974.
Village Voice, January 14, 1981.
Virginia Quarterly Review, winter, 1981.
Washington Post, November 16, 1969; May 2, 1979; September 4, 1980; May 12, 1984.*

*   *   *

BRUIN, John
See BRUTUS, Dennis

*   *   *

BRUTUS, Dennis 1924-
(John Bruin)

PERSONAL: Born November 28, 1924, in Salisbury, Southern Rhodesia (now Harare, Zimbabwe); came to the United States, 1971, granted political asylum, 1983; son of Francis Henry (a teacher) and Margaret Winifred (a teacher; maiden name, Bloemetjie) Brutus; married May Jaggers, May 14, 1950; children: Jacinta, Marc, Julian, Antony, Justina, Cornelia, Gregory, Paula. *Education:* Fort Hare University, B.A. (with distinction), 1947; City of the Witwatersrand, Johannesburg, South Africa, study of law, 1963-64.

ADDRESSES: Office—Department of Black Community Education Research and Development, University of Pittsburgh, 230 S. Bouquet St., Forbes Quad 3T01, Pittsburgh, PA 15260.

CAREER: Poet and political activist. High school teacher of English and Afrikaans in Port Elizabeth, South Africa, 1948-61; journalist in Port Elizabeth, South Africa, 1960-61; imprisoned for anti-apartheid activities, Robben Island Prison, 1964-65; teacher and journalist in London, England, 1966-70; Northwestern University, Evanston, IL, professor of English, 1971-85; Swarthmore College, Swarthmore, PA, Cornell Professor of English Literature, 1985-86; University of Pittsburgh, Pittsburgh, PA, professor of black studies and English, chairman of department of black community education research and development, 1986—. Visiting professor, University of Denver, 1970, University of Texas at Austin, 1974-75, Amherst College, 1981-82, Dartmouth College, 1983, and Northeastern University, 1984; Oxford Center for Africa Studies, International Summer school, lecturer, 1990; University of Durban, Westville, South Africa, visiting fellow, 1992; University of Colorado, Boulder, distinguished visiting humanist, 1992-93. Founder of Troubadour Press. South African Sports Association (now South African Non-Racial Olympic Committee), founding secretary, 1958, president, 1963—; United Nations representative, International Defense and Aid Fund (London), 1966-71; chairman of International Campaign against Racism in Sport, 1972—; member of advisory board, ARENA: Institute for the Study of Sport and Social Analysis, 1975—; chairman, International Advisory Commission to End Apartheid in Sport, 1975—; member of board of directors, Black Arts Celebration (Chicago), 1975—; member, Emergency Committee for World government, 1978—; member of Working Committee for Action against Apartheid (Evanston), 1978—; chairman, Africa Network, 1984—; advisory board member, African Arts Fund, 1985—; board member, Nicaragua Cultural Alliance, 1987—; advisory board member, American Poetry Center, 1988—; member of advisory committee, National Coalition to Abolish the Death Penalty, 1989; coordinator, Union of Writers of the African Peoples, 1986—; program director, Program on African Writers in Africa and the Diaspora, 1988—; president of Third World Energy Resources Institute; director, World Campaign for Release of South African Political Prisoners (London).

MEMBER: International Poetry Society (fellow), International Platform Association, Union of Writers of the African People (Ghana; vice-president, 1974—), Modern Language Association, National Writers Union, Congress of South African Writers (patron 1989—), African Literature Association (founding chairman, 1975—member of executive committee, 1979—), United Nations Association of Illinois and Greater Chicago (member of board of directors, 1978), American Poetry Centre (advisory board 1989—).

AWARDS, HONORS: Chancellor's prize, University of South Africa, 1947; Mbari Award, CCF, 1963, for *Sirens, Knuckles, Boots;* Freedom Writers Award, Society of Writers and Editors, 1975; Kenneth Kaunda Humanism Award, 1979; awarded key to city of Sumter, SC, 1979; Steve Biko Award, TransAfrica, 1985; First Outstanding Teacher Award, Institute for Policy Studies, 1987; Langston Hughes Award, City University of New York, 1987; Paul Robeson Award for excellence, political conscience, and integrity, 1989; honorary doctorates from Worcester State College, Massachusetts, 1982, University of Massachusetts, 1984, Northeastern University, 1990, and University of D. C., 1994.

WRITINGS:

POETRY

Sirens, Knuckles, Boots, Mbari Publications, 1963.
Letters to Martha and Other Poems from a South African Prison, Heinemann, 1968.
Poems from Algiers, African and Afro-American Research Institute, University of Texas at Austin, 1970.
(Under pseudonym John Bruin) *Thoughts Abroad,* Troubadour Press, 1970.
A Simple Lust: Selected Poems Including "Sirens, Knuckles, Boots," "Letters to Martha," "Poems from Algiers," "Thoughts Abroad," Hill & Wang, 1973.
Strains, edited by Wayne Kamin and Chip Dameron, Troubadour Press, 1975, revised edition, 1982.
China Poems, translations by Ko Ching Po, African and Afro-American Studies and Research Center, University of Texas at Austin, 1975.
Stubborn Hope: New Poems and Selections from "China Poems" and "Strains," Three Continents Press, 1978.
Salutes and Censures, Fourth Dimension Publishers (Nigeria), 1984, Africa World Press, 1985.
Airs and Tributes, edited by Gil Ott, Whirlwind Press, 1989.

(Editor with Hal Wylie and Juris Silenieks) *African Literature, 1988: New Masks,* Three Continents/African Literature Association, 1990.

OTHER

The American-South African Connection (sound recording), Iowa State University of Science and Technology, 1975.
Informal Discussion in Third World Culture Class (sound recording), Media Resources Center, Iowa State University of Science and Technology, 1975.

Work represented in anthologies, including *Seven South African Poets,* edited by Cosmo Pieterse, Heinemann, 1966, Humanities, 1973; *From South Africa: New Writing, Photographs, and Art,* edited by David Bunn and Jane Taylor, University of Chicago Press, 1988; and *Words on the Page: The World in Your Hand,* edited by Catherine Lipkin and Virginia Solotaroff, Harper, 1989. Contributor to journals. Member of editorial board, *Africa Today,* 1976—, and *South and West.* Guest editor, *The Gar,* 1978.

WORK IN PROGRESS: Still the Sirens, a chapbook, for Pennywhistle Press.

SIDELIGHTS: Describing Dennis Brutus as a "soft-spoken man of acerbic views," Kevin Klose suggests in the *Washington Post* that "he is one of English-speaking Africa's best-known poets, and also happens to be one of the most successful foes of the apartheid regime in South Africa." Born in Southern Rhodesia of racially mixed parentage, Brutus spent most of his early life in South Africa.

Dismissed from his teaching post and forbidden to write by the South African government as a result of anti-apartheid activities, he was arrested in 1963 for attending a meeting in defiance of a ban on associating with any group. Seeking refuge in Swaziland following his release on bail, Brutus was apprehended in Mozambique by Portuguese secret police, who surrendered him to South African secret police.

Fearing that he would be killed in Johannesburg, where he was subsequently taken, he again tried to escape. Pursued by police, Brutus was shot in the back, tortured, and finally sentenced to eighteen months of hard labor at Robben Island Prison—"the escape-proof concentration camp for political prisoners off the South African coast," remarks Klose in another *Washington Post* article. The time Brutus spent there, says Klose, "included five months in solitary confinement, which brought him to attempt suicide, slashing at his wrists with sharp stones."

After Brutus's release from prison, he was placed under house arrest and was prohibited from either leaving his home or receiving visitors. He was permitted to leave South Africa, however, "on the condition that he not return, according to court records, and he took his family to England," states William C. Rempel in the *Los Angeles Times*. Granted a conditional British passport because of Rhodesia's former colonial status, Brutus journeyed to the United States, where temporary visas allowed him to remain. Rempel notes, however, that Brutus's "passport became snarled in technical difficulties when Rhodesia's white supremacist government was overthrown and Zimbabwe was created." In the process of applying for a new passport, Brutus missed his application deadline for another visa; and the United States government began deportation proceedings immediately. Brutus was ultimately granted political asylum because a return to Zimbabwe, given its proximity to South Africa, would place his life in imminent danger. Klose indicates that Brutus's efforts to remain in the United States have been at the expense of his art, though: "He has written almost no poetry, which once sustained him through the years of repression and exile."

Suggesting that Brutus's "poetry draws its haunting strength from his own suffering and from the unequal struggle of 25 million blacks, 'coloreds,' Indians and Orientals to throw off the repressive rule by the 4.5 million South African whites," Klose remarks that "there is no doubt in Brutus' mind of the power and relevance of his poetry to the struggle." Brutus's works are officially banned in South Africa. When, for example, his *Thoughts Abroad,* a collection of poems concerned with exile and alienation, was published under the pseudonym of John Bruin, it was immediately successful and was even taught in South African colleges; but when the government discovered that Brutus was the author, all copies were confiscated. The effectiveness of the South African government's censorship policies is evidenced by the degree to which Brutus's writing is known there. Colin Gardner, who thinks that "it seems likely that many well-read South Africans, even some of those with a distinct interest in South African poetry, are wholly or largely unacquainted with his writing," declares in *Research in African Literatures* that "Brutus as a writer exists, as far as the Pretoria government is concerned, as a vacuum, an absence; in

the firmament of South African literature, such as it is, Brutus could be described as a black hole. But it is necessary to find him and read him, to talk and write about him, to pick up the light which in fact he does emit, because he is at his best as important as any other South African who has written poetry in English."

Deeming Brutus's poetry "the reaction of one who is in mental agony whether he is at home or abroad," R. N. Egudu suggests in Christopher Heywood's *Aspects of South African Literature* that "this agony is partly caused by harassments, arrests, and imprisonment, and mainly by Brutus's concern for other suffering people." Brutus's first volume of poetry, *Sirens, Knuckles, Boots,* which earned him the Mbari Award, includes a variety of verse, including love poems as well as poems of protest against South Africa's racial policies. Much of his subsequent poetry concerns imprisonment and exile. For example, *Letters to Martha and Other Poems from a South African Prison* was written under the guise of letters—the writing of which, unlike poetry, was not prohibited—and is composed of poems about his experiences as a political prisoner. His *Simple Lust: Selected Poems Including "Sirens, Knuckles, Boots," "Letters to Martha," "Poems from Algiers," "Thoughts Abroad"* represents "a collection of all Brutus' poetry relating to his experience of jail and exile," notes Paul Kameen in *Best Sellers.* Similarly, *Stubborn Hope: New Poems and Selections from "China Poems" and "Strains"* "contains several poems which deal directly with the traumatic period of his life when he was imprisoned on the island," states Jane Grant in *Index on Censorship.* Discussing the "interaction between the personal and political" in Brutus's poetry, Gardner points out that "the poet is aware that he has comrades in his political campaigns and struggles, but under intense government pressure, there is no real sense of mass movement. The fight for liberation will be a long one, and a sensitive participant cannot but feel rather isolated. This isolation is an important aspect of the poet's mode and mood." Chikwenye Okonjo Ogunyemi thinks that although Brutus's writing is inspired by his imprisonment, it is "artistic rather than overtly propagandistic"; the critic observes in *Ariel* that "he writes to connect his inner life with the outside world and those who love him. . . . That need to connect with posterity, a reason for the enduring, is a genuine artistic feeling." Perceiving an early "inner conflict between Brutus, the activist against *apartheid,* and Brutus, the highly literate writer of difficult, complex and lyrical poetry," Grant suggests that "the months in solitary confinement on Robben Island seem to have led him to a radical reassessment of his role as poet." Moving toward a less complex poetry, "the trend culminates in the extreme brevity and economy of the *China Poems* (the title refers both to where they were written and to the delicate nature of the poems)," says Grant. "They are seldom more than a few lines long, and are influenced by the Japanese *haiku* and its Chinese ancestor, the *chueh chu*." These poems, according to Hans Zell's *New Reader's Guide to South African Literature,* evolved from Brutus's trip to the Republic of China and were composed "in celebration of the people and the values he met there." Calling him "learned, passionate, skeptical," Gessler Moses Nkondo says in *World Literature Today* that "Brutus is a remarkable poet, one of the most distinguished South Africa has produced." Nkondo explains that "the lucidity and precision which he is at pains to develop in his work are qualities he admires from artistic conviction, as a humanist opposed both to romantic cultivation of spirit, a certain wholeness and harmony of nature, as they do too to a fine independence of literary fashion."

Influenced by the seventeenth-century metaphysical poets, Brutus employs traditional poetic forms and rich language in his work; Nkondo proposes that what "Brutus fastens on is a composite sensibility made up of the passionate subtleties and the intellectual sensuousness of the metaphysical poets and the masculine, ironic force of [John] Donne." Noting that Brutus assumes the persona of a troubadour throughout his poetry, Tanure Ojaide writes in *Ariel* that while it serves to unify his work, the choice of "the persona of the troubadour to express himself is particularly significant as the moving and fighting roles of the medieval errant, though romantic, tally with his struggle for justice in South Africa, a land he loves dearly as the knight his mistress. The movement contrasts with the stasis of despair and enacts the stubborn hope that despite the suffering, there shall be freedom and justice for those *now* unfree." And Gardner believes that "Brutus's best poetry has a resonance which both articulates and generalizes his specific themes; he has found forms and formulations which dramatize an important part of the agony of South Africa and of contemporary humanity."

Brutus "has traveled widely and written and testified extensively against the Afrikaner-run government's policies," remarks Klose. "In the world of activism, where talk can easily outweigh results, his is a record of achievement." For instance, Klose states that Brutus's voice against apartheid is largely responsible for South Africa's segregated sports teams having

been "barred from most international competitions, including the Olympics since 1964." Egudu observes that in Brutus's "intellectual protest without malice, in his mental agony over the apartheid situation in South Africa, in his concern for the sufferings of the others, and in his hope which has defied all despair— all of which he has portrayed through images and diction that are imbued with freshness and vision— Brutus proves himself a capable poet fully committed to his social responsibility." And according to Klose, Brutus maintains: "You have to make it a two-front fight. You have to struggle inside South Africa to unprop the regime, and struggle in the United States— to challenge the U.S. role, and if possible, inhibit it. Cut off the money, the flow of arms, the flow of political and military support. You have to educate the American people. And that is what I think I'm doing."

BIOGRAPHICAL/CRITICAL SOURCES:

BOOKS

Beier, Ulli, editor, *Introduction to African Literature,* Northwestern University Press, 1967.
Black Literature Criticism, Gale, 1992, pp. 307-20.
Contemporary Authors Autobiography Series, Volume 14, Gale, 1991, pp. 53-64.
Contemporary Literary Criticism, Volume 43, Gale, 1987.
Heywood, Christopher, editor, *Aspects of South African Literature,* Africana Publishing, 1976.
A History of Africa, Horizon Press, 1971.
Legum, Colin, editor, *The Bitter Choice,* World Publishing, 1968.
McLuckie, Craig W. and Patrick J. Colbert, *Critical Perspectives on Dennis Brutus,* Three Continents Press (Colorado Springs, CO), 1995.
Pieterse, Cosmo, and Dennis Duerden, editors, *African Writers Talking,* Africana Publishing, 1972.
Twentieth-Century Caribbean and Black African Writers, Gale, 1992, pp. 98-106.
Zell, Hans M., and others, *A New Reader's Guide to African Literature,* 2nd revised and expanded edition, Holmes & Meier, 1983.

PERIODICALS

Ariel, October, 1982; January, 1986.
Best Sellers, October 1, 1973.
Index on Censorship, July/August, 1979.
Los Angeles Times, September 7, 1983.
New York Times, January 29, 1986.
Research in African Literatures, fall, 1984.

Washington Post, August 13, 1983; September 7, 1983.

World Literature Today, spring, 1979; autumn, 1979; winter, 1981.*

* * *

BUEHLER, Evelyn Judy 1953-
(Evelyn Judy Regulus)

PERSONAL: Surname is pronounced *Byoo*-ler; born March 18, 1953, in Chicago, IL; daughter of Marzell W. and Ida Mae (maiden name, Rubbia; present surname, Fields) Regulus; married Henry Eric Buehler, August 23, 1985; children: Ashley Leonard, Evelyn Judy. *Ethnicity:* "African American." *Education:* Attended Harold Washington College, Chicago, IL. *Politics:* Democrat. *Religion:* Baptist. *Avocational interests:* Art, music, hiking, biking, travel.

ADDRESSES: Home and office—5658 South Normal Blvd., Chicago, IL 60621-2966. *E-mail*—muffin@ameritech.net.

CAREER: Poet and writer.

MEMBER: International Society of Poets (life member).

AWARDS, HONORS: Seven Golden Poet Awards, World of Poetry, 1985-91; three Editor's Choice Awards, International Society of Poets, 1993, and two Editor's Choice Awards, 1994.

WRITINGS:

Tales of Summer (poems), FirstBooks (Indiana), 1998.

Work represented in about fifty anthologies of poetry and short fiction, including *Love's Greatest Treasures: Today's Poets Speak from the Heart,* Volume II, Robert Nelson, 1989; *Calm Winds,* Drury's Publishing, 1997, and *The Best Writers of 1997,* Drury's Publishing, 1998. Work published prior to 1986 appeared under the name Judy Evelyn Regulus.

SIDELIGHTS: Evelyn Judy Buehler told *CA:* "As a child, I was somewhat quiet, and I liked to reflect on various things. I must have been something of a dreamer and have always had a real appreciation of the beauty of nature. I think that this part of my

personality is one of the things that led to my becoming a poet and writer.

"I feel that my love of music also shaped me. This is fitting, because nearly all music begins as verse. Music filled me with feelings that I longed to express. As a 'flower child' of the sixties, I began to write poetry for the first time. You might say that poetry is another kind of music.

"Writing is my way of expressing appreciation and sharing insights, whether through a poem or a short story. It is like sunshine—I want to share it."

* * *

BULLINS, Ed 1935-
(Kingsley B. Bass, Jr.)

PERSONAL: Born July 2, 1935, Philadelphia, PA; son of Edward and Bertha Marie (Queen) Bullins; married; wife's name, Trixie. *Education:* Attended Los Angeles City College, San Francisco State College (now University), New York School of Visual Arts, New School Extension, Vista College, and University of California Berkeley Extension; William Penn Business Institute, general business certificate; Antioch University, B.A., 1989; Sonoma State University, B.A. candidate; San Francisco State University, M.F.A., 1994.

ADDRESSES: Home—3629 San Pablo Ave., Emeryville, CA 94608. *Agent*—Helen Merrill, 435 West 23rd St., No. 1A, New York, NY 10011.

CAREER: Left Philadelphia, PA, for Los Angeles, CA, 1958, moved to San Francisco, CA, in 1964; Black Arts/West, San Francisco, cofounder and producer, 1965-67; co-founder of the Black Arts Alliance, Black House (Black Panther Party headquarters in San Francisco), cultural director until 1967, also serving briefly as Minister of Culture of the Party. Joined The New Lafayette Theatre, New York City, in 1967, becoming playwright in residence, 1968, associate director, 1971-73; writers unit coordinator, New York Shakespeare Festival, 1975-82; playwright in residence, American Place Theatre, beginning 1973; producing director, The Surviving Theatre, beginning 1974; public relations director, Berkeley Black Repertory, 1982; promotion director, Magic Theatre, 1982-83; group sales coordinator, Julian Theatre, 1983. Instructor in playwriting and black theater at various colleges, universities, and work-shops, 1971-79; instructor, School for Continuing Education, New York University, 1979; instructor, Dramatic Writing Department, New York University, 1981; instructor, Summer Playwrights Conference, Hofstra University, New York, 1982; playwriting teacher, People's School of Dramatic Arts, San Francisco, 1983; summer drama workshop leader, Bay Area Playwrights Festival, Mill Valley, CA, 1983; instructor in dramatic performance, play directing, and playwriting, City College of San Francisco, 1984-88; instructor in playwriting and administrative assistant in public information and recruitment, Antioch University, 1986-87; producer and playwright, Bullins Memorial Theatre, Emeryville, CA, 1988; student instructor in playwriting, Antioch University, San Francisco, 1986-87; lecturer, American Multicultural Studies Department, Sonoma State University, Rohnert Park, CA, 1988—; lecturer, Afro-American Studies Department, University of California at Berkeley, 1988—; instructor, African American Humanities/Afro-American Theatre, Contra Costa College, 1989-94; Professor of Theater, Northeastern University, Boston, 1995—.

MEMBER: Dramatists Guild.

AWARDS, HONORS: American Place Theatre grant, 1967; Vernon Rice Drama Desk Award, 1968, for plays performed at American Place Theatre; four Rockefeller Foundation grants, including 1968, 1970, and 1973; Obie Award for distinguished playwriting, and Black Arts Alliance award, both 1971, for *The Fabulous Miss Marie* and *In New England Winter;* Guggenheim fellowship for playwriting, 1971 and 1976; grant from Creative Artists Public Service Program, 1973, in support of playwriting; National Endowment for the Arts playwriting grant, 1972, 1989; Obie Award for distinguished playwriting and New York Drama Critics Circle Award, both 1975, for *The Taking of Miss Janie;* also recipient of a third Obie award and an AUDELCO award from the Harlem Theater; Litt.D., Columbia College, Chicago, 1976.

WRITINGS:

PUBLISHED PLAYS

How Do You Do?: A Nonsense Drama (one-act; first produced as *How Do You Do* in San Francisco at Firehouse Repertory Theatre, August 5, 1965; produced off-Broadway at La Mama Experimen-tal Theatre Club, February, 1972), Illuminations Press, 1967.

(Editor and contributor) *New Plays from the Black Theatre* (includes *In New England Winter* [one-act; first produced off-Broadway at New Federal Theatre of Henry Street Playhouse, January 26, 1971]), Bantam, 1969.

Five Plays (includes: *Goin'a Buffalo* [three-act; first produced in New York City at American Place Theatre, June 6, 1968], *In the Wine Time* [three-act; first produced at New Lafayette Theatre, December 10, 1968], *A Son, Come Home* [one-act; first produced off-Broadway at American Place Theatre, February 21, 1968; originally published in *Negro Digest,* April, 1968], *The Electronic Nigger* [one-act; first produced at American Place Theatre, February 21, 1968], and *Clara's Ole Man* [one-act; first produced in San Francisco, August 5, 1965; produced at American Place Theatre, February 21, 1968]), Bobbs-Merrill, 1969 (published in England as *The Electronic Nigger, and Other Plays,* Faber, 1970).

Ya Gonna Let Me Take You Out Tonight, Baby? (first produced off-Broadway at Public Theatre, May 17, 1972), published in *Black Arts,* Black Arts Publishing (Detroit), 1969.

The Gentleman Caller (one-act; first produced in Brooklyn, NY, with other plays as part of *A Black Quartet,* Chelsea Theatre Center at Brooklyn Academy of Music, April 25, 1969), published in *A Black Quartet,* New American Library, 1970.

The Duplex: A Black Love Fable in Four Movements (one-act; first produced at New Lafayette Theatre, May 22, 1970; produced at Forum Theatre of Lincoln Center, New York, NY, March 9, 1972), Morrow, 1971.

The Theme Is Blackness: The Corner, and Other Plays (includes: *The Theme Is Blackness* [first produced in San Francisco by San Francisco State College, 1966], *The Corner* [one-act; first produced in Boston by Theatre Company of Boston, 1968, produced off-Broadway at Public Theatre, June 22, 1972], *Dialect Determinism* [one-act; first produced in San Francisco, August 5, 1965; produced at La Mama Experimental Theatre Club, February 25, 1972], *It Has No Choice* [one-act; first produced in San Francisco by Black Arts/West, spring, 1966, produced at La Mama Experimental Theatre Club, February 25, 1972], *The Helper* [first produced in New York by New Dramatists Workshop, June 1, 1970], *A Minor Scene* [first produced in San Francisco by Black Arts/West, spring, 1966; produced at La Mama

Experimental Theatre Club, February 25, 1972], *The Man Who Dug Fish* [first produced by Theatre Company of Boston, June 1, 1970], *Black Commercial #2, The American Flag Ritual, State Office Bldg. Curse, One Minute Commercial, A Street Play, Street Sounds* [first produced at La Mama Experimental Theatre Club, October 14, 1970], *A Short Play for a Small Theatre,* and *The Play of the Play*), Morrow, 1972.

Four Dynamite Plays (includes: *It Bees Dat Way* [one-act; first produced in London, September 21, 1970; produced in New York at ICA, October, 1970], *Death List* [one-act; first produced in New York by Theatre Black at University of the Streets, October 3, 1970], *The Pig Pen* [one-act; first produced at American Place Theatre, May 20, 1970], and *Night of the Beast* [screenplay]), Morrow, 1972.

(Editor and contributor) *The New Lafayette Theatre Presents; Plays with Aesthetic Comments by Six Black Playwrights: Ed Bullins, J. E. Gaines, Clay Gross, Oyamo, Sonia Sanchez, Richard Wesley,* Anchor Press, 1974.

The Taking of Miss Janie (first produced in New York at New Federal Theatre, May 4, 1975), published in *Famous American Plays of the 1970s,* edited by Ted Hoffman, Dell, 1981.

New/Lost Plays by Ed Bullins: An Anthology, That New Publishing Co. (Honolulu), 1993.

Also author of "Malcolm:'71 or Publishing Blackness," published in *Black Scholar,* June, 1975. Plays represented in anthologies, including *New American Plays,* Volume III, edited by William M. Hoffman, Hill & Wang, 1970.

UNPUBLISHED PLAYS

(With Shirley Tarbell) *The Game of Adam and Eve,* first produced in Los Angeles at Playwrights' Theatre, spring, 1966.

(Under pseudonym Kingsley B. Bass, Jr.) *We Righteous Bombers* (adapted from Albert Camus's *The Just Assassins*), first produced in New York at New Lafayette Theatre, April, 1969.

A Ritual to Raise the Dead and Foretell the Future, first produced in New York at New Lafayette Theatre, 1970.

The Devil Catchers, first produced at New Lafayette Theatre, November 27, 1970.

The Fabulous Miss Marie, first produced at New Lafayette Theatre, March 5, 1971; produced at Mitzi E. Newhouse Theatre of Lincoln Center, May, 1979.

Next Time . . . , first produced in Bronx, NY, at Bronx Community College, May 8, 1972.

The Psychic Pretenders (A Black Magic Show), first produced at New Lafayette Theatre, December, 1972.

House Party, a Soul Happening, first produced at American Place Theatre, fall, 1973.

The Mystery of Phyllis Wheatley, first produced at New Federal Theatre, February 4, 1976.

I Am Lucy Terry, first produced at American Place Theatre, February 11, 1976.

Home Boy, first produced in New York at Perry Street Theatre, September 26, 1976.

JoAnne! first produced in New York at Theatre of the Riverside Church, October 7, 1976.

Storyville, first produced in La Jolla at the Mandeville Theatre, University of California, May 1977.

DADDY!, first produced at the New Federal Theatre, June 9, 1977.

Sepia Star, first produced in New York at Stage 73, August 20, 1977.

Michael, first produced in New York at New Heritage Repertory Theatre, May, 1978.

C'mon Back to Heavenly House, first produced in Amherst, MA, at Amherst College Theatre, 1978.

Leavings, first produced in New York at Syncopation, August, 1980.

Steve and Velma, first produced in Boston by New African Company, August, 1980.

Boy x Man, first produced at the Samuel Beckett Theater, June, 1997.

OTHER

The Hungered One: Early Writings (collected short fiction), Morrow, 1971.

The Reluctant Rapist (novel), Harper, 1973.

Also author of article "The Polished Protest: Aesthetics and the Black Writer," published in *Contact,* 1963. Editor of *Black Theatre,* 1968-73; editor of special black issue of *Drama Review,* summer, 1968. Contributor to *Negro Digest, New York Times,* and other periodicals.

SIDELIGHTS: Ed Bullins is one of the most powerful black voices in contemporary American theater. He began writing plays as a political activist in the mid-1960s and soon emerged as a principal figure in the black arts movement that surfaced in that decade. First as Minister of Culture for California's Black Panther Party and then as associate director of Harlem's New Lafayette Theatre, Bullins helped shape a revolutionary "theater of black experience" that took drama to the streets. In more than fifty dramatic works, written expressly for and about blacks, Bullins probed the disillusionment and frustration of ghetto life. At the height of his militancy, he advocated cultural separatism between races and outspokenly dismissed white aesthetic standards. Asked by *Race Relations Reporter* contributor Bernard Garnett how he felt about white critics' evaluations of his work, Bullins replied: "It doesn't matter whether they appreciate it. It's not for them." Despite his disinterest, by the late 1960s establishment critics were tracking his work, more often than not praising its lyricism and depth and commending the playwright's ability to transcend narrow politics. As C. W. E. Bigsby points out in *The Second Black Renaissance: Essays in Black Literature,* Bullins "was one of the few black writers of the 1960s who kept a cautious distance from a black drama which defined itself solely in political terms." In the 1970s, Bullins won three Obie Awards for distinguished playwriting, a Drama Critics Circle Award, and several prestigious Guggenheim and Rockefeller playwriting grants.

Bullins's acceptance into the theatrical mainstream, which accelerated as the black arts movement lost momentum, presents some difficulty for critics trying to assess the current state of his art. The prolific output of his early years has been replaced by a curious silence. One possible explanation, according to *Black American Literature Forum* contributor Richard G. Scharine, is that Bullins is facing the same artistic dilemma that confronts Steve Benson, his most autobiographical protagonist: "As an artist he requires recognition. As a revolutionary he dare not be accepted. But Bullins has been accepted. . . . The real question is whether, severed from his roots and his hate, Bullins can continue to create effectively." In a written response published with the article, Bullins answered the charge: "I was a conscious artist before I was a conscious artist-revolutionary, which has been my salvation and disguise. . . . I do not feel that I am severed from my roots."

Bullins's desire to express the reality of ordinary black experience reflects the philosophy he developed during his six-year association with the New Lafayette Theatre, a community-based playhouse that was a showpiece of the black arts movement until it closed for lack of funds in 1973. During its halcyon days, the New Lafayette provided a sanctuary wherein the black identity could be assuaged and nurtured, a crucial goal of Bullins and all the members of that theatrical family. "Our job," former New Lafayette director Robert Macbeth told Jervis Anderson in a *New Yorker* interview, "has always been to show black people who they are, where they are, and what condition they are in. . . . Our function, the healing function of theatre and art, is absolutely vital."

Bullins was born and raised in a North Philadelphia ghetto, but was given a middle-class orientation by his mother, a civil servant. He attended a largely white elementary school, where he was an excellent student, and spent his summers vacationing in Maryland farming country. As a junior high student, he was transferred to an inner-city school and joined a gang, the Jet Cobras. During a street fight, he was stabbed in the heart and momentarily lost his life (as does his fictional alter-ego Steve Benson in *The Reluctant Rapist*). The experience, as Bullins explained to *New York Times* contributor Charles M. Young, changed his attitude: "See, when I was young, I was stabbed in a fight. I died. My heart stopped. But I was brought back for a reason. I was gifted with these abilities and I was sent into the world to do what I do because that is the only thing I can do. I write."

Bullins did not immediately recognize his vocation, but spent several years at various jobs. After dropping out of high school, he served in the Navy from 1952-55, where he won a shipboard lightweight boxing championship and started a program of self-education through reading. Not much is known about the years he spent in North Philadelphia after his discharge, but in the *Dictionary of Literary Biography* Leslie Sanders says "his 1958 departure for Los Angeles quite literally saved his life. When he left Philadelphia, he left behind an unsuccessful marriage and several children." In California, Bullins earned a GED high school equivalency degree and started writing. He turned to plays when he realized that the black audience he was trying to reach did not read much fiction and also that he was naturally suited to the dramatic form. But even after moving to San Francisco in 1964, Bullins found little encouragement for his talent. "Nobody would produce my work," he recalled of his early days in the *New Yorker.* "Some people said my language was too obscene, and others said the stuff I was writing was not theatre in the traditional sense." Bullins might have been discouraged had he not chanced upon a production of two plays by LeRoi Jones, *Dutchman* and *The Slave,* that reminded him of his own. "I could see that an experienced playwright like Jones was dealing with the same qualities and conditions of black life that moved me," Bullins explained.

Inspired by Jones's example, Bullins and a group of black revolutionaries joined forces to create a militant cultural-political organization called Black House. Among those participating were Huey Newton and Bobby Seale, two young radicals whose politics of revolution would soon coalesce into the Black Panther Party.

Between 1967 and 1973 Bullins created and/or produced almost a dozen plays, some of which are still considered his finest work. He also edited the theater magazine, *Black Theatre,* and compiled and edited an anthology of six New Lafayette plays. During this time, Bullins was active as a playwriting teacher and director as well. Despite Bullins's close ties to the New Lafayette, his plays were also produced off-Broadway and at other community theaters, notably the American Place Theatre, where he became playwright in residence after the New Lafayette's demise.

Bullins's plays of this period share common themes. "Clara's Ole Man," an early drama that established the playwright's reputation in New York during its 1968 production, introduces his concerns. Set in the mid-fifties, it tells the story of 20-year-old Jack, an upwardly mobile black who goes to the ghetto to visit Clara one afternoon when her "ole man" is at work. Not realizing that Clara's lover is actually Big Girl, a lesbian bully who is home when Jack calls, he gets brutally beaten as a result of his ignorance. Leslie Sanders believes that "in *Clara's Ole Man,* Bullins's greatest work is foreshadowed. Its characters, like those in many of his later plays, emerge from brutal life experiences with tenacity and grace. While their language is often crude, it eloquently expresses their pain and anger, as well as the humor that sustains them."

By and large, Bullins's plays of this period have fared well artistically while being criticized, by both black and white critics, for their ideology. Some blacks have objected to what Bigsby calls the "reductive view of human nature" presented in these dramas, along with "their sense of the black ghetto as lacking in any redeeming sense of community or moral values." Other blacks, particularly those who have achieved material success, resent their exclusion from this art form. "I am a young black from a middle-class family and well-educated," reads a letter printed in the *New York Times Magazine* in response to a black arts article. "What sense of self will I ever have if I continue to go to the theatre and movies and never see blacks such as myself in performance?" For the white theater going community, Bullins's exclusively black drama has raised questions of cultural elitism that seems "to reserve for black art an exclusive and,

in some senses, a sacrosanct critical territory," Jervis Anderson believes.

In the 1990s Ed Bullins's presence was once again felt in the theater world. He came out with an anthology, *New/Lost Plays by Ed Bullins,* making available his work from the past decades. In 1997, a new play, *Boy x Man* (pronounced "boy times man") was presented by the Negro Ensemble Company, produced at New York's Samuel Beckett Theater. The play concerns family, class, and memory. Though sometimes difficult to perform, its dialogue, in the words of *New York Times* theater reviewer Anita Gates, contains Bullins's brand of "down-home poetry." "*Boy x Man* gets off to a slow start," Brooks wrote, "but eventually it subtly pays off."

Bullins some time ago distanced himself from the critical fray, saying that if he had listened to what critics have told him, he would have stopped writing long ago. "I don't bother too much what anyone thinks," he told Jervis Anderson. "When I sit down in that room by myself, bringing in all that I ever saw, smelled, learned, or checked out, I am the chief determiner of the quality of my work. The only critic that I really trust is me."

BIOGRAPHICAL/CRITICAL SOURCES:

BOOKS

Bigsby, C. W. E., *The Second Black Renaissance: Essays in Black Literature,* Greenwood Press, 1980.

Black Literature Criticism, Gale, 1992.

Contemporary Authors Autobiography Series, Volume 16, Gale, 1992.

Contemporary Literary Criticism, Gale, Volume 1, 1973; Volume 5, 1976; Volume 7, 1977.

Dictionary of Literary Biography, Gale, Volume 7: *Twentieth-Century American Dramatists,* 1981; Volume 38: *Afro-American Writers after 1955-Dramatists and Prose Writers,* 1985.

Gayle, Addison, editor, *The Black Aesthetic,* Doubleday, 1971.

Hay, Samuel A., *Ed Bullins: A Literary Biography,* Wayne State University Press, 1997.

Sanders, Leslie C., *The Development of Black Theater in America: From Shadows to Selves,* Louisiana State University Press, 1988.

PERIODICALS

Black American Literature Forum, fall, 1979.

Black Creation, winter, 1973.

Black World, April, 1974.
CLA Journal, June, 1976.
Dance, April, 1992, p. 86.
Nation, November 12, 1973; April 5, 1975.
Negro Digest, April, 1969.
Newsweek, May 20, 1968.
New Yorker, June 16, 1973.
New York Times, September 22, 1971; May 18, 1975;
    June 17, 1977; May 31, 1979; June 4, 1997, p. B2.
New York Times Book Review, June 20, 1971; Sep-
    tember 30, 1973.
New York Times Magazine, September 10, 1972.
Plays and Players, May, 1972; March, 1973.
Race Relations Reporter, February 7, 1972.

*   *   *

BUNKLEY, Anita Richmond

PERSONAL: Married; children: two daughters.

ADDRESSES: Agent—c/o HarperCollins Publishers,
10 E. 53 St., New York, NY 10022.

CAREER: Writer and public speaker. Also worked as
a language teacher in middle schools and adult education programs and as a director of nonprofit organizations. Workshops include "Steppin' Out with Attitude."

AWARDS, HONORS: Excellence in Achievement
Award, United Negro College Fund; *Wild Embers*
was cited by *Publishers Weekly* as one of the ten best
romances of 1995.

WRITINGS:

ROMANCE NOVELS

Emily, the Yellow Rose, privately printed, then Rinard
    Publishing (Houston, TX), 1989.
Black Gold, Dutton, 1994.
Wild Embers, Dutton, 1995.
(With Sandra Kitt and Eva Rutland) *Sisters,* Signet,
    1996.
Starlight Passage, Dutton, 1996.
Balancing Act, Dutton, 1997.

OTHER

Steppin' Out with Attitude: Sister, Sell Your Dream,
    Harper-Perennial, 1998.

Work represented in anthologies, including *Girl-
friends,* Rinard.

BIOGRAPHICAL/CRITICAL SOURCES:

PERIODICALS

Booklist, February 15, 1995, p. 1059; July, 1997, p.
    1794.
Ebony, December, 1998, p. 22.
Emerge, July-August, 1997, p. 88.
Essence, July, 1997, p. 75.
Library Journal, April 15, 1996, p. 120; April 15,
    1997, p. 116.
Publishers Weekly, April 8, 1996, p. 56; June 9,
    1997, p. 37; August 10, 1998, p. 375.

OTHER

Anita Richmond Bunkley Online, http://www.rinard.
    com/arbunkley, April 11, 1999.
Romantic Times, http://www.romantictimes.com.
    data.books.697.html, April 11, 1999.*

*   *   *

BURTON, LeVar 1957-

PERSONAL: Born Levardis Robert Martin Burton,
February 16, 1957, in Landstuhl, Germany; son of
Levardis Robert and Erma (Christian) Burton; mar-
ried Stephanie Cozart, October 3, 1992; children:
Michaela. *Education:* Attended the University of
Southern California.

ADDRESSES: Office—Peaceful Warrior Productions,
13601 Ventura Blvd., Ste. 209, Sherman Oaks, CA
91423-3701.

CAREER: Actor and director. Film actor: *Almos' a
Man,* 1976; *Looking for Mr. Goodbar,* Paramount,
1977; *The Hunter,* Paramount, 1980; *The Supernaturals,* 1986; *Parallel Lives,* Showtime, 1994; *Star
Trek: Generations,* Paramount, 1994; *Yesterday's
Target,* 1996; *Star Trek: First Contact,* Paramount,
1996; *Star Trek: Insurrection,* Paramount, 1998.

Television actor: *Rebop,* 1976; *Billy: Portrait of a
Street Kid,* 1977; *Roots,* 1977; *One in a Million: The
Ron LeFlore Story,* 1978; *Battered,* 1978; *Dummy,*
Konigsberg Company, 1979; *Guyana Tragedy: The
Story of Jim Jones,* 1980; *Grambling's White Tiger,*

1981; *The Acorn People,* Rollins-Joffe-Morra-Breszner Productions, 1981; *Emergency Room,* 1983; *Reading Rainbow,* 1983; *The Jesse Owens Story,* Howe Bennett Productions, 1984; *The Midnight Hour,* 1985; *And the Children Shall Lead,* 1985; *The Supernaturals,* 1986; *Liberty,* 1986; *Star Trek: The Next Generation,* Paramount, 1987-94; *A Special Friendship,* 1987; *Roots: The Gift,* 1988; *Captain Planet and the Planeteers,* 1990; *Firestorm: 72 Hours in Oakland,* 1993; *Christy,* 1994. TV Guest Appearances: *Deadly Games,* 1995; *Gargoyles,* 1994; *Batman: The Animated Series,* 1992.

AWARDS, HONORS: Emmy Award nomination, best actor, 1977, for *Roots.*

WRITINGS:

Aftermath (novel), Warner (New York City), 1997.

Contributor of an introduction to *Reading Rainbow Guide to Children's Books: The One-Hundred-and-One Best Titles,* 1996.

ADAPTATIONS: Aftermath was adapted for an audio version.

SIDELIGHTS: Actor and director LeVar Burton is best known for his roles in such television series as *Roots* and *Star Trek: The Next Generation,* and in the motion pictures *Star Trek: Generations* and *Looking for Mr. Goodbar.* After directing episodes of the three *Star Trek* television series, Burton delved into creating a science fiction world of his own in *Aftermath.*

On a near-future Earth devastated by race riots, earthquakes, and other natural and unnatural disasters, only Dr. Rene Reynolds, the inventor of an important medical device, can change a bleak future. About to be kidnapped by people trying to stop her, Reynolds hurriedly trusts the computer disks containing her research to indigent Leon Crane. Crane, with the help of a homeless child and a Sioux shaman, seeks to rescue the doctor and the future. *Aftermath* caught the attention of commentators. Calling Burton's prose "workmanlike" and the fictional universe "less than credible," a *Publishers Weekly* reviewer judged the novel to be "terribly earnest and straightforward," and said the novel had "humane and caring moral message." *Library Journal* Susan Hamburger complained that *Aftermath* is similar to a television-show-like format and found Burton's characterizations "shallow." Roland Green of *Booklist* wrote that al-

though *Aftermath* sometimes has the "awkwardness" of a first novel, it also has "much solid writing" and is "thoroughly readable." Burton, Green concluded, "has already mastered the art of keeping readers turning pages."

BIOGRAPHICAL/CRITICAL SOURCES:

BOOKS

Contemporary Black Biography, Volume 8, Gale (Detroit), 1995.
Contemporary Theatre, Film, and Television, Volume 7, Gale (Detroit), 1989.

PERIODICALS

Booklist, November 1, 1996, p. 459.
Bookwatch, March, 1997, p. 8.
Kirkus Reviews, December 1, 1996, p. 1707.
Library Journal, December, 1996, p. 152.
Publishers Weekly, December 9, 1996, p. 64.*

*   *   *

BUTLER, Octavia E(stelle) 1947-

PERSONAL: Born June 22, 1947, in Pasadena, CA; daughter of Laurice and Octavia Margaret (Guy) Butler. *Education:* Pasadena City College, A.A., 1968; attended California State University, Los Angeles, 1969, and University of California, Los Angeles.

ADDRESSES: Home—P.O. Box 6604, Los Angeles, CA 90055.

CAREER: Freelance writer, 1970—.

MEMBER: Science Fiction Writers of America.

AWARDS, HONORS: Fifth Prize, *Writer's Digest* Short Story Contest, 1967; Creative Arts Achievement Award, Los Angeles YWCA, 1980; Hugo Award, World Science Fiction Convention, 1984, for short story "Speech Sounds"; Hugo Award, and Nebula Award, Science Fiction Writers of America, Locus Award, *Locus* magazine, and award for best novelette, *Science Fiction Chronicle Reader,* all 1985, all for novelette *Bloodchild;* Nebula Award nominations, 1987, for novelette "The Evening and the Morning and the Night," 1994 for *Parable of the Sower;* MacArthur fellowship, 1995.

WRITINGS:

SCIENCE FICTION

Patternmaster, Doubleday (New York City), 1976.
Mind of My Mind, Doubleday, 1977.
Survivor, Doubleday, 1978.
Kindred, Doubleday, 1979, second edition, Beacon
  Press (Boston), 1988.
Wild Seed, Doubleday, 1980.
Clay's Ark, St. Martin's Press (New York City), 1984.
Dawn: Xenogenesis (first novel in "Xenogenesis" tril-
  ogy), Warner Books (New York City), 1987.
Adulthood Rites (second novel in "Xenogenesis" tril-
  ogy), Warner Books, 1988.
Imago (third novel in "Xenogenesis" trilogy), Warner
  Books, 1989.
Parable of the Sower, Warner Books, 1995.
Bloodchild, and Other Stories, Four Walls Eight
  Windows (New York City), 1995.

Contributor to anthologies, including *Clarion,* 1970,
and *Chrysalis 4,* 1979; contributor to *Isaac Asimov's
Science-Fiction Magazine, Future Life, Transmission,*
and other publications.

WORK IN PROGRESS: Parable of the Talents, a sequel to *Parable of the Sower.*

SIDELIGHTS: Concerned with genetic engineering,
psionic powers, advanced alien beings, and the nature
and proper use of power, Octavia E. Butler's science
fiction presents these themes in terms of racial and
sexual awareness. "Butler consciously explores the
impact of race and sex upon future society," Frances
Smith Foster explains in *Extrapolation.* As one of the
few African American writers in the science-fiction
field, and the only black woman, Butler's racial and
sexual perspective is unique. This perspective, however, does not limit her fiction or turn it into mere
propaganda. "Her stories," Sherley Anne Williams
writes in *Ms.,* "aren't overwhelmed by politics, nor
are her characters overwhelmed by racism or sexism." Speaking of how Butler's early novels deal with
racial questions in particular, John R. Pfeiffer of
Fantasy Review maintains that "nevertheless, and
therefore more remarkably, these are the novels of
character that critics so much want to find in science
fiction—and which remain so rare. Finally, they are
love stories that are mythic, bizarre, exotic and heroic
and full of doom and transcendence."

Among Butler's strengths as a writer, according to
several reviewers, is her creation of believable, inde-

pendent female characters. "Her major characters are
black women," Foster explains, and through these
characters Butler explores the possibilities for a society open to true sexual equality. In such a society
Butler's female characters, "powerful and purposeful in their own right, need not rely upon eroticism
to gain their ends." Williams also believes that Butler
posits "a multiracial society featuring strong
women characters." Still, her characters' race and
gender are not Butler's primary concerns, according to a 1993 *Publishers Weekly* interview with the
author. "I'm just interested in telling a story, hopefully a good one," the author told Lisa See. Indeed,
in addition to her unique characters, critics praise
Butler's controlled, economical prose style. Writing
in the *Washington Post Book World,* Elizabeth A.
Lynn calls the author's prose "spare and sure, and
even in moments of great tension she never loses
control over her pacing or over her sense of story."
"Butler," Dean R. Lambe of *Science Fiction Review*
similarly attests, "has a fine hand with lean, well-
paced prose."

Butler's stories have been well received by science-
fiction fans. In 1985 she won three of the genre's top
honors—the Nebula Award, the Hugo Award, and the
Locus Award—for her novella *Bloodchild,* the story
of human males on another planet who bear the children of an alien race. *"Bloodchild,"* Williams explains, "explores the paradoxes of power and inequality, and starkly portrays the experience of a class
who, like women throughout most of history, are
valued chiefly for their reproductive capacities." The
novella was reprinted in 1995's *Bloodchild and Other
Stories,* which also includes the remainder of Butler's
previously published short fiction, with afterwords,
and two essays. The short stories explore some science-fiction themes—"Speech Sounds" and "The
Evening and the Morning and the Night," for instance, envision a troubled future in California—and
some family ones, as in "Near of Kin," which focuses
on a strained mother-daughter relationship. One of the
essays deals with Butler's life, the other with her
craft. Chicago's *Tribune Books* reviewer Danille Taylor-Guthrie deems the afterwords to the short stories
valuable: "The author's commentaries on her works
are as pleasurable to read as the fiction itself." She
also finds that the essays contribute much to the volume. *"Bloodchild and Other Stories* is not only vintage Butler, it permits the reader to look beyond the
pen," Taylor-Guthrie remarks. Elizabeth Hand, writing in the *Washington Post Book World,* says the
collection will provide "a useful signpost" to Butler's
novels.

It is through her novels that Butler reaches her largest audience; and, of these, she is best known for her books set in the world of the "Patternists," including *Patternmaster, Mind of My Mind, Survivor,* and *Wild Seed*. The Patternist series tells of a society dominated by an elite, specially bred group of telepaths who are mentally linked together into a hierarchical pattern. Originally founded by a four-thousand-year-old immortal Nubian named Doro who survives by killing and then taking over younger bodies, these telepaths seek to create a race of superhumans. But Doro's plans are repeatedly thwarted in *Wild Seed* by Anyanwu, an immortal woman who does not need to kill to survive; and in *Mind of My Mind* Mary, Doro's daughter, organizes all the other telepaths to defeat him, thus giving the Patternists an alternative to Doro's selfish and murderous reign. As *Dictionary of Literary Biography* contributor Margaret Anne O'Connor says, "this novel argues for the collective power of man as opposed to individual, self-interested endeavor."

The Patternist novels cover hundreds of years of human history. *Wild Seed* takes place in the eighteenth and nineteenth centuries and *Mind of My Mind* is set in a Los Angeles of the near future, but the other books in the series are set in the distant future. *Patternmaster,* like *Mind of My Mind,* addresses the theme of the importance of compassion and empathy between people over the ambitions of the individual. In this tale Butler describes an agrarian society now ruled by the telepaths whose communities are at constant risk of attack from humans who have been monstrously mutated by a genetic disease—just how this disease is brought to Earth by an astronaut is explained in *Clay's Ark*. During one of these raids, a Patternist ruler is wounded and becomes an invalid. His two sons vie for his position, and Butler shows how the younger son, Teray, learns from a woman healer named Amber that compassion is necessary to maintain and control the communal Pattern. By learning—as Mary did in *Mind of My Mind*—the benefits of the community over the individual, Teray defeats his brother and takes his father's place.

Although many of Butler's protagonists in the Patternist books are black women, the novelist does not display any particular favoritism towards either African Americans or women. Instead, she emphasizes the need for breaking down race and gender barriers by illustrating the inability of those hindered by prejudice and narrow vision to progress and evolve. According to Foster, for "the feminist critic, Octavia Butler may present problems. Her female characters are undeniably strong and independent; but whether, as Joanna Russ insists is crucial, 'the assumptions underlying the entire narrative are feminist,' is uncertain, for 'who wins and who loses' is less clear than that a compromise has been made which unifies the best of each woman and man. For Afro-American literary critics, Butler can present problems as well, for their attention has been focused upon the assumptions and depictions about the black experience of the past and the present; yet the implications of Butler's vision should be a significant challenge."

In *Survivor,* another Patternist novel, and Butler's more recent "Xenogenesis" trilogy, the author uses alien beings to help illustrate her themes: the differences between humans and aliens magnifies the issue of cultural misunderstanding and prejudice-inspired antipathy. With *Survivor,* the character Alanna survives on a distant world by learning to understand and love one of the alien Kohns. Butler's "Xenogenesis" books explore the interrelationships between two peoples in greater depth by creating a race called the Oankali, nomadic aliens who interbreed with other sentient species in order to improve their gene pool. Arriving on Earth after a nuclear holocaust has wiped out almost all of humanity, the Oankali offer mankind a second chance through the combination of the best characteristics of both species. They accomplish this through a third sex called ooloi, whose function is to manipulate the two races' genes into a new species. Here, according to *Analog* reviewer Tom Easton, "we may have Butler's [main] point: The ooloi are the means for gene transfer between species, but they also come between, they are intermediaries, moderators, buffers, and Butler says that the human tragedy is the unfortunate combination of intelligence and hierarchy."

One book that Butler has written that has nothing to do with either her Patternist or her Xenogenesis series is *Kindred,* which, except for its time-travel theme, diverges enough from the science-fiction genre that her publisher marketed it as a mainstream novel. *Kindred* concerns Dana, a contemporary African American woman who is pulled back in time by her great-great-grandfather, a white plantation owner in the antebellum American South. To insure that he will live to father her great-grandmother—and thus provide the means for her own birth in the twentieth century—Dana is called upon to save the slave owner's life on several occasions. "Butler makes new and eloquent use of a familiar science-fiction idea, protecting one's own past, to express the tangled interdependency of black and white in the United States," Joanna Russ writes in the *Magazine of Fantasy and Science Fiction.* Williams calls *Kindred* "a startling and engrossing commentary on the complex actuality and continuing heritage of American slavery."

Parable of the Sower also deals with the racial and social concerns typical of Butler's work. Set in a dystopian California in the years 2024 and 2025, the 1995 novel is written in the form of a journal by a young black woman named Lauren Olamina. In Butler's horrific future, a dearth of jobs has created such hostility between haves and have-nots that middle-class towns like the one where Lauren lives have become armed fortresses. Lauren's hometown is eventually attacked and destroyed, but she becomes a leader of survivors who seek to establish a society built on a new religion and nontraditional values. The question of whether or not this society will endure is left unresolved.

Critiquing the novel for *Women's Review of Books,* Hoda Zaki notes that there are echoes of the African American past in Butler's tale of the future. For instance, Zaki observes, "Lauren's band of survivors recalls the Underground Railroad." She adds that the book, in common with Butler's other works, is a "celebration of racial differences and the coming together of diverse individuals to work, live and build community." Some reviewers point out that in this tale of a world gone awry—according to Zaki, "an exaggerated reflection of what is occurring today"— Butler does not take the expected or obvious approach. "Many other science fiction writers would take this setting and spin out an adventure story following the usual schematics," writes Thomas Wiloch in the *Bloomsbury Review.* "Many already have. Butler turns her story into a character study of a young woman."

In a 1997 interview, Butler told *Poets & Writers Magazine* she was working on a "continuation" of *Parable of the Sower,* with the planned title *Parable of the Talents.* "I examined a lot of the problems in *Parable of the Sower,* and now I'd like to consider some of the solutions," the novelist commented. "Not *propose* solutions, you understand—what I want to do is look at some of the solutions that human beings can come up with when they're feeling uncertain and frightened."

Butler currently enjoys a solid reputation among both readers and critics of science fiction, and Williams notes that Butler has a "cult status among many black women readers." She also notes that "Butler's work has a scope that commands a wide audience." Many of her books have been recommended by critics as examples of the best that science fiction has to offer. For example, speaking of *Kindred* and *Wild Seed,* Pfeiffer argues that with these books Butler "produced two novels of such special excellence that critical appreciation of them will take several years to assemble. To miss them will be to miss unique novels in modern fiction." And Easton asserts that with *Dawn* "Butler has gifted SF with a vision of possibility more original than anything we have seen since [Arthur C.] Clarke's *Childhood's End.*"

Nevertheless, Foster believes that Butler's novels deserve more recognition because they fill a void in the science fiction genre, which often neglects to explore sexual, familial, and racial relationships. "Since Octavia Butler is a black woman who writes speculative fiction which is primarily concerned with social relationships, where rulers include women and nonwhites," Foster concludes, "the neglect of her work is startling." For her part, Butler does not discount the unique place she occupies as a black female science-fiction writer, but she has no wish to be typecast by her race or gender, or even by her genre. "I write about the things that interest me, and I'm not the most unique person on earth," *Publishers Weekly* quoted her as stating. "So I figure what will interest me will interest other people."

BIOGRAPHICAL/CRITICAL SOURCES:

BOOKS

Contemporary Literary Criticism, Volume 38, Gale (Detroit), 1986.
Dictionary of Literary Biography, Volume 33: *Afro-American Fiction Writers after 1955,* Gale, 1984.

PERIODICALS

African American Review, summer, 1994, pp. 223-35, 259-71.
Analog: Science Fiction/Science Fact, January 5, 1981; November, 1984; December 15, 1987; December, 1988.
Black American Literature Forum, summer, 1984.
Black Scholar, March/April, 1986.
Bloomsbury Review, May/June, 1994, p. 24.
Emerge, June, 1994, p. 65.
Equal Opportunity Forum Magazine, no. 8, 1980.
Essence, April, 1979; May, 1989, pp. 74, 79, 132, 134.

Extrapolation, spring, 1982.

Fantasy Review, July, 1984.

Janus, winter, 1978-79.

Los Angeles Times, January 30, 1981.

Los Angeles Times Book Review, November 26, 1995, p. 14.

Magazine of Fantasy and Science Fiction, February, 1980; August, 1984.

Ms., March, 1986; June, 1987.

New York Times Book Review, January 2, 1994, p. 22; October 15, 1995, p. 33.

Poets & Writers Magazine, March/April, 1997, pp. 58-69.

Publishers Weekly, December 13, 1993, pp. 50-51.

Salaga, 1981.

Science Fiction Review, May, 1984.

Science Fiction Studies, November, 1993, pp. 394-408.

Thrust: Science Fiction in Review, summer, 1979.

Tribune Books (Chicago), March 31, 1996, p. 5.

Washington Post Book World, September 28, 1980; June 28, 1987; July 31, 1988; June 25, 1989; October 29, 1995, p. 8.

Women's Review of Books, July, 1994, pp. 37-38.

C

CADE, Toni
   See **BAMBARA, Toni Cade**

*   *   *

CAMPBELL, Bebe Moore 1950-

PERSONAL: Born in 1950; daughter of George Linwood Peter and Doris (a social worker; maiden name, Carter) Moore; married Tiko F. Campbell (divorced); married Ellis Gordon, Jr. (a banker); children: Maia. *Education:* University of Pittsburgh, B.A. (summa cum laude).

ADDRESSES: Agent—Beth Swofford, William Morris Agency, 151 El Camino Dr., Beverly Hills, CA 90212.

CAREER: Freelance writer. Schoolteacher for five years; commentator on *Morning Edition,* National Public Radio. Guest on television talk shows, including *Donahue, Oprah, Sonya Live,* and *Today,* and numerous radio talk shows.

MEMBER: Alpha Kappa Alpha, Delta Sigma Theta.

AWARDS, HONORS: Body of Work Award, National Association of Negro Business and Professional Women, 1978; National Endowment for the Arts grant, 1980; Golden Reel Award, Midwestern Radio Theatre Workshop Competition, for *Sugar on the Floor;* Certificate of Appreciation, from the mayor of Los Angeles, CA; NAACP Image Award for outstanding literary work (fiction).

WRITINGS:

Successful Women, Angry Men: Backlash in the Two-Career Marriage, Random House (New York City), 1986.
Sweet Summer: Growing Up with and without My Dad, Putnam (New York City), 1989.
Your Blues Ain't Like Mine, Putnam, 1992.
Brothers and Sisters, Putnam, 1994.
Singing in the Comeback Choir, Putnam, 1998.

Also author of nonfiction short story "Old Lady Shoes" and a radio play based on it, and of the radio play *Sugar on the Floor.* Contributor to periodicals, including *Ebony, Lear's, Ms., New York Times Book Review, New York Times Magazine, Publishers Weekly, Savvy, Seventeen, Washington Post,* and *Working Mother.* Contributing editor of *Essence.*

RECORDINGS

Singing in the Comeback Choir, Books on Tape, 1998.

ADAPTATIONS: Film rights to *Sweet Summer* were bought by Motown Productions in 1989; film rights to *Brothers and Sisters* were bought by Touchstone Pictures in 1995.

WORK IN PROGRESS: A novel, *Where I Useta Live.*

SIDELIGHTS: Bebe Moore Campbell's fiction and nonfiction has earned her widespread acclaim for her insights on racism and divorce. Campbell worked as a teacher for several years before turning to a career in freelance journalism following the birth of her daughter. It was an article for *Savvy* magazine that led to the development of her first book, *Successful Women, Angry Men: Backlash in the Two-Career Marriage.* An article about Father's Day prompted the 1989 book, *Sweet Summer: Growing Up with and without My Dad,* her memoir as a child of divorce.

Since her parents had separated when she was quite young, Campbell lived a divided existence, spending the school year in Pennsylvania with her mother and the summer in North Carolina with her father. Campbell draws a sharp contrast between the two worlds. According to *Sweet Summer,* her Philadelphia home was dominated by women—notably her mother, aunt, and grandmother—who urged her to speak well, behave properly, study hard, and generally improve herself. Life with her father, his mother, and his male friends, on the other hand, she describes as a freer one full of cigar and pipe smoke, beer, loud laughter, "roughness, gruffness, awkward gentleness," and a father's abiding love. Wheelchair-bound by a car accident, Campbell's father was nonetheless her hero, a perfect dad who loved her just for herself. When she learned that he was responsible, through speeding, not only for his own crippling accident but also for one that killed a boy, her image of him became tarnished, and Campbell had to come to terms with him as a flawed human being, no longer the dream-father she had idolized.

Critics hailed *Sweet Summer* for its poignant, positive look at a father-daughter relationship and especially for showing such a loving relationship in the black community. *Times Literary Supplement* contributor Adeola Solanke observed that in Campbell's memoir "a black father is portrayed by his daughter as a hero, instead of as the monster stalking the pages of many black American women writers." Similarly, poet Nikki Giovanni, writing in the *Washington Post Book World,* praised the book for providing "a corrective to some of the destructive images of black men that are prevalent in our society." Campbell also earned approval for her treatment of ordinary black life and for the vitality and clarity of her writing. Some reviewers expressed reservations about her work, however, suggesting that she was too hard on women; Martha Southgate of the *Village Voice* found "the absolute dichotomy Campbell perceives between men and women . . . disturbing." A few critics pointed out Campbell's lack of emphasis on social context and analysis, which some deemed a drawback, others an advantage. Stated Solanke, "One of the book's main strengths is that the political and social tumult it presents never eclipses the vitality and immediacy of personal experience."

By sharing her story, Campbell gives readers "the opportunity to reflect on our own fathers," mused Melissa Pritchard in Chicago *Tribune Books,* "to appreciate their imperfect, profound impact on our lives." The importance of fathers and other men in girls' lives is in fact "perhaps the crucial message in her book," related Itabari Njeri in the *Los Angeles Times,* "one still not fully understood by society." As Campbell explained to Njeri, "Studies show that girls without that nurturing from a father or surrogate father are likely to grow up with damaged self-esteem and are more likely to have problems with their own adult relationships with men." She hoped that reading her book might inspire more divorced fathers to increase their participation in their children's lives. Reflecting on the flurry of Campbell's talk show appearances, the competition for paperback rights, and the interest shown in the book by film producers, Njeri suggested that she was indeed reaching her audience. Noted the critic, "Campbell's gentle, poignant story about her relationship with her father has struck a nerve."

Campbell turned to fiction in 1992 with her novel *Your Blues Ain't Like Mine.* It tells of a young black man, murdered in 1955, whose white killer was acquitted by an all-white jury. The novel goes on to trace what happens to the families of the killer and the victim over following years. Campbell told the *New York Times:* "I wanted to give racism a face. . . . African-Americans know about racism, but I don't think we really know the causes. I decided it's first of all a family problem." The care with which the book's characters are drawn has been cited as one of its greatest strengths. Clyde Edgerton, writing for the *New York Times,* felt that much of the power of the novel "results from Ms. Campbell's subtle and seamless shifting of point of view. She wears the skin and holds in her chest the heart of each of her characters, one after another, regardless of the character's race or sex, response to fear and hate, or need for pity, grace, punishment or peace."

The rioting that broke out in Los Angeles after the 1992 Rodney King trial was the impetus behind Campbell's next novel, *Brothers and Sisters.* Explained Veronica Chambers in the *New York Times:* "While many saw the Los Angeles riots as the curtain falling on the myth of racial unity, Campbell . . . saw them as an opportunity to write about race and gender." The setting is a Los Angeles bank during the days after the riots, and the author explores the conflicting loyalties held by two women friends, one black, the other white. The author used her characters very differently than she had in her previous novel; *New York Times* reviewer Elizabeth Fleich dubbed them "a fairly conventional batch," and a *Publisher Weekly* contributor noted that they were "intriguing (if not always three-dimensional)." Instead, the novel focuses on the complexities of their relations. *Time* contributor Christopher John Farley praised the work accordingly: "Writing with wit and grace, Campbell shows how all our stories—white, black, male, female—ultimately intertwine." *Ms.* reviewer Retha Powers commended Campbell for her "astute observations about the subtleties of race and race relations in the U.S." The popular success of the novel was proven by its appearance on the *New York Times* bestseller list two weeks after its release.

Writing in the *New York Times*, Pamela Newkirk placed Campbell "among a growing number of black women whose writing has mass crossover appeal. One reason for that appeal—to readers as well as to talk show hosts—is that in her characters, and in person, she manages to articulate deftly both black and white points of view."

With *Singing in the Comeback Choir*, Campbell "returns to the heart of our culture, the family," states a contributor to *Essence* magazine. "Maxine Lott McCoy, a strong-willed but vulnerable television executive producer in L.A., struggles to maintain her relationship with her once-wayward husband, Satchel; her place in the high-stakes TV game; and the care of Lindy, her aging grandmother who reared her up and out of a declining Philadelphia neighborhood." Maxine has to return to her roots in Philadelphia to confront the dangers threatening her grandmother and the neighborhood in which she lives—and to find the healing that will mend Maxine and her troubled marriage. "Maxine's relationship with her grandmother . . . is the key to the healing Maxine needs to redefine her life and rebuild her marriage on a foundation of forgiveness and renewed trust," declares Nancy Paul in *Library Journal.* "Campbell . . . weaves the strands of her story with a skilled hand; it is energizing, engaging, and uplifting. She gently touches on the issues of community, enduring values, and the need to reconnect with one's roots."

BIOGRAPHICAL/CRITICAL SOURCES:

BOOKS

Campbell, Bebe Moore, *Sweet Summer: Growing Up with and without My Dad*, Putnam, 1989.
Newsmakers 96, Gale (Detroit), 1996, pp. 76-77.

PERIODICALS

African American Review, summer, 1997, p. 369.
American Visions, October/November, 1994, p. 38.
Black Enterprise, February, 1995, p. 224.
Booklist, June 1, 1994, p. 1725; December 15, 1997, p. 666.
Entertainment Weekly, September 9, 1994, p. 78.
Essence, January, 1998, p. 92.
Jet, March 30, 1998, p. 39.
Library Journal, August, 1994, p. 124; December, 1994, p. 154; February 15, 1998, p. 169; April 15, 1999, p. 164.
Los Angeles Times, July 25, 1989; December 1, 1989.
Ms., September/October, 1994, p. 78.
Newsweek, April 29, 1996, p. 79.
New York Times, November 15, 1995, p. C6.
New York Times Book Review, June 11, 1989, p. 47; September 20, 1992, p. 13; October 16, 1994, p. 18; April 12, 1998, p. 17.
New York Times Magazine, December 25, 1994, p. 16.
People Weekly, November 21, 1994, p. 32; February 23, 1998, p. 22.
Publishers Weekly, June 30, 1989, pp. 82-83; July 4, 1994, p. 51; December 15, 1997, p. 49; April 6, 1998, p. 35.
School Library Journal, February, 1995, p. 134.
Southwest Review, spring, 1996, p. 195.
Time, October 17, 1994, p. 81.
Times Literary Supplement, October 26, 1990, p. 1148.
Tribune Books (Chicago), June 18, 1989, p. 7.
U.S. Catholic, September, 1987, p. 48.
Village Voice, July 4, 1989, p. 63.
Washington Post Book World, June 18, 1989, pp. 1, 8.

*   *   *

CAMPBELL, Rhonda 1962-
   (Denise Turney)

PERSONAL: Born September 4, 1962; daughter of Richard and Doris Turney; children: Gregory.

ADDRESSES: Home—2500 Knights Rd., No. 19-01, Bensalem, PA 19020.

CAREER: U.S. Navy, staff writer, 1984-88; currently freelance writer. Merrill Lynch, Princeton, NJ, administrative assistant.

WRITINGS:

Portia (novel), Chistell Publishing (Bensalem, PA), 1997.

Contributor of articles, stories, and reviews to periodicals, including *Moondance, Bucks County Writer, Today's Black Woman, HeartBeat, Sisters in Style,* and *Your Church.* Some writings appear under the pseudonym Denise Turney.

SIDELIGHTS: Rhonda Campbell told *CA:* "I am a single mother of a son. I work full-time as an administrative assistant. I am the niece of Norris Turney, for years the leading saxophonist in Duke Ellington's band. My writing career started when I was ten years old. My first work was a five-act play. After the play I started on my first novel—*Spiral.* With college, work, and a ton of daydreaming, I didn't finish the novel until I was eighteen. By that time I had typed more than four-hundred pages while leaning over a sky-blue manual typewriter. My goal is to entertain, teach, and encourage through the written word."

*   *   *

CARSON, Ben
  See CARSON, Benjamin S(olomon) Sr.

*   *   *

CARSON, Benjamin S(olomon), Sr. 1951-
  (Ben Carson)

PERSONAL: Born September 18, 1951, in Detroit, MI; son of Robert Solomon (a Baptist minister) and Sonya (Copeland) Carson; married Lacena (Candy) Rustin, July 6, 1975; children: Murray Nedlands, Benjamin Jr., Rhoeyce Harrington. *Ethnicity:* "African American." *Education:* Yale University, B.A. (psychology), 1973; University of Michigan, M.D., 1977. *Religion:* Seventh Day Adventist.

ADDRESSES: Home—West Friendship, MD. *Office*—Johns Hopkins Hospital, 600 North Wolfe, Baltimore, MD 21287-0005

CAREER: Neurosurgeon. Johns Hopkins University, Baltimore, MD, surgical intern, 1977-78, neuro-sur-

gical resident, 1978-82, chief resident in neurosurgery, 1982-83, assistant professor of neurosurgery, 1984—, assistant professor of oncology, 1984—, director of pediatric neurosurgery, 1985-91, assistant professor of pediatrics, 1987—, associate professor, 1991—; Queen Elizabeth II Medical Center, Perth, Australia, senior registrar of neurosurgery, 1983-84. Served on Kellogg Co. board of directors. Has appeared on television in numerous programs. Gives presentations, especially to adolescents, about fulfilling personal potential.

MEMBER: American Association for the Advancement of Science, National Pediatric Oncology Group, National Medical Association, Regional Red Cross Cabinet (honorary chair, 1987), Children's Cancer Foundation (medical advisory board, 1987—), American Association of Neurological Surgeons, Congress of Neurological Surgeons, Academy of Pediatric Neurosurgeons; USA Scholars Fund (president), Maryland Congress of Parents and Teachers.

AWARDS, HONORS: Cum Laude award, American Radiological Society, Chicago, 1982; citations for Excellence, Detroit City Council, 1987, Philadelphia City Council, 1987, Michigan State Senate, 1987, Detroit Medical Society, 1987, Pennsylvania House of Representatives, 1989; American Black Achievement Award, Business and Professional, Ebony and Johnson Publications, 1988; Paul Harris fellow Rotary International, 1988; Clinical Practitioner of the Year, National Medical Association Region II, 1988; Certificate of Honor for Outstanding Achievement in the Field of Medicine, National Medical Fellowship, Inc., 1988; Candle Award for Science and Technology, Morehouse College, 1989; Blackbook Humanitarian Award, Blackbook Publishing, 1991; Horatio Alger Association Award, 1994; numerous honorary doctor of science degrees, including honorary doctor of medical sciences from Gettysburg College, 1988, North Carolina A & T, 1989, Andrews University, 1989, Sojourner-Douglas College, 1989, Shippenburg University, 1990, Jersey City State College, 1990, Southwestern Adventist College, 1992, University of Massachusetts, Boston, 1992, Marygrove College, 1993, University of Detroit-Mercy, 1994, Long Island University, 1994, North Carolina State University, 1994, Tuskegee University, 1995, Yale University, 1996, Delaware State University, 1996, Medical University of South Africa, Medunsa, 1997, GMI Engineering and Management Institute, 1997, University of Delaware, 1997, and College of William and Mary, 1998.

WRITINGS:

(With Cecil Murphey) *Gifted Hands: The Ben Carson Story,* Zondervan (Grand Rapids, MI), 1990.

(With Cecil Murphey) *Think Big: Unleashing Your Potential for Excellence,* Zondervan, 1992.

(Editor with Craig R. Dufresne and S. James Zinreich) *Complex Craniofacial Problems: A Guide to Analysis and Treatment,* illustrated by Carmella Clifford, Churchill Livingstone (New York City), 1992.

(As Ben Carson, with Gregg Lewis Zondervan) *The Big Picture: Getting Perspective on What's Really Important in Life,* Cahners, 1999.

Also author of *Pediatric Neurooncology,* 1987; *Achondroplasia,* 1988; and, with Cecil Murphy and Nathan Aaseng, *Ben Carson,* 1992. Contributor to periodicals. Member of editorial board, *Voices of Triumph,* Time-Life Books.

SIDELIGHTS: Benjamin S. Carson, Sr. is an internationally acclaimed neurosurgeon perhaps best known for leading a surgical team in a twenty-two hour successful operation to separate conjoined twins who shared some of their brain matter. He is also recognized for his expertise in performing hemispherectomies, where half the brain is removed to stop seizures. Carson is director of pediatric neurosurgery at Johns Hopkins University Hospital, as well as associate professor of neurosurgery, oncology, plastic surgery, and pediatrics at the institution's School of Medicine.

Born on September 18, 1951, Carson came from a poor family in Detroit. He was the second son of Robert Solomon Carson, a Baptist minister, and Sonya Copeland Carson. His father was twenty-eight when he married, but his mother was only thirteen; she married in order to escape a difficult home situation. "After his mother discovered that his father was a bigamist, his father—given an ultimatum—abandoned the family to live with his other wife," reported an essay in *Current Biography Yearbook.* Carson was only eight years old, and his brother Curtis was ten when their parents divorced. His mother took them to live with relatives in a Boston tenement, while she rented out their house in Detroit. Working as many as three domestic jobs at a time, she earned enough money to move her family back to Detroit two years later.

Both Carson and his brother had a difficult time in school, and their low grades fanned the racial preju-

dice against them. But their mother took charge of their education, even though she herself had not gone past the third grade. By limiting the television they could watch and insisting they both read two books a week and report on them, she helped them raise their grades considerably. Carson discovered he enjoyed learning, and by the time he reached junior high school he had risen from the bottom to the top of his class.

But even then he continued to face racial prejudice; in the eighth grade, he listened to a teacher scold his class for allowing him, a black student, to win an achievement award. These early difficulties left Carson with a violent temper as a young man. He was often in fights: "I would fly off the handle," he told *People* contributors Linda Dramer and Joe Treen. Once he almost killed a friend in an argument. Carson tried to stab him in the stomach with a knife, but luckily the boy was wearing a heavy belt buckle, which stopped the blade. Only fourteen at the time, Carson was shocked at what he had almost done, and he saw the direction his life could have taken. Following his near murderous act, Carson locked himself in the bathroom with a Bible and "by his own account," according to *Current Biography,* "he emerged from the bathroom a changed person: '[God] took away my temper and I can honestly say I have never been troubled with anger since.'" This experience drove him more deeply into his religion—he is still a Seventh-Day Adventist.

Carson studied hard and did so well during high school that he won a scholarship to Yale University, where he received his bachelor's degree in 1973. He had always dreamed of becoming a doctor and was very interested in psychiatry, but once in medical school at the University of Michigan, he realized he was good with his hands and set his sights on neurosurgery. After completing medical school in 1977, he was one of the few graduates and the first black person accepted into the residency program at Johns Hopkins Hospital in Baltimore. In 1983, because of a shortage of neurosurgeons in Australia, Carson was offered a chief neurosurgical residency at Queen Elizabeth II Medical Center in Perth, where he gained a great deal of operating experience. He returned to Johns Hopkins in 1984, and after a year he was promoted to director of pediatric neurosurgery, becoming one of the youngest doctors in the country to head such a division.

One of Carson's accomplishments is his revival of a procedure called a hemispherectomy, an operation that removes half the patient's brain to cure diseases such as Rassmussen's encephalitis, which causes seizures. These operations had been stopped because of their high mortality rate, but with Carson's skills the procedure has been highly successful.

Perhaps Carson's best-known accomplishment is the operation he performed in September, 1987, to separate seven-month-old German conjoined twins, who were joined at the head. Carson was the lead surgeon on the team that performed "perhaps the most complex surgical feat in the history of mankind," as he described the operation in *Ebony*. There was a team of seventy medical staff members, including five neurosurgeons, seven pediatric anesthesiologists, five plastic surgeons, two cardiac surgeons, and dozens of nurses and technicians, and it took five months of preparation, including five three-hour dress rehearsals. A crowd of media people waited outside the operating room for Carson and his medical team to emerge, triumphant, at the end of the twenty-two-hour operation.

In 1988 Carson was awarded both the Certificate of Honor for Outstanding Achievement in the Field of Medicine by the National Medical Fellowship and the American Black Achievement Award. He has received honorary doctor of science degrees from several universities, and the Candle Award for Science and Technology from Morehouse College in 1989.

Carson's surgical achievements are not limited to performing hemispherectomies and separating the infant conjoined twins. His patients range in age from fetus to adults, and suffer from "abnormalities or disorders of the brain or nervous system, among them tumors, vascular malformations, congenital dwarfism, congenital spinal deformities, conditions that result in unremitting facial pain and . . . seizures that cannot be controlled with medication," according to *Current Biography*. In 1995, the press recognized Carson for performing yet another difficult surgery on a brain tumor. The patient, seven-year-old Matthew Anderson, was not offered surgical treatment for his cancer because his doctors felt that it was an unrealistic option. "Three days before Matthew was to begin radiation treatments, he brought a note home from his Sunday school teacher, who thought the Andersons would be interested in a book she had read. It was the autobiography of a brain surgeon who thrived on cases other doctors deemed hopeless," stated *U.S. News & World Report* contributor Rita Rubin.

The autobiography that Mr. Anderson read was *Gifted Hands: The Ben Carson Story,* a book co-written with

Cecil Murphey that the *Current Biography* essayist said "has been described as 'a story of how love, faith, and hard work can help overcome seemingly insurmountable odds.'" Carson, a "surgeon with moxie," averred Rubin, is known for his surgical courage as well as his talent. "He tackles difficult cases that not every surgeon [will]," noted the *Current Biography* contributor, later noting that "'Do your best, and let God do the rest,' is a favorite maxim of Carson's." The essayist continued, "Twice each month at Johns Hopkins, with the aim of inspiring young people to make use of their intellects and resist the lures of what he terms 'media-oriented values,' Carson speaks to groups of 700 junior high and high school students. He advises them to 'THINK BIG: Recognize your *T*alents; lead an *H*onest life; gain *I*nsight by learning from others' triumphs and mistakes; be *N*ice to others (they'll be nice to you in return); acquire *K*nowledge; read *B*ooks; learn *I*n-depth (not to impress others but to gain knowledge and understanding); and rely on *G*od.'" This approach to successful living is discussed in Carson's book *Think Big: Unleashing Your Potential for Excellence,* which he co-authored with Murphey.

Carson married Lacena Rustin—whom he met at Yale—in 1975; she holds an M.B.A. degree and is an accomplished musician. They have three sons. Carson feels strongly about motivating young people to fulfill their potential, as he did, and he often lectures to students around the nation. Carson is also on the editorial advisory board of the Time-Life series *Voices of Triumph,* about the history and achievements of African Americans.

BIOGRAPHICAL/CRITICAL SOURCES:

BOOKS

Blacks in Science and Medicine, Hemisphere Publishing Co., 1990.
Schick, Elizabeth A., editor, *Current Biography Yearbook, 1997* H. W. Wilson (New York City), 1997.

PERIODICALS

Black Enterprise, October, 1988.
Christianity Today, May 27, 1991.
Ebony, January, 1988.
Jet, September 8, 1997.
New York Times, June 8, 1993.
People, fall, 1991.

Publishers Weekly, January 11, 1999.
U.S. News & World Report, July 24, 1995, p. 46.*

* * *

CASEY, Bernard Terry 1939-
   (Bernie Casey)

PERSONAL: Born in 1939, in Wyco, WV. *Education:*
Bowling Green State University, B.A., M.F.A., 1966.

ADDRESSES: Agent—c/o Doubleday, 1540 Broadway, New York, NY 10036.

CAREER: Painter, screen actor, writer, and former
star flanker back for Los Angeles Rams football team.
Co-founder of Negro Industrial and Economic Union;
president of Community Arts Foundation. Actor in
films, including *The Man Who Fell to Earth,* 1976;
Never Say Never Again, 1983; and *Steele Justice,*
1987. Has had artwork exhibited at La Jolla Museum
of Art, La Jolla, CA, 1970; University of Iowa
Museum of Art, 1972; Ankrum Gallery (permanent
collection), Los Angeles, CA; John Bolles Gallery,
San Francisco, CA.

WRITINGS:

UNDER NAME BERNIE CASEY

Look at the People (poetry), self-illustrated, Doubleday, 1969.

Also author of *My Point of View—Poems and Drawings,* 1971, *You Can Win the Game, If It's Your Turn,
In Little Ways, Schizophrenic Moon Folly, White
Bird, Some Rainy Days, Saturday's Nightscape,
Shadow in the Bright Sun, Barbara,* and *An Excerpt
from a Terry Trip.* Contributor to periodicals, including the *Los Angeles Herald* and *Los Angeles Times.*

BIOGRAPHICAL/CRITICAL SOURCES:

PERIODICALS

American Artist, February, 1970, p. 70.
Black World, September, 1970, pp. 51-52.
Booklist, December 1, 1969, p. 432.
Ebony, May, 1987, p. 138.
Kirkus Reviews, August 1, 1969, p. 813.
Library Journal, November 15, 1969, p. 4309; December 1, 1969, p. 4439.*

CASEY, Bernie
   See CASEY, Bernard Terry

* * *

CASEY, Patrick
   See THURMAN, Wallace (Henry)

* * *

CESAIRE, Aime (Fernand) 1913-

PERSONAL: Born June 25, 1913, in Basse-Pointe,
Martinique; son of Fernand (a comptroller with the
revenue service) and Marie (Hermine) Cesaire; married Suzanne Roussi (a teacher), July 10, 1937; children: Jacques, Jean-Paul, Francis, Ina, Marc, Michelle.
Education: Attended Ecole Normale Superieure,
Paris; Sorbonne, University of Paris, licencie es
lettres.

ADDRESSES: Office—Assemblee Nationale, 75007
Paris, France; and La Mairie, 97200 Fort-de-France,
Martinique, West Indies.

CAREER: Lycee of Fort-de-France, Martinique,
teacher, 1940-45; member of the two French constituent assemblies, 1945-46; mayor of Fort-de-France,
1945; deputy for Martinique in the French National
Assembly, 1946. Conseiller general for the fourth
canton (district) of Fort-de-France; president of the
Parti Progressiste Martiniquais.

MEMBER: Society of African Culture (Paris; president).

*AWARDS, HONORS: Aime Cesaire: The Collected
Poetry* was nominated for the *Los Angeles Times* Book
Award, 1984.

WRITINGS:

(With Gaston Monnerville and Leopold Sedar-
   Senghor) *Commemoration du centenaire de
   l'abolition de l'esclavage: Discours pronounces a
   la Sorbonne le 27 avril 1948* (title means "Commemoration of the Centenary of the Abolition of
   Slavery: Speeches Given at the Sorbonne on April
   27, 1948"), Presses Universitaires de France,
   1948.

Discours sur le colonialisme, Reclame, 1950, 5th edition, Presence Africaine (Paris), 1970, translation by Joan Pinkham published as *Discourse on Colonialism,* Monthly Review Press, 1972.

Lettre a Maurice Thorez, 3rd edition, Presence Africaine, 1956, translation published as *Letter to Maurice Thorez,* 1957.

Toussaint L'Ouverture: La revolution francaise et le probleme coloniale (title means "The French Revolution and the Colonial Problem"), Club Francais du Livre, 1960, revised edition, Presence Africaine, 1962.

Ouvres completes (title means "Complete Works"), three volumes, Editions Desormeaux, 1976.

(Contributor) *Studies in French,* William Marsh Rice University, 1977.

Culture and Colonization, University of Yaounde, 1978.

Also author of *Textes,* edited by R. Mercier and M. Battestini, French and European Publications.

POETRY

Cahier d'un retour au pays natal, published in the Paris periodical *Volontes,* 1939, published by Presence Africaine, 1956, 2nd edition, 1960, translation by Emil Snyders published as *Return to My Native Land,* Presence Africaine, 1968, translation by John Berger and Anna Bostock published under same title, Penguin Books, 1969, translation by Mireille Rosello and Annie Pritchard published as *Notebook of a Return to My Native Land = Cahier d'un Retour au Pays Natal,* Bloodaxe Books (Newcastle upon Tyne, England), 1995.

Les armes miraculeuses (title means "The Miracle Weapons"; also see below), Gallimard, 1946, reprinted, 1970.

Soleil cou-coupe (title means "Solar Throat Slashed"), K (Paris), 1948, reprinted (bound with *Antilles a main armee* by Charles Calixte under title *Poems from Martinique*), Kraus, 1970.

Corps perdu, illustrations by Pablo Picasso, 1949, translation by Clayton Eshleman and Annette Smith published as *Lost Body,* Braziller, 1986.

Ferrements (title means "Shackles"; also see below), Editions du Seuil, 1960.

Cadastre (also see below), Editions du Seuil, 1961, translation by Gregson Davis published as *Cadastre,* Third Press, 1972, translation by Snyders and Sanford Upson published under same title, Third Press, 1973.

State of the Union, translation by Eshleman and Dennis Kelly of selections from *Les armes miracu-*leuses, *Ferrements,* and *Cadastre,* [Bloomington, IL], 1966.

Moi, Laminaire (title means "I, Laminarian"), first published in 1982, published by French & European Publications, 1991.

Aime Cesaire: The Collected Poetry, translation and with an introduction by Eshleman and Smith, University of California Press, 1983.

Non-Vicious Circle: Twenty Poems, translation by Davis, Stanford University Press, 1985.

Lyric and Dramatic Poetry, 1946-82 (includes English translations of *Et les Chiens se taisaient* and *Moi, laminaire*), translation by Eshleman and Smith, University Press of Virginia, 1990.

PLAYS

Et les chiens se taisaient: tragedie (title means "And the Dogs Were Silent: A Tragedy"), Presence Africaine, 1956.

La tragedie du roi Christophe, Presence Africaine, 1963, revised edition, 1973, translation by Ralph Manheim published as *The Tragedy of King Christophe,* Grove, 1970.

Une saison au Congo, Editions du Seuil, 1966, translation by Manheim published as *A Season in the Congo* (produced in New York at the Paperback Studio Theatre, July, 1970), Grove, 1969.

Une tempete: d'apres "le tempete" de Shakespeare. Adaptation pour un theatre negre, Editions du Seuil, 1969, translation by Richard Miller published as *A Tempest,* Ubu Repertory, 1986.

OTHER

Editor of *Tropiques,* 1941-45, and of *L'Afrique.*

SIDELIGHTS: Because of his role in creating and promoting negritude, a cultural movement which calls for black people to renounce Western society and adopt the traditional values of black civilization, Aime Cesaire is a prominent figure among blacks in the Third World. A native of the Caribbean island of Martinique, where he has served as mayor of the city of Fort-de-France since 1945, Cesaire also enjoys an international literary reputation for his poems and plays. His 1,000-line poem *Return to My Native Land,* a powerful piece written in extravagant, surreal language and dealing with the reawakening of black racial awareness, is a major work in contemporary French-language literature. Cesaire is, Serge Gavronsky states in the *New York Times Book Review,* "one of the most powerful French poets of this century."

At the age of eighteen Cesaire left his native Martinique, at that time a colony of France, to attend school in Paris. The city was the center for a number of political and cultural movements during the 1930s, several of which especially influenced the young Cesaire and his fellow black students. Marxism gave them a revolutionary perspective, while surrealism provided them with a modernist esthetic by which to express themselves. Together with Leon-Goutran Damas and Leopold Sedar Senghor, who later became president of Senegal, Cesaire founded the magazine *L'Etudiant Noir,* in which the ideology of negritude was first developed and explained. "Negritude . . . proclaimed a pride in black culture and, in turning their contemporaries' gaze away from the notion of things French, these young students began a revolution in attitudes which was to make a profound impact after the war," Clive Wake explains in the *Times Literary Supplement.* The influence of the movement on black writers in Africa and the Caribbean was so pervasive that the term negritude has come to refer to "large areas of black African and Caribbean literature in French, roughly from the 1930s to the 1960s," Christopher Miller writes in the *Washington Post Book World.*

The first use of the word negritude occurred in Cesaire's poem *Return to My Native Land* (*Cahier d'un retour au pays natal*), first published in the magazine *Volontes* in 1939. In this poem, Cesaire combines an exuberant wordplay, an encyclopedic vocabulary, and daring surreal metaphors with bits of African and Caribbean black history to create an "exorcism . . . of the poet's 'civilized' instincts, his lingering shame at belonging to a country and a race so abject, servile, petty and repressed as is his," Marjorie Perloff writes in the *American Poetry Review.* Gavronsky explains that the poem "is a concerted effort to affirm [Cesaire's] stature in French letters by a sort of poetic one-upmanship but also a determination to create a new language capable of expressing his African heritage." *Return to My Native Land,* Perloff maintains, is "a paratactic catalogue poem that piles up phrase upon phrase, image upon image, in a complex network of repetitions, its thrust is to define the threshold between sleep and waking— the sleep of oppression, the blind acceptance of the status quo, that gives way to rebirth, to a new awareness of what is and may be."

Written as Cesaire himself was leaving Paris to return to Martinique, *Return to My Native Land* reverberates with both personal and racial significance. The poet's definition of his own negritude comes to symbolize the growing self-awareness of all blacks of their cultural heritage. Judith Gleason, writing in the *Negro Digest,* believes that Cesaire's poetry is "grounded in the historical sufferings of a chosen people" and so "his is an angry, authentic vision of the promised land." Jean Paul Sartre, in an article for *The Black American Writer: Poetry and Drama,* writes that "Cesaire's words do not describe negritude, they do not designate it, they do not copy it from the outside like a painter with a model: they create it; they compose it under our very eyes."

Several critics see Cesaire as a writer who embodies the larger struggles of his people in all of his poetry. Hilary Okam of *Yale French Studies,* for example, argues that "Cesaire's poetic idiosyncrasies, especially his search for and use of uncommon vocabulary, are symptomatic of his own mental agony in the search for an exact definition of himself and, by extension, of his people and their common situation and destiny." Okam concludes that "it is clear from [Cesaire's] use of symbols and imagery, that despite years of alienation and acculturation he has continued to live in the concrete reality of his Negro-subjectivity." Writing in the *CLA Journal,* Ruth J. S. Simmons notes that although Cesaire's poetry is personal, he speaks from a perspective shared by many other blacks. "Poetry has been for him," Simmons explains, "an important vehicle of personal growth and self-revelation, [but] it has also been an important expression of the will and personality of a people. . . . [It is] impossible to consider the work of Cesaire outside of the context of the poet's personal vision and definition of his art. He defines his past as African, his present as Antillean and his condition as one of having been exploited. . . . To remove Cesaire from this context is to ignore what he was and still is as a man and as a poet."

The concerns found in *Return to My Native Land* ultimately transcend the personal or racial, addressing liberation and self-awareness in universal terms. Gleason calls *Return to My Native Land* "a masterpiece of cultural relevance, every bit as 'important' as *The Wasteland,* its remarkable virtuosity will ensure its eloquence long after the struggle for human dignity has ceased to be viewed in racial terms." Andre Breton, writing in *What Is Surrealism?: Selected Writings,* also sees larger issues at stake in the poem. "What, in my eyes, renders this protest invaluable," Breton states, "is that it continually transcends the anguish which for a black man is inseparable from the lot of blacks in modern society, and unites with the protest of every poet, artist and thinker worthy of the name . . . to embrace the entire intolerable though amendable condition created for *man* by this society."

Cesaire's poetic language was strongly influenced by the French surrealists of the 1930s, but he uses familiar surrealist poetic techniques in a distinctive manner. Breton claims that Cesaire "is a black man who handles the French language as no white man can handle it today." Alfred Cismaru states in *Renascence* that Cesaire's "separation from Europe makes it possible for him to break with clarity and description, and to become intimate with the fundamental essence of things. Under his powerful, poetic eye, perception knows no limits and pierces appearances without pity. Words emerge and explode like firecrackers, catching the eye and the imagination of the reader. He makes use of the entire dictionary, of artificial and vulgar words, of elegant and forgotten ones, of technical and invented vocabulary, marrying it to Antillean and African syllables, and allowing it to play freely in a sort of flaming folly that is both a challenge and a tenacious attempt at mystification." Poetic language is seen by some critics as a form of literary violence, with the jarring images and forceful rhythms of the poetry assaulting the reader. Perloff finds that Cesaire's "is a language so violently charged with meaning that each word falls on the ear (or hits the eye) with resounding force." Gleason explains this violence as the expression of an entire race, not just of one man: "Cesaire's is the turbulent poetry of the spiritually dislocated, of the damned. His images strike through the net. . . . Cesaire's is the Black Power of the imagination."

This violent energy is what first drew Cesaire to surrealism. The surrealist artists and writers of the 1930s saw themselves as rebels against a stale and outmoded culture. Their works were meant to revive and express unconscious, suppressed, and forbidden desires. Politically, they aligned themselves with the revolutionary left. As Gavronsky explains, "Cesaire's efforts to forge a verbal medium that would identify him with the opposition to existing political conditions and literary conventions [led him to] the same camp as the Surrealists, who had combined a new poetics that liberated the image from classical restraints with revolutionary politics influenced by Marx and his followers." Cesaire was to remain a surrealist for many years, but he eventually decided that his political concerns would best be served by more realistic forms of writing. "For decades," Karl Keller notes in the *Los Angeles Times Book Review,* "[Cesaire] found the surreal aesthetically revolutionary, but in the face of the torture and the suffering, he has pretty well abandoned it as a luxury."

In the late 1950s Cesaire began to write realistic plays for the theatre, hoping in this way to attract a larger audience to his work. These plays are more explicitly political than his poetry and focus on historical black nationalist leaders of the Third World. *The Tragedy of King Christophe*(*La tragedie du roi Christophe*) is a biographical drama about King Henri Christophe of Haiti, a black leader of that island nation in the early nineteenth century. After fighting in a successful revolution against the French colonists, Christophe assumed power and made himself king. But his cruelty and arbitrary use of power led to a rebellion in turn against his own rule, and Christophe committed suicide. Writing in *Studies in Black Literature,* Henry Cohen calls *The Tragedy of King Christophe*"one of French America's finest literary expressions." *A Season in the Congo* (*Une saison au Congo*) follows the political career of Patrice Lumumba, first president of the Republic of the Congo in Africa. Lumumba's career was also tragic. With the independence of the Congo in 1960, Lumumba became president of the new nation. But the resulting power struggles among black leaders led in 1961 to Lumumba's assassination by his political opponents. The reviewer for *Prairie Schooner* calls *A Season in the Congo* "a passionate and poetic drama." Wake remarks that Cesaire's plays have "greatly widened [his] audience and perhaps tempted them to read the poetry." Gavronsky claims that "in the [1960s, Cesaire] was . . . the leading black dramatist writing in French."

Despite the international acclaim he has received for his poetry and plays, Cesaire is still best known on Martinique for his political career. Since 1945 he has served as mayor of Fort-de-France and as a member of the French National Assembly. For the first decade of his career Cesaire was affiliated with the Communist bloc of the assembly, then moved to the Parti du Regroupement Africain et des Federalistes for a short time, and is now president of the Parti Progressiste Martiniquais, a leftist political organization. Cesaire's often revolutionary rhetoric is in sharp contrast to his usually moderate political actions. He opposes independence for Martinique, for example, and was instrumental in having the island declared an oversea department of France—a status similar to that of Puerto Rico to the United States. And as a chief proponent of negritude, which calls for blacks to reject Western culture, Cesaire nonetheless writes his works in French, not in his native black language of creole.

But what may seem contradictory in Cesaire's life and work is usually seen by critics as the essential tension that makes his voice uniquely important. A. James

Arnold, in his *Modernism and Negritude: The Poetry and Poetics of Aime Cesaire,* examines and accepts the tension between Cesaire's European literary sources and his black subject matter and between his modernist sensibility and his black nationalist concerns. Miller explains that "Arnold poses the riddle of Cesaire with admirable clarity" and "effectively defuses . . . either a wholly African or a wholly European Cesaire." This uniting of the European and African is also noted by Clayton Eshleman and Annette Smith in their introduction to *Aime Cesaire: The Collected Poetry.* They describe Cesaire as "a bridge between the twain that, in principle, should never meet, Europe and Africa. . . . It was by borrowing European techniques that he succeeded in expressing his Africanism in its purest form." Similarly, Sartre argues that "in Cesaire, the great surrealist tradition is realized, it takes on its definitive meaning and is destroyed: surrealism—that European movement—is taken from the Europeans by a Black man who turns it against them and gives it vigorously defined function."

It is because of his poetry that Cesaire is primarily known worldwide, while in the Third World he is usually seen as an important black nationalist theoretician. Speaking of his poetry, Gavronsky explains that Cesaire is "among the major French poets of this century." Cismaru believes that Cesaire "is a poet's poet when he stays clear of political questions, a tenacious and violent propagandist when the theme requires it. His place in contemporary French letters . . . is assured in spite of the fact that not many agree with his views on Whites in general, nor with his opinions on Europe, in particular." *Return to My Native Land* has been his most influential work, particularly in the Third World where, Wake notes, "by the 1960s it was widely known and quoted because of its ideological and political significance." To European and American critics, *Return to My Native Land* is a masterpiece of surrealist literature. Cesaire's coining of the term negritude and his continued promotion of a distinctly black culture separate from Western culture has made him especially respected in the emerging black nations. Eshleman and Smith report "although Cesaire was by no means the sole exponent of negritude, the word is now inseparable from his name, and largely responsible for his prominent position in the Third World."

BIOGRAPHICAL/CRITICAL SOURCES:

BOOKS

Aime Cesaire: The Collected Poetry, translated and with an introduction by Clayton Eshleman and Annette Smith, University of California Press, 1983.

Aime Cesaire: Ecrivain Martiniquais, Fernand Nathan, 1967.

Antoine, R., *Le Tragedie du roi Christophe d'Aime Cesaire,* Pedagogie Moderne, 1984.

Arnold, A. James, *Modernism and Negritude: The Poetry and Poetics of Aime Cesaire,* Harvard University Press, 1981.

Bhalla, Alok, editor, *Garcia Marquez and Latin America,* Sterling Publishers, 1987, pp. 161-68.

Bigsby, C. W. E., editor, *The Black American Writer: Poetry and Drama,* Volume 2, Penguin Books, 1971.

Black Literature Criticism, Gale, Volume 1, 1992.

Bouelet, Remy Sylvestre, *Espaces et dialectique du heros cesairien,* L'Harmattan, 1987.

Breton, Andre, *What Is Surrealism?: Selected Writings,* edited by Franklin Rosemont, Monad Press, 1978.

Contemporary Literary Criticism, Gale, Volume 19, 1981, Volume 32, 1985.

Davies, Gregson, *Aime Cesaire,* Cambridge University Press, 1997.

Dennis, Philip A., and Wendell Aycock, editors, *Literature and Anthropology,* Texas Tech University Press, 1989, pp. 113-32.

Frutkin, Susan, *Aime Cesaire: Black between Worlds,* Center for Advanced International Studies: University of Miami, 1973.

Kesteloot, Lilyan, *Aime Cesaire,* P. Seghers, 1962, new edition, 1970.

Kubayanda, Josaphat B., *The Poet's Africa: Africanness in the Poetry of Nicolas Guillen and Aime Cesaire,* Greenwood, 1990.

Leiner, Jacqueline, *Soleil eclate: Melanges offerts a Aime Cesaire a l'occasion de son soixante-dixieme anniversaire par une equipe internationale d'artiste et de chercheurs,* Gunter Narr Verlag (Tubingen), 1985.

Ngal, M., editor, *Cesaire 70,* Silex, 1985.

Owusu-Sarpong, Albert, *Le Temps historique dans l'oeuvre theatrale a'Aime Cesaire,* Naaman, 1987.

Pallister, Janis L., *Aime Cesaire,* Twayne, 1991.

Scharfman, Ronnie Leah, *Engagement and the Language of the Subject in the Poetry of Aime Cesaire,* University Presses of Florida, 1980.

Songolo, Aliko, *Aime Cesaire: Une Poetique de la decouverte,* L'Harmattan, 1985.

PERIODICALS

African Journal, spring, 1974, pp. 1-29.
Afro-Hispanic Review, January, 1985, p. 1.
American Poetry Review, January-February, 1984.

Black Images, spring, 1973, pp. 7-15.

Callaloo, February, 1983, pp. 61-136; summer, 1989, p. 612.

Choice, March, 1991, p. 1141.

CLA Journal, March, 1976; September, 1984; December, 1986, pp. 144-53.

Comparative Literature Studies, summer, 1978.

Concerning Poetry, fall, 1984.

Culture et Developpement, Volume 15, number 1, 1983, pp. 57-63.

Diagonales, October 12, 1989, pp. 5-6.

French Review, May, 1949, pp. 443-47; December, 1982, pp. 272-80; February, 1983, pp. 411-23; March, 1983, pp. 572-78; December, 1983, pp. 224-30.

French Studies Bulletin, 1990.

Hemispheres, fall-winter, 1943-44, pp. 8-9.

Journal of Ethnic Studies, spring, 1981, pp. 69-74.

Journal of West Indian Literature, October, 1986; June, 1987.

Kentucky Foreign Language Quarterly, 1967, pp. 71-9.

Kentucky Romance Quarterly, no. 3, 1969, pp. 195-208.

La Licorne, number 9, 1985, pp. 153-160.

Le Monde, December, 1981.

L'Esprit Createur, fall, 1970, pp. 197-212; spring, 1992, p. 110.

Los Angeles Times Book Review, December 4, 1983.

Negro Digest, May, 1968, pp. 53-61; January, 1970.

New Scholar, number 8, 1982, pp. 1-2.

New York Times Book Review, February 19, 1984, p. 14.

Notre Librairie, number 74, 1984, pp. 9-13.

Prairie Schooner, spring, 1972.

Quadrant, November, 1984, pp. 50-3.

Renascence, winter, 1974.

Revue de Litterature Comparee, April/June, 1986.

Revue Francophone de Louisiane, spring, 1988, p. 1.

San Francisco Review of Books, Volume 15, number 3, 1990, p. 36.

Studies in Black Literature, winter, 1974.

Studies in the Humanities, June, 1984.

Times Literary Supplement, July 19, 1985.

Twentieth Century Literature, July, 1972.

Washington Post Book World, February 5, 1984.

Yale French Studies, no. 46, 1971, pp. 41-7; no. 53, 1976.

*   *   *

CHAMBERS, Charles, Sr.   1927-

PERSONAL: Born September 10, 1927, in Baltimore, MD; son of James D., Sr. (a steel worker) and Carsie

T. (a homemaker) Chambers; married Agnes Williams, September 18, 1954; children: Carol Chambers Lewis, Charles, Jr., Sharon Chambers Williams, Keith. *Ethnicity:* "Black." *Education:* Hampton University, B.S., 1952; University of Maryland at College Park, M.Ed., 1974. *Politics:* Democrat. *Religion:* Baptist. *Avocational interests:* Gardening.

*ADDRESSES: Home—*5602 Belle Ave., Baltimore, MD 21207.

CAREER: Department of Education, Baltimore, MD, guidance counselor, c. 1960-83. Active with local neighborhood association.

MEMBER: American Association of Retired Persons, Maryland Retired Teachers Association, Grove Park Civic Association.

WRITINGS:

Sunlight on Verse, 1stBooks Library (Bloomington, IN), 1998.

WORK IN PROGRESS: A religious book, *Gems of the Spirit.*

*   *   *

CHESNUTT, Charles W(addell)   1858-1932

PERSONAL: Born June 20, 1858, in Cleveland, OH; died November 15, 1932, Cleveland, OH; son of Andrew Jackson (in grocery business) and Ann (one source says Anne) Maria (Sampson) Chesnutt; married Susan Utley Perry (a teacher), June 6, 1878; children: Ethel, Helen Maria, Edwin, Dorothy. *Education:* Educated at schools in Cleveland, OH, and Fayetteville, NC.

CAREER: Teacher, lawyer, businessman, and writer. Taught at public schools in Spartanburg, SC, Charlotte, NC, and Fayetteville, NC, 1872-77; New State Normal School, Fayetteville, assistant principal, 1877-80, principal, 1880-83; worked as a reporter for Dow Jones & Co., 1883; *New York Mail and Express,* New York City, stenographer, reporter, and author of daily column "Wall Street Gossip," 1883; Nickel Plate Railroad Co., Cleveland, OH, 1884-89, began as clerk, became stenographer for the firm's legal counsel; admitted to the Bar of Ohio, 1887; private practice of court reporting, beginning in 1890. Active in community affairs and social causes; served on General Committee of National Association for the Advancement of Colored People (NAACP).

AWARDS, HONORS: Spingarn Medal from NAACP, 1928.

WRITINGS:

The Conjure Woman (short stories; contains "The Goophered Grapevine," "Po'Sandy," "Mars Jeems's Nightmare," "The Conjurer's Revenge," "Sis' Becky's Pickaninny," "The Gray Wolf's Ha'nt," and "Hot-Foot Hannibal"), Houghton, 1899, deluxe edition with a foreword by Joel Elias Spingarn, 1929, retold for young readers by Ray Anthony Shepard as *Conjure Tales,* with illustrations by John Ross and Clare Romano, Dutton, 1973.

The Wife of His Youth, and Other Stories of the Color Line (short stories; contains "The Wife of His Youth," "Her Virginia Mammy," "The Sheriff's Children," "A Matter of Principle," "Cicely's Dream," "The Passing of Grandison," "Uncle Wellington's Wives," "The Bouquet," and "The Web of Circumstance"), Houghton, 1899, reprinted with illustrations by Clyde O. DeLand, Gregg, 1967.

Frederick Douglass (biography), Small, Maynard, 1899.

The House behind the Cedars (novel), Houghton, 1900, reprinted with an introduction by Darwin Turner, P. F. Collier, 1969.

The Marrow of Tradition (novel), Houghton, 1901.

The Colonel's Dream (novel), Doubleday, Page, 1905.

The Short Fiction of Charles W. Chesnutt, edited with an introduction by Sylvia Lyons Render, Howard University Press, 1974.

The Journals of Charles W. Chesnutt, Duke University Press, 1993.

Collected Stories of Charles Chesnutt, Amereon Ltd., 1996.

Mandy Oxendine, (novel), edited by Charles Hackenberry, University of Illinois Press, 1997.

Paul Marchand, F.M.C., edited by Dean Mc-Williams, Princeton University Press, 1999.

The Quarry, edited by Dean McWilliams, Princeton University Press, 1999.

Contributor to periodicals, including *Alexander's Magazine, Boston Evening Transcript, Family Fiction, Puck, Youth's Companion, Cleveland News and Herald, Atlantic Monthly, Crisis, Overland Monthly, Chicago Ledger, Century, New Haven Register, New York Independent, Outlook,* and *Southern Workman.*

SIDELIGHTS: In her biography, *Charles W. Chesnutt: Pioneer of the Color Line,* Helen M. Chesnutt describes her father as "a pioneer Negro author, the first to exploit in fiction the complex lives of men and women of mixed blood." Similarly, Sylvia Lyons Render writes admiringly in her introduction to *The Short Fiction of Charles W. Chesnutt* of his "extraordinary ability to blend his African and European heritages into distinctly American forms." Because of his fair complexion, Render pointed out, Chesnutt could have "passed" for white; instead "he chose to remain identified as an Afro-American and sought to remove rather than to avoid various forms of discrimination." Chesnutt also merits recognition as one of the first black American fiction writers to receive serious critical attention and acclaim for portraying blacks realistically and sensitively, shunning condescending characterizations and nostalgia for antebellum days of slavery in the South.

Chesnutt was born in 1858 in Cleveland, Ohio, the son of free Negro parents who had moved from Fayetteville, North Carolina, before the Civil War in flight from increasingly severe restrictions imposed on the free colored population of North Carolina. In 1866 the family returned to Fayetteville, and Chesnutt's father started a grocery store there. When young Charles wasn't working in the store, he attended the Howard School for blacks, founded by the Freedman's Bureau in 1865. Pressed to help support his family, Chesnutt was forced to end his formal education when he was only fourteen. However, Robert Harris, the school's principal, prevailed upon Charles's father to let his son stay at the school as a pupil-teacher and turn his modest salary over to his father. At sixteen Chesnutt went to Charlotte as a full-time teacher, and in 1877 he returned to Fayetteville as assistant principal of Howard School, becoming upon Harris's death three years later its principal. Concomitantly Chesnutt commenced a vigorous program of reading and study that led to his proficiency in Latin, German, French, mathematics, and stenography. In 1883 Chesnutt resigned his school administrator post and struck out alone in search of more lucrative employment in the North. He found a job in New York City as a stenographer and journalist on Wall Street, then later returned to Cleveland, where he was hired as a railway clerk and, in 1884, settled with his family.

Chesnutt eventually became a stenographer for the railway company's lawyer, Judge Samuel E.

Williamson, in whose office he studied law, and in 1887 he passed the Ohio Bar at the top of his class. Judge Williamson offered to finance a law practice for Chesnutt in Europe, which was less racist than the United States, but Chesnutt declined the offer. He also turned down the invitation of George Washington Cable, a prominent American writer, to become his private secretary.

Instead, in 1890 Chesnutt chose to support his growing family by establishing a court reporting business and devoting his evenings to his longtime avocation, writing fiction. His first stories were generally light in tone and dealt with conventional subjects of appeal to lesser magazines ranging from *Puck* to *Youth's Companion* and to newspaper syndicates such as S. S. McClure's. These early efforts were crowned by *Atlantic Monthly*'s acceptance of his stories "The Goophered Grapevine" in 1887 and "Po' Sandy" in 1888. At Cable's urging he also contributed commentary to the *New York Independent* and other liberal publications, and by 1889 Chesnutt had completed his first novel, eventually published in 1900 as *The House Behind the Cedars.*

Chesnutt's first published volume, *The Conjure Woman*-issued in 1899 by Houghton Mifflin-was a collection of dialect stories told by an old Negro gardener, "Uncle" Julius McAdoo, to his Northern employer. Ostensibly simple tales of metamorphosis, voodoo, and conjuring, they nonetheless illuminate the dynamics of master-slave relationships and the injustices of slavery. One slaveholder, for instance, resorts to conjuring his grapevine to protect his grapes from thieving slaves. That idea misfires when a new slave mistakenly eats some of the "goophered" grapes. Even after he has tried a magic antidote, the unlucky slave has strange tendrils of grapes growing all over his head-grapes that appear every spring and die down in the winter along with his strength and youth, which also wax and wane with the seasons. Yet his owner profits from this, selling the slave in the spring, when he is young and vigorous, and buying him back cheaply in the fall, when he looks about to die. As several critics noted, these stories convey a very different picture of Southern society from those in the Uncle Remus stories of Joel Chandler Harris, in which happy slaves cheerfully tell animal fables about mischievous Brer Rabbit.

In *The Wife of His Youth, and Other Stories of the Color Line,* a second collection of short stories also published in 1899, Chesnutt portrays the dilemma of mulattoes who felt alien in the black community and excluded from the white. Chesnutt satirized the race-conscious Blue Veins of Cleveland-people of Negro descent with skin light enough to show the blueness of their veins-for snubbing their darker-skinned relatives and mimicking middle-class whites. A third 1899 Chesnutt publication was *Frederick Douglass,* a biography of the prominent abolitionist, for the series "Beacon Biographies of Eminent Americans."

In September, 1900, buoyed by the favorable initial reception given *The Conjure Woman, The Wife of His Youth,* and *Frederick Douglass,* Chesnutt closed down his stenography business so that he could write and lecture full time. Financial success, however, did not match critical acclaim and recognition. His first two novels, *The House Behind the Cedars* and *The Marrow of Tradition,* published in 1900 and 1901 respectively, attracted more controversy than sales. Reviewers who had applauded *The Conjure Woman* became disenchanted with Chesnutt when he began to treat taboo themes such as miscegenation and racial hatred. His sympathetic treatment of erotic love in *The House Behind the Cedars* and his pessimism toward the likelihood of racial harmony in *The Marrow of Tradition* outraged critics. Even William Dean Howells, the distinguished American novelist and critic who in 1900 had praised Chesnutt for "sound[ing] a fresh note, boldly, not blatantly" and placed him in the top rank of American short story writers, declared in a 1901 issue of *North American Review* that "at his worst, [Chesnutt] is no worse than the higher average of the ordinary novelists, but he ought always to be very much better, for he began better."

Chesnutt's earnings from the sales of his two novels and from his freelance journalism and speaking engagements proved inadequate to the financial needs of his family. Consequently in 1902 he reopened the stenography firm he had closed two years earlier. Chesnutt continued writing, however, and in 1905 he published *The Colonel's Dream,* a novel examining the futility of amoral schemes for the economic regeneration of the South. *The Colonel's Dream* received less attention than *The Marrow of Tradition* and garnered even fewer sales. It was to be Chesnutt's last book-length work to appear during his lifetime.

Chesnutt's last published work was an article titled "Post-Bellum-Pre-Harlem" that appeared in *Colophon* a year before his death in 1932. In the article Chesnutt reflected on his literary life and on the history of Afro-American writing in general. He summarized his various books and commented on the ambivalence of his publishers toward revealing his racial identity during the early years of his career. He accepted the fact that literary fashion had passed him by, but he proudly noted that Afro-American literature and the attitude of the white literary world had advanced considerably since the days of his earliest publications. Once possibly the only black American to write serious fiction about Negroes, Chesnutt had devoted his art to reorienting his readers toward what he considered the real issues of race in America.

BIOGRAPHICAL/CRITICAL SOURCES:

BOOKS

Andrews, William L., *The Literary Career of Charles W. Chesnutt,* Louisiana State University Press, 1980.

Bigsby, C. W. E., editor, *The Black American Writer,* Everett/Edwards, 1969.

Chesnutt, Helen M., *Charles Waddell Chesnutt: Pioneer of the Color Line,* University of North Carolina Press, 1952.

Dictionary of Literary Biography, Volume 12: *American Realists and Naturalists,* Gale, 1982; Volume 50: *Afro-American Writers Before the Harlem Renaissance,* Gale, 1986.

Ellison, Curtis W. and E. W. Metcalf, Jr., *Charles W. Chesnutt: A Reference Guide,* G. K. Hall, 1977.

Keller, Frances Richardson, *An American Crusade: The Life of Charles Waddell Chesnutt,* Brigham Young University Press, 1978.

McElrath, Jr., Joseph R., and Robert C. Leitz III, *"To Be an Author": Letters of Charles W. Chesnutt, 1889-1905,* Princeton University Press (Princeton, NJ), 1996.

Pickens, Ernestine Williams, *Charles W. Chesnutt and the Progressive Movement,* Pace University Press (New York City), 1994.

Render, Sylvia Lyons, editor, *The Short Fiction of Charles W. Chesnutt,* Howard University Press, 1974.

Twentieth-Century Literary Criticism, Gale, Volume 5, 1981.

Wonham, Henry B., *Charles W. Chesnutt: A Study of the Short Fiction,* Twayne Publishers, 1998.

PERIODICALS

American Literature, May, 1975.
American Scholar, winter, 1972.
American Visions, April-May, 1994, p. 30.
Atlantic Monthly, May, 1900.
Books and Bookmen, December, 1975.
CLA Journal, March, 1972; December, 1974.
Colophon, Volume II, number 5, 1931.
Crisis, January, 1933.
Growing Point, January, 1976.
Kirkus Reviews, September 15, 1973; December 15, 1973.
Kliatt, winter, 1979.
New Republic, March 1, 1975.
New York Times Book Review, November 4, 1973; January 17, 1974.
Observer, December 7, 1975.
Phylon, spring, 1971.
Saturday Review, June 21, 1969; October 25, 1969.
Southern Literary Journal, fall, 1982.
Spectator, March 21, 1969; August 16, 1979.
Times Literary Supplement, December 5, 1975.*

* * *

CHILDRESS, Alice 1920-1994

PERSONAL: Surname is pronounced *"Chil*-dress"; born October 12, 1920, in Charleston, SC; died of cancer, August 14, 1994, Queens, NY; first husband unknown; married second husband, Nathan Woodard (a musician), July 17, 1957; children: (first marriage) Jean (Mrs. Richard Lee). *Education:* Attended public schools in New York, NY.

ADDRESSES: Office—Beacon Press, 25 Beacon St., Boston, MA 02108-2824. *Agent*—c/o Flora Roberts Inc., 157 West 57th St, New York, NY 10019.

CAREER: Playwright, novelist, actress, and director. Began career in theater as an actress, with her first appearance in *On Strivers Row,* 1940; actress and director with American Negro Theatre, New York City, for eleven years, featured in the plays *Natural Man,* 1941, *Anna Lucasta,* 1944, and *Florence,* which she also wrote and directed, 1949; also performed on Broadway and television; made her film appearance in *Uptight,* in 1968. Lecturer at universities and schools; member of panel discussions and conferences on Black American theater at numerous institutions, including New School for Social Research, 1965, and Fisk University, 1966; visiting scholar at Radcliffe Institute for Independent Study (now Mary Ingraham Bunting Institute), Cambridge, MA, 1966-68. Member of governing board of Frances Delafield Hospital.

MEMBER: PEN, Dramatists Guild (member of council), American Federation of Television and Radio

Artists, Writers Guild of America East (member of council), Harlem Writers Guild.

AWARDS, HONORS: Obie Award for best original off-Broadway play, *Village Voice,* 1956, for *Trouble in Mind;* John Golden Fund for Playwrights grant, 1957; Rockefeller grant, 1967; Outstanding Book of the Year, *New York Times Book Review,* Best Young Adult Book of 1975, Woodward School Book Award, 1974, Jane Addams Children's Book Honor Award for young adult novel, 1974, National Book Award nomination, 1974, and Lewis Carroll Shelf Award, University of Wisconsin, 1975, all for *A Hero Ain't Nothin' but a Sandwich;* Sojourner Truth Award, National Association of Negro Business and Professional Women's Clubs, 1975; Virgin Islands film festival award for best screenplay, and first Paul Robeson Award for Outstanding Contributions to the Performing Arts, Black Filmmakers Hall of Fame, both 1977, both for *A Hero Ain't Nothin' but a Sandwich;* "Alice Childress Week" officially observed in Charleston and Columbia, SC, 1977, to celebrate opening of *Sea Island Song;* Paul Robeson Award, 1980; Best Book, *School Library Journal,* 1981, one of the Outstanding Books of the Year, *New York Times,* 1982, notable children's trade book in social studies, National Council for the Social Studies and Children's Book Council, 1982, and honorable mention, Coretta Scott King Award, 1982, all for *Rainbow Jordan;* Radcliffe Graduate Society Medal, 1984; Audelco Pioneer Award, 1986; Lifetime Achievement Award, Association for Theatre in Higher Education, 1993.

WRITINGS:

Like One of the Family: Conversations from a Domestic's Life, Independence Publishers, 1956, reprinted with an introduction by Trudier Harris, Beacon Press (Boston), 1986.
(Editor) *Black Scenes* (collection of scenes from plays written by African Americans), Doubleday (New York City), 1971.
A Hero Ain't Nothin' but a Sandwich (novel; also see below), Coward (London), 1973.
A Short Walk (novel), Coward, 1979.
Rainbow Jordan (novel), Coward, 1981.
Many Closets, Coward, 1987.
Those Other People, Putnam (New York City), 1989.

PLAYS

Florence (one-act), first produced in New York City at American Negro Theatre, 1949.

Just a Little Simple (based on Langston Hughes's short story collection *Simple Speaks His Mind*), first produced in New York City at Club Baron Theatre, September, 1950.
Gold through the Trees, first produced at Club Baron Theatre, 1952.
Trouble in Mind, first produced off-Broadway at Greenwich Mews Theatre, November 3, 1955, revised version published in *Black Theatre: A Twentieth-Century Collection of the Work of Its Best Playwrights,* edited by Lindsay Patterson, Dodd (New York City), 1971.
Wedding Band: A Love/Hate Story in Black and White (first produced in Ann Arbor, MI, at University of Michigan, December 7, 1966; produced off-Broadway at New York Shakespeare Festival Theatre, September 26, 1972; also see below), Samuel French (New York City), 1973.
String (one-act; based on Guy de Maupassant's story "A Piece of String"; also see below), first produced off-Broadway at St. Mark's Playhouse, March 25, 1969.
Mojo: A Black Love Story (one-act; also see below), produced in New York City at New Heritage Theatre, November, 1970.
Mojo [and] *String,* Dramatists Play Service (New York City), 1971.
When the Rattlesnake Sounds: A Play (juvenile), illustrated by Charles Lilly, Coward, 1975.
Let's Hear It for the Queen: A Play (juvenile), Coward, 1976.
Sea Island Song, produced in Charleston, SC, 1977, produced as *Gullah* in Amherst, MA, at University of Massachusetts, Amherst, 1984.
Moms: A Praise Play for a Black Comedienne (based on the life of Jackie "Moms" Mabley), music and lyrics by Childress and her husband, Nathan Woodard, first produced by Green Plays at Art Awareness, 1986, produced off-Broadway at Hudson Guild Theatre, February 4, 1987.

Also author of *Martin Luther King at Montgomery, Alabama,* music by Woodard, 1969; *A Man Bearing a Pitcher,* 1969; *The Freedom Drum,* music by Woodard, produced as *Young Man Martin Luther King* by Performing Arts Repertory Theatre, 1969-71; *The African Garden,* music by Woodard, 1971; and *Vashti's Magic Mirror.*

SCREENPLAYS

Wine in the Wilderness: A Comedy-Drama (first produced in Boston by WGBH-TV, March 4, 1969), Dramatists Play Service, 1969.

Wedding Band (based on her play of the same title), American Broadcasting Companies (ABC-TV), 1973.

A Hero Ain't Nothin' but a Sandwich (based on her novel of the same title), New World Pictures, 1978.

String (based on her play of the same title), Public Broadcasting Service (PBS-TV), 1979.

Author of "Here's Mildred" column in *Baltimore Afro-American,* 1956-58. Contributor of plays, articles, and reviews to *Masses and Mainstream, Black World, Freedomways, Essence, Negro Digest, New York Times,* and other publications.

SIDELIGHTS: Alice Childress's work is noted for its frank treatment of racial issues, its compassionate yet discerning characterizations, and its universal appeal. Because her books and plays often deal with such controversial subjects as interracial relationships and teenage drug addiction, her work has been banned in certain locations. She recalled that some affiliate stations refused to carry the nationally televised broadcasts of *Wedding Band* and *Wine in the Wilderness,* and in the case of the latter play, the entire state of Alabama banned the telecast. In addition, Childress noted that as late as 1973 the novel *A Hero Ain't Nothin' but a Sandwich* "was the first book banned in a Savannah, Georgia school library since *Catcher in the Rye.*" Despite such regional resistance, Childress won praise and respect for writings that a *Variety* reviewer termed "powerful and poetic."

A talented writer and performer in several media, Childress began her career in the theater, initially as an actress and later as a director and playwright. Although "theater histories make only passing mention of her, . . . she was in the forefront of important developments in that medium," wrote *Dictionary of Literary Biography* contributor Trudier Harris. Rosemary Curb pointed out in another *Dictionary of Literary Biography* essay that Childress's 1952 drama *Gold through the Trees* was "the first play by a black woman professionally produced on the American stage." Moreover, Curb added, "As a result of successful performances of [*Just a Little Simple* and *Gold through the Trees*], Childress initiated Harlem's first all-union off-Broadway contracts recognizing the Actors Equity Association and the Harlem Stage Hand Local."

Partly because of her pioneering efforts, Childress is considered a crusader by many. But she is also known as "a writer who resists compromise," explained Doris E. Abramson in *Negro Playwrights in the American Theatre: 1925-1959.* "She tries to write about [black] problems as honestly as she can," thus, the problems Childress addressed most often were racism and its effects. Her *Trouble in Mind,* for example, is a play within a play that focuses on the anger and frustration experienced by a troupe of black actors as they try to perform stereotyped roles in a play that has been written, produced, and directed by whites. As Sally R. Sommer explained in the *Village Voice,* "The plot is about an emerging rebellion begun as the heroine, Wiletta, refuses to enact a namby-Mammy, either in the play or for her director." In the *New York Times,* Arthur Gelb stated that Childress "has some witty and penetrating things to say about the dearth of roles for [black] actors in the contemporary theatre, the cutthroat competition for these parts and the fact that [black] actors often find themselves playing stereotyped roles in which they cannot bring themselves to believe." And of *Wedding Band,* a play about an interracial relationship that takes place in South Carolina during World War I, Clive Barnes wrote in the *New York Times,* "Childress very carefully suggests the stirrings of black consciousness, as well as the strength of white bigotry."

Both Sommer and the *New York Times*'s Richard Eder found that Childress's treatment of the themes and issues in *Trouble in Mind* and *Wedding Band* gives these plays a timeless quality. "Writing in 1955, . . . Alice Childress used the concentric circles of the play-within-the-play to examine the multiple roles blacks enact in order to survive," Sommer remarked. She found that viewing *Trouble in Mind* years later enables one to see "its double cutting edge: It predicts not only the course of social history but the course of black playwriting." Eder stated: "The question [in *Wedding Band*] is whether race is a category of humanity or a division of it. The question is old by now, and was in 1965, but it takes the freshness of new life in the marvelous characters that Miss Childress has created to ask it."

The strength and insight of Childress's characterizations have been widely commented upon; critics contend that the characters who populate her plays and novels are believable and memorable. Eder called the characterizations of *Wedding Band: A Love/Hate Story in Black and White* "rich and lively." Similarly impressed, Harold Clurman wrote in the *Nation* that "there is an honest pathos in the telling of this simple story, and some humorous and touching thumbnail sketches reveal knowledge and understanding of the people dealt with." In the novel *A Short Walk,*

Childress chronicled the life of a fictitious black woman, Cora James, from her birth in 1900 to her death in the middle of the century, illustrating, as *Washington Post* critic Joseph McLellan described it, "a transitional generation in black American society." McLellan noted that the story "wanders considerably" and that "the reader is left with no firm conclusion that can be put into a neat sentence or two." What is more important, he asserted, is that "the wandering has been through some interesting scenery, and instead of a conclusion the reader has come to know a human being-complex, struggling valiantly and totally believable." In her play *Moms,* Childress drew a portrait of real-life comic Jackie "Moms" Mabley, a popular black comedienne of the 1960s and 1970s. Dressed as a stereotypical shopping-bag lady, Moms Mabley was a television staple with her stand-up routine as a feisty woman with a sharp tongue. Childress, Mel Gussow writes in the *New York Times,* "shrewdly gives Moms center stage and lets her comic sensibility speak for itself."

In several novels aimed at a young adult audience, Childress displayed her talent for believable characterization. In the novel *A Hero Ain't Nothin' but a Sandwich,* the author creates a portrait of a teenaged heroin addict by giving us his story not only from his point of view but from several of his friends and family as well. The *Lion and the Unicorn*'s Miguel Oritz stated, "The portrait of whites is more realistic in this book, more compassionate, and at the same time, because it is believable, more scathing." In *Those Other People,* Childress tells of a group of young friends who are all outsiders: a homosexual, a wealthy black sister and brother, a teacher who has molested one of his students, and a psychiatric patient who was sexually abused as a girl. Each character tells his or her story in separate chapters. The result is a multifaceted look at a pivotal incident at their school which calls into question matters of race and sexual preference. Kathryn Havris, writing in the *School Library Journal,* called *Those Other People* "a disturbing, disquieting novel that reflects another side to life." A *Publishers Weekly* critic concluded that the novel was "a penetrating examination of bigotry and racism."

Many have acclaimed Childress's work for its honesty, insight, and compassion. In his review of *A Hero Ain't Nothin' but a Sandwich,* Oritz wrote: "The book conveys very strongly the message that we are all human, even when we are acting in ways that we are somewhat ashamed of. The structure of the book grows out of the personalities of the characters, and

the author makes us aware of how much the economic and social circumstances dictate a character's actions." Loften Mitchell concluded in *Crisis:* "Childress writes with a sharp, satiric touch. Character seems to interest her more than plot. Her characterizations are piercing, her observations devastating."

BIOGRAPHICAL/CRITICAL SOURCES:

BOOKS

Abramson, Doris E., *Negro Playwrights in the American Theatre, 1925-1959,* Columbia University Press (New York City), 1969.

Betsko, Kathleen, and Rachel Koenig, *Interviews with Contemporary Women Playwrights,* Beech Tree Books (Taylors, SC), 1987.

Brown, Janet, *Feminist Drama: Definition and Critical Analysis,* Scarecrow Press, 1979, pp. 56-70.

Brown-Guillory, Elizabeth, *Their Place on the Stage: Black Women Playwrights in America,* Greenwood Press, 1988, pp. 25-49.

Children's Literature Review, Volume 14, Gale (Detroit), 1988.

Contemporary Dramatists, fifth edition, St. James Press (Detroit), 1993.

Contemporary Literary Criticism, Gale, Volume 12, 1980; Volume 15, 1980; Volume 96, 1997.

Dictionary of Literary Biography, Gale, Volume 7: *Twentieth-Century American Dramatists,* 1981; Volume 38: *Afro-American Writers after 1955: Dramatists and Prose Writers,* 1985.

Donelson, Kenneth L. and Aleen Pace Nilson, *Literature for Today's Young Adults,* Scott, Foresman (Glenview, IL), 1980, 2nd edition, 1985.

Drama Criticism, Volume 4, Gale, 1994.

Evans, Mari, editor, *Black Women Writers (1950-1980): A Critical Evaluation,* Doubleday-Anchor (New York City), 1984.

Feminist Theatre: An Introduction to Plays of Contemporary British and American Women, Macmillan, 1984, pp. 22-52.

Hatch, James V., *Black Theater, U.S.A.: Forty-five Plays by Black Americans,* Free Press (New York City), 1974.

Jennings, La Vinia Delois, *Alice Childress,* Twayne (New York City), 1995.

Miller, R. Baxter, editor, *Black American Literature and Humanism,* University Press of Kentucky, 1981, pp. 8-10.

Mitchell, Loften, editor, *Voices of the Black Theatre,* James White (Clifton, NJ), 1975.

Schlueter, June, editor, *Modern American Drama: The Female Canon,* Fairleigh Dickinson University Press, 1990, pp. 184-197.

Street, Douglas, editor, *Children's Novels and the Movies,* Ungar (New York City), 1983.

PERIODICALS

Atlanta Constitution, March 27, 1986, p. 1.

CLA Journal, June, 1977, pp. 494-507.

Crisis, April, 1965.

Daily Worker, November 8, 1955, p. 7.

Freedomways, Volume 14, number 1, 1974.

Horn Book Magazine, May-June, 1989, p. 374.

Interracial Books for Children Bulletin, Volume 12, numbers 7-8, 1981.

Lion and the Unicorn, fall, 1978.

Los Angeles Times, November 13, 1978; February 25, 1983.

Los Angeles Times Book Review, July 25, 1982.

MELUS, winter, 1980, pp. 57-68.

Ms., December, 1979.

Nation, November 13, 1972.

Negro American Literature Forum, fall, 1976, pp. 93-95.

Negro Digest, April, 1967; January, 1968.

New Republic, November 25, 1972, pp. 22, 36.

Newsweek, August 31, 1987.

New York, November 13, 1972, p. 134.

New Yorker, November 4, 1972, p. 105; November 19, 1979.

New York Times, November 5, 1955, p. 23; February 2, 1969; April 2, 1969; October 27, 1972; November 5, 1972; February 3, 1978; January 11, 1979; January 23, 1987; February 10, 1987, p. 16; March 6, 1987; August 18, 1987; October 22, 1987.

New York Times Book Review, November 4, 1973; November 11, 1979; April 25, 1981.

Publishers Weekly, November 25, 1988, p. 67.

SAGE: A Scholarly Journal on Black Women, spring, 1987, pp. 66-68.

School Library Journal, February, 1989, p. 99.

Show Business, April 12, 1969.

Southern Quarterly, spring, 1987, pp. 53-62.

Variety, December 20, 1972.

Village Voice, January 15, 1979.

Washington Post, May 18, 1971; December 28, 1979.

Wilson Library Bulletin, September, 1989, p. 14.

OBITUARIES:

PERIODICALS

Jet, September 5, 1994, p. 18.

Time, August 29, 1994, p. 25.*

CHINWEIZU 1943-

PERSONAL: Born March 26, 1943, in Eluama-Isuikwuato, Nigeria; son of Obediah Dimgba (in business) and Oluchi Akuji (Ejinwa) Ibekwe. *Education:* Massachusetts Institute of Technology, S.B., 1967; State University of New York at Buffalo, M.A., 1975; Ph.D., 1976.

ADDRESSES: Office—Okike, P.O. Box 53, Nsukka, Nigeria.

CAREER: Biafra Review, Cambridge, MA, founder and editor, 1969-70; *Okike,* Nsukka, Nigeria, associate editor, 1973—; San Jose State University, San Jose, CA, associate professor, 1978-79.

AWARDS, HONORS: Rockefeller Foundation fellow in the United States, 1976; prize from the Association of Nigerian Authors, 1985, for *Invocations and Admonitions: 49 Poems and a Triptych of Parables.*

WRITINGS:

The West and the Rest of Us: White Predators, Black Slavers, and the African Elite (history), Random House (New York City), 1975.

Energy Crisis and Other Poems, NOK Publishers (New York City), 1978.

(With Onwuchekwa Jemie and Ihechukwu Madubuike) *Toward the Decolonization of African Literature* (literary history and criticism), Fourth Dimension Publishers (Enugu, Nigeria), Volume I, 1980, Volume II, 1981, Howard University Press (Washington, DC), 1983.

The Footrace and Other Satires, Fourth Dimension Publishers, 1981.

Invocations and Admonitions: 49 Poems and a Triptych of Parables, Pero Press (Lagos, Nigeria), 1986.

The Black World and the Nobel, Pero Press, 1987.

Decolonising the African Mind, Pero Press, 1987.

(Compiler and author of introduction) *Voice from Twentieth-Century Africa: Griots and Towncriers,* Faber (Boston), 1988.

Anatomy of Female Power: A Masculinist Dissection of Matriarchy, Pero Press, 1990.

Contributor to journals, including *Africa, Black Scholar, First World, East African Journal,* and *New Age.* Contributing editor, *American Rag,* 1978—.

WORK IN PROGRESS: Poems; research on ecology and culture and on African development.

SIDELIGHTS: Chinweizu is a Nigerian poet, historian, economist, and literary critic whose work draws on numerous disciplines in the social sciences and humanities in order to explore Africa's current political, social, and cultural condition. *Dictionary of Literary Biography* essayist Chris Dunton credited Chinweizu with significantly extending "the analysis of colonialism and neocolonialism carried out by African, African American, and Caribbean writers such as Kwame Nkrumah, Walter Rodney, and Frantz Fanon. Its significance lies not in the development of new theoretical insights, since Chinweizu's often highly polemical writing serves to recharge the stimuli provided by earlier writers, but his insistence on reading culture through an understanding of political and economic history was influential in alerting other writers to the value of an interdisciplinary approach to the study of Africa. The vehemence of much of his writing and his eagerness to engage in fierce, sometimes abusive, personal debate created many enmities. It also ensured . . . that his work maintained high visibility . . . and helped keep alive a radical critique of the colonial and neo-colonial experience."

"Chinweizu demands of literature," wrote G. G. Darah of *Punch,* "the mental preparation of the people for the task of nation-building." Since literature, as Chinweizu believes, has a fundamental role in shaping a people's consciousness, it is a central concern in African cultural autonomy. "For centuries," the author told Darah, "Africa has been under attack by colonialists. It needs to free itself in autonomous ways. Our writers have to do serious rethinking of their themes, styles, and centrally in our view, the audience for which they write. They should write about issues fundamental to Africa today and bear in mind the literary traditions of pre-colonial era." Chinweizu suggests that African authors write for their countrymen using the official language, English, and that they explore contemporary issues the average individual can appreciate. Darah explained: "The writer should grasp the essence of political events and their impact on, say, the farmer, taxi driver and factory worker."

The author's first book, *The West and the Rest of Us: White Predators, Black Slavers, and the African Elite,* is a historical look at the Western world's relationship with the underdeveloped countries, particularly those in Africa. In it, Chinweizu speculates about possible ways to bring about political, economic, and cultural renewal. The book's scope is sweeping, beginning with a history of Western imperialism from 1415 to the present day, then moving on to analyze African economies and to explain the need for Africans to cultivate their own cultural awareness. According to Dunton, Chinweizu sees lack of cultural awareness as "inseparable from . . . political subordination to the West, and . . . the malfunction of African political institution."

Another of Chinweizu's books, *Toward the Decolonization of African Literature* (written with Onwuchekwa Jemie and Ihechukwu Madubuike), is considered one of the most influential and controversial studies of African literature. This volume urges writers to use techniques for modern poetry and fiction that are drawn from African oral tradition. It also examines existing criticism of African literature and points out the Eurocentric prejudice in most of it. It was the first book to urge African writers to look to their African heritage rather than striving to emulate European models. Dunton noted that "its impact on teaching faculty, especially in Nigeria, was to shift the parameters through which theory of cultural production was discussed, and it stimulated a new appraisal of the nature of African literatures and of the cultural and intellectual interaction of Africa and the West."

In attacking the existing Eurocentric cultural establishment of Nigeria, Chinweizu reserved a great deal of venom for Nobel Prize-winning author Wole Soyinka. In a 1981 short story entitled "Simple Simon Learns About Art-AS-ART," he referred to Soyinka as "the panther pontiff of African ART—The nemesis of Ebonism," and a puppet of the British elite, according to Dunton. After Soyinka won the Nobel in 1986, Chinweizu published "one of his most vitriolic pieces," said Dunton, "in which Soyinka is denounced as a 'Nigger Tom' and the Nobel as a 'Neocolonial O.B.E. Lollipop,' whose award prompts Africa to 'give vent to a boundless joy: Massa says we smart! Massas says we smart! Rejoice, all you niggers, rejoice!'" The conflict between the two men even gave rise to a "caustically funny satire" by Esiaba Irobi entitled *Gold, Frankincense and Myrrh.* In it, Dunton reported, "Chinweizu and Soyinka battle it out—and the latter emerges as clear winner."

Chinweizu once told *CA:* "I write because it is the way of contributing to my society that I find most appropriate to my talents and temperament. My primary audience is the Pan-African world—i.e., Africans of both the continental homeland and the diaspora. Most of my writing comes out of a consciousness shaped by the anti-colonial movement in

Africa. Political, economic, and cultural nationalism saturated the very air in which I grew up in Nigeria. The great unfinished business of African decolonization and development is my theme, and my writing is devoted to raising consciousness about the sources of, the nature of, and the possible remedies for our condition. I am particularly concerned with helping to clean up the colonial cataracts and the hangover that still prevents us from seeing what our condition calls for.

"In the last few years, my interest has enlarged to include ecology. My focus is on the quest for ecological values, a quest guided by the question: What values, if any, are appropriate for both the survival of the human species and the health of the biosphere? If and when we discover ecologically valid values, we must work very hard to create a culture consistent with them, seeing as values and habits are extremely difficult to alter. Whether we can do all that before catastrophe overtakes us is in much doubt. However, I do see cause for some hope. If we do discover ecological values, we ought not have too much difficulty adopting them, for, after all, any species that could sell itself the virgin birth could sell itself anything.

"All that grave and serious stuff aside, I write satires for fun."

BIOGRAPHICAL/CRITICAL SOURCES:

BOOKS

Amuta, Chidi, *The Theory of African Literature,* Zed (Atlantic Highlands, NJ), 1989.
Appiah, Kwame Anthony, *Canonization and Teaching of African Literatures,* Rodopi (Atlanta, GA), 1990, pp. 57-89.
Appiah, Kwame Anthony, *In My Father's House: Africa in the Philosophy of Culture,* Oxford University Press (New York City), 1992.
Dictionary of Literary Biography, Volume 157: *Twentieth-Century Caribbean and Black African Writers, Third Series,* Gale (Detroit), 1995.
Soyinka, Wole, *Art, Dialogue and Outrage,* New Horn (Ibadan, Nigeria), 1988, pp. 86-109.

PERIODICALS

African Concord, November 5, 1990, pp. 50-53.
African Literature Today, volume 10, 1979, pp. 32-56.
Alkebu-Lan, volume 2, number 1, 1988, pp. 9-13; Volume 2, number 2, 1988, pp. 8-12.

BBC Arts and Africa, number 699, 1987, pp. 1-5.
Canadian Journal of African Studies, volume 8, number 2, 1974, pp. 385-410.
Crown Prince, May, 1991, pp. 26-28, 30, 36, 44, 56, 58.
Daily Times (Lagos), May 16, 1980, p. 3; May 17, 1980; May 19, 1980, pp. 3, 13; July 13, 1991, p. 14; July 20, 1991, p. 16.
Guardian (Lagos), December 7, 1985, p. 9; April 6, 1986, p. 8; April 13, 1986, p. 6; April 27, 1986, p. 6.
International Fiction Review, winter, 1988, pp. 54-57.
Journal of Caribbean Studies, volume 8, numbers 1-2, 1990-1991, pp. 89-104.
Odu, January, 1990, pp. 126-146.
Punch, March 21, 1981.
Quality, May 4, 1989, pp. 43-49.
Research in African Literatures, spring, 1986, pp. 39-47; summer, 1986, pp. 317-322; summer, 1987, pp. 259-265; summer, 1991, pp. 5-20.
Saiwa, number 4, 1987, pp. 68-71.
South, April-May, 1981, pp. 33-37.
Ufahamu, volume 14, number 3, 1985, pp. 139-155.
West Africa, December 5, 1988, p. 2292.

*   *   *

CHUCK D
See RIDENHOUR, Carlton

*   *   *

CLARK, Al C.
See GOINES, Donald

*   *   *

CLEAVER, (Leroy) Eldridge 1935-1998

PERSONAL: Born August 31, 1935, in Wabbaseka (some sources say June 5, 1935), AK, died May 1, 1998, in Pomona, CA; son of Leroy (a dining car waiter) and Thelma (a janitress) Cleaver; married Kathleen Neal, December, 1967; children: Maceo (son), Joju (daughter). *Education:* Attended junior college; also educated in Soledad.

CAREER: Prisoner at Soledad Prison, 1954-57, 1958-66; *Ramparts* (magazine), San Francisco, Calif., assistant editor and contributing writer, 1966-68; Black Panther Party, Oakland, Calif., minister of information, 1967-71; presidential candidate, Peace and Freedom Party, 1968; in exile in Cuba, Algeria, and France, 1968-75; owner of boutique in Hollywood, Calif., 1978-79; founder of Eldridge Cleaver Crusades, 1979; independent candidate for Congress in 8th Congressional District, Calif., 1984. Lecturer at universities.

AWARDS, HONORS: Martin Luther King Memorial Prize, 1970, for *Soul on Ice.*

WRITINGS:

Soul on Ice, introduction by Maxwell Geismar, McGraw, 1968.
Eldridge Cleaver: Post-Prison Writings and Speeches, edited by Robert Scheer, Random House, 1969. 1969.
(Author of introduction) Jerry Rubin, *Do It!,* Simon & Schuster, 1970.
(With others) *Revolution in the Congo, Stage 1 for the Revolutionary Peoples' Network,* 1971.
(Contributor) G. Louis Heath, editor, *The Black Panther Leaders Speak: Huey P. Newton, Bobby Seale, Eldridge Cleaver, and Company Speak Out through the Black Panther Party's Official Newspaper,* Scarecrow, 1976.
Soul on Fire, Word Inc., 1978.

Also author, with others, of *War Within: Violence or Non-violence in Black Revolution,* 1971, of *Education and Revolution,* Center for Educational Reform, and of pamphlets for the Black Panther Party and People's Communication Network. Work appears in anthologies, including *Prize Stories, 1971: The O. Henry Awards.* Contributor to *Ramparts, Commonweal, National Review,* and other periodicals.

SIDELIGHTS: Speaking of his days as a leader of the revolutionary Black Panther Party, Eldridge Cleaver told Lynne Baranski and Richard Lemon of *People* that at that time he felt "there was no hope of effecting real freedom within the capitalistic system. I was the guy who demanded we go down shooting." Cleaver's radical exhortations endeared him to the militant nationalists who made up the Black Panthers. During the Party's short and turbulent history, nineteen Panthers were killed in gun battles with the police. "It was exhilarating. . . ," Cleaver's wife

Kathleen told Baranski and Lemon about that period. "But it was also terrible—people getting killed."

Cleaver joined the Black Panther Party shortly after his release from prison in 1966. He had served nine years for drug dealing and rape and was only released on parole after a number of literary figures petitioned the government on his behalf. *Soul on Ice,* a book Cleaver rary campaign. A collection of essays about the situation of black people in America and about Cleaver's own life, *Soul on Ice* is "an original and disturbing report on what a black man, reacting to a society he detests, reacting to life behind bars for nine years, finally becomes," as Gertrude Samuels wrote in *Saturday Review.* Charlayne Hunter of the *New York Times Book Review* judged Cleaver to be "not a nihilist like so many of his contemporaries who share his revolutionary zeal more than his sense of history. He can tear the system apart, but, unlike them, he has a few ideas about how to put it back together again." In *Soul on Ice,* Jervis Anderson of *Commentary* believed, Cleaver expressed "the profound alienation from America which black nationalists feel and the extreme political and cultural view of its future which they take."

The inspiration for *Soul on Ice* came from a number of writers Cleaver read while in prison, including Thomas Paine, Karl Marx, Nikolai Lenin, and James Baldwin. The most important influence, however, was Malcolm X, a leader of the Black Muslims. Cleaver joined the Muslims in the early 1960s and, when Malcolm X broke away from Elijah Muhammad's leadership of the group, Cleaver followed. Shortly after this break, Malcolm X was assassinated. "I have, so to speak," Cleaver wrote in *Soul on Ice,* "washed my hands in the blood of the martyr, Malcolm X, whose retreat from the precipice of madness created new room for others to turn about in, and I am now caught up in that tiny space, attempting a maneuver of my own."

Shortly after his release from prison, Cleaver became the minister of information for the Black Panther Party. Calling for an armed insurrection to overthrow the United States government and establish a black socialist government in its place, the Panthers were described by F.B.I. director J. Edgar Hoover, *People* notes, as the nation's "greatest threat." The Panthers ran free lunch programs for poor children and operated other service-oriented programs in several cities; but they were also heavily armed for "self-defense" and had frequent problems with the police, including a number of gun battles. *Playboy* noted at the time that Cleaver "has been called the first black leader since Malcolm X with the potential to organize a militant mass movement of 'black liberation.' Whether he will succeed in forging it, whether he will remain free—or even alive—to lead it, and whether, if he does, it will be a force for racial reconciliation or division remains to be seen."

The extent of support Cleaver and the Panthers enjoyed in the white liberal and black communities became clear when Cleaver's parole was revoked in 1968 after he was involved in a gun battle with the police in Oakland, California. One Panther was killed and a police officer and Cleaver were wounded in the battle. He was charged with assault and attempted murder. Support for Cleaver came from around the world. A demonstration in New York City on his behalf included participants such as writer Susan Sontag and actor Gary Merrill. In Europe, French film director Jean-Luc Godard urged his audience to donate to Cleaver's defense fund. Later that same year, while he was still fighting these charges, his wide liberal support became even more clear when Cleaver was chosen as the presidential candidate of the Peace and Freedom Party, an organization of both black and white radicals. "I never exactly dreamed of waking up in the White House after the November election," Cleaver told Nat Hentoff in a *Playboy* interview, "but I took part in that campaign because I think it's necessary to pull a lot of people together, black and white."

Rather than face charges over the gun battle Cleaver fled the country in late 1968. Over the next seven years he lived in Cuba, Algeria, and France and was warmly welcomed on his visits to the Soviet Union, China, North Vietnam, and North Korea. During this time, wrote Richard Gilman in the *New Republic,* "Cleaver played a complicated role from afar in the troubled internal politics of the Black Panthers, served as an unofficial emissary of American radicalism to various communist regimes . . . , fathered two children with his wife Kathleen and found himself growing more and more disenchanted with both his life as an expatriate and his former political beliefs."

This disenchantment stemmed from his realization, after actually visiting and living in many Communist countries, that Communism did not work as well as he had thought. "I had heard," Cleaver writes in *Soul on Fire,* "so much rhetoric about their glorious leaders and their incredible revolutionary spirit that even to this very angry and digruntled American, it was absurd and unreal." Cleaver now "derides Cuba's

system as 'voodoo socialism,'" Baranski and Lemon reported, "and says North Korea and Algeria are 'even worse, because they have been doing it longer.'" Parallel to this political awakening was Cleaver's conversion to Christianity, the result of a mystical vision. Cleaver saw his own face on the moon, then the faces of "my former heroes . . . Fidel Castro, Mao Tsetung, Karl Marx, Friedrich Engels. . . . Finally, at the end of the procession, in dazzling, shimmering light, the image of Jesus Christ appeared . . . ," Cleaver explains in *Soul on Fire.* "I fell to my knees."

In 1975, Cleaver returned to the United States and surrendered to the F.B.I. Although he faced up to seventy-two years in prison, Cleaver struck a deal with the government. By pleading guilty to the assault charge, he had the attempted murder charge dropped and was sentenced to 1,200 hours of commmunity service. One reason for the lenient treatment was the feeling that Cleaver's religious conversion had changed him. Baranski and Leon quoted Earl Anthony, an ex-Panther, who believed: "Eldridge changed from one of the most vicious dudes against the system into a person who is reaching out. He's become a nice human being."

Cleaver was involved in a number of ventures after returning to the United States. In 1978, he opened a boutique in Hollywood featuring men's trousers with a codpiece, his own design. The following year he founded the Eldridge Cleaver Crusades, an evangelical organization with plans to open a headquarters in the Nevada desert. Cleaver returned to politics in 1984 as an independent conservative candidate for Congress; his bid for election was unsuccessful. Denying charges that he had somehow mellowed since his return, Cleaver told Baranski and Lemon: "That implies [my] ideas have changed because of age. I've changed because of new conclusions."

BIOGRAPHICAL/CRITICAL SOURCES:

BOOKS

Cleaver, Eldridge, *Soul on Ice,* McGraw, 1968.

Cleaver, Eldridge, *Soul on Fire,* Word Inc., 1978.

Contemporary Literary Criticism, Volume 30, Gale, 1984.

Cranston, Maurice, editor, *The New Left,* Library Press, 1971.

Hemenway, Robert, editor, *Black Novelist,* Merrill, 1970.

Lockwood, Lee, *Conversation with Eldridge Cleaver: Algiers,* McGraw, 1970.

Oliver, John A., *Eldridge Cleaver: Ice and Fire!*, Bible Voice, 1977.

Parks, Gordon, *Born Black*, Lippincott, 1971.

PERIODICALS

Antioch Review, fall, 1968.

Atlantic, June, 1968.

Best Sellers, February, 1979.

Christianity Today, March 23, 1977; July 8, 1977; December 7, 1979; April 20, 1984.

Commentary, December, 1968.

Communication Quarterly, winter, 1986, pp. 24-40.

Critic, June-July, 1969; August 30, 1976.

Dissent, July/August, 1969.

Economist, November 22, 1975.

Evergreen Review, October, 1968.

Humanist, September/October, 1976.

Jet, August 20, 1984; September 3, 1984.

Life, February 6, 1970.

Look, January, 1969.

Nation, May 13, 1968; January 20, 1969; August 11, 1969; December 6, 1975.

National Review, December 5, 1975; February 10, 1984.

Negro American Literature Forum, March, 1970.

Negro Digest, June, 1968; October, 1969.

New Leader, March 25, 1968.

New Letters, winter, 1971.

New Republic, March 9, 1968; March 13, 1968; November 30, 1968; January 20, 1979.

Newsweek, December 9, 1968; December 1, 1975; September 11, 1978; August 13, 1979; December 3, 1979.

New York Review of Books, December 19, 1968; May 8, 1969.

New York Times, March 13, November 1, 1968; October 7, 1969; November 1, 1970; September 9, 1972.

New York Times Book Review, March 24, 1968; April 27, 1969.

New York Times Magazine, September 7, 1969; January 16, 1977.

People, March 22, 1982.

Playboy, May, 1968; December, 1968.

Progressive, May, 1968; July, 1969.

Ramparts, May, 1968; June, 1968; December, 1968; September, 1969.

Reader's Digest, September, 1976.

Saturday Evening Post, November 16, 1968.

Saturday Review, March 9, 1968; March 1, 1969.

Spectator, February 2, 1969; September 13, 1969.

Time, April 5, 1968; September 20, 1968.

Times Literary Supplement, February 27, 1969.

Village Voice, April 11, 1968; March 6, 1969.

Washington Post, December 11, 1968.

Yale Review, October, 1968.*

* * *

CLIFTON, (Thelma) Lucille 1936-

PERSONAL: Born June 27, 1936, in Depew, NY; daughter of Samuel Louis, Sr. (a laborer) and Thelma (a laborer; maiden name, Moore) Sayles; married Fred James Clifton (an educator, writer, and artist), May 10, 1958 (died November 10, 1984); children: Sidney, Fredrica, Channing, Gillian, Graham, Alexia. *Education:* Attended Howard University, 1953-55, and Fredonia State Teachers College (now State University of New York College at Fredonia), 1955.

ADDRESSES: Office—Distinguished Professor of Humanities, St. Mary's College of Maryland, St. Mary's City, MD 20686. *Agent*—Marilyn Marlow, Curtis Brown Ltd., 10 Astor Pl., New York, NY 10003.

CAREER: New York State Division of Employment, Buffalo, claims clerk, 1958-60; U.S. Office of Education, Washington, DC, literature assistant for CAREL (Central Atlantic Regional Educational Laboratory), 1969-71; Coppin State College, Baltimore, MD, poet in residence, 1971-74; University of California, Santa Cruz, professor of literature and creative writing, 1985-89; St. Mary's College of Maryland, St. Mary's City, MD, distinguished professor of humanities, 1989—; Columbia University, professor of writing, 1994—; Visiting writer, Columbia University School of the Arts; Jerry Moore Visiting Writer, George Washington University, 1982-83; Trustee, Enoch Pratt Free Library, Baltimore.

MEMBER: International PEN, Authors Guild, Authors League of America.

AWARDS, HONORS: Discovery Award, New York YW-YMHA Poetry Center, 1969; *Good Times: Poems* was cited as one of the year's ten best books by the *New York Times*, 1969; National Endowment for the Arts awards, 1969, 1970, and 1972; Poet Laureate of the State of Maryland, 1979-82; Juniper Prize, University of Massachusetts, 1980; Pulitzer prize nominations for poetry, 1980, 1988; Coretta Scott King Award, American Library Association, 1984, for *Everett Anderson's Goodbye*; honorary degrees from University of Maryland and Towson State University; Lannan Literary Award for poetry, 1996, for *The Terrible Stories.*

WRITINGS:

ADULT

Good Times: Poems, Random House, 1969.
Good News about the Earth: New Poems, Random House, 1972.
An Ordinary Woman (poetry), Random House, 1974.
Generations: A Memoir (prose), Random House, 1976.
Two-Headed Woman (poetry), University of Massachusetts Press, 1980.
Good Woman: Poems and a Memoir, 1969-1980, Boa Editions, 1987.
Next: New Poems, Boa Editions, 1987.
Ten Oxherding Pictures, Moving Parts Press, 1988.
Quilting: Poems 1987-1990, Boa Editions, 1991.
The Book of Light, Copper Canyon Press, 1993.

Also author of *The Terrible Stories,* BOA Editions.

JUVENILE

The Black BCs (alphabet poems), illustrations by Don Miller, Dutton, 1970.
Good, Says Jerome, illustrations by Stephanie Douglas, Dutton, 1973.
All Us Come Cross the Water, pictures by John Steptoe, Holt, 1973.
Don't You Remember?, illustrations by Evaline Ness, Dutton, 1973.
The Boy Who Didn't Believe in Spring, pictures by Brinton Turkle, Dutton, 1973, translation into Spanish by Alma Flor Ada, E. P. Dutton, 1976.
The Times They Used to Be, illustrations by Susan Jeschke, Holt, 1974.
My Brother Fine with Me, illustrations by Moneta Barnett, Holt, 1975.
Three Wishes, illustrations by Douglas, Viking, 1976, illustrations by Michael Hays, Delacorte, 1992.
Amifika, illustrations by Thomas DiGrazia, Dutton, 1977.
The Lucky Stone, illustrations by Dale Payson, Delacorte, 1979.
My Friend Jacob, illustrations by DiGrazia, Dutton, 1980.
Sonora Beautiful, illustrations by Michael Garland, Dutton, 1981.
Dear Creator: A Week of Poems for Young People and Their Teachers, illustrations by Gail Gordon Carter, Doubleday (New York City), 1997.

"EVERETT ANDERSON" SERIES; JUVENILE

Some of the Days of Everett Anderson, illustrations by Ness, Holt, 1970.
Everett Anderson's Christmas Coming, illustrations by Ness, Holt, 1971, illustrations by Jan Spivey Gilchrist, Holt, 1991.
Everett Anderson's Year, illustrations by Ann Grifalconi, Holt, 1974.
Everett Anderson's Friend, illustrations by Grifalconi, Holt, 1976.
Everett Anderson's 1 2 3, illustrations by Grifalconi, Holt, 1977.
Everett Anderson's Nine Month Long, illustrations by Grifalconi, Holt, 1978.
Everett Anderson's Goodbye, illustrations by Grifalconi, Holt, 1983.

OTHER

(Compiler with Alexander MacGibbon) *Composition: An Approach through Reading,* Harcourt, 1968.
(Contributor) Langston Hughes and Arna Bontemps, *Poetry of the Negro, 1746-1970,* Doubleday, 1970.
(Contributor) Marlo Thomas and others, *Free to Be . . . You and Me,* McGraw-Hill, 1974.

Also contributor to *Free to Be a Family,* 1987, *Norton Anthology of Literature by Women, Coming into the Light,* and *Stealing the Language.* Contributor of poetry to the *New York Times.* Contributor of fiction to *Negro Digest, Redbook, House and Garden,* and *Atlantic.* Contributor of nonfiction to *Ms.* and *Essence.*

SIDELIGHTS: Lucille Clifton "began composing and writing stories at an early age and has been much encouraged by an ever-growing reading audience and a fine critical reputation," writes Wallace R. Peppers in a *Dictionary of Literary Biography* essay. "In many ways her themes are traditional: she writes of her family because she is greatly interested in making sense of their lives and relationships; she writes of adversity and success in the ghetto community; and she writes of her role as a poet." Clifton's work emphasizes endurance and strength through adversity. Ronald Baughman suggests in his *Dictionary of Literary Biography* essay that "Clifton's pride in being black and in being a woman helps her transform difficult circumstances into a qualified affirmation about the black urban world she portrays."

Clifton's first volume of poetry, *Good Times: Poems,* which was cited by the *New York Times* as one of

1969's ten best books, is described by Peppers as a "varied collection of character sketches written with third person narrative voices." Baughman notes that "these poems attain power not only through their subject matter but also through their careful techniques; among Clifton's most successful poetic devices . . . are the precise evocative images that give substance to her rhetorical statements and a frequent duality of vision that lends complexity to her portraits of place and character." Calling the book's title "ironic," Baughman indicates, "Although the urban ghetto can, through its many hardships, create figures who are tough enough to survive and triumph, the overriding concern of this book is with the horrors of the location, with the human carnage that results from such problems as poverty, unemployment, substandard housing, and inadequate education."

In Clifton's second volume of poetry, *Good News about the Earth: New Poems,* "the elusive good times seem more attainable," remarks Baughman, who summarizes the three sections into which the book is divided: the first section "focuses on the sterility and destruction of 'white ways,' newly perceived through the social upheavals of the early 1970s"; the second section "presents a series of homages to black leaders of the late 1960s and early 1970s"; and the third section "deals with biblical characters powerfully rendered in terms of the black experience." Harriet Jackson Scarupa notes in *Ms.* that after having read what Clifton says about blackness and black pride, some critics "have concluded that Clifton hates whites. [Clifton] considers this a misreading. When she equates whiteness with death, blackness with life, she says: 'What I'm talking about is a certain kind of white arrogance—and not all white people have it—that is not good. I think airs of superiority are very dangerous. I believe in justice. I try not to be about hatred.'" Writing in *Poetry,* Ralph J. Mills, Jr., says that Clifton's poetic scope transcends the black experience "to embrace the entire world, human and nonhuman, in the deep affirmation she makes in the teeth of negative evidence."

An Ordinary Woman, Clifton's third collection of poems, "abandons many of the broad racial issues examined in the two preceding books and focuses instead on the narrower but equally complex issues of the writer's roles as woman and poet," says Baughman. Peppers notes that "the poems take as their theme a historical, social, and spiritual assessment of the current generation in the genealogical line" of Clifton's great-great-grandmother, who had been taken from her home in Dahomey, West Africa,

and brought to America in slavery in 1830. Peppers notes that by taking an ordinary experience and personalizing it, "Clifton has elevated the experience into a public confession" which may be shared, and "it is this shared sense of situation, an easy identification between speaker and reader, that heightens the notion of ordinariness and gives . . . the collection an added dimension." Helen Vendler writes in the *New York Times Book Review* that "Clifton recalls for us those bare places we have all waited as ordinary women, with no choices but yes or no, no art, no grace, no words, no reprieve." "Written in the same ironic, yet cautiously optimistic spirit as her earlier published work," observes Peppers, the book is "lively, full of vigor, passion, and an all-consuming honesty."

In *Generations: A Memoir,* "it is as if [Clifton] were showing us a cherished family album and telling us the story about each person which seemed to sum him or her up best," says a *New Yorker* contributor. Calling the book an "eloquent eulogy of [Clifton's] parents," Reynolds Price writes in the *New York Times Book Review* that, "as with most elegists, her purpose is perpetuation and celebration, not judgment. There is no attempt to see either parent whole; no attempt at the recovery of history not witnessed by or told to the author. There is no sustained chronological narrative. Instead, clusters of brief anecdotes gather round two poles, the deaths of father and mother." Price, however, believes that *Generations* stands "worthily" among the other modern elegies that assert that "we may survive, some lively few, if we've troubled to *be* alive and loved." However, a contributor to *Virginia Quarterly Review* thinks that the book is "more than an elegy or a personal memoir. It is an attempt on the part of one woman to retrieve, and lyrically to celebrate, her Afro-American heritage."

Clifton's books for children are designed to help them understand their world. *My Friend Jacob,* for instance, is a story "in which a black child speaks with affection and patience of his friendship with a white adolescent neighbor . . . who is retarded," writes Zena Sutherland in *Bulletin of the Center for Children's Books.* "Jacob is Sam's 'very very best friend' and all of his best qualities are appreciated by Sam, just as all of his limitations are accepted. . . . It is strong in the simplicity and warmth with which a handicapped person is loved rather than pitied, enjoyed rather than tolerated." Critics find that Clifton's characters and their relationships are accurately and positively drawn. Ismat Abdal-Haqq notes in *Interracial Books for Children Bulletin* that "the two boys have a strong relationship filled with trust and affection. The author depicts this relationship and their everyday adventures in a way that is unmarred by the mawkish sentimentality that often characterizes tales of the mentally disabled." And a contributor to *Reading Teacher* states that "in a matter-of-fact, low-keyed style, we discover how [Sam and Jacob] help one another grow and understand the world."

Clifton's children's books also facilitate an understanding of black heritage specifically, which in turn fosters an important link with the past generally. *All Us Come Cross the Water,* for example, "in a very straight-forward way . . . shows the relationship of Africa to Blacks in the U.S. without getting into a heavy rap about 'Pan-Africanism,'" states Judy Richardson in the *Journal of Negro Education,* adding that Clifton "seems able to get inside a little boy's head, and knows how to represent that on paper." An awareness of one's origins figures also in *The Times They Used to Be.* Called a "short and impeccable vignette-laced with idiom and humor of rural Black folk," by Rosalind K. Goddard in *School Library Journal,* it is further described by Lee A. Daniels in the *Washington Post* as a "story in which a young girl catches her first glimpse of the new technological era in a hardware store window, and learns of death and life." "Most books that awaken adult nostalgia are not as appealing to young readers," says Sutherland in *Bulletin of the Center for Children's Books,* "but this brief story has enough warmth and vitality and humor for any reader."

In addition to quickening an awareness of black heritage, Clifton's books for children frequently include an element of fantasy as well. Writing about *Three Wishes,* in which a young girl finds a lucky penny on New Year's Day and makes three wishes upon it, Christopher Lehmann-Haupt in the *New York Times Book Review* calls it "an urbanized version of the traditional tale in which the first wish reveals the power of the magic object . . . the second wish is a mistake, and the third undoes the second." Lehmann-Haupt adds that "too few children's books for blacks justify their ethnicity, but this one is a winning blend of black English and bright illustration." And *The Lucky Stone,* in which a lucky stone provides good fortune for all of its owners, is described by Ruth K. MacDonald in *School Library Journal* as: "Four short stories about four generations of Black women and their dealings with a lucky stone. . . . Clifton uses as a frame device a grandmother telling the history of the stone to her granddaughter; by the end, the granddaughter has inherited the stone herself."

Barbara Walker writes in *Interracial Books for Children Bulletin* that "Clifton is a gifted poet with the greater gift of being able to write poetry for children." But in a *Language Arts* interview with Rudine Sims, Clifton indicated that she doesn't think of it as poetry especially for children, though. "It seems to me that if you write poetry for children, you have to keep too many things in mind other than the poem. So I'm just writing a poem." *Some of the Days of Everett Anderson* is a book of nine poems, about which Marjorie Lewis observes in *School Library Journal,* "Some of the days of six-year-old 'ebony Everett Anderson' are happy; some lonely—but all of them are special, reflecting the author's own pride in being black." In the *New York Times Book Review,* Hoyt W. Fuller thinks that Clifton has "a profoundly simple way of saying all that is important to say, and we know that the struggle is worth it, that the all-important battle of image is being won, and that the future of all those beautiful black children out there need not be twisted and broken." *Everett Anderson's Christmas Coming* concerns Christmas preparations in which "each of the five days before Everett's Christmas is described by a verse," says Anita Silvey in *Horn Book,* observing that "the overall richness of Everett's experiences dominates the text." Jane O'Reilly suggests in the *New York Times Book Review* that "Everett Anderson, black and boyish, is glimpsed, rather than explained through poems about him." *Everett Anderson's Year* celebrates "a year in the life of a city child . . . in appealing verses," says Beryl Robinson in *Horn Book,* adding that "mischief, fun, gaiety, and poignancy are a part of his days as the year progresses. The portrayals of child and mother are lively and solid, executed with both strength and tenderness."

Language is important in Clifton's writing. In answer to Sim's question about the presence of both black and white children in her work, Clifton responds specifically about *Sonora Beautiful,* which is about the insecurities and dissatisfaction of an adolescent girl and which has only white characters: "In this book, I *heard* the characters as white. I have a tendency to *hear* the language of the characters, and then I know something about who the people are." However, regarding objections to the black vernacular she often uses, Clifton tells Sims: "I do not write out of weakness. That is to say, I do not write the language I write because I don't know any other. . . . But I have a certain integrity about my art, and in *my* art you have to be honest and you have to have people talking the way they really talk. So all of my books are not in the same language." Asked by Sims whether or not she feels any special pressures or special opportunities as a black author, Clifton responds: "I do feel a responsibility. . . . First, I'm going to write books that tend to celebrate life. I'm about that. And I wish to have children see people like themselves in books. . . . I also take seriously the responsibility of not lying. . . . I'm not going to say that life is wretched if circumstance is wretched, because that's not true. So I take that responsibility, but it's a responsibility to the truth, and to my art as much as anything. I owe everybody that. . . . It's the truth as I see it, and that's what my responsibility is."

In Clifton's 1991 title, *Quilting: Poems 1987-1990,* the author uses a quilt as a poetic metaphor for life. Each poem is a story, bound together through the chronicles of history and figuratively sewn with the thread of experience. The result is, as Roger Mitchell in *American Book Review* describes it, a quilt "made by and for people." Each section of the book is divided by a conventional quilt design name such as "Eight-Pointed Star" and "Tree of Life," which provides a framework within which Clifton crafts her poetic quilt. Clifton's main focus is on women's history; however, according to Mitchell her poetry has a far broader range: "Her heroes include nameless slaves buried on old plantations, Hector Peterson (the first child killed in the Soweto riot), Fannie Lou Hamer (founder of the Mississippi Peace and Freedom Party), Nelson and Winnie Mandela, W. E. B. DuBois, Huey P. Newton, and many other people who gave their lives to Black people from slavery and prejudice."

Enthusiasts of *Quilting* include critic Bruce Bennett in the *New York Times Book Review,* who praises Clifton as a "passionate, mercurial writer, by turns angry, prophetic, compassionate, shrewd, sensuous, vulnerable and funny. . . . The movement and effect of the whole book communicate the sense of a journey through which the poet achieves an understanding of something new." Pat Monaghan in *Booklist* admires Clifton's "terse, uncomplicated" verse, and judges the poet "a fierce and original voice in American letters." Mitchell finds energy and hope in her poems, referring to them as "visionary." He concludes that they are "the poems of a strong woman, strong enough to . . . look the impending crises of our time in the eye, as well as our customary limitations, and go ahead and hope anyway."

Clifton's 1993 poetry collection, *The Book of Light,* examines "life through light in its various manifestations," comments Andrea Lockett in a *Belles Lettres* review of the collection. Among the poetic subjects of the collection are bigotry and intolerance, epitomized by a poem about U.S. Senator Jesse Helms; destruction, including a poem about the tragic bombing by police of a MOVE compound in Philadelphia in 1985; religion, characterized by a sequence of poems featuring a dialogue between God and the Devil; and mythology, rendered by poems about figures such as Atlas and Superman. "If this poet's art has deepened since . . . *Good Times,* it's in an increased capacity for quiet delicacy and fresh generalization," remarks *Poetry*'s Calvin Bedient. Bedient criticizes the poems in the collection that take an overtly political tone, taking issue with" Clifton's politics of championing difference-except, of course, where the difference opposes her politics." However, Bedient commends the more personal poems in *The Book of Light,* declaring that when Clifton writes without "anger and sentimentality, she writes at her remarkable best." Lockett concludes that the collection is" a gift of joy, a truly illuminated manuscript by a writer whose powers have been visited by grace."

BIOGRAPHICAL/CRITICAL SOURCES:

BOOKS

Beckles, Frances N., *20 Black Women,* Gateway Press, 1978.
Black Literature Criticism, Gale, 1992.
Children's Literature Review, Volume 5, Gale, 1983.
Contemporary Literary Criticism, Gale, Volume 9, 1981; Volume 66, 1991.
Dictionary of Literary Biography, Gale, Volume 5: *American Poets since World War II,* 1980; Volume 41: *Afro-American Poets since 1955,* 1985.
Dreyer, Sharon Spredemann, *The Bookfinder: A Guide to Children's Literature about the Needs and Problems of Youth Aged 2-15,* Volume 1, American Guidance Service, 1977.
Evans, Mari, editor, *Black Women Writers (1950-1980): A Critical Evaluation,* Doubleday-Anchor, 1984.

PERIODICALS

America, May 1, 1976.
American Book Review, June, 1992, p. 21.
Belles Lettres, summer, 1993, p. 51.
Black Scholar, March, 1981.
Black World, July, 1970; February, 1973.
Booklist, June 15, 1991, p. 1926; May 1, 1997, p. 1506; August, 1996, p. 187.
Book World, March 8, 1970; November 8, 1970; November 11, 1973; November 10, 1974; De-

cember 8, 1974; December 11, 1977; September 14, 1980; July 20, 1986; May 10, 1987.

Bulletin of the Center for Children's Books, March, 1971; November, 1974; March, 1976; September, 1980.

Christian Science Monitor, February 5, 1988, p. B3; January 17, 1992, p. 14.

Horn Book, December, 1971; August, 1973; February, 1975; December, 1975; October, 1977; March, 1993, p. 229.

Interracial Books for Children Bulletin, Volume 5, numbers 7 and 8, 1975; Volume 7, number 1, 1976; Volume 8, number 1, 1977; Volume 10, number 5, 1979; Volume 11, numbers 1 and 2, 1980; Volume 12, number 2, 1981.

Journal of Negro Education, summer, 1974.

Journal of Reading, February, 1977; December, 1986.

Kirkus Reviews, April 15, 1970; October 1, 1970; December 15, 1974; April 15, 1976; February 15, 1982.

Language Arts, January, 1978; February 2, 1982.

Ms., October, 1976.

New Yorker, April 5, 1976.

New York Times, December 20, 1976.

New York Times Book Review, September 6, 1970; December 6, 1970; December 5, 1971; November 4, 1973; April 6, 1975; March 14, 1976; May 15, 1977; February 19, 1989, p. 24; March 1, 1992; April 18, 1993, p. 15.

Poetry, May, 1973; March, 1994, p. 344.

Reading Teacher, October, 1978; March, 1981.

Redbook, November, 1969.

Saturday Review, December 11, 1971; August 12, 1972; December 4, 1973.

School Library Journal, May, 1970; December, 1970; September, 1974; December, 1977; February, 1979; March, 1980.

Tribune Books (Chicago), August 30, 1987.

Virginia Quarterly Review, fall, 1976; winter, 1997, p. 41.

Voice of Youth Advocates, April, 1982.

Washington Post, November 10, 1974; August 9, 1979.

Washington Post Book World, February 10, 1980; February 13, 1994, p. 8.

Western Humanities Review, summer, 1970.*

*   *   *

COLE, Nora (Marie)   1953-

PERSONAL: Born September 10, 1953, in Louisville, KY; daughter of Lattimore Walls (a postal supervisor) and Mary Lue (an assembly line worker; maiden name, Bradford) Cole. *Education:* Art Institute of Chicago, Goodman School of Drama, B.F.A., 1978; attended Beloit College; studied acting with Wynn Handman at the American Place Theatre. *Religion:* Christian.

ADDRESSES: Agent—c/o Bret Adams Agency, 448 West 44th St., New York, NY 10036.

CAREER: Actor and playwright. Appeared in theatrical productions, including *Alice in Wonderland,* Louisville Children's Theatre, Louisville, KY, 1965; *The Ups and Downs of Theophilus Maitland,* Urban Arts Corporation, New York City, 1976; *Movie Buff,* Actors' Playhouse, New York City, 1977; *Boogie-Woogie Rumble,* Urban Arts Corporation, 1982; *Medea,* Vinnette Carroll Repertory Theatre, Fort Lauderdale, FL; *Tamer of Horses,* Penguin Repertory, 1987; *Joe Turner's Come and Gone,* Studio Arena Theatre, Buffalo, NY, 1989-90; *Birdsend,* Studio Arena Theatre, 1990-91; *A Christmas Carol,* Studio Arena Theatre, 1990-91; *The Good Times Are Killing Me,* Minetta Lane Theatre, New York City, 1991; *Groundhog,* Stage II, New York City, 1992; *Avenue X,* O'Neill Theatre Center, 1992; *Olivia's Opus,* Primary Stages, then Negro Ensemble Company at Tribeca Performing Arts Center both in New York City, and National Black Theatre Festival, and Winston-Salem, NC, all 1993; *On the Town,* New York Shakespeare Festival, 1996; *The Colored Museum,* Hartford Stage, 1997; and *. . . Love, Langston,* Hartford Stage, Hartford Stage, CT, 1998. Appeared on Broadway in *Runaways,* New York Shakespeare Festival, 1978; *Inacent Black,* Biltmore Theatre, 1981; *Your Arms Too Short to Box Gold,* Alvin Theatre, 1982; and *Jelly's Last Jam;* Also appeared in *Alice in Wonderland* and *I'm Laughin' but I Ain't Tickled,* both at Urban Arts Corporation; in *El Hajj Malik,* Gene Frankel Theatre, New York City; in *Cartoons for a Lunch Hour,* Perry Street Theatre, New York City; in *The Peanut Man* and in *Beowulf,* both at AMAS Repertory Theatre, New York City; and in *Trojan Women,* Black Theatre Alliance.

Toured in stage productions, including *Jelly's Last Jam,* 1994-95; *The Wiz,* 1980-81; *Your Arms Too Short to Box with God,* 1982-83; *When Hell Freezes Over I'll Skate,* 1984; and in *The All-Night Strut,* 1984-85. Appeared as a featured soloist at Radio City Music Hall, New York City, 1980-81. Appeared in an episode of the television series *The Cosby Mysteries* (also known as *Guy Hanks I*), NBC, c. 1994, as well as numerous soap operas. Her reading of Alice

Schell's "Kingdom of the Sun" has been broadcast on National Public Radio affiliate KMUW in Wichita, KS.

MEMBER: Actors' Equity Association, American Federation of Television and Radio Artists, Screen Actors Guild, American Guild of Variety Artists.

AWARDS, HONORS: Joseph Jefferson Award nominee, for *Jelly's Last Jam;* Connecticut Critics Award nominee, for . . . *Love, Langston;* Theatre of Renewal Award, for *Boogie-Woogie Rumble.*

WRITINGS:

PLAYS

Olivia's Opus, produced at Primary Stages, then Negro Ensemble Company at Tribeca Performing Arts Center, both New York City, 1993, National Black Theatre Festival, Winston-Salem, NC, 1993, African-American Cultural Center, Charlotte, NC, 1994, Hartford Stage, Hartford, CT, 1998, Eastern Connecticut State University, 1999.

WORK IN PROGRESS: "A musically based one woman performance piece and a collection of essay about living in Harlem."

SIDELIGHTS: Cole told *CA:* "Aside from writing and performing, I am enthralled whenever I have time to research my family tree and history. My grandfather, I. Willis Cole owned, published and was the editor of a weekly newspaper, the *Louisville Ledger,* from 1917 to 1950. Piecing it all together is like working on a giant, never-ending puzzle and preserving my grandfather's memory and memorabilia is quite an experience getting to know a man I never knew, but always heard about when I was growing up."

BIOGRAPHICAL/CRITICAL SOURCES:

PERIODICALS

Variety, January 19, 1998, p. 97.

* * *

COLEMAN, Emmett
See REED, Ishmael

COLEMAN, Wanda 1946-

PERSONAL: Born November 13, 1946, in Los Angeles, CA; daughter of George (in advertising) and Lewana (a seamstress and domestic worker) Evans; married and divorced twice before she married Austin Straus (poet); children: Anthony, Tunisia, Ian Wayne Grant. *Education:* Has attended several colleges.

ADDRESSES: Home—P.O. Box 29154, Los Angeles, CA 90029.

CAREER: Writer and performer. Worked as production editor, proofreader, magazine editor, waitress, and assistant recruiter for Peace Corps/Vista, 1968-75; staff writer for *Days of Our Lives,* National Broadcasting Co. (NBC-TV), 1975-76; medical transcriber and insurance billing clerk, 1979-84. Writer in residence at Studio Watts, 1968-69; co-host of interview program for Pacific Radio, 1981—.

MEMBER: PEN.

AWARDS, HONORS: Named to Open Door Program Hall of Fame, 1975; Emmy Award, Academy of Television Arts and Sciences, best writing in a daytime drama, 1976, for *Days of Our Lives;* fellowships from National Endowment for the Arts, 1981-82, and Guggenheim Foundation, 1984.

WRITINGS:

Art in the Court of the Blue Fag (chapbook), Black Sparrow Press, 1977.
Mad Dog Black Lady, Black Sparrow Press (Santa Barbara, CA), 1979.
Imagoes, Black Sparrow Press, 1983.
A War of Eyes and Other Stories, Black Sparrow Press (Santa Rosa, CA), 1988.
(Editor) *Women for All Seasons: Poetry and Prose about the Transitions in Women's Lives,* Woman's Building, 1988.
Dicksboro Hotel & Other Travels, Ambrosia Press, 1989.
(Editor) Susannah Foster, *Earthbound in Betty Grable's Shoes,* Chiron Review Press, 1990.
African Sleeping Sickness: Stories and Poems, Black Sparrow Press, 1990.
Heavy Daughter Blues: Poems and Stories, Black Sparrow Press, 1991.
Hand Dance, Black Sparrow Press, 1993.
Native in a Strange Land: Trials and Tremors, Black Sparrow Press, 1996.
Bathwater Wine, Black Sparrow Press, 1998.

Also author of "The Time Is Now" episode, *The Name of the Game,* NBC-TV, 1970. Wrote text of *24 Hours in the Life of Los Angeles* with Jeff Spurrier. Contributor to periodicals, including *An Afro American* and *African Journal of Arts and Letters.*

SIDELIGHTS: Poet and short story writer Wanda Coleman is a blatantly political artist who has won much critical acclaim for her work but who has often struggled to make a living from her craft. With eight books of collected writings published by the small Black Sparrow Press by 1998, as well as numerous other publications, she has created a body of work that is first of all focused on racism and that, secondly, ponders the "outcast" status of poor blacks living in Los Angeles. Thus her stories and poems are often angry and treat unhappy, hateful, and violent themes. Her subjects and tone are what separate her from the publishing mainstream. But if such things are avoided by the average reader—and, arguably, by other more successful African American writers— many critics have found a wealth of insight and fine writing skills in Coleman's work.

Writing in *Black American Literature Forum,* Tony Magistrale summarized, "Coleman frequently writes to illuminate the lives of the underclass and the disenfranchised, the invisible men and women who populate America's downtown streets after dark, the asylums and waystations, the inner city hospitals and clinics. . . . Wanda Coleman, like Gwendolyn Brooks before her, has much to tell us about what it is like to be a poor black woman in America." Praise has also come from reviewers in a number of prominent magazines. Stephen Kessler wrote in *Bachy* that Coleman "shows us scary and exciting realms of ourselves," and Holly Prado noted in the *Los Angeles Times* that Coleman's "heated and economical language and head-on sensibility take her work beyond brutality to fierce dignity." Tamar Lehrich wrote in *The Nation:* "Wanda Coleman consistently confronts her readers with images, ideas and language that threaten to offend or at least to excite." Lehrich concluded that "Wanda Coleman's poetry and prose have been inspired by her frustration and anger at her position as a black woman and by her desire to translate those feelings into action."

Coleman loved books as a child and published her first poems in a local newspaper at age thirteen. However, she never enjoyed school and considered it "dehumanizing," according to Kathleen K. O'Mara in the *Dictionary of Literary Biography.* Coleman attended several colleges but has never earned a degree.

Married and the mother of two children by age twenty, she worked many different kinds of jobs during the 1970s and 1980s. By 1969 she had divorced her first husband and had determined to become professional writer, but she was forced to turn her energies to more pragmatic concerns. After a brief stint on welfare, she supported her family by waiting tables and typing, among other jobs. In part, the difficulty of finding time to write while working other jobs led Coleman to concentrate on writing poems.

The writer published her first short story "Watching the Sunset" in *Negro Digest* in 1970. During the 1970s Coleman experimented in theater, dance, television, and journalism. She won an Emmy for her work as a writer for the television soap opera *Days of Our Lives* during the 1975-76 season. But Coleman's passion for non-commercial writing was undiminished. Her interest in poetry was deepened by the opportunity to make dramatic public performances. As she participated in the Los Angeles poetry scene, Coleman was influenced by poets Diane Wakoski, John Thomas, Clayton Eshleman, and Charles Bukowski, and mentored by Black Sparrow Press publisher "Papa" John Martin. Her first poetry manuscript was published as the chapbook *Art in the Court of the Blue Fag* in 1977.

Within a few years, Coleman's work gained her attention from outside of the local literary circle. *Mad Dog Black Lady* (1979) and *Imagoes* (1983) earned her a National Endowment for the Arts grant and a Guggenheim Fellowship for Poetry. In 1987 the author published her first collection to include short stories as well as poetry, *Heavy Daughter Blues.* According to O'Mara, the book received "mixed reviews" with the "negative criticism centered on the poems and stories as overpoweringly grim and inadequately edited." An all-fiction volume published the next year, *A War of Eyes and Other Stories,* fared better and strengthened a surge of critical attention and praise focused on Coleman during the 1980s.

The collection of autobiographical stories and prose poems titled *African Sleeping Sickness* came out in 1990. It included the story "Where the Sun Don't Shine," which won the 1990 Harriette Simpson Arnow Prize for fiction. Following this publication, O'Mara summarized, "What little negative criticism she has drawn has focused on her fragmentary vignettes as sketches that leave the reader wanting more, or her violence-laden plots as sometimes too predictable. Her finest skill is making human pain poetically concrete and devising dialogue that allows the reader under the skin of 'the other.'"

Coleman's 1996 book of essays and articles, *Native in a Strange Land: Trials and Tremors,* offered readers a selection of nonfiction by Coleman. The writings had first been published over a thirty-year span and were now modified for republication. Like Coleman's fiction, they were mostly based on personal experience in Los Angeles. "She gives us L.A. as a microcosm of what America is today and where it is heading," a *Publishers Weekly* critic said. "The picture is not always hopeful." The review also noted the author's "wry sense of humor" and called some of her ideas "Swiftian" for their gruesomely humorous bent. The book was described by Janice E. Braun in *Library Journal* as a "nonlinear memoir"; Braun concluded, "Whether one identifies with Coleman or objects to her views, the writing is positively outstanding." The 1998 poetry collection, *Bathwater Wine,* returned Coleman's readers to a more familiar form. It was described by a *Publishers Weekly* contributor as "an encyclopedic, moment-by-moment accounting of left coast rage, witness and transcendence. . . . [It is a] large somewhat sprawling, formally diverse, yet occasionally lose, book of poetry."

After some thirty years of writing, Wanda Coleman remains devoted to the themes of racism and female experience, as well as to Los Angeles. The city has been a vital part of her writings and an important outlet for her poetry readings. "As a poet," she once told *CA,* "I have gained a reputation, locally, as an electrifying performer/reader, and have appeared at local rock clubs, reading the same poetry that has taken me into classrooms and community centers for over five hundred public readings since 1973." Coleman added, "Words seem inadequate in expressing the anger and outrage I feel at the persistent racism that permeates every aspect of black American life. Since words are what I am best at, I concern myself with this as an urban actuality as best I can."

BIOGRAPHICAL/CRITICAL SOURCES:

BOOKS

Dictionary of Literary Biography, Volume 130: *American Short-Story Writers since World War II,* Gale, 1993.

PERIODICALS

African American Review, summer 1992, pp. 355-57.
Bachy, fall, 1979, spring, 1980.
Black American Literature Forum, fall 1989, pp. 539-54.

Library Journal, February 1, 1997, p. 97.
Los Angeles, April, 1983.
Los Angeles Times, September 15, 1969; November 26, 1973; January 31, 1982; November 13, 1983.
Los Angeles Times Book Review, August 14, 1988, pp. 1, 9.
Michigan Quarterly Review, fall, 1991, pp. 717-31.
Nation, February 20, 1988, pp. 242-43.
Publishers Weekly, July 1, 1988; October 28, 1996, p. 73; June 29, 1998, p. 54.
Stern, May 16, 1974.

*   *   *

COLLINS, Merle 1950-

PERSONAL: Born September 29, 1950; daughter of John and Helena Collins. *Education:* University of West Indies, Mona, Jamaica, B.A., 1972; Georgetown University, M.A. (Latin American Studies), 1981; University of London, School of Economics and Political Science, Ph.D., 1990.

ADDRESSES: Office—University of Maryland, Department of Comparative Literature, 4136 Susquehanna Hall, College Park, MD 20742.

CAREER: Poet and educator, 1985—.

WRITINGS:

POETRY

Because the Dawn Breaks! Poems Dedicated to the Grenadian People, Karia Press (London), 1985.
Rotten Pomerack, Virago (London), 1992.
Lady in a Boat: Poems, Azul Editions, 1999.

NOVELS

Angel, The Women's Press (London), 1987.
The Color of Forgetting, Virago, 1995.

ANTHOLOGIES

(Editor, with Rhonda Cobham) *Watchers and Seekers: Creative Writing by Black Women in Britain,* The Women's Press, 1987.
(Editor) Nellie Payne and Jean Buffong, *Jump-Up-and-Kiss Me: Two Stories of Grenadian Childhood,* The Women's Press, 1990.

SHORT STORIES

Rain Darling: Stories, The Women's Press, 1990.

Also contributor to anthologies, including *Callaloo: A Grenada Anthology,* Young World Books (London), 1984; and *From My Guy to Sci-Fi: Genre and Women's Writing in the Postmodern World,* edited by Helen Carr, Pandora (London), 1989.

Contributor to periodicals. including *Wasafiri, Caribbean Quarterly,* and *Artrage.*

SIDELIGHTS: Merle Collins's poetry and writings focus mostly on her native country of Grenada, including the politics of revolution that she supported in that country. The author is also known for her use of language, as well as for demonstrating the significance of language in Caribbean culture. Collins is a believer in the theatrical elements of poetry and feels that the effectiveness of a poem is enhanced with vocal participation from its audience. Much of Collins's poetry has a rhythmic, energetic beat similar to the languages and dialects of the Caribbean.

Collins spent most of her childhood in Grenada, which she considers a major influence on her work. She completed undergraduate and graduate degrees in the 1970s and early 1980s. It was at about this time that Collins began to get interested in the Grenadian revolutionary movement, which later influenced her work. Though the People's Revolutionary Government was later overthrown when the United States invaded Grenada in 1983, the period of revolution gave a voice to many artists who supported its cause, such as Collins. Collins left the country for Britain shortly after the invasion, claiming in a later interview that the end of the movement "made it difficult [for her] to focus emotionally on Grenada," according to a profile of Collins by Patricia Joan Saunders in *Dictionary of Literary Biography.* In Britain she earned a doctorate as she continued to study the history and politics leading up to colonialism in her country.

Some of Collins's first published poems illustrate the characteristics that were to become hallmarks of her writing, according to Saunders. A recurring theme in the poetry and later works involves the role of women in Caribbean culture who tell stories, an important influence early in Collins's life. According to Saunders, the poem "The Lesson" illustrates the rhythm, storytelling, and use of language that are so typical of Collins's work: "I/could remember/Great Grand-mammy/Brain tired/And wandering/Walkin' an' talkin'/Mind empty and filled/Bright/Retaining/ And skillfully twisted/By a sin/Unequaled by Eve's." According to Saunders, other lines of this poem also make a statement about the impact of colonialist teachings upon citizens of Grenada. Collins uses symbolism in an early poem titled "Callaloo," which compares the thick, rich Caribbean soup of the title to the varied ethnicity of Grenada.

Collins's first published collection, *Because the Dawn Breaks!: Poems Dedicated to the Grenadian People,* was written to acknowledge the people of the Grenadian revolution and in the author's own words, to represent "specific moments, different responses, the pain and joy and beauty and doubt and hope of a total, still developing, defiantly positive experience." An exiled Kenyan writer, Ngugi wa Thiong'o, commented in his introduction to *Because the Dawn Breaks!* that Collins captured not only the dreams and hopes of revolution, but the realities and conquest.

In the collection *Watchers and Seekers,* Collins continued to write about how language defines life. In her poem "Images," Saunders remarked that this poem "traces the way that women have been defined through the words of others." Another poem in the collection titled "No Dialects, Please" was inspired by a statement using those words which appeared in the guidelines for a British poetry contest. According to Collins, the statement made too apparent the elitist colonial motivations of Great Britain to homogenize its colonies.

Collins's novel *Angel* explores the use of language as an instrument of power, according to Saunders. The story covers three generations of Grenadian women and uses proverbs, letters, and rich dialects including French creole, patois, Grenadian English, and Standard English. Collins also portrays the experience of moving to London and losing a "collective cultural voice" in the poem "It Grow Fire" (from *Rotten Pomerack*), cited in Saunders' *Dictionary of Literary Biography* essay. A narrator visits an uncle who migrated to London and finds that "I went to see uncle in a London flat/no step of its own/no space for beginning/not even for happy remembering/ses mwen oh!/and my uncle lifted his head/looked at the darkening corner/listened/seemed to see nothing/must have heard nothing/said nothing." Such poetry illustrates not only Collins's appeal for recognizing cultural voice, but her attempt to preserve the oral tradition of the Caribbean through her use of language.

BIOGRAPHICAL/CRITICAL SOURCES:

BOOKS

Dictionary of Literary Biography, Volume 157: *Twentieth-Century Caribbean and Black African Writers, Third Series,* Gale Research (Detroit), 1995.*

*   *   *

CONDE, Maryse
  See BOUCOLON, Maryse

*   *   *

CORNWELL, Anita (R.) 1923-

PERSONAL: Born in 1923.

ADDRESSES: Office—c/o New Seed Press, P. O. Box
9488, Berkeley, CA 94709-7556.

CAREER: Freelance writer and novelist. Former employee at Pennsylvania State Department of Public
Welfare. Judge, Lambda Book Awards, 1990—.

WRITINGS:

Black Lesbian in White America, Naiad Press (Talla-
hassee, FL), 1983.
The Girls of Summer (juvenile), illustrated by Kelly
Caines, New Seed Press (San Francisco), 1989.

Work appears in anthologies, including *The Lavender
Herring: Lesbian Essays from 'The Ladder,'* Diana
Press (Baltimore), 1976; *For Lesbians Only: A Separatist Anthology,* Onlywomen Press (London), 1988;
and *Revolutionary Tales: African-American Women's
Short Stories,* Dell (New York City), 1995. Contributor of essays and fiction to *Negro Digest, Liberator,
Dyke: A Quarterly, Gay Alternative, Feminary, Griot,*
and other publications.

SIDELIGHTS: Anita Cornwell, according to Tina
Gianoulis in *Gay and Lesbian Literature,* "is no less
than a pioneer of radical lesbian feminist thought. . . .
Cornwell examines the interaction of the United
States' interventionist policies, sexism, racism, and
classism in an unflinching style. . . . Cornwell took
her place as one of the early spokeswomen of feminist

theory in her essays about black women. . . .
Cornwell dealt with being a black, a lesbian, and a
woman by recognizing that these aspects of herself
are inseparable in her identity, and by remaining just
slightly outside each group, strongly loving, yet critical of each, and slightly alienated from each because
of that criticism. . . . Perhaps Cornwell's greatest
contributions to the body of lesbian feminist writing
are her explorations of racism, especially as it occurs
within the feminist and the lesbian communities."

BIOGRAPHICAL/CRITICAL SOURCES:

BOOKS

Gay and Lesbian Literature, Volume 2, St. James
Press (Detroit), 1998.

PERIODICALS

Off Our Backs, December, 1983.

*   *   *

CORTEZ, Jayne 1936-

PERSONAL: Born May 10, 1936, in Fort Huachuca,
AZ; married Ornette Coleman (a jazz musician), 1954
(divorced, 1964); married Melvin Edwards (a sculptor
and illustrator), 1975; children: (first marriage)
Denardo Coleman.

ADDRESSES: Home—c/o Bola Press, Box 96, Village
Station, New York, NY 10014.

CAREER: Poet and performance artist. Watts Repertory Theatre Company, Los Angeles, co-founder,
1964; Bola Press, New York City, founder, 1972; has
lectured and read her poetry alone and with musical
accompaniment at universities, including Dartmouth
College, Howard University, Queens College,
Wesleyan University, and throughout Europe, Africa,
Latin America, and the Caribbean.

AWARDS, HONORS: Creative Artists Program Ser-
vice poetry awards, New York State Council on the
Arts, 1973 and 1981; National Endowment for the
Arts fellowship in creative writing, 1979-86; Ameri-
can Book Award, 1980; New York Foundation for the
Arts Award, 1987; Before Columbus Foundation
Award, 1987; Fannie Lou Hammer Award, 1994;
Afrikan Poetry Theatre tribute and award, 1994.

MEMBER: Organization of Women Writers of Africa (co-founder).

WRITINGS:

POETRY

Pissstained Stairs and the Monkey Man's Wares, Phrase Text (New York City), 1969.
Festivals and Funerals, illustrated by husband, Mel Edwards, Bola Press (New York City), 1971.
Scarifications, illustrated by Edwards, Bola Press, 1973.
Mouth on Paper, Bola Press, 1977.
Firespitter, illustrated by Mel Edwards, Bola Press, 1982.
Coagulations: New and Selected Poems, Thunder's Mouth Press (New York City), 1982.
Poetic Magnetic, illustrated by Edwards, Bola Press, 1991.
Somewhere in Advance of Nowhere, Serpent's Tail (London), 1997.

OTHER

Celebrations and Solitudes: The Poetry of Jayne Cortez (sound recording), Strata-East Records, 1975.
Unsubmissive Blues (sound recording), Bola Press, 1980.
There It Is (sound recording), Bola Press, 1982.
War against War (performance piece), UNESCO (Paris), 1982.
Poetry in Motion (screenplay), Sphinx Productions (Toronto, Ontario, Canada), 1983.
Maintain Control (sound recording), Bola Press, 1986.
Everywhere Drums (sound recording), Bola Press, 1991.
Mandela Is Coming (music video), Globalvision, 1991.
Taking the Blues Back Home (sound recording), with band the Firespitters, Harmolodic/Verve, 1997.

Contributor to anthologies, including *We Speak as Liberators,* edited by Orde Coombs, Dodd, 1970; *The Poetry of Black America,* edited by Arnold Adoff, Harper, 1972; *Homage a Leon Gontran Damas,* Presence Africaine, 1979; *Black Sister,* edited by Erlene Stedson, Indiana University Press, 1981; *Women on War,* edited by Daniela Gioseffi, Simon & Schuster, 1988; and *Daughters of Africa,* Pantheon, 1992. Contributor to numerous periodicals, including *Free Spirits, Mother Jones, UNESCO Courier, Black Scholar, Heresies,* and *Mundus Artium.* Guest editor, *Black Scholar,* 1988, and *Drumvoices Revue,* 1994.

SIDELIGHTS: Poet and performance artist Jayne Cortez began her creative explorations as an actress, publishing her first volume of poetry, *Pissstained Stairs and the Monkey Man's Wares,* in 1969. Her work, which reflects the politics and culture of African Americans, is characterized by a dramatic intensity, causing D. H. Melhem to note in an introduction to an interview with Cortez published in *Heroism in the New Black Poetry,* that "Her fine ear for music, her dynamic imagery, and her disposition to orchestrate in a broad cultural span, both African and American, have led her social and political concerns into unique and risk-taking forms." Recording and performing around the world, often with backing by blues musicians, Cortez "has forged connections . . . that help us see how our histories . . . whether we life in Chile, Harlem or Nigeria, are related," in the opinion of Barbara T. Christian, writing in *Callaloo.* "The result is a poetry as wide in its scope as it is compelling in its craft."

In a review of Cortez's debut work, *Pissstained Stairs and the Monkey Man's Wares* for *Negro Digest* Nikki Giovanni remarks: "We haven't had many jazz poets who got inside the music and the people who created it. We poet about them, but not of them. And this is Cortez's strength. She can wail from Theodore Navarro and Leadbelly to Ornette [Coleman, Cortez' first husband] and never lose a beat and never make a mistake. She's a genius and all lovers of jazz will need this book—lovers of poetry will want it." The jazz elements threaded throughout Cortez' body of work have caused *Dictionary of Literary Biography* essayist Jon Woodson to remark that she remains "a creative artist uniquely able to reach audiences for whom books of poetry have little appeal."

Although the influence of music is evident throughout Cortez's body of work, the poet also pointedly seeks to convey a message. Reviewing the 1984 collection *Coagulations,* Barbara T. Christian states in *Callaloo* that "it is eminently clear . . . that Jayne Cortez is a blatantly political poet—that her work intends to help us identify those who control our lives and the devastating effects such control has on our lives, and she rouses us to do something about it. . . . Like the poets and warriors whose words and actions it celebrates, Jayne Cortez's *Coagulations* is a work of resistance."

Citing influences such as Amiri Bakara, Langston Hughes, Aime Cesaire, Margaret Walker, and Pablo

Neruda, John F. Roche notes in an essay in *Contemporary Women Poets* that Cortez' free verse is characterized by its "impassioned crescendo," as well as the use of anaphora, repetition, alliteration, and modulated spoken tones. "She often combines African iconology, American colloquialisms, and leftist political themes with surrealist body imagery," explains Roche, adding that her more recent verse has begun to explore the patterned typesetting characteristic of the concrete poetry of the 1960s. Commenting on Cortez' 1996 collection, *Somewhere in Advance of Nowhere,* a *Publishers Weekly* critic comments on Cortez' ability to write in a manner that remains rhythmic while providing "an unflinching glimpse at life's ugliness" that nonetheless ends with the ability to survive. "This resilience animates Cortez's work and supports the unwavering, and compelling directness with which she confronts the world," the critic adds.

In an interview with Melhem, Cortez outlined what she believes to be the responsibilities inherent in her craft: "I think that poets have the responsibility to be aware of the meaning of human rights, to be familiar with history, to point out distortions, and to bring their thinking and their writing to higher levels of illumination." An acknowledgement of Cortez' success at meeting these standards was made in 1994, when she received the Fannie Lou Hammer award for her "outstanding contribution through her poetry to the struggle for justice, equality, and the freedom of the human spirit."

In addition to her work as a published author, Cortez has distinguished herself as an internationally acclaimed performance artist, and has several recorded performances to her credit, including *Everywhere Drums* (1990), *Cheerful and Optimistic* (1994), and 1996's *Taking the Blues Back Home.* Commenting on *Unsubmissive Blues,* a 1980 recording of the poet reading her works accompanied jazz musicians Bill Cole, Joe Daley, Bern Nix, and Cortez's son Denardo Coleman, Warren Woessner asserts in *Small Press Review* that the record "is the most accomplished collaboration between a poet and jazz group that I've listened to in recent years." He continues: "*Unsubmissive Blues* is an unqualified success. The sum of this collaboration is always greater than its individual pieces."

BIOGRAPHICAL/CRITICAL SOURCES:

BOOKS

American Women Writers: From Colonial Times to the Present, Volume 5, Continuum, 1994.

Contemporary Women Poets, St. James Press (Detroit), 1997.
Dictionary of Literary Biography, Volume 41: *Afro-American Poets since 1955,* Gale (Detroit), 1985.
Melhem, D. H., *Heroism in the New Black Poetry,* University Press of Kentucky, 1990.

PERIODICALS

Black World, March, 1975.
Callaloo, winter, 1986, pp. 235-39.
Greenfield Review, summer/fall, 1983.
MELUS, spring, 1996, pp. 71-79.
Negro Digest, December, 1969.
Publishers Weekly, June 3, 1996, p. 74.
Small Press Review, March, 1981.

OTHER

Jane Cortez Biography, www.harmolodic.com/jayne/ portrait.html (May 31, 1997).

*   *   *

COSBY, Bill
  See COSBY, William Henry Jr.

*   *   *

COSBY, William Henry, Jr. 1937-
  (Bill Cosby)

PERSONAL: Born July 12, 1937, in Philadelphia, PA; son of William Henry (a U.S. Navy mess steward) and Anna (a domestic worker) Cosby; married Camille Hanks, January 25, 1964; children: Erika Ranee, Erinn Chalene, Ennis William (deceased), Ensa Camille, Evin Harrah. *Education:* Attended Temple University, 1961-62; University of Massachusetts, M.A., 1972, Ed.D., 1977.

ADDRESSES: Agent—The Brokaw Co., 9255 Sunset Blvd., Los Angeles, CA 90069.

CAREER: Comedian, actor, and recording artist. Performer in nightclubs, including The Cellar, Philadelphia, PA, Gaslight Cafe, New York City, Bitter End, New York City, and Hungry i, San Francisco, CA, 1962—; performer in television series including *I Spy,* National Broadcasting Co. (NBC-TV), 1965 68, *The*

Bill Cosby Show, NBC-TV, 1969-71, *The New Bill Cosby Show,* Columbia Broadcasting System (CBS-TV), 1972-73, *Cos,* American Broadcasting Co. (ABC-TV), 1976, *The Cosby Show,* NBC-TV, 1984-92, and *Cosby,* 1996—; host of syndicated game show, *You Bet Your Life,* 1992-93; actor in motion pictures, including *Hickey and Boggs,* 1972, *Man and Boy,* 1972, *Uptown Saturday Night,* 1974, *Let's Do It Again,* 1975, *Mother, Jugs, and Speed,* 1976, *A Piece of the Action,* 1977, *California Suite,* 1978, *The Devil and Max Devlin,* 1981, *Bill Cosby Himself,* 1985, *Leonard Part VI,* 1987, and *Ghost Dad,* 1990; creator of animated children's programs *The Fat Albert Show* and *Fat Albert and the Cosby Kids,* CBS-TV, 1972-84. Performer on *The Bill Cosby Radio Program,* television specials *The First Bill Cosby Special* and *The Second Bill Cosby Special,* in animated feature *Aesop's Fables,* in *An Evening with Bill Cosby* at Radio City Music Hall, 1986, and on videocassette *Bill Cosby: 49,* sponsored by Kodak, 1987. Guest on Public Broadcasting Co. (PBS-TV) children's programs *Sesame Street* and *The Electric Company,* and NBC-TV's *Children's Theatre;* host of Picture Pages segment of CBS-TV's *Captain Kangaroo's Wake Up.* Commercial spokesperson for Jell-O Pudding (General Foods Inc.), Coca-Cola Co., Ford Motor Co., Texas Instruments, E. F. Hutton, and Kodak Film.

President of Rhythm and Blues Hall of Fame, 1968. Member of Carnegie Commission for the Future of Public Broadcasting, board of directors of National Council on Crime and Delinquency, Mary Holmes College, and Ebony Showcase Theatre, board of trustees of Temple University, advisory board of Direction Sports, communications council at Howard University, and steering committee of American Sickle Cell Foundation. *Military service:* U.S. Navy Medical Corps, 1956-60.

AWARDS, HONORS: Eight Grammy awards for best comedy album, National Society of Recording Arts and Sciences, including 1964, for *Bill Cosby Is a Very Funny Fellow . . . Right!,* 1965, for *I Started Out as a Child,* 1966, for *Why Is There Air?,* 1967, for *Revenge,* and 1969, for *To Russell, My Brother, Whom I Slept With;* Emmy Award for best actor in a dramatic series, Academy of Television Arts and Sciences, 1965-66, 1966-67, and 1967-68, for *I Spy;* named "most promising new male star" by *Fame* magazine, 1966; Emmy Award, 1969, for *The First Bill Cosby Special;* Seal of Excellence, Children's Theatre Association, 1973; Ohio State University award, 1975, and Gold Award for Outstanding Children's Program, International Film and Televi-

sion Festival, 1981, both for *Fat Albert and the Cosby Kids;* NAACP Image Award, 1976; named "Star Presenter of 1978" by *Advertising Age;* Emmy Award for best comedy series, 1985, for *The Cosby Show;* inducted to TV Hall of Fame, Academy of Television Arts and Sciences, 1992; Founder's Award, 19th International Emmy Awards, 1992; honorary degree, Brown University; Golden Globe Award, Hollywood Foreign Press Association; four People's Choice Awards; voted "most believable celebrity endorser" three times in surveys by Video Storyboard Tests, Inc.

WRITINGS:

UNDER NAME BILL COSBY

The Wit and Wisdom of Fat Albert, Windmill Books, 1973.
Bill Cosby's Personal Guide to Tennis Power; or, Don't Lower the Lob, Raise the Net, Random House (New York City), 1975.
(Contributor) Charlie Shedd, editor, *You Are Somebody Special,* McGraw, 1978, 2nd edition, 1982.
Fatherhood, Doubleday (Garden City, NY), 1986.
Time Flies, Doubleday, 1987.
Love and Marriage, Doubleday, 1989.
Childhood, Putnam (New York City), 1991.
Kids Say the Darndest Things, Bantam, 1998.
Congratulations! Now What? A Book for Graduates, Hyperion, 1999.

"LIL BOOKS FOR BEGINNING READERS" SERIES; ILLUSTRATED BY VARNETTE P. HONEYWOOD; ALL PUBLISHED BY SCHOLASTIC, INC. (NEW YORK CITY)

The Meanest Thing to Say, 1997.
Treasure Hunt, 1997.
The Best Way to Play, 1997.
One Dark and Scary Night, 1998.
Super-Fine Valentine, 1998.
The Day I Was Rich, 1999.
The Big Fib, 1999.

Also author of *Fat Albert's Survival Kit* and *Changes: Becoming the Best You Can Be.*

RECORDINGS

Recordings by Cosby include *Bill Cosby Is a Very Funny Fellow . . . Right!,* 1964; *I Started Out as a Child,* 1965; *Why Is There Air?,* 1966; *Wonderfulness,* 1967; *Revenge,* 1967; *To Russell, My Brother, Whom I Slept With,* 1969; *Bill Cosby Is Not Himself*

These Days, Rat Own, Rat Own, Rat Own, 1976; *My Father Confused Me . . . What Must I Do? What Must I Do?,* 1977; *Disco Bill,* 1977; *Bill's Best Friend,* 1978; *It's True, It's True; Bill Cosby Himself, 200 MPH; Silverthroat; Hooray for the Salvation Army Band; 8:15; 12:15; For Adults Only; Bill Cosby Talks to Kids about Drugs;* and *Inside the Mind of Bill Cosby.*

SIDELIGHTS: "When I was a kid I always used to pay attention to things that other people didn't even think about," claims comedian, actor, and author Bill Cosby. "I'd remember funny happenings, just little trivial things, and then tell stories about them later. I found I could make people laugh, and I enjoyed doing it because it gave me a sense of security. I thought that if people laughed at what you said, that meant they like you." As an adult, Cosby has developed his childhood behavior into a comedic talent that earns him millions of dollars annually for his work in films, television, and commercials. In 1988 Cosby was ranked the second-highest-paid entertainer in the world. "Despite his wealth," Brian D. Johnson notes in *Maclean's,* "Cosby manages to pass himself off as a clownish Everyman, treating his life as a bottomless well of folk wisdom."

What Cosby calls his "storytelling knack" may have had its roots in his mother's nightly readings of Mark Twain and the Bible to her three sons. Their father, a Navy cook, was gone for long stretches of time, but Anna Cosby did her best to provide a strong moral foundation for the family she raised in Philadelphia's housing projects. Bill helped with the family's expenses by delivering groceries and shining shoes. His sixth-grade teacher described him as "an alert boy who would rather clown than study"; nevertheless, he was placed in a class for gifted students when he reached high school. His activities as captain of the track and football teams and member of the baseball and basketball teams continued to distract him from academics, however, and when his tenth-grade year ended, Cosby was told he'd have to repeat the grade. Instead of doing so, he quit school to join the Navy. It was a decision he soon came to regret, and during his four-year hitch in the Navy, Cosby earned his high school diploma through a correspondence course. He then won an athletic scholarship to Temple University in Philadelphia, where he entered as a physical education major in 1961.

After amusing his schoolmates and shipmates with his tales, Cosby turned professional comedian while a student at Temple, showcasing his humor in a five-dollar-a-night job telling jokes and tending bar at the Cellar, a Philadelphia coffee-house. More engagements soon followed, and before long his budding career as an entertainer was conflicting with his school schedule. Forced to choose between the two, Cosby dropped out of Temple, although the university eventually awarded him a bachelor's degree on the basis of "life experience." His reputation as a comic grew quickly as he worked in coffee-houses from San Francisco to New York City. Soon he was playing the biggest nightclubs in Las Vegas, and shortly after signing a recording contract in 1964, he became the best-selling comedian on records, with several of his albums earning over one million dollars in sales.

While Cosby's early performances consisted of about thirty-five percent racial jokes, he came to see this kind of humor as something that perpetuated racism rather than relieving tensions, and he dropped all such jokes from his act. "Rather than trying to bring the races together by talking about the differences, let's try to bring them together by talking about the similarities," he urges. Accordingly, he developed a universal brand of humor that revolved around everyday occurrences. A long-time jazz devotee, the comedian credits the musical improvisations of Miles Davis, Charles Mingus, and Charlie Parker with inspiring him to come up with continually fresh ways of restating a few basic themes. "The situations I talk about people can find themselves in . . . it makes them glad to know they're not the only ones who have fallen victims of life's little ironies," states Cosby.

The comedian first displayed his skill as an actor when he landed the co-starring lead in *I Spy,* a popular NBC-TV program of the late 1960s that featured suspense, action, and sometimes humor. Cosby portrayed Alexander Scott, a multilingual Rhodes scholar working as part of a spy team for the United States. Scott and his partner (played by Robert Culp) traveled undercover in the guises of a tennis pro and his trainer. The Alexander Scott role had not been created especially for a black actor, and Cosby's casting in the part was hailed as an important breakthrough for blacks in television.

The Bill Cosby Show followed *I Spy.* In this half-hour comedy, Cosby portrayed Chet Kincaid, a high-school gym teacher—a role closer to his real-life persona than that of Alexander Scott. In fact, at this time Cosby announced that he was considering quitting show business to become a teacher. Although he never followed through on that statement, Cosby did return to college and earned a doctorate in education in 1977. His doctoral thesis, "An Integration of the Visual Media via Fat Albert and the Cosby Kids into the Elementary School Curriculum as a Teaching Aid and Vehicle to Achieve Increased Learning," analyzed an animated Saturday-morning show that Cosby himself had created. *Fat Albert and the Cosby Kids* had its roots in the comedy routines about growing up in Philadelphia. It attempted to entertain children while encouraging them to confront moral and ethical issues, and it has been used as a teaching tool in schools.

During the 1970s, Cosby teamed with Sidney Poitier and several other black actors to make a highly successful series of comedies, including *Uptown Saturday Night, Let's Do It Again,* and *A Piece of the Action.* These comedies stood out in a time when most of the films for black audiences were oriented to violence. Critics are generous in their praise of Cosby's acting; Tom Allen notes his "free-wheeling, jiving, put-down artistry," and Alvin H. Marritt writes that, in *Let's Do It Again,* Cosby "breezes through the outrageous antics."

Concern over his family's television viewing habits led Cosby to return to prime-time in 1984. "I got tired of seeing TV shows that consist of a car crash, a gunman and a hooker talking to a black pimp," the actor states in an article by Jane Hall in *People.* "It was cheaper to do a series than to throw out my family's six TV sets." But Cosby found that network executives were resistant to his idea for a family-oriented comedy. He was turned down by both CBS and ABC on the grounds that a family comedy—particularly one featuring a black family—could never succeed on modern television. NBC accepted his proposal and *The Cosby Show* very quickly became the top-rated show on television, drawing an estimated sixty million weekly viewers.

Like most of Bill Cosby's material, *The Cosby Show* revolved around everyday occurrences and interactions between siblings and parents. Cosby played obstetrician Cliff Huxtable, who with his lawyer wife, Claire, had four daughters and one son—just as Cosby and wife Camille do in real life. Besides entertaining audiences, Cosby aimed to project a positive image of a family whose members love and respect one another. The program was hailed by some as a giant step forward in the portrayal of blacks on television. Writes Lynn Norment in *Ebony,* "This show pointedly avoids the stereotypical Blacks often seen on TV. There are no ghetto maids or butlers wisecracking about Black life. Also, there are no fast cars and

helicopter chase scenes, no jokes about sex and boobs and butts. And, most unusual, both parents are present in the home, employed and are Black."

The Cosby Show was not unanimously acclaimed, however. As Norment explains, "Despite its success, the show [was] criticized by a few for not being 'Black enough,' for not dealing with more controversial issues, such as poverty and racism and interracial dating, for focusing on a Black middle-class family when the vast majority of Black people survive on incomes far below that of the Huxtables." Cosby finds this type of criticism racist in itself. "Does it mean only white people have a lock on living together in a home where the father is a doctor and the mother is a lawyer and the children are constantly being told to study by their parents?" Hall quotes Cosby in *People:* "This is a black American family. If anybody has difficulty with that, it's their problem, not ours."

The paternal image of Cliff Huxtable led a publisher to ask Cosby for a humorous book to be called *Fatherhood.* Cosby obliged, making notes for the project with shorthand and tape recorder between his entertainment commitments. The finished book sold a record 2.6 million hardcover copies and was quite well received by critics. *Newsweek* book reviewer Cathleen McGuigan states that it "is like a prose version of a Cosby comedy performance—informal, commiserative anecdotes delivered in a sardonic style that's as likely to prompt a smile of recognition as a belly laugh. . . . [But] it's not all played for laughs. There's a tough passage in which he describes the only time he hit his son, and a reference to a drinking-and-driving incident involving a daughter and her friends that calls upon him to both punish and forgive. Cosby's big strength, though, is his eye and ear for the everyday event—sibling squabbles, children's excuses." Jonathan Yardley concurs in the *Washington Post Book World:* "Cosby has an extraordinarily keen ear for everyday speech and everyday event, and knows how to put just enough of a comic spin on it so that even as we laugh we know we are getting a glimpse of the truth."

Tragically, Cosby's role as a father would be affected by the murder of his son, Ennis, in 1997. Twenty-seven years old, the younger Cosby was teaching children with learning disabilities when he was killed in a shooting. Coping with the loss was difficult for Bill Cosby—made more difficult, ironically, by an attempt at extortion by a young woman who claimed to be his daughter and demanded forty million dollars to keep quiet just days before his son's death—but he has remained optimistic that the violence that caused his son's untimely death will eventually be eradicated from society. "I am very hopeful because there are people out there trying to find the answers [to the problems plaguing society,]" he told Allison Samuels in *Newsweek*. "Like educators, they must have power. . . . The answer is in hardworking people finding answers and fighting for change in the system. Ennis was one of those people. He was going to make changes. . . . And that's why he was my hero."

Following the huge success of *Fatherhood*, Doubleday published *Time Flies*, in which Cosby treats the subject of aging in the same style as his earlier book. Toronto *Globe & Mail* reviewer Leo Simpson comments, "Decay and the drift into entropy wouldn't get everyone's vote as a light-hearted theme, yet *Time Flies* is just as illuminating, witty and elegantly hilarious as . . . *Fatherhood*." The book sold over 1.7 million hardcover copies.

For his 1989 book, *Love and Marriage*, Cosby draws upon his own long marriage to wife Camille for an advice book on maintaining domestic tranquility. As he explains to Johnson in *Maclean's*, "The book is to make people laugh, make them identify and have a good time." Some of the truths revealed by the author is that "the wife is in charge" and "even the deepest love doesn't stop a marriage from being a constant struggle for control." For any husband who believes himself to be the boss of his own house, Cosby advises that he buy some wallpaper and redecorate a room without consulting his wife first. Calling the book a "diverting but forgettable" work, Leah Rozen of *People* nonetheless finds *Love and Marriage* to be "gently amusing." Johnson finds the book "by turns tender, amusing and coy," while a *New York Times Book Review* critic calls it "a scrapbook of the happier side of romance. . . . Cosby captures the give and take of happy marriages."

Cosby reminisces about his own youth in Philadelphia in 1991's *Childhood*, comparing that time in his life with the experiences of the present generation of children. His remembrances of childhood pranks, family advice, and schoolyard games form the bulk of the memoir. Dulcie Leimbach of the *New York Times Book Review* finds that Cosby presents a "rough-and-tumble (but never spoiled or weary) childhood." Because of his ability to reconstruct those times, she calls Cosby "a man trapped inside a child's mind."

The mid-1990s would find Cosby at the helm of yet another television sitcom, *Cosby*, which takes place in Queens, New York and finds its sixty-something protagonist suddenly downsized from his job with a major airlines and left to his own devices in and around home. Although Cosby had complained in *Time Flies* that he was slowing down with age, his continued performing, directing, and writing efforts—he has written several books for young readers published by Scholastic—as well as his devotion to numerous charitable projects, would tend to contradict him. As he told the *Los Angeles Times,* "I think one of the most important things to understand is that my mother, as a domestic, worked 12 hours a day, and then she would do the laundry, and cook the meals and serve them and clean them up, and for this she got $7 a day. So 12 hours a day of whatever I do is as easy as eating a Jell-O Pudding Pop."

BIOGRAPHICAL/CRITICAL SOURCES:

BOOKS

Adams, Barbara Johnston, *The Picture Life of Bill Cosby,* F. Watts (New York City), 1986.
Conord, Bruce W., *Bill Cosby,* Chelsea Juniors (New York City), 1993.
Johnson, Robert E., *Bill Cosby: In Words and Pictures,* Johnson Publishing (Chicago), 1987.
Ruth, Marianne, *Bill Cosby,* Melrose Square (Los Angeles), 1992.
Schuman, Michael A., *Bill Cosby: Actor and Comedian,* Enslow Publishers (Springfield, NJ), 1995.
Smith, R. L., *Cosby,* St. Martin's Press, 1986.
Woods, H., *Bill Cosby, Making America Laugh and Learn,* Dillon, 1983.

PERIODICALS

Chicago Tribune, September 14, 1987.
Ebony, May, 1964; June, 1977; April, 1985; February, 1986; February, 1987.
Films in Review, November, 1975.
Globe & Mail (Toronto), July 5, 1986; October 24, 1987.
Good Housekeeping, February, 1991.
Jet, January 12, 1987; January 19, 1987; February 9, 1987; February 23, 1987; March 9, 1987.
Kliatt, January 1993, p. 27.
Ladies Home Journal, June, 1985.
Los Angeles Times, September 25, 1987; December 20, 1987; January 24, 1988.
Los Angeles Times Book Review, June 15, 1986; June 18, 1989.
Maclean's, May 1, 1989.
National Observer, January 6, 1964.

Newsweek, November 5, 1984; September 2, 1985; May 19, 1986; September 14, 1987; March 17, 1997, p. 58.
New Yorker, October 14, 1996, pp. 104-07.
New York Post, February 23, 1964.
New York Times Book Review, September 20, 1987; May 14, 1989; October 27, 1991, p. 20.
New York Times Magazine, March 14, 1965.
People, December 10, 1984; September 14, 1987; July 10, 1989.
Playboy, December, 1985.
Publishers Weekly, April 10, 1987, p. 92; September 13, 1991, p. 69.
Reader's Digest, November, 1986; November, 1987.
Saturday Evening Post, April, 1985; April, 1986.
Time, September 28, 1987.
Tribune Books (Chicago), May 3, 1987, p. 5.
Village Voice, November 3, 1975.
Washington Post, September 7, 1987.
Washington Post Book World, April 27, 1986.*

*   *   *

COUCH, William, Jr.

PERSONAL: Married Ola B. Criss (a gerontologist and officer in U.S. State Department), September 7, 1980; children: (previous marriage) William, another son; Gregg Antonio Jackson (stepson). *Education:* Received doctorate.

ADDRESSES: Agent—c/o Louisiana State University Press, P.O. Box 25053, Baton Rouge, LA 70894-5053.

CAREER: North Carolina College (now North Carolina Central University), Durham, NC, 1962-78, became professor of English; Federal City College (now University of the District of Columbia), Washington, DC, academic vice-president, 1968-90, became chair of English department, then full-time teaching faculty member; in Africa, 1991—.

WRITINGS:

(Editor and author of introduction) *New Black Playwrights: An Anthology,* Louisiana State University Press, 1968.

Contributor of articles and poems to periodicals, including *CLA Journal, Negro Story,* and *Phylon.*

BIOGRAPHICAL/CRITICAL SOURCES:

PERIODICALS

Drama: The Quarterly Theatre Review, summer, 1969, p. 66.
Negro Digest, September, 1969, p. 96.
Negro History Bulletin, March, 1969, p. 22.*

*   *   *

CRUMP, Paul (Orville) 1930(?)-

PERSONAL: Born c. 1930. *Education:* Attended school to ninth grade. *Religion:* Catholic.

CAREER: Novelist. Sentenced to death and incarcerated in Cook County Jail, IL, c. 1953, for role in a robbery-murder, had sentence commuted to 199 years in prison and was transferred to Illinois State Prison in Joliet, IL, 1962; released in 1993.

WRITINGS:

Burn, Killer, Burn! (novel), Johnson Publishing, 1962.

WORK IN PROGRESS: Walk in Fury, a novel.

SIDELIGHTS: Fatherless in the Chicago ghetto from the age of six, jailed for armed robbery at sixteen and again, for murder, at twenty-three, Paul Crump went to death row in 1953. He was described as "savage" at that time, according to a 1962 *Time* article, but during his imprisonment a gradual change took place. His prison warden, Jack Johnson, believed that "men, if treated as men, would respond as men," reported an *Ebony* writer. Under Johnson's leadership, which de-emphasized punishment, prisoners like Crump were given responsibility and a chance to feel needed. Chaplain James Jones got to know Crump by joining the prisoners' card games, and eventually Crump took hold of the Christian faith that turned his life around. Again and again he strove to win clemency. His case made the newspapers, and popular support for his cause began to build. Arguing that he was truly reformed, people from his own state and beyond wrote letters, editorials, or affidavits on his behalf, including internationally known evangelist Billy Graham. In 1962, after nine years in prison and fourteen reprieves, Crump won a commutation of his sentence; forty years after his imprisonment he was finally released.

While fighting off his death sentence, Crump realized that he wanted to write about his experience, to try to prevent others from following his own criminal path. Crump, however, didn't know enough about writing. He started with an intense study of Herman Melville's classic novel *Moby Dick* under the tutelage of the assistant warden and went on to read a wide variety of other esteemed authors. A fellow inmate who was himself a writer critiqued his emerging manuscript. The publication of Crump's novel, *Burn, Killer, Burn!,* came the same year his sentence was commuted.

In the *Ebony* article Crump called his main character, Guy Morgan, Jr., "a child of action and not thought, impulsive, quick to anger, quick to be sorry, resentful of slights, real or imagined. . . . Fearing ideals are indications of weakness, he covers up with a facade of tough-guy sneers and violence." As the *Ebony* writer related, this description fits many urban youths, rich or poor, "whose spiritual, social, educational and emotional needs are not met, or even recognized until they have engaged in an overt act of antisocial behavior—and been caught. . . . The tragedy of Guy Morgan, Jr. is in this sense the tragedy of urban American life."

BIOGRAPHICAL/CRITICAL SOURCES:

BOOKS

Nizer, Louis, *The Jury Returns,* Doubleday, 1966, pp. 1-137.

PERIODICALS

Ebony, July, 1962, pp. 31-34; November, 1962, pp. 88-90.
Life, July 27, 1962, pp. 26-31.
Newsweek, August 13, 1962, p. 17.
New York Times Book Review, June 16, 1963, p. 8.
Time, July 20, 1962, p. 22; August 10, 1962, p. 12.

OTHER

The People versus Paul Crump, Facets Video, 1988.

*   *   *

CRUZ, Ricardo Cortez 1964-

PERSONAL: Born August 10, 1964, in Decatur, IL; son of Theodore and Carol M. (Belue) Cruz; married Carol M. Milling, 1994; children: Ricardo Cortez, II. *Ethnicity:* "Black-Hispanic." *Education:* Richland Community College, A.A.; Illinois State University, B.S. (English), completed coursework towards Doctor of Philosophy in English. *Politics:* "Democratic, liberal." *Religion:* "Belief in God and the importance of spirituality." *Avocational interests:* Stereo mixing, film, basketball.

ADDRESSES: Home—Bloomington, IL. *Office*—Department of English, Stevenson Hall, Campus Box 4240, Illinois State University, Normal, IL 61790-4240. *E-mail*—rccruz@ilstu.edu.

CAREER: Herald & Review, Decatur, IL, sportswriter, intern, and clerk, 1982-88; *Pantagraph,* Bloomington, IL, sportswriter and clerk, 1988-89; Heartland Community College, Bloomington, IL, English instructor, 1992-93; Southern Illinois University, Carbondale, assistant and associate professor, 1993-98; Illinois State University, Normal, IL, guest and assistant professor, 1998—.

AWARDS, HONORS: Charles H. and N. Mildred Nilon Excellence in Minority Fiction Award, for *Straight Outta Compton;* Distinguished Alumnus Award, Illinois Community College, 1996.

WRITINGS:

NOVELS

Straight Outta Compton: A Dive into Living Large, a Work Where Characters Trip, Talk Out the Side of Their Neck, and Cuss Like It Was Nothing, Fiction Collective Two (Normal, IL), 1992.
Five Days of Bleeding, Fiction Collective Two/Black Ice, 1992.

Also contributor to literary journals, including the *Kenyon Review, Iowa Review, Postmodern Culture,* and the *African-American Review.*

WORK IN PROGRESS: Premature Autopsies, a novel.

SIDELIGHTS: Ricardo Cortez Cruz writes about the lives of African Americans in a fast, gritty style. His first novel, *Straight Outta Compton,* which borrows from the rap music genre, is considered to be the first notable rap novel published. Cruz worked as a sportswriter and intern at several publications before publishing the novel. He then went on to teach English at the college level. Cruz has contributed to many literary journals.

The author's second work, *Five Days of Bleeding,* takes its title from a reggae song. The story takes place in modern-day Harlem and involves a homeless woman named Zu-Zu and a narrator who has fallen in love with her. A *Publishers Weekly* review noted that much of the story consists of transcribed song lyrics from rap, reggae, and other popular music. The critic claimed that Cruz's narrative style "entirely overwhelms the characterizations" and that some readers will have difficulty understanding the language and life in the modern urban setting. Cruz should have developed the plot more fully, and leaned less on song sketches to hold the plot up, claimed the *Publishers Weekly* reviewer. Nonetheless, the critic gave Cruz credit for "the innovative way in which he describes his city scenarios."

Cruz told *CA:* "I write (s)language, creating dark, urban landscapes replete with hard cadences, riffs, muted voices, magic realism, black comedy, sampling, postmodern conditions, rap, madness and violence, raging energy, asides, pop culture references, and characters talking smack out the side of the necks. My hope is to represent. And, I recommend fiction(s) for the study of sociolinguistics. My heroes livin in/for the city. My villains are people who might have been heroes under different circumstances.

"I am a 'cultural worker.' My goal is to move the crowd."

BIOGRAPHICAL/CRITICAL SOURCES:

BOOKS

The Schomburg Center Guide to Black Literature, Gale Research (Detroit, MI), 1996.

PERIODICALS

Publishers Weekly, July 31, 1995, p. 77.

*   *   *

CURTIS, Christopher Paul 1954(?)-

PERSONAL: Born May 10, 1954(?), in Flint, MI; son of Herman (an auto worker) and Leslie Curtis; married Kaysandra (a nurse); children: Steven, Cydney. *Education:* University of Michigan—Flint, B.A., 1996.

ADDRESSES: Home—Windsor, Ontario, Canada. *Agent*—c/o Delacorte Press, 1540 Broadway, New York, NY 10036-4039.

CAREER: Writer. Fisher Body Plant, Flint, MI, assembly line worker, 1972-85; assistant to Senator Don Riegle, Lansing, MI; employed at Automatic Data Processing, Allen Park, MI. Previously worked as a maintenance man, a warehouse clerk, and a purchasing clerk.

AWARDS, HONORS: Best Books, *Publishers Weekly* and *New York Times Books Review,* both 1995, Coretta Scott King Text Honor, and Newbery Honor Book, American Library Association Best Books for Young Adults, and Golden Kite Award, all 1996, all for *The Watsons Go to Birmingham—1963*; Newbery Honor Book, 1999, for *Bud, Not Buddy.*

WRITINGS:

The Watsons Go to Birmingham—1963, Delacorte (New York City), 1995.
Bud, Not Buddy, Delacorte, 1999.

ADAPTATIONS: The Watsons Go to Birmingham—1963 has been recorded on audiocassette, Ingram, 1996.

SIDELIGHTS: Christopher Paul Curtis wrote his first book, *The Watsons Go to Birmingham—1963,* at a table in the children's section of his local library. His award-winning story tells of a closely knit African American family that travels to the racially divided South during the civil rights era. Curtis's novel has literally changed the author's life. Praised by readers and reviewers and awarded a Newbery honor in 1996, *The Watsons Go to Birmingham* has allowed Curtis to fulfill his dream of becoming a full-time writer. Curtis's debut novel has been praised for its warmly drawn characters and its vivid settings. "When the 'Weird Watsons' drive to Birmingham . . . to visit Grandma," related Ann Valentine Martino in the *Ann Arbor News,* "you feel like you're riding along in the back seat—with Kenny's little sister drooling in your lap." The entertaining tale includes the author's memories of his own childhood, as well as an historic event—the bombing of Birmingham's Sixteenth Avenue Baptist Church in September, 1963.

Because he was not a witness to the church bombing, Curtis did research for the novel. However, he did not consciously prepare his tale for a particular audience. "Perhaps because Curtis didn't think the novel would be for children when he started it, there's nothing heavy-handed or preachy about the Watsons' brush with the civil rights movement," noted Linnea Lannon in an article on Curtis for the *Detroit Free Press*. "By telling his tale through the eyes of Kenny Watson, a fourth grader, Curtis illustrates the way that momentous social events and political movements can impact the lives of even the youngest children. Moreover," observed Gwen A. Tarbox in the *St. James Guide to Young Adult Writers*, "like Mildred Taylor before him, Curtis provides a detailed and poignant description of the inner life of an African-American family, but he uses a humorous style that is unique and geared to appeal to young adults as well as to children."

The Watsons Go to Birmingham recounts everyday events in the life of Kenny Watson, a ten-year-old African American boy. Blessed with a quick wit and a crossed eye, Kenny lives in the industrialized city of Flint, Michigan, along with his parents, little sister, and older brother. "The relationships [between characters] aren't idealized," indicated *Booklist*'s Hazel Rochman. "Curtis's accurate description of the living conditions in Flint, as well as his use of actual business names and places, lend a realistic quality to the text," observed Tarbox, continuing: "This realism is carried over in Curtis's depiction of childhood experience as seen through the eyes of his narrator, Kenny."

Kenny believes that everyone in his neighborhood must think his family is nuts—the "Weird Watsons." Kenny learns a "life lesson . . . from observing the actions of his far less ambitious brother, thirteen year old Byron 'Daddy Cool' Watson," remarked Tarbox. Byron makes the transformation from bossy older brother into teenage juvenile delinquent almost overnight. He starts to behave very badly: flushing flaming tissue parachutes down the toilet, dying his hair bright red and then getting it "conked" (straightened), and generally bullying his younger siblings around, including little sister Joetta, a kindergartner trying to keep up with her older brothers. "In addition to chronicling Byron's maturation," analyzed Tarbox, "Curtis is also interested in depicting the way that younger children process complex and frightening events. . . . Curtis considers . . . the way that some events in life are mystifying, even to adults."

During the summer of 1963, Kenny's parents decide to take a vacation to Birmingham, Alabama, the home of Grandma Sands, to see if she can discipline the obstinate and unruly Byron. After packing, everyone

piles into the family car, the "Brown Bomber," to begin the long journey. In Birmingham, the mood of the novel shifts—the lighthearted hijinks of the Watson brood suddenly become overshadowed by the racial tensions of the era. Kenny and his family experience racial violence first-hand when four teens are killed after a bomb explodes in the Sunday school classroom where little Joetta has been. "Curtis doesn't exploit the horror" of the church bombing, noted Rochman. Although the young girl is physically unharmed, she and the rest of her family return to Michigan transformed by their experiences.

Remarking on the shift between the lighthearted first part of Curtis's novel and its tragic ending, Betsy Hearne wrote in the *Bulletin of the Center for Children's Books:* "The contrast is startling, innovative, and effective . . . showing how—and why—the Civil Rights movement affected individual African Americans." *Horn Book* reviewer Martha V. Parravano similarly asserted that "Curtis's control of his material is superb as he unconventionally shifts tone and mood, as he depicts the changing relationship between the two brothers, and as he incorporates a factual event into his fictional story." "Evoking a full spectrum of emotions, this exceptional first novel is certain to reverberate within the reader's psyche," proclaimed a reviewer for *Publishers Weekly*. Kermit Frazier of the *New York Times Book Review* concluded that *The Watsons Go to Birmingham-1963* is "both comic and deeply moving. . . . [It is] a marvelous debut, a fine novel about a solid and appealing family." "I've read a lot of Chris' writing over the years," the author's sister Cydney told Lannon in the *Detroit Free Press,* recalling the "fibs" that her brother told as a child. "This is good," she exclaimed of *The Watsons,* "but I don't think it's his best. His best is yet to come."

Like the characters in his first novel, Curtis was raised in Flint, Michigan. He worked in a local automotive assembly plant for more than a decade after graduating from high school. After putting his dreams of a college education on hold for several long years, he began attending classes at the University of Michigan part time, while holding down another job, and finally graduated in 1996. During that time, encouraged by winning the University's Hopwood prize for a rough draft of his story, Curtis agreed with his wife Kaysandra's suggestion that he take a year off and see what he could do as a writer. With the strong support of his family—his wife assumed many of their financial responsibilities, while son Steven typed his father's handwritten manuscript into the family's computer every night—the story was completed by the end of 1993. Curtis entered his manuscript in a national writing contest, where it came to the attention of Delacorte editors. Although his story did not meet the contest's content guidelines, Delacorte editor Wendy Lamb responded favorably to the novel and began making arrangements to publish it.

BIOGRAPHICAL/CRITICAL SOURCES:

BOOKS

St. James Guide to Young Adult Writers, St. James Press (Detroit), 1999.

PERIODICALS

Ann Arbor News, April 8, 1996, p. D1.
Booklist, August, 1995, p. 1946; July, 1997, p. 1830.
Bulletin of the Center for Children's Books, January, 1996, pp. 157-58.
Detroit Free Press, December 27, 1995, pp. C1, C5.
Horn Book, March-April, 1996, pp. 195-96.
Kirkus Reviews, October 1, 1995, p. 1426.
Library Journal, February 1, 1997, p. 127.
New York Times Book Review, November 12, 1995, p. 23.
Publishers Weekly, October 16, 1995, p. 62; December 18, 1995, pp. 28-30.
School Library Journal, October, 1995, p. 152.*

D

DANGAREMBGA, Tsitsi 1959-

PERSONAL: Born 1959 (some sources say 1958), in Mutoko, Zimbabwe. *Education:* Studied medicine at Oxford University and psychology at the University of Zimbabwe; studied at the German Film and Television Academy, Berlin.

ADDRESSES: Agent—c/o The Women's Press, 34 Great Sutton St. London EC1V ODX England.

CAREER: Author and filmmaker.

AWARDS, HONORS: Commonwealth Writer's Prize (Africa section) for *Nervous Conditions,* 1988.

WRITINGS:

She No Longer Weeps (play), College Press (Harare, Zimbabwe), 1987.
Nervous Conditions (novel), Seal Press (Seattle), 1989.
(With John Riber and Andrew Whaley; and director) *Everyone's Child* (screenplay), Media for Development Trust, 1996.

Also author of screenplay *The Lost of the Soil,* 1983, and short story "The Letter," 1985.

SIDELIGHTS: A former medical and psychology student, Tsitsi Dangarembga is the first black Zimbabwean woman to direct a feature film and is the author of the prize-winning novel *Nervous Conditions.* After joining Zambuko, an African student theater group, and beginning to write fiction, Dangarembga chose to study film in Berlin. She has written in several genres, including a work of short fiction, a novel, a stage play, and two screenplays. The novel, *Nervous Conditions,* was first published in Zimbabwe in 1987, but soon thereafter was also issued in England and the United States. While studying at the German Film and Television Academy, Dangarembga produced films including a documentary for German television. She wrote and directed the feature film *Everyone's Child,* which was released in 1996.

Nervous Conditions is a tale centering on family dynamics, colonization, and the female role in Zimbabwean society. Tambu, an adolescent girl from the country, is sent to her rich uncle's missionary school. Her formal education is part of a larger transformation, as she is distanced from the rural, traditional lifestyle she had previously known. She feels a new awareness of the suffering of such women as her mother, who are poor, black and uneducated. Astonished by the wealth and comforts of her uncle's home, she feels a conflict between her upbringing and Western values. She senses a loss when she cannot comfortably return home, as her new experiences have changed her perception of village life.

The semi-autobiographical account won several warm reviews. A *Publishers Weekly,* reviewer called the novel "a resonant, eloquent tribute to the women in [Tambu's] life, and to their losses." Alice Walker reviewed the work in *Ms.* magazine, valuing the book for its self-possessed voice and memorable characters, and calling it "an expression of liberation not to be missed." Likewise, Charlotte H. Bruner noted in *World Literature Today* that Dangarembga's "excellent style and power of characterization make the book outstanding," and hoped that the author would continue the young woman's story.

Dangarembga turned her authorial talents to writing for the screen with *Everyone's Child*. The film presents, like *Nervous Conditions,* an examination of a social-cultural crisis in contemporary Zimbabwe. It is the story of a brother and sister, Itai and Tamari, who lose their parents to AIDS. While two younger siblings are helped by relatives, the boy and girl must support themselves; Itai moves to the big city, while Tamari stays at home in the village. The adults who observe them struggling eventually feel compelled to respond compassionately, recognizing the community responsibility to such individuals—to everyone's child. The film was very popular in Africa and features a soundtrack of contemporary Zimbabwean music.

BIOGRAPHICAL/CRITICAL SOURCES:

BOOKS

Buck, Claire, editor, *The Bloomsbury Guide to Women's Literature,* Prentice Hall General Reference (New York), 1992, p. 457.
Murphy, Bruce, editor, *Benet's Reader's Encyclopedia,* fourth edition, Harper (New York), 1996, p. 249.

PERIODICALS

Booklist, June 15, 1989, p. 1779.
Ms. Magazine, July-August, 1990, p. 61.
Publishers Weekly, February 3, 1989, p. 102.
World Literature Today, spring, 1990, pp. 353-54.*

*   *   *

DARDEN, Christopher   1957(?)-

PERSONAL: Born c. 1957, in Texas; son of Edward (a welder) and Jean Darden; children: Jenee. *Education:* Earned degrees at San Jose State University and Hastings College of Law, San Francisco.

ADDRESSES: Agent—c/o HarperCollins, 1000 Keystone Industrial Park, Scranton, PA 18512.

CAREER: Has worked for the Los Angeles County District Attorney's Office as an attorney; Southwestern University School of Law, instructor.

WRITINGS:

(With Jess Walter) *In Contempt* (memoir), Harper Collins (Scranton, PA), 1996.

ADAPTATIONS: In Contempt was simultaneously released on an audiotape read by Darden.

SIDELIGHTS: Attorney Christopher Darden was thrust into the national spotlight in 1995 when he replaced the ailing Bill Hodgman in the number two slot of the prosecuting team in the famous O. J. Simpson murder trial. Prior to this trial, Darden worked for the Los Angeles County District Attorney's office for fourteen years and successfully prosecuted nineteen murderers. By 1994, though, Darden had become somewhat disenchanted with the legal system and was thinking of leaving the district attorney's office when he was chosen to work on the O. J. Simpson case. He first worked behind the scenes, investigating Al Cowlings, Simpson's friend and the driver of Simpson's white Bronco in a lengthy, low-speed police chase. Convinced of Simpson's guilt, Darden took over Hodgman's role when it became available. Darden then became a lightning rod and target for criticism by defense attorneys, who suggested that he was a "token black" on the DA's team, placed there to influence a largely black jury. He was perceived by some as a traitor to his race for his role in the trial, and he even received death threats.

After the jury returned a not guilty verdict, Darden was angry to the point of exploding. He needed to vent his anger. "I was full of contempt for some people, and it was easy to purge myself of all of this," Darden confessed in a *People* magazine interview. *In Contempt,* which he co-authored with Jess Walter, a journalist from Spokane, Washington, tells not only the story of the trial but of Darden's coming of age as a black man and lawyer. Darden describes his childhood and college and law school years, dramatizes how he believes the murders of Nicole Brown Simpson and Ronald Goldman took place, portrays the various participants in the trial, and discusses his reactions to being called an "Uncle Tom" for his work for the District Attorney's office.

In Contempt elicited favorable reviews. According to Michiko Kakutani, writing in the *New York Times,* Darden's work results in a "powerful and affecting new book." "In a trial peopled with glib demagogues and carefully coiffed publicity hounds, Mr. Darden stood out as an earnest, conflicted presence—alternately brooding and impassioned, introspective and acerbic. That same voice comes through in *In Contempt,"* Kakutani added. Likewise, Adam Hochschild commented in the *New York Times Book Review:* "During the trial Mr. Darden seemed, unlike many on view, as if he might be a decent human being. *In Contempt* leaves you convinced of this." "While some of his remarks read like a rationalization of his team's mistakes. . . , he is as tough on himself as he is on his colleagues," observed Kakutani, who added, "Darden's portraits of the main players in the trial are colorful and blunt."

Hochschild voiced some misgivings about celebrity books in general: "On the whole, Mr. Darden's book is disappointing, because it, too, is touched by the disease of celebrity. . . . With books like this, you never really know whose voice you're hearing." In a review for *Entertainment Weekly,* Gene Lyons assessed the work's value: "The real importance of *In Contempt* lies not in the Simpson trial, but in its powerful self-portrait of a proud, complex individual confronting racial group-think and refusing to bow down. Chris Darden is indeed a genuine American hero."

BIOGRAPHICAL/CRITICAL SOURCES:

PERIODICALS

Entertainment Weekly, April 12, 1996, pp. 58-59.
New Yorker, April 15, 1996, pp. 40-44.
New York Times, March 26, 1996, p. C18.
New York Times Book Review, April 28, 1996, p. 14.
People, April 1, 1996, pp. 50, 52, 55.*

*   *   *

DATHORNE, O(scar) R(onald) 1934-

PERSONAL: Born November 19, 1934, in Georgetown, British Guiana (now Guyana); son of Oscar Robertson and Rosalie Belona (Peazer) Dathorne; married Hildegard Ostermaier, 1959; children: Shade Cecily and Alexander Franz Keith. *Education:* University of Sheffield, B.A. (honors), 1958, M.A., 1960, Ph.D., 1966; University of London, Grad. Cert. in Ed., 1959, Diploma in Ed., 1967; University of Miami, M.B.A., M.P.A., 1984.

ADDRESSES: Office—Department of English, University of Kentucky, Lexington, KY 40506.

CAREER: Ahmadu Bello University, Zaria, Nigeria, lecturer in English, 1959-63; University of Ibadan, Ibadan, Nigeria, lecturer in English, 1963-66; UNESCO., Paris, France, adviser to Government of Sierra Leone, 1967-68; University of Sierra Leone, Njala University College, Freetown, professor of English and chairman of department, 1968-70; professor of Afro-American studies at Howard University, Washington, DC and University of Wisconsin, Madison, 1970-71; Ohio State University, Columbus, professor of English and black studies, 1971-74, 1975-77; visiting professor of literature, Florida International University, 1974-75; University of Miami, Coral Gables, FL, professor of English and director of American Studies, beginning 1977; University of Kentucky, Lexington, professor of English, 1977—. Has given radio lectures and poetry readings for Nigerian Broadcasting Corp., B.B.C. (London), and several university-owned radio stations. Part-time teacher at Western Nigerian Training College, 1963-66, University of Sierra Leone, 1967-68; visiting professor at Yale University, 1970.

WRITINGS:

Dumplings in the Soup (novel), Cassell (London), 1963.
The Scholar-Man (novel), Cassell, 1964.
The Black Mind: A History of African Literature, University of Minnesota Press (Minneapolis), 1974, abridged edition published as *African Literature in the Twentieth Century,* 1976.
Kelly Poems (verse), privately printed, 1977.
Dark Ancestor: The Literature of the Black Man in the Caribbean, Louisiana State University Press (Baton Rouge), 1981.
Dele's Child (novel), Three Continents Press (Washington, DC), 1986.
In Europe's Image: The Need for American Multiculturalism, Bergin & Garvey (Westport, CT), 1994.
Imagining the World: Mythical Belief Versus Reality in Global Encounters, Bergin & Garvey, 1994.
Asian Voyages: Two Thousand Years of Constructing the Other, Bergin & Garvey, 1996.

EDITOR

(With others) *Young Commonwealth Poets '65,* Heinemann (London), 1965.
(And author of introduction) *Caribbean Narrative: An Anthology of West Indian Writing,* Heinemann, 1966.
(And author of introduction) *Caribbean Verse: An Anthology,* Heinemann, 1967.
(With Willfried Feuser) *Africa in Prose,* Penguin (London), 1969.
(And author of introduction) *African Poetry for Schools and Colleges,* Macmillan (Yaba, Nigeria), 1969.

Derek Walcott, *Selected Poems,* Heinemann, 1977.

Afro World: Adventures in Ideas, University of Wisconsin Press (Milwaukee), 1984.

Caribbean Aspirations and Achievements, Association of Caribbean Studies (Coral Gables, FL), 1985.

OTHER

(Author of introduction) Donald St. John-Parsons, compiler, *Our Poets Speak,* University of London Press, 1966.

(Author of introduction) Mongo Beti, *King Lazarus,* Collier-Macmillan, 1971.

Contributor of verse to *Black Orpheus, Transition, Outposts,* and *Presence Africaine;* contributor of stories to *Nigerian Radio Times,* Ibadan, 1967; contributor of critical articles to *Journal of Commonwealth Literature, Times Literary Supplement, New African, Phylon, London Magazine,* and other periodicals. Editor, *Journal of Caribbean Studies.*

SIDELIGHTS: O. R. Dathorne often focuses in his fiction on the predicaments of immigrants, particularly of African and West Indian immigrants to England. His first two novels are comedies about African immigrants, while his third novel takes a more serious look at immigration and the search for one's racial ancestry.

In *Dumplings in the Soup,* Dathorne writes of Boffo, a conman among the London African immigrant community whose comic antics provide the book's humorous moments. "The book," writes Louis James in *Contemporary Novelists,* "is lively and readable, but the comic exaggeration undermines the more serious undertones, and, ultimately, some of the comedy itself."

With *The Scholar-Man* Dathorne tells of a West Indian man who goes to Africa in search of a mentor who made a strong impression on him as a child. While in an African village, he undergoes a native cult ceremony which gives him visions of his slave ancestors. The novel is, according to James, "a more complex and thoughtful work. . . . Some of the humour is somewhat forced, but in this second work the comedy also touches wider themes of identity and the wider reality."

Dele's Child moves from comedy to a serious exploration of African heritage. "The novel shows Dathorne's deepening interest in aspects of African culture, including Yoruba religion and poetic form, as he experiments with ways to move beyond the conventions

of European narrative into a form appropriate for an African-oriented consciousness," writes James.

BIOGRAPHICAL/CRITICAL SOURCES:

BOOKS

Contemporary Novelists, 6th edition, St. James Press (Detroit), 1996.

James, Louis, *The Islands in Between Us,* Oxford University Press (London), 1969.

Ngugi, James T., *Homecoming,* Heinemann, 1972, Hill (New York City), 1973.

PERIODICALS

Choice, October, 1986.

New World, 1966.

New Yorker, February 28, 1970.

Times Literary Supplement, July 28, 1966; April 2, 1982.

World Literature Today, winter, 1965; autumn, 1965; spring, 1977; winter, 1987.

*   *   *

DAVIS, Angela (Yvonne) 1944-

PERSONAL: Born January 26, 1944, in Birmingham, AL; daughter of B. Frank (a teacher and businessman) and Sally E. (a teacher) Davis. *Education:* Attended Sorbonne, University of Paris, 1963-64; Brandeis University, B.A. (magna cum laude), 1965; University of Frankfurt, graduate study, 1965-67; University of California, San Diego, M.A., 1968, graduate study, 1968-69.

ADDRESSES: Office—c/o Random House, Inc., 201 East 50th St., New York, N.Y. 10022.

CAREER: University of California, Los Angeles, acting assistant professor of philosophy, 1969-70; currently works with National Alliance against Racist and Political Repression. Communist Party candidate for vice-president of the United States, 1980.

AWARDS, HONORS: Ph.D. (honorary), Lenin University.

WRITINGS:

(With Ruchell Magee, the Soledad Brothers, and others) *If They Come in the Morning: Voices of*

Resistance, foreword by Julian Bond, Third Press, 1971.

Angela Davis: An Autobiography, Random House, 1974, revised edition, 1990.

Women, Race and Class, Random House, 1982.

Women, Culture and Politics, Random House, 1989.

The Angela Y. Davis Reader, edited by Joy James, Blackwell (Cambridge, MA), 1998.

Blues Legacies and Black Feminism: Gertrude "Ma" Rainey, Bessie Smith, and Billie Holiday, Pantheon Books, 1998.

Also author of phonodisc, *Angela Davis Speaks,* Folkways, 1971. Contributor of articles to *Ebony* and other periodicals.

SIDELIGHTS: Long known as a political activist, Angela Davis has committed her life to the eradication of oppression and poverty, especially among blacks. A controversial figure in the American public eye, Davis's political convictions propel her to fight for the rights of minority groups. Through her active involvement in the American Communist Party, she has worked ceaselessly and often militantly to guarantee political freedom for repressed peoples.

Although she didn't formally espouse communism until the age of twenty-four, Davis experienced exposure to multiple socio-economic systems throughout her youth. She participated in civil rights demonstrations and helped from interracial study groups while a Birmingham, Alabama, teenager. Her family had numerous Communist friends; she joined a Communist youth group, Advance, while a scholarship student (from the American Friends Service Committee) at Elizabeth Irwin High School in New York. In addition, while in college, she studied under political philosopher Herbert Marcuse, who considered her the best student he ever taught. At the University of California, San Diego, she participated in several activist organizations, including the San Diego Black Conference and the Student Nonviolent Coordinating Committee; she also helped found the Black Students Council. Elinor Langer of the *New York Times Book Review* asserts that Davis's later political philosophies reflect her early influences of socialism and communism: "Both the anticapitalist theory she studied and the interracial Communist community to which she was accustomed must have affected her negative analysis of the American black political scene."

Davis believes that blacks have traditionally lacked the same rights fundamentally available to whites in the United States. In *If They Come in the Morning:*

Voices of Resistance, she states, "Needless to say, the history of the United States has been marred from its inception by an enormous quantity of unjust laws, far too many expressly bolstering the oppression of Black people." As a result, she believes, numerous minority members fall prey to the very political and economic conditions that support the upper classes. She explains in *If They Come in the Morning:* "Prisoners—especially Blacks, Chicanos, and Puerto Ricans—are increasingly advancing the proposition that they are political prisoners. They contend that they are political prisoners in the sense that they are largely the victims of an oppressive politico-economic order, swiftly becoming conscious of the causes underlying their victimization."

Davis further characterizes political prisoners as not merely "victims" but rather actual pioneers in the fight against repression. She argues that these prisoners' actions demonstrate a protest against the "oppressive politico-economic order" of which she speaks. She defines the political prisoner in *If They Come in the Morning:* "The offense of the political prisoner is his political boldness, his persistent lenging—legally or extra-legally—of fundamental social wrongs fostered and reinforced by the state. He has opposed unjust laws and exploitative, racist social conditions in general, with the ultimate aim of transforming these laws and this society into an order harmonious with the material and spiritual needs and interests of the vast majority of its members."

Davis views her work with political prisoners as an outgrowth of her personal devotion "to defend our embattled humanity," she states in *Angela Davis: An Autobiography.* She contends that she did not want to write her autobiography, but comments in it: "When I decided to write the book after all, it was because I had come to envision it as a *political* autobiography that emphasized the people, the events and the forces in my life that propelled me to my present commitment." Her autobiography details how her aims to help oppressed individuals found expression in the political ideals of communism. About her early introduction to communism, she states in her autobiography: "The *Communist Manifesto* hit me like a bolt of lightning. I read it avidly, finding in it answers to many of the seemingly unanswerable dilemmas which had plagued me. . . . I began to see the problems of Black people within the context of a large working-class movement. My ideas about Black liberation were imprecise, and I could not find the right concepts to articulate them; still, I was acquiring some understanding about how capitalism could be abolished." She continues, explaining the connection between communism and minority liberation, "What struck me so emphatically was the idea that once the emancipation of the proletariat became a reality, the foundation was laid for the emancipation of all oppressed groups in society."

Within the Communist Party, U.S.A., Davis allied herself primarily with the Che-Lumumba Club, a black faction of the Los Angeles Party membership. The black Communists of the Che-Lumumba Club had already declared their goal as the liberation of black peoples in the Los Angeles area through application of Marxist-Leninist philosophies when Davis officially joined the party in July, 1968. Her search for a revolutionary community with which to involve herself did not end with her membership in the Communist Party, however. She actively initiated militant demonstrations and protests designed to focus public attention on the plight of minorities. Her radical views eventually interfered with her career as an educator as well. In 1969, the Board of Regents of the University of California dismissed her from the faculty; a court order reinstated her shortly thereafter. However, the University of California, Los Angeles, did not renew her contract in 1970, despite her rating as an "excellent" and reasonably unbiased teacher by the administration. The American Association of University Professors censured the institution for its decision, and a final attempt by the philosophy department to reinstate her in 1972 failed.

Concurrent with her professional difficulties, Davis's radical beliefs led to her involvement in a 1970 prison break. Political prisoner George Jackson and others attempted to escape from the Marin County, California, courthouse. The situation deteriorated into a shoot-out. In connection with the incident, Angela Davis was charged with kidnapping, conspiracy, and murder. Her subsequent imprisonment and trial aroused international concern and interest; she was ultimately acquitted of all charges.

Davis's controversial behavior has not lessened since her prison and courtroom experiences. She adopts, however, more conventional methods for spreading her ideologies than she perhaps once did. She has immersed herself in the Communist Party, lecturing around the world. Even within the Communist Party, her activities have followed more traditional political avenues to effect change: in the 1980 U.S. Presidential election, Angela Davis was the vice-presidential candidate of the Communist Party.

About *If They Come in the Morning: Voices of Resistance,* Steven V. Roberts of *Commonweal* observes, "In essence, . . . this is a book written by revolutionaries, true believers, who can justify anything in the name of their cause." Although he finds that "the book bristles with contradictions," Roberts adds, "The best parts of [the collection] are several essays by Miss Davis."

Angela Davis: An Autobiography "is less an autobiography than a preliminary probe of her own fiber, her humble realization that she is made of stern stuff," according to the *New Republic*'s Ivan Webster. "She is eloquent, tough and stubborn in her moral integrity." Yet, Webster a failing: "It's when she moves away from hard, stark issues that the book falters." Julius Lester of the *Progressive* comments: "One is left with the impression of a woman who lives as she thinks it necessary to live and not as she would like to, if she allowed herself to have desires. She seems to be a woman of enormous self-discipline and control, who willed herself to a total political identity. Her will is so strong that, at times, it is frightening." Lester continues, "Davis has used her politics to eradicate everything in her which would interfere with her commitment to revolutionary change."

Paula Giddings, in *Black World,* shares Lester's view of Davis's intensity and autonomous vision: "[After] reading the last page, one's immediate reaction is, but what have we learned about Angela Davis? The answer is a great deal. . . . She has little desire to project as a singularly charismatic figure; . . . the primary purpose of her book is to illuminate the political causes and concerns central to her life." George F. Kent, writing in *PHYLON: The Atlanta University Review of Race and Culture,* also remarks upon Davis's devotion to her aims, noting, "Despite its single-minded emphasis upon proper ideological response, the passion with which this political autobiography is written enhances its educational objective."

Davis's *Women, Race and Class* traces and documents the historical development of feminism. Carolly Erickson of the *Los Angeles Times Book Review* states that the book "is as useful an exposition of the current dilemmas of the women's movement as one could hope for." She adds, "Women, Race and Class offers a view from the underside of 19th-Century feminism, and argues that the profound differences that estranged black and white women in the early days of the women's movement still estrange them today." Ann Jones of the *New York Times Book Review* explains further, "Against this intricate background of the separate and unequal histories of black and white women, Miss Davis sets in perspective some contemporary women's issues: rape, reproductive freedom, housework and child care." Jones continues: "I wish she had spoken to us here, as she has so movingly in the past, in a voice less tuned at times to the Communist Party, more insistently her own. But she is herself a woman of undeniable courage. She should be heard."

The collection *Women, Culture and Politics* includes essays based on speeches Davis gave from 1983 to 1987. In them, Davis examines racism and classism in American culture and social movements, while arguing for the ideals of communism. In *Belles Lettres* Eleanor J. Bader notes that "Davis's commitment is passionate and vigorous" but finds that "Although most of Davis's arguments are supported with irrefutable information and figures, her conclusions are often glib and somewhat weak." Bader continues, "Davis indicts capitalism successfully. . . . Yet the book does not convince us that socialism is, in fact, better suited to meeting human needs." However, in his article for *New Statesman & Society,* Toks Williams supports Davis's words: "Angela Davis's single-minded dedication and hard-headed idealism provide more than enough positive encouragement for those who may think there is little left to fight for in the civil rights movement." Commenting on the continued controversy surrounding Davis's writings and actions, Michele Wallace in the *Village Voice Literary Supplement* writes, "Just think of Davis as a latter-day Joan of Arc who didn't perish in the fire."

Angela Davis's political commitments keep her involved in an unending fight against oppression. Her communist beliefs alienate her from many American citizens, yet she continues to lecture and write in support of her philosophies. Although Davis's ideologies garner much opposition in the United States, Jones remarks upon her tenacity, describing Davis as one "who has never shied from impossible tasks."

BIOGRAPHICAL/CRITICAL SOURCES:

BOOKS

The Angela Davis Trial (microfilm), Oceana, 1974.
Ashman, Charles R., *The People vs. Angela Davis,* Pinnacle Books, 1972.
Contemporary Issues Criticism, Volume I, Gale, 1982.

Davis, Angela, "Angela Davis Speaks" (phonodisc), Folkways, 1974.
Davis, *Angela Davis: An Autobiography,* Random House, 1974.
Davis, Ruchell Magee, the Soledad Brothers, and others, *If They Come in the Morning: Voices of Resistance,* Third Press, 1971.
Lund, Caroline, *The Czechoslovak Frame-Up Trials,* Pathfinder Press, 1973.

PERIODICALS

Advocate, October 31, 1995, p. 57.
Belles Lettres, summer, 1989, p. 20.
Essence, August, 1995, p. 50; May, 1996, p. 82.
Los Angeles Times Book Review, April 4, 1982.
New Statesman & Society, March 16, 1990, p. 39.
New York Times Book Review, January 10, 1982; March 18, 1990, p. 32.
Village Voice Literary Supplement, June, 1982; November, 1995.*

* * *

DAVIS, Frank Marshall 1905-1987

PERSONAL: Born December 31, 1905, in Arkansas City, KS; died July 26, 1987, in Honolulu, HI; married; children: Lynn, Beth, Jeanne, Jill, Mark. *Education:* Attended Friends University, 1923; attended Kansas State Agricultural College (now Kansas State University of Agricultural and Applied Science), 1924-27, 1929.

CAREER: Worked for various newspapers in Illinois, including the *Chicago Evening Bulletin, Whip,* and *Gary American,* 1927-29; *Atlanta Daily World,* Atlanta, GA, editor and co-founder, 1931-34; Associated Negro Press, Chicago, IL, executive editor, 1935-47; *Chicago Star,* Chicago, executive editor, 1946-48; owned wholesale paper business in Honolulu, HI, beginning c. 1948. Worked as a jazz radio disc jockey in the early 1940s. Toured black colleges as a lecturer, 1973.

MEMBER: League of American Writers, Allied Arts Guild, Southside Chicago Writers Group.

AWARDS, HONORS: Julius Rosenwald Foundation grant, 1937.

WRITINGS:

Black Man's Verse, Black Cat (Chicago), 1935.
I Am the American Negro, Black Cat, 1937.
Through Sepia Eyes, illustrated by William Fleming, Black Cat, 1938.
47th Street: Poems, Decker (Prairie City, IL), 1948.
Awakening, and Other Poems, Black Cat, 1978.
Livin' the Blues: Memoirs of a Black Journalist and Poet, edited by John Edgar Tidwell, University of Wisconsin Press (Madison, WI), 1992.

Also contributor to anthologies, including *The Negro Caravan,* Dryden, 1942; *Kaleidoscope: Poems by American Negro Poets,* Harcourt, 1967; *Black Voices: An Anthology of Afro-American Literature,* New American Library, 1968; *The Poetry of the Negro, 1746-1970,* Anchor Books, 1970; *Black Insights,* Ginn, 1971; *Understanding the New Black Poetry,* Morrow, 1973; and *The New Negro Renaissance: An Anthology,* Holt, 1975. Contributor to periodicals, including *National, Light and Heebie Jeebies, Voices,* and *Cottonwood Magazine.* Weekly columnist for *Honolulu Record.*

SIDELIGHTS: Frank Marshall Davis's poetry "not only questioned social ills in his own time but also inspired Blacks in the politically charged 1960s," according to John Edgar Tidwell in the *Dictionary of Literary Biography.* Sometimes likened to poets such as Carl Sandburg, Edgar Lee Masters, and Langston Hughes, Davis published his first volume, *Black Man's Verse,* in 1935. The book met with much applause from critics, including Harriet Monroe, who concluded in *Poetry* that its author was "a poet of authentic inspiration, who belongs not only among the best of his race, but who need not lean upon his race for recognition as an impassioned singer with something to say." Davis concerned himself with portraying Black life, protesting racial inequalities, and promoting Black pride. The poet described his work thus in the poem "Frank Marshall Davis: Writer" from his *I Am the American Negro:* "When I wrote / I dipped my pen / In the crazy heart / Of mad America."

Davis grew up in Arkansas City, Kansas, surrounded by racism. Tidwell reported that when the poet was five years old he was nearly killed by some older White children who had heard stories of lynchings and wanted to try one for themselves. The result of this incident and others was that Davis hated whites in his youth. He gained some relief, according to Tidwell, when he left the prejudiced, small town atmosphere of Arkansas City in 1923 to attend Friends

University in Wichita; he eventually transferred to Kansas State Agricultural College's school of journalism. There, because of a class assignment, Davis received his first introduction to writing free verse—his preferred poetic form. When he left Kansas State, he traveled to Chicago, where he wrote freelance articles for magazines and worked for several Black newspapers while continuing to produce poems. After a brief return to Kansas State, Davis moved to Atlanta, Georgia, to take an editing post on a semiweekly paper. With the help of his leadership, the periodical became the *Atlanta Daily World,* the first successful Black daily newspaper in America. Meanwhile, one of Davis's published poems, "Chicago's Congo," which concerns the underlying similarities between the Blacks of Chicago and those still living the tribal life of the African Congo, attracted the attention of bohemian intellectual Frances Norton Manning. When Davis returned to Chicago, Manning introduced him to Norman Forgue, whose Black Cat Press subsequently published four of Davis's books of poetry, beginning with *Black Man's Verse.*

A critical success, *Black Man's Verse* "is experimental, cacophonous, yet sometimes harmonious," according to Tidwell. The volume includes poems such as "Giles Johnson, Ph.D.," in which the title character starves to death in spite of his four college degrees and knowledge of Latin and Greek because he does not wish to teach and is incapable of doing the manual labor that made up the majority of work available to Blacks. Other pieces in *Black Man's Verse*—"Lynched," "Mojo Mike's Beer Garden," and "Cabaret," for example—make use of Davis's expertise on the subject of jazz to combine "the spirit of protest in jazz and free verse with . . . objections to racial oppression, producing a poetry that loudly declaims against injustice," explained Tidwell. Another well-known part of the volume is entitled "Ebony Under Granite." Likened to author Edgar Lee Masters's *Spoon River Anthology,* this section discusses the lives of various Black people buried in a cemetery. Characters include Reverend Joseph Williams, who used to have sex with most of the women in his congregation; Goldie Blackwell, a two-dollar prostitute; George Brown, who served life in prison for voting more than once, although in Mississippi he had seen white voters commit the same crime many times without punishment; and Roosevelt Smith, a Black writer who was so frustrated by literary critics that he became a postman.

I Am the American Negro, Davis's second collection of poems, was published two years after his first.

While drawing generally favorable reviews, it did not attract as much attention as *Black Man's Verse,* and some critics complained that it was too similar to the earlier book. For example, Tidwell quoted Black critic Alain Locke's assertion that *I Am the American Negro* "has too many echoes of the author's first volume . . . it is not a crescendo in the light of the achievement of *Black Man's Verse.*" One of the obvious similarities between the two collections is that Davis also included an "Ebony Under Granite" section in the second. Members of this cast are people like the two Greeley sisters—the first's earlier promiscuous lifestyle did not prevent her from marrying respectably, while the second's lack of sexual experience caused her husband to be unfaithful; Nicodemus Perry, killed by loiterers for accidentally bumping into a white woman while, ironically, lost in memories of the sexual abuse his female relatives suffered at the hands of White men; and Mrs. Clifton Townsend, prejudiced against the darker-skinned members of her own race, who dies after giving birth to a baby much blacker than herself. Other poems featured in *I Am the American Negro* are "Modern Man—The Superman," which laments the state of modern civilization and has mock musical notations in its margins such as "Eight airplane motors, each keyed to a different pitch, are turned on and off to furnish musical accompaniment within the range of an octave"; and the title poem, which is a diatribe against Southern laws treating Blacks differently from Whites. Davis also placed love poems such as "Flowers of Darkness" and "Come to Me" in this book.

"The culmination of Davis's thought and poetic development," is found in Davis's 1948 collection of poems, *47th Street,* according to Tidwell. Davis himself remarked on the time span between his first book, *I Am,* and his fourth book, *47th Street,* in a 1973 interview for *Black World:* "I was going through a number of changes during that particular time and I had to wait for these changes to settle and jell before I produced other work which I thought would be suitable to appear in a volume. And, of course, some critics naturally have thought that I would have been better off had I just continued to jell indefinitely." *47th Street* is composed of poems such as "Coincidence," which narrates the life stories of Donald Woods, a White man, and Booker Scott, a Black man, who shared their dates of birth and death—by the poem's end the reader discovers that they also shared the same white biological father. The title poem, "unlike Davis's previous descriptions of Southside Chicago as exclusively Black," noted Tidwell, "presents a 'rainbow race' of people." Indeed, Tidwell saw the whole

of *47th Street* as having more universal concerns than his earlier works. When questioned about this issue Davis declared: "I am a Black poet, definitely a Black poet, and I think that my way of seeing things is the result of the impact of our civilization upon what I like to think of as a sensitive Black man. . . . But I do not think the Black poet should confine himself exclusively to Black readership. I think poetry, if it is going to be any good, should move members of all groups, and that is what I hope for." In the same year that *47th Street* was published, Davis left Chicago for Honolulu, Hawaii. What began as a vacation turned into permanent residency.

Except for a few poems that appeared in *Voices* in 1950, Davis virtually disappeared from the literary world. Ironically, Davis moved to Hawaii at approximately the same time, in which notes Tidwell, "The House Un-American Activities Committee, the Senate's Eastland Committee, and the Federal Bureau of Investigation" were seeing Davis' social realism as "politically subversive material." Thus, while Davis' poems were being translated and read internationally, his work was being removed from libraries and schools.

During the Black Arts Movement of the 1960s, Frank Davis was "rediscovered" by literary critic Stephen Henderson and Dudley Randall, poet and publisher of the important Broadside press which launched the careers of African American poets Nikki Giovanni, Etheridge Knight, and others. Davis was presented as the "mystery poet" and as the "father of modern Black poetry" by Randall who arranged for Davis to go on a college lecture tour in 1973. Following his resurfacing, in 1978 Davis published another volume of poetry, *Awakening, and Other Poems.*

At the time of his death in 1987, Davis was working on a manuscript called "That Incredible Waikiki Jungle" about his Hawaiian experiences. In Hawaii, Davis raised his five children where, instead of the racial and social polarity of post-war American, he experienced the cultural diversity that derived from the mix of Whites, Blacks, Japanese, Chinese, Filipinos, Puerto Ricans, Samoans, Tongans, and Hawaiians. When asked why he decided to remain in Hawaii, Davis cited the relative lack of racial problems and added, "I think one of the reasons why was that this [was] the first time that I began to be treated as a man instead of a Black curiosity. That was important to me, for my feeling of dignity and self-respect."

Livin' the Blues: Memoirs of a Black Journalist and Poet, published posthumously in 1992, was edited by John Edgar Tidwell from the surviving manuscripts of Davis. The book details the struggles of growing up in racially-restricted early twentieth century America, especially as it chronicles the difficulties which challenged Black magazines and newspapers which championed and served as advocates for "the Black voice in both art and society," notes Judy Solberg in *Library Journal.* As much as the book tells Davis' story, Solberg comments upon how it concurrently presents "a vivid portrayal of African American cultural history of the 1930s and 1940s." Written in a kind of "jazz" structure, *Kirkus Review* praised *Livin' the Blues* for the "writing voice, with its throaty, soft cornet style," and Solberg points out how Davis' "love of language and his poetic voice shine through in this creative representation of his life as a blues narrative." Documenting the experiences of a working journalist and a poet in Chicago and Atlanta, places not commonly studied in the context of the importance of the Harlem Renaissance, Davis' autobiography *Livin' the Blues* is "an important addition to the recovery of significant American voices," states Solberg.

Davis' poetry is "generally that of an advocate urging social change," noted Tidwell in *Dictionary of Literary Biography.* In an interview with Tidwell in *Black American Literature Forum,* Davis stated that "To me, poetry is a subjective way of looking at the world. All poetry worthy of the name is propaganda," adding as a qualification that "Since I take pride in being considered a social realist, my work will be looked upon as blatant propaganda by some not in sympathy with my goals and as fine poetry by others of equal discernment who agree with me." Still, it was the blues and jazz, which has also inspired Langston Hughes and Sterling Brown, which characterize much of Davis' work. Davis told Tidwell that "When I heard my first blues and early jazz at the age of eight years, I felt the same kind of exultant kinship with this music that I felt when I read my first free verse in college." Yet his poetry will be remembered for more than its sound and its social commentary, observes Helena Kloder in *CLA Journal,* who believes that Davis' greatest strength lies in his creation of visual art, calling his poetry "a force of verbal kodacolor snapshots and reels of spliced, almost always precisely edited, motion pictures" which offer readers "an assortment of colorful, realistic portraits of Americans (black and white), their lifestyles, their visions."

Although critics have disagreed about the value of Davis' poetry—whether at times he is presenting po-

etry or propaganda, poetry or prose—as *Black Literature Criticism* concludes, "few dispute the sociological and historical value of his works." His death in 1987 silenced one of the last living chroniclers of the Harlem Renaissance era. The "rediscovery" of Davis, and his work, as well as the posthumously autobiography *Livin' the Blues,* add an important piece to the growing quilt that is African American literature.

BIOGRAPHICAL/CRITICAL SOURCES:

BOOKS

Black Literature Criticism, Gale (Detroit), 1992.
Davis, Frank Marshall, *I Am the American Negro,* Black Cat, 1937.
Davis, Frank Marshall, *Livin' the Blues: Memoirs of a Black Journalist and Poet,* University of Wisconsin Press, 1992.
Dictionary of Literary Biography, Volume 51: *Afro-American Writers from the Harlem Renaissance to 1940,* Gale, 1987.
Selected Black American Authors: An Illustrated Bio-Bibliography, G. K. Hall (Boston), 1977.
Wagner, Jean. *Black Poets of the United States: From Paul Laurence Dunbar to Langston Hughes,* University of Illinois Press (Champaign, IL), 1973.

PERIODICALS

American Literature, December, 1993, p. 833.
Black American Literature Forum, fall, 1985, pp. 105-108.
Black Scholar, spring, 1993, p. 59.
Black World, January, 1974, pp. 37-48.
Booknews, August 1, 1993.
Chicago Tribune, August 9, 1987.
CLA Journal, September, 1971, pp. 59-63.
Journal of American History, March, 1994, p. 1520.
Kirkus Review, December 1, 1992, p. 1477.
Library Journal, February 1, 1993, p. 90.
Nation, March 11, 1936, p. 328.
Poetry, August, 1936, pp. 293-295.
Reference and Research Book News, August, 1993, p. 38.
Saturday Review of Literature, January 18, 1936, p. 19.*

* * *

DAVIS, Ossie 1917-

PERSONAL: Born December 18, 1917, in Cogdell, GA; son of Kince Charles (a railway construction engineer) and Laura (Cooper) Davis; married Ruby Ann Wallace (an actress and writer under name Ruby Dee), December 9, 1948; children: Nora, Guy, La Verne. *Education:* Attended Howard University, 1935-39, and Columbia University, 1948; trained for the stage with Paul Mann and Lloyd Richards.

ADDRESSES: Office—Emmalyn II Productions, P.O. Box 1318, New Rochelle, NY 10802. *Agent*—Artists Agency, 10000 Santa Monica Blvd., Suite 305, Los Angeles, CA 90067.

CAREER: Actor, playwright, screenwriter, novelist, director and producer of stage productions and motion pictures, civil rights activist. Worked as janitor, shipping clerk, and stock clerk in New York City, 1938-41. Actor in numerous stage productions, 1941—, including *Joy Exceeding Glory,* 1941, *Jeb,* 1946, *Anna Lucasta,* 1948, *Stevedore,* 1949, *The Green Pastures,* 1951, *No Time for Sergeants,* 1957, *A Raisin in the Sun,* 1959, *Purlie Victorious,* 1961, *Take It from the Top,* 1979, and *I'm Not Rappaport,* 1986. Actor in motion pictures and teleplays, including *The Joe Louis Story,* 1953, *The Emperor Jones,* 1955, *The Cardinal,* 1963, *Gone Are the Days,* 1963, *Man Called Adam,* 1966, *Teacher, Teacher* for Hallmark Hall of Fame, 1969, *Let's Do It Again,* 1976, *For Us the Living* for American Playhouse, 1983, *School Daze,* 1988, *Do the Right Thing,* 1989, *Jungle Fever,* 1991, *No Way Out, Harry and Son, Gladiator, Malcolm X, Grumpy Old Men, The Client,* 1994, and *Get on the Bus,* 1996; actor in television series *Evening Shade,* 1990-93, miniseries Alex Haley's *Queen,* 1993, and Stephen King's *The Stand,* 1994, television specials *The Ernest Green Story,* 1993 and *The Ray Alexander Mystery,* 1994; other television appearances include *Name of the Game, Night Gallery, Bonanza,* and *B. L. Stryker.* Director of motion pictures, including *Cotton Comes to Harlem,* 1970, *Kongi's Harvest,* 1971, *Black Girl,* 1972, *Gordon's War,* 1973, and *Countdown at Kusini,* 1976. Co-host of radio program *Ossie Davis and Ruby Dee Story Hour,* 1974-78, and of television series *With Ossie and Ruby,* Public Broadcasting System (PBS-TV), 1981. Co-producer of stage production *Ballad for Bimshire,* 1963. Narrator of motion picture *From Dreams to Reality: A Tribute to Minority Inventors,* 1986, and of television movie *The American Experience: Goin' Back to T'Town,* 1993. Chairperson of the board, Institute for New Cinema Artists; founder with wife Ruby Dee of Emmalyn II Productions. Performer on recordings for Caedmon and Folkways Records. *Military service:* U.S. Army, 1942-45;

served as surgical technician in Liberia, West Africa, and with Special Services Department.

MEMBER: Actor's Equity Association, Screen Actors Guild, American Federation of Radio and Television Artists, Director's Guild of America, National Association for the Advancement of Colored People (advisory board), Southern Christian Leadership Conference (advisory board), Congress of Racial Equality, Masons.

AWARDS, HONORS: First Mississippi Freedom Democratic Party Citation, 1965; Emmy Award nomination from Academy of Television Arts and Sciences, best actor in a special, 1969, for *Teacher, Teacher,* and nomination, c. 1978, for *King;* Antoinette Perry Award nomination, best musical, 1970, for *Purlie;* recipient with Dee of Frederick Douglass Award from New York Urban League, for "distinguished leadership toward equal opportunity," 1970; Paul Robeson Citation from Actor's Equity Association, 1975, for "outstanding creative contributions in the performing arts and in society at large"; Coretta Scott King Book Award from American Library Association, and Jane Addams Children's Book Award from Jane Addams Peace Association, both 1979, for *Escape to Freedom: A Play about Young Frederick Douglass;* Jury Award from Neil Simon Awards, 1983, for *For Us the Living;* Father of the Year Award, 1987; Image Award from National Association for the Advancement of Colored People, for best performance by a supporting actor, and Hall of Fame Award for outstanding artistic achievement, both 1989, both for *Do The Right Thing;* Monarch Award, 1990; inducted into Theater Hall of Fame, 1994.

WRITINGS:

PLAYS

(And director) *Goldbrickers of 1944,* first produced in Liberia, West Africa, 1944.
Alice in Wonder (one-act), first produced in New York City at Elks Community Theatre, September 15, 1952; revised and expanded version produced as *The Big Deal in New York* at New Playwrights Theatre, March 7, 1953.
Purlie Victorious (first produced on Broadway at Cort Theatre, 1961; also see below), Samuel French (New York City), 1961.
Curtain Call, Mr. Aldridge, Sir (first produced in Santa Barbara at the University of California, summer, 1968), published in *The Black Teacher and the Dramatic Arts: A Dialogue, Bibliography,*

and Anthology, edited by William R. Reardon and Thomas D. Pawley, Negro Universities Press, 1970.

(With Philip Rose, Peter Udell, and Gary Geld) *Purlie* (adaptation of *Purlie Victorious;* first produced on Broadway at Broadway Theatre, March 15, 1970), Samuel French, 1971.

Escape to Freedom: A Play about Young Frederick Douglass (first produced in New York City at the Town Hall, March 8, 1976), Viking (New York City), 1978.

Langston: A Play (first produced in New York City in 1982), Delacorte (New York City), 1982.

(With Hy Gilbert, and director) *Bingo* (baseball musical based on novel *The Bingo Long Traveling All-Stars and Motor Kings* by William Brashler), first produced in New York City at AMAS Repertory Theater, November, 1985.

Also author of *Last Dance for Sybil.*

SCREENPLAYS AND TELEPLAYS

Gone Are the Days (adaptation of *Purlie Victorious;* also released as *Purlie Victorious* and *The Man from C.O.T.T.O.N.),* Trans Lux, 1963.

(With Arnold Perl, and director) *Cotton Comes to Harlem* (based on a novel by Chester Himes), United Artists, 1970.

(And director) *Kongi's Harvest* (adapted from work by Wole Soyinka), Calpenny Films Nigeria Ltd., 1970.

Today Is Ours, Columbia Broadcasting System (CBS-TV), 1974.

(With Ladi Ladebo and Al Freeman, Jr.) *Countdown at Kusini* (based on a story by John Storm Roberts), CBS-TV, 1976.

Also writer of television episodes of *East Side/West Side,* 1963, *The Negro People,* 1965, *Just Say the Word,* 1969, *The Eleventh Hour, Bonanza,* and *N.Y.P.D.;* and for special *Alice in Wonder,* 1987.

OTHER

(With others) *The Black Cinema: Foremost Representatives of the Black Film World Air Their Views* (sound recording), Center for Cassette Studies, 1975.

(Author of foreword) Langston Hughes, *Black Magic: A Pictorial History of the African-American in the Performing Arts,* Da Capo (New York City), 1990.

(Author of foreword) G. William Jones, *Black Cinema Treasures: Lost and Found,* University of North Texas (Denton), 1991.

(Author of afterword) Malcolm X, *The Autobiography of Malcom X* (with the assistance of Alex Haley; introduction by M. S. Handler; epilogue by Alex Haley), Ballantine (New York City), 1992.

Just Like Martin (young adult novel), Simon & Schuster (New York City), 1992.

(Author of foreword with wife, Ruby Dee) Barbara Brandon, *Where I'm Coming From,* Andrews and McMeel (Kansas City), 1993.

Purlie Victorious: A Commemorative (with commentary by Dee), Emmalyn Enterprises (New Rochelle, NY), 1993.

(With wife, Ruby Dee) *Hands upon the Heart* (two-volume videotape), Emmalyn Enterprises, 1994.

(With Grace Lee Boggs) *Living for Change: An Autobiography,* University of Minnesota Press, 1998.

(With wife, Ruby Dee) *With Ossie and Ruby: In This Life Together,* Morrow, 1998.

(Author of foreword) Ruby Dee, *My One Good Nerve,* Wiley and Sons, 1998.

Also author of "Ain't Now But It's Going to Be" (song), for *Cotton Comes to Harlem,* 1970. Contributor to journals and periodicals, including *Negro History Bulletin, Negro Digest,* and *Freedomways.*

SIDELIGHTS: "Ossie Davis is best known as an actor, but his accomplishments extend well beyond the stage," writes Michael E. Greene in the *Dictionary of Literary Biography.* "In the theater, in motion pictures, and in television he has won praise both for his individual performances and those he has given with his wife, Ruby Dee. He has, however, also been a writer, director, producer, social activist, and community leader." The bond uniting all of Davis's work, according to Jayne F. Mulvaney in the *Dictionary of Literary Biography,* is Davis's commitment to "creating works that would truthfully portray the black man's experience."

Long active in the cause of racial justice, Davis was a prominent figure in the civil rights movement of the 1960s. He gave the eulogies at the funerals of black leaders Malcolm X and Dr. Martin Luther King, Jr., and he acted as master of ceremonies at the famous "March on Washington" in 1963-the site of Dr. King's "I Have a Dream" speech. Throughout his life, Davis has used his many talents and experiences to expose wide audiences to his views. As the actor explains to Calvin Reid in *Publishers Weekly:* "I am essentially a storyteller, and the story I want to tell is about black people. Sometimes I sing the story, sometimes I dance it, sometimes I tell tall tales about it, but I always want to share my great satisfaction at being a black man at this time in history."

A native of Cogdell, Georgia, Davis began his career after enrolling at Howard University, where Alain Locke, a drama critic and professor of philosophy, spurred his budding interest in the theater. On Locke's counseling, Davis became involved in several facets of stage life, including maintenance and set construction, while biding time as an actor. He first appeared on the stage as a member of Harlem's Ross McClendon Players in a 1941 production of *Joy Exceeding Glory*. Few offers followed, however, and Davis was reduced to sleeping in parks and scrounging for food.

In 1942 in the midst of World War II, Davis was inducted into the U.S. Army, where he served as a medical technician in Liberia, West Africa. After his transfer to Special Services, he began writing and producing stage works to entertain military personnel. Upon discharge, though, Davis returned to his native Georgia. There he was reached by McClendon director Richard Campbell, who encouraged Davis to return to New York City and audition for Robert Ardrey's *Jeb*. Davis accepted Campbell's encouragement and eventually secured the title role in Ardrey's work. The play, which concerns a physically debilitated veteran's attempt to succeed as an adding machine operator in racist Louisiana, was poorly received, but Davis was exempted for his compelling performance.

Davis married fellow *Jeb* performer Ruby Dee in 1948 after they completed a stint with the touring company of *Anna Lucasta*. The pace of his acting career then accelerated as Davis received critical praise for his work in *Stevedore,* in which he played a servant who assumes a misplaced worldliness following a visit to Paris, and *The Green Pastures,* in which he portrayed one of several angels in a black-populated Heaven.

While acting, Davis also continued to devote attention to his writing. "As a playwright Davis was committed to creating works that would truthfully portray the black man's experience," says Mulvaney. In 1953, his play *Alice in Wonder,* which focused on McCarthy-era issues of integrity and blacklisting, was dimly received in Harlem; however, his 1961 opus *Purlie Victorious* generated a more favorable response.

Mulvaney describes the play as a comedy about the schemes of an eloquent itinerant preacher who returns to his Georgia home with hopes of buying the old barn that once served as a black church, and establishing an integrated one. To realize his plan, he must secure the inheritance of his deceased aunt, a former slave, whose daughter has also died. Because Captain Cotchipee, the play's antagonist and holder of the inheritance, is unaware of the death of Purlie's cousin, Purlie plans to have a pretty young black girl impersonate his cousin so that he can claim the inheritance to finance the church of his dreams. "The action of the play involves the hilarious efforts of Purlie, his family, and the captain's liberal son, Charlie, to outwit the captain," says Mulvaney. Many critics were especially pleased with Davis's humorous portrayal of the black preacher's efforts to swipe the $500 inheritance from the white plantation owner.

Greene calls *Purlie Victorious* a "Southern fable of right against wrong with Purlie's faith in the cause of equality triumphing over the bigotry of Ol' Cap'n Cotchipee, the local redneck aristocrat." Considering the comedy's brilliance to derive "chiefly from how cliches and stereotypes are blown out of proportion," Mulvaney suggests that *Purlie Victorious* is "satire which proceeds toward reconciliation rather than bitterness. Its invective is not venomous." "Unfortunately, despite the reviews, the endorsement of the National Association for the Advancement of Colored People, and the play's seven-and-a-half month run, neither playwright nor producer made money," notes Mulvaney. "The financial support of the black community was not enough; the white audiences did not come." Greene suggests that the play would have been considerably more successful had it been written either ten years before or after it was. "Davis himself recognized that his handling of stereotypes, black and white, would have been offensive had a white writer created them," Greene observes. He adds that Davis "argues that one of his purposes in the play was to present justice as an ideal, as something that is not always the same as traditional law-and-order, which allows the Ol' Cap'ns of American society to win too often."

Purlie Victorious was adapted by Davis as the motion picture *Gone Are the Days.* A. H. Weiler, writing in the *New York Times,* complains that the film rarely availed itself of cinematic techniques, but adds that the work "is still speaking out against injustice in low, broad, comic fashion." Weiler praises the performances of Davis, who played the preacher Purlie Victorious, and Ruby Dee, the title character's lover.

Race relations are at the core of Davis's novel for young adults, *Just Like Martin.* A *Kirkus Reviews* contributor describes the story as "dramatic and simply told, with a cast of strong personalities." Set in 1963, the tale finds Isaac "Stone" and his father, Ike, struggling with their involvement in the civil rights movement. Ike will not let Stone, an all-A student, leave their Alabama home to go with a church youth group to a civil rights march in Washington, D.C. Ike's fear that Stone would be harmed is compounded by his wife's recent death. Ike is also opposed to his son's devotion to nonviolence and belittles the boy's admiration of Martin Luther King. Stone, who hopes to become a preacher "just like Martin," eventually organizes a children's march after two friends are killed and another is maimed when a church youth meeting room is bombed.

In *Just Like Martin,* the church's Reverend Cable asks Stone and other members in the Creative Nonviolence Workshop for Children if they have the strength to let people strike them and not strike back. Stone believes he can endure a beating without resorting to violence, yet finds himself "fist fighting in the house of the Lord," according to Reverend Cable. Anne Scott in *Washington Post Book World* praises Davis's characters, despite their flaws, as they fight off "injustice . . . not always knowing how to respond to the history in which they find themselves."

Other reviewers of Davis's novel comment on Ike's coming to terms with the values of his son. Watching the youth's efforts, along with the shock of hearing of President John F. Kennedy's assassination, prompt Ike to resolve his inner conflict and lend his support to Stone. Lauding Davis's development of father and son, Lyn Miller-Lachmann notes in *Junior High Up* that the author "realistically portrays the boy's struggle to apply King's values in his personal life, and the ending is hopeful but not happy." *Booklist* contributor Hazel Rochman points out some minor flaws in the story, but deemed that "what is riveting here is the sense of history being made-of struggle and commitment in one community."

Davis was also prominently featured in films such as Spike Lee's *School Daze, Do the Right Thing, Jungle Fever,* and *Malcolm X,* and the careers of Dee and Davis have remained intertwined as well. They have performed together in stage productions, films, and recordings; shared duties as hosts/performers on the brief PBS-TV series *With Ossie and Ruby;* and co-founded Emmalyn II Productions. When not on location, they live in New Rochelle, New York.

In addition to his career and his status as a role model, Davis has also been a direct source of encouragement and support for other African American artists. He founded the Institute of Cinema Artists in 1973, providing black students with training for careers in television and film. In recognition of his achievements in this area, Mulvaney calls Davis "a force in the development of black culture." Davis explains his commitment to nurturing other artists in the *Dictionary of Literary Biography:* "For if we can, in fact, create for our own people; work for our own people; belong to our own people; we will no longer be forced into artistic prostitution and self-betrayal in the mad scramble, imposed upon us far too long, to belong to some other people. . . . Only then can we begin to take a truly independent position within the confines of American culture, a black position."

BIOGRAPHICAL/CRITICAL SOURCES:

BOOKS

Abramson, Doris E., *Negro Playwrights in the American Theatre, 1925-1959,* Columbia University Press (New York City), 1969.
Dictionary of Literary Biography, Gale (Detroit), Volume 7: *Twentieth-Century American Dramatists,* 1981; Volume 38: *Afro-American Writers after 1955: Dramatists and Prose Writers,* 1985.
Funke, Lewis, *The Curtain Rises-The Story of Ossie Davis,* Grosset & Dunlap (New York City), 1971.
Patterson, Lindsay, editor, *Anthology of the American Negro in the Theatre,* Association for the Study of Life and History/Publishers Company, 1967.

PERIODICALS

Booklist, September 1, 1992.
Detroit Free Press, November 11, 1983.
Ebony, February, 1961; December, 1979.
Essence, December, 1994, p. 76.
Freedomways, spring, 1962; summer, 1965; summer, 1968.
Junior High Up, October, 1992.
Kirkus Reviews, September 15, 1992, p. 1185.
Modern Maturity, July-August, 1994, p. 64.
Nation, April 6, 1970; July 24-31, 1989, pp. 144-48.
National Observer, March 22, 1970.
Negro Digest, February, 1966; April, 1966.
Negro History Bulletin, April, 1967.
Newsweek, March 30, 1970; December 17, 1990, p. 64.
New York, April, 1970; February 13, 1989, p. 71.

New Yorker, October 7, 1961; July 24, 1989, p. 78; March 26, 1990, p. 79.

New York Times, September 24, 1963; May 5, 1968; October 12, 1969; March 10, 1970; November 11, 1985.

People Weekly, February 13, 1989, p. 13; September 24, 1990, p. 7; August 1, 1994, p. 16.

Publishers Weekly, December 28, 1992, p. 27.

Variety, March 5, 1969; January 28, 1970; March 28, 1970.

Voice of Youth Advocates, April, 1993, p. 24.

Washington Post Book World, December 6, 1992, p. 20.*

*   *   *

DAVIS, Thulani

PERSONAL: Female.

ADDRESSES: Office—c/o *Village Voice,* 842 Broadway, New York, NY 10003.

CAREER: Journalist, poet, and novelist.

WRITINGS:

The Renegade Ghosts Rise (poems), Anemone, 1978.

Playing the Changes (poems), Wesleyan University Press (Middletown, PA), 1985.

(Author of libretto) *X: The Life and Times of Malcolm X* (opera), Nani Press, 1986.

1959 (novel), Grove Weidenfeld, 1992.

(With Howard Chapnick) *Malcolm X: The Great Photographs,* Stewart, Tabori & Chang (New York City), 1993.

Maker of Saints (novel), Scribner (New York City), 1996.

Contributor to periodicals, including *The Village Voice.*

SIDELIGHTS: Thulani Davis's journalism in the *Village Voice* ranges widely over the black experience. While her first novel, *1959,* sees black history from a small-town perspective, her poetry and second novel, *Maker of Saints,* shows her urban sensibility. Of her poems in the 1985 collection, *Playing the Changes,* a *Publishers Weekly* reviewer commented that Davis's work is "vibrant" with "the immediacy of spontaneous composition." Her poems contain random impressions, violence, and well-known person-

alities that are part of city life, as well as the mistrust and danger that are part of racial and, most frequently, sexual relationships from a woman's point of view. "Davis' style," wrote a contributor for *Parnassus,* "may reflect the fragmented psychological attitude of the poet herself and of the impersonal, alienating, dog-eat-dog forces operating on and within people living in big cities."

In 1992, Davis wrote her first novel, *1959,* which Lucasta Miller, writing in the *Times Saturday Review,* called "more readily sympathetic" than her poetry. Though it concerns an important moment in the civil rights movement, that national phenomena is seen through the feelings of certain citizens of a small town in Virginia, such as a barber who has a deep relationship with his Dexter Gordon records. The protagonist, Willie Turant, is a fairly typical twelve-year-old girl who changes significantly after being chosen to guide Martin Luther King around the local black college and, later, to be one of the first black children to enroll at a white high school. Soon, college students stage sit-in protests at the lunch counter of the local Woolworth's. The characters in the novel are in this way reflecting the historic events of the civil rights movement. Despite the fact that the town's black neighborhood is eventually bulldozed and its residents scattered, Davis intimates that the movement will carry on.

"Ms. Davis has a masterly sense of time and place," wrote Beth Levine in the *New York Times Book Review,* "using the history of the town and Willie's aunt's diary to create a raw and moving testament to the power that rests within a community." Michiko Kakutani also commended Davis in her *New York Times* review, particularly enjoying the "captivating heroine." Kakutani remarked, "When she keeps the focus on her heroine . . . [Davis] demonstrates her gift for conjuring up a vanished time and place, her gift for characterization." Kakutani concluded that Davis had skillfully recreated an important moment in history: "By allowing the reader to experience . . . events through Willie's eyes, Ms. Davis is able to avoid sounding like a social studies teacher; she is able to show the consequences of integration on a single family and community with insight, sympathy and grace."

Davis's second novel, *Maker of Saints,* was published in 1996. The book is thematically very different from *1959.* It is a contemporary murder mystery set in Manhattan and is presumably based on the real story of artist Ana Mendieta and her sculptor husband, who was a suspect in her 1985 death. *Maker of Saints* tells the story of two friends, performance artist Alex Decatur and her best friend Cynthia "Bird" Kincaid. When Alex is found dead after falling from the window of her eighth-floor apartment, Bird is not convinced that she committed suicide, as is determined by the police. Rather, she suspects Alex's lover, Frank, an art critic who effectively ended Bird's former career as a painter with a rabid review. Bird sets out to catalog the dead artist's work and to prove that Frank is a murderer. These tasks are complicated by Bird's feelings about her aborted artistic career and secrets in Alex's life that she uncovers, including the fact that Alex had presented some of Bird's experiences as her own.

Lillian Lewis, writing for *Booklist,* noted influences from African American and Spanish traditions in Davis's writing, "including mystical and spiritual conventions." Lewis commended the book for being different from others of the "homegirl variety" and for having "engaging characters and complex situations." In contrast, Lise Funderburg did not commend the mystery elements of the plot in her *New York Times* review. Funderburg remarked that the "hapless investigation . . . is more tedious than suspenseful" and felt that the strongest points in the book were Bird's "melancholy musings," such as a poetic description of her father as a man who went through life with clenched fists. The reviewer regretted that these "rich pulses are too far apart to build a rhythm." In a more positive assessment, however, a critic for *Publishers Weekly* called the novel "a riveting crime story that enters some of the darker corners of the artistic soul." The reviewer also asserted that Davis "reveals truths" about being an African American artist and concluded, "her narrative pulses with a multiethnic chorus of lively urban voices."

BIOGRAPHICAL/CRITICAL SOURCES:

PERIODICALS

American Libraries, February, 1992, p. 192.
Booklist, January 1, 1992, p. 810; September 15, 1996, p. 219.
Essence, May, 1992, p. 60.
Hungry Mind Review, summer, 1992, p. 15.
Kirkus Reviews, November 1, 1991, p. 1361.
Library Journal, February 15, 1985, p. 171.
Los Angeles Times Book Review, March 1, 1992, p. 1.
New Statesman and Society, June 5, 1992, p. 40.
Newsweek, March 9, 1992, p. 60.

New York Times, February 11, 1992, p. C15; November 17, 1996.
New York Times Book Review, March 15, 1992, p. 18.
Observer (London), June 28, 1992, p. 66.
Parnassus: Poetry in Review, spring, 1985, p. 518.
Publishers Weekly, January 11, 1985, p. 69; December 6, 1991; August 26, 1996, p. 76.
Times Literary Supplement, May 29, 1992, p. 21.
Times Saturday Review, August 1, 1992, p. 33.
Village Voice Literary Supplement, March, 1992, p. 7.
Washington Post Book World, January 26, 1992, p. 12.
Women's Review of Books, May, 1992, p. 6.

*   *   *

DELANY, A(nnie) Elizabeth 1891-1995 (Bessie Delany)

PERSONAL: Born in 1891; died September 25, 1995, in Mount Vernon, NY; daughter of Henry Beard (an Episcopal bishop) and Nanny (an Episcopal school matron; maiden name, Logan) Delany. *Education:* School of Dental and Oral Surgury, Columbia University, D.D.S., 1923.

CAREER: Teacher, Boardman, NC, 1911-13; teacher, Brunswick, GA; dentist, Harlem, NY, 1923-50.

WRITINGS:

(With Sarah Delany and Amy Hill Hearth) *Having Our Say: The Delany Sisters' First 100 Years,* Kodansha International, 1993.

SIDELIGHTS: Much is remarkable about A. Elizabeth Delany's life, as well as that of her sister, Sarah Delany, as *Having Our Say: The Delany Sister' First 100 Years* reveals. Both sisters lived to be over one hundred years old, and as African American women (a term which Delany dislikes, preferring to be called simply "American") experienced many things in life, including segregation and sexism. The sisters are also unique for the fact that both were able to earn college degrees during a period when neither females nor African Americans were encouraged to pursue higher education.

Since childhood, Delany had always been the feistier of the two sisters, who both employed different methods to get their way. According to their memoir, Delany had no fear of confrontation, while her sister took a more subtle approach, smiling sweetly and doing what she wanted anyway. The sisters remained close throughout life and attributed their longevity to having never married. In articles about the Delanys, one sister would often joke that they had lived so long because they did not have to worry about taking care of a man.

In their book, which they wrote with Amy Hill Hearth, Delany and her sister relate that worked summers to earn money to go to college. They were encouraged from an early age to pursue higher education, even though the family had little money to spare. It never occurred to Delany that she would get married—she assumed that she would devote her attention to the career of her choice. All ten of the Delany children graduated from college at a time in history when most people of any race did not get beyond high school, especially women.

Much of the poise that came naturally to the Delany family was taught by their parents. Delany's father had been a slave in a good household, where he was taught to read and write, an act that was illegal at the time. When emancipation occurred, he was glad to be freed but missed the good people he had worked for, according to the Delany sisters. In adulthood their father became an Episcopal bishop, one of the first African Americans to serve in that capacity.

Regardless of their father's status, the Delany family still did not have extra money. The Delany children grew up on the campus of St. Augustine School, the Episcopal institution their father administered. Their mother ran the school's daily operations. Delany remembered being punished severely by her father only once as a child, when she and her sister wandered a little too far from home. At the time, African American girls who wandered too far from safety were often molested or raped with no possibility of seeking justice against the offenders. Delany's father wanted to make sure they did not forget that such an outcome was possible.

Delany's life changed considerably as a child when the Jim Crow laws—which enforced segregation—were enacted in 1896. Being referred to as black confused Delany, who had though she and her siblings represented every skin shade from "nearly white to brown sugar." Suddenly the sisters were faced with new and unpleasant experiences, such as being ordered to drink from different water faucets than white

people, to sit in designated sections in restaurants, or to go to the back of the trolley. Delany remembered sneaking a sip of water from the fountain for white people, concluding that the white water did not taste any different from her own.

After completing high school, Delany left home before her sister did and took two teaching jobs, first in North Carolina and then in Georgia. But the sisters missed each other, and when Sarah moved to New York to study at the Pratt Institute, Delany joined her shortly and entered the dentistry program at Columbia University. Graduating in 1923, she opened a practice in Harlem, becoming the second practicing African American woman dentist in the city. Her rates remained the same until she retired in 1950, since she felt she didn't need to charge extra and wanted to provide a service. Delany claimed that she never turned anyone away who needed dental assistance, regardless of income or skin color.

During the 1920s Delany got involved in the fight for equal rights, with a passion for advocacy that her sister did not share. While Delany's sister supported civil rights strides, she was usually less confrontative in her approach than Delany. Delany marched in a number of protests, particularly after she endured threats at a Ku Klux Klan gathering.

Delany's father died in 1928 and at that point, her mother came to live with her and her sister, remaining with them until she died at the age of ninety-five. Delany retired early to help care for her mother. Delany's sister had been particularly close to their mother, and after her death the sisters moved to the New York suburb of Mount Vernon (and were the first to integrate it), where they remained until Delany's death in 1995. Even after reaching one hundred years in age, they continued to practice yoga daily, ate healthfully, made their own soap, and avoided having a telephone, which Delany called "the biggest nuisance invented by mankind."

As *Having Our Say* reveals, Delany and her sister were opinionated and followed current events closely. They were adamant supporters of voting because, as Delany said, "It's true you can't change the world with your one vote, but if you don't vote, you don't have the right to complain. And honey, I surely do not want to give up my right to complain." Delany said that Hillary Clinton was the one First Lady she had paid attention to since Eleanor Roosevelt; Roosevelt was her favorite First Lady because of the respect she showed the Delany's mother at a gathering. Delany and her sister were fascinated by talk shows, and one interviewer was amazed that the sisters could recite Ross Perot's fiscal policy almost verbatim, even though they had no idea how certain modern-day conveniences such as answering machines worked.

In 1993 Delany and her sister published their memoir, *Having Our Say*. It became a bestseller and catapulted the sisters into sudden fame, going into a third printing that year. The sisters became well known via extensive media publicity and appearances on talk shows. The book, according to *Washington Post Book World* review Sherley Anne Williams, was a welcome celebration of sharing and service. While the book captures each sister's unique voice (Delany's narration is outspoken and her sentences peppered with slang, while her sister Sarah has a softer, measured approach), Williams found it a "fascinating glimpse of an almost hidden racial class." Delany reinforced that idea, according to a *New York* magazine review of the book, saying "I am the kind of Negro that most white people don't know about." A *Publishers Weekly* reviewer gave co-author Hearth credit for "deftly shap[ing] and contextualiz[ing] the sisters' reflections." While reviewer Rhoda Koenig, writing for *New York,* found the book a bit too cute and contrived in places, she also conceded that most readers would be moved by the sisters' lives, which were full of generosity, service, and hard work—and characterized by equal treatment of all, black or white.

BIOGRAPHICAL/CRITICAL SOURCES:

BOOKS

Delany, Annie Elizabeth, Sarah Delany, and Amy Hill Hearth, *Having Our Say: The Delany Sisters' First 100 Years,* Kodonsha International, 1993.

PERIODICALS

American Heritage, October, 1993, pp. 68-79.
Entertainment Weekly, October 6, 1995, p. 16.
Jet, October 16, 1995, pp. 54-55.
Journal and Constitution (Atlanta), September 19, 1993, p. 13.
New York, September 20, 1993, pp. 66-67.
New York Times, September 8, 1993, p. B3; September 23, 1993, p. B1.
New York Times Book Review, December 5, 1993, pp. 15-16.
People Weekly, September 5, 1994, p. 34; October 9, 1995, pp. 48-49.

Publishers Weekly, July 5, 1993, p. 54; February 7, 1994, p. 39.
Smithsonian, October, 1993, pp. 144-164.
Washington Post, September 12, 1993, p. 1; October 25, 1993.
Washington Post Book World, September 12, 1993, p. 1.*

* * *

DELANY, Bessie
See DELANY, A(nnie) Elizabeth

* * *

DELANY, Samuel R(ay, Jr.) 1942-
(K. Leslie Steiner)

PERSONAL: Born April 1, 1942, in New York, NY; son of Samuel R. (a funeral director) and Margaret Carey (a library clerk; maiden name, Boyd) Delany; married Marilyn Hacker (a poet), August 24, 1961 (divorced, 1980); children: Iva Alyxander. *Education:* Attended City College (now of the City University of New York), 1960 and 1962-63.

ADDRESSES: Agent—Henry Morrison, Inc., Box 235, Bedford Hills, NY 10507.

CAREER: Writer. State University of New York at Buffalo, Butler Professor of English, 1975; University of Wisconsin—Milwaukee, senior fellow at the Center for Twentieth Century Studies, 1977; Cornell University, Ithaca, NY, senior fellow at the Society for the Humanities, 1987; University of Massachusetts—Amherst, professor of comparative literature, 1988—.

AWARDS, HONORS: Nebula Awards, Science Fiction Writers of America, 1966, for best novel *Babel-17,* 1967, for best novel *The Einstein Intersection,* 1967, for best short story *"Aye and Gomorrah,"* and 1969, for best novelette *"Time Considered as a Helix of Semi-Precious Stones";* Hugo Award for best short story, World Science Fiction Convention, 1970, for *"Time Considered as a Helix of Semi-Precious Stones";* American Book Award nomination, 1980, for *Tales of Neveryon;* Pilgrim Award, Science Fiction Research Association, 1985; Bill Whitehead Award for Lifetime Achievement in Gay Literature, 1993.

WRITINGS:

SCIENCE FICTION

The Jewels of Aptor (abridged edition bound with *Second Ending* by James White), Ace Books, 1962, hardcover edition, Gollancz, 1968, complete edition published with an introduction by Don Hausdorff, Gregg Press, 1976.

Captives of the Flame (first novel in trilogy; bound with *The Psionic Menace* by Keith Woodcott), Ace Books, 1963, revised edition published under author's original title *Out of the Dead City* (also see below), Sphere Books, 1968.

The Towers of Toron (second novel in trilogy; also see below; bound with *The Lunar Eye* by Robert Moore Williams), Ace Books, 1964.

City of a Thousand Suns (third novel in trilogy; also see below), Ace Books, 1965.

The Ballad of Beta-2 (also see below; bound with *Alpha Yes, Terra No!* by Emil Petaja), Ace Books, 1965, hardcover edition published with an introduction by David G. Hartwell, Gregg Press, 1977.

Empire Star (also see below; bound with *The Three Lords of Imeten* by Tom Purdom), Ace Books, 1966, hardcover edition published with an introduction by Hartwell, Gregg Press, 1977.

Babel-17, Ace Books, 1966, hardcover edition, Gollancz, 1967, published with an introduction by Robert Scholes, 1976.

The Einstein Intersection, slightly abridged edition, Ace Books, 1967, hardcover edition, Gollancz, 1968, complete edition, Ace Books, 1972.

Nova, Doubleday, 1968.

The Fall of the Towers (trilogy; contains *Out of the Dead City, The Towers of Toron,* and *City of a Thousand Suns*), Ace Books, 1970, hardcover edition published with introduction by Joseph Milicia, Gregg Press, 1977.

Driftglass: Ten Tales of Speculative Fiction, Doubleday, 1971.

The Tides of Lust, Lancer Books, 1973.

Dhalgren, Bantam, 1975, hardcover edition published with introduction by Jean Mark Gawron, Gregg Press, 1978.

The Ballad of Beta-2 [and] *Empire Star*, Ace Books, 1975.

Triton, Bantam, 1976.

Empire: A Visual Novel, illustrations by Howard V. Chaykin, Berkley Books, 1978.

Distant Stars, Bantam, 1981.

Stars in My Pocket Like Grains of Sand, Bantam, 1984.

The Complete Nebula Award-Winning Fiction, Bantam, 1986.

The Star Pits (bound with *Tango Charlie and Foxtrot Romeo* by John Varley), Tor Books, 1989.

They Fly at Ciron, Incunabula, 1992.

Equinox, Masquerade, 1994.

The Mad Man, Masquerade, 1994.

Atlantis: Three Tales, Wesleyan University (Middletown, CT), 1995.

Trouble on Triton: An Ambiguous Heterotopia, University Press of New England (Hanover, NH), 1996.

"RETURN TO NEVERYON" SERIES; SWORD AND SORCERY NOVELS

Tales of Neveryon, Bantam, 1979.

Neveryona; or, The Tale of Signs and Cities, Bantam, 1983.

Flight from Neveryon, Bantam, 1985.

The Bridge of Lost Desire, Arbor House, 1987.

OTHER

The Jewel-Hinged Jaw: Notes on the Language of Science Fiction, Dragon Press, 1977, revised edition, Berkley Publishing, 1978.

The American Shore: Meditations on a Tale of Science Fiction by Thomas M. Disch—"Angouleme" (criticism), Dragon Press, 1978.

Heavenly Breakfast: An Essay on the Winter of Love (memoir), Bantam, 1979.

Starboard Wine: More Notes on the Language of Science Fiction, Dragon Press, 1984.

The Motion of Light in Water: Sex and Science Fiction Writing in the East Village, 1957-1965, Arbor House, 1988.

Wagner/Artaud: A Play of Nineteenth and Twentieth Century Critical Fictions, Ansatz Press, 1988.

Straits of Messina (essays; originally published in magazines under pseudonym K. Leslie Steiner), Serconia Press, 1989.

Silent Interviews; On Language, Race, Sex, Science Fiction, and Some Comics: A Collection of Written Interviews, Wesleyan University Press, 1994.

Longer Views: Extended Essays, University Press of New England (Hanover, NH), 1996.

Bread & Wine: An Erotic Tale of New York City; An Autobiographical Account, Juno Books (New York City), 1998.

Times Square Red, Times Square Blue, New York University Press, 1999.

Also author of scripts, director, and editor for two short films, *Tiresias,* 1970, and *The Orchid,* 1971; author of two scripts for the *Wonder Woman Comic Series,* 1972, and of the radio play *The Star Pit,* based on his short story of the same title. Editor, *Quark,* 1970-71.

Contributor to periodicals, including *The New York Review of Science Fiction.*

SIDELIGHTS: "Samuel R. Delany is one of today's most innovative and imaginative writers of science-fiction," comments Jane Branham Weedman in her study of the author, *Samuel R. Delany.* In his science fiction, which includes over fifteen novels and several collections of short stories, the author "has explored what happens when alien world views intersect, collide, or mesh," writes Greg Tate in the *Voice Literary Supplement.* Delany first appeared on the science fiction horizon in the early 1960s, and in the decade that followed he established himself as one of the stars of the genre. Like many of his contemporaries who entered science fiction in the 1960s, he is less concerned with the conventions of the genre, more interested in science fiction as literature, literature which offers a wide range of artistic opportunities. As a result, maintains Weedman, "Delany's works are excellent examples of modern science-fiction as it has developed from the earlier and more limited science-fiction tradition, especially because of his manipulation of cultural theories, his detailed futuristic or alternate settings, and his stylistic innovations."

"One is drawn into Delany's stories because they have a complexity," observes Sandra Y. Govan in the *Black American Literature Forum,* "an acute consciousness of language, structure, and form; a dexterous ability to weave together mythology and anthropology, linguistic theory and cultural history, gestalt psychology and sociology as well as philosophy, structuralism, and the adventure story." At the center of the complex web of personal, cultural, artistic, and intellectual concerns that provides the framework for all of his work is Delany's examination of how language and myth influence reality. "According to [the author]," writes Govan in the *Dictionary of Literary Biography,* "language identifies or negates the self. It is self-reflective; it shapes perceptions." By shaping perceptions, language in turn has the capacity to shape reality. Myths can exercise much the same power. In his science fiction, Delany "creates new myths, or inversions of old ones, by which his protagonists measure themselves and their societies against the traditional myths that Delany includes,"

Weedman observes. In this way, as Peter S. Alterman comments in the *Dictionary of Literary Biography,* the author confronts "the question of the extent to which myths and archetypes create reality."

In societies in which language and myth are recognized as determinants of reality, the artist—one who works in language and myth—plays a crucial part. For this reason, the protagonist of a Delany novel is often an artist of some sort. "The role which Delany defines for the artist is to observe, record, transmit, and question paradigms in society," explains Weedman. But Delany's artists do more than chronicle and critique the societies of which they are a part. His artists are always among those at the margin of society; they are outcasts and often criminals. "The criminal and the artist both operate outside the normal standards of society," observes Alterman, "according to their own self-centered value systems." The artist/criminal goes beyond observation and commentary. His actions at the margin push society's values to their limits and beyond, providing the experimentation necessary to prepare for eventual change.

Delany entered the world of science fiction in 1962 with the publication of his novel *The Jewels of Aptor.* Over the next six years, he published eight more, including *Babel-17, The Einstein Intersection,* and *Nova,* his first printed originally in hardcover. Douglas Barbour, writing in *Science Fiction Writers,* describes these early novels as "colorful, exciting, entertaining, and intellectually provocative to a degree not found in most genre science fiction." Barbour adds that although they do adhere to science fiction conventions, they "begin the exploration of those literary obsessions that define [Delany's] oeuvre: problems of communication and community; new kinds of sexual/love/family relationships; the artist as social outsider. . . ; cultural interactions and the exploration of human social possibilities these allow; archetypal and mythic structures in the imagination."

With the publication of *Babel-17* in 1966, Delany began to gain recognition in the science fiction world. The novel, which earned its author his first Nebula Award, is a story of galactic warfare between the forces of the Alliance, which includes the Earth, and the forces of the Invaders. The poet Rydra Wong is enlisted by Alliance intelligence to decipher communications intercepted from its enemy. When she discovers that these dispatches contain not a code but rather an unknown language, her quest becomes one of learning this mysterious tongue labeled *Babel-17.* While leading an interstellar mission in search of clues, Rydra gains insights into the nature of language and, in the process, discovers the unique character of the enigmatic new language of the Invaders.

Babel-17 itself becomes an exploration of language and its ability to structure experience. A central image in the novel, as George Edgar Slusser points out in his study *The Delany Intersection: Samuel R. Delany Considered as a Writer of Semi-Precious Words,* is that of "the web and its weaver or breaker." The web, continues Slusser, "stands, simultaneously, for unity and isolation, interconnectedness and entanglement." And, as Alterman points out in *Science-Fiction Studies,* "the web is an image of the effect of language on the mind and of the mind as shaper of reality." Weedman elaborates in her essay on the novel: "The language one learns necessarily constrains and structures what it is that one says." In its ability to connect and constrain is the power of the language/web. "Language . . . has a direct effect on how one thinks," explains Weedman, "since the structure of the language influences the processes by which one formulates ideas." At the center of the language as web "is one who joins and cuts—the artist-hero," comments Slusser. And, in *Babel-17,* the poet Rydra Wong demonstrates that only she is able to master this new language weapon and turn it against its creators.

Delany followed *Babel-17* with another Nebula winner, *The Einstein Intersection.* This novel represents a "move from a consideration of the relationship among language, thought, action and time to an analytic and imaginative investigation of the patterns of myths and archetypes and their interaction with the conscious mind," writes Alterman. Slusser sees this development in themes as part of a logical progression: "[Myths] too are seen essentially as language constructs: verbal scenarios for human action sanctioned by tradition or authority." Comparing this novel to *Babel-17,* he adds that "Delany's sense of the language act, in this novel, has a broader social valence."

The Einstein Intersection relates the story of a strange race of beings that occupies a post-apocalyptic Earth. This race assumes the traditions—economic, political, and religious—of the extinct humans in an attempt to make sense of the remnant world in which they find themselves. "While they try to live by the myths of man," writes Barbour in *Foundation,* "they cannot create a viable culture of their own. . . . Their more profound hope is to recognize that they do not have to live out the old myths at all, that the 'difference' they

seek to hide or dissemble is the key to their cultural and racial salvation."

"Difference is a key word in this novel," Weedman explains, "for it designates the importance of the individual and his ability to make choices, on the basis of being different from others, which affect his life, thus enabling him to question the paradigms of his society." The artist is the embodiment of this difference and in *The Einstein Intersection* the artist is Lobey, a musician. The power of Lobey's music is its ability to create order, to destroy the old myths and usher in the new. At its core, then, "*The Einstein Intersection* is . . . a novel about experiments in culture," Weedman comments.

Delany's next novel, *Nova,* "stands as the summation of [his] career up to that time," writes Barbour in *Science Fiction Writers: Critical Studies of the Major Authors from the Early Nineteenth Century to the Present Day.* "Packing his story full of color and incident, violent action and tender introspective moments, he has created one of the grandest space operas ever written." In this novel, Delany presents a galaxy divided into three camps, all embroiled in a bitter conflict caused by a shortage of the fuel illyrion on which they all depend. In chronicling one group's quest for a new source of the fuel, the author examines, according to Weedman, "how technology changes the world and philosophies for world survival. Delany also explores conflicts between and within societies, as well as the problems created by people's different perceptions and different reality models."

"In developing this tale," notes Slusser, "Delany has inverted the traditional epic relationship, in which the human subject (the quest) dominates the 'form.' Here instead is a 'subjunctive epic.' Men do not struggle against an inhuman system so much as inside an unhuman one." The system inside which these societies struggle is economic; the goal of the quester, who is driven by selfishness, is a commodity. Whether the commodity is abundant or scarce, as Jeanne Murray Walker points out in *Extrapolation,* this "is a world where groups are out of alignment, off balance, where some suffer while others prosper, where the object of exchange is used to divide rather than to unite." Walker concludes in her essay that "by ordering the action of *Nova* in the quest pattern, but assuming a value system quite different from that assumed by medieval romance writers, Delany shows that neither pattern nor action operate as they once did. Both fail." Even so, as she continues, "individuals must continue to quest. Through their quests they find meaning for themselves."

After the publication of *Nova,* Delany turned his creative urges to forms other than the novel, writing a number of short stories, editing four quarterlies of speculative fiction, and dabbling in such diverse media as film and comic books. Also at this time, he engaged himself in conceiving, writing, and polishing what would become his longest, most complex, and most controversial novel, *Dhalgren*—a work that would earn him national recognition. On its shifting surface, this novel represents the experience of a nameless amnesiac, an artist/criminal, during the period of time he spends in a temporally and spatially isolated city scarred by destruction and decay. As Alterman relates in the *Dictionary of Literary Biography,* "it begins with the genesis of a protagonist, one so unformed that he has no name, no identity, the quest for which is the novel's central theme." The critic goes on to explain that "at the end Kid has a name and a life, both of which are the novel itself; he is a persona whose experience in *Dhalgren* defines him."

Dhalgren's length and complexity provide a significant challenge to readers, but as Gerald Jonas observes in the *New York Times Book Review,* "the most important fact about Delany's novel . . . is that nothing in it is clear. Nothing is meant to be clear." He adds: "An event may be described two or three times, and each recounting is slightly disconcertingly different from the one before." What is more, continues the reviewer, "the nameless narrator experiences time discontinuously; whole days seem to be excised from his memory." According to Weedman, "Delany creates disorientation in *Dhalgren* to explore the problems which occur when reality models differ from reality." And in Jonas's estimation, "If the book can be said to be *about* anything, it is about nothing less than the nature of reality."

"*Dhalgren* has drawn more widely divergent critical response than any other Delany novel," comments Govan in her *Dictionary of Literary Biography* essay. "Some reviewers deny that it is science fiction, while others praise it for its daring and experimental form." For instance, *Magazine of Fantasy and Science Fiction* book reviewer Algis Budrys contends that "this book is not science fiction, or science fantasy, but allegorical quasi-fantasy on the [James Gould] Cozzens model. Thus, although it demonstrates the breadth of Delany's education, and many of its passages are excellent prose, it presents no new literary

inventions." In his *Science Fiction Writers* essay, Barbour describes the same novel as "the very stuff of science fiction but lacking the usual structural emblems of the genre." "One thing is certain," offers Jonas, "*Dhalgren* is not a conventional novel, whether considered in terms of S.F. or the mainstream."

Following the exhaustive involvement with Kid necessary to complete *Dhalgren,* Delany chose to do a novel in which he distanced himself from his protagonist, giving him a chance to look at the relationship between an individual and his society in a new light. "I wanted to do a psychological analysis of someone with whom you're just not in sympathy, someone whom you watch making all the wrong choices, even though his plight itself is sympathetic," Delany explained in an interview with Larry McCaffery and Sinda Gregory published in their book *Alive and Writing: Interviews with American Authors of the 1980s.* The novel is *Triton;* its main character is Bron.

"*Triton* is set in a sort of sexual utopia, where every form of sexual behavior is accepted, and sex-change operations (not to mention 'refixations,' to alter sexual preference) are common," observes Michael Goodwin in *Mother Jones.* In this world of freedom lives Bron, whom Govan describes in *Black American Literature Forum* as "a narrow-minded, isolated man, so self-serving that he is incapable of reaching outside himself to love another or even understand another despite his best intentions." In an attempt to solve his problems, he undergoes a sex-change operation, but finds no happiness. "Bron is finally trapped in total social and psychological stasis, lost in isolation beyond any help her society can offer its citizens," comments Barbour in *Science Fiction Writers.*

In this novel, once again Delany creates an exotic new world, having values and conventions that differ from ours. In exploring this fictional world, he can set up a critique of our present-day society. In *Triton,* he casts a critical eye, as Weedman points out, on "sexual persecution against women, ambisexuals, and homosexuals." She concludes that the work is "on the necessity of knowing one's self despite sexual identification, knowing one's sexual identity is not one's total identity."

In the 1980s, Delany continued to experiment in his fiction writing. In his *Neveryon* series, which includes *Tales of Neveryon, Neveryona; or, The Tale of Signs and Cities, Flight from Neveryon,* and *The Bridge of Lost Desire,* he chooses a different setting. "Instead of being set in some imagined future, [they] are set in some magical, distant past, just as civilization is being created," observes McCaffery in a *Science-Fiction Studies* interview with Delany. Their focus, suggests Gregory in the same interview, is "power—all kinds of power: sexual, economic, even racial power via the issue of slavery."

Throughout these tales of a world of dragons, treasures, and fabulous cities Delany weaves the story of Gorgik, a slave who rises to power and abolishes slavery. In one story, the novel-length *"Tale of Plagues and Carnivals,"* he shifts in time from his primitive world to present-day New York and back to examine the devastating effects of a disease such as acquired immune deficiency syndrome (AIDS). And, in the appendices that accompany each of these books, he reflects on the creative process itself. Of the four, it is *Neveryona,* the story of Pryn—a girl who flees her mountain home on a journey of discovery—that has received the most attention from reviewers. *Science Fiction and Fantasy Book Review* contributor Michael R. Collings calls it "a stirring fable of adventure and education, of heroic action and even more heroic normality in a world where survival itself is constantly threatened." Faren C. Miller finds the book groundbreaking; she writes in *Locus:* "Combining differing perspectives with extraordinary talent for the *details* of a world—its smells, its shadows, workaday furnishings, and playful frills—Delany has produced a sourcebook for a new generation of fantasy writers." The book also "presents a new manifestation of Delany's continuing concern for language and the magic of fiction, whereby words become symbols for other, larger things," Collings observes.

In *Stars in My Pocket Like Grains of Sand,* Delany returns to distant worlds of the future. The book is "a densely textured, intricately worked out novelistic structure which delights and astonishes even as it forces a confrontation with a wide range of thought-provoking issues," writes McCaffery in *Fantasy Review.* Included are "an examination of interstellar politics among thousands of far flung worlds, a love story, a meandering essay on the variety of human relationships and the inexplicability of sexual attractiveness, and a hypnotic crash-course on a fascinating body of literature which does not yet exist," notes H. J. Kirchhoff in the Toronto *Globe and Mail.*

Beneath the surface features, as Jonas suggests in the *New York Times Book Review,* the reader can discover the fullness of this Delany novel. The reviewer writes: "To unpack the layers of meaning in seem-

ingly offhand remarks or exchanges of social pleasantries, the reader must be alert to small shifts in emphasis, repeated phrases or gestures that assume new significance in new contexts, patterns of behavior that only become apparent when the author supplies a crucial piece of information at just the proper moment." Here in the words and gestures of the characters and the subtle way in which the author fashions his work is the fundamental concern of the novel. "I take the most basic subject here to be the nature of information itself," McCaffery explains, "the way it is processed, stored and decoded symbolically, the way it is distorted by the present and the past, the way it has become a commodity . . . the way that the play of textualities defines our perception of the universe."

"This is an astonishing new Delany," according to Somtow Sucharitkul in the *Washington Post Book World,* "more richly textured, smoother, more colorful than ever before." Jonas commends the novel because of the interaction it encourages with the reader. "Sentence by sentence, phrase by phrase, it invites the reader to collaborate in the process of creation, in a way that few novels do," writes the reviewer. "The reader who accepts this invitation has an extraordinarily satisfying experience in store for him/her." " *Stars in My Pocket Like Grains of Sand* . . . confirms that [Delany] is American SF's most consistently brilliant and inventive writer," McCaffery claims.

Delany's 1992 novel *They Fly at Ciron* grew out of a short story Delany wrote in 1962. Although a version of the story, produced in collaboration with James Sallis, was published in 1971, Delany was not satisfied with it and subsequently reworked it into a novel. The action takes place in a nameless world that consists of small, independent village-states living in isolated harmony. However, this harmony is shattered when a fierce, technologically advanced people known as the Myetrans begin pillaging the land, overpowering and slaughtering the inhabitants of every village they encounter. It is left to a pair of men—Kire, a former member of the Myetrans, and Rahm—to thwart the warring Myetrans. The two men eventually overcome their nemesis by joining forces with the Winged Ones, a species of intelligent, flying beings. *New York Times Book Review* critic Gerald Jones calls the novel "a biting parable about the bloody roots of civilization" and praises the "spare beauty" of Delany's prose. Likewise, an *Analog Science Fiction and Fact* contributor notes that "Delany is a fine, expressive, thoughtful writer."

Critics often comment on Delany's use of fiction as a forum to call for greater acceptance of women's rights and gay rights; yet, as Govan maintains in her *Dictionary of Literary Biography* contribution, "a recurring motif frequently overlooked in Delany's fiction is his subtle emphasis on race. Black and mixed-blood characters cross the spectrum of his speculative futures, both as a testimony to a future Delany believes will change to reflect human diversity honestly and as a commentary on the racial politics of the present."

In novels such as *Babel-17,* Delany demonstrates how language can be used to rob the black man of his identity. "White culture exerts a great influence because it can force stereotypic definitions on the black person," writes Weedman. She adds that "if the black person capitulates to the definition imposed on him by a force outside of his culture, then he is in danger of losing his identity." In his other novels, Govan points out, "Delany utilizes existing negative racial mythologies about blacks, but, in all his works, he twists the commonplace images and stereotypes to his own ends." In using his fiction to promote awareness of the race issue, he and other black writers like him "have mastered the dominant culture's language and turned it against its formulators in protest," writes Weedman.

"Delany is not only a gifted writer," claims Barbour in his *Foundation* article, "he is one of the most articulate theorists of sf to have emerged from the ranks of its writers." In such critical works as *The Jewel-Hinged Jaw, The American Shore,* and *Starboard Wine,* "he has done much to open up critical discussion of sf as a genre, forcefully arguing its great potential as art," adds the reviewer. In his nonfiction, Delany offers a functional description of science fiction and contrasts it with other genres such as naturalistic fiction and fantasy. He also attempts to expand "the domain of his chosen genre by claiming it the modern mode of fiction *par excellence,*" comments Slusser, "the one most suited to deal with the complexities of paradox and probability, chaos, irrationality, and the need for logic and order."

With the publication of *The Motion of Light in Water,* Delany turned to writing about himself. This memoir of his early days as a writer in New York's East Village is "an extraordinary account of life experienced by a precocious black artist of the 1960s," as E. Guereschi writes in *Choice.* The book reveals much of Delany's sexual adventures, with partners of both sexes at the time, his nervous breakdown, and the general sense of living on the edge in an exciting and innovative period. Moreover, the book tells of Delany's realization and eventual acceptance of his homosexuality. Thomas M. Disch, writing in the *American Book Review,* finds that Delany "can't help creating legends and elaborating myths. Indeed, it is his forte, the open secret of his success as an SF writer. [Delany's] SF heroes are variations of an archetype he calls The Kid. . . . In his memoir, the author himself [is] finally assuming the role in which his fictive alter-egos have enjoyed their success. That is the book's strength even more than its weakness." Guereschi believes that the memoir "defines an arduous search for identity," while Disch concludes that *The Motion of Light in Water* "has the potential of being as popular, as representative of its era, as *On the Road.*"

Silent Interviews contains ten written interviews with Delany as well as one interview by him (of composer Anthony Davis) and features Delany discussing topics such as the state of science fiction, race, sexuality, language, and literary criticism. Paul Miller, reviewing the work in the *Village Voice,* remarks that "the most interesting parts of *Silent Interviews* are not when [Delany] talks about the obvious aspects of sexuality and race, but when he discusses the ways they are encoded into our lives."

Samuel R. Delany is not a simple man: a black man in a white society, a writer who suffers from dyslexia, an artist who is also a critic. His race, lifestyle, chosen profession, and chosen genre keep him far from the mainstream. "His own term 'multiplex' probably best describes his work (attitudes, ideas, themes, craftsmanship, all their inter-relations, as well as his relation as artist, to them all)," Barbour suggests. And, adds the reviewer, "His great perseverance in continually developing his craft and never resting on his past achievements is revealed in the steady growth in [his] artistry." In Weedman's estimation, "Few writers approach the lyricism, the command of language, the powerful combination of style and content that distinguishes Delany's works. More importantly," she concludes, "few writers, whether in science fiction or mundane fiction, so successfully create works which make us question ourselves, our actions, our beliefs, and our society as Delany has helped us do." Writing in the *Washington Post Book World,* John Clute places Delany in a central position in modern science fiction. In his best work, Clute believes, Delany "treated the interstellar venues of space opera as analogues of urban life in the decaying hearts of the great American cities. As a black gay

New Yorker much too well educated for his own good, Delany . . . illuminated the world the way a torch might cast light in a cellar."

Sexuality and urban life are also major themes of Delany's work. "New York," explains *Publishers Weekly* critic Michael Bronski, "shines through all of Delany's writing ... even in such intergalactic tales as the Neveryon novels and *Dhalgren* (1975), which are infused with the intensity and momentum of New York, and reflections on AIDS and gay life." Delany's autobiographical graphic novel *Bread and Wine: An Erotic Tale of New York,* writes Bronski, "uses illustrations by Mia Wolff to recount how he and [his partner] Dennis [Ricketts], a New Yorker from a working-class Irish background, met seven years ago, when the latter was homeless and selling old books from a shopping cart on 72nd Street and Broadway." In the volume *Times Square Red, Times Square Blue,* Delany takes a closer look at the area that has defined the seedy side of the city for decades. "Delany cogently argues that the gentrification and Disnification of Times Square—which was achieved through rezoning and enforcement of new 'safe sex' health codes—had far less to do with the officially stated goals of containing AIDS and promoting public safety," Bronski continues, "than it did with fulfilling a well-established, four-decades-long master plan of real estate development." Although most tourists and local people welcome the changes that have regardless of its inspiration, Delany views it as a net loss in neighborhood values. "Now casual contact"—the basis for much city socializing and community feeling—"is being replaced by 'networking'—people with similar interests meeting intentionally to further those interests, which tend to be professional and motive driven," Bronski concludes. "According to Delany, it narrows the common discourse, cutting us off from the broader—and more democratic—aspects of urban living."

BIOGRAPHICAL/CRITICAL SOURCES:

BOOKS

Bleiler, E. F., editor, *Science Fiction Writers: Critical Studies of the Major Authors from the Early Nineteenth Century to the Present Day,* Scribner, 1982.

Contemporary Literary Criticism, Gale, Volume 8, 1978, Volume 14, 1980, Volume 38, 1986.

Dictionary of Literary Biography, Gale, Volume 8: *Twentieth-Century American Science Fiction Writers,* 1981, Volume 33: *Afro-American Fiction Writers after 1955,* 1984.

Kostelanetz, Richard, editor, *American Writing Today,* Whitston, 1991.

McCaffery, Larry, and Sinda Gregory, editors, *Alive and Writing: Interviews with American Authors of the 1980s,* University of Illinois Press, 1987.

McEvoy, Seth, *Samuel R. Delany,* Ungar, 1984.

Peplow, Michael W., and Robert S. Bravard, *Samuel R. Delany: A Primary and Secondary Bibliography, 1962-1979,* G. K. Hall, 1980.

Platt, Charles, editor, *Dream Makers: The Uncommon People Who Write Science Fiction,* Berkley Books, 1980.

Sallis, James, *Ash of Stars: On the Writing of Samuel R. Delaney,* University Press of Mississippi (Jackson), 1996.

Slusser, George Edgar, *The Delany Intersection: Samuel R. Delany Considered as a Writer of Semi-Precious Words,* Borgo, 1977.

Smith, Nicholas D., editor, *Philosophers Look at Science Fiction,* Nelson-Hall, 1982.

Weedman, Jane Branham, *Samuel R. Delany,* Starmont House, 1982.

PERIODICALS

African American Review, spring, 1999, p. 172.

American Book Review, January, 1989.

Analog Science Fiction/Science Fact, April, 1985; June, 1995, p. 168.

Black American Literature Forum, summer, 1984.

Choice, February, 1989.

Commonweal, December 5, 1975.

Extrapolation, fall, 1982; winter, 1989; fall, 1989; fall, 1995, p. 198.

Fantasy Review, December, 1984.

Foundation, March, 1975.

Globe and Mail (Toronto), February 9, 1985.

Locus, summer, 1983; October, 1989; January, 1995, p. 54.

Los Angeles Times Book Review, March 13, 1988.

Magazine of Fantasy and Science Fiction, November, 1975; June, 1980; May, 1989.

Mother Jones, August, 1976.

Nation, October 28, 1996, p. 60.

New York Review of Books, January 29, 1991.

New York Times Book Review, February 16, 1975; March 28, 1976; October 28, 1979; February 10, 1985; January 1, 1995, p. 22; October 29, 1995, p. 42; December 29, 1996, p. 15.

Publishers Weekly, January 29, 1988; October 19, 1992; May 6, 1996, p. 74; July 12, 1999, p. 68.

Science Fiction and Fantasy Book Review, July/August, 1983.

Science Fiction Chronicle, November, 1987; February, 1990.

Science-Fiction Studies, November, 1981; July, 1987; November, 1990.

Village Voice, January 24, 1995, p. 78.

Voice Literary Supplement, February, 1985.

Washington Post Book World, January 27, 1985; August 25, 1991; November 29, 1992, p. 11. *

*   *   *

DEL RIO, Rikki
See GORDON, Lewis Ricardo

*   *   *

DEMBY, William 1922-

PERSONAL: Born December 25, 1922, in Pittsburgh, PA; son of William and Gertrude (Hendricks) Demby; married Lucia Drudi (a novelist); children: James Gabriel. *Education:* Attended West Virginia State College; Fisk University, Nashville, B.A., 1947; additional study at University of Rome, Italy.

ADDRESSES: Home—Box 363, Sag Harbor, NY 11963. *Office*—College of Staten Island of the City University of New York, Staten Island, New York.

CAREER: Novelist. Screenwriter and translator for film and television industry in Rome, Italy. College of Staten Island of the City University of New York, associate professor of English, 1969-89. *Military service:* Served in North Africa during World War II.

MEMBER: European Community of Writers, Alpha Phi Alpha.

WRITINGS:

NOVELS

Beetlecreek, Rinehart, 1950.

The Catacombs, Pantheon, 1965.

Love Story Black, Reed, Cannon & Johnson, 1978.

Blueboy, Pantheon, 1979.

Work represented in anthologies, including *Soon One Morning: New Writing by American Negroes, 1940-1962,* edited by Herbert Hill, Knopf, 1963; *A Native Sons Reader,* edited by Edward Margolies, Lippincott, 1970; *Cavalcade: Negro American Writing From 1760 to the Present,* Houghton, 1971.

SIDELIGHTS: In an interview with John O'Brien in *Studies in Black Literature,* William Demby spoke of writing and the novelist's function: "It must be very, very difficult not to write because there's certainly plenty of things to write, but the whole context of the novel seems to have moved into another ball field. You can do almost anything you want. . . yet, you have to remain in contact with the consciousness of your reader, at the same time you are seeing things yourself. . . . How much can we feed back, how much should we feed back. . .? The novelist must have this function of seeing connections." Demby assessed that "he also has the responsibility (and this may be true for all artists), to make some connection with the past. That is, to illustrate how much of the past is living in the present and how much of the present is only the future and the past. All these things he must bring to life, all the connections, or 'myths' if you will, by which people will imagine things to survive. I suppose that that may be the artist's function, as you say, to make all the connections," he concluded, "because if we disavow the chronological progression idea of history, then it must be something like that tapestry, it must be made up at the same moment of the past, present and future."

Nancy Y. Hoffman wrote: "Demby re-creates himself as a descendant of Michelangelo, of the Renaissance man, whose goal is to be that most elusive of human beings, a whole man—or even in Demby's terms, the Yang-Yin of the whole man-woman. While Demby writes in an age where the anti-hero is king, he himself writes in the Michelangelo tradition of the artist as hero."

BIOGRAPHICAL\CRITICAL SOURCES:

BOOKS

Bone, Robert, *The Negro Novel in America,* revised edition, Yale University Press, 1965.

Lee, A. Robert, editor, *Black Fiction: New Studies in the Afro-American Novel since 1945,* Vision Press, 1980.

Margolies, Edward, *Native Sons: A Critical Study of Twentieth Century Negro American Authors,* Lippincott, 1968.

O'Brien, John, *Interviews with Black Writers,* Liveright, 1973.

Whitlow, Roger, *Black American Literature,* Nelson Hall, 1973.

PERIODICALS

American Quarterly, Summer, 1968.
Chicago Tribune, February 12, 1950.
CLA Journal, June, 1983.
Nation, February 11, 1950.
Negro American Literature Forum, fall, 1976.
Negro Digest, November, 1969.
New York Herald Tribune Book Review, June 27, 1965.
New York Times Book Review, February 26, 1950; July 11, 1965.
Saturday Review of Literature, March 4, 1950.
Studies in Black Literature, number 2, 1972; number 3, 1972.
TriQuarterly, spring, 1969.
Washington Post Book World, December 1, 1986.*

*   *   *

DENG, Francis Mading 1938-

PERSONAL: Born January 1, 1938, in Abyei, Sudan; son of Majok Deng (a Paramount chief); married Dorothy Ludwig; children: Donald, Daniel, David, Dennis. *Education:* Khartoum University, LL.B. (with honors), 1962; Yale Law School, LL.M. 1965, J.S.D., 1967; attended graduate courses at King's College and School of Oriental and African Studies in Jurisprudence and African Law, Islamic and Civil Procedure, 1962-64.

ADDRESSES: Home—708 Highland Ave., NW, Washington, DC 20012. *Office*—The Brookings Institution, 1775 Massachusetts Ave. NW, Washington, DC 20036.

CAREER: Sudanese Ambassador to Scandinavia, 1972-74; Sudanese Ambassador to the United States, 1974-76; Minister of State for Foreign Affairs (Sudan), Khartoum, Sudan, 1976-80; Sudanese Ambassador to Canada (Minister of State), 1980-83; Brookings Institution, Washington, DC, senior fellow, 1988—. Yale Law School, visiting lecturer; representative of the United Nations Secretary-General on Internally Displaced Persons, 1992—.

MEMBER: African Studies Association, African-American Institute, SYNERGOS Institute, African Leadership Forum, Yale Club of New York, Cosmos Club (Washington, DC).

AWARDS, HONORS: Excellence in Publishing Award, Association of American Publishers, 1990.

WRITINGS:

Tradition and Modernization: A Challenge for Law among the Dinka of the Sudan, foreword by Harold D. Lasswell, Yale University Press (New Haven, CT), 1971.
The Dinka of the Sudan, Holt (New York City), 1972.
The Dinka and Their Songs, Clarendon Press (Oxford, England), 1973.
Dynamics of Identification: A Basis for National Integration in the Sudan, Khartoum University Press (Khartoum, Sudan), 1973.
Dinka Folktales: African Stories from the Sudan, illustrated by Martha Reisman, Africana (New York City), 1974.
Africans of Two Worlds: The Dinka in Afro-Arab Sudan, Yale University Press, 1978, published with a foreword by Andre Young, Institute of Asian and African Studies, University of Khartoum (Khartoum), 1978.
Dinka Cosmology, Ithaca Press (London), 1980.
Recollections of Babo Nimir, Ithaca Press, 1982.
(As Francis Deng) *Seed of Redemption: A Political Novel,* Lilian Barber Press (New York City), 1986.
The Man Called Deng Majok: A Biography of Power, Polygyny, and Change, Yale University Press, 1986.
(Editor with Prosser Gifford) *The Search for Peace and Unity in the Sudan,* Wilson Center Press (Washington, DC), 1987.
Cry of the Owl (novel), Lilian Barber Press, 1989.

AS FRANCIS M. DENG

Security Problems: An African Predicament, Indiana University (Bloomington, IN), 1981.
(Editor with Robert O. Collins) *The British in the Sudan, 1898-1956: The Sweetness and the Sorrow,* Hoover Institution Press, Stanford University (Stanford, CA), 1984.
(With M. W. Daly) *Bonds of Silk: The Human Factor in the British Administration of the Sudan,* Michigan State University Press (East Lansing, MI), 1989.
(Editor with Ahmed An-Naim) *Human Rights in Africa: Cross-Cultural Perspectives,* Brookings Institution (Washington, DC), 1990.
(Editor with I. William Zartman) *Conflict Resolution in Africa,* Brookings Institution, 1991.

(With Larry Minear) *The Challenges of Famine Relief: Emergency Operations in the Sudan,* Brookings Institution, 1992.

Protecting the Dispossessed: A Challenge for the International Community, Brookings Institution, 1993.

War of Visions: Conflict of Identities in the Sudan, Brookings Institution, 1995.

(With others) *Sovereignty as Responsibility: Conflict Management in Africa,* Brookings Institution, 1996.

OTHER

Contributor of numerous articles to periodicals, including *Current, Middle East Journal,* and *Brookings Review.*

WORK IN PROGRESS: Internally Displaced Persons: An Agenda for Protection, Assistance and Development, and *Sovereignty, Responsibility and Accountability: An African Challenge.*

SIDELIGHTS: During his career Francis Mading Deng has served in several ambassadorial positions for Sudan, including representing Sudan in the United States and Canada. In 1988 he became a senior fellow at the Brookings Institution in Washington, D.C. Deng has contributed regularly to such journals as the *Brookings Review, Current,* and the *Middle East Journal,* as well as editing and authoring a number of books on Africa in general and Sudan in particular. Deng's prolific and varied output of writing includes both fiction and nonfiction. In 1986 his novel of the Sudanese Civil War, *Seeds of Redemption,* was published. David Dorsey, writing in *World Literature Today,* called the book "an honorably biased account of Sudanese politics since independence. . . . [It is] effective and original, with romantic idealism, well-crafted suspenseful episodes, cyclical plot patterns, subtle humor, and delayed revelations of authorial irony." *Best Sellers* contributor Bernard D. Williams called the *Seeds of Redemption* "a realistic account . . . of the political developments of the civil war in the Sudan."

In Deng's 1990 nonfiction work *Bonds of Silk: The Human Factor in the British Administration of the Sudan,* which he coauthored with M. W. Daly and which is based on a collection of interviews, Deng investigated the nationalist movement in Sudan. Deng's 1992 volume, *The Challenge of Famine Relief: Emergency Operations in the Sudan,* coauthored with international development specialist Larry Minear, is a study of two famines in Sudan during the 1980s—one drought-induced and one conflict-related—and the efforts by various non-governmental relief organizations and government agencies to alleviate the suffering. In a review of *Famine Relief, African Studies Review* contributor Carl C. Mabbs-Zeno maintained, "The strength of this book lies in the compelling insights shared by two, well informed perspectives on the process of relief." Mabbs-Zeno concluded, "The challenge of coordinating a wide variety of relief initiatives is covered particularly well by this book."

Deng proposes in 1995's *War of Visions: Conflict of Identities in the Sudan* that Sudan's internal problems stem from "the state trying to impose a single identity on the entire population," related Williams B. Quandt in a *Foreign Affairs* review; he called *War of Visions* an "important" work. "Deng has done Sudan a great favour," exclaimed an *Economist* contributor, "The world has been told [of its internal crisis]." "Sudan is . . . a state which has a deep ethnic divide," explained the reviewer, lauding *War of Vision* as "an excellent analysis of this division that actually offers some solutions." For *Sovereignty as Responsibility: Conflict Management in Africa,* noted Gail M. Gerhart's *Foreign Affairs* assessment, Deng collaborated with others to "lucidly" present "concepts and arguments [for] . . . prevent[ing], manag[ing], and resolv[ing] conflicts," as well as "promot[ing] norms of responsibility within and among states."

Deng has also written several books on the law, culture, and folklore of Sudan's Dinka people, including a biography of his own father, who was one of their important leaders. Reviewing *The Man Called Deng Majok,* Lina Fruzetti wrote in *Africa Today:* "Entering the world of Deng Majok, the reader is confronted with levels of contradictions, some of which are delicately balanced by the author."

BIOGRAPHICAL/CRITICAL SOURCES:

PERIODICALS

African Studies Review, September, 1995, pp. 150-52.
Africa Today, volume 35, number 1, 1988, p. 81; volume 36, numbers 3 and 4, 1989, p. 88.
Best Sellers, February, 1987, p. 414.
Choice, March, 1992, p. 1150.
Economist, March 16, 1996.
Foreign Affairs, March/April, 1994, pp. 141-42; March/April, 1996, p. 166; May-June, 1997, p. 147.

Times Literary Supplement, March 8, 1991, p. 8.
World Literature Today, summer, 1987, p. 483.*

*   *   *

De VEAUX, Alexis   1948-

PERSONAL: Born September 24, 1948, in New York, NY; daughter of Richard Hill and Mae De Veaux. *Education:* State University of New York Empire State College, B.A., 1976. *Avocational interests:* Studying Egyptian mythology and ancient culture, astrology, art history, "development of a new language composed of musical sounds and derived from African, Haitian, American Black, and neo-sexual sources."

ADDRESSES: Agent—Charlotte Sheedy Literary Agency, 65 Bleeker St., New York, NY 10012.

CAREER: Writer and illustrator. New York Urban League, New York, NY, assistant instructor in English for WIN Program, 1969-71; Frederick Douglass Creative Arts Center, New York City, instructor in creative writing, 1971-72; Bronx Office of Probations, New York City, community worker, 1972-73; Project Create, New York City, instructor in reading and creative writing, 1973-74; teacher of creative writing and literature at Sara Lawrence College, New York City, 1979-80, Vermont College, 1984-85, Wabash College, 1986-87, and State University of New York at Buffalo, 1991—. Intern for Roundabout Theatre/Stage One, 1974; cultural coordinator of Black Expo for the Black Coalition of Greater New Haven, 1975. Poetry editor, *Essence* magazine. Has given readings at colleges, churches, and theaters; has appeared on radio and television programs in New York City, Washington, DC, and New Haven, CT, Artist and co-founder of Coeur de l'Unicorne Gallery, 1975—.

MEMBER: Screen Writers Guild of America (East), Poets and Writers, Inc., American Theatre Association, Black Theatre Alliance, Afro-American Cultural Center (Yale University).

AWARDS, HONORS: First prize from Black Creation, 1972, for short story; best production award from Westchester Community College Drama Festival, 1973, for *Circles;* Art Books for Children awards from Brooklyn Museum, 1974 and 1975, for *Na-ni; Don't Explain: A Song of Billie Holiday* appeared on the American Library Association's Best Books for Young Adults list in 1981; National Endowment for the Arts fellow, 1981; Unity in Media Award, 1982, 1983; MADRE Humanitarian Award, 1984; Fannie Lou Hammer Award, 1984; Coretta Scott King Honor Award, 1988, for *An Enchanted Hair Tale.*

WRITINGS:

(And illustrator) *Na-ni* (juvenile), Harper (New York City), 1973.
(And illustrator) *Spirits in the Street* (novel), Doubleday (New York City), 1973.
Li Chen/Second Daughter First Son (prose poem), Ba Tone Press, 1975.
Don't Explain: A Song of Billie Holiday, Harper, 1980.
Adventures of the Dread Sisters, privately printed, 1982.
Blue Heat: A Portfolio of Poems and Drawings, Diva Enterprises (Brooklyn), 1985.
An Enchanted Hair Tale (juvenile), Harper, 1987.

PLAYS

Circles (one-act), first produced in New York City at the Frederick Douglass Creative Arts Center, March, 1973.
A Little Play and Whip Cream, produced in Harlem at the Young People's Workshop of All Souls Church, 1973.
The Tapestry, first broadcast on KCET-TV (PBS), March, 1976, produced in New York City at the Harlem Performance Center, May, 1976.
A Season to Unravel, first produced Off-Broadway at St. Mark's Playhouse, January 27, 1979.
No, produced in New York City at the New Federal Theatre, 1981.

Also author of *The Fox Street War,* 1979.

OTHER

Contributor of poems and stories to *Sunbury II, Encore, Black Creation, Iowa Review, Open Places, Confirmations, Essence, Village Voice,* and *New Haven Advocate.*

SIDELIGHTS: Writer and illustrator Alexis De Veaux believes that "art should confront head-on the racial and economic inequities in American life," writes *Dictionary of Literary Biography* contributor Priscilla R. Ramsey. As Richard Morris writes in *Gay and Lesbian Literature,* "For Alexis De Veaux, art is not separate from living; art is life, and life is art." In her self-illustrated children's story *Na-ni,* for example, De Veaux writes about a poor Harlem child, Na-ni, whose dream of a new bicycle goes unfulfilled when the family's welfare check is stolen. Reviews of *Na-ni* praised both the storyline and illustrations. "The style is spare, poetic—a performance startlingly personal and alive," Margaret F. O'Connell writes in the *New York Times Book Review.* A *Library Journal* contributor comments, "this is a unique, poignant, and poetic book, illustrated with line drawings of haunting power." Concludes a *Horn Book* reviewer: "Powerful and stark, the text itself has such a poetic quality that the reader is simultaneously aware of the tragedy and the beauty in Na-ni's life."

De Veaux also has a particular interest in addressing the image of the black woman in her work. Ramsey relates that De Veaux once stated: "In all of the work I've done, there is a certain and deliberate care I've taken with laying out the image of the black woman as I have seen or experienced her, which indicates that there is a clear and conscious desire to address myself to her." In *Don't Explain: A Song of Billie Holiday* De Veaux recreates, in lyric form, the life of the renowned jazz singer. *Ms.* contributor June Jordan writes: "De Veaux gives you the life of Billie Holiday fitted into its time, the music of Billie Holiday traced back to its source, the voice of Billie Holiday fathomed for its meaning." *Don't Explain* is written for young adults, and reviewers note that the book will enlighten this audience in several ways. A *Publishers Weekly* contributor believes that *Don't Explain* "can help young people understand inequity and iniquity and arm themselves against the deadly lure of drugs." Mary Laka Cannella concludes in *Best Sellers:* "[*Don't Explain*] is melodic, gripping and emotional. It could turn on some young readers to poetry."

De Veaux's lesbianism also figures into a number of her works. In her poem "Sister Love," for example, De Veaux writes: "But to be silent is to collaborate with my own oppression. To agree—by omission—to generations of negative sexual myths, piled histrionic and solid against me. Against my pussy. And worse: the acceptance of second-class colored/female/leper-status." "Women loving women," notes Morris, "arises in different contexts and various forms, but it is generally not the central motif for De Veaux's projects. The issues surrounding race, gender, and class are more demanding: the violence, poverty, alienation, and, perhaps most of all, the threat of losing hope are De Veaux's main concerns. . . . De Veaux clearly demonstrates that issues of sexuality,

while present and important, are very much intertwined with other issues, some of which can be far more pressing when the survival of the individual and the community are at stake."

BIOGRAPHICAL/CRITICAL SOURCES:

BOOKS

Dictionary of Literary Biography, Volume 38: *Afro-American Writers after 1955: Dramatists and Prose Writers,* Gale (Detroit), 1985.
Gay and Lesbian Literature, Volume 2, St. James Press (Detroit), 1998.

PERIODICALS

Best Sellers, October, 1980.
Booklist, May 15, 1980.
Children's Literature in Education, winter, 1986.
Essence, June, 1981; April, 1995, p. 68.
Horn Book, June, 1973.
Library Journal, May 15, 1973.
Ms., June, 1980.
New York Times, January 26, 1979.
New York Times Book Review, April 1, 1973.
Publishers Weekly, February 5, 1973; May 30, 1980.
School Library Journal, August, 1980.*

* * *

DHLOMO, H(erbert) I(saac) E(rnest) 1903-1956

PERSONAL: Born February 26, 1903, in Siyamu, Edendale, Natal, South Africa; died of complications of heart trouble, October 20, 1956; son of Ezra (a miner and descendent of the royal Zulu house) Dhlomo; married Ethel Kunene, 1931. *Ethnicity:* "African." *Education:* Attended American Board Mission School, Doornfontein, and Amanzimtoti Training Institute (Adams College), Natal. *Politics:* African National Congress.

CAREER: Writer, c. 1935-56. Teacher in Umzumbe, Natal, and then principal of American Board Mission School, Doornfontein, South Africa, 1924-34; assistant editor, *Ilanga Lase Natal,* 1934; journalist, *Bantu World,* 1935-37; librarian, Carnegie Non-European Library, 1937-40; broadcaster, South African Broadcasting Company, 1940.

MEMBER: Bantu Men's Social Centre, Bantu Dramatic and Operatic Society.

WRITINGS:

The Girl Who Killed to Save (Nongqause the Liberator), Lovedale Press (Lovedale, South Africa), 1935.
Moshoeshoe (play), first produced at Bantu Men's Social Centre, Johannesberg, May 2, 1939.
Valley of a Thousand Hills: A Poem, Knox Publishing Co. (Durban, South Africa), 1941.
Dingana (play; limited edition of less than fifty copies), privately printer, 1954.
H. I. E. Dhlomo: Collected Works, edited by Nick Visser and Tim Couzens, Ravan Press (Johannesburg, South Africa), 1985.

Also author of other plays, including *Ntsikana, Cetshwayo, Shaka, Men and Women, Ruby and Frank* (musical), *The Living Dead, Workers Boss Bosses, Ruby, Malaria, The Expert, Mfolozi,* and *Arrested and Discharged* (also known as *The Pass*).

SIDELIGHTS: H. I. E. Dhlomo was born in 1903 in Siymau, Edendale, in the Natal province of South Africa. His parents were Christians, but on his father's side his ancestors were the royal family of the Dhlomos, and—according to *Dictionary of Literary Biography* contributor Tim Couzens—his father may have been raised "in the house of Bambatha, which led the last Zulu resistance movement in 1906." His mother's grandfather was the first person converted to Christianity by the Reverend James Allison, whose followers formed the Edendale community in 1851. Other members of Dhlomo's family would become well known for their talents; his older brother, Rolfes Robert Reginald Dhlomo, known as R. R. R Dhlomo, was a well-known novelist and newspaper editor, and his cousin, Reuben Caluza, was one of South Africa's most famous musicians.

In 1912, Dhlomo's family moved to Johannesburg, where his father worked for a life insurance company and then got a job in mining. Dhlomo's mother took in washing. She encouraged him to attend school; he went first to the American Board Mission School in Doornfontein, and then trained as a teacher at the Amanzimtoti Training Institute, also known as Adams College. About 1924, he completed his studies and obtained a teaching position at Umzumbe on the south coast of the province of Natal. After five years, he moved back to Doornfontein and became principal of the American Board Mission School he had attended.

In 1931, Dhlomo married Ethel Kunene, whom he had met at the Amanzimtoti Training Institute. His interest in journalism grew after his marriage, and in 1935 he quit teaching and began writing for *Bantu World.* He also joined the Bantu Men's Social Center (BMSC), an organization of black, middle-class men. In addition to holding social events, the club gave room to other organizations, such as the African National Congress (ANC), which held meetings in the club's hall. In July of 1932 Dhlomo and others founded the Bantu Dramatic and Operatic Society, and he appeared in several of their productions. It is not known whether he had already begun writing his own plays, or if this experience stimulated him to begin writing them. Dhlomo was devoted to his writing, but his career and education were marred by prejudice: at that time, blacks were not allowed into libraries, and could not attend public theaters. Therefore, he was unable to see any plays, except a very few school performances, and had few models for his own writing.

Dhlomo's first two plays were based on historical characters: *Ntsikana* and *The Girl Who Killed to Save.* These plays both revealed Dhlomo's optimistic belief in progress and improvement. In *The Girl Who Killed to Save,* the AmaXhosa tribe slaughtered all its livestock in order to fulfill a prophecy, ultimately leading to the death of 20,000 people. Dhlomo viewed the catastrophe as good in the long run, because it destroyed old tribal traditions and prepared the people for the new, modern world. Dhlomo also wrote a historical play, *Cetshwayo,* which examined the origins of segregation; it directly attacked current events and politics.

In 1937 Dhlomo became a librarian at the Carnegie Non-European Library, and continued to write plays, which he produced and directed using local actors and resources. Dhlomo was a serious person, not known for having a sense of humor; he believed in his destiny as a genius. This high opinion of himself caused trouble both in his marriage and in his work, and when he lost both he began to suffer financially. He left his wife and moved to Durban, where he slept on the beach, and looked for a job. He eventually got a job with the South African Broadcasting Company, but it did not last, due in part to his bitterness. Dhlomo's experiences with his wife and job, and the bitterness they engendered, led him to become more radical politically. He turned his disappointment outward, believing that the reason he was not appreciated or understood was related to the oppression of blacks.

Dhlomo's second book, a collection of poems titled *Valley of a Thousand Hills,* was published in 1941. The title poem was an epic that celebrated the legacy of the Zulu tribe, and tried to integrate their great past and the present, as well as the future. Dhlomo was one of the first African literary critics. Between 1936 and 1946, he wrote many articles on drama and poetry, and expressed his belief that modern African writers should go back to their roots, to their tribal ancestors, and gather material from these sources. He believed that the tribal cultures should be preserved and continued, and that this preservation, integrated with modern life, would lead to a great flowering of literature. He drew on traditional tribal songs of war, hunting, love, agriculture, and lullabies, as well as folk poetry and incantations. He believed that modern poetry and drama could spring from this rich matrix and draw strength from it. However, he did not believe that poetry and drama should spring only from African roots, but that it should integrate the traditions and forms of European arts. Couzens quoted him as saying, "Great art or thought is more than racial or national. It is universal, reflecting the image, the spirit, of the All-Creative Being who knows neither East nor West, Black nor White, Jew nor Gentile, time nor space, life nor death."

Although Dhlomo had been a nonsmoker and nondrinker for most of his life, in the 1940s he began smoking and drinking heavily, perhaps in response to his marital and employment difficulties. These excesses may have led to his early death at age 53, in 1956, and he was soon largely forgotten until the early 1970s, when a collection of his manuscripts was discovered. A collection of his major works was published in 1985.

BIOGRAPHICAL/CRITICAL SOURCES:

BOOKS

Dictionary of Literary Biography, Volume 157: *Twentieth-Century Caribbean and Black African Writers, Third Series,* Gale (Detroit, MI), 1996.*

*　　*　　*

DIOP, Birago (Ismael) 1906-1989
(Max, d'Alain Provist)

PERSONAL: Some sources spell middle name "Ismail"; born December 11, 1906, in Ouakam (some sources say Dakar), Senegal; died November 25, 1989, in Dakar, Senegal; son of Ismael (a master mason) and Sokhna (Diawara) Diop; married Marie-Louise Pradere (an accountant), 1934 (deceased); children: Renee, Andree. *Education:* Received doctorate from Ecole Nationale Veterinaire de Toulouse, 1933; attended Institut de Medecine Veterinaire Exotique, c. 1934, and Ecole Francaise des Cuirs et Peaux.

CAREER: Head of government cattle inspection service in Senegal and French Sudan (now Mali), c. 1934-42; employed at Institut de Medecine Veterinaire Exotique in Paris, France, 1942-44; interim head of zoological technical services in Ivory Coast, 1946; head of zoological technical services in Upper Volta (now Burkina Faso), 1947-50, in Mauritania, 1950-54, and in Senegal, 1955; administrator for Societe de la Radio-diffusion d'Outre-Mer (broadcasting during early 1960s; veterinarian in private practice in Dakar, Senegal, beginning c. 1964. Vice- president of Confederation Internationale des Societes d'Auteurs et Compositeurs, 1982; president of reading board of Nouvelles Editions Africaines (publisher); official of Institut des Hautes Etudes de ' Defense Nationale (French national defense institute). *Military service:* Nurse in military hospital in St.-Louis, Senegal, 1928-29.

MEMBER: Association des Ecrivains du Senegal (president), Bureau Senegalais des Droits d'Auteur (president of administrative council), Societe des Gens de Lettres de France, Pen-Club, Rotary-Club de Dakar, Anemon.

AWARDS, HONORS: Grand Prix Litteraire de l'Afrique-Occidentale Francaise, for *Les Contes d'Amadou Koumba;* Grand Prix Litteraire de l'Afrique Noire from Association des Ecrivains d'Expression Francaise de la Mer et de l'Outre Mer (now or *Contes et lavanes*). Officier de la Legion d'Honneur; commandeur des Palmes Academiques; chevalier de l'Etoile Noire; chevalier du Merite Agricole; chevalier des Arts et des Lettres; grand-croix de l'Ordre National Senegalais; grand officier de l'Ordre de la Republique Tunisienne; grand officier de l'Ordre National Ivoirien.

WRITINGS:

STORY COLLECTIONS

Les Contes d'Amadou Koumba (includes "Maman-Caiman," "Les Mamelles," and "Sarzan"), Fasquelle, 1947, reprinted, Presence Africaine, 1978.

Les Nouveaux Contes d'Amadou Koumba (title means "The New Tales of Amadou Koumba"; includes "L'Os de Mor Lam"), preface by Leopold Sedar Senghor, Presence Africaine, 1958.

Contes et lavanes (title means "Tales and Commentaries"), Presence Africaine, 1963, (Includes "A Judgment"), translation and introduction by Dorothy S. Blair, Oxford University Press, 1966.

Contes choisis, edited with an introduction by Joyce A. Hutchinson, Cambridge University Press, 1967.

Contes d'Awa, illustrations by A. Diallo, Nouvelles Editions Africaines, 1977.

Mother Crocodile: Maman-Caiman, translation and adaptation by Rosa Guy, illustrations by John Steptoe, Delacorte Press, 1981.

PLAYS; ADAPTED FROM HIS SHORT STORIES

Sarzan, performed in Dakar, Senegal, 1955.

L'Os de Mor Lam (performed at Theatre National Daniel Sorano, Senegal, 1967-68), Nouvelles Editions Africaines, 1977.

Also adapted "Maman-Caiman" and "Les Mamelles."

OTHER

Leurres et lueurs (poems; title means "Lures and Lights"; includes "Viatique"), Presence Africaine, 1960.

Birago Diop, ecrivain senegalais (collection), ry by Roger Mercier and M. and S. Battestini, F. Nathan, 1964.

Memoires (autobiography), Volume 1: *La Plume raboutee* (title means "The Piecemeal Pen"), Presence Africaine, 1978, Volume 2: *A Rebrousse-temps* (title means "Against the Grain of Time"), Presence Africaine, 1982, Volume 3: *A Rebrousse-gens: Epissures, entrelacs, et reliefs,* Presence Africaine, 1985, Volume 4: *Senegal du temps de,* L'Harmattan, c. 1989, Volume 5, *Et les yeux pour me dire,* L'Harmattan, 1989.

Work represented in anthologies, including *Anthologie de la nouvelle poesie negre et malagache de langue francaise,* edited by Leopold Sedar Senghor, Presses Universitaires de France, 1948; *A Book of African Verse,* Heinemann, 1964; and *An Anthology of African and Malagasy 5.*

Contributor to periodicals, including *L'Echo des etudiants* (sometimes under pseudonyms Max and d'Alain Provist), *L'Etudiant noir,* and *Presence africaine.*

SIDELIGHTS: Birago Diop was an author and poet best known for short stories inspired by the folktales of West Africa. Born and raised in Senegal, formerly a French colony, Diop wrote in French, although some of his works have been translated into English and other languages. As a young man Diop left Senegal for France, where he studied veterinary science at the Ecole Nationale Veterinaire in Toulouse. After receiving his doctorate in 1933 he went to Paris, where he encountered a community of black writers from the French colonial empire that included Aime Cesaire of Martinique and Leopold Sedar Senghor of Senegal. Senghor and Cesaire led the Negritude movement, which rejected the assimilation of black colonial peoples into French culture, asserting the value of the black heritage. Inspired by the movement, Diop wrote poems such as "Viatique," a vivid portrayal of the initiation ceremony of an African tribe. His work appeared in two of Senghor's groundbreaking efforts at publishing Franco-African authors: the journal *L'Etudiant noir* and the book *Anthologie de la nouvelle poesie negre et malagache de langue francaise.*

Later in the 1930s Diop returned to French West Africa, and in his work as a government veterinarian he traveled widely throughout the region, sometimes into remote areas of the interior. He turned from poetry to the short story, "the most traditional form of African literature," as Joyce A. Hutchinson observed in her introduction to *Contes choisis.* For centuries African literature was primarily spoken, and storytellers such as the *griots* of West Africa found the short story a convenient form in which to provide moral p published his first collection of stories, *Les Contes d'Amadou Koumba,* he said they were drawn verbatim from a *griot* named Amadou whom he had met during his travels. In a later interview for *Le Soleil,* however, he acknowledged that Amadou was a composite of many storytellers he had encountered, including members of his own family.

In fact many commentators, including Senghor, have suggested that Diop's stories succeed on the printed page because they are a skillful combination of African oral tradition and the author's own considerable talent as a writer. Diop "uses tradition, of which he is proud," Hutchinson wrote in 1967, "but he does not insist in an unintelligent fashion on tradition for tradition's sake. He resuscitates the spirit and the style of the traditional *conte* [tale] in beautiful French, without losing all the qualities which were in the vernacular version." ed for their varied and skillful observations on human nature. In "L'Os de Mor

Lam," for instance, a selfish man prefers to be buried alive rather than share his supper with a neighbor. The author often drew upon traditional animal tales, which put human foibles on display by endowing animals with exaggerated forms of human characteristics. In one African story cycle, which Diop used extensively, a physically strong but foolish hyena is repeatedly bested by a hare who relies on intelligence rather than strength.

Reviewers generally note that Diop preferred laughter to melodrama in his stories, and in *The African Experience in Literature and Ideology* Abiola Irele stressed the "gentle" quality of Diop's humor. But other commentators agreed with Dorothy S. Blair, who in her foreword to *Tales of Amadou Koumba* held that some stories contain a sharper element of social satire. "Sarzan," for example, who returns from service in the French Army and tries to impose French culture on his people. And in "A Judgment," according to John Field of *Books and Bookmen,* a couple with marital problems must endure first the "pompous legalism" of the village elders and then the "arbitrary and callous" judgment of a Muslim lord.

In adapting the oral folktale to a written form, Diop strove to maintain the spontaneity of human speech, and to do so he interspersed his prose with dialogue, songs, and poems—all part of the African storyteller's technique, as Hutchinson noted. "Diop's use of dialogue is masterly," she remarked. "He uses the whole range of human emotional expression: shouts, cries, tears, so vividly that one can without difficulty imagine and supply the accompanying gestures and the intonation of the voice." Diop adapted several of his stories for the stage, including "Sarzan" and "L'Os de Mor Lam." Writing in *World Literature Today,* Eileen Julien praised Diop's adaptation of "L'Os" for "depict[ing] in a warm and colorful style the manners of an African village," including "gatherings, prayers, communal rites and . . . ubiquitous, compelling chatter." "All of these," she averred, "are the matter of which theatre is made."

Diop's adaptations of the folktale have made him one of Africa's most widely read authors, and he received numerous awards and distinctions. His first volume of tales promptly won the Grand Prix Litteraire de l'Afrique-Occidentale Francaise; for Diop's second volume, Senghor, who had become one of Senegal's most prominent writers and political leaders, wrote a laudatory preface. After Senghor led Senegal to independence in 1960 he sought Diop as the country's first ambassador to Tunisia. Between 1978 and 1985 Diop produced three highly account of the early days of the Negritude movement in Paris. Summarizing Diop's literary achievement, Hutchinson praised the author for showing that short stories in the traditional African style are "not just children's tales, not just sociological or even historical material, but a work of art, part of Africa's cultural heritage."

BIOGRAPHICAL\CRITICAL SOURCES:

BOOKS

Diop, Birago, *Les Nouveaux Contes d'Amadou Koumba,* preface by Leopold Sedar Senghor, Presence Africaine, 1958.

Diop, Birago, *Tales of Amadou Koumba,* translation and introduction by Dorothy S. Blair, Oxford University Press, 1966.

Diop, Birago, *Contes choisis,* edited with an introduction by Joyce A. Hutchinson, Cambridge University Press, 1967.

Diop, Birago, *Memoires,* three volumes, Presence Africaine, 1978.

Irele, Abiola, *The African Experience in Literature and Ideology,* Heinemann, 1981.

PERIODICALS

Books and Bookmen, October, 1986.
Le Soleil, December 11, 1976.
World Literature Today, winter, 1979; autumn, 1986.

OBITUARIES:

PERIODICALS

New York Times, November 29, 1989.*

*   *   *

DJOLETO, (Solomon Alexander) Amu 1929-

PERSONAL: Born July 22, 1929, in Manyakpogunor, Ghana; son of Frederick Badu (a Presbyterian minister) and Victoria Shome Tetteh ("a modest trader") Djoleto; married Ann Augusta Wulff (a school administrator), May 27, 1961; children: Ofeibia Lomotey, Nii Amu, Manaa Otobia. *Education:* University of Ghana, B.A. (with honors), 1958, postgraduate degree, 1960; studied book production at University of London, 1965-66. *Politics:* "Nil." *Religion:* Presbyterian.

ADDRESSES: Home—P.O. Box C2217, Cantonments Communications Centre, Accra, Ghana. *Office*—Ministry of Education, P.O. Box M45, Accra, Ghana. *Agent*—Heinemann Publishers, Halley Court, Jordan Hill, Oxford OX2 8EJ, England.

CAREER: Ghana Ministry of Education, Government Secondary Technical School, Takoradi, education officer, 1958, became both senior education officer and head of the English department, 1963, assistant headmaster, 1964; affiliated with a publishing firm, London, England, 1965-66; Ghana Ministry of Education, editor of *Ghana Teachers Journal,* 1966, became principal education officer in charge of information, public relations, and publications, 1967, deputy chief education officer and head of the planning division, 1973, executive director of the Ghana Book Development Council, 1975-89. Ghana Publishing Corporation, board member, beginning 1968; United Nations Educational, Scientific and Cultural Organization, consultant on book development councils to several African countries, 1981-88; United Nations University, consultant, 1988-89; Ghana Ministry of Education, textbooks consultant, 1989—; Authorship Development Fund, vice-chairperson of board.

AWARDS, HONORS: Commonwealth Bursary Award, 1965; Amu Djoleto Award instituted by Ghana Book Publishers Association, 1990.

WRITINGS:

NONFICTION

English Practice for the African Student (textbook), Macmillan (London), 1967, revised and updated as *English Practice,* Macmillan, 1990.
(Editor with T. H. S. Kwami) *West African Prose Anthology,* Heinemann (London), 1974.
(Editor) *Ten Stories from Chaucer,* Ghana Publishing, 1979.
Books and Reading in Ghana, United Nations Educational, Scientific and Cultural Organization (Paris), 1985.
(Editor) *Chaucer's Prologue and Five Stories,* Sedco Publishing, 1987.

Also contributor to *Publishing in the Third World: Knowledge and Development,* Heinemann, 1985.

FICTION

The Strange Man, Heinemann (London), 1967.
Money Galore, Heinemann, 1975.
Hurricane of Dust, Longman, 1988.

POETRY

Amid the Swelling Act, Heinemann, 1992.

CHILDREN'S BOOKS

Obodai Sai (novel), Heinemann, 1990.
Twins in Trouble, Heinemann, 1991.
The Frightened Thief, Heinemann, 1992.

Also author of *Kofi Loses His Way,* 1996; *The Girl Who Knows about Cars,* 1996; and *Akos and the Fir Ghost,* 1997.

SIDELIGHTS: Amu Djoleto has held a variety of positions in the Ministry of Education of his native country, Ghana. He also has a substantial background in the world of publishing. Djoleto has published books in several genres. In the nonfiction field, he has edited some of the works of Geoffrey Chaucer; put together a report entitled *Books and Reading in Ghana* for the United Nations Educational, Scientific and Cultural Organization; and written a textbook on the English language for use by African students. He has written several books for children, a book of poetry, and three novels for adult readers. His first novel, *The Strange Man,* depicts the life of Mensa, a Ghanaian boy who suffers terribly under various school headmasters. As an adult, Mensa grapples with village jealousies and troubles within his own family. *Money Galore* is a serious yet witty satire, also set in Ghana.

Djoleto told *CA:* "I write for four principal reasons. First, I feel I should write, that's all. Second, I desperately need the money from writing. In Ghana, government salaries as I have endured are uneconomic. Third, and more important, I have always strongly held that Africans must write for Africans in the first place. Besides, Africans must write textbooks for Africans at all levels of education to begin the process of the development of the indigenous and, of course, the endogenous African intellectual. Fourth, I write both prose and poetry to record my reaction to my time and circumstance in hope that it might be useful primary source material."*

*   *   *

DOMINI, Rey
   See LORDE, Audre (Geraldine)

DRIVER, David E. 1955-

PERSONAL: Born October 17, 1955, in Chicago, IL; son of Edward (a postman) and Esther (a homemaker; maiden name, Williams) Driver. *Ethnicity:* "African American." *Education:* Bradley University, B.A., 1976; University of Chicago Business School, M.B.A., 1984.

ADDRESSES: Office—The Noble Press, Inc., 213 West Institute Place, Suite 508, Chicago, IL 60610.

CAREER: Book publisher, social activist, and investor. Staff accountant at Arthur Young & Company, 1976-78; finance manager at International Hospital Supply Corporation, 1978-80; account executive at Merrill Lynch Capital Markets, 1980-82, vice president, 1982-88; founder and president of Noble Press, Inc., 1988—; author, 1989—.

MEMBER: Black Literary Society (founder), National Association of Black Book Publishers (founding member), Society of Illinois Book Publishers (secretary).

WRITINGS:

The Good Heart Book: A Guide to Volunteering, Noble Press (Chicago), 1989, 2nd edition, 1991.
Defending the Left: An Individual's Guide to Fighting for Social Justice, Individual Rights, and the Environment, Noble Press, 1992.
Bronzeville, Noble Press, 1999.

SIDELIGHTS: Thriving in spite of childhood poverty, David E. Driver's career successes have ranged from institutional investing in the booming 1980s to book publishing in the 1990s. In all these ventures, he has committed himself to giving something back to his community by engaging in various forms of social activism. These activities include working with the Boys and Girls Clubs of America and various speaking engagements.

As a child, Driver's small stature did not lend itself to athletic activities; therefore, he was "a real bookworm type," as he told a *Chicago Tribune* contributor. This did not preclude such high ambitions, however, as becoming a race car driver. With his grandfather's admonition that he instead become a professional, such as a doctor or an attorney, Driver set his sights on the latter—not in the least because he could not stand the sight of blood. But growing up on public assistance in an inner-city neighborhood on Chicago's West Side did not pave an easy path to a

legal career. "I always had high aspirations, though I never really doubted that I was going to make it at something," he stated in an interview published in *Contemporary Black Biography (CBB)*.

This confidence, along with excellent grades, garnered Driver admission to Lindblom High School, an elite public trade school. It was there that Driver first became aware of his family's poverty. "At Lindblom you had a lot of kids from middle-class black families. My clothes were not as nice looking [as those of the other kids], and so I became very fashion conscious for awhile!," he stated fondly in *CBB*. Though Driver and his siblings were raised by their single mother and were the first generation to attend college, it has always been an unstated assumption that they would seek a higher education despite the family's shaky financial situation. Determined to earn degrees, Driver and his siblings managed to find grants and loans that enabled them to attend college.

At Bradley University in Peoria, Illinois, Driver confronted his immersion into an almost all-white student body by running successfully for sophomore class president, becoming the first black to do so. He also joined groups, such as the Black Student Union and a black fraternity, Phi Beta Sigma, both of which involved him in volunteer work that was to play a significant role in his life and career. Among the projects Driver was associated with- -or initiated— were an inner-city literacy tutoring program and numerous food drives. Having decided to become a business attorney, Driver followed the advice of a counselor who suggested that he change his major from political science to accounting.

In 1976, upon receiving his B.A. from Bradley and a CPA license from the State of Illinois, Driver accepted a position as a staff accountant at Arthur Young & Company. He worked there for two years, until a client contact led him to a job at the International Hospital Supply Corporation. As a finance manager from 1978 to 1980, Driver dealt with foreign currency markets, where companies buy and sell money from other countries in order to protect their foreign investments from exchange rate fluctuations.

With this experience in foreign currencies, Driver landed a job at Merrill Lynch Capital Markets in 1980, where he served as an account executive until becoming vice president in 1982. He became a pioneer in the emerging field of stock and bond futures, wherein an investor speculates on what the price of these securities will be at a specified date in the future. Because it was such a new field, Driver spent nearly two years trying to convince clients of the value of such investments—difficult in an industry that worked primarily on commission—but Driver's supervisors had faith in his judgment. When it turned out that these new kinds of investments were extremely lucrative, he was, for some time, Chicago's only institutional futures broker, or "the only one in town playing the game," as he put it in *CBB* interview. Driver parlayed this advantage into huge profits for Merrill Lynch—and himself—while the competition scurried to catch up. Meanwhile he received his M.B.A. in economics from the prestigious University of Chicago Business School in 1984.

By 1988, Driver told *Publishers Weekly,* "It was time to take the money and run." In fact, he had been plotting his departure from the world of corporate finance since about 1985. As Driver told *CBB,* he found the brokering to be "self-serving and lacking in social significance," a drawback he was finding increasingly unacceptable as corporate demands on his time and energy left less room for his varied volunteer efforts. These activities included working with the Boys and Girls Clubs of America, coaching a basketball team of homeless children, and speaking to black M.B.A.s as the head of a United Way recruitment committee.

A long-standing interest in writing prompted Driver to take a number of creative writing classes at the University of Chicago, and this, coupled with his community activism, gave him the idea to start his own publishing company, one that would focus on books with social or environmental significance. Driver hoped that certain business tools he had acquired, including the use of demographic surveys and databases, would help overcome the marketing obstacles such titles traditionally face.

In 1988, Driver founded The Noble Press, and its first title was his own, *The Good Heart Book: A Guild to Volunteering.* This book detailed the issues surrounding a number of social ills, ranging from illiteracy to inner-city poverty, and it provided a step-by-step approach to becoming an effective volunteer. He started the company with an initial outlay of $250,000. Able to live off the interest on investments he had made during his previous career, Driver received no salary, but hired a small staff and initially ran the operation out of his apartment.

By 1991 the Noble Press had a full-time staff of five working in the refurbished loft of a former bicycle factory, and a number of its titles had received critical notice. *The Parents' Guide to Innovative Education,* by Ann W. Dodd, for example, received a *Child* magazine award in 1992. However, the company struggled financially as it released titles true to its social mission but lacking sufficient sales, including *Eco-Warriors, A Just and Lasting Peace,* and books tackling the issues of homelessness and child abuse. Driver concluded that such titles were perhaps better suited to college presses and decided to take a more market-driven approach by shifting Noble's focus to general interest titles for the black community- at-large, including fiction and even romance novels.

The Noble Press' breakthrough book, *Volunteer Slavery: My Authentic Negro Experience,* had significant popular appeal and a social message, as well. The book gave an irreverent and unforgiving account of black author Janet Nelson's four years as a liberal activist struggling to make her voice heard as a writer for the *Washington Post Magazine.* It also explored the meaning of black identity in the United States. Released in the spring of 1993, *Volunteer Slavery* sold more than forty thousand hardcover copies before Noble sold it to Penguin for a paperback release that became a national bestseller. It also won an American Book Award in 1994. "It's changed our lives around here a lot," Driver told the *Chicago Tribune.* "We were always well-thought-of in our little literary circle as a progressive, high-quality publishing company, but this book has risen us to new levels." Other publications, such as *Black and Single* by Larry E. Davis, sold equally as well for Noble.

These and other successes proved the wisdom of diversifying the company's catalog and targeting a black audience. Noble turned its first profit in 1993, as annual sales reached nearly one million dollars, and its distribution outlets increased to six thousand. Unwilling to let the opportunities of new technology pass by the Noble Press, Driver began exploring avenues for Internet applications, which included placing the firm's catalog on-line. He also founded the Black Literary Society, a book club that places its reading list of Noble Press and other black-oriented books on the Internet. In 1995, Driver explored the possibility of a CD-ROM that would document a traveling museum exhibit featuring black architects.

Unsatisfied with simply publishing significant and entertaining books and helping to manifest the potential of a once underestimated and under-served African American reading public, Driver continues the volunteer work that has always been his marker of personal success. He founded and runs a program called Young Chicago Authors that provides Saturday morning workshops for aspiring high school-age writers. Driver invites accomplished writers and others well-versed in the trade to speak to the students and help them hone their skills.

BIOGRAPHICAL/CRITICAL SOURCES:

BOOKS

Contemporary Black Biography, Gale (Detroit), 1996.

PERIODICALS

American Banker, December 6, 1990.
Booklist, December 1, 1992.
Chicago Tribune, April 11, 1990; July 25, 1993.
Essence, November, 1993.
Library Journal, February 15, 1995.
Los Angeles Sentinel, April 19, 1990.
Publishers Weekly, March 15, 1992; March 15, 1993; May 2, 1994.
Time, October 10, 1994.

*   *   *

Du BOIS, W(illiam) E(dward) B(urghardt) 1868-1963

PERSONAL: Born February 23, 1868, in Great Barrington, MA; immigrated to Ghana, 1960; naturalized Ghanaian citizen, 1963; died August 27, 1963, in Accra, Ghana; buried in Accra; son of Alfred and Mary (Burghardt) Du Bois; married Nina Gomer, 1896 (died, 1950); married Shirley Graham (an author), 1951 (died, 1977); children: Burghardt (deceased), Yolande Du Bois Williams (deceased). *Education:* Fisk University, B.A., 1888; Harvard University, B.A. (cum laude) 1890, M.A., 1891, Ph.D., 1896; graduate study at University of Berlin, 1892-94. *Politics:* Joined Communist Party, 1961.

CAREER: Wilberforce University, Wilberforce, OH, professor of Greek and Latin, 1894-96; University of Pennsylvania, Philadelphia, assistant instructor in sociology, 1896-97; Atlanta University, Atlanta, GA, professor of history and economics, 1897-1910, professor and chairman of department of sociology, 1934-44; National Association for the Advancement of Colored People (NAACP), New York City, director of publicity and research and editor of *Crisis,*

1910-34, director of special research, 1944-48; Peace Information Center, New York City, director, 1950. Co-founder and general secretary of Niagra Movement, 1905-09.

Organizer of the Pan-African Congress, 1919. Vice-chairman of the Council of African Affairs, 1949. American Labor Party candidate for U.S. Senator from New York, 1950.

AWARDS, HONORS: Spingarn Medal, NAACP, 1932; elected to the National Institute of Arts and Letters, 1943; Lenin International Peace Prize, 1958; Knight Commander of the Liberian Humane Order of African Redemption conferred by the Liberian Government; Minister Plenipotentiary and Envoy Extraordinary conferred by President Calvin Coolidge; LL.D., Howard University, 1930, and Atlanta University, 1938; Litt.D., Fisk University, 1938; L.H.D. from Wilberforce University, 1940; also recipient of honorary degrees from Morgan State College, University of Berlin, and Charles University (Prague).

WRITINGS:

NOVELS

The Quest of the Silver Fleece, A. C. McClurg, 1911.
Dark Princess: A Romance, Harcourt, 1928.
The Ordeal of Mansart (first novel in trilogy), Mainstream Publishers, 1957.
Mansart Builds a School (second novel in trilogy), Mainstream Publishers, 1959.
Worlds of Color (third novel in trilogy), Mainstream Publishers, 1961.
The Black Flame (trilogy collection; includes *The Ordeal of Mansart, Mansart Builds a School,* and *Worlds of Color*), Kraus Reprint, 1976.

POETRY

Selected Poems, Ghana University Press, c. 1964.

PLAYS

Haiti, included in *Federal Theatre Plays,* edited by Pierre De Rohan, Works Progress Administration, 1938.

Also author of pageants, "The Christ of the Andes," "George Washington and Black Folk: A Pageant for the Centenary, 1732-1932," and "The Star of Ethiopia."

WORKS EDITED IN CONJUNCTION WITH THE ANNUAL CON-FERENCE FOR THE STUDY OF NEGRO PROBLEMS

Mortality Among Negroes in Cities, Atlanta University Press, 1896.

Social and Physical Condition of Negroes in Cities, Atlanta University Press, 1897.

Some Efforts of American Negroes for Their Own Social Benefit, Atlanta University Press, 1898.

The Negro in Business, Atlanta University Press, 1899.

A Select Bibliography of the American Negro: For General Readers, Atlanta University Press, 1901.

The Negro Common School, Atlanta Univ. Press, 1901.

The Negro Artisan, Atlanta University Press, 1902.

The Negro Church, Atlanta University Press, 1903.

Some Notes on Negro Crime, Particularly in Georgia, Atlanta University Press, 1904.

A Select Bibliography of the Negro American, Atlanta University Press, 1905.

The Health and Physique of the Negro American, Atlanta University Press, 1906.

Economic Co-operation among Negro Americans, Atlanta University Press, 1907.

The Negro American Family, Atlanta University Press, 1908.

Efforts for Social Betterment Among Negro Americans, Atlanta University Press, 1909.

(With Augustus Granville Dill) *The College-Bred Negro American,* Atlanta University Press, 1910.

(With Dill) *The Common School and the Negro American,* Atlanta University Press, 1911.

(With Dill) *The Negro American Artisan,* Atlanta University Press, 1912.

(With Dill) *Morals and Manners among Negro Americans,* Atlanta University Press, 1914.

Atlanta University Publications, two volumes, Hippocrene, 1968.

NONFICTION

The Suppression of the African Slave-Trade to the United States of America, 1638-1870, Longmans, Green, 1896.

The Conservation of Races, American Negro Academy, 1897.

The Philadelphia Negro: A Special Study, (bound with *A Special Report on Domestic Service,* by Isobel Eaton), University of Pennsylvania, 1899.

The Souls of Black Folk: Essays and Sketches (young adult), A. C. McClurg, 1903.

(With Booker Taliaferro Washington) *The Negro in the South: His Economic Progress in Relation to His Moral and Religious Development* (lectures), G. W. Jacobs, 1907.

John Brown (biography), G. W. Jacobs, 1909, 2nd revised edition, International Publishing, 1974.

The Negro, Holt, 1915.

Darkwater: Voices from Within the Veil (semi-autobiographical), Harcourt, 1920.

The Gift of Black Folk: The Negroes in the Making of America, Stratford Co., 1924.

Africa: Its Geography, People and Products, Haldeman-Julius Publications, 1930.

Africa: Its Place in Modern History, Haldeman-Julius Publications, 1930, reprinted in a single volume with *Africa: Its Geography, People and Products,* Unipub-Kraus International, 1977.

Black Reconstruction: An Essay Toward a History of the Part Which Black Folk Played in the Attempt to Reconstruct Democracy in America, 1860-1880, Harcourt, 1935, published as *Black Reconstruction in America, 1860-1880,* Atheneum, 1969.

Black Folk, Then and Now: An Essay in the History and Sociology of the Negro Race, Holt, 1939.

Dusk of Dawn: An Essay Toward an Autobiography of a Race Concept, Harcourt, 1940.

Color and Democracy: Colonies and Peace, Harcourt, 1945.

The World and Africa: An Inquiry Into the Part Which Africa Has Played in World History, Viking, 1947, revised edition, 1965.

(Editor) *An Appeal to the World: A Statement on the Denial of Human Rights to Minorities in the Case of Citizens of Negro Descent in the United States of America and an Appeal to the United Nations for Redress,* [New York], 1947.

In Battle for Peace: The Story of My 83rd Birthday (autobiography), Masses and Mainstream, 1952.

The Autobiography of W. E. Burghardt Du Bois: A Soliloquy on Viewing My Life From the Last Decade of Its First Century, edited by Herbert Aptheker, International Publishers, 1968.

Black North in 1901: A Social Study, Ayer, 1970.

COLLECTIONS AND CORRESPONDENCE

An ABC of Color: Selections From Over Half a Century of the Writings of W. E. B. Du Bois, Seven Seas Publishers (Berlin), 1963.

Three Negro Classics, edited by John H. Franklin, Avon, 1965.

W. E. B. Du Bois Speaks: Speeches and Addresses, edited by Philip S. Foner, Pathfinder Press, 1970.

The Selected Writings of W. E. B. Du Bois, edited by Walter Wilson, New American Library, 1970.

W. E. B. Du Bois: A Reader, edited by Meyer Weinberg, Harper, 1970.

The Seventh Son: The Thought and Writings of W. E. B. Du Bois, edited by Julius Lester, Random House, 1971.

A W. E. B. Du Bois Reader, edited by Andrew G. Paschal, Macmillan, 1971.

W. E. B. Du Bois: The Crisis Writings, edited by Daniel Walden, Fawcett Publications, 1972.

The Emerging Thought of W. E. B. Du Bois: Essays and Editorials from "The Crisis," edited by Harvey Lee Moon, Simon & Schuster, 1972.

The Correspondence of W. E. B. Du Bois, edited by Aptheker, University of Massachusetts Press, Volume I: *1877-1934,* 1973, Volume II: *1934-1944,* 1976, Volume III: *1944-1963,* 1978.

The Education of Black People: Ten Critiques, 1906-1960, edited by Aptheker, University of Massachusetts Press, 1973.

The Writings of W. E. B. Du Bois, edited by Virginia Hamilton, Crowell, 1975.

Book Reviews, edited by Aptheker, KTO Press, 1977.

Prayers for Dark People, edited by Aptheker, University of Massachusetts Press, 1980.

(And editor) *Writings in Periodicals,* UNIPUB-Kraus International, 1985.

Creative Writings by W. E. B. Du Bois: A Pageant, Poems, Short Stories and Playlets, UNIPUB-Kraus International, 1985.

Pamphlets and Leaflets by W. E. B. Du Bois, UNIPUB-Kraus International, 1985.

Against Racism: Unpublished Essays, Papers, Addresses, 1887-1961, edited by Aptheker, University of Massachusetts Press, 1985.

W. E. B. Du Bois on Sociology and the Black Community, edited by Dan S. Greene and Edwin D. Driver, University of Chicago Press, 1987.

W F B Writings, Library of America, 1987.

W.E.B. DuBois: A Reader, H. Holt and Company (New York City), 1995.

The Oxford W.E.B. DuBois Reader, Oxford University Press (New York City), 1996.

The Selected Speeches of W.E.B. DuBois, Modern Library (New York City), 1996.

OTHER

Columnist for newspapers, including *Chicago Defender, Pittsburgh Courier, New York Amsterdam News,* and *San Francisco Chronicle.* Contributor to numerous periodicals, including *Atlantic Monthly* and *World's Work.* Founder and editor of numerous periodicals, including *Moon,* 1905-06, *Horizon,* 1908-10, *Brownies' Book,* 1920-21, and *Phylon Quarterly,* 1940. Editor in chief of *Encyclopedia of the Negro,* 1933-46. Director of *Encyclopaedia Africana.*

Some of Du Bois's books have been published in French and Russian.

SIDELIGHTS: W. E. B. Du Bois was at the vanguard of the civil rights movement in America. Of French and African descent, Du Bois grew up in Massachusetts and did not begin to comprehend the problems of racial prejudice until he attended Fisk University in Tennessee. Later he was accepted at Harvard, but while he was at that institution he voluntarily segregated himself from white students. Trained as a sociologist, Du Bois began to document the oppression of black people and their strivings for equality in the 1890s. By 1903 he had learned enough to state in *The Souls of Black Folk* that "the problem of the twentieth century is the problem of the color line," and he spent the remainder of his long life trying to break down racial barriers.

The Souls of Black Folk was not well received when it first came out. Houston A. Baker, Jr. explained in his *Black Literature in America* that white Americans were not "ready to respond favorably to Du Bois's scrupulously accurate portrayal of the hypocrisy, hostility, and brutality of white America toward black America." Many blacks were also shocked by the book, for in it Du Bois announced his opposition to the conciliatory policy of Booker T. Washington and his followers, who argued for the gradual development of the Negro race through vocational training. Du Bois declared: "So far as Mr. Washington apologizes for injustice, North or South, does not rightly value the privilege and duty of voting, belittles the emasculating effects of caste distinctions, and opposes the higher training and ambition of our brighter minds—so far as he, the South, or the Nation, does this—we must unceasingly and firmly oppose him. By every civilized and peaceful method we must strive for the rights which the world accords to men." In retrospect, many scholars have pointed to *The Souls of Black Folk* as a prophetic work. Harold W. Cruse and Carolyn Gipson noted in the *New York Review of Books* that "nowhere else was DuBois's description of the Negro's experience in American Society to be given more succinct expression. . . . *Souls* is probably his greatest achievement as a writer. Indeed, his reputation may largely rest on this remarkable document, which had a profound effect on the minds of black people."

A few years after *The Souls of Black Folk* was published, Du Bois banded with other black leaders and began the Niagra Movement, which sought to abolish all distinctions based on race. Although this movement disintegrated, it served as the forerunner of the

National Association for the Advancement of Colored People (NAACP). Du Bois helped to establish the NAACP and worked as its director of publicity and research for many years. As the editor of *Crisis,* a journal put out by the NAACP, he became a well-known spokesman for the black cause. In 1973 Henry Lee Moon gathered a number of essays and articles written by Du Bois for *Crisis* and published them in a book, *The Emerging Thought of W. E. B. Du Bois.*

In addition to the articles and editorials he wrote for *Crisis,* Du Bois produced a number of books on the history of the Negro race and on the problems of racial prejudice. In *Black Reconstruction,* Du Bois wrote about the role that blacks played in the Reconstruction, a role that had been hitherto ignored by white historians. The history of the black race in Africa and America was outlined in *Black Folk: Then and Now.* H. J. Seligmann found the book impressive in the *Saturday Review of Literature:* "No one can leave it without a deepened sense of the part the Negro peoples have played and must play in world history." An even higher compliment was paid by Barrett Williams reviewing for the *Boston Transcript:* "Professor Du Bois has overlooked one of the strongest arguments against racial inferiority, namely, this book itself. In it, a man of color has proved himself, in the complex and exacting field of scholarship, the full equal of his white colleagues."

Although Du Bois's novels did not attract as much notice as his scholarly works, they also were concerned with the plight of the black race. His first novel, *The Quest of The Silver Fleece,* dramatizes the difficulties created by the low economic status of the Southern Negro. *Dark Princess* dealt with miscegenation. After reading *Dark Princess,* a reviewer for the *Springfield Republican* observed: "The truth is, of course, that DuBois is not a novelist at all, and that the book judged as a novel has only the slightest merit. As a document, as a program, as an exhortation, it has its interest and value."

Du Bois gradually grew disillusioned with the moderate policies of the NAACP and with the capitalistic system in the United States. When he advocated black autonomy and "non-discriminatory segregation" in 1934, he was forced to resign from his job at the NAACP. Later he returned to the NAACP and worked there until another rift developed between him and that organization's leaders in 1944. More serious conflicts arose between Du Bois and the U.S. government. Du Bois had become disenchanted with capitalism relatively early. In *Darkwater: Voices From*

Within the Veil, he had depicted the majority of mankind as being subjugated by an imperialistic white race. In the 1940s he returned to this subject and examined it in more detail. *Color and Democracy: Colonies and Peace* presented a case against imperialism. "This book by Dr. Du Bois is a small volume of 143 pages," critic H. A. Overstreet observed in the *Saturday Review of Literature,* "but it contains enough dynamite to blow up the whole vicious system whereby we have comforted our white souls and lined the pockets of generations of free-booting capitalists." *The World and Africa* contained a further indictment of the treatment of colonials. Du Bois "does not seek exaggeration of Africa's role, but he insists the role must not be forgotten," Saul Carson remarked in the *New York Times.* "And his insistence is firm. It is persuasive, eloquent, moving. Considering the magnitude of the provocation, it is well-tempered, even gentle."

Du Bois not only wrote about his political beliefs; he acted upon them. He belonged to the Socialist party for a brief time in the early 1900s. Later he conceived a program of Pan-Africanism, a movement that he called "an organized protection of the Negro world led by American Negroes." In 1948 he campaigned for the Progressive Party in national elections, and in 1950 he ran for senator from New York on the American Labor Party ticket. Du Bois's radical political stance provoked some run-ins with the U.S. government, the first of which occurred in 1949, when he accepted an honorary position as vice-chairman of the Council on African affairs. This organization was labeled "subversive" by the attorney general. His work with the Peace Information Center, a society devoted to banning nuclear weapons, also embroiled him in controversy. Along with four other officers from the Peace Information Center, Du Bois was indicted for "failure to register as an agent of a foreign principal." The case was brought to trial in 1951 and the defendants were acquitted.

After the trial was over, Du Bois wanted to travel outside the United States, but he was denied a passport on the grounds that it was not in "the best interests of the United States" for him to journey abroad. Later the State Department refused to issue a passport to him unless he stated in writing that he was not a member of the Communist Party, a condition that Du Bois rejected. In 1958 the Supreme Court handed down a decision which declared that "Congress had never given the Department of State any authority to demand a political affidavit as prerequisite to issuing a passport." This decision enabled Du Bois and his wife to leave the country the same year. For several months they traveled in Europe, the U.S.S.R., and China.

Du Bois's travels abroad had a profound influence on his thinking. In 1961 he joined the Communist Party. He explained in his autobiography how he reached this decision: "I have studied socialism and communism long and carefully in lands where they are practiced and in conversation with their adherents, and with wide reading. I now state my conclusion frankly and clearly: I believe in communism. . . . I believe that all men should be employed according to their ability and that wealth and services should be distributed according to need. Once I thought that these ends could be attained under capitalism, means of production privately owned, and used in accord with free individual initiative. After earnest observation I now believe that private ownership of capital and free enterprise are leading the world to disaster."

After joining the Communist party, Du Bois moved to Ghana at the invitation of President Nkrumah. While there he served as the director of the *Encyclopaedia Africana* project. In August, 1963, the ninety-five-year-old leader inspired a protest march on the U.S. embassy in Accra to show support for the historic "March for Jobs and Freedom" taking place in Washington, D.C., that same month. Shortly afterward, Du Bois died. Although Du Bois was a controversial figure in his lifetime, his reputation has grown in the past decade. A large number of books and scholarly studies about him have recently appeared. In a discussion of the revival of interest in Du Bois, Cruse and Gipson wrote: "It is important to remember that he continued to plead for a truly pluralistic culture in a world where the superiority of whites is still an *a priori* assumption. In so far as he grasped the basic dilemma of Western blacks as being a people with 'two souls, two thoughts, two unreconciled strivings,' Du Bois's attitudes have been vindicated. He was, as we can now see, one of those unique men whose ideas are destined to be reviled and then revived, and then, no doubt, reviled again, haunting the popular mind long after his death."

BIOGRAPHICAL/CRITICAL SOURCES:

BOOKS

Baker, Houston A., Jr., *Black Literature in America,* McGraw, 1971.

Bell, Bernard W.; Emily Grosholz; and James B. Stewart; *The Critique of Custom: W. E. B. DuBois and Philosophical Questions,* Routledge (New York), 1996.

Bone, Robert A., *The Negro Novel in America,* Yale University Press, revised edition, 1965.

Byerman, Keith Eldon, *Seizing the Word: History, Art, and Self in the Work of W. E. B. DuBois,* University of Georgia Press (Athens), 1994.

Concise Dictionary of American Literary Biography: Realism, Naturalism, and Local Color, 1865-1917, Gale, 1988.

Contemporary Literary Criticism, Gale, Volume 1, 1973, Volume 2, 1974.

Dictionary of Literary Biography, Gale, Volume 47: *American Historians, 1866-1912,* 1986, Volume 50: *Afro-American Writers Before the Harlem Renaissance,* 1986.

Du Bois, Shirley Graham, *His Day Is Marching On: A Memoir of W. E. B. Du Bois,* Lippincott, 1971.

Du Bois, W. E. B., *Darkwater: Voices from Within the Veil,* Harcourt, 1920, reprinted, Kraus Reprint, 1975.

Du Bois, W. E. B., *Dusk of Dawn: An Essay Toward an Autobiography of Race Concept,* Harcourt, 1940, reprinted, Kraus Reprint, 1975.

Du Bois, W. E. B., *In Battle for Peace: The Story of My 83rd Birthday,* Masses & Mainstream, 1952, reprinted, Kraus Reprint, 1976.

Du Bois, W. E. B., *The Autobiography of W. E. B. DuBois: A Soliloquy on Viewing My Life from the Last Decade of Its First Century,* International Publishers, 1968.

Hawkins, Hugh, editor, *Booker T. Washington and His Critics: Black Leadership in Crisis,* Heath, 1974.

Katz, Michael B., and Thomas J. Sugrue, *W. E. B. DuBois, Race, and the City: The Philadelphia Negro and Its Legacy,* University of Pennsylvania Press, 1998.

Logan, Rayford W., editor, *W. E. B. DuBois: A Profile,* Hill & Wang, 1971.

Moss, Nathaniel, *W. E. B. DuBois: Civil Rights Leader,* Chelsea Juniors (New York), 1996.

Pobi-Asamani, Kwadwo, *W. E. B. DuBois: His Contribution to Pan-Africanism,* Borgo Press (San Bernardino), 1994.

Rampersad, Arnold, *Art and Imagination of W. E. B. DuBois,* Harvard University Press, 1976.

Reed, Adolph L., *Fabianism and the Color Line: W. E. B. DuBois and American Political Thought in Black and White,* Oxford University Press (New York City), 1997.

Rudwick, Elliott M., *W. E. B. DuBois: Propagandist of the Negro Protest,* Atheneum, 1968.

Sterne, Emma Gelders, *His Was the Voice: The Life of W. E. B. DuBois,* Crowell-Collier, 1971.

Wintz, Cary D., *African-American Political Thought,* M.E. Sharpe (Armonk, NY), 1996.

Zamir, Shamoon, *Dark Voices: W. E. B. DuBois and American Thought, 1888-1903,* University of Chicago Press (Chicago), 1995.

PERIODICALS

American Visions, February-March, 1994, p. 24.
Boston Transcript, June 24, 1939.
Ebony, August, 1972; August, 1975; November, 1994, p. 102.
Forbes, December 5, 1994, p. 84.
Jet, November 14, 1994, p. 20.
Los Angeles Times Book Review, January 25, 1987.
New Republic, February 26, 1972; August 4, 1994, p. 28.
Newsweek, August 23, 1971.
New York Review of Books, November 30, 1972.
New York Times, March 9, 1947; October 24, 1979.
New York Times Book Review, September 29, 1985.
Saturday Review of Literature, July 29, 1939; June 23, 1945.
Springfield Republican, May 28, 1928.*

*   *   *

DUNBAR, Paul Laurence 1872-1906

PERSONAL: Born June 27, 1872, in Dayton, OH; died of tuberculosis, February 9, 1906, in Dayton, OH; buried in Woodland Cemetery, Dayton; son of Joshua (a former slave, Union soldier, and plasterer) and Matilda Glass Murphy (a former slave and laundress; maiden name, Burton) Dunbar; married Alice Ruth Moore (a writer and teacher), March 6, 1898 (separated, 1902). *Education:* Attended school in Dayton, OH.

CAREER: Poet, novelist, and short story writer. Worked as elevator operator; *Dayton Tattler,* Dayton, OH, founder and editor, 1889-1890; *Indianapolis World,* Indianapolis, IN, temporary editor, 1895; court messenger, 1896; Library of Congress, Washington DC, assistant clerk, 1897-98. Served as guest editor, *Chicago Tribune,* 1903.

MEMBER: American Social Science Association (member of the Executive Council, Western Association of Writers.

AWARDS, HONORS: Honorary M.A. from Atlanta University.

WRITINGS:

POETRY

Oak and Ivy (also see below), Press of United Brethren Publishing House, 1893.
Majors and Minors (also see below), Hadley & Hadley, 1896.
Lyrics of Lowly Life (includes poems from *Oak and Ivy* and *Majors and Minors*), introduction by William Dean Howells, Dodd, 1896.
Lyrics of the Hearthside, Dodd, 1899.
Poems of Cabin and Field (collection of eight previously published poems), illustrated by wife, Alice Morse, photographs by Hampton Institute Camera Club, Dodd, 1899.
Candle-lightin' Time, Dodd, 1901.
Lyrics of Love and Laughter, Dodd, 1903.
When Malindy Sings, Dodd, 1903.
Li'l Gal, Dodd, 1904.
Chris'mus Is a Comin', and Other Poems, Dodd, 1905.
Howdy, Howdy, Howdy, Dodd, 1905.
Lyrics of Sunshine and Shadow, Dodd, 1905.
A Plantation Portrait, Dodd, 1905.
Joggin' Erlong, Dodd, 1906.
The Complete Poems of Paul Laurence Dunbar, Dodd, 1913.
Speakin' o' Christmas, and Other Christmas and Special Poems, Dodd, 1914.
Little Brown Baby: Poems for Young People, edited and with biographical sketch by Bertha Rodgers, illustrated by Erick Berry, Dodd, 1940.
I Greet the Dawn: Poems, edited and with an introduction by Ashley Bryan, Atheneum, 1978.

FICTION

The Uncalled (semi-autobiographical novel), Dodd, 1898.
Folks From Dixie (short stories), Dodd, 1898.
The Love of Landry (novel), Dodd, 1900.
The Strength of Gideon, and Other Stories, illustrated by Edward Windsor Kemble, Dodd, 1900.
The Fanatics (novel), Dodd, 1901.
The Sport of the Gods (novel), Dodd, 1902, reprinted, with an introduction by Kenny J. Williams, 1981, published in England as *The Jest of Fate: A Story of Negro Life,* Jarrold, 1902.
In Old Plantation Days (short stories), illustrated by B. Martin Justice, Dodd, 1903.
The Heart of the Happy Hollow (short stories), Dodd, 1904.

The Best Stories of Paul Laurence Dunbar, edited and with an introduction by Benjamin Brawley, Dodd, 1938.

OTHER

Dream Lovers: An Operatic Romance (libretto for operetta with music by Samuel Coleridge-Taylor), Boosey, 1898.

(Author of lyrics) *In Dahomey* (stage show), with music by Will Marion Cook, produced in Boston, then at Buckingham Palace, England, in honor of the birthday of the Prince of Wales, 1903.

(Contributor) *The Negro Problem: A Series of Articles by Representative American Negroes,* James Pott, 1903.

(Contributor) *Selected Songs Sung by Students of Tuskegee Normal and Industrial Institute* (contains "The Tuskegee Song"), Tuskegee Institute, 1904.

The Life and Works of Paul Laurence Dunbar, edited and with biography by Lida Keck Wiggins, J. L. Nichols, 1907.

The Letters of Paul and Alice Dunbar: A Private History, two volumes, edited by Eugene Wesley Metcalf, University Microfilms, 1974.

The Paul Laurence Dunbar Reader, edited by Jay Martin and Gossie H. Hudson, Dodd, 1975.

The Collected Poetry of Paul Laurence Dunbar, edited and with introduction by Joanne M. Braxton, University Press of Virginia (Charlottesville), 1993.

Selected Poems, Dover Publications, 1997.

Also author of *Uncle Eph's Christmas* (one-act musical), produced in 1900. Author of lyrics to songs such as "Jes Lak White Folk," "Down De Lover's Lane: Plantation Croon," and "Who Knows."

Contributor to newspapers and periodicals, including *Atlantic Monthly, Blue and Gray, Bookman, Chicago News Record, Century, Dayton Herald, Denver Post, Detroit Free Press, Harper's Weekly, Independent, Lippincott's, Nation, New York Times,* and *Saturday Evening Post.* Work represented in anthologies.

Author's papers and letters are included in collections at the Ohio Historical Society, the Schomburg Collection of the New York Public Library, and the Houghton Library, Harvard University.

ADAPTATIONS: Portions of Dunbar's work were adapted by Pauline Myers for the stage production *The World of My America: A One Woman Dramatiza-*
tion, and by Vinette Carroll for the stage production *When Hell Freezes Over, I'll Skate.*

SIDELIGHTS: Paul Laurence Dunbar is widely acknowledged as the first important black poet in American literature. He enjoyed his greatest popularity in the early twentieth century following the publication of dialectic verse in collections such as *Majors and Minors* and *Lyrics of Lowly Life.* But the dialectic poems constitute only a small portion of Dunbar's canon, which is replete with novels, short stories, essays, and many poems in standard English. In its entirety, Dunbar's literary body has been acclaimed as an impressive representation of black life in turn-of-the-century America. As Dunbar's friend James Weldon Johnson noted in the preface to his *Book of American Poetry:* "Paul Laurence Dunbar stands out as the first poet from the Negro race in the United States to show a combined mastery over poetic material and poetic technique, to reveal innate literary distinction in what he wrote, and to maintain a high level of performance. He was the first to rise to a height from which he could take a perspective view of his own race. He was the first to see objectively its humor, its superstitions, its short-comings; the first to feel sympathetically its heart-wounds, its yearnings, its aspirations, and to voice them all in a purely literary form."

Dunbar began showing literary promise while still in high school in Dayton, Ohio, where he lived with his widowed mother. The only black in his class, he became class president and class poet. By 1889, two years before he graduated, he had already published poems in the *Dayton Herald* and worked as editor of the short-lived *Dayton Tattler,* a newspaper for blacks published by classmate Orville Wright, who later gained fame with brother Wilbur Wright as inventors of the airplane.

Dunbar aspired to a career in law, but his mother's meager financial situation precluded his university education. He consequently sought immediate employment with various Dayton businesses, including newspapers, only to be rejected because of his race. He finally settled for work as an elevator operator, a job that allowed him time to continue writing. At this time Dunbar produced articles, short stories, and poems, including several in the black-dialect style that later earned him fame.

In 1892 Dunbar was invited by one of his former teachers to address the Western Association of Writers then convening in Dayton. At the meeting Dunbar befriended James Newton Matthews, who subsequently praised Dunbar's work in a letter to an Illinois newspaper. Matthews's letter was eventually reprinted by newspapers throughout the country and thus brought Dunbar recognition outside Dayton. Among the readers of this letter was poet James Whitcomb Riley, who then familiarized himself with Dunbar's work and wrote him a commendatory letter. Bolstered by the support of both Matthews and Riley, Dunbar decided to publish a collection of his poems. He obtained additional assistance from Orville Wright and then solicited a Dayton firm, United Brethren Publishing, that eventually printed the work, entitled *Oak and Ivy,* for a modest sum.

In *Oak and Ivy* Dunbar included his earliest dialect poems and many works in standard English. Among the latter is one of his most popular poems, "Sympathy," in which he expresses, in somber tone, the dismal plight of blacks in American society. In another standard English poem, "Ode to Ethiopia," he records the many accomplishments of black Americans and exhorts his fellow blacks to maintain their pride despite racial abuse. The popularity of these and other poems inspired Dunbar to devote himself more fully to writing.

Shortly after the publication of *Oak and Ivy* Dunbar was approached by attorney Charles A. Thatcher, an admirer sympathetic to Dunbar's college education. Dunbar, however, was greatly encouraged by sales of *Oak and Ivy* and so rejected Thatcher to pursue a literary career. Thatcher then applied himself to promoting Dunbar in nearby Toledo, Ohio, and helped him obtain work there reading his poetry at libraries and literary gatherings. Dunbar also found unexpected support from psychiatrist Henry A. Tobey, who helped distribute *Oak and Ivy* in Toledo and occasionally sent Dunbar much needed financial aid.

Tobey eventually teamed with Thatcher in publishing Dunbar's second verse collection, *Majors and Minors.* In this book Dunbar produced poems on a variety of themes and in several styles. He grouped the more ambitious poems, those written in standard English, under the heading "Majors," and he gathered the more superficial, dialect works as "Minors." Although Dunbar invested himself most fully in his standard poetry—which bore the influences of such poets as the English romantics and Americans such as Riley—it was the dialect verse that found greater favor with his predominantly white readership, and it was by virtue of these dialect poems that Dunbar gained increasing fame throughout the country. Instrumental to Dunbar's growing popularity was a

highly positive, though extremely patronizing, review by eminent novelist William Dean Howells. Writing in *Harper's Weekly,* Howells praised Dunbar as "the first man of his color to study his race objectively" and commended the dialect poems as faithful representations of the black race.

Through Thatcher and Tobey, Dunbar met an agent and secured more public readings and a publishing contract. He then published *Lyrics of Lowly Life,* a poetry collection derived primarily from verse already featured in *Oak and Ivy* and *Majors and Minors.* This new volume sold impressively across America and established Dunbar as the nation's foremost black poet. On the strength of his recent acclaim Dunbar commenced a six- month reading tour of England. There he found publishers for a British edition of *Lyrics of Lowly Life* and befriended musician Samuel Coleridge-Taylor, with whom he then collaborated on the operetta "Dream Lovers."

When Dunbar returned to the United States in 1897 he obtained a clerkship at the Library of Congress in Washington, D.C. Soon afterwards he married fellow writer Alice Ruth Moore. Although his health suffered during the two years he lived in Washington, the period nonetheless proved fruitful for Dunbar. In 1898 he published his first short story collection, *Folks From Dixie,* in which he delineated the situation of blacks in both pre-and post-emancipation United States. Although these tales, unlike some of his dialect verse, were often harsh examinations of racial prejudice, *Folks From Dixie* was well received upon publication.

Not so Dunbar's first novel, *The Uncalled,* which recalled Nathaniel Hawthorne's *The Scarlet Letter* in probing the spiritual predicament of a minister. Critics largely rejected *The Uncalled* as dull and unconvincing in its portrait of Frederick Brent, a pastor who had, in childhood, been abandoned by an alcoholic father and then raised by a zealously devout spinster, Hester Prime (Hawthorne's protagonist in *The Scarlet Letter* was named Hester Prynne). After securing a pastor's post, Brent alienated church-goers by refusing to reproach an unwed mother. He resigns from his pastorship and departs for Cincinnati. After further misadventure—he ends his marriage engagement and encounters his father, now a wandering preacher—Brent finds fulfillment and happiness as minister in another congregation.

At the end of 1898, his health degenerating still further, Dunbar left the Library of Congress and commenced another reading tour. He published another verse collection, *Lyrics of the Hearthside,* and recovered any status he may have jeopardized with *The Uncalled.* In the spring of 1899, however, his health lapsed sufficiently to threaten his life. Ill with pneumonia, the already tubercular Dunbar was advised to rest in the mountains. He therefore moved to the Catskills in New York State, but he continued to write while recovering from his ailments.

In 1900, after a brief stay in Colorado, Dunbar returned to Washington, D.C. Shortly before his return he published another collection of tales, *The Strength of Gideon,* in which he continued to recount black life both before and after slavery. Reviewers at the time favored his pre-emancipation stories full of humor and sentiment, while ignoring more volatile accounts of abuse and injustice. More recently these latter stories have gained greater recognition from critics eager to substantiate Dunbar's opposition to racism.

Dunbar followed *The Strength of Gideon* with his second novel, *The Love of Landry,* about an ailing woman who arrives in Colorado for convalescence and finds true happiness with a cowboy. Like the earlier *Uncalled, The Love of Landry* was deemed unconvincing in its presentation of white characters and was dismissed as inferior to Dunbar's tales of blacks. Dunbar suffered further critical setback with his next novel, *The Fanatics,* about America at the beginning of the Civil War. Its central characters are from white families who differ in their North-South sympathies and spark a dispute in their Ohio community. *The Fanatics* was a commercial failure upon publication, and in the ensuing years it has continued to be regarded as a superficial, largely uncompelling work. Among the novel's many detractors is Robert Bone, who wrote in *The Negro in America* that Dunbar resorted to "caricature in his treatment of minor Negro characters" and that his stereotypic portraits of black characters only served to reinforce prejudice.

The Sport of the Gods, Dunbar's final novel, presents a far more critical and disturbing portrait of black America. The work centers on butler Berry Hamilton and his family. After Berry is wrongly charged with theft by his white employers, he is sentenced to ten years of prison labor. His remaining family—wife, son, and daughter—consequently find themselves targets of abuse in their southern community, and after being robbed by the local police they head north to Harlem. There they encounter further hardship and strife: the son becomes embroiled in the city's seamy

nightlife and succumbs to alcoholism and crime; the naive daughter is exploited by fellow blacks and begins a questionable dancing career; and the mother, convinced that her husband's prison sentence has negated their marriage, weds an abusive profligate. A happy resolution is achieved only after Berry's accuser confesses, while dying, that his charge was fabricated, whereupon Berry is released from prison. He then travels north and finds his family in disarray. But the cruel second husband is then, conveniently, murdered, and the parental Hamiltons are reunited in matrimony.

Although its acclaim was hardly unanimous, *The Sport of the Gods* nonetheless earned substantial praise as a powerful novel of protest. By this time, however, Dunbar was experiencing considerable turmoil in his own life. Prior to writing *The Sport of the Gods* he had suffered another lapse of poor health, and he compounded his problems by resorting to alcohol. And after *The Sport of the Gods* appeared in 1902, Dunbar's marital situation—always troublesome—degenerated further due to his continued reliance on alcohol and to antagonism from his wife's parents.

Dunbar and his wife separated in 1902, but that separation only contributed to his continued physical and psychological decline. The next year, following a nervous breakdown and another bout of pneumonia, Dunbar managed to assemble another verse collection, *Lyrics of Love and Laughter,* and another short story collection, *In Old Plantation Days.* With *Lyrics of Love and Laughter* he confirmed his reputation as America's premier black poet. The volume contains both sentimental and somberly realistic expressions and depictions of black life, and it features both dialect and standard English verse. *In Old Plantation Days* is comprised of twenty-five stories set on a southern plantation during the days of slavery. Here Dunbar once again resorted to caricaturing his own race, portraying black slaves as faithful and obedient, slow-witted but good-natured workers appreciative of their benevolent white owners. Dunbar drew the ire of many critics for his stereotyped characters, and some of his detractors even alleged that he contributed to racist concepts while simultaneously disdaining such thinking.

If *In Old Plantation Days* was hardly a pioneering work, it was at least a lucrative publication and one that confirmed the preferences of much of Dunbar's public. With the short story collection *The Heart of Happy Hollow* he presented a greater variety of perspectives on aspects of black life in America, and he even included a tale on the moral filly of lynching. Dunbar followed *The Heart of Happy Hollow* with two more poetry collections, *Lyrics of Sunshine and Shadow* and *Howdy, Honey, Howdy,* both of which featured works from previous volumes.

Dunbar's health continued to decline even as he persisted in producing poems. But his reliance on alcohol to temper his chronic coughing only exacerbated his illness, and by the winter of 1905 he was fatally ill. He died on February 9, 1906, at age thirty-three.

In the years immediately following his death, Dunbar's standing as America's foremost black poet seemed assured, and his dialect poems were prized as supreme achievements in black American literature. In the ensuing decades, however, his reputation was damaged by scholars questioning the validity of his often stereotypic characterizations and his apparent unwillingness to sustain an anti-racist stance. Among his most vehement detractors from this period was Victor Lawson, whose *Dunbar Critically Examined* remains a provocative, if overly aggressive, study.

More recently Dunbar's stature has increased markedly. He is once again regarded as America's first great black poet, and his standard English poems are now, perhaps surprisingly, prized as his greatest achievements in verse. Contemporary champions include Addison Gayle, Jr., whose *Oak and Ivy: A Biography of Paul Laurence Dunbar,* is considered a key contribution to Dunbar studies, and black poet Nikki Giovanni, whose prose contribution to *A Singer in the Dawn: Reinterpretations of Paul Laurence Dunbar,* edited by Jay Martin, hails Dunbar as "a natural resource of our people." For Giovanni, as for other Dunbar scholars, his work constitutes both a history and a celebration of black life. "There is no poet, black or nonblack, who measures his achievement," she declared. "Even today. He wanted to be a writer and he wrote."

BIOGRAPHICAL/CRITICAL SOURCES:

BOOKS

Best, Felton O., *Crossing the Color Line: A Biography of Paul Laurence Dunbar,* Kendall/Hunt Pub. Co. (Dubuque, IA), 1996.
Black Literature Criticism, Gale, 1992.
Brawley, Benjamin, *Paul Laurence Dunbar: Poet of His People,* University of North Carolina Press, 1936.

Contemporary Black Biography, Gale, Volume 8, 1995.
Cunningham, Virginia, *Paul Laurence Dunbar and His Song,* Dodd, 1947.
Dictionary of Literary Biography, Gale, Volume 51: *Afro-American Writers From the Harlem Renaissance to 1940,* 1987, Volume 54: *American Poets, 1880-1945, Third Series,* 1987.
Gayle, Addison, Jr., *Oak and Ivy: A Biography of Paul Laurence Dunbar,* Anchor/Doubleday, 1971.
Gentry, Tony, *Paul Laurence Dunbar,* Melrose Square Pub., (Los Angeles), 1993.
Gould, Jean, *That Dunbar Boy,* Dodd, 1958.
Inge, M. Thomas, Maurice Duke, and Jackson R. Bryer, editors, *Black American Writers: Bibliographical Essays,* Volume 1, St. Martin's Press, 1978.
Lawson, Victor, *Dunbar Critically Examined,* Associated Publishers, 1941.
Martin, Jay, editor, *A Singer in the Dawn: Reinterpretations of Paul Laurence Dunbar,* Dodd, 1975.
Metcalf, E. W., *Paul Lawrence Dunbar: A Bibliography,* Scarecrow Press, 1975.
Poetry Criticism, Gale, Volume 5, 1992.
Revell, Peter, *Paul Laurence Dunbar,* Twayne, 1979.
Short Story Criticism, Gale, Volume 8, 1991.
Twentieth-Century Literary Criticism, Gale, Volume 2, 1979, Volume 12, 1984.
Wagner, Jean, *Black Poets of the United States,* University of Illinois Press, 1973, pp. 73-125.

PERIODICALS

A. M. E. Church Review, April, 1902, pp. 320-327.
Denver Daily News, September 24, 1899.
Journal of Negro History, January, 1967, pp. 1-13.
Ohio Historical Quarterly, April, 1958, pp. 95-108.
Texas Quarterly, summer, 1971.
Voice of the Negro, January, 1906, p. 50.*

*   *   *

DUPLECHAN, Larry 1956-

PERSONAL: Surname pronounced *"doo* pluh shahn"; born December 30, 1956, in Los Angeles, CA; son of Lawrence, Sr. (an electronics liaison engineer) and Margie Nell (a postal clerk, office administrator, and homemaker; maiden name, Andrus) Duplechan; life partner of Greg Harvey (a banker), 1976. *Education:* University of California, Los Angeles, B.A., 1978.

Politics: "Registered Democrat with feminist leanings and particular interest in the rights of gays and lesbians, women and African Americans." *Religion:* "Raised Southern Baptist. Currently vaguely Christian with a side-order of reincarnation and karma." *Avocational interests:* Reading (histories, biographies, fiction), singing, guitar playing, flute playing, drawing, bodybuilding, and twentieth-century American popular culture (music, film, theater, advertising, comic strips) pertaining particularly to African Americans and gays.

ADDRESSES: Home—Woodland Hills, CA. *Office*—c/o Cooper, Epstein & Hurewitz, 345 North Maple Drive, Suite 200, Beverly Hills, CA 90210.

CAREER: Pop/jazz vocalist (solo and with jazz vocal group String of Pearls), Los Angeles, CA, 1975-82;University of California, Los Angeles, librarian's assistant, 1976-80; word processor and secretary, various real estate-oriented companies, 1980-90; real estate legal secretary, 1990—. Taught fiction writing through the University of California at Los Angeles Continuing Education program.

WRITINGS:

NOVELS

Eight Days a Week, Alyson, 1985.
Blackbird, St. Martin's Press, 1986.
Tangled up in Blue, St. Martin's Press, 1989.
Captain Swing, Alyson, 1993.

Contributor to anthologies, including *Black Men/White Men,* Gay Sunshine Press, 1983; *Revelations: A Collection of Gay Male Coming out Stories,* Alyson, 1988; *Certain Voices: Short Stories about Gay Men,* Alyson, 1991; *Hometowns,* Dutton, 1991; *A Member of the Family,* Dutton, 1992; and *Calling the Wind: Twentieth-Century African American Short Stories,* HarperCollins, 1993. Contributor to periodicals, including *L.A. Style,Advocate, New York Native,* and *Black American Literature Forum.*

SIDELIGHTS: Larry Duplechan is credited with writing one of the first gay "coming-out" novels to feature an African American protagonist. *Blackbird,* which Duplechan published in 1986, drew a great deal of attention from the black community for the efforts of its youthful protagonist, Johnnie Ray Rosseau, to come to terms with and openly declare his homosexuality. Published seven years later, his *Captain Swing* finds the same protagonist, now older, facing a similar rejection from his close-knit,conservative, and

socially conscious family while a younger male family member's sexual preference for men is tolerated. While poetry and shorter writings by gay black men had been accepted by critics and the general reading public since the Harlem Renaissance of the 1920s made popular the work of such writers as Langston Hughes, novel-length works continued to be dominated by a white cast of characters until the mid-1980s. *Gay and Lesbian Literature* essayist Robert B. Marks Ridinger praised Duplechan's "willingness to give voice to the often monolithic homophobia, deliberate incomprehension and active rejection faced by openly gay African American men" through such novels as *Blackbird, Tangled up in Blue,* and *Captain Swing.*

Duplechan told *CA:* "It was not my dream to become a novelist. My childhood dream was to be a singing star—sort of Johnny Mathis with a dash of Bette Midler. I'd once heard Carol Burnett advise someone to give show business five years and if it didn't look as if a viable career was in the works, give it up. So, after languishing in the extreme lower end of show business for nearly seven years without a record contract in sight, I gave it up and decided to attempt to write. It was the early 1980s and the first flowering of novels aimed at a gay readership was underway. Pleased though I was at the existence of a rapidly growing body of gay-themed literature (both serious and popular), it soon occurred tome that there were nearly no black characters in any of the gay books I found. I searched in vain for a young, black, openly gay, middle-class, college-educated protagonist with a penchant for girl group music, 1930s movie musicals and the well-placed wisecrack. Someone not unlike myself. Finding none, I decided to create one.

"Thus was born Johnnie Ray Rousseau, my literary alter ego and mouthpiece, the protagonist of three of my four published novels. When people ask me how much of Johnnie Ray Rousseau is really Larry Duplechan, my answer can vary greatly with my mood. The fact is, Johnny Ray Rousseau is almost entirely me. A bit better looking, perhaps, and a good half-inch taller, but otherwise very much me. The circumstances and events of his life are completely fictional as often as not (my own relatively happy suburban life would likely make truly soporific reading), but Johnnie's attitudes, his likes and dislikes, his sense of humor—all me.

"Blissfully ignorant of the fact that it's all but impossible to get a novel published without the benefit of an agent, I did. *Eight Days a Week,* an interracial gay love story loosely based upon the first few years of my relationship with my life partner (and my abortive singing career), was generally treated very kindly by the gay press, utterly ignored by the mainstream press, and lambasted by a few African American gay critics who took exception to what was perceived to be Johnnie Ray Rousseau's lack of 'Afrocentricity,' particularly concerning Johnnie's outspoken preference for white men as lovers. The field of openly gay African American novelists writing for the gay audience remains very small, and unfortunately burdens each and any book with a black gay protagonist with inordinate political importance. I had not created Johnnie Ray Rousseau as a role model, only as an interesting and amusing character. To be accused of being ashamed of my African descent by someone who'd never met me was angering and painful, both to myself and Johnnie Ray.

"But we recovered. *Blackbird,* my next book, is the story of Johnnie Ray's coming out at the age of seventeen. The people who longed for a more Afrocentric protagonist were likely not won over, but the late author, film historian and critic Vito Russo wrote 'I fell in love with Johnnie Ray,' and the late African American writer and editor Joseph Beam wrote in the *Advocate,* 'We have all been waiting for this novel for a long time.' It is generally acknowledged as the first black, gay coming-out novel.

"In 1985, the year *Blackbird* was published, Rock Hudson died of AIDS, and a dear friend of mine tested positive for HIV—the first of many friends I was to lose to AIDS. His experiences in coping with the deadly syndrome were among the things that led to the writing of *Tangled up in Blue,* a love triangle in which the threat of AIDS is a catalyst for emotional upheaval. Written in the third person from three different points of view—a young woman, her secretly bisexual husband, and their gay friend—*Tangled up in Blue* was in large part an attempt to answer questions I'd asked myself after the completion of *Blackbird:* Could I write in a voice other than Johnnie Ray's first-person narrative? Could I write believable Caucasian characters? Could I write from the point of view of a woman? Could I write a comic novel concerning AIDS?

"With *Captain Swing,* I return to the first person, and to Johnnie Ray (who made a brief appearance in *Tangled up in Blue*—I couldn't get rid of him). He's in his mid-thirties now and has lost the love of his life and several friends to premature death. *Captain Swing* concerns both Johnnie's coping with the dying of his estranged father and his learning to love again.

"With the exceptions of James Baldwin (whose influence on me has more to do with subject matter than style) and Tom Robbins (whose wild flights of verbal fancy I admire but only rarely attempt to imitate, and whose *Even Cowgirls Get the Blues* is my favorite novel and the shining example toward which I ever aspire), I have no conscious literary influences. Or rather, I am influenced by everything I read—novels, biographies, magazines, cereal boxes.

"I don't make my living as a novelist—I work a forty-hour week in a law firm. As the chances of my ever making a living writing black gay novels are quite slender, I write each book purely as self-expression. When I feel like writing, I write; if not, not. If my books get published (which, so far, they have), wonderful. If not, I'll pass the manuscripts around among my friends. If I have any advice for aspiring writers, it would be the advice I give my writing students: don't write fiction for money—there very likely won't be much. If you want to make money, write for television or feature films. Only write fiction if that's how you really want to express yourself, because the work itself may be its own sole reward."

BIOGRAPHICAL/CRITICAL SOURCES:

BOOKS

Contemporary Gay American Novelists: A Bio-Bibliographical Critical Sourcebook, Greenwood Press, 1993.
Hemphill, Essex, editor, *Brother to Brother: New Writings by Black Gay Men,* Alyson, 1991.
Pendergast, Sara, and Tom Pendergast, editors, *Gay and Lesbian Literature,* Volume 2, St. James Press, 1998.

PERIODICALS

Christopher Street, Volume 10, 1987.
Los Angeles Times, May 8, 1989.
Publishers Weekly, January 6, 1989.
Village Voice, July 18, 1989.*

*   *   *

DYSON, Michael Eric 1958-

PERSONAL: Born October 23, 1958, in Detroit, MI; son of Addie Mae Leonard (a public school teacher's aide), adopted by Everett Dyson (employee of Kelsey-

Hayes Wheelbrake and Crum Company) following Everett's marriage to Addie Mae, c. 1960; married and divorced first wife (model, actor, dancer, waitress), c. 1978; married Brenda Joyce Dyson (nurse), 1982 (divorced); married Marcia Louise Dyson (public relations specialist, marketing consultant, and author), June 24, 1992; children: Michael II, Maisha. *Education:* Became licensed Baptist preacher, 1979, ordained as a minister, 1981; attended Knoxville College beginning, 1979, transferred to Carson-Newman, B.A. (magna cum laude; philosophy), 1985; Princeton University, M.A., 1991, Ph.D., 1993. *Politics:* Democratic Socialists of America. *Religion:* Baptist.

ADDRESSES: Office—c/o Columbia University, Institute for Research in African-American Studies, Mail Code 5514, 760B Schermerhorn Extension, 1200 Amsterdam Ave., New York, NY 10027.

CAREER: Preacher and minister at various Baptist churches, including Thankful Baptist Church, Tennessee; Mathy College, Princeton University, Princeton, NJ, assistant master; Hartford Seminary, CT, assistant director of a poverty project, 1988-89; Chicago Theological Seminary, instructor of ethics and cultural criticism, later assistant professor, c. 1989-92; Brown University, Providence, RI, assistant professor, taught American civilization and Afro-American studies, c. 1993-1995; University of North Carolina, Chapel Hill, professor of communication studies and director of Institute of African-American Research, c. 1995-1997; Columbia University, New York City, visiting distinguished professor of African-American studies, 1997—. Guest on Good Morning America, Nightline, Oprah Winfrey Show, and National Public Radio Broadcasts.

AWARDS, HONORS: National Magazine Award from the National Association of Black Journalism, 1992.

WRITINGS:

Reflecting Black: African-American Cultural Criticism (essays), University of Minnesota Press (Minneapolis, MN), 1993.
Making Malcolm: The Myth and Meaning of Malcolm X, Oxford University Press (New York City), 1995.
Between God and Gangsta Rap: Bearing Witness to Black Culture (essays), Oxford University Press, 1996.
Race Rules: Navigating the Color Line (essays), Addison-Wesley (Reading, MA), 1996.
I May Not Get There with You, Free Press, 1999.

Contributor to various journals and periodicals, including *New York Times, Nation, Chicago Tribune, Vibe,* and *Rolling Stone.*

SIDELIGHTS: An educator and ordained Baptist minister, Michael Eric Dyson has published several collections of writings on a range of African American cultural issues. "Raised in a ghetto in Detroit, Michigan," reported a writer for the 1997 *Current Biography Yearbook (CBY),* Dyson "overcame poverty to become one of those few African-American academics deemed 'public intellectuals'—people consulted regularly by the media establishment for their insights into racial issues." Some of his major influences, according to *CBY,* were his childhood experiences of "the powerful sermonizing of black ministers and . . . poems, plays, and set pieces that were performed during Sunday school." "Ministers," remarked *CBY,* "were the first 'public intellectuals' he encountered." "Books and learning served as an escape route for Dyson," explained *CBY,* noting that some of Dyson's childhood hobbies included "reading works by such philosophers as Blaise Pascal and Jean-Paul Sarte . . . read[ing] dictionaries. . . . [and skipping] school . . . [to go] to the local library, because he didn't think he was getting a good education."

Following high school Dyson not only became an ordained Baptist minister, he also completed an ivy league education, receiving both a masters and a doctorate degree from Princeton University. Among his career accomplishments are appointments at well-known universities, numerous appearance on television and radio, contributions to periodicals and journals, and a number of book publications. Following the release of his fourth book, *Race Rules: Navigating the Color Line,* Wray Herbert summarized some of Dyson's published beliefs in a *U.S. News and World Report* article: "Dyson . . . has developed a theory regarding the complexity of racial identity. To Dyson, identity is something that is constantly changing and evolving, and that all societal subcurrents, like rap music, should be taken seriously. . . . For Dyson, grasping the complexity of racial identity is the key to understanding everything from our fascination with O. J. [Simpson] and deep ambivalence about black nationalism to our uneasiness about gangsta culture and—most important—the apparent self-destructiveness of many young black men living in American cities today."

Reflecting Black: African-American Cultural Criticism collects Dyson's journalistic writings from 1989 to 1993 on such figures as Michael Jackson, Michael

Jordan, and Spike Lee, and concerning such topics as racism, sexism, film, politics, and music. While critic George Packer complained in the *Chicago Tribune Books* that jargon obscures the argument in several cases, he praised Dyson's analytical ability, particularly in his critique of religious issues. According to Patricia Hill Collins in *Contemporary Sociology,* "Dyson manages to merge sophisticated theoretical analysis with a comprehensible and plausible interpretation of contemporary black culture," and Jonathan Scott, writing in *Modern Fiction Studies,* called the work "in a fundamental sense . . . an autobiographical account of a good man's intellectual formation and moral activity in the world."

In his 1995 work *Making Malcolm: The Myth and Meaning of Malcolm X,* Dyson examines the appeal of the controversial political leader to the current generation of African American males and locates Malcolm's legacy in the development of alliances between African Americans and other racial and social minorities within the United States. *Nation* reviewer Lawrence Muhammad questioned Dyson's assessment of Malcolm's influence among black youth of the rap generation. According to Muhammad, "Making Malcolm carefully separates the legacy from any antisocial implications, but Dyson doesn't say if Malcolm's evolution to virtue has positively influenced today's troubled teens." A *Publishers Weekly* contributor declared that Dyson's work comprises a "thoughtful, scholarly essay."

Dyson's Between God and Gangsta Rap: Bearing Witness to Black Culture, published in 1995, offers a collection of essays on subjects ranging from his brother's imprisonment for murder to the music of singers Mariah Carey and Vanessa Williams, and offers a consideration of racial issues in the O. J. Simpson murder trial. *Time* magazine reviewer Christopher John Farley called the work "provocative," and in *Booklist* Mike Tribby praised Dyson's critique of gangsta rap music, noting his "literate and compelling argument that cultural warfare over popular music . . . is just a convenient way for society to avoid dealing with larger issues of race and class."

Race Rules, Dyson's fourth book, is comprised of six essays that touch on a range of topics, such as O. J. Simpson's criminal trial, Lois Farrakhan, Colin Powell, the Million Man March, the movie *Waiting to Exhale,* and sexual issues such as homophobia and promiscuity. A *Publishers Weekly* critic reviewed the "somewhat disjointed essay collection," asserting that Dyson "writes with rhythm and power, even if he sometimes travels well-trod ground." *New York Times Book Review* contributor Allen D. Boyer was disappointed that "the writing seems regrettably hasty," yet maintained that *Race Rules* accomplished what it intended: to give direction to "deal with white people's newfound resentment of black people's continuing rage."

BIOGRAPHICAL/CRITICAL SOURCES:

BOOKS

Current Biography Yearbook, H.W. Wilson (New York), 1997.

PERIODICALS

Booklist, December 15, 1995, pp. 671, 692; October 15, 1996, p. 384; May 15, 1997, p. 1596.
Chicago Tribune Books, August 8, 1993, pp. 6-7.
Christian Century, June 7, 1995, p. 59.
Chronicle of Higher Education, January 26, 1996.
Contemporary Sociology, July, 1994, pp. 607-08.
Emerge, November, 1996.
Herald-Sun (Durham, NC), May 18, 1997.
Journal of American History, June, 1996.
Library Journal, January, 1996, p. 126; October 1, 1996, p. 108.
Los Angeles Times Book Review, March 26, 1995.
Modern Fiction Studies, winter, 1994, pp. 923-25.
Nation, September 27, 1993, pp. 320-23; February 13, 1995, pp. 213-15.
New Yorker, January 9, 1995.
New York Times Book Review, November 27, 1994, p. 13; December 10, 1995, p. 26; November 4, 1996, p. 56.
Philadelphia Inquirer, April 12, 1995.
Publishers Weekly, October 10, 1994, pp. 55-56; October 2, 1995, p. 59; August 12, 1996, p. 108.
School Library Journal, March, 1995, p. 238.
Tikkun, March-April, 1995.
Time, December 18, 1995, p. 80.
U.S. News & World Report, November 4, 1996.*

E

EDELMAN, Marian Wright 1939-

PERSONAL: Born June 6, 1939, in Bennettsville, SC; daughter of Arthur J. and Maggie (Bowen) Wright; married Peter Benjamin Edelman, July 14, 1968; children: Joshua Robert, Jonah Martin, Ezra Benjamin. *Education:* Attended University of Paris and University of Geneva, 1958-59; Spelman College, B.A., 1960; Yale University, LL.B., 1963.

ADDRESSES: Office—Children's Defense Fund, 122 C St. N.W., Washington, DC 20001.

CAREER: National Association for the Advancement of Colored People (NAACP), Legal Defense and Education Fund, Inc., New York City, staff attorney, 1963-64, director of office in Jackson, MS, 1964-68; partner of Washington Research Project of Southern Center for Public Policy, 1968-73; Children's Defense Fund, Washington, DC, founder and president, 1973—. W. E. B. Du Bois Lecturer at Harvard University, 1986. Member of Lisle Fellowship's U.S.-U.S.S.R. Student Exchange, 1959; member of executive committee of Student Non-Violent Coordinating Committee (SNCC), 1961-63; member of Operation Crossroads Africa Project in Ivory Coast, 1962; congressional and federal agency liaison for Poor People's Campaign, summer, 1968; director of Harvard University's Center for Law and Education, 1971-73. Member of Presidential Commission on Americans Missing and Unaccounted for in Southeast Asia (Woodcock Commission), 1977, United States-South Africa leadership Exchange Program, 1977, National Commission on the International Year of the Child, 1979, and President's Commission for a National Agenda for the Eighties, 1979; member of board of directors of Carnegie Council on Children,

1972-77, Aetna Life and Casualty Foundation, Citizens for Constitutional Concerns, U.S. Committee for UNICEF, and Legal Defense and Education Fund of the NAACP; member of board of trustees of Martin Luther King, Jr., Memorial Center, and Joint Center for Political Studies.

MEMBER: Council on Foreign Relations, Delta Sigma Theta (honorary member).

AWARDS, HONORS: Merrill scholar in Paris and Geneva, 1958-59; honorary fellow of Law School at University of Pennsylvania, 1969; Louise Waterman Wise Award, 1970; Presidential Citation, American Public Health Association, 1979; Outstanding Leadership Award, National Alliance of Black School Educators, 1979; Distinguished Service Award, National Association of Black Women Attorneys, 1979; National Award of Merit, National Council on Crime and Delinquency, 1979; named Washingtonian of the Year, 1979; Whitney M. Young Memorial Award, Washington Urban League, 1980; Professional Achievement Award, Black Enterprise magazine, 1980; Outstanding Leadership Achievement Award, National Women's Political Caucus and Black Caucus, 1980; Outstanding Community Service Award, National Hookup of Black Women, 1980; Woman of the Year Award, Big Sisters of America, 1980; Award of Recognition, American Academy of Pedodontics, 1981; Rockefeller Public Service Award, 1981; Gertrude Zimand Award, National Child Labor Committee, 1982; Florina Lasker Award, New York Civil Liberties Union, 1982; Anne Roe Award, Graduate School of Education at Harvard University, 1984; Roy Wilkins Civil Rights Award, National Association for the Advancement of Colored People (NAACP), 1984; award from Women's Legal Defense Fund, 1985; Hubert H. Humphrey Award, Leadership Conference on Civil Rights, 1985; fellow of MacArthur Foundation, 1985; Grenville Clark Prize from Dartmouth College, 1986; Compostela Award of St. James Cathedral, 1987; Gandhi Peace Award, 1989; Fordham Stein Prize, 1989; Murray-Green-Meany Award, AFL-CIO, 1989; Frontrunner Award, Sara Lee Corporation, 1990; Jefferson Award, American Institute for Public Service, 1991; recipient of more than thirty honorary degrees.

WRITINGS:

Families in Peril: An Agenda for Social Change, Harvard University Press, 1987.
The Measure of Our Success: A Letter to My Children and Yours, Beacon Press (Boston, MA), 1992.
Guide My Feet: Prayers and Meditations on Loving and Working for Children, Beacon Press, 1995.
Stand for Children, Hyperion Books for Children (New York City), 1998.

Also author of *School Suspensions: Are They Helping Children?,* 1975, and *Portrait of Inequality: Black and White Children in America,* 1980. Contributor to books, including *Raising Children in Modern America: Problems and Prospective Solutions,* edited by Nathan B. Talbot, Little, Brown, 1975; and *Toward New Human Rights: The Social Policies of the Kennedy and Johnson Administrations,* edited by David C. Warner, Lyndon B. Johnson School of Public Affairs, University of Texas at Austin, 1977.

SIDELIGHTS: Dubbed "the 101st Senator on children's issues" by Senator Edward Kennedy, Marian Wright Edelman left her law practice in 1968, just after the assassination of civil rights leader Martin Luther King, Jr., to work toward a better future for American children. She was the first black woman on the Mississippi bar and had been a civil rights lawyer with the National Association for the Advancement of Colored People (NAACP). "Convinced she could achieve more as an advocate than as a litigant for the poor," wrote Nancy Traver in *Time,* Edelman moved to Washington, D.C., and began to apply her researching and rhetorical skills in Congress. She promotes her cause with facts about teen pregnancies, poverty, and infant mortality and—with her Children's Defense Fund—has managed to obtain budget increases for family and child health care and education programs. In *Ms.* magazine Katherine Bouton described Edelman as "the nation's most effective lobbyist on behalf of children . . . an unparalleled strategist and pragmatist."

Edelman's book, *Families in Peril: An Agenda for Social Change,* was judged "a powerful and necessary document" of the circumstances of children by *Washington Post* reviewer Jonathan Yardley, and it urges support for poor mothers and children of all races. The book is based on the 1986 W. E. B. Du Bois Lectures that Edelman gave at Harvard University. In making her case for increased support for America's children, Edelman offers numerous statistics that paint a grim portrait of life for the country's poor. Don Wycliff, reviewing the book for the *New York Times Book Review,* questioned Edelman's solutions as overly dependent on government support and neglectful of parental responsibility for children: "Governmental exertions . . . are indispensable. But . . . Edelman doesn't satisfactorily address how [parents] can be induced to behave wisely and responsibly *for their child's benefit.*" A *Kirkus Review* contributor, however, termed the book "graphic and eloquent."

In *Measure of Our Success: A Letter to My Children and Yours,* Edelman again deals with the problems and possible solutions of poverty and the neglect of children, in part by discussing her own experience as a parent. The book is divided into five sections: "A Family Legacy"; "Passing on the Legacy of Service"; "A Letter to My Sons"; "Twenty-five Lessons for Life"; and "Is the Child Safe?" Writing in the *New York Times Book Review* about the "Twenty-five Lessons for Life" chapter, Clifton L. Taulbert commented, "In the twenty-five lessons for life that she presents here, she issues a call for parental involvement, a commitment of personal time on behalf of others, the primacy of service over self, and the assumption of individual responsibility for our nation's character."

Edelman once commented: "I have been an advocate for disadvantaged Americans throughout my professional career. The Children's Defense Fund, which I have been privileged to direct, has become one of the nation's most active organizations concerned with a wide range of children's and family issues, especially those which most affect America's children: our poorest Americans.

"Founded in 1968 as the Washington Research Project, the Children's Defense Fund monitors and proposes improvements in federal, state, and local budgets, legislative and administrative policies in the areas of child and maternal health, education, child care, child welfare, adolescent pregnancy prevention, youth employment, and family support systems. In 1983 the Children's Defense Fund initiated a major long-term national campaign to prevent teenage pregnancy and provide positive life options for youth. Since then, we have launched a multimedia campaign that includes transit advertisements, posters, and television and radio public service announcements, a national prenatal care campaign, and Child Watch coalitions in more than seventy local communities in thirty states to combat teen pregnancy.

"The Children's Defense Fund also has been a leading advocate in Congress, state legislatures, and courts for children's rights. For example, our legal actions blocked out-of-state placement of hundreds of Louisiana children in Texas institutions, guaranteed access to special education programs for tens of thousands of Mississippi's children, and represented the interests of children and their families before numerous federal administrative agencies."

BIOGRAPHICAL/CRITICAL SOURCES:

PERIODICALS

Ebony, July, 1987.
Harper's, February, 1993, p. 154.
Kirkus Reviews, February 1, 1987, p. 189.
Library Journal, March 1, 1987, p. 66.
Ms., July/August, 1987.
New Republic, March 4, 1996, p. 33.
Newsweek, June 10, 1996, p. 32.
New York Times Book Review, June 7, 1987, p. 12; August 23, 1992, p. 13.
Psychology Today, July-August, 1993, p. 26.
School Library Journal, September, 1992, p. 290; December, 1992, p. 29.
Time, March 23, 1987.
Washington Post, March 4, 1987.
Washington Post Book World, April 19, 1992, p. 13.*

*   *   *

EDWARDS, Deborah R. 1945-

PERSONAL: Born September 24, 1945, in St. Louis, MO; daughter of Earnest L. (a minister) and Anna E. (a homemaker) Carter; married Freddie Edwards (divorced March 8, 1983); children: Neuil A., Nyron E. "Black." *Education:* Lincoln University, Jefferson City, MO, graduated, 1967; St. Louis University, M.A.Ed., 1972, Ed.S., 1993, Ed.D., 1994. *Religion:*

Christian. *Avocational interests:* Reading, bowling, travel.

ADDRESSES: Home—St. Louis, MO. *Office*—Eboni, Inc., P.O. Box 38308, St. Louis, MO 63138. *E-mail*—MentorEdD@aol.com.

CAREER: Teacher of enrichment classes in writing at public schools in St. Louis, MO, for thirteen years; schoolteacher in Florence, MO, for two years; St. Louis Public Schools, classroom teacher, for eleven years; Eboni, Inc., executive director.

MEMBER: Christian Educators Association International, Publishers' Marketing Association, Metropolitan St. Louis Alliance of Black School Educators.

WRITINGS:

Wrap It Up, I'll Take It!, Teachers' Load Press, 1980.
ABCs for Beginning Teachers, Teachers' Load Press, 1994.
Colors, Colors, Colors! (juvenile), Teachers' Load Press, 1996.
The Mentor Center by Eboni, Teachers' Load Press, in press.

SIDELIGHTS: Deborah R. Edwards told *CA:* "My primary motivation for writing is to help others. Guided by the Holy Spirit, I am inspired to write about people that I have met and places where I have been, either personally or vicariously. I also write about my experiences in the hope that they will be of help to others.

"Given a subject, I often do some research on it. This may involve reading books and/or articles, interviewing people, and taking notes. Next I write the first draft, then I put it aside for a day, and then I begin to edit it. Finally, I rewrite the material in its final form.

"For the subject that I have chosen to write about, I have been inspired by the many children, parents, and teachers that I have worked with over the years."

*   *   *

EDWARDS, Eli
See McKAY, Festus Claudius

EDWENSI, C. O. D.
See EKWENSI, Cyprian (Odiatu Duaka)

* * *

EKWENSI, Cyprian (Odiatu Duaka) 1921-
(C. O. D. Ekwensi)

PERSONAL: Born September 26, 1921, in Minna, Nigeria; son of Ogbuefi David Duaka and Uso Agnes Ekwensi; married Eunice Anyiwo; children: five. *Education:* Attended Achimota College, Ghana, and Ibadan University; received B.A.; further study at Chelsea School of Pharmacy, London, and University of Iowa. *Avocational interests:* Hunting game, swimming, photography, motoring, weightlifting.

ADDRESSES: Home—12 Hillview, Independence Layout, P.O. Box 317, Enugu, Anambra, Nigeria.

CAREER: Novelist and writer of short stories and stories for children. Igbodi College, Lagos, Nigeria, lecturer in biology, chemistry, and English, 1947-49; School of Pharmacy, Lagos, lecturer in pharmacognosy and pharmaceutics, 1949-56; pharmacist superintendent for Nigerian Medical Services, 1956-57; head of features, Nigerian Broadcasting Corporation, 1957-61; Federal Ministry of Information, Lagos, director of information, 1961-66; chair of Bureau for External Publicity during Biafran secession, 1967-69, and director of an independent Biafran radio station; chemist for plastics firm in Enugu, Nigeria; managing director of Star Printing & Publishing Co. (publishers of *Daily Star*), 1975-79; managing director of Niger Eagle Publishing Company, 1980-81; managing director of Ivory Trumpet Publishing Co. Ltd., 1981-83. Owner of East Niger Chemists and East Niger Trading Company. Chair of East Central State Library Board, 1972-75. Newspaper consultant to *Weekly Trumpet* and *Daily News* of Anambra State and to *Weekly Eagle* of Imo State, 1980-83; consultant on information to the executive office of the president; consultant to Federal Ministry of Information; public relations consultant.

MEMBER: PEN, Society of Nigerian Authors, Pharmaceutical Society of Great Britain, Institute of Public Relations (London), Institute of Public Relations (Nigeria; fellow).

AWARDS, HONORS: Dag Hammarskjold International Prize for Literary Merit, 1969.

WRITINGS:

NOVELS

People of the City, Andrew Dakers, 1954, Northwestern University Press, 1967, revised edition, Fawcett, 1969.
Jagua Nana, Hutchinson, 1961.
Burning Grass, Heinemann, 1962.
Beautiful Feathers, Hutchinson, 1963.
Divided We Stand, Fourth Dimension Publishers, 1980.

JUVENILE

(Under name C. O. D. Ekwensi) *Ikolo the Wrestler and Other Ibo Tales,* Thomas Nelson, 1947.
(Under name C. O. D. Ekwensi) *The Leopard's Claw,* Thomas Nelson, 1950.
The Drummer Boy, Cambridge University Press, 1960.
The Passport of Mallam Ilia, Cambridge University Press, 1960.
An African Night's Entertainment (folklore), African Universities Press, 1962.
Yaba Roundabout Murder (short novel), Tortoise Series Books (Lagos, Nigeria), 1962.
The Great Elephant-Bird, Thomas Nelson, 1965.
Juju Rock, African Universities Press, 1966.
The Boa Suitor, Thomas Nelson, 1966.
Trouble in Form Six, Cambridge University Press, 1966.
Coal Camp Boy, Longman, 1971.
Samankwe in the Strange Forest, Longman, 1973.
The Rainbow Tinted Scarf and Other Stories (collection), Evans Africa Library, 1975.
Samankwe and the Highway Robbers, Evans Africa Library, 1975.
Masquerade Time, Heinemann Educational Books, 1992.
King Forever!, Heinemann Educational Books, 1992.

OTHER

(Under name C. O. D. Ekwensi) *When Love Whispers* (novella), Tabansi Bookshop (Onitsha, Nigeria), 1947.
The Rainmaker and Other Short Stories (short story collection), African Universities Press, 1965.
Lokotown and Other Stories(short story collection), Heinemann, 1966.
Iska, Hutchinson, 1966.
The Restless City and Christmas Gold, Heinemann, 1975.

Survive the Peace, Heinemann, 1976.

(Editor) *Festac Anthology of Nigerian Writing,* Festac, 1977.

Motherless Baby (novella), Fourth Dimension Publishers, 1980.

For a Roll of Parchment, Heinemann, 1987.

Jagua Nana's Daughter, Spectrum, 1987.

Gone to Mecca, Heinemann, 1991.

Also author of *Behind the Convent Wall,* 1987. Writer of plays and scripts for BBC radio and television, Radio Nigeria, and other communication outlets. Contributor of stories, articles, and reviews to magazines and newspapers in Nigeria and England, including *West African Review, London Times, Black Orpheus, Flamingo,* and *Sunday Post.* Several of Ekwensi's novels have been translated into other languages, including Russian, Italian, German, Serbo-Croatian, Danish, and French. His novellas have been used primarily in schools as supplementary readers.

SIDELIGHTS: "Cyprian Ekwensi is the earliest and most prolific of the socially realistic Nigerian novelists," according to Martin Tucker in his *Africa in Modern Literature: A Survey of Contemporary Writing in English.* "His first writings were mythological fragments and folk tales. From these African materials he turned to the city and its urban problems, which he now feels are the major issues confronting his people." Reviewing Cyprian Ekwensi's *Beautiful Feathers* in *Critique: Studies in Modern Fiction,* John F. Povey writes: "The very practice of writing, the developing professionalism of his work, makes us find in Ekwensi a new and perhaps important phenomenon in African writing. . . . Other Nigerian novelists have sought their material from the past, the history of missionaries and British administration as in Chinua Achebe's books and the schoolboy memoirs of Onuora Nzekwu. Ekwensi faces the difficult task of catching the present tone of Africa, changing at a speed that frighteningly destroys the old certainties. In describing this world, Ekwensi has gradually become a significant writer."

Born in Northern Nigeria in 1921, Ekwensi grew up in various cities and had ample opportunity to observe what one critic called the "urban politics" of Nigeria. He went to schools in Ibadan, Lagos, and the Gold Coast, excelling in English, mathematics, and science; a high school record indicates that only his temper and occasional sullen moods kept him from being the ideal student. In the early-1940s he enrolled at the School of Forestry in Western Nigeria; successfully completing his degree requirements in 1944, he began

his work as a forestry officer. According to biographer Ernest Emenyonu, "it was . . . while wandering in the domains of animals and trees that ekwensi decided to become a writer. Taking advantage of his wild and lonely environment he began to create adventure stories with forest backgrounds." Among his early works are the short stories "Banana Peel," "The Tinted Scarf," and "Land of Sani," which he published together with a collection of Igbo folk tales under the title *Ikolo the Wrestler and Other Ibo Tales* in 1947. Other early works include *When Love Whispers* and *The Leopard's Claw;* he also published several adventure stories for children. In addition to being a professional writer, Ekwensi has worked as a pharmacist and a teacher. Most recently he has been involved with the Nigerian Broadcasting Corporation and various newspaper and publishing organizations.

Despite his popularity as folklorist and writer of children's literature, Ekwensi's fans frequently cite his urban novels as their favorites. *People of the City, Jagua Nana, Beautiful Feathers,* and *Iska* are all set in the city of Lagos, and according to Juliet Okonkwo, Ekwensi "revels in the excitement of city life and loves to expose its many faces of modernity. He writes about . . . its criminals, prostitutes, band-leaders, ministers of state, businessmen, civil servants, professionals, policemen on duty, thugs, thieves, and many other types that are found in the city. . . . Employing a naturalistic narrative technique reminiscent of Emile Zola, Ekwensi has been able to capture both the restless excitement and the frustrations of life in the city." *Burning Grass: A Story of the Fulani of Northern Nigeria* and *Survive the Peace* are exceptions to his "city novels." The former centers on Mai Sunsaye, a Fulani cattleman living on the grassy plains of Nigeria, and the latter on James Oduga, a radio journalist who tries to rebuild his life after a war.

Of Ekwensi's city novels, *Jagua Nana* is considered his best work. It focuses on Jagua Nana, an aging prostitute who thrives on Lagos nightlife—"They called her Jagua because of her good looks and stunning fashions. They said she was Ja-gwa, after the famous British prestige car." When the novel opens she is in love with Freddie Namme, an ambitious young teacher. She continues to sleep with other men for money, to Freddie's dismay, because she wants to "wear fine cloth": "She loved Freddie well, but his whole salary would not buy that dress. He must understand that taking money from the Syrian did not mean that she loved him less." Freddie claims to despise Jagua's lifestyle but doesn't refuse the luxuries that her income provides. Seeking consolation, Freddie has an affair with a younger woman, but before Jagua can unleash her jealous rage, he leaves for England. When Jagua and Freddie meet again, Freddie is running for office against Uncle Taiwo, a large, crass, power-hungry politician "who has chosen to absorb and use all that is worst in European ways," according to critic John Povey. The novel ends with Freddie and Uncle Taiwo both murdered and Jagua fleeing Lagos for her life. "Through Jagua, her career, her pursuits and her fluctuating fortune," Okonkwo observed, "Ekwensi reveals the common wickedness, squalor, materialism and immorality of the city, together with its crimes and violence." Since its publication in 1961, *Jagua Nana* has attracted bitter controversy. Church organizations and women's groups vehemently attacked it, prompting some schools to ban it from their libraries. The Nigerian Parliament refused an Italian studio's request to film the book. Some readers called it "obscene" and "pornographic," while others praised it as a masterpiece. Similarly, literary critics were equally divided in their opinions: some were impressed with *Jagua Nana,* particularly by Ekwensi's use of language and depth of characterization, but others dismissed it as another "whorewith-a-heart-of-gold" story commonly found in bad American movies and books.

Controversy appears to follow all of Ekwensi's fiction; while *Jagua Nana* has received the most attention, his other books have also been scrutinized. Assessing Ekwensi as a writer, critic Bernth Lindfors declared: "not one [of his works] is entirely free of amateurish blots and blunders, not one could be called the handiwork of a careful, skilled craftsman." Ekwensi's supporters, most notably Povey, have argued otherwise. Acknowledging Ekwensi's weaknesses as a writer, Povey explained: "He often dangerously approaches the senstimental, the vulgar and melodramatic. Behind his work stands a reading of American popular fiction and paperback crime stories. Yet Ekwensi's writing cannot be dismissed wtih such assertions. . . . Ekwensi is interesting because he is concerned with the present, with the violence of the new Lagos slums, the dishonesty of the new native politicians. . . . Only Ekwensi has dared to approach the contemporary scene with critical satire."

Ekwensi states that his life in government and quasi-government organizations like the Nigerian Broadcasting Corporation has prevented him from expressing any strong political opinions, but adds, "I am as much a nationalist as the heckler standing on the soapbox, with the added advantage of objectivity." During the late-1960s Biafran war, in which the eastern region of Biafra seceded temporarily from the rest of Nigeria, Ekwensi visited the United States more than once to help raise money for Biafra and to purchase radio equipment for the independent Biafran radio station of which he was director. He has also traveled in western Europe.

J. O. J. Nwachukwu-Agbada, in *World Literature Today,* describes Ekwensi as the "Nigerian Defoe": "Ekwensi has been writing fiction since the 1940s. He is prolific and versatile, especially in the subject matter of his works, which can range from sex to science. . . . The 'new' work [*For a Roll of Parchment*] also reveals considerable artistic development, particularly in language and descriptive power."

In a later issue of *World Literature Today,* Nwachukwu-Agbada talks of "Cyprian Ekwensi's Rabelaisian jeu d'esprit whose obscene flavor sparked considerable outrage among Nigerian readers of the sixties [upon the release of *Jagua Nana* in 1961]. The new novel's [*Jagua Nana's Daughter*] bawdiness twenty-five years later has not attracted similar attention, probably due to the increased permissiveness and decreased influence of tradition in modern-day Nigeria."

Ekwensi's stature as a novelist is still debated. Emenyonu believes that Ekwensi's commitment "to portray the naked truth about the life of modern man" is the reason for the existing controversy over *Jagua Nana* and all of Ekwensi's fiction. "When one looks at his works over the past three decades," he observed, "one sees the deep imprints of a literature of social awareness and commitment, and this is Ekwensi's greatest achievement in the field of modern African writing."

BIOGRAPHICAL/CRITICAL SOURCES:

BOOKS

Contemporary Literary Criticism, Volume 4, Gale (Detroit), 1975.
Emenyonu, Ernest N., *The Essential Ekwensi: A Literary Celebration of Cyprian Ekwensi's Sixty-Fifth Birthday,* Heinemann, 1987.
Tucker, Martin, *Africa in Modern Literature: A Survey of Contemporary Writing in English,* Ungar, 1967.

PERIODICALS

Books Abroad, autumn, 1967.

Critique: Studies in Modern Fiction, October, 1965.
Times Literary Supplement, June 4, 1964.
World Literature Today, autumn, 1988; winter, 1989.

*   *   *

ELDER, Lonne III 1931-1996

PERSONAL: Born December 26, 1931, in Americus, GA; died June 11, 1996, in Woodland Hills, CA; son of Lonne, Jr., and Quincy Elder; married Betty Gross, 1963 (divorced, 1967); married Judith Ann Johnson (an actress), February 14, 1969; children: (first marriage) David DuBois; (second marriage) Christian, Loni. *Education:* Attended Yale University School of Drama, 1965-67. *Religion:* Episcopalian.

CAREER: Playwright, screenwriter, and freelance writer. Has worked as a political activist, phone clerk, waiter, professional gambler, and dock worker; actor in *A Raisin in the Sun* in New York City, 1959, and on tour, 1960-61; actor in *A Day of Absence* in New York City, 1965; Negro Ensemble Company, New York City, director of playwrights division, 1967-69; Talent Associates, New York City, writer, 1968; Cinema Center Films, Hollywood, CA, writer and producer, 1969-70; Universal Pictures, Hollywood, writer, 1970-71; Radnitz/Mattel Productions, Hollywood, writer, 1971; Talent Associates, Hollywood, writer and producer, 1971; Metro-Goldwyn-Mayer, Hollywood, writer, 1971; Columbia Pictures Industries, Inc., Hollywood, writer, 1972; American Broadcasting Co., New York City, scriptwriter, 1972. Co-founder, Banneker Productions (a filmmaking company), 1969; founder, Black Artists Alliance. *Military service:* Served in U.S. Army, 1952-54.

MEMBER: Black Academy of Arts and Letters, Writers Guild of America, West, New Dramatists, Harlem Writer's Guild.

AWARDS, HONORS: Stanley Drama Award in playwriting, 1965, Pulitzer Prize nomination, 1969, Outer Drama Critics Circle Award, 1970, Vernon Rice Drama Desk Award, 1970, Stella Holt Memorial Playwrights Award, 1970, Los Angeles Drama Critics Award, 1970, and Christopher Award, 1975, all for *Ceremonies in Dark Old Men;* John Hay Whitney fellowship, 1965-66; ABC fellowship in television writing, 1965-66; Hamilton K. Bishop Award in playwriting; American National Theatre Academy Award, 1967; Joseph E. Levine fellowship in film-making Yale University School of Drama, 1966-67; John Golden fellowship, 1966-67; Award of Merit, University of Southern California Film Conference, 1971; Academy Award nomination for best screenplay based on material from another medium, from Academy of Motion Picture Arts and Sciences, Christopher Award, Atlanta Film Festival Silver Award, and Image Award, all 1972, all for *Sounder,* which was also nominated for an Academy Award for best picture; Award of Merit, California Association of Teachers of English, 1973.

WRITINGS:

Ceremonies in Dark Old Men (two-act; first produced in New York City at Wagner College, July, 1965; revised version produced in New York City at St. Mark's Playhouse, February 4, 1969; also see below), Farrar, Straus, 1969.
Charades on East Fourth Street (one-act; commissioned by New York City Mobilization for Youth, Inc.), first produced at Expo-67 Montreal, Quebec, 1967, published in *Black Drama Anthology,* edited by Woodie King and Ron Milner, New American Library, 1971.
Splendid Mummer (monodrama), first produced Off-Broadway at American Place Theater, April 24, 1988.

Also author of plays: *A Hysterical Turtle in a Rabbit Race,* 1961; *Kissing Rattlesnakes Can Be Fun* (one-act), 1966; and *Seven Comes Up, Seven Comes Down* (one-act), 1966.

SCREENPLAYS AND TELEVISION DRAMAS

The Terrible Veil, National Broadcasting Corporation (NBC-TV), 1964.
Sounder (adaptation of novel of same title by William H. Armstrong), Twentieth Century-Fox, 1972.
Melinda, Metro-Goldwyn-Mayer, 1972.
Ceremonies in Dark Old Men (based on his play of same title), American Broadcasting Co. (ABC-TV), 1975.
Sounder, Part 2, ABC-TV, 1976.
A Woman Called Moses, NBC-TV, 1978.
Bustin' Loose (adaptation of story by Richard Pryor), Universal Pictures, 1981.

Also author of screenplay about the life of Ethel Waters for World Wide Pictures, and of television drama, *Deadly Circle of Violence.* Author of scripts for *Number One with a Bullet,* an expose on the recording industry, for a film version of Richard

Wright's novel, *Native Son,* and for television series, *Camera Three,* CBS-TV, 1963, *N.Y.P.D.,* ABC- TV, 1967-68, and *McCloud,* NBC-TV, 1970-71.

OTHER

(Contributor) Lindsay Patterson, editor, *Black Theater: A 20th-Century Collection of the Works of the Best Playwrights,* Dodd, 1971.

(Contributor) Clive Barnes, editor, *Best American Plays, Seventh Series, 1967-1973,* Crown, 1974.

The Responsibilities of the Black Writer (sound recording), Center for Cassette Studies, 1975.

Contributor to *New York Times, Black Creation,* and *Freedomways.*

SIDELIGHTS: "Lonne Elder III is a talented and creative actor, playwright, and screenwriter whose career has evolved from acting and writing for the stage to acting and writing for the screen," stated Joseph Millichap in a *Dictionary of Literary Biography* essay. "Elder has remained committed to a program of raising audience consciousness of racial tensions through his analysis of the black identity in modern America. In particular, his vision has stressed the personal dedication necessary for Afro-Americans to overcome the handicaps imposed by generations of white prejudice and black fear. He has also used his writing to help change the portrayal of blacks in films and on television."

In an interview with Liz Gant in *Black World,* Elder indicated that t the early age of six or seven, he had no particular inclination to make writing his career. Elder recalled: "I don't think I even knew what a writer was. I just liked the idea of writing to myself; it was a way of expressing feelings that I didn't know how to express in other ways, like talking. There was no one to whom I could convey those kinds of thoughts and emotions in the environment I grew up in." Soon after Elder's birth in Georgia, his family moved to New Jersey and, orphaned in adolescence, Elder was raised by an aunt and uncle. Although Elder's formal education was not extensive, he indicated to Gant that the education he did receive was "good and well-balanced." And while he was stationed with the Army near Fisk University, he was introduced to the poet and teacher Robert Hayden, with whom he spent much time. "I gave him my wotk to read and he was very, very encouraging," recalled Elder in his interview with Gant, adding that Hayden helped him to "handle and structure" what he was

trying to write. "He really made a tremendous impact on my life that has lasted up to this day."

"Elder's encounters with dramatist and actor Douglas Turner Ward moved him away from short stories and poetry and in the direction of playwriting," wrote Wilsonia E. D. Cherry in a *Dictionary of Literary Biography* essay. Elder and Ward shared an apartment during the 1950s; and it was during this time that Ward wrote his first play, to which Elder reacted with both wonder and determination. "It was a gigantic thing, one of the longest plays I'd ever seen," Elder told Gant. "I read it and all I could do was shake my head. Damn! I thought. He wrote this whole thing! And he was one of my peers. . . . The most I'd ever written was maybe a 15-page short story or a ge poem. So I said, well, I can do that too! And that's when I started writing plays." Explaining that it was "the immediacy of expressing a feeling or an emotion" that most excited him about drama, Elder also told Gant, "I started going to the theater and I was impressed with playwrights who were being produced in small theaters. . . . There was something about it that just got to me. And no matter what I saw, I thought I could do better."

"Like other black dramatists of the last three decades—a period marked by an upsurge of plays by, about, and for black people—Lonne Elder articulates the sorrows, angers, and joys that characterize black life in America," stated Cherry; and although Elder's dramatic canon was small, "the plays that he has written strongly emphasize his belief in the survival of a people traumatized both from without and from within." In a *Dictionary of Literary Biography* essay, William Bryan Hart noted that Elder weaves his "multifaceted" personal life into his plays. "For a number of years the struggling playwright supported himself as a professional political activist, dock worker, waiter, phone clerk, professional poker dealer, and actor." Elder gained valuable insights into the theater through his experience as an actor, which "reinforced his positive feelings about writing for the stage," noted Cherry. And when his award-winning play *Ceremonies in Dark Old Men* was first produced, says Megan Rosenfeld in the *Washington Post,* "Lonne Elder III immediately entered the ranks of young black playwrights who sounded a new voice in the theater." The play was warmly received by critics such as the *New York Post*'s Richard Watts, who praised it as the "best American play of the season." Echoing the assessment that it was "one of the more notable plays to come out of the eruption of black theater in the late 1960s," David Richards added in the *Washington Post* that it had weathered the years well, "Its compassion for the dispossessed and its insights into the souls of the misguided remain undimmed by time."

In the *New York Times,* Richard F. Shepard called *Ceremonies in Dark Old Men* "a tragedy gleefully shrouded in comedy." And in the *Washington Post,* Joe Brown described the cast of various Parker family members. The father "is an unemployed barber, a charming dreamer and yarn-spinner who spends his days playing ritual checker games and telling stories so well he even deceives himself." One of Parker's sons is "a restless schemer" while the other is "a light-fingered loafer," Brown continued; and the daughter "is full of righteous resentment about supporting three grown men, as her mother did before her." The family tries to "escape the poverty-stricken treadmill of their Harlem home by selling illegally made corn liquor . . . and by stealing from white Harlem store owners," said Cherry. According to Hart, Elder emphasized that the greatest adversity threatening the Parker family to black Americans generally—"individual weakness compounded by the frustration of being incapable of prospering in a white-oriented society." Cherry suggested, however, that the play also "points toward the resilience of the American black family." Interviewed by C. W. E. Bigsby in his *The Black American Writer,* Elder indicated that he did not specifically aim the play at a black audience, "If I do that I think I'm crippling myself in terms of what I am and what I can do with the material before me. I write out of the black frame of reference, which is different from saying that I am writing for all black people."

Affirming the "overwhelmingly positive" critical response to *Ceremonies in Dark Old Men,* Cherry continued: "Although a few critics saw the play as inept, formulaic, and dated, the majority found it well wrought, rich, powerful, and meritorious. And rewarded it was." Having placed second in the Pulitzer Prize, the work was honored with several other dramatic awards, including a Christopher for the teleplay. Disagreeing with the assessment of some critics that the play was "naturalistic in the traditional or conventional sense of the word," Elder explained to Bigsby that it is only naturalistic "out of necessity in areas where it had to be. I would call it more akin to exalted realism." Elder told Bigsby that "it's naturalism to [the critics] mainly because they're unacquainted with the flow and the various colours of life in the black ghetto." *Ceremonies in Dark Old Men,* Elder continued, "really is based on the daily ritual of

survival in the black community, which does not necessarily have anything to do with black/white confrontation or any clenched fist anger." Writing in the *New York Times* about the play's recent revival, Mel Gussow held that it "is marked breadth of its vision of interdependent, mutually harmful lives, and it is written with humor and a depth of understanding," and concluded that Elder's "absence has been a loss for the theater."

Despite his success with both theater and television, Elder journeyed west to launch a career as a screenwriter. Explaining to Gant that he decided to leave New York City because it "just became a mentally unbearable place to live in," Elder added: "I'm just not made of the stuff to walk around with daggers in my eyes and a clenched fist. I just can't live like that." In his interview with Gant, Elder also spoke about the sense of closure that he experienced with *Ceremonies in Dark Old Men,* recalling: "It was well received in New York and I felt that, in terms of what I had set out to do, I'd accomplished do it anymore. I said I wasn't going to write any more Black 'kitchen sink' dramas. From that point on, it was not exactly my choice." Nevertheless, Dan Sullivan pointed out in the *New York Times* that "as a black writer, [Elder] has had to deal with the particular temptations of the 'blaxploitation' film and the neo-Amos 'n' Andy TV comedy series, two genres that he has little respect for but that do offer good money and, what is almost as important in Hollywood, highly visible credits."

Regarding *Melinda,* Elder's screenwriting debut and the only "blaxploitation" film with which he was associated, Elder told Sullivan: "I went in under the delusion that I could write a crime melodrama that wouldn't just titillate. I wasn't able to do it. No, I wouldn't say I'm proud of that picture. But I'm not ashamed of it either." The film is a mystery about a disc jockey who is wrongly accused of killing his girlfriend d pursues the actual murderer himself. Elder acknowledged to Gant that, although he was not "anxious" to get involved with the film, he was prompted by commercial rather than artistic reasons; and Millichap recognized in the film a "blending of Elder's commercial efforts for television and his more serious efforts at probing the effects of deprivation on black personality."

Released coincidentally at the same time as his critically deplored *Melinda* was Elder's award-winning *Sounder,* a film about the difficulties endured by a black sharecropping family during the Depression, starring Cicely Tyson and Paul Winfield. Millichap believed that "Elder created a moving film which received much critical acclaim and provided an artistic counterpoint to the exploitation trend." "About 95 percent of what I wrote was represented on screen—a miracle by Hollywood standards," Elder related to Gant. A *Chicago Sun-Times* contributor, who called it "one of the most that "the story is so simple because it involved, not so much what people do, but how they change and grow." Elder's other film work included a sequel to *Sounder* and an adaptation of Richard Pryor's screen story *Bustin' Loose*. Most of Elder's writing, however, was for television and included the well-received mini-series, *A Woman Called Moses,* based on the life of Harriet Tubman.

"Elder has had to adjust to what he calls 'the whore mentality' that smogs the film-TV industry, the assumption that one's talent is on call to an inscrutable client who will drop you the minute you fail to give pleasure," commented Sullivan. Admitting to Gant that he is a "perfectionist," Elder added that "contrary to what a lot of Black artists say, I don't think you have to create new standards and values. They're already there, on anybody's terms. But structure and craftsmanship are all- important. And this is something that I've en myself to. I intend for whatever I write to be excellent. I'm not going to just shove things out." Perceiving an obligation to correct the industry's stereotyped depictions of black life, "Elder maintains that he is willing to play the Hollywood charade if it means changing the way black people are portrayed on television and film," Hart wrote. "Elder says that these media have become rigid and resistant to authentic characterizations of black American life." Expressing his belief that "no one wants to really believe that black people are human," Elder remarked to Sullivan that "if the black man did emerge as a human entity, it would mean that he should participate in the culture, that he should own a part of it. That still bothers people."

Elder's *Splendid Mummer* signaled his return to the theater. Calling the monodrama "an act of homage to his theatrical past and the little-known cultural history of his race," Steven Erlanger explained in the *New York Times* that the play is about Ira Frederick Aldridge, a black actor who left America in the 1820s for the "more racially tolerant England, Europe and Russia" to become a Shakespearean actor. Believed to have been the first black actor to perform the role of Othello, Aldridge headed his own touring company and was recognized as "one of the foremost interpreters of Shakespeare," notes Erlanger. According to Gussow in the *New York Times,* "he had an astonish-

ing career in the English theater, one that has not been equaled by any other American classical actor." Describing Elder as "more at ease with himself than in the interviews of 20 years ago, when *Ceremonies in Dark Old Men* became a sudden hit, thrusting him forward into the capricious world of New York theater," Erlanger related Elder's response to a question concerning "his sense of responsibility to the black theater: 'My responsibility basically starts with me, in terms of what I do and how I carry out whatever mission I take on.'"

Transcripts of Elder's one-act plays are housed in the Hatch-Billops Archives in New York, and a collection of his manuscripts is maintained by Boston University. However, despite a canon that includes other plays and significant contributions to film and television, Hart noted that Elder's "reputation as a dramatist rests primarily upon this single, major work [*Ceremonies in Dark Old Men*]." Assessing the entirety of his writing, though, Millichap considered Elder "a committed, intelligent writer whose work is shaped by a responsible vision of black experience as an important part of modern American life." Similarly, Hart believed that Elder "celebrates the humanity of blacks and does not conveniently avoid the ironies and difficulties that are a part of his life." As Elder related to Shepard: "I think I have a lot of respect for people, especially black people. I know there has always glorious and adventurous thing constantly unfolding in every day life in its beauty, speech, walk, dance and even in its anger."

BIOGRAPHICAL\CRITICAL SOURCES:

BOOKS

Arata, Esther Spring, *More Black American Playwrights: A Bibliography,* Scarecrow, 1979.

Arata, Esther Spring, and Nicholas John Rotoli, *Black American Playwrights: 1800 to the Present; A Bibliography,* Scarecrow, 1976.

Bigsby, C. W. E., editor, *The Black American Writer,* Volume 2: *Poetry and Drama,* Penguin Books, 1969.

Dictionary of Literary Biography, Gale, Volume 7: *Twentieth-Century American Dramatists,* 1981, Volume 38: *Afro-American Writers after 1955: Dramatists and Prose Writers,* 1985, Volume 44: *American Screenwriters,* 1986.

Harrison, Paul Carter, *The Drama of the Nommo,* Grove, 1972, pp. 27-8.

Hatch, James Vernon, and Amanii Abdullah, *Black Playwrights 1823-1977,* Bowker, 1977, p. 83.

Vinson, James, editor, *Contemporary Dramatists,* St. Martin's Press, 1973, pp. 239-41.

PERIODICALS

Arts in Society, summer, 1971.
Black Creation, summer, 1973; winter, 1973.
Black World, April, 1973.
Chicago Sun-Times, December 18, 1972.
CLA Journal, September, 1971; September, 1972; December, 1972; December, 1976.
Dialog on Film, May, 1973.
Dissent, winter, 1973; summer, 1976.
English Journal, April, 1970.
Freedomways, Volume 19, 1979.
MELUS, spring, 1980.
Nation, May 14, 1988, p. 689-90.
Negro History Bulletin, January, 1973.
New York Daily News, February 6, 1969.
New York Post, February 6, 1969.
New York Times, February 8, 1969; February 16, 1969; January 5, 1975.
Partisan Review, volume 36, 1969.
Village Voice, November 12, 1972.
Wall Street Journal, February 19, 1969.
Washington Post, September 23, 1972; February 8, 1985; February 11, 1985.

OBITUARIES:

PERIODICALS

New York Times, June 13, 1996, p. B6.*

*   *   *

ELLISON, Ralph (Waldo) 1914-1994

PERSONAL: Born March 1, 1914, in Oklahoma City, OK; died of cancer, April 16, 1994, in New York, NY; son of Lewis Alfred (a construction worker and tradesman) and Ida (Millsap) Ellison; married Fanny McConnell, July, 1946. *Education:* Attended Tuskegee Institute, 1933-36. *Avocational interests:* Jazz and classical music, photography, electronics, furniture-making, bird-watching, gardening.

CAREER: Writer, 1937-94. Worked as a researcher and writer on Federal Writers' Project in New York City, 1938-42; edited *Negro Quarterly,* 1942; lecture tour in Germany, 1954; lecturer at Salzburg Seminar, Austria, fall, 1954; U.S. Information Agency, tour of

Italian cities, 1956; Bard College, Annandale-on-Hudson, NY, instructor in Russian and American literature, 1958-61; New York University, New York City, Albert Schweitzer Professor in Humanities, 1970-79, professor emeritus, 1979-94. Alexander White Visiting Professor, University of Chicago, 1961; visiting professor of writing, Rutgers University, 1962-64; visiting fellow in American studies, Yale University, 1966. Gertrude Whittall Lecturer, Library of Congress, January, 1964; delivered Ewing Lectures at University of California, Los Angeles, April, 1964. Lecturer in African-American culture, folklore, and creative writing at other colleges and universities throughout the United States, including Columbia University, Fisk University, Princeton University, Antioch University, and Bennington College. Member of Carnegie Commission on Educational Television, 1966-67; honorary consultant in American letters, Library of Congress, 1966-72. Trustee, Colonial Williamsburg Foundation, John F. Kennedy Center for the Performing Arts, 1967-77, Educational Broadcasting Corp., 1968-69, New School for Social Research, 1969-83, Bennington College, 1970-75, and Museum of the City of New York, 1970-86. Charter member of National Council of the Arts, 1965-67, and of National Advisory Council, Hampshire College. *Military service:* U.S. Merchant Marine, World War II.

MEMBER: PEN (vice president, 1964), Authors Guild, Authors League of America, American Academy and Institute of Arts and Letters, Institute of Jazz Studies (member of board of advisors), Century Association (resident member).

AWARDS, HONORS: Rosenwald grant, 1945; National Book Award and National Newspaper Publishers' Russwurm Award, both 1953, both for *Invisible Man;* Certificate of Award, *Chicago Defender,* 1953; Rockefeller Foundation award, 1954; Prix de Rome fellowships, American Academy of Arts and Letters, 1955 and 1956; *Invisible Man* selected as the most distinguished postwar American novel and Ellison as the sixth most influential novelist by *New York Herald Tribune Book Week* poll of two hundred authors, editors, and critics, 1965; recipient of award honoring well-known Oklahomans in the arts from governor of Oklahoma, 1966; Medal of Freedom, 1969; Chevalier de l'Ordre des Arts et Lettres (France), 1970; Ralph Ellison Public Library, Oklahoma City, named in his honor, 1975; National Medal of Arts, 1985, for *Invisible Man* and for his teaching at numerous universities; honorary doctorates from Tuskegee Institute, 1963, Rutgers University, 1966, Grinnell College,

1967, University of Michigan, 1967, Williams College, 1970, Long Island University, 1971, Adelphi University, 1971, College of William and Mary, 1972, Harvard University, 1974, Wake Forest College, 1974, University of Maryland, 1974, Bard College, 1978, Wesleyan University, 1980, and Brown University, 1980.

WRITINGS:

Invisible Man (novel), Random House (New York City), 1952, published in a limited edition with illustrations by Steven H. Stroud, Franklin Library, 1980, thirtieth-anniversary edition with new introduction by author, Random House, 1982, edited and with an introduction by Harold Bloom, Chelsea House (New York City), 1996.

(Author of introduction) Stephen Crane, *The Red Badge of Courage and Four Great Stories,* Dell (New York City), 1960.

Shadow and Act (essays), Random House, 1964.

(With Karl Shapiro) *The Writer's Experience* (lectures; includes "Hidden Names and Complex Fate: A Writer's Experience in the U.S.," by Ellison, and "American Poet?," by Shapiro), Gertrude Clarke Whittall Poetry and Literature Fund for Library of Congress, 1964.

(With Whitney M. Young and Herbert Gans) *The City in Crisis,* introduction by Bayard Rustin, A. Philip Randolph Education Fund, 1968.

(Author of introduction) Romare Bearden, *Paintings and Projections* (catalogue of exhibition, November 25-December 22, 1968), State University of New York at Albany, 1968.

(Author of foreword) Leon Forrest, *There Is a Tree More Ancient than Eden,* Random House, 1973.

Going to the Territory (essays), Random House, 1986.

The Collected Essays of Ralph Ellison, Modern Library, 1995.

Flying Home and Other Stories, edited by John F. Callahan, preface by Saul Bellow, Random House (New York City), 1996.

Juneteenth (novel), edited by Callahan, Random House, 1999.

OTHER

Ralph Ellison: An Interview with the Author of Invisible Man (sound recording), Center for Cassette Studies, 1974.

(With William Styron and James Baldwin) *Is the Novel Dead?: Ellison, Styron and Baldwin on*

Contemporary Fiction (sound recording), Center for Cassette Studies, 1974.

Conversations with Ralph Ellison, edited by Maryemma Graham and Amritjit Singh, University Press of Mississippi (Jackson), 1995.

Contributor to books, including *The Living Novel: A Symposium,* edited by Granville Hicks, Macmillan (New York City), 1957; *Education of the Deprived and Segregated* (report of seminar on education for culturally-different youth, Dedham, MA, September 3-15, 1963), Bank Street College of Education, 1965; *Who Speaks for the Negro?,* by Robert Penn Warren, Random House, 1965; *To Heal and to Build: The Programs of Lyndon B. Johnson,* edited by James MacGregor Burns, prologue by Howard K. Smith, epilogue by Eric Hoffer, McGraw (New York City), 1968; and *American Law: The Third Century, the Law Bicentennial Volume,* edited by Bernard Schwartz, F. B. Rothman for New York University School of Law, 1976. Work represented in numerous anthologies, including *American Writing,* edited by Hans Otto Storm and others, J. A. Decker, 1940; *Best Short Stories of World War II,* edited by Charles A. Fenton, Viking (New York City), 1957; *The Angry Black,* edited by John Alfred Williams, Lancer Books, 1962, 2nd edition published as *Beyond the Angry Black,* Cooper Square (Totowa, NJ), 1966; *Soon, One Morning: New Writing by American Negroes, 1940-1962* (includes previously unpublished section from original manuscript of *Invisible Man*), edited by Herbert Hill, Knopf (New York City), 1963, published in England as *Black Voices,* Elek Books (London), 1964; *Experience and Expression: Reading and Responding to Short Fiction,* edited by John L. Kimmey, Scott, Foresman (Glenview, IL), 1976; and *The Treasury of American Short Stories,* compiled by Nancy Sullivan, Doubleday (New York City), 1981.

SIDELIGHTS: Growing up in Oklahoma, a "frontier" state that "had no tradition of slavery" and where "relationships between the races were more fluid and thus more human than in the old slave states," Ralph Ellison became conscious of his obligation "to explore the full range of American Negro humanity and to affirm those qualities which are of value beyond any question of segregation, economics or previous condition of servitude." This sense of obligation, articulated in his 1964 collection of critical and biographical essays, *Shadow and Act,* led to his staunch refusal to limit his artistic vision to the "uneasy sanctuary of race" and commit instead to a literature that explores and affirms the complex, often contradictory frontier of an identity at once black and American and universally human. For Ellison, whom John F. Callahan in a *Chant of Saints: A Gathering of Afro-American Literature, Art, and Scholarship* essay called a "moral historian," the act of writing was fraught with both great possibility and grave responsibility. As Ellison asserted, writing "offers me the possibility of contributing not only to the growth of the literature but to the shaping of the culture as I should like it to be. The American novel is in this sense a conquest of the frontier; as it describes our experience, it creates it."

For Ellison, then, the task of the novelist was a moral and political one. In his preface to the thirtieth anniversary edition of *Invisible Man,* Ellison argued that the serious novel, like the best politics, "is a thrust toward a human ideal." Even when the ideal is not realized in the actual, he declared, "there is still available that fictional *vision* of an ideal democracy in which the actual combines with the ideal and gives us representations of a state of things in which the highly placed and the lowly, the black and the white, the Northerner and the Southerner, the native-born and the immigrant are combined to tell us of transcendent truths and possibilities such as those discovered when Mark Twain set Huck and Jim afloat on the raft." Ellison saw the novel as a "raft of hope" that may help readers stay above water as they try "to negotiate the snags and whirlpools that mark our nation's vacillating course toward and away from the democratic ideal."

Early in his career, Ellison conceived of his vocation as a musician, as a composer of symphonies. When he entered Alabama's Tuskegee Institute in 1933 he enrolled as a music major; he wonders in *Shadow and Act* if he did so because, given his background, it was the only art "that seemed to offer some possibility for self-definition." The act of writing soon presented itself as an art through which he could link the disparate worlds he cherished, could verbally record and create the "affirmation of Negro life" he knew was so intrinsic a part of the universally human. To move beyond the old definitions that separated jazz from classical music, vernacular from literary language, the folk from the mythic, he would have to discover a prose style that could equal the integrative imagination of the "Renaissance Man."

Because Ellison did not get a job that paid him enough to save money for tuition, he stayed in New York, working and studying composition until his mother died in Dayton, Ohio. After his return to Dayton, he and his brother supported themselves by hunting. Though Ellison had hunted for years, he did not know how to wing-shoot; it was from Hemingway's fiction that he learned this process. Ellison studied Hemingway to learn writing techniques; from the older writer he also learned a lesson in descriptive accuracy and power, in the close relationship between fiction and reality. Like his narrator in *Invisible Man,* Ellison did not return to college; instead he began his long apprenticeship as a writer, his long and often difficult journey toward self-definition.

Ellison's early days in New York, before his return to Dayton, provided him with experiences that would later translate themselves into his theory of fiction. Two days after his arrival in "deceptively 'free' Harlem," he met black poet Langston Hughes who introduced him to the works of Andre Malraux, a French writer defined as Marxist. Though attracted to Marxism, Ellison sensed in Malraux something beyond a simplistic political sense of the human condition. Said Ellison: Malraux "was the artist-revolutionary rather than a politician when he wrote *Man's Fate,* and the book lives not because of a political position embraced at the time, but because of its larger concern with the tragic struggle of humanity." Ellison began to form his definition of the artist as a revolutionary concerned less with local injustice than with the timelessly tragic.

Ellison's view of art was furthered after he met black novelist Richard Wright. Wright urged him to read Joseph Conrad, Henry James, James Joyce, and Feodor Dostoevsky and invited Ellison to contribute a review essay and then a short story to the magazine he was editing. Wright was then in the process of writing *Native Son,* much of which Ellison read, he declared in *Shadow and Act,* "as it came out of the typewriter." Though awed by the process of writing and aware of the achievement of the novel, Ellison, who had just read Malraux, began to form his objections to the "sociological," deterministic ideology which informed the portrait of the work's protagonist, Bigger Thomas. In *Shadow and Act,* which Arthur P. Davis in *From the Dark Tower: Afro-American Writers, 1900 to 1960* described as partly an *apologia provita sua* (a defense of his life), Ellison articulated the basis of his objection: "I, for instance, found it disturbing that Bigger Thomas had none of the finer qualities of Richard Wright, none of the imagination, none of the sense of poetry, none of the gaiety." Ellison thus refuted the depiction of the black individual as an inarticulate victim whose life is one only of despair, anger, and pain. He insisted that art must capture instead the complex reality, the pain and the pleasure of black existence, thereby challenging the definition of the black person as something less than fully human. Such a vision of art, which is at the heart of *Invisible Man,* became the focal point of an extended debate between Ellison and Irving Howe, who in a 1963 *Dissent* article accused Ellison of disloyalty to Wright in particular and to "protest fiction" in general.

From 1938 to 1944, Ellison published a number of short stories and contributed essays to journals such as *New Masses.* As with other examples of Ellison's work, these stories have provoked disparate readings. In an essay in *Black World,* Ernest Kaiser called the earliest stories and the essays in *New Masses* "the healthiest" of Ellison's career. The critic praised the economic theories that inform the early fiction, and he found Ellison's language pure, emotional, and effective. Lamenting a change he attributed to Ellison's concern with literary technique, Kaiser charged the later stories, essays, and novels with being no longer concerned with people's problems and with being "unemotional." Other critics, like Marcus Klein in *After Alienation: American Novels in Mid-Century,* saw the early work as a progressive preparation for Ellison's mature fiction and theory. In the earliest of these stories, "Slick Gonna Learn," Ellison drew a character shaped largely by an ideological, naturalistic conception of existence, the very type of character he later repudiated. From this imitation of proletarian fiction, Ellison's work moved towards psychological and finally metaphysical explorations of the human condition. His characters thus were freed from restrictive definitions as Ellison developed a voice that was his own, Klein maintains.

In the two latest stories of the 1938-1944 period, "Flying Home" and "King of the Bingo Game," Ellison created characters congruent with his sense of pluralism and possibility and does so in a narrative style that begins to approach the complexity of *Invisible Man.* As Arthur P. Davis noted, in "Flying Home" Ellison combined realism, folk story, symbolism, and a touch of surrealism to present his protagonist, Todd. In a fictional world composed of myriad levels of the mythic and the folk, the classical and the modern, Todd fights to free himself of imposed definitions. In "King of the Bingo Game," Ellison experimented with integrating sources and techniques. As in all of Ellison's early stories, the protagonist is a young black man fighting for his freedom against forces and people that attempt to deny it. In "King of the Bingo Game," Robert G. O'Meally argued in *The Craft of Ralph Ellison,* "the struggle is seen in its most abstracted form." This abstraction results from

the "dreamlike shifts of time and levels of consciousness" that dominate the surrealistic story and also from the fact that "the King is Ellison's first character to sense the frightening absurdity of everyday American life." In an epiphany which frees him from illusion and which places him, even if for only a moment, in control, the King realizes "that his battle for freedom and identity must be waged not against individuals or even groups, but against no less than history and fate," O'Meally declared. The parameters of the fight for freedom and identity have been broadened. Ellison saw his black hero as one who wages the oldest battle in human history: the fight for freedom to be timelessly human, to engage in the "tragic struggle of humanity," as the writer asserted in *Shadow and Act.*

Whereas The King achieves awareness for a moment, the Invisible Man not only becomes aware but is able to articulate fully the struggle. As Ellison noted in his preface to the anniversary edition of the novel, too often characters have been "figures caught up in the most intense forms of social struggle, subject to the most extreme forms of the human predicament but yet seldom able to articulate the issues which tortured them." The Invisible Man is endowed with eloquence; he is Ellison's radical experiment with a fiction that insists upon the full range and humanity of the black character.

Ellison began *Invisible Man* in 1945. Although he was at work on a never-completed war novel at the time, Ellison recalled in his 1982 preface that he could not ignore the "taunting, disembodied voice" he heard beckoning him to write *Invisible Man.* Published in 1952 after a seven-year creative struggle, and awarded the National Book Award in 1953, *Invisible Man* received critical acclaim. Although some early reviewers were puzzled or disappointed by the experimental narrative techniques, many now agree that these techniques give the work its lasting force and account for Ellison's influence on later fiction. The novel is a fugue of cultural fragments—echoes of Homer, Joyce, Eliot, and Hemingway join forces with the sounds of spirituals, blues, jazz, and nursery rhymes. The Invisible Man is as haunted by Louis Armstrong's "What did I do / To be so black / And blue?" as he is by Hemingway's bullfight scenes and his matadors' grace under pressure. The linking together of these disparate cultural elements allows the Invisible Man to draw the portrait of his inner face that is the way out of his wasteland.

In the novel, Ellison clearly employed the traditional motif of the *Bildungsroman,* or novel of education:

the Invisible Man moves from innocence to experience, darkness to light, from blindness to sight. Complicating this linear journey, however, is the narrative frame provided by the Prologue and Epilogue which the narrator composes after the completion of his above-ground educational journey. Yet readers begin with the Prologue, written in his underground chamber on the "border area" of Harlem where he is waging a guerrilla war against the Monopolated Light & Power Company by invisibly draining their power. At first denied the story of his discovery, readers must be initiated through the act of re-experiencing the events that led them and the narrator to this hole. Armed with some suggestive hints and symbols, readers then start the journey toward a revisioning of the Invisible Man, America, and themselves.

The act of writing, of ordering and defining the self, is what gives the Invisible Man freedom and what allows him to manage the absurdity and chaos of everyday life. Writing frees the self from imposed definitions, from the straitjacket of all that would limit the productive possibilities of the self. Echoing the pluralism of the novel's form, the Invisible Man insists on the freedom to be ambivalent, to love and to hate, to denounce and to defend the America he inherits. Ellison himself was well-acquainted with the ambivalence of his American heritage; nowhere is it more evident than in his name. Named after the nineteenth-century essayist and poet Ralph Waldo Emerson, whom Ellison's father admired, the name created for Ellison embarrassment, confusion, and a desire to be the American writer his namesake called for. And Ellison placed such emphasis on his unnamed yet self-named narrator's breaking the shackles of restrictive definitions, of what others call reality or right, he also freed himself, as Robert B. Stepto in *From Behind the Veil: A Study of Afro-American Narrative* argued, from the strictures of the traditional slave narratives of Frederick Douglas and W. E. B. Du Bois. By consciously invoking this form but then not bringing the motif of "ascent and immersion" to its traditional completion, Ellison revoiced the form, made it his own, and stepped outside it.

In her 1979 *PMLA* essay, Susan Blake argued that Ellison's insistence that black experience be ritualized as part of the larger human experience results in a denial of the unique social reality of black life. Because Ellison so thoroughly adapted black folklore into the Western tradition, Blake found that the definition of black life becomes "not black but white"; it "exchanges the self-definition of the folk for the definition of the masters." Thorpe Butler, in a 1984

College Language Association Journal essay, defended Ellison against Blake's criticism. He declared that Ellison's depiction of specific black experience as part of the universal does not "diminish the unique richness and anguish" of that experience and does not "diminish the force of Ellison's protest against the blind, cruel dehumanization of black Americans by white society." This debate extends arguments that have appeared since the publication of the novel. Underlying these controversies is the old, uneasy argument about the relationship of art and politics, of literary practice and social commitment.

Although the search for identity is the major theme of *Invisible Man,* other aspects of the novel have also received critical attention. Among them, as Joanne Giza noted in her essay in *Black American Writers: Bibliographical Essays,* are literary debts and analogies, comic elements, the metaphor of vision, use of the blues, and folkloric elements. Although all of these concerns are part of the larger issue of identity, Ellison's use of blues and folklore has been singled out as a major contribution to contemporary literature and culture. Since the publication of *Invisible Man,* scores of articles have appeared on these two topics, a fact which in turn has led to a rediscovery and revisioning of the importance of blues and folklore to American literature and culture in general.

Much of Ellison's groundbreaking work is presented in *Shadow and Act.* Published in 1964, this collection of essays, said Ellison, is "concerned with three general themes: with literature and folklore, with Negro musical expression—especially jazz and the blues—and with the complex relationship between the Negro American subculture and North American culture as a whole." This volume has been hailed as one of the more prominent examples of cultural criticism of the century. Writing in *Commentary,* Robert Penn Warren praised the astuteness of Ellison's perceptions; in *New Leader,* Stanley Edgar Hyman proclaimed Ellison "the profoundest cultural critic we have." In the *New York Review of Books,* R. W. B. Lewis explored Ellison's study of black music as a form of power and found that "Ellison is not only a self-identifier but the source of self-definition in others." Published in 1986, *Going to the Territory* is a second collection of essays reprising many of the subjects and concerns treated in *Shadow and Act*—literature, art, music, the relationships of black and white cultures, fragments of autobiography, tributes to such noted black Americans as Richard Wright, Duke Ellington, and painter Romare Beardon. With the exception of "An Extravagance of Laughter," a lengthy examination of Ellison's response to Jack Kirkland's dramatization of Erskine Caldwell's novel *Tobacco Road,* the essays in *Going to the Territory* are reprints of previously published articles or speeches, most of them dating from the 1960s.

Ellison's influence as both novelist and critic, as artist and cultural historian, has been enormous. In special issues of *Black World* and *College Language Association Journal* devoted to Ellison, strident attacks appear alongside equally spirited accolades. Perhaps another measure of Ellison's stature and achievement was his readers' vigil for his long-awaited second novel. Although Ellison often refused to answer questions about the work-in-progress, there was enough evidence during Ellison's lifetime to suggest that the manuscript was very large, that all or part of it was destroyed in a fire and was being rewritten, and that its creation was a long and painful task. Most readers waited expectantly, believing that Ellison, who said in *Shadow and Act* that he "failed of eloquence" in *Invisible Man,* intended to wait until his second novel equaled his imaginative vision of the American novel as conqueror of the frontier, equaled the Emersonian call for a literature to release all people from the bonds of oppression.

Eight excerpts from this novel-in-progress were originally published in journals such as *Quarterly Review of Literature, Massachusetts Review,* and *Noble Savage.* Set in the South in the years spanning the Jazz Age to the Civil Rights movement, these fragments seemed an attempt to recreate modern American history and identity. The major characters are the Reverend Hickman, a one-time jazz musician, and Bliss, the light-skinned boy whom he adopts and who later passes into white society and becomes Senator Sunraider, an advocate of white supremacy. As O'Meally noted in *The Craft of Ralph Ellison,* the major difference between Bliss and Ellison's earlier young protagonists is that despite some harsh collisions with reality, Bliss refuses to divest himself of his illusions and accept his personal history. Said O'Meally: "Moreover, it is a renunciation of the blackness of American experience and culture, a refusal to accept the American past in all its complexity."

After Ellison's death on April 16, 1994, speculation about the existence of the second novel reignited. In an article in the *New York Times,* William Grimes assembled the information available on the subject. "Joe Fox, Mr. Ellison's editor at Random House, and close friends of the novelist say that Mr. Ellison has

left a manuscript of somewhere between 1,000 and 2,000 pages," Grimes reported. "At the time of his death, he had been working on it every day and was close to completing the work, whose fate now rests with his widow, Fanny." A close friend of Ellison's, John F. Callahan, a college dean from Portland, Oregon, told Grimes that he had seen parts of the manuscript not already published in other sources. "From what I've read, if *Invisible Man* is akin to Joyce's *Portrait of the Artist,* then the novel in progress may be his *Ulysses.*" Callahan added that "it's a weaving together of all kinds of voices, and not simply voices in the black tradition, but white voices, too: all kinds of American voices." As Grimes suggested, "If Mr. Ellison, as his final creative act, were to top *Invisible Man,* it would be a stunning bequest," given that the first novel is considered a literary classic. *Invisible Man* "has never been out of print," Grimes pointed out. "It has sold millions of copies worldwide. On college campuses it is required reading in twentieth-century American literature courses, and it has been the subject of hundreds of scholarly articles."

In 1999, five years after his death, the longtime rumors surrounding this second novel were finally answered—at least in part—with the publication of *Juneteenth.* The novel was culled from Ellison's voluminous manuscript by Callahan, who became Ellison's literary executor after the author's death. According to Callahan, the published form of *Juneteenth* consists of several distinct elements: a 1959 published story titled "And Hickman Arrives"; one of three long narratives (referred to as "Book 2" in Ellison's notes) in the novel that Ellison had been working on for years before he died; a thirty-eight page draft titled "Bliss's Birth"; and a single paragraph from a short fictional piece titled "Cadillac Flambe." The chief characters remain the same as those from the earlier published excerpts: the white, race-baiting Senator Sunraider (also called "Bliss") and the black minister Alonzo Hickman, who raised Bliss as a child. The novel's action is set in motion via a visit by Hickman to the Senate chambers to hear Bliss speak. During the speech, Bliss is mortally wounded by a gunman, and the remainder of the novel features a dying Bliss and a watchful Hickman—the only person whom Bliss allows to see him—reminiscing about their earlier relationship. Much like *Invisible Man,* the novel addresses such themes as the black-white divide in America; the nature of identity; and the interaction between politics and religion. The novel's title, in fact, comes from a combined religious/political holiday celebrated by African Americans to commemorate a day in June 1865, when black slaves in Texas finally discovered that they were free—more than two years after Abraham Lincoln issued the Emancipation Proclamation.

Given the unusual circumstances of the book's publication, reviewers perhaps inevitably focused as much on these circumstances as on the merits of the work itself. Specifically, critics focused on Callahan's role in shaping a single narrative out of Ellison's sprawling manuscript despite the lack of any instructions from the author himself about what he intended the novel to be. Lamenting that Callahan had excised two of the three narratives that made up Ellison's manuscript, *New York Times Book Review* contributor Louis Menand noted, "It seems unfair to Ellison to review a novel he did not write. . . . A three-part work implies counterpoint: whatever appears in a Book 2 must be designed to derive its novelistic significance from whatever would have appeared in a Book 1 and a Book 3." According to Gerald Early in the Chicago *Tribune Books,* the new work "reads very much like the pastiche it is, with uneven characterization, clashing styles of writing and shifting points of view, and a jumbled narrative. The reader should be warned that this is a very unfinished product." Some reviewers reserved praise for certain prose sections that reflect Ellison's dazzling technical ability; Early, for instance, remarked on the "passages of affecting, sometimes tour-de-force writing and some deft wordplay," while a *Publishers Weekly* reviewer commented that the book's "flashbacks showcase Ellison's stylized set pieces, among the best scenes he has written." In the end, though, critics expressed reservations that the book should ever have been released. Menand concluded forcefully, "This is not Ralph Ellison's second novel," while Early averred that "I wonder if the world and Ralph Ellison have been best served by the publication of this work." Despite these concerns, critics noted that Ellison's literary reputation—relying heavily on the landmark *Invisible Man*—remains secure.

BIOGRAPHICAL/CRITICAL SOURCES:

BOOKS

Benstion, Kimberly W., editor, *Speaking for You: The Vision of Ralph Ellison,* Howard University Press (Washington, DC), 1987.

Bishop, Jack, *Ralph Ellison,* Chelsea House (New York City), 1988.

Bloom, Harold, editor, *Ralph Ellison: Modern Critical Views,* Chelsea Publishing, 1986.

Busby, Mark, *Ralph Ellison,* Twayne (Boston), 1991.

Callahan, John F., *In the African-American Grain: The Pursuit of Voice in Twentieth-Century Black Fiction,* University of Illinois Press (Urbana, IL), 1988.

Concise Dictionary of American Literary Biography: The New Consciousness, 1941-1948, Gale (Detroit), 1987.

Contemporary Literary Criticism, Gale, Volume 1, 1973; Volume 3, 1975; Volume 11, 1979; Volume 54, 1989.

Cooke, Michael, *Afro-American Literature in the Twentieth Century: The Achievement of Intimacy,* Yale University Press, 1984.

Davis, Arthur P., *From the Dark Tower: Afro-American Writers, 1900 to 1960,* Howard University Press, 1974.

Davis, Charles T., *Black Is the Color of the Cosmos: Essays on Afro-American Literature and Culture, 1942-1981,* edited by Henry Louis Gates, Jr., Garland Publishing (New York City), 1982.

Dictionary of Literary Biography, Gale, Volume 2: *American Novelists since World War II,* 1978; Volume 76: *Afro-American Writers, 1940-1955,* 1988.

Graham, Maryemma, and Amritjit Singh, editors, *Conversations with Ralph Ellison,* University Press of Mississippi (Jackson, MS), 1995.

Inge, M. Thomas, editor, *Black American Writers: Bibliographic Essays, Volume 2: Richard Wright, Ralph Ellison, James Baldwin, and Amiri Baraka,* St. Martin's, 1978.

Jothiprakash, R., *Commitment as a Theme in African American Literature: A Study of James Baldwin and Ralph Ellison,* Wyndham Hall Press (Bristol, IN), 1994.

Klein, Marcus, *After Alienation: American Novels in Mid-Century,* World Publishing, 1964.

Kostelanetz, Richard, *Politics in the African-American Novel: James Weldon Johnson, W. E. B. Du Bois, Richard Wright, and Ralph Ellison,* Greenwood Press (New York City), 1991.

Lynch, Michael F., *Creative Revolt: A Study of Wright, Ellison, and Dostevsky,* P. Lang (New York City), 1990.

McSweeney, Kerry, *Invisible Man: Race and Identity,* Twayne (Boston), 1988.

Nadel, Alan, *Invisible Criticism: Ralph Ellison and the American Canon,* University of Iowa Press (Iowa City, IA), 1988.

O'Meally, Robert G., *New Essays on Invisible Man,* Cambridge University Press (Cambridge, England), 1988.

O'Meally, Robert G., *The Craft of Ralph Ellison,* Harvard University Press, 1980.

Parr, Susan Resneck, and Pancho Savery, editors, *Approaches to Teaching Ellison's "Invisible Man,"* Modern Language Associates of America, 1989.

Schor, Edith, *Visible Ellison: A Study of Ralph Ellison's Fiction,* Greenwood Press, 1993.

Stepto, Robert B., *From Behind the Veil: A Study of Afro-American Narrative,* University of Illinois Press, 1979.

Sundquist, Eric J., editor, *Cultural Contexts for Ralph Ellison's Invisible Man,* Bedford Books (Boston), 1995.

Watts, Jerry Gafio, *Heroism and the Black Intellectual: Ralph Ellison, Politics, and Afro-American Intellectual Life,* University of North Carolina Press (Chapel Hill, NC), 1994.

PERIODICALS

America, August 27, 1994, p. 26.

Atlantic Monthly, July, 1952; December, 1970; August, 1986.

Black American Literature Forum, summer, 1978.

Black World, December, 1970 (special Ellison issue).

Carleton Miscellany, winter, 1980 (special Ellison issue).

Chicago Review, Volume 19, number 2, 1967.

Chicago Tribune, June 18, 1992, p. 1.

Chicago Tribune Book World, August 10, 1986.

College Language Association Journal, December, 1963; June, 1967; March, 1970 (special Ellison issue); September, 1971; December, 1971; December, 1972; June, 1973; March, 1974; September, 1976; September, 1977; Number 25, 1982; Number 27, 1984.

Commentary, November, 1953; Number 39, 1965.

English Journal, September, 1969; May, 1973; November, 1984.

Harper's, October, 1959; March, 1967; July, 1967.

Los Angeles Times, August 8, 1986.

Massachusetts Review, autumn, 1967; autumn, 1977.

Modern Fiction Studies, winter, 1969-70.

Nation, May 10, 1952; September 9, 1964; November 9, 1964; September 20, 1965.

Negro American Literature Forum, July, 1970; summer, 1973; Number 9, 1975; spring, 1977.

Negro Digest, May, 1964; August, 1967.

Negro History Bulletin, May, 1953; October, 1953.

New Criterion, September, 1983.

New Leader, October 26, 1964.

New Republic, November 14, 1964; August 4, 1986.

Newsweek, August 12, 1963; October 26, 1964; May 2, 1994, p. 58.

New Yorker, May 31, 1952; November 22, 1976; March 14, 1994, p. 34.

New York Herald Tribune Book Review, April 13, 1952.

New York Review of Books, January 28, 1964; January 28, 1965.

New York Times, April 13, 1952; April 24, 1985; April 17, 1994, p. A38; April 20, 1994, p. C13; April 18, 1996, pp. B1, B2.

New York Times Book Review, April 13, 1952; May 4, 1952; October 25, 1964; January 24, 1982; August 3, 1986; June 20, 1999, p. 4.

New York Times Magazine, November 20, 1966; January 1, 1995, p. 22.

PMLA, January, 1979.

Publishers Weekly, March 22, 1999, p. 68.

Renascence, spring, 1974; winter, 1978.

Saturday Review, April 12, 1952; March 14, 1953; December 11, 1954; January 1, 1955; April 26, 1958; May 17, 1958; July 12, 1958; September 27, 1958; July 28, 1962; October 24, 1964.

Southern Humanities Review, winter, 1970.

Southern Literary Journal, spring, 1969.

Southern Review, fall, 1974; summer, 1985.

Studies in American Fiction, spring, 1973.

Studies in Black Literature, autumn, 1971; autumn, 1972; spring, 1973; spring, 1975; spring, 1976; winter, 1976.

Time, April 14, 1952; February 9, 1959; February 1, 1963; April 6, 1970.

Times Literary Supplement, January 18, 1968.

Tribune Books (Chicago), April 24, 1994, p. 3; June 13, 1999, p. 1.

Village Voice, November 19, 1964.

Washington Post, August 19-21, 1973; April 21, 1982; February 9, 1983; March 30, 1983; July 23, 1986; April 18, 1994, p. C1; April 25, 1994, p. C2.

Washington Post Book World, May 17, 1987.*

*   *   *

**EL-SHABAZZ, El-Hajj Malik
See LITTLE, Malcolm**

*   *   *

EMECHETA, (Florence Onye) Buchi 1944-

PERSONAL: Born July 21, 1944, in Yaba, Lagos, Nigeria; daughter of Jeremy Nwabudike (a railway worker and molder) and Alice Ogbanje (Okwuekwu)

Emecheta; married Sylvester Onwordi, 1960 (separated, 1966); children: Florence, Sylvester, Jake, Christy, Alice. *Education:* University of London, B.Sc. (with honors), 1972. *Religion:* Anglican. *Avocational interests:* Gardening, attending the theatre, listening to music, reading.

ADDRESSES: Home—7 Briston Grove, Crouch End, London N8 9EX, England.

CAREER: British Museum, London, England, library officer, 1965-69; Inner London Education Authority, London, youth worker and sociologist, 1969-76; community worker, Camden, NJ, 1976-78. Writer and lecturer, 1972—. Visiting professor at several universities throughout the United States, including Pennsylvania State University, University of California, Los Angeles, and University of Illinois at Urbana-Champaign, 1979; senior resident fellow and visiting professor of English, University of Calabar, Nigeria, 1980-81; lecturer, Yale University, 1982, London University, 1982—; fellow, London University, 1986. Proprietor, Ogwugwu Afor Publishing Company, 1982-83. Member of Home Secretary's Advisory Council on Race, 1979—, and of Arts Council of Great Britain, 1982-83.

AWARDS, HONORS: Jock Campbell Award for literature by new or unregarded talent from Africa or the Caribbean, *New Statesman,* 1978; selected as the Best Black British Writer, 1978, and one of the Best British Young Writers, 1983.

WRITINGS:

In the Ditch, Barrie & Jenkins, 1972.
Second-Class Citizen (novel), Allison & Busby, 1974, Braziller, 1975.
The Bride Price: A Novel (paperback published as *The Bride Price: Young Ibo Girl's Love; Conflict of Family and Tradition*), Braziller, 1976.
The Slave Girl: A Novel, Braziller, 1977.
The Joys of Motherhood: A Novel, Braziller, 1979.
Destination Biafra: A Novel, Schocken, 1982.
Naira Power (novelette directed principally to Nigerian readers), Macmillan (London), 1982.
Double Yoke (novel), Schocken, 1982.
The Rape of Shavi (novel), Ogwugwu Afor, 1983, Braziller, 1985.
Adah's Story: A Novel, Allison & Busby, 1983.
Head above Water (autobiography), Ogwugwu Afor, 1984, Collins, 1986.
A Kind of Marriage (novelette), Macmillan, 1987.
The Family (novel), Braziller, 1990.

Gwendolen (novel), Collins, 1990.
Kehinde, Heinemann (Portsmouth, NH), 1994.

JUVENILE

Titch the Cat (based on story by daughter, Alice Emecheta), Allison & Busby, 1979.
Nowhere to Play (based on story by daughter, Christy Emecheta), Schocken, 1980.
The Moonlight Bride, Oxford University Press in association with University Press, 1981.
The Wrestling Match, Oxford University Press in association with University Press, 1981, Braziller, 1983.
Family Bargain (publication for schools), British Broadcasting Corp., 1987.

OTHER

(Author of introduction and commentary) Maggie Murray, *Our Own Freedom* (book of photographs), Sheba Feminist (London), 1981.
A Kind of Marriage (teleplay; produced by BBC-TV), Macmillan (London), 1987.

Also author of teleplays *Tanya, a Black Woman,* produced by BBC-TV, and *The Juju Landlord.* Contributor to journals, including *New Statesman, Times Literary Supplement,* and *Guardian.*

SIDELIGHTS: Although Buchi Emecheta has resided in London since 1962, she is "Nigeria's best-known female writer," comments John Updike in the *New Yorker.* "Indeed, few writers of her sex . . . have arisen in any part of tropical Africa." Emecheta enjoys much popularity in Great Britain, and she has gathered an appreciative audience on this side of the Atlantic as well. Although Emecheta has written children's books and teleplays, she is best known for her historical novels set in Nigeria, both before and after independence. Concerned with the clash of cultures and the impact of Western values upon agrarian traditions and customs, Emecheta's work is strongly autobiographical; and, as Updike observes, much of it is especially concerned with "the situation of women in a society where their role, though crucial, was firmly subordinate and where the forces of potential liberation have arrived with bewildering speed."

Born to Ibo parents in Yaba, a small village near Lagos, Nigeria, Emecheta indicates that the Ibos "don't want you to lose contact with your culture," writes Rosemary Bray in the *Voice Literary Supple-*

ment. Bray explains that the oldest woman in the house plays an important role in that she is the "big mother" to the entire family. In Emecheta's family, her father's sister assumed this role. says Bray: "She was very old and almost blind," Buchi recalls, "And she would gather the young children around her after dinner and tell stories to us." The stories the children heard were about their origins and ancestors; and, according to Bray, Emecheta recalls: "I thought to myself 'No life could be more important than this.' So when people asked me what I wanted to do when I grew up I told them I wanted to be a storyteller—which is what I'm doing now."

In the Ditch, her first book, originally appeared as a series of columns in the *New Statesman.* Written in the form of a diary, it "is based on her own failed marriage and her experiences on the dole in London trying to rear alone her many children," state Charlotte and David Bruner in *World Literature Today.* Called a "sad, sonorous, occasionally hilarious . . . extraordinary first novel," by Adrianne Blue of the *Washington Post Book World,* it details her impoverished existence in a foreign land, as well as her experience with racism, and "illuminates the similarities and differences between cultures and attitudes," remarks a *Times Literary Supplement* contributor, who thinks it merits "special attention."

Similarly autobiographical, Emecheta's second novel, *Second-Class Citizen,* "recounts her early marriage years, when she was trying to support her student-husband—a man indifferent to his own studies and later indifferent to her job searches, her childbearing, and her resistance to poverty," observe the Bruners. The novel is about a young, resolute and resourceful Nigerian girl who, despite traditional tribal domination of females, manages to continue her own education; she marries a student and follows him to London, where he becomes abusive toward her. "Emecheta said people find it hard to believe that she has not exaggerated the truth in this autobiographical novel," reports Nancy Topping Bazin in *Black Scholar.* "The grimness of what is described does indeed make it painful to read." Called a "brave and angry book" by Marigold Johnson in the *Times Literary Supplement,* Emecheta's story, however, "is not accompanied by a misanthropic whine," notes Martin Levin in the *New York Times Book Review.* Alice Walker, who thinks it is "one of the most informative books about contemporary African life" that she has read, observes in *Ms.* that "it raises fundamental questions about how creative and prosaic life is to be lived and to what purpose."

"Emecheta's women do not simply lie down and die," observes Bray. "Always there is resistance, a challenge to fate, a need to renegotiate the terms of the uneasy peace that exists between them and accepted traditions." Bray adds that "Emecheta's women know, too, that between the rock of African traditions and the hard place of encroaching Western values, it is the women who will be caught." Concerned with the clash of cultures, in *The Bride Price: A Novel,* Emecheta tells the story of a young Nigerian girl "whose life is complicated by traditional attitudes toward women," writes Richard Cima in *Library Journal.* The young girl's father dies when she is thirteen; and, with her brother and mother, she becomes the property of her father's ambitious brother. She is permitted to remain in school only because it will increase her value as a potential wife. However, she falls in love with her teacher, a descendant of slaves; and because of familial objections, they elope, thereby depriving her uncle of the "bride price." When she dies in childbirth, she fulfills the superstition that a woman would not survive the birth of her first child if her bride price had not been paid; and Susannah Clapp maintains in the *Times Literary Supplement,* that the quality of the novel "depends less on plot or characterization than on the information conveyed about a set of customs and the ideas which underlay them." Calling it "a captivating Nigerian novel lovingly but unsentimentally written, about the survival of ancient marriage customs in modern Nigeria," Valerie Cunningham adds in *New Statesman* that this book "proves Buchi Emecheta to be a considerable writer."

Emecheta's *Slave Girl: A Novel* is about "a poor, gently raised Ibo girl who is sold into slavery to a rich African marketwoman by a feckless brother at the turn of the century," writes a *New Yorker* contributor. Educated by missionaries, she joins the new church where she meets the man she eventually marries. In *Library Journal,* Cima thinks that the book provides an "interesting picture of Christianity's impact on traditional Ibo society." Perceiving parallels between marriage and slavery, Emecheta explores the issue of "freedom within marriage in a society where slavery is supposed to have been abolished," writes Cunningham in the *New Statesman,* adding that the book indicts both "pagan and Christian inhumanity to women." And although a contributor to World Literature Today suggests that the "historical and anthropological background" in the novel tends to destroy its "emotional complex," another contributor to the same journal believes that the sociological detail has been "unobtrusively woven into" it and that *The Slave Girl* represents Emecheta's "most accomplished work so far. It is coherent, compact and convincing."

"Emecheta's voice has been welcomed by many as helping to redress the somewhat one-sided picture of African women that has been delineated by male writers," according to *A New Reader's Guide to African Literature.* Writing in *African Literature Today,* Eustace Palmer indicates that "the African novel has until recently been remarkable for the absense of what might be called the feminine point of view." Because of the relatively few female African novelists, "the presentation of women in the African novel has been left almost entirely to male voices . . . and their interest in African womanhood . . . has had to take second placeto numerous other concerns," continues Palmer. "These male novelists, who have presented the African woman largely within the traditional milieu, have generally communicated a picture of a male-dominated and male-oriented society, and the satisfaction of the women with this state of things has been . . . completely taken for granted." Palmer adds that the emergence of Emecheta and other "accomplished female African novelists . . . seriously challenges all these cosy assumptions. The picture of the cheerful contented female complacently accepting her lot is replaced by that of a woman who is powerfully aware of the unfairness of the system and who longs to be else's appendage." For instance, Palmer notes that *The Joys of Motherhood: A Novel* "presents essentially the same picture of traditional society . . . but the difference lies in the prominence in Emecheta's novel of the female point of view registering its disgust at male chauvinism and its dissatisfaction with what it considers an unfair and oppressive system."

The Joys of Motherhood is about a woman "who marries but is sent home in disgrace because she fails to bear a child quickly enough," writes Bazin. "She then is sent to the city by her father to marry a man she has never seen. She is horrified when she meets this second husband because she finds him ugly, but she sees no alternative to staying with him. Poverty and repeated pregnancies wear her down; the pressure to bear male children forces her to bear child after child since the girls she has do not count." Palmer observes that "clearly, the man is the standard and the point of reference in this society. It is significant that the chorus of countrymen say, not that a woman without a child is a failed woman, but that a woman without a child *for her husband* is a failed woman." Bazin observes that in Emecheta's novels, "a woman must accept the double standard of sexual freedom: it permits polygamy and infidelity for both Christian and non-Christian men but only monogamy for women. These books reveal the extent to which the African woman's oppression is engrained in the African mores."

Acknowledging that "the issue of polygamy in Africa remains a controversial one," Palmer states that what Emecheta stresses in *The Joys of Motherhood* is "the resulting dominance, especially sexual, of the male, and the relegation of the female into subservience, domesticity and motherhood." Nonetheless, despite Emecheta's "angry glare," says Palmer, one can "glean from the novel the economic and social reasons that must have given rise to polygamy. . . . But the author concentrates on the misery and deprivation polygamy can bring." Palmer praises Emecheta's insightful psychological probing of her characters's thoughts: "Scarcely any other African novelist has succeeded in probing the female mind and displaying the female personality with such precision." Blue likewise suggests that Emecheta "tells this story in a plain style, denuding it of exoticism, displaying an impressive, embracing compassion." Calling it a "graceful, touching, ironically titled tale that bears a plain feminist message," Updike adds that "in this compassionate but slightly distanced and stylized story of a life that comes to seem wasted, [Emecheta] sings a dirge for more than African pieties. The lives within *The Joys of Motherhood* might be, transposed into a different cultural key, those of our own rural ancestors."

Emecheta's "works reveal a great deal about the lives of African women and about the development of feminist perspectives," observes Bazin, explaining that one moves beyond an initial perspective of "personal experience," to perceive "social or communal" oppression. This second perspective "demands an analysis of the causes of oppression within the social mores and the patriarchal power structure," adds Bazin. Finding both perspectives in Emecheta's work, Bazin thinks that through her descriptions of "what it is like to be for 'millions of black African women.'" Although her feminist perspective is anchored in her own personal life, says Bazin, Emecheta "grew to understand how son preference, bride price, polygamy, menstrual taboos, . . . wife beating, early marriages, early and unlimited pregnancies, arranged marriages, and male dominance in the home functioned to keep women powerless." The Bruners write that "obviously Emecheta is concerned about the plight of women, today and yesterday, in both technological and traditional societies, though she rejects a feminist label." Emecheta told the Bruners: "The main themes of my novels are African society and family; the historical, social, and political life in Africa as seen by a woman through events. I always try to show that the African male is oppressed and he too oppresses the African women. . . . I have not committed myself to the cause of African women only. I write about Africa as a whole."

Emecheta's *Destination Biafra: A Novel* is a story of the "history of Nigeria from the eve of independence to the collapse of the Biafran secessionist movement," writes Robert L. Berner in *World Literature Today*. The novel has generated a mixed critical response, though. In the *Times Literary Supplement,* Chinweizu feels that it "does not convey the feel of the experience that was Biafra. All it does is leave one wondering why it falls so devastatingly below the quality of Buchi Emecheta's previous works." Noting, however, that Emecheta's publisher reduced the manuscript by half, Berner suggests that "this may account for what often seems a rather elliptical narrative and for the frequently clumsy prose which 'different from any of her others . . . larger and more substantive,'" the Bruners state: "Here she presents neither the life story of a single character nor the delineation of one facet of a culture but the whole perplexing canvas of people from diverse ethnic groups, belief systems, levels of society all caught in a disastrous civil war." Moreover, the Bruners feel that the "very objectivity of her reporting and her impartiality in recounting atrocities committed by all sides, military and civilian, have even greater impact because her motivation is not sadistic."

The Rape of Shavi represents somewhat of a departure in that "Emecheta attempts one of the most difficult of tasks: that of integrating the requirements of contemporary, realistic fiction with the narrative traditions of myth and folklore," writes Somtow Sucharitkul in the *Washington Post Book World*. Roy Kerridge describes the novel's plot in the *Times Literary Supplement:* "A plane crashes among strange tribespeople, white aviators are made welcome by the local king, they find precious stones, repair their plane and escape just as they are going to be forcibly married to native girls. The king's son and heir stows away and has adventures of his own in England." Called a "wise and haunting tale" by a *New Yorker* contributor, *The Rape of Shavi* "recounts the ruination of this small African society by voracious white interlopers," says Richard Eder in the *Los Angeles Times*. A few critics suggest that in *The Rape of Shavi,*

Emecheta's masterful portrayal of her Shavian community is not matched by her depiction of the foreigners. Eder, for instance, calls it a "lopsided fable," and declares: "It is not that the Shavians are noble and the whites monstrous; that is what fables are for. It is that the Shavians are finely drawn and the Westerners very clumsily. It is a duet between a flute and a kitchen drain." However, Sucharitkul thinks that portraying the Shavians as "complex individuals" and the Westerners as "two dimensional, mythic types" presents a refreshing, seldom expressed, and "particularly welcome" point of view.

Although in the *New York Times* Michiko Kakutani calls *The Rape of Shavi* "an allegorical tale, filled with ponderous morals about the evils of imperialism and tired aphorisms about nature and civilization," Sucharitkul believes that "the central thesis of [the novel] is brilliantly, relentlessly argued, and Emecheta's characters and societies are depicted with a bittersweet, sometimes painful honesty." The critic also praises Emecheta's "persuasive" prose: "It is prose that appears unusually simple at first, for it is full of the kind of rhythms and sentence structures more often found in folk tales than in contemporary novels. Indeed, in electing to tell her multilayered and often very contemporary story within a highly mythic narrative framework, the author walks a fine line between the pitfalls of preciosity and pretentiousness. By and large, the tightrope act is a success."

"Emecheta has reaffirmed her dedication to be a full-time writer," say the Bruners. "Her culture and her education at first were obstacles to her literary inclination. She had to struggle against precedent, against reluctant publishers, and later against minated audiences and readership." Her fiction is intensely autobiographical, drawing on the difficulties she has both witnessed and experienced as a woman, and most especially as a Nigerian woman. Indicating that in Nigeria, however, "Emecheta is a prophet without honor," Bray adds that "she is frustrated at not being able to reach women—the audience she desires most. She feels a sense of isolation as she attempts to stake out the middle ground between the old and the new." Remarking that "in her art as well as in her life, Buchi Emecheta offers another alternative," Bray quotes the author: "What I am trying to do is get our profession back. Women are born storytellers. We keep the history. We are the true conservatives—we conserve things and we never forget. What I do is not clever or unusual. It is what my aunt and my grandmother did, and their mothers before them."

BIOGRAPHICAL\CRITICAL SOURCES:

BOOKS

Allan, Tuzyline Jita, *Womanist and Feminist Aesthetics: A Comparative Review,* Ohio University Press (Athens), 1995.
Contemporary Literary Criticism, Gale (Detroit, MI), Volume 14, 1980, Volume 28, 1984.
Fishburn, Katherine, *Reading Buchi Emecheta: Cross-Cultural Conversations,* Greenwood Press (Westport, CT), 1995.
Umeh, Marie, *Emerging Perspectives on Buchi Emecheta,* Africa World Press (Trenton, NJ), 1995.
Zell, Hans M., and others, *A New Reader's Guide to African Literature,* 2nd revised and expanded edition, Holmes & Meier, 1983.

PERIODICALS

African Literature Today, Number 3, 1983.
Atlantic, May, 1976.
Black Scholar, November/December, 1985; March/April, 1986.
Library Journal, September 1, 1975; April 1, 1976; January 15, 1978; May 1, 1979; May 15, 1994, p. 98.
Listener, July 19, 1979.
Los Angeles Times, October 16, 1983; March 6, 1985; January 16, 1990.
Ms., January, 1976; July, 1984; March, 1985.
New Statesman, June 25, 1976; October 14, 1977; June 2, 1978; April 27, 1979.
New Yorker, May 17, 1976; January 9, 1978; July 2, 1979; April 23, 1984; April 22, 1985.
New York Times, February 23, 1985; June 2, 1990.
New York Times Book Review, September 14, 1975; November 11, 1979; January 27, 1980; February 27, 1983; May 5, 1985; April 29, 1990.
School Library Journal, September, 1994, p. 255.
Times Literary Supplement, August 11, 1972; January 31, 1975; June 11, 1976; February 26, 1982; February 3, 1984; February 27, 1987; April 20, 1990.
Voice Literary Supplement, June, 1982.
Washington Post Book World, May 13, 1979; April 12, 1981; September 5, 1982; September 25, 1983; March 30, 1985.
World Literature Today, spring, 1977; summer, 1977; spring, 1978; winter, 1979; spring, 1980; winter, 1983; autumn, 1984.

ESEKI, Bruno
See MPHAHLELE, Ezekiel

*   *   *

ESKRIDGE, Ann E. 1949-

PERSONAL: Born July 17, 1949, in Chicago, IL; daughter of Arnett E. V. and Marguerite (Hinds) Eskridge. *Education:* University of Oklahoma, B.A., 1971; Michigan State University, M.A., 1981; attended Ferris State College and Recording Institute of Detroit.

ADDRESSES: Home and office—17217 Fairfield, Detroit, MI 48221. *Agent*—Marie Dutton Brown, 625 Broadway, No. 902, New York, NY 10012.

CAREER: WXYZ-TV, Detroit, MI, reporter, 1972-76; freelance public relations agent, Detroit, 1976-78; executive assistant to the Lieutenant Governor of Michigan, 1978-79; administrator to the Michigan State Treasurer, 1979-81, and for the Statewide (Michigan) Nutrition Commission, 1982-83; administrative assistant to Detroit Council President Erma Henderson, 1983; Golightly Vocational Technical Center, Detroit, instructor in mass media, 1983-90; freelance writer and teaching consultant, Detroit, 1990-92; speechwriter for Michigan Consolidated Gas Company, 1992-95; freelance writer, 1995—. *Chicago Daily Defender,* reporter, summers, 1968-69; *Oklahoma Daily,* reporter, 1970; *Oklahoma Journal,* reporter, 1970; KWTV, Oklahoma City, OK, reporter, 1970-71; WBEN-TV, Buffalo, NY, reporter, 1971-72. Has conducted various workshops, including a creative scriptwriting workshop for Henry Ford High School, Detroit, MI, 1991, and playwriting for the theater program portion of a youth training program for Urban Arts Corporation, 1992; has given numerous lectures and demonstrations on scriptwriting at local colleges; has also served on a variety of boards, including the Michigan Film and Video Production Industry Council (president), Detroit Producers Association, Black Professionals in Film and Video (vice president), and WTVS-TV; appointed vice president of the Public Benefit Corporation by Detroit Mayor Dennis Archer.

MEMBER: Detroit Women Writers.

AWARDS, HONORS: Distinguished Service Award, Detroit City Council, 1974; Mayor's Award of Merit,

Detroit, 1975; Alpha Kappa Alpha Award, 1975; grants from Detroit Public Education Fund and New Detroit, 1984-85, Michigan Council of the Arts, 1986 and 1988, Wayne County Intermediate School District, 1987-88, Women's Scriptwriting Project Funding Exchange, 1991, Center for New Television, 1992, and Arts Foundation of Michigan, 1992; award from National Black Programming Consortium, teen category, Ohio State University award, and Communications Excellence to Black Audiences (CEBA) Award of Distinction, all 1991, for "Brother Future."

WRITINGS:

The Sanctuary (for children), Cobblehill Books (New York City), 1994.
The Sanctuary (play; based in part on the author's book of the same title), Child's Play (West Orange, NJ), 1995.

Contributor of numerous articles to periodicals, including *American Visions, Michigan Chronicle, Detroit Free Press, Detroit News,* and *Monthly Detroit Magazine.*

SCREENPLAYS

Brother Future, first broadcast on *Wonderworks,* PBS, 1991.

Also author of *Echoes across the Prairie* (mini-series), optioned by Longbow Productions. Has created various commercial and industrial video tapes for companies, including Ford Motor Company, Wayne County Foster Care, and Adult Well Being Services.

ADAPTATIONS: The Sanctuary was optioned for a television movie.

WORK IN PROGRESS: A Black historical saga.

SIDELIGHTS: Ann E. Eskridge once commented, "I have worked as a television reporter, public relations consultant, political appointee, and teacher. Writing was an integral part of all the jobs I had. However, I didn't take my writing seriously until I began teaching high school students how to write for the media. I started writing about my students.

"One work produced in this period was *Brother Future,* a *Wonderworks* family movie airing on PBS in 1991. I have won numerous writing grants and was chosen to participate in various writing workshops. My first children's book, *The Sanctuary,* published by Cobblehill Books, an imprint of Penguin, has received critical acclaim. Currently, it is being optioned for a TV movie, and a mini-series I wrote is also being developed for television. Although I was born and raised in Chicago, I have made Detroit my home for many years. I hope to continue writing for television and for children."

BIOGRAPHICAL/CRITICAL SOURCES:

PERIODICALS

Kirkus Reviews, June 1, 1994, p. 773.
Publishers Weekly, May 2, 1994, p. 310.
Quill & Quire, May, 1994, p. 38.
School Library Journal, May, 1994, p. 112.*

F

FARAH, Nuruddin 1945-

PERSONAL: Born November 24, 1945, in Baidoa, Somalia; son of Hassan (a merchant) and Aleeli (a poet; maiden name, Faduma) Farah; married Chitra Muliyil Farah (divorced); married Amina Mama (a doctor), July 21, 1992; children: (first marriage) Koschin Nuruddin (son). *Education:* Attended Panjab University, Chandigarh, India, 1966-70, University of London, 1974-75, and University of Essex, 1975-76. *Religion:* "Born Muslim."

ADDRESSES: Home—Kaduna, Nigeria. *Agent*—Curtis Brown, 162-168 Regent St., London W1R 5TB, England.

CAREER: Free-lance writer, translator, and broadcaster. Clerk-typist for Ministry of Education in Somalia, 1964-66; teacher at secondary school in Mogadishu, Somalia, 1969-71; lecturer in comparative literature at Afgoi College of Education, and at Somali National University, Mogadishu, 1971-74; Royal Court Theatre, London, England, resident writer, 1976; University of Ibadan, Jos Campus, Jos, Nigeria, associate professor, 1981-83, Makerere University, Kampala, Uganda, professor, 1990—.

Guest professor and lecturer at universities in the United States, Europe, and Africa.

MEMBER: Union of Writers of the African Peoples.

AWARDS, HONORS: United Nations Educational, Scientific and Cultural Organization (UNESCO) fellowship, 1974-76; literary award from English-Speaking Union, 1980, for *Sweet and Sour Milk*.

WRITINGS:

Why Dead So Soon? (short story), 1965.
A Dagger in Vacuum (play), produced in Mogadishu, Somalia, 1970.
From a Crooked Rib (novel), Heinemann, 1970.
The Offering (play), produced in Colchester, Essex, England, 1975.
A Naked Needle (novel), Heinemann, 1976.
A Spread of Butter (radio play), 1978.
Sweet and Sour Milk (novel; volume 1 of "Variations on the Theme of an African Dictatorship"), Allison & Busby, 1979, Graywolf Press, 1992.
Tartar Delight (radio play), broadcast in Germany, 1980.
Sardines (novel; volume 2 of "Variations on the Theme of an African Dictatorship"), Allison & Busby, 1981, Graywolf Press, 1992.
Close Sesame (novel; volume 3 of "Variations on the Theme of an African Dictatorship"), Allison & Busby, 1982, Graywolf Press, 1992.
Yussuf and His Brothers (play), produced in Jos, Nigeria, 1982.
Maps (novel), Pan Book, 1986, Pantheon, 1987.
Gavor (novel), 1990.
Secrets (novel), Little Brown & Company, 1998.

Contributor to a variety of periodicals, including *Suitcase: A Journal of Transcultural Traffic* (1998).

SIDELIGHTS: An African writer best known for novels that champion the oppressed, particularly women, Nuruddin Farah sets his plots in twentieth-century Somalia, with most of the action occurring in the capital, Mogadishu. Farah is best-known for a trilogy on an African dictatorship led by the fictional Major General Muhammad Siyad, referred to as the "General," and the subsequent demise of democracy in Somalia. The first volume, *Sweet and Sour Milk,* focuses upon a political activist who attempts to unravel the mysterious circumstances involving the death of his twin brother. The second novel, *Sardines,* depicts life under the General's repressive regime while also examining the social barriers that limit Somalian women and their quest for individuality and equality. The novel's central character is Medina, a young woman who, after losing her job as editor of a state-run newspaper, refuses to support the General's domestic policies. The final volume in the trilogy is *Close Sesame,* the story of an elderly man who spent many years in prison for opposing both colonial and postrevolutionary governments. When the man's son plots to overthrow the General's regime, the man attempts to stop the coup himself.

Farah has written two other novels that have met with high acclaim from critics. *Maps* is set during Somalia's war against Ethiopia in the late 1970s and examines the conflict between nationalism and personal commitment through the story of Askar. A Somalian orphan, Askar is raised by an Ethiopian woman. As Askar approaches adulthood, he is forced to choose between his loyalties to the ailing adoptive mother—who is suspected of being a spy—and enlisting in the army.

Farah's *A Naked Needle* is the story of a single, key day in the life of Koschin, a man on the edge of a nervous breakdown who passively accepts the arrival of an Englishwoman, a former lover, who is determined to marry him. In *A Naked Needle,* Farah explores not only Somalian politics, but the preference, at least of some elite Somalian men, for Western white women—a fact which arouses the discomfort of Koschin.

A central theme in all of Farah's unique works is the depiction of women meeting and solving challenges cast upon them by an African society which has traditionally stymied the intellectual growth of women. For example, in *From a Crooked Rib,* Ebla, the main character, sets out to extricate herself from the imprisoning women's role in traditional society. Ebla's moral and intellectual growth is detailed initially in her artful escape from an arranged marriage, then her steady progress as she searches for personal freedom and dignity.

A feature of Farah's portrayal of women is their ability to take an active part in the environment which surrounds them. Because Farah presents his women from this perspective, he is unique among African creative writers. Farah's depiction of progress made by African women in their bid for personal freedom from outdated values is typified by Medinia in *Sweet and Sour Milk.* Conscious that sacrifice is indispensable in any concerted struggle against established authority, Medinia, despite a privileged background, rises up against the General in a blow for the silent majority. As an active member of a revolutionary group, Medinia offers counsel and protection to young students who participate in protests of the General's tyrannical form of government.

Another example of Farah's portrayal of women taking an active role in the world around them is Qumman in *Sweet and Sour Milk.* A suppressed, second-class citizen of traditional Muslim culture, Qumman is the typical mother, loving, all-caring, and patient. The victim of physical abuse by her husband, Qumman lives only for her children. But despite being cast in the traditional mold, Qumman organizes the religious rituals involved with her son Soyaan's funeral while arranging for the presence of the sheikhs watching over the corpse. Though such arrangements would not be not uncommon in Western culture, this clearly exemplifies the changing role of women in African society. "Through his portrayal of educated women like Medina, Segal, Amina and their associates, Farah presents a penetrating study of conflict between traditional Muslim culture and the encroaching Western influence," writes J. I. Okonkwo in *World Literature Today.*

Though sometimes criticized for substandard stylistic and technical writing, Farah is generally acknowledged, along with Sembene Ousmane and Ayi Kwei Armah, whose female characters also possess the same vision as Farah's women, as the African writers who have done the greatest justice in championing human rights. The political tone of his novels is evident as Farah attempts to show the pressure of the Somalian regime on individual psyches, but his writings concentrate on characters who, despite the system, slowly grow as individuals.

Critics have praised the uniqueness of Farah's writing. "The novels are, in the widest sense, political but are never simplistic or predictable," declares Angela Smith in *Contemporary Novelists.* "Farah is not politically naive or specifically anti-Soviet; his implicit theme is the imprisoning effect of outside intervention in Somalian life." Kirsten Holst Petersen, writing in *Ariel: A Review of International English Literature,* says of Farah, "Pushed by his own sympathy and sensitivity, but not pushed too far, anchored to a modified Western bourgeois ideology, he battles valiantly, not for causes but for individual freedom, for a slightly larger space round each person, to be filled as he or she chooses."

BIOGRAPHICAL\CRITICAL SOURCES:

BOOKS

Kenneth Little, *Women and Urbanization in African Literature*, Macmillan, 1981.
Wright, Derek, *The Novels of Nuruddin Farah*, Bayreuth University (Germany), 1994.

PERIODICALS

Ariel, summer, 1981.
Bananas, March-April, 1981.
Index, May, 1981.
International Fiction Review, winter, 1984.
Journal of Commonwealth Literature, Volume 24, number 1, 1989.
Modern Fiction Studies, spring, 1989.
Neue Zuricher Zeitung, July 3, 1981.
New York Times Book Review, July 12, 1992, p. 18.
Ufahamu, Volume 17, number 2, 1989.
Utne Reader, January-February, 1993, p. 118.
World Literature Written in English Volume 24, number 1, 1984.

*   *   *

FISHER, Rudolph   1897-1934

PERSONAL: Born May 9, 1897, in Washington, DC; died of a chronic intestinal ailment, December 26, 1934. *Education:* Brown University, B.A. (with honors), 1919, M.A., 1920; Howard University, earned degree (summa cum laude); further study at Columbia University.

CAREER: Physician and writer. Superintendent of the International Hospital, 1929-32; roentgenologist with Department of Health in New York City, 1930-34; teacher and lecturer. *Military service:* U.S. Army, Medical Division of the 369th Infantry, 1931-34, first lieutenant.

MEMBER: Phi Beta Kappa, Sigma Psi, Delta Sigma Rho.

AWARDS, HONORS: Spingarn Prize, 1925, for "High Yaller."

WRITINGS:

NOVELS

The Walls of Jericho, Knopf, 1928, reprinted with preface by William Robinson, Jr., Arno Press/ New York Times, 1969.
The Conjure-Man Dies: A Mystery Tale of Dark Harlem, Covici, Friede, 1932, reprinted with introduction by Stanley Ellin, Arno Press/New York Times, 1971 (also see below).

SHORT STORIES

"The City of Refuge" in *Atlantic Monthly,* February, 1925; anthologized in *American Negro Short Stories,* edited by John Henrik Clark, Hill & Wang, 1966; and in *Black Literature in America,* edited by Houston A. Baker, Jr., McGraw, 1971.
"The South Lingers On" in *Survey Graphic,* March, 1925.
"Ringtail" in *Atlantic Monthly,* May, 1925.
"High Yaller" in two parts in *Crisis,* October, 1925, November, 1925; anthologized in *Cavalcade: Negro American Writing from 1760 to the Present,* edited by Arthur P. Davis and Saunders Redding, Houghton, 1971.
"The Promised Land" in *Atlantic Monthly,* January, 1927.
"The Backslider" in *McClure's,* August, 1927.
"Blades of Steel" in *Atlantic Monthly,* August, 1927; anthologized in *Anthology of American Negro Literature,* edited by Victor F. Calverton, Modern Library, 1929.
"The Caucasian Storms Harlem" in *American Mercury,* August, 1927.
"Fire by Night" in *McClure's,* December, 1927.
"Common Meter" in *Baltimore Afro-American,* February, 1930; anthologized in *Best Short Stories by Afro-American Writers,* edited by Nick Aaron Ford and H. L. Faggett, Meador Publishing, 1950; and in *Black Voices: An Anthology of Afro-American Literature,* edited by Abraham Chapman, Mentor Books, 1968.
"Dust" in *Opportunity,* February, 1931.
"Ezekiel" in *Junior Red Cross News,* March, 1932.
"Ezekiel Learns" in *Junior Red Cross News,* February, 1933.
"Guardian of the Law" in *Opportunity,* March, 1933.
"Miss Cynthie" in *Story,* June, 1933; anthologized in *The Best Short Stories by Negro Writers,* edited by Langston Hughes, Little, Brown, 1967; in *Dark Symphony: Negro Literature in America,* edited by James A. Emanuel and Theodore L.

Gross, Free Press, 1968; and in *On Being Black: Writings by Afro-Americans from Frederick Douglass to the Present,* edited by Charles T. Davis and Daniel Walden, Fawcett, 1970.

"John Archer's Nose" in *Metropolitan,* January, 1935.

The City of Refuge: The Collected Stories, edited by John McCluskey, Jr., University of Missouri Press (Columbia, MO), 1987.

The Short Fiction of Rudolph Fisher, edited and introduced by Margaret Perry, Greenwood Press (New York City), 1987.

Also author of *The Collected Stories of Rudolph Fisher,* "The South Lingers On," and unpublished stories "Across the Airshaft," "The Love Lost Blues," "The Man Who Passed," and "The Lindy Hop" held at Brown University Archives.

OTHER

Conjur' Man Dies (play; adapted by Fisher from his novel *The Conjure-Man Dies: A Mystery Tale of Dark Harlem;* also see above), first produced on March 11, 1936, at the Lafayette Theatre in Harlem.

Contributor of nonfiction to periodicals, including *American Mercury, Survey Graphic Number,* and (with Earl B. McKinley) *Journal of Infectious Diseases.* Contributor of book reviews to *Book League Monthly* and *New York Herald Tribune Books.*

SIDELIGHTS: Rudolph Fisher was among the writers who sparked interest in black literature during the Harlem Renaissance of the 1920s. Within that group, he was notable for addressing the conditions of Harlem blacks and for adopting an incisively satiric approach in depicting that community. For these reasons, Fisher is widely regarded as one of the first writers to provide significant insights into the urban black society, and he is respected for both the realistic and humorous aspects of his short stories and novels. As Leonard J. Deutsch wrote in a 1979 issue of *Phylon:* "Fisher was an insider who scratched deeply. The stories reveal his love for the people of Harlem and the diversity of talents they represent. They also help us to understand the quality of life of Harlem during the Renaissance period."

Unlike the blacks that frequently populated his fiction, Fisher was sophisticated and extensively educated. He was born in Washington, D.C., and received his early education in New York and Rhode Island. He earned both undergraduate and graduate degrees from Brown University, where he distinguished himself for his academic prowess. He subsequently pursued a medical education at Howard University, from which he graduated with further honors, and at Columbia University.

It was during his time in medical school that Fisher published his first story, "The City of Refuge," in the *Atlantic Monthly.* Abjuring the stereotypical portraiture that fellow blacks Claude McKay and Jean Toomer had appropriated from leading white writers, Fisher presented fully developed, sympathetic black characters. In "The City of Refuge" he recounted the experiences of King Solomon Gillis, a naive out-of-towner who arrives enthusiastically in Harlem only to find himself exploited by his fellow blacks. This story, which Edward J. O'Brien selected for inclusion in the volume *Best Short Stories of 1925,* readily established Fisher as an iconoclast within the budding Harlem Renaissance.

Fisher quickly followed "The City of Refuge" with three more tales: "High Yaller," "Ringtail," and "The South Lingers On." In "High Yaller" he continued exploring exploitation and antagonism within the black community by focusing on a light-skinned black's predicament among abusive peers. As Arthur P. Davis noted in his volume *From the Dark Tower,* prejudice among blacks was a prevalent theme in Fisher's work. "Fisher . . . does not overplay the issue," Davis observed, "but he does not ignore or sidestep it." In "Ringtail" Fisher mined the same theme, only this time focusing on the abuses endured by a West Indian from Native Americans. A more humorous approach was taken by Fisher in "The South Lingers On," where he depicts Harlem as an extension of the South. Notable among the tale's five vignettes is the concluding portion, in which a transplanted Southern black regresses while attending a tent revival. As Davis noted in *From the Dark Tower,* the character "has not lost as much of his Southern upbringing as he had thought."

The more violent aspects of Harlem life are addressed by Fisher in tales such as "Blades of Steel" and "The Promised Land," both published in 1927. In "Blades of Steel" a gambler named Eight-Ball undoes the unsavory Dirty Cozzens by means of a clever, and grisly, trick with a razor. "The Promised Land," like other Fisher stories, deals with the plight of Southern blacks in the unfamiliar and unfriendly Harlem environs. Here a grandmother vainly attempts to reconcile two grandsons. Her efforts are futile, though, and one fellow eventually kills the other. Writing of "The

Promised Land" in his book *Down Home,* Robert A. Bone noted Harlem's destructive effect on the unity of Southern blacks in Fisher's works. "Divisiveness," Bone wrote, "is the price the black community must pay to enter in the promised land."

Fisher's next important work is probably *The Walls of Jericho,* his satiric novel about a wealthy black's shattering experiences in a white portion of New York City. The novel's protagonist is Fred Merrit, a prosperous lawyer who moves into a strictly white neighborhood and consequently finds himself ostracized by both whites and blacks. Merrit, however, delights in distressing whites, and is only distressed by his own fellow blacks' reactions to his move. Unfortunately for Merrit, it is the antagonism he has generated within the black community that eventually undermines his life when a fellow black, hostile to Merrit's actions, torches his home.

The tone of *The Walls of Jericho* is largely satirical, with Fisher mocking aspiring blacks, out-of-towners, and—of course—righteous whites. When *The Walls of Jericho* was first published in 1928, reviewers focused on the work's humorous perspective. A critic for *Crisis* declared that Fisher's novel was "finely worked out with a delicate knowledge of human reactions." The critic added, however, that secondary characters were only "moderately funny" and speculated that Fisher's humor might mask his cynicism. "Perhaps he really laughs at all life and believes nothing," the reviewer considered. More impressed was a critic for the *Times Literary Supplement* who reported that *The Walls of Jericho* was "a sympathetic and extraordinarily impressive account" of black life. The reviewer added that Fisher "holds the reader's attention from the first to last" and that the tale is told "with unfailing and pungent humor."

Fisher followed *The Walls of Jericho* with "Common Meter," which appeared in the *Baltimore Afro-American* in 1930. "Common Meter" tells of two jazz musicians—drumming bandleader Bus Williams, who celebrates his music's strong ties to black culture; and light-skinned trumpeter Fess Baxter, who merely uses jazz as a forum for self-promotion and social climbing. The two musicians are rivals for the affections of a young woman, Jean. At a ballroom show, where the musicians' respective bands are engaged in a contest for "the jazz championship of the world," the loathsome Fess attempts to sabotage Bus's performance by slashing his drums. Jean then realizes that Bus possesses greater integrity and self-awareness, and she rescues his band by leading everyone—musicians and

audience—in a foot stomping session that sustains the music's rhythm. Afterwards she rewards Bus with her love and the championship trophy.

In *Down Home,* Bone found "Common Meter" to be Fisher's reminder to fellow blacks of their heritage and rightful pride of achievement. "At bottom," wrote Bone, "Fisher is warning the black community to guard itself against a certain kind of spiritual loss. Don't abandon your ancestral ways when you move to the big city; don't discard the authentic blues idiom for the shallow, trivial, flashy, meretricious values of the urban world." Similarly, Thomas Friedman wrote in *Studies in Black Literature* that "Common Meter" was a superb example of black positivism. He declared: "By fully fifty years, Fisher anticipates the notion of 'Black is beautiful,' and uses the blackness of a man's skin to indicate his goodness. . . . As such, 'Common Meter' is a valuable source for those who look for early indications of the change in Black consciousness and for those who search literature for positive uses of the color black."

In 1932 Fisher published his second novel, *The Conjure-Man Dies.* This quasi-supernatural mystery concerns the efforts of two sleuths—police sergeant Perry Dart and physician John Archer—to fathom the possible demise of N'Gana Frimbo, an African king who indulges in fortune-telling in his capacity as a Harlem psychiatrist. *The Conjure-Man Dies* is remarkable in that it is probably the first American mystery novel entirely populated by black characters. In the *New York Times Book Review,* Isaac Anderson described Fisher's novel as an entertaining and enlightening volume. Anderson cited the work's "lively picture of Harlem" and praised Fisher's skills as a comedic writer. Hugh M. Gloster, in his 1948 volume *Negro Voices in American Fiction,* also noted the novel's humor as well as its strengths as a mystery. He called *The Conjure-Man Dies* "a refreshing creation."

Fisher apparently found great pleasure in recording the antics of sleuths Dart and Archer, and he had intentions of writing at least two more novels featuring the characters. Unfortunately he was able to write the pair in only one more work, the short story "John Archer's Nose," before his untimely death in 1934. The story, appraised by Deutsch in his *Phylon* essay, amusingly details the devastating effect of superstition in the black community. Deutsch deemed the tale "supremely clever and witty."

Of Fisher's last works, the most important is probably "Miss Cynthie," his often-anthologized tale of a grandmother's initial disappointment, and eventual pride, in her grandson's success as a musician. Like many of Fisher's previous tales, "Miss Cynthie" contrasts the values of Southern traditionalists and Northern blacks. Also consistent with Fisher's prior writings, "Miss Cynthie," uses music as a device for exploring these different values. In *Down Home,* Bone called "Miss Cynthie" "the best of Fisher's stories," and he noted that the story constituted an artistic breakthrough for Fisher. "Having given us a gallery of static characters," Bone contended, "he suddenly discovers how to *interiorize* his dramatic conflicts, so that his characters have an opportunity to grow."

"Miss Cynthie" and "John Archer's Nose" proved to be Fisher's last published works. His final writing was an adaptation, for the stage, of *The Conjure-Man Dies.* The play was produced in 1936, four years after Fisher's death. In the ensuing decades, his stature as a key black writer waned. In the early 1960s, however, critical interest in his work was revived, and today he is recognized as a unique and innovative artist.

BIOGRAPHICAL/CRITICAL SOURCES:

BOOKS

Abrahamson, Doris E., *Negro Playwrights in the American Theatre, 1925-1959,* Columbia University Press, 1969, pp. 59-63.
Black Literature Criticism, Gale, Volume 2, 1992.
Bone, Robert A., *Down Home: A History of Afro-American Short Fiction from Its Beginnings to the End of the Harlem Renaissance,* Putnam, 1975.
Bone, Robert A., *The Negro Novel in America,* Yale University Press, 1965.
Bontemps, Arna, editor, *The Harlem Renaissance Remembered,* Dodd, 1972.
Brawley, Benjamin, *The Negro Genius: A New Appraisal of the Achievement of the American Negro in Literature and the Fine Arts,* Biblo & Tannen, 1937.
Brown, Sterling, *The Negro in American Fiction: Negro Poetry and Drama,* Arno Press, 1969.
Davis, Arthur P., *From the Dark Tower,* Howard University Press, 1974, pp. 98-103.
Dictionary of Literary Biography, Gale, Volume 51: *Afro-American Writers from the Harlem Renaissance to 1940,* 1987; Volume 102: *American Short-Story Writers, 1910-1945, Second Series,* 1991.

Emanuel, James A. and Theodore L. Gross, editors, *Dark Symphony: Negro Literature in America,* Free Press, 1968.
Gayle, Addison, Jr., *The Way of the New World: The Black Novel in America,* Anchor Press, 1976, pp. 135-40.
Gross, Theodore L., *The Heroic Ideal in American Literature,* Free Press, 1971.
Hill, Herbert, editor, *Anger and Beyond,* Harper, 1966.
Huggins, Nathan Irvin,*Harlem Renaissance,* Oxford University Press, 1971.
Kramer, Victor, editor, *The Harlem Renaissance Reexamined,* AMS, 1987, pp. 253-63.
Littlejohn, David, *Black on White: A Critical Survey of the Writings by Negroes,* Viking, 1966.
Perry, Margaret, *Silence to the Drums,* Greenwood, 1976, pp. 64-8 and 112-16.
Short Story Criticism, Volume 25, Gale, 1997.
Twentieth-Century Literary Criticism, Gale, Volume 11, 1983.

PERIODICALS

African American Review, fall, 1992, p. 524.
Afro-American, August 11, 1928.
Amsterdam News, August 10, 1932.
CLA Journal, December 26, 1982, pp. 191-203.
Cleveland Open Shelf, December, 1928.
Crisis, November, 1928, September, 1932, July 1971.
New York Evening Post, July 30, 1932.
New York Herald Tribune, August 26, 1928, August 14, 1932.
New York Times, March 12, 1936.
New York Times Book Review, July 31, 1932.
Philadelphia Tribune, September 29, 1932.
Phylon, June, 1979.
Pittsburgh Courier, September 24, 1932.
Saturday Review of Literature, September 8, 1928, August 13, 1932.
Spectator, August 25, 1928.
Studies in Black Literature, spring, 1976.
Times Literary Supplement, September 6, 1928.*

*   *   *

FLOURNOY, Valerie (Rose) 1952-

PERSONAL: Born April 17, 1952, in Camden, NJ; daughter of Payton I. Flournoy, Sr. (a chief of police), and Ivie Mae (Buchanan) Flournoy; divorced.

Education: William Smith College, teacher's certificate and B.A., 1974. *Politics:* Independent. *Religion:* Roman Catholic.

ADDRESSES: Office—Vis a Vis Publishing, 505 Arch St., Palmyra, NJ 08065.

CAREER: Dial Books for Young Readers, New York City, assistant editor, 1977-79; Pocket Books, New York City, senior editor for the Silhouette Books division, 1979-82; Berkley Publishing Group, New York City, consulting editor for Second Chance at Love, 1982-83; Vis a Vis Publishing Co., Palmyra, NJ, editor in chief, 1985—.

MEMBER: Black Women in Publishing, Romance Writers of America.

AWARDS, HONORS: The Patchwork Quilt was named an American Library Association Notable Book, 1985; Christopher Award, 1985, for *The Patchwork Quilt;* Ezra Jack Keats New Writer Award, Ezra Jack Keats Foundation and New York Public Library, 1986.

WRITINGS:

CHILDREN'S BOOKS, EXCEPT AS INDICATED

The Best Time of Day, illustrated by George Ford, Random House (New York City), 1978.
The Twins Strike Back, illustrated by Diane deGroat, Dial (New York City), 1980.
The Patchwork Quilt, illustrated by Jerry Pinkney, Dial Books for Young Readers (New York City), 1985.
Until Summer's End (young adult), Doubleday (Garden City, NY), 1986.
Tanya's Reunion, illustrated by Jerry Pinkney, Dial Books for Young Readers, 1995.
(With Vanessa Flournoy) *Celie and the Harvest Fiddler,* illustrated by James E. Ransome, Tambourine Books (New York City), 1995.

ADAPTATIONS: The Patchwork Quilt was adapted to video by Great Plains National Instructional Television Library, 1985.

SIDELIGHTS: Valerie Flournoy's books for children and young adults have won high praise from book reviewers, but she is probably best recognized for her award-winning novel *The Patchwork Quilt.* Published in 1985, the work tells of Tanya, a young black girl enthralled by her grandmother's dedication to sewing a quilt. When the family matriarch becomes sick, Tanya and her family cooperate to continue the task for their grandmother. In addition to recognizing the book's merit when recited orally, Tony Bradman said in a *Times Literary Supplement* review that *The Patchwork Quilt* "is very well written, and manages to convey . . . important themes in a totally painless way." *School Library Journal* reviewer Susan Powers commented that "this story of the completion of a year-long project—a quilt that has brought a family together in a new way, with a new understanding of each other—will leave children moved and satisfied."

In 1995, Flournoy continued the story of Tanya and her family in *Tanya's Reunion.* In this book, Tanya accompanies her grandmother to the farm in Virginia—where Grandma spent her childhood—to prepare for a family reunion. Grandma is thrilled to go home, but the old farmhouse and bad weather leave Tanya feeling bored and lonely. Grandma eases the girl's disappointment by sharing her memories of the place, "helping the child to visualize the past, learn of the family's continuity, and feel the ever-present love to which Tanya is connected," according to *Horn Book* reviewer Maria B. Salvadore. Calling *Tanya's Reunion* "a special, heartwarming book," Lauralyn Persson of *School Library Journal* added that "Flournoy is a graceful writer who lets readers discover things on their own." Ilene Cooper commented in *Booklist* that *Tanya's Reunion* was not quite as "fresh" as *The Patchwork Quilt,* but she added: "Still, you can't argue too much with themes of love, family, and home running through a story, and the essence of the grandmother-grandchild relationship is nicely captured."

Flournoy went back in time for her next book, *Celie and the Harvest Fiddler,* which is set in the 1870s. Celie is an African-American girl who hopes to win a prize for the scariest costume at an All Hallows' Eve party. When her costume falls apart, she runs from the laughing crowd into the woods, where a mysterious fiddler gives her an African mask capable of granting wishes to the one who wears it. Returning to the party, she does indeed win the coveted prize, but when her brother and a friend grab her mask, they inadvertently turn themselves into wolves and chase Celie back into the forest. There, the fiddler transforms the boys back into human form and disappears with the mask, leaving Celie with her prize and a tale worth telling. Julie Yates, writing in *Booklist,* found merit in the book's "appealing spookiness and its historical value."

BIOGRAPHICAL/CRITICAL SOURCES:

PERIODICALS

American Visions, December-January, 1995, p. 36.
Booklist, April 1, 1985, p. 1119; September 1, 1995, p. 85; September 15, 1995, p. 169.
Bulletin of the Center for Children's Books, May, 1980, p. 171; April, 1985, p. 146.
Children's Playmate, October-November, 1996, p. 20.
Horn Book, September-October, 1995, p. 587.
Kirkus Reviews, August 1, 1980, p. 977.
New York Times Book Review, October 20, 1985, p. 18.
Publishers Weekly, April 18, 1980, p. 89; May 10, 1985, p. 231; September 18, 1995, pp. 131-32.
School Library Journal, April, 1985, p. 78; September, 1995, p. 175; November, 1995, p. 71.
Times Literary Supplement, August 2, 1985, p. 862.*

* * *

FOSTER, Cecil (A.) 1954-

PERSONAL: Born September 26, 1954, in Bridgetown, Barbados, West Indies; son of Fred and Doris Goddard; married Glenys Cadogan; children: Munyonzwe, Michelio, Mensah. *Education:* Harrison College of Barbados, diploma in mass communications; York University, B.B.A., B.A. (with honors).

ADDRESSES: Home—25 Greenbush Cres., Thornhill, Ontario L4J 5M3, Canada.

CAREER: Caribbean News Agency, senior reporter and editor, 1975-77; *Barbados Advocate News,* reporter and columnist, 1977-79; *Toronto Star,* Toronto, Ontario, Canada, reporter, 1979-82; *Contrast,* Toronto, editor, 1979-82; *Transportation Business Management,* editor, 1982-83; *Globe and Mail,* Toronto, reporter, 1983-89; *Financial Post,* senior editor, 1989—.

MEMBER: PEN Canada (director, 1992—), Writer's Union of Canada, Glen Shield Soccer Club (executive member and fundraiser, 1991-93), Harambee Cultural Centres, Canadian Artist Network, Blacks in Action.

WRITINGS:

Distorted Mirror: Canada's Racist Face, Harper Collins (Toronto), 1991.

No Man in the House (novel), Random House (Toronto), 1991, Ballantine (New York), 1992.
Sleep On, Beloved (novel), Ballantine (New York), 1995.

Also author of *A Place Called Heaven: The Meaning of Being Black in Canada,* HarperCollins (Toronto). Contributor of articles and reviews to periodicals, including *Chatelaine, Maclean's,* and *Canadian Business.*

SIDELIGHTS: A native of the West Indies, Cecil Foster is the author of several books, all of which describe both the hardships and achievements of blacks in the West Indies and Canada. He has garnered the most attention for his novels *No Man in the House* and *Sleep On, Beloved.*

Foster's native Barbados forms the backdrop for *No Man in the House,* the story of 10-year-old Howard Prescod and his family's struggle to survive their impoverished world in the early 1960s, during their country's fight for independence from Britain. Howard's parents have left him and his brothers to begin a new, and hopefully brighter, life in England. In the meantime, Howard's God-fearing grandmother and his aunts work to feed the family and hold it together. Howard's salvation from his desperate existence comes in the form of a man, Humphrey Bradshaw, the first black headmaster of Howard's school. From Bradshaw, Howard learns that education is his ticket out of poverty and oppression by others, and also realizes the importance of personal and political independence.

No Man in the House is loosely based on Foster's own life in Barbados. In an interview with Donna Nurse published in *Books in Canada,* Foster commented on the similarities between Howard Prescod and himself, responding: "I grew up in a very poor neighbourhood, Lodge Road, where I set the book. There was me and two brothers and as in *No Man in the House,* my parents had gone off to England to live. I was the last of the three, somewhat like Howard himself. By the time you get into the third chapter or so, the resemblance to me has to some degree disappeared." Foster told Nurse of the influence of his family and grandmothers before adding: "I also got a strong sense of the importance of education—it was seen as a way out. When I was growing up the ambitious ones among us saw ourselves as emigrants in the making."

Critics applauded *No Man in the House,* which a *Publishers Weekly* reviewer deemed a "finely crafted, affecting debut novel of triumph over social and historical inequities." Michael Harris, writing in the *Los Angeles Times Book Review,* commented on Foster's depictions of women in *No Man in the House,* opining: "The beleaguered grandmother, Howard's young aunts and the other village women are vividly drawn; their angry, loving voices are riches in an impoverished world." Further praise was issued by M. G. Vassanji, a contributor to *Canadian Forum:* "It is the major strength of Foster's novel, and the mark of its honesty that it celebrates the human spirit and acknowledges the humanity of its characters as it describes their weaknesses and struggles."

Foster followed *No Man in the House* with *Sleep On, Beloved,* a novel about a Jamaican woman who emigrates to Canada. Foster's protagonist, Ona Morgan, is a dancer with Kingston's National Dance Troupe, but must leave the company when she becomes pregnant with the troupe's married director's child. She later leaves her homeland and her infant daughter, Suzanne, to seek a new life in Canada. Ona obtains work in a garment factory, where she must yield to the sexual advances of her boss, who controls her with his threats of deportation. By the time Ona can send for Suzanne, the girl is nearly a teen, and the years of separation between mother and daughter, coupled with Suzanne's difficulty in assimilating to a new culture, prove troubling.

Foster told Nurse that he wrote *Sleep On, Beloved* to illustrate "that multiculturalism can work. That multiculturalism worked in the Caribbean where we had people from different places getting along and that the best form of multiculturalism is when you allow people to be natural." Some reviewers of *Sleep On, Beloved* maintained that Foster's lectures on the difficulties West Indians face in white culture diminish the success of his story. For example, reviewer Lynne Van Luven responded negatively to Foster's "extra lectures" and wrote in *Quill and Quire* that although Foster's novel "tells a sad and unsettling story of the bigotry faced by a struggling black family, . . . Foster should have trusted that his characters' lives would speak for themselves. They do, and eloquently." Donna Nurse, reviewing *Sleep On, Beloved* for *Maclean's,* found flaws existing in the story line, but applauded the novel as "a poignant and disturbing portrait of the formidable impediments that may constrain Caribbean immigrants, barriers that make the dream of a new family life in Canada so difficult to achieve." Uma Parameswaran in a review in *Books in Canada,* declared: "*Sleep On, Beloved* speaks from the inside of the community, and some

details are disturbing. . . . The novel's merit lies in being a record of Caribbean experience in Canada."

BIOGRAPHICAL/CRITICAL SOURCES:

PERIODICALS

Books in Canada, May, 1995, pp. 36-37; September, 1995, pp. 18-21.
Boston Globe, October 19, 1992, p. 40.
Canadian Forum, August, 1991, pp. 28-29.
Library Journal, May 1, 1995, p. 65.
Los Angeles Times Book Review, November 8, 1992, p. 6.
Maclean's, May 22, 1995, p. 65.
Publishers Weekly, August 24, 1992, pp. 62-63.
Quill and Quire, March, 1995, p. 72.
School Library Journal, April, 1993, p. 149.*

*   *   *

FRENCH, Albert   1943-

PERSONAL: Born in 1943.

ADDRESSES: Home—7219 Thomas Blvd., Pittsburgh, Pa 15208. *Agent*—c/o Anchor Books, Doubleday & Co., Inc., 1540 Broadway, New York, NY 10036-4094.

CAREER: Pittsburgh Post-Gazette, Pittsburgh, PA, photographer, c. 1971-83; *Pittsburgh Preview Magazine,* Pittsburgh, publisher, c. 1980-88; writer. *Military service:* U.S. Marine Corps, 1963-67, attained rank of corporal; wounded in Vietnam, 1965.

AWARDS, HONORS: New York Times Book Review Notable Book of 1994, for *Billy.*

WRITINGS:

Billy (novel), Viking (New York City), 1993.
Holly (novel), Viking (New York City), 1995.
Patches of Fire: A Story of War and Redemption (autobiography), Anchor (New York City), 1996.
I Can't Wait on God (novel), Anchor (New York City), 1998.

SIDELIGHTS: Albert French, author of the critically-acclaimed novel *Billy,* reportedly spent three years holed up in an apartment, only coming out occasionally for a pack of cigarettes, prior to the publication of the book. A Vietnam War veteran, French came to terms with his struggle with depression to emerge as a singular literary voice.

Billy, based on life in rural Mississippi during the Great Depression, is set in fictional Banes County, and focuses on the horrors, trauma, and racism that engulf a small town. While wading in a pond, ten-year-old Billy Lee Turner and his friend Gumpy are attacked by two white girls for trespassing; during the struggle, Billy fatally stabs one of the girls with his pocket knife. The town is enraged, a mob demands vengeance, and eventually Billy is tracked down with hounds. After a one-day trial, he is sentenced to death by electrocution. "The story, once in motion, gathers momentum like a landslide; at first a few pebbles disturb the quiet and then, inexorably, the earth itself seems to collapse into catastrophe," commented Michael Dorris in the *New York Times Book Review.* "*Billy* is a tragedy in the classical mode . . . here we are confirmed in our worst dreads as destiny immutably and shockingly unfolds."

Billy was noted by critics for its earthy dialect, an authentic depiction of the Deep South, and a convincing portrayal of the twisted psychology of racism and injustice. Inspiration for *Billy* came from French's intense experiences during the Vietnam War as well as time he spent as a Marine in a southern training camp and a youth spent observing the civil rights movement of the 1960s. A *Publishers Weekly* contributor noted that *Billy* "pulses with its unnerving vision of inhumanity legalized under the name of justice." Donna Seaman observed in *Booklist* that the work is a "stunning first novel. . . . An American tragedy, stark and resonant."

"Without racism, the book would not have occurred, so it was a vital part of the book, but not my main focus when I started writing. I wasn't thinking, 'let's go attack racism,'" French told Polly Vedder in the *Contemporary Literary Criticism Yearbook.* The author stated that his focus was on the many characters in the book, including Billy's mother, Cinder, and Lori Pasko, the fifteen-year-old white girl killed by Billy.

French wrote *Billy* in a six-week period, using a one-page outline, an old typewriter and some whiteout. French described himself as desperately fighting a depression incurred from the Vietnam War; he had been shot in the throat in 1965, sent home, and spent the next two decades in various jobs, including twelve years as a newspaper photographer. He later became

publisher of a magazine, but when the publication failed, French isolated himself. "I wanted to fit in—God knows I tried," the author confided to Nicci Gerrard of the *Observer.* "But I kept running into Vietnam." Rarely emerging from his apartment, French began to write some accounts of his Vietnam experience. "I had nothing to do, there was no hope in my life or anything, and what I started to do is to—and I don't remember why—but I started writing different stories—short stories about Vietnam," he told Vedder in the *Contemporary Literary Criticism Yearbook.*

Those short stories eventually became more than one hundred pages of manuscript. When he showed them to his cousin, esteemed writer John Edgar Wideman, Wideman passed them on to his agent. Although it would be a few years before it became published, that manuscript—later titled *Patches of Fire*—helped to French gain recognition as a writer, and he began work on *Billy.*

"*Billy* permits me to believe that nothing is impossible; that one grows in the darkest of times. If it hadn't been for Vietnam, I wouldn't be able to see what I can now see, write what I write," French told Gerrard in the *Observer.* "*Billy* will be here long after I'm gone. That's my contribution. That's mine. That makes my life count."

Following the success of *Billy* in 1993, French began to work on his next novel, *Holly.* Like its predecessor, *Holly* addresses the theme of racism. Set during the 1940s in the town of Supply, North Carolina, the work focuses on the relationship between Holly, a nineteen-year-old white girl whose life had been changed when her fiance is killed in service during World War II, and a black artist, a veteran of the war who has lost an arm in battle. "There's this system that says as a black man, as a black writer, you cannot write about a nineteen-year-old white girl," French informed Ervin Dyer in *Emerge.* "So that's why I did it. And I really liked Holly, her energy, her person." Although Seaman in *Booklist* remarked that the pace of *Holly* was slow, she stated that "French's provocative power . . . is undeniable." David Dodd in *Booklist* described the novel as "beautifully written."

Patches of Fire: A Story of War and Redemption is a first-hand narrative of war, tragedy, senselessness, and the rebuilding process that follows such trauma. The book recounts "strange" Vietnam incidents, and walks the reader through French's return home, his struggle with the magazine, and his accomplishment as a successful writer.

French is also the author of a third novel, *I Can't Wait on God,* published in 1998. Set in the period following World War II, the novel opens in the black ghetto of Pittsburgh. There Willet Mercer and Jeremiah Henderson scheme to gather enough money to move to New York. However, when their plans fall awry the couple finds themselves on the run from the law. The novel is peopled with numerous colorful characters.

Albert French discussed his writing in an interview with the online literary magazine *Bold Type.* He commented, "With *I Can't Wait on God,* as in *Billy* and *Holly,* and *Patches of Fire,* the most important thing to me is to feel that I've been honest with the characters in that book. Respectful to their lives. My real accomplishment is that I made that contribution with my art, giving the book the chance to live, allowing these people this time to live again."

BIOGRAPHICAL/CRITICAL SOURCES:

BOOKS

Contemporary Literary Criticism Yearbook, Volume 86, Gale, 1995.

PERIODICALS

American Visions, April, 1994, p. 31.
Black Scholar, spring, 1995, p. 69.
Booklist, October 1, 1993, p. 254; January 15, 1994, p. 867; February 15, 1994, p. 1043; April 1, 1995, p. 1403; April 15, 1995, p. 1479; December 15, 1996, p. 695.
Bookwatch, spring, 1995, p. 8.
Emerge, June, 1995, p. 58.
Kirkus Reviews, August 15, 1993, p. 1017; February 15, 1995, p. 171; November 15, 1996, p. 1650.
Kliatt, July, 1996, p. 10.
Library Journal, April 15, 1995, p. 114; November 1, 1996, p. 80; January, 1997, p. 108.
New York, December 13, 1993, p. 90.
New York Times Book Review, December 19, 1993, p. 7; December 4, 1994, p. 70; February 12, 1995, p. 36; June 4, 1995, p. 12; May 26, 1996, p. 20; January 26, 1997, p. 10.
Observer, February 6, 1994, p. 18.
Publishers Weekly, August 30, 1993, p. 73; February 27, 1995, p. 85; April 8, 1996, p. 66; November 25, 1996, p. 64.

Washington Post Book World, July 9, 1995, p. 12; May 26, 1996, p. 12.

OTHER

Barnes & Noble, http://www.barnesandnoble.com (September, 1998).
Bold Type, http://www.boldtype.com/0898/french/ index.html (September, 1998).*

*   *   *

FRYE, Charles A(nthony)   1946-1994

PERSONAL: Born March 18, 1946, in Washington, DC; died of lymphoma, October 8, 1994, in New Orleans, LA; divorced; children: Odeyo J., Sekou C., Anthony F., Lia M. *Education:* Howard University, B.A., 1968, M.A., 1970; University of Pittsburgh, Ph.D., 1976.

CAREER: Washington, DC, Public Library, librarian, 1968-69; Washington, DC, Public Schools, teacher, 1969-70; Howard University, Washington, DC, assistant professor, 1970-77; Fayetteville State University, director of interdisciplinary studies, 1977-78; Hampshire College, associate dean of students and associate professor of education, beginning c. 1978; Five College Black Studies Executive Committee, chair and journal editor, 1983-85; taught at University of Massachusetts at Amherst; Southern University, New Orleans, professor of African philosophy and humanities, director of Center for African and African-American studies, until 1994.

MEMBER: National Council for Black Studies (chair and editor of council journal, 1980-82; member of board of directors), Association for Supervision and Curriculum Development.

AWARDS, HONORS: Advanced Study Fellowship, Ford Foundation, 1972-73.

WRITINGS:

The Impact of Black Studies on the Curricula of Three Universities, University Press of America, 1976.
Towards a Philosophy of Black Studies, R & E Research Associates, 1978.
(Editor) *Level Three: A Black Philosophy Reader,* University Press of America, 1980.

(Editor) *Values in Conflict: Blacks and the American Ambivalence toward Violence,* University Press of America, 1980.

From Egypt to Don Juan: The Anatomy of Black Philosophy, preface by August Coppola, University Press of America, 1988.

The Peter Pan Chronicles (novella), University Press of Virginia, 1989.

Contributor of reviews to periodicals, including *Journal of Negro History.*

SIDELIGHTS: A glance at Charles A. Frye's publications reveals his varied interests and areas of expertise. His first three books—*The Impact of Black Studies on the Curricula of Three Universities, Towards a Philosophy of Black Studies,* and *Level Three: A Black Philosophy Reader*—reflect his graduate training in both philosophy and higher education. Another of Frye's concerns is evident in his fourth text, *Values in Conflict: Blacks and the American Ambivalence toward Violence,* which not only addresses the contemporary phenomenon of violence but also examines social values as they relate to African Americans. His fifth text, *From Egypt to Don Juan: The Anatomy of Black Philosophy,* treats similar themes of blacks, race identity, and philosophy.

Though his mode of presentation for his sixth book, *The Peter Pan Chronicles,* shifts from analytic to creative writing, his thematic concern with contemporary black issues remains constant. The story is told through the unreliable eyes of a black patient, Raynard Parker, in an insane asylum. Parker was once assigned to sabotage the efforts of black civil rights activists in the 1960s, especially those of his friend Tommy Rollins, who Parker betrayed to government authorities. Unable to deal with the guilt of his actions, Parker suffers from severe time and space disorientation. Throughout the book he transforms figures in the asylum into people from his past, yielding a disjointed recreation of his activities in the 1960s.

Some reviewers of *The Peter Pan Chronicles* complained that they found it difficult to derive meaning from the novel's unorthodox narration. Others, however, found it a refreshing deviance from traditional fictional conventions. Charles C. Nash, writing in *Library Journal,* felt that Frye's technique resulted in a "brilliant collage of images" and that the book presented a terrifying yet convincing portrait of blacks in the United States.

BIOGRAPHICAL/CRITICAL SOURCES:

PERIODICALS

Library Journal, June 15, 1989.
Publishers Weekly, June 2, 1989, p. 78.*

*   *   *

FULANI, Lenora (Branch)   1950-

PERSONAL: Born April 25, 1950, in Chester, PA; daughter of Charles (a railroad worker) and Pearl (a licensed practical nurse) Branch; name changed to Lenora Branch Fulani, 1973; divorced; children: Ainka (daughter), Amani (son). *Ethnicity:* "African American." *Education:* Hofstra University, B.A.; Columbia University, Teachers College, M.A.; City University of New York, Graduate Center, Ph.D.; New York Institute for Social Therapy and Research, post-graduate training in social therapy.

ADDRESSES: Agent—Castillo International, 500 Greenwich St., Suite 201, New York, NY 10013.

CAREER: Political party leader, psychologist, and social therapist. Associated with Rockefeller Institute, New York City, 1970s; associated with New York Institute for Social Therapy and Research; East Side Center for Short Term Psychotherapy, New York City, psychotherapist; National Alliance Party, founder, presidential candidate, 1988 and 1992; "This Way for Black Empowerment" (newspaper column), columnist; All-Stars Talent Show Network, founder; *Fulani!* (television show), host.

MEMBER: Transnational Radical Party (member of general council), Committee for a Unified Independent Party (chair), Patriot Party (co-founder, 1994).

WRITINGS:

(Editor) *The Politics of Race and Gender in Therapy,* Haworth Press (New York), 1988.

(Editor) *The Psychopathology of Everyday Racism and Sexism,* Harrington Park Press (New York), 1988.

The Making of a Fringe Candidate, 1992, Castillo International Publications (New York), 1993.

Contributor to books, including *Independent Black Leadership in America,* Castillo International, 1990.

Author of newspaper column "This Way for Black Empowerment," 1996.

SIDELIGHTS: For more than twenty years, Lenora Fulani has established herself as one of the leading voices in national independent politics and working-class advocacy. She is the first woman and first African American to have appeared as a presidential candidate on all U.S. ballots. She is also a community organizer against discrimination and violence. Furthermore, Fulani makes a difference on a more individual level through her practice of social therapy.

Fulani was one of the founders of the Barbara Taylor school in New York City. This independent school adopted the social development model first outlined by Soviet psychologist Lev Vygotski. She is a main supporter of the Castillo Cultural Center in Manhattan, founded in 1984, which supports multicultural art and theater. A multi-talented woman, Fulani is also the founder and co-producer of the *All Stars Talent Show Network,* an anti-violence television program for urban children in the United States.

Lenora Fulani was born just outside of Philadelphia in the working-class city of Chester, Pennsylvania. She spent her first eighteen years in Chester progressing through the public school system and attending church. According to an article published in *Ms. Black Shopper International Network,* Fulani first became interested in changing the world at the age of twelve, when her father, Charles Branch, "died of a seizure after her family could not get an ambulance to come into their neighborhood in Chester." Even at such a young age, she was aware that the economic considerations of others had an effect on the health and well-being of African Americans.

In her book, *The Making of a Fringe Candidate, 1992,* Fulani explained that the firing of her church's choir director also convinced her to assist people whom she terms "disenfranchised." "Everybody sort of knew [the choir director] was gay, but nobody said anything about it until they decided to replace him so they could do something else with his salary line. They used his homosexuality as an excuse to get rid of him." The injustice of the situation enraged the young Fulani so much that she advocated his retention, even against the urging of her mother to simply participate in "'prayer meetings . . . like everyone else.'"

Another example of Fulani's early activism was related in the *Philadelphia Inquirer Daily Magazine.*

"As a senior at predominantly black Chester High in 1968, she [threatened] to organize a walkout if her class were forced to integrate its all black class cabinet, the first in the school's history. The administration backed down." Fulani's cousin, Yvonne Mann, was quoted as saying in the article: "All her life she knew she was going somewhere. . . . She thought about 'when,' not 'if.'"

Fulani told of her time at Hofstra University in *The Making of a Fringe Candidate, 1992* as one of growth. While there she learned about her own prejudices and how to overcome them. She noticed that women and their contributions to society and the civil rights movement remained in the shadows of men. Fulani did not enjoy this unequal treatment, but she was unsure about what she could do to change anything as prevalent as sexism.

During the early 1970s Fulani married. The two children from this relationship—a daughter, Ainka, and a son, Amani—received the majority Fulani's attention while she also worked to support the family and complete her various degrees. As she acknowledged in her book, the effort was taxing, but it made her stronger. The hard work and desire for change led Fulani in new directions.

Fulani began exploring activism and social change in the 1970s. While completing her doctorate work and working at the Rockefeller Institute in New York City, she attended a therapy group run by Dr. Fred Newman, a psychologist who practices what he calls social therapy. The group helped her eradicate her prejudices against different kinds of people. She wrote in *The Making of a Fringe Candidate, 1992* that "what I had learned about [people different from myself] was a pile of bull and very hurtful. I worked aggressively to do something about that." With Dr. Newman's help, she recognized that she had been raised with "certain expressions [and] attitudes" that were unfair assessments of people she did not know. "[Prejudices are] so deeply embedded in how you think that they make you insensitive and hurtful even to people you love very much. I worked hard in that group to provide leadership around these issues."

Dr. Newman has continued to play an important role in Fulani's life outside of the therapy group by serving as campaign manager during most of her political campaigns. As Fulani admitted in her book, she consults Newman about her most pressing concerns because he shares Fulani's hope of improving the lot of disenfranchised people through political means.

After finishing her doctoral work, Fulani furthered her association with the New York Institute for Social Therapy and Research. She began her therapy practice working with people in Harlem. Fulani also founded a political party known as the National Alliance Party (NAP) in order to effect political change without resorting to the policies of the Republican or Democratic parties. As an independent party, the NAP looked for support wherever it could find it, but the majority of NAP's original followers were women and African Americans from Fulani's work-place and the local community.

As a political starting point, the NAP described itself, according to the *Philadelphia Inquirer,* as "black-led, multiracial, pro-gay, and pro-socialist." Over the years Fulani often served the party as its standard-bearer in elections. She campaigned for lieutenant governor of New York in 1982, mayor of New York City in 1985, governor of New York in 1986 and 1990, and president of the United States in 1988 and 1992. In her run for the presidency, she distinguished herself by becoming the first woman and the first African American to qualify for the ballot in all 50 states. She also became the first woman to qualify for federal primary matching funds during her 1992 bid. In fact, she was so successful in 1992 that she garnered more in matching funds than mainstream candidates Jerry Brown and Douglas Wilder.

Fulani's brand of independent politics has involved many tactics. She has led drives for voter registration. She has initiated lawsuits to open up ballot access to independent parties. Fulani has fought to be included in debates with major candidates on the state and national levels. She gained much attention in the 1992 New Hampshire presidential primary by fighting for the inclusion of Larry Agran and Eugene McCarthy in the Democratic Party debates, so that they could provide a more independent voice to the event. She later led Agran and McCarthy's fight to be included on the New York primary ballot.

During her bids for public office, Fulani received endorsements from disparate people and groups. One of her supporters over the years has been the controversial minister Louis Farrakhan. Fulani has endured a great deal of criticism from more mainstream politicians because she has refused to denounce Farrakhan. Fulani stated in *The Making of a Fringe Candidate, 1992,* however, that "black leaders—like white leaders—have the right to have differences without having to repudiate each other." She also received a great deal of bad publicity for her support of gay rights.

Fulani insists, though, that it is possible to derive support from these very different sectors of the country and build a movement that is unified in its thinking. In her run for the Democratic Party's nomination for governor of New York in 1994, she showed this statement to be true by collecting twenty-one percent of the total vote in the primary elections. She gathered more than thirty percent of the vote in many black majority areas and more than forty percent of the vote in the six northern New York counties where industrialist Ross Perot scored very high percentages of the vote in the 1992 presidential election.

In addition to her grassroots runs for political office, Fulani has often taken to the streets to push for action issues or solve problems of the working class. She played a major role in attempting to serve justice in the rape case of fifteen-year-old Tawana Brawley in which Brawley originally implicated three white men, was defended by black social activist Reverend Al Sharpton, but eventually admitted that she fabricated the story. Fulani organized marches, again with Sharpton, in regards to the Howard Beach, New York, incident in which three black men with car problems were severely beaten, one fatally, by whites in a white neighborhood for just being there. Fulani took to the streets for more than twenty-five marches through the predominantly white Bensonhurst section of Brooklyn, New York, in which Yusuf Hawkins, a black youth, was killed. She spent several hours in the streets of the Crown Heights section of Brooklyn "helping to avert a bloodbath [between African American and Jewish residents] in the wake of the death of Gavin Cato [a black child run over by a car]," according to *Ms. Black Shopper International Network.* This event led to her endorsement in the 1990 gubernatorial race by the Guardian Association of the New York City Police Department.

Fulani continues her work with what she calls "the overtaxed and under served population" in her political activities, said her spokesperson Madelyn Chapman. In 1994, Fulani assisted in forming a unified front of the disenfranchised and other independent voters who supported the presidential campaign of Ross Perot. At a meeting that year of the Federation of Independent Voters in Arlington, Virginia, the Patriot Party was born through this organizing effort. The NAP has since folded itself into the Patriot Party for the 1996 elections, hoping to strengthen the power of independent voters.

Although Fulani has achieved great success in organizing independent voters, it has not been without obstacles. Both Political Research Associates of Cambridge, Massachusetts, and *Nation* magazine have published material highly critical of Fulani and the NAP. *Nation* likened the party to a cult run by Dr. Newman. According to the *Philadelphia Inquirer,* however, "Fulani's followers have heard all the criticism and remain fiercely loyal. Many of the most ardent, from the most disaffected quarters of society, say she has revived their interest in politics."

Fulani continues to work hard for independent politics and the reform of the current system. In 1996 she reached out to people through a newspaper column carried in more than 140 newspapers, titled "This Way for Black Empowerment." She also is the host of her own cable television show, *Fulani!,* seen in more than twenty cities each week. In these ways, Lenora Fulani has expanded her efforts to include everyone in the democratic process.

BIOGRAPHICAL/CRITICAL SOURCES:

PERIODICALS

Ms., May/June, 1992, pp. 86-88.
Ms. Black Shopper International Network, January, 1995, p. 3.
Nation, May 4, 1992, pp. 385-94; May 30, 1994, pp. 746-47.
New York Amsterdam News, January 30, 1993, p. 4.
Philadelphia Inquirer Daily Magazine, April 6, 1992, p. C1.

OTHER

Press release, Castillo International Publications, November, 1995.

G

GAINES, Ernest J(ames) 1933-

PERSONAL: Born January 15, 1933, in Oscar (some sources cite River Lake Plantation, near New Roads, Pointe Coupee Parish), LA; son of Manuel (a laborer) and Adrienne J. (Colar) Gaines. *Education:* Attended Vallejo Junior College; San Francisco State College (now University), B.A., 1957; graduate study at Stanford University, 1958-59.

ADDRESSES: Office—Department of English, University of Southwestern Louisiana, P.O. Box 44691, Lafayette, LA 70504. *Agent*—JCA Literary Agency, Inc., 242 West 27th St., New York, NY 10001.

CAREER: "Writing, five hours a day, five days a week." Denison University, Granville, OH, writer in residence, 1971; Stanford University, Stanford, CA, writer in residence, 1981; University of Southwestern Louisiana, Lafayette, professor of English and writer in residence, 1983-. Whittier College, visiting professor, 1983, and writer in residence, 1986. Subject of the film, *Louisiana Stories: Ernest Gaines,* which aired on WHMM-TV in 1993. *Military service:* U.S. Army, 1953-55.

AWARDS, HONORS: Wallace Stegner fellow, Stanford University, 1957; Joseph Henry Jackson Award from San Francisco Foundation, 1959, for "Comeback" (short story); award from National Endowment for the Arts, 1967; Rockefeller grant, 1970; Guggenheim fellow, 1971; award from Black Academy of Arts and Letters, 1972; fiction gold medal from Commonwealth Club of California, 1972, for *The Autobiography of Miss Jane Pittman,* and 1984, for *A Gathering of Old Men;* award from Louisiana Library Association, 1972; honorary doctorate of letters from Denison University, 1980, Brown University, 1985, Bard College, 1985, and Louisiana State University, 1987; award for excellence of achievement in literature from San Francisco Arts Commission, 1983; D.H.L. from Whittier College, 1986; literary award from American Academy and Institute of Arts and Letters, 1987; John D. and Catherine T. MacArthur Foundation fellowship, 1993; inducted into Literary Hall of Fame for Writers of African Descent, Chicago State University, 1998.

WRITINGS:

FICTION

Catherine Carmier (novel), Atheneum, 1964.
Of Love and Dust (novel), Dial, 1967.
Bloodline (short stories; also see below), Dial, 1968, Vintage Contemporaries (New York City), 1997.
A Long Day in November (story originally published in *Bloodline*), Dial, 1971.
The Autobiography of Miss Jane Pittman (novel), Dial, 1971.
In My Father's House (novel), Knopf, 1978.
A Gathering of Old Men (novel), Knopf, 1983.
A Lesson before Dying (novel), Knopf, 1993.
Conversations with Ernest Gaines, edited by John Lowe, University Press of Mississippi (Jackson, MS), 1995.

ADAPTATIONS: The Autobiography of Miss Jane Pittman, adapted from Gaines's novel, aired on the Columbia Broadcasting System (CBS-TV), January 31, 1974, starring Cicely Tyson in the title role; the special won nine Emmy Awards. "The Sky Is Gray," a short story originally published in *Bloodline,* was adapted for public television in 1980. *A Gathering of*

Old Men, adapted from Gaines's novel, aired on CBS-TV, May 10, 1987, starring Lou Gossett, Jr. and Richard Widmark.

SIDELIGHTS: The fiction of Ernest J. Gaines, including his 1971 novel *The Autobiography of Miss Jane Pittman,* is deeply rooted in the black culture and storytelling traditions of rural Louisiana where the author was born and raised. His stories have been noted for their convincing characters and powerful themes presented within authentic, often folk-like, narratives that tap into the complex world of Southern rural life. Gaines depicts the strength and dignity of his black characters in the face of numerous struggles: the dehumanizing and destructive effects of racism; the breakdown in personal relationships as a result of social pressures; and the choice between secured traditions and the sometimes radical measures necessary to bring about social change. Although the issues presented in Gaines's fiction are serious and often disturbing, "this is not hot-and-breathless, burn-baby-burn writing," Melvin Maddocks points out in *Time;* rather, it is the work of "a patient artist, a patient man." Expounding on Gaines's rural heritage, Maddocks continues: "[Gaines] sets down a story as if he were planting, spreading the roots deep, wide and firm. His stories grow organically, at their own rhythm. When they ripen at last, they do so inevitably, arriving at a climax with the absolute rightness of a folk tale."

Gaines's boyhood experiences growing up on a Louisiana plantation provide many of the impressions upon which his stories are based. Particularly important, he told Paul Desruisseaux in the *New York Times Book Review,* were "working in the fields, going fishing in the swamps with the older people, and, especially, listening to the people who came to my aunt's house, the aunt who raised me." Although Gaines moved to California at the age of fifteen and subsequently went to college there, his fiction has been based in an imaginary Louisiana plantation region named Bayonne, which a number of critics have compared to William Faulkner's Yoknapatawpha County. Gaines has acknowledged looking to Faulkner, in addition to Ernest Hemingway, for language, and to French writers such as Gustave Flaubert and Guy de Maupassant for style. A perhaps greater influence, however, has been the writings of nineteenth-century Russian authors.

Gaines's first novel, *Catherine Carmier,* is "an apprentice work more interesting for what it anticipates than for its accomplishments," notes William E. Grant in the *Dictionary of Literary Biography.* The novel chronicles the story of a young black man, Jackson Bradley, who returns to Bayonne after completing his education in California. Jackson falls in love with Catherine, the daughter of a Creole sharecropper who refuses to let members of his family associate with anyone darker than themselves, believing Creoles racially and socially superior. The novel portrays numerous clashes of loyalty: Catherine torn between her love for Jackson and love for her father; Jackson caught between a bond to the community he grew up in and the experience and knowledge he has gained in the outside world. "Both Catherine and Jackson are immobilized by the pressures of [the] rural community," writes Keith E. Byerman in the *Dictionary of Literary Biography,* which produces "twin themes of isolation and paralysis [that] give the novel an existential quality. Characters must face an unfriendly world without guidance and must make crucial choices about their lives." The characters in *Catherine Carmier*—as in much of Gaines's fiction—are faced with struggles that test the conviction of personal beliefs. Winifred L. Stoelting in *CLA Journal* explains that Gaines is concerned more "with how they [his characters] handle their decisions than with the rightness of their decisions—more often than not predetermined by social changes over which the single individual has little control."

Gaines sets *Catherine Carmier* in the time of the Civil Rights movement, yet avoids making it a primary force in the novel. Grant comments on this aspect: "In divorcing his tale from contemporary events, Gaines declares his independence from the political and social purposes of much contemporary black writing. Instead, he elects to concentrate upon those fundamental human passions and conflicts which transcend the merely social level of human existence." Grant finds Gaines "admirable" for doing this, yet also believes Jackson's credibility marred because he remains aloof from contemporary events. For Grant, the novel "seems to float outside time and place rather than being solidly anchored in the real world of the modern South." Byerman concurs, stating that the novel "is not entirely successful in presenting its major characters and their motivations." Nonetheless, he points out that in *Catherine Carmier,* "Gaines does begin to create a sense of the black community and its perceptions of the world around it. Shared ways of speaking, thinking, and relating to the dominant white society are shown through a number of minor characters."

Gaines's next novel, *Of Love and Dust,* is also a story of forbidden romance, and, as in *Catherine Carmier,* a "new world of expanding human relationships erodes the old world of love for the land and the acceptance of social and economic stratification," writes Stoelting. *Of Love and Dust* is the story of Marcus Payne, a young black man bonded out of prison by a white landowner and placed under the supervision of a Cajun overseer, Sidney Bonbon. Possessed of a rebellious and hostile nature, Marcus is a threat to Bonbon, who in turn does all that he can to break the young man's spirit. In an effort to strike back, Marcus pays special attention to the overseer's wife; the two fall in love and plot to run away. The novel ends with a violent confrontation between the two men, in which Marcus is killed. After the killing, Bonbon claims that to spare Marcus would have meant his own death at the hands of other Cajuns. Grant notes a similarity between *Of Love and Dust* and *Catherine Carmier* in that the characters are "caught up in a decadent social and economic system that determines their every action and limits their possibilities." Similarly, the two novels are marked by a "social determinism [which] shapes the lives of all the characters, making them pawns in a mechanistic world order rather than free agents."

Of Love and Dust demonstrates Gaines's development as a novelist, offering a clearer view of the themes and characters that dominate his later work. Stoelting writes that "in a more contemporary setting, the novel . . . continues Gaines's search for human dignity, and when that is lacking, acknowledges the salvation of pride," adding that "the characters themselves grow into a deeper awareness than those of [his] first novel. More sharply drawn . . . [they] are more decisive in their actions." Byerman writes that the novel "more clearly condemns the economic, social, and racial system of the South for the problems faced by its characters." Likewise, the first-person narrator in the novel—a co-worker of Marcus—"both speaks in the idiom of the place and time and instinctively asserts the values of the black community."

Gaines turns to a first-person narrator again in his next novel, *The Autobiography of Miss Jane Pittman,* which many consider to be his masterwork. Miss Jane Pittman—well over 100-years-old—relates a personal history that spans the time from the Civil War and slavery up through the Civil Rights movement of the 1960s. "To travel with Miss Pittman from adolescence to old age is to embark upon a historic journey, one staked out in the format of the novel," writes Addison Gayle, Jr., in *The Way of the World: The Black Novel in America.* "Never mind that Miss Jane Pittman is fictitious, and that her 'autobiography,'

offered up in the form of taped reminiscences, is artifice," adds Josh Greenfield in *Life,* "the effect is stunning." Gaines's gift for drawing convincing characters reaches a peak in *The Autobiography of Miss Jane Pittman.* "His is not . . . an 'art' narrative, but an authentic narrative by an authentic ex-slave, authentic even though both are Gaines's inventions," Bryant comments. "So successful is he in *becoming* Miss Jane Pittman, that when we talk about her story, we do not think of Gaines as her creator, but as her recording editor."

The character of Jane Pittman could be called an embodiment of the black experience in America. "Though Jane is the dominant personality of the narrative-observer and commentator upon history, as well as participant—in her odyssey is symbolized the odyssey of a race of people; through her eyes is revealed the grandeur of a people's journey through history," writes Gayle. "The central metaphor of the novel concerns this journey: Jane and her people, as they come together in the historic march toward dignity and freedom in Sampson, symbolize a people's march through history, breaking old patterns, though sometimes slowly, as they do." The important historical backdrop to Jane's narrative—slavery, Reconstruction, the Civil Rights movement, segregation—does not compromise, however, the detailed account of an individual. "Jane captures the experiences of those millions of illiterate blacks who never had a chance to tell their own stories," Byerman explains. "By focusing on the particular yet typical events of a small part of Louisiana, those lives are given a concreteness and specificity not possible in more general histories."

In his fourth novel, *In My Father's House,* Gaines focuses on a theme which appears in varying degrees throughout his fiction: the alienation between fathers and sons. As the author told Desruisseaux: "In my books there always seems to be fathers and sons searching for each other. That's a theme I've worked with since I started writing. Even when the father was not in the story, I've dealt with his absence and its effects on his children. And that is the theme of this book." *In My Father's House* tells of a prominent civil rights leader and reverend (Phillip Martin) who, at the peak of his career, is confronted with a troubled young man named Robert X. Although Robert's identity is initially a mystery, eventually he is revealed to be one of three offspring from a love affair the reverend had in an earlier, wilder life. Martin hasn't seen or attempted to locate his family for more than twenty years. Robert arrives to confront and kill the father whose neglect he sees as responsible for the family's disintegration: his sister has been raped, his brother imprisoned for the murder of her attacker, and his mother reduced to poverty, living alone. Although the son's intent to kill his father is never carried out, the reverend is forced "to undergo a long and painful odyssey through his own past and the labyrinthine streets of Baton Rouge to learn what really happened to his first family," writes William Burke in the *Dictionary of Literary Biography Yearbook.* Larry McMurtry, in the *New York Times Book Review,* notes that as the book traces the lost family, "we have revealed to us an individual, a marriage, a community and a region, but with such an unobtrusive marshaling of detail that we never lose sight of the book's central thematic concern: the profoundly destructive consequences of the breakdown of parentage, of a father's abandonment of his children and the terrible and irrevocable consequences of such an abandonment."

A Gathering of Old Men, Gaines's fifth novel, presents a cast of aging Southern black men who, after a life of subordination and intimidation, make a defiant stand against injustice. Seventeen of them, together with the 30-year-old white heiress of a deteriorating Louisiana plantation, plead guilty to murdering a hostile member (Beau Boutan) of a violent Cajun clan. While a confounded sheriff and vengeful family wait to lynch the black they've decided is guilty, the group members-toting recently fired shotguns-surround the dead man and "confess" their motives. "Each man tells of the accumulated frustrations of his life—raped daughters, jailed sons, public insults, economic exploitation—that serve as sufficient motive for murder," writes Byerman. "Though Beau Boutan is seldom the immediate cause of their anger, he clearly represents the entire white world that has deprived them of their dignity and manhood. The confessions serve as ritual purgings of all the hostility and self-hatred built up over the years." Fifteen or so characters—white, black, and Cajun—advance the story through individual narrations, creating "thereby a range of social values as well as different perspectives on the action," notes Byerman. Reynolds Price writes in the *New York Times Book Review* that the black narrators "are nicely distinguished from one another in rhythm and idiom, in the nature of what they see and report, especially in their specific laments for past passivity in the face of suffering." The accumulated effect, observes Elaine Kendall in the *Los Angeles Times Book Review,* is that the "individual stories coalesce into a single powerful tale of subjugation, exploitation and humiliation at the hands of landowners."

Another theme of *A Gathering of Old Men,* according to Ben Forkner in *America,* is "the simple, natural dispossession of old age, of the traditional and well-loved values of the past, the old trades and the old manners, forced to give way to modern times." Sam Cornish writes in the *Christian Science Monitor* that the novel's "characters—both black and white—understand that, before the close of the novel, the new South must confront the old, and all will be irrevocably changed. Gaines portrays a society that will be altered by the deaths of its 'old men,' and so presents an allegory about the passing of the old and birth of the new."

A Lesson before Dying, issued ten years after *A Gathering of Old Men,* continues the author's historical reflections on the Southern world captured in all of his novels to date. The setting remains relatively the same-a plantation and jail in Bayonne during a six-month span in 1948. The unlikely hero is Jefferson, a scarcely literate, twenty-one-year-old man-child who works the cane fields of the Pichot Plantation. Trouble finds the protagonist when he innocently hooks up with two men, who rob a liquor store and are killed in the process along with the shop's proprietor, leaving Jefferson as an accomplice. The young man's naivete in the crime is never recognized as he is brought to trial before a jury of twelve white men and sentenced to death. Jefferson's defense attorney ineffectively attempts to save his client by presenting him as a dumb animal, as "a thing that acts on command. A thing to hold the handle of a plow, a thing to load your bales of cotton." When Jefferson's godmother learns of this analogy, she determines that her nephew will face his execution as a man, not as an animal. Thus, she enlists the help of a young teacher named Grant Wiggins, who is initially resistant but works to help Jefferson achieve manhood in his final days.

According to Sandra D. Davis in the *Detroit Free Press,* "*A Lesson before Dying* begins much like many other stories where racial tension brews in the background." Yet, as in Gaines's other works, the racial tension in this novel is more of a catalyst for his tribute to the perseverance of the victims of injustice. Unexpectantly, pride, honor, and manhood in a dehumanizing environment emerge as the themes of this novel. Through Wiggins, the young narrator and unwilling carrier of the "burden" of the community, and his interaction with the black community, as represented by Jefferson's godmother and the town's Reverend Ambrose, Gaines "creates a compelling, intense story about heroes and the human spirit," contends

Davis. Ironically, Jefferson and Reverend Ambrose ultimately emerge as the real teachers, showing Wiggins that, as Davis asserts, "education encompasses more than the lessons taught in school." Wiggins is also forced to admit, according to Jonathan Yardley in *Washington Post Book World,* "his own complicity in the system of which Jefferson is a victim."

Of that community which yields the lessons of Gaines' fiction and his relation to it, Alice Walker writes in the *New York Times Book Review* that Gaines "claims and revels in the rich heritage of Southern Black people and their customs; the community he feels with them is unmistakable and goes deeper even than pride . . . Gaines is mellow with historical reflection, supple with wit, relaxed and expansive because he does not equate his people with failure." Gaines has been criticized by some, however, who feel his writing does not more directly focus on problems facing blacks. Gaines responds to Desruisseaux that he feels "too many blacks have been writing to tell whites all about 'the problems,' instead of writing something that all people, including their own, could find interesting, could enjoy." Gaines has also remarked that more can be achieved than strictly writing novels of protest. In an interview for *San Francisco,* the author states: "So many of our writers have not read any farther back than [Richard Wright's] *Native Son.* So many of our novels deal only with the great city ghettos; that's all we write about, as if there's nothing else." Gaines continues: "We've only been living in these ghettos for 75 years or so, but the other 300 years—I think this is worth writing about."

In *Conversations with Ernest Gaines,* the author reveals to editor John Lowe some of the factors behind his popularity and critical acclaim. "While a notable consistency in themes and setting is evident within the body of his writing," states critic Valerie Babb, writing about *Conversations with Ernest Gaines* in the *African American Review,* "in novel ways this talented writer consistently re-envisions and reworks the material that inspires him. . . . The best commentary is Gaines's own . . . as he assesses his art." "Critiques of racial essentialism are many," Babb concludes, "and there is increased scholarly emphasis on finding voice and telling story, two elements that imbue Gaines's works with their own unique pyrotechnics. With greater appreciation of how small details make great fiction, it seems our critical age is indeed ready to appreciate the fiction of Ernest Gaines."

BIOGRAPHICAL/CRITICAL SOURCES:

BOOKS

Babb, Valerie-Melissa, *Ernest Gaines,* Twayne, 1991.
Beavers, Herman, *Wrestling Angels into Song: The Fictions of Ernest J. Gaines and James Alan McPherson,* University of Pennsylvania Press (Philadelphia), 1995.
Bruck, Peter, editor, *The Black American Short Story in the Twentieth Century: A Collection of Critical Essays,* B. R. Gruner (Amsterdam), 1977.
Carmean, Karen, *Ernest J. Gaines: A Critical Companion,* Greenwood Press, 1998.
Concise Dictionary of American Literary Biography: Broadening Views, 1968-1988, Gale (Detroit), 1989.
Contemporary Literary Criticism, Gale, Volume 3, 1975; Volume 11, 1979; Volume 18, 1981.
Conversations with Ernest Gaines, University Press of Mississippi (Jackson), 1995.
Dictionary of Literary Biography, Gale, Volume 2: *American Novelists since World War II,* 1978; Volume 33: *Afro-American Fiction Writers after 1955,* 1984.
Dictionary of Literary Biography Yearbook: 1980, Gale, 1981.
Estes, David C., *Critical Reflections on the Fiction of Ernest J. Gaines,* University of Geogia Press (Athens), 1994.
Gaudet, Marcia, and Carl Wooton, *Porch Talk with Ernest Gaines: Conversations on the Writer's Craft,* Louisiana State University Press, 1990.
Gayle, Addison, Jr., *The Way of the New World: The Black Novel in America,* Doubleday, 1975.
Hicks, Jack, *In the Singer's Temple: Prose Fictions of Barthelme, Gaines, Brautigan, Piercy, Kesey, and Kosinski,* University of North Carolina Press, 1981.
Hudson, Theodore R., *The History of Southern Literature,* Louisiana State University Press, 1985.
Lowe, John, editor, *Conversations with Ernest Gaines,* University Press of Mississippi, 1995.
O'Brien, John, editor, *Interview with Black Writers,* Liveright, 1973.

PERIODICALS

African American Review, fall, 1994, p. 489; February, 1998, p. 350.
America, June 2, 1984.
Atlanta Journal and Constitution, October 26, 1997.
Black American Literature Forum, Volume 11, 1977; Volume 24, 1990.

Callaloo, Volume 7, 1984; Volume 11, 1988.
Chicago Tribune Book World, October 30, 1983.
Christian Science Monitor, December 2, 1983.
Chronicle of Higher Education, May 11, 1994, p. 23A.
CLA Journal, March, 1971; December, 1975.
Detroit Free Press, June 6, 1993, p. 7J.
Essence, August, 1993, p. 52.
Iowa Review, winter, 1972.
Life, April 30, 1971.
Los Angeles Times, March 2, 1983.
Los Angeles Times Book Review, January 1, 1984.
Meleus, Volume 11, 1984.
Nation, February 5, 1968; April 5, 1971; January 14, 1984.
Negro Digest, November, 1967; January, 1968; January, 1969.
New Orleans Review, Volume 1, 1969; Volume 3, 1972; Volume 14, 1987.
New Republic, December 26, 1983.
New Statesman, September 2, 1973; February 10, 1984.
Newsweek, June 16, 1969; May 3, 1971.
New Yorker, October 24, 1983.
New York Times, July 20, 1978.
New York Times Book Review, November 19, 1967; May 23, 1971; June 11, 1978; October 30, 1983.
Observer (London), February 5, 1984.
Publishers Weekly, March 21, 1994, p. 8.
San Francisco, July, 1974.
Southern Review, Volume 10, 1974; Volume 21, 1985.
Studies in Short Fiction, summer, 1975.
Time, May 10, 1971, December 27, 1971.
Times Literary Supplement, February 10, 1966; March 16, 1973; April 6, 1984.
Voice Literary Supplement, October, 1983.
Washington Post, January 13, 1976.
Washington Post Book World, June 18, 1978; September 21, 1983; March 28, 1993, p. 3; May 23, 1993.
Writer, May, 1999, p. 4.*

*   *   *

GATES, Henry Louis, Jr. 1950-

PERSONAL: Born September 16, 1950, Keyser, WV; son of Henry Louis and Pauline Augusta (Coleman) Gates; married Sharon Lynn Adams (a potter), September 1, 1979; children: Maude Augusta Adams, Elizabeth Helen-Claire. *Education:* Yale University,

B.A. (summa cum laude), 1973; Clare College, Cambridge, M.A., 1974, Ph.D., 1979. *Religion:* Episcopalian. *Avocational interests:* Jazz, pocket billiards.

ADDRESSES: Office—Dept. of English, 302 Allen Bldg., Duke University, Durham, NC, 27706. *Agent*—Carl Brandt, Brandt & Brandt Literary Agents, Inc., 1501 Broadway, New York, NY 10036.

CAREER: Anglican Mission Hospital, Kilimatinde, Tanzania, general anesthetist, 1970-71; John D. Rockefeller gubernatorial campaign, Charleston, WV, director of student affairs, 1971, director of research, 1972; *Time,* London Bureau, London, England, staff correspondent, 1973-75; Yale University, New Haven, CT, lecturer, 1976-79, assistant professor, 1979-84, associate professor of English and Afro-American Studies, 1984-85, director of undergraduate Afro-American studies, 1976-79; Cornell University, Ithaca, NY, professor of English, comparative literature, and African studies, 1985-88, W. E. B. DuBois Professor of Literature, 1988-90; Duke University, Durham, NC, John Spencer Bassett Professor of English and Literature, 1990-; Harvard University, Cambridge, MA, W. E. B. DuBois Professor of the Humanities, professor of English, chair of Afro-American studies, and director of W. E. B. DuBois Institute for Afro-American Research, 1991-. Virginia Commonwealth, visiting professor, 1987. Created the television series *The Image of the Black in the Western Imagination,* Public Broadcasting Service (PBS), 1982.

MEMBER: Council on Foreign Relations; American Antiquarian Society; Union of Writers of the African Peoples; Association for Documentary Editing; African Roundtable; African Literature Association; Afro-American Academy; American Studies Association; Trans Africa Forum Scholars Council; Association for the Study of Afro-American Life and History (life); Caribbean Studies Association; College Language Association (life); Modern Language Association; Stone Trust; Zora Neale Hurston Society; Cambridge Scientific Club; American Civil Liberties Union National Advisory Council; German American Studies Association; National Coalition Against Censorship; American Philosophical Society; Saturday Club; New England Historic Genealogical Society; Phi Beta Kappa.

AWARDS, HONORS: Carnegie Foundation Fellowship for Africa, 1970-71; Phelps Fellowship, Yale University, 1970-71; Mellon fellowships, Cambridge University, 1973-75, and National Humanities Center,

1989-90; grants from Ford Foundation, 1976-77 and 1984-85, and National Endowment for the Humanities, 1980-86; A. Whitney Griswold Fellowship, 1980; Rockefeller Foundation fellowships, 1981 and 1990; MacArthur Prize Fellowship, MacArthur Foundation, 1981-86; Yale Afro-American teaching prize, 1983; award from Whitney Humanities Center, 1983-85; Princeton University Council of the Humanities lectureship, 1985; Award for Creative Scholarship, Zora Neale Hurston Society, 1986; associate fellowship from W. E. B. DuBois Institute, Harvard University, 1987-88 and 1988-89; John Hope Franklin Prize honorable mention, American Studies Association, 1988; Woodrow Wilson National Fellow, 1988-89 and 1989-90; Candle Award, Morehouse College, 1989; American Book Award and Anisfield-Wolf Book Award for Race Relations, both 1989, both for *The Signifying Monkey: Towards a Theory of Afro-American Literary Criticism;* recipient of honorary degrees from Dartmouth College, 1989, University of West Virginia, 1990, University of Rochester, 1990, Pratt Institute, 1990, University of Bridgeport, 1991 (declined), University of New Hampshire, 1991, Bryant College, 1992, Manhattan Community College, 1992, George Washington University, 1993, University of Massachusetts at Amherst, 1993, Williams College, 1993, Emory University, 1995, Colby College, 1995, Bard College, 1995, and Bates College, 1995; Richard Wright Lecturer, Center for the Study of Black Literature and Culture, University of Pennsylvania, 1990; Potomac State College Alumni Award, 1991; Bellagio Conference Center Fellowship, 1992; Clarendon Lecturer, Oxford University, 1992; Best New Journal of the Year award (in the humanities and the social sciences), Association of American Publishers, 1992; elected to the American Academy of Arts and Sciences, 1993; Golden Plate Achievement Award, 1993; African American Students Faculty Award, 1993; George Polk Award for Social Commentary, 1993; Heartland Prize for Nonfiction, 1994, for *Colored People: A Memoir;* Lillian Smith Book Award, 1994; West Virginian of the Year, 1995; Humanities Award, West Virginia Humanities Council, 1995; Ethics Award, Tikun (magazine), 1996; Distinguished Editorial Achievement, *Critical Inquiry,* 1996; W. D. Weatherford Award.

WRITINGS:

Figures in Black: Words, Signs, and the Racial Self, Oxford University Press (New York City), 1987.
The Signifying Monkey: Towards a Theory of Afro-American Literary Criticism, Oxford University Press, 1988.

Loose Canons: Notes on the Culture Wars (essays), Oxford University Press, 1992.
Colored People: A Memoir, Knopf (New York City), 1994.
Speaking of Race: Hate Speech, Civil Rights, and Civil Liberties, New York University Press, 1995.
(With Cornel West) *The Future of the Race,* Knopf, 1996.
Thirteen Ways of Looking at a Black Man, Random House (New York City), 1997.
(Author of introduction) Douglass, Frederick, *Narrative of the Life of Frederick Douglass, an American Slave,* Laurel Leaf, 1997.

EDITOR

(And author of introduction) *Black Is the Color of the Cosmos: Charles T. Davis's Essays on Afro-American Literature and Culture, 1942-1981,* Garland Publishing (New York City), 1982.
(And author of introduction) Harriet E. Wilson, *Our Nig; or, Sketches from the Life of a Free Black,* Random House (New York City), 1983.
(And author of introduction) *Black Literature and Literary Theory,* Methuen (New York City), 1984.
(And author of introduction with Charles T. Davis) *The Slave's Narrative: Texts and Contexts,* Oxford University Press, 1986.
(And author of introduction) *"Race," Writing, and Difference,* University of Chicago Press (Chicago), 1986.
(And author of introduction) *The Classic Slave Narratives,* New American Library (New York City), 1987.
(And author of introduction) *In the House of Oshugbo: A Collection of Essays on Wole Soyinka,* Oxford University Press, 1988.
(Series editor) *The Oxford-Schomburg Library of Nineteenth-Century Black Women Writers,* 30 volumes, Oxford University Press, 1988.
W. E. B. DuBois, *The Souls of Black Folk,* Bantam Books (New York City), 1989.
James Weldon Johnson, *The Autobiography of an Ex-Coloured Man,* Vintage, 1989.
Three Classic African American Novels, Vintage, 1990.
Zora Neale Hurston, *Their Eyes Were Watching God* (introduction by Mary Helen Washington), Harper (New York City), 1990.
Hurston, *Jonah's Gourd Vine* (introduction by Rita Dove), Harper, 1990.

Hurston, *Tell My Horse* (introduction by Ishmael Reed), Harper, 1990.

Hurston, *Mules and Men* (introduction by Arnold Rampersad), Harper, 1990.

Reading Black, Reading Feminist: A Critical Anthology, Meridian Book, 1990.

Voodoo Gods of Haiti (introduction by Ishmael Reed), Harper, 1991.

The Schomburg Library of Nineteenth-Century Black Women Writers, 10 volume supplement, Oxford University Press, 1991.

(With Randall K. Burkett and Nancy Hall Burkett) *Black Biography, 1790-1950: A Cumulative Index,* Chadwyck-Healey (Teaneck, NJ), 1991.

(With George Bass) Langston Hughes and Zora Neale Hurston, *Mulebone: A Comedy of Negro Life,* HarperPerennial (New York City), 1991.

Bearing Witness: Selections from African American Autobiography in the Twentieth Century, Pantheon Books (New York City), 1991.

(With Anthony Appiah) *Gloria Naylor: Critical Perspectives Past and Present,* Amistad (New York City), 1993.

(With Appiah) *Alice Walker: Critical Perspectives Past and Present,* Amistad, 1993.

(With Appiah) *Langston Hughes: Critical Perspectives Past and Present,* Amistad, 1993.

(With Appiah) *Richard Wright: Critical Perspectives Past and Present,* Amistad, 1993.

(With Appiah) *Toni Morrison: Critical Perspectives Past and Present,* Amistad, 1993.

(With Appiah) *Zora Neale Hurston: Critical Perspectives Past and Present,* Amistad, 1993.

The Amistad Chronology of African American History from 1445-1990, Amistad, 1993.

(And annotations) *Frederick Douglass: Autobiographies,* Library of America, 1994.

(With Appiah) *The Dictionary of Global Culture,* Knopf, 1995.

The Complete Stories of Zora Neale Hurston, Harper Collins, 1995.

(With Appiah) *Identities,* University of Chicago, 1996.

Ann Petry: Critical Perspectives Past and Present, Amistad, 1997.

Chinua Achebe: Critical Perspectives Past and Present, Amistad, 1997.

Harriet A. Jacobs: Critical Perspectives Past and Present, Amistad, 1997.

Ralph Ellison: Critical Perspectives Past and Present, Amistad, 1997.

Wole Soyinka: Critical Perspectives Past and Present, Amistad, 1997.

Frederick Douglass: Critical Perspectives Past and Present, Amistad, 1997.

The Essential Soyinka: A Reader, Pantheon, 1998.

Also editor, with Appiah, of "Amistad Critical Studies in African American Literature" series, 1993, and editor of the Black Periodical Literature Project. Advisory editor of "Contributions to African and Afro-American Studies" series for Greenwood Press (Westport, CT), "Critical Studies in Black Life and Culture" series for Garland Press, and "Perspectives on the Black World" series for G. K. Hall (Boston). General editor of *A Dictionary of Cultural and Critical Theory; Middle-Atlantic Writers Association Review.* Coeditor of *Transition.* Associate editor of *Journal of American Folklore.* Member of editorial boards including, *Critical Inquiry, Studies in American Fiction, Black American Literature Forum, PMLA, Stanford Humanities Review,* and *Yale Journal of Law and Liberation.*

OTHER

(Compiler with James Gibb and Ketu H. Katrak) *Wole Soyinka: A Bibliography of Primary and Secondary Sources,* Greenwood Press, 1986.

(With N. Y. McKay) *The Norton Anthology of African American Literature,* Norton (New York City), 1996.

SIDELIGHTS: Henry Louis Gates, Jr., is one of the most controversial and respected scholars in the field of African-American studies. Gates was recognized early on by an English instructor at Potomac State Community College, who encouraged his student to transfer to Yale University. Gates graduated from that institution with highest honors in 1973. While in Africa on a Carnegie Foundation Fellowship and a Phelps Fellowship during 1970-1971, he visited fifteen countries and became familiar with various aspects of African culture. His knowledge of Africa deepened when the celebrated African writer Wole Soyinka became his tutor at Cambridge University, where Gates worked on his master's and doctoral degrees. In 1981 he was awarded one of the so-called "genius grants" from the MacArthur Foundation. He moved quickly from a teaching post at Yale to a full professorship at Cornell to an endowed chair at Duke, and in 1991, he became the W. E. B. DuBois Professor of the Humanities at Harvard and head of its Afro-American Studies program. Gates breathed new life and enthusiasm into the program and hired lecturers, such as film director Spike Lee and authors Jamaica Kincaid and Wole Soyinka. Under Gates's leadership, the number of students in the program tripled within a few years.

Gates has his detractors as well as his admirers, however. Some of his colleagues have faulted him for being insufficiently Afro-centric, while others have criticized his high-profile activities—such as publicly testifying at the obscenity trial of rap group 2 Live Crew—as inappropriate self-promotion. Yet even those who take exception to Gates's showmanship cannot argue with his credentials or deny his prolific contributions to Afro-American scholarship, as he has written and edited numerous books of literary and social criticism. According to James Olney in the *Dictionary of Literary Biography,* Gates's mission is to reorder and reinterpret "the literary and critical history of Afro-Americans in the context of a tradition that is fully modern but also continuous with Yoruba modes of interpretation that are firmly settled and at home in the world of black Americans."

In his approach to literary criticism, Gates is avowedly eclectic and defines himself as a centrist who rejects extreme positions, whether they be on the right (guardians of a Western tradition) or on the left (Afrocentricists). Gates insists that we need to transcend "ethnic absolutism" of all kinds. Like the American novelist Ralph Ellison, Gates sees the fluid, indeed porous, relationship between black and white culture in the United States. Gates argues that our conception of the literary canon needs to be enlarged accordingly.

Gates's *Black Literature and Literary Theory,* which he edited, is considered by many reviewers to be an important contribution to the study of black literature. Calling it "an exciting, important volume," Reed Way Dasenbrock wrote in *World Literature Today:* "It is a collection of essays . . . that attempts to explore the relevance of contemporary literary theory, especially structuralism and poststructuralism, to African and Afro-American literature. . . . Anyone seriously interested in contemporary critical theory, in Afro-American and African literature, and in black and African studies generally will need to read and absorb this book." R. G. O'Meally wrote in *Choice* that in *Black Literature and Literary Theory* Gates "brings together thirteen superb essays in which the most modern literary theory is applied to black literature of Africa and the U.S. . . . For those interested in [the] crucial issues—and for those interested in fresh and challenging readings of key texts in black literature—this book is indispensable." Finally, Terry Eagleton remarked in the *New York Times Book Review* that "the most thought-provoking contributions to [this] collection are those that not only enrich our under-

standing of black literary works but in doing so implicitly question the authoritarianism of a literary 'canon.'"

One of Gates's best-known works is *Loose Canons: Notes on the Culture Wars,* in which he discusses gender, literature, and multiculturalism and argues for greater diversity in American arts and letters. Writing in the *Virginia Quarterly Review,* Sanford Pinsker noted that according to Gates "the cultural right . . . is guilty of 'intellectual protectionism,' of defending the best that has been thought and said within the Western Tradition because they are threatened by America's rapidly changing demographic profile; while the cultural left 'demands changes to accord with population shifts in gender and ethnicity.' *Loose Canons* makes it clear that Gates has problems with both positions." "The society we have made," Gates argues in *Loose Canons,* "simply won't survive without the values of tolerance. And cultural tolerance comes to nothing without cultural understanding. . . . If we relinquish the ideal of America as a plural nation, we've abandoned the very experiment that America represents." Writing in the *Los Angeles Times,* Jonathan Kirsch praised the humor and wit that infused Gates's arguments. *Loose Canons,* Kirsch concluded, is "the work of a man who has mastered the arcane politics and encoded language of the canon makers; it's an arsenal of ideas in the cultural wars. But it is also the outpouring of a humane, witty and truly civilized mind."

Colored People: A Memoir played to a wider audience than did *Loose Canons.* In it, Gates recalls his youth in Piedmont, West Virginia, at a time when the town was becoming integrated. It "explores the tension between the racially segregated past and the integrated modernity that the author himself represents," commented David Lionel Smith in *America.* While affirming the progress brought by desegregation, Gates also laments the loss of the strong, united community feeling that segregation created among blacks—a feeling epitomized in the annual all-black picnic sponsored by the paper mill that provided jobs to most of Piedmont's citizens. Numerous reviewers pointed out the gentle, reminiscent tone of Gates's narrative, but some considered this a weakness in light of the momentous changes Gates lived through. Smith remarked: "From an author of Gates's sophistication, we expect more than unreflective nostalgia." Comparing it to other recent African-American memoirs and autobiographies, he concluded, "Some of them address social issues more cogently and others are more self-analytical, but none is more vivid and pleasant to read than *Colored People.*" *Los Angeles Times Book Review* contributor Richard Eder affirmed that *Colored People* was an "affecting, beautifully written and morally complex memoir," and Joyce Carol Oates, in her *London Review of Books* assessment, described it as an "eloquent document to set beside the grittier contemporary testimonies of black male urban memoirists; in essence a work of filial gratitude, paying homage to such virtues as courage, loyalty, integrity, kindness; a pleasure to read and, in the best sense, inspiring."

Gates wrote *The Future of the Race* with Cornel West, a professor of Afro-American studies at Harvard University. This work contains an essay by Gates, an essay by West, and two essays by black intellectual W. E. B. DuBois, the latter of which are preceded by a foreword by Gates. Writing in the *New York Times Book Review*, Gerald Early noted: "The question . . . that the authors wish to answer—what is their duty to the lower or less fortunate class of blacks?—indicates the black bourgeoisie's inability to understand precisely what their success means to themselves or blacks generally." Early also observed that while "the pieces seem hastily written," Gates's essay is "engagingly witty and journalistic" as well as "charming and coherent."

Gates offers insight into the position of the black male in American society in *Thirteen Ways of Looking at a Black Man.* Through a series of discussions recorded over several years and documented in various magazine articles, Gates brings a broad cross-section of African-American hopes and ideals to the reader's attention. Interviewees include such major black American figures as James Baldwin, Harry Belafonte, Colin Powell, and Bill T. Jones. Writing in *Library Journal*, Michael A. Lutes refers to *Thirteen Ways of Looking at a Black Man* as a "riveting commentary on race in America."

BIOGRAPHICAL/CRITICAL SOURCES:

BOOKS

Dictionary of Literary Biography, Volume 67: *Modern American Critics since 1955,* Gale (Detroit), 1988.

PERIODICALS

America, December 31, 1994, p. 24.

American Spectator, April-May, 1994, p. 69.
Boston Globe, October 20, 1990, p. 3; May 12, 1991, p. 12; April 23, 1992, p. 70; November 7, 1992, p. 15; December 1, 1992, p. 23; April 29, 1993, p. 53; May 29, 1994, p. A13.
Callaloo, spring, 1991.
Chicago Tribune, February 18, 1993, section 5, p. 3; November 18, 1993, section 1, p. 32; July 17, 1994, section 14, p. 3; August 24, 1994, section 5, p. 1.
Choice, May, 1985; March, 1995, p. 1059.
Christian Century, January 19, 1994, p. 53-54.
Christian Science Monitor, April 10, 1992, p. 11; June 7, 1994, p. 13.
Commonweal, December 18, 1992, pp. 22-23.
Criticism, winter, 1994, pp. 155-61.
Emerge, November, 1990, p. 76.
Humanities Magazine, July/August, 1991, pp. 4-10.
Library Journal, February, 1997.
London Review of Books, July 21, 1994, p. 22-23; January 12, 1995, p. 14.
Los Angeles Times, October 29, 1990, p. A20; March 25, 1992, p. E2; June 3, 1994, p. E1.
Los Angeles Times Book Review, May 8, 1994, pp. 3, 12.
New Leader, September 12, 1994, pp. 12-13.
New Literary History, autumn, 1991.
New Republic, July 4, 1994, p. 33; June 16, 1997.
New Statesman & Society, February 10, 1995, p. 43.
New York Times, December 6, 1989, p. B14; April 1, 1990, section 6, p. 25; June 3, 1992, p. B7; May 16, 1994, p. C16.
New York Times Book Review, December 9, 1984; August 9, 1992, p. 21; June 19, 1994, p. 10; April 21, 1996, p. 7; February 9, 1997.
New York Times Magazine, April 1, 1990.
Spectator, February 18, 1995, pp. 31-32.
Time, April 22, 1991, pp. 16, 18; May 23, 1994, p. 73.
Times Literary Supplement, May 17, 1985; February 24, 1995, p. 26.
Tribune Books (Chicago), July 17, 1994, pp. 3, 5; October 9, 1994, p. 11.
U.S. News and World Report, March, 1992.
Village Voice, July 5, 1994, p. 82.
Virginia Quarterly Review, summer, 1993, pp. 562-68.
Voice Literary Supplement, June, 1985.
U. S. News and World Report, March, 1992.
Washington Post, October 20, 1990, p. D1; August 11, 1992, p. A17.
Washington Post Book World, July 3, 1983; June 7, 1992, p. 6; May 15, 1994, p. 3.
World Literature Today, summer, 1985.*

GIOVANNI, Nikki 1943-

PERSONAL: Birth name, Yolande Cornelia Giovanni, Jr.; born June 7, 1943, in Knoxville, TN; daughter of Jones (a probation officer) and Yolande Cornelia (a social worker; maiden name, Watson) Giovanni; children: Thomas Watson. *Education:* Fisk University, B.A. (with honors), 1967; postgraduate studies at University of Pennsylvania, Social Work School, and Columbia University, School of the Arts.

ADDRESSES: Office—English Department, Virginia Polytechnic Institute and State University, Blacksburg, Virginia, 24061.

CAREER: Poet, writer, lecturer, and educator. Queens College of the City University of New York, Flushing, NY, assistant professor of black studies, 1968; Rutgers University, Livingston College, New Brunswick, NJ, associate professor of English, 1968-72; Ohio State University, Columbus, visiting professor of English, 1984; College of Mount St. Joseph on the Ohio, Mount St. Joseph, Ohio, professor of creative writing, 1985-87; Virginia Polytechnic Institute and State University, Blacksburg, VA, professor, 1987—; Texas Christian University, visiting professor in humanities,1991. Founder of publishing firm, Niktom Ltd., 1970. Has given numerous poetry readings and lectures at universities in the United States and Europe; has made numerous television appearances on talk shows; participated in "Soul at the Center," Lincoln Center for the Performing Arts, 1972. Co-chair of Literary Arts Festival for State of Tennessee Homecoming, 1986. Duncanson artist-in-residence, Taft Museum, Cincinnati, 1986. Ohio Humanities Council, 1987. Warm Hearth Writer's Workshop, director, 1988—. Virginia Foundation for Humanities and Public Policy (member of board of directors), 1990-93.

MEMBER: National Council of Negro Women, Society of Magazine Writers, National Black Heroines for PUSH, Winnie Mandela Children's Fund Committee, Delta Sigma Theta.

AWARDS, HONORS: Grants from Ford Foundation, 1967, National Endowment for the Arts, 1968, and Harlem Cultural Council, 1969; named one of ten "Most Admired Black Women," *Amsterdam News,* 1969; outstanding achievement award, *Mademoiselle,* 1971; Omega Psi Phi Fraternity Award, 1971; Service, Cook County Jail, 1971; Prince Matchabelli Sun Shower Award,1971; life membership and scroll, National Council of Negro Women, 1972; National Association of Radio and Television Announcers

Award, 1972, for *Truth Is on Its Way;* Woman of the Year Youth Leadership Award, *Ladies' Home Journal,* 1972; National Book Award nomination, 1973, for *Gemini;* "Best Books for Young Adults" citation, American Library Association,1973, for *My House;* "Woman of the Year" citation, Cincinnati Chapter of YWCA, 1983; elected to Ohio Women's Hall of Fame, 1985; "Outstanding Woman of Tennessee" citation, 1985; Post-Corbett Award, 1986; Woman of the Year, NAACP (Lynchburg chapter), 1989; inducted into Literary Hall of Fame for Writers of African Descent, Chicago State University, 1998.

Honorary Doctorate of Humanities, Wilberforce University, 1972, Fisk University, 1988; Honorary Doctorate of Literature, University of Maryland (Princess Anne Campus), 1974, Ripon University, 1974, and Smith College, 1975; Honorary Doctorate of Humane Letters, The College of Mount St.Joseph on the Ohio, 1985, Indiana University, 1991, Otterbein College, 1992, Widener University, 1993, Albright College, 1995, Cabrini College, 1995, and Allegheny College, 1997. Keys to numerous cities, including Lincoln Heights, OH, Dallas, TX, and Gary, IN, all 1972; New York City, 1975; Buffalo, NY, and Cincinnati, OH, both 1979; Savannah, GA, and Clarksdale, Fort Lauderdale, FL, and Los Angeles, CA, all 1984; Ohioana Book Award, 1988; Jeanine Rae Award for the Advancement of Women's Culture, 1995; Langston Hughes Award, 1996.

WRITINGS:

POETRY

Black Feeling, Black Talk (also see below), Broadside Press (Highland Park, MI), 1968, third edition, 1970.

Black Judgement (also see below), Broadside Press, 1968.

Black Feeling, Black Talk/Black Judgement (contains *Black Feeling, Black Talk,* and *Black Judgement*), Morrow (New York City), 1970.

Re: Creation, Broadside Press, 1970.

Poem of Angela Yvonne Davis, Afro Arts, 1970.

Spin a Soft Black Song: Poems for Children, illustrations by Charles Bible, Hill & Wang (New York City), 1971, reprinted, illustrations by George Martins, Lawrence Hill (Westport, CT), 1985, revised edition, Farrar, Straus (New York City), 1987.

My House, foreword by Ida Lewis, Morrow, 1972.

Ego Tripping and Other Poems for Young People, illustrations by George Ford, Lawrence Hill, 1973.

The Women and the Men, Morrow, 1975.

Cotton Candy on a Rainy Day, introduction by Paula Giddings, Morrow, 1978.

Vacation Time: Poems for Children, illustrations by Marisabina Russo, Morrow, 1980.

Those Who Ride the Night Winds, Morrow, 1983.

Knoxville, Tennessee, Scholastic (New York City), 1994.

Shimmy Shimmy Shimmy Like My Sister Kate: Looking at the Harlem Renaissance through Poems, Holt (New York City), 1995.

The Genie in the Jar, Holt, 1996.

The Selected Poems of Nikki Giovanni (1968-1995), Morrow, 1996.

The Sun Is So Quiet: Poems, Holt, 1996.

Love Poems, Morrow, 1997.

Blues: For All the Changes: New Poems, Morrow, 1999.

NONFICTION

Gemini: An Extended Autobiographical Statement on My First Twenty-five Years of Being a Black Poet, Bobbs- Merrill (New York City), 1971.

(With James Baldwin) *A Dialogue: James Baldwin and Nikki Giovanni,* Lippincott (Philadelphia), 1973.

(With Margaret Walker) *A Poetic Equation: Conversations between Nikki Giovanni and Margaret Walker,* Howard University Press (Washington, DC), 1974.

Sacred Cows . . . and Other Edibles (essays; includes "Reflections on My Profession," "Four Introductions," and "An Answer to Some Questions on How I Write"), Morrow, 1988.

Racism 101, Morrow, 1994.

OTHER

Grand Fathers: Reminiscences, Poems, Recipes, and Photos of the Keepers of Our Traditions, Holt (New York City), 1999.

SOUND RECORDINGS

Truth Is on Its Way, Right-On, 1971.

Like a Ripple on a Pond, Niktom, 1973.

The Way I Feel, Atlantic, 1974.

Legacies: The Poetry of Nikki Giovanni, Folkways, 1976.

The Reason I Like Chocolate, Folkways, 1976.

OTHER

(Editor) *Night Comes Softly: An Anthology of Black Female Voices,* Medic (Redmond, WA), 1970.

(Author of introduction) Adele Sebastian, *Intro to Fine* (poems), Woman in the Moon, 1985.

(Editor) *Appalachian Elders: A Warm Hearth Sampler,* Pocahontas Press, 1991.

(Author of foreword) *The Abandoned Baobob: The Autobiography of a Woman,* Chicago Review Press, 1991.

Grand Mothers: Poems, Reminiscences, and Short Stories about the Keepers of Our Traditions, Holt, 1994.

Knoxville, Tennessee, Scholastic, 1994.

Contributor to numerous anthologies. Also contributor of columns to newspapers and magazines, including *Black Creation, Black World, Ebony, Essence, Freedom Ways, Journal of Black Poetry, Negro Digest,* and *Umbra.* Editorial consultant, *Encore American* and *Worldwide News.*

A selection of Giovanni's public papers are at Mugar Memorial Library, Boston University.

ADAPTATIONS: Spirit to Spirit: The Poetry of Nikki Giovanni (television film), 1986, produced by Public Broadcasting Corporation, Corporation for Public Broadcasting, and Ohio Council on the Arts.

SIDELIGHTS: One of the most prominent poets to emerge from the black literary movement of the late 1960s, Nikki Giovanni is famous for strongly voiced poems that testify to her own evolving awareness and experience: as a daughter and young girl, a black woman, a revolutionary in the Civil Rights movement, and a mother. A popular reader and lecturer in both the United States and Europe, Giovanni has been nicknamed "The Princess of Black Poetry," a title warranted by the crowds of fans which gather at her speaking engagements. Popular for her adult poetry and essays, as well as best-selling recorded albums of her poetry, Giovanni has also published three books of acclaimed verse for children: *Spin a Soft Black Song, Ego Tripping and Other Poems for Young People,* and *Vacation Time.* Like her adult works, "Nikki Giovanni's poems for children . . . exhibit a combination of casual energy and sudden wit," wrote Nancy Klein in the *New York Times Book Review.* Giovanni "explores the contours of childhood with honest affection, sidestepping both nostalgia and condescension. Her poems focus on the experiences of children—naps and baths and getting bigger, dreams and fears and growing up."

Giovanni was born in 1943 in Knoxville, Tennessee, a city nestled in the Smoky Mountains. "The mountains cause you to raise your eyes upward and ponder the heavens," she wrote in *Fifth Book of Junior Authors and Illustrators*. "They help to create a larger vision. You are small but not alone." Her family life was a happy one, and Nikki, a strong-willed and independent child, was particularly close to her older sister Gary, who studied music, and her maternal grandmother, Louvenia Terrell Watson. Her grandmother—an outspoken women—instilled in the young Nikki an intense admiration and appreciation for her race. Other members of her family influenced her in the oral tradition of poetry. "I come from a long line of storytellers," she once commented. "My grandfather was a Latin scholar and he loved the myths, and my mother is a big romanticist, so we heard a lot of stories growing up. . . . I appreciated the quality and the rhythm of the telling of the stories, and I know when I started to write that I wanted to retain that—I didn't want to become the kind of writer that was stilted or that used language in ways that could not be spoken."

When Giovanni was still young, she moved with her family to a suburb of Cincinnati, Ohio, but remained close to her grandmother and spent several of her teen years in Knoxville. As a teenager, she was conservative in her outlook— a supporter of Republican presidential candidate Barry Goldwater and a follower of writer Ayn Rand, who was famous for her philosophy of objectivism. In 1960, at the age of seventeen, Giovanni enrolled in Nashville's all-black Fisk University, yet her independent nature caused her to abide by her own rules, and she was eventually asked by school officials to leave. After several years, however, she returned to Fisk in 1964 and became a dedicated student—one focused on both political and literary activities. She edited a campus literary magazine, *Elan,* and also participated in writing workshops. Politically awakened to the changes occurring on the American social scene in the 1960s, she helped restore Fisk's chapter of the SNCC (Student Non-Violent Coordinating Committee) at a time when SNCC was pressing the concept of "black power" to bring about social and economic reform. In 1967, Giovanni graduated from Fisk with an honors degree in history, as well as a commitment to become a poet herself and voice of the black movement.

Giovanni's first three books of poetry—*Black Feeling, Black Talk; Black Judgement;* and *Re: Creation*—display a strongly black perspective as she recounts her growing political awareness. According to Mozella G. Mitchell in the *Dictionary of Literary Biography,* these early poems, published between 1968 and 1970,

are "a kind of ritualistic exorcism of former nonblack ways of thinking and an immersion in blackness. Not only are they directed at other black people whom [Giovanni] wanted to awaken to the beauty of blackness, but also at herself as a means of saturating her own consciousness." These early books quickly established Giovanni as a prominent new voice in black poetry; her books sold numerous copies and she became an increasingly popular figure on the reading and speaking circuit. In 1971, she recorded the first of several poetry albums, *Truth Is on Its Way,* featuring Giovanni reading her poetry to a background of gospel music. *Truth Is on Its Way* became the best-selling spoken-word album of the year, furthering her nationwide celebrity status as a poet.

Giovanni's personal life, meanwhile, underwent changes which would affect her future evolution as a writer. In 1969, she accepted a teaching position at Rutgers University, and during the summer of that year decided to bear a child out of wedlock. She explained her stance to Peter Bailey in *Ebony:*"I had a baby at 25 because I *wanted* to have a baby and I could *afford* to have a baby. I did not get married because I didn't want to get married and I could afford not to get married." As the single mother of her son (Thomas), Giovanni realized that her priorities had changed from complete commitment to the black movement. She told Gwen Mazer in *Harper's Bazaar:* "To protect Tommy there is no question I would give my life. I just cannot imagine living without him. But I can live without the revolution." Giovanni's writing in the early 1970s began to reflect this change. In addition to a collection of autobiographical essays on her early life as a poet, *Gemini,* she published her first book of children's verse, *Spin a Soft Black Song*. These were then followed by two new books of adult verse (*My House* and *The Women and the Men*) which showed a change in Giovanni's work. Mitchell described it as "a more developed individualism and greater introspection, and a sharpening of [Giovanni's] creative and moral powers, as well as of her social and political focus and understanding."

Spin a Soft Black Song was followed by two other books of poetry for young readers, *Ego Tripping* and *Vacation Time*. *Spin a Soft Black Song* focuses on the everyday experiences of black children; "some of the poems deal with universal childhood feelings and concerns while others are unique to the black experience," wrote a contributor to *Booklist,* "but all are honest and nonsentimental in concept and expression." *Ego Tripping* contains poems "directed at older readers able to handle heavier subjects and more ambitious poetry," wrote Nancy Rosenberg in the *New York Times Book Review.* "They are sly and seductive, freewheeling and winsome, tough, sure and proud." Giovanni expressed personal fondness towards her 1980 collection of children's verse, *Vacation Time:* "Mostly I'm aware, as the mother of a reader, that I read to him. I think all of us know that your first line to the child is going to be his parent, so you want to write something that the parent likes and can share. I love *Vacation Time* because it's romantic,and I think black children have not had a lot of romantic literature. It's very soft, very gentle. And I like the Victorians. I wanted to do something modern, but with that kind of soft feel to it."

Giovanni's later adult poetry shows a continuing evolution from her earlier work. Her 1978 book, *Cotton Candy on a Rainy Day,* according to Alex Batman in *Dictionary of Literary Biography,* stands out for its "poignancy. . . . One feels throughout that here is a child of the 1960s mourning the passing of a decade of conflict, of violence, but most of all, of hope." While such an outlook, Batman continues, might "lend itself too readily to sentimentality and chauvinism, . . . Giovanni is capable of countering the problems with a kind of hard matter-of-factness about the world that has passed away from her and the world she now faces."

In her 1983 book, *Those Who Ride the Night Winds,* Giovanni takes an altered political stance, offering sketches and tributes to various characters in Afro-American history, including Phillis Wheatley, Martin Luther King, Jr., and Rosa Parks. "In most cases," notes Mitchell, "the poems are meditation pieces that begin with some special quality in the life of the subject, and with thoughtful, clever, eloquent and delightful words amplify and reconstruct salient features of her or his character."

In addition to her books of poetry, Giovanni has co-authored acclaimed books of critical essays with two other noted black writers, James Baldwin and Margaret Walker. She is also a frequent teacher of poetry, which, as she told Ross, "enriches" the "lonely profession" of being a poet by "reminding . . . that there are other concerns out there." In the introduction to *Cotton Candy on a Rainy Day,* Paula Giddings praises Giovanni's commitment to her work: "Nikki Giovanni is a witness. Her intelligent eye has caught the experience of a generation and dutifully recorded it. . . . I have never known anyone who cares so much and so intensely about the things she sees around her as Nikki." In a profile by Lois Rosenthal for *Writer's*

Digest, Giovanni offered comments that uphold this aspect of her work. "I use poetry as an outlet for my mind. It's my justification for living. . . . Everyone has a right to the dictates of her own heart. The one thing you cannot take away from people is their own sense of integrity. I don't want my integrity impinged upon nor will I impinge on the integrity of someone else. . . . This is a great profession. If everybody became a poet, the world would be so much better."

Giovanni returned to combining the personal and political in a collection of essays titled *Racism 101.* Published in 1994, it ruminates over lessons learned in the 1960s, in light of her more recent experience teaching at Virginia Polytechnic. Giovanni rails against icons such as Spike Lee, whom she finds "self-serving", while reflecting on her own career path. A contributor to *Kirkus Reviews* finds Giovanni, "mellower with age, but (her) ability to provoke with barbed comments remains much in evidence." A reviewer for *Publishers Weekly* comments that the essays are "often perceptive musings" but that they "beg for more substance." Giovanni also included advice to black students on academics and racism, "outlining . . . how the black collegian can become not merely certified as 'educated,' but *educated,"* notes Dale Edwyna Smith in *Belles Lettres.* Smith praises the work, confessing, "It seems to me that I have always loved the writing of Nikki Giovanni. I still do."

Grandmothers: Poems, Reminiscences and Short Stories About the Keepers of Our Traditions, edited by Giovanni and also published in 1994, is a collection of contributions on the figure of the grandmother, from a number of known and lesser-known writers. Established contributors include Maxine Hong Kingston, Gloria Naylor, and Gwendolyn Brooks;however, a *Publishers Weekly* contributor comments that "the real treasures here are offered by relatively unknown authors," noting Susan Power and Anna Esaki-Smith in particular. The collection also includes works by Giovanni's writing students at a retirement home that provide "the feel of spontaneous personal reminiscences, the rough-edged, homespun manner of their telling contributing to their power, their charm," notes a *Voya* contributor. The work was aimed at children, but the *Children's Book Review Service* contributor remarks that the stories are "a disappointment because they do not actively address young adults." Kathleen Krull, however, writing for the *Los Angeles Times Book Review,* feels that *Grandmothers* is "full of revelations for all ages."

Giovanni's work continued to focus on the image of strong women in 1996 with the publication of *The Genie in the Jar*. This children's poem, which Giovanni wrote for the singer Nina Simone, depicts a young black girl surrounded and supported by the love of her mother and a circle of women, creating a "loom of love" that "spins the notes of life's song," as a contributor to the *Children's Book Review Service* notes. But, comments a *Kirkus Reviews* contributor, "Readers don't need to know anything about Simone to hear this book sing." Kate McClelland, writing for *School Library Journal* finds the book to be "Symbolic on many levels . . . its message is undeniably universal. It is as cautionary and as reassuring as a creative life, lived with both risk and self-fulfillment."

Giovanni returns to the themes originally presented in *Grand Mothers* in *Grand Fathers: Reminiscences, Poems, Recipes, and Photos of the Keepers of Our Traditions*. "While some of the 47 writers of these poems and reminiscences ... celebrate the relationship between grandfather and grandchild," says a *Publishers Weekly* reviewer, "the majority focus on documenting the lives of the men who came before them, setting down details of births, marriages, children and careers as a testament to their courage, strong wills and, occasionally, to their failures." "Most," states *Booklist* contributor Hazel Rochman, "are ordinary people from many backgrounds with memories that range from the sweet and inspirational ... to the sad and even angry." "I'm sure you've said to yourself, Who do I owe this to? Who am I going to answer to?" Giovanni tells *Essence* interviewer Evelyn C. White. "It's the Lena Hornes, the Leontyne Prices, it's your grandparents who've paved the way. They created. The Harlem Renaissance is still the prototype for everything in American pop culture. But what I love about us, about Black people, is that we keep going to the next level."

BIOGRAPHICAL\CRITICAL SOURCES:

BOOKS

Authors in the News, Volume 1, Gale (Detroit), 1976.

Black Literature Criticism, Gale, 1992.

Children's Literature Review, Volume 6, Gale, 1984.

Contemporary Authors Autobiography Series, Volume 6, Gale, 1988.

Contemporary Literary Criticism, Gale, Volume 2, 1974, Volume 4, 1975, Volume 19, 1981, Volume 64, 1991.

Dictionary of Literary Biography, Gale, Volume 5: *American Poets since World War II, 1980, Volume 41: Afro-American Poets since 1955*, 1985.

Evans, Mari, editor, *Black Women Writers, 1950-1980: A Critical Evaluation*, Doubleday (New York City), 1984.

Fowler, Virginia, *Nikki Giovanni*, Twayne (Boston), 1992.

Fowler, *Conversations with Nikki Giovanni*, University Press of Mississippi (Jackson), 1992.

Giovanni, Nikki, *Cotton Candy on a Rainy Day*, Morrow, 1978.

Giovanni, *Gemini: An Extended Autobiographical Statement on My First Twenty-five Years of Being a Black Poet*, Bobbs-Merrill, 1971.

Giovanni and James Baldwin, *A Dialogue: James Baldwin and Nikki Giovanni*, Lippincott, 1973.

Tate, Claudia, editor, *Black Women Writers at Work*, Crossroad Publishing (New York City), 1983.

Twentieth-Century Children's Writers, St. Martin's (New York City), 1978.

PERIODICALS

Advocate, June 22, 1999, p. 131.

African American Review, summer, 1993, p. 318.

America, February 19, 1972.

Belles Lettres, spring, 1995, p. 68-70.

Booklist, May 1, 1972, p. 770; November 15, 1992, p. 572; June 1, 1999, p. 1807.

Children's Book Review Service, March, 1994, p. 87; September, 1994, p. 11; April, 1996, p. 102.

Ebony, February, 1972, pp. 48-50.

Essence, May, 1999, p. 122.

Harper's Bazaar, July, 1972, p. 50.

Horn Book, September-October, 1994, p. 575.

Jet, April 4, 1994, p. 29.

Kirkus Reviews, December 1, 1993, p. 1503; March 15, 1996, p. 447; April 1, 1996, p. 529.

Library Journal, January, 1996, p. 103.

Los Angeles Times Book Review, December 18, 1994, p. 9.

New York Times Book Review, November 28, 1971, p. 8; February 13, 1972, pp. 6, 26; May 5, 1974, p. 38.

Publishers Weekly, December 13, 1993, p. 54; January 24, 1994, p. 54; August 8, 1994, p. 450; December 18, 1995, p. 51-52; July 12, 1999, p. 96.

School Library Journal, April, 1994, p. 119; October, 1994, p. 152; May, 1996, p. 103-104, 139.

Voice of Youth Advocates, December, 1994, p. 298.

Washington Post Book World, February 13, 1994, p. 4-5; July 3, 1994, p. 11.

Writer, May, 1999, p. 4.

Writer's Digest, February, 1989, pp. 30-34.

* * *

GOINES, Donald 1937-1974
(Al C. Clark)

PERSONAL: Born December 15, 1937 (some sources indicate 1935 or 1936), in Detroit, MI; died of gunshot wounds, October 21, 1974, in Highland Park, MI; married (common law) Shirley Sailor; children: nine, including Donna and Camille from common-law marriage. *Education:* Educated in Detroit, MI.

CAREER: Writer and convicted criminal. *Military service:* U.S. Air Force, 1951-54; served in Japan during Korean War.

WRITINGS:

NOVELS

Dopefiend: The Story of a Black Junkie, Holloway House (Los Angeles), 1971.

Whoreson: The Story of a Ghetto Pimp, Holloway House, 1972.

Black Gangster, Holloway House, 1972, revised edition, 1983.

Street Players, Holloway House, 1973.

White Man's Justice, Black Man's Grief, Holloway House, 1973.

Black Girl Lost, Holloway House, 1973.

(Under pseudonym Al C. Clark) *Cry Revenge!,* Holloway House, 1974.

Eldorado Red, Holloway House, 1974.

Swamp Man, Holloway House, 1974.

Never Die Alone, Holloway House, 1974.

Daddy Cool, Holloway House, 1974.

Inner City Hoodlum, Holloway House, 1975.

UNDER PSEUDONYM AL C. CLARK; "KENYATTA" SERIES

Crime Partners, Holloway House, 1974.

Death List, Holloway House, 1974.

Kenyatta's Escape, Holloway House, 1974.

Kenyatta's Last Hit, Holloway House, 1975.

SIDELIGHTS: Donald Goines was known for his grim novels about drug users and prostitutes in Detroit, Michigan. He was born in Detroit in 1937 and attended Catholic schools there, proving himself an earnest and cooperative student. In his midteens, however, he abruptly left school and joined the Air Force. In order to join the service he lied about his age, an act that may account for the later discrepancy regarding his actual birthdate. During the Korean War, Goines was stationed in Japan. There he became a frequent drug user, and when he returned home in 1955 he was a heroin addict.

For the next fifteen years Goines supported his drug habit by pimping, robbing, and smuggling. He was arrested fifteen times, and served seven prison terms. While in jail—where he apparently remained free of heroin addiction—he was introduced to the writings of Robert "Iceberg Slim" Beck, a pimp-novelist who enjoyed substantial popularity among inmate readers. Inspired by Slim's *Trick Baby,* Goines—who had earlier attempted to write westerns—produced *Whoreson: The Story of a Ghetto Pimp,* a semi-autobiographical novel about a pimp and his clashes with other seedy criminals. The world of *Whoreson* is an unsparing one where weakness or error inevitably leads to death. It is, perhaps, the raw, unyielding vision of *Whoreson* that made it popular with inmates whose opinions Goines solicited. Upon the advice of one particularly enthusiastic convict, Goines sent *Whoreson* to Iceberg Slim's publisher, the California-based Holloway House. The company, which specialized in black literature, readily accepted Goines's manuscript and requested additional works.

Though still in prison, Goines quickly produced *Dopefiend: The Story of a Black Junkie,* which became his first published work. In *Dopefiend* he presented a graphic account of the drug addict's sordid life, tracing the degeneration of two middle-class blacks. In a *Village Voice* assessment of Goines's writings, Michael Covino described *Dopefiend* as a "relentless" depiction of loathsome and disgusting individuals. Particularly memorable is Porky, a vicious drug dealer first presented examining a pornographic magazine amid bloody squalor while a desperate addict jabs a syringe into her groin. *Dopefiend* abounds in such repellent situations: In one episode a pimp taunts a syphilitic prostitute, threatening to incorporate her into a sex show featuring animals; another passage details Porky's plan for killing two addicts who had robbed him. For Covino, the unsettling *Dopefiend* was "Goines's best book."

With advances from Holloway House for both *Dopefiend* and *Whoreson,* Goines could afford to concentrate on writing after he left prison in 1970. But by 1971 he had resumed drug use, and he consequently wrote only in the mornings, then spent the rest of each day indulging his heroin habit. In 1972 he nonetheless published a third novel, *Black Gangster,* about a cynical hoodlum who establishes a civil-rights organization as a front for prostitution and extortion. After publishing this novel, Goines moved to Los Angeles for greater access to Holloway House and to the nearby film industry, which he hoped to interest in his works.

In 1973 Goines published three more novels, including *White Man's Justice, Black Man's Grief,* an indictment of the American judicial system he termed racist. The novel tells of two inmates who conspire to commit a burglary after leaving prison. When one inmate is freed, he attempts the crime unassisted and kills a witness. Upon apprehension the killer names his black co-conspirator as the mastermind of the robbery and thus his accomplice in murder. The black convict is then tried and sentenced for murder even though he was in prison when the crime transpired.

Goines wrote eight more novels in 1974, including several works under the name of his friend Al C. Clark. Four of Goines's novels as Clark feature the ambitious militant Kenyatta, who rises from small-time hoodlum to leader of a two-thousand-member organization. With his military gang, Kenyatta hopes to eliminate all white police officers and rid the black ghetto of drugs and prostitution. Through considerable violence, he nearly succeeds. But in *Kenyatta's Last Hit*—the final work in a series that also features *Crime Partners, Death List,* and *Kenyatta's Escape*—he is killed while plotting the murder of a wealthy Los Angeles businessman dealing drugs.

Before writing *Kenyatta's Last Hit,* Goines returned to Detroit, having apparently disliked vast, unfamiliar Los Angeles. He settled with his common-law wife in nearby Highland Park. They were murdered there in October, 1974. Police suspected that robbery was the motive behind the slayings, though there were indications that Goines had once again involved himself in drug use.

In the years following his death Goines's novels continued to prove profitable for Holloway House, which reprinted his entire canon and reported total sales surpassing five million copies. Critical recognition, however, has been minimal. Mainstream publications ignore Goines's work, and more offbeat periodicals and literary journals rarely acknowledge his achievements. Covino's article in the *Village Voice* may promote greater recognition of Goines's talents as "a

writer of unmediated raw realism, a chronicler of the black ghetto."

BIOGRAPHICAL/CRITICAL SOURCES:

BOOKS

Authors in the News, Volume 1, Gale (Detroit), 1976.
Dictionary of Literary Biography, Volume 33: Afro-American Fiction Writers After 1955, Gale, 1984.
Stone, Eddie, *Donald Writes No More: A Biography of Donald Goines,* Holloway House, 1974.

PERIODICALS

Detroit Free Press, November 28, 1974.
Detroit News, November 15, 1974.
MELUS, summer, 1984.
Village Voice, August 4, 1987.*

*   *   *

GOLDEN, Marita 1950-

PERSONAL: Born April 28, 1950, in Washington, DC; daughter of Francis Sherman (a taxi driver) and Beatrice (a landlord; maiden name, Reid) Golden; divorced; children: Michael Kayode. *Education:* American University, B.A., 1972; Columbia University, M.Sc., 1973.

ADDRESSES: Home—Washington, DC. *Agent*—Carol Mann, 168 Pacific St., Brooklyn, NY 11201.

CAREER: Writer. WNET-Channel 13, New York City, associate producer, 1974-75; University of Lagos, Lagos, Nigeria, assistant professor of mass communications, 1975-79; Roxbury Community College, Roxbury, MA, assistant professor of English, 1979-81; Emerson College, Boston, MA, assistant professor of journalism, 1981-83; George Mason University, senior writer of the Creative Writing Program. Executive director of the Institute for the Preservation and Study of African American Writing, 1986-87; consultant for the Washington DC Community Humanities Council, 1986-89; member of nominating committee for the George K. Polk Awards.

MEMBER: Afro-American Writer's Guild (president, 1986—).

WRITINGS:

(Contributor) Beatrice Murphy, editor, *Today's Negro Voices,* Messner, 1970.

(Contributor) *Keeping the Faith: Writings by Contemporary Black American Women,* Fawcett, 1974.

Migrations of the Heart (autobiography), Doubleday (New York), 1983.

A Woman's Place (novel), Doubleday, 1986.

Long Distance Life (novel), Doubleday, 1989.

And Do Remember Me (novel), Doubleday, 1992.

(Editor) *Wild Women Don't Wear No Blues,* Doubleday, 1993.

Saving Our Sons: Raising Black Children in a Turbulent World, Doubleday, 1995.

(Editor with Susan Richards Shreve) *Skin Deep: Black Women and White Women Write about Race,* Nan A. Talese (New York), 1995.

The Edge of Heaven (novel), Doubleday, 1998.

A Miracle Every Day: Triumph and Transformation in the Lives of Single Mothers, Doubleday, 1999.

Contributor of poetry to several anthologies, and contributor to periodicals, including *Essence, Daily Times* (Nigeria), *National Observer, Black World,* and *Amsterdam News.*

SIDELIGHTS: A former teacher who became a full-time writer in 1983, Marita Golden is perhaps best known as a novelist. Beginning in the 1990s she has also served as the editor for collections of poetry and essays, and has published two books about parenting. She also serves as the senior writer for the Creative Writing Program at George Mason University, where she established the nonprofit Zora Neale Hurston/ Richard Wright Foundation. The foundation gives awards to African American writers to help recruit more black students to the university's master's degree program.

Golden enjoys writing in many different forms. "I was trained to be a journalist at Columbia's graduate school of journalism," she once remarked, "but I was born, I feel, to simply write, using whatever medium best expresses my obsession at a particular time. I have written poetry and have been included in several anthologies and want in the future to write more. I use and need journalism to explore the external world, to make sense of it. I use and need fiction to give significance to and to come to terms with the internal world of my own particular fears, fantasies, and dreams, and to weave all of that into the texture of the outer, tangible world. I write essentially to complete myself and to give my vision a significance that the world generally seeks to deny."

Marita Golden began writing her autobiography, *Migrations of the Heart,* when she was only twenty-nine years old. When asked about her motivation for the book, Golden told *Washington Post* reporter Jacqueline Trescott that she "stumbled into" it, adding that "I wanted to meditate on what it meant to grow in the '60's, what it meant to go to Africa the first time, what it meant to be a modern black woman living in that milieu. I had to bring order to the chaos of memory. . . . What I wanted to do was write a book that would take my life and shape it into an artifact that could inform and possibly inspire."

The book met with generally favorable reviews and was described by Diane McWhorter in the *New York Times Book Review* as "interesting" and "told in a prose that often seems possessed by some perverse genius." Reviewer Elayne B. Byman Bass commended Golden in the *Washington Post Book World* for her account of how "the love of a girl for her father evolves through several migrations into a woman's love for her man, her child and finally herself," while in *Ms.* magazine, critic Carole Bovoso suggested that Golden has earned a place among those black women writers who share a "greater and greater commitment . . . to understand self, multiplied in terms of the community, the community multiplied in terms of the nation, and the nation multiplied in terms of the world."

Golden's novel *A Woman's Place*—a "truncated *herstory*" according to Wanda Coleman in the *Los Angeles Times Book Review*—follows the lives of three black women who meet and become friends at an elite Boston university. Each of them confronts problems facing women of color in today's society. One cannot adjust to the pressures her possessive Islamic husband puts on her, another suffers from guilt related to her love of a white man, and the third tries to lose herself working in a developing African nation. "By refusing to offer easy answers to the predicaments of women, and black women in particular," said *Washington Post Book World* contributor Susan Wood, "Golden makes us believe in her characters and care about them."

Long Distance Life, Golden's second novel, takes the reader into the black streets of Washington, D.C., where she was raised. Beginning in the 1920s, the story follows Naomi, a southern farmer's daughter, as she moves north in search of opportunity, marries, prospers, and loses part of her spirituality along the way. The tale then turns to the family's subsequent generations, their involvement in the civil rights movement, and one grandson's drug-related death. *Newsweek* writer Laura Shapiro lauded *Long Distance Life,* commenting that Golden "writes about the city with understanding and a sense of commitment." The critic added that within these borders the author "traces a web of determination, suffering, and renewal."

Golden's third novel, *And Do Remember Me,* charts the lives of two black women, Jesse and Macon, whose search to better themselves leads to their involvement in the civil rights movement. Jesse leaves her poor, abusive home in the south and later finds fame as an actress. And Macon, a professor at a predominantly white college, tries to help her African American students contend with the racism that has become prevalent on campus. According to Ellen Douglas in the *Washington Post Book World,* the novel "addresses the political upheavals of the '60s and '70s and the personal difficulties and tragedies of these lives with a seriousness which one must respect." Commending *And Do Remember Me,* Douglas concluded, "We need to be reminded that young people were murdered in Mississippi in 1964 for taking black people to register to vote. . . . And we need to be reminded that racism is again or still a deep national problem."

During the 1990s Golden completed several nonfiction projects. She served as editor for *Wild Women Don't Wear No Blues,* a collection of writings by black women about their thoughts on sexuality. Critic Lynda M. Hill, writing in *African American Review,* called the range of ideas and experiences to be "vastly different." She explained, "Collectively, the essays illustrate a 'stages of life' theme pertaining to black female rites of passage." Hill commended Golden's work, saying her "introduction and commentaries provide a tone and context to unify the varied perspectives." Together with Susan Richards Shreve, Golden was also an editor and contributor to *Skin Deep: Black Women and White Women Write about Race.* The book is comprised of writings by twenty different authors, some famous and others less well-known, whom *Booklist* reviewer Mary Carroll described as "brave disconcerting, moving, funny, and challenging" as they discuss successes and failures in dealing with "the multifarious barriers of race."

In two solo projects, Golden addressed different aspects of parenting. Using her own experience as a springboard, she penned *Saving Our Sons: Raising Black Children in a Turbulent World* and *A Miracle Every Day: Triumph and Transformation in the Lives of Single Mothers.* The first book was inspired by a crisis in the author's own life, as she feared for the life of her teenage son in their Washington, D.C., neighborhood. Golden decided to write a book about Michael's life and her concerns as a single mother, including providing male role models for him. *Entertainment Weekly* reviewer Suzanne Ruta complimented Golden for a book that was "complex and heartfelt" and asserted that "Golden's close-ups of young men on the edge will haunt you." Veronica Chambers commented on the book in *Essence,* concluding, "In sharing their lives so honestly, Marita and Michael bring us closer to empowering both ourselves and our sons."

In *A Miracle Every Day* Golden addresses the related topic of being a single mother. This work acknowledges the difficulties of being a single parent; moreover, it applauds the remarkable resources women have found in themselves. As reviewer Mary Carroll noted in *Booklist,* Golden asserts that both children and mothers have the ability to deal with the challenges they face, especially if they have "faith and family and a willingness to ask for help." Carroll called the book "inspiring and encouraging."

Golden also penned the more recent novel, *The Edge of Heaven,* a complex story of a family facing the return of a mother, Lena, who has been in prison. Adele and Teresa, her mother and daughter, are at home awaiting Lena's release. These two women are left to welcome Lena, because Teresa's father long ago left the family and because Lena's imprisonment involves the death of her other daughter, Kenya. Golden examines the denial, guilt, and grief that are central to the story, as she gradually reveals the details of Kenya's death.

In a *New York Times* review, Janet Kaye called it "an often affecting story," but found that "confusion rather than mystery results from her decision to withhold key information about the specifics of Lena's crime." A *Publishers Weekly* reviewer similarly deemed it "uneven" but said that Golden had "a compelling gift for plotting." Stronger recommendations came from *Booklist* reviewer Mary Carroll, who noted that Golden "skillfully displays the contradictory emotions they experience," and from *Library Journal* contributor Shannon Haddock, who summarized that Golden "compassionately peels away the layers of a family's grief to reveal one woman's passage from repentance to renewal."

BIOGRAPHICAL/CRITICAL SOURCES:

BOOKS

Migrations of the Heart, Doubleday, 1983.

PERIODICALS

African American Review, winter, 1995, p. 691.
Antioch Review, winter, 1984.
Booklist, July 1995, p. 1844; November 15, 1997, p. 24; February 15, 1995, p. 1010.
Entertainment Weekly, February 3, 1995, p. 49.
Essence, February 1995, p. 52.
Los Angeles Times Book Review, April 17, 1983; September 7, 1986.
Ms., June, 1983; September, 1988.
Newsweek, November 20, 1989, p. 79.
New Yorker, February 21, 1983.
New York Times, April 15, 1998.
New York Times Book Review, May 1, 1983; September 14, 1986; December 27, 1987.
Publishers Weekly, June 20, 1986; September 1, 1989; April 27, 1992; October 27, 1997, p. 52.
Village Voice Literary Supplement, May, 1990.
Voice Literary Supplement, June, 1983.
Washingtonian, October, 1990; November, 1990.
Washington Post, May 22, 1983; December 13, 1987.
Washington Post Book World, June 4, 1983; July 30, 1986; December 13, 1987; September 17, 1989; December 3, 1989; May 24, 1992, p. 12; June 21, 1992.*

*   *   *

GORDON, Lewis Ricardo 1962-
(Rikki del Rio)

PERSONAL: Born May 12, 1962, in Jamaica; permanent resident of the U.S.; son of Lewis Calwood Gordon and Yvonne Patria Garel (Solomon); married Lisa C. (a researcher and teacher), April 25, 1987; children: Mathieu A., Jennifer S. *Ethnicity:* "African-American." *Education:* Lehman College, City University of New York, B.A. (magna cum laude); received M.A. (aesthetics), 1988; Yale University, M.Phil. and M.A. (philosophy), 1991; Ph.D. (philosophy; with distinction), 1993. *Politics:* "Radical (Progressive)." *Religion:* "Spiritual." *Avocational*

interests: Performing piano and percussion, jazz, rhythm and blues, and reggae music.

ADDRESSES: Office—Department of Afro-American Studies, Brown University, Box 1904, 155 Angell St., Providence, RI 02912; Department of Religious Studies, Brown University, Box 1927, Steiger House, 59 George St., Providence, RI 02912. *E-mail*—Lewis_ Gordon@Brown.edu.

CAREER: Lehman High School, Bronx, NY, social studies teacher, 1985-89, Second Chance Program founder and coordinator, 1987-89; Yale University, New Haven, CT, teaching fellow in philosophy and classics, 1990-93; University of Hartford, West Hartford, CT, adjunct professor of philosophy, 1992; Lehman College, City University of New York, Bronx, adjunct assistant professor in Lehman Scholars Program, 1993; Purdue University, West Lafayette, IN, assistant professor of philosophy and African American studies, 1993-95; Indiana University—Purdue University at Indianapolis, Indianapolis, IN, adjunct assistant professor of philosophy and American studies, summer, 1994; Purdue University, West Lafayette, associate professor of philosophy and African-American studies, 1996; Brown University, Providence, RI, visiting professor of Afro-American studies and religion, fall 1996, became associate professor of Afro-American studies, contemporary religious thought, Latin-American studies, modern culture and media, and ethnic studies, 1997—; *Radical Philosophy Review,* editor, 1997—.

MEMBER: American Philosophical Association, Radical Philosophy Association, Society for Phenomenological and Existential Philosophy, Sartre Society of North America, Association of Caribbean Studies, International Association of Philosophy and Literature.

AWARDS, HONORS: Hess Memorial Prize, 1983, for best essay in English and American literature; Danforth-Compton fellow, 1989-93; Society for Values in Higher Education fellow, 1991—; African American Studies and Research Center Faculty Award, 1994; Certificado, Universidad de la Habana, Facultad de Filosofia e Historia, 1994; Book Honor, African American Studies and Research Center at Purdue University, 1995, for *Bad Faith and Antiblack Racism;* Service Award, Yale Afro-American Cultural Center, 1992; Alumni Achievement Award, Lehman College, City University of New York, 1995, "for outstanding work in his profession"; Presidential

Faculty fellow, Pembroke Center for the Study and Teaching of Women, 1997-98.

WRITINGS:

Bad Faith and Antiblack Racism, Humanities Press (Atlantic Highlands, NJ), 1995.

Fanon and the Crisis of European Man: An Essay on Philosophy and the Human Sciences, Routledge (New York City), 1995.

(Editor and translator, with T. Denean Sharpley-Whiting and Renee T. White) *Fanon: A Critical Reader,* Blackwell (Oxford, England), 1996.

Her Majesty's Other Children: Sketches of Racism from a Neocolonial Age, Rowman and Littlefield (Lanham, MD), 1997.

(Editor) *Existence in Black: An Anthology of Black Existential Philosophy,* Routledge, 1997.

(Editor, with Renee T. White) *Black Texts and Textuality: Constructing and De-Constructing Blackness,* Rowman and Littlefield, 1998.

(Editor) *Key Figures in African American Thought,* Blackwell, 1998.

(Contributing editor) Simon Glendenning, editor, *The Edinburgh Encyclopedia of Continental Philosophy: Philosophy of Existence,* Edinburgh University Press (Edinburgh, Scotland), 1998.

What Fanon Really Said: An Introduction to His Life and Thought, Schocken/Knopf (New York City), 1998.

Contributor of numerous chapters to books, among them *The Prism of the Self: Essays in Honor of Maurice Natanson* (1995), *Men's Bodies, Men's Gods: Male Identities in a (Post-)Christian Culture* (1996), *Soulfires: Young Black Men on Love and Violence* (1996), and *Spoils of War: Women, Culture, and Revolution* (1997); author of articles and reviews in such journals as *Black Scholar, Differences, Political Affairs, Political Commentary, Radical Philosophy Review of Books,* and *Social Identities;* author of essays under pseudonym Rikki Del Rio.

WORK IN PROGRESS: Existence and Spirit, Essence and Social Theory, Existentia Africana, and *Identity and Liberation;* various articles.

SIDELIGHTS: Focusing on the work of Jean-Paul Sartre and Frantz Fanon, professor and philosopher Lewis R. Gordon has published extensively in the areas of philosophy of existence, phenomenology, philosophy of human sciences, critical race theory, philosophy of culture, and aesthetics. He cites among his influences, Frantz Fanon, William R. Jones,

Soren Kierkegaard, Karl Marx, Maurice Merleau-Ponty, Jean-Paul Sartre, and Alfred Schutz.

In his first book, *Bad Faith and Antiblack Racism,* Gordon deals with the concept of bad faith as Sartre expressed it as a clue to understanding antiblack racism and "problems of rigor and evasion of human beings in human studies." As Gordon told *CA:* "I have also managed to advance several arguments that are regarded as original arguments in Sartre studies, Fanon studies, ethics, black theology, and critical race theory. In Sartre studies, I have shown that the concept of bad faith is central for the understanding of the Sartrean quest to understand human reality, and that it exemplifies a special argument that remains throughout his entire corpus." In addition, Gordon proposed a new type of bad faith, which he called *the body in bad faith.* Gordon enumerated his "original contributions" to critical race theory: the model of the "anti-black world," the theory of color premised upon a radical phenomenology rooted in a historical schema, a demonstration that the eradication of race as a social construction will not lead to the eradication of racism, a demonstration of racism as rooted in an *existential* reality, a demonstration of racism's leading to denial of ambiguity, where designations of "slimy" people emerge, a demonstration of the importance of a critical ontology for the study of racism, and demonstration of why racism (and all forms of oppression) is compelled to construct prosthetic gods, and a demonstration of the importance of theodicy for understanding racism and oppression in general.

Fanon and the Crisis of European Man is Gordon's exploration of human studies in "an inhumane world." He focuses on the historical context for human invisibility, as seen in the work of Fanon, a philosopher who has considered this problem in its manifestations of racism and colonialism. Among the topics Gordon discusses are Fanon as a philosopher of the human sciences, his phenomenology, connections between his work and European thinkers—Kierkegaard, Schopenhauer, Marx, Husserl, Merleau-Ponty, and Schutz—and his philosophy of history. Gordon also proposes his own concept of "perverted anonymity" to define antiblack racism and asserts that Fanon's writings on violence "can best be understood not through classical ethical and political categories alone, but fundamentally through the classical conception of tragedy."

Discussing another of his books, Gordon told *CA:* "*Her Majesty's Other Children* is a critical study of postcolonial thought and what I call 'black antiblack philosophy' as manifestations of neocolonial dynamics of evading race and progressive revolutionary thought. Guided by Frantz Fanon's theory of sociogenesis, the book is divided into three parts, each of which relates the relation between the social and the existentially situational. The first, "Philosophy and Racism," presents my views of race and racism, sex, gender, and sexuality, and identity and theory (especially Africana philosophy) in opposition to neoliberal and conservative presentations of the same in philosophy, cultural studies, and postmodern thought. The second part examines how neocolonial and racist dynamics have an impact on our understanding of the engaged intellectual. Thinkers discussed include Antonio Gramsci, Lorraine Hansberry, Edward Said, and Cornel West. The third part, 'Aisthesis democrate,' presents a case for the importance of aesthetics in contemporary radical progressive thought through an examination of African American classical music (jazz), rap and hip hop, and film on Frantz Fanon. The book closes with a short anti-colonial tale titled, 'The Lion and the Spider.'"

Gordon has also served as an editor and contributed introductions, translations, and essays to collections dealing with antiblack racism. He said: "My subsequent plans are to continue my work in Africana philosophy, particularly with regards to developing my work on black aesthetic productions, and to go into the next stage of my exploration of the dynamics of radicality and rigor, by exploring in great detail, the importance of the phenomenological treatment of spirituality for an understanding of metaphysical dimensions of human reality."

*   *   *

GORDONE, Charles 1925-1995

PERSONAL: Born October 12, 1925, in Cleveland, OH; died of cancer, November 17, 1995, in College Station, TX; son of William Lee and Camille (Morgan) Gordon; married Jeanne Warner (a stage and film producer), 1959 (marriage ended); married Susan Kouyomjian; children: (first marriage) Stephen, Judy, Leah Carla, David. *Education:* Los Angeles State College of Applied Arts and Sciences (now California State University, Los Angeles), B.A., 1952; also attended University of California, Los Angeles.

CAREER: Playwright, actor, and director. As actor, appeared in plays, including *Fortunato,* 1952, *The*

Climate of Eden, 1952, *Of Mice and Men,* 1953, *The Blacks,* 1961-65, and the *Trials of Brother Jero,* 1967. Appeared as actor on television in *The Climate of Eden,* 1961. Director of about twenty-five plays, including *Rebels and Bugs,* 1958, *Peer Gynt,* 1959, *Tobacco Road,* 1960, *Detective Story,* 1960, *No Place to Be Somebody,* 1967, *Cures,* 1978, and *Under the Boardwalk,* 1979. Co-founder and chair of Committee for the Employment of Negro Performers, 1962; member of Commission on Civil Disorders, 1967; instructor at Cell Block Theatre, Yardville and Bordontown Detention Centers, New Jersey, 1977-78; judge, Missouri Arts Council Playwriting Competition, 1978; instructor at New School for Social Research, 1978-79; Texas A & M University, College Station, instructor of English and theater, 1986-95; member of Ensemble Studio Theatre and Actors Studio. *Military service:* U.S. Air Force.

AWARDS, HONORS: Obie Award for best actor, 1953, for performance in *Of Mice and Men;* Vernon Rice award, 1970; Pulitzer Prize for Drama, Los Angeles Critics Circle Award, and Drama Desk Award, all 1970, all for *No Place to Be Somebody;* American Academy award, 1971; National Institute of Arts and Letters grant, 1971; National Endowment for the Humanities grant, 1978; D. H. Lawrence fellow, 1987.

WRITINGS:

PLAYS

(With Sidney Easton) *A Little More Light Around the Place* (adaptation of Easton's novel), first produced in New York City at Sheridan Square Playhouse, 1964.

No Place to Be Somebody: A Black-Black Comedy (first produced in New York City at Sheridan Square Playhouse, November, 1967; produced Off-Broadway at New York Shakespeare Festival Public Theatre, May, 1969; produced on Broadway at American National Theatre and Academy (ANTA) Theatre, December 30, 1969), introduction by Joseph Papp, Bobbs-Merrill (Indianapolis), 1969.

Willy Bignigga [and] *Chumpanzee,* first produced together in New York City at Henry Street Settlement New Federal Theatre, July, 1970.

Gordone Is a Muthah (collection of monologues; first produced in New York City at Carnegie Recital Hall, May, 1970), published in *The Best Short Plays of 1973,* edited by Stanley Richards, Chilton (Radnor, PA), 1973.

Baba-Chops, first produced in New York City at Wilshire Ebel Theatre, 1975.

The Last Chord, first produced in New York City at Billie Holliday Theatre, 1977.

A Qualification for Anabiosis, first produced in New York City, 1978; revised as *Anabiosis* and produced in St. Louis, 1979.

Also author of an unproduced musical, *The Block,* and of the following screenplays: *No Place to Be Somebody* (adapted from the play); *The W.A.S.P.* (adapted from the novel by Julius Horwitz); *From These Ashes 2; Under the Boardwalk;* and *Liliom.*

Gordone's manuscripts are housed in the Schomburg Collection, New York.

SIDELIGHTS: Charles Gordone was the first black playwright to win the Pulitzer Prize. His race-conscious work, usually marked by heated drama, was exemplified in his first play *No Place to Be Somebody,* which won him the Pulitzer. The subject matter was largely drawn from his own life. Robin Pogrebin quoted Gordone as saying in the *New York Times* that he was "part Indian, part Irish, part French and part nigger." Born and reared in the Midwest, he moved to New York City in 1952. There, he waited tables to support himself while working as an actor and putting together his first play.

In 1970, *No Place to Be Somebody* opened on Broadway to rave reviews. Walter Kerr hailed Gordone as "the most astonishing new American playwright since Edward Albee," while other critics compared him to Eugene O'Neill. According to Norman Nadel, Gordone found, as did O'Neill, "the gritty truths in bars, where pretense is too much trouble and deceit too futile." Set in a tawdry bar in Greenwich Village, *No Place* belongs in the category of American saloon dramas, and followed in the tradition of such plays as *The Iceman Cometh* and *The Time of Your Life.* But, as a *Time* critic pointed out, "'Johnny's Bar' is no oasis for gentle day-dreamers. It is a foxhole of the color war—full of venomous nightmares, thwarted aspirations and trigger-quick tempers."

The owner of the bar, Johnny Williams, is also a pimp who takes on the syndicate in an effort to obtain control of the local rackets. His ambition is to organize his own black mafia, and he uses the affections of a white female student to further his aims. Although he has "learned early to hate white society and not to trust anybody," Johnny supports an out-of-work actor and retains an incompetent white employee.

Other characters include a bartender who has "drug-induced daydreams of having once been a jazz musician," Johnny's two whores, a disillusioned ex-dancer and short-order cook, and Gabe Gabriel, an unemployed, light-skinned black actor who is too white for black roles. Gabe functioned as Gordone's spokesman, introducing the acts of the play, and reciting monologues that "use humor and candor to express the absurdity and tragedy of racism." He was also, as Molly Haskell observed, "by nature witness rather than activist." At the end of the play, however, he shoots Johnny, at the request of Machine Dog, a black militant who exists only in Gabe's mind.

Although many critics noted that the play had some flaws, all praised Gordone's ability for characterization and dialogue. Some indicated that the play's only problem came from Gordone's ambition of trying to say too much in one work. As Edith Oliver noted: "There are several plots . . .and subplots running through the script, but what is more important is the sense of life and intimacy of people in a place, and of the diversity of their moods—the sudden, sometime inexplicable, spurts of anger and wildness and fooling—and their understanding of one another." Kerr highlighted Gordone's "excellent habit" of pressing "his confrontations until they become reversals, until the roles are changed."

"Written with a mixture of white heat and intellectual clarity," wrote Jack Kroll, "it is necessarily and brilliantly grounded in realism but takes off from there with high courage and imagination; it is funny and sad and stoical, revolutionary and conciliatory." Brendon Gill concurred: "Mr. Gordone is as fearless as he is ambitious, and such is the speed and energy with which he causes his characters to assault each other—every encounter is, in fact, a collision—that we have neither the time nor the will to catch our breath and disbelieve. The language is exceptionally rough and exceptionally eloquent; it is a proof of Mr. Gordone's immense talent that the excrementitious gutterances of his large cast of whores, gangsters, jailbirds, and beat-up drifters stamp themselves on the memory as beautiful."

Criticism from black reviewers was not, however, totally favorable. Along with Clayton Riley and Peter Bailey, some black critics found evidence of self-hate—"a hint of contempt for black people"—in Gordone's play. But Jeanne-Marie Miller disagreed: "[The play] depicts the black experience, but it is also concerned with people, black and white, who are filled with despair but who continue to hold on to their dreams, dreams shaped by their surroundings." Other reviewers were also quick to stress Gordone's concern with the total human experience. "In Gordone's work," declared Ross Wetzsteon, "rage and wit and dignity are ultimately aspects not so much of black consciousness as of humanity."

The extraordinary success of *No Place to Be Somebody* was in many ways a dream come true, yet Gordone was never again able to reach such heights. He wrote a few more plays, and worked as a director in many locations around the country, but as the years went by, his name slowly faded from the mainstream theatrical world. While his involvement in theater diminished, his passionate commitment to activist causes never abated. He served as the chairman of the Congress of Racial Equality's committee for employment of black actors, worked with prison inmates in drama workshops, and came out strongly in favor of nontraditional casting. He also taught English and drama at Texas A & M University for many years.

In a 1979 interview with *Contemporary Authors*, Gordone was asked about a controversial comment he once made that there was no such thing as "black theatre." In reply, he declared that he did not understand what the term "black theatre" meant. "We know what we mean when we say white people in this country; that means anyone that is not a Caucasian would not be white. . . . White people—that is not their identity. Are we talking about Russians? Are we talking about the Irish? Are we talking about the British? Are we talking about Germans? On the other side, do we have a whole world of blacks? The opposite of white here is not black. There are many opposites of what is white. . . . It's very hard in this world to find a skin that is absolutely black. So we obscure it." He gave other examples to illustrate his point: "Are there black painters? Is there black basketball? I went to see the Nicks and the Lakers. The teams are predominantly black, to use the term black here. Does that mean I went to see black basketball subsidized by white money?. . . . Black music, we say, when everybody knows that jazz is still formulated on the musicology of the so-called white people in the Western culture. So the music is now Occidental music. All art borrows. We borrow; we are influenced; we respect. That's what makes it art."

Gordone summarized his philosophy: "This is a multiracial country; and certainly anytime there is a culture that is born out of this country, it is American culture. . . . For myself, I write out of an American experience. I don't write out of a black experience or a white experience; it's American. If my color happens to be different from someone else's, that doesn't make any difference. I write for whites just as well as I write for blacks. I write out of the American experience as I observe it and as I live it."

BIOGRAPHICAL\CRITICAL SOURCES:

PERIODICALS

Black World, December, 1972, pp. 4-29.
Christian Science Monitor, September 21, 1970.
Critic's Choice, September, 1969.
Ebony, July, 1970, pp. 29-32, 36-37.
Journal of Negro Education, spring, 1971, pp. 185-86.
Los Angeles Magazine, October, 1987, p. 244.
Los Angeles Times, July 17, 1987, section 6, p. 1; July 24, 1987.
Negro Digest, April, 1970.
Newsweek, June 2, 1969; May 25, 1970, p. 95.
New York, June 9, 1969, p. 56.
New Yorker, May 17, 1969; January 10, 1970.
New York Times, May 18, 1969; December 31, 1969; January 25, 1970; May 17, 1970; September 9, 1971; May 17, 1976.
Saturday Review, May 31, 1969.
Time, May 16, 1969.
Variety, May 28, 1969; January 14, 1970; June 10, 1970; August 26, 1970; September 15, 1971.
Village Voice, May 8, 1969; May 22, 1969.
Wall Street Journal, May 6, 1969.

OBITUARIES:

PERIODICALS

Los Angeles Times, November 21, 1995, p. A14.
New York Times, November 19, 1995, p. 51; November 20, 1995, p. A2.
Time, December 4, 1995, p. 29.
Washington Post, November 20, 1995, p. B4.*

*   *   *

GOSS, Clay(ton E.) 1946-

PERSONAL: Born May 26, 1946, in Philadelphia, PA; son of Douglas P. (a counselor) and Alfreda (a teacher; maiden name, Ivey) Jackson; married Linda McNear (a teacher and performer), March 25, 1969;

children: Aisha, Uhuru (daughters). *Education:* Howard University, B.F.A., 1972.

ADDRESSES: Agent—Dorothea Oppenheimer, 866 United Nations Plaza, New York, NY 10017.

CAREER: Department of Recreation, Washington, DC, drama specialist, 1969; Howard University, Washington, DC, playwright-in-residence in drama department, 1970-73, playwright-in-residence at Institute for the Arts and Humanities, 1973-75; poet, playwright, and writer. Instructor in poetry and development of Afro-American theater, Antioch College, Washington and Baltimore campuses, 1971-73.

MEMBER: Theatre Black, Kappa Alpha Psi.

WRITINGS:

JUVENILE

Bill Pickett: Black Bulldogger (novel), illustrated by Chico Hall, Hill and Wang (New York City), 1970.
(With wife, Linda Goss) *The Baby Leopard: An African Folktale,* illustrated by Suzanne Bailey-Jones and Michael R. Jones, Bantam Books (New York City), 1989.
(With L. Goss) *It's Kwanzaa Time!,* Philomel Books (New York City), 1993.

PLAYS

Hip Rumpelstiltskin, first produced in Washington, DC, by Department of Recreation, 1969.
Ornette (three-act), produced in Washington, DC, at Howard University, 1970.
On Being Hit (one-act), produced in Washington, DC, at Howard University, 1970, produced as *Of Being Hit* in Brooklyn, NY, at Billie Holiday Theater, 1973.
Homecookin' (one-act), produced in Washington, DC, at Howard University, 1970.
Andrew (one-act), produced in Baltimore, MD, c. 1970, first produced in New York City at New York Shakespeare Festival Theatre, 1972.
Mars: Monument to the Last Black Eunuch, first produced in Washington, DC, at Howard University, 1972.
Oursides (one-act), first produced in New York City at New Federal Theatre, 1972.
Spaces in Time, produced in Washington, DC, by D. C. Black Repertory Company, 1973.

Homecookin': Five Plays, Howard University Press (Washington, DC), 1974.

Also author of *Keys to the Kingdom.* Plays represented in anthologies, including *Transition,* Department of Afro-American Studies, Howard University (Washington, DC), 1972; *Kuntu Drama,* edited by Paul Carter Harrison, Grove (New York City), 1974; and *The New Lafayette Theatre Presents: Six Black Playwrights,* edited by Ed Bullins, Anchor Press (New York City), 1974.

OTHER

(Editor with L. Goss) *Jump Up and Say! A Collection of Black Storytelling,* Simon & Schuster (New York City), 1995.

Author of the television play *Billy McGhee,* for *The Place,* broadcast by WRC-TV (Washington, DC), 1974. Contributor to books, including *We Speak as Liberators: Young Black Poets,* edited by Orde Coombs, Dodd (New York City), 1970; *The Drama of Nommo,* edited by Paul Carter Harrison, Grove, 1972; and *The Sheet,* edited by Carol Kirkendall, Compared to What, Inc. (Washington, DC), 1974. Contributor of short fiction, articles, and reviews to periodicals, including *Liberator, Reflect, Black Books Bulletin, Blackstage,* and *Black World.*

SIDELIGHTS: Clay Goss writes primarily as a dramatist, but he has also done his part to preserve African-American traditions through the books *It's Kwanzaa Time!* And *Jump Up and Say! A Collection of Black Storytelling,* both of which were produced collaboratively with his wife, Linda Goss. *It's Kwanzaa Time!* is a comprehensive volume aimed at young readers. It includes a brief history of Kwanzaa; one story for each of the seven days of the Kwanzaa festival; African recipes appropriate for celebrating the holiday; full-page paintings by award-winning artists such as Jerry Pinkney, Floyd Cooper, and Leo and Diane Dillon; songs; contemporary writings; and crafts projects suitable for families or classrooms to do together. A *Publishers Weekly* reviewer found the book's design rather "stark," but added that "the information, upbeat mood and encouragement of participation raise this book above its ordinary appearance." Chris Sherman, writing in *Booklist,* found that of all the elements included in *It's Kwanzaa Time!,* "the real reason to buy this book is for the wonderful stories that have been selected to match the seven principles of the Kwanzaa celebration. . . . [They] read aloud beautifully and offer a mix of humor and insight."

In *Jump Up and Say! A Collection of Black Storytelling,* the Gosses showcase "the diversity of black stories by encompassing various continents, styles, genders, and time," reported Lillian Lewis in *Booklist.* Eight sections cover the themes of morals, freedom, family and friends, rhythm talking, ghost stories, superstitions, humor, and songs and poems. Well-known authors such as Toni Morrison, Langston Hughes, and Amiri Baraka are included along with lesser-known storytellers like Serious Bizness and Harriette Bias Insignares. *American Visions* contributor Sharon E. Wilkins noted that the black storytelling tradition goes back to the "griots" of African society, who were responsible for keeping alive the stories of the past. *Jump Up and Say!,* Wilkins believed, "pays tribute to this heritage" and, at times, "will have you laughing out loud!"

Goss once told *CA:* "What we must first do is to make our goals become our models instead of models becoming our goals. Then build from there."

BIOGRAPHICAL/CRITICAL SOURCES:

PERIODICALS

American Visions, October-November, 1995, p. 37.
Booklist, October 15, 1995, p. 385; December 15, 1995, p. 700.
Choice, January, 1976, p. 1444.
Emerge, December, 1995, p. 74.
Grade Teacher, February, 1971, p. 147.
Jet, October 15, 1970.
Kirkus Reviews, October 1, 1970, p. 1096.
Library Journal, March 15, 1971, p. 1114; June 15, 1975, p. 1236; September 15, 1995, p. 96.
Publishers Weekly, September 18, 1995, p. 94.
School Library Journal, October, 1995, p. 94.
Washington Post, March 21, 1971; March 1, 1973.

*   *   *

GREEN, Daryl D. 1966-
(Dewayne Green)

PERSONAL: Born February 5, 1966, in Shreveport, LA; son of Edward and Annette (Green) Elias; married Estraletta Andrews; children: Mario, Sharlita, Demetrius. *Education:* Southern University A & M,

B.S., 1989; Tusculum College, M.A., 1997. *Politics:* Independent. *Religion:* Baptist.

ADDRESSES: Home—1713 Hitching Post Dr., Knoxville, TN 37931. *Office*—Performance Management and Logistics Associates, P.O. Box 32733, Knoxville, TN 37931-2733; fax 423-670-0653. *E-mail*—darylg@hotmail.com.

CAREER: Tennessee Department of Energy, Oak Ridge, TN, program manager, 1994-97, account executive, 1997, technology-development manager, 1997—; writer; Performance Management and Logistics Associates (PMLA), Knoxville, TN, president, 1997—.

MEMBER: Toastmaster International, Blacks in Government (served as vice-president), Knoxville Urban League, Pi Tau Sigma.

AWARDS, HONORS: Martin Luther King, Jr., Humanitarian Award, 1991; Community Service Award, Department of Energy, 1992; Pollution Prevention Award, Department of Energy, 1997.

WRITINGS:

My Cup Runneth Over: Setting Goals for Single Parents and Working Couples, Triangle Publications, 1998.

Author of column "Family Vision" in the *Knoxville Enlightener,* 1998. Also author of works published under the name Dewayne Green.

WORK IN PROGRESS: An audio version of *My Cup Runneth Over: Setting Goals for Single Parents and Working Couples;* collaborating with sister-in-law Lydia Vogel on *A Lily among Thorns,* a book for single parents; plays; *Tell It Like It Tis,* a screenplay; establishing a reading program for children.

SIDELIGHTS: Daryl D. Green is the author of *My Cup Runneth Over: Setting Goals for Single Parents and Working Couples,* which he once described as a "'how-to' aimed at assisting families in setting goals for themselves." Green, who works as a program manager for the Tennessee Department of Energy, applied his organizational skills to his family life in order to establish goals and realize greater stability and optimism. "America is being destroyed from the inside out," Green commented. "Our children feel alienated in many of our families. Many couples are selfish and do not provide the healthy, nurturing environment for their children. . . . If our country is to be healed, we need to fix the problem at the very core—the family. Our children need hope. Hope is a very spiritual concept."

According to Jacqueline Brown, writing in the *Knoxville News-Sentinel,* Green also used the Bible to provide ideas for the family. This model, Brown noted, is only part of a large plan that includes the establishing of "a family mission statement" and the developing of "a plan to accomplish [family] goals." Green told the *Shreveport Sun* that *My Cup Runneth Over* "tells you how to give your family vision for life." He added, "Priorities are important to have in a family. They must have goals."

Green told *CA:* "I'm a natural goal-setter. I read lots of self-help books to improve my learning and knowledge. I read 'how-to' books and textbooks just for the pleasure. I'm probably one of the few students in college who enjoyed reading his textbooks.

"I give God the credit for my writing ability. God directs my footsteps. This is definitely the case with *My Cup Runneth Over.* I felt this project was part of my destiny. I wrote *My Cup Runneth Over* in two months, found a publisher, and published it in ten months. I believe what has happened to me is not just chance. There are a lot of people that have more talent than I. However, most of them don't realize how important it is to take advantage of the opportunity given. I feel an obligation to use all of my talents and gifts in life."

BIOGRAPHICAL/CRITICAL SOURCES:

PERIODICALS

Knoxville News-Sentinel, March 18, 1998, p. N3.
Shreveport Sun, February 12, 1998.

*   *   *

GREEN, Dewayne
   See GREEN, Daryl D.

*   *   *

GREGORY, J. Dennis
   See WILLIAMS, John A(lfred)

GUNN, Bill
   See GUNN, William Harrison

*   *   *

GUNN, William Harrison   1934-1989
   (Bill Gunn)

PERSONAL: Original name, William Harrison Gunn; born July 15, 1934, in Philadelphia, Pa.; died April 5, 1989; son of William Harrison (an entertainer) and Louise (Alexander) Gunn. *Ethnicity:* African American. *Education:* Studied art.

CAREER: Actor, director, and writer. Began acting professionally during the 1950s; wrote plays beginning in the 1960s; began screen writing and directing in the 1970s. Writer for commercial and educational television. *Military service:* Served in the U.S. Navy.

AWARDS, HONORS: Emmy Award, 1972, for best teleplay for *Johnnas;* Cannes Film Festival, 1973, *Ganja and Hess* selected for showing during Critics' Week; Audelco awards, 1975, for best play of the year and for best playwright of the year for *Black Picture Show.*

WRITINGS:

PLAYS

Marcus in the High Grass, first produced in Connecticut at the Westport Theater by the Theater Guild, 1958.
Johnnas, first produced off-Broadway at the Chelsea Theatre, 1968, published in *Drama Review,* summer 1968, teleplay produced in Washington, D.C., by NBC, 1972.
Black Picture Show, first produced on Broadway at the Vivian Beaumont Theater, Lincoln Center, for the New York Shakespeare Festival, January 1975, published by Reed, Cannon & Johnson, 1975.
Rhinestone Sharecropping, first produced at the Richard Allen Centre, October 1982, published by I. Reed Books, 1981.
Family Employment, first produced in New York at Joseph Papp's Public Theatre, 1985.

SCREENPLAYS

Fame Game, Columbia Pictures, 1968.

Friends, Universal Studios, 1968.

Stop, Warner Brothers, 1969.

(Adapter with Ronald Ribman) *Angel Levine,* story by Bernard Malamud, United Artists, 1970.

Don't the Moon Look Lonesome, Chuck Barris Productions, 1970.

(Adapter) *The Landlord,* novel by Kristin Hunter, United Artists, 1970.

Ganja and Hess, Kelly-Jordan, 1973, re-edited and released as *Blood Couple,* Heritage Enterprises, 1973.

The Greatest: The Muhammed Ali Story, Columbia Pictures, 1976.

OTHER

All the Rest Have Died (novel), Delacorte Press, 1964.

The Alberta Hunter Story (teleplay), produced by Southern Pictures/British Broadcasting Corp., 1982.

The Forbidden City, Theatre Communications, 1987.

SIDELIGHTS: Bill Gunn was born into a creative family. His father was a songwriter, musician, comedian, and poet. His mother, an actress, operated a theater group. Given this background, a career as an actor seemed a natural choice for Gunn. His first major role came in 1954, at the age of 20, when Gunn appeared in *Take a Giant Step,* a production of the New York Theater Company. Gunn continued acting on Broadway and in off-Broadway productions throughout the 1950s and 1960s. He performed in a variety of shows, including *The Immortalist* with James Dean and in Shakespeare's *Antony and Cleopatra, The Winter's Tale,* and *Troilus and Cressida.* Gunn expanded his acting jobs to include television roles during the 1960s.

Like many African Americans in the performing arts, Gunn felt that the few meaningful roles for minority actors compromised his acting opportunities. He once commented: "When a good part for a Negro actor does come along, they always offer it to Sidney Poitier. If he turns it down, they rewrite it for a white actor."

Since theater companies and studios resisted plays and films about African-American culture, Gunn began writing to supplement his income as an actor. The actor wrote for movies and television during the 1970s, and he appeared in many of his own screenplays. Much of his writing gave voice to the artist in conflict with society. Later he refined his focus, using the restrictions of African-American culture and life to relate his frustration as an artist. Thus, much of Gunn's writing proved autobiographical in nature.

At first, Gunn handled race in a fairly benign matter. Allusion to race in one of his early works, the play *Marcus in High Grass*—performed at the Westport Theater in Connecticut in 1958—were transparent. In fact, *Marcus in High Grass* contained no racial overtones or issues. Two well-known white actors, David Wayne and Elizabeth Ashley, were cast in the leading roles. Even many theater critics were unaware that the play was written by an African American.

Over time, though, Gunn's work revealed his disillusionment as an artist using society's repression of African-American culture as a framework. Gunn's first novel, for example, the Bildungsroman *All the Rest Have Died,* profiled an African-American man's search for self-discovery and for a fulfilled life. The main character utters such lines as "I am not concerned with what I am racially. . . . I am victimized and I am responsible." Nearly ten years later, Gunn has the hero of his *Black Picture Show*—a suffering African-American writer—sell out to white ideals. This compromised artist comes to believe that "white heaven is colored hell." At the time, *Newsweek* critic Jack Kroll reflected on the shift in the playwright's perception. "Maybe Gunn's consciousness has been raised," the critic suggested, "but I think . . . [the main character's] words represent Gunn's real feelings as a writer, and I think the real theme of this play is the agony of the artist in a world where art is a dirty word."

The film *Ganja and Hess,* perhaps Gunn's most acclaimed work, also exemplified his personal struggles as a serious African-American writer contending with commercially oriented, white-controlled studios and production companies. A vampire film, *Ganja and Hess* was an introspective work through which Gunn explored his own obsessions and compulsions; for example, black fundamentalist Christianity, African myths, drugs, and wealth. *Ganja and Hess* was called "the most complicated, intriguing, subtle, sophisticated, and passionate black film of the seventies." The renowned Cannes Film Festival selected the movie for showing during Critics' Week, an honor for any film maker. Just as the movie came to the attention of the public, though, its production studio removed it from circulation. Studio executives had *Ganja and Hess* re-edited to the point of changing the intent, scope, and focus of the film. The original version, however, circulated in the underground film world and gained recognition for Gunn as a writer and film maker. Eventually, *Ganja and Hess* became part of a collection at the Museum of Modern Art.

Gunn ultimately won his battle as an artist in a uncultivated world. He died a respected actor and writer in 1989.

BIOGRAPHICAL/CRITICAL SOURCES:

BOOKS

Contemporary Literary Criticism, Volume 5, Gale, 1976.
Dictionary of Literary Biography, Volume 38: *Afro-American Writers After 1955,* Gale, 1985.
Monaco, James, *American Film Now,* Oxford University Press, 1979.
Schraufnagel, Noel, *From Apology to Protest: The Black American Novel,* Everett/Edwards, 1973.

PERIODICALS

Essence, October 1973, pp. 27, 96.
Nation, January 25, 1975.
New Yorker, January 20, 1975.
New York Magazine, January 27, 1975.
Newsweek, January 20, 1975, p. 83.
Time, January 20, 1975, p. 76.

*   *   *

GUTHRIE, Thomas Anstey   1856-1934
(F. Anstey)

PERSONAL: Born August 8, 1856, in London, England; died March 10, 1934, of pneumonia; son of Thomas Anstey (a tailor) and Augusta Amherst (a pianist; maiden name, Austen) Guthrie. *Education:* Attended Trinity Hall, Cambridge.

CAREER: Writer. Called to the bar, 1880; worked as barrister. *Military service:* Served in Court Reserve Corps during World War I.

WRITINGS:

UNDER PSEUDONYM F. ANSTEY; CHILDREN BOOKS

Vice Versa; or, A Lesson to Fathers (fantasy novel), Appleton (New York City), 1882, revised edition, 1884, revised and corrected edition, Newnes (London), 1901.
The Black Poodle, and Other Tales, Appleton, 1884.
The Giant's Robe (novel), Appleton, 1884.
The Tinted Venus: A Farcical Romance, Lovell (New York City), 1885.
A Fallen Idol (novel), Munro (New York City), 1886.
Burglar Bill, and Other Pieces for the Use of the Young Reciter, Bradbury, Agnew (London), 1888.
The Pariah (novel), Lippincott (Philadelphia, PA), 1889.
Voces Populi, Reprinted from "Punch," Longmans, Green, Volume 1, 1890, Volume 2, 1892.
The Talking Horse, and Other Tales, Lovell, 1891.
Tourmalin's Time Cheques (fantasy novel), Appleton, 1891, reprinted as *The Time Bargain; or, Tourmalin's Cheque Book,* Arrowsmith, 1905.
Mr. Punch's Model MusicHall Songs and Dramas, National Book Company (New York City), 1892.
Mr. Punch's Young Reciter: Burglar Bill and Other Pieces, Bradbury, Agnew, 1892, enlarged edition, 1897.
The Traveling Companions: A Story in Scenes, Longmans, Green, 1892.
The Man From Blankley's, and Other Sketches, Longmans, Green, 1893.
Mr. Punch's Pocket Ibsen: A Collection of Some of the Master's Best Known Dramas Condensed, Revised, and Slightly Rearranged for the Benefit of the Earnest Student, Macmillan, 1893, enlarged edition published as *The Pocket Ibsen,* Heinemann, 1895.
Under the Rose: A Story in Scenes, Bradbury, Agnew, 1894.
Lyre and Lancet: A Story in Scenes, Macmillan, 1895.
The Statement of Stella Maberly, Written by Herself (novel), Appleton, 1896.
Baboo Hurry Bungsho Jabberjee, B.A., Appleton, 1897 (published in England as *Baboo Jabberjee, B.A.*), Dent (London), 1897.
Puppets at Large: Scenes and Subjects from Mr. Punch's Show, Bradbury, Agnew, 1897.
Paleface and Redskin, and Other Stories for Boys and Girls, Richards (London), 1898, Appleton, 1912.
Love Among the Lions: A Matrimonial Experience, Dent, 1898, Appleton, 1899.
The Brass Bottle (fantasy novel), Appleton, 1900.
A Bayard from Bengal, Appleton, 1902.
Only Toys! (for children), Richards, 1903.
Salted Almonds, Smith, Elder, 1906.
Vice Versa: A Farcical Fantastic Play in Three Acts (adapted from Anstey's *Vice Versa; or, A Lesson to Fathers*), Baker (Boston), 1910.

The Brass Bottle: A Farcical Fantastic Play in Three Acts (adapted from Anstey's book), Heinemann, 1911.

In Brief Authority, Smith, Elder, 1915, Doran, 1916.

Percy and Others: Sketches Mainly from "Punch," Methuen, 1915.

The Last Load: Stories and Essays, Methuen, 1925.

The Would Be Gentleman (adapted from Moliere's play), Secker (London), 1926.

The Man from Blankley's: A Comedy of the Early Nineties, Hodder & Stoughton (London), 1927.

The Imaginary Invalid (adapted from Moliere's play), Hodder & Stoughton, 1929.

Four Moliere Comedies (adapted from Moliere's plays), Hodder & Stoughton, 1931.

Humor and Fantasy (includes *Vice Versa, The Tinted Venus, A Fallen Idol, The Talking Horse, Salted Almonds,* and *The Brass Bottle*), Dutton (New York City), 1931.

Three Moliere Plays: Tartuf, Scapin the Trickster, The School for Wives (adapted from Moliere's plays), Oxford University Press (London), 1933.

A Long Retrospect (autobiography), Oxford University Press, 1936.

Work represented in anthologies, including *In a Good Cause,* edited by Margaret Susan Tyson Amherst, Wells Gardner, Darton (London), 1885; *Alma Mater's Mirror,* edited by Thomas Spencer Baynes and Lewis Campbell, Edinburgh University Press (Edinburgh, Scotland), 1887; *The Press Album,* edited by Thomas Catling, John Murray (London), 1909; and *Another Book of Miniature Plays,* edited by Theodore Johnson, Baker (Boston), 1934.

Contributor to periodicals, including *Punch* and *Strand.*

ADAPTATIONS: The Brass Bottle was adapted for the stage and for film.

SIDELIGHTS: F. Anstey, the pseudonym of Thomas Anstey Guthrie, was a prolific English writer whose publications include several fantasy tales that are sometimes regarded as children's fiction. Anstey was born in 1856 in London, where his father worked as a tailor and his mother performed as a pianist. Jacqueline L. Gmuca, writing in the *Dictionary of Literary Biography,* affirmed that Anstey's childhood "was replete with toys and children's parties, theatricals, and exhibitions." Reluctantly, Anstey became a boarding school student, an experience he later recalled in his autobiography, *A Long Retrospect,* as one replete with conniving classmates, unappealing

food, and awkward instructors. Anstey later studied at Trinity Hall, Cambridge, where he trained for a legal profession and contributed stories and poems to school publications. After leaving Cambridge, Anstey passed his bar examination and began working as a barrister. But he also continued with his literary endeavors, and in 1882, after *Vice Versa; or, A Lesson to Fathers,* his first significant work was accepted for publication, he abandoned the law profession and devoted himself to writing.

Anstey's *Vice Versa,* in which the author recalls his dismal boarding school days, concerns a father who magically exchanges physical identities with his son and, thus, experiences student life. For the father, the self-inflated Mr. Bultitude, this means enduring poor food and dull lectures, but it also means reexperiencing the traumas of socialization. The stubborn Bultitude initially refuses to modify his adult behavior, which appears grotesque when generating from his adolescent persona, and he soon runs afoul of his fellow students and even alienates his that is, his son's girlfriend. But by novel's end Bultitude has gained some significant realizations about his son's life. As Gmuca observed in the *Dictionary of Literary Biography,* "Mr. Bultitude . . . comes closer to understanding his son's vulnerability and need for affection" and "has learned the lessons indicated by the novel's title."

Upon publication in 1882, *Vice Versa* won Anstey considerable acclaim and success. According to Gmuca, the novel's "critical reception . . . was overwhelmingly favorable," and its appeal with the book-buying public was quite impressive, sparking many further editions in the ensuing decades. In addition, it inspired several stage productions and, in later years, various film adaptations.

Vice Versa would remain Anstey's most notable work throughout the remainder of the 1880s and 90s, though he continued to publish prolifically. Among his immediately ensuing novels are *The Giant's Robe,* which charts the rise and fall of a plagiarist; *The Tinted Venus,* wherein a prominent hairdresser is the unwilling target of affection from the goddess Aphrodite; *The Fallen Idol,* in which a painter suffers considerable misfortune while in possession of a haunted idol; *The Pariah,* wherein a young man grows increasingly maladjusted following his father's marriage to an heiress; and *The Statement of Stella Maberly Written by Herself,* wherein a matchmaker unites her employer with a dashing bachelor, dies, recovers through the employer's occult endeavor, then dies again at the employer's hands. None of these works matched the acclaim and success of *Vice Versa,* and for several years Anstey refused to publish further novels.

Instead of continuing as a novelist, Anstey published *The Black Poodle, and Other Tales* and *The Talking Horse, and Other Tales,* two collections of stories for children. In addition, he found favor in *Punch* with his funny tales relating the escapades of a distinguished Indian, Baboo Jabberjee. These tales were eventually collected in *Baboo Hurry Bungsho Jabberjee, B.A.* (published in England as *Baboo Jabberjee, B.A.*).

In 1900 Anstey published *The Brass Bottle,* which ranks with Vice Versa among his most memorable works. In *The Brass Bottle* novice architect Horace Ventimore unleashes a genie who thereupon bestows his gratitude with such extravagance that the hero finds himself with unexplainable wealth. But only after luring the genie back into captivity does Horace find true love and success. Gmuca described *The Brass Bottle* as "clearly a study of gratitude, right and wrongly expressed, rightly and wrongly motivated." As such, it secured further recognition and success for Anstey, and like the earlier *Vice Versa* it inspired both stage and film adaptations.

After completing *The Brass Bottle,* Anstey produced many additional volumes, including another children's book, *Only Toys!;* adaptations of Moliere's plays; and his own plays of both *The Brass Bottle* and Vice *Versa.* Only in his final decade did his output noticeably diminish. But even after his death in 1934, he drew attention with his posthumously published autobiography, *A Long Retrospect,* in which he candidly reflected on both the triumphs and disappointments of his long and notable literary career.

BIOGRAPHICAL/CRITICAL SOURCES:

BOOKS

Dictionary of Literary Biography, Volume 141: *British Children's Writers, 1880-1914,* Gale, 1994, pp. 311.
Green, Roger Lancelyn, *Tellers of Tales,* Ward, 1946.
Twentieth-Century Children's Writers, St. James Press, 1995, p. 1071.

PERIODICALS

English, summer, 1957, pp. 178-181.
Living Age, April 28, 1917, pp. 204-209.*

H-I

HALEY, Alex(ander Murray Palmer) 1921-1992

PERSONAL: Born August 11, 1921, in Ithaca, NY; died of cardiac arrest, February 10, 1992, in Seattle, WA; son of Simon Alexander (a professor) and Bertha George (a teacher; maiden name, Palmer) Haley; married Nannie Branch, 1941 (divorced, 1964); married Juliette Collins, 1964 (divorced); children: (first marriage) Lydia Ann, William Alexander; (second marriage) Cynthia Gertrude. *Education:* Attended Alcorn Agricultural & Mechanical College (now Alcorn State University); attended Elizabeth City Teachers College, 1937-39.

CAREER: U.S. Coast Guard, 1939-59, retiring as chief journalist; freelance writer, 1959-92. Founder and president of Kinte Corporation, Los Angeles, CA, 1972-92. Board member of New College of California, 1974; member of King Hassan's Royal Academy. Script consultant for television miniseries *Roots, Roots: The Next Generations,* and *Palmerstown, U.S.A.;* has lectured extensively and appeared frequently on radio and television; adviser to African American Heritage Association, Detroit, MI.

MEMBER: Authors Guild, Society of Magazine Writers.

AWARDS, HONORS: Litt.D. from Simpson College, 1971, Howard University, 1974, Williams College, 1975, and Capitol University, 1975; honorary doctorate from Seton Hall University, 1974; special citation from National Book Award committee, 1977, for *Roots;* special citation from Pulitzer Prize committee, 1977, for *Roots;* Spingarn Medal from NAACP, 1977; nominated to Black Filmmakers Hall of Fame, 1981, for producing *Palmerstown, U.S.A.,* 1981.

WRITINGS:

(With Malcolm X) *The Autobiography of Malcolm X,* Grove, 1965.
Roots: The Saga of an American Family, Doubleday, 1976.
Alex Haley Speaks (recording), Kinte Corporation, 1980.
A Different Kind of Christmas, Doubleday, 1988, abridged edition, Literacy Volunteers of New York City, 1991.
Alex Haley: The Playboy Interviews (edited with an introduction by Murray Fisher), Ballantine Books, 1993.
(With David Stevens) *Queen* (screenplay adapted from dictation tapes), Columbia Broadcasting System (CBS-TV), 1993.
(With David Stevens) *Mama Flora's Family: A Novel,* Scribner (New York City), 1998.

Author of forewords, *Somerset Homecoming,* by Dorothy Redford and Michael D'Orso, Anchor/Doubleday, 1988; *Marva Collins' Way: Returning to Excellence in Education,* by Marva Collins, J. P. Tarcher, 1990; and *They That Go Down to the Sea: A Bicentennial Pictorial History of the United States Coast Guard,* by Paul A. Powers, United States Coast Guard Chief Petty Officers Association, 1990. Initiated "Playboy Interviews" feature for *Playboy,* 1962. Contributor to periodicals, including *Reader's Digest, New York Times Magazine, Smithsonian, Harper's,* and *Atlantic.*

WORK IN PROGRESS: Haley was working on the following projects at the time of his death: *My Search for Roots,* an account of how *Roots* was researched and written; a study of Henning, Tennessee, where Haley was raised.

ADAPTATIONS: Roots was adapted as two television miniseries by American Broadcasting Companies (ABC), as *Roots,* 1977, and *Roots: The Next Generations* (also known as *Roots II*), 1979; Haley served as script consultant for both productions. Filmmaker Spike Lee used *The Autobiography of Malcolm X* as the source for his 1992 film biography *Malcolm X. Queen,* a novel based an outline and research left by Haley, was published by Morrow in 1993.

SIDELIGHTS: Alex Haley's reputation in the literary world largely rests upon his much acclaimed historical novel, *Roots: The Saga of an American Family.* Haley's tracing of his African ancestry to the Mandinka tribe in a tiny village in Juffure of the Gambia region of West Africa, spawned one of the most ambitious American television productions ever undertaken and inspired a generation of ancestry-seeking Americans. Eleven years prior to the appearance of *Roots,* Haley had gained recognition for writing Malcolm X's "as-told-to" autobiography, which was released shortly after the charismatic leader was gunned down while giving a speech in New York. After Spike Lee released the movie *Malcolm X* in 1992, bookstore owners had difficulty keeping the autobiography in stock.

Haley was born in 1921 in Ithaca, New York, and reared in the small town of Henning, Tennessee. He was the eldest of three sons born to Bertha George Palmer and Simon Alexander Haley, and when he was born, both his parents were in their first years of graduate school—his mother at the Ithaca Conservatory of Music, and his father at Cornell University. After finishing school, his parents took young Alex to Henning, where he grew up under the influence of his grandmother and aunts Viney, Mathilda, and Liz, who perpetuated stories about his African ancestor Kunte Kinte. These stories became the impetus for *Roots,* with which hundreds of thousands of African Americans would identify.

Before Haley became famous for this autobiographical work, however, he earned his living as a journalist. He was the first interviewer for *Playboy* magazine, and the volume *Alex Haley: The Playboy Interviews* collects eleven of his conversations with notable and controversial public figures, including Miles Davis, Muhammad Ali, Dr. Martin Luther King, Jr., George Lincoln Rockwell—a leader of the American Nazi Party—and Malcolm X. The interview with Malcolm X predates and resulted in the book *The Autobiography of Malcolm X. The Playboy Interviews* also includes an excerpt from *Roots.*

Although it took Haley twelve years to research and write *Roots,* success quickly followed its publication. Recipient of numerous awards, including a citation from the judges of the 1977 National Book Awards and the Pulitzer Prizes, the book is recognized as one of the most successful bestsellers in American publishing history, having sold millions of copies worldwide in 37 languages. Combined with the impact of the televised miniseries, *Roots* has become a "literary-television phenomenon" and a "sociological event," according to *Time.* By April, 1977, almost 2 million people had seen all or part of the first eight-episode series; and seven of those eight episodes ranked among the top ten shows in TV ratings, attaining an average of 66 percent of audience share.

Although critics generally lauded Haley for his accomplishment, they seemed unsure whether to treat *Roots* as a novel or as a historical account. While it is based on factual events, the dialogue, thoughts, and emotions of the characters are fictionalized. Haley himself described the book as "faction," a mixture of fact and fiction. Most critics concurred and evaluated *Roots* as a blend of history and entertainment. And despite the fictional characterizations, Willie Lee Rose suggested in the *New York Review of Books* that Kunta Kinte's parents Omoro and Binte "could possibly become the African proto-parents of millions of Americans who are going to admire their dignity and grace." *Newsweek* found that Haley's decision to fictionalize was the right approach: "Instead of writing a scholarly monograph of little social impact, Haley has written a blockbuster in the best sense—a book that is bold in concept and ardent in execution, one that will reach millions of people and alter the way we see ourselves."

Some concern was voiced, especially at the time of the first television series, that racial tension in America would be aggravated by *Roots.* But while *Time* reported several incidents of racial violence following the telecast, it commented that "most observers thought that in the long term, *Roots* would improve race relations, particularly because of the televised version's profound impact on whites. . . . A broad consensus seemed to be emerging that *Roots* would spur black identity, and hence black pride, and eventually pay important dividends." Some black leaders viewed *Roots* "as the most important civil rights event since the 1965 march on Selma," according to *Time.* Vernon Jordan, executive director of the National Urban League, called it "the single most spectacular educational experience in race relations in America."

Haley has heard only positive comments from both blacks and whites. He told William Marmon in a *Time* interview: "The blacks who are buying books are not buying them to go out and fight someone, but because they want to know who they are. *Roots* is all of our stories. It's the same for me or any black. It's just a matter of filling in the blanks—which person, living in which village, going on what ship across the same ocean, slavery, emancipation, the struggle for freedom. . . . The white response is more complicated. But when you start talking about family, about lineage and ancestry, you are talking about every person on earth. We all have it; it's a great equalizer. . . . I think the book has touched a strong, subliminal chord."

But there was also concern, according to *Time,* that "breast-beating about the past may turn into a kind of escapism, distracting attention from the present. Only if *Roots* turns the anger at yesterday's slavery into anger at today's ghetto will it really matter." And James Baldwin wrote in the *New York Times Book Review:* "*Roots* is a study of continuities, of consequences, of how a people perpetuate themselves, how each generation helps to doom, or helps to liberate, the coming one—the action of love, or the effect of the absence of love, in time. It suggests, with great power, how each of us, however unconsciously, can't but be the vehicle of the history which has produced us. Well, we can perish in this vehicle, children, or we can move on up the road."

For months after the publication of *Roots* in October, 1976, Haley signed at least 500 books daily, spoke to an average of 6,000 people a day, and traveled round trip coast-to-coast at least once a week, according to *People.* Stardom took its toll on Haley. *New Times* reported that on a trip to his ancestral village in Africa, Haley complained: "You'll find that people who celebrate you will kill you. They forget you are blood and flesh and bone. I have had days and weeks and months of schedules where everything from my breakfast to my last waking moment was planned for me. . . . Someone has you by the arm and is moving you from room to room. Then people *grab* at you. You're actually pummeled—hit with books—and you ask yourself, My God, what *is* this?"

Roots was so successful that ABC produced a sequel, *Roots: The Next Generations,* a $16.6-million production that ran for 14 hours. The story line of *Roots II,* as it was called, begins in 1882, twelve years after the end of the *Roots I,* and it concludes in 1967. During the 85-year span, Haley's family is depicted against the backdrop of the Ku Klux Klan, world wars, race riots, and the Great Depression; the commonalities between black and white middle-class life are dramatized as well.

Haley also researched his paternal heritage; and in 1993, CBS aired a three-episode miniseries, *Queen,* about his paternal great-grandmother, Queen, the daughter of a mulatto slave girl and a white slave owner. Writing in the *New York Times,* John J. O'Connor noted that although "the scope is considerably more limited . . . the sense of unfolding history, familial and national, is still compelling." Accusations surfaced about the historical accuracy of *Queen,* though, which recalled the charges of plagiarism and authenticity leveled at *Roots* by the author of *The Africans,* Harold Courtlander, who was subsequently paid $650,000 in an out-of-court settlement. Critics questioned whether a romance had actually existed between Queen and her slave-owning master. According to Melinda Henneberger in the *New York Times,* the tapes left by Haley did not mention a romance between his paternal great-grandparents, and David Stevens, who worked with Haley's research and outline, recalled Haley's intent to soften the relationship. Producer Mark Wolper indicated that "Haley had become convinced by his later inquiries . . . that his great-grandparents had actually been in love," wrote Henneberger, adding that "several scholars, all of whom said they would never contradict Haley's research into his own family, added that consensual, lifelong relationships between slaves and owners were exceedingly rare." Esther B. Fein noted in the *New York Times* that the book was published as a novel "partly because Mr. Haley could not verify all the family folklore that inspired it and died before the project was completed."

In 1985, Haley was working on a novel set in the Appalachian culture that he had researched extensively. The novel was centered around the relationships among a mountain father, son, and grandson. Because this book was not about blacks but primarily about whites, Haley said of the project, "I think one of the most fascinating things you can do after you learn about your own people is to study something about the history and culture of other people." Haley also planned to write a book detailing the life of Madame C. J. Walker and her daughter A'Lelia. Haley had signed a three-book contract with Ballantine for its new multicultural publishing program, for which his first title was to be a comprehensive history of his hometown, Henning. Those who knew Haley well say his research on Henning predated the writing of *Roots*. Haley was buried on the grounds of his Henning homestead, but in 1992, his estate auctioned off virtually all his possessions to pay a $1.5 million debt.

BIOGRAPHICAL/CRITICAL SOURCES:

BOOKS

The Black Press U.S.A., Iowa State University Press, 1990.

Contemporary Literary Criticism, Gale, Volume 8, 1978, Volume 12, 1980, Volume 76, 1993.

Dictionary of Literary Biography, Volume 38: *Afro-American Writers After 1955: Dramatists and Prose Writers,* Gale, 1985.

Gonzales, Doreen, *Alex Haley: Author of Roots,* Enslow Publishers (Hillside, NJ), 1994.

Shirley, David, *Alex Haley,* Chelsea House (New York City), 1994.

Williams, Sylvia B., *Alex Haley,* Abdo & Daughters (Edina, MN), 1996.

PERIODICALS

Black Collegian, September/October, 1985.
Booklist, July, 1993, p. 1938.
Christianity Today, May 6, 1977.
Ebony, April, 1977.
Forbes, February 15, 1977.
Library Journal, June 1, 1993, p. 144.
Los Angeles Times Book Review, December 25, 1988, p. 1.
Ms., February, 1977.
National Review, March 4, 1977.
Negro History Bulletin, January, 1977.
New Republic, March 12, 1977.
Newsweek, September 27, 1976; February 14, 1977.
New Yorker, February 14, 1977.
New York Review of Books, November 11, 1976.
New York Times, October 14, 1976; February 12, 1993, p. C34; February 14, 1993, p. H1; March 3, 1993, p. C18.
New York Times Book Review, September 26, 1976, January 2, 1977, February 27, 1977.
People, March 28, 1977.
Publishers Weekly, September 6, 1976; March 2, 1992; October 12, 1992, p. 10.
San Francisco Review of Books, February-March, 1994.
Saturday Review, September 18, 1976.
Time, October 18, 1976; February 14, 1977; February 19, 1979.

Today's Educator, September, 1977.
Washington Post Book World, July 25, 1993, p. 12.

OBITUARIES:

PERIODICALS

Chicago Tribune, February 11, 1992, sec. 1, pp. 1, 10; February 16, 1992, sec. 2, p. 10.
Essence, February, 1992, pp. 88-92.
New York Times, February 11, 1992, p. B8.
Times (London), February 11, 1992, p. 15.
Washington Post, February 11, 1992, pp. A1, A10, and p. E1.*

* * *

HAMILTON, Virginia 1936-

PERSONAL: Born March 12, 1936, Yellow Springs, OH; daughter of Kenneth James (a musician) and Etta Belle (Perry) Hamilton; married Arnold Adoff (an anthologist and poet), March 19, 1960; children: Leigh Hamilton, Jaime Levi. *Education:* Studied at Antioch College, 1952-55, Ohio State University, 1957-58, and New School for Social Research, 1958-60.

ADDRESSES: Agent—Arnold Adoff Agency, Box 293, Yellow Springs, OH 45387.

CAREER: "Every source of occupation imaginable, from singer to bookkeeper."

AWARDS, HONORS: Notable Children's Book citation, American Library Association, 1967, and Nancy Block Memorial Award, Downtown Community School Awards Committee, New York, both for *Zeely;* Edgar Allan Poe Award for best juvenile mystery, Mystery Writers of America, 1969, for *The House of Dies Drear;* Ohioana Literary Award, 1969; John Newbery Honor Book Award, 1971, for *The Planet of Junior Brown;* Lewis Carroll Shelf Award, *Boston Globe-Horn Book* Award, 1974, John Newbery Medal, and National Book Award, both 1975, and Gustav-Heinemann-Friedinspreis fur kinder und Lugendbucher (Dusseldorf, Germany), 1991, all for *M. C. Higgins, the Great;* John Newbery Honor Book Award, Coretta Scott King Award, *Boston Globe-Horn Book* Award, and American Book Award nomination, all 1983, all for *Sweet Whispers, Brother Rush;* Horn Book Fanfare Award in fiction, 1985, for *A Little Love;*

Coretta Scott King Award, *New York Times* Best Illustrated Children's Book citation, Children's Book Bulletin Other Award, and *Horn Book* Honor List selection, all 1986, all for *The People Could Fly: American Black Folktales;* Boston Globe-Horn Book Award, 1988, and Coretta Scott King Award, 1989, both for *Anthony Burns: The Defeat and Triumph of a Fugitive Slave;* John Newbery Honor Book Award, 1989, for *In the Beginning: Creation Stories from around the World;* D.H.L., Bank St. College, 1990; Regina Medal for lifetime achicvement, Catholic Library Association, 1990; Hans Christian Andersen Award, U.S. nominee, 1992, for body of work; Laura Ingalls Wilder Award for lifetime achievement, American Library Association, 1995; Coretta Scott King Award, 1996, for *Her Stories;* L.L.D., Wright State University.

WRITINGS:

FICTION FOR CHILDREN

Zeely, illustrated by Symeon Shimin, Macmillan, 1967.

The House of Dies Drear, illustrated by Eros Keith, Macmillan, 1968.

The Time-Ago Tales of Jahdu, Macmillan, 1969.

The Planet of Junior Brown, Macmillan, 1971.

Time-Ago Lost: More Tales of Jahdu, illustrated by Ray Prather, Macmillan, 1973.

M. C. Higgins, the Great, Macmillan, 1974, published with teacher's guide by Lou Stanek, Dell, 1986.

Arilla Sun Down, Greenwillow, 1976.

Justice and Her Brothers (first novel in the Justice Trilogy), Greenwillow, 1978.

Jahdu, pictures by Jerry Pinkney, Greenwillow, 1980.

Dustland (second novel in the Justice Trilogy), Greenwillow, 1980.

The Gathering (third novel in the Justice Trilogy), Greenwillow, 1981.

Sweet Whispers, Brother Rush, Philomel, 1982.

The Magical Adventures of Pretty Pearl, Harper, 1983.

Willie Bea and the Time the Martians Landed, Greenwillow, 1983.

A Little Love, Philomel, 1984.

Junius over Far, Harper, 1985.

The People Could Fly: American Black Folktales, illustrated by Leo and Diane Dillon, Knopf, 1985, published with cassette, 1987.

The Mystery of Drear House: The Conclusion of the Dies Drear Chronicle, Greenwillow, 1987.

A White Romance, Philomel, 1987.

In the Beginning: Creation Stories from around the World, Harcourt, 1988.

Anthony Burns: The Defeat and Triumph of a Fugitive Slave (an historical reconstruction based on fact), Knopf, 1988.

Bells of Christmas, illustrated by Davis, Harcourt, 1989.

The Dark Way: Stories from the Spirit World, illustrated by Lambert Davis, Harcourt, 1990.

Cousins, Putnam, 1990.

The All Jahdu Storybook, illustrated by Barry Moser, Harcourt, 1991.

Drylongso, illustrated by Jerry Pinkney, Harcourt Brace Jovanovich, 1992.

Many Thousand Gone: African Americans from Slavery to Freedom, illustrated by L. Dillon and D. Dillon, Knopf, 1992.

Plain City, Blue Sky/Scholastic, 1993.

Her Stories: African American Folktales, Fairy Tales and True Tales, Scholastic, 1995.

Jaguarundi, Blue Sky Press, 1995.

When Birds Could Talk and Bats Could Sing: The Adventures of Bruh Sparrow, Sis Wren, and Their Friends, illustrated by Barry Moser, Blue Sky Press, 1995.

A Ring of Tricksters: Animal Tales from America, the West Indies, and Africa, Blue Sky Press, 1997.

Second Cousins, Scholastic, 1998.

BIOGRAPHIES FOR CHILDREN

W. E. B. Du Bois: A Biography, Crowell, 1972.

Paul Robeson: The Life and Times of a Free Black Man, Harper, 1974.

OTHER

(Editor) W. E. B. Du Bois, *The Writings of W. E. B. Du Bois,* Crowell, 1975.

(Author of introduction) Martin Greenberg, editor, *The Newbery Award Reader,* Harcourt, 1984.

ADAPTATIONS: The House of Dies Drear was adapted for the Public Broadcasting Service series "Wonderworks" in 1984.

SIDELIGHTS: Virginia Hamilton is one of the most influential authors of children's books writing today. Not only have many of her works received awards such as the National Book Award, but her novel *M. C. Higgins, the Great* was the first work ever to win both the National Book Award and the Newbery Medal. Hamilton, winner of the 1995 Laura Ingalls

Wilder Award for lifetime achievement, is recognized as a gifted and demanding storyteller. Ethel L. Heins, for example, writes in *Horn Book*: "Few writers of fiction for young people are as daring, inventive, and challenging to read-or to review-as Virginia Hamilton. Frankly making demands on her readers, she nevertheless expresses herself in a style essentially simple and concise." Hamilton's writing is a mix of realism, history, myth, and folklore, which, according to *Horn Book* contributor Paul Heins, results in "some exterior manifestation-historical and personal-that she has examined in the light of her feelings and her intelligence."

Hamilton's vision has been deeply influenced by her background. Her mother's side of the family was descended from a fugitive slave, Levi Perry, who settled in the southern Ohio Miami valley town of Yellow Springs. The Perry family grew and prospered by farming the rich Ohio soil. "I grew up within the warmth of loving aunts and uncles, all reluctant farmers but great storytellers," Hamilton recalls in a *Horn Book* article by Lee Bennett Hopkins. "I remember the tales best of all. My own father, who was an outlander from Illinois, Iowa, and points west, was the finest of the storytellers besides being an exceptional mandolinist. Mother, too, could take a slice of fiction floating around the family and polish it into a saga."

While attending Antioch College on a scholarship, Hamilton majored in writing and composed short stories. One of her instructors liked her stories enough to encourage the young student to leave college and test her skills in New York City. Hamilton was eager to experience the excitement of city life, and so in 1955 she began spending her summers in New York working as a bookkeeper. Later, she moved to the city permanently. "I don't have a clear recollection of the day I officially left home to go to New York," she tells Marguerite Feitlowitz in *Something About the Author*. "My plan was to find a cheap apartment, a part-time job, write and have a good time. And it all came together."

An important influence on the creation of *Zeely* came after Hamilton married poet and anthologist Arnold Adoff, whom she met not long after arriving in New York City. The two newlyweds traveled to Spain and then to northern Africa. "Going to Africa had been an enduring dream of Hamilton's," according to *Dictionary of Literary Biography* contributor Jane Ball, "and the land of dark-skinned people had 'a tremendous impression' on her, she said, even though her stay was brief. The impact is apparent on her first

book." According to John Rowe Townsend in his *A Sounding of Storytellers: New and Revised Essays on Contemporary Writers for Children*, *Zeely* exemplifies the type of writing that Hamilton would produce throughout her career: there "is not taint of racism in her books. . . . All through her work runs an awareness of black history, and particularly of black history in America. And there is a difference in the furniture of her writing mind from that of most of her white contemporaries: dream, myth, legend and ancient story can be sensed again and again in the background of naturalistically-described present-day events."

Zeely is about a girl called Geeder who, fascinated by a tall, regal-looking woman she sees tending pigs on a farm, obsessively imagines her to be a Watusi queen. By the end of the tale, Zeely convinces Geeder she is nothing of the sort, "and with the aid of a parable she helps Geeder [accept herself for who she is, too]. She is not a queen; and perhaps there is an implication that for black Americans to look back towards supposed long-lost glories in Africa is unfruitful."

In books like the Jahdu tales, including *The Time-Ago Tales of Jahdu, Time-Ago Lost: More Tales of Jahdu, Jahdu,* and *The All Jahdu Storybook*, Hamilton takes an approach that mimics the style of the traditional folk tale. These works tell of the fantastic adventures of Jahdu and his "encounters [with] the allegorical figures Sweetdream, Nightmare, Trouble, Chameleon, and others," writes Marilyn F. Apseloff in the *Dictionary of Literary Biography*. "These original tales have a timeless quality about them; in addition, they reveal racial pride, as Jahdu discovers in [*The Time-Ago Tales of Jahdu*] that he is happiest when he becomes a part of a black family in Harlem." Similarly, in the collections *The People Could Fly: American Black Folktales, In the Beginning: Creation Stories from around the World,* and *The Dark Way: Stories from the Spirit World* Hamilton retells old myths and folk tales from her own black ancestry-as well as many other cultures-in an attempt to restore pride in this diverse and rich literary heritage.

One ethnic group in particular, Native Americans, has influenced Hamilton's writing in books like the Edgar Award-winning *The House of Dies Drear*. "The references to Indians in her books," observes Apseloff, "are probably the result of two factors: Hamilton knew that many Shawnees lived in the Yellow Springs area originally, with Cherokees further south, and her grandmother claimed to be part American Indian." Despite this element in the story, however, *The House of Dies Drear* is a mystery novel centered around the history of the Underground Railroad, the route that fugitive blacks took to escape slavery in the South before the Civil War. It "is a taut mystery, one which youngsters gulp down quickly and find hard to forget," attests Hopkins. "Miss Hamilton remarked, *'The House of Dies Drear* is [one of] my favorite books, I think, because it is so full of all the things I love: excitement, mystery, black history, the strong, black family. In it I tried to pay back all those wonderful relatives who gave me so much in the past.'"

Hamilton's *M. C. Higgins, the Great* emphasizes the importance of family. The story portrays the Higginses, a close-knit family that resides on Sarah's Mountain in southern Ohio. The mountain has special significance to the Higginses, for it has belonged to their family since M. C.'s great-grandmother Sarah, an escaped slave, settled there. The conflict in the story arises when a huge spoil heap, created by strip mining, threatens to engulf their home. M. C. is torn between his love for his home and his concern for his family's safety, and he searches diligently for a solution that will allow him to preserve both. *M. C. Higgins, the Great* was highly praised by critics, including poet Nikki Giovanni, who writes in the *New York Times Book Review:* "Once again Virginia Hamilton creates a world and invites us in. *M. C. Higgins, the Great* is not an adorable book, not a lived-happily-ever-after kind of story. It is warm, humane and hopeful and does what every book should do—creates characters with whom we can identify and for whom we care."

Hamilton chronicles slavery in *Anthony Burns: The Defeat and Triumph of a Fugitive Slave* and in *Many Thousand Gone: African Americans from Slavery to Freedom.* In *Anthony Burns,* Hamilton relates the true story of an escaped slave who was captured and tried under the Fugitive Slave Act. The trial triggered riots and ended with Burns's return to his former owner. Hamilton based her account on court records, newspaper reports, biographies, and other primary sources. "Told in an appropriately restrained, unadorned style, incorporating verbatim the speeches of counsel for both sides, *Anthony Burns* is a work of simple, but noble, eloquence," praises Elizabeth Ward in *Washington Post Book World.* A reviewer for *Children's Book Review Service* remarks, "Black history comes alive in this striking, gripping, personalized account." Based on information found in nineteenth century archives and oral histories, *Many Thousand Gone* contains biographical profiles of celebrated and obscure individuals that reveal their personal experiences with

slavery. The stories provide insight on slavery in America from the early 1600s to its abolishment in 1865 with the ratification of the Thirteenth Amendment to the Constitution. "All of these profiles drive home the sickening realities of slavery in a personal way," asserts David Haward Bain in the *New York Times Book Review,* who adds that "many also show how the experiences of individuals in the legal system worked in the larger struggle for freedom." Michael Dirda concludes in *Washington Post Book World* that "as a kind of portrait gallery of the brave and resourceful, *Many Thousand Gone* deserves many thousand readers."

In the *New York Times Book Review,* Veronica Chambers characterizes Hamilton's *Her Stories: African American Folktales, Fairy Tales and True Tales* as "possibly the first collection of such folk literature to focus exclusively on African-American women and girls." She recasts stories dealing with animals, fairy tales, the supernatural, folkways, and true experiences that were passed down through oral history and in several African languages, Spanish, and English. "Hamilton's retellings of these stories strike a nice balance between dialect and accessibility, modernizing just enough to make the stories easily readable without sacrificing the flavor of the originals," credits Jennifer Howard in *Washington Post Book World.*

BIOGRAPHICAL/CRITICAL SOURCES:

BOOKS

Children's Literature Review, Gale (Detroit), Volume 1, 1976; Volume 8, 1985; Volume 11, 1986.
Contemporary Literary Criticism, Volume 26, Gale, 1983.
Dictionary of Literary Biography, Gale, Volume 33: *Afro-American Fiction Writers after 1955,* 1984; Volume 52: *American Writers for Children since 1960: Fiction,* 1986.
Egoff, Sheila A., *Thursday's Child: Trends and Patterns in Contemporary Children's Literature,* American Library Association, 1981, pp. 31-65, 130-158.
Mikkelsen, Nina, *Virginia Hamilton,* Twayne (New York City), 1994.
Rees, David, *Painted Desert, Green Shade: Essays on Contemporary Writers of Fiction for Children and Young Adults,* Horn Book, 1984, pp. 168-184.
Sims, Rudine, *Shadow and Substance: Afro-American Experience in Contemporary Children's Fiction,* National Council of Teachers of English, 1982, pp. 79-102.

Something About the Author, Volume 56, Gale, 1990.

Townsend, John Rowe, *A Sounding of Storytellers: New and Revised Essays on Contemporary Writers for Children,* Lippincott, 1979, pp. 97-108.

Wheeler, Jill C., *Virginia Hamilton,* ABDO & Daughters (Minneapolis, MN), 1997.

PERIODICALS

Best Sellers, January, 1983.

Booklist, August, 1982, p. 1525; April 1, 1983, pp. 1034-1035; July, 1985, p. 1554; April 1, 1994, p. 1464; December 15, 1994, p. 753.

Bulletin of the Center for Children's Books, September, 1978, p. 9; March, 1981, p. 134; July-August, 1982, p. 207; November, 1983, pp. 50-51; April, 1985, p. 148; June, 1988.

Chicago Tribune Book World, November 10, 1985, pp. 33-34.

Children's Book Review Service, April, 1985, p. 97; July, 1988, p. 146; October, 1992, p. 22; March, 1995, p. 90; October, 1995, p. 22; March, 1996, p. 91.

Children's Literature Association Quarterly, fall, 1982, pp. 45-48; winter, 1983, pp. 10-14, 25-27; spring, 1983, pp. 17-20; fall, 1986, pp. 134-42; winter, 1995-96, pp. 168-74.

Children's Literature in Education, winter, 1983; summer, 1987, pp. 67-75.

Christian Science Monitor, May 4, 1972, p. B5; March 12, 1979, p. B4; May 12, 1980, p. B9; March 2, 1984, p. B7; August 3, 1984.

Horn Book, October, 1968, p. 563; February, 1970; February, 1972; October, 1972, p. 476; December, 1972, pp. 563-569; June, 1973; October, 1974, pp. 143-144; April, 1975; August, 1975, pp. 344-348; December, 1976, p. 611; December, 1978, pp. 609-619; June, 1980, p. 305; October, 1982, pp. 505-506; June, 1983; February, 1984, pp. 24-28; September-October, 1984, pp. 597-598; September-October, 1985, pp. 563-564; March-April, 1986, pp. 212-213; January-February, 1988, pp. 105-106; March-April, 1989, pp. 183-185; July-August, 1993, p. 437; September-October, 1993, p. 621; March-April, 1994, p. 204; July-August, 1995, pp. 436-445.

Interracial Books for Children Bulletin, Numbers 1 and 2, 1983, p. 32; Number 5, 1984; Volume 15, number 5, 1984, pp. 17-18; Volume 16, number 4, 1985, p. 19.

Kirkus Reviews, July 1, 1974; October 15, 1980, pp. 1354-1355; April 1, 1983; October 1, 1985, pp. 1088-1089; March 1, 1996, p. 375.

Lion and the Unicorn, Volume 9, 1985, pp. 50-57; Volume 10, 1986, pp. 15-17.

Los Angeles Times Book Review, March 23, 1986; May 22, 1988, p. 11; December 17, 1989, p. 8; November 18, 1990, p. 8.

New York Times Book Review, October 13, 1968, p. 26; October 24, 1971, p. 8; September 22, 1974, p. 8; December 22, 1974, p. 8; October 31, 1976, p. 39; December 17, 1978, p. 27; May 4, 1980, pp. 26, 28; September 27, 1981, p. 36; November 14, 1982, pp. 41, 56; September 4, 1983, p. 14; March 18, 1984, p. 31; April 17, 1985, p. 20; November 10, 1985, p. 38; November 8, 1987, p. 36; October 16, 1988, p. 46; November 13, 1988, p. 52; December 17, 1989, p. 29; November 11, 1990, p. 6; November 22, 1992, p. 34; February 21, 1993, p. 23; November 12, 1995, p. 23.

Publishers Weekly, January 18, 1993, p. 470; February 19, 1996, p. 214.

School Library Journal, December 1968, pp. 53-54; September, 1971, p. 126; December, 1978, p. 60; March, 1980, p. 140; April, 1981, p. 140; April, 1983, p. 123; August, 1985, p. 97; December, 1994, p. 75.

Times (London), November 20, 1986.

Times Literary Supplement, May 23, 1975; July 11, 1975, p. 766; March 25, 1977, p. 359; September 19, 1980, p. 1024; November 20, 1981, p. 1362; August 30, 1985, p. 958; February 28, 1986, p. 230; October 30, 1987, p. 1205; November 20, 1987, p. 1286; July 29, 1988, p. 841.

Tribune Books (Chicago), October 16, 1988, p. 9; November 13, 1988, p. 6; February 26, 1989, p. 8; November 11, 1990; February 14, 1993.

Voice of Youth Advocates, August, 1980, pp. 31-32; October, 1983, p. 215; June, 1985, p. 130; October, 1988, p. 201; February, 1994, p. 367.

Washington Post Book World, June 25, 1967, p. 12; November 10, 1974; November 7, 1976, p. G7; November 11, 1979; September 14, 1980, p. 6; November 7, 1982, p. 14; November 10, 1985; July 10, 1988, p. 11; April 8, 1990, p. 8; November 4, 1990, p. 19; December 9, 1990, p. 14; February 14, 1993, p. 10; December 10, 1995, p. 17.*

*   *   *

HANDY, W(illiam) C(hristopher) 1873-1958

PERSONAL: Born November 16, 1873, in Florence, AL; died of a stroke, March 28, 1958, in New York, NY; son of Charles B. Handy; married Elizabeth

Price, July 19, 1898; children: six. *Education:* Attended Florence District School for Negroes.

CAREER: Worked in the McNabb Iron Furnace as a teenager; teacher, at Crittendon Cross Road School and in Bethel, AL, c. early 1890s; Howard and Harrison Pipe Works, Bessemer, Alabama, molder's helper, 1892; served in odd jobs and band work, c. 1893-96; played with "Mahara's Minstrels," 1896-1900; Alabama A&M University, music teacher, 1900-02; "Knights of Pythias," band leader, Clarksdale, MS, 1903; played in various bands, 1903-14; Pace & Handy Music Company, later Handy Brothers, cofounder, beginning 1914.

WRITINGS:

Negro Authors and Composers of the United States, Handy Brothers Music Company (New York City), 1938.
W. C. Handy's Collection of Negro Spirituals, Handy Brothers Music Company (New York City), 1938.
Father of the Blues, Macmillan (New York City), 1941.
Unsung Americans Sung, [New York City], 1944.
A Treasury of the Blues, C. Boni (New York City), 1949.

EDITOR

Blues, A. & C. Boni (New York City), 1926.

OTHER

Author of blues compositions, including "St. Louis Blues," "Memphis Blues," and "Beale Street Blues."

SIDELIGHTS: W. C. Handy, known by some scholars of jazz music as the "father of the blues," is credited with the popular songs "St. Louis Blues," "Memphis Blues," and "Beale Street Blues." In addition, Handy is the author of a number of books, including the autobiography *Father of the Blues* and *Negro Authors and Composers of the United States.*

Handy was born in Florence, Alabama, on November 16, 1873. His grandfather, William Wise Handy, had been the first African-American to own property in the area, which came to be known as Handy's Hill. His parents were both freed slaves; his father, a Methodist preacher, intended him for Wilberforce University and a career in the ministry, and strongly

disapproved of his early interest in music. From a local teacher, former Fisk University professor Y. A. Wallace, he learned to sing and was taught perfect pitch on tuning forks and pitch pipes: "When I was no more than ten," he wrote in his autobiography, "I could catalogue almost any sound that came to my ears, using the tonic *sol-fa* system."

Handy absorbed the ambient blues avidly, and saved enough money to buy a cornet, on which he practiced in secret. Soon he was playing with other local musicians, and then found himself performing for money in nearby towns. However, Handy did not abandon his studies, and continued to excel in school. Upon finishing, he took the County Teacher's Examination and passed it with the highest marks of any of his classmates and second only to the top white student applying to the State Normal College. By this time, Handy had already done some teaching in local village schools, and decided they were a dead end. Not only was the pay very low, but, since most of the students were required to work on their family farms for the greater part of the year, school sessions were extremely short, sometimes as little as three months. Handy decided to try his luck teaching in Birmingham, only to discover that he could earn more money as an industrial laborer in nearby Bessemer. When economic depression hit the area shortly thereafter, the pipe works that had employed Handy closed down, and he found himself out of work, with dwindling savings, on the streets of Birmingham.

Handy's Bessemer years had seen the formation of his first brass band, and his love of and interest in music continued unabated. He organized a vocal group and hitched a ride to Chicago on freight trains in the hopes of performing at the 1893 World's Fair, only to discover on arrival that the fair had been postponed until the following year. An attempt to sustain themselves in St. Louis failed as well. The group disbanded, and Handy found himself penniless and on the street. He lived a hobo's life in the period that followed, eventually drifting to Evansville, Indiana. There, he met, auditioned for, and began to play with the Hampton Band. His playing attracted attention, and when he joined a band in Henderson, Kentucky, his career as a professional musician began. It was also in Henderson that he met and fell in love with Elizabeth Price, who would later become his wife.

On August 4, 1896, he received a letter from a friend he had once played with, inviting him to come to Chicago and join "Mahara's Minstrels," which combined the cream of the musical crop among black musicians. This was the group that made his fortune, established him enough to marry Elizabeth and raise a family. Handy toured around the country, playing with the minstrels, often encountering intolerance and sometimes barely escaping outright violence, including a lynch mob in Missouri. The minstrels played a number of gigs in Havana, a place Handy speaks of fondly in his memoirs.

Finally, in 1900, Handy left the band and returned to Florence with his wife. His first child was born shortly thereafter, and he accepted a position teaching vocal and orchestral music, and leading the band, at Alabama A & M University. But Handy's insistent interest in American music did not sit well with the rest of the faculty, and Handy was receiving letters asking him to return to Mahara, which he ultimately did after his second year. Again the whirlwind of touring took over his life, and Handy visited Canada and Mexico, California and Cuba, polishing his skills as both a performer and a band leader. In 1903, he accepted an invitation to lead the "Knights of Pythias" band in Clarksdale, Mississippi. It proved a momentous decision.

All throughout his career, Handy had been performing versions of established classics, show tunes, bowing to "the authority of printed notes." His band had been asked to perform in Cleveland, Mississippi, and, during a break, a local group got up to play blues-influenced dance music. Handy was galvanized by what he heard. "That night a composer was born," he wrote. He immediately changed the itinerary of the band to blues, arranged a number of locally-circulating tunes for his players, and watched their popularity soar. Unlike most other blues musicians of his time, Handy had the classical training, the sense of perfect pitch, and the knowledge of notation, to capture and score blues music. In short order, he was not only arranging, but composing the blues.

In 1912, after considerable difficulties, Handy released his own song, "Memphis Blues." At a time when there was no electric media of any kind, the release of a song was primarily a matter of the publication of its sheet music—the more in demand the song might be, the greater the sales of its printed parts. As this was a considerably quieter sort of popularity, it took some time for Handy to realize that he had written one of the most widely clamoured-after pieces of his day. While he was delighted at its success, he received no part of its proceeds—he had been forced to sell the copyright to get it published at all, for which he was paid one hundred dollars.

Handy continued to compose and play with his latest band, now centered in Memphis. In 1914, at the age of forty, he composed his signature tune: the "St. Louis Blues." But this was only one of a great many songs from this period; Handy would start in on a new piece before the ink was dry on the last. Several years before, in 1907, Handy had met and collaborated with Harry H. Pace, cashier of the Solvent Savings Bank, an all African American enterprise. Together, they had written "In the Cotton Fields of Dixie," and, in the years that followed, the pair formed a joint enterprise: Pace & Handy Music Company—Publishers. Slow to start, with the explosion of interest in blues music and piano rolls, Handy soon found himself piloting a highly successful business.

But financial success cannot be fully realized in an atmosphere of repression—Handy found that banking and other necessary business services were hard to come by in the south. His checks were not accepted, he found it difficult to attain insurance, and he found it difficult even to maintain the mortgage on his home. Handy relocated briefly to Chicago, then, at Pace's urging, moved a second time, to New York, arriving in 1918. They brought with them their next hit, "A Good Man Is Hard to Find," as sung by Sophie Tucker, which sold half a million copies. But Handy's fortune was far from made—the market for this music was becoming highly competitive, so much so that eventually Harry Pace left the firm to start his own. Suddenly, Handy found himself nearing bankruptcy. Still worse, while his general health was good, Handy found himself slowly losing his sight.

In the end, Handy's business, now the Handy Brothers Music Company (which he shared with his younger brother Charles), picked up again, while his competitors began to slide. The blues was becoming "glorified": Gershwin had performed his "Rhapsody in Blue," and Handy himself had the opportunity to orchestrate a program around his "St. Louis Blues" which was performed at the Metropolitan Opera House.

In his later years, Handy wrote several books about gospel and blues music, singing the praises of unsung African-American composers. In 1941, he produced his own autobiography, *Father of the Blues*. There is little dispute as to the appropriateness of this title: according to commentators, Handy did perhaps more than anyone else to bring the blues to a wide popular audience and to demonstrate its legitimacy as an original American art form.

BIOGRAPHICAL/CRITICAL SOURCES:

BOOKS

The ASCAP Biographical Dictionary of Composers, Authors, and Publishers, fourth edition, Bowker, 1980.
Three Jazz Greats, Garrard Publishing, 1973.

PERIODICALS

Times (London), March 29, 1958.*

*   *   *

HANSBERRY, Lorraine (Vivian)   1930-1965

PERSONAL: Born May 19, 1930, in Chicago, IL; died of cancer, January 12, 1965, in New York, NY; buried in Beth-El Cemetery, Croton-on-Hudson, NY; daughter of Carl Augustus (a realtor and banker) and Nannie (Perry) Hansberry; married Robert B. Nemiroff (a music publisher and songwriter), June 20, 1953 (divorced March, 1964). *Education:* Attended University of Wisconsin, Art Institute of Chicago, Roosevelt College, New School for Social Research, and studied in Guadalajara, Mexico, 1948-50. *Avocational interests:* Ping-pong, skiing, walking in the woods, reading biographies, conversation.

CAREER: Playwright. Worked variously as a clerk in a department store, a tag girl in a fur shop, an aide to a theatrical producer, and as a waitress, hostess, and cashier in a restaurant in Greenwich Village run by the family of Robert Nemiroff; associate editor, *Freedom* (monthly magazine), 1952-53.

MEMBER: Dramatists Guild, Ira Aldrich Society, Institute for Advanced Study in the Theater Arts.

AWARDS, HONORS: New York Drama Critics Circle Award for best American play, 1959, for *A Raisin in the Sun;* named "most promising playwright" of the season, *Variety,* 1959; Cannes Film Festival special award and Screen Writers Guild nomination, both 1961, both for screenplay *A Raisin in the Sun.*

WRITINGS:

PLAYS

A Raisin in the Sun (three-act; produced on Broadway, 1959), Random House (New York City),

1959, with introduction by Robert Nemiroff, Vintage (New York City), 1994.
The Sign in Sidney Brustein's Window (three-act; produced on Broadway, 1964), Random House, 1965.
Les Blancs (two-act; produced on Broadway, 1970), Hart Stenographic Bureau, 1966, published as *Lorraine Hansberry's "Les Blancs",* adapted by Nemiroff, Samuel French (New York City), 1972.
To Be Young, Gifted, and Black: A Portrait of Lorraine Hansberry in Her Own Words (produced Off-Broadway, 1969), adapted by Nemiroff, Samuel French, 1971.
Les Blancs: The Collected Last Plays of Lorraine Hansberry (includes *The Drinking Gourd* and *What Use Are Flowers?*), edited by Nemiroff, Random House, 1972, published as *Lorraine Hansberry: The Collected Last Plays,* New American Library (New York City), 1983.
A Raisin in the Sun (expanded twenty-fifth anniversary edition)[and] *The Sign in Sidney Brustein's Window,* New American Library, 1987.

OTHER

A Raisin in the Sun (screenplay), Columbia, 1960.
(Author of text) *The Movement: Documentary of a Struggle for Equality* (collection of photographs), Simon & Schuster (New York City), 1964, published as *A Matter of Colour: Documentary of the Struggle for Racial Equality in the U.S.A.,* Penguin (London), 1965.
(Self-illustrated) *To Be Young, Gifted and Black: Lorraine Hansberry in Her Own Words,* edited by Nemiroff, introduction by James Baldwin, Prentice-Hall, 1969.
Lorraine Hansberry Speaks Out: Art and the Black Revolution (recording), Caedmon, 1972.

Contributor to anthologies, including *American Playwrights on Drama,* 1965; *Three Negro Plays,* Penguin, 1969; and *Black Titan: W. E. B. Du Bois.* Also contributor to periodicals, including *Negro Digest, Freedomways, Village Voice,* and *Theatre Arts.*

ADAPTATIONS: A musical version of *The Sign in Sidney Brustein's Window* was produced on Broadway in 1972; *Raisin,* a musical version of *A Raisin in the Sun,* was produced on Broadway in 1973. *A Raisin in the Sun* was recorded on audiocassette, Caedmon, 1972.

SIDELIGHTS: The first African-American woman to have a play produced on Broadway, Lorraine Hansberry dedicated both her short life and her literary output to pursuing racial and sexual equality in the United States. Written during the Civil Rights Era, her works reflect the non-militant approach of such black leaders as Dr. Martin Luther King, Jr. Although published as the women's movement of the 1960s and 1970s was only beginning to rally supporters, Hansberry's plays portray strong female characters who stand up for themselves in a male-dominated society. "Ultimately life—and love—affirming," her works "focus on the bonds and conflicts of family and romantic relationships," according to Leslie-Ann Skolnik in *Feminist Writers,* "the pursuit of individual fulfillment, and the clashes between traditions and modern life."

Hansberry was born into a middle-class black family on the south side of Chicago in 1930. She recalled that her childhood was basically a happy one: "The insulation of life within the Southside ghetto, of what must have easily been half a million people, protected me from some of the harsher and more bestial aspects of white-supremacist culture," the playwright stated in *Portraits in Color.* At the age of seven or eight, Hansberry and her upwardly mobile family deliberately attempted to move into a restricted white neighborhood. Her father fought the civil-rights case all the way to the U.S. Supreme Court, eventually winning his claim to a home within the restricted area. "The Hansberrys' determination to continue to live in this home in spite of intimidation and threats from their angry, rock-throwing white neighbors is a study in courage and strength," Porter Kirkwood assessed in *Freedomways.* "Lorraine's character and personality were forged in this atmosphere of resistance to injustice." "Both of my parents were strong-minded, civic-minded, exceptionally race-minded people who made enormous sacrifices on behalf of the struggle for civil rights throughout their lifetimes," Hansberry remembered.

While in high school, Hansberry first became interested in the theater. "Mine was the same old story—" she recollected, "sort of hanging around little acting groups, and developing the feeling that the theater embraces everything I liked all at one time." While attending the University of Wisconsin, she became further acquainted with great theater, including the works of August Strindberg, Henrik Ibsen, and Sean O'Casey. She was particularly taken with O'Casey's ability to express in his plays the complex and transcendent nature of humans, to achieve "the emotional transformation of people on stage."

After studying painting in Chicago and abroad, Hansberry eschewed her artistic plans and moved to New York City in 1950 to begin her career as a writer. Politically active in New York, Hansberry wrote for Paul Robeson's *Freedom* magazine and participated in various liberal crusades. During one protest concerning practices of discrimination at New York University, she met Robert Nemiroff, himself a writer and pursuer of liberal politics. Although Nemiroff was white, a romance developed between the two, and in 1953 they married.

Nemiroff encouraged Hansberry in her writing efforts, going so far as to salvage her discarded pages from the wastebasket. One night in 1957, while the couple was entertaining a group of friends, they read a scene from Hansberry's play in progress, *A Raisin in the Sun.* The impact left by the reading prompted Hansberry, Nemiroff, and friends to push for the completion, financing, and production of the drama within the next several months.

Enjoying solid success at tryout performances on the road, *A Raisin in the Sun* made its New York debut at the Ethel Barrymore Theater, becoming the first play written by a black woman to be produced on Broadway; it was the first to be directed by a black director in more than fifty years. When *A Raisin in the Sun* won the New York Drama Critics Circle Award, Hansberry became the youngest writer and the first black artist ever to receive the honor, competing that year with such theater luminaries as Tennessee Williams, Eugene O'Neill, and Archibald MacLeish. In June, 1959, Hansberry was named the "most promising playwright" of the season by *Variety*'s poll of New York drama critics.

A Raisin in the Sun tells the story of a black family attempting to escape the poverty of the Chicago projects by buying a house in the suburbs with the money left from the insurance policy of their dead father. Conflict erupts when the son, Walter Lee, fights to use the money instead to buy his own business—a life's ambition. Yet, when a white representative from the neighborhood that the family plans to integrate attempts to thwart their move, the young man submerges his materialistic aspirations—for a time, at least—and rallies to support the family's dream. Still Hansberry wonders, as expressed in the lines of poet Langston Hughes from which she takes her title, what will become of Walter Lee's frustrated desires: "What happens to a dream deferred? / Does it dry up like a raisin in the sun? / Or fester like a sore—and then run?"

Because the play explored a universal theme—the search for freedom and a better life—the majority of its audience loved it. According to Gerald Weales in *Commentary,* it reflected neither the traditional Negro show, folksy and exotic, or the reactionary protest play, with black characters spouting about the injustices of white oppression. Rather, *A Raisin in the Sun* was a play about a family that just happened to be black. "The thing I tried to show," Hansberry told Ted Poston in the *New York Post,* "was the many gradations in even one Negro family, the clash of the old and the new."

New York Times critic Brooks Atkinson admired *A Raisin in the Sun* because it explored serious problems without becoming academic or ponderous. Hansberry "has told the inner as well as outer truth about a Negro family in Chicago," the critic observed. "The play has vigor as well as veracity and is likely to destroy the complacency of anyone who sees it." Weales labeled *Raisin* "a good play" whose "basic strength lies in the character and the problem of Walter Lee, which transcends his being a Negro. If the play were only the Negro-white conflict that crops up when the family's proposed move is about to take place, it would be editorial, momentarily effective, and nothing more. Walter Lee's difficulty, however, is that he has accepted the American myth of success at its face value, that he is trapped, as Willy Loman was trapped, by a false dream. In planting so indigenous an American image at the center of her play, Miss Hansberry has come as close as possible to what she intended—a play about Negroes which is not simply a Negro play." The reviewer also found the play "genuinely funny and touching," with the dialogue between family members believable.

Despite its long run, *A Raisin in the Sun* did not achieve universal acclaim by critics. Dubbing the work "old fashioned," *New Republic* drama critic Tom F. Driver wrote that "much of its success is due to our sentimentality over the 'Negro question,'" and wondered whether "it may have been Miss Hansberry's objective to show that the stage stereotypes will fit Negroes as well as white people." And Henry Cruse, voicing the opinion of several critics in his *The Crisis of the Negro Intellectual,* contended that the fact that the leading characters of the play are African-American is the sole basis on which the work was valued by racially conscious U.S. audiences; "If this play—," wrote Cruse, "which is so 'American' that many whites did *not* consider it a 'Negro play'—had ever been staged by *white actors* it would be judged second rate. . . . The truth is that *A Raisin in the Sun* . . . was the artistic, aesthetic and class-inspired culmination of the efforts of the Harlem left- wing literary

and cultural in-group to achieve integration of the Negro in the arts."

Despite its dismissal by some critics, including C. W. E. Bigsby, who called the work "disappointing" and "an unhappy crossbreed of social protest and re-assuring resolution" in his *Confrontation and Commitment: A Study of Contemporary American Drama, 1959-66, A Raisin in the Sun* ran for 530 performances. Shortly thereafter a film version of the drama was released; Hansberry won a special award at the Cannes Film Festival and was nominated for an award from the Screen Writers Guild for her screenplay. She then began working on a second play about a Jewish intellectual who vacillates between social commitment and paralyzing disillusionment. Titled *The Sign in Sidney Brustein's Window,* the play ran on Broadway for 101 performances despite mixed reviews and poor sales. "Its tenure on Broadway parallels the playwright's own failing health," Kirkwood noted. The play closed on January 12, 1965, the day Hansberry died of cancer at the age of thirty-five.

According to Steven R. Carter in the *Dictionary of Literary Biography,* the reason for the lack of critical success of *The Sign in Sidney Brustein's Window* was "possibly because it had to be seen twice to be justly appreciated, possibly because it challenged too many preconceptions about what subjects were appropriate for Afro-American writers." Expanding her social vision beyond the problems within the black ghetto, Hansberry portrayed an individual whose sophistication in literature and other manifestations of high culture extended far beyond that of much of her audience. "In spite of its difficulty," maintained Carter of the play, "it should be considered a major work for its fascinating characters, witty dialogue, and superb portrayal of the social and intellectual currents of its time." Hansberry would return to illuminating the conditions faced by her fellow African Americans in *Les Blancs,* which, although unfinished at her death, would be produced in 1970.

Although Hansberry and her husband divorced in 1964, Nemiroff remained dedicated to the playwright and her work. Appointed her literary executor, he collected his ex-wife's writings and words after her death and presented them in the autobiographical montage *To Be Young, Gifted, and Black.* He also edited and published her three unfinished plays, which were subsequently produced: *Les Blancs,* a psychological and social drama of a European-educated African who returns home to join the fight against colonialism; *The Drinking Gourd,* a drama on slavery and emancipation expressed through the story of a black woman; and *What Use Are Flowers?*, an anti-war fable about an aging hermit who, in a ravaged world, tries to impart to children his remembrances of the past civilization he had once renounced. "It's true that there's a great deal of pain for me in this," Nemiroff told Arlynn Nellhaus of the *Denver Post* about his custodianship, "but there's also a great deal of satisfaction. There is first-class writing and the joy of seeing [Lorraine's] ideas become a contemporary force again . . . [is] rewarding. . . . She was proud of black culture, the black experience and struggle. . . . But she was also in love with all cultures, and she related to the struggles of other people. . . . She was tremendously affected by the struggle of ordinary people—the heroism of ordinary people and the ability of people to laugh and transcend."

To Be Young, Gifted, and Black was made into a play that ran Off-Broadway in 1969, keeping the memory of Hansberry and critical examination of her small body of work alive. Martin Goffried hypothesized in *Women's Wear Daily* that "Hansberry's tragically brief playwriting career charted the postwar steps in the racial movement, from working within the system (*A Raisin in the Sun*) to a burgeoning distrust of white liberals (*The Sign in Sidney Brustein's Window*) to the association with Africa in *Les Blancs* that would evolve, after her death, from the ashes of passive resistance into the energy and danger of militant activism." Writing in *Beautiful, Also, Are the Souls of My Black Sisters*, Jeanne L. Noble examined the author in a similar sociological light, wondering where, in the political continuum of the late-twentieth century, Hansberry would stand in comparison with newer breeds of black writers. Yet she concluded: "Certainly for [Hansberry's] works to leave a continuing legacy—though she died at age 35, just before the fiercest testing period of the black revolution—is itself monumental. And we will always ponder these among her last words: 'I think when I get my health back I shall go into the South to find out what kind of revolutionary I am.'"

But most critics did not perceive Hansberry as a particularly political or "black" writer, but rather as one who dealt more with human universals. Gerald Weales speculated in *Commonweal* that "it is impossible to guess how she might have grown as a writer, but her two [finished] plays indicate that she had wit and intelligence, a strong sense of social and political possibility and a respect for the contradictions in all men; that she could create a milieu (the family in *Raisin*, the Greenwich Village circle in *Sign*) with

both bite and affection; that she was a playwright—like Odets, like Miller— with easily definable flaws but an inescapable talent that one cannot help admiring." And *Life* magazine's Cyclops concluded that Hansberry's gentle and intelligent sensibilities could best be read in these lines from *The Sign in Sidney Brustein's Window*, when Sidney describes himself: "A fool who believes that death is a waste and love is sweet and that the earth turns and men change every day and that rivers run and that people wanna be better than they are and that flowers smell good and that I hurt terribly today, and that hurt is desperation and desperation is energy and energy can *move* things."

BIOGRAPHICAL/CRITICAL SOURCES:

BOOKS

Authors in the News, Volume 2, Gale (Detroit), 1976.

Bigsby, C. W. E., and others, *Confrontation and Commitment: A Study of Contemporary American Drama,* MacGibbon & Kee (London), 1967.

Bigsby, *Confrontation and Commitment: A Study of Contemporary American Drama,* University of Missouri Press, 1968.

Bigsby, editor, *The Black American Writer,* Volume 2, Penguin (London), 1969.

Black Literature Criticism, Gale, 1992.

Carter, Steven R., *Hansberry's Drama: Commitment amid Complexity,* University of Illinois Press (Urbana), 1991.

Cherry, Gwendolyn, and others, *Portraits in Color,* Pageant Press, 1962.

Concise Dictionary of American Literary Biography: The New Consciousness, 1941-1968, Gale, 1987.

Contemporary Authors Bibliography Series, Volume 3: *American Dramatists,* Gale, 1989.

Contemporary Literary Criticism, Gale, Volume 17, 1981, Volume 62, 1991.

Cruse, Harold, *The Crisis of the Negro Intellectual,* Morrow (New York City), 1967.

Dictionary of Literary Biography, Gale, Volume 7: *Twentieth-Century American Dramatists,* 1981, Volume 38: *Afro-American Writers after 1955: Dramatists and Prose Writers,* 1985.

Drama Criticism, Volume 2, Gale, 1992.

Feminist Writers, St. James Press (Detroit), 1996.

Keppel, Ben, *The Work of Democracy: Ralph Bunche, Kenneth B. Clarke, Lorraine Hansberry, and the Cultural Politics of Race,* Harvard University Press (Cambridge, MA), 1995.

McKissack, Patricia C., and Fredrick L. McKissack, *Young, Black, and Determined: A Biography of*

Lorraine Hansberry, Holiday House (New York City), 1997.

Nemiroff, Robert, *The 101 Final Performances of "Sidney Brustein": Portrait of a Play and Its Author,* [published with *A Raisin in the Sun* and *The Sign in Sidney Brustein's Window*], New American Library, 1966.

Noble, Jeanne L., *Beautiful, Also, Are the Souls of My Black Sisters: A History of the Black Women in America,* Prentice-Hall, 1978.

Scheader, Catherine, *They Found a Way: Lorraine Hansberry,* Children's Press, 1978.

Scheader, Catherine, *Lorraine Hansberry: Playwright and Voice of Justice,* Enslow Publishers, 1998.

Tripp, Janet, *Lorraine Hansberry,* Lucent Books, 1998.

PERIODICALS

Antiquarian Bookman, January 25, 1965.
Books Abroad, spring, 1966.
Commentary, June, 1959.
Commonweal, September 5, 1969; January 22, 1971.
Denver Post, March 14, 1976.
Esquire, November, 1969.
Freedomways, winter, 1963; summer, 1965; fourth quarter, 1978.
Life, January 14, 1972.
New Republic, June 9, 1959.
Newsweek, January 25, 1965.
New Yorker, May 9, 1959.
New York Post, March 22, 1959.
New York Times, March 8, 1959; March 12, 1959; April 9, 1959; January 13, 1965; November 9, 1983; August 15, 1986.
Publishers Weekly, February 8, 1965.
Theatre Journal, December 1986, p. 441-52.
Washington Post, November 16, 1986; December 2, 1986; November 16, 1989, pp. F1-3.
Women's Wear Daily, November 16, 1970.*

*   *   *

HANSBERRY, William Leo 1894-1965

PERSONAL: Born February 25, 1894, in Gloster, MS; died of a cerebral hemorrhage, November 3, 1965, in Chicago, IL; son of Elden Hayes and Pauline (Bailey) Hansberry; married Myrtle Kelso, 1937; children: Gail Adelle, Myrtle Kay. *Ethnicity:* "African American." *Education:* Harvard University, B.A., 1921, M.A., 1932; attended Oriental Institute, Uni-

versity of Chicago, 1936, Oxford University, 1937-38, and Cairo University, 1953.

CAREER: Historian and professor. Howard University, professor of history, 1922-59; University of Nigeria, visiting professor, 1963.

AWARDS, HONORS: Award of Honor, African Student Association of the U.S. and Africa, 1951, 1959, 1963; Fullbright scholarship, 1953; Bronze Citation for "Forty Years of Service in the Cause of African Freedom," United Friends of Africa, 1961; Achievement Award, Omega Psi Phi Fraternity, 1961; Hansberry Institute of African Studies, University of Nigeria, established in his name, 1963; First African Research Award, Haile Selassie I Prize Trust, 1964. Honorary degrees include Doctor of Letters, University of Nigeria; Doctor of Laws, Morgan College.

WRITINGS:

Africana at Nsukka: Inaugural Address Delivered at the Hansberry College of African Studies, Nsukka, Eastern Nigeria, September 22, 1963, Howard University Department of History (Washington), 1972.

Pillars in Ethiopian History: The William Leo Hansberry African History Notebook, Volume I, edited by Joseph E. Harris, Howard University Press (Washington), 1974.

Africa and Africans as Seen by Classical Writers: The William Leo Hansberry History Notebook, Volume II, edited by Harris, Howard University Press, 1977.

SIDELIGHTS: William Leo Hansberry was a man born one generation too soon. A pioneer in the study of ancient African history, he started his career at Howard University in 1922. It was a time when the black academic community was far more concerned with creating a livable present than with resurrecting an ancestral past. It was also a time when many white scholars were still mired in the racist tradition that saw all blacks as intellectual inferiors. Therefore, Hansberry's insistence on studying long-gone communities at first earned him little support from either camp.

Recognition finally came in the early 1950s. During this time, many African countries, long held under colonial rule, began their conversion to self-governance. Searching for proof that African societies had, at one time, a sophisticated cultural history and could reach these heights again, these new regimes treated

Hansberry's research into their societies with deep respect. The international attention he received prompted his U.S. colleagues to take a second look at his work and to acknowledge, at last, his contribution to the study of ancient African culture.

The direction of Hansberry's life was set by his father, Elden Hansberry, who taught history at Alcorn College in Gloster, Mississippi. The elder Hansberry died when his son was scarcely three years old, but he left him the priceless legacy of a library on culture and customs of the ancient world. Young Leo enjoyed reading his late father's collection of books. He could not help wondering, however, why they held so much information about the glorious histories of Greece, Rome, and even faraway China, but so little about Africa, the home of his own ancestors.

In 1915 Hansberry entered Atlanta University as a freshman. The history of the ancient world continued to fascinate him, but the mystery of Africa's shadowy past was not solved by his course work. Extra-curricular reading proved no more enlightening, for only two types of information seemed to be available. The first, as represented by the Old Testament of the Bible, mentioned such countries as Kush and Ethiopia, but gave no details of their inhabitants' lives. The second category of African history tended to emphasize either the supposedly civilizing influence of the slave trade or the rescue of the indigenous population from hopeless ignorance by white colonial missionaries.

An example of this parochial thinking appears in a book called *Howard University Department of History, 1913-1973,* written by faculty member Michael Winston. To show how the Jim Crow laws of the late nineteenth century perpetuated such so-called white superiority, Winston resurrected the following opinion of "the archetypal black person" aired during a U.S. Senate session of February 1914 by then-Senator James K. Vardaman of Mississippi. "He has never had any civilization except that which has been inculcated by a superior race," said Vardaman. "And it is lamentable that his civilization lasts only so long as he is in the hands of the white man who inculcates it."

Hansberry was unconvinced by Vardaman's assertion that Africa's entire indigenous population owed all the wisdom they possessed to their European conquerors. He could find no respected social scientist to support his own dissent until 1916, when a new volume of essays on race was published by Atlanta University's Department of Sociology. In two of the essays, "Old

African Civilizations" by Franz Boas, then an anthropology professor at Columbia University, and "The Contribution of the Negro to Human Civilization" by A. F. Chamberlain, did Hansberry finally find confirmation of his opinion that the modern march of progress owed much to Africa and her ancient societies. Later that year he found another source of support in the work of activist W. E. B. Du Bois. The first black scholar to gain a Ph.D. from Harvard University, Du Bois was well known nation-wide as a founder of the National Association for the Advancement of Colored People (NAACP) and editor of the NAACP's journal titled *The Crisis.*

Du Bois had also recently gained attention as the author of a new book called *The Negro.* A devoted follower of Du Bois' trailblazing work, Hansberry bought a copy of the new book and read it immediately. As he had hoped, Du Bois mentioned not only the Greek historian Herodotus, but also several Latin writers who had acknowledged the existence of Kushite, Ethiopian, and other sophisticated African kingdoms predating their own Roman Empire by centuries. Eagerly he rushed to the library to request each precious reference that Du Bois had cited. But Atlanta University was not equipped for detailed study of the more obscure antiquities. Its shelves offered a meager selection so disappointing to him that he decided to transfer to the best-equipped academic institution open to blacks that he could find. Two weeks into his sophomore year he left Atlanta to attend Harvard University in Cambridge, Massachusetts.

Hansberry arrived in Cambridge in February of 1917, and plunged immediately into the work that was to occupy him for the rest of his life. African archeology, anthropology, ethnology, and paleontology became the focus of his existence, with courses in the history of science providing a systematic backbone for future research. Yet, while he found encouragement and friendship from Dr. E. A. Hooton of Harvard's renowned Peabody Museum, he found little support for his conviction that indigenous African people had played the most important roles in the shaping of their own communities. Even at Harvard, he noted, the prevailing scholarly belief of the time was that the Africans who had made contributions to civilization were not blacks at all. Instead, it was thought that they, similar to the inhabitants of India, were members of predominantly brown races.

In 1921 Hansberry left Harvard with a bachelor's degree in anthropology and a burning determination to stamp out American ignorance of what was derogatorily known as the Dark Continent. As a first step he designed a flier called "Announcing an Effort to Promote the Study and Facilitate the Teaching of the Fundamentals of Negro Life and History." He mailed it to several black schools and colleges to express his interest in helping those institutions replace what he considered to be the dangerous revisionist history they were teaching. He wanted to encourage educators to teach black students about their real roots. He felt such instruction could lift students out of the humiliating bigotry that was a part of their lives, and give them some badly needed pride in their heritage.

Hansberry picked a good time to launch his project. A consciousness surrounding black-influenced culture was awakening, thanks to the emergence of the back-to-Africa movement of Marcus Garvey, the newly popular, black-inspired jazz music and dance scene, and the Harlem Renaissance period of talented writers and artists. Nevertheless, many white Americans who enjoyed these novel additions to their culture were unaware of the ancient African roots from which they sprang. Several recipients of Hansberry's flier conceded this point and offered him cordial invitations to visit their schools and colleges.

Among the invitations Hansberry received were three offers of long-term employment. One offer, which was impossible to pass up, came from Howard University. Situated just a stone's throw from the great Library of Congress in Washington, D.C., well entrenched on the educational front since 1867, and reasonably well funded, the university informed him that they were planning to expand their history curriculum by adding a new section on African studies. Howard added that a teaching post would soon be available if Hansberry chose to consider it.

Pausing only to honor a year-long teaching contract at Straight College in Atlanta, Hansberry arrived at Howard University in 1922, and quickly established three new courses. "Negro Peoples in the Cultures and Civilizations of Prehistoric and Proto-Historic Times" was a general survey, based partly on archeological and anthropological finds in Paleolithic and Neolithic cultures of Africa. "The Ancient Civilizations of Ethiopia" covered the present-day Sudan and Egyptian areas, while "The Civilization of West Africa in Medieval and Early Modern Times" moved the student ahead to the fifteenth century and beyond. Each of these programs was based on his profound belief that the earliest beginnings of higher human culture sprang not from Asia, as the prevailing theory of the time specified, but from Africa. His theory

proved vastly popular with Howard's history students, and by 1925 the department's new section of African Studies boasted upward of eight hundred undergraduates.

Hansberry's success did not bring universal approval, however. In fact, two distinguished faculty members went to then-Howard University president Stanley Durkee and accused Hansberry of endangering Howard's reputation by teaching subject matter for which he had no proof. As a result the university's board of trustees came perilously close to closing his program. To prevent this, Hansberry justified his opinions with a sheaf of detailed documents, among them a meticulously annotated bibliography he had amassed while chronicling the passing centuries of Africa's history. Arranged by subject, the list covered a dazzling array of primary sources ranging from the diaries of Roman travelers such as Pliny the Elder through the Amharic and Coptic accounts of the Middle Ages. His documents also included up-to-the-minute papers written by the modern Egyptologists responsible for the excavation of the tomb of Egyptian pharaoh King Tutankhamen in 1922. His list was an impressive achievement. Hansberry knew, however, that it was not enough to prove his academic integrity so he also took care to spell out for the board his long-term goal—to use these sources to produce a narrative, chronological history of ancient and medieval Africa. This effort to save his career, though diligent, was only moderately successful.

In the end, the Howard board of trustees rescinded its decision to discontinue African Studies, but refused to reinstate Hansberry's former financial support. His tainted status marred the rest of his thirty-plus years at Howard. As a little-respected member of the university faculty, he found reimbursements for classroom equipment suddenly unavailable. Study grants and work-related travel expenses became bureaucratically impossible to obtain. Even a hard-earned promotion was systematically denied him until 1938, when he was at last elevated to an assistant professorship. Still, he refused to let these problems intimidate him. Philosophically, he put the opposition down to public ignorance of the widely scattered and extremely technical sources he had used to reach his conclusions. Therefore, he set for himself the mammoth task of bringing the contents of his research out of arcane obscurity, so that anyone interested could understand what he was trying to achieve.

While the 1920s could be characterized as the direction-finding decade of Hansberry's career, the 1930s signaled a concern with his own continuing education. In 1932 he went back to Harvard University for a master's degree in anthropology and history, following up in 1936 to 1937 with further post-graduate study at the University of Chicago's renowned Oriental Institute. Next, he was awarded a two-year Rockefeller Foundation grant that enabled him to study at Oxford University in England. This small breakthrough proved temporary, however, for the grant was abruptly terminated without explanation after just one year. Hansberry chose to regard this unexpected free time as a bonus, attending European conferences and visiting museums, where he carried out in-depth studies of artifacts gathered by the Leakey family and other eminent scholars of the time.

Hansberry tried to get other financial grants that would support him while he furthered his research, but he was largely unsuccessful. Two possible reasons have been cited for this frustrating failure. The first may have been due to the general academic trend, which was still following the tenets of *A Study of History* by the influential Arnold Toynbee. First published in 1934, it expressed his blunt opinion that "the only primary race that has not made a creative contribution to any civilization is the Black Race," a view that stood unaltered on page 233 of a condensed 1962 edition, in proud defiance of the growing civil rights movement.

The second possible obstacle to grant money for Hansberry resulted from the new modus operandi of the universities that catered to African American students. The accreditation of these schools became a crucial issue in terms of both federal funding and the post-graduate opportunities open to their alumnae. For these reasons, these colleges became increasingly unwilling to employ faculty members who had not earned Ph.D. degrees. Lacking this tangible badge of academic excellence, Hansberry was at a competitive disadvantage when grant money was being awarded.

The situation seemed unfair. It was not as if Hansberry had not tried to fill this gap, as a supporting letter from his loyal Harvard mentor, Earnest Hooton, showed. "He [Hansberry] has been unable to take the Ph.D. degree . . . because . . . there is no university or institution that has manifested a really profound interest in this subject," wrote Hooton to the generous Rosenwald Foundation. He added, "no present day scholar has developed anything like the knowledge of this field that Hansberry has developed." Nevertheless, like several others, this grant did not materialize.

Stymied on two fronts, Hansberry was still an associate professor without tenure as World War II came to an end. But when the century-long colonial stranglehold on Africa began to loosen in the 1950s, his value to the university began to rise. Howard University had long been an educational leader with an international reputation, which made it a natural choice for black undergraduates coming to the United States to study. Now, as nationalism became a closer reality for many African countries and the need for an educated leadership increased, the numbers of foreign students escalated, adding to both Howard's coffers and its luster.

Unfortunately, not all the newcomers found this adventure to be a happy one. Many foreign students did not have enough money to live on. Most faced the challenges of fitting themselves into an educational and social system completely different from their own, and then transporting their new knowledge into the completely virgin territory of their homelands. Upon return to Africa, they then had to readjust socially, and fit their new cultural knowledge into their former indigenous setting.

Nobody understood these students' dilemma better Hansberry, who had studied their customs since his youth. His expertise now made him indispensable to the university authorities, who assigned him to the position of faculty advisor to African students in 1946, and followed up in 1950 by appointing him to Howard's Emergency Aid to the African Students' Committee. Quietly he took on these added responsibilities. For example, without benefit of secretarial help or typewriter, he wrote hundreds of letters and smoothed out emergencies. In one case, as requested, he even saw to it that the heart of a deceased undergraduate was excised and returned to his Nigerian homeland. Hansberry's proteges called him the "father of African students," and several made sure they kept in touch with him after graduation.

With the dawn of the U.S. civil rights movement in the 1950s, knowledge of African American roots became essential to Howard University. Finally, Hansberry's vast knowledge of Africa and her history became more valuable to the university than his role as the "father of African students." This may have been the reason why the Fulbright scholarship for 1953 was awarded to him, finally giving him the means to do fieldwork in Egypt, the Sudan, and Ethiopia, to deliver lectures requested by former students in many parts of Africa, and to serve as a team member on trips to Kenya, Uganda, and the mighty

Zimbabwe Ruins in what was then Southern Rhodesia. On the negative side however, in his absence, the Ford Foundation had awarded the university a grant to further its African Studies program, from which he had been excluded, despite his twenty-seven years of service.

It is not surprising that his retirement in 1959 brought Hansberry the first real distinction he had ever known. Free to travel as he wished, in 1960 Hansberry accepted an invitation by the government of Ghana to the ceremonies celebrating the establishment of the Republic. That same year, he also made a point of accepting an invitation to visit Nigeria when the country received its independence, and watched with pride as a former student named Nndami Azikiwe became that country's first president. Ties with Nigeria remained so close that Hansberry was on hand in 1963 as a distinguished visiting professor to inaugurate the Hansberry College of African Studies.

Hansberry took great pleasure in traveling until, in November, 1965, he died as a result of a cerebral hemorrhage while visiting relatives in Chicago. He never knew of the honor finally paid him by Howard University—a lecture hall bearing his name, dedicated in 1972 to mark his fifty years of association with the university's Department of History. Regardless, the great contributions he made to the historical study of African culture will live on to the benefit of all future generations.

BIOGRAPHICAL/CRITICAL SOURCES:

PERIODICALS

Current Bibliography on African Affairs, November/December, 1970, p. 25.
Daedalus, summer, 1971, p. 678.
Ebony, February, 1961, p. 62; October, 1964, p. 28.
Freedomways, second quarter, 1966, p. 161.
Negro History Bulletin, December, 1965, p. 63.*

*   *   *

HARPER, F. E. W.
    See HARPER, Frances Ellen Watkins

*   *   *

HARPER, Frances E. W.
    See HARPER, Frances Ellen Watkins

HARPER, Frances E. Watkins
    See HARPER, Frances Ellen Watkins

*   *   *

HARPER, Frances Ellen
    See HARPER, Frances Ellen Watkins

*   *   *

HARPER, Frances Ellen Watkins   1825-1911
    (F. E. W. Harper, Frances Ellen Harper, Frances E. W. Harper, Frances E. Watkins Harper, Mrs. F. E. W. Harper, Frances Ellen Watkins; Effie Afton, a pseudonym)

PERSONAL: Born September 24, 1825, in Baltimore, MD; died of heart failure, February 22, 1911, in Philadelphia, PA; buried at Eden Cemetery in Philadelphia; married Fenton Harper (a farmer), November 22, 1860 (died, May, 1864); children: Mary. *Education:* Educated in Baltimore, MD, and in Pennsylvania and Ohio. *Religion:* Unitarian.

CAREER: Writer, social reformer, and public lecturer. Worked as a nursemaid and domestic; Union Seminary, Columbus, OH, sewing teacher, 1850-52; elementary school teacher in Little York, PA, 1852-53; Underground Railroad worker in Little York, 1853-54; lecturer for Maine Anti-Slavery Society, 1854-56, and other organizations, 1856-60, and reader of antislavery verse; lecturer and poetry reader advocating freed-men's rights, Christian temperance, and women's suffrage, men's Christian Association (YMCA) Sabbath School, 1872; director of American Association of Education of Colored Youth, 1894. Associated with American Woman Suffrage Association conventions, 1875 and 1887; speaker at international Council of Women in Washington, 1888, National Council of Women, 1891, and World Congress of Representative Women at Columbian Exposition in Chicago, 1893.

MEMBER: National Council of Women in the United States, National Association of Colored Women (founding member, 1886; vice-president, 1897), National Women's Christian Temperance Union (executive committee member; superintendent of Philadelphia and Pennsylvania chapters of Colored Branch, 1875-

82; head of northern U.S. division, 1883-93), American Equal Rights Association.

WRITINGS:

(Under name Frances Ellen Watkins) *Forest Leaves* (also referred to as *Autumn Leaves;* poems and prose), [Baltimore, MD], c. 1845.

(Under name Frances Ellen Watkins) *Poems on Miscellaneous Subjects* (poems and essays), preface by William Lloyd Garrison, J. B. Yerrinton & Son (Boston, MA), 1854, reprinted, Kraus, 1971, enlarged edition, [Philadelphia, PA], 1855, 2nd enlarged edition, Merrihew & Thompson (Philadelphia), 1857, reprinted with new introduction by Maxwell Whiteman, Historic Publications, 1969, 20th edition, Merrihew & Son (Philadelphia), 1871.

(Under pseudonym Effie Afton) *Eventide* (poems and tales), Ferridge & Co. (Boston), 1854.

(Under name Mrs. F. E. W. Harper) *Moses: A Story of the Nile* (poems and essay), 2nd edition, Merrihew, 1869, 3rd edition, 1870, enlarged edition, [Philadelphia], 1889.

(Under name Frances E. Watkins Harper) *Poems,* Merrihew & Son, 1871, reprinted, AMS Press (New York City), 1975.

Poems on Miscellaneous Subjects, Merrihew & Thompson, 1857.

(Under name Frances E. Watkins Harper) *Sketches of Southern Life* (poems), George S. Ferguson (Philadelphia), 1891.

Light beyond the Darkness, Donohue & Henneberry (Chicago), [189?].

(Under name Frances E. W. Harper) *Iola Leroy; or, Shadows Uplifted* (novel), Garrigues Bros. (Philadelphia), 1892, 2nd edition, with introduction by William Still, James H. Earle, 1893, new introduction by Hazel V. Carby, Beacon Press (Boston), 1987, new introduction by Frances Smith Foster, Oxford University Press (New York City), 1988.

Enlightened Motherhood: An Address by Mrs. Frances E. W. Harper, Before the Brooklyn Literary Society, November 15th, 1892, The Society (Brooklyn), 1892.

(Under name Frances Ellen Harper) *Atlanta Offering: Poems* (contains *The Sparrow's Fall and Other Poems* and *The Martyr of Alabama and Other Poems*), George S. Ferguson, 1895, reprinted, Mnemosyne, 1969.

(Under name Frances E. Watkins Harper) *Poems,* George S. Ferguson, 1895, Books for Libraries, 1970, 2nd enlarged edition, [Philadelphia], 1900.

(Under name F. E. W. Harper) *Idylls of the Bible* (contains *Moses: A Story of the Nile*), [Philadelphia], 1901, reprinted, AMS Press, 1975.

(Annotator) John Bartram, *Diary of a Journey Through the Carolina, Georgia, and Florida, July 1, 1775—April 10, 1776,* Philosophical Society (Philadelphia), 1942.

The Poems of Frances E. W. Harper, Books for Libraries, 1970.

(Under name Frances E. Watkins Harper) *Poems,* AMS Press, 1975.

Complete Poems of Frances E.W. Harper, edited by Maryemma Graham, Oxford University Press, 1988.

A Brighter Coming Day: A Frances Ellen Watkins Harper Reader, edited and introduced by Frances Smith Foster, Feminist Press at the City University of New York (New York City), 1990.

Minnie's Sacrifice; Sowing and Reaping; Trial and Triumph: Three Rediscovered Novels, edited by Frances Smith Foster, Beacon Press, 1994.

Also author of poem collections *The Sparrow's Fall and Other Poems,* c. 1890, *The Martyr of Alabama and Other Poems,* c. 1894, and *Light Beyond Darkness,* Donohue & Henneberry (Chicago, IL). Poems and essays represented in anthologies and sociological/historical studies, including *The Black Man: His Antecedents, His Genius, and his Achievements,* edited by William Wells Brown, Hamilton/Wallcut, 1863; *The Negro Caravan,* edited by Sterling A. Brown, Arthur Davis, and Ulysses Lee, Dryden, 1941; *In Their Own Words: A History of the American Negro, 1619-1865,* edited by Milton Meltzer, Crowell, 1964; and *Kaleidoscope: Poems by American Negro Poets,* edited by Robert Hayden, Harcourt, 1967. Contributor to periodicals, including *African Methodist Episcopal Church Review, Anglo-African Magazine, Crisis, Englishwoman's Review, Frederick Douglass's Paper, Liberator,* and *National Anti- Slavery Standard.*

The largest collections of Harper's books and papers are housed at the Moorland-Spingarn Research Center at Howard University in Washington, DC, and at the Schomburg Center for Research in Black Culture at the New York Public Library.

SIDELIGHTS: Frances Ellen Watkins Harper was the outstanding black woman poet of the nineteenth century. Known as the "Bronze Muse" to her public, Harper captivated black and white audiences alike with dramatic recitations of her antislavery and social reform verse. Harper's verse was conventional lyric poetry with familiar themes and imagery; according to a contemporary, Phebe A. Hanaford in the *Daughters of America; or, Women of the Century,* it gained much from the orator/poets "clear, plaintive, melodious voice" and "the flow of her musical speech." Many critics have stated that the greatest significance of Harper's work is its social value, rather than its literary merit. She was a lecturer whose long life was devoted to abolition, freedmen's rights, Christian temperance, and women's suffrage. Harper used prose and poetry to enhance her message and stir audience emotions. "Mrs. Harper's verse is frankly propagandist, a metrical extension of her life dedicated to the welfare of others," Joan R. Sherman decided in *Invisible Poets: Afro-Americans of the Nineteenth Century.* "She believed in art for humanity's sake." "Her writing resonates with the social, moral, political, and racial causes to which she dedicated herself," added Meryemma Graham in *Dictionary of Literary Biography.*

Born of free parents in the slave state of Maryland, Harper was raised by an aunt and uncle after her parents' early deaths and educated at her uncle's school for free blacks. Her first job at thirteen was caring for the children of a bookseller; there she began writing, composing poems, and reading the popular literature of the period. Intent on living in a free state, Harper moved to Ohio, where she worked as a teacher.

The 1850 Fugitive Slave Act had greatly increased the number of slaves running North for freedom. After moving from Ohio to Little York, Pennsylvania, Harper became acquainted with the workings of the Underground Railroad. At about the same time, her home state of Maryland passed a law denying free blacks from the North to enter the state. If they did, they could be seized and sold into slavery. Harper and all others in her situation immediately became exiles. One free black man who reentered his native Maryland was captured and sold. He attempted to escape while being shipped down the Mississippi, was recaptured, cruelly treated, and eventually died of overwork and exposure. Hearing of this incident charged Harper with the determination to leave teaching behind and devote herself to the cause of social justice. She wrote to a friend: "Upon that grave I pledged myself to the Anti-Slavery cause."

Harper's first abolitionist speech was a marked success; preaching social and political reform and moral betterment, Harper spent the next several years lecturing for antislavery societies throughout the North

and included readings from her *Poems on Miscellaneous Subjects.* The poet's most popular book, the collection sold several thousand copies and saw at least twenty editions. Containing her most-acclaimed abolitionist poem, "Bury Me in a Free Land," it firmly established Harper's literary reputation.

Thought to resemble the poetry of Henry Wadsworth Longfellow, John Greenleaf Whittier, and Felicia Dorothea Hemans, Harper's largely narrative verse uses rhymed tetrameter and the ballad stanza, both "well suited to some of her material" and creating "an excellent elocutionary patter," commented J. Saunders Redding in *To Make a Poet Black.* Emotionally charged and frequently didactic (with authorial intrusions), the poems mirrored the conventions of the day and were tailored to Harper's social intent and to audience expectations. Varying little in form, language, or technique, the verse is simple, direct, and lyrical. Writing in *Drumvoices: The Mission of Afro-American Poetry,* Eugene B. Redmond observed: "Up until the Civil War, Mrs. Harper's favorite themes were slavery, its harshness, and the hypocrisies of America. She is careful to place graphic details where they will get the greatest result, especially when the poems are read aloud." He continued: "Critics generally agree that Mrs. Harper's poetry is not original or brilliant. But she is exciting and comes through with powerful flashes of imagery and statement."

Married to a farmer when she was thirty-five, Harper retired from public life and bore a child but soon returned to lecturing when she was widowed. Following the Civil War she traveled south for the first time and was appalled by the unfair treatment of freed blacks; she saw flagrant voting rights violations, meager educational opportunities, and overt physical abuse. Particularly stirred by the plight of black women—whose subjection had not only continued, but had grown worse with emancipation—the poet determined that "a free people could be a moral people only when the women were respected," according to Larsen Scruggs, quoted in an article in *Black American Literature Forum,* and Harper appealed to women of all colors to work towards social equality. For the remaining decades of her life, Harper spoke and wrote for social and reform organizations that supported her ideals of racial justice, women's rights, and Christian humanism; her notable posts included director of the American Association of Education of Colored Youth, executive member of the National Women's Christian Temperance Union, and founding member and vice-president of the National Association of Colored Women.

Redding maintained that by addressing a spectrum of social ills in her writings, Harper broke free of the "willful (and perhaps necessary) monopticism" that had confined other black authors. "If our talents are to be recognized we must write less of issues that are particular and more of feelings that are general," the poet once acknowledged to an editor acquaintance, Redding related. "We are blessed with hearts and brains that compass more than ourselves in our present plight." Sherman, too, saw Harper as an innovator who combined race issues with national and universal concerns, inspiring succeeding black writers. Like the majority of critics, Sherman also proclaimed Harper's post-Civil War verse "more objective and intellectual" and informed with a strong optimism.

The poet breaks with conventional meter and sentiment, creating a correspondence between subject and technique, in *Moses: A Story of the Nile,* considered her best work. This volume is an extended blank-verse biblical allegory without overt racial references; recounting the life of the Hebrew patriarch and focusing on his leadership and self-sacrifice, Harper urges similar leadership and sacrifice among blacks. "The poem's elevated diction, concrete imagery, and formal meter harmoniously blend to magnify the noble adventure of Moses' life and the mysterious grandeur of his death," related Sherman, discussing the work's artistic merits. "Mrs. Harper maintains the pace of her long narrative and its tone of reverent admiration with scarcely a pause for moralizing. *Moses* is Mrs. Harper's most original poem and one of considerable power."

Referring to a second critically praised Harper work, Sherman added that the poet "shows a similar talent for matching technique and subject in the charming series of poems which make up most of *Sketches of Southern Life.*" Narrated by politically aware ex-slaves Aunt Chloe and Uncle Jacob, the poems provide a commentary on the concerns of southern blacks: family, education, religion, slavery, and Reconstruction. Admired for their wit and irony, the narratives are written in Afro-American vernacular speech—"a new idiom in black poetry," Sherman elaborated, "which ripens into the dialect verse of [James Edwin] Campbell, [Daniel Webster] Davis, and [Paul Laurence] Dunbar in the last decades of the century." "Serious issues sketched with a light touch are rare in Mrs. Harper's work," the critic added, "and it is unfortunate that Aunt Chloe's fresh and lively observations were not enlarged."

A writer of prose as well as poetry, Harper produced essays, articles, short stories, and a novel. "Her prose is frankly propagandic," remarked Redding, joining the consensus that the writer's prose is "less commendable" than her poetry. Harper's reform essays and articles appeared frequently in journals and periodicals, however, and her short story "The Two Offers" was the first to be published by a black American. In addition, her novel *Iola Leroy; or Shadows Uplifted* pleased contemporary readers and critics, although current assessments consider it a contrived and sentimental piece unable to transcend the conventions of its age. The story of light-skinned Negroes who reject "passing" as whites in order to work and live among their people, *Iola Leroy* expresses its author's belief that sacrifice is essential to black progress. Considered a transitional novel because it treats both antebellum and post-bellum periods, the story is particularly significant for featuring educated, socially committed black characters. Redding concluded that "as a writer of prose [Harper] is to be remembered rather for what she attempted than for what she accomplished."

A figure of more historic than artistic importance, Harper has sparked renewed interest among later twentieth-century scholars. Described variously as an early feminist, one of the first African American protest poets, and—in the words of *Black American Literature Forum* writer Patricia Liggins Hill—"a major healer and race-builder of nineteenth-century America," Harper nonetheless made aesthetic contributions of pioneer significance. In a *Crises* editorial following the poet's death, W. E. B. DuBois reflected: "It is, however, for her attempts to forward literature among colored people, that Frances Harper deserves most to be remembered. She was not a great singer, but she had some sense of song; she was not a great writer, but she wrote must worth reading. She was, above all, sincere. She took her writing soberly and earnestly; she gave her life to it."

BIOGRAPHICAL/CRITICAL SOURCES:

BOOKS

Barksdale, Richard and Kenneth Kinnamon, *Black Writers of America: A Comprehensive Anthology,* Macmillan (New York City), 1972.

Bell, Roseann P. and others, editors, *Sturdy Black Bridges: Visions of Black Women in Literature,* Anchor Books (New York City), 1979.

Black Literature Criticism, Gale (Detroit), 1992.

Bone, Robert, *The Negro Novel in America,* revised edition, Yale University Press (New Haven, CT), 1965.

Boyd, Melba Joyce, *Discarded Legacy: Politics and Poetics in the Life of Frances E.W. Harper,* Wayne State University Press (Detroit, MI), 1994.

Brawley, Benjamin, *The Negro in Literature and Art in the United States,* Duffield, 1929.

Brown, Hallie Q., *Homespun Heroines and Other Women of Distinction,* Aldine (Hawthorne, NY), 1926.

Carby, Hazel V., *Reconstructing Womanhood: The Emergence of the Afro-American Woman Novelist,* Oxford University Press, 1987.

Christian, Barbara, *Black Feminist Criticism: The Development of a Tradition, 1892-1976,* Greenwood Press (Westport, CT), 1980.

Christian, Barbara, *Black Feminist Criticism: Perspectives of Black Women Writers,* Pergamon (Elmsford, NY), 1985.

Christian, Barbara, *Black Women Novelists: The Development of a Tradition, 1892-1976,* Greenwood Press, 1980.

Dannett, Sylvia G. L., *Profiles of Negro Womanhood: Volume I: 1619-1900,* M. W. Lads, 1964.

Dictionary of Literary Biography, Volume 50: *Afro-American Writers before the Harlem Renaissance,* Gale, 1986.

"Doers of the Word": African-American Women Speakers and Writers in the North (1830-1880), Oxford University Press, 1995.

Foster, Frances Smith, *A Brighter Coming Day: A Frances Ellen Watkins Harper Reader,* Feminist Press at City University of New York (New York City), 1990.

Foster, Frances Smith, *Written by Herself: Literary Production by African American Women, 1746-1892,* Indiana University Press (Bloomington, IN), 1993.

Giddings, Paula, *When and Where I Entered: The Impact of Black Women on Race and Sex in America,* Morrow (New York City), 1984.

Gloster, Hugh M., *Negro Voices in American Fiction,* University of North Carolina Press (Chapel Hill, NC), 1948.

Goldstein, Rhoda L., *Black Life and Culture in the United States,* Crowell (New York City), 1971.

Hanaford, Phebe A., *Daughters of America: or, Women of the Century,* B. B. Russell, 1882.

Kerlin, Robert T., *Negro Poets and Their Poems,* Associated Publishers (White Plains, NY), 1923, revised third edition, 1935.

Loggins, Vernon, *The Negro Author: His Development in America,* Columbia University Press (New York City), 1931.

Lowenberg, Bert James and Ruth Bogin, *Black Women in Nineteenth-Century American Life: Their Words, Their Thoughts, Their Feelings,* Pennsylvania State University Press (University Park, PA), 1976.

Majors, M. A., *Noted Negro Women: Their Triumphs and Activities,* Donohue & Henneberry, 1893.

The Negro Genius: A New Appraisal of the Achievement of the American Negro in Literature and the Fine Arts, Dodd (New York City), 1937.

O'Connor, Lillian, *Pioneer Women Orators,* Columbia University Press, 1954.

The Pen Is Ours: A Listing of Writings by and about African-American Women before 1910 with Secondary Bibliography to the Present, Oxford University Press (New York City), 1991.

Poetry Criticism, Volume 21, Gale, 1998.

Redding, J. Saunders, *To Make a Poet Black,* University of North Carolina Press, 1939.

Redmond, Eugene B., *Drumvoices: The Mission of Afro American Poetry, A Critical History,* Anchor/Doubleday, 1976.

Reference Guide to American Literature, St. James Press (Detroit), 1994.

Richings, G. F., *Evidences of Progress among Colored People,* George S. Ferguson, 1896, AFRO-AM Press, 1969.

Robinson, William H., Jr., editor, *Early Black American Poets: Selections With Biographical and Critical Introductions,* W. C. Brown, 1969.

Scruggs, Lawson A., *Women of Distinction,* L. A. Scruggs (Raleigh, NC), 1893.

Sherman, Joan R., *Invisible Poets: Afro-Americans of the Nineteenth Century,* University of Illinois Press (Urbana), 1974.

Sillen, Samuel, *Women against Slavery,* Masses & Mainstream, 1955.

Still, William Grant, *The Underground Railroad,* Porter & Coates (Philadelphia), 1872, reprinted, Arno/New York Times (New York City), 1968.

Twentieth-Century Literary Criticism, Volume 14, Gale, 1984.

Wagner, Jean, *Black Poets of the United States from Paul Laurence Dunbar to Langston Hughes,* translation by Kenneth Douglas, University of Illinois Press, 1973.

Whiteman, Maxwell, *A Century of Fiction by American Negroes, 1853-1952: A Descriptive Bibliography,* Albert Saifer, 1955.

Williams, Kenny J., *They Also Spoke: An Essay on Negro Literature in America, 1787-1930,* Townsend, 1970.

Woodson, Carter G. and Charles H. Wesley, *The Negro in Our History,* Associated Publishers, 1922.

PERIODICALS

African Methodist Episcopal Church Review, April, 1892.
Anglo-Saxon Magazine, May, 1859.
Black American Literature Forum, summer, 1981, pp. 60-65.
Black World, December, 1972.
Crisis, April, 1911.
Jet, February 23, 1961; February 24, 1966.
Journal of Negro History, October, 1917.
Legacy, spring, 1988.
Massachusetts Review, winter/spring, 1972.
Messenger, February, 1927.
Nation, February, 1893.
Negro History Bulletin, December, 1938; January, 1942.
Pennsylvania Magazine of History & Biography, No. 1, 1989, pp. 21-43.

OTHER

Daniel, Theodora Williams, *The Poems of Frances E. W. Harper* (masters thesis), Howard University, 1937.
Graham, Maryemma, *The Threefold Cord: Blackness, Womanness, and Art: A Study of the Life and Work of Frances Ellen Watkins Harper* (masters thesis), Cornell University, 1973.
Montgomery, Janey Weinhold, *A Comparative Analysis of the Rhetoric of Two Negro Women Orators: Sojourner Truth and Frances E. Watkins Harper* (masters thesis), Fort Hays Kansas State College, 1968.*

*   *   *

HARPER, Mrs. F. E. W.
   See HARPER, Frances Ellen Watkins

*   *   *

HARRIS, (Theodore) Wilson 1921-
   (Kona Waruk)

PERSONAL: Born March 24, 1921, in New Amsterdam, British Guiana (now Guyana); immigrated to England, 1959; son of Theodore Wilson (an insurer and underwriter) and Millicent Josephine (Glasford) Harris; married Cecily Carew, 1945 (divorced); married Margaret Nimmo Burns (a writer), April 2, 1959. *Education:* Queen's College, Georgetown, British Guiana, 1934-39; studied land surveying and geomorphology under government auspices, 1939-42.

ADDRESSES: Home—London, England. *Office*—c/o Faber & Faber, 3 Queen Sq., London WC1N 3AU, England.

CAREER: British Guiana Government, assistant government surveyor, 1942-44, government surveyor, 1944-54, senior surveyor, 1955-58; full-time writer in London, England, 1958—. Visiting lecturer, State University of New York at Buffalo, 1970, Yale University, 1970; guest lecturer, Mysore University (India), 1978; regents' lecturer, University of California, 1983. Writer-in-residence, University of West Indies, 1970, University of Toronto, 1970, Newcastle University, Australia, 1979, University of Queensland, Australia, 1986. Visiting professor, University of Texas at Austin, 1972, 1981-82, and 1983, University of Aarhus, Denmark, 1973, and in Cuba. Delegate for U.N. Educational, Scientific, and Cultural Organization (UNESCO) symposium in Cuba on Caribbean literature, 1968, and National Identity Conference in Brisbane, Australia, 1968.

AWARDS, HONORS: English Arts Council grants, 1968 and 1970; Commonwealth fellow at University of Leeds, 1971; Guggenheim fellow, 1972-73; Henfield writing fellow at University of East Anglia, 1974; Southern Arts fellow, Salisbury, 1976; D.Litt., University of West Indies, 1984; Guyana Prize for Fiction, 1985-87; D.Litt., University of Kent at Canterbury, 1988.

WRITINGS:

FICTION

Palace of the Peacock (first novel in "Guyana Quartet"; also see below), Faber (London), 1960.
The Far Journey of Oudin (second novel in "Guyana Quartet"; also see below), Faber, 1961.
The Whole Armour (third novel in "Guyana Quartet"; also see below), Faber, 1962.
The Secret Ladder (fourth novel in "Guyana Quartet"; also see below), Faber, 1963.
The Whole Armour [and] *The Secret Ladder,* Faber, 1963.
Heartland, Faber, 1964.

The Eye of the Scarecrow, Faber, 1965.
The Waiting Room, Faber, 1967.
Tamatumari, Faber, 1968.
Ascent to Omai, Faber, 1970.
The Sleepers of Roraima (short stories), Faber, 1970.
The Age of the Rainmakers (short stories), Faber, 1971.
Black Marsden: A Tabula Rasa Comedy, Faber, 1972.
Companions of the Day and Night, Faber, 1975.
Da Silva da Silva's Cultivated Wilderness [and] *Genesis of the Clowns* (also see below), Faber, 1977.
Genesis of the Clowns, Faber, 1978.
The Tree of the Sun, Faber, 1978.
The Angel at the Gate, Faber, 1982.
The Guyana Quartet (boxed set), Faber, 1985.
Carnival (first novel in "Carnival" trilogy; also see below), Faber, 1985.
The Infinite Rehearsal (second novel in "Carnival" trilogy; also see below), Faber, 1987.
The Four Banks of the River of Space (third novel in "Carnival" trilogy; also see below), Faber, 1990.
Resurrection at Sorrow Hill, Faber, 1993.
The Carnival Trilogy, Faber, 1993.
Jonestown, Faber, 1996.

POETRY

(Under pseudonym Kona Waruk) *Fetish,* privately printed (Georgetown, British Guiana [now Guyana]), 1951.
The Well and the Land, [British Guiana], 1952.
Eternity to Season, privately printed (Georgetown, British Guiana), 1954, second edition, New Beacon (London), 1978.

OTHER

Tradition and the West Indian Novel (lecture), New Beacon, 1965.
Tradition, the Writer and Society: Critical Essays, New Beacon, 1967.
History, Fable and Myth in the Caribbean and Guianas (booklet), National History and Arts Council (Georgetown, Guyana), 1970.
Fossil and Psyche (criticism), African and American Studies and Research Center, University of Texas (Austin), 1974.
Explorations: A Series of Talks and Articles, 1966-1981, edited with an introduction by Hena Maes-Jelinek, Dangaroo Press (Aarhus, Denmark), 1981.
The Womb of Space: The Cross-Cultural Imagination (criticism), Greenwood Press (Westport, CT), 1983.

The Radical Imagination (essays, lectures, and interview), edited by Alan Riach and Mark Williams, University of Liege (Liege, Belgium), 1991.

Contributor to anthologies, including *Caribbean Rhythms,* 1974, and *Critics on Caribbean Literature,* 1978; contributor to periodicals, including *Literary Half-Yearly, Kyk-over-al,* and *New Letters.*

SIDELIGHTS: The novels of Wilson Harris incorporate philosophy, poetic imagery, symbolism, and myth, creating new and unique visions of reality. His fiction shows the reader a world where the borders between physical and spiritual reality, life and death, have become indistinguishable. In *World Literature Today,* Richard Sander states that Harris has "realized a new, original form of the novel that in almost all respects constitutes a radical departure from the conventional novel." Reed Way Dasenbrock, also writing in *World Literature Today,* claims that Harris "has always operated at a very high level of abstraction, higher than any of his fellow West Indian novelists, higher perhaps than any other contemporary novelist in English. . . . And whether one regards Harris's evolution as a rich and exciting development or a one-way trip down an abstractionist cul-de-sac, there is no denying his unique vision or dedication to that vision." The use of abstraction has brought Harris both praise and criticism; while some regard his work as challenging and rewarding, others find his unorthodox methods alienate the reader.

Harris is perhaps best known for the four novels in his "Guyana Quartet"—*Palace of the Peacock, The Far Journey of Oudin, The Whole Armour,* and *The Secret Ladder. Palace of the Peacock* begins the journey of the narrator and his brother, Donne, through Guyana. The narrator and his brother represent opposites in a novel wherein paradox and allegory play central roles. As the two brothers and their attendants continue their journey through the remainder of the novel, they meet with obstacles that often lead to death, a necessary prequel to the rebirth of the psyche that serves as Harris's central focus. In *The Whole Armour,* the restoration of life provides the basis for Harris's story, as a young man named Cristo flees in the face of an accusation of murder, destined to live on in the form of his yet unborn child as his temporal form is captured and condemned to death.

Important to all four works of the quartet is the landscape of Guyana, which Harris came to know well during his years as a government surveyor. Hena Maes-Jelinek writes in *West Indian Literature,* "Two major elements seem to have shaped Harris's approach to art and his philosophy of existence: the impressive contrasts of the Guyanese landscapes . . . and the successive waves of conquest which gave Guyana its heterogeneous population polarised for centuries into oppressors and their victims." Furthermore, she comments, "The two, landscape and history, merge in his work into single metaphors symbolising man's inner space saturated with the effects of historical—that is, temporal—experiences."

The plots of Harris's works are frequently difficult for critics to summarize since they are comprised of events, dreams, hallucinations, and psychic experiences, which are frequently not clearly distinguished from one another. In addition, time in Harris's works is often nonlinear. Such works move so far from the accepted definition of a novel that critics are often compelled to invent a genre in order to discuss them. Michael Thorpe in *World Literature Today* calls the author's more recent books "psychical 'expeditions'." And an *Encounter* contributor describes Harris's work as "a metaphysical shorthand on the surface of a narrative whose point cannot readily be grasped by any but those thoroughly versed in his previous work and able at once to recognise the recurrent complex metaphors."

Many reviewers note that to fully appreciate Harris's work the reader must be familiar with his metaphors, since the elaborately written passages and complex symbolism can make the writing nearly impenetrable for readers accustomed to more traditional fiction. A *Times Literary Supplement* contributor warns, "no reader should attempt Mr. Harris's novels unless he is willing to work at them." But according to Jean-Pierre Durix, also a *Times Literary Supplement* contributor, the reader who stays with Harris is rewarded by his "dense style and meticulous construction, his attention to visual and rhythmic effects, [which] are matched by an inventiveness which few contemporary novelists can equal."

Another Harris achievement is his "Carnival" trilogy, which encompasses *Carnival* (1985), *The Infinite Rehearsal* (1987), and *The Four Banks of the River of Space* (1990). *Carnival* one of Harris's lengthiest works, is a reconstruction of the life and death of Everyman Masters, a South American plantation owner who eventually moves to England, meeting the narrator, Jonathan Weyl, aboard ship during that trip. Accounts of violent interactions, witnessed by Masters, that often involve the exploitation of women by men, and the interplay of memory and remembrance,

are scattered throughout the novel, making the novel almost a summary of Harris's earlier prose works. *The Infinite Rehearsal,* a fictional autobiography of Robin Redbreast Glass, is more reflective, as the author intersperses scenes from earlier novels with reflection and what *Dictionary of Literary Biography* essayist Jean-Pierre Durix calls "literary memories" of such diverse writers as T. S. Eliot, James Joyce, Samuel Beckett, Robert Burns, Joseph Conrad, and Shakespeare. "The fictional text progresses through metaphoric echoes, side plots, and paradoxes in a constant revisionary process that precludes the possibility of any final statement," Durix adds. Explaining Harris's oeuvre as "attempt[ing] to offer a radical methodology whereby postcolonial societies can create their own cultures through a return to myth," A. L. McLeod maintains in *World Literature Today* that *The Infinite Rehearsal* "comprises all of Harris's idiosyncratic approaches to narrative, exposition, and thematic development."

In the trilogy's final volume, *The Four Banks of the River of Space,* Harris's protagonist is Anselm, a Guyanese land surveyor who functions as the author's alter ego. Anselm searches for God through a series of dreams. Once again an exploration of the past, *The Four Banks* is both a journey of rediscovery for the protagonist and a thematic reworking of several of Harris's earlier works. Characteristically complex and demanding, the entire trilogy has been praised for its poetic prose style and has been compared to Homer's *Odyssey.* Brian Morton concludes in his essay for *Listener* that Harris is "difficult, often maddeningly so, but he is also funny and humane, and he really must be read."

Resurrection at Sorrow Hill, which Harris published in 1993, is characterized by *New Statesman & Society* reviewer Brian Morton as "perhaps the nearest thing [Harris] will ever write to a developed novel of manners and psychology." Set in a mental asylum whose patients—imitating Montezuma, Leonardo da Vinci, Socrates, Buddha, and Karl Marx, they are symbols of some of the world's greatest cultures—act out parables of the problems that have repeatedly plagued mankind's existence. A love affair between patients Hope and Butterfly that is brought to an end by the shooting attack on the lovers by Butterfly's jealous lover, Christopher D'eath, can be read as "the sacrifice of innocence to meaningless violence," according to Abdulrazak Gurnah in the *Times Literary Supplement.* Other issues surface, including the relationship between guilt and conscience, the transformative power of knowledge, and the ceaseless battle between faith in the future and nihilism. Gurnah comments that in *Resurrection at Sorrow Hill,* Harris's "metaphors come heavily laden, and his narrative, though full of striking images and phrases, is constructed from a language which is obstinate and difficult." However, Stephen Breslow argues in *World Literature Today* that the novel's prose is its strongest attraction. "Like Joyce's, Harris's prose is difficult reading," admits Breslow, "yet tremendously stimulating to the pertinacious reader who can cast aside all desire for realism and can take the time to savor many rich new conceptual flavors exuded phrase by phrase, sentence by sentence, stirred by the hand of a master poetic chef."

In his 1996 novel, *Jonestown,* Harris turns his unique gifts to the one recent event that comes to the minds of people all over the world whenever the land of Guyana is mentioned, the Jonestown Massacre. Jonestown conjures up images of the more than nine hundred followers of the messianic Jim Jones lying face down in the cult's compound, poisoned by the grape kool-aid distributed to them. Jones himself lay dead with a gunshot in his head. "Harris transforms the banner headline of Jonestown into something rich and strange, weaving a new pattern from ancient and contemporary threads," writes Paula Burnett in the *New Statesman and Society.* In a story that follows two survivors of Jonestown, Harris combines threads from this twentieth-century tragedy with threads from the fall of the Maya in pre-Columbian times. Through these survivors, two of Jim Jones's lieutenants, Harris explores the themes of death and hope that emerge from both the historic and modern tragedies. "Harris entwines these two paths, of nemesis and imaginative insight," observes Burnett. "Thought and action, life and death, are turned inside out like a sleeve. He calls Jones 'Jonah,'" continues the reviewer, "making him an inverted Christ . . . and a tragic figure like *Moby Dick*'s hero." Burnett concludes, "Readers interested in mind-altering substances, without a rainforest to hand, could find a session with *Jonestown* a truly consciousness-raising experience."

In addition to his fiction, Harris has also written several studies in literary criticism. In *The Womb of Space,* he expands upon many of the ideas expressed in his novels. Harris's goal in the work is to establish parallels between writers of various cultural backgrounds. He observes in *The Womb of Space* that "literature is still constrained by regional and other conventional but suffocating categories." His vision is of a new world community, based on cultural hetero-geneity, not homogeneity, which, "as a cultural model, exercised by a ruling ethnic group, tends to become an organ of conquest and division because of imposed unity that actually subsists on the suppression of others." Sander believes that *The Womb of Space* is "an attack on the traditional critical establishment." A *Choice* contributor agrees, claiming, "*The Womb of Space* issues a direct challenge to the intellectual provincialism that often characterises literary study in the U.S." In his literary theory as well as in his fictional works, some critics find Harris's ideas difficult to discern. For instance, Steven G. Kellman writes in *Modern Fiction Studies,* "I take it that Wilson Harris' theme is the ability of consciousness to transcend a particular culture. But his articulation of that theme is so turgid, so beset by mixed and obscure metaphors and by syntactical convolutions that much of the book simply remains unintelligible even to a sympathetic reader." However, *Choice* elected *The Womb of Space* as the best critical study published in 1983.

This degree of difficulty is recognized in all of Harris's works, be they fiction or nonfiction. Yet, as Alan Riach explains in *Contemporary Novelists:* "Harris is a visionary, and his work is the complex literary expression of a vision which offers redemptive hope. For Harris," Riach continues, "creativity is an intrinsic value in all the forms taken by the expressions of the intuitive imagination. Harris's prose is not seductively mimetic, like that of a realist novel. Rather," notes the critic, "it demands concentrated attention through continual disclosures of its own ambivalence." For all these reasons, Harris's works continue to draw praise from many critics who believe he has made a significant contribution to our understanding of art and consciousness. John Hearne writes in *The Islands in Between,* "No other British Caribbean novelist has made quite such an explicitly and conscious effort as Harris to reduce the material reckonings of everyday life to the significance of myth." And speaking of the breadth of Harris's work, Louis James states in the *Times Literary Supplement,* "The novels of Wilson Harris . . . form one ongoing whole. Each work is individual; yet the whole sequence can be seen as a continuous, ever-widening exploration of civilization and creative art."

Harris once remarked that he has "moved away from the framework of the conventional novel and sought a different architecture of the Imagination and of space within an endangered, biased world, that is still susceptible to cross-cultural capacities and to subtle, dramatic, far-reaching, testing changes within a civilisation in dialogue with changes in reality reflected in quantum physics, quantum mechanics, and chaos theory." Jean-Pierre Durix characterizes the author's works thus: "Wilson Harris is a modern version of the Renaissance humanist: his concern as an artist bears on all aspects of life, and, in his style of expression, he transcends all notions of genre. . . . His respect for the complexity of his art is only equalled by his faith in the reader's intelligence."

BIOGRAPHICAL/CRITICAL SOURCES:

BOOKS

Baugh, Edward, editor, *Critics on Caribbean Literature: Readings in Literary Criticism,* St. Martin's (New York City), 1978.

Contemporary Literary Criticism, Volume 25, Gale (Detroit), 1983.

Contemporary Novelists, 6th edition, St. James Press (Detroit), 1996.

Dictionary of Literary Biography, Volume 117: *Twentieth-Century Caribbean and Black African Writers, First Series,* Gale, 1992.

Drake, Sandra E., *Wilson Harris and the Modern Tradition: A New Architecture of the World,* Greenwood Press (Westport, CT), 1986.

Gilkes, Michael, *The Literate Imagination,* Macmillan (London), 1989

Gilkes, Michael, *The West Indian Novel,* Twayne (Boston), 1981.

Gilkes, Michael, *Wilson Harris and the Caribbean Novel,* .Longmans, 1975.

Griffiths, Gareth, *A Double Exile,* Boyars (London), p. 171.

Harris, Wilson, *The Tree of the Sun,* Faber, 1978.

Harris, Wilson, *The Womb of Space: The Cross-Cultural Imagination,* Greenwood Press, 1983.

James, Louis, editor, *The Islands in Between,* Oxford University Press, 1968.

Maes-Jelinek, Hena, *The Naked Design,* Dangaroo Press, 1976.

Maes-Jelinek, Hena, *Wilson Harris,* Twayne, 1982.

Munro, Ian, and Reinhard Sander, editors, *Kas-Kas: Interviews with Three Caribbean Writers in Texas,* African and Afro-American Research Institute, University of Texas at Austin, 1972.

Wilson Harris: The Uncompromising Imagination, Dangaroo Press, 1991.

Webb, Barbara J., *Myth and History in Caribbean Fiction: Alejo Carpentier, Wilson Harris, and Edouard Glissant,* University of Massachusetts Press (Amherst), 1992.

PERIODICALS

Canadian Literature, summer, 1992, p. 195.

Choice, March, 1984.

Encounter, May, 1987.

Journal of Commonwealth Literature, July, 1969, p. 20; June, 1971, p. 113; April, 1979, p. 71; Volume 22, number 1, 1987, p. 87; Volume 24, number 1, 1989, p. 88.

Listener, September, 1990.

Modern Fiction Studies, summer, 1984.

New Statesman & Society September 7, 1990, pp. 46-47; November 12, 1993, p. 39; July 12, 1996, p. 48.

Observer, July 7, 1985.

Publishers Weekly, February 7, 1994, p. 73.

Quill and Quire, October, 1985.

Spectator, March 25, 1978.

Times Literary Supplement, December 9, 1965; July 4, 1968; May 21, 1970; October 10, 1975; May 25, 1977; May 19, 1978; October 15, 1982; July 12, 1985; September 25-October 1, 1987; November 12, 1993, p. 22.

World Literature Today, winter, 1984; summer, 1985; spring, 1986; summer, 1988, pp. 498-99; winter, 1995.

*   *   *

HASKINS, James
  See HASKINS, James S.

*   *   *

HASKINS, James S. 1941-
  (Jim Haskins, James Haskins)

PERSONAL: Born September 19, 1941, in Demopolis, AL; son of Henry and Julia (Brown) Haskins. *Education:*Georgetown University, B.A. (psychology), 1960; Alabama State University, B.S. (history), 1962; University of New Mexico, M.A. (social psychology), 1963; graduate study at New School for Social Research, 1965-67, and Queens College of the City University of New York, 1968-70.

ADDRESSES: Home—325 West End Ave., Apt. 7D, New York, NY 10023. *Office*—Department of English, University of Florida, Gainesville, FL 32611.

CAREER: Smith Barney & Co., New York, NY, stock trader, 1963-65; New York City Board of Education, New York City, teacher, 1966-68; New School for Social Research, New York City, visiting lecturer, 1970-72; Staten Island Community College of the City University of New York, Staten Island, NY, associate professor, 1970-77; University of Florida, Gainesville, professor of English, 1977—. New York *Daily News,* reporter, 1963-64. Visiting lecturer at Elisabeth Irwin High School, 1971-73, Indiana University/Purdue University—Indianapolis, 1973-76, and College of New Rochelle, 1977. Director, Union Mutual Life, Health and Accident Insurance, 1970-73; member of board of directors, Psi Systems, 1971-72, and Speedwell Services for Children, 1974-76. Member of Manhattan Community Board No. 9, 1972-73, academic council for the State University of New York, 1972-74, New York Urban League Manhattan Advisory Board, 1973-75, and National Education Advisory Committee and vice director of Southeast Region of Statue of Liberty—Ellis Island Foundation, 1985-86. Consultant, Education Development Center, 1975—, Department of Health, Education and Welfare, 1977-79, Ford Foundation, 1977-78, National Research Council, 1979-80, and Grolier, Inc., 1979-82. Member of National Education Advisory Committee, Commission on the Bicentennial of the Constitution, 1987-92.

MEMBER: National Book Critics Circle, Authors League of America, Authors Guild, New York Urban League, 100 Black Men, Civitas, Phi Beta Kappa, Kappa Alpha Psi.

AWARDS, HONORS: Notable children's book in the field of social studies citations from *Social Education,* 1971, for *Revolutionaries: Agents of Change,* from *Social Studies,* 1972, for *Resistance: Profiles in Nonviolence* and *Profiles in Black Power,* and 1973, for *A Piece of the Power: Four Black Mayors,* from National Council for the Social Studies—Children's Book Council book review committee, 1975, for *Fighting Shirley Chisholm,* and 1976, for *The Creoles of Color of New Orleans* and *The Picture Life of Malcolm X,* and from Children's Book Council, 1978, for *The Life and Death of Martin Luther King, Jr.;* World Book Year Book literature for children citation, 1973, for *From Lew Alcindor to Kareem Abdul Jabbar;* Books of the Year citations, Child Study Association of America, 1974, for *Adam Clayton Powell: Portrait of a Marching Black* and *Street Gangs: Yesterday and Today;* Books for Brotherhood bibliography citation, National Council of Christians and Jews book review committee, 1975, for *Adam Clayton Powell;* Spur Award finalist, Western Writers of America, 1975, for *The Creoles of Color of New Orleans;* Coretta Scott King Award, and children's choice citation, Children's Book Council, both 1977, both for *The Story of Stevie Wonder;* Carter G. Woodson Outstanding Merit Award, National Council for the Social Studies, 1980, for *James Van DerZee: The Picture Takin' Man;* Deems Taylor Award, American Society of Composers, Authors and Publishers, 1980, for *Scott Joplin: The Man Who Made Ragtime;* Ambassador of Honor Book, English-Speaking Union Books-Across-the-Sea, 1983, for *Bricktop;* Coretta Scott King honorable mention, 1984, for *Lena Horne;* American Library Association (ALA) best book for young adults citation, 1987, and Carter G. Woodson Award, 1988, both for *Black Music in America: A History through Its People;* Alabama Library Association best juvenile work citation, 1987, for "Count Your Way" series; Coretta Scott King honor book, 1991, for *Black Dance in America: A History through Its People;* Parents Choice picture book award, 1992, and Hungry Mind YA nonfiction award, 1993, for *Rosa Parks: My Story;* Carter G. Woodson Award, 1994, for *The March on Washington; Washington Post*/Children's Book Guild award, 1994, for body of work in nonfiction for young people; Coretta Scott King honor book for text, 1997, for *The Harlem Renaissance* and 1998, for *Bayard Rustin: Behind the Scenes of the Civil Rights Movement;* Carter G. Woodson merit books, 1998, for *I Am Rosa Parks* and *Bayard Rustin: Behind the Scenes of the civil Rights Movement.* "Bicentennial Reading, Viewing, Listening for Young Americans" selections, ALA and National Endowment for the Humanities, for *Street Gangs, Ralph Bunche: A Most Reluctant Hero,* and *A Piece of the Power;* certificate of appreciation, Joseph P. Kennedy Foundation, for work with Special Olympics.

WRITINGS:

JUVENILE

Resistance: Profiles in Nonviolence, Doubleday (New York City), 1970.

Revolutionaries: Agents of Change, Lippincott (Philadelphia), 1971.

The War and the Protest: Vietnam, Doubleday, 1971.

Religions, Lippincott, 1971, revised edition as *Religions of the World,* Hippocrene (New York City), 1991.

Witchcraft, Mysticism and Magic in the Black World, Doubleday, 1974.

Street Gangs: Yesterday and Today, Hastings House (New York City), 1974.

Jobs in Business and Office, Lothrop (New York City), 1974.

The Creoles of Color of New Orleans, Crowell (New York City), 1975.

The Consumer Movement, F. Watts (New York City), 1975.

Who Are the Handicapped?, Doubleday, 1978.

(With J. M. Stifle) *The Quiet Revolution: The Struggle for the Rights of Disabled Americans,* Crowell, 1979.

The New Americans: Vietnamese Boat People, Enslow Pubs. (Hillside, NJ), 1980.

Black Theatre in America, Crowell, 1982.

The New Americans: Cuban Boat People, Enslow Pubs., 1982.

The Guardian Angels, Enslow Pubs., 1983.

(With David A. Walker) *Double Dutch,* Enslow Pubs., 1986.

Black Music in America: A History through Its People, Crowell, 1987.

(With Kathleen Benson) *The Sixties Reader,* Viking (New York City), 1988.

India under Indira and Rajiv Gandhi, Enslow Pubs., 1989.

Black Dance in America: A History through Its People, Crowell, 1990.

(With Rosa Parks) *The Autobiography of Rosa Parks,* Dial (New York City), 1990.

The Methodists, Hippocrene, 1992.

The March on Washington, introduction by James Farmer, HarperCollins (New York City), 1993.

(Reteller) *The Headless Haunt and Other African-American Ghost Stories,* illustrated by Ben Otera, HarperCollins, 1994.

(With Joann Biondi) *From Afar to Zulu: A Dictionary of African Cultures,* Walker (New York City), 1995.

The Freedom Rides: Journey for Justice, Hyperion Books for Children (New York City), 1995.

Distinguished African American Political and Governmental Leaders, Oryx Press (Phoenix, AZ), 1999.

(With Kathleen Benson) *Bound for America: The Forced Migration of Africans to the New World,* illustrated by Floyd Cooper, Lothrop, 1999.

History of Rap, Hyperion, in press.

History of Reggae, Hyperion, in press.

JUVENILE BIOGRAPHIES

From Lew Alcindor to Kareem Abdul Jabbar, Lothrop, 1972.

A Piece of the Power: Four Black Mayors, Dial, 1972.

Profiles in Black Power, Doubleday (New York City), 1972.

Deep Like the Rivers: A Biography of Langston Hughes, 1902-1967, Holt (New York City), 1973.

Adam Clayton Powell: Portrait of a Marching Black, Dial, 1974.

Babe Ruth and Hank Aaron: The Home Run Kings, Lothrop, 1974.

Fighting Shirley Chisholm, Dial, 1975.

The Picture Life of Malcolm X, F. Watts, 1975.

Dr. J: A Biography of Julius Irving, Doubleday, 1975.

Pele: A Biography, Doubleday, 1976.

The Story of Stevie Wonder, Doubleday, 1976.

Always Movin' On: The Life of Langston Hughes, F. Watts, 1976, revised edition, Africa World Press (Trenton, NJ), 1992.

Barbara Jordan, Dial, 1977.

The Life and Death of Martin Luther King, Jr., Lothrop, 1977.

George McGinnis: Basketball Superstar, Hastings House, 1978.

Bob McAdoo: Superstar, Lothrop, 1978.

Andrew Young: Man with a Mission, Lothrop, 1979.

I'm Gonna Make You Love Me: The Story of Diana Ross, Dial, 1980.

"Magic": A Biography of Earvin Johnson, Enslow Pubs., 1981.

Katherine Dunham, Coward-McCann, 1982.

Sugar Ray Leonard, Lothrop, 1982.

Donna Summer, Atlantic Monthly Press, 1983.

About Michael Jackson, Enslow Pubs., 1985.

Diana Ross: Star Supreme, Viking, 1985.

Leaders of the Middle East, Enslow Pubs., 1985.

Corazon Aquino: Leader of the Philippines, Enslow Pubs., 1988.

The Magic Johnson Story, Enslow Pubs., 1988.

Shirley Temple Black: From Actress to Ambassador, illustrated by Donna Ruff, Puffin Books (New York City), 1988.

Sports Great Magic Johnson, Enslow Pubs., 1989, revised and expanded edition, 1992.

Thurgood Marshall: A Life for Justice, Holt, 1992.

Colin Powell: A Biography, Scholastic (New York City), 1992.

I am Somebody! A Biography of Jesse Jackson, Enslow Pubs., 1992.

The Scottsboro Boys, Holt, 1994.

The First Black Governor, Pinckney Benton Stewart Pinchback, Africa World Press (Trenton, NJ), 1996.

Bayard Rustin: Behind the Scenes of the Civil Rights Movement, Hyperion Books for Children (New York City), 1997.

JUVENILE; UNDER NAME JIM HASKINS

Jokes from Black Folks, Doubleday, 1973.

Ralph Bunche: A Most Reluctant Hero, Hawthorne (New York City), 1974.

Your Rights, Past and Present: A Guide for Young People, Hawthorne, 1975.

Teen-Age Alcoholism, Hawthorne, 1976.

The Long Struggle: The Story of American Labor, Westminster (Philadelphia), 1976.

Real Estate Careers, F. Watts, 1978.

Gambling—Who Really Wins, F. Watts, 1978.

James Van DerZee: The Picture Takin' Man, illustrated by James Van DerZee, Dodd (New York City), 1979.

(With Pat Connolly) *The Child Abuse Help Book,* Addison Wesley (Reading, MA), 1981.

Werewolves, Lothrop, 1982.

(Editor) *The Filipino Nation,* three volumes, Grolier (Danbury, CT), 1982.

(With Stifle) *Donna Summer: An Unauthorized Biography,* Little, Brown (Boston), 1983.

(With Benson) *Space Challenger: The Story of Guion Bluford, an Authorized Biography,* Carolrhoda (Minneapolis, MN), 1984.

Break Dancing, Lerner Publications (Minneapolis, MN), 1985.

The Statue of Liberty: America's Proud Lady, Lerner, 1986.

Bill Cosby: America's Most Famous Father, Walker, 1988.

(With Helen Crothers) *Scatman: An Authorized Biography of Scatman Crothers,* Morrow (New York City), 1991.

Christopher Columbus: Admiral of the Ocean Sea, Scholastic, 1991.

Outward Dreams: Black Inventors and Their Inventions, Walker, 1991.

I Have a Dream: The Life and Words of Martin Luther King, Millbrook Press (Brookfield, CT), 1992.

The Day Martin Luther King, Jr. Was Shot: A Photo History of the Civil Rights Movement, Scholastic, 1992.

Amazing Grace: The Story behind the Song, Millbrook Press, 1992.

Against All Opposition: Black Explorers in America, Walker, 1992.

One More River to Cross: The Story of Twelve Black Americans, Scholastic, 1992.

Get On Board: The Story of the Underground Railroad, Scholastic, 1993.

Black Eagles: African Americans in Aviation, Scholastic, 1995.

The Day They Fired on Fort Sumter, Scholastic, 1995.

Louis Farrakhan and the Nation of Islam, Walker and Co. (New York City), 1996.

The Harlem Renaissance, Millbrook Press, 1996.

Power to the People: The Rise and Fall of the Black Panther Party, Simon and Schuster Books for Young Readers (New York City), 1997.

Spike Lee: By Any Means Necessary, Walker, 1997.

Separate, But Not Equal: The Dream and the Struggle, Scholastic, 1997.

(With Rosa Parks) *I Am Rosa Parks,* pictures by Wil Clay, Dial Books for Young Readers (New York City), 1997.

(Reteller) *Moaning Bones: African-American Ghost Stories,* illustrated by Felicia Marshall, Lothrop, 1998.

Black, Blue, & Grey: African Americans in the Civil War, Simon & Schuster, 1998.

(Editor) Otha Richard Sullivan, *African American Inventors,* Wiley (New York City), 1998.

African American Military Heroes, Wiley, 1998.

African American Entrepreneurs, Wiley, 1998.

The Exodusters, Millbrook Press, 1999.

Blacks in Colonial America, Lothrop, 1999.

(Editor) Brenda Wilkinson, *African American Women Writers,* Wiley, 1999.

The Geography of Hope: Black Exodus from the South after Reconstruction, Millbrook Press, 1999.

"COUNT YOUR WAY" SERIES; UNDER NAME JIM HASKINS

Count Your Way through China, illustrated by Martin Skoro, Carolrhoda (Minneapolis), 1987.

Count Your Way through Japan, Carolrhoda, 1987.

Count Your Way through Russia, Carolrhoda, 1987.

Count Your Way through the Arab World, illustrated by Skoro, Carolrhoda, 1987.

Count Your Way through Mexico, illustrations by Helen Byers, Carolrhoda, 1989.

Count Your Way through Canada, illustrations by Steve Michaels, Carolrhoda, 1989.

Count Your Way through Africa, illustrations by Barbara Knutson, Carolrhoda, 1989.

Count Your Way through Korea, illustrations by Dennis Hockerman, Carolrhoda, 1989.

Count Your Way through Israel, illustrations by Rick Hanson, Carolrhoda, 1990.

Count Your Way through India, illustrations by Liz Brenner Dodson, Carolrhoda, 1990.

Count Your Way through Italy, illustrations by Beth Wright, Carolrhoda, 1990.

Count Your Way through Germany, illustrations by Byers, Carolrhoda, 1990.

(With Kathleen Benson) *Count Your Way Through Greece,* illustrated by Janice Lee Porter, Carolrhoda, 1996.

(With Benson) *Count Your Way Through France,* illustrated by Andrea Shine, Carolrhoda, 1996.

(With Benson) *Count Your Way Through Ireland,* illustrated by Beth Wright, Carolrhoda, 1996.

(With Benson) *Count Your Way Through Brazil,* illustrated by Liz Brenner Dodson, Carolrhoda, 1996.

NONFICTION; UNDER NAME JIM HASKINS

Diary of a Harlem School Teacher, Grove (New York City), 1969, 2nd edition, Stein & Day (Briarcliff Manor, NY), 1979.

(Editor) *Black Manifesto for Education,* Morrow, 1973.

(With Hugh F. Butts) *The Psychology of Black Language,* Barnes & Noble (New York City), 1973, enlarged edition, Hippocrene, 1993.

Snow Sculpture and Ice Carving, Macmillan (New York City), 1974.

The Cotton Club, Random House (New York City), 1977, 2nd edition, New American Library (New York City), 1984, revised edition, Hippocrene, 1994.

(With Benson and Ellen Inkelis) *The Great American Crazies,* Condor Publishing (Ashland, MA), 1977.

Voodoo and Hoodoo: Their Tradition and Craft as Revealed by Actual Practitioners, Stein & Day, 1978.

(With Benson) *The Stevie Wonder Scrapbook,* Grosset & Dunlap, 1978.

Richard Pryor, a Man and His Madness: A Biography, Beaufort Books (New York City), 1984.

Queen of the Blues: A Biography of Dinah Washington, Morrow, 1987.

NONFICTION; UNDER NAME JAMES HASKINS

Pinckney Benton Stewart Pinchback: A Biography, Macmillan, 1973.

A New Kind of Joy: The Story of the Special Olympics, Doubleday, 1976.

(With Benson) *Scott Joplin: The Man Who Made Ragtime,* Doubleday, 1978.

(With Benson) *Lena: A Personal and Professional Biography of Lena Horne,* Stein & Day, 1983.

(With Bricktop) *Bricktop,* Atheneum (New York City), 1983.

(With Benson) *Nat King Cole,* Stein & Day, 1984, updated and revised edition, Scarborough House, 1990.

(With Benson) *Aretha: A Personal and Professional Biography of Aretha Franklin,* Stein & Day, 1986.

Mabel Mercer: A Life, Atheneum, 1988.

Winnie Mandela: Life of Struggle, Putnam (New York City), 1988.

Mr. Bojangles: The Biography of Bill Robinson, Morrow, 1988.

(With Lionel Hampton) *Hamp: An Autobiography* (with discography), Warner Books (New York City), 1989, revised edition, Amistad Press, 1993.

(With Benson) *Nat King Cole: A Personal and Professional Biography,* Scarborough House, 1990.

(With Joann Biondi) *Hippocrene U.S.A. Guide to the Historic Black South: Historical Sites, Cultural Centers, and Musical Happenings of the African-American South,* Hippocrene, 1993.

(With Biondi) *Hippocrene U.S.A. Guide to Black New York,* Hippocrene, 1994.

(With Kathleen Benson) *African Beginnings,* illustrated by Floyd Cooper, Lothrop (New York City), 1995.

OTHER

Editor of Hippocrene's "Great Religions of the World" series. Contributor to books, including *Children and Books,* 4th edition, 1976; Emily Mumford, *Understanding Human Behavior in Health and Illness,* 1977; *New York Kid's Catalog,* 1979; *Notable American Women Supplement,* 1979; Jerry Brown, *Clearings in the Thicket: An Alabama Humanities Reader,* 1985; and *Author in the Kitchen.*

Contributor of articles and reviews to periodicals, including *American Visions, Now, Arizona English Bulletin, Rolling Stone, Children's Book Review Service, Western Journal of Black Studies, Elementary English, Amsterdam News, New York Times Book Review, Afro-Hawaii News,* and *Gainesville Sun.*

ADAPTATIONS: Diary of a Harlem Schoolteacher has been recorded by Recordings for the Blind; *The Cotton Club* inspired Francis Ford Coppola's film of the same name, produced by Orion in 1984.

SIDELIGHTS: Born in the rural South at a time when African Americans did not receive the full rights of American citizenship, James S. Haskins absorbed the hard realities of life around him, translated them into a fascination with fact, and, as an adult, became the author of over 100 works of nonfiction. "It has always seemed to me that truth is not just 'stranger than fiction,' but also more interesting," Haskins explained in an essay for *Something about the Author Autobiography Series (SAAS)*. Haskins also cites the desire to provide information as another reason for writing only nonfiction, and further explains his commitment to facts by writing: "I was born into a society in which blacks were in deep trouble if they forgot about the real world. For if they daydreamed and were caught off-guard, they could pay dearly."

Demopolis, Alabama, in 1941, the year of Haskins's birth, was a segregated community. Because there were no adequate medical facilities for African Americans, Haskins was born at home, where, appropriately, he locates the literary lessons of his early childhood. Haskins recalled for *SAAS* that a strong tradition of storytelling existed in his family and among his relatives. "My Aunt Cindy was the greatest storyteller who ever lived," he declared, describing her mixed-up versions of traditional folktales as ones in which Hansel and Gretel meet the Three Little Pigs. Haskins credits these stories with stimulating an interest in the unseen, complex "goings on under the surface of the real world." Among these interests was Voodoo, which the Haskins family regarded with skepticism, but which was a real part of everyday life for many people in the black community. Like other interests he developed as child, Haskins continued to think about the belief and practice of such mysticism, and later wrote a book about the subject.

Once he began reading, however, Haskins encountered obstacles to the pursuit of his interests. "There was not a lot of money for books, and the Demopolis Public Library was off limits to blacks," Haskins remembered in *SAAS*. His mother managed to get him an encyclopedia, one volume at a time, from a local supermarket. This constituted the majority of his reading, until a white woman for whom his mother worked learned of his interest in books. With access to the library, the woman checked out books for Haskins once a week, which she passed along through his mother. In this way, Haskins was able to read a wide assortment of fiction. "I enjoyed these stories," Haskins noted in *SAAS,* "but since my first major reading was the encyclopedia, this is probably another reason why I prefer nonfiction."

Haskins attended a segregated elementary school. The district did not have the most recent textbooks or best sports equipment, but, Haskins points out, there was an atmosphere of respect between teachers and students that transcended the limits of the environment. Because teaching was the highest profession African Americans had entry to at the time, they were greatly respected in black community. They "earned that respect," Haskins reasoned in *SAAS,* "by caring about their students as if it were their mission in life to educate us." In particular, Haskins's teachers departed from standard lessons and emphasized African-American contributions to American history. "In fact, if my teachers had followed the official curriculum, I would have grown up thinking that blacks had never done anything in the history of the world except be slaves," he wrote. "But they taught us that there had been many important black heroes in history."

As a teenager, Haskins and his mother moved to Boston, where he was admitted to the prestigious Boston Latin School. While attending school with a majority of white students was a new experience for Haskins, he quickly made the adjustment, and did well academically. After graduating from high school, Haskins decided to return to Alabama to attend Alabama State University in Montgomery. Haskins admitted in his autobiographical essay to being somewhat lonely in Boston, and he wanted once again to be surrounded by people like himself. He drew additional incentive to return to Alabama from the recent activities of the civil rights movement, which had its roots in that state.

As Haskins explained, the protests began over the segregation of Montgomery city buses, and gained such momentum that leaders of the cause formed the Montgomery Improvement Association to unite African Americans on issues of common concern. A young Martin Luther King Jr. was chosen to head the association, and his charismatic leadership attracted Haskins and others to Montgomery to take part in the struggle for equal rights for all. Haskins contacted King shortly after his enrollment at Alabama State. The young student was soon "putting leaflets under doors in the dormitories at Alabama State and stuffing envelopes and doing other fairly innocent tasks," he recalled in *SAAS*. Even this level of activism, however, was met with opposition by the university administration, and when Haskins was arrested for marching on downtown Montgomery, he was expelled from Alabama State.

Haskins then went to Georgetown University in Washington, D.C., where he graduated with a bachelor's degree in psychology in 1960. In the years since his expulsion from Alabama State, public sentiment toward the civil rights movement had improved, and Haskins returned to Montgomery to pick up the work he had left behind. Haskins also returned to Alabama State, where he earned a second bachelor's degree, this time in history. Haskins continued his education at the University of New Mexico, earning a graduate degree in social psychology.

Haskins worked for a time in New York City at the brokerage house of Smith Barney & Co. as a stock trader, but found that he wasn't quite satisfied with his career. "And then, gradually, it dawned on me that what I wanted to be was like the people who had made the strongest impression on me," Haskins commented in his *SAAS* essay, "and those people were teachers." Haskins took a job teaching special education at Public School 92 in Harlem. His students were challenged by a variety of handicaps, he noted, but most simply lacked the kind of supportive environment necessary to develop as individuals. Haskins undertook a variety of alternative teaching methods, including bringing newspapers to class for his students to read in place of outdated textbooks, and taking his students on learning excursions outside school.

"While I could not do much about their home lives, I worried about my students constantly and wondered what kind of future awaited them," Haskins confessed in his *SAAS* essay. He shared his concerns with friends and associates, and one, a social worker named Fran Morill, suggested that he keep a record of his feelings. She gave him a diary, and Haskins kept a daily journal of his experiences at P.S. 92. The result was Haskins's first publication, *Diary of a Harlem School Teacher*. Ronald Gross of the *New York Times Book Review* characterized the work as "plain, concrete, unemotional, and unliterary. . . . By its truthfulness alone does it command our concern. The book is like a weapon—cold, blunt, painful."

Following the publication of *Diary of a Harlem School Teacher*, Haskins was approached by publishers who wondered if he might be interested in writing books for children. "I knew exactly the kind of books I wanted to do—books about current events and books about important black people so that students could understand the larger world around them through books written at a level they could understand," Haskins told *SAAS*.

Published in 1970, *Resistance: Profiles in Nonviolence* was Haskins' first book for children. With this work Haskins tried to place nonviolence in a historical context culminating in, but not exclusive to, Mar-

tin Luther King, Jr. Shortly after *Resistance*, Haskins published *A Piece of the Power: Four Black Mayors*, which chronicles the political successes of Carl Stokes, Richard Hatcher, Charles Evers, and Kenneth Gibson. In addition to telling how these men began their careers and ultimately came to hold power, "James Haskins tells us something about what happens next and it is interesting and useful information," asserted Fred and Lucille Clifton in the *New York Times Book Review*. A *Kirkus Reviews* writer took issue, however, with the fact that the book provides little guidance to the complex issues surrounding the men profiled, calling the work "competent but totally non-interpretive."

In 1975 Haskins published another work with a historical emphasis, *The Creoles of Color of New Orleans*. In this book Haskins examines the culture of Louisiana's Creoles, a mixed population of African-American descent which was exempt from slavery. In the absence of any definitive political freedom, the Creoles embraced the values of slave-owning whites, and set themselves up in differentiation and opposition to black slaves. In an *Interracial Books for Children Bulletin*, Patricia Spence credited Haskins for dealing openly with the prejudices of the Creoles, but faulted him for failing to locate Creoles in the larger context of a racially segregated society: "Such a framework is necessary to foster understanding of the Creole's value system as the product of a racist environment." *The Creoles of Color of New Orleans* attracted the attention of other readers and critics, and was selected as a Spur Award finalist by the Western Writers of America.

In *Street Gangs: Yesterday and Today* Haskins studies the history of organized violence among adolescents and teenagers to explain the gang culture which absorbs so many young Americans. Haskins concludes that gang membership brings a sense of inclusion and a feeling of worth that is otherwise lacking in the gang member's life. This has been true, he claims, throughout American history. "The strength of Haskins' book is in its historical material," wrote Colman McCarthy in a *Washington Post Book World* review. McCarthy notes, in particular, the descriptions of street gangs that formed in the new states following the revolutionary war, and the notorious Bowery Boys of nineteenth-century New York City. In a *Bulletin of the Center for Children's Books* review, Zena Sutherland praised the "strong direct prose" of *Street Gangs*, and credited the book with linking the problems of contemporary youth to the past. For the insight it provided into a disturbing aspect of American urban life, *Street Gangs* received a Books of the Year citation from the Child Study Association of America.

Haskins has, since 1970, taught writing and lectured on literature for young readers at several colleges and universities. Haskins began teaching at this level at the New School for Social Research, in New York City. He then taught at Staten Island Community College of the City University of New York, Indiana University—Purdue University in Indianapolis, and the State University of New York at New Paltz. In 1977, Haskins assumed his current post as a professor of English at the University of Florida in Gainesville. Commenting on the development of his career in his *SAAS* essay, Haskins observed that he really has two careers. Teaching is Haskins' primary career, while writing remains a fascinating sideline that allows him to simultaneously pursue his own interests, and share them with others.

In 1977 Haskins published an adult book, *The Cotton Club,* an in-depth account of a nightclub in Harlem that showcased African-American entertainers for a white audience during the 1920s. Among the luminaries that performed in this segregated setting were Cab Calloway, Lena Horne, and Duke Ellington. In the *New York Times Book Review,* Jervis Anderson concluded that the *Cotton Club* "memorializes that Harlem nightspot—one of the classiest joints in the history of New York late-night entertainment. It is a detailed, instructive and entertaining work." *The Cotton Club* inspired a 1984 movie of the same name. Although the melodramatic film departed greatly from Haskins's book, he was invited to visit the movie set, and also met the actors and actresses who starred in the film. "I even got a director's chair with my name on it," he recalled fondly in *SAAS,* "though I had nothing really to do with the movie."

Among Haskins's more recent historical works for young readers is *The Sixties Reader,* which he co-wrote with Kathleen Benson. The reader is an attempt to present some of the major social movements of the 1960s through documentary evidence, with little interpretation. In a *Voice of Youth Advocates* review of the book, Patrick Jones compared it to other works which deal with the same period for young readers, pointing out that the strength of *The Sixties Reader* is a reliance on fact and a desire to present information rather than anecdotes. "The book is a starting point," Jones wrote. "Each of the chapters focuses on a movement, then important documents, statements, lyrics, or interviews are presented." This allows readers to appreciate not only the events of the period, but how those events were shaped in the minds of those present, concluded Jones.

As a writer, Haskins has a professed interest in biography. "It seemed to me that young people ought to have some living black heroes to read about," he noted in *SAAS,* "and because of the gains made by black people there were more black heroes to write about." Haskins was reluctant at first to write about African-American sports stars, however, because he felt that children needed role models other than athletes. But when professional baseball player Hank Aaron was on the verge of breaking Babe Ruth's career mark for home runs, Haskins noticed a debate emerging over who was the better athlete and the better person. Inspired by the need for fairness in this dialogue, Haskins wrote his first sports biography, *Babe Ruth and Hank Aaron: The Home Run Kings.* Several other sports biographies followed, and they have been among Haskins's more popular works, a fact the writer has come to accept. "I realized that it doesn't matter so much *what* kids read as it does *that* they read," he proclaimed.

Among Haskins's later sports biographies is *Sports Great Magic Johnson.* From high school championships in Lansing, Michigan, to professional championships with the Los Angeles Lakers, basketball superstar Earvin "Magic" Johnson has a remarkable record of winning. Well before the emergence of Michael Jordan as the dominant player in the National Basketball Association (NBA), critics and fans hailed Magic Johnson as the greatest player ever to play the game. In a *School Library Journal* review, Tom S. Hurlbut characterized Haskins's work as straightforward, and noted that Johnson's personal and family life are covered, "keeping the biography focused on the person rather than just the athlete." In 1992 Haskins updated the volume to reflect the emergence of Johnson, who is infected with HIV, as an activist in the fight against AIDS.

Haskins has also written biographies of entertainment celebrities as well. His biography of the rock singer Diana Ross, *I'm Gonna Make You Love Me,* brings the reader not only into the singer's professional life, but also into the era that shaped her. "Haskins creates a vivid picture of Detroit," noted Diane Haas in *School Library Journal.* Likewise lauded was Haskins's biography of Lena Horne which Voice of Youth Advocates dubbed a "moving story of a beautiful and sensitive dancer, singer, and actress."

To research *The Story of Stevie Wonder,* Haskins traveled to Los Angeles to spend a couple of days with the musician. "He made music all the time and everywhere," Haskins recalled of Wonder in *SAAS,* "beating on the table with a fork or making rhythms with his feet on the steps." Haskins has also written a biography of pop superstar Michael Jackson. In *About Michael Jackson,* Haskins provides a glimpse of the childhood and personal life of the intensely private and reclusive star. In a *Voice of Youth Advocates* review, Jerry Grim wrote that although he found the writing "trite" in places, "the artist comes out looking like a human being and not a two-dimensional poster." Hurlbut's *School Library Journal* review of the book faulted Haskins, however, for skirting the more controversial issues of Jackson's life, including his plastic surgery and family difficulties, saying they are "only dealt with in passing."

Haskins's biography of Bill Cosby, *Bill Cosby: America's Most Famous Father,* attempts to reveal the early influences that gave direction to the comedian's life. "Young people will relate to the impatience with school that brought on bad grades and dropping out of high school," commented Luvada Kuhn in a *Voice of Youth Advocates* review. They will also respect the struggle Cosby faced to pass his GED (General Equivalency Diploma) test and go on to college, Kuhn concluded. In a *School Library Journal* review Todd Morning noted that Cosby's career is surveyed in detail, and credits Haskins for presenting the charge that "there is a certain amount of anger and arrogance beneath the affable surface" of the actor.

From his early work *The Creoles of Color in New Orleans* to more recent titles such as *Black Theater in America,* Haskins has frequently examined various aspects of black culture. In the award-winning *Black Music in America,* he traced musical roots from slave days through spirituals, ragtime, blues, jazz, gospel and soul. Jeffrey Cooper, writing in *Kliatt,* announced that "it's difficult to imagine the library that could not find a place in its shelves for this clear and concise history of African-American music." Haskins and co-author Kathleen Benson took a clear-eyed view at the horrifying facts surrounding the origin of African-Americans in *Bound for America: The Forced Migration of Africans to the New World. Booklist* reviewer Hazel Rochman noted with approval the detailed historical facts and statistics that give a grim picture of the slave trade and its victims, calling the book's effect "intensely personal."

Some of his biographies also provide insight into social and cultural trends, such as those about Scott Joplin and Mr. Bojangles. He has written studies of reggae and rap, and took an in-depth look at one of the world's most popular hymns in the 1992 publication *Amazing Grace: The Story behind the Song,* a book which *Booklist*'s Ilene Cooper called "unique and uplifting."

Haskins's recent profiles of blacks in positions of leadership include books about Jesse Jackson, Winnie Mandela, Colin Powell, and Thurgood Marshall. *I Am Somebody! A Biography of Jesse Jackson* tells of Jackson's childhood in rural Greenville, South Carolina, of the determination that led Jackson to succeed in sports and academics and win a college scholarship, of his rise to the forefront of the civil rights movement, and his eventual prominence among black political figures. Jeanette Lambert, in a *School Library Journal* review, called the book "incisive," and credited Haskins with providing a fair portrait of Jackson, in which both strengths and flaws of character are discussed "in a balanced manner." In a *Voice of Youth Advocates* review of *I Am Somebody,* Alice M. Johns appreciated Haskins's depiction of Jackson as a leader who increased his power and influence by helping "people to participate in full citizenship."

Winnie Mandela: Life of Struggle is similar to the Jackson biography in that its subject has been intimately involved in a civil rights struggle, this time in South Africa. Born in a remote village, Winnie Mandela became the first black medical social worker in South African history. In the process of her education she was introduced to the ideology of African nationalism, which she soon advocated. This advocacy became the determining factor in her life after her marriage to the former leader of the once-outlawed African National Congress, Nelson Mandela. After his imprisonment, Winnie continued to oppose apartheid and to keep the vision of a democratic South Africa alive. To promote her cause, Winnie has "endured police harassment, numerous arrests, physical mistreatment, solitary confinement, and banishment to a community with a language different from her own," pointed out Virginia B. Moore in a *Voice of Youth Advocates* review, making for an "easy-to-read, fast-paced and gripping profile." In a *School Library Journal* review Nancy J. Schmidt praised Haskins's facility for connecting "Mandela's personal story with that of milestones in the black South African struggle." In the "moving" portrayal that results, Schmidt remarked, Mandela is both a person and the leader of a globally significant social movement.

Colin Powell takes a look at the life of the first African American to head the Joint Chiefs of Staff of the

United States. Hazel Moore, in a *Voice of Youth Advocates* review, found the description of Powell's struggle to succeed academically sufficiently inspiring to recommend the book. "The person, more than the military leader, emerges from the portrait Haskins paints," she added. *Thurgood Marshall: A Life for Justice* follows a similar format, emphasizing Marshall's beginnings in the Civil Rights movement, then following him through his years as attorney to the National Association for the Advancement of Colored People (NAACP), and finally, to the bench of the United States Supreme Court. In a *School Library Journal* review, Mary Mueller particularly appreciated the "discussion of the difference between Marshall's constitutional tactics and those used by the Direct Actions Civil Rights Movement, led by Martin Luther King, Jr."

Haskins returned to the subject of overall black contributions to history with *Against All Opposition: Black Explorers in America.* From the seafaring adventurers of the African nation of Mali in the 1300s, to the Arctic travels of Matthew Henson, and the experiences of astronauts Ronald McNair and Guion Stewart Bluford, Jr., Haskins sheds light on accomplishments which racism has suppressed. In *Voice of Youth Advocates,* Diane Yankelevitz found the work informative, but asserted that the specificity that makes the work valuable as a reference prevents it from being "very interesting as general reading." A similar work, *Get on Board: The Story of the Underground Railroad,* recounts the history of the network of abolitionists and free African-American men and women who helped escaped slaves flee north. In addition to describing the organization and structure of the railroad, the roles played by the "conductors," who provided safe passage, and the "station masters," who provided shelter, Haskins includes accounts from men and women who "rode" the railroad to freedom. "Although the firsthand stories are interesting on their own, the book is not successful" because of its organization, wrote Elizabeth M. Reardon in a *School Library Journal* review. A reviewer for Chicago *Tribune Books* concluded, however, that the book was successful in evoking the "significant" courage of those involved, especially the fugitives themselves.

Haskins captures one of the greatest days of the Civil Rights movement in *The March on Washington.* Haskins points out that a nonviolent march on Washington, D.C., had been proposed as early as 1941 by labor organizer A. Phillip Randolph, but it was not until 1963, after enormous coordination and compromise, that 250,000 people marched from the Washing-

ton Monument to the Lincoln Memorial. While the nation watched, Martin Luther King, Jr., delivered his famous "I Have a Dream" speech. Haskins also goes into the planning and logistics of the march, from provisions for sanitation and food to the cleanup following one of the country's largest public demonstrations. Offering high praise in a *Booklist* review, Sheilamae O'Hara wrote, "the narrative is eminently readable as a story of what may be regarded as one of the great days in American history." Similarly, Judy Silverman remarked in a *Voice of Youth Advocates* review that "Haskins manages to make this history come very much alive." "Haskins provides a lucid, in-depth, and moving study of the 1963 March on Washington for jobs and freedom," Helen Fader declared in a *Horn Book* review.

Haskins often uses his credibility as a writer to support personal causes, such as the restoration of the Statue of Liberty. It is his writing for children, however, that Haskins gives greatest importance. In his *SAAS* essay he wrote: "Most of my books are about black subjects—black history, black people. Partly that's because I remember being a child and not having many books about black people to read. I want children today, black and white, to be able to find books about black people and black history in case they want to read them. . . . And when, some day, the missing second date after that '1941-' gets filled in, I will know that I have not only done something worthwhile in the years between, but also that I have had a good time doing it."

BIOGRAPHICAL/CRITICAL SOURCES:

BOOKS

Brown, Jerry, *Clearings in the Thicket: An Alabama Humanities Reader,* Mercer University Press (Macon, GA), 1985.

Children's Literature Review, Volume 3, Gale (Detroit), 1978, pp. 63-69.

Something about the Author Autobiography Series, Volume 4, Gale, 1987, pp. 197-209.

Twentieth-Century Young Adult Writers, St. James Press (Detroit), 1994.

PERIODICALS

American Visions, December-January, 1995, p. 36.

Booklist, September 15, 1974, p. 100; January 1, 1977, p. 666; July 15, 1979, p. 1618; February 1, 1982, pp. 709-10; January 15, 1983, p. 676; September 1, 1984, p. 65; January 15, 1992, p.

115; February, 1992, p. 1024; February 15, 1992, p. 1097; July, 1992, p. 1939; May 15, 1993, p. 1691; January 1, 1995, p. 818; September 1, 1996, p. 116; February 15, 1997, p. 1020; March 15, 1997, p. 1233; May 1, 1997, p. 1488; February 15, 1998, pp. 995, 1002; February 15, 1999, p. 1068.

Bulletin of the Center for Children's Books, January, 1975, p. 78; September, 1983, p. 9; June, 1988, p. 205; July, 1988, p. 229; July, 1996, p. 375; May, 1997, p. 323; April, 1998, p. 281.

Chicago Tribune Book World, April 13, 1986.

Christian Science Monitor, March 12, 1970, p. 9; February 21, 1990, p. 13.

Horn Book, August, 1993, pp. 477-478.

Interracial Books for Children Bulletin, Volume 7, No. 5, 1976, pp. 12-13.

Kirkus Reviews, June 1, 1972, p. 631; May 1, 1974, p. 492; June 15, 1979, p. 692; August 1, 1979, p. 862; November 1, 1984, p. 1036; April 15, 1988, p. 618; December 1, 1997, pp. 1775-76; January 15, 1998, pp. 111-12; April 15, 1998, p. 618; June 1, 1998, pp. 827-28.

Kliatt, May, 1993, p. 36.

Los Angeles Times Book Review, July 24, 1983, p. 8; March 11, 1984, p. 9; January 20, 1985, p. 6; July 17, 1988, p. 10; February 23, 1992, p. 10.

New York Times Book Review, February 8, 1970, pp. 6-7; December 6, 1970; May 7, 1972, Part 2, p. 30; May 5, 1974, p. 22; August 4, 1974, p. 8; September 23, 1979, p. 26; November 20, 1977, pp. 13, 58; October 7, 1979, p. 34; January 25, 1981, p. 31; March 4, 1984; May 17, 1987, p. 51; September 13, 1987, p. 48; February 28, 1988, p. 21; June 26, 1988, p. 45; February 16, 1997, p. 25.

Publishers Weekly, July 20, 1992, p. 252; December 8, 1997, p. 74; February 2, 1998, p. 92.

School Library Journal, November, 1980, p. 86; January, 1986, pp. 67-68; June-July, 1988, pp. 111, 123, 130; July, 1989, pp. 85-86; August, 1992, p. 181; February, 1993, p. 98; April, 1995, p. 162; March, 1997, p. 201; April, 1997, p. 149.

Skipping Stones, November, 1998, p. 32.

Times Literary Supplement, May 24, 1985, p. 583.

Tribune Books (Chicago), February 14, 1993, p. 5.

Voice Literary Supplement, October, 1988, p. 5.

Voice of Youth Advocates, April, 1984, pp. 46-47; February, 1986, p. 40; August, 1988, p. 146; April, 1989, p. 58; June, 1992, p. 125; August, 1992, p. 188; December, 1992, pp. 300-301; August, 1993, p. 177; October, 1994, p. 230; February, 1995, p. 358; June, 1995, p. 132; August, 1995, p. 182; August, 1996, p. 150; December, 1996, p. 288; August, 1997, p. 202; October, 1997, p. 264; February, 1998, p. 402.

Washington Post Book World, November 10, 1974, p. 8; September 11, 1977, p. E6; February 5, 1978, p. G4; August 17, 1983; December 9, 1984, p. 15; January 16, 1985; May 10, 1987; May 13, 1990, p. 17; September 1, 1991, p. 13.*

*   *   *

HASKINS, Jim
See HASKINS, James S.

*   *   *

HAWKINS, W(alter) Lincoln   1911-1992

PERSONAL: Born March 21, 1911, in Washington, DC; died of heart failure, August 20, 1992, in CA; son of William Langston (a lawyer for the Census Bureau) and Maude Johnson (a science teacher) Hawkins; married Lilyan Varina Bobo, August 19, 1939; children: two sons. *Education:* Rensselaer Polytechnic Institute, graduated, 1932; Howard University, M.S. (chemistry), 1934; McGill University, Ph.D. (chemistry), 1938.

CAREER: Chemical engineer and writer. Taught at a trade school, c. 1934; Columbia University, instructor, 1938-42; Bell Laboratories, Murray Hills, NJ, began as researcher and inventor, became assistant director of the Chemical Research Laboratory, 1942-76, consultant on the education and employment of minorities, beginning in 1976; Plastics Institute of America, Hoboken, NJ, research director, 1976-83. American Chemical Society's Project SEED (a campaign to promote science careers to minority students around the country), chair, 1981; worked with the National Action Council for Minorities in Engineering (NACME), a committee set up by several major companies to get minorities into the field; member and chair of the board of trustees of Montclair State College, New Jersey.

AWARDS, HONORS: Fellowship in chemistry, 1938, from McGill University; National Research Council Fellowship in alkaloid chemistry, 1938; Honor Scroll, 1970, from the American Institute of Chemistry; Percy Julian Award, 1977, from the National Organization of Black Chemists and Chemical Engineers; International Medal, 1984, from the Society of Plastics Engineering; National Medal of Technology, 1992, for his work in chemical engineering and for his efforts to bring minorities into the sciences.

WRITINGS:

Polymer Degradation and Stabilization, Springer Verlag, 1984.

SIDELIGHTS: A longtime employee of Bell Laboratories, W. Lincoln Hawkins was a chemical engineer whose work helped make universal telephone service possible. Until the late 1940s telephone cables were insulated with a lead coating, which was very expensive; this coating was also too heavy for use in the multi-cable conduits which would be required if most homes were to have telephones. It was clear to many that plastics could be a cheaper and lighter insulating alternative, but every plastic then in existence broke down rapidly when exposed to the elements. Hawkins, working at Bell Laboratories, helped to solve the problem by co-inventing a plastic coating that withstood heat and cold and had a life span of many decades.

Hawkins was always a tinkerer. Born Walter Lincoln Hawkins on March 21, 1911, in Washington D.C., he was the son of William Langston Hawkins, a lawyer for the Census Bureau, and Maude Johnson Hawkins, a science teacher. As a child, he was fascinated with how things worked, and he made spring-driven model boats to sail on Washington's Reflecting Pool. He also constructed a simple radio to listen to baseball games. "I always loved building things," he told Kim E. Pearson in a 1983 interview for *Crisis*. "When I was about eleven years old, a friend and I tried to build a perpetual motion machine. We didn't know anything about thermodynamics—we had no idea that it couldn't be done." Hawkins's parents hoped their son would pursue a career in medicine, but it was engineering that captured his imagination. He attended Dunbar High School in Washington, a segregated public school renowned for its science and engineering programs—the faculty consisted primarily of African Americans with doctoral degrees who could not get a job elsewhere because of their race. One of his teachers had a new car every year, and when Hawkins learned it was partial compensation for the man's patent on a component of the car's self-starter, he realized that tinkering could actually earn a person a living.

After graduation from Dunbar High School, Hawkins and one other African American student attended the well-known engineering school in Troy, New York, Rensselaer Polytechnic Institute. They were the only black students in the school. The next year they were followed by two more African American students from Dunbar. While nearly two out of three students dropped out of Rensselaer, Hawkins and the three other black students completed their studies in four years. But the Depression awaited Hawkins upon graduation in 1932, so he continued his studies, and by 1934 he had earned a master's degree in chemistry at Howard University in Washington. Following this, he taught for a time in a trade school and then was convinced by a counselor at Howard University to apply for a fellowship in chemistry at McGill University in Canada. He won the fellowship and completed his Ph.D. in chemistry at McGill in 1938. That same year he won a National Research Council Fellowship in alkaloid chemistry and he accepted a position at Columbia University, where he would remain until 1942. During his time at Columbia he met Lilyan Varina Bobo, whom he married on August 19, 1939. They would have two sons.

In 1942 Hawkins joined Bell Laboratories in Murray Hills, New Jersey, the first African American scientist to be hired there. Hawkins would stay at Bell for the next thirty- four years, researching and inventing new materials and products for the preservation and recycling of plastics; he completed his career as assistant director of the Chemical Research Laboratory. "I had a ball," Hawkins told Pearson, describing his years of service at the research lab. "There's a world of excitement there that's like nowhere else." Of the eighteen domestic and 129 foreign patents Hawkins himself held, by far the most important was that to replace the lead insulation of telephone cables with a new weather-resistant plastic coating. Working together with Vincent Lanza in the late 1940s, he developed additives to create a new polymer that could resist both thermal degradation and the effects of oxidation and last up to seventy years in the elements. "Hawkins's work is arguably one of the major achievements which made universal telephone service economical," a colleague at Bell Laboratories told John Burgess of the *Washington Post*.

But engineering was only part of Hawkins's long and distinguished career. Retiring at age sixty-five, he remained a consultant to Bell on the education and employment of minorities. He also became research director for the Plastics Institute of America in Hoboken, New Jersey, from 1976 to 1983, and he worked privately as a materials consultant. In addition, he often spoke to minority youth about the importance of education. In 1981, he became the first chairman of the American Chemical Society's Project SEED, a campaign to promote science careers to minority students around the country. Hawkins worked for many years with the National Action Council for Minorities in Engineering (NACME), a committee set up by several major companies to get minorities into the field. He was also a member and chair of the board of trustees of Montclair State College in New Jersey. This second career in counseling was as successful as his first in engineering, and the kids listened to him as if he were a member of their own family. Robert Stephens of Montclair State College told Burgess of the *Washington Post* that the students said to themselves: "This guy is my uncle, this guy is my grandfather, but this guy is also somebody important."

Hawkins was widely honored for his pioneering work in polymers, winning the Honor Scroll of the American Institute of Chemistry in 1970, the Percy Julian Award from the National Organization of Black Chemists and Chemical Engineers in 1977, and the International Medal of the Society of Plastics Engineering in 1984. But by far his most important honor was the 1992 National Medal of Technology, awarded to him not only for his work in chemical engineering, but also for his labors in attempting to bring minorities into the sciences.

Hawkins remained vital and active through his eighth decade. He and his wife traveled around the world and then moved to San Marcos, California, to be near one of their sons. On August 20, 1992, Hawkins died of heart failure at the age of eighty-one. Shortly after his death, an undergraduate research fellowship was established in his name by the National Action Council for Minorities in Engineering.

BIOGRAPHICAL/CRITICAL SOURCES:

BOOKS

Sammons, Vivian Ovelton, *Blacks in Science and Medicine,* Hemisphere Publishing Corporation, 1990, pp. 114- 15.

PERIODICALS

About . . . Time, March, 1993, p. 9.
American Chemical Society Chemunity News, September, 1992, p. 3.

Crisis, April, 1983, pp. 192-93.
New York Times, August 23, 1992, p. L46.
Washington Post, June 24, 1992, pp. F1-F2.*

*   *   *

HAWKINS, Walter Everette   1883-(?)

PERSONAL: Born November 17, 1883, in Warrenton, NC; date of death unknown; son of farmers. *Education:* Kittrell College, graduated in 1901. *Politics:* "Anarchist." *Religion:* "Agnostic."

CAREER: Poet. Also worked as a mail clerk in the post office in Washington, DC.

MEMBER: Negro Society for Historical Research.

WRITINGS:

Chords and Discords, introduction by Freeman H. M. Murray, Murray Brothers (Washington, DC), 1909, revised edition published by Richard G. Badger (Boston, MA), 1920.
Petals from the Poppies, Fortuny's (New York City), 1936.

Contributor to books, including *Black and White,* edited by J. C. Byars, 1927, republished by Books for Libraries Press (Freeport, NY), 1971; *Negro Anthology,* edited by Nancy Cunard, Wishart (London, England), 1934, republished by Negro Universities Press (New York City), 1969. Contributor to periodicals, including the *African Times and Orient Review, Crisis, Messenger,* and the *Negro History Bulletin.* Personal papers located at the Schomburg Center for Research in Black Culture, New York Public Library, New York City.

SIDELIGHTS: Poet Walter Everette Hawkins was a transitional figure in African American literature during the late nineteenth century and early twentieth century. His work, according to *Dictionary of Literary Biography* contributor Dickson D. Bruce, Jr., moves "from the genteel modes of the latter nineteenth century to the flowering of black militancy." In later works, Hawkins and his African American literary contemporaries express their social and political viewpoints, attacking many of the injustices that existed in America. Their works became more frank and militant as a larger audience embraced their work. Ultimately, their writings influenced the African

American writers of the Harlem Renaissance that flourished after World War I. Scholars of African American literature, such as Benjamin Brawley and Sterling A. Brown, have noted the significance of Hawkins's poems, particularly for their discussion of a unique black identity.

Though Hawkins was not a figure in the cultural movement known as the Harlem Renaissance, he was familiar with its leaders, and the themes in his works are consistent with some of their themes. Hawkins's poems have a strong social consciousness, addressing the racial issues of his day. His poems decry racial prejudice and segregation and affirm the importance of black pride. They tackle a number of subjects, including religion and capitalism, because these subjects contribute to a system that permits racism. Hawkins ardently supported black leader W. E. B. Du Bois, and was a member of the Negro Society for Historical Research, an organization founded in 1912 to research African American history and promote African American identity. Hawkins achieved notoriety in 1919 when the United States Department of Justice maintained that his poem "Mob Victim" displays a "radical" political ideology. Although nothing came of these charges, they did bring greater awareness to Hawkins's work.

Hawkins was born in Warrenton, North Carolina, in 1883, a generation after the days of slavery in the American South. In fact, both of his parents were former slaves who became independent farmers. One of his elder siblings, John R. Hawkins, served as a teacher and the president of Kittrell College in North Carolina before moving to Washington, D.C. John R. Hawkins ultimately served as the financial secretary of the African Methodist Episcopal Church and the president of the Association for the Study of Negro Life and History. Like his elder brother, Walter Everette Hawkins attended Kittrell, and graduated in 1901. He emulated his brother once again by moving to Washington, D.C. There he worked as a mail clerk and wrote much of his poetry. Outside of his political convictions, his sentimental views of nature and family became the other dominant themes of his poetry. These themes occur in Hawkins's earliest poems, most of which were published in the collection *Chords and Discords.*

Chords and Discords contains the controversial "Mob Victim," a condemnation of the widespread lynching of southern black men, and of the "Christian land" that could tolerate such injustice. In another poem in the collection, "Too Much Religion," Hawkins ex-

presses his dismay with religious institutions. Like other black writers of the time, Hawkins felt that it was his duty to bring public awareness to existing racial problems. Some of the poems from *Chords and Discords,* along with a new poem called "Child of the Night," were published in the London periodical *African Times and Orient Review.* Before their publication in *Chords and Discords,* "Mob Victim" and "Too Much Religion" were originally published in the *Messenger,* a Harlem-based magazine investigated by the Justice Department in the aforementioned study of "radical" works. Hawkins also contributed other poems to the *Messenger,* an organ known for its discussion of African American political, social, and intellectual issues. Due to his contributions to the periodical, editors at the *Messenger* sometimes called Hawkins "the *Messenger* Poet." Sterling A. Brown discussed the Hawkins poem "I Am Africa" in *Negro Poetry and Drama* (1937), a study of the African American literary voice. The poem appeared in *Crisis,* a National Association for the Advancement of Colored People publication edited for a time by W. E. B. Du Bois, as well as in the anthology *Black and White.*

In 1920 Hawkins significantly revised *Chords and Discords,* and it was issued by another publisher. He included "The Mob Victim," but changed its title to "A Festival in Christendom," and also included the *Chords and Discords* poem "Credo." Hawkins declined to include many of the poems with racial themes. Instead, the book tackles class issues, evidence of Hawkins's increasingly leftist political views. Yet many of the poems are sentimental reflections on love and nature.

Hawkins's socialist nature and sentimental leanings are also evident in the volume *Petals from the Poppies,* a book published after Hawkins moved to New York City. In his piece in the *Dictionary of Literary Biography,* Dickson D. Bruce, Jr. observed that Hawkins's "political poems in *Petals from the Poppies* were probably more persistently leftist than the work of any other black poet through the 1930s. But he framed his radicalism in a context that looked steadfastly backward to an earlier time, to a poetry of sentimentality and even gentility."

BIOGRAPHICAL/CRITICAL SOURCES:

BOOKS

Hawkins, Walter Everette, *Chords and Discords,* introduction by Freeman H. M. Murray, Murray

Brothers, 1909, revised edition published by Richard G. Badger, 1920.

Dictionary of Literary Biography: Volume 50: *Afro-American Writers before the Harlem Renaissance,* Gale (Detroit, MI), 1986.

PERIODICALS

Wilson Library Journal, March, 1995, p. 128.*

*   *   *

HAYDEN, Robert E(arl) 1913-1980

PERSONAL: Name originally Asa Bundy Sheffey; name legally changed by foster parents; born August 4, 1913, in Detroit, MI; died February 25, 1980, in Ann Arbor, MI; son of Asa and Gladys Ruth (Finn) Sheffey; foster son of William and Sue Ellen (Westerfield) Hayden; married Erma I. Morris, June 15, 1940; children: Maia. Detroit City College (now Wayne State University), B.A., 1936; University of Michigan, M.A., 1944. *Religion:* Baha'i.

CAREER: Federal Writers' Project, Detroit, MI, researcher, 1936-40; University of Michigan, Ann Arbor, teaching fellow, 1944-46; Fisk University, Nashville, TN, 1946-69, began as assistant professor, became professor of English; University of Michigan, professor of English, 1969-80. Bingham Professor, University of Louisville, 1969; visiting poet, University of Washington, 1969, University of Connecticut, 1971, and Denison University, 1972. Member, Michigan Arts Council, 1975-76; Consultant in Poetry, Library of Congress, 1976-78.

MEMBER: American Academy and Institute of Arts and Letters, Academy of American Poets, PEN, American Poetry Society, Authors Guild, Authors League of America, Phi Kappa Phi.

AWARDS, HONORS: Jules and Avery Hopwood Poetry Award, University of Michigan, 1938 and 1942; Julius Rosenwald fellow, 1947; Ford Foundation fellow in Mexico, 1954-55; World Festival of Negro Arts grand prize, 1966, for *A Ballad of Remembrance;* Russell Loines Award, National Institute of Arts and Letters, 1970; National Book Award nomination, 1971, for *Words in the Mourning Time;* Litt.D., Brown University, 1976, Grand Valley State College, 1976, Fisk University, 1976, Wayne State University, 1977, and Benedict College, 1977; Acad-

emy of American Poets fellow, 1977; Michigan Arts Foundation Award, 1977; National Book Award nomination, 1979, for *American Journal.*

WRITINGS:

POEMS

Heart-Shape in the Dust, Falcon Press (Detroit), 1940.

(With Myron O'Higgins) *The Lion and the Archer,* Hemphill Press (Nashville), 1948.

Figure of Time: Poems, Hemphill Press, 1955.

A Ballad of Remembrance, Paul Breman (London), 1962.

Selected Poems, October House, 1966.

Words in the Mourning Time, October House, 1970.

The Night-Blooming Cereus, Paul Breman, 1972.

Angle of Ascent: New and Selected Poems, Liveright, 1975.

American Journal, limited edition, Effendi Press, 1978, enlarged edition, Liveright, 1982.

Robert Hayden: Collected Poems, edited by Frederick Glaysher, Liveright, 1985, with an introduction by Arnold Rampersad, Liveright, 1996.

OTHER

(Editor and author of introduction) *Kaleidoscope: Poems by American Negro Poets* (juvenile), Harcourt, 1967.

(With others) *Today's Poets* (recording), Folkways, 1967.

(Author of preface) Alain LeRoy Locke, editor, *The New Negro,* Atheneum, 1968.

(Editor with David J. Burrows and Frederick R. Lapides) *Afro-American Literature: An Introduction,* Harcourt, 1971.

(Editor with James Edwin Miller and Robert O'Neal) *The United States in Literature,* Scott, Foresman, 1973, abridged edition published as *The American Literary Tradition, 1607-1899,* 1973.

(Contributor) *The Legend of John Brown,* Detroit Institute of Arts, 1978.

Collected Prose, edited by Glaysher, University of Michigan Press, 1984.

Contributor to periodicals, including *Atlantic, Negro Digest,* and *Midwest Journal.* Drama and music critic, *Michigan Chronicle,* late 1930s.

SIDELIGHTS: Robert E. Hayden was the first black poet to be chosen as Consultant in Poetry to the Library of Congress, a position described by Thomas W. Ennis of the *New York Times* as "the American equivalent of the British poet laureate designation." Hayden's formal, elegant poems about the black historical experience earned him a number of other major awards as well. "Robert Hayden is now generally accepted," Frederick Glaysher stated in Hayden's *Collected Prose,* "as the most outstanding craftsman of Afro-American poetry."

The historical basis for much of Hayden's poetry stemmed from his extensive study of American and black history. Beginning in the 1930s, when he researched black history for the Federal Writers' Project in his native Detroit, Hayden studied the story of his people from their roots in Africa to their present condition in the United States. "History," Charles T. Davis wrote in *Modern Black Poets: A Collection of Critical Essays,* "has haunted Robert Hayden from the beginning of his career as a poet." As he once explained to Glenford E. Mitchell of *World Order,* Hayden saw history "as a long, tortuous, and often bloody process of becoming, of psychic evolution."

Other early influences on Hayden's development as a poet were W. H. Auden, under whom Hayden studied at the University of Michigan, and Stephen Vincent Benet, particularly Benet's poem "John Brown's Body." That poem describes the black reaction to General Sherman's march through Georgia during the Civil War and inspired Hayden to also write of that period of history, creating a series of poems on black slavery and the Civil War that won him a Hopwood Award in 1942.

After graduating from college in 1944, Hayden embarked on an academic career. He spent some twenty-three years at Fisk University, where he rose to become a professor of English, and ended his career with an eleven-year stint at the University of Michigan. Hayden told Mitchell that he considered himself to be "a poet who teaches in order to earn a living so that he can write a poem or two now and then."

Although history plays a large role in Hayden's poetry, many of his works are also inspired by the poet's adherence to the Baha'i faith, an Eastern religion which believes in a coming world civilization. Hayden served for many years as the poetry editor of the group's *World Order* magazine. The universal outlook of the Baha'is also moved Hayden to reject any narrow racial classification for his work.

James Mann of the *Dictionary of Literary Biography* claimed that Hayden "stands out among poets of his

race for his staunch avowal that the work of black writers must be judged wholly in the context of the literary tradition in English, rather than within the confines of the ethnocentrism that is common in contemporary literature written by blacks." As Lewis Turco explained in the *Michigan Quarterly Review,* "Hayden has always wished to be judged as a poet among poets, not one to whom special rules of criticism ought to be applied in order to make his work acceptable in more than a sociological sense."

This stance earned Hayden harsh criticism from other blacks during the polarized 1960s. He was accused of abandoning his racial heritage to conform to the standards of a white, European literary establishment. "In the 1960s," William Meredith wrote in his foreword to *Collected Prose,* "Hayden declared himself, at considerable cost in popularity, an American poet rather than a black poet, when for a time there was posited an unreconcilable difference between the two roles. . . . He would not relinquish the title of American writer for any narrower identity."

Ironically, much of Hayden's best poetry is concerned with black history and the black experience. "The gift of Robert Hayden's poetry," Vilma Raskin Potter remarked in *MELUS,* "is his coherent vision of the black experience in this country as a continuing journey both communal and private." Hayden wrote of such black historical figures as Nat Turner, Frederick Douglass, Malcolm X, Harriet Tubman, and Cinquez. He also wrote of the Underground Railroad, the Civil War, and the American slave trade. Edward Hirsch, writing in the *Nation,* called Hayden "an American poet, deeply engaged by the topography of American myth in his efforts to illuminate the American black experience."

Though Hayden wrote in formal poetic forms, his range of voices and techniques gave his work a rich variety. "Hayden," Robert G. O'Meally wrote in the *Washington Post Book World,* "is a poet of many voices, using varieties of ironic black folk speech, and a spare, ebullient poetic diction, to grip and chill his readers. He draws characters of stark vividness as he transmutes cardinal points and commonplaces of history into dramatic action and symbol." "His work," Turco wrote, "is unfettered in many ways, not the least of which is in the range of techniques available to him. It gives his imagination wings, allows him to travel throughout human nature."

Speaking of Hayden's use of formal verse forms, Mann explained that Hayden's poems were "formal in a nontraditional, original way, strict but not straight-jacketed" and found that they also possessed "a hard-edged precision of line that molds what the imagination wants to release in visually fine-chiseled fragmental stanzas that fit flush together with the rightness of a picture puzzle."

It wasn't until 1966, with the publication of *Selected Poems*, that Hayden first enjoyed widespread attention from the nation's literary critics. As the *Choice* critic remarked at the time, *Selected Poems* showed Hayden to be "the surest poetic talent of any Negro poet in America; more importantly, it demonstrated a major talent and poetic coming-of-age without regard to race or creed." With each succeeding volume of poems his reputation was further enhanced until, in 1976 and his appointment as Consultant in Poetry to the Library of Congress, Hayden was generally recognized as one of the country's leading black poets. Critics often point to Hayden's unique ability to combine the historical and the personal when speaking of his own life and the lives of his people. Writing in *Obsidian: Black Literature in Review*, Gary Zebrun argued that "the voice of the speaker in Hayden's best work twists and squirms its way out of anguish in order to tell, or sing, stories of American history—in particular the courageous and plaintive record of Afro-American history—and to chart the thoughts and feelings of the poet's own private space. . . . Hayden is ceaselessly trying to achieve . . . transcendence, which must not be an escape from the horror of history or from the loneliness of individual mortality, but an ascent that somehow transforms the horror and creates a blessed permanence."

BIOGRAPHICAL/CRITICAL SOURCES:

BOOKS

Concise Dictionary of Literary Biography, Volume 1: *The New Consciousness, 1941-1968,* Gale, 1987.

Contemporary Authors Bibliographical Series, Volume 2, Gale, 1986.

Contemporary Literary Criticism, Gale, Volume 5, 1976, Volume 9, 1978, Volume 14, 1980, Volume 37, 1986.

Conversations with Writers, Volume 1, Gale, 1977.

Dictionary of Literary Biography, Gale, Volume 5: *American Poets since World War II,* 1980, Volume 76: *Afro-American Writers, 1940-1955,* 1988.

Fetrow, Fred M., *Robert Hayden,* Twayne, 1984.

Gibson, Donald B., editor, *Modern Black Poets: A Collection of Critical Essays,* Prentice-Hall, 1973.

Hatcher, John, *From the Auroral Darkness: The Life and Poetry of Robert Hayden,* George Ronald, 1984.

Hayden, Robert E., *Collected Prose,* edited by Frederick Glaysher, University of Michigan Press, 1984.

O'Brien, John, *Interviews with Black Writers,* Liveright, 1973.

PERIODICALS

AB Bookman's Weekly, April 21, 1980.

Black Scholar, March/April, 1980.

Chicago Tribune, February 27, 1980.

Choice, May, 1967; December, 1984.

Encore, April, 1980.

Los Angeles Times, March 3, 1980.

MELUS, spring, 1980; spring, 1982.

Michigan Quarterly Review, spring, 1977; winter, 1982; fall, 1983.

Nation, December 21, 1985.

New York Times, February 27, 1980.

New York Times Book Review, January 17, 1971; February 22, 1976; October 21, 1979.

Obsidian: Black Literature in Review, spring, 1981.

Time, March 10, 1980.

Virginia Quarterly Review, autumn, 1982.

Washington Post, February 27, 1980.

Washington Post Book World, June 25, 1978.

World Order, spring, 1971; summer, 1975; winter, 1976; fall, 1981.*

*   *   *

HAYGOOD, Johnnie   1924-

PERSONAL: Born December 6, 1924, in Irondale, AL; son of Marvin Haygood (a minister). *Ethnicity:* "African American."

ADDRESSES: Home—16651 Lahser, Apt. 101, Detroit, MI 48219.

CAREER: Writer. Success through Self-Awareness, founder and director. Worked as motivational speaker in Chicago, IL, and Detroit, MI, and as sales techniques trainer, Chicago. *Military service:* U.S. Navy.

WRITINGS:

Success through Self-Awareness, privately printed.

WORK IN PROGRESS: Research on "man/woman relationships."

SIDELIGHTS: Johnnie Haygood told *CA:* "Through extensive studies of philosophy, psychology, sociology, metaphysics, Islam, and the teachings of Jesus and the masters of the Far East, I have lifted my state of consciousness. I portend that truth of self, knowledge of self, and a positive mental attitude are the keys to the betterment of society and humanity.

"Since 1979 I have published *Success through Self-Awareness* and poetry. I have also been an instructor, motivator, and sales trainer for such organizations as Lewis University, Chicago Metropolitan Insurance Company, Osun Art Gallery, PRIDE Community Center, Project Reconciliation, and Operation Push. I have demonstrated my talents in group sessions, training seminars, and lectures."

* * *

HAYWOOD, Gar Anthony 1954-

PERSONAL: Born 1954; married Lynnette, 1981 (divorced); children: Courtney, Erin.

ADDRESSES: Home—Venice, CA. *Agent*—c/o Putnam Berkley Group, 200 Madison Ave., New York, NY 10016.

CAREER: Novelist. Bell Atlantic, field engineer, 1976-88; freelance novelist, 1988—.

MEMBER: Mystery Writers of America, Private Eye Writers of America, American Crime Writers League.

AWARDS, HONORS: Shamus Award for Best First Private Eye Novel of the Year, Private Eye Writers of America, 1988, for *Fear of the Night.*

WRITINGS:

Fear of the Night, St. Martin's (New York City), 1988.
Not Long for This World, St. Martin's, 1990.
You Can Die Trying, St. Martin's, 1993.
Going Nowhere Fast, Putnam, 1994.
Bad News Travels Fast, Putnam, 1995.
It's Not a Pretty Sight, Putnam, 1996.
When Last Seen Alive, Putnam, 1997.
All the Lucky Ones Are Dead, Putnam, 2000.

SIDELIGHTS: Gar Haywood started his career as a mystery novelist with considerable aplomb, as his first private eye novel, 1988's *Fear of the Night,* was named best first private eye novel of the year. This award, from the Private Eye Writers of America, confirmed Haywood's emergence as a fresh face on the mystery-writing market, one who provides a searing look into America's gang-led inner city culture.

In *Fear of the Dark,* black P.I. Aaron Gunner is hired to find the killer who burst into a south central Los Angeles bar and gunned down both the bar's owner and a patron who turns out to be a black activist. The sister of one of the victims feels police are not pursuing the case with vigor, so at her request Gunner—somewhat reluctantly—enters the world of gangs, bars, drugs and crooked politicians to search for the murderer. He soon discovers the killer is a white supremacist working on the campaign of a law-and-order candidate, but before Gunner can question him, the supremacist is found dead—in Gunner's car. Now the P.I.'s concerns shift to saving his own neck, as he is naturally considered a prime suspect for the murder. A critic for *Publishers Weekly* in a review of *Fear of the Dark* wrote that "Haywood has a good ear for the sour voice of the true private eye and the sense of tired hopelessness of the underclass they have always served."

Gunner returns in Haywood's second book, *Not Long for This World.* In this novel, the African American P.I. finds himself defending someone he absolutely detests: a cocky-mouthed gang member accused of murdering someone in a drive-by shooting. Gunner uncovers evidence that the accused, Toby Mills, may have actually been framed, since the key witness is really a crack addict who exchanges testimony for drugs. Gunner's job is to find the driver of the car in the shooting, a man who has since left the gang.

Racism, murder, bad cops, and lawsuits are the theme of Haywood's third mystery novel, *You Can Die Trying,* as P.I. Gunner is lured into clearing up a messy case of suicide. Racist L.A. cop Jack McGovern gunned down a twelve-year-old liquor store thief, insisting that the robber shot first. Eight months later McGovern, disliked both within and outside the L.A.P.D., commits suicide due to overwhelming agony and an impending lawsuit by the dead boy's family. Only then does a witness come forward to corroborate McGovern's story, and Gunner sets out to exonerate the dead cop despite great resistance from both the police department and the local African American community.

Haywood takes an abrupt turn in his fourth book, as he temporarily puts Gunner to rest and introduces a new set of characters: retired police officer Joe Loudermilk and his witty, earthy wife Dottie. In *Going Nowhere Fast,* Joe and Dottie begin to realize their dream of a lifetime—selling their house, buying an Airstream trailer, and traveling around the country. The truth is, they do it partially to get away from their five adult, yet childish, offspring. While visiting the Grand Canyon, Joe and Dottie return from a morning walk to find one of their children, Bad Dog, at their doorstep, and soon discover a dead man in the toilet room of the trailer. Soon the police, the FBI, the mob, and phony reporters are snooping around their trailer, while a suspended N.F.L. football player is chasing Bad Dog. Dottie sets out to find the truth in this fast-paced and sometimes humorous thriller. *Library Journal* contributor Rex E. Klett praised the novel, noting that "deft, descriptive touches and humorous family interaction provide credibility."

Joe and Dottie Loudermilk return for more madcap Airstream adventures in *Bad News Travels Fast.* Deciding to visit Washington, D.C., Dottie makes plans to see one of their children, Eddie. Joe is not happy about the idea, as he is a black conservative, and Eddie would be considered left-of-center. During their visit, one of Eddie's roommates is murdered, and Eddie becomes a prime suspect. Joe and Dottie hit the investigative trail again, this time uncovering a blackmail plot involving the missing diary of a U.S. senator accused of sexual harassment. Joe uses his street smarts to find clues, while Dottie uses her seeming innocence and persistence to make dead leads open up.

Gunner returns to the job in Haywood's sixth book, *It's Not a Pretty Sight.* When the P.I. investigates the murder of his former girlfriend, Nina Pearson, he finds an ugly past that is indicative of the title. His search takes him to a home for abused women, where Nina had spent her last days, as well as the law firm that had recently fired her. There are a whole slew of suspects, including the lawyer, two women who once threatened Nina with a gun, Nina's abusive husband, and a photographer documenting battered women. Gunner's search reveals no lack of possibilities and, as always, he navigates the dangers and threats to his own life to find the guilty party. Haywood's 1997 Gunner episode, *When Last Seen Alive,* finds the African American P.I. once again on the streets of L.A. showing his incredible sleuth tactics.

Haywood and fictional character Gunner have become an established dynamic-duo. Charles Champlin, com-menting on the novel series in the *Los Angeles Times Book Review,* writes that "Crime-fiction writing has been a white near-monopoly, but there are exceptions, and Gar Anthony Haywood is a recent one—an able black writer with a black hero."

BIOGRAPHICAL/CRITICAL SOURCES:

PERIODICALS

Booklist, September 1, 1988, p. 41; September 1, 1996, p. 67.
Kirkus Reviews, May 15, 1993, p. 625; June 1, 1994, p. 738; August 1, 1996, p. 1099.
Library Journal, June 1, 1993, p. 196; July, 1994, p. 133; July, 1995, p. 127.
Los Angeles Times Book Review, September 9, 1990, p. 10.
Publishers Weekly, July 8, 1988, p. 43; April 27, 1990, p. 55; May 10, 1993, p. 55; June 27, 1994, p. 59; July 15, 1996, p. 58.
Washington Post Book World, June 17, 1990, p. 8; August 20, 1995, p. 11.
Wilson Library Bulletin, February, 1989, p. 88.*

*   *   *

HEAD, Bessie 1937-1986

PERSONAL: Original name Bessie Amelia Emery; born July 6, 1937, in Pietermaritzburg, South Africa; died of hepatitis April 17, 1986, in Botswana; married Harold Head (a journalist), September 1, 1961 (divorced); children: Howard. *Education:* Educated in South Africa as a primary teacher. *Politics:* None ("dislike politics"). *Religion:* None ("dislike formal religion").

CAREER: Teacher in primary schools in South Africa and Botswana for four years; journalist at Drum Publications in Johannesburg for two years; writer. Represented Botswana at international writers conference at University of Iowa, 1977-78, and in Denmark, 1980.

AWARDS, HONORS: The Collector of Treasures and Other Botswana Village Tales was nominated for the Jock Campbell Award for literature by new or unregarded talent from Africa or the Caribbean, *New Statesman,* 1978.

WRITINGS:

When Rain Clouds Gather (novel), Simon & Schuster, 1969.

Maru (novel), McCall, 1971.

A Question of Power (novel), Davis Poynter, 1973, Pantheon, 1974.

The Collector of Treasures and Other Botswana Village Tales (short stories), Heinemann, 1977.

Serowe: Village of the Rain Wind (historical chronicle), Heinemann (Portsmouth, NH), 1981.

A Bewitched Crossroad: An African Saga (historical chronicle), Donker (Craighall), 1984, Paragon House, 1986.

A Gesture of Belonging: Letters from Bessie Head, 1965-1979, edited by Randolph Vigne, Heinemann, 1990.

A Woman Alone: Autobiographical Writings, edited by Craig MacKenzie, Heinemann, 1990.

Tales of Tenderness and Power, Heinemann, 1990.

The Cardinals, with Meditations and Short Stories, David Philip (Cape Town), 1993, Heinemann, 1996.

Contributor to periodicals, including the London *Times, Presence Africaine, New African* and *Transition.*

SIDELIGHTS: "Unlike many exiled South African writers," wrote a London *Times* contributor, "[Bessie Head] was able to root her life and her work anew in a country close to her tormented motherland." Born of racially-mixed parentage in South Africa, Head lived and died in her adopted Botswana, the subject of much of her writing; in 1979, after fifteen years as part of a refugee community located at Bamangwato Development Farm, she was granted Botswanan citizenship. In *World Literature Written in English,* Betty McGinnis Fradkin described Head's meager existence after a particularly lean year: "There is no electricity yet. At night Bessie types by the light of six candles. Fruit trees and vegetables surround the house. Bessie makes guava jam to sell, and will sell vegetables when the garden is enlarged." Despite her impoverished circumstances, Head acknowledged to Fradkin that the regularity of her life in the refugee community brought her the peace of mind she sought: "In South Africa, all my life I lived in shattered little bits. All those shattered bits began to grow together here. . . . I have a peace against which all the turmoil is worked out!" "Her novels strike a special chord for the South African diaspora, though this does not imply that it is the only level at which they work or produce an impact as novels," observed Arthur

Ravenscroft in *Aspects of South African Literature.* "They are strange, ambiguous, deeply personal books which initially do not seem to be 'political' in any ordinary sense of the word."

Head's racially-mixed heritage profoundly influenced both her work and her life, for an element of exile as well as an abiding concern with discrimination, whatever its guise, permeate her writing. Noting in *Black Scholar* that Head has "probably received more acclaim than any other black African woman novelist writing in English," Nancy Topping Bazin added that Head's works "reveal a great deal about the lives of African women and about the development of feminist perspectives." According to Bazin, Head's analysis of Africa's "patriarchal system and attitudes" enabled her to make connections between the discrimination she experienced personally from racism and sexism, and the root of oppression generally in the insecurity that compels one to feel superior to another. Head is "especially moving on the position of women, emerging painfully from the chrysalis of tribalist attitudes into a new evaluation of their relationship to men and their position in society," stated Mary Borg in a *New Statesman* review of Head's first novel, *When Rain Clouds Gather.* Considered "intelligent and moving" by one *Times Literary Supplement* contributor, it was described by another as combining "a vivid account of village life in Botswana with the relationship between an Englishman and an embittered black South African who try to change the traditional farming methods of the community."

The black male flees South African apartheid only to experience discrimination from other blacks as a refugee in Botswana. For this novel, Head drew upon her own experience as part of a refugee community, which she indicated in *World Literature Written in English* had been "initially, extremely brutal and harsh." Head explained that she had not experienced oppression by the Botswanan government itself in any way, but because South African blacks had been "stripped bare of every human right," she was unaccustomed to witnessing "human ambition and greed . . . in a black form." Calling *When Rain Clouds Gather* "a tale of innocence and experience," Ravenscroft acknowledged that "there are moments of melodrama and excessive romanticism, but the real life of the novel is of creativity, resilience, reconstruction, fulfillment." Most of the major characters "are in one sense or another handicapped exiles, learning how to mend their lives," said Ravenscroft, adding that "it is the vision behind their effortful embracing of exile that gives Bessie Head's first novel an unusual maturity." Ravenscroft found that in addition to the collective, cooperative enterprise that the village itself represents in *When Rain Clouds Gather,* it speaks to an essential concern of Head's writing by offering a solution for personal fulfillment: "Against a political background of self-indulgent, self-owning traditional chiefs and self-seeking, new politicians more interested in power than people, the village of Golema Mmidi is offered as a difficult alternative: not so much a rural utopia for the Africa of the future to aim at, as a means of personal and economic independence and interdependence, where the qualities that count are benign austerity, reverence for the lives of ordinary people (whether university-educated experts or illiterate villagers), and, above all, the ability to break out of the prison of selfhood without destroying individual privacy and integrity."

Head's second novel, *Maru,* is also set in a Botswanan village. According to Ravenscroft, though, in this book "workaday affairs form the framework for the real novel, which is a drama about inner conflict and peace of mind and soul." *Maru* is about the problems that accompany the arrival of the well-educated new teacher with whom two young chiefs fall in love. It is "about interior experience, about thinking, feeling, sensing, about control over rebellious lusts of the spirit," said Ravenscroft, who questioned whether or not "the two chief male characters . . . who are close, intimate friends until they become bitter antagonists, are indeed two separate fictional characters, or . . . symbolic extensions of contending character-traits within the same man?" Although the new teacher has been raised and educated by a missionary's wife, she belongs to the "lowliest and most despised group in Botswana, the bushmen," explained the London *Times* contributor. "Problems of caste and identity among black Africans are explored with sensitivity," remarked Martin Levin in the *New York Times Book Review.* Ravenscroft suggested that while the novel is a more personal one than Head's first, it is also a more political one, and he was "much impressed and moved by the power . . . in the vitality of the enterprise, which projects the personal and the political implications in such vivid, authentic parallels that one feels they are being closely held together."

Head's critically well-received third novel, *A Question of Power,* relates the story of a young woman who experiences a mental breakdown. In a *Listener* review, Elaine Feinstein observed that "the girl moves through a world dominated by strange figures of supernatural good and evil, in which she suffers torment and enchantment in turn: at last she reaches the point where she can reject the clamorous visions which beset her and assert that there is 'only one God and his name is Man.'"

According to Bazin, Head acknowledged in an interview with Lee Nichols in her *Conversations with African Writers: Interviews with Twenty-six African Authors* that *A Question of Power* is largely autobiographical. "Like Elizabeth, the protagonist in *A Question of Power,* Bessie Head was born in a South African mental hospital," explained Bazin. "Her mother, a wealthy, upperclass, white woman, was to spend the rest of her life there, because in an apartheid society, she had allowed herself to be made pregnant by a black stableman. Until age thirteen, Bessie Head, like Elizabeth, was raised by foster parents and then put in a mission orphanage." Paddy Kitchen pointed out in the *New Statesman,* though, that the novel merely "contains parallels and winnowings from life, not journalist records," adding that "the incredible part is the clarity of the terror that has been rescued from such private, muddled nightmares." Similarly, Ravenscroft discerned no "confusion of identity" between the character and her creator: "Head makes one realize often how close is the similarity between the most fevered creations of a deranged mind and the insanities of deranged societies."

Lauded for the skill with which she recreated the hellish world of madness, Head was also credited by critics such as Jean Marquard in *London Magazine* with having written "the first metaphysical novel on the subject of nation and a national identity to come out of southern Africa." In his *The Novel in the Third World,* Charles R. Larson credits the importance of *A Question of Power* not just to the introspection of its author, but to her exploration of subjects hitherto "foreign to African fiction as a sub-division of the novel in the Third World: madness, sexuality, guilt." Noting that the protagonist's "coloured classification, her orphan status at the mission, and her short-lived marriage" represent the origin of most of her guilt, Larson attributed these factors directly to "the South African policy of apartheid which treats people as something other than human beings." Further, Larson felt that Head intended the reader to consider all the "variations of power as the evils that thwart each individual's desire to be part of the human race, part of the brotherhood of man." *A Question of Power,* wrote Roberta Rubenstein in the *New Republic,* "succeeds as an intense, even mythic, dramatization of the mind's struggle for autonomy and as a symbolic protest against the political realities of South Africa." And in *Books Abroad,* Robert L. Berner considered it "a remarkable attempt to escape from the limitations of mere 'protest' literature in which Black South African writers so often find themselves." Berner recognized that Head could have "written an attack on the indignities of apartheid which have driven her into exile in Botswana," but instead chose to write a novel about the "response to injustice—first in madness and finally in a heroic struggle out of that madness into wholeness and wisdom." Ravenscroft perceived in *A Question of Power* "an intimate relationship between an individual character's private odyssey of the soul and public convulsions that range across the world and from one civilization to another," and deemed the novel "a work of striking virtuosity—an artistically shaped descent into the linked hells of madness and oppression, and a resolution that provides the hope of both internal and external reconciliation."

Critics have analyzed Head's first three novels, *When Rain Clouds Gather, Maru,* and *A Question of Power,* collectively in terms of their thematic concerns and progression. Suggesting that the three novels "deal in different ways with exile and oppression," Marquard noted that "the protagonists are outsiders, new arrivals who try to forge a life for themselves in a poor, under-populated third world country, where traditional and modern attitudes to soil and society are in conflict." Unlike other African writers who are also concerned with such familiar themes, said Marquard, Head "does not idealize the African past and . . . she resists facile polarities, emphasizing personal rather than political motives for tensions between victim and oppressor." Ravenscroft recognized "a steady progression from the first novel to the third into ever murkier depths of alienation from the currents of South African, and African, matters of politics and power." Similarly, Marquard detected an inward movement "from a social to a metaphysical treatment of human insecurities and in the last novel the problem of adaptation to a new world, or new schemes of values, is located in the mind of a single character." Ravenscroft posited that "it is precisely this journeying into the various characters' most secret interior recesses of mind and (we must not fight shy of the word) of soul, that gives the three novels a quite remarkable cohesion and makes them a sort of trilogy."

Considering *When Rain Clouds Gather, Maru,* and *A Question of Power* to be "progressive in their philosophical conclusion about the nature and source of racism," Cecil A. Abrahams suggested in *World Literature Written in English* that "ultimately, Head examines . . . sources of evil and, conversely, of poten-

tial goodness. The most obvious source is the sphere of political power and authority; it is clear that if the political institutions which decree and regulate the lives of the society are reformed or abolished a better or new society can be established." According to Ravenscroft, the elements of imprisonment and control provide thematic unity among the novels. Pointing to the "loneliness and despair of exile" in each of them, Ravenscroft found the resilience of their characters "even more remarkable," and concluded that "what the three novels do say very clearly is that whoever exercises political power, however laudable his aims, will trample upon the faces and limbs of ordinary people, and will lust in that trampling. That horrible obscenity mankind must recognize in its collective interior soul." And Head, said Ravenscroft, "refuses to look for the deceiving gleam that draws one to expect the dawn of liberation in the South, but accepts what the meagre, even parched, present offers."

Head's collection of short stories, *The Collector of Treasures and Other Botswana Village Tales,* which was considered for the *New Statesman*'s Jock Campbell Award, explores several aspects of African life, especially the position of women. Linking Head to the "village storyteller of the oral tradition," Michael Thorpe noted in *World Literature Today* that her stories are "rooted, folkloristic tales woven from the fabric of village life and intended to entertain and enlighten, not to engage the modern close critic." In the *Listener,* John Mellors related Head's statement that "she has 'romanticised and fictionalized' data provided by old men of the tribe whose memories are unreliable." In its yoking of present to past, the collection also reveals the inevitable friction between old ways and new. The world of Head's work "is not a simply modernizing world but one that seeks, come what may, to keep women in traditionally imprisoning holes and corners," said Valerie Cunningham in the *New Statesman.* "It's a world where whites not only force all blacks into an exile apart from humanity but where women are pushed further still into sexist exile." In *The Collector of Treasures and Other Botswana Village Tales,* added Cunningham, "Head puts a woman's as well as a black case in tales that both reach back into tribal legend and cut deep into modern Africa."

Head's *The Cardinals, with Meditations and Short Stories* contains a novella (written before her exile) and seven short pieces set in South Africa. A *Publishers Weekly* reviewer remarked that the stories "read . . . like scattershot historical information mixed with outdated ideas" and that the introduction was "far more interesting than the work itself." The central novella concerns a woman called Mouse who was sold by her mother for five shillings when she was a child. Later, she perseveres to become a newspaper reporter. As a reporter, Mouse struggles in a male-dominated world and becomes involved with a man who, unbeknownst to either of them, is her father. Adele S. Newson remarked in *World Literature Today* that "Drawing from the experiences of her South African existence, Head provides something of a poetic rendering of what it means to be a woman and a writer in the male-dominated, racist, and sexist South Africa of her formative years as a writer." In the *New York Times Book Review,* Scott Martelle noted that the book "bears the unpolished marks of an immature writer, particularly in long stretches of improbable dialogue. But the work overcomes these weaknesses to stand as a clearsighted snapshot of people trying to pursue their lives within a system that seeks to deny their existence."

Two books by Head, *Serowe: Village of the Rain Wind* and *A Bewitched Crossroad: An African Saga,* are categorized as historical chronicles and combine historical accounts with the folklore of the region. The collected interviews in *Serowe* focus on a time frame that spans the eras of Khama the Great (1875-1923) and Tshekedi Khama (1926-1959) through the Swaneng Project beginning in 1963 under Patrick Van Rensburg, "a South African exile who, like Head herself, has devoted his life in a present-day Botswana to make some restitution for white rapacity," wrote Thorpe. Larson, who considers "reading any book by Bessie Head . . . always a pleasure," added that *Serowe* "falls in a special category." Calling it a "quasi-sociological account," Larson described it as "part history, part anthology and folklore." "Its citizens give their testimonies, both personal and practical, in an unselfconscious way," said Paddy Kitchen in the *Listener,* "and Bessie Head—in true African style—orders the information so that, above all, it tells a story." *Serowe* is "a vivid portrait of a remarkable place . . . one wishes there were many more studies of its kind," remarked a *British Book News* contributor. Kitchen believed it to be "a story which readers will find themselves using as a text from which to meditate on many aspects of society." And discussing her book, *A Bewitched Crossroad,* which examines on a broader scope the African tribal wars in the early nineteenth century, Thorpe found that "in her moral history humane ideals displace ancestor-worship, and peace-loving strength displaces naked force." Questioned by Fradkin about the manner in

which she worked, Head explained: "Every story or book starts with something just for myself. Then from that small me it becomes a panorama—the big view that has something for everyone." Head "stresses in her novels the ideals of humility, love, truthfulness, freedom, and, of course, equality," wrote Bazin. At the time of her death, she had achieved an international reputation and had begun to write her autobiography. Head obviously endured much difficulty during her life; despite her rejection of South Africa as well as the hardships of her exiled existence, however, she emerged from the racist and sexist discrimination that she both witnessed and experienced, to the affirmation she told Fradkin represented the only two themes present in her writing—"that love is really good . . . and . . . that it is important to be an ordinary person." She added, "More than anything I want to be noble." According to Kitchen, "a great deal has been written about black writers, but Bessie Head is surely one of the pioneers of brown literature—a literature that includes everybody."

Published posthumously, *Tales of Tenderness and Power* and *A Woman Alone: Autobiographical Writings* are companion collections of short pieces. Some of the material appears in both volumes, including stories that critics think are inappropriately included in the autobiographical volume. The stories in *Tales of Tenderness and Power* date from the early 1960s, when Head lived in South Africa, to the 1980s, when Head had lived in Serowe for years. The pieces in *A Woman Alone* date from 1937 to 1986. "Head concentrated on black people, living together. Her stories are small descriptions of how traditions change over time, of how colonialism appears to the colonized, of chiefly justice and political corruption, of neighbors helping each other through famines and of villagers attacking deviants, of lovers and families," summed up Gay W. Seraman in *Women's Review of Books.* A *Publishers Weekly* reviewer stated: "The stories in [*Tales of Tenderness and Power*] . . . offer a rare insight into African history, culture and lore from a black perspective." In the *Times Literary Supplement* Maya Jaggi declared that the stories "testify to Head's subtlety, versatility and prowess as a story-teller. . . . All are enriched by Head's distinctive vision, whether in their scornful exposure of corruption and abuses of power, or their epiphanic moments of generosity and tenderness." According to Charles Larson in *Washington Post Book World,* Head's stories "were not only humane but genuinely hopeful about the human condition." But he added that Head's memoir in *A Woman Alone* "reads like a horror tale, filled not only with the most appalling acts of inhumanity but also with one of the most agonizing accounts of loneliness one is likely to encounter." Jaggi characterized *A Woman Alone* as "brief, fragmentary and sometimes repetitive," yet called it a work that "builds a surprisingly coherent portrait of a sensitive, compassionate and talented writer transcending an onerous legacy. . . . These notes and sketches yield valuable insights into Head's views on politics, literature and feminism."

A Gesture of Belonging: Letters from Bessie Head, 1965-1979 provides further insight into Head and her works. She wrote the letters to editor Randolph Vigne, who puts them into context with explanatory notes regarding the author's circumstances and clarifying her references. Vigne shared Head's interests in political activism and journalism in Cape Town; she referred to him as "my papa" in many of the letters. "Of significant literary interest is the light the letters shed on the composition and reception of her works. Present also, however, is a disquieting strain of paranoia and contradictory responses," remarked A. A. Elder in *Choice*. Despite her concerns about the extent to which Vigne bowdlerized the letters, Arlene A. Elder maintained in *Callaloo:* "*A Gesture of Belonging* will help satisfy those clamoring for more biographical information about the writer as well as those hoping to put her works within the contexts of her own assessment of them and their relationship to the political and personal issues with which she was struggling as she composed them." Desiree Lewis concluded in *World Literature Today:* "Head's restless struggles both against and with available narratives, forms, and discourses were rarely univocal, linear, or intentional ones. Her lesser-known fiction encodes traces of her complex battle to construct identities beyond dominant fictions and to discover the conditions for her own creativity."

BIOGRAPHICAL/CRITICAL SOURCES:

BOOKS

Abrahams, Cecil, editor, *The Tragic Life: Bessie Head and Literature in Southern Africa,* Africa World Press (Trenton, NJ), 1990.

Black Literature Criticism, Gale, 1992.

Contemporary Literary Criticism, Gale, Volume 25, 1983; Volume 67, 1992.

Dictionary of Literary Biography, Volume 117: *Twentieth-Century Caribbean and Black African Writers, First Series,* Gale, 1992.

Eilersen, Gilliam Stead, *Bessie Head: Thunder Behind Her Ears: Her Life and Writing,* Heinemann (Portsmouth, NH), 1996.

Heywood, Christopher, editor, *Aspects of South African Literature,* Heinemann, 1976.

Ibrahim, Humam, *Bessie Head: Subversive Identities in Exile,* University Press of Virginia (Charlottesville), 1996.

Larson, Charles R., *The Novel in the Third World,* Inscape Publishers, 1976.

Nichols, Lee, editor, *Conversations with African Writers: Interviews with Twenty-six African Writers,* Voice of America (Washington, D.C.), 1981.

Ola, Virginia, *The Life and Works of Bessie Head,* E. Mellen Press (Lewiston, NY), 1994.

Olaussen, Maria, *Forceful Creation in Harsh Terrain: Place and Identity in Three Novels by Bessie Head,* Peter Lang (New York City), 1997.

Zell, Hans M., and others, *A New Reader's Guide to African Literature,* Holmes & Meier, 2nd edition, 1983.

PERIODICALS

Best Sellers, March 15, 1969.

Black Scholar, March/April, 1986.

Books Abroad, winter, 1975.

British Book News, November, 1981.

Callaloo, winter, 1993, p. 277.

Choice, July/August, 1991, p. 1788; December, 1991, p. 592.

Journal of Commonwealth Literature, Volume 21, number 1, 1986.

Listener, February 4, 1971; November 22, 1973; April 20, 1978; July 2, 1981.

London Magazine, December/January, 1978-79.

Ms., January, 1987.

New Republic, April 27, 1974.

New Statesman, May 16, 1969; November 2, 1973; June 2, 1978.

New York Times Book Review, September 26, 1971; March 31, 1996.

Publishers Weekly, October 12, 1990, p. 56; January 1, 1996, p. 68.

Times (London), May 1, 1986.*

Times Literary Supplement, May 2, 1969; February 5, 1971; December 7, 1990, p. 1326.

Washington Post Book World, February 17, 1991, p. 4.

Women's Review of Books, January, 1991, p. 1.

World Literature Today, winter, 1982; summer, 1983; winter, 1983; winter, 1986; autumn, 1994, p. 869; winter, 1996, p. 73.

World Literature Written in English, Volume 17, number 1, 1978; Volume 17, number 2, 1978; Volume 18, number 1, 1979.

HEARNE, John (Edgar Caulwell) 1926-
(John Morris, a joint pseudonym)

PERSONAL: Born February 4, 1926, in Montreal, Quebec, Canada; son of Maurice Vincent and Doris (May) Hearne; married Joyce Veitch, September 3, 1947 (divorced); married Leeta Mary Hopkinson (a teacher), April 12, 1955; children: two. *Education:* Attended Jamaica College; Edinburgh University, M.A., 1950; University of London, teaching diploma, 1950. *Religion:* Christian.

ADDRESSES: Home—P.O. Box 335, Kingston 8, Jamaica. *Office*—Creative Arts Centre, University of the West Indies, Kingston 7, Jamaica. *Agent*—Claire Smith, Harold Ober Associates, Inc., 40 East 49th St., New York, NY 10017.

CAREER: Teacher at schools in London, England, and in Jamaica, 1950-59; information officer, Government of Jamaica, 1962; University of the West Indies, Kingston, Jamaica, resident tutor in extramural studies, 1962-67, head of Creative Arts Centre, 1968-92. Visiting Gregory Fellow in Commonwealth Literature at University of Leeds, England, 1967; Colgate University, New York, visiting O'Conner Professor in Literature, 1969-70, and visiting professor in literature, 1973. Royal Air Force, air gunner, 1943-46.

MEMBER: International PEN.

AWARDS, HONORS: John Llewelyn Rhys Memorial Prize, 1956, for *Voices under the Window;* Silver Musgrave Medal from Institute of Jamaica, 1964.

WRITINGS:

NOVELS

Voices under the Window, Faber, 1955, reprinted, 1985.
Stranger at the Gate, Faber, 1956.
The Faces of Love, Faber, 1957, published as *The Eye of the Storm,* Little, Brown, 1958.
The Autumn Equinox, Faber, 1959, Vanguard Press, 1961.
Land of the Living, Faber, 1961, Harper, 1962.
(With Morris Cargill, under joint pseudonym John Morris) *Fever Grass,* Putnam, 1969.
(With Cargill, under joint pseudonym John Morris) *The Candywine Development,* Collins, 1970, Lyle Stuart, 1971.
The Sure Salvation, Faber, 1981, St. Martin's, 1982.

SHORT STORIES

Contributor of short stories to anthologies, including *West Indian Stories,* edited by Andrew Salkey, Faber, 1960, and *Stories from the Caribbean,* edited by Salkey, Elek, 1965, published as *Island Voices: Stories from the West Indies,* Liveright, 1970.

Contributor of short stories and articles to periodicals, including *Atlantic Monthly, New Statesman,* and the *Trinidad Guardian.*

OTHER

(With Rex Nettleford) *Our Heritage,* University of the West Indies, 1963.
(Editor and author of introduction) *Carifesta Forum: An Anthology of Twenty Caribbean Voices,* Carifesta 76 (Kingston, Jamaica), 1976.
(Editor and author of introduction) *The Search for Solutions: Selections from the Speeches and Writings of Michael Manley,* Maple House Publishing Co., 1976.
(With Lawrence Coote and Lynden Facey) *Testing Democracy through Elections: A Tale of Five Elections,* edited by Marie Gregory, Bustamante Institute of Public and International Affairs (Kingston, Jamaica), 1985.

Also author of teleplays, including *Soldiers in the Snow,* with James Mitchell, 1960, and *A World Inside,* 1962; author of stage play *The Golden Savage,* 1965.

Work represented in anthologies, including O. R. Dathorne's *Caribbean Narrative: An Anthology of West Indian Writing,* Heinemann, 1966, and Barbara Howes's *From the Green Antilles: Writings of the Caribbean,* Macmillan, 1966.

SIDELIGHTS: A West Indian writer who sometimes collaborates with Morris Cargill as the pseudonymous John Morris, John Hearne is known for his vivid depictions of life among the West Indies and their people. In particular, several of his writings focus on Jamaica—the native land of his parents—and address complex social and moral issues affecting both individual relationships and, to a lesser extent, the cultural and political aspects of the island. Much of Hearne's fiction—including the novels *Stranger at the Gate, The Faces of Love, The Autumn Equinox,* and *Land of the Living*—also takes place on Cayuna, a mythical counterpart of Jamaica. More generally, his work relates a broad, first-hand account of the Caribbean experience and features elements of racial and social inequities as well as recurrent themes of betrayal and disenchantment. Especially noteworthy are Hearne's acclaimed narrative skill and descriptive style, which distinguish his fiction as characteristically evocative and lifelike.

Hearne's 1981 novel, *The Sure Salvation,* takes place in the southern Atlantic Ocean aboard a sailing ship of the same name. Set in the year 1860, the story chronicles the illegal buying and selling of negroes more than fifty years after England first enacted laws prohibiting the practice commonly known as slave trade. Through a "series of deft flashbacks," observed *Times Literary Supplement* critic T. O. Treadwell, Hearne recounts individual circumstances that led to his characters' unlawful fraternity on board the *Sure Salvation.* Risking constant danger and the death penalty if they are caught, the captain and crew hope to amend their ill-fated lives with monies paid for the vessel's charge of five hundred Africans. While the "beastliness isn't played down," Treadwell noted, we come "to understand, and even sympathize with" these men and their despicable dealings due to Hearne's successful literary craftsmanship and execution. Treadwell further announced that the "author's gift for irony . . . that the slavers are no freer than" their shackled cargo, provides this "absorbing" tale with its utmost pleasures, and he concluded that *The Sure Salvation* proves the "power of the sea story . . . as potent as ever."

Hearne commented that his writing is influenced by his growing up in an island society large enough to be interesting but small enough for "characters" to be known intimately. He added: "I have been much concerned with politics (as a commentator) as Jamaica has tried to fashion itself into a newly independent society since the early 1960s."

BIOGRAPHICAL/CRITICAL SOURCES:

BOOKS

James, Louis, editor, *The Islands in Between: Essays on West Indian Literature,* Oxford University Press, 1968.
Ramchand, Kenneth, *The West Indian Novel and Its Background,* Barnes & Noble, 1970.

PERIODICALS

Times Literary Supplement, June 19, 1981.*

HEATH, Roy A(ubrey) K(elvin) 1926-

PERSONAL: Born August 13, 1926, in Georgetown, British Guiana (now Guyana); son of Melrose A. (a teacher) and Jessie R. (a teacher) Heath; married Aemilia Oberli; children: three. *Education:* University of London, B.A., 1956.

ADDRESSES: Agent—Bill Hamilton, A. M. Heath and Company. Ltd., 40-42 William IV St., London WC2N 4DD, England.

CAREER: Called to the Bar, Lincolns Inn, 1964. Worked in civil service in British Guiana, 1942-50; held various clerical jobs in London, England, 1951-58; teacher of French and German in London, 1959—.

AWARDS, HONORS: Drama award, Theatre Guild of Guyana, 1971, for *Inez Combray;* fiction prize, London *Guardian,* 1978, for *The Murderer;* Guyana Award for Literature, 1989, for *The Shadow Bride.*

WRITINGS:

NOVELS

A Man Come Home, Longman (Port of Spain), 1974.
The Murderer, Allison & Busby (London), 1978, Persea (New York City), 1992.
From the Heat of the Day (also see below), Allison & Busby, 1979, Persea, 1993.
One Generation (also see below), Allison & Busby (New York City), 1980.
Genetha (also see below), Allison & Busby, 1981.
Kwaku; or, The Man Who Could Not Keep His Mouth Shut, Allison & Busby, 1982.
Orealla, Allison & Busby, 1984.
The Shadow Bride, Collins (London), 1988.
The Armstrong Trilogy (contains *From the Heat of the Day, One Generation,* and *Genetha*), Persea, 1994.
The Ministry of Hope, or, The Metamorphosis of Kwaku: A Novel, Marion Boyars (New York City), 1996.

OTHER

The Reasonable Adventurer, University of Pittsburgh Press (Pittsburgh, PA), 1964.
Inez Combray (stage play), produced in Georgetown, Guyana, 1972.
Princeton Retrospectives: Twenty-Fifth-Year Reflections on a College Education, Darwin Press, 1979.

Art and History (lectures), Ministry of Education (Georgetown, Guyana), 1983.
Shadows round the Moon: Caribbean Memoirs, Collins, 1990.

Contributor of short stories to anthologies, including *Firebird 2,* edited by T. J. Binding, Penguin (London), 1983; *Colours of a New Day: New Writing for South Africa,* edited by Sarah Lefanu and Stephen Hayward, Pantheon (New York City), 1990; and *So Very English,* edited by Marsha Rowe, Serpents Tail, 1991.

Contributor of short stories to periodicals, including *London, Savacou,* and *Kaie.*

SIDELIGHTS: Though a London resident since 1951, Roy A. K. Heath sets his fiction in Georgetown, British Guiana (now Guyana), where he was born in 1926. "My work is intended to be a chronicle of twentieth-century Guyana," he once told *CA.* By providing detailed descriptions of Georgetown streets, slums, brothels, and suburbs, combined with insights on local colonial roots, Heath not only educates readers about life in contemporary Guyana but also reveals a deeper, more historical concern. "His reference to ancestors illustrates a vital aspect of Heath's vision as a novelist," comments Ian H. Munro in the *Dictionary of Literary Biography,* "for though the surface of his work is naturalistic, his narrative technique relentlessly probes the hidden realities of Guyanese life, the complex web of myths, dreams, customs, and prejudices arising from the aboriginal, African, and East Indian legacies."

Published in 1974, Heath's first novel, *A Man Come Home,* is a tale "pungent with the sex, sweat and wit of Georgetown's 'yard society,'" explains Sally Emerson in *Books and Bookmen.* Loutish protagonist Bird Foster relies for a living on the financial generosity of his mistress. Seeking to escape this dependence, he is finally motivated to gain monetary independence and vanishes from the area, only to return as a wealthy man. Given his reputation as a layabout, local wisdom credits Foster's fortune to the magic of Fair Maid, a local river spirit. In the nature of such tales, Foster's happiness is short-lived; his mistress discovers and removes a gold chain given to her lover by the river spirit, thus enraging Fair Maid, who conjures forth the circumstances of Foster's death. A multilayered novel, *A Man Come Home* sets Foster's tale against that of his father, whose hopes for independence for both his children and for Guyana are destroyed by violence and a breakdown of morality.

Interweaving contemporary drama with the harsh, uncompromising justice born of ancient myths, Heath's "occasional allusions to Guyana's tormented history are reminders that the explosive, unexamined emotions [of his characters] have counterparts in the larger world," observes Munro.

The Murderer, winner of the 1978 *Guardian* prize for fiction, depicts the mental turmoil of one Galton Flood, a man who kills his wife, Gemma, after discovering that she had engaged in a sexual relationship with another man before their marriage. Heath's protagonist battles "the web of domination and subservience lying at the heart of Guyanese society," according to Munro, as "the flood of repressed emotion he feels when he kills her is his one moment of emotional truth." "It is the geography of Guyana . . . that determines the disposition of her people," adds Shena Mackay, also commenting on the political allegory inherent in Heath's work in the *Times Educational Supplement.* "Trapped between the oceans and the forest, . . . people are isolated and frustrated; friendships founder, resentments and misunderstandings smoulder, good intentions explode into violence; love and regrets cannot be expressed."

Heath's *The Armstrong Trilogy,* which was released in a single volume in 1994, focuses on "irredeemably paranoid men and the women they destroy in their madness," according to James Polk in the *Washington Post Book World.* Tracing Guyanese culture from the 1920s to the 1950s, the trilogy begins with 1979's *From the Heat of the Day,* which opens during the wedding of Sonny Armstrong and Gladys Davis. *One Generation,* published in 1980, focuses on the life of the couple's son, Rohan; *Genetha,* published a year later, charts the life of their daughter. *From the Heat of the Day* presents a foredoomed marriage: Gladys comes from an upper-class family that scorns Sonny, a mere civil servant. He, in turn, reacts by being abusive to Gladys, riding the emotional pendulum between his natural compassion and the urge to belittle her because of his feelings of inferiority. The novel "is nicely evocative of the mood of [the 1930s,] that paralysed decade," comments John Naughton in *Listener,* "and nicely evocative also of the sultry hopelessness of a society where few people have anything, and where the men have the lion's share of what little is going."

One Generation continues the history of Sonny and his family following the death of his wife. The novel focuses on his son, Rohan, who becomes an aimless civil servant and a frequenter of pool halls alongside a ne'er-do-well calling himself Fingers. After Fingers gets involved with Rohan's sister, Genetha, Rohan flees from Georgetown society and recoils into a tragic affair with an East Indian woman. *Genetha* explores the dysfunctional relationship between Rohan's sister and Fingers, which results in her growing poverty and degradation. Sheltered by a prostitute who once worked as Sonny's servant, Genetha is drawn down into the ultimate degradation afforded in the world of sex-for-money. Although she is aware of the depravity she has fallen into, Genetha finds it strangely satisfying.

The protagonist of Heath's 1982 novel *Kwaku; or, The Man Who Could Not Keep His Mouth Shut* is a shoemaker who lives with his wife and eight children in a small Guyanese village and dreams of one day becoming successful. He leaves his family and travels to the town of New Amsterdam, where he passes himself off as a medicine man. The recovery of several patients, which accidentally coincides with their use of one of his concoctions, transforms Kwaku into an instant success. A variant of the Native American trickster character, Kwaku is able to ride the crest of this fluke of fate through cleverness and sheer brazenness. His newfound success and social status are challenged, however, after Kwaku returns to his native village: His wife succumbs to an illness her husband cannot cure, and a new medicine man begins to challenge Kwaku's monopoly on the enterprise. Ultimately, the once distant Kwaku learns to appreciate family, both supporting and gaining support from his wife. "Heath puts all of his considerable skills—of narration, characterization and description—on display in a book that conveys its comic vision with wisdom as well as wit," concludes Alan Bold in the *Times Literary Supplement*. *Orealla* takes place in 1920's Georgetown, a capitalist society where "the aura of gas lamps, shadows, burning sun, and horses passing on rain-sodden streets provides a haunting background to this most disturbing of Heath's novels," comments Munro.

In *Orealla* Heath tells the story of Ben, a black freelance journalist who craves freedom but is forced by circumstance to sideline as a private coachman. Ben also moonlights as a burglar. Robbing the homes of wealthy citizens is, in fact, his way of striking out against the class and racial prejudice rife in Guyanese society. Caught and forced to work for a petty civil servant, Ben dreams of attaining his freedom by traveling to the village of Orealla. Instead, he kills his overbearing employer, thereby gaining a measure of freedom without making the dreamed-of journey.

Taking as its subject the condition of East Indians living in Guyana, Heath's 1988 novel, *The Shadow Bride,* focuses on the well-to-do Singh family. One of the children, Betta, dedicates his life to healing the poor and sickly. However, the young man's noble efforts are sabotaged by the efforts of his widowed mother, who emerges as the novel's destructive force. Brought from India to Guyana by her husband, the widowed mother is the "shadow bride" who rages against her exile, influencing her hapless son to identify with his Indian heritage and destroy his compassion for his fellow Guyanese. Although torn by this conflict, Betta ultimately comes to accept the contradictions of his birth and avoids ultimate despair. Calling the novel a tale of "the tragic isolation of this Indian version of Medea," John Spurling in the London *Observer* notes that the mother character "is as fully explored and credible as that of the place, time and people amongst which he sets her." Although his works focus on his native country, Heath's appeal as a novelist has extended to his adopted home of England. While sometimes criticized for his dry prose style, Clive Davis praises Heath's work in *New Statesman and Society*. "At his best," notes Davis, "he evokes the arbitrary, almost fantastical atmosphere of life in a British possession teetering on the edge of South America." Evoking compassion for the land of his birth—its language, its vistas, and its society—through his fiction, Heath continues to enlighten readers' understanding of his homeland; he has, in Munro's opinion, "added a new dimension to the literary map of Guyana."

BIOGRAPHICAL/CRITICAL SOURCES:

PERIODICALS

American Book Review, August/September, 1993, p. 25.
Booklist, September, 1982.
Books and Bookmen, April, 1975.
Library Journal, April 1, 1994, p. 131.
Listener, December 13, 1979.
London Review of Books, July 12, 1990, pp. 19-20.
Los Angeles Times, January 21, 1993, p. E5.
Los Angeles Times Book Review, April 12, 1992.
New Statesman and Society, December 7, 1979; May 11, 1990, p. 38.
New York Times, June 22, 1994, p. C12.
New York Times Book Review, January 15, 1984; August 23, 1992, p. 9; June 27, 1993, p. 19.
Observer (London), April 17, 1988.
Publishers Weekly, June 25, 1982; January 6, 1992.
Times Educational Supplement, February 22, 1985, p. 22.

Times Literary Supplement, December 27, 1974; November 12, 1982; July 27, 1984; September 14, 1990, p. 979.

Washington Post Book World, August 21, 1994, p. 4; February 18, 1996, p. 7.

World Literature Today, winter, 1989, pp. 151-52; autumn, 1991, pp. 753-54; spring, 1993, pp. 427-28.

World Literature Written in English, spring, 1989, pp. 103-10.

*   *   *

HEMPHILL, Essex 1956(?)-

PERSONAL: Born in c. 1956.

CAREER: Editor, poet, and essayist.

WRITINGS:

(Editor) *Brother to Brother: New Writings by Black Gay Men* (anthology), Alyson Publications, 1991.

Ceremonies: Prose and Poetry, New American Library, 1992.

Standing in the Gap, Dutton, 1999.

Also author of two self-published chapbooks of poetry, *Earth Life* and *Conditions,* both 1985; contributed to the films *Looking for Langston,* by Isaac Julien, and *Tongues Untied,* by Marlon Riggs.

SIDELIGHTS: Since the beginning of the modern gay liberation movement in the 1970s, a steadily growing body of literature by gay and lesbian writers has explored issues of gay identity, the gay community, and the place of gay men and lesbians in mainstream society. As an editor, poet, and essayist, Essex Hemphill has been a key figure in the emergence of a distinctive African American perspective in the field of gay literature.

Hemphill grew up in a working-class neighborhood in Washington, D.C., gradually becoming aware of the racism that proliferated around him. And as he entered adolescence and became increasingly aware of his own homosexuality, he had to contend with yet another kind of oppression. As Hemphill writes in his book *Ceremonies,* "My sexual curiosity would have blossomed in any context, but in Southeast Washington, where I grew up, I had to carefully allow my petals to unfold. If I had revealed them too soon they would have been snatched away, brutalized, and scattered down alleys. I was already alert enough to know what happened to the flamboyant boys at the school who were called 'sissies' and 'faggots.' I could not have endured then the violence and indignities they often suffered."

In his twenties, Hemphill was attracted to the ideas embodied in the black nationalist movement that flourished in the 1960s and 1970s. But as he got older, he began to question the rhetoric that had previously inspired him. "I moved away from black nationalism," Hemphill writes in *Ceremonies,* "as being too narrow a politic for the interests that reside in me." But he also found that a narrowly defined lesbian and gay political ideology could not adequately accommodate his personal vision, and went on to develop his own political and literary ideas.

Hemphill's literary voice had to accommodate the numerous conflicts that he faced, both as an African American male in a predominantly white society afflicted by racism and as a gay man in a predominantly heterosexual society afflicted by homophobia. And as many black gay writers, including Hemphill, have expressed repeatedly in recent years, being both black and gay carries a special burden. Throughout American history, the culture of slavery and racism often encouraged white men to bolster their own sense of masculinity by asserting their dominance over black men. In response to this violent and abusive history, the black community placed a high premium on strong male images. Homosexuality, understood only through stereotypes of effeminacy and submissiveness, was particularly repugnant in this context. Thus, where many white Americans were reluctant to tolerate homosexuals, many blacks were reluctant even to acknowledge that homosexuals existed in their community. Moreover, the racism that prevailed in mainstream American society could also be found in the newly emerging and predominantly white gay community, an especially frustrating and disheartening fact for the many black gay men and lesbians seeking to participate in the newfound gay liberation of the past 25 years.

Given these multiple layers of oppression and rejection, black gay and lesbian writers were truly courageous in staking out a new literary terrain for themselves. The writings of 35 such black gay men were gathered by Hemphill in *Brother to Brother,* an anthology of poetry and prose. The pieces in this collection are primarily autobiographical, and lend a personal immediacy to discussions of racism, religious intolerance, homophobia, and life in the age of AIDS. Given the sensitivity of these topics, *Brother to Brother* could not help but be controversial. The book is divided into four sections, each with a distinct theme. The first section, called "When I Think of Home," focuses on varying notions of home and family, from those we grow up in to those we choose and create for ourselves as adults. The second section, called "Baby, I'm for Real," explores the false identities that black gay men create for themselves and hide behind, identities that often represent what they wish they could truly be or could truly have, including white skin or heterosexuality. The third section, called "Hold Tight, Gently," considers life in the age of AIDS, and includes personal accounts of dealing with the epidemic. The final section, "The Absence of Fear," contrasts the way black men are represented in mainstream culture with the way black men represent themselves. It includes discussions of homoerotic images of black men by the gay white photographer Robert Mapplethorpe, as well as recent films by and about black gay men, like Isaac Julien's *Looking for Langston* and Marlon Riggs's *Tongues Untied*. Hemphill himself contributes poetry which, according to Donald Suggs in his *Village Voice* review of the book, "effectively brackets and enlarges many of the conflicts in the anthology."

Ceremonies, an anthology of Hemphill's poetry and prose, spans the author's entire writing career, and includes pieces from his self-published 1985 chapbooks *Earth Life* and *Conditions* as well as previously unpublished work. As did the writings by Hemphill and others in *Brother to Brother,* the poems and essays in *Ceremonies* continue to explore the double burden of being a minority within a minority. "One of Hemphill's most persistent themes [is] the outsider confronting the dominant culture," wrote David Trinidad in his *Village Voice Literary Supplement* review of the book. Hemphill "has forged—with few role models to emulate, and with little or no support from the white gay literary establishment—an identity and a style characterized by anger and point-blank honesty," according to Trinidad. In addition to overtly political pieces, Hemphill includes love poems, celebrations of sexuality, and affirmations of gay identity, along with heartfelt and moving accounts of the fears and dangers of growing up black and gay. "He makes passionate common sense," wrote Thomas Tavis in his *Library Journal* review, concluding that "this is urgent, fiercely telling work." According to Craig Allen Seymour II, writing in the *Advocate,* Hemphill "is poised to become the most widely known black gay writer since James Baldwin."

BIOGRAPHICAL/CRITICAL SOURCES:

PERIODICALS

Advocate, June 2, 1992, p. 38.
Library Journal, October 1, 1992, p. 88.
Los Angeles Times Book Review, September 8, 1991, p. 18.
Village Voice, October 1, 1991, p. 74.
Village Voice Literary Supplement, June 1992, pp. 7-8.

*   *   *

HOLLINS, Etta R(uth)

PERSONAL: Daughter of Ruben and Willie Mae (Wilbon) Stevenson; children: Kimberly S., Karla D. *Ethnicity:* "African American." *Education:* Kansas State College of Pittsburg (now Pittsburg State University), B.S., 1964; University of Washington, Seattle, M.Ed., 1972; University of Texas at Austin, Ph.D., 1983.

ADDRESSES: Home—7700 John Elwood Dr., Centerville, OH 45459. *Office*—College of Education and Human Services, Wright State University, Dayton, OH 45435.

CAREER: Elementary schoolteacher in Parsons, KS, 1964-65; California State Department of Youth Authority, Paso Robles, classroom teacher, 1966-69; social studies teacher and department head at middle schools in Seattle, WA, 1969-72; primary resource teacher at public schools in Sacramento, CA, 1972-73; full-time consultant in multicultural education for public schools in San Mateo, CA, 1973-75; administrator of public schools in Palo Alto, CA, 1975-79; Education Service Center, Region XIII, Austin, TX, full-time consultant in social studies and multicultural education, 1979-82; coordinator of teacher training program for public schools in Austin, 1982-84; University of Utah, Salt Lake City, assistant professor of educational studies, 1984-86; Weber State College, Ogden, UT, assistant professor of teacher education, 1986-87; Delaware State University, Dover, associate professor of education and head of department, 1987-88; California State University, Hayward, professor of teacher education, 1988-95, and member of board of directors, Urban Teacher Academy, beginning in 1989; Washington State University, Pullman, professor of teaching and learning and department head,

1995-98; Wright State University, Dayton, OH, professor of education and associate dean, College of Education and Human Services, 1998—. Pacific Lutheran Seminary, lecturer, 1990; University of California, Berkeley, member of council of teachers, Center for the Study of Writing, 1989-90, member of advisory board, 1990-91; Jackson State University, Joseph H. Jackson Distinguished Lecturer, 1994.

MEMBER: American Educational Research Association (division vice-president, 1997-99), National Council for the Social Studies (and African American Special Interest Group), National Association of Black School Educators, Association for Supervision and Curriculum Development, National Council for Negro Women, Phi Delta Kappa, Kappa Delta Pi, Pi Lambda Theta.

AWARDS, HONORS: Martin Luther King, Jr. Humanitarian Award, Citizens Committee, Austin, TX, 1984; Teacher Diversity Award, California State University, 1989; grant from Ford Foundation, 1990-91; Outstanding Writing Award, American Association of Colleges of Teacher Education, 1997.

WRITINGS:

A Conceptual Framework for Selecting Instructional Approaches and Materials for Inner City Black Youngsters, California Department of Education, 1989.

(With K. Spencer) *Schooling in a Context of Cultural Isolation: African American Students in Utah* (monograph), Mid-Continent Regional Educational Laboratory Center for Educational Equity (Aurora, CO), 1991.

(Editor with J. E. King and W. A. Hayman, and contributor) *Teaching Diverse Populations: Formulating a Knowledge Base,* State University of New York Press (Albany, NY), 1994.

(Contributor) Helene Hodges, editor, *Educating Everybody's Children,* Association for Supervision and Curriculum Development (Washington, DC), 1994.

(Contributor) Benjamin Bowser, Terry Jones, and Gale Auletta, editors, *Toward the Multicultural University,* Greenwood Press (Westport, CT), 1995.

Culture in School Learning, Lawrence Erlbaum (Mahwah, NJ), 1996.

(Editor) *Transforming Curriculum for a Culturally Diverse Society,* Lawrence Erlbaum, 1996.

(Editor with King and Hayman, and contributor) *Preparing Teachers for Cultural Diversity,* Teachers College Press (New York City), 1997.

(Editor with R. H. Sheets, and contributor) *Racial-Ethnic Identity and Aspects of Human Development in School Practices,* Lawrence Erlbaum, in press.

(Editor with E. I. Oliver, and contributor) *Reflective Teaching in a Culturally Diverse Society: Finding Pathways to Success,* Lawrence Erlbaum, in press.

(Contributor) D. A. Gabbard, editor, *Power/Knowledge and the Politics of Educational Meaning: A Teacher's Guide,* Lawrence Erlbaum, in press.

Contributor of articles and reviews to academic journals, including *Action in Teacher Education, Theory into Practice, American Behavioral Scientist, Current Directions, Journal of Education,* and *Journal of Teacher Education.* Member of editorial board, *American Educational Research Journal,* 1997—.

*   *   *

HOLLY, Ellen (Virginia) 1931-

PERSONAL: Born January 16, 1931, in New York, NY; daughter of William (a chemical engineer) and Grayce (a librarian; maiden name, Arnold) Holly. *Ethnicity:* "African American." *Education:* Hunter College (now Hunter College of the City University of New York), B.A., 1952; studied acting at Perry-Mansfield School of the Theater, and with Barney Brown, Uta Hagen, Charlotte Perry, Eli Rill, and Mira Rostova. *Avocational interests:* Writing.

ADDRESSES: Agent—Starkman Agency, 1501 Broadway, Suite 301A, New York, NY 10036.

CAREER: Actor and writer. Actor in theatrical productions, including *The Anniversary* and *A Switch in Time, Two for Fun* (double-bill), Greenwich Mews Theatre, New York City, 1955; *A Florentine Tragedy* and *Salome,* Davenport Theatre, New York City, 1955; *Too Late the Phalarope* (Broadway debut), Belasco Theatre, New York City, 1956; *Tevya and His Daughters,* Carnegie Hall Playhouse, New York City, 1957; *Othello,* Belvedere Lake Theatre, 1958; *Face of a Hero,* Eugene O'Neill Theatre, New York City, 1960; *Moon on a Rainbow Shawl,* East Eleventh Street Theatre, New York City, 1962; *Tiger, Tiger, Burning Bright,* Booth Theatre, New York City, 1962; *Antony and Cleopatra,* New York Shakespeare Festival, Delacorte Theatre, New York City, 1963; *Funny House of a Negro,* East End Theatre, New York City, 1964; *A Midsummer Night's Dream,* New

York Shakespeare Festival, Delacorte Mobile Theatre, 1964; *King Henry V* and *The Taming of the Shrew,* New York Shakespeare Festival, Delacorte Mobile Theatre, 1965; *The Owl Answers,* White Barn Theatre, Westport, CT, then Theatre de Lys, New York City, 1965; *An Evening of Negro Poetry and Folk Music,* Delacorte Theatre, 1966, produced as *A Hand Is on the Gate,* Longacre Theatre, New York City, 1966; *Macbeth,* New York Shakespeare Festival, Delacorte Mobile Theatre, 1966; *The Comedy of Errors,* National Repertory Theatre, U.S. cities, 1967; *Camino Real,* Playhouse in the Park, Cincinnati, OH, 1968; *The Comedy of Errors,* Ford's Theatre, Washington, DC, 1968; *Crime on Goat Island,* Playhouse in the Park, Cincinnati, OH, 1968; *The Cherry Orchard,* New York Shakespeare Festival, Public/Anspacher Theatre, New York City, 1973; *King Lear,* New York Shakespeare Festival, Delacorte Theatre, 1973; *'Tis Pity She's a Whore,* U.S. cities, 1974-75. Also appeared in stage productions of *Orchids in the Moonlight,* American Repertory Theatre, Cambridge, MA, and in *John Brown's Body.* Member of Playhouse in the Park, Cincinnati, OH, 1968. Actor in films, including *Take a Giant Step,* United Artists, 1959; *Cops and Robbers,* United Artists, 1973; *School Daze,* Columbia, 1988. Actor in television series, including *One Life to Live,* ABC, 1968-81 and 1983-85; *Guiding Light* (also known as *The Guiding Light*), CBS, 1989—; and *Love of Life,* CBS. Actor in television episodes, including *Odyssey,* CBS, 1957; "King Lear," *Great Performances* (also known as *Theatre in America*), PBS, 1974; "High School Narc," *ABC Afterschool Special,* ABC, 1985; *The Big Story,* NBC; *Confidential File,* syndicated; *The Defenders,* CBS; *Dr. Kildare,* NBC; *Look Up and Live,* CBS; *The Nurses,* CBS; *Sam Benedict,* ABC. Actor in television movies, including *Sergeant Matlovich vs. the U.S. Air Force,* NBC, 1978.

MEMBER: Actors Equity Association, Screen Actors Guild, American Federation of Television and Radio Artists, Delta Sigma Theta.

WRITINGS:

One Life: The Autobiography of an African American Actress, Kodansha (New York City), 1996.

SIDELIGHTS: Ellen Holly turned to writing relatively late in life, after working over forty years as an actress. *One Life: The Autobiography of an African American Actress* depicts her struggles to succeed as an African American woman in the entertainment industry. Throughout much of Ellen Holly's career

there were few acting jobs for women of color, and Holly did not win many of them because she was considered too fair-skinned for African American roles. Hence, the acclaim she received for her acting abilities, both on stage and film, never materialized into concrete opportunities to perform.

Holly made her acting debut on a New York Stage in 1955, but she did not climb into the national spotlight until 1968. That year she won the part of Carla Benari on the daytime television drama *One Life to Live.* This character would be a fixture on the show for the next seventeen seasons, until a dispute with the soap's director pushed her to move to a competitor's drama. Noting the many facets of Ellen Holly's career, a reviewer for *Publishers Weekly* noted how Holly "depicts the mercurial world of show biz" and "displays a vivid sense of justice in this outspoken memoir." Writing in *Booklist,* Ilene Cooper shared similar opinions, remarking on the "raw emotion behind Holly's often quite elegant prose."

BIOGRAPHICAL/CRITICAL SOURCES:

BOOKS

Contemporary Theatre, Film, and Television, Volume 10, Gale (Detroit, MI), 1993.

PERIODICALS

Booklist, November 15, 1996, p. 563.
Publishers Weekly, October 28, 1996, p. 69.*

*   *   *

HOPKINS, Pauline Elizabeth 1859-1930 (Sarah A. Allen)

PERSONAL: Born in 1859, in Portland, ME; died in a fire, August 13, 1930, in Boston, MA.

CAREER: Novelist, dramatist, journalist, and editor. Worked throughout much of her life as a stenographer; performed her own musicals and those of others with family troupe, The Hopkins' Colored Troubadours, 1880-92; *Colored American* magazine, Boston, editorial staff member and frequent contributor, 1900-04.

AWARDS, HONORS: First Prize, Congregational Publishing Society of Boston essay contest, 1874, for *Evils of Intemperance and Their Remedies.*

WRITINGS:

Slaves' Escape: or, the Underground Railroad (play), produced in Boston, MA, at Oakland Garden, July 5, 1880, revised as *Peculiar Sam, or the Underground Railroad.*

Contending Forces: A Romance Illustrative of Negro Life North and South (novel), Colored Co-operative Publishing Company, 1900, Southern Illinois University Press, 1978.

A Primer of Facts Pertaining to the Greatness of Africa (nonfiction), P.E. Hopkins, 1905.

The Magazine Novels of Pauline Hopkins, with an introduction by Hazel V. Carby, Oxford University Press, 1988.

Also author, under pseudonym Sarah A. Allen, of the novel *Hagar's Daughter: A Story of Southern Caste Prejudice,* serialized in *Colored American* magazine, 1901-02. Author of the novels *Winona: A Tale of Negro Life in the South and Southwest,* serialized in *Colored American* magazine, 1902; and *Of One Blood; or, The Hidden Self,* serialized in *Colored American* magazine, 1902-03. Also author of the short story "The Mystery within Us," published in *Colored American* magazine, 1900. Author of the novella *Topsy Templeton,* published in *New Era* magazine, 1916. Author of the biographical sketches *Famous Men of the Negro Race* and *Famous Women of the Negro Race,* both published in *Colored American,* 1901-02. Author of the essay *Evils of Intemperance and Their Remedies.* Contributor of additional articles, editorials, and short stories to *Colored American,* 1900-04, and *Voice of the Negro,* 1904-05.

SIDELIGHTS: A minor black author of the late nineteenth and early twentieth centuries, Pauline Elizabeth Hopkins was one of the first writers to introduce racial and social themes into the framework of traditional nineteenth-century romance novels. In her most important publication, *Contending Forces: A Romance Illustrative of Negro Life North and South* (1900), she propounded the ideology of W. E. B. Du Bois, an early advocate of liberal education and political rights for black Americans. Throughout her work Hopkins examined racial injustice, challenged widely held notions about her race, and emphasized self-reliance as an important component of social advancement for black Americans.

Hopkins was born in Portland, Maine, and grew up in Boston, Massachusetts, where she attended public schools and graduated from Girls' High School. She was twenty-one when her musical drama *Slaves' Escape; or, The Underground Railroad* (1880) was produced, with Hopkins and members of her family in the cast. For several years following this production Hopkins toured as a singer with her family's performing group, the Hopkins' Colored Troubadours. During the 1890s she worked at various clerical jobs and as a public lecturer. In 1900 Hopkins's short story "The Mystery within Us" appeared in the first issue of *Colored American* magazine. The same year her first novel, *Contending Forces: A Romance Illustrative of Negro Life North and South,* was published. During the early 1900s Hopkins served on the editorial staff of *Colored American* and eventually became the magazine's literary editor. Her subsequent novels, short stories, and nonfiction appeared primarily in the *Colored American* between 1901 and 1903. Three of her novels, *Hagar's Daughter: A Story of Southern Caste Prejudice* (1901-02), *Winona: A Tale of Negro Life in the South and Southwest* (1902), and *Of One Blood; or, The Hidden Self* (1902-03), were first serialized in the magazine. Ill health caused Hopkins to leave the magazine's staff in 1904, but she continued writing and occasionally published fiction and nonfiction in black-owned journals while supporting herself largely through clerical work. She died in a fire in 1930.

Contending Forces is a historical romance tracing the experiences of one black family throughout the nineteenth century, from slavery in the West Indies and the American South to freedom in Boston and New Orleans. The novel illuminates the political, economic, and social problems encountered by blacks in antebellum America. Hopkins stated that she wrote *Contending Forces* in order to "faithfully portray the inmost thoughts and feelings of the Negro with all the fire and romance which lie dormant in our history" and to help "raise the stigma of degradation" from her race—something that she maintained black people had to do for themselves. *Contending Forces* earned Hopkins neither literary fame nor financial success during her lifetime, and it began to receive critical attention only after her death. In an early survey of black American authors titled *The Negro Author: His Development in America to 1900,* Vernon Loggins considered *Contending Forces* overly complicated and sensational. In *Negro Voices in American Fiction,* Hugh M. Gloster also pronounced Hopkins an untalented narrator, but he commended *Contending Forces* for providing "interesting sidelights on the struggles of a middle-class Negro family for education, employment, and social adjustment in post-bellum Boston."

Throughout her career Hopkins protested the inequities suffered by her race, advocating assimilation and integration with the white community as a remedy to racial injustice. Hopkins's presumption of the superior value of white culture and her advocacy of assimilation have been of particular interest to modern critics. In her afterword to the 1978 edition of *Contending Forces,* Gwendolyn Brooks, for example, criticized Hopkins for her assimilationist outlook and admiration of the dominant culture, and Joseph Rosenbaum of *Reprint Bulletin Book Reviews* has observed that in *Contending Forces* "beauty and success are judged by the white man's standard." Most commentators agree that *Contending Forces* is overplotted and confusingly constructed; nevertheless, they consider it an important historical and sociological document that portrays the effect of Du Bois's social and educational programs on the black community and sheds light on the role of black women in nineteenth-century America.

Hopkins remains an obscure figure in American literature. The critical neglect of her work has most often been attributed to her unexceptional narrative technique, although the relative unavailability of her works and the general neglect suffered by female authors have also been cited as reasons for her obscurity. Nevertheless, a number of commentators have argued that her fiction merits wider attention, and many have praised *Contending Forces* as a poignant reflection of Hopkins's era.

BIOGRAPHICAL/CRITICAL SOURCES:

BOOKS

Berzon, Judith R., *Neither White nor Black: The Mulatto Character in American Fiction,* New York University Press, 1978.

Black Literature Criticism, Gale, 1992, pp. 1023-1037.

Bone, Robert, *The Negro Novel in America,* Yale University Press, 1965.

Carby, Hazel V., *Reconstructing Womanhood: The Emergence of the Afro-American Woman Novelist,* Oxford University Press, 1987, pp. 121-44.

Dictionary of Literary Biography, Volume 50: *Afro-American Writers before the Harlem Renaissance,* Gale, 1987, pp. 182-189.

Gloster, Hugh M., *Negro Voices in American Fiction,* University of North Carolina Press, 1948.

Gruesser, John Cullen (Editor), *The Unruly Voice: Rediscovering Pauline Elizabeth Hopkins,* University of Illinois Press, 1996.

Hopkins, Pauline Elizabeth, *Contending Forces: A Romance Illustrative of Negro Life North and South* (novel), Colored Co-operative Publishing Company, 1900, Southern Illinois University Press, 1978.

Loggins, Vernon, *The Negro Author: His Development in America to 1900,* Columbia University Press, 1931.

Pryse, Marjorie, and Hortense J. Spillers, editors, *Conjuring: Black Women, Fiction, and Literary Tradition,* Indiana University Press, 1985, pp. 53-66.

Rush, Theressa Gunnels, Carol Fairbanks Myers, and Esther Spring Arata, *Black American Writers Past and Present: A Biographical and Bibliographical Dictionary,* Scarecrow Press, 1975, Vol. 1, pp. 389-90.

Schomburg Guide to Black Literature, Gale, 1996.

Twentieth-Century Literary Criticism, Volume 28, Gale, 1988.

PERIODICALS

Choice, January, 1979, p. 1518.

Kliatt, September, 1980, p. 7.

Reprint Bulletin Book Reviews, Volume XXIV, No. 1, 1979, p. 35.

Voice Literary Supplement, November, 1988, p. 16.*

* * *

HOWARD, Vanessa 1955-

PERSONAL: Born in 1955, in Brooklyn, NY.

CAREER: Poet and fiction writer. Participant in the Fort Greene Writing Workshop.

WRITINGS:

A Screaming Whisper (poetry), photographs by J. Pinderhughes, Holt, 1972.

Work represented in anthologies, including *Soulscript, Voice of the Children,* and *Tales and Stories.*

SIDELIGHTS: Vanessa Howard was still a teenager when *A Screaming Whisper,* a book of forty-four poems, was published. Among the works collected in the volume is "Observations of a Subway Train," in which Howard perceives both the projected images and the true personalities of other passengers on the train. Despite Howard's youth, Margaret A. Dorsey, a critic for the *Library Journal,* commended the author for her "maturity of understanding." In the *English Journal* John W. Conner found that Howard's "observations are poignant and real. She is restless and impatient with the age-old restlessness and impatience of youth."

BIOGRAPHICAL/CRITICAL SOURCES:

PERIODICALS

English Journal, May, 1973, p. 829.
Library Journal, December 15, 1972, p. 4078.*

*   *   *

HUBBARD, Dolan   1949-

PERSONAL: Born February 20, 1949, in Wingate Township, NC; son of Olin (a farmer, cook, textile worker, and furniture worker) and Elizabeth (a homemaker, domestic worker, and seamstress; maiden name, Kendall) Hubbard; married Jennie Ruth Hampton, July 15, 1973; children: Aisha Katherine Elizabeth, Desmond Jelani. *Ethnicity:* "Black American." *Education:* Catawba College, B.A., 1971; University of Denver, M.A., 1974; University of Illinois at Urbana-Champaign, Ph.D., 1986; University of North Carolina at Chapel Hill, postdoctoral study, 1986-88. *Religion:* African Methodist Episcopal. *Avocational interests:* Reading, travel, antique furniture, gardening, old movies, sports.

ADDRESSES: Home—2413 Hartfell Rd., Timonium, MD 21093-2514. *Office*—Department of English and Language Arts, Morgan State University, 1700 East Cold Spring Lane, Baltimore, MD 21251; fax 410-319-3743. *E-mail*—dhubbard@moac.morgan.edu.

CAREER: Frederick County Board of Education, Frederick County, MD, teacher, 1971-72, 1974-76; Catawba College, Salisbury, NC, minority counselor and admissions counselor, 1976-77; Winston-Salem State University, Winston-Salem, NC, instructor, 1977-82; University of Cincinnati, Cincinnati, OH, assistant professor, 1988-89; University of Tennessee, Knoxville, assistant professor, 1989-94; University of Georgia, Athens, associate professor of English, 1994-98; Morgan State University, Baltimore, MD, professor of English and chairperson of Department of English and Language Arts, 1998—. Catawba Col-

lege, member of board of trustees, 1994—. Big Brothers/Big Sisters of Winston-Salem, volunteer, 1980-82.

MEMBER: Modern Language Association of America (chairperson of Division on Black American Literature and Culture, 1996), American Literature Association, Association of Governing Boards of Colleges and Universities, College Language Association (president, 1994-96), MELUS, Richard Wright Circle, Langston Hughes Society (vice-president, 1998—), Middle Atlantic Writers Association, South Atlantic Modern Language Association.

AWARDS, HONORS: National Endowment for the Humanities, fellowship, 1985, grant, 1991; Carolina minority postdoctoral scholar, 1986-88; *The Sermon and the African American Literary Imagination* was selected by *Choice* as an "outstanding academic book" for 1995.

WRITINGS:

The Sermon and the African American Literary Imagination, University of Missouri Press (Columbia, MO), 1994.
(Contributor) Julie Brown, editor, *American Short Story Writers: A Collection of Critical Essays,* Garland Publishing (New York City), 1994.
(Editor) *Recovered Writers/Recovered Texts: Race, Class, and Gender in Black Women's Literature,* University of Tennessee Press (Knoxville, TN), 1997.
(Contributor) Gloria L. Cronin, editor, *Critical Essays in American Literature: Zora Neal Hurston,* G. K. Hall (New York City), in press.

General editor (with others) of the series "The Collected Works of Langston Hughes," University of Missouri Press. Contributor of articles and reviews to academic journals, including *CLA Journal, Black Issues in Higher Education, Obsidian II, Centennial Review, Black American Literature Forum,* and *Franklin Pierce Studies in Literature.* Editor, *Langston Hughes Review,* 1994-98; member of editorial board, *Texas Studies in Literature and Language,* 1996-2002; advisory editor, *African American Review,* 1993—.

WORK IN PROGRESS: Editing *Critical Essays on W. E. B. DuBois' The Souls of Black Folk,* for University of Missouri Press, completion expected in 1999; *Wallace Thurman and the Harlem Renaissance: Negotiating Modernism.*

SIDELIGHTS: Dolan Hubbard told *CA:* "I was inspired to write by my teachers at Granite Quarry (North Carolina) Colored Elementary School, from 1957 to 1963. In a rigidly segregated America, these teachers challenged us to be our best and told us that we could achieve anything that we wanted. Rosebud Aggrey, my fourth-grade teacher, from a distinguished Ghanian-American family, always gave her best students extra work and also had us serve as tutors for the slower students. She humanized the learning experience for me.

"When I write, I write to tell the untold stories of these faceless American heroes. By this, I mean that my criticism situates blacks in the American experience as actors and not as reactors. Stylistically, I want my writing to sing, for I feel that criticism need not be dull or dry. For me, criticism is a narrative, and I try to illuminate the drama involved in the critical moment."

*   *   *

HUDSON, Wade   1946-

PERSONAL: Born October 23, 1946, in Mansfield, LA; son of Wade and Lurline (Jones) Hudson; married Cheryl Willis (a publisher and writer), June 24, 1972; children: Katura, Stephan. *Education:* Attended Southern University and Agricultural and Mechanical College, 1964-68. *Politics:* Democrat. *Religion:* Baptist.

ADDRESSES: Home—202 Dodd St., East Orange, NJ 07017. *Office*—Just Us Books, 356 Glenwood Ave., 3rd Floor, East Orange, NJ 07017.

CAREER: Just Us Books, East Orange, NJ, co-owner, 1987—; writer.

MEMBER: Multicultural Publishers Exchange (board member), African American Publishers, Writers and Booksellers Association.

WRITINGS:

(With Valerie Wilson Wesley) *Afro-Bets Book of Black Heroes from A to Z: An Introduction to Important Black Achievers,* illustrated by Cheryl W. Hudson, Just Us Books (Orange, NJ), 1988.
Afro-Bets Alphabet Rap Song, Just Us Books, 1990.
Jamal's Busy Day, illustrated by George Ford, Just Us Books, 1991.

Afro-Bets Kids: I'm Gonna Be!, illustrated by Culverson Blair, Just Us Books, 1992.
(With Debbi Chocolate) *NEATE: To the Rescue,* Just Us Books, 1992.
I Love My Family, illustrated by Cal Massey, Scholastic (New York City), 1993.
(Editor) *Pass It On: African-American Poetry for Children,* illustrated by Floyd Cooper, Scholastic, 1993.
(Editor with wife, Cheryl Hudson) *How Sweet the Sound: African-American Songs for Children,* Scholastic, 1995.
Five Brave Explorers, Scholastic, 1995.
Five Notable Inventors, Scholastic, 1995.
(Editor with C. Hudson) *Kids' Book of Wisdom: Quotes from the African American Tradition,* Just Us Books, 1996.
(Editor with C. Hudson) *In Praise of Our Fathers and Our Mothers: A Black Family Treasury by Outstanding Authors and Artists,* Just Us Books, 1997.

Also author of the children's book *Beebe's Lonely Saturday,* New Dimension Publishing, and the stage plays *Freedom Star,* Macmillan, *Sam Carter Belongs Here, The Return, A House Divided. . . , Black Love Story,* and *Dead End.*

SIDELIGHTS: Wade Hudson's children's books present uplifting portraits of African American family life and historical black figures. Co-owner with his wife, Cheryl, of Just Us Books, Hudson is committed to publishing positive books for a young black audience. Hudson's stories provide subtle self-affirmation for his readers. His story *Jamal's Busy Day* has been praised for its use of a clever conceit that draws parallels between the daily activities of a young boy, Jamal, and those of his accountant mother and architect father. Like them, he gets himself ready for his "work," takes a crowded bus, works with numbers, attends meetings, does drawings, and so on. "The upbeat message," according to *Publishers Weekly,* "is that both parents and children can 'work hard' and accomplish much in their respective arenas: all have something to contribute and all work has value."

In 1988 Wade Hudson and Valerie Wilson Wesley collaborated on *Afro-Bets Book of Black Heroes from A to Z,* which presents profiles of forty-nine black men and women who have achieved success in the face of adversity and have made important contributions to society. Although the "information is uneven," *Afro-Bets* has been called by a *Booklist* critic "a useful item for black history collections." Included in the book are entries on such diverse people as Shaka, the Zulu king, to Thurgood Marshall, the Supreme Court justice, boxer Muhammad Ali, activist Martin Luther King, Jr., and writer Zora Neal Hurston. Some reviewers noted that the work offers hard-to-find information on individuals such as sculptress Edmonia Lewis and educator Fanny Coppin, who are often overlooked in reference works.

Hudson and his wife paid tribute to the African American family with their highly-praised collection *In Praise of Our Fathers and Our Mothers: A Black Family Treasury by Outstanding Authors and Artists.* The anthology includes poetry, essays, paintings, photographs, interviews, and memoirs from nearly 50 artists and writers, including Gwendolyn Brooks, Candy Dawson Boyd, Brian Pinkney, and Walter Dean Myers. Hazel Rochman, reviewing *In Praise of Our Fathers and Our Mothers* in *Booklist,* called it a "fine" book whose "tone is upbeat but neither sentimental nor nostalgic. . . . The design is clear and spacious, and the large-size volume will lend itself to sharing across generations at home, in the library, and at school." In addition, Rochman commented, "This collection may encourage young people to draw on their own family stories."

Horn Book critic Rudine Sims Bishop similarly believed the book could "appeal to readers across generations and across cultural boundaries as well." Bishop noted that "certain themes run through these pieces like ribbons woven through braided hair." A strong fatherly presence throughout the collection belies the stereotype of the fatherless black family; the strength of women too is celebrated in stories about mothers, grandmothers, sisters, and aunts. "Even the black church is honored as a metaphorical mother," reported Bishop. "Shared values are also woven through these works, including an emphasis on creating and surrounding oneself with beauty; a high regard for education; the necessity to maintain a life of the spirit; and the need for familial and cultural continuity. . . . [The contributors] span at least three generations, and while their voices are varied, their works affirm the perseverance of those values across time and circumstances."

In all his books, Hudson hopes to fill a shortage in black-oriented children's books. Speaking of his Just Us Books publishing house to Claire Serant of *Black Enterprise,* Hudson states: "There's an age-old belief in publishing that blacks don't read. But it's actually the mainstream market that hasn't devised a strategy to reach that audience." Hudson also told *CA:* "One

can never take any image for granted. Images, whether in print, film, television, or on stage, are constantly shaping the way we feel and what we think and believe. This is particularly crucial to the African-American community which has been deliberately given negative images of its history and culture. I find it rewarding to help reshape and change those negative images to reflect truth. I think the struggle to present the correct images, the truth, is the most crucial one facing us all."

BIOGRAPHICAL/CRITICAL SOURCES:

PERIODICALS

Black Enterprise, March, 1991, p. 21.
Booklist, January 1, 1989, p. 788; September 15, 1995, p. 165; April 1, 1997, p. 132.
Bookwatch, January, 1989, p. 7.
Emerge, October, 1996, p. 26.
Horn Book, March-April, 1997, p. 217.
Publishers Weekly, December 6, 1991, p. 71; January 20, 1997, p. 400.
School Library Journal, December, 1988, p. 117; February, 1992, p. 74; November, 1995, p. 90; June, 1997, p. 138.
Social Education, April, 1992, p. 262.

* * *

HUGHES, (James) Langston 1902-1967

PERSONAL: Born February 1, 1902, in Joplin, MO; died May 22, 1967, of congestive heart failure in New York, NY; son of James Nathaniel (in business, and a lawyer and rancher) and Carrie Mercer (a teacher; maiden name, Langston) Hughes. *Education:* Attended Columbia University, 1921-22; Lincoln University, A.B., 1929.

CAREER: Poet, novelist, short story writer, playwright, song lyricist, radio writer, translator, author of juvenile books, and lecturer. In early years worked as assistant cook, launderer, busboy, and at other odd jobs; worked as seaman on voyages to Africa and Europe. Lived at various times in Mexico, France, Italy, Spain, and the Soviet Union. Madrid correspondent for *Baltimore Afro-American,* 1937; visiting professor in creative writing, Atlanta University, 1947; poet in residence, Laboratory School, University of Chicago, 1949.

MEMBER: Authors Guild, Dramatists Guild, American Society of Composers, Authors, and Publishers, PEN, National Institute of Arts and Letters, Omega Psi Phi.

AWARDS, HONORS: Opportunity magazine literary contest, first prize in poetry, 1925; Amy Spingarn Contest, *Crisis* magazine, poetry and essay prizes, 1925; Witter Bynner undergraduate poetry prize contests, first prize, 1926; *Palms* magazine Intercollegiate Poetry Award, 1927; Harmon Gold Medal for Literature, 1931; Guggenheim fellowship for creative work, 1935; Rosenwald fellowship, 1941; Litt.D., Lincoln University, 1943, Howard University, 1960, Western Reserve University, 1964; National Institute and American Academy of Arts and Letters grant, 1947; Anisfeld-Wolfe Award for best book on racial relations, 1954; Spingarn Medal, National Association for the Advancement of Colored People (NAACP), 1960.

WRITINGS:

POETRY; PUBLISHED BY KNOPF, EXCEPT AS INDICATED

The Weary Blues, 1926.
Fine Clothes to the Jew, 1927.
The Negro Mother and Other Dramatic Recitations, Golden Stair Press, 1931.
Dear Lovely Death, Troutbeck Press, 1931.
The Dream Keeper and Other Poems, 1932.
Scottsboro Limited: Four Poems and a Play, Golden Stair Press, 1932.
A New Song, International Workers Order, 1938.
(With Robert Glenn) *Shakespeare in Harlem,* 1942.
Jim Crow's Last Stand, Negro Publication Society of America, 1943.
Freedom's Plow, Musette Publishers, 1943.
Lament for Dark Peoples and Other Poems, Holland, 1944.
Fields of Wonder, 1947.
One-Way Ticket, 1949.
Montage of a Dream Deferred, Holt, 1951.
Ask Your Mama: 12 Moods for Jazz, 1961.
The Panther and the Lash: Poems of Our Times, 1967, reprinted, Vintage Books, 1992.
The Collected Poems of Langston Hughes, Knopf (New York City), 1994.
The Block: Poems, Viking (New York City), 1995.
Carol of the Brown King: Poems, Atheneum Books (New York City), 1997.
The Pastebaord Bandit, Oxford University Press (New York City), 1997.

NOVELS

Not Without Laughter, Knopf, 1930, Macmillan, 1986.
Tambourines to Glory, John Day, 1958, reprinted, Hill & Wang, 1970.

SHORT STORIES

The Ways of White Folks, Knopf, 1934, reprinted, Random House, 1971.
Simple Speaks His Mind, Simon & Schuster, 1950.
Laughing to Keep from Crying, Holt, 1952.
Simple Takes a Wife, Simon & Schuster, 1953.
Simple Stakes a Claim, Rinehart, 1957.
Something in Common and Other Stories, Hill & Wang, 1963.
Simple's Uncle Sam, Hill & Wang, 1965.
The Return of Simple Hill & Wang, 1994.
Short Stories of Langston Hughes, Hill & Wang (New York City), 1996.

AUTOBIOGRAPHY

The Big Sea: An Autobiography, Knopf, 1940, reprinted, Thunder's Mouth, 1986.
I Wonder as I Wander: An Autobiographical Journey, Rinehart, 1956, reprinted, Thunder's Mouth, 1986.

NONFICTION

A Negro Looks at Soviet Central Asia, Co-operative Publishing Society of Foreign Workers in the U.S.S.R., 1934.
(With Roy De Carava) *The Sweet Flypaper of Life,* Simon & Schuster, 1955, reprinted, Howard University Press, 1985.
(With Milton Meltzer) *A Pictorial History of the Negro in America,* Crown, 1956, 4th edition published as *A Pictorial History of Black Americans,* 1973, 6th edition published as *A Pictorial History of African Americans,* 1995.
Fight for Freedom: The Story of the NAACP, Norton, 1962.
(With Meltzer) *Black Magic: A Pictorial History of the Negro in American Entertainment,* Prentice-Hall, 1967.
Black Misery, Paul S. Erickson, 1969, reprinted, Oxford University Press, 1994.

JUVENILE

(With Arna Bontemps) *Popo and Fifina: Children of Haiti,* Macmillan, 1932, reprinted, Oxford University Press, 1993.

The First Book of Negroes, F. Watts, 1952.

The First Book of Rhythms, F. Watts, 1954, also published as *The Book of Rhythms,* Oxford University Press (New York City), 1995.

Famous American Negroes, Dodd, 1954.

Famous Negro Music Makers, Dodd, 1955.

The First Book of Jazz, F. Watts, 1955, revised edition, 1976.

The First Book of the West Indies, F. Watts, 1956 (published in England as *The First Book of the Caribbean,* E. Ward, 1965).

Famous Negro Heroes of America, Dodd, 1958.

The First Book of Africa, F. Watts, 1960, revised edition, 1964.

The Sweet and Sour Animal Book, Oxford University Press (New York City), 1994.

EDITOR

Four Lincoln University Poets, Lincoln University, 1930.

(With Bontemps) *The Poetry of the Negro, 1746-1949,* Doubleday, 1949, revised edition published as *The Poetry of the Negro, 1746-1970,* 1970.

(With Waring Cuney and Bruce M. Wright) *Lincoln University Poets,* Fine Editions, 1954.

(With Bontemps) *The Book of Negro Folklore,* Dodd, 1958, reprinted, 1983.

An African Treasury: Articles, Essays, Stories, Poems by Black Africans, Crown, 1960.

Poems from Black Africa, Indiana University Press, 1963.

New Negro Poets: U.S., foreword by Gwendolyn Brooks, Indiana University Press, 1964.

The Book of Negro Humor, Dodd, 1966.

The Best Short Stories by Negro Writers: An Anthology from 1899 to the Present, Little, Brown, 1967.

TRANSLATOR

(With Mercer Cook) Jacques Roumain, *Masters of Dew,* Reynal & Hitchcock, 1947, second edition, Liberty Book Club, 1957.

(With Frederic Carruthers) Nicolas Guillen, *Cuba Libre,* Ward Ritchie, 1948.

Selected Poems of Gabriela Mistral, Indiana University Press, 1957.

OMNIBUS VOLUMES

Selected Poems, Knopf, 1959, reprinted, Vintage Books, 1974.

The Best of Simple, Hill & Wang, 1961.

Five Plays by Langston Hughes, edited by Webster Smalley, Indiana University Press, 1963.

The Langston Hughes Reader, Braziller, 1968.

Don't You Turn Back (poems), edited by Lee Bennett Hopkins, Knopf, 1969.

Good Morning Revolution: The Uncollected Social Protest Writing of Langston Hughes, edited by Faith Berry, Lawrence Hill, 1973.

The Collected Poems of Langston Hughes, Knopf, 1994.

OTHER

(With Bontemps) *Arna Bontemps-Langston Hughes Letters: 1925-1967,* edited by Charles H. Nichols, Dodd, 1980.

Mule Bone: A Comedy of Negro Life (play; with Zora Neale Hurston), HarperCollins, 1991.

Langston Hughes and the Chicago Defender: Essays on Race, Politics, and Culture, 1942-62, edited by Christopher C. De Santis, University of Illinois Press, 1995.

Author of numerous plays (most have been produced), including *Little Ham,* 1935, *Mulatto,* 1935, *Emperor of Haiti,* 1936, *Troubled Island,* 1936, *When the Jack Hollers,* 1936, *Front Porch,* 1937, *Joy to My Soul,* 1937, *Soul Gone Home,* 1937, *Little Eva's End,* 1938, *Limitations of Life,* 1938, *The Em-Fuehrer Jones,* 1938, *Don't You Want to Be Free,* 1938, *The Organizer,* 1939, *The Sun Do Move,* 1942, *For This We Fight,* 1943, *The Barrier,* 1950, *The Glory Round His Head,* 1953, *Simply Heavenly,* 1957, *Esther,* 1957, *The Ballad of the Brown King,* 1960, *Black Nativity,* 1961, *Gospel Glow,* 1962, *Jericho-Jim Crow,* 1963, *Tambourines to Glory,* 1963, *The Prodigal Son,* 1965, *Soul Yesterday and Today, Angelo Herndon Jones, Mother and Child, Trouble with the Angels,* and *Outshines the Sun.*

Also author of screenplay, *Way Down South,* 1942. Author of libretto for operas, *The Barrier,* 1950, and *Troubled Island.* Lyricist for *Just Around the Corner,* and for *Kurt Weill's Street Scene,* 1948. Columnist for *Chicago Defender* and *New York Post.* Poetry, short stories, criticism, and plays have been included in numerous anthologies. Contributor to periodicals, including *Nation, African Forum, Black Drama, Players Magazine, Negro Digest, Black World, Freedomways, Harlem Quarterly, Phylon, Challenge, Negro Quarterly,* and *Negro Story.*

Some of Hughes's letters, manuscripts, lecture notes, periodical clippings, and pamphlets are included in the James Weldon Johnson Memorial Collection, Beinecke Library, Yale University. Additional materials are in the Schomburg Collection of the New York Public Library, the library of Lincoln University in Pennsylvania, and the Fisk University library.

SIDELIGHTS: Langston Hughes was first recognized as an important literary figure during the 1920s, a period known as the "Harlem Renaissance" because of the number of emerging black writers. Du Bose Heyward wrote in the *New York Herald Tribune* in 1926: "Langston Hughes, although only twenty-four years old, is already conspicuous in the group of Negro intellectuals who are dignifying Harlem with a genuine art life. . . . It is, however, as an individual poet, not as a member of a new and interesting literary group, or as a spokesman for a race that Langston Hughes must stand or fall. . . . Always intensely subjective, passionate, keenly sensitive to beauty and possessed of an unfaltering musical sense, Langston Hughes has given us a 'first book' that marks the opening of a career well worth watching."

Despite Heyward's statement, much of Hughes's early work was roundly criticized by many black intellectuals for portraying what they thought to be an unattractive view of black life. In his autobiographical *The Big Sea,* Hughes commented: "*Fine Clothes to the Jew* was well received by the literary magazines and the white press, but the Negro critics did not like it at all. The Pittsburgh *Courier* ran a big headline across the top of the page, *LANGSTON HUGHES' BOOK OF POEMS TRASH.* The headline in the New York *Amsterdam News* was *LANGSTON HUGHES— THE SEWER DWELLER.* The Chicago *Whip* characterized me as 'the poet low-rate of Harlem.' Others called the book a disgrace to the race, a return to the dialect tradition, and a parading of all our racial defects before the public. . . . The Negro critics and many of the intellectuals were very sensitive about their race in books. (And still are.) In anything that white people were likely to read, they wanted to put their best foot forward, their politely polished and cultural foot—and only that foot."

An example of the type of criticism of which Hughes was writing is Estace Gay's comments on *Fine Clothes to the Jew.* "It does not matter to me whether every poem in the book is true to life," Gay wrote. "Why should it be paraded before the American public by a Negro author as being typical or representative of the Negro? Bad enough to have white authors holding up our imperfections to public gaze. Our aim ought to be [to] present to the general public, already

misinformed both by well meaning and malicious writers, our higher aims and aspirations, and our better selves." Commenting on reviewers like Gay, Hughes wrote: "I sympathized deeply with those critics and those intellectuals, and I saw clearly the need for some of the kinds of books they wanted. But I did not see how they could expect every Negro author to write such books. Certainly, I personally knew very few people anywhere who were wholly beautiful and wholly good. Besides I felt that the masses of our people had as much in their lives to put into books as did those more fortunate ones who had been born with some means and the ability to work up to a master's degree at a Northern college. Anyway, I didn't know the upper class Negroes well enough to write much about them. I knew only the people I had grown up with, and they weren't people whose shoes were always shined, who had been to Harvard, or who had heard of Bach. But they seemed to me good people, too."

Hoyt W. Fuller commented that Hughes "chose to identify with plain black people—not because it required less effort and sophistication, but precisely because he saw more truth and profound significance in doing so. Perhaps in this he was inversely influenced by his father—who, frustrated by being the object of scorn in his native land, rejected his own people. Perhaps the poet's reaction to his father's flight from the American racial reality drove him to embrace it with extra fervor." (Langston Hughes's parents separated shortly after his birth and his father moved to Mexico. The elder Hughes came to feel a deep dislike and revulsion for other American blacks.) In Hughes's own words, his poetry is about "workers, roustabouts, and singers, and job hunters on Lenox Avenue in New York, or Seventh Street in Washington or South State in Chicago—people up today and down tomorrow, working this week and fired the next, beaten and baffled, but determined not to be wholly beaten, buying furniture on the installment plan, filling the house with roomers to help pay the rent, hoping to get a new suit for Easter—and pawning that suit before the Fourth of July."

In fact, the title *Fine Clothes to the Jew,* which was misunderstood and disliked by many people, was derived from the Harlemites Hughes saw pawning their own clothing; most of the pawn shops and other stores in Harlem at that time were owned by Jewish people. Lindsay Patterson, a novelist who served as Hughes's assistant, believed that Hughes was "critically, the most abused poet in America. . . . Serious white critics ignored him, less serious ones compared his poetry to Cassius Clay doggerel, and most black critics only grudgingly admired him. Some, like James Baldwin, were downright malicious about his poetic achievement. But long after Baldwin and the rest of us are gone, I suspect Hughes' poetry will be blatantly around growing in stature until it is recognized for its genius. Hughes' tragedy was double-edged: he was unashamedly black at a time when blackness was demode, and he didn't go much beyond one of his earliest themes, black *is* beautiful. He had the wit and intelligence to explore the black human condition in a variety of depths, but his tastes and selectivity were not always accurate, and pressures to survive as a black writer in a white society (and it was a miracle that he did for so long) extracted an enormous creative toll. Nevertheless, Hughes, more than any other black poet or writer, recorded faithfully the nuances of black life and its frustrations."

Although Hughes had trouble with both black and white critics, he was the first black American to earn his living solely from his writing and public lectures. Part of the reason he was able to do this was the phenomenal acceptance and love he received from average black people. A reviewer for *Black World* noted in 1970: "Those whose prerogative it is to determine the rank of writers have never rated him highly, but if the weight of public response is any gauge then Langston Hughes stands at the apex of literary relevance among Black people. The poet occupies such a position in the memory of his people precisely because he recognized that 'we possess within ourselves a great reservoir of physical and spiritual strength,' and because he used his artistry to reflect this back to the people. He used his poetry and prose to illustrate that 'there is no lack within the Negro people of beauty, strength and power,' and he chose to do so on their own level, on their own terms."

Hughes brought a varied and colorful background to his writing. Before he was twelve years old he had lived in six different American cities. When his first book was published, he had already been a truck farmer, cook, waiter, college graduate, sailor, and doorman at a nightclub in Paris, and had visited Mexico, West Africa, the Azores, the Canary Islands, Holland, France, and Italy. As David Littlejohn observed in his *Black on White: A Critical Survey of Writing by American Negroes:* "On the whole, Hughes' creative life [was] as full, as varied, and as original as Picasso's, a joyful, honest monument of a career. There [was] no noticeable sham in it, no pretension, no self-deceit; but a great, great deal of de-

light and smiling irresistible wit. If he seems for the moment upstaged by angrier men, by more complex artists, if 'different views engage' us, necessarily, at this trying stage of the race war, he may well outlive them all, and still be there when it's over. . . . Hughes' [greatness] seems to derive from his anonymous unity with his people. He *seems* to speak for millions, which is a tricky thing to do."

Hughes reached many people through his popular fictional character, Jesse B. Semple (shortened to Simple). Simple is a poor man who lives in Harlem, a kind of comic no-good, a stereotype Hughes turned to advantage. He tells his stories to Boyd, the foil in the stories who is a writer much like Hughes, in return for a drink. His tales of his troubles with work, women, money, and life in general often reveal, through their very simplicity, the problems of being a poor black man in a racist society. "White folks," Simple once commented, "is the cause of a lot of inconvenience in my life." Simple's musings first appeared in 1942 in "From Here to Yonder," a column Hughes wrote for the *Chicago Defender* and later for the *New York Post.* According to a reviewer for *Kirkus Reviews,* their original intent was "to convince black Americans to support the U.S. war effort." They were later published in several volumes.

A more recent collection, 1994's *The Return of Simple,* contains previously unpublished material but remains current in its themes, according to a *Publishers Weekly* critic who noted Simple's addressing of such issues as political correctness, children's rights, and the racist undercurrent behind contraception and sterilization proposals. Donald C. Dickinson wrote in his *Bio-Bibliography of Langston Hughes* that the "charm of Simple lies in his uninhibited pursuit of those two universal goals, understanding and security. As with most other humans, he usually fails to achieve either of these goals and sometimes once achieved they disappoint him. . . . Simple has a tough resilience, however, that won't allow him to brood over a failure very long. . . . Simple is a well-developed character, both believable and lovable. The situations he meets and discusses are so true to life everyone may enter the fun. This does not mean that Simple is in any way dull. He injects the ordinary with his own special insights. . . . Simple is a natural, unsophisticated man who never abandons his hope in tomorrow." A reviewer for *Black World* commented on the popularity of Simple: "The people responded. Simple lived in a world they knew, suffered their pangs, experienced their joys, reasoned in their way, talked their talk, dreamed their dreams, laughed their laughs, voiced their fears—and all the while underneath, he affirmed the wisdom which anchored at the base of their lives. It was not that ideas and events and places and people beyond the limits of Harlem—all of the Harlems—did not concern him; these things, indeed, were a part of his consciousness; but Simple's rock-solid commonsense enabled him to deal with them with balance and intelligence. . . . Simple knows *who* he is and *what* he is, and he knows that the status of expatriate offers no solution, no balm. The struggle is here, and it can only be won here, and no constructive end is served through fantasies and illusions and false efforts at disguising a basic sense of inadequacy. Simple also knows that the strength, the tenacity, the commitment which are necessary to win the struggle also exist within the Black community." Hoyt W. Fuller believed that, like Simple, "the key to Langston Hughes . . . was the poet's deceptive and *profound* simplicity. Profound because it was both willed and ineffable, because some intuitive sense even at the beginning of his adulthood taught him that humanity was of the essence and that it existed undiminished in all shapes, sizes, colors and conditions. Violations of that humanity offended his unshakable conviction that mankind is possessed of the divinity of God."

It was Hughes' belief in humanity and his hope for a world in which people could sanely and with understanding live together that led to his decline in popularity in the racially turbulent latter years of his life. Unlike younger and more militant writers, Hughes never lost his conviction that "*most* people are generally good, in every race and in every country where I have been." Reviewing *The Panther and the Lash: Poems of Our Times* in *Poetry,* Laurence Lieberman recognized that Hughes's "sensibility [had] kept pace with the times," but he criticized his lack of a personal political stance. "Regrettably, in different poems, he is fatally prone to sympathize with starkly antithetical politics of race," Lieberman commented. "A reader can appreciate his catholicity, his tolerance of all the rival—and mutually hostile—views of his outspoken compatriots, from Martin Luther King to Stokely Carmichael, but we are tempted to ask, what are Hughes' politics? And if he has none, why not? The age demands intellectual commitment from its spokesmen. A poetry whose chief claim on our attention is moral, rather than aesthetic, must take sides politically."

Despite some recent criticism, Langston Hughes's position in the American literary scene seems to be secure. David Littlejohn wrote that Hughes is "the one sure Negro classic, more certain of permanence than even Baldwin or Ellison or Wright. . . . His voice is as sure, his manner as original, his position as secure as, say Edwin Arlington Robinson's or Robinson Jeffers'. . . . By molding his verse always on the sounds of Negro talk, the rhythms of Negro music, by retaining his own keen honesty and directness, his poetic sense and ironic intelligence, he maintained through four decades a readable newness distinctly his own."

The Block and *The Sweet and Sour Animal Book* are posthumously published collections of Hughes's poetry for children that position his words against a backdrop of visual art. *The Block* pairs Hughes's poems with a series of six collages by Romare Bearden that bears the book's title. *The Sweet and Sour Animal Book* contains previously unpublished and repeatedly rejected poetry of Hughes from the 1930s. Here, the editors have combined it with the artwork of elementary school children at the Harlem School of the Arts. The results, noted Veronica Chambers in the *New York Times Book Review,* "reflect Hughes's childlike wonder as well as his sense of humor." Chambers also commented on the rhythms of Hughes's words, noting that "children love a good rhyme" and that Hughes gave them "just a simple but seductive taste of the blues." Hughes's poems have been translated into German, French, Spanish, Russian, Yiddish, and Czech; many of them have been set to music.

Donald B. Gibson noted in the introduction to *Modern Black Poets: A Collection of Critical Essays* that Hughes "has perhaps the greatest reputation (worldwide) that any black writer has ever had. Hughes differed from most of his predecessors among black poets, and (until recently) from those who followed him as well, in that he addressed his poetry to the people, specifically to black people. During the twenties when most American poets were turning inward, writing obscure and esoteric poetry to an ever decreasing audience of readers, Hughes was turning outward, using language and themes, attitudes and ideas familiar to anyone who had the ability simply to read. He has been, unlike most nonblack poets other than Walt Whitman, Vachel Lindsay, and Carl Sandburg, a poet of the people. . . . Until the time of his death, he spread his message humorously—though always seriously—to audiences throughout the country, having read his poetry to more people (possibly) than any other American poet."

BIOGRAPHICAL/CRITICAL SOURCES:

BOOKS

Baker, Houston A., Jr., *Black Literature in America,* McGraw, 1971.

Berry, Faith, *Langston Hughes, Before and Beyond Harlem,* Wings Books (New York City), 1995.

Berry, S. L., *Langston Hughes,* Creative Education (Mankato, MN), 1994.

Black Literature Criticism, Gale, 1992.

Bone, Robert A., *The Negro Novel in America,* Yale University Press, 1965.

Bonner, Pat E., *Sassy Jazz and Slo' Draggin' Blues: Music in the Poetry of Langston Hughes,* P. Lang (New York City), 1996.

Children's Literature Review, Volume 17, Gale, 1989.

Concise Dictionary of Literary Biography: The Age of Maturity, 1929-1941, Gale, 1989.

Contemporary Literary Criticism, Gale (Detroit), Volume 1, 1973, Volume 5, 1976, Volume 10, 1979, Volume 15, 1980, Volume 35, 1985, Volume 44, 1987.

Cooper, Floyd, *Coming Home: From the Life of Langston Hughes,* Philomel Books (New York City), 1994.

(Dace, Tish, editor) *Langston Hughes: The Contemporary Reviews,* Cambridge University Press (New York City), 1997.

Davis, Arthur P. and Saunders Redding, editors, *Cavalcade,* Houghton, 1971.

Dekle, Bernard, *Profiles of Modern American Authors,* Charles E. Tuttle, 1969.

Dickinson, Donald C., *A Bio-Bibliography of Langston Hughes, 1902-1967,* Archon Books, 1967.

Dictionary of Literary Biography, Gale, Volume 4: *American Writers in Paris, 1920-1939,* 1980, Volume 7: *Twentieth-Century American Dramatists,* 1981, Volume 48: *American Poets, 1880-1945, Second Series,* 1986, Volume 51: *Afro-American Writers From the Harlem Renaissance to 1940,* 1987.

Dunham, Montrew, *Langston Hughes: Young Black Poet,* Aladdin (New York City), 1995.

Emanuel, James, *Langston Hughes,* Twayne, 1967.

Gibson, Donald B., editor, *Five Black Writers,* New York University Press, 1970.

Gibson, Donald B., editor and author of introduction, *Modern Black Poets: A Collection of Critical Essays,* Prentice-Hall, 1973.

Harper, Donna Sullivan, *Not So Simple: The "Simple" Stories by Langston Hughes,* University of Missouri Press (Columbia), 1995.

Hart, W., editor, *American Writers' Congress,* International, 1935.

Hill, Christine, H., *Langston Hughes: Poet of the Harlem Renaissance,* Hanslow Pub. (Springfield, NJ), 1997.

Hughes, Langston, *The Big Sea: An Autobiography,* Knopf, 1940.

Hughes, Langston, *I Wonder as I Wander: An Autobiographical Journey,* Rinehart, 1956.

Jackson, Blyden and Louis D. Rubin, Jr., *Black Poetry in America: Two Essays in Historical Interpretation,* Louisiana State University, 1974.

Jahn, Janheinz, *A Bibliography of Neo-African Literature from Africa, America and the Caribbean,* Praeger, 1965.

Littlejohn, David, *Black on White: A Critical Survey of Writing by American Negroes,* Viking, 1966.

McLaren, Joseph, *Langston Hughes, Folk Dramatist in the Protest Tradition, 1921-1943,* Greenwood Press (Westport, CT), 1996.

Meltzer, Milton, *Langston Hughes: A Biography,* Crowell, 1968.

Myers, Elizabeth P., *Langston Hughes: Poet of His People,* Garrard, 1970.

Nazel, Joseph, *Langston Hughes,* Melrose Square (Los Angeles), 1994.

Neilson, Kenneth, *To Langston Hughes, With Love,* All Seasons Art (Hollis, NY), 1996.

O'Daniel, Thermon B., editor, *Langston Hughes: Black Genius, a Critical Evaluation,* Morrow, 1971.

Osofsky, Audrey, *Free to Dream: The Making of a Poet,* Lothrop, Lee & Shepard Books (New York City), 1996.

Rollins, Charlamae H., *Black Troubador: Langston Hughes,* Rand McNally, 1970.

Something about the Author, Gale, Volume 4, 1973, Volume 33, Gale, 1983.

Trotman, C. James, *Langston Hughes: The Man, His Art, and His Continuing Influence,* Garland (New York City), 1995.

Walker, Alice, *Langston Hughes, American Poet,* HarperCollins (New York City), 1988.

PERIODICALS

African American Review, fall, 1994, p. 333.

American Mercury, January, 1959.

Black Scholar, June, 1971; July, 1976.

Black World, June, 1970; September, 1972; September, 1973.

Booklist, November 15, 1976; January 1, 1991, p. 889.

Bulletin of the Center for Children's Books, January, 1995, p. 168; January, 1996, p. 162.

CLA Journal, June, 1972.

Chicago Tribune Book World, April 13, 1980.

Choice, February 1996, p. 951.

Crisis, August-September, 1960; June, 1967; February, 1969.

Ebony, October, 1946.

Emerge, May, 1995, p. 58.

English Journal, March, 1977.

Horn Book, September-October, 1994, p. 603; January-February, 1996, p. 86.

Kirkus Reviews, May 1, 1994, p. 578.

Library Journal, February 1, 1991, p. 78.

Life, February 4, 1966.

Los Angeles Times Book Review, February 26, 1995, p. 1.

Nation, December 4, 1967.

Negro American Literature Forum, winter, 1971.

Negro Digest, September, 1967, November, 1967; April, 1969.

New Leader, April 10, 1967.

New Republic, January 14, 1974; March 6, 1995, p. 37.

New Yorker, December 30, 1967.

New York Herald Tribune, August 1, 1926.

New York Herald Tribune Books, November 26, 1961.

New York Times, May 24, 1967; June 1, 1968; June 29, 1969; December 13, 1970; February 8, 1995, p. C17.

New York Times Book Review, November 3, 1968; December 25, 1994, p. 15; February 12, 1995, p. 18; November 12, 1995, p. 38.

Philadelphia Tribune, February 5, 1927.

Poetry, August, 1968.

Publishers Weekly, May 9, 1994, p. 62; October 3, 1994, p. 30; October 31, 1994, p.54; November 13, 1995, p. 60.

San Francisco Chronicle, April 5, 1959.

Saturday Review, November 22, 1958; September 29, 1962.

School Library Journal, February, 1995, p. 92.

Smithsonian, August, 1994, p. 49.

Washington Post, November 13, 1978.

Washington Post Book World, February 2, 1969; December 8, 1985.*

*   *   *

HUNT, Marsha 1946-

PERSONAL: Born in 1946, in Europe; children (with Mick Jagger, a musician): Karis (daughter).

CAREER: Model, actress, singer, and writer.

WRITINGS:

Real Life (autobiography), Chatto & Windus (London), 1986.

Joy (novel), Dutton (New York City), 1990.

Free (novel), Dutton, 1993.

The Way We Wore: Styles of the 1930s and "40s and Our World since Then, Fallbrook (Fallbrook, CA), 1993.

Repossessing Ernestine: A Granddaughter Uncovers the Secret History of Her American Family, HarperCollins (New York City), 1996 (published in England as *Repossessing Ernestine: The Search for a Lost Soul,* HarperCollins, 1996).

SIDELIGHTS: Marsha Hunt's books frequently concern hidden truths. Her novels *Joy* and *Free* are both, in a sense, voyages of self-discovery—voyages during which blinders are lifted from the eyes of the main characters, with both humorous and tragic effects. The main characters of the books are African Americans who have for some time failed to notice changes in the world around them, at the same time ignoring terrible truths concerning the people to whom they have been closest. The same themes occur in one of Hunt's nonfiction titles, *Repossessing Ernestine: A Granddaughter Uncovers the Secret History of Her American Family.*

Hunt's first book, *Real Life,* was an autobiography. She has worked as a singer, songwriter, and actress, gaining her greatest fame for the starring role in the London production of *Hair.* Her experiences in the entertainment industry also provided a great deal of background for her first novel, *Joy.* The central character and narrator of that book is Baby Palatine, an elderly, church-going woman who is travelling from California to New York to assist in the funeral of Joy Bang, one of three sisters she helped raise. The three had gained brief stardom in the sixties as a girl group calling itself Bang Bang Bang. The group crashed as quickly as it had become famous, leaving the sisters free to pursue the excesses of their respective personalities. Joy was Baby's favorite, her "God-sent child;" Baby ignored Joy's corruption while she was alive and continues to do so as she recollects Joy's life during the trip eastward. It is not until the very end of the novel that Baby realizes the unpleasant truth and her own part in creating it. At that point a bloodfest ends the novel, leaving many critics agreeing with Jewelle Gomez, who wrote in the *Women's Review of Books* that "the additional deaths in the final pages seem gratuitous and completely at odds with the humorous bantering style of Baby P.'s narrative."

Teenotchy, the protagonist of *Free,* Hunt's second novel, carries a weightier repression: that of the rape and murder of his mother. As a teenager in turn of the century Germantown, Pennsylvania, he is "a slave to habit," working as a servant for the same man his mother had worked for—a man who had a role in her murder and afterward had become Teenotchy's kindly protector. Teenotchy's journey of self-discovery comes when an upper-class Englishman visits and takes him to England. He falls in love with his benefactor and also learns a great deal about himself, though the novel ends tragically.

In *Repossessing Ernestine: A Granddaughter Uncovers the Secret History of Her American Family,* Hunt tells a compelling story from her own life, in which a grandmother thought long dead was revealed to be alive. Hunt further discovered that this forgotten relative had spent much of her life locked away in mental hospitals and other institutions. As a *Publishers Weekly* reviewer explained, Hunt "suspects the reason may have had more to do with racism and sexism than insanity," and she set out on a quest for the truth behind the matter. The result, according to the reviewer, is "a compelling memoir" that "reads like an edge-of-your-seat mystery."

Andrea Stuart, writing in *New Statesman & Society,* concurred that *Repossessing Ernestine* is a gripping personal story but added that "bubbling beneath all this is the even greater tragedy of race. Its stain is impressed across every page of the book. Hunt, who hasn't lived in America since the civil rights conflicts of the 1960s, is a paranoid witness, a constant reminder of the attitudes that existed in the years when Ernestine was institutionalised—the threat of rednecks with rifle-racks, of lonely Southern roads, of the shade prejudice within the black community."

BIOGRAPHICAL/CRITICAL SOURCES:

BOOKS

Contemporary Literary Criticism Yearbook 1991, Volume 70, Gale (Detroit), 1991.
Hunt, Marsha, *Real Life,* Chatto & Windus, 1986.

PERIODICALS

Booklist, December 1, 1990, p. 717; May 15, 1996, p. 1563.

Books, May, 1991, p. 16; July, 1992, p. 11.
Emerge, July-August, 1996, p. 76.
Entertainment Weekly, November 15, 1996, p. 82.
Essence, July, 1991, p. 36.
Kirkus Reviews, November 15, 1990, p. 1559.
Lambda Book Report, May, 1991, p. 40.
Library Journal, January, 1991, p. 152; May 15, 1996, p. 67.
Listener, April 12, 1990, p. 25.
Los Angeles Times, January 21, 1991, p. E6.
New Statesman and Society, April 13, 1990, p. 36; February 16, 1996, p. 38.
Publishers Weekly, December 7, 1990, p. 69; April 22, 1996, p. 52.
Punch, June 8, 1990, p. 37.
Spectator, May 12, 1990, p. 38.
Times Literary Supplement, August 7, 1992, p. 18.
Women's Review of Books, June, 1991, pp. 20-21.

*   *   *

HURSTON, Zora Neale   1903-1960

PERSONAL: Born January 7, 1903, in Eatonville, FL; died January 28, 1960, in Fort Pierce, FL; daughter of John (a preacher and carpenter) and Lucy (a seamstress; maiden name, Potts) Hurston; married Herbert Sheen, May 19, 1927 (divorced, 1931); married Albert Price III, June 27, 1939 (divorced). Attended Howard University, 1923-24; Barnard College, B.A., 1928; graduate study at Columbia University.

CAREER: Writer and folklorist. Collected folklore in the South, 1927-31; Bethune-Cookman College, Daytona, FL, instructor in drama, 1933-34; collected folklore in Jamaica, Haiti, and Bermuda, 1937-38; collected folklore in Florida for the Works Progress Administration, 1938-39; Paramount Studios, Hollywood, CA, staff writer, 1941; collected folklore in Honduras, 1946-48; worked as a maid in Florida, 1950; freelance writer, 1950-56; Patrick Air Force Base, FL, librarian, 1956-57; writer for *Fort Pierce Chronicle* and part-time teacher at Lincoln Park Academy, both in Fort Pierce, FL, 1958-59. Librarian at the Library of Congress, Washington, DC; professor of drama at North Carolina College for Negroes (now North Carolina Central University), Durham; assistant to writer Fannie Hurst.

MEMBER: American Folklore Society, American Anthropological Society, American Ethnological Society, Zeta Phi Beta.

AWARDS, HONORS: Guggenheim fellowship, 1936 and 1938; Litt.D. from Morgan College, 1939; Annisfield Award, 1943, for *Dust Tracks on a Road.*

WRITINGS:

(With Clinton Fletcher and Time Moore) *Fast and Furious* (musical play), published in *Best Plays of 1931-32,* edited by Burns Mantle and Garrison, Sherwood, 1931.

(With Langston Hughes) *Mule Bone: A Comedy of Negro Life in Three Acts,* HarperPerennial, 1931, reprint, 1991.

Jonah's Gourd Vine (novel), with an introduction by Fanny Hurst, Lippincott, 1934, reprinted with a new introduction by Rita Dove, Perennial, 1990.

Mules and Men (folklore), with an introduction by Franz Boas, Lippincott, 1935, reprinted with a new foreword by Arnold Rampersad, Perennial, 1990.

Their Eyes Were Watching God (novel), Lippincott, 1937, reprinted, University of Illinois Press, 1991.

Tell My Horse (nonfiction), Lippincott, 1938, reprinted, Turtle Island Foundation, 1981, published as *Voodoo Gods: An Inquiry into Native Myths and Magic in Jamaica and Haiti,* Dent, 1939, reprint published as *Tell My Horse: Voodoo and Life in Haiti and Jamaica,* with an introduction by Ishmael Reed, Perennial, 1990.

Moses, Man of the Mountain (novel), Lippincott, 1939, reprint, HarperPerennial, 1991.

Dust Tracks on a Road (autobiography), Lippincott, 1942, reprinted with an introduction by Neal, 1971, reprinted with a foreword by Maya Angelou, HarperPerennial, 1991.

(With Dorothy Waring) *Stephen Kelen-d'Oxylion Presents Polk County: A Comedy of Negro Life on a Sawmill Camp with Authentic Negro Music* (three-act play), [New York], c. 1944.

Seraph on the Suwanee (novel), Scribner, 1948, reprint, HarperPerennial, 1991.

I Love Myself When I Am Laughing . . . And Then Again When I Am Looking Mean And Impressive, edited by Alice Walker, Feminist Press, 1979.

The Sanctified Church, Turtle Island Foundation, 1983.

Spunk: The Selected Stories of Zora Neale Hurston, Turtle Island Foundation, 1985, reprint, Dramatists Play Service, 1992.

The Gilded Six-Bits, Redpath Press, 1986.

The Complete Stories, HarperCollins, 1994.

Folklore, Memoirs, and Other Writings, Library of America, 1995.

Novels and Stories, Library of America, 1995.

Sweat, edited and with an introduction by Cheryl A. Wall, (New Brunswick, NJ), Rutgers University Press, 1997.

Collected Essays, HarperCollins, 1998.

Also author of *The First One* (one-act play), published in *Ebony and Topaz,* edited by Johnson, and of *Great Day* (play). Work represented in anthologies, including *Black Writers in America,* edited by Barksdale and Kinnamon; *Story in America,* edited by E. W. Burnett and Martha Foley, Vanguard, 1934; *American Negro Short Stories,* edited by Clarke; *The Best Short Stories by Negro Writers,* edited by Hughes; *From the Roots,* edited by James; *Anthology of American Negro Literature,* edited by Watkins. Contributor of stories and articles to periodicals, including *American Mercury, Negro Digest, Journal of American Folklore, Saturday Evening Post,* and *Journal of Negro History.*

SIDELIGHTS: Zora Neale Hurston is considered one of the greats of twentieth-century African-American literature. Although Hurston was closely associated with the Harlem Renaissance and has influenced such writers as Ralph Ellison, Toni Morrison, Gayl Jones, Alice Walker, and Toni Cade Bambara, interest in her has only recently been revived after decades of neglect. Hurston's four novels and two books of folklore are important sources of black myth and legend. Through her writings, Robert Hemenway wrote in *The Harlem Renaissance Remembered,* Hurston "helped to remind the Renaissance—especially its more bourgeois members—of the richness in the racial heritage; she also added new dimensions to the interest in exotic primitivism that was one of the most ambiguous products of the age.

"Hurston was born and raised in the first incorporated all-black town in America, and was advised by her mother to "jump at de sun." At the age of thirteen she was taken out of school to care for her brother's children. At sixteen, she joined a traveling theatrical troupe and worked as a maid for a white woman who arranged for her to attend high school in Baltimore. Hurston later studied anthropology at Barnard College and Columbia University with the anthropologist Franz Boas, which profoundly influenced her work. After graduation she returned to her hometown for anthropological study. The data she collected would be used both in her collections of folklore and her fictional works.

"I was glad when somebody told me: 'You may go and collect Negro folklore,'" Hurston related in the introduction to *Mules and Men*. "In a way it would not be a new experience for me. When I pitched headforemost into the world I landed in the crib of Negroism. From the earliest rocking of my cradle, I had known about the capers Br'er Rabbit is apt to cut and what the Squinch Owl says from the housetop. But it was fitting me like a tight chemise. I couldn't see it for wearing it. It was only when I was off in college, away from my native surroundings, that I could see myself like somebody else and stand off and look at my garment. Then I had to have the spyglass of anthropology to look through at that."

Hurston was an ambiguous and complex figure. She embodied seemingly antipodal traits, and Hemenway described her in his *Zora Neale Hurston: A Literary Biography* as being "flamboyant yet vulnerable, self-centered yet kind, a Republican conservative and an early black nationalist." Hurston was never bitter and never felt disadvantaged because she was black. Henry Louis Gates, Jr., explained in the *New York Times Book Review:* "Part of Miss Hurston's received heritage—and perhaps the traditional notion that links the novel of manners in the Harlem Renaissance, the social realism of the 30s, and the cultural nationalism of the Black Arts movement—was the idea that racism had reduced black people to mere ciphers, to beings who react only to an omnipresent racial oppression, whose culture is 'deprived' where different, and whose psyches are in the main 'pathological'. . . . Miss Hurston thought this idea degrading, its propagation a trap. It was against this that she railed, at times brilliantly and systematically, at times vapidly and eclectically."

Older black writers criticized Hurston for the frequent crudeness and bawdiness of the tales she told. The younger generation criticized her propensity to gloss over the injustices her people were dealt. According to Judith Wilson, Hurston's greatest contribution was "to all black Americans' psychic health. The consistent note in her fieldwork and the bulk of her fiction is one of celebration of a black cultural heritage whose complexity and originality refutes all efforts to enforce either a myth of inferiority or a lie of assimilation." Wilson continued, "Zora Neale Hurston had figured out something that no other black author of her time seems to have known or appreciated so well—that our home-spun vernacular and street-corner cosmology is as valuable as the grammar and philosophy of white, Western culture.

"Hurston herself wrote in 1928: "I am not tragically colored. There is no great sorrow dammed up in my soul, nor lurking behind my eyes. I do not mind at all. I do not belong to the sobbing school of Negrohood who hold that nature somehow has given them a lowdown dirty deal and whose feelings are all hurt about it. . . . No, I do not weep at the world—I am too busy sharpening my oyster knife."

Their Eyes Were Watching God is generally acknowledged to be Hurston's finest work of fiction. Still, it was controversial. Richard Wright found the book to be "counter-revolutionary" in a *New Masses* article. June Jordan praised the novel for its positiveness. She declared in a *Black World* review: "Unquestionably, *Their Eyes Were Watching God* is the prototypical Black novel of affirmation; it is the most successful, convincing, and exemplary novel of Blacklove that we have. Period. But the book gives us more: the story unrolls a fabulous, written-film of Blacklife freed from the constraints of oppression; here we may learn Black possibilities of ourselves if we could ever escape the hateful and alien context that has so deeply disturbed and mutilated our rightly efflorescence—*as people*. Consequently, this novel centers itself on Blacklove—even as *Native Son* rivets itself upon white hatred."

Hurston's autobiography, *Dust Tracks on a Road,* was reissued in 1985 with many chapters that had been deleted restored. The publication of this book coincided with the rediscovery by many contemporary black writers—especially Alice Walker—of the excellence of Hurston's work. The work is lengthy and tends to ramble; Hurston organized the tome around several visions she had that signified her life as an artist. In the work she delves into her childhood, when the death of her mother sent her to a boarding school where she was ignored by her family. The autobiography also traces Hurston's out-of-fashion views of racial issues, such as her opposition to desegregation and her belief that blacks should not consider themselves victims of racism. At the time of the original release of this book in 1942, she was soundly criticized for these views from leading black authors of the day, including Richard Wright, a fact which perhaps led to her fading popularity. However, with the new material in this book, Hurston is able to explain further many of her ideas.

"*Dust Tracks on a Road* suffers from weak structure, a tone that is too conciliatory, too many concessions to the publisher and an anticipated audience, and not enough concern with narrative development and proportion," commented Joanne M. Braxton in the *Women's Review of Books.* While Henry Louis Gates,

Jr., noted in the *New York Times Book Review* that there were flaws in the book, namely with Hurston's clever prose overshadowing the interesting details of her life, he related that "Hurston's achievement in *Dust Tracks* is twofold. First, she gives us a *writer's life*—rather than an account of 'the Negro Problem'—in a language [that is] dazzling. . . . [And] a verbal analogue of her double experiences as a woman in a male-dominated world and as a black person in a non-black world—strikes me as her second great achievement." He concluded that "black male writers caricatured Hurston as the fool. For protection, she made up significant parts of herself."

Hurston's collection of short stories, *Spunk,* was published in 1985. She entered the title story in an *Opportunity* (the publication most central to the Harlem Renaissance) contest and won second prize. It concerns the huge and intimidating Spunk Banks, a man who has power over an entire town because of his intimidation. Banks has a public affair with Lena Kanty. Her husband, Joe, seeks revenge on Banks and attempts to kill him, but is shot to death by Banks instead. Eventually, Banks is haunted by a black bobcat, which many of the townspeople suspect is the ghost of Joe Kanty. Finally, Banks is killed in a grisly accident at the town mill, and the villagers quickly forget his reign of terror. In "Muttsy," another *Opportunity* contest winner, the tragic relationship of sheltered Pinkie and worldly Muttsy Owens is chronicled. Pinkie has been forced to live in a brothel after she runs away from home; after seeing her in the brothel, Muttsy falls for her immediately. Pinkie tries to change Muttsy's gambling addiction, forcing him to get a job before she'll become romantically involved with him. While he does get a respectable job and the two marry, Muttsy eventually resumes his gambling. Grace Ingoldby, writing in *New Statesman,* praised the collection, saying that "the stories in *Spunk* transcend the particular without any sense that Hurston knows how far she's leaping: unselfconscious, exuberant, tragi-comic, they are, to wipe the grime of overuse from a good word, brilliant."

In 1995, the Library of America collected and combined much of Hurston's writings into two volumes: *Folklore, Memoirs, and Other Writings,* and *Novels and Stories.* Critics commented that her inclusion into this prestigious collection of American writers has done much to cement her work in the minds of Americans. "That we remember her today is due, of course, to the untiring work of women like Alice Walker and the literary critic Mary Helen Washington," remarked David Nicholson in the *Washington Post Book World.* "Black women reclaimed her. Now, with her inclusion in the Library of America, Zora Neale Hurston belongs to all of us." Joyce Irene Middleton commended both works in the *Women's Review of Books:* "a sustained reading of the chronology of her life . . . in this beautiful, two-volume Library of America collection, reanimates the complex cultural and political forces that shaped the world in which we see Zora Hurston laughing and lying, fighting and loving, speaking and writing."

"She was full of sidesplitting anecdotes, humorous tales, and tragicomic stories," Langston Hughes wrote of Hurston, "remembered out of her life in the South as a daughter of a traveling minister of God. She could make you laugh one minute and cry the next. . . . But Miss Hurston was clever, too—a student who didn't let college give her a broad 'a' and who had great scorn for all pretensions, academic or otherwise. That is why she was such a fine folklore collector, able to go among the people and never act as if she had been to school at all. Almost nobody else could stop the average Harlemite on Lenox Avenue and measure his head with a strange-looking, anthropological device and not get bawled out for the attempt, except Zora, who used to stop anyone whose head looked interesting, and measure it."

BIOGRAPHICAL/CRITICAL SOURCES:

BOOKS

Black Literature Criticism, Gale, 1992.
Bloom, Harold, editor, *Zora Neale Hurston,* Chelsea House, 1986.
Bone, Robert, *Down Home: A History of Afro-American Short Fiction from Its Beginnings to the End of the Harlem Renaissance,* Putnam, 1975.
Carter-Sigglow, Janet, *Making Her Way With Thunder: A Reappraisal of Zora Neale Hurston's Narrative Art,* P. Lang (New York City), 1994.
Contemporary Literary Criticism, Gale, Volume 7, 1977, Volume 30, 1984; Volume 61, 1990.
Cronin, Gloria L., ed., *Critical Essays on Zora Neale Hurston,* G. K. Hall, 1998.
Davis, Arthur P., *From the Dark Tower,* Howard University Press, 1974.
Davis, Rose Parkman, *Zora Neale Hurston: An Annotated Bibliography and Reference Guide,* Greenwood Press, 1997.
Dictionary of Literary Biography, Gale, Volume 51: *Afro-American Writers From the Harlem Renaissance to 1940,* 1987; Volume 86: *American Short-Story Writers, 1910-1945,* 1989.

Harris, Trudier, *The Power of the Porch: the Storyteller's Craft in Zora Neale Hurston, Gloria Naylor, and Randall Kenan,* University of Georgia Press (Athens), 1996.

Hemenway, Robert E., *Zora Neale Hurston: A Literary Biography,* University of Illinois Press, 1977.

Hill, Lynda Marion, *Social Rituals and the Verbal Art of Zora Neale Hurston,* Howard University Press (Washington, DC), 1996.

Howard, Lillie P., *Zora Neale Hurston,* G. K. Hall, 1980.

Hughes, Langston, *The Big Sea,* Knopf, 1940.

Hughes, Langston and Arna Bontemps, editors, *The Harlem Renaissance Remembered,* Dodd, 1972.

Hurston, Zora Neale, *Dust Tracks on a Road* (autobiography), Lippincott, 1942.

Johnson, Yvonne, *The Voices of African American Women: The Use of Narrative and Authorial Voice in the Works of Harriet Jacobs, Zora Neale Hurston, and Alice Walker,* P. Lang (New York City), 1996.

Kaplan, Carla, *The Erotics of Talk: Women's Writing and Feminist Paradigms,* Oxford University Press (New York City), 1996.

Karanja, Ayana I., *Zora Neale Hurston: Dialogue in Spirit and in Truth,* P. Lang (New York City), 1996.

Lowe, John, *Jump at the Sun: Zora Neale Hurston's Cosmic Comedy,* University of Illinois Press (Urbana), 1994.

Peters, Pearlie Mae Fisher, *The Assertive Woman in Zora Neale Hurston's Fiction, Folklore, and Drama,* Garland, 1997.

Plant, Deborah G., *Every Tub Must Sit on Its Own Bottom: The Philosophy and Politics of Zora Neale Hurston,* University of Illinois Press (Urbana), 1995.

Turner, Darwin T., *In a Minor Chord: Three Afro-American Writers and Their Search for Identity,* Southern Illinois University Press, 1971.

Wall, Cheryl A., *Women of the Harlem Renaissance,* Indiana University Press (Bloomington), 1995.

Witcover, Paul, *Zora Neale Hurston,* Melrose Square (Los Angeles), 1994.

Yannuzzi, Della A., *Zora Neale Hurston: Southern Storyteller,* Enslow (Springfield, NJ), 1996.

PERIODICALS

African American Review, summer, 1994, p. 283; spring, 1995, p. 17.
Black World, August, 1972; August, 1974.
Entertainment Weekly, March 17, 1995, p. 82.
Ms., March, 1975; June, 1978.

National Review, April 3, 1995, p. 58.
Negro American Literature Forum, spring, 1972.
Negro Digest, February, 1962.
New Masses, October 5, 1937.
New Republic, February 11, 1978; July 3, 1995, p. 30.
New Statesman, July 3, 1987, pp. 29-30.
Newsweek, February 15, 1960.
New York Times, February 5, 1960.
New York Times Book Review, February 19, 1978; April 21, 1985, p. 43, 45.
Observer, February 16, 1986.
Publishers Weekly, February 15, 1960.
Time, February 15, 1960.
Times Literary Supplement, May 2, 1986, p. 479.
Village Voice, August 17, 1972.
Washington Post Book World, July 23, 1978; May 12, 1985, p. 10; March 5, 1995, p. 4.
Wilson Library Bulletin, April, 1960.
Women's Review of Books, July, 1985, p. 5; November, 1995, p. 28.*

*   *   *

IKE, Chukwuemeka
See IKE, Vincent Chukwuemeka

*   *   *

IKE, Vincent Chukwuemeka 1931-
(Chukwuemeka Ike)

PERSONAL: Born April 28, 1931, in Ndikelionwu, Awka, Nigeria; son of Charles and Dinah (Ezeani) Ike; married Adebimpe Olurinsola Abimbolu, December 13, 1959; children: Osita Naanyelugo Adeolu Olusanya (son). *Education:* Attended Government College, Umuahia, Nigeria; University College, Ibadan, Nigeria, B.A., 1955; Stanford University, M.A., 1966.

ADDRESSES: Office—Chinwuba House, Ndikelionwu Postal Agency, Via Awka, Anambra State, Nigeria.

CAREER: Nigerian novelist, short-story writer, educator, and administrator. Teacher in Nigeria, 1950-51, girls' secondary school, Nkwerre, 1955-56; University College, Ibadan, Nigeria, administrative assistant and assistant registrar, 1957-60; University of Nigeria, Nsukka, deputy registrar, 1960-63, registrar and secretary to council, 1963-71; West African Examinations Council, Accra, Ghana, registrar and secretary to council, 1971-79; University Press Ltd., director, 1978—. Chair, planning and management committee, University of Nigeria, 1970; director, *Daily Times of Nigeria Ltd.*, 1971-77(?); chair, Times Leisure Services Ltd., 1977-1979; executive chair, Emekike and Co., 1979—; founding editorial committee, *Okike* (literary journal). Provincial refugee officer, Umuahia Province, 1968-69; headquarters scout commander in charge of Nsukka Province, 1970-71. Trustee, Nigerian Universities Joint Superannuation Scheme, Nsukka, 1964-71; and West African Examinations Council Provident Fund Scheme.

MEMBER: Nigerian Institute of Management, International Association for Educational Assessment (member of executive committee).

AWARDS, HONORS: UNESCO travel grantee, 1954; USAID participant fellow, 1962; Ford Foundation grantee, 1966; honorary fellow, City and Guilds of London Institute of Publishers.

WRITINGS:

FICTION

Toads for Supper, Harvill Press (London), 1965, Fontana (London), 1970.
The Naked Gods, Harvill Press (London), 1970.
The Potter's Wheel, Harvill Press (London), 1973, Fontana (London), 1974.
Sunset at Dawn: A Novel About Biafra, Collins and Harvill Press (London), 1976, University Press PLC (Ibadan, Nigeria), 1993.
The Chicken Chasers, Fontana (Douglas, Isle of Man), 1980.
The Bottled Leopard, University Press (Ibadan), 1985.
Our Children Are Coming, Spectrum Books (Ibadan), 1990.
The Search, Heinemann Educational Books Nigeria, (Ibadan), 1991.

NONFICTION

University Development in Africa: The Nigerian Experience, Oxford University Press (Ibadan), 1976.
Expo '77, Fontana (London), 1980.
How to Become a Published Writer, Heinemann Educational Books Nigeria (Ibadan), 1991.

EDITOR

(As Chukwuemeka Ike; with Emmanuel Obiechina and John Anenechukwu Umeh) *The University of*

Nigeria, 1960-1985: An Experiment in Higher Education, University of Nigeria Press (Nsukka, Nigeria), 1986.

ADAPTATIONS: The Potter's Wheel, adapted as textbook for foreign speakers of English, abridged by Lewis Jones, with illustrations by Anthea Eames, Collins (Glasgow, Scotland), 1986.

SIDELIGHTS: Vincent Chukwuemeka Ike has been a successful novelist both within Nigeria and beyond its borders since the release of his first novel, *Toads for Supper,* in 1965. That debut was a comedy with strongly realistic elements, about a young man from a village who goes to the University of Nigeria and finds his head turned. Protagonist Amobi has been groomed and financed by his whole village to become its first university-educated resident; the village has even built him a special hut to study in, and the girl to whom he has been betrothed since childhood has been sent to a teacher training college in order to be a better match for him. Once at the university, however, Amobi decides to change his major from English and medicine to history; worse, in the view of his Ibo family, he falls in love with, and betroths himself to, a pretty Yoruba girl he meets on campus. Complicating matters is the fact that a Lagos prostitute named Sweetie accuses him of fathering her child.

Returning to his village, Amobi encounters the displeasure of the entire village, especially in the person of his father, an uneducated but wise and powerful figure who bombards Amobi with what a (London) *Times Literary Supplement* reviewer called "paternal homilies." The trouble with the prostitute is easily smoothed out since Amobi is in fact not the father of the child; his romantic entanglements, however, require a more difficult resolution that did not satisfy either the *Times Literary Supplement* reviewer or another British critic, the *New Statesman*'s Edwin Morgan. Nevertheless, the last page was, for Morgan, the only flaw in the otherwise "unassuming, humorous," and "well-observed" novel, in which satirical insights blended neatly with "warm feeling for the realities of village life."

The critic for the *Times Literary Supplement,* appreciating the "wry poetry" with which Ike illustrated generational conflict, called the "unpretentious" novel "a pleasing comedy, animated by a fluent, good-humoured intelligence." The preeminent flaw pointed to by the *Times Literary Supplement* reviewer was an unevenness and a rushed quality in parts of the book, particularly the ending. Novelist Shiva Naipaul, reviewing *Toads for Supper* for *Books & Bookmen*, enjoyed its "steadying realism" and its "fine writing," noting that the latter was to be found in the descriptions of village life and in the "moving" characterizations of Amodi's father, mother, and friends. Like the other two reviewers, Naipaul had reservations about the ending, which he termed a "plunge . . . into sudden tragedy and melodrama." Naipaul had words of praise, however, for Ike's cataloguing of "the dissonances in modern Nigerian society": tensions between tribes, between villagers and university graduates, between Christianity and native religion, between white professors and black students, and even between "the girls who can dance the high life and the girls who can't."

After his reputation had been made by *Toads for Supper,* Ike continued in his already-established career in educational administration, which had begun with his first teaching experiences in the early 1950s. In the 1970s he branched out into newspaper publishing and other businesses while continuing to produce a steady stream of novels, short stories, and occasional nonfiction books. The latter genre includes a study of Nigerian higher education, in 1976, and a book on how to become a published writer, in 1991.

BIOGRAPHICAL/CRITICAL SOURCES:

PERIODICALS

Books & Bookmen, February, 1971, p. 41.
New Statesman, May 14, 1965, p. 772.
Times Literary Supplement, April 8, 1965, p. 269.*

*   *   *

IROH, Eddie

PERSONAL: Born in Nigeria.

ADDRESSES: Home—London, England. *Agent*—c/o Heinemann Educational Publishing, Halley Court, Jordan Hill, Oxford OX2 8EJ, England.

CAREER: Novelist. *The Guardian,* Lagos, Nigeria, cofounder and former managing editor; radio and television broadcaster and writer and producer for ENTV (Nigerian television network); USAfrica Median Networks, executive editor of international projects and columnist for *USAfricaonline; Black Business Journal,* columnist.

AWARDS, HONORS: Recipient of fiction awards.

WRITINGS:

NOVELS; NIGERIAN CIVIL WAR TRILOGY

Forty-Eight Guns for the General, Heinemann (London, England), 1976.
Toads of War, Heinemann (London, England), 1979.
The Siren in the Night, Heinemann (London, England), 1982.

OTHER NOVELS

Without a Silver Spoon, Spectrum Books (Ibadan, Nigeria), 1981.

SIDELIGHTS: Nigerian novelist Eddie Iroh is known for his trilogy of novels about his country's civil war of 1967-1970, a war begun when Biafra attempted to secede and ended when the Biafran rebellion collapsed amid starvation and violence. The first novel of the three, *Forty-Eight Guns for the General* (1976), focuses on white mercenaries who are hired by the Biafran side, and in particular, a colonel named Rudolph. These mercenaries delay fighting in order to increase their revenues; when fighting does come, they lose men and materials and thus prestige. They attempt to mutiny against their employers, but the attempt is quashed with the help of Rudolph's Biafran second-in-command.

Reviewing Iroh's fictional account of these events in *World Literature Today,* Ossie Onuora Enekwe of Columbia University expressed admiration for a pervasive sense of "irony and paradox" that was "skillfully heightened by punning and repetition." However, Enekwe also commented on the book's "melodrama and sensationalism" and stereotyped characters. The novel, the reviewer concluded, was a work of journalistic fiction, "superb" as a thriller rather than a work of literary art. Nigerian novelist Chikwnye Okonjo Ogunyemi, in a scholarly assessment of Nigerian war novels in *Comparative Literature Studies,* called *Forty-Eight Guns for the General* "brutally funny in the style of *Catch-22*" and called attention to Iroh's preference for short, action-packed scenes, "racy" dialogue, and straightforwardly narrated episodes of sex and drinking.

The second novel in the trilogy, *Toads of War,* appeared in 1979; it was called "a *roman a these*" in Ogunyemi's article, the thesis being that the promise of Biafra had deteriorated into a reality of war propagandaa and social-class tension. The first-person narrator is a Biafran soldier who has lost an arm; much of the novel is devoted, however, to a good-hearted prostitute. According to David Dorsey, in *World Literature Today,* "The novel is essentially a simple suspense story, but its many features of daring originality and earnest didacticism merit serious attention." Its structure, consisting of forty-four brief, titled chapters, among which are sections in the third person, quotations from poetry (including footnotes), and a six-page summary of a play the characters see, was for Dorsey "at once ambitious and naive." These devices, as well as the device of foreshadowing, made for increased suspense, in Dorsey's view. That critic found *Toads of War* well-blended in different forms and intents, artistically liberating, craftsmanlike, and successful in depending on "its sardonic but sympathetic moral vision."

The trilogy concludes with *The Siren in the Night* (1982), which Dorsey, again in *World Literature Today,* called "less ambitious" than its two predecessors, "but a greater artistic success." The novel's protagonist and antagonist, respectively, are two colonels who never meet: Ben Udaja, who becomes disenchanted with the rebels and successfully moves his allegiance to the federal army; and villainous security chief Mike Kolawole, whose mistress has been killed in an operation led by Udaja. Kolawole hatches a complicated scheme to assassinate Udaja, which is only foiled at the novel's end. For Dorsey, this was "a plot of elaborate intrigue with laudably spare violence." He remarked favorably on the "mordant humor" of Iroh's social commentary. The reviewer commented that he was most impressed by the characterizations, particular of Kolawole and his expatriate daughter. Kolawole, Dorsey attested, was "believable, sometimes even admirable." All in all, Dorsey wrote, *Siren in the Night* was "shorn of most idiosyncrasies which marred the other two novels," and both "an engaging example of popular fiction" and "a conscious tribute to the spirit of reconciliation." For *Library Journal* reviewer Peter Sabor, *The Siren in the Night* was a "tense, chilling" reading experience.

BIOGRAPHICAL/CRITICAL SOURCES:

PERIODICALS

Comparative Literature Studies, summer, 1983, pp. 203-216.
Library Journal, November 15, 1982, p. 2190.
World Literature Today, winter, 1978, p. 166; winter, 1980, p. 161; autumn, 1983, p. 679.

OTHER

Black Business Journal Online, http://www.bbjonline. com (February 5, 1999).
USAfricaonline, http://www.usafricaonline.com (February 5, 1999).*

J

JACKSON, Angela 1951-

PERSONAL: Born July 25, 1951, in Greenville, MS; daughter of George and Angeline Jackson. *Ethnicity:* "African-American." *Education:* Graduated from Northwestern University.

ADDRESSES: Agent—c/o Northwestern University Press, 625 Colfax St., Evanston, IL 60208.

CAREER: Poet. Organization of Black American Culture (OBAC) Workshop, Chicago, IL, coordinator, 1976—. Active in the Poets-in-the-Schools Program in the state of Illinois throughout the 1970s.

MEMBER: Organization of Black American Culture.

AWARDS, HONORS: Conrad Kent Rivers Memorial Award from *Black World,* 1973; Edwin Schulman Fiction Prize, and Academy of American Poets Prize, both from Northwestern University, 1974; Illinois State Arts Council Award, for "Witchdoctor," 1978.

WRITINGS:

POETRY

Voo Doo/Love Magic, Third World Press (Chicago, IL), 1974.

The Greenville Club (chapbook), published in *Four Black Poets,* Bk Mk Press (Kansas City, MO), 1977.

Solo in the Boxcar Third Floor E, OBAhouse (Chicago, IL), 1985.

The Man with the White Liver, Contact II (New York City), 1987.

Dark Legs and Silk Kisses: The Beatitudes of the Spinners, Triquarterly Books (Evanston, IL), 1993.

And All These Roads Be Luminous: Poems Selected and New, Northwestern University Press (Evanston, IL), 1997.

Contributor of poetry to periodicals, including *Callaloo, Obsidian, Black Collegian,* and *Open Places.*

OTHER

Witness! (play), produced at the Showcase Theatre, Chicago, 1978.

Shango Diaspora: An African-American Myth of Womanhood and Love (play), produced at the Parkway Community House Theatre, Chicago, 1980.

When the Wind Blows (play), produced in Chicago, 1984.

Author of the short stories "Witchdoctor," *Chicago Review,* winter, 1977, and "Dreamer," *First World,* 1977. Also contributor of short stories to other periodicals, including *TriQuarterly.*

SIDELIGHTS: Though she has shown great versatility throughout her writing career, author Angela Jackson is most recognized for her poetry. An African-American who grew up in urban Chicago after having spent her earliest years in rural Mississippi, Jackson expresses a great concern for racial equality in her poems, as well as her other works, which include short stories and dramas. A graduate of Chicago's prestigious Northwestern University, where she won several literary awards in 1974, Jackson went on to become an instrumental member of the city's Organization of Black American Culture (OBAC) Writers

Workshop. The influence of this organization, which also produced such writers as Carolyn Rodgers and Johari Amini (Jewel Latimore), informed the themes that dominate Jackson's work. In the early 1970s, Hoyt Fuller, who was also the publisher of the periodical *Black World,* directed OBAC, helping to shape its strong political and social consciousness. The community-based group was formed with the goal of advancing "the conscious development and articulation of a Black Aesthetic." The member writers were encouraged to find ways to express in words the "Black Experience," as well as focusing their attention on the works of other African-American authors.

In the midst of this experience, Jackson published her first volume of poetry entitled *Voo Doo/Love Magic* in 1974. In the book, which she dedicated to her family, Fuller, and OBAC, she expressed her debt to the group. Jackson declared in a poem included in the volume: "i am more than grateful for the grooming and growth allowed me in the workshop; for the dedications i have gained as a Blackperson and the commitment to Black / craftsmanship and Black / communication." Marked by its experimental use of rhythmic patterns and inflection, the collection of 15 poems incorporates the themes of love, family, and the black experience.

With this experimental style in *Voo Doo/Love Magic,* Jackson attempted, among other things, to mimic the accent of African-American dialect, a fact not lost on critics. "[S]he exhibits a distinctive, highly personal voice. No one has developed a more complex and subtly modulated vernacular-based poetic diction than she," D. L. Smith remarked in *Dictionary of Literary Biography.* Another of the collection's poems that strives to imitate Afro-American vernacular is "Make/n My Music." Because of her mastery with pause and rhythm, Jackson has been one of the most sought after readers and performers in the Chicago area. Throughout the 1970s, she was a participant in the Poets-in-the-Schools Program that traveled throughout Illinois.

After some of her poems were included in the 1976 anthology *15 Chicago Poets,* Jackson published her next collection, *The Greenville Club* (she was born in Greenville, Mississippi), in 1977. The work was included and published in a volume called *Four Black Poets,* which was made up of several chapbooks. Although the title suggests a rural setting, most of the poems revolve around Jackson's urban upbringing in Chicago. Some of these same concerns were echoed in Jackson's 1985 volume of poetry, *Solo in the Boxcar Third Floor E.*

In her 1997 volume, *And All These Roads Be Luminous: Poems Selected and New,* Jackson offers a collection of poems—some published between 1969 and 1993 and some new—that treat a broad spectrum of topics, including the advent of language, sexuality, and the experience of the homeless. *Booklist* contributor Donna Seaman offered high praise for the volume, calling the poems "sinuous and inexhaustible exhalations, complex riffs rich in sensuous detail and resonant with psychological insight." Seaman concluded that "Jackson reanimates myth and history, scrutinizes life from unexpected perspectives, and shares her keen irony, seasoned humor, and hard-won wisdom in poems that conjure diverse times and places, and tell many stories."

In addition to her works of poetry, Jackson has found success with her fiction, in the form of short stories and drama. In fact, she spent much of the late 1970s and 1980s working on her fiction. Some of her most recognized short stories are "Dreamer," a work that was published in the 1977 inaugural issue of *First World,* and "Witchdoctor," which appeared in 1977 in the *Chicago Review,* and for which Jackson received a 1978 Illinois State Arts Council Award. Smith observed: "The power of these stories derives not from the movement of plot, but from the vividly present consciousness of her characters and their sense of themselves, of each other, and of the world."

BIOGRAPHICAL/CRITICAL SOURCES:

BOOKS

Dictionary of Literary Biography, Volume 41: *Afro-American Poets since 1955,* edited by Trudier Harris and Thadious M. Davis, Gale (Detroit, MI), 1985.
Jackson, Angela, *Voo Doo/Love Magic,* Third World Press (Chicago, IL), 1974.

PERIODICALS

Booklist, February 15, 1998, p. 970.*

*   *   *

JACKSON, Sheneska   1970-

PERSONAL: Born c. 1970, in CA; daughter of Etna Jackson (a phone company supervisor). *Education:*

California State University at Northridge, B.A., 1992.

ADDRESSES: Home—Sherman Oaks, CA. *Agent*—c/o Simon & Schuster, 1230 Ave. of the Americas, New York, NY 10020.

CAREER: Novelist. UCLA Extension Program, writing instructor; worked as a medical secretary, 1992-95.

WRITINGS:

Caught up in the Rapture, Simon & Schuster (New York City), 1996.
Li'l Mama's Rules, Simon & Schuster, 1997.
Blessings, Simon & Schuster, 1998.

SIDELIGHTS: Sheneska Jackson is the author of two novels centering on young African American women striving for satisfying personal relationships and professional success in the 1990s. Employed as a secretary following her graduation from the University of California at Northridge, Jackson was inspired to write a novel after hearing a lecture by the highly acclaimed author of *Waiting to Exhale,* Terry McMillan.

Jackson worked on her manuscript before leaving for work each morning—from 3:00 a.m. to 7:00 a.m.—for six weeks, completing the first draft of what became her 1996 debut novel, *Caught up in the Rapture.* The novel focuses on Jazmine Deems, a twenty-six-year-old African American pop singer from Los Angeles who is the daughter of a religious minister. After gaining her long-held ambition to sign a recording contract, Jazmine becomes involved with a rap artist who has been recently signed to the same record label and who is, in the words of Dan Bogey in *Library Journal,* "as streetwise as Jazmine is naive." In the novel Jazmine's singing career is threatened by the cocaine habit of one of the record company executives, while her personal relationship is jeopardized by the gang activities of her new boyfriend, X-Man.

Described as "lively" by a reviewer for *People Weekly, Caught up in the Rapture* won the praises of a *Kirkus Reviews* critic, who called the novel "seamless, convincing, and gruelingly honest." That reviewer noted that the book's portrayal the glamorous music business world contrasted effectively with the grittiness of the ghetto street scenes, and added that *Caught up in the Rapture* is "an impressive debut novel that never lets its message overwhelm the

story." Anita B. Short, writing in *School Library Journal,* called the book "a bold, often humorous tale," and concluded that *Caught up in the Rapture* offers "an insightful look at the street life, loyalty, and ties of the hood."

Jackson's follow-up novel, *Li'l Mama's Rules,* was published in 1997. The plot centers on Madison McGuire, a thirty-year-old private school teacher whose understanding of love relationships and of her own self-worth are transformed when a test reveals that she is HIV-positive. Disappointed by an early, unfaithful lover, Madison has developed a list of "rules," or dating situations to avoid based on her experiences with a series of unsuitable men. Ultimately Madison is reunited with her former lover who helps her to accept her situation and to recognize value in herself. According to a commentator in *Kirkus Reviews,* Jackson's novel offers "some wry—and eminently universal—observations on the battle between the sexes." Lillian Lewis in *Booklist* remarked that the seriousness of Madison's medical condition "forces her to make choices and decisions that are not self-destructive; she finally learns that the rules to follow are of things 'to do'." While generally finding favor with the novel, the *Kirkus Reviews* critic complained that "the end of the book succumbs to triteness in the form of safe-sex messages." Fannette H. Thomas wrote approvingly in *Library Journal,* calling it a "gripping story."

BIOGRAPHICAL/CRITICAL SOURCES:

PERIODICALS

Booklist, May 1, 1997, p. 1479.
Kirkus Reviews, March 1, 1996, pp. 318-19; April 1, 1997, p. 488.
Library Journal, April 16, 1996, p. 122; November 15, 1996, p. 116; May 1, 1997, p. 140.
People Weekly, June 10, 1996, p. 125.
Publishers Weekly, March 18, 1996, p. 56; April 21, 1997, p. 60.
School Library Journal, August, 1996, p. 184.*

*   *   *

JOHNSON, Charles (Richard) 1948-

PERSONAL: Born April 23, 1948, in Evanston, IL; son of Benjamin Lee and Ruby Elizabeth (Jackson) Johnson; married Joan New (an elementary school teacher), June, 1970; children: Malik, Elizabeth. *Education:* Southern Illinois University, B.A., 1971, M.A., 1973; post-graduate work at State University of New York at Stony Brook, 1973-76.

ADDRESSES: Office—Department of English, University of Washington, Seattle, WA 98105.

CAREER: Chicago Tribune, Chicago, IL, cartoonist and reporter, 1969-70; *St. Louis Proud,* St. Louis, MO, member of art staff, 1971-72; University of Washington, Seattle, assistant professor, 1976-79, associate professor, 1979-82, professor of English, 1982—. Writer and cartoonist. Fiction editor of *Seattle Review,* 1978—. Director of Associated Writing Programs Awards Series in Short Fiction, 1979-81, member of board of directors, 1983—.

AWARDS, HONORS: Named journalism alumnus of the year by Southern Illinois University, 1981; Governors Award for Literature from State of Washington, 1983, for *Oxherding Tale;* Callaloo Creative Writing Award, 1983, for short story "Popper's Disease"; citation in *Pushcart Prize'*s Outstanding Writers section, 1984, for story "China"; National Book Award, 1990, for *Middle Passage.*

WRITINGS:

NOVELS

Faith and the Good Thing, Viking (New York City), 1974.
Oxherding Tale, Indiana University Press, 1982.
Middle Passage, Macmillan (New York City), 1990.
Dreamer, Scribners, 1998.

CARTOON COLLECTIONS

Black Humor (self-illustrated), Johnson Publishing, 1970.
Half-Past Nation Time (self-illustrated), Aware Press, 1972.

Contributor of cartoons to periodicals, including *Ebony, Chicago Tribune, Jet, Black World,* and *Players.*

TELEVISION SCRIPTS

Charlie's Pad (fifty-two-part series on cartooning), PBS, 1970.
Charlie Smith and the Fritter Tree, PBS "Visions" series, 1978.

(With John Alman) *Booker,* PBS, 1983.

Contributor of scripts to numerous television series, including *Up and Coming,* PBS, 1981, and *Y.E.S., Inc.,* PBS, 1983.

OTHER

The Sorcerer's Apprentice (short stories), Atheneum, 1986.
(Contributor) Jeff Henderson, editor, *Thor's Hammer: Essays on John Gardner,* Arkansas Philological Association, 1986.
Being and Race: Black Writing since 1970, Indiana University Press, 1988.
Pieces of Eight, Discovery Press, 1989.
(Author of foreword) *Rites of Passage: Stories about Growing up by Black Writers from Around the World,* Hyperion, 1993.
(Author of introduction) *On Writers and Writing,* Addison-Wesley, 1994.

Work represented in anthologies, including *Best American Short Stories, 1982,* edited by John Gardner and Shannon Ravenel, Houghton, 1982. Contributor of short stories and essays to periodicals, including *Mother Jones, Callaloo, Choice, Indiana Review, Nimrod, Intro 10, Obsidian,* and *North American Review.*

SIDELIGHTS: "Charles Johnson has enriched contemporary American fiction as few young writers can," observed *Village Voice* critic Stanley Crouch, adding that "it is difficult to imagine that such a talented artist will forever miss the big time." A graduate of Southern Illinois University, Johnson studied with the late author John Gardner, under whose guidance he wrote *Faith and the Good Thing.* Though Johnson had written six "apprentice" novels prior to his association with Gardner, *Faith* was the first to be accepted for publication. Johnson professes to "share Gardner's concern with 'moral fiction'" and believes in the "necessity of young (and old) writers working toward becoming technicians of language and literary form."

Faith and the Good Thing met with an enthusiastic response from critics such as Garrett Epps of *Washington Post Book World,* who judged it "a brilliant first novel" and commended its author as "one of this country's most interesting and inventive younger writers." Roger Sale, writing in the *Sewanee Review,* had similar praise for the novel. He commented: "Johnson, it is clear, is a writer, and if he works too hard at it at times, or if he seems a little too pleased with it at other times, he is twenty-six, and with prose and confidence like his, he can do anything."

The book is a complex, often humorous, folktale account of Faith Cross, a Southern black girl traveling to Chicago in search of life's "Good Thing," which she has learned of from her dying mother. In her quest, noted *Time*'s John Skrow, Faith "seeks guidance from a swamp witch, a withered and warty old necromancer with one green and one yellow eye," who nonetheless "spouts philosophy as if she were Hegel." Skrow deemed the work a "wry comment on the tension felt by a black intellectual," and Annie Gottlieb of the *New York Times Book Review* called *Faith and the Good Thing* a "strange and often wonderful hybrid—an ebullient philosophical novel in the form of a folktale-cum-black-girl's odyssey." She noted that the novel's "magic falls flat" on occasion, "when the mix . . . is too thick with academic in-jokes and erudite references," but she added that "fortunately, such moments are overwhelmed by the poetry and wisdom of the book." In conclusion, Gottlieb found the novel "flawed yet still fabulous."

Johnson described his second novel, *Oxherding Tale,* as "a modern, comic, philosophical slave narrative— a kind of dramatization of the famous 'Ten Oxherding Pictures' of Zen artist Kakuan-Shien," which represent the progressive search of a young herdsman for his rebellious ox, a symbol for his self. The author added that the novel's style "blends the eighteenth-century English novel with the Eastern parable."

Like his first novel, Johnson's *Oxherding Tale* received widespread critical acclaim. It details the coming of age of Andrew Hawkins, a young mulatto slave in the pre-Civil War South. Andrew is conceived when, after much drinking, plantation owner Jonathan Polkinghorne convinces his black servant, George Hawkins, to swap wives with him for the evening. Unaware that the man sharing her bed is not her husband, Anna Polkinghorne makes love with George and consequentially becomes pregnant with Andrew. After the child is born Anna rejects him as a constant reminder of her humiliation, and he is taken in by George's wife, Mattie. Though he is raised in slave quarters, Andrew receives many privileges, including an education from an eccentric tutor who teaches him about Eastern mysticism, socialism, and the philosophies of Plato, Schopenhauer, and Hegel.

Writing in *Literature, Fiction, and the Arts Review,* Florella Orowan called Andrew "a man with no social place, caught between the slave world and free white society but, like the hapless hero Tom Jones, he gains from his ambiguous existence the timeless advantage of the Outsider's omniscience and chimerism: he can assume whatever identity is appropriate to the situation." *Oxherding Tale* accompanies its hero on a series of adventures that include an exotic sexual initiation, an encounter with the pleasures of opium, escape from the plantation, "passing" as white, and eluding a telepathic bounty hunter called the Soulcatcher. As Michael S. Weaver observed in *Gargoyle,* Andrew "lives his way to freedom through a succession of sudden enlightenments. . . . Each experience is another layer of insight into human nature" that has "a touch of Johnson's ripe capacity for laughter." The book's climax, noted Crouch, is "remarkable for its brutality and humble tenderness; Andrew must dive into the briar patch of his identity and risk destruction in order to express his humanity."

Weaver admitted that "at times *Oxherding Tale* reads like a philosophical tract, and may have been more adequately billed as Thus Spake Andrew Hawkins." But he concluded that the novel "is nonetheless an entertaining display of Johnson's working knowledge of the opportunities for wisdom afforded by the interplay between West and East, Black and White, man and woman, feeling and knowing—all of them seeming contradictions." According to Crouch, the novel is successful "because Johnson skillfully avoids melodramatic platitudes while creating suspense and comedy, pathos and nostalgia. In the process, he invents a fresh set of variations on questions about race, sex, and freedom."

In the short story collection *The Sorcerer's Apprentice,* Johnson continued to examine spiritual, mystical, and philosophical matters through the essentially realistic filter of historical African-American experience. Magic, however, particularly African voodoo practices, plays an essential role in most of the stories, lending these tales an element of the fantastic "without," as Michael Ventura noted in the *New York Times Book Review,* "getting lost in fantasy." Johnson's overriding concern in this volume is with transcending the self, examining the importance of and terror involved in surrendering to nonrational forces. For example, in the title story, an older former slave in South Carolina—the Sorcerer—tries unsuccessfully to pass his abilities on to a young man born in freedom. He laments the fact that the youth has become too American, rational, to accept African magic. Johnson writes that "magic did not reside in ratiocination, education, or will. Skill was of no service. . . . God or creation, or the universe—it had several names— had to *seize* you, *use* you, as the Sorcerer said, because it needed a womb, shake you down, speak through you until the pain pearled into a beautiful spell that snapped the world back together." Ventura concluded that "Mr. Johnson's spell of a book comes on with the authority of a classic."

In 1990, Johnson's literary stature was officially recognized when he won the National Book Award for his novel *Middle Passage.* Set in 1830, the story concerns the newly freed slave Rutherford Calhoun, an ardent womanizer, an admitted liar, and a thief who runs from New Orleans ahead of bill collectors and away from an ill-fated romance. He stows away on a ship, the Republic, that is setting out on a round-trip voyage to Africa where it will fill its hold with slaves. As the novel progresses, the ship's captain is revealed to be a kind of mad genius, the crew is shown to be comprised of a variety of unsavory seagoing types, and the slaves who are eventually transported are—like the Sorcerer in *The Sorcerer's Apprentice*—members of the (fictional) Allmuseri tribe of wizards. *Middle Passage,* like much of Johnson's fiction, relates the many aspects of the African-American experience through a fantastically tinted literary realism. Writing in *African American Review,* Daniel M. Scott III concluded of *Middle Passage:* "As Johnson sings the world, he searches experience and perception for the roots of reality and the doorways to transformation. Writing, understood as a mode of thought, *is* the middle passage, between what has been and what will be, between the word and the world."

Johnson told *CA:* "As a writer I am committed to the development of what one might call a genuinely systematic philosophical black American literature, a body of work that explores classical problems and metaphysical questions against the background of black American life. Specifically, my philosophical style is phenomenology, the discipline of Edmund Husserl, but I also have a deep personal interest in the entire continuum of Asian philosophy from the Vedas to Zen, and this perspective inevitably colors my fiction to some degree.

"I have been a martial artist since the age nineteen and a practicing Buddhist since about 1980. So one might also say that in fiction I attempt to interface Eastern and Western philosophical traditions, always with the hope that some new perception of experience—especially 'black experience'—will emerge from these meditations."

BIOGRAPHICAL/CRITICAL SOURCES:

BOOKS

Contemporary Authors Autobiography Series, Volume 18, Gale (Detroit), 1994.
Contemporary Literary Criticism, Gale, Volume 7, 1977, Volume 51, 89, Volume 65, 1991.
Dictionary of Literary Biography, Volume 33: *Afro-American Fiction Writers After 1955,* Gale, 1984.

PERIODICALS

African American Review, winter, 1995; spring, 1995.
Callaloo, October, 1978.
CLA Journal, June, 1978.
Commonweal, December 2, 1994.
Gargoyle, June, 1978.
Kliatt, March, 1995.
Literature, Fiction, and the Arts Review, June 30, 1983; January 22, 1995.
Los Angeles Times Book Review, November 21, 1982.
New Yorker, December 20, 1982.
New York Times Book Review, January 12, 1975; January 9, 1983; February 5, 1986; March 30, 1986.
Publishers Weekly, February 28, 1994, p. 65.
Sewanee Review, January, 1975.
Time, January 6, 1975.
Times Literary Supplement, January 6, 1984.
Village Voice, July 19, 1984.
Washington Post Book World, December 15, 1982; February 16, 1986.*

* * *

JOHNSON, Charles S(purgeon) 1893-1956

PERSONAL: Born July 24, 1893, in Bristol, VA; died following a heart attack, October 27, 1956, in Louisville, KY; son of Charles Henry (a minister) and Winifred (Branch) Johnson; married Marie Antoinette Burgette, November 6, 1920; children: Charles, Jr., Robert Burgette, Jeh Vincent, Patricia Marie Clifford. *Education:* Virginia Union University, B.A., 1916; University of Chicago, Ph.B., 1918. *Politics:* Democrat. *Religion:* Congregationalist.

CAREER: Director of Department of Research and Investigations for Chicago Urban League, 1917-19; associate executive secretary for Chicago Commission on Race Relations, 1919-21; National Urban League, New York, NY, director of Department of Research and Investigations, 1921-28; Fisk University, Nashville, TN, professor of sociology and chairman of department of social sciences, beginning in 1928, president of the university, 1946-56. Delegate to United Nations Educational, Scientific, and Cultural Organization (UNESCO) conferences in Paris in 1946 and in Mexico City in 1947. Delegate to World Council of Churches in Amsterdam in 1948 and to Conference on Indian-American Relations in New Delhi in 1949. Member of numerous government committees on sociological matters, including the commission appointed by the League of Nations to investigate forced labor in Liberia in 1930, the commission sent to Japan in 1946 by the State Department to organize the Japanese educational system, and the commission established by the Eisenhower administration in 1952 to study the health needs of the nation. Participant in several private organizations, including director in 1933 and co-director from 1934 to 1938 of the Institute of Race Relations at Swarthmore College, co-director of the race relations program and a member of the board of trustees from 1943 to 1948 of the Julius Rosenwald Fund, and a director from 1944 to 1950 of the Race Relations Division of the American Missionary Association of the Congregational and Christian Churches of America. *Military service:* U.S. Army, 1918-19, served as a sergeant with the 893d Pioneer Infantry.

AWARDS, HONORS: Recipient of many awards and honors, including the William E. Harmon Gold Medal from the Harmon Foundation, 1930, for his achievements in the field of social science, the Anisfield-Wolf Award from *Saturday Review,* 1938, for his book *The Negro College Graduate,* the Russwurm Award for Public Service from the Negro Newspaper Publishers' Association, and the Social Action Churchmanship Award of the General Council of the Congregational Christian Churches. Honorary Litt.D. degrees conferred by Virginia Union University in 1938 and Columbia University in 1947, an honorary L.H.D. degree by Howard University in 1941, the honorary LL.D. degree by Harvard University in 1948, the University of Glasgow, Scotland, in 1952, Lincoln University in 1955, and Central State College, Xenia, Ohio, in 1956.

WRITINGS:

(Editor) *Ebony and Topaz: A Collectanea,* Urban League, 1927, reprinted, Books for Libraries, 1971.

The Negro in American Civilization: A Study of Negro Life and Race Relations in the Light of Social Research, Holt, 1930, reprinted, Johnson, 1970.

Negro Housing: Report of the Committee on Negro Housing, edited by John M. Gries and James Ford, President's Conference on Home Building and Home Ownership (Washington, D.C.), 1932, reprinted, Negro Universities Press, 1969.

The Economic Status of Negroes: Summary and Analysis of the Materials Presented at the Conference on the Economic Status of the Negro, Held in Washington, D.C., May 11-13, 1933, Under the Sponsorship of the Julius Rosenwald Fund, Fisk University Press, 1933, reprinted, New York Public Library, 1974.

Shadow of the Plantation, University of Chicago Press, 1934, reprinted, 1966.

(With Willis Duke Weatherford) *Race Relations: Adjustment of Whites and Negroes in the United States,* Heath, 1934, reprinted, Negro Universities Press, 1969.

(With Edwin R. Embree and W.W. Alexander) *The Collapse of Cotton Tenancy: Summary of Field Studies and Statistical Surveys, 1933-1935,* University of North Carolina Press, 1935, reprinted, Books for Libraries, 1972.

A Preface to Racial Understanding, Friendship, 1936.

The Negro College Graduate, University of North Carolina Press, 1938, reprinted, Negro Universities Press, 1969.

Growing Up in the Black Belt: Negro Youth in the Rural South, with an introduction by St. Clair Drake, American Council on Education, 1941, reprinted, Schocken, 1967.

(Co-author) *Statistical Atlas of Southern Counties: Listing and Analysis of Socio-Economic Indices of 1,104 southern Counties,* University of North Carolina Press, 1941.

Patterns of Negro Segregation, Harper, 1943, reprinted as *Backgrounds to Patterns of Negro Segregation,* Crowell, 1970.

(Co-author) *To Stem This Tide: A Survey of Racial Tension Areas in the United States,* Pilgrim Press, 1943, reprinted, AMS Press, 1969.

(Editor) *Education and the Cultural Process: Papers Presented at Symposium Commemorating the Seventy-fifth Anniversary of the Founding of Fisk University, April 29-May 4, 1941,* University of Chicago Press, 1943, reprinted, Negro Universities Press, 1970.

(With Herman H. Long) *People Versus Property: Race Restrictive Covenants in Housing,* Fisk University Press, 1947.

(Co-author) *Into the Main Stream: A Survey of Best Practices in Race Relations in the South,* University of North Carolina Press, 1947, reprinted, 1967.

Bitter Canaan: The Story of the Negro Republic, with an introduction by John Stanfield, Transaction Books, 1987.

Contributor to *Recent Gains in American Civilization,* edited by Kirby Page, Harcourt, 1928. Contributor of articles to periodicals, including *Opportunity, Journal of Negro History,* and *New York Times.*

SIDELIGHTS: For four decades Charles S. Johnson worked quietly but steadfastly in his efforts to improve race relations between blacks and whites in the United States. As the chief black sociologist of his period Johnson wrote the scholarly books that documented the causes of race riots, the effects of racism on the personalities of black youths, and the necessity for blacks to become a part of the mainstream of American life. As the first black president of Fisk University Johnson was the driving force behind the establishment of Fisk as a first-rate institution the rival of Booker T. Washington's Tuskegee Institute. And, most of all, as founder and editor of the National Urban League's *Opportunity: A Journal of Negro Life,* Johnson helped generate one of the most impressive cultural movements in American history, the Harlem Renaissance of the 1920s.

It was in 1923 that, in addition to his duties as director of the National Urban League's Department of Research and Investigations, Johnson assumed the task of editing the league's new magazine, *Opportunity.* Eugene Kinckle Jones, executive secretary of the league, set the tone of *Opportunity* when in the first issue he wrote that it would "depict Negro life as it is with no exaggerations. We shall try to set down interestingly but without sugar-coating or generalization the findings of careful scientific surveys and the facts gathered from research." Johnson, while supporting Jones's position, noted an additional dimension that *Opportunity* would report, when in the next issue he wrote: "There are aspects of the cultural side of Negro life that have been long neglected." Very quickly *Opportunity* became more than a house organ of the Urban League.

Like W. E. B. Du Bois's *Crisis* magazine, *Opportunity* provided an outlet for publication to young black writers and scholars whose work was not acceptable to other established media. Although *Crisis* was older and had a larger circulation than *Opportunity,* the orientation of its editor, W. E. B. Du Bois, was more political than Johnson's. *Opportunity* did not neglect political issues: it too reported on scientific surveys of discrimination and conditions in the black community in housing, health, employment, and other economical and sociological areas. *Opportunity,* however, made its most enduring contribution in reporting black culture in the United States and the world at large. In the May, 1924, issue, for instance, black scholars Alain Locke, Albert C. Barnes, and Paul Guillaume all contributed articles to a special issue on African art. And in the November, 1926, issue, *Opportunity* presented a special "Caribbean issue." Among other features it included poems by Claude McKay, an article on West Indian composers musicians, and W. A. Domingo's "The West Indies."

It was in the popular *Opportunity* dinners and contests, however, that Johnson was most successful in promoting the new awakening of black culture. An early observer of the creative genius of the many black artists of the 1920s, Johnson, along with the Urban League administration, moved deliberately to bring the white publishers and the black writers together. The dinners, which gathered together white editors and black artists, served to showcase black literary and artistic talent and to secure patronage for the Renaissance movement from white publishers. The contests, which awarded first, second, and third prizes for short stories, poems, plays, and essays as well as a guarantee of publication, were open not only to black contributors but also to non-blacks on topics about blacks. Many of the contest winners, for the most part unknown to white publishers, were well known within black literary circles. Among them were short-story writers John F. Matheus, Zora Neale Hurston, and Eric D. Walrond, poets Langston Hughes and Countee Cullen, essayists E. Franklin Frazier, Sterling A. Brown, and Laura D. Wheatley, and playwright Warren A. MacDonald.

The first *Opportunity* dinners and contests were the most successful. In subsequent years there were more contestants, but the submissions were of a lesser quality, causing Johnson's enthusiasm to wane. In 1927, the year before he left the Urban League, Johnson gathered what he judged to be the best of the work published in *Opportunity* and collected it in *Ebony and Topaz, A Collectanea.* A diverse sampling of Johnson's conception of Afro-American artistic pursuits in the 1920s, the volume contained poetry, short fiction, drama, essays, translations, paintings, and drawings. Represented are the best known artists and writers of the Harlem Renaissance, including Gwendolyn Bennett,

Arna Bontemps, Sterling A. Brown, Countee Cullen, Langston Hughes, Zora Neale Hurston, and Helene Johnson.

Years later Johnson had occasion in "The Negro Renaissance and Its Significance," a speech given at Howard University and later assembled by Fisk University Library into a special collection, to look back at the Harlem Renaissance. Even though more than a quarter of a century had passed since its heyday, Johnson seemed more convinced than ever of its success. He said of the 1920s: "It was a period, not only of the quivering search for freedom but of a cultural, if not a social and racial emancipation. It was unabashedly self-conscious and race conscious. But it was race consciousness with an extraordinary facet in that it had virtues that could be incorporated into the cultural bloodstream of the nation."

BIOGRAPHICAL/CRITICAL SOURCES:

BOOKS

Anderson, Jervis, *This Was Harlem: A Cultural Portrait, 1900-1950,* Farrar, Straus, 1981.

Blackwell, James E. and Morris Janowitz, editors, *Black Sociologists: Historical and Contemporary Perspectives,* University of Chicago Press, 1974.

Bone, Robert A., *The Negro Novel in America,* Yale University Press, 1958.

Bontemps, Arna, editor, *The Harlem Renaissance Remembered,* Dodd, 1972.

Charke, John Henrik, editor, *Harlem: A Community in Transition,* Citadel, 1964.

Cruse, Harold, *The Crisis of the Negro Intellectual,* Apollo, 1968.

Dictionary of Literary Biography, Volume 51: *Afro-American Writers From the Harlem Renaissance to 1940,* Gale, 1987.

Embree, Edwin R., *Thirteen against the Odds,* Viking, 1945.

Huggins, Nathan I., *Harlem Renaissance,* Oxford University Press, 1971.

Lewis, David Levering, *When Harlem Was in Vogue,* Knopf, 1981.

Locke, Alain, *The New Negro,* Atheneum, 1969.

Meier, August, *Negro Thought in America, 1880-1915,* University of Michigan Press, 1963.

Richardson, Joe M., *A History of Fisk University, 1865-1946,* University of Alabama Press, 1980.

PERIODICALS

Black World, November, 1970.

Ebony, February, 1957.
Massachusetts Review, autumn, 1979.
Negro History Bulletin, April, 1968.
Opportunity, Volume I, number 1, January, 1923; Volume I, number 2, February, 1923.
Phylon, Volume 17, fourth quarter, 1956.*

*   *   *

JOHNSON, James Weldon   1871-1938

PERSONAL: Born June 17, 1871, in Jacksonville, FL; died following an automobile accident, June 26, 1938, in Wiscasset, ME; buried in Brooklyn, New York; son of James (a restaurant headwaiter) and Helen Louise (a musician and schoolteacher; maiden name, Dillette) Johnson; married Grace Nail, February 3, 1910. *Education:* Atlanta University, A.B., 1894, A.M., 1904; graduate study at Columbia University, c. 1902-05.

CAREER: Poet, novelist, songwriter, editor, historian, civil rights leader, diplomat, lawyer, and educator. Stanton Central Grammar School for Negroes, Jacksonville, Florida, teacher, later principal, 1894-1901; *Daily American* (newspaper), Jacksonville, founder and co-editor, 1895-96; admitted to the Bar of the State of Florida, 1898; private law practice, Jacksonville, 1898-1901; songwriter for the musical theater in partnership with brother, J. Rosamond Johnson, and Bob Cole, New York City, 1901-06; United States Consul to Puerto Cabello, Venezuela, 1906-09, and to Corinto, Nicaragua, 1909-13; *New York Age* (newspaper), New York City, editorial writer, 1914-24; National Association for the Advancement of Colored People (NAACP), New York City, field secretary, 1916-20, executive secretary, 1920-30; Fisk University, Nashville, Tennessee, professor of creative literature and writing, 1931-38; elected treasurer of the Colored Republican Club, New York City, and participated in Theodore Roosevelt's presidential campaign, both in 1904; lectured on literature and black culture at numerous colleges and universities during the 1930s, including New York, Northwestern, and Yale Universities, Oberlin and Swarthmore Colleges, and the Universities of North Carolina and Chicago. Served as director of the American Fund for Public Service and as trustee of Atlanta University.

MEMBER: American Society of Composers, Authors, and Publishers (charter member), Academy of Political Science, Ethical Society, Civic Club (New York City).

AWARDS, HONORS: Spingarn Medal from NAACP, 1925, for outstanding achievement by an American Negro; Harmon Gold Award for *God's Trombones;* Julius Rosenwald Fund grant, 1929; W.E.B. Du Bois Prize for Negro Literature, 1933; named first incumbent of Spence Chair of Creative Literature at Fisk University; honorary doctorates from Talladega College and Howard University.

WRITINGS:

The Autobiography of an Ex-Coloured Man (novel), Sherman, French, 1912, Arden Library, 1978, reprinted, Dover, 1995.

(Translator) Fernando Periquet, *Goyescas; or, The Rival Lovers* (opera libretto), G. Schirmer, 1915.

Fifty Years and Other Poems, Cornhill, 1917, AMS Press, 1975.

(Editor) *The Book of American Negro Poetry,* Harcourt, 1922, revised edition (publisher unknown), 1969.

(Editor) *The Book of American Negro Spirituals,* Viking, 1925.

(Editor) *The Second Book of Negro Spirituals* Viking, 1926.

God's Trombones: Seven Negro Sermons in Verse (poetry), illustrations by Aaron Douglas, Viking, 1927, Penguin, 1976.

Black Manhattan (nonfiction), Knopf, 1930, Arno, 1968.

Along This Way: The Autobiography of James Weldon Johnson, Viking, 1933, Da Capo, 1973.

Negro Americans, What Now? (nonfiction), Viking, 1934, Da Capo, 1973.

Saint Peter Relates an Incident: Selected Poems, Viking, 1935, AMS Press, 1974.

The Great Awakening, Revell, 1938.

(Editor) *The Books of American Negro Spirituals* (contains *The Book of American Negro Spirituals* and *The Second Book of Negro Spirituals*), Viking, 1940, reprinted, 1964.

The Creation (poetry), illustrated by James Ransome, Holiday House, 1994.

The Selected Writings of James Weldon Johnson, edited by Sondra K. Wilson, Oxford University Press, 1995.

Lift Ev'ry Voice and Sing (songs), illustrated by Jan Spivey Gilchrist, Scholastic, 1995.

Also author of *Selected Poems,* 1936.

Contributor of articles and poems to numerous newspapers and magazines, including the *Chicago Defender, Times-Union* (Jacksonville, FL), *New York Age, New York Times, Pittsburgh Courier, Savannah Tribune, Century, Crisis, Nation, Independent, Harper's, Bookman, Forum,* and *Scholastic.* Poetry represented in many anthologies; songs published by Joseph W. Stern & Co., Edward B. Marks Music Corp., and others; author of numerous pamphlets on current events published by the NAACP, *Nation, Century,* and others.

SIDELIGHTS: James Weldon Johnson distinguished himself equally as a man of letters and as a civil rights leader in the early decades of the twentieth century. A talented poet and novelist, Johnson is credited with bringing a new standard of artistry and realism to black literature in such works as *The Autobiography of an Ex-Coloured Man* and *God's Trombones.* His pioneering studies of black poetry, music, and theater in the 1920s also helped introduce many white Americans to the genuine Afro-American creative spirit, hitherto known mainly through the distortions of the minstrel show and dialect poetry. Meanwhile, as head of the National Association for the Advancement of Colored People (NAACP) during the 1920s, Johnson led determined civil rights campaigns in an effort to remove the legal, political, and social obstacles hindering black achievement.

Johnson's multi-faceted career, which also included stints as a diplomat in Latin America and a successful Tin Pan Alley songwriter, testified to his intellectual breadth, self-confidence, and deep-rooted belief that the future held unlimited new opportunities for black Americans.

Johnson was born in Jacksonville, Florida, in 1871, and his upbringing in this relatively tolerant Southern town may help explain his later political moderation. Both his father, a resort hotel headwaiter, and his mother, a schoolteacher, had lived in the North and had never been enslaved, and James and his brother John Rosamond grew up in broadly cultured and economically secure surroundings that were unusual among Southern black families at the time. Johnson's mother stimulated his early interests in reading, drawing, and music, and he attended the segregated Stanton School, where she taught, until the eighth grade. Since high schools were closed to blacks in Jacksonville, Johnson left home to attend both secondary school and college at Atlanta University, where he took his bachelor's degree in 1894. It was during his college years, as Johnson recalled in his autobiography, *Along This Way,* that he first became aware of the depth of the racial problem in the United States. Race questions were vigorously debated on campus, and Johnson's experience teaching black schoolchildren in a poor district of rural Georgia during two summers deeply impressed him with the need to improve the lives of his people. The struggles and aspirations of American blacks form a central theme in the thirty or so poems that Johnson wrote as a student.

Returning to Jacksonville in 1894, Johnson was appointed a teacher and principal of the Stanton School and managed to expand the curriculum to include high school-level classes. He also became an active local spokesman on black social and political issues and in 1895 founded the *Daily American,* the first black-oriented daily newspaper in the United States. During its brief life, the newspaper became a voice against racial injustice and served to encourage black advancement through individual effort—a "self-help" position that echoed the more conservative civil rights leadership of the day. Although the newspaper folded for lack of readership the following year, Johnson's ambitious publishing effort attracted the attention of such prominent black leaders as W. E. B. Du Bois and Booker T. Washington.

Meanwhile Johnson read law with the help of a local white lawyer, and in 1898 he became the first black lawyer admitted to the Florida Bar since Reconstruction. Johnson practiced law in Jacksonville for several years in partnership with a former Atlanta University classmate while continuing to serve as the Stanton School's principal. He also continued to write poetry and discovered his gift for songwriting in collaboration with his brother Rosamond, a talented composer. Among other songs in a spiritual-influenced popular idiom, Johnson penned the lyrics to "Lift Every Voice and Sing," a tribute to black endurance, hope, and religious faith that was later adopted by the NAACP and dubbed "the Negro National Anthem."

In 1901, bored by Jacksonville's provincialism and disturbed by mounting incidents of racism there, the Johnson brothers set out for New York City to seek their fortune writing songs for the musical theater. In partnership with Bob Cole they secured a publishing contract paying a monthly stipend and over the next five years composed some two hundred songs for Broadway and other musical productions, including such hit numbers as "Under the Bamboo Tree," "The Old Flag Never Touched the Ground," and "Didn't He Ramble." The trio, who soon became known as

"Those Ebony Offenbachs," avoided writing for racially exploitative minstrel shows but often found themselves obliged to present simplified and stereotyped images of rural black life to suit white audiences. But the Johnsons and Cole also produced works like the six-song suite titled "The Evolution of Ragtime" that helped document and expose important black musical idioms.

During this time James Weldon Johnson also studied creative literature formally for three years at Columbia University and became active in Republican party politics. He served as treasurer of New York's Colored Republican Club in 1904 and helped write two songs for Republican candidate Theodore Roosevelt's successful presidential campaign that year. When the national black civil rights leadership split into conservative and radical factions—headed by Booker T. Washington and W. E. B. Du Bois, respectively—Johnson backed Washington, who in turn played an important role in getting the Roosevelt Administration to appoint Johnson as United States consul in Puerto Cabello, Venezuela, in 1906. With few official duties, Johnson was able to devote much of his time in that sleepy tropical port to writing poetry, including the acclaimed sonnet "Mother Night" that was published in *The Century* magazine and later included in Johnson's verse collection *Fifty Years and Other Poems.*

The consul also completed his only novel, *The Autobiography of an Ex-Coloured Man,* during his three years in Venezuela. Published anonymously in 1912, the novel attracted little attention until it was reissued under Johnson's own name more than a decade later. Even then, the book tended to draw more comment as a sociological document than as a work of fiction. (So many readers believed it to be truly autobiographical that Johnson eventually wrote his real life story, *Along This Way,* to avoid confusion.)

The Autobiography of an Ex-Coloured Man bears a superficial resemblance to other "tragic mulatto" narratives of the day that depicted, often in sentimental terms, the travails of mixed-race protagonists unable to fit into either racial culture. In Johnson's novel, the unnamed narrator is light-skinned enough to pass for white but identifies emotionally with his beloved mother's black race. In his youth, he aspires to become a great black American musical composer, but he fearfully renounces that ambition after watching a mob of whites set fire to a black man in the rural South. Though horrified and repulsed by the whites' attack, the narrator feels an even deeper shame and humiliation for himself as a black man and he subsequently allows circumstances to guide him along the easier path of "passing" as a middle-class white businessman. The protagonist finds success in this role but ends up a failure in his own terms, plagued with ambivalence over his true identity, moral values, and emotional loyalties.

Early criticism of *The Autobiography of an Ex-Coloured Man* tended to emphasize Johnson's frank and realistic look at black society and race relations more than his skill as a novelist. Carl Van Vechten, for example, found the novel "an invaluable sourcebook for the study of Negro psychology," and the *New Republic's* Edmund Wilson judged the book "an excellent, honest piece of work" as "a human and sociological document" but flawed as a work of literature. In the 1950s and 1960s, however, something of a critical reappraisal of the *Autobiography* occurred that led to a new appreciation of Johnson as a crafter of fiction. In his critical study *The Negro Novel in America,* Robert A. Bone called Johnson "the only true artist among the early Negro novelists," who succeeded in "subordinating racial protest to artistic considerations." Johnson's subtle theme of moral cowardice, Bone noted, set the novel far above "the typical propaganda tract of the day." In a 1971 essay, Robert E. Fleming drew attention to Johnson's deliberate use of an unreliable narrative voice, remarking that *The Autobiography of an Ex-Coloured Man* "is not so much a panoramic novel presenting race relations throughout America as it is a deeply ironic character study of a marginal man." Johnson's psychological depth and concern with aesthetic coherence anticipated the great black literary movement of the 1920s known as the Harlem School, according to these and other critics.

In 1909, before the *Autobiography* had been published, Johnson was promoted to the consular post in Corinto, Nicaragua, a position that proved considerably more demanding than his Venezuelan job and left him little time for writing. His three-year term of service occurred during a period of intense political turmoil in Nicaragua, which culminated in the landing of U.S. troops at Corinto in 1912. In 1913, seeing little future for himself under President Woodrow Wilson's Democratic administration, Johnson resigned from the foreign service and returned to New York to become an editorial writer for the *New York Age,* the city's oldest and most distinguished black newspaper. The articles Johnson produced over the next ten years tended toward the conservative side, combining a strong sense of racial pride with a deep-

rooted belief that blacks could individually improve their lot by means of self-education and hard work even before discriminatory barriers had been removed. This stress on individual effort and economic independence put Johnson closer to the position of black educator Booker T. Washington than that of the politically militant writer and scholar W. E. B. Du Bois in the great leadership dispute on how to improve the status of black Americans, but Johnson generally avoided criticizing either man by name and managed to maintain good relations with both leaders.

During this period Johnson continued to indulge his literary love. Having mastered the Spanish language in the diplomatic service, he translated Fernando Periquet's grand opera *Goyescas* into English and the Metropolitan Opera produced his libretto version in 1915. In 1917, Johnson published his first verse collection, *Fifty Years and Other Poems,* a selection from twenty years' work that drew mixed reviews. "Fifty Years," a sonorous poem commemorating the half-century since the Emancipation Proclamation, was generally singled out for praise, but critics differed on the merits of Johnson's dialect verse written after the manner of the great black dialect poet Paul Laurence Dunbar. The dialect style was highly popular at the time, but has since been criticized for pandering to sentimental white stereotypes of rural black life. In addition to his dialect work, Johnson's collection also included such powerful racial protest poems as "Brothers," about a lynching, and delicate lyrical verse on non-racial topics in the traditional style.

In 1916, at the urging of W. E. B. Du Bois, Johnson accepted the newly created post of national field secretary for the NAACP, which had grown to become the country's premier black rights advocacy and defense organization since its founding in 1910. Johnson's duties included investigating racial incidents and organizing new NAACP branches around the country, and he succeeded in significantly raising the organization's visibility and membership through the years following World War I. In 1917, Johnson organized and led a well-publicized silent march through the streets of New York City to protest lynchings, and his on-site investigation of abuses committed by American marines against black citizens of Haiti during the U.S. occupation of that Caribbean nation in 1920 captured headlines and helped launch a congressional probe into the matter. Johnson's in-depth report, which was published by the *Nation* magazine in a four-part series titled "Self-Determining Haiti," also had an impact on the presidential race that year, helping to shift public sentiment from the interventionist policies associated with the Wilson Democrats toward the more isolationist position of the Republican victor, Warren Harding.

Johnson's successes as field secretary led to his appointment as NAACP executive secretary in 1920, a position he was to hold for the next ten years. This decade marked a critical turning point for the black rights movement as the NAACP and other civil rights organizations sought to defend and expand the social and economic gains blacks had achieved during the war years, when large numbers of blacks migrated to the northern cities and found industrial and manufacturing jobs. These black gains triggered a racist backlash in the early years of the decade that found virulent expression in a sharp rise in lynchings and the rapid growth of the white supremacist Ku Klux Klan terror organization in the North as well as the South. Despite this violent reaction, Johnson was credited with substantially increasing the NAACP's membership strength and political influence during this period, although his strenuous efforts to get a federal anti-lynching bill passed proved unsuccessful.

Johnson's personal politics also underwent change during the postwar years of heightened black expectations. Disappointed with the neglectful minority rights policies of Republican presidents Harding and Calvin Coolidge, Johnson broke with the Republican party in the early 1920s and briefly supported Robert LaFollette's Progressive party. LaFollette also lost the NAACP leader's backing, however, when he refused to include black demands in the Progressives' 1924 campaign platform. Though frustrated in his political objectives, Johnson opposed Marcus Garvey's separatist "Back to Africa" movement and instead urged the new black communities in the northern cities to use their potentially powerful voting strength to force racial concessions from the country's political establishment.

Even with the heavy demands of his NAACP office, the 1920s were a period of great literary productivity for Johnson. He earned critical acclaim in 1922 for editing a seminal collection of black verse, titled *The Book of American Negro Poetry*. Johnson's critical introduction to this volume provided new insights into an often ignored or denigrated genre and is now considered a classic analysis of early black contributions to American literature. Johnson went on to compile and interpret outstanding examples of the black religious song form known as the spiritual in his pioneering *The Book of American Negro Spirituals* and *The Second Book of Negro Spirituals* . These renditions of

black voices formed the background for *God's Trombones,* a set of verse versions of rural black folk sermons that many critics regard as Johnson's finest poetic work. Based on the poet's recollections of the fiery preachers he had heard while growing up in Florida and Georgia, Johnson's seven sermon-poems about life and death and good and evil were deemed a triumph in overcoming the thematic and technical limitations of the dialect style while capturing, according to critics, a full resonant timbre. In *The Book of American Negro Poetry,* Johnson had compared the traditional Dunbar-style-dialect verse to an organ having only two stops, one of humor and one of pathos, and he sought with *God's Trombones* to create a more flexible and dignified medium for expressing the black religious spirit. Casting out rhyme and the dialect style's buffoonish misspellings and mispronunciations, Johnson's clear and simple verses succeeded in rendering the musical rhythms, word structure, and vocabulary of the unschooled black orator in standard English. Critics also credited the poet with capturing the oratorical tricks and flourishes that a skilled preacher would use to sway his congregation, including hyperbole, repetition, abrupt mood juxtapositions, an expert sense of timing, and the ability to translate biblical imagery into the colorful, concrete terms of everyday life. "The sensitive reader cannot fail to hear the rantings of the fire-and-brimstone preacher; the extremely sensitive reader may even hear the unwritten 'Amens' of the congregation," declared Eugenia W. Collier in a 1960 essay for *Phylon.*

Johnson's efforts to preserve and win recognition for black cultural traditions drew praise from such prominent literary figures as H. L. Mencken and Mark Van Doren and contributed to the spirit of racial pride and self- confidence that marked the efflorescence of black music, art, and literature in the 1920s known as the Harlem Renaissance. This period of intense creative innovation forms the central subject of *Black Manhattan,* Johnson's informal survey of black contributions to New York's cultural life beginning as far back as the seventeenth century. The critically well-received volume focuses especially on blacks in the theater but also surveys the development of the ragtime and jazz musical idioms and discusses the earthy writings of Harlem Renaissance poets Langston Hughes, Countee Cullen, and Claude McKay. "*Black Manhattan* is a document of the 1920's—a celebration, with reservations, of both the artistic renaissance of the era and the dream of a black metropolis," noted critic Allan H. Spear in his preface to the 1968 edition of Johnson's book.

In December 1930, fatigued by the demands of his job and wanting more time to write, Johnson resigned from the NAACP and accepted a part-time teaching post in creative literature at Fisk University in Nashville, Tennessee. In 1933, he published his much-admired autobiography *Along This Way,* which discusses his personal career in the context of the larger social, political, and cultural movements of the times. Johnson remained active in the civil rights movement while teaching at Fisk, and in 1934 he published a book-length argument in favor of racial integration titled *Negro Americans, What Now?* The civil rights struggle also figures in the title poem of Johnson's last major verse collection, *Saint Peter Relates an Incident: Selected Poems.* Inspired by an outrageous act of public discrimination by the federal government against the mothers of black soldiers killed in action, Johnson's satirical narrative poem describes a gathering of veterans' groups to witness the Resurrection Day opening of the Tomb of the Unknown Soldier. When this famous war casualty is finally revealed, he turns out to be black, a circumstance that provokes bewilderment and consternation among the assembled patriots. Despite this original conceit, the poem is generally regarded as one of Johnson's lesser efforts, hampered by structural flaws and somewhat bland writing.

Johnson died tragically in June 1938 after a train struck the car he was riding in at an unguarded rail crossing in Wiscasset, Maine. The poet and civil rights leader was widely eulogized and more than two thousand mourners attended his Harlem funeral. Known throughout his career as a generous and invariably courteous man, Johnson once summed up his personal credo as a black American in a pamphlet published by the NAACP: "I will not allow one prejudiced person or one million or one hundred million to blight my life. I will not let prejudice or any of its attendant humiliations and injustices bear me down to spiritual defeat. My inner life is mine, and I shall defend and maintain its integrity against all the powers of hell." Johnson was buried in Brooklyn's Greenwood Cemetery dressed in his favorite lounging robe and holding a copy of *God's Trombones* in his hand.

BIOGRAPHICAL/CRITICAL SOURCES:

BOOKS

Bone, Robert A., *The Negro Novel in America,* Yale University Press, 1958.

Fleming, Robert E., *James Weldon Johnson and Arna Wendell Bontemps: A Reference Guide,* G.K. Hall, 1978.

Johnson, James Weldon, *Along This Way: The Autobiography of James Weldon Johnson,* Viking, 1933, Da Capo, 1973.

Levy, Eugene, *James Weldon Johnson: Black Leader, Black Voice,* Chicago University Press, 1973.

Price, Kenneth M. and Lawrence J. Oliver, *Critical Essays on James Weldon Johnson,* G.K. Hall, 1997.

Twentieth-Century Literary Criticism, Volume 19, Gale, 1986.

Wagner, Jean, *Les poetes negres des Etats Unis,* Librairie Istra, 1962, translation by Kenneth Doublas published as *Black Poets of the United States: From Paul Laurence Dunbar to Langston Hughes,* University of Illinois Press, 1973.

PERIODICALS

African American Review, spring, 1996, p. 17.

American Literature, March, 1971.

Crisis, June, 1971.

Journal of Popular Culture, spring, 1968.

Nation, July 2, 1938.

New Republic, February 1, 1928; February 21, 1934.

Newsweek, July 4, 1938.

Phylon, December, 1960; winter, 1971.

Publishers Weekly, December 12, 1994, p. 61.

School Library Journal, May, 1994, p. 108; February, 1995, p. 92.

Time, July 4, 1938.*

* * *

JOHNSON, Linton Kwesi 1952-

PERSONAL: Born in 1952, in Chapeltown, Jamaica; immigrated to England in 1963. *Education:* Goldsmith's College, University of London, B.A. (sociology), 1973.

ADDRESSES: Office—c/o Island Records Ltd., 22 St. Peters Sq., London W6 9NW, England.

CAREER: Race Today Collective, London, founding member; *Race Today* magazine, arts editor; Keskidee Arts Centre, library resource and education officer; London Borough of Lambeth, writer-in-residence. University of Warwick, Coventry, fellow. Producer of a ten-part program about Jamaican music, BBC Television. Has made several recordings, including *Poet and the Roots,* Virgin, 1977; *Dread, Beat, and Blood,* Virgin, 1978; *Forces of Victory,* Island, 1979; *Bass Culture,* Island, 1980; *Making History,* Island,

1984; *In Concert with the Dub Band,* Rough Trade, 1985; *Dread Beat an' Blood,* Heartbeat, 1989.

AWARDS, HONORS: C. Day Lewis fellowship, 1977.

WRITINGS:

POETRY

Voices of the Living and the Dead (includes play), Towards Racial Justice (London), 1974.
Dread, Beat, and Blood, Bogle L'Ouverture (London), 1975.
Inglan Is a Bitch, Race Today (London), 1980.
Tings an Times: Selected Poems, Bloodaxe (Newcastle upon Tyne), 1991.
Voices of the Living and the Dead (produced in London, 1973), included in *Voices of the Living and the Dead* (also contains poetry), Towards Racial Justice, 1974.

SIDELIGHTS: Linton Kwesi Johnson is among England's most prominent contemporary black poets. His poetry is politically charged and deeply influenced by his Caribbean roots, giving it a rhythmic quality. In the 1970s, Johnson began blending elements of black music (jazz, soul, calypso, and reggae) into the dialect of his West Indian and British language. Anthony G. Stocks of *Contemporary Poets* observed, "The result has been a distinguished body of work that mixes compelling narratives of black British life, sophisticated political analysis, and passionate demands for racial justice and cultural harmony." One of Johnson's unique achievements is his demonstration that poetry can be simultaneously political, popular, and linguistically complex.

In *Dictionary of Literary Biography,* Fred D'Aguiar wrote, "Linton Kwesi Johnson is known as the world's first Dub poet, a term he coined to describe the poets that evolved from the practice of Jamaican DJs dubbing their own voices to wordless recordings of reggae records at dance parties. . . . There are Dub poets from Germany to Japan and conferences and anthologies dedicated specifically to Dub poetry. He remains at the top of his profession and is generally believed to be the best exponent of his chosen art form. A close look at the man, his poetry, and music is tantamount to a critical history of the newest and most original poetic form to have emerged in the English language in the last quarter century.

"Johnson's poetry was generated by his extended residence in England and an experience that took as its basis a culture from Jamaica that found expression in the English setting. The black youths Johnson describes are for all intents and purposes British by birth or residence, though their parents and/or grandparents came from the Caribbean. It is not surprising that the tension between the twin heritages of Britain and the Caribbean should have produced an outstanding poet, but the racism experienced by Caribbean youth in British society undoubtedly inhibited many. Johnson often witnessed blatant discrimination against black people that impoverished their lives and relegated their economic status to that of second-class citizens. He saw the mostly unskilled and semiskilled jobs into which the older generation of blacks were funneled, and he experienced firsthand the counseling of limited career choices in a school system that expected little of black people except menial roles. All this was a source of anger and resentment. Mixed with an actively prejudiced police force, the result was a cocktail of explosive and combustible emotions.

"Johnson's first book, *Voices of the Living and the Dead* (1974), is mostly taken up by a long dramatic poem of the same title whose main thrust is to forecast a cataclysm involving black people in struggles worldwide against poverty and racism. The poem's first public airing was in a dramatic form as a poem for four voices in June 1973 at the Keskidee Center in London. This format suggests the influence on Johnson of call and response, a communal practice of Africa continued in the Caribbean. In its imagery Johnson's poem is also indebted to Surrealism. These influences are common to the work of writers such as Okigbo, Tchicaya U Tam'si, and Kamau Brathwaite, all of whom Johnson has read. . . .

"Although he had included it in his first collection, Johnson also chose 'Five Nights of Bleeding,' a representative poem in terms of its range of tones, for *Dread, Beat, and Blood.* While the twenty-seven poems in the five sections of the book still exhibit Johnson's early penchant for surreal imagery, apocryphal statements, and didactic tracts of thought, *Dread, Beat, and Blood* triumphed as a catalog of the experience of black people, and in particular black youth, in Britain at a time when few examples of that experience ended up as art. There is also an organic blend of Johnson's voice with the reggae rhythm and beat not previously evident in British poetry.

"In the period between the two books [*Dread, Beat, and Blood* and *Inglan is a Bitch*] Johnson recorded four long-playing records, setting his published poems to reggae music—a natural step given the reggae base of his compositions and his involvement in performance with drummers in the group Rasta Love before and after he published his first book. His first album, *Poet and the Roots* (1977), was originally made as a demo for Virgin Records. A year later it was reconceived as the full-length 1978 album *Dread Beat an' Blood.* The difference in sound between the two recordings has much less to do with quality than it has to do with Johnson's own understanding of the relationship of his voice to the music. In the first recording Johnson allows the music to dominate. Music and voice seem to work independently of one another and sometimes against each other. In the second Johnson's voice is foregrounded, and the music serves more to enhance the meaning of the poems.

"The antagonism in the title *Inglan Is a Bitch* is toward a country with which Johnson appears to be losing patience. Subtleties and niceties are jettisoned for the mode of direct address. A hard social realism typifies the poems on this collection, which catalog injustices against blacks from all quarters of British society. Seven of the book's twelve poems express anger with Britain and offer testimonies of ruined lives and unfulfilled dreams. Two poems, 'Man Free' and 'It Dread Ina Inglan,' celebrate victories over unjust imprisonment, and 'Forces of Victory' marks a victory of the people. One poem written in Standard English is a Jamaican lullaby, a lament. The last poem in the collection attacks a new class of blacks in Britain, the so-called black petty bourgeois, as opportunists who flourish at the expense of the well-being of the black community as a whole.

"Johnson shows more of a sense of humor and reveals more of a personal side to his art in his collection of poems *Tings an Times: Selected Poems.* His overhaul of the use of Jamaican English, which has evolved over the course of his career, is evident in his spelling of words and his use of punctuation. Successive revisions of poems such as the much anthologized 'Five Nights of Bleeding,' 'Dread, Beat, and Blood,' 'Bass Culture,' and 'Reggae Sounds' illustrate these changes. In 1992 Johnson asserted that his guiding principle for spelling is a phonetic rule: 'as it sounds so I spell it.' Johnson also moved away from the conventions of punctuation, preferring line breaks, indentations, spacing, and capitalization of words for emphasis. While the version of 'Bass Culture' published in *Dread, Beat, and Blood* is punctuated, sixteen years later in *Tings an Times* all punctuation is omitted and some spellings are altered from Standard English to Jamaican English in keeping with the rest of the poem.

"The only poem in *Tings an Times* that is written in Standard English is 'Beacon of Hope,' a song of praise for John La Rose, Johnson's friend and mentor, a fellow activist and poet from the days of Panther involvement who is now a distinguished publisher and still active politically and culturally in London. The inspirational light of La Rose's life and thought— 'the fire fly / fine florescent gift of night'—illuminates the way for Johnson. Unabashed affection mixed with evaluation of a friendship is sustained through the metaphor of the firefly shedding light in the darkness. Johnson appears to keep his abundant skill as a poet able to write in Standard English in reserve for the more reflective and private occasions, such as this one."

BIOGRAPHICAL/CRITICAL SOURCES:

BOOKS

Contemporary Poets, 6th edition, St. James Press, 1996.
Dictionary of Literary Biography, Volume 157: *Twentieth-Century Caribbean and Black African Writers, Third Series,* Gale, 1996.*

*   *   *

JOHNSON, Robert   1911-1938
(Robert Lockwood, Robert Sax, Robert Saxton)

PERSONAL: Born May 8, 1911, near Hazelhurst, MS; died of probable poisoning, August 16, 1938, near Greenwood, MS; son of Noah Johnson (a plantation worker) and Julia Ann Majors (a plantation worker); married Virginia Travis, 1929 (died, 1930); married Calletta Craft, 1931 (separated); companion of Estella Coleman; children: (first marriage) Claude Lee Johnson; stepchildren: (second marriage) three; (with Estella Coleman) Robert Junior Lockwood. *Education:* Studied music with Willie Brown, Charlie Patton, Son House, Lonnie Johnson, and Ike Zinnerman.

CAREER: Singer, musician, and songwriter. Also used the names Robert Lockwood, Robert Sax, and Robert Saxton.

WRITINGS:

ALBUMS

Robert Johnson: King of the Delta Blues Singers, Vol. 1, Columbia, 1961.

Robert Johnson: King of the Delta Blues Singers, Vol. 2, Columbia, 1970.
Robert Johnson: The Complete Recordings, Columbia, 1990.

Also author of the music singles "I Believe I'll Dust My Broom" (also known as "Dust My Broom"), American Record Company, 1936; "Kind Hearted Woman Blues," American Record Company, 1936; "Sweet Home Chicago," American Record Company, 1936; and "Terraplane Blues," American Record Company, 1936.

Recorded other songs released by the American Record Company, 1936; recorded songs released by the American Record Company, 1937. Other songs include "Come on in My Kitchen," "Crossroads Blues," "Hellhound on My Trail," "If I Had Possession over Judgment Day," "The Last Fair Deal Gone Down," "Love in Vain," "Me and the Devil Blues," "Phonograph Blues," "Stop Breakin' Down," "Traveling Riverside Blues," and "Walking Blues."

SIDELIGHTS: Although his short life has been shrouded in myth and mystery, Robert Johnson remains one of the most famous and influential blues artists. Known for his innovative guitar playing and evocative singing and lyrics, Johnson's work inspired fellow blues musicians Muddy Waters and Johnny Shines, as well as musicians in other genres such as Bob Dylan. Johnson only recorded twenty-nine compositions, but some are blues standards. Songs such as "Sweet Home Chicago" and "I Believe I'll Dust My Broom" (also known as "Dust My Broom") have been performed and recorded by several other performers. Johnson learned music by performing with and watching older players around his Mississippi home, and eventually became a master of the Delta blues. The Delta blues take their name from where they developed, the Mississippi River Delta region, and evolved from African American chants, religious music, work-related field hollers, and other distinct cultural melodies. Johnson's musical proficiency earned him the nickname "King of the Delta Blues Singers."

Because his guitar playing and singing had improved markedly over a short period of time, a story circulated that Johnson had sold his soul to the devil at a mythical "crossroads" to become a successful blues musician. The story persisted up until the time of his death, partially because Johnson never actually denied it, and continues to be told today. Scholars believe that Johnson improved his musical skills by studying more attentively with accomplished musicians such as Willie Brown, Charlie Patton, Son House, Lonnie Johnson, and Ike Zinnerman. Johnson toured small venues in the Delta region and had even occasionally traveled north to cities such as Chicago and Detroit before being noticed by representatives from the American Record Company (ARC). ARC scout H. C. Speir invited Johnson to San Antonio, Texas, where he recorded his first batch of songs. These songs included "Terraplane Blues," a tune that became his signature song. A year later, Johnson recorded more songs for ARC in Dallas, Texas.

According to Johnson researcher Stephen C. LaVere, many of Johnson's compositions portray a lifestyle of drinking, romantic encounters with a host of women, traveling, and often painful introspection, a lifestyle Johnson knew from personal experience. Critics have noted that Johnson's songs contain a considerable amount of depth. "There is no end of quoting and no end of reading into the lyrics, but unlike other equally eloquent blues, this is not random folk art, hit or miss, but rather carefully selected and honed detail, carefully considered and achieved effect," wrote Peter Guralnick in *Searching for Robert Johnson.* The events surrounding Johnson's death are sketchy, and there are three accounts of how he died. The most likely is that he was poisoned by a jealous husband at a house party.

Despite his short life and relatively small body of recorded work, Johnson is known as a blues great. Later generations became aware of his work through the release of three posthumous albums: *Robert Johnson: King of the Delta Blues Singers, Vol. 1* (1961), *Robert Johnson: King of the Delta Blues Singers, Vol. 2* (1970), and *Robert Johnson: The Complete Recordings* (1990).

BIOGRAPHICAL/CRITICAL SOURCES:

BOOKS

Contemporary Musicians, Volume 6, Gale (Detroit, MI), 1992.
Dictionary of Twentieth-Century Culture, Volume 5: *African American Culture,* Gale (Detroit, MI), 1996.
Guralnick, Peter, *Searching for Robert Johnson,* Dutton (New York City), 1989.
Twentieth-Century Literary Criticism, Volume 69, Gale, 1997.*

JOHNSON, Whittington B. 1931-

PERSONAL: Born April 29, 1931, in Miami, FL; son of Joseph Blake (a mattress maker) and Lucille Marie (a domestic worker; maiden name, Bain; present surname, Milton) Johnson; married Juanita Simkins, September, 1955 (divorced, March, 1959); married Vivian Page, May, 1959 (divorced, June, 1966); married Imogene Smith, June 26, 1966; children: Terrance (deceased), Toni Thomas, Traci-Leigh, Todd. *Ethnicity:* "African American." *Education:* West Virginia State College, B.S., 1953; Indiana University—Bloomington, M.A.T., 1957; University of Georgia, Ph.D., 1970. *Politics:* Democrat. *Religion:* Episcopalian.

ADDRESSES: Home—Miami, FL. *Office*—Department of History, University of Miami, Coral Gables, FL 33124.

CAREER: Edward Waters College, Jacksonville, FL, instructor in social science, 1957-62; Savannah State College (now University), Savannah, GA, assistant professor of social science, 1962-67; University of Miami, Coral Gables, FL, associate professor, 1970-95, professor of history, 1995—, department head, 1976-77, director of Afro-American Studies Center, 1972-73. Wisconsin State University (now University of Wisconsin—Superior), guest lecturer, 1972. Civil Rights Museum, Savannah, member of board of directors. *Military service:* U.S. Army, airborne marksman, 1953-55; became first lieutenant.

MEMBER: Society for Historians of the Early American Republic, Southern Historical Association, Phi Kappa Phi (president, 1986-87), Omicron Delta Kappa, Phi Alpha Theta, Golden Key, Iron Arrow.

AWARDS, HONORS: Recipient of plaque for dedicated service to education, Dade County Commission, 1972; Educator of the Year, Zeta Phi Beta Sorority, 1975; Professor of the Year, Phi Eta Sigma Freshman Honorary Fraternity, 1979; Max Orovitz summer fellow, 1981, 1987, 1988; Social Science Professor of the Year, 1984; Professor of the Year, College of Arts and Sciences Alumni Association, 1984; Southern Regional Education fellow, 1988; Mac Lamore summer award, 1995.

WRITINGS:

The Promising Years, 1750-1830: The Emergence of Black Labor and Business, Garland Publishing (New York City), 1993.

Black Savannah, 1788-1864, University of Arkansas Press (Fayetteville, AR), 1996.

Contributor of articles and reviews to periodicals, including Journal of the Early American Republic, *Gulf Coast Historical Review, Journal of Negro History, Georgia Historical Quarterly, Southern University Law Review,* and *Journal of the Bahamas Historical Society.*

WORK IN PROGRESS: Race Relations in the Bahamas, 1784-1834.

SIDELIGHTS: Whittington B. Johnson told *CA:* "I entered graduate school at the University of Georgia in the fall of 1967 with the goal of earning a doctorate and returning to Savannah State College, where I worked, to continue teaching history to students who may enroll at that institution. By the time I had completed my course work, however, I knew that just teaching history would not be enough for me; I want to both teach and write history, because creating knowledge is as important to me as disseminating it. In short, I write history to contribute to the corpus of knowledge on the subject. In this small way, I hope to justify the time God has given to me, on this wonderful planet we call earth."

*   *   *

JONES, Edward P. 1950-

PERSONAL: Born October 5, 1950. *Education:* Attended College of the Holy Cross, Worcester, MA, and University of Virginia.

ADDRESSES: Home—4300 Old Dominion Dr., No. 914, Arlington, VA 22207.

CAREER: Columnist for *Tax Notes.*

AWARDS, HONORS: National Book Award finalist, National Book Foundation, 1992, for *Lost in the City.*

WRITINGS:

Lost in the City (short stories), photographs by Amos Chan, Morrow (New York), 1992.

SIDELIGHTS: Called "a poignant and promising first effort" by *Publishers Weekly,* Edward P. Jones's first book, *Lost in the City,* was greeted with both critical and popular acclaim. The work was nominated for the 1992 National Book Award, the first short story collection to do so in six years. In addition, the book's first printing sold out.

The appeal of the 14 stories collected in *Lost in the City* lies in the realness of the people and the experiences that Jones presents. Each of the stories profiles African-American life in Washington, D.C. The characters are all lost in the nation's capital—some literally, some figuratively. They are black working-class heroes who struggle to preserve their families, communities, neighborhoods, and themselves amid drugs, violence, divorce, and other crises. Jones's assortment of characters include a mother whose son buys her a new home with drug money, a husband who repeatedly stabs his wife as their children sleep, and a girl who watches her pigeons fly from her home after their cages are destroyed by rats. They are all stories that "affirm humanity as only good literature can," remarked Michael Harris in the *Los Angeles Times Book Review.* "There's no secret to it, or only the final, most elusive secret: Jones has near-perfect pitch for people. . . . Whoever they are, he reveals them to us from the inside out." *Washington Post* writer Mary Ann French noted that "he creates sympathy through understanding—a sadly needed service that is too seldom performed."

Washington Post Book World reviewer Jonathan Yardley noted that Jones's stories are set in the 1950s, 1960s, and 1970s, "so there is little sense of the drug-and-crime haunted place that the inner city has become," yet he added that nevertheless, "danger and death are never far in the background." While the stories usually convey a sense of hope despite some bleak settings and horrible events, "Jones is no sentimentalist," found Yardley. Rather, he is "a lucid, appealing writer. He puts on no airs, tells his stories matter-of-factly and forthrightly, yet his prose is distinctive and carries more weight than first impressions might suggest."

Numerous critics have pointed out that while Jones skirts no racial issues, his stories ultimately transcend race, "even those that seem most particularly fixed on black life and culture," as Yardley insisted. "Edward P. Jones writes about black people, to be sure, but it is more accurate to say that he writes about people who happen to be black. For that reason his stories will touch chords of empathy and recognition in all readers, which is exactly what fiction is supposed to do."

BIOGRAPHICAL/CRITICAL SOURCES:

BOOKS

Contemporary Literary Criticism, Yearbook 1992, Volume 76, Gale (Detroit), 1992.

PERIODICALS

Los Angeles Times Book Review, July 12, 1992, p. 6.
New York Times, June 11, 1992, p. C18; August 23, 1992, section 7, p. 16.
Publishers Weekly, March 23, 1992, p. 59.
Washington Post, July 22, 1992, pp. G1, G4; October 6, 1992, p. B4.
Washington Post Book World, June 21, 1992, p. 3.

*   *   *

JONES, Gayl 1949-

PERSONAL: Born November 23, 1949, in Lexington, KY; daughter of Franklin (a cook) and Lucille (Wilson) Jones. *Education:* Connecticut College, B.A., 1971; Brown University, M.A., 1973, D.A., 1975.

ADDRESSES: Agent—Beacon Press, 25 Beacon St., Boston, MA 02108.

CAREER: University of Michigan, Ann Arbor, 1975-83, began as assistant professor, became professor of English; writer.

MEMBER: Authors Guild, Authors League of America.

AWARDS, HONORS: Award for best original production in the New England region, American College Theatre Festival, 1973, for *Chile Woman;* grants from Shubert Foundation, 1973-74, Southern Fellowship Foundation, 1973-75, and Rhode Island Council on the Arts, 1974-75; fellowships from Yaddo, 1974, National Endowment of the Arts, 1976, and Michigan Society of Fellows, 1977-79; award from Howard Foundation, 1975; fiction award from *Mademoiselle,* 1975; Henry Russell Award, University of Michigan, 1981.

WRITINGS:

Chile Woman (play), Shubert Foundation, 1974.
Corregidora (novel), Random House, 1975.

Eva's Man (novel), Random House, 1976.
White Rat (short stories), Random House, 1977.
Song for Anninho (poetry), Lotus Press, 1981.
The Hermit-Woman (poetry), Lotus Press, 1983.
Xarque and Other Poems, Lotus Press, 1985.
Liberating Voices: Oral Tradition in African American Literature (criticism), Harvard University Press, 1991.
The Healing (novel), Beacon Press, 1998.
Mosquito (novel), Beacon Press, 1999.

Contributor to anthologies, including *Confirmation,* 1983, *Chants of Saints, Keeping the Faith, Midnight Birds,* and *Soulscript.*

Contributor to *Massachusetts Review.*

WORK IN PROGRESS: Research on sixteenth- and seventeenth-century Brazil and on settlements of escaped slaves, such as Palmares.

SIDELIGHTS: Gayl Jones's novels *Corregidora* and *Eva's Man,* in addition to many of the stories in her collection *White Rat,* offer stark, often brutal accounts of black women whose psyches reflect the ravages of accumulated sexual and racial exploitation. In *Corregidora* Jones reveals the tormented life of a woman whose female forebears—at the hands of one man—endured a cycle of slavery, prostitution, and incest over three generations. *Eva's Man* explores the deranged mind of a woman institutionalized for poisoning and sexually mutilating a male acquaintance. And in "Asylum," a story from *White Rat,* a young woman is confined to a mental hospital for a series of bizarre actions that, in her mind, protests a society she sees as bent on her personal violation. "The abuse of women and its psychological results fascinate Gayl Jones, who uses these recurring themes to magnify the absurdity and the obscenity of racism and sexism in everyday life," comments Jerry W. Ward, Jr., in *Black Women Writers (1950-1980): A Critical Evaluation.* "Her novels and short fictions invite readers to explore the interior of caged personalities, men and women driven to extremes." Keith Byerman elaborates: "Jones creates worlds radically different from those of 'normal' experience and of storytelling convention. Her tales are gothic in the sense of dealing with madness, sexuality, and violence, but they do not follow in the Edgar Allan Poe tradition of focusing of private obsession and irrationality. Though her narrators are close to if not over the boundaries of sanity, the experiences they record reveal clearly that society acts out its own obsessions often violently."

Corregidora, Jones's first novel, explores the psychological effects of slavery and sexual abuse on a modern black woman. Ursa Corregidora, a blues singer from Kentucky, descends from a line of women who are the progeny, by incest, of a Portuguese slaveholder named Corregidora—the father of both Ursa's mother and grandmother. "All of the women, including the great-granddaughter Ursa, keep the name Corregidora as a reminder of the depredations of the slave system and of the rapacious natures of men," Byerman explains in the *Dictionary of Literary Biography.* "The story is passed from generation to generation of women, along with the admonition to 'produce generations' to keep alive the tale of evil." Partly as a result of this history, Ursa becomes involved in abusive relationships with men. The novel itself springs from an incident of violence; after being thrown down a flight of stairs by her first husband and physically injured so that she cannot bear children, Ursa "discharges her obligation to the memory of Corregidora by speaking [the] book," notes John Updike in the *New Yorker.* The novel emerges as Ursa's struggle to reconcile her heritage with her present life. *Corregidora* "persuasively fuses black history, or the mythic consciousness that must do for black history, with the emotional nuances of contemporary black life," Updike continues. "The book's innermost action . . . is Ursa's attempt to transcend a nightmare black consciousness and waken to her own female, maimed humanity."

Corregidora was acclaimed as a novel of unusual power and impact. "No black American novel since Richard Wright's *Native Son* (1940)," writes Ivan Webster in *Time,* "has so skillfully traced psychic wounds to a sexual source." Darryl Pinckney in *New Republic* calls *Corregidora* "a small, fiercely concentrated story, harsh and perfectly told. . . . Original, superbly imagined, nothing about the book was simple or easily digested. Out of the worn themes of miscegenation and diminishment, Gayl Jones *excavated* the disturbingly buried damage of racism." Critics particularly praised Jones's treatment of sexual detail and its illumination of the central character. "One of the book's merits," according to Updike, "is the ease with which it assumes the writer's right to sexual specifics, and its willingness to explore exactly how our sexual and emotional behavior is warped within the matrix of family and race." In the book's final scene, Ursa comes to a reconciliation with her first husband, Mutt, by envisioning an ambivalent sexual relationship between her great-grandmother and the slavemaster Corregidora. *Corregidora* is a novel "filled with sexual and spiritual pain," writes Margo

Jefferson in *Newsweek;* "hatred, love and desire wear the same face, and humor is blues-bitter. . . . Jones's language is subtle and sinewy, and her imagination sure."

Jones's second novel, *Eva's Man,* continues her exploration into the psychological effects of brutality, yet presents a character who suffers greater devastation. Eva Medina Canada, incarcerated for the murder and mutilation of a male acquaintance, narrates a personal history that depicts the damaging influences of a sexually aggressive and hostile society. Updike describes the exploitative world that has shaped the mentally deranged Eva: "Evil permeates the erotic education of Eva Canada, as it progresses from Popsicle-stick violations to the witnessing of her mother's adultery and a growing awareness of the whores and 'queen bees' in the slum world around her, and on to her own reluctant initiation through encounters in buses and in bars, where a man with no thumb monotonously propositions her. The evil that emanates from men becomes hers." In a narrative that is fragmented and disjointed, Eva gives no concrete motive for the crime committed; furthermore, she neither shows remorse nor any signs of rehabilitation. More experimental than *Corregidora, Eva's Man* displays "a sharpened starkness, a power of ellipsis that leaves ever darker gaps between its flashes of rhythmic, sensuously exact dialogue and visible symbol," according to Updike. John Leonard adds in the *New York Times* that "not a word is wasted" in Eva's narrative. "It seems, in fact, as if Eva doesn't have enough words, as if she were trying to use the words she has to make a poem, a semblance of order, and fails of insufficiency." Leonard concludes: "*Eva's Man* may be one of the most unpleasant novels of the season. It is also one of the most accomplished."

Eva's Man was praised for its emotional impact, yet some reviewers found the character of Eva extreme or inaccessible. June Jordan in the *New York Times Book Review* calls *Eva's Man* "the blues that lost control. This is the rhythmic, monotone lamentation of one woman, Eva Medina, who is nobody I have ever known." Jordan explains: "Jones delivers her story in a strictly controlled, circular form that is wrapped, around and around with ambivalence. Unerringly, her writing creates the tension of a problem unresolved." In the end, however, Jordan finds that the fragmented details of Eva's story "do not mesh into illumination." On the other hand, some reviewers regard the gaps in *Eva's Man* as appropriate and integral to its meaning. Pinckney calls the novel "a tale of madness; one exacerbated if not caused by frustration, accumu-

lated grievances" and comments on aspects that contribute to this effect: "Structurally unsettled, more scattered than *Corregidora, Eva's Man* is extremely remote, more troubling in its hallucinations. . . . The personal exploitation that causes Eva's desperation is hard to appreciate. Her rage seems never to find its proper object, except, possibly, in her last extreme act." Updike likewise holds that the novel accurately portrays Eva's deranged state, yet he points out that Jones's characterization skills are not at their peak: "Jones apparently wishes to show us a female heart frozen into rage by deprivation, but the worry arises, as it did not in *Corregidora,* that the characters are dehumanized as much by her artistic vision as by their circumstances."

Jordan raises a concern that the inconclusiveness of *Eva's Man* harbors a potentially damaging feature. "There is the very real, upsetting accomplishment of Gayl Jones in this, her second novel: sinister misinformation about women—about women, in general, about black women in particular." Jones comments in *Black Women Writers (1950-1980)* on the predicament faced in portraying negative characters: "To deal with such a character as Eva becomes problematic in the way that 'Trueblood' becomes problematic in [Ralph Ellison's] *Invisible Man.* It raises the questions of possibility. Should a Black writer ignore such characters, refuse to enter 'such territory' because of the 'negative image' and because such characters can be misused politically by others, or should one try to reclaim such complex, contradictory characters as well as try to reclaim the idea of the 'heroic image'?" In an interview with Claudia Tate for *Black Women Writers at Work,* Jones elaborates: "'Positive race images' are fine as long as they're very complex and interesting personalities. Right now I'm not sure how to reconcile the various things that interest me with 'positive race images.' It's important to be able to work with a range of personalities, as well as with a range within one personality. For instance, how would one reconcile an interest in neurosis or insanity with positive race image?"

Although Jones's subject matter is often charged and intense, a number of critics have praised a particular restraint she manages in her narratives. Regarding *Corregidora,* Updike remarks: "Our retrospective impression of *Corregidora* is of a big territory—the Afro-American psyche—rather thinly and stabbingly populated by ideas, personae, hints. Yet that such a small book could seem so big speaks well for the generous spirit of the author, unpolemical where there has been much polemic, exploratory where rhetoric and outrage tend to block the path." Similarly, Jones maintains an authorial distance in her fiction which, in turn, makes for believable and gripping characters. Byerman comments: "The authority of [Jones's] depiction of the world is enhanced by [her] refusal to intrude upon or judge her narrators. She remains outside the story, leaving the reader with none of the usual markers of a narrator's reliability. She gives these characters the speech of their religion, which, by locating them in time and space, makes it even more difficult to easily dismiss them; the way they speak has authenticity, which carries over to what they tell. The results are profoundly disturbing tales of repression, manipulation, and suffering."

Reviewers have also noted Jones's ability to innovatively incorporate Afro-American speech patterns into her work. In *Black Women Writers (1950-1980),* Melvin Dixon contends that "Gayl Jones has figured among the best of contemporary Afro-American writers who have used Black speech as a major aesthetic device in their works. Like Alice Walker, Toni Morrison, Sherley Williams, Toni Cade Bambara, and such male writers as Ernest Gaines and Ishmael Reed, Jones uses the rhythm and structure of spoken language to develop authentic characters and to establish new possibilities for dramatic conflict within the text and between readers and the text itself." In her interview with Tate, Jones remarks on the importance of storytelling traditions to her work: "At the time I was writing *Corregidora* and *Eva's Man* I was particularly interested—and continue to be interested—in oral traditions of storytelling—Afro-American and others, in which there is always the consciousness and importance of the hearer, even in the interior monologues where the storyteller becomes her own hearer. That consciousness or self-consciousness actually determines my selection of significant events."

Jones's 1977 collection of short stories, *White Rat,* received mixed reviews. A number of critics noted the presence of Jones's typical thematic concerns, yet also felt that her shorter fiction did not allow enough room for character development. Diane Johnson comments in the *New York Review of Books* that the stories in *White Rat* "were written in some cases earlier than her novels, so they confirm one's sense of her direction and preoccupations: sex is violation, and violence is the principal dynamic of human relationships." Mel Watkins remarks in the *New York Times,* however, on a drawback to Jones's short fictions: "The focus throughout is on desolate, forsaken characters struggling to exact some snippet of gratification from their lives. . . . Although her prose here is as

starkly arresting and indelible as in her novels, except for the longer stories such as 'Jeveta' and 'The Women,' these tales are simply doleful vignettes—slices of life so beveled that they seem distorted."

While Jones's writing often emphasizes a tormented side of life—especially regarding male-female relationships—it also raises the possibility for more positive interactions. Jones points out in the Tate interview that "there seems to be a growing understanding—working itself out especially in *Corregidora*—of what is required in order to be genuinely tender. Perhaps brutality enables one to recognize what tenderness is." Some critics have found ambivalence at the core of Jones's fiction. Dixon remarks: "Redemption . . . is most likely to occur when the resolution of conflict is forged in the same vocabulary as the tensions which precipitated it. This dual nature of language makes it appear brutally indifferent, for it contains the source and the resolution of conflicts. . . . What Jones is after is the words and deeds that finally break the sexual bondage men and women impose upon each other."

In 1991, Jones published her first book of literary criticism. In this volume, entitled *Liberating Voices: Oral Tradition in African American Literature,* Jones argues that all literatures, not just African-American, develop in relation to and must come to terms with their own culture's oral storytelling practices. With this point in mind, she compares the poetry, short fiction, and novels of African-American authors—including Paul Lawrence Dunbar, Jean Toomer, Zora Neale Hurston, Ralph Ellison, Amiri Baraka, Alice Walker, Langston Hughes, and Toni Morrison—with the works of long-standing canonical authors from a wide variety of historical eras and cultures, from Chaucer and Cervantes to Joyce. M. Giulia Fabi, in *American Literature,* calls this a "daring and insightful study."

BIOGRAPHICAL/CRITICAL SOURCES:

BOOKS

Contemporary Literary Criticism, Gale, Volume 6, 1976; Volume 9, 1978.

Coser, Stelamaris, *Bridging the Americas: The Literature of Paule Marshall, Toni Morrison, and Gayl Jones,* Temple University Press, 1995.

Dictionary of Literary Biography, Volume 33: *Afro-American Fiction Writers after 1955,* Gale, 1984.

Evans, Mari, editor, *Black Women Writers (1950-1980): A Critical Evaluation,* Anchor Books, 1984.

Tate, Claudia, editor, *Black Women Writers at Work,* Continuum, 1986.

PERIODICALS

African American Review, winter, 1994, p. 559; spring, 1994, p. 141; summer, 1994, p. 223.
American Literature, June, 1993.
Belles Lettres, summer, 1992.
Black World, February, 1976.
Book World, February 22, 1987.
Canadian Literature, winter, 1992.
Choice, November, 1991.
College Literature, February, 1992.
Esquire, December, 1976.
Journal of American Folklore, winter, 1993.
Kliatt, spring, 1986.
Literary Quarterly, May 15, 1975.
Massachusetts Review, winter, 1977.
Modern Fiction Studies, fall, 1993, p. 825.
National Review, April 14, 1978.
New Republic, June 28, 1975; June 19, 1976.
Newsweek, May 19, 1975; April 12, 1976.
New Yorker, August 18, 1975; August 9, 1976.
New York Review of Books, November 10, 1977.
New York Times, April 30, 1976; December 28, 1977.
New York Times Book Review, May 25, 1975; May 16, 1976; March 15, 1987.
Time, June 16, 1975.
Washington Post, October 21, 1977.
Yale Review, autumn, 1976.*

*   *   *

JONES, LeRoi
  See BARAKA, Amiri

*   *   *

JORDAN, Emma Coleman 1946-

PERSONAL: Born November 29, 1946, in Berkeley, CA; daughter of Earl and Myrtle Coleman; married Don Jordan; children: Kristen Elena, Allison Elizabeth. *Education:* California State University, B.A., 1969; Howard University, J.D., 1973.

ADDRESSES: Office—School of Law, Georgetown University, 600 New Jersey Ave., Washington, DC 20001-2075.

CAREER: Stanford Law School, teaching fellow, 1973-74; University of Santa Clara, assistant professor, 1974-75; Georgetown University Law Center, professor; University of California School of Law, acting professor, 1975-80, professor, 1980—. Special assistant to the Attorney General of the United States, 1981.

MEMBER: National Conference of Black Lawyers, National Bar Association, American Society of International Law, California State Board of Dental and Examiners, American Association of Law Schools (sections on Commercial Law and Contracts, Minority Groups), Charles Houston Bar Association, California Association of Black Lawyers (board of directors), Society of American Law Teachers (president, 1986-88), California State Bar Financial Institution Committee (chair), American Agricultural Law Association (AALA), Financial Institute and Consumer Financial Service Section (chair), Consumer Action (board member), National Consumer Union of Northern California (advisory committee), American Law Institute, Association of American Law Schools (executive committee, 1988-91, president-elect, 1991-92, president, 1992-93).

AWARDS, HONORS: Outstanding academic achievement award, Phi Alpha Delta, 1973; graduated first in class, Howard Law School, 1973.

WRITINGS:

(Editor, with Anita Faye Hill) *Race, Gender, and Power in America: The Legacy of the Hill-Thomas Hearing,* Oxford University Press (New York), 1995.

Has published several articles in state law reviews, including *Nebraska Law Review.*

SIDELIGHTS: Emma Coleman Jordan is a law school professor whose legal writings pertain predominantly to the area of affirmative action, the branch of the law that seeks to redress the historic inequality of opportunity for non-whites in the United States. Jordan is also the co-editor, with Anita Faye Hill, of the 1995 volume *Race, Gender, and Power in America: The Legacy of the Hill-Thomas Hearing.* An anthology of essays written by legal scholars and lawyers, *Race, Gender, and Power in America* grew out of a conference sponsored by the Georgetown University Law Center in 1992, one year after the controversial nomination hearings of Clarence Thomas to the United States Supreme Court. During those hearings, one of Thomas's former employees, Anita Hill, testified that the nominee had sexually harassed her, inciting intense public debate and nearly derailing Thomas's nomination. Jordan and Hill jointly edit this collection of essays, which seeks to assess the ramifications of the hearings.

The contributors to *Race, Gender, and Power in America* examine why the American public, as represented by the members of the Senate Judicial Committee, were unable to either believe or to take seriously the charge of sexual harassment made by a single, black, professional woman against a married, black, male professional. The reasons offered include society's historically suspicious treatment of a black woman lacking patronage or marriage; a belief among some African Americans that because she is African American Hill should have supported Thomas—also African American—and not disclosed her claims of sexual harassment; and one contributor traces the treatment of both Thomas and Hill as a consequence of the historical relationship between blacks and whites in the United States, dating back to the age of slavery.

Race, Gender, and Power in America was generally well-received as an important contribution to the on-going debates on race and gender in America. Reviewers noted that the essays were of varying quality, from thoughtful, scholarly analyses to essays of less merit. "Ms. Hill's own essay . . . is required reading for those interested in this historic confrontation," maintained Neil A. Lewis in *New York Times Book Review.* Although *Boston Globe* reporter Sandy Coleman maintained that the volume "makes no attempt to be balanced," calling it "an all-out rally around Hill," she concluded: "*Race, Gender, and Power in America* is an important book that conjures up the haunting realities of the past and shows readers the ghosts that will continue to stalk the present if not faced and dealt with head on."

BIOGRAPHICAL/CRITICAL SOURCES:

PERIODICALS

Booklist, October 1, 1995.
Boston Globe, October 26, 1995, p. 63.
New York Times Book Review, November 5, 1995, p. 22.
Publishers Weekly, October 2, 1995, p. 60.
Washington Post Book World, November 26, 1995, p. 8.*

JORDAN, June 1936-
(June Meyer)

PERSONAL: Born July 9, 1936, in Harlem, NY; daughter of Granville Ivanhoe (a postal clerk) and Mildred Maude (Fisher) Jordan (a nurse); married Michael Meyer, 1955 (divorced, 1966); children: Christopher David. *Education:* Attended Barnard College, 1953-55 and 1956-57, and University of Chicago, 1955-56. *Politics:* "Politics of survival and change." *Religion:* "Humanitarian."

ADDRESSES: Office—Department of Afro-American Studies, University of California, 3335 Dwinelle Hall, Berkeley, CA 94720. *Agent*—Victoria Sanders, 241 Avenue of the Americas, Suite 11H, New York, NY 10014.

CAREER: Poet, novelist, essayist, and writer of children's books. Assistant to producer for motion picture *The Cool World,* New York City, 1963-64; Mobilization for Youth, Inc., New York City, associate research writer in technical housing department, 1965-66; City College of the City University of New York, New York City, instructor in English and literature, 1966-68; Connecticut College, New London, teacher of English and director of Search for Education, Elevation, and Knowledge (SEEK Program), 1967-69; Sarah Lawrence College, Bronxville, NY, instructor in literature, 1969-74; City College of the City University of New York, assistant professor of English, 1975-76; State University of New York at Stony Brook, professor of English, 1982-89, director, Poetry Center and Creative Writing Program, 1986-89; University of California, Berkeley, professor of Afro-Amcrican studies and women's studies, 1989-93, professor of African-American studies, 1994—, founder and director of Poetry for the People, 1991—. Visiting poet-in-residence at MacAlester College, 1980; writer-in-residence at City College of the City University of New York; playwright-in-residence, New Dramatists, New York City, 1987-88, poet-in-residence, 1988. Visiting lecturer in English and Afro-American studies, Yale University, 1974-75; chancellor's distinguished lecturer, University of California, Berkeley, 1986; visiting professor, Department of Afro-American Studies, University of Wisconsin, Madison, summer 1988; poet-in-residence, Walt Whitman Birthplace Association, 1988. Has given poetry readings in schools and colleges around the country and at the Guggenheim Museum. Founder and co-director, Voice of the Children, Inc.; co-founder, Afro-Americans against the Famine, 1973—. Member of board of directors, Teachers and

Writers Collaborative, Inc., 1978—, and Center for Constitutional Rights, 1984—; member of board of governors, New York Foundation for the Arts, 1986—.

MEMBER: American Writers Congress (member of executive board), PEN American Center (member of executive board), Poets and Writers, Inc. (director).

AWARDS, HONORS: Rockefeller grant for creative writing, 1969-70; Prix de Rome in Environmental Design, 1970-71; Nancy Bloch Award, 1971, for *The Voice of the Children; New York Times* selection as one of the year's outstanding young adult novels, 1971, and nomination for National Book Award, 1971, for *His Own Where—;* New York Council of the Humanities award, 1977; Creative Artists Public Service Program poetry grant, 1978; Yaddo fellowship, 1979; National Endowment for the Arts fellowship, 1982; achievement award for international reporting from National Association of Black Journalists, 1984; New York Foundation for the Arts fellow in poetry, 1985; MacDowell Colony fellowship, 1987; Nora Astorga Leadership award, 1989; PEN West Freedom to Write Award, 1991; Ground Breakers-Dream Makers Award, The Women's Foundation (San Francisco, CA), 1994; Lila Wallace Writers Award, *Reader's Digest,* 1995; The Critics Award and The Herald Angel Award, Edinburgh Arts Festival, 1995, for *I Was Looking at the Ceiling and Then I Saw the Sky;* President's Certificate of Service and Contribution to the Arts, Harvard University, 1997; Student's Choice Louise Patterson African American Award, University of California, Berkeley, 1998, for most outstanding African American faculty.

WRITINGS:

POETRY

Some Changes, Dutton (New York City), 1971.
New Days: Poems of Exile and Return, Emerson Hall (New York City), 1973.
Things That I Do in the Dark: Selected Poetry, Random House (New York City), 1977, revised, Beacon Press (Boston), 1981.
Okay Now, Simon & Schuster (New York City), 1977.
Passion: New Poems, 1977-1980, Beacon Press, 1980.
Living Room: New Poems, 1980-84, Thunder's Mouth Press (New York City), 1985.
High Tide—Marea Alta, Curbstone (Willimantic, CT), 1987.

Naming Our Destiny: New and Selected Poems, Thunder's Mouth Press, 1989.
Lyrical Campaigns: Selected Poems, Virago, 1989.
The Haruko: Love Poetry of June Jordan, Serpent's Tail (New York City), 1994.
Kissing God Goodbye: New Poems, Scribners (New York City), 1997.

FOR CHILDREN

Who Look at Me?, Crowell (New York City), 1969.
His Own Where— (young adult novel), Crowell, 1971.
Dry Victories, Holt (New York City), 1972.
Fannie Lou Hamer (biography), Crowell, 1972.
New Life: New Room, Crowell, 1975.
Kimako's Story, illustrated by Kay Burford, Houghton (Boston), 1981.

PLAYS

In the Spirit of Sojourner Truth, produced in New York City at the Public Theatre, May, 1979.
For the Arrow that Flies by Day (staged reading), produced in New York City at the Shakespeare Festival, April, 1981.
I Was Looking at the Ceiling and Then I Saw the Sky (opera libretto), music by John Adams, Scribners, 1995.

Composer of lyrics and libretto, *Bang Bang Ueber Alles,* 1985.

OTHER

(Editor) *Soulscript: Afro-American Poetry,* Doubleday (Garden City, NY), 1970.
(Editor with Terri Bush) *The Voice of the Children* (reader), Holt, 1970.
Civil Wars: Selected Essays, 1963-1980 (essays, articles, and lectures), Beacon Press, 1981, revised edition with a new introductory essay, Scribners, 1996.
Bobo Goetz a Gun, Curbstone Press, 1985.
On Call: New Political Essays, 1981-1985, South End Press (Boston), 1985.
Moving towards Home: Political Essays, Virago (London), 1989.
Technical Difficulties: African-American Notes on the State of the Union, Pantheon (New York City), 1994.
(Editor with Lauren Muller) *June Jordan's Poetry for the People: A Revolutionary Blueprint,* Routledge (New York City), 1995.

Affirmative Acts: New Political Essays, Doubleday, 1998.

Portrait of a Poet as a Little Black Girl (childhood memoir), Doubleday, in press.

Regular columnist to the *Progressive Magazine,* 1989-97. Also contributor to *Double Stitch: Black Women Write about Mothers and Daughters,* edited by Patricia Bell-Scott, HarperPerennial, 1992. Contributor of stories and poems, prior to 1969 under name June Meyer, to various periodicals, including *Esquire, Nation, Evergreen, Partisan Review, Black World, Black Creation, Essence, Village Voice, New York Times,* and *New York Times Magazine.* Contributing editor to the *San Francisco Bay Guardian,* 1992-94.

SIDELIGHTS: June Jordan is an accomplished poet, novelist, playwright, and essayist. Called one of the most versatile and prolific late twentieth-century African American writers by *Contemporary Women Poets* contributor Saundra Towns, Jordan's written works, taken as a whole, "chart the artistic concerns of a poet who successfully maintains a sense of spiritual wholeness and the vision of a shared humanity," while frequently confronting and addressing a less-than-appealing reality.

Jordan grew up in Brooklyn, New York, where she was the only black student at Midwood High School. She then attended the Northfield School for Girls in Massachusetts, where her interest in writing was encouraged, although her constant exposure to white male poets undermined her confidence in her own abilities. Jordan's family also presented difficulties, since her father beat her regularly and her mother was complicit in the violence. In 1953 Jordan entered Barnard College, where she met Michael Meyer, a white student; the two were married in 1955. Jordan's *Civil Wars* offers a vivid glimpse of the author's problematic relationship with her husband and the problem of public intolerance of interracial marriages. Jordan and Meyer divorced in 1965, and Jordan took full responsibility for supporting their son, Christopher, who was born in 1958. During the early-to mid-1960s, Jordan worked as a research associate and writer for the Technical Housing Department of Mobilization for Youth in New York City. Then, in the fall of 1967, she began a teaching career at City College of New York, the first in a series of positions that led to her appointment as a tenured professor at the State University of New York at Stony Brook. Her first book, *Who Look at Me?,* was published in 1969.

A collection of essays published in periodicals between 1964 to 1980, 1981's *Civil Wars* is an important source of biographical information on Jordan, as it serves as a record of her development as a writer and addresses each of the author's main concerns: feminism, the black experience, children, and education, including her personal experience as a mother. The book is regarded as an autobiographical testament to Jordan's commitment to the black community. Toni Cade Bambara comments in a *Ms.* review of Jordan's *Civil Wars* that Jordan has written a "chilling but profoundly hopeful vision of living in the USA. Jordan's vibrant spirit manifests itself throughout this collection of articles, letters, journal entries, and essays. What is fundamental to that spirit is caring, commitment, a deep-rooted belief in the sanctity of life. . . . 'We are not powerless,' she reminds us. 'We are indispensable despite all atrocities of state and corporate power to the contrary.'" And as Patricia Jones points out in the *Village Voice:* "Whether speaking on the lives of children, or the victory in Nicaragua, or the development of her poetry, or the consequences of racism in film Jordan brings her faithfulness to bear; faith in her ability to make change. . . . You respect June Jordan's quest and her faith. She is a knowing woman."

Later essay collections by Jordan have included *On Call: New Political Essays, 1981-1985,* wherein the author turns to nonfiction to discuss a variety of international and domestic political subjects ranging from U.S. policy concerning Nicaragua to Israeli foreign policy in relation to South Africa. "What emerges, for Jordan," comments Dorothy Abbott in *Women's Review of Books* "is an affirmation of her faith in the possibility of a truly democratic society." In another essay collection, *Technical Difficulties: African-American Notes on the State of the Union,* Jordan articulates her progressive views on racial, sexual, and feminist issues. Joseph Jordan in *Antioch Review* remarks that the collection "aspires to capture Jordan's passion for justice, which is a constant and conscious part of her language."

As with *Civil Wars* and other of her essays, critics have also detected autobiographical elements in Jordan's young adult novel *His Own Where—,* which portrays Buddy and Angela, two teenaged lovers searching for a secure future in Harlem. Critics have emphasized the novel's concern with the physical, economic, and cultural structures of an urban environment, along with the significance of Black English as a valid and highly expressive means of communication. "The language [used in *His Own Where—*] moves freely, violating syntax to get to deeper levels of meaning," comments Sarah Webster Fabio in the *New York Times Book Review.* "At first the speech patterns might seem to create a barrier for the reader, but not for long."

Jordan writes for a variety of audiences, from young children to adults, and in genres that include poetry, fiction, essays, and plays. In all of her writings, she powerfully and skillfully explores the black experience in America. "The reader coming to June Jordan's work for the first time can be overwhelmed by the breadth and diversity of her concern, and by the wide variety of literary forms in which she expresses them," writes Peter B. Erickson in the *Dictionary of Literary Biography.* "But the unifying element in all her activities is her fervent dedication to the survival of black people."

Chad Walsh writes of Jordan in the *Washington Post Book World:* "Exploring and expressing black consciousness, [Jordan] speaks to everyman, for in his heart of hearts every man is at times an outsider in whatever society he inhabits." Susan Mernit writes in *Library Journal* that "Jordan is a poet for many people, speaking in a voice they cannot fail to understand about things they will want to know." In a *Publishers Weekly* interview with Stella Dong, Jordan explains: "I write for as many different people as I can, acknowledging that in any problem situation you have at least two viewpoints to be reached. I'm also interested in telling the truth as I know it, and in telling people, 'Here's something new that I've just found out about.' I want to share discoveries because other people might never know the thing, and also to get feedback. That's critical."

Reviewers have generally praised Jordan for uniquely and effectively uniting in poetic form the personal, everyday struggle and the political oppression of blacks. For example, Mernit believes that Jordan "elucidates those moments when personal life and political struggle, two discrete elements, suddenly entwine. . . . [Jordan] produces intelligent, warm poetry that is exciting as literature." Honor Moore comments in *Ms.* that Jordan "writes ragalike pieces of word-music that serve her politics, both personal and public." And Peter B. Erickson remarks: "Given her total commitment to writing about a life beset on all sides, Jordan is forced to address the whole of experience in all its facets and can afford to settle for nothing less. Jordan accepts, rises to, the challenge."

Jordan sees poetry as a valid and useful vehicle to express her personal and political ideas while at the same time masterfully creating art. Among her verse collections have been *New Days: Poems of Exile and Return, Things That I Do in the Dark,* and *Naming Our Destiny: New and Selected Poems.* While combining humane concerns with somewhat strident political views, Honor Moore states in *Ms.* that Jordan "never sacrifices poetry for politics. In fact, her craft, the patterning of sound, rhythm, and image, make her art inseparable from political statement, form inseparable from content. [She] uses images contrapuntally to interweave disparate emotions."

Jordan's 1989 work *Naming Our Destiny* represents the range of the poet's political concerns and poetic techniques over three decades, while 1994's *The Haruko: Love Poems* presents poems concerned with the theme of love and the emotions of joy and loss that accompany it. Praising the strength and effectiveness of the voice manifested in the poems of the latter collection, Margaret Randall of the *American Book Review* comments: "She says exactly what she means to say, and says it so powerfully that the reader (or fortunate listener) hears each phrase: isolated, made specific, an essential part of the whole."

Jordan is also noted for the intense passion with which she writes about the struggles against racism. Susan McHenry remarks in *Nation* that "Jordan's characteristic stance is combative. She is exhilarated by a good fight, by taking on her antagonists against the odds. . . . However, Jordan [succeeds] in effectively uniting her impulse to fight with her need and 'I' desire to love." Jascha Kessler comments in *Poetry* that Jordan's literary "expression is developed out of, or through, a fine irony that manages to control her bitterness, even to dominate her rage against the intolerable, so that she can laugh and cry, be melancholic and scornful and so on, presenting always the familiar faces of human personality, integral personality." Kessler adds that Jordan "adapts her poems to the occasions that they are properly, using different voices, and levels of thought and diction that are humanly germane and not disembodied rages or vengeful shadows; thus she can create her world, that is, people it for us, for she has the singer's sense of the dramatic and projects herself into a poem to express its special subject, its individuality. Of course it's always her voice, because she has the skill to use it so variously: but the imagination it needs to run through all her changes is her talent." Faith and optimism are perhaps the two common threads that weave through all of Jordan's work, whether it be prose or poetry, for juvenile readers or for a more mature audience.

BIOGRAPHICAL/CRITICAL SOURCES:

BOOKS

Alexander, Amy, *Fifty Black Women Who Changed America,* Birch Lane Press, 1998.
Authors and Artists for Young Adults, Volume 2, Gale (Detroit), 1989.
Children's Literature Review, Volume 10, Gale, 1986.
Contemporary Literary Criticism, Gale, Volume 5, 1976, Volume 11, 1979, Volume 23, 1983.
Contemporary Women Poets, St. James Press (Detroit), 1997.
Dictionary of Literary Biography, Volume 38: *Afro-American Writers after 1955: Dramatists and Prose Writers,* Gale, 1985.
Twentieth-Century Children's Writers, third edition, St. James Press, 1989.

PERIODICALS

American Book Review, March, 1995, p. 1545; May, 1995, p. 26.
Antioch Review, summer, 1993, p. 459.
Belles Lettres, spring, 1995, p. 68.
Black Scholar, January-February, 1981.
Booklist, October 1, 1992; May 1, 1995, p. 1545.
Callaloo, Volume 9, number 1, 1986.
Choice, October, 1985.
Christian Science Monitor, November 11, 1971.
Chronicle of Higher Education, February 23, 1996, p. 87.

Essence, April, 1981; July, 1995, p. 56.
Kirkus Reviews, September 15, 1971; September 15, 1992, p. 1167.
Library Journal, December 1, 1980; November 1, 1989, p. 92; September 15, 1992; January, 1994; May 15, 1995, p. 73.
Los Angeles Times, September 3, 1986; January 21, 1993.
Ms., April, 1975; April, 1981.
Nation, April 11, 1981; January 29, 1990; July 5, 1993.
Negro Digest, February, 1970.
New Statesman, June 5, 1987, p. 38.
New York, July 31, 1995, p. 46.
New Yorker, May 29, 1995, p. 94.
New York Times, April 25, 1969.
New York Times Book Review, November 7, 1971, pp. 6, 34; April 20, 1972, pp. 13-14; October 9, 1977; August 9, 1981.
Partisan Review, 1969.
Poetry, February, 1973.
Progressive, May, 1994.
Publishers Weekly, February 21, 1972; May 1, 1981; January 17, 1994, p. 428.
Quarterly Black Review of Books, summer, 1994, p. 42.
San Francisco Examiner, December 7, 1977.
Saturday Review, April 17, 1971.
Village Voice, May 27-June 2, 1981.
Virginia Quarterly Review, winter, 1978.
Washington Post, October 13, 1977.
Washington Post Book World, July 4, 1971.
Wilson Library Bulletin, October, 1978.
Women's Review of Books, June, 1986.

K

KEARSE, Amalya (Lyle) 1937-

PERSONAL: Born June 11, 1937, in Vauxhall, NJ; daughter of Robert Freeman (a postmaster) and Myra Lyle (a doctor; maiden name, Smith) Kearse. *Ethnicity:* "African American." *Education:* Wellesley College, B.A., 1959; University of Michigan Law School, J.D., 1962.

ADDRESSES: Office—U.S. Court of Appeals, U.S. Courthouse, Foley Square, New York, NY 10007-1501.

CAREER: Lawyer, federal judge, and author. Hughes, Hubbard, and Reed, New York City, associate, 1962-69, partner, 1969-79; U.S. Court of Appeals, Second Circuit, judge, 1979—. Adjunct lecturer, New York University Law School, 1968-69; member of editorial board, Charles Goren (bridge expert), 1974—. Member, American Law Institute, 1977—; fellow, American College of Trial Lawyers, 1979—.

MEMBER: American Bar Association, New York Bar Association, National Association of Women Judges.

AWARDS, HONORS: Order of the Coif; Jason L. Honigman Award for Outstanding Contribution to *Law Review* Editorial Board, University of Michigan; women's pairs bridge champion, national division, 1971, 1972, world division, 1986; "Bridge Personality of the Year" from International Bridge Press Association, 1980; Outstanding Achievement Award from University of Michigan, 1982; Golden Plate Award from American Academy of Achievement, 1984; National Women's Teams Bridge Champion, 1987, 1990, 1991.

WRITINGS:

(Translator and editor, with Alan Truscott) *Championship Bridge,* 1974.
Bridge Conventions Complete, Hart Publishing (New York City), 1975, 3rd edition, 1990.
(Editor, with others) *The Official Encyclopedia of Bridge,* 3rd edition, Crown (New York City), 1976.
(Translator and editor) *Bridge Analysis,* 1979.
Bridge at Your Fingertips, A & W Visual Library (New York City), 1979.

Also author of *Federal Minimum Wage Standards,* October, 1973; and *Employers and Social Security,* November, 1973.

SIDELIGHTS: Appointed to the U.S. Court of Appeals, Second Circuit, by President Carter in 1979, Amalya Kearse is distinguished as the first woman and only the second black to sit on that court. Kearse was considered for a possible Supreme Court appointment by the Reagan, Bush, and Clinton administrations, and she was also considered as a possible nominee to the post of U.S. Attorney General in 1992. Although she remains on the U.S. Appeals Court bench, she has won the approval of both liberal and conservative law professors. She was the first choice for a seat on the high court by fifty top lawyers in a 1993 poll conducted by the *Los Angeles Daily Journal,* a legal newspaper. In addition to her legal career, Kearse is a world-class bridge player and has been a five-time national bridge champion. She has written, translated, and edited several books on bridge.

Called "enigmatic" and "fiercely private" by a *Wall Street Journal* reporter in 1993, Kearse has kept most details of her family and childhood to herself. She was born on June 11, 1937, in Vauxhall, New Jersey. Her father, Robert Freeman Kearse, was Vauxhall's postmaster. He was supportive of his daughter's career choice. "My father always wanted to be a lawyer," Kearse told the *New York Times* in 1979. "The Depression had a lot to do with why he didn't. I got a lot of encouragement." Profiled in *Ebony* in 1966 as an up-and-coming corporate law attorney, Kearse revealed that her legal aspirations began in childhood. "I became an attorney," she stated, "because I once wanted [as a child] to be an FBI agent." Kearse's mother, Myra Lyle (Smith) Kearse, was a medical doctor in Vauxhall—although later she served as the anti-poverty director of Union County—and hoped her daughter would pursue a career in medicine. "But I couldn't," Kearse explained in the *New York Times*. "I was too squeamish. Besides, I liked going through old law books."

Kearse attended elite Wellesley College, where she took a course in international law, reinforcing her desire to be a lawyer and sparking her interest in litigation. "I decided I wanted to be a litigator," she recalled in the *New York Times*. "There was a moot court and I found that very enjoyable." She earned her bachelor of arts degree in philosophy in 1959. Against the advice of counselors at Wellesley, Kearse went on to enroll in law school at the University of Michigan in Ann Arbor. One of only eight women in her class, she graduated cum laude in 1962. While at Michigan she was editor of the law review and won the Jason L. Honigman Award for her outstanding contributions. According to a *New York Times* correspondent, "even before she received her degree, she received job offers from several Wall Street firms." Kearse ultimately chose to join the corporate law firm of Hughes, Hubbard, and Reed in 1962 as an associate trial lawyer. In addition to her work with the firm, she was also an adjunct lecturer in evidence at New York University Law School for two years. She also served on the board of Big Sisters, which assisted Family Court. In 1969 she was invited to become a partner at Hughes, Hubbard.

Kearse was one of three women profiled by the *New York Times* in a 1970 article applauding their status as the only female partners in Wall Street firms. Kearse herself was the first female black partner in a Wall Street firm. Orville Schell, a senior partner at Hughes, Hubbard, offered high praise for his pioneering colleague in 1979. "She became a partner here not because she is a woman, not because she is black, but because she is just so damned good—no question about it," he told the *New York Times*. Kearse was certified to appear before the benches of New York's Federal District Courts, the U.S. Court of Appeals (Second and Fourth Circuits), and the U.S. Supreme Court. A *Wall Street Journal* reporter noted in 1993 that while at Hughes, Hubbard, "Kearse built her reputation on antitrust and other business litigation. In one of her biggest victories, she represented Broadcast Music, Inc., the music licensing organization, before the U.S. Supreme Court in the late 1970s. In the decision, the court backed away from the use of strict statistical standards, such as similarity of prices, in determining whether a business has a monopoly."

In June, 1979, Democratic President Jimmy Carter named Kearse, a Republican at the time, to the Second U.S. Circuit Court of Appeals, which serves New York, Connecticut, and Vermont. A *New York Times* correspondent observed at the time that she was "the first woman ever to sit on the Federal appeals court in Manhattan and only the second black in the court's history." Thurgood Marshall was the first, appointed in 1961. And at the age of forty-two, Kearse was also one of the youngest judges in the history of that court, which the *New York Times* further noted, "is considered by many lawyers to be the most important court in the country, after the United States Supreme Court."

As a federal judge, Kearse has impressed liberals and conservatives alike, partly because of her command of the law, and partly because her decisions do not allow her to be predictably categorized. In a *Washington Post* profile in 1994, a reporter observed that Kearse "has a reputation for a sharp intellect, even on complicated business issues that confound some other judges. Her votes on social issues please the liberal-leaning groups." On the other hand, conservatives were pleased in 1984 when Kearse rendered an opinion that restricted circumstances under which private plaintiffs can seek triple damages in lawsuits brought under the RICO act. A decision in 1990 "approved a stricter statute of limitations for bringing securities-fraud suits. The standard was adopted by the Supreme Court in another case," wrote Jonathan Moses in the *Wall Street Journal* in 1993.

Kearse's positions on social issues are illustrated by her dissenting opinion in the 1989 case Rust v. Sullivan, which upheld President Bush's gag order prohibiting federally funded clinics from dispensing abortion information. The *Los Angeles Times* quoted her opinion, which stated in part: "The present regulations deny a woman her constitutionally protected right to choose. She cannot make an informed choice between two options when she cannot obtain information as to one of them." In a 1984 majority opinion Kearse wrote that prosecutors should not be allowed to exclude minorities from juries with peremptory challenges.

Kearse has been considered several times for possible appointment to the U.S. Supreme Court. In the early 1980s she was one of eight candidates put forward by the National Women's Political Caucus for consideration by President Reagan for possible replacement of Justice Potter Stewart. In 1991 the Bush administration appraised Kearse, along with Clarence Thomas and others, for high court appointment. Her name appeared on a 1992 list of possible nominees being considered by the Clinton administration for the position of U.S. Attorney General, but she was passed over in favor of Janet Reno. Kearse's record was reviewed in 1993 as President Clinton looked for a replacement for Supreme Court Justice Byron White, and again in 1994 when Justice Harry Blackmun announced his retirement. Insiders speculated that, although considered a moderate with centrist views, Kearse was likely viewed as too liberal in her leanings by the Republicans, and considered too conservative by the Clinton administration.

A *Wall Street Journal* reporter wrote in 1993 that "by all accounts Judge Kearse is brilliant," noting further that she is described by colleagues as "demanding and precise." In another article, a *Wall Street Journal* staff member observed: "Judge Kearse's towering intellect is recognized by her colleagues, who call her 'our resident genius.'" She is much admired as well by fellow judges, who hold her exacting constructions of legal precedent in high regard.

Kearse is also highly respected in the world of tournament bridge. She is a top national and world class player who won the Women's Pairs Bridge Championships National Division twice, its World Division once, and was the National Women's Teams Bridge Champion in 1987, 1990, and 1991. She was named Bridge Personality of the Year by the International Bridge Press Association in 1980. Kearse has authored *Bridge Conventions Complete* (1975) and *Bridge at Your Fingertips* (1980) and has translated two other books on bridge from French to English. She is also a member of the editorial board of Charles Goren, the recognized bridge authority.

BIOGRAPHICAL/CRITICAL SOURCES:

PERIODICALS

Ebony, September, 1966, p. 6.
Essence, May, 1995, p. 146.
Jet, March 27, 1980, p. 9; July 9, 1981, p. 7.
Los Angeles Times, June 29, 1991, p. A18.
New York Times, June 22, 1970; June 25, 1979; September 10, 1981; December 9, 1992; May 5, 1994.
Scholastic Update, November 30, 1984, p. 2.
Wall Street Journal, May 19, 1993, p. A15; June 14, 1993, p. B5.
Washington Post, April 13, 1994, p. A10.

*   *   *

KENAN, Randall (G.) 1963-

PERSONAL: Born March 12, 1963, in Brooklyn, NY. *Education:* University of North Carolina, B.A., 1985.

ADDRESSES: Office—Lecturer in Writing, Sarah Lawrence College, Bronxville, NY 10708.

CAREER: Alfred A. Knopf, New York City, editor, 1985-89; lecturer at Sarah Lawrence College, Bronxville, NY, 1989—, Vassar College, Poughkeepsie, NY, 1989—, and Columbia University, New York City, 1990—.

AWARDS, HONORS: New York Foundation of the Arts grant, 1989; MacDowell Colony Fellowship, 1990.

WRITINGS:

A Visitation of Spirits (novel), Grove Press (New York), 1989.
Let the Dead Bury Their Dead and Other Stories, Harcourt (San Diego), 1992.
James Baldwin, Chelsea House (New York), 1994.
Walking on Water: Black American Lives at the Turn of the Twenty-First Century, Knopf (New York), 1999.

SIDELIGHTS: Randall Kenan has provided his readers with fascinating fiction and nonfiction pictures of black America. Kenan's first two publications were books of fiction that drew much attention for their stylistic virtuosity and thematic richness. They work together, as well as singly, in bringing to life a small African American community in North Carolina called Tims Creek. Critics have been impressed by Kenan's skill in filling that community with magical as well as realistic imagery and complex individuals within racial and sexual types.

Readers were first introduced to Tims Creek in the novel *A Visitation of Spirits.* Horace Thomas Cross, a brilliant student, is led to relive much of his life, and generations of his family's history, through a long night in April, 1984, that ends in tragedy. Taking him on this tour toward doom are demons that may be real or figurative—for Cross is full of confusion and guilt, and disgusted by his own homosexuality. Interspersed with this narrative is one in which Cross's older cousin, the Reverend James Malachai Green, takes his aunt and uncle to visit a dying relative in December, 1985. On the way, the trio provide perspective on Cross and the town's history. Besides these time leaps, the narrative also shifts between various third- and first-person narrations, including discourses on subjects from chicken plucking to contemporary music. "Truth is," George Garrett wrote in *Chicago Tribune Books,* "Kenan tries pretty much of everything and pretty much gets away with all of it, too."

Kenan continues to explore Tims Creek, and the human condition, from an even greater variety of perspectives in *Let the Dead Bury the Dead and Other Stories.* "Each of these stories," said Valerie Miner in the *Nation,* "builds on and resonates with the others, giving readers a textured appreciation for Tims Creek, pious and witty, poor and affluent, black and white." In the title novella, Horace Cross's surname turns out to be that of the plantation owner whose slaves escaped and founded the town in a then-isolated swamp. A history of the founding and development of the town—from which myth and chronicle are hard to separate—is related in the novella through a variety of prisms: oral history, diary entries, and letters, all recorded by Reverend Green, whose unfinished opus is incorporated into a heavily annotated academic treatise by the narrator "RK" in the late 1990s. "The result," commented Jean Hanff Korelitz in the *Washington Post Book World,* "is a conjuring at once specific to one imaginary corner of the south and yet somehow evocative of the entire region and period." The conjuring as well as sensuality—lost, recovered, genuine, manipulative, hetero- and homo-erotic—runs throughout the remaining stories in the collection, as do humourous and enlightening (but non-didactic) encounters, such as that between Booker T. Washington and two former schoolmates in 1909.

The liveliness, variety, and dexterity of the writer has been impressive to many. "Kenan explores the territories in between the living and the dead, between the fantastic and mundane in an energetic, inventive prose that never descends to contrivance or sentimentality," concluded Miner.

Kenan has also published *Walking on Water: Black American Lives at the Turn of the Twenty-First Century,* a personal and social exploration of black culture in the United States. The book is based on several years of research, during which Kenan interviewed black individuals across the country. This included farmers in Idaho and Iowa, a Montana state senator, and other ordinary individuals. Kenan's subjects were chosen to show a wide geographic range and to include both blacks who live in relative isolation and those who live in large urban black communities. The book incorporates Kenan's reflections on his own place within black culture, recounting his experiences during his travels and his upbringing in rural North Carolina. Kenan also conjectures on the emerging shape of black culture in the new century.

In a review for *Booklist,* Vernon Ford noted that Kenan was in part motivated to write *Walking on Water* as a contradictory response to black youth who believe "that ambition and achievement are antithetical to black identity." Ford was struck by the fact that Kenan's subjects "all reflect on the impact of racism on how they live" and called the book "a valuable look" at the effects of "racial isolation or concentration" on current black culture. Thomas J. Davis commented on the book in *Library Journal,* concluding that it "offers fertile commentary" and was not only valuable as an examination of being black, but also for its insight into "what it means to be American and to be human." A *Publishers Weekly* review, however, found fault with Kenan's approach to his subject and asserted that the author was "determined to think about black culture as monolithic," while his material showed "that black American life is multifaceted, shaped as much by class and region as by race." The *Publishers Weekly* reviewer found the book's greatest strength to be its inclusion of local histories, such as information about black cowboys and the Black American West Museum in Denver.

BIOGRAPHICAL/CRITICAL SOURCES:

PERIODICALS

Booklist, March 15, 1992, p. 1336; February 15, 1999, p. 1010.

Callaloo, fall, 1990, p. 913.

Essence, September, 1989, p. 28; August, 1992, p. 44.

Kirkus Reviews, May 1, 1989, p. 650; January 15, 1992, p. 67.

Lambda Book Report, January, 1991, p. 37.

Library Journal, February 15, 1992, p. 199; February 1, 1999, p. 111.

Los Angeles Times Book Review, October 28, 1990, p. 14; September 13, 1992, p. 14.

Nation, July 6, 1992, p. 28.

New York Times Book Review, June 14, 1992.

Publishers Weekly, May 12, 1989, p. 283; January 13, 1992, p. 45; January 4, 1999, p. 79.

Tribune Books (Chicago), August 13, 1989, p. 6; May 3, 1992, p. 6.

Virginia Quarterly Review, winter, 1990, p. 14.

Washington Post Book World, August 2, 1992, pp. 1, 11.*

*   *   *

KENNEDY, Adrienne (Lita) 1931-

PERSONAL: Born September 13, 1931, in Pittsburgh, PA; daughter of Cornell Wallace (an executive secretary of the YMCA) and Etta (a teacher, maiden name, Haugabook) Hawkins; married Joseph C. Kennedy, May 15, 1953 (divorced, 1966); children: Joseph C., Adam Patrice. *Education:* Ohio State University, B.A., 1953; graduate study in creative writing at Columbia University, 1954-56; also studied playwriting, New School for Social Research, American Theatre Wing, Circle in the Square Theatre School, and Edward Albee's workshop.

ADDRESSES: Agent—Bridget Aschenberg, 40 West 57th St., New York, NY 10019.

CAREER: Playwright. Yale University, New Haven, CT, lecturer, 1972-74; School of Drama, New York City, CBS fellow, 1973; Princeton University, Princeton, NJ, lecturer, 1977; Brown University, Providence, RI, visiting associate professor, 1979-80; University of California, Berkeley, distinguished lecturer, 1980, 1986; Harvard University, Cambridge, MA, visiting lecturer, 1990-91; Signature Theatre Company, New York City, playwright-in-residence, 1995-96. Member of playwriting unit, Actors Studio, New York, 1962-65. International Theatre Institute representative, Budapest, 1978.

MEMBER: PEN (member of board of directors, 1976-77).

AWARDS, HONORS: Obie Award from *Village Voice,* 1964, for *Funnyhouse of a Negro;* Guggenheim memorial fellowship, 1967; Rockefeller grants, 1967-69, 1974, 1976; National Endowment for the Arts grant, 1973; CBS fellow, School of Drama, 1973; Creative Artists Public Service grant, 1974; Yale fellow, 1974-75; Stanley Award for play writing; New England Theatre Conference grant; Manhattan Borough President's award, 1988, for *People Who Led to My Plays;* National Endowment for the Arts award, 1993; Pierre Lecomte du Novy Award, Lincoln Center, 1994; American Academy of Arts and Letters Award, 1994; Lila Wallace Award, *Reader's Digest.*

WRITINGS:

PLAYS

Funnyhouse of a Negro (one-act; first produced Off-Broadway at Circle in the Square Theatre, 1962), Samuel French (New York City), 1969.

The Owl Answers (one-act; also see below), first produced in Westport, CT, at White Barn Theatre, 1963, produced Off-Broadway at Public Theatre, January 12, 1969.

A Lesson in a Dead Language, first produced in 1964.

A Rat's Mass, first produced in Boston, MA, by the Theatre Company, April, 1966, produced Off-Broadway at La Mama Experimental Theatre Club, November, 1969.

A Beast Story (one-act; also see below), first produced in 1966, produced Off-Broadway at Public Theatre, January 12, 1969.

(With John Lennon and Victor Spinetti) *The Lennon Play: In His Own Write* (adapted from Lennon's books *In His Own Write* and *A Spaniard in the Works;* first produced in London by National Theatre, 1967; produced in Albany, NY, at Arena Summer Theatre, August, 1969), Simon & Schuster (New York City), 1969.

Sun: A Poem for Malcolm X Inspired by His Murder, first produced on the West End, London, at Royal Court Theatre, 1968, produced in New York at La Mama Experimental Theatre Club, 1970.

Cities in Bezique (contains *The Owl Answers* and *A Beast Story;* first produced in New York at Shakespeare Festival, 1969), Samuel French, 1969.

Boats, first produced in Los Angeles at the Forum, 1969.

An Evening with Dead Essex, first produced in New York by American Place Theatre Workshop, 1973.

A Movie Star Has to Star in Black and White, first produced in New York by Public Theatre Workshop, 1976.

A Lancashire Lad (for children), first produced in Albany, NY, at Governor Nelson A. Rockefeller Empire State Plaza Performing Arts Center, May, 1980.

Orestes and Electra, first produced in New York at Juilliard School of Music, 1980.

Black Children's Day, first produced in Providence, RI, at Brown University, November, 1980.

Diary of Lights, first produced at City College in New York, June 5, 1987.

The Alexander Plays (contains *She Talks to Beethoven, The Ohio State Murders, The Film Club,* and *The Dramatic Circle*), University of Minnesota Press (Minneapolis), 1992.

(With son, Adam Patrice Kennedy) *Sleep Deprivation Chamber,* Theatre Communications Group, 1996.

Also author of *In One Act,* a collection of plays. Contributor to numerous anthologies, including *New American Plays,* edited by William M. Hoffman, Hill & Wang (New York City), 1968; *New Black Playwrights,* edited by William Couch, Jr., Louisiana State University Press (Baton Rouge), 1968; *Kuntu Drama,* edited by Paul C. Harrison, Grove (New York City), 1974; and *Wordplay 3,* Performing Arts Journal (New York City), 1984. Contributor of plays to periodicals, including *Scripts 1.*

OTHER

People Who Led to My Plays (memoir), Knopf (New York City), 1987.

Deadly Triplets: A Theatre Mystery and Journal (novel), University of Minnesota Press, 1990.

ADAPTATIONS: Solo Voyages, an adaptation by Joseph Chaikin of three monologues from *The Owl Answers, A Rat's Mass,* and *A Movie Star Has to Star in Black and White,* was produced in New York and Washington, 1985.

SIDELIGHTS: "While almost every black playwright in the country is fundamentally concerned with realism . . . Miss [Adrienne] Kennedy is weaving some kind of dramatic fabric of poetry," Clive Barnes comments in the *New York Times.* "What she writes is a mosaic of feeling, with each tiny stone stained with the blood of the gray experience. Of all our black writers, Miss Kennedy is most concerned with white, with white relationship, with white blood. She thinks black, but she remembers white. It gives her work an eddying ambiguity."

In her complex and introspective plays, Martin Duberman remarks in *Partisan Review,* Kennedy is "absorbed by her private fantasies, her interior world. She disdains narrative, 'everyday' language and human interaction; the dream, the myth, the poem are her domain." James Hatch and Ted Shine also note that "in a tradition in which the major style has long been realism, Adrienne Kennedy has done what few black playwrights have attempted: used form to project an interior reality and thereby created a rich and demanding theatrical style."

Kennedy's first play, *Funnyhouse of a Negro,* examines the psychological problems of Sarah, a young mulatto woman who lives with a Jewish poet in a boarding house run by a white landlady. Dealing with the last moments before Sarah's suicide, the play consists of scenes of the young woman's struggle with herself. Tortured by an identity crisis, Sarah is "lost in a nightmare world where black is evil and white is good, where various personages, including Queen Victoria, Patrice Lumumba, and Jesus Himself, materialize to mock her," says *New Yorker*'s Edith Oliver. *Funnyhouse of a Negro* earned Kennedy an Obie award, and, notes a *Variety* reviewer, a reputation as "a gifted writer with a distinctive dramatic imagination."

Oliver describes *The Owl Answers* as another fantasy of "a forbidden and glorious white world, viewed with a passion and frustration that shred the spirit and nerves and mind of the dispossessed heroine." The illegitimate child of a black cook and the wealthiest white man in Georgia, the heroine is riding on a New York subway. The subway doors become the doors to the chapel of the Tower of London through which appear masked historical characters, including Chaucer, Shakespeare, Anne Boleyn, and the Virgin Mary, who at times unmask to become other characters, such as the heroine's mother and father.

A Beast Story, produced with *The Owl Answers* under the title *Cities in Bezique,* was described as more elaborate, hallucinatory and obscure than the first play. It draws analogies, says Steve Tennen in *Show Business,* "between inhuman beings and man's bestial tendencies." Kennedy's later play, *A Rat's Mass,* staged as a parody mass, is also abstract, centering around the relationship between a black brother and sister and their childhood involvement with the white girl next door.

In all of these plays, Kennedy's writing is poetic and symbolic; plot and dialogue are secondary to effect. Her reliance on such devices as masks, characters who become other characters, characters played by more than one actor, and Christian symbolism makes her work difficult to understand, and her plays have been seen as both nightmarish rituals and poetic dances. Marilyn Stasio explains in *Cue:* "Kennedy is a poet, working with disjointed time sequences, evocative images, internalized half-thoughts, and incantatory language to create a netherworld of submerged emotions surfacing only in fragments. Events are crucial only for the articulated feelings they evoke."

During 1971, Kennedy joined five other women playwrights to found the Women's Theatre Council, a theatre cooperative devoted to producing the works of women playwrights and providing opportunities for women in other aspects of the theatre, such as directing and acting. Mel Gussow of the *New York Times* notes that the council's "founding sisters all come from Off Off Broadway. . . . Each has a distinctive voice, but their work is related in being largely nonrealistic and experimental. The women feel unified as innovators and by their artistic consciousness."

Kennedy branched out into juvenile theatre in 1980 after being commissioned by the Empire State Youth Theatre Institute. *A Lancashire Lad,* her first play for children, is a fictionalized version of Charles Chaplin's childhood. Narrated by the hero, the play traces his life growing up in Dickensian England and beginning his career in the British music halls. Although an entertaining musical, the show confronts the poverty and pain of Chaplin's youth. Praising Kennedy's language for achieving "powerful emotional effects with the sparest of means," *New York Times* reviewer Frank Rich concludes: "The difference between *A Lancashire Lad* and an adult play is, perhaps, the intellectual simplicity of its ambitions. Yet that simplicity can also be theater magic in its purest and most eloquent form."

During the latter half of the 1980s, Kennedy worked on a quartet of plays illuminating the life of a woman named Suzanne Alexander—a character several commentators believe is a fictionalized version of Kennedy herself. *She Talks to Beethoven, The Ohio*

State Murders, The Film Club, and *The Dramatic Circle* were collected in 1992 under the title *The Alexander Plays.* According to *Theatre Journal* reviewer Nicole R. King, this collection of one-acts "will further [Kennedy's] brilliant reputation and characteristically introduce the theatre world to something altogether new."

In *The Ohio State Murders,* which some critics have singled out as the best of the Alexander plays, Suzanne recalls her tenure as a student at an Ohio college. Kennedy has often related that her years at Ohio State University during the early period of integration were an ordeal; in the play, Alexander summons up memories of trauma similar to Kennedy's, and worse. During the course of the drama, it is revealed that Alexander was seduced by a professor and gave birth to twins, who were later murdered. Years later, after becoming a successful writer, she returns to the college to lecture on the origins of her work's frequently violent imagery. King relates: "Typically, the answer is imbedded in the multiple experiences of violence, racism and emotional abuse." *She Talks to Beethoven, The Dramatic Circle,* and *The Film Club* show Alexander in England and Africa, where her husband mysteriously vanishes. There are references to various aspects of African and European culture, and the contrast between the two; through it all, the power of love and the fight against oppression provide the plays' grounding, critics observe.

King notes that while these plays are typical of Kennedy's work in that they are highly unconventional, they also "demonstrate a palpable shift in [her] creative style." There is little action, points out Rosemary Keefe Curb in *Belles Lettres;* instead, Suzanne is seen "waiting, dreading, hoping, remembering, and reading aloud from literature and letters. Since nothing happens in the dramatized present except a layering of voices, spectators must create a dramatic context."

Like all of Kennedy's best work, each of *The Alexander Plays* is "short and powerful," relates King. Kennedy's style in these plays is "no less powerful" but "markedly less frenetic" than in her previous efforts, King comments. The critic finds that many of Kennedy's trademark techniques, such as the use of striking and contrasting images, are present in *The Alexander Plays,* but they are used in fresh, startling ways. "For Kennedy fans," King summarizes, "the poignancy of this quartet will seem new although the multiple levels of consciousness and instability of time frame will not."

BIOGRAPHICAL/CRITICAL SOURCES:

PERIODICALS

African American Review, summer, 1994, p. 293.
Belles Lettres, spring, 1989, p. 23; summer, 1993, pp. 49-50.
City Arts Monthly, February, 1982.
CLA Journal, December, 1976, pp. 235-44.
Cue, January 18, 1969; October 4, 1969.
Drama Review, December, 1977, pp. 41-48.
International Times, September 22, 1968.
Library Journal, August, 1992, p. 99.
Los Angeles Times Book Review, July 12, 1987.
Modern Drama, December, 1989, pp. 520-39.
Ms., June, 1987.
Multicultural Review, April, 1992, p. 76.
New York, October 9, 1995, p. 82; December 4, 1995, p. 134.
New Yorker, January 25, 1964, pp. 76-78; January 25, 1969.
New York Times, January 15, 1964; June 20, 1968; July 9, 1968; January 13, 1969, p. 26; January 19, 1969; November 1, 1969; February 22, 1972; May 21, 1980; February 15, 1981; September 11, 1985; September 20, 1985; January 27, 1991, p. CN12; July 25, 1995, pp. C13, C14.
New York Times Book Review, October 14, 1990, p. 48.
Observer Review, June 23, 1968.
Partisan Review, Number 3, 1969.
Show Business, January 25, 1969; October 4, 1969.
Studies in Black Literature, summer, 1975, pp. 1-5.
Theatre Journal, October, 1985, pp. 302-316; March, 1991, pp. 125-28; March, 1992, pp. 67-86; October, 1993, pp. 406-408.
Variety, January 29, 1969.
Village Voice, August 14, 1969; September 25, 1969; November 3, 1987, pp. 61, 65.
Voice Literary Supplement, October, 1990, p. 2.
Washington Post Book World, November 20, 1988, p. 12.
Women's Review of Books, October, 1987, pp. 14-15.*

*   *   *

KENNEDY, Florynce (Rae) 1916-

PERSONAL: Born February 11, 1916, in Kansas City, MO; daughter of Wiley (a Pullman porter and taxi owner) and Zella Kennedy; married Charles Dudley

Dye (a writer), 1957 (deceased). *Ethnicity:* "African American." *Education:* Columbia University, B.A., 1948, J.D., 1951.

ADDRESSES: Home—San Francisco, CA.

CAREER: Lawyer, political activist, lecturer, and author. Hartman, Sheridan, and Tekulsky, law clerk, c. 1951-54; lawyer in private practice, New York City, 1954-66; Media Workshop and Consumer Information Service, founder and director, 1966; Feminist Party, founder and director, 1970; Voters, Artists, Anti-Nuclear Activist and Consumers for Political Action and Communication Coalition (VAC-PAC), national director; Ladies Aid and Trade Crusade, national director.

MEMBER: New York Bar Association.

WRITINGS:

(With Diane Schulder) *Abortion Rap,* McGraw Hill (New York), 1971.
Color Me Flo: My Hard Life and Good Times, Prentice-Hall (Englewood Cliffs, NJ), 1976.
(With William F. Pepper) *Sex Discrimination in Employment: An Analysis and Guide for Practitioner and Student,* Michie Co. (Charlottesville, VA), 1981.

SIDELIGHTS: Florynce Kennedy has had a remarkably long and visible career as a lawyer, militant activist, and feminist. Since the 1950s, when as an attorney she fought for royalty rights due the estates of musical legends Billie Holiday and Charlie Parker, Kennedy has unflinchingly attacked racism, inequity, and hypocrisy wherever she has found it. An original member of the National Organization for Women (NOW) and the founder of the Feminist Party, Kennedy has been a vocal spokesperson for women, blacks, homosexuals, and other minorities, and a staunch defender of civil rights. Variously called outspoken, outrageous, profane, and a woman of "immeasurable spirit," Kennedy was once described in *People* as "the biggest, loudest, and indisputably, the rudest mouth on the battleground where feminist activists and radical politics join in mostly common cause." Fellow feminist and friend Gloria Steinem has said that for those in the black movement, the women's movement, the peace movement, and the consumer movement, "Flo was a political touchstone—a catalyst."

Born Florynce Rae Kennedy on February 11, 1916 in Kansas City, Missouri, she was the second of Wiley and Zella Kennedy's five daughters. Wiley was first a Pullman porter with the railroad and later owned a taxi business. Zella worked outside the home only during the Depression. Neither parent was very strict, and Kennedy wrote in her autobiography, *Color Me Flo: My Hard Life and Good Times,* that her parents' protective attitudes combined to make her and her sisters feel very special. "All of us had such a sense of security because we were almost never criticized," she recalled. She has suggested that her upbringing contributed significantly to her anti-Establishment outlook. "I suspect that that's why I don't have the right attitude toward authority today, because we were taught very early in the game that we didn't have to respect the teachers, and if they threatened to hit us we could just act as if they weren't anybody we had to pay any attention to," she wrote.

Kennedy's childhood, while not always prosperous, was a happy time. Zella instilled both tenacity and optimism in her daughter. "Zella never accepted poverty, and yet she didn't resent it either, and we laughed a lot when we were really desperately poor," Kennedy wrote of her mother in *Color Me Flo.* "She always made an effort to maintain some kind of esthetic surroundings. . . . She was determined to have rose bushes, although our yard had too much shade. . . . But every year Zella decided she was going to have grass and roses. . . . We never had a single rose from any of those bushes, yet she persisted in going out and buying them. It was Zella who epitomized hope for us—she never gave up."

Kennedy graduated from Lincoln High School in Kansas City at the top of her class, but she did not immediately go on to college. Although she felt that one day she probably would attend college, opportunities for higher education for blacks were limited, "really kind of unheard-of," she stated. Instead, Kennedy opened a hat shop in Kansas City with her sisters, an enterprise that was fun, if not exceptionally prosperous. While Kennedy admitted she may have been "a little more outspoken, a little crazier than the rest" in high school, she was more interested in boys than politics. Within a few years of graduation, however, she was involved in her first political action. She helped organize a boycott when the local Coca Cola bottler refused to hire black truck drivers.

Following her mother's death from cancer, Kennedy and her sister Grayce moved to New York City in 1942. Ignoring those who advised her to become a teacher or a nurse at City College, Kennedy enrolled at Columbia University in 1944 as a pre-law student.

She supported herself working at various part-time jobs. She explained her decision in 1976: "I thought anybody with the brains and energy to become a teacher ought to want to become something better." She elaborated, "I find that the higher you aim the better you shoot, and even if it seems you're way beyond yourself . . . it always turns out that you can do a lot more than you thought you could." When in her senior year she again aimed high, attempting a concurrent enrollment at Columbia Law School, she was refused admission. Told she had been rejected not because she was black but because she was a woman, Kennedy was no less incensed. She promptly wrote the dean a letter suggesting the move was racially motivated and hinting that a lawsuit might follow. In 1948 she was admitted to the law school, one of eight women and the only black member of her class. She received her B.A. in 1948 and was awarded her law degree in 1951.

After law school Kennedy clerked with the law firm of Hartman, Sheridan, and Tekulsky, and she was admitted to the bar in 1952. By 1954 she had opened an office on Madison Avenue. It was rough going at times, and she had to take a job at Bloomingdale's one Christmas in order to pay the rent.

The late 1950s brought Don Wilkes, a law partner, and Charles "Charlie" Dye, a Welsh writer ten years her junior whom she married in 1957. Neither relationship was to last long. After several disappointing legal defeats, Wilkes ran off with most of the firm's assets, leaving Kennedy over $50,000 in debt. Although Dye was very supportive during this crisis, the marriage was rocky due to his alcoholism, and he died soon after.

Before Wilkes left, the firm had taken on a case for blues singer Billie Holiday. When Holiday died, Kennedy continued to represent the estate, and later she represented the estate of jazz great Charlie Parker as well. In both situations Kennedy successfully fought the record companies to recover money from royalties and sales due the estates. Kennedy's experience with this estate work signaled the beginning of her disillusionment with law. "Handling the Holiday and Parker estates taught me more than I was really ready for about government and business delinquency and the hostility and helplessness of the courts," she wrote in her memoir. She continued: "Not only was I not earning a decent living, there began to be a serious question in my mind whether practicing law could ever be an effective means of changing society or even of simple resistance to oppression."

As a result of these experiences, as well as her conviction that a government conspiracy shrouded the assassination of President Kennedy, the enterprising attorney began to reassess her ability to effect social change through the judicial system. In 1966 Kennedy set up the Media Workshop in order to fight racism in media and advertising. When Benton and Bowles, a large ad agency, refused to provide the Workshop with requested hiring and programming information, the group picketed the Fifth Avenue office. "After that they invited us upstairs," Kennedy recalled, "and ever since I've been able to say, 'When you want to get to the suites, start in the streets.'"

Thus began Kennedy's career as an activist. She was highly visible in this role during the 1960s, picketing the Colgate-Palmolive building with members of NOW, and also protesting at WNEW-TV. The group's media protest led them to CBS, where they were arrested for refusing to leave the building. Eventually CBS withdrew the complaint.

In 1966 Kennedy represented activist H. Rap Brown and was present at the four Black Power Conferences, and at the Black political caucuses as well. She also attended the first meeting of the fledgling National Association for Women, but she was soon disappointed by NOW's reluctance to go head-to-head with the issues of the day. "I saw the importance of a feminist movement, and stayed in there because I wanted to do anything I could to keep it alive, but when I saw how retarded NOW was, I thought, 'My God, who needs this?'" In November of 1971 Kennedy founded the Feminist Party. Its first action was to support Shirley Chisholm's presidential candidacy.

The speaking career that would take Kennedy through the next two decades began in 1967 at an anti-war convention in Montreal. She became incensed when Black Panther Bobby Seale was not allowed to speak. She wrote in her memoir: "I went berserk. I took the platform and started yelling and hollering." An invitation to speak in Washington followed, and her lecturing career was born. Kennedy's activist and speaking careers continued throughout the 1970s and 1980s, and included the Coat Hanger Farewell Protest on the abortion issue, anti-Nixon demonstrations, picketing Avon International for support for the three-hour Celebrate Women TV program, the MAMA March— the March against Media Arrogance—and the organization of a demonstration at Harvard University protesting the lack of women's restrooms. In 1971 Kennedy co-authored *Abortion Rap* with Diane Schulder, and in 1981 she wrote *Sex Discrimination* *in Employment: An Analysis and Guide for Practitioner and Student,* with William F. Pepper. She was national director of Voters, Artists, Anti-Nuclear Activists and Consumers for Political Action and Communications Coalition (VAC-PAC) and also national director of the Ladies Aid and Trade Crusade. According to a *Jet* magazine article published in 1986, these organizations' "commandments" include "Thou Shall Not Use Our Dollars to Finance Racism and Sexism on Network Television."

In 1986 Kennedy was "roasted" by friends and colleagues at a 70th birthday party in New York City. Among those honoring her at the event were activist Dick Gregory and civil rights attorney William Kunstler. That Flo Kennedy's career has lengthened to four decades is no surprise when one considers her approach to activism. She described her philosophy about her struggles and victories in her autobiography as being "like a successful bath; you don't expect not to take another bath. . . . Countermovements among racists and sexists and nazifiers are just as relentless as dirt on a coffee table. . . . Every housewife knows that if you don't sooner or later dust . . . the whole place will be dirty again."

BIOGRAPHICAL/CRITICAL SOURCES:

PERIODICALS

Essence, May, 1995, p. 140.
Jet, March 31, 1986, p. 6.
People, April 14, 1974, p. 54.

*   *   *

KENYATTA, Jomo 1891(?)-1978

PERSONAL: Name originally Kamau wa Ngengi; baptized as Johnstone Kamau, 1914; known subsequently as Johnstone Kenyatta and Jomo Kenyatta; born c. October 20, 1891 (some sources say 1889, 1890, 1893, 1897, or 1898), in Ichaweri (some sources say Ngenda), British East Africa Protectorate (now Kenya); died August 21 (some sources say August 22), 1978, in Mombasa, Kenya; son of Muigai (a small farmer and herdsman) and Wambui; married Grace Wahu, November 28, 1922; married Edna Grace Clarke (a schoolteacher and governess), May 11, 1942; married third wife, Grace; married fourth wife, Ngina; children: (first marriage) Peter Mugai, Margaret Wambui; (second marriage) Peter Magana; (third marriage)

Jane Wambui; (fourth marriage) Uhuru, Muhoho, Nyokabi (some sources say a total of four sons and four daughters). *Education:* Attended Woodbroke College, 1931-32; studied in Moscow, U.S.S.R., c. 1932; attended London School of Economics and Political Science, c. 1936.

CAREER: Courier for sisal company in Nairobi, British East Africa Protectorate (now Kenya), c. 1915; interpreter for Supreme Court in Nairobi, 1919; stores clerk and water meter reader for city of Nairobi, 1922-28; Kikuyu Central Association, general secretary beginning in 1928, envoy in London, England, beginning in 1929; University of London, London, England, assistant in phonetics at School of Oriental and African Studies, beginning in 1933; farm worker in England and lecturer for British Army and Workers' Educational Association, c. 1939-45; Independent Teachers' College, Githunguri, Kenya, vice-principal, 1946-47, principal, beginning in 1947; president of Kenya African Union (political party), beginning in 1947; imprisoned at Lokitaung, Kenya, 1953-59; detained in Lodwar, Kenya, 1959-61, and Maral, Kenya, 1961; president of Kenya African National Union (political party), beginning in 1961; Government of Kenya, Nairobi, member of Legislative Council representing Fort Hall, beginning in 1962, minister of state for constitutional affairs and economic planning, 1962-63, prime minister and minister for internal security and defense, 1963-64, president, 1964-78. Helped organize fifth Pan-African Congress in Manchester, England, 1945; co-founder of Organization of African Unity. Actor in film "Sanders of the River," 1935.

MEMBER: International African Friends of Abyssinia (co-founder and honorary secretary), International African Service Bureau.

AWARDS, HONORS: Knight of Grace in Order of St. John of Jerusalem, 1972; Order of Golden Ark from World Wildlife Fund, 1974; honorary fellow of London School of Economics and Political Science; honorary doctorates from Victoria University of Manchester and University of East Africa.

WRITINGS:

(Contributor) Nancy Cunard, editor, *Negro Anthology,* privately printed, 1934.

Facing Mount Kenya: The Tribal Life of the Gikuyu, introduction by Bronislaw Malinowski, Secker & Warburg, 1938, Vintage, 1962, AMS Press, 1978.

(With Lilias E. Armstrong) *The Phonetic and Tonal Structure of Kikuyu,* Oxford University Press, 1940.

My People of Kikuyu and the Life of Chief Wangombe, United Society for Christian Literature, 1942, Oxford University Press, 1966.

Kenya: The Land of Conflict, Panaf Service, 1945, International African Service Bureau, 1971.

Harambee! The Prime Minister of Kenya's Speeches, 1963-1964, From the Attainment of Internal Self-Government to the Threshold of the Kenya Republic, foreword by Malcolm MacDonald, edited by Anthony Cullen, Oxford University Press, 1964.

Suffering without Bitterness: The Founding of the Kenya Nation, East African Publishing House, 1968.

The Challenge of Uhuru: The Progress of Kenya, 1968 to 1970; Selected and Prefaced Extracts From the Public Speeches of Jomo Kenyatta, President of the Republic of Kenya, East African Publishing House, 1971.

Founder and editor of *Muigwithania,* 1928-30. Contributor to periodicals, including *Daily Worker, Labour Monthly, Manchester Guardian, Negro Worker,* and *Sunday Worker.*

SIDELIGHTS: Jomo Kenyatta led the newly independent African nation of Kenya from 1964 until his death in 1978. He grew up in a traditional African culture as a member of Kenya's largest ethnic group, the Kikuyu. (His exact age is a matter of conjecture because the Kikuyu classified themselves by age-group, ignoring an individual's birthday.) Son of a small farmer and herdsman, Kenyatta saw firsthand how black Africans suffered when white settlers took over their land. As a young man Kenyatta moved to the capital city of Nairobi, where he held a succession of minor jobs. In 1928 he became general secretary of the Kikuyu Central Association (KCA), which sought to improve the living conditions of the Kikuyu under British rule, and as part of his job he traveled widely among his people. The periodical he edited for the association, *Muigwithania,* is believed to be the first black journal in Kenya. The next year Kenyatta went to England as a KCA representative, lobbying successfully for independent Kikuyu schools and unsuccessfully for land reform. Kenyatta spent most of the next seventeen years in England, promoting the cause of black Kenyans in a wide variety of forums. He wrote letters to the Colonial Office and articles for British periodicals, joined Pan-African groups such as the International African Service Bureau, and lobbied influential guests at London cocktail parties. He commiserated with black activists such as Paul Robeson, famous American singer and actor; W. E. B. Du Bois, a leader of America's National Association for the Advancement of Colored People; and Kwame Nkrumah, future president of Ghana. Traveling widely in Europe, Kenyatta studied for several months at an institute in Moscow that hoped to inspire Communist revolutionaries. (When he later became president of Kenya, however, he declared his country unsuitable for communism.) Some of Kenyatta's political concerns are summarized in the short work *Kenya: Land of Conflict.*

Although Kenyatta never earned a bachelor's degree, he became a graduate student in anthropology at the London School of Economics and Political Science in the mid-1930s, turning a series of papers he wrote about Kikuyu culture into the book *Facing Mount Kenya.* The work uses the format and terminology of a Western scholarly study, devoting chapters to religion, education, sexual practices, and land ownership. But *Facing Mount Kenya* is also a defense of Kenyatta's African background, for it suggests that European influence had harmed the Kikuyu, whose culture at its most untouched was as worthy of respect as that of Europe. In the *New York Times Book Review,* John Barkham said that Kenyatta's eagerness to defend his people had compromised his work, but the *Times Literary Supplement* praised the book as "very readable and highly instructive," noting that Kenyatta had maintained professional standards and had stated his opinions with "due restraint." *Facing Mount Kenya* has been reprinted several times since it first appeared, and in 1953 *Christian Science Monitor* reviewer Marian Sorenson suggested that the book remained a useful background source for understanding black complaints against colonial rule. Kenyatta returned to Kenya in 1946 and was elected president of a prominent political party, the Kenya African Union. He championed a reform program that included voting rights for blacks, an end to racial discrimination, and a more equitable distribution of land. At the same time, however, a black clandestine movement known as the Mau Mau began efforts to force the British from Kenya, murdering a small number of white settlers and many blacks suspected of collaborating with the white regime.

British authorities, already concerned by Kenyatta's political prominence, became convinced that he was involved with the Mau Mau despite his public repudiation of its violence. Arrested in 1952, Kenyatta was tried and sentenced to prison as a Mau Mau organizer. Many sources cast doubt on the state's case

against him. As opposition to the colonial regime continued, the British resigned themselves to Kenya's eventual independence. Kenyatta, who remained highly popular while in prison and detention, was released from exile in a remote province in 1961. He was soon elected president of Kenya's largest political party, the African National Union, and led his country to independence in 1964.

Kenyatta's national agenda, which included giving blacks a more balanced share of the Kenyan economy and creating a sense of social unity, is reflected in *Harambee,* a collection of his speeches. The book was named for Kenyatta's political rallying cry—Swahili for "let us all pull together!" Although Kenyatta insisted that Kenya become a one-party state and suppressed rivals to his personal rule, his political philosophy was notably pragmatic. Certain speeches in *Suffering without Bitterness* outline Kenyatta's doctrine of "African socialism"—an eclectic mixture of individual initiative and concern for the common good. Assessing Kenyatta's career in *New Times,* Charles Mohr wrote that the Kenyan leader's "admirers and critics alike had come to see him as perhaps the leading exponent in Africa of moderate politics and laissez-faire economics." Kenyatta allowed nonblacks to remain and contribute their skills to the new country. The economy prospered, and with government encouragement blacks increasingly entered the fields of business and large-scale farming, helping to create Africa's largest black middle class. The press was "nearly free," as Kenneth Labich and James Pringle wrote in *Newsweek.* Kenyatta remained interested in Pan-Africanism, helping to found the Organization of African Unity and a short-lived common market with the neighboring states of Uganda and Tanzania.

Although Kenyatta faced recurrent political discontent—including complaints that he countenanced nepotism and official corruption—when he died in 1978 commentators generally held that he was a great asset to his country and would be difficult to replace. "The Kenya he governed," Mohr asserted, "is today one of the most . . . free societies on the continent."

BIOGRAPHICAL/CRITICAL SOURCES:

BOOKS

Arnold, Guy, *Kenyatta and the Politics of Kenya,* Dent, 1974.

Aseka, Eric Masinde, *Jomo Kenyatta: A Biography,* East African Educational Publishers, 1992.

Assensoh, A. B., *African Political Leadership: Jomo Kenyatta, Kwame Nkrumah, and Julius K. Nyerere,* Krieger, 1998.

Macharia, Rawson, *The Truth about the Trial of Jomo Kenyatta,* Longman Kenya, 1991.

Malhotra, Veena, *Kenya Under Kenyatta,* Kalinga (Delhi), 1990.

Murray-Brown, Jeremy, *Kenyatta,* Allen & Unwin, 1972, Dutton, 1973, 2nd edition, Allen & Unwin, 1979.

Thompson, Dudley, *From Kingston to Kenya: The Making of a Pan-Africanist Lawyer,* Majority Press, 1993.

PERIODICALS

Christian Science Monitor, August 27, 1953.
New York Times, August 22, 1978.
New York Times Book Review, September 6, 1953.
Times Literary Supplement, March 11, 1939.

OBITUARIES:

PERIODICALS

Newsweek, September 4, 1978.
New Times, September 18, 1978.
New York Times, November 6, 1978.
Time, September 4, 1978.*

*   *   *

KINCAID, Jamaica   1949-

PERSONAL: Born Elaine Potter Richardson, May 25, 1949, in St. Johns, Antigua; daughter of a carpenter/cabinet maker and Annie Richardson; married Allen Shawn (a composer and professor at Bennington College); children: Annie Shawn and Harold. *Education:* Studied photography at the New School for Social Research in New York; attended Franconia College, NH. *Religion:* Jewish.

ADDRESSES: Home—P.O. Box 822, North Bennington, VT 05257.

CAREER: Writer. *New Yorker,* New York City, staff writer, 1976-95. Visiting professor, Harvard University, Cambridge, MA.

AWARDS, HONORS: Morton Dauwen Zabel Award, American Academy and Institute of Arts and Letters, 1983, for *At the Bottom of the River;* honorary degrees from Williams College and Long Island College, both in 1991, Colgate University, Amherst College, and Bard College; Lila Wallace-*Reader's Digest* Fund annual writer's award, 1992; *The Autobiography of My Mother* was a finalist for the National Book Critics Circle Award for fiction and the PEN Faulkner Award, both 1997; National Book Award nomination, 1997, for *My Brother.*

WRITINGS:

At the Bottom of the River (short stories), Farrar, Straus (New York City), 1983.
Annie John (novel), Farrar, Straus, 1985.
A Small Place (essays), Farrar, Straus, 1988.
Annie, Gwen, Lilly, Pam and Tulip, illustrations by Eric Fischl, Knopf (New York City) and Whitney Museum of American Art, 1989.
Lucy (novel), Farrar, Straus, 1990.
The Autobiography of My Mother (novel), Farrar, Straus, 1995.
My Brother, Farrar, Straus, 1997.
(Editor and author of introduction) *My Favorite Plant: Writers and Gardeners on the Plants They Love,* Farrar, Straus, 1998.
(With Lynn Geesaman) *Poetics of Place: Photographs by Lynn Geesaman,* Umbrage Editions, 1998.
(Author of introduction) *Generations of Women: In Their Own Words,* photographs by Mariana Cook, Chronicle Books, 1998.

Also contributor to periodicals. *At the Bottom of the River* has been recorded by the Library of Congress Archive of Recorded Poetry and Literature.

SIDELIGHTS: Jamaica Kincaid gained wide acclaim with her first two works, *At the Bottom of the River* and *Annie John.* In these and other books about life on the Caribbean island of Antigua, where she was born, Kincaid employs a highly poetic literary style celebrated for its rhythms, imagery, characterization, and elliptic narration. As Ike Onwordi wrote in *Times Literary Supplement:* "Jamaica Kincaid uses language that is poetic without affectation. She has a deft eye for salient detail while avoiding heavy symbolism and diverting exotica. The result captures powerfully the essence of vulnerability." "Everyone thought I had a way with words, but it came out as a sharp tongue. No one expected anything from me at all. Had I just sunk in the cracks it would not have been noted. I would have been lucky to be a secretary somewhere," Kincaid told Leslie Garis in the *New York Times Magazine.* When she was seventeen, Kincaid, whose given name was Elaine Potter, left the rural island to become an *au pair* in New York City. By the time she returned, almost twenty years later, she had become a successful writer for the *New Yorker* magazine under her chosen name.

In her first collection of stories, *At the Bottom of the River,* Kincaid shows an imposing capacity for detailing life's mundane aspects. This characteristic of her writing is readily evident in the oft-cited tale "Girl," which consists almost entirely of a mother's orders to her daughter: "Wash the white clothes on Monday and put them on the stone heap; wash the color clothes on Tuesday and put them on the clothesline to dry; don't walk barehead in the hot sun; cook pumpkin fritters in very hot sweet oil . . . ; on Sundays try to walk like a lady, and not like the slut you are so bent on becoming." Anne Tyler, in a review for *New Republic,* declared that this passage provides "the clearest idea of the book's general tone; for Jamaica Kincaid scrutinizes various particles of our world so closely and so solemnly that they begin to take on a nearly mystical importance." "The Letter from Home," also from *At the Bottom of the River,* serves as further illustration of Kincaid's style of repetition and her penchant for the mundane. In this tale a character recounts her daily chores in such a manner that the story resembles an incantation: "I milked the cows, I churned the butter, I stored the cheese, I baked the bread, I brewed the tea," Kincaid begins. In *Ms.,* Suzanne Freeman cited this tale as evidence that Kincaid's style is "akin to hymn-singing or maybe even chanting." Freeman added that Kincaid's "singsong style" produces "images that are as sweet and mysterious as the secrets that children whisper in your ear."

With the publication of *At the Bottom of the River,* Kincaid was hailed as an important new voice in American fiction. Edith Milton wrote in the *New York Times Book Review* that Kincaid's tales "have all the force of illumination, and even prophetic power," and David Leavitt noted in the *Village Voice* that they move "with grace and ease from the mundane to the enormous." He added that "Kincaid's particular skill lies in her ability to articulate the internal workings of a potent imagination without sacrificing the rich details of the external world on which that imagination thrives." Doris Grumbach expressed similar praise in a review for the *Washington Post Book World.* She declared that the world of Kincaid's narrators "hovers between fantasy and reality," and she asserted that Kincaid's prose "results not so much in stories as in states of consciousness." Grumbach also noted that

Kincaid's style, particularly its emphasis on repetition, intensifies "the feelings of poetic jubilation Kincaid has . . . for all life."

That exuberance for life is also evident in Kincaid's second book, *Annie John,* which contains interrelated stories about a girl's maturation in Antigua. In *Annie John* the title character evolves from a young girl to an aspiring nurse and from innocent to realist: she experiences her first menstruation, buries a friend, gradually establishes a life independent of her mother, and overcomes a serious illness. She is ultimately torn by her pursuit of a career outside her life in Antigua, and Kincaid renders that feeling so incisively that, as Elaine Kendall noted in her review for the *Los Angeles Times,* "you can almost believe Kincaid invented ambivalence." Critically acclaimed as a coming-of-age novel, *Annie John* was praised by a number of reviewers for expressing qualities of growing up that transcend geographical locations. "Her work is recollections of childhood," Paula Bonnell remarked in the *Boston Herald.* "It conveys the mysterious power and intensity of childhood attachments to mother, father and friends, and the adolescent beginnings of separation from them." Susan Kenney, writing in the *New York Times Book Review,* noted Annie John's ambivalence about leaving behind her life in Antigua and declared that such ambivalence was "an inevitable and unavoidable result of growing up." Kenney concluded that Kincaid's story is "so touching and familiar . . . so inevitable [that] it could be happening to any of us, anywhere, any time, any place. And that's exactly the book's strength, its wisdom, and its truth."

Kincaid's second novel, *Lucy,* is a first-person narrative in which nineteen-year-old Lucy not only expresses feelings of rage, but struggles with separation from her homeland and especially her mother. *Lucy* is about a young woman from Antigua who comes to an unnamed American city to work as an *au pair* girl. She is employed by a wealthy, white couple—Mariah and Lewis—to take care of their four young daughters. In the *Washington Post Book World,* Susanna Moore commented: "Lucy is unworldly. She has never seen snow or been in an elevator. . . . Written in the first person, [the novel] is Lucy's story of the year of her journey—away from her mother, away from home, away from the island and into the world." Richard Eder mused in the *Los Angeles Times Book Review* that "The anger of Lucy . . . is an instrument of discovery, not destruction. It is lucid and cool, but by no means unsparing." The novel ends with Lucy writing in a journal given to her by Mariah, the woman for whom she works, and weeping over the very first line: "'I wish I could love someone so much that I would die from it.' And then as I looked at this sentence a great wave of shame came over me and I wept and wept so much that the tears fell on the page and caused all the words to become one great blur." Eder ended his review saying, "she will turn the page and go on writing." Derek Walcott, a West Indian poet, talked with Garis in the *New York Times Magazine* about Kincaid's identification with issues that thread through all people's lives: "That relationship of mother and daughter—today she loves her mother, tomorrow she hates her, then she admires her—that is so true to life, without any artificiality, that it describes parental and filial love in a way that has never been done before. [Kincaid's] work is so full of spiritual contradictions clarified that it's extremely profound and courageous." Thulani Davis, writing in the *New York Times Book Review* said, "Ms. Kincaid is a marvelous writer whose descriptions are richly detailed; her sentences turn and surprise even in the bare context she has created, in which there are few colors, sights or smells and the moments of intimacy and confrontation take place in the wings, or just after the door closes. . . . Lucy is a delicate, careful observer, but her rage prevents her from reveling in the deliciousness of a moment. At her happiest, she simply says, 'Life isn't so bad after all.'"

The Autobiography of My Mother, Kincaid's third novel, follows her previous fictional efforts in its West Indies setting and vivid, poetic prose. The book's narrator, Xuela, is an elderly woman who recounts her difficult life, beginning with the death of her mother at Xuela's birth. In what reviewers termed a chilling, unsparing tone, Xuela describes her childhood abuse at the hands of a stepmother; the corruption of her father, a policeman; and the abortion of her unborn child, after she realizes that the baby is intended for the baby's father and his barren wife. At the end of the novel, the narrator calls her account a story of the mother she never knew, of her unborn baby, and of "the voices that should have come out of me, the faces I never allowed to form, the eyes I never allowed to see me," as quoted by Dale Peck in the *London Review of Books.* As with the author's earlier works, *The Autobiography of My Mother* received significant critical praise, especially for Kincaid's lyrical writing style. "Kincaid has written a truly ugly meditation on life in some of the most beautiful prose we are likely to find in contemporary fiction," averred Cathleen Schine in the *New York Times Book Review. Maclean's* reviewer Diane Turbide concurred, noting, "Kincaid employs an almost incantatory tone, using repetition and unusual syntax to give the book a hypnotic rhythm." Several reviewers commented that Kincaid's striking prose was not matched by the novel's thematic development. Schine wrote that "there is . . . something dull and unconvincing about Xuela's anguish." And according to Peck, "The prose is lovely . . . and, I would argue, distinctly, beautifully American, yet the sentiments expressed by the words themselves are trite, falsely universalising, and often just muddled." However, *Time* reviewer John Skow stated, "The reward here, as always with Kincaid's work, is the reading of her clear, bitter prose." The novel was a finalist for the National Book Critics Circle Award for fiction in 1997.

Henry Louis Gates, Jr., a distinguished critic and black studies scholar, told Emily Listfield in *Harper's Bazaar* that he felt comfortable comparing Kincaid's work to that of Toni Morrison and Wole Soyinka: "There is a self-contained world which they explore with great detail. Not to chart the existence of that world, but to show that human emotions manifest themselves everywhere." Gates said that an important contribution of Kincaid is that "she never feels the necessity of claiming the existence of a black world or a female sensibility. She assumes them both. I think it's a distinct departure that she's making, and I think that more and more black American writers will assume their world the way that she does. So that we can get beyond the large theme of racism and get to the deeper themes of how black people love and cry and live and die. Which, after all, is what art is all about."

With her memoir, *My Brother,* Kincaid recounts the last years of life of her brother, Devon Drew, who died of AIDS at the age of 33. Kincaid left the island of Antigua when her brother was three; when she returns, they are strangers to each other. She only learns about her brother's bisexuality after his death. Kincaid reveals that during the period in which she was buying medication from the United States for him, her brother was still engaging in unprotected sex. The reader also learns that her brother was a drug addict and that he had served time in prison for his involvement in a murder. While *My Brother* provides a portrait of the author's sibling, it also explores Kincaid's own reactions to her brother's life and death. The book returns to ground that was made familiar in Kincaid's earlier works, offering another look at Antigua, which here she describes as homophobic, and revisiting her difficult relationship with her mother. *My Brother* received significant praise from critics. As with the author's previous works, reviewers pointed to her distinctive writing style.

Anna Quindlen in the *New York Times Book Review* noted that Kincaid's "endless incantatory sentences [are] a contrast to the simple words and images—a tower built of small bricks." Even though she pointed out that "the unadorned, often flat style of Kincaid's prose can occasionally feel perfunctory," Quindlen argued that "its great advantage is that within the simple setting the observations glow." Regarding the memoir's narrative structure, Gay Wachman in the *Nation* maintained that "the lucid, assertive, deceptively simple voice takes its time in fleshing out the figures of the memoir, both in their present and in the past, circling around Devon and the multiple meanings of his life, illness and death." Referring to "the measured and limpid simplicity of her prose," Deborah E. McDowell in the *Women's Review of Books* linked *My Brother* to earlier works by the author in declaring that "despite the grimness of her work, few writers have made the aesthetics of death and darkness more luminous than has Jamaica Kincaid."

BIOGRAPHICAL/CRITICAL SOURCES:

BOOKS

Black Literature Criticism, Volume 2, Gale, 1991.

Bloom, Harold, editor, *Jamaica Kincaid,* Chelsea House, 1998.

Contemporary Literary Criticism, Gale, Volume 43, 1987, Volume 68, 1991.

Cudjoe, Selwyn R., editor, *Caribbean Women Writers: Essays from the First International Conference,* Callaloo, 1990.

Dance, D. Cumber, editor, *Fifty Caribbean Writers,* Greenwood (Westport, CT), 1986.

Ferguson, Moira, *Jamaica Kincaid: Where the Land Meets the Body,* University Press of Virginia (Charlottesville), 1994.

Kincaid, Jamaica, *At the Bottom of the River,* Farrar, Straus, 1983.

Kincaid, *Lucy,* Farrar, Straus, 1990.

Kincaid, *The Autobiography of My Mother,* Farrar, Straus, 1995.

Mistron, Deborah E., *Understanding Jamaica Kincaid's "Annie John": A Student Casebook to Issues, Sources, and Historical Documents,* Greenwood Press, 1998.

Simmons, Diane, *Jamaica Kincaid,* Macmillan (New York City), 1994.

PERIODICALS

Atlantic, May, 1985.
Boston Herald, March 31, 1985.
Christian Science Monitor, April 5, 1985.
Essence, March, 1996, p. 98.
Harper's Bazaar, October, 1990; January, 1996, p. 66.
Hudson Review, autumn, 1996, p. 483.
Interview, October, 1997, p. 94.
Library Journal, December 1, 1989.
Listener, January 10, 1985.
London Review of Books, February 6, 1997, p. 25.
Los Angeles Times, April 25, 1985.
Los Angeles Times Book Review, October 21, 1990.
Maclean's, May 20, 1985; April 8, 1996, p. 72.
Mother Jones, September-October, 1997, p. 28.
Ms., January, 1984.
Nation, June 15, 1985; February 5, 1996, p. 23; November 3, 1997, p. 43.
New Republic, December 31, 1983.
New Statesman, September 7, 1984; October 11, 1996, p. 45.
New York Times Book Review, January 15, 1984; April 7, 1985; July 10, 1988; October 28, 1990; February 4, 1996, p. 5; October 19, 1997, p. 7.
New York Times Magazine, October 7, 1990.
People, February 19, 1996, p. 27; December 15, 1997, p. 109.
Time, February 5, 1996, p. 71.
Times Literary Supplement, November 29, 1985; September 20, 1996, p. 22.
Village Voice, January 17, 1984.
Virginia Quarterly Review, summer, 1985.
Voice Literary Supplement, April, 1985; February, 1996, p. 11.
Washington Post, April 2, 1985.
Washington Post Book World, October 7, 1990.
Women's Review of Books, January, 1998, p. 1.
World Literature Today, autumn, 1985.

OTHER

Interview with Jamaica Kincaid, conducted by Kay Bonetti, recorded for American Audio Prose Library (Bennington, VT), 1991.*

*   *   *

KING, Martin Luther, Jr. 1929-1968

PERSONAL: Given name, Michael, changed to Martin; born January 15, 1929, in Atlanta, GA; assassinated April 4, 1968, in Memphis, TN; originally buried in South View Cemetery, Atlanta; reinterred at Martin Luther King, Jr., Center for Nonviolent Social

Change, Atlanta; son of Martin Luther (a minister) and Alberta Christine (a teacher; maiden name, Williams) King; married Coretta Scott (a concert singer), June 18, 1953; children: Yolanda Denise, Martin Luther III, Dexter Scott, Bernice Albertine. *Education:* Morehouse College, B.A., 1948; Crozer Theological Seminary, B.D., 1951; Boston University, Ph.D., 1955, D.D., 1959; Chicago Theological Seminary, D.D., 1957; attended classes at University of Pennsylvania and Harvard University.

CAREER: Ordained Baptist minister, 1948; Dexter Avenue Baptist Church, Montgomery, AL, pastor, 1954-60; Southern Christian Leadership Conference (S.C.L.C.), Atlanta, GA, founder, 1957, and president, 1957-68; Ebenezer Baptist Church, Atlanta, co-pastor with his father, 1960-68. Vice-president, National Sunday School and Baptist Teaching Union Congress of National Baptist Convention; president, Montgomery Improvement Association.

MEMBER: National Association for the Advancement of Colored People (NAACP), Alpha Phi Alpha, Sigma Pi Phi, Elks.

AWARDS, HONORS: Selected one of ten outstanding personalities of 1956 by *Time* magazine, 1957; Spingarn Medal, NAACP, 1957; L.H.D., Morehouse College, 1957, and Central State College, 1958; L.L.D., Howard University, 1957, and Morgan State College, 1958; Anisfield-Wolf Award, 1958, for *Stride Toward Freedom; Time* Man of the Year, 1963; Nobel Prize for Peace, 1964; Judaism and World Peace Award, Synagogue Council of America, 1965; Brotherhood Award, 1967, for *Where Do We Go from Here: Chaos or Community?;* Nehru Award for International Understanding, 1968; Presidential Medal of Freedom, 1977; received numerous awards for leadership of Montgomery Movement; two literary prizes were named in his honor by National Book Committee and Harper & Row.

WRITINGS:

Stride toward Freedom: The Montgomery Story, Harper, 1958.
The Measure of a Man, Christian Education Press (Philadelphia), 1959, memorial edition, Pilgrim Press, 1968.
Pilgrimage to Nonviolence (monograph; originally published in *Christian Century*), Fellowship of Reconciliation, 1960.
Letter from Birmingham City Jail, American Friends Service Committee, 1963, published as *Letter*

from Birmingham Jail (also see below), Overbrook Press, 1968, reprinted, Harper, 1994.
Why We Can't Wait (includes *Letter from Birmingham Jail*), Harper, 1964.
Where Do We Go from Here: Chaos or Community?, Harper, 1967, memorial edition with an introduction by wife, Coretta Scott King, Bantam, 1968 (published in England as *Chaos or Community?,* Hodder & Stoughton, 1968).
(Author of introduction) William Bradford Huie, *Three Lives for Mississippi,* New American Library, 1968.
(Contributor) John Henrik Clarke and others, editors, *Black Titan: W. E. B. Du Bois,* Beacon Press, 1970.
I've Been to the Mountaintop, HarperSanFrancisco, 1994.
The Autobiography of Martin Luther King, Jr., edited by Clayborne Carson, Warner Books, 1998.
A Knock at Midnight: Inspiration from the Great Sermons of Reverend Martin Luther King, Jr., edited by Clayborne Carson and Peter Holloran, Intellectual Properties Management in association with Warner Books, 1998.

Works represented in anthologies. Contributor to periodicals, including *Harper's, Nation,* and *Christian Century.*

SPEECHES

The Montgomery Story, [San Francisco, CA], 1956.
I Have a Dream, John Henry and Mary Louise Dunn Bryant Foundation (Los Angeles), 1963.
Nobel Lecture, Harper, 1965.
Address at Valedictory Service, University of the West Indies (Mona, Jamaica), 1965.
The Ware Lecture, Unitarian Universalist Association (Boston), 1966.
Conscience for Change, Canadian Broadcasting Co., 1967.
Beyond Vietnam, Altoan Press, 1967.
Declaration of Independence from the War in Vietnam, [New York], 1967. *A Drum Major for Justice,* Taurus Press, 1969.
A Testament of Hope (originally published in *Playboy,* January, 1969), Fellowship of Reconciliation, 1969.

OMNIBUS VOLUMES

Unwise and Untimely? (letters; originally appeared in *Liberation,* June, 1963), Fellowship of Reconciliation, 1963.

Strength to Love (sermons), Harper, 1963, large print edition, Walker, 1996.

A Martin Luther King Treasury, Educational Heritage (New York City), 1964.

The Wisdom of Martin Luther King in His Own Words, edited by staff of Bill Alder Books, Lancer Books, 1968.

"I Have a Dream": The Quotations of Martin Luther King, Jr., edited and compiled by Lotte Hoskins, Grosset, 1968.

The Trumpet of Conscience (transcripts of radio broadcasts), introduction by C. S. King, Harper, 1968.

We Shall Live in Peace: The Teachings of Martin Luther King, Jr., edited by Deloris Harrison, Hawthorn, 1968.

Speeches about Vietnam, Clergy and Laymen Concerned About Vietnam (New York City), 1969.

A Martin Luther King Reader, edited by Nissim Ezekiel, Popular Prakashan (Bombay), 1969.

Words and Wisdom of Martin Luther King, Taurus Press, 1970.

Speeches of Martin Luther King, Jr., commemorative edition, Martin Luther King, Jr., Memorial Center (Atlanta), 1972.

Loving Your Enemies, Letter from Birmingham Jail [and] *Declaration of Independence from the War in Vietnam,* A. J. Muste Memorial Institute, 1981.

The Words of Martin Luther King, Jr., edited and with an introduction by C. S. King, Newmarket Press, 1983.

A Testament of Hope: The Essential Writings of Martin Luther King, Jr., edited by James Melvin Washington, Harper, 1986.

The Papers of Martin Luther King, Jr.: Birth of a New Age, December 1955—December 1956 (Volume 3), University of California Press, 1997.

SIDELIGHTS: "We've got some difficult days ahead," civil rights activist Martin Luther King, Jr., told a crowd gathered at Memphis's Clayborn Temple on April 3, 1968, in a speech now collected in *The Words of Martin Luther King, Jr.* "But it really doesn't matter to me now," he continued, "because I've been to the mountaintop. . . . And I've seen the promised land. I may not get there with you. But I want you to know tonight that we as a people will get to the promised land." Uttered the day before his assassination, King's words were prophetic of his death. They were also a challenge to those he left behind to see that his "promised land" of racial equality became a reality; a reality to which King devoted the last twelve years of his life.

Just as important as King's dream was the way he chose to achieve it: through nonviolent resistance. He embraced nonviolence as a method for social reform after being introduced to the nonviolent philosophy of Mahatma Gandhi while doing graduate work at Pennsylvania's Crozer Seminary. Gandhi had led a bloodless revolution against British colonial rule in India. According to Stephen B. Oates in *Let the Trumpet Sound: The Life of Martin Luther King, Jr.,* King became "convinced that Gandhi's was the only moral and practical way for oppressed people to struggle against social injustice."

What King achieved during the little over a decade that he worked in civil rights was remarkable. "Rarely has one individual," noted Flip Schulke and Penelope O. McPhee in *King Remembered,* "espousing so difficult a philosophy, served as a catalyst for so much significant social change. . . . There are few men of whom it can be said their lives changed the world. But at his death the American South hardly resembled the land where King was born. In the twelve years between the Montgomery bus boycott and King's assassination, Jim Crow was legally eradicated in the South."

The first public test of King's adherence to the nonviolent philosophy came in December, 1955, when he was elected president of the Montgomery [Alabama] Improvement Association (M.I.A.), a group formed to protest the arrest of Rosa Parks, a black woman who refused to give up her bus seat to a white passenger. Planning to end the humiliating treatment of blacks on city bus lines, King organized a bus boycott that was to last more than a year. Despite receiving numerous threatening phone calls, being arrested, and having his home bombed, King and his boycott prevailed. Eventually, the U.S. Supreme Court declared Montgomery's bus segregation laws illegal and, in December, 1956, King rode on Montgomery's first integrated bus.

"Montgomery was the soil," wrote King's widow in her autobiography, *My Life with Martin Luther King, Jr.,* "in which the seed of a new theory of social action took root. Black people found in nonviolent, direct action a militant method that avoided violence but achieved dramatic confrontation which electrified and educated the whole nation."

King was soon selected president of an organization of much wider scope than the M.I.A., the Southern Christian Leadership Conference (S.C.L.C.). The members of this group were black leaders from throughout the South, many of them ministers like King. Their immediate goal was for increased black voter registration in the South with an eventual elimination of segregation.

1957 found King drawn more and more into the role of national and even international spokesman for civil rights. In February a *Time* magazine cover story on King called him "a scholarly . . . Baptist minister . . . who in little more than a year has risen from nowhere to become one of the nation's remarkable leaders of men." In March, he was invited to speak at the ceremonies marking the independence from Great Britain of the new African republic of Ghana.

The following year, King's first book, *Stride toward Freedom: The Montgomery Story,* which told the history of the boycott, was published. *New York Times* contributor Abel Plenn called the work "a document of far-reaching importance for present and future chroniclings of the struggle for civil rights in this country." A *Times Literary Supplement* writer quoted U.S. Episcopalian Bishop James Pike's reaction to the book: *Stride toward Freedom* "may well become a Christian classic. It is a rare combination: sound theology and ethics, and the autobiography of one of the greatest men of our time."

In 1959, two important events happened. First, King and his wife were able to make their long-awaited trip to India where they visited the sites of Gandhi's struggle against the British and met with people who had been acquainted with the Indian leader. Second, King resigned as pastor of Dexter Avenue Baptist Church in Montgomery so he could be closer to S.C.L.C.'s headquarters in Atlanta and devote more of his time to the civil rights effort.

King's trip to India seemed to help make up his mind to move to Atlanta. The trip greatly inspired King, as Oates observed: "He came home with a deeper understanding of nonviolence and a deep commitment as well. For him, nonviolence was no longer just a philosophy and a technique of social change; it was now a whole way of life."

Despite his adherence to the nonviolent philosophy, King was unable to avoid the bloodshed that was to follow. Near the end of 1962, he decided to focus his energies on the desegregation of Birmingham, Alabama. Alabama's capital was at that time what King called in his book *Why We Can't Wait,* "the most segregated city in America," but that was precisely why he had chosen it as his target.

In *Why We Can't Wait* King detailed the advance planning that was the key to the success of the Birmingham campaign. Most important was the training in nonviolent techniques given by the S.C.L.C.'s Leadership Training Committee to those who volunteered to participate in the demonstrations. "The focus of these training sessions," King noted in his book, "was the socio-dramas designed to prepare the demonstrators for some of the challenges they could expect to face. The harsh language and physical abuse of the police and self-appointed guardians of the law were frankly presented, along with the non-violent creed in action: to resist without bitterness; to be cursed and not reply; to be beaten and not hit back."

One of the unusual aspects of the Birmingham campaign was King's decision to use children in the demonstrations. When the protests came to a head on May 3, 1963, it was after nearly 1,000 young people had been arrested the previous day. As another wave of protestors, mostly children and teenagers, took to the streets, they were hit with jets of water from fire hoses. Police dogs were then released on the youngsters.

The photographs circulated by the media of children being beaten down by jets of water and bitten by dogs brought cries of outrage from throughout the country and the world. U.S. president John F. Kennedy sent a Justice Department representative to Birmingham to work for a peaceful solution to the problem. Within a week negotiators produced an agreement that met King's major demands, including desegregation of lunch counters, restrooms, fitting rooms, and drinking fountains in the city and the hiring of blacks in positions previously closed to them.

Although the Birmingham campaign ended in triumph for King, at the outset he was criticized for his efforts. Imprisoned at the beginning of the protest for disobeying a court injunction forbidding him from leading any demonstrations in Birmingham, King spent some of his time in jail composing an open letter answering his critics. This document, called *Letter from Birmingham Jail,* appeared later in his book *Why We Can't Wait.* Oates viewed the letter as "a classic in protest literature, the most elegant and learned expression of the goals and philosophy of the nonviolent movement ever written."

In the letter King addressed those who said that as an outsider he had no business in Birmingham. King reasoned: "I am in Birmingham because injustice is here. . . . I cannot sit idly by in Atlanta and not be concerned about what happens in Birmingham. Injustice anywhere is a threat to justice everywhere. We are caught in an inescapable network of mutuality, tied in a single garment of destiny."

Another important event of 1963 was a massive march on Washington, D.C., which King planned together with leaders of other civil rights organizations. When the day of the march came, an estimated 250,000 people were on hand to hear King and other dignitaries speak at the march's end point, the Lincoln Memorial. While King's biographers noted that the young minister struggled all night writing words to inspire his people on this historic occasion, when his turn came to speak, he deviated from his prepared text and gave a speech that Schulke and McPhee called "the most eloquent of his career." In the speech, which contained the rhythmic repetition of the phrase "I have a dream," King painted a vision of the "promised land" of racial equality and justice for all, which he would return to often in speeches and sermons in the years to come, including his final speech in Memphis. Schulke and McPhee explained the impact of the day: "The orderly conduct of the massive march was an active tribute to [King's] philosophy of non-violence. Equally significant, his speech made his voice familiar to the world and lives today as one of the most moving orations of our time."

On January 3, 1964, King was proclaimed "Man of the Year" by *Time* magazine, the first black to be so honored. Later that same year, King's book, *Why We Can't Wait,* was published. In the book King gave his explanation of why 1963 was such a critical year for the civil rights movement. He believed that celebrations commemorating the 100-year-anniversary of Lincoln's Emancipation Proclamation reminded American blacks of the irony that while Lincoln made the slaves free in the nineteenth century, their twentieth-century grandchildren still did not feel free.

Reviewers generally hailed the work as an important document in the history of the civil rights movement. In *Book Week,* J. B. Donovan called it "a basic handbook on non-violent direct action." *Critic* contributor C. S. Stone praised the book's "logic and eloquence" and observed that it aimed a death blow "at two American dogmas—racial discrimination, and the even more insidious doctrine that nourishes it, gradualism."

In December of 1964, King received the Nobel Peace Prize, becoming the twelfth American, the third black, and the youngest—he was thirty-five—person

ever to receive the award. He donated the $54,600 prize to the S.C.L.C. and other civil rights groups. The Nobel Prize gave King even wider recognition as a world leader. "Overnight," commented Schulke and McPhee, "King became . . . a symbol of world peace. He knew that if the Nobel Prize was to mean anything, he must commit himself more than ever to attaining the goals of the black movement through peace."

The next two years were marked by both triumph and despair. First came King's campaign for voting rights, concentrating on a voters registration drive in Selma, Alabama. Selma would be, according to Oates, "King's finest hour." Voting rights had been a major concern of King's since as early as 1957 but, unfortunately, little progress had been made. In the country surrounding Selma, for example, only 335 of 32,700 blacks were registered voters. Various impediments to black registration, including poll taxes and complicated literacy tests, were common throughout the South.

Demonstrations continued through February and on into early March, 1965, in Selma. One day nearly 500 school children were arrested and charged with juvenile delinquency after they cut classes to show their support for King. In another incident, more than 100 adults were arrested when they picketed the county courthouse. On March 7, state troopers beat nonviolent demonstrators who were trying to march from Selma to Montgomery to present their demands to Alabama governor George Wallace.

Angered by such confrontations, King sent telegrams to religious leaders throughout the nation calling for them to meet in Selma for a "ministers' march" to Montgomery. Although some 1,500 marchers assembled, they were again turned back by a line of state troopers, but this time violence was avoided. King was elated by the show of support he received from the religious leaders from around the country who joined him in the march, but his joy soon turned to sorrow when he learned later that same day that several of the white ministers who had marched with him had been beaten by club-wielding whites. One of them died two days later.

The brutal murder of a clergyman seemed to focus the attention of the nation on Selma. Within a few days, President Lyndon B. Johnson made a televised appearance before a joint session of Congress in which he demanded passage of a voting rights bill. In the speech Johnson compared the sites of revolutionary war battles such as Concord and Lexington with their modern-day counterpart, Selma, Alabama. Although Johnson had invited King to be his special guest in the Senate gallery during the address, King declined the honor, staying instead in Selma to complete plans to again march on Montgomery. A federal judge had given his approval to the proposed Selma-to-Montgomery march and had ordered Alabama officials not to interfere. The five-day march finally took place as hundreds of federal troops stood by overseeing the safety of the marchers.

Later that year, Johnson signed the 1965 Voting Rights Act into law, this time with King looking on. The act made literacy tests as a requirement for voting illegal, gave the Attorney General the power to supervise federal elections in seven southern states, and urged the Attorney General to challenge the legality of poll taxes in state and local elections in four Southern states. "Political analysts," Oates observed, "almost unanimously attributed the voting act to King's Selma campaign. . . . Now, thanks to his own political sagacity, his understanding of how nonviolent, direct-action protest could stimulate corrective federal legislation, King's long crusade to gain southern Negroes the right to vote . . . was about to be realized."

By this time, King was ready to embark on his next project, moving his nonviolent campaign to the black ghettoes of the North. Chicago was chosen as his first target, but the campaign did not go the way King had planned. Rioting broke out in the city just two days after King initiated his program. He did sign an open-housing agreement with Chicago mayor Richard Daley but, according to Oates, many blacks felt it accomplished little.

Discord was beginning to be felt within the civil rights movement. King was afraid that advocates of "black power" would doom his dream of a nonviolent black revolution. In his next book, *Where Do We Go from Here: Chaos or Community?,* published in 1967, he explored his differences with those using the "black power" slogan.

According to *New York Times Book Review* contributor Gene Roberts, while King admitted in the volume that black power leaders "foster[ed] racial pride and self-help programs," he also expressed regret that the slogan itself produced "fear among whites and [made] it more difficult to fashion a meaningful interracial political coalition. But above all, he [deplored] . . . an acceptance of violence by many in the movement."

In the *Saturday Review* Milton R. Knovitz noted other criticisms of the movement which King voiced in the book. King saw black power as "negative, even nihilistic in its direction," "rooted in hopelessness and pessimism," and "committed to racial—and ethical—separatism." In *America,* R. F. Drinan wrote, "Dr. King's analysis of the implications of the black power movement is possibly the most reasoned rejection of the concept by any major civil rights leader in the country."

Where Do We Go from Here touched on several issues that became King's major concerns during the last two years of his life. He expressed the desire to continue nonviolent demonstrations in the North, to stop the war in Vietnam, and to join underprivileged persons of all races in a coalition against poverty.

His first wish never materialized. Instead of nonviolent protest, riots broke out in Boston, Detroit, Milwaukee and more than thirty other U.S. cities between the time King finished the manuscript for the book and when it was published in late summer. By that time, King had already spoken out several times on Vietnam. His first speech to be entirely devoted to the topic was given on April 15, 1967, at a huge antiwar rally held at the United Nations Building in New York City. Even though some of King's followers begged him not to participate in antiwar activities, fearful that King's actions would antagonize the Johnson administration which had been so supportive in civil rights matters, King could not be dissuaded.

In *The Trumpet of Conscience,* a collection of radio addresses published posthumously, King explained why speaking out on Vietnam was so important to him. He wrote: "I cannot forget that the Nobel Prize for Peace was also a commission—a commission to work harder than I ever worked before for the 'brotherhood of man.' This is a calling which takes me beyond national allegiances." Commenting on King's opposition to the war, Coretta King observed that her husband's "peace activity marked incontestably a major turning point in the thinking of the nation. . . . I think history will mark his boldness in speaking out so early and eloquently—despite singularly virulent opposition—as one of his major contributions."

When King was assassinated in Memphis on April 4, 1968, he was in the midst of planning his Poor People's Campaign. Plans called for recruitment and training in nonviolent techniques of 3,000 poor people from each of fifteen different parts of the country. The campaign would culminate when they were brought to Washington, D.C., to disrupt government operations until effective antipoverty legislation was enacted.

On hearing of King's death, angry blacks in 125 cities across the nation rioted. As a result, thirty people died, hundreds suffered injuries, and more than $30 million worth of property damage was incurred. But, fortunately, rioting was not the only response to his death. Accolades came from around the world as one by one world leaders paid their respects to the martyred man of peace. Eventually, King's widow and other close associates saw to it that a permanent memorial—the establishment of Martin Luther King, Jr.'s birthday as a national holiday in the United States—would assure that his memory would live on forever.

In her introduction to *The Trumpet of Conscience,* Coretta King quoted from one of King's most famous speeches as she gave her thoughts on how she hoped future generations would remember her husband. "Remember him," she wrote, "as a man who tried to be 'a drum major for justice, a drum major for peace, a drum major for righteousness.' Remember him as a man who refused to lose faith in the ultimate redemption of mankind."

BIOGRAPHICAL/CRITICAL SOURCES:

BOOKS

Abernathy, Donzaleigh, *Partners to History: Martin Luther King, Jr., Ralph David Abernathy, and the Civil Rights Movement,* foreword by Robert F. Kennedy, Jr., General, 1998.

Daldwin, Lewis V., *Toward the Beloved Community: Martin Luther King Jr. and South Africa,* Pilgrim Press, 1995.

Bennett, Lerone, Jr., *What Manner of Man,* Johnson Publishing (Chicago, IL), 1964.

Bishop, Jim, *The Days of Martin Luther King, Jr.,* Putnam, 1971.

Bleiweiss, Robert M., editor, *Marching to Freedom: The Life of Martin Luther King, Jr.,* New American Library, 1971.

Branch, Taylor, *Pillar of Fire: America in the King Years, 1963-65,* Simon & Schuster, 1998.

Chinula, Donald M., *Building King's Beloved Community: Foundations for Pastoral Care and Counseling with the Oppressed,* United Church Press, 1997.

Clayton, Edward T., *Martin Luther King, Jr.: The Peaceful Warrior,* Prentice-Hall, 1968.

Colbert, Jan, and Ann McMillan Harms, editors, *Dear Dr. King: Letters from Today's Children to Dr. Martin Luther King, Jr.,* photographs by Ernest C. Withers and Roy Cajero, Hyperion Books for Children, 1998.

Collins, David R., *Not Only Dreamers: The Story of Martin Luther King, Sr., and Martin Luther King, Jr.,* Brethren Press, 1986.

Cook, Anthony E., *The Least of These: Race, Law, and Religion in American Culture,* Routledge, 1997.

Davis, Lenwood G., *I Have a Dream: The Life and Times of Martin Luther King, Jr.,* Adams Book Co., 1969.

Daynes, Gary, *Making Villains, Making Heroes: Joseph R. McCarthy and Martin Luther King, Jr. in American Memory,* Garland, 1997.

Erskine, Noel Leo, *King among the Theologians,* Pilgrim Press, 1994.

Fairclough, Adam, *Martin Luther King, Jr.,* University of Georgia Press, 1995.

Frank, Gerold, *An American Death: The True Story of the Assassination of Dr. Martin Luther King, Jr., and the Greatest Manhunt of Our Time,* Doubleday, 1972.

Franklin, V. P., *Martin Luther King, Jr.,* Park Lane Press, 1998.

Garrett, George P., *The King of Babylon Shall Not Come against You,* Harcourt Brace, 1996.

Garrow, David J., *Bearing the Cross: Martin Luther King, Jr., and the Southern Christian Leadership Conference,* Morrow, 1986.

Harding, Vincent, *Martin Luther King, The Inconvenient Hero,* Orbis Books, 1996.

Harrison, Deloris, editor, *We Shall Live in Peace: The Teachings of Martin Luther King, Jr.,* Hawthorn, 1968.

Huie, William Bradford, *He Slew the Dreamer: My Search, with James Earl Ray, for the Truth about the Murder of Martin Luther King, Jr.,* Black Belt Press, 1997.

Ivory, Luther D., *Toward a Theology of Radical Involvement: The Theological Legacy of Martin Luther King, Jr.,* Abingdon Press (Nashville, TN), 1997.

Johnson, Charles Richard, *Dreamer: A Novel,* Scribners, 1998.

King, Coretta Scott, *My Life with Martin Luther King, Jr.,* Holt, 1969.

King, Martin Luther, Jr., *The Trumpet of Conscience,* with an introduction by Coretta Scott King, Harper, 1968.

King, Martin Luther, Jr., *The Words of Martin Luther King, Jr.,* edited and with an introduction by Coretta Scott King, Newmarket Press, 1983.

Lewis, David, L., *King: A Critical Biography,* Praeger, 1970.

Lincoln, Eric C., editor, *Martin Luther King, Jr.: A Profile,* Hill & Wang, 1970, revised edition, 1984.

Lischer, Richard, *The Preacher King: Martin Luther King, Jr. and the Word that Moved America,* Oxford University Press, 1995.

Lokos, Lionel, *House Divided: The Life and Legacy of Martin Luther King,* Arlington House, 1968.

Lomax, Louis E., *To Kill a Black Man,* Holloway, 1968.

Martin Luther King, Jr.: The Journey of a Martyr, Universal Publishing & Distributing, 1968.

Martin Luther King, Jr., 1929-1968, Johnson Publishing (Chicago, IL), 1968.

Martin Luther King, Jr., Norton, 1976.

McKnight, Gerald D., *The Last Crusade: Martin Luther King, Jr., the FBI, and the Poor People's Campaign,* Westview Press (Boulder, CO), 1997.

Miller, Keith D., *Voice of Deliverance: The Language of Martin Luther King, Jr., and Its Sources,* University of Georgia Press, 1998.

Miller, William Robert, *Martin Luther King, Jr.: His Life, Martyrdom, and Meaning for the World,* Weybright, 1968.

Moses, Greg, *Martin Luther King, Jr., and the Logic of Nonviolence,* Guilford Press (New York City), 1996.

Moses, Greg, *Revolution of Conscience: Martin Luther King, Jr., and the Philosophy of Nonviolence,* Guilford Press, 1997.

Murray, Peter, *Dreams: The Story of Martin Luther King, Jr.,* Child's World (Plymouth, MN), 1996.

Oates, Stephen B., *Let the Trumpet Sound: The Life of Martin Luther King, Jr.,* Harper, 1982.

Odey, John Okwoeze, *Nigeria, Search for Peace and Social Justice: The Relevance of the Philosophical and Theological Foundations of the Nonviolent Resistance of Martin Luther King, Junior,* Snaap Press, 1997.

Paulsen, Gary and Dan Theis, *The Man Who Climbed the Mountain: Martin Luther King,* Raintree, 1976.

Pepper, William, *Conspiracy: The Truth behind Martin Luther King Jr.'s Murder,* HarperCollins, 1995.

Pepper, William, *Orders to Kill: The Truth behind the Murder of Martin Luther King,* Carroll & Graf, 1995.

Playboy Interviews, Playboy Press, 1967.

Posner, Gerald L., *Killing the Dream: James Earl Ray and the Assassination of Martin Luther King, Jr.,* Random House, 1998.

Ray, James Earl, *Who Killed Martin Luther King?: The True Story by the Alleged Assassin,* Marlowe, 1997.

Roop, Peter and Connie, *Dr. Martin Luther King Jr.,* Heinemann Interactive Library, 1997.

Schulke, Flip, editor, *Martin Luther King, Jr.: A Documentary . . . Montgomery to Memphis,* with an introduction by Coretta Scott King, Norton, 1976.

Schulke, Flip and Penelope O. McPhee, *King Remembered,* with a foreword by Jesse Jackson, Norton, 1986.

Schuman, Michael, *Martin Luther King, Jr.: Leader for Civil Rights,* Enslow (Springfield, NJ), 1996.

Small, Mary Luins, *Creative Encounters with "Dear Dr. King": A Handbook of Discussions, Activities, and Engagements on Racial Injustice, Poverty, and War,* edited by Saunders Redding, Buckingham Enterprises, 1969.

Smith, Kenneth L. and Ira G. Zepp, Jr., *Search for the Beloved Community: The Thinking of Martin Luther King, Jr.,* Judson, 1974.

Stein, R. Conrad, *The Assassination of Martin Luther King, Jr.,* Children's Press (New York City), 1996.

Tucker, Deborah J., and Carrolyn A. Davis, *Unstoppable Man: A Bibliography,* Wayne State University (Detroit), 1994.

Vaughn, Wally G., and Richard W. Wills, editors, *Reflections on Our Pastor: Dr. Martin Luther King, Jr. at Dexter Avenue Baptist Church, 1954-1960,* Majority Press, 1998.

Westin, Alan, and Barry Mahoney, *The Trial of Martin Luther King,* Crowell, 1975.

Witherspoon, William Roger, *Martin Luther King, Jr.: To the Mountaintop,* Doubleday, 1985.

PERIODICALS

AB Bookman's Weekly, April 22, 1968.

America, August 17, 1963; October 31, 1964; July 22, 1967; April 20, 1968.

American Vision, January/February, 1986.

Antioch Review, spring, 1968.

Black Scholar, summer, 1992.

Books Abroad, autumn, 1970.

Book World, July 9, 1967; September 28, 1969.

Choice, February, 1968; June, 1995.

Christian Century, August 23, 1967; January 14, 1970; August 26, 1970.

Christian Science Monitor, July 6, 1967.

Commonweal, November 17, 1967; May 3, 1968; January 14, 1994, p. 10.

Critic, August, 1964.

Ebony, April, 1961; May, 1968; July, 1968; April, 1984; January, 1986; January, 1987; April, 1988; January, 1994, p. 21; February, 1994, p. 68; November, 1995, p. 54; January, 1996, p. 44.

Economist, April 6, 1968.

Esquire, August, 1968.

Harper's, February, 1961.

Jet, September 19, 1994, p. 6.

Life, April 19, 1968; January 10, 1969; September 12, 1969; September 19, 1969.

Listener, April 11, 1968; April 25, 1968.

Los Angeles Times Book Review, December 11, 1983.

National Review, February 13, 1987; February 27, 1987.

Negro Digest, August, 1968.

Negro History Bulletin, October, 1956; November, 1956; May, 1968.

New Republic, February 3, 1986; January 5, 1987.

New Statesman, March 22, 1968.

Newsweek, January 27, 1986.

New Yorker, June 22, 1967; July 22, 1967; April 13, 1968; February 24, 1986; April 6, 1987.

New York Herald Tribune, October 16, 1964.

New York Post, October 15, 1964.

New York Review of Books, August 24, 1967; January 15, 1987.

New York Times, October 12, 1958; October 15, 1964; July 12, 1967; April 12, 1968; April 13, 1968.

New York Times Book Review, September 3, 1967; February 16, 1969; February 16, 1986; November 30, 1986.

Punch, April 3, 1968.

Ramparts, May, 1968.

Saturday Review, July 8, 1967; April 20, 1968.

Time, February 18, 1957; January 3, 1964; February 5, 1965; February 12, 1965; April 19, 1968; October 3, 1969; January 27, 1986; January 19, 1987.

Times (London), April 6, 1968.

Times Literary Supplement, April 18, 1968.

Virginia Quarterly Review, autumn, 1968.

Washington Post, January 14, 1970.

Washington Post Book World, January 19, 1986; January 18, 1987.

OBITUARIES:

PERIODICALS

New York Times, April 5, 1968.

Time, April 12, 1968.

Times (London), April 5, 1968.*

KNIGHT, Etheridge 1931(?)-1991

PERSONAL: Born April 19, 1931 (one source says c. 1934), in Corinth, MS; died of lung cancer on March 10, 1991, in Indianapolis, IN; son of Bushie and Belzora (Cozart) Knight; married Sonia Sanchez (divorced); married Mary Ann McAnally, June 11, 1973 (divorced); married Charlene Blackburn; children: (second marriage) Mary Tandiwe, Etheridge Bambata; (third marriage) Isaac Bushie; (stepchildren) Morani Sanchez, Mongou Sanchez, Anita Sanchez. *Education:* Attended high school for two years; self-educated at "various prisons, jails." *Politics:* "Freedom." *Religion:* "Freedom."

CAREER: Poet. Writer-in-residence, University of Pittsburgh, Pittsburgh, PA, 1968-69, and University of Hartford, Hartford, CT, 1969-70; Lincoln University, Jefferson City, MO, poet-in-residence, 1972. Inmate at Indiana State Prison, Michigan City, 1960-68. *Military service:* U.S. Army, 1947-51, served in Guam, Hawaii, and Korea; became medical technician.

AWARDS, HONORS: National Endowment for the Arts grants, 1972 and 1980; National Book Award and Pulitzer Prize nominations, both 1973, for *Belly Song and Other Poems;* Self- Development through the Arts grant, for local workshops, 1974; Guggenheim fellowship, 1974.

WRITINGS:

(Contributor) *For Malcolm,* Broadside Press, 1967.

Poems from Prison, preface by Gwendolyn Brooks, Broadside Press, 1968.

(With others) *Voce Negre dal Carcere* (anthology), [Laterza, Italy], 1968, original English edition published as *Black Voices from Prison,* introduction by Roberto Giammanco, Pathfinder Press, 1970.

A Poem for Brother/Man (after His Recovery from an O.D.), Broadside Press, 1972.

Belly Song and Other Poems, Broadside Press, 1973.

Born of a Woman: New and Selected Poems, Houghton, 1980.

The Essential Etheridge Knight, University of Pittsburgh Press, 1986.

Work represented in many anthologies, including *Norton Anthology of American Poets, Black Poets, A Broadside Treasury,Broadside Poet, Dices and Black Bones* and *A Comprehensive Anthology of Black Poets.* Contributor of poems and articles to many magazines and journals, including *Black Digest, Essence, Motive, American Report* and *American Poetry.* Poetry editor, *Motive,* 1969- 71; contributing editor, *New Letters,* 1974.

SIDELIGHTS: Etheridge Knight began writing poetry while an inmate at the Indiana State Prison and published his first collection, *Poems from Prison* in 1968. "His work was hailed by black writers and critics as another excellent example of the powerful truth of blackness in art," writes Shirley Lumpkin in the *Dictionary of Literary Biography.* "His work became important in Afro-American poetry and poetics and in the strain of Anglo- American poetry descended from Walt Whitman." Since then, Knight has attained recognition as a major poet, earning both Pulitzer Prize and National Book Award nominations for *Belly Song and Other Poems* as well as the acclaim of such fellow practitioners as Gwendolyn Brooks, Robert Bly, and Galway Kinnell.

When Knight entered prison, he was already an accomplished reciter of "toasts"—long, memorized, narrative poems, often in rhymed couplets, in which "sexual exploits, drug activities, and violent aggressive conflicts involving a cast of familiar folk . . . are related . . . using street slang, drug and other specialized argot, and often obscenities," explains Lumpkin. Toast-reciting at Indiana State Prison not only refined Knight's expertise in this traditional Afro-American art form but also, according to Lumpkin, gave him a sense of identity and an understanding of the possibilities of poetry. "Since toast-telling brought him into genuine communion with others, he felt that poetry could simultaneously show him who he was and connect him with other people." In an article for the *Detroit Free Press* about Dudley Randall, the founder of Broadside Press, Suzanne Dolezal, indicates that Randall was impressed with Knight and visited him frequently at the prison: "In a small room reserved for consultations with death row inmates, with iron doors slamming and prisoners shouting in the background, Randall convinced a hesitant Knight of his talent." And says Dolezal, Randall feels that because Knight was from the streets, "He may be a deeper poet than many of the others because he has felt more anguish."

Much of Knight's prison poetry, according to Patricia Liggins Hill in *Black American Literature Forum* focuses on imprisonment as a form of contemporary enslavement and looks for ways in which one can be free despite incarceration. Time and space are significant in the concept of imprisonment, and Hill indi-

cates that "specifically, what Knight relies on for his prison poetry are various temporal/spatial elements which allow him to merge his personal consciousness with the consciousness of Black people." Hill believes that this merging of consciousness "sets him apart from the other new Black poets . . . [who] see themselves as poets/priests. . . . Knight sees himself as being one with Black people." Randall observes in *Broadside Memories: Poets I Have Known* that "Knight does not objure rime like many contemporary poets. He says the average Black man in the streets defines poetry as something that rimes, and Knight appeals to the folk by riming." Randall notes that while Knight's poetry is "influenced by the folk," it is also "prized by other poets."

Knight's *Born of a Woman: New and Selected Poems* includes work from *Poems from Prison, Black Voices from Prison* and *Belly Song and Other Poems.* Although David Pinckney states in *Parnassus: Poetry in Review* that the "new poems do not indicate much artistic growth," a *Virginia Quarterly Review* contributor writes that Knight "has distinguished his voice and craftsmanship among contemporary poets, and he deserves a large, serious audience for his work." Moreover, H. Bruce Franklin suggests in the *Village Voice* that with *Born of a Woman,* "Knight has finally attained recognition as a major poet." Further, Franklin credits Knight's leadership "in developing a powerful literary mode based on the rhythms of black street talk, blues, ballads, and 'toasts.'"

Reviewing *Born of a Woman* for *Black American Literature Forum* Hill describes Knight as a "masterful blues singer, a singer whose life has been 'full of trouble' and thus whose songs resound a variety of blues moods, feelings, and experiences and later take on the specific form of a blues musical composition." Lumpkin suggests that an "awareness of the significance of form governed Knight's arrangement of the poems in the volume as well as his revisions. . . . He put them in clusters or groupings under titles which are musical variations on the book's essential theme— life inside and outside prison." Calling this structure a "jazz composition mode," Lumpkin also notes that it was once used by Langston Hughes in an arrangement of his poetry. Craig Werner observes in *Obsidian: Black Literature in Review:* "Technically, Knight merges musical rhythms with traditional metrical devices, reflecting the assertion of an Afro-American cultural identity within a Euro-American context. Thematically, he denies that the figures of the singer . . . and the warrior . . . are or can be separate." Lumpkin finds that "despite the pain and evil described and attacked, a celebration and an affirmation of life run through the volume." And in the *Los Angeles Times Book Review* Peter Clothier considers the poems to be "tools for self- discovery and discovery of the world—a loud announcement of the truths they pry loose."

Lumpkin points out that "some critics find Knight's use of . . . [language] objectionable and unpoetic and think he does not use verse forms well," and some believe that he "maintains an outmoded, strident black power rhetoric from the 1960s." However, Lumpkin concludes: "Those with reservations and those who admire his work all agree . . . upon his vital language and the range of his subject matter. They all agree that he brings a needed freshness to poetry, particularly in his extraordinary ability to move an audience. . . . A number of poets, Gwendolyn Brooks, Robert Bly, and Galway Kinnell among them . . . consider him a major Afro-American poet because of his human subject matter, his combination of traditional techniques with an expertise in using rhythmic and oral speech patterns, and his ability to feel and to project his feelings into a poetic structure that moves others."

Knight told *Contemporary Authors* he believes a definition of art and aesthetics assumes that "every man is the master of his own destiny and comes to grips with the society by his own efforts. The 'true' artist is supposed to examine his own experience of this process as a reflection of his self, his ego." Knight feels "white society denies art, because art unifies rather than separates; it brings people together instead of alienating them." The western/European aesthetic dictates that "the artist speak only of the beautiful (himself and what *he sees*); his task is to edify the listener, to make him see *beauty* of the world." Black artists must stay away from this because "the red of this aesthetic rose got its color from the blood of black slaves, exterminated Indians, napalmed Vietnamese children." According to Knight, the black artist must "perceive and conceptualize the collective aspirations, the collective vision of black people, and through his art form give back to the people the truth that he has gotten from them. He must sing to them of their own deeds, and misdeeds."

BIOGRAPHICAL/CRITICAL SOURCES:

BOOKS

Contemporary Literary Criticism, Volume 40, Gale, 1986.

Dictionary of Literary Biography, Volume 41: *Afro-American Poets since 1955,* Gale, 1985.
Randall, Dudley, *Broadside Memories: Poets I Have Known,* Broadside Press, 1975.

PERIODICALS

Black American Literature Forum, fall, 1980, summer, 1981.
Black World, September, 1970; September, 1974.
Detroit Free Press, April 11, 1982.
Hollins Critic, December, 1981.
Los Angeles Times Book Review, August 10, 1980.
Negro Digest, January, 1968; July, 1968.
Obsidian: Black Literature in Review, summer and winter, 1981.
Parnassus: Poetry in Review, spring-summer, 1981.
Village Voice, July 27, 1982.
Virginia Quarterly Review, winter, 1981.

*   *   *

KUNENE, Mazisi (Raymond) 1930-

PERSONAL: Born in 1930, in Durban, South Africa. *Education:* Received M.A. from Natal University; attended School of Oriental and African Studies, London, 1959.

ADDRESSES: Office—Department of African Literature and Language, University of California, Los Angeles, 405 Hilgard, Los Angeles, CA 90024.

CAREER: Head of department of African studies at University College at Rome, Lesotho; director of education for South African United Front; African National Congress in Europe and United States, chief representative, 1962, director of finance, 1972; visiting professor of African literature at Stanford University, Palo Alto, CA; began as associate professor, became professor of African literature and language at University of California, Los Angeles.

AWARDS, HONORS: Winner of Bantu Literary Competition, 1956.

WRITINGS:

(And translator from the Zulu) *Zulu Poems,* Africana, 1970.
(And translator from the Zulu) *Emperor Shaka the Great: A Zulu Epic,* Heinemann, 1979.

(And translator from the Zulu) *Anthem of the De-cades: A Zulu Epic,* Heinemann, 1981.

The Ancestors and the Sacred Mountain: Poems, Heinemann, 1982.

Work represented in anthologies, including *Modern Poetry From Africa,* edited by Gerald Moore and Ulli Beier, Penguin, 1963; *African Writing Today,* edited by Ezekiel Mphahlele, Penguin, 1967. Contributor of short stories to *Drum.*

SIDELIGHTS: Drawing on the oral tradition of Zulu literature, Mazisi Kunene writes poetry expressing Zulu culture, religion, and history. He has translated much of his work, originally written in Zulu, into English. *Emperor Shaka the Great* is Kunene's verse narrative about the life and achievements of the nine-teenth-century Zulu leader who unified various Zulu chiefdoms and attempted to deal diplomatically with English settlers. Deeming it "an African epic equal to *The Iliad* and *The Odyssey,*" *World Literature Today* contributor Charles R. Larson judged the poem "a monumental undertaking and achievement by any standards." *Anthem of the Decades* details the Zulu account of how death came to mankind, and Kunene's collection *The Ancestors and the Sacred Mountain,* containing more than one hundred poems, promotes humanity, appreciation of nature, ancestral wisdom, and social action.

BIOGRAPHICAL/CRITICAL SOURCES:

PERIODICALS

Times Educational Supplement, January 28, 1983.
Times Literary Supplement, May 14, 1982.
World Literature Today, summer, 1981; summer, 1983.

L

La GUMA, (Justin) Alex(ander) 1925-1985

PERSONAL: Born February 20, 1925, in Cape Town, South Africa; immigrated to London, England, 1966; died October 11, 1985, in Havana, Cuba; son of Jimmy and Wilhelmina (Alexander) La Guma; married Blanche Valerie Herman (an office manager and former midwife), November 13, 1954; children: Eugene, Bartholomew. *Education:* Cape Technical College, student, 1941-42, correspondence student, 1965; London School of Journalism, correspondence student.

CAREER: New Age (weekly newspaper), Cape Town, South Africa, staff journalist, 1955-62; free-lance writer and journalist, 1962-85. Member of African National Congress, 1955-85. Member of editorial board, Afro-Asian Writers Bureau, 1965-85.

MEMBER: Afro-Asian Writers Association (deputy secretary-general, 1973-85).

AWARDS, HONORS: Afro-Asian Lotus Award for literature, 1969.

WRITINGS:

NOVELS

And a Threefold Cord, Seven Seas Publishers (East Berlin), 1964.

The Stone Country, Seven Seas Publishers (East Berlin), 1967, Heinemann, 1974.

In the Fog of the Season's End, Heinemann, 1972, Third Press, 1973.

Time of the Butcherbird, Heinemann, 1979.

OTHER

A Walk in the Night (novelette), Mbari Publications (Ibadan, Nigeria), 1962, expanded as *A Walk in the Night and Other Stories* (includes "The Gladiators," "At the Portagee's," "The Lemon Orchard," "A Matter of Taste," "Tattoo Marks and Nails," and "Blankets"), Northwestern University Press, 1967.

(Editor) *Apartheid: A Collection of Writings on South African Racism by South Africans,* International Publishers, 1971.

A Soviet Journey (travel), Progress Publishers (Moscow), 1978.

Contributor of short stories to anthologies, including *Quartet: New Voices from South Africa* (includes "Nocturne" [originally published as "Etude"], "A Glass of Wine," and "Out of Darkness"), edited by Richard Rive, Crown, 1963, new edition, Heinemann, 1968; *Modern African Stories,* edited by Ellis Ayitey Komey and Ezekiel Mphahlele, Faber, 1964; *African Writing Today,* edited by Mphahlele, Penguin, 1967; *Africa in Prose,* edited by O. R. Dathorne and Willfried Feuser, Penguin, 1969; *Modern African Stories* (includes "Coffee for the Road"), edited by Charles R. Larson, Collins, 1971.

Contributor of short stories to magazines, including *Black Orpheus* and *Africa South.*

SIDELIGHTS: Until his death in 1985, fiction writer Alex La Guma was among South Africa's most noted anti-apartheid activists, combining autobiographical elements with pointed criticism of his country's treatment of native blacks within his novels and short fiction. Imprisoned in the early 1960s for his continued vocal opposition to the South African government's racist policies, La Guma began a self-imposed exile in London, England in 1966, remaining there until 1979 when he moved to Cuba. Among his novels are *And a Threefold Cord* and the critically acclaimed *In the Fog of the Season's End,* both of which were banned in South Africa during their author's lifetime.

La Guma's active opposition to the South African government's racist policies permeates his fiction as it did his life. Growing up in an impoverished black neighborhood, he was aware of the social and economic inequities that surrounded him through the work of his father, a local politician. A member of the CapeTown district Communist party until it went underground in 1950, La Guma attended technical college for a year and then worked for a time on the staff of the leftist newspaper *New Age.* He came to the government's notice in 1955, when he helped draw up the Freedom Charter, a declaration of rights; in 1956, he and over 150 others were accused of treason; in 1961 he was arrested for helping to organize a strike and was subsequently imprisoned.

Various acts passed by the South African government kept La Guma either in prison or under twenty-four-hour house arrest for some years, including time in solitary confinement. La Guma spent this time writing; he composed the novel *And a Threefold Cord* while he was under house arrest in the early 1960s. He left South Africa in 1966 and moved to London where he remained until 1979, writing and working as a journalist. At the time of his death, La Guma was serving as the African National Congress representative to Cuba and working on his autobiography and his sixth novel.

Much of La Guma's work treats the situations and problems he encountered in his native Cape Town and which fueled his journalism career. The short novel *A Walk in the Night* "concerns the social, economic, and political purpose of the colored community" in Cape Town, according to *Dictionary of Literary Biography* essayist Cecil A. Abrahams. La Guma tells the story of Michael Adonis, a factory worker who has just lost his job because he talked back to his white supervisor. Frustrated, Michael commits a senseless crime; he kills the decrepit old ex-actor Doughty. Intertwined with Michael's fate are the lives of Raalt, a white constable on duty in the district where the murder is committed, and Willieboy, a malingerer and occasional criminal. The novelette, says Shatto Arthur Gakwandi in his *The Novel and Contemporary Experience in Africa,* avoids "being a sermon of despair [while also evading] advocating sentimental solutions to the problems that it portrays. Without pathos, it creates a powerful impression of that rhythm of violence which characterizes South African life." Gakwandi concludes: "All these characters are victims of a system that denies them the facility of living in harmony with fellow human beings and their frustrations find release in acts of violence against weaker members of their society."

In 1964's *And a Threefold Cord,* La Guma again examines his native Cape Town, particularly the slum that serves as the novel's setting. Winter has begun, bringing with it rain and illness and discomfort to slum residents like the Pauls family, who live in a cardboard shack woefully inadequate in keeping out the rain. Slum life is portrayed in all its squalor, as prostitution, alcoholism, violence, famine, joblessness, and sickness are an accepted part of daily life. La Guma's protagonists can be distinguished by their ability to perceive the inadequacies of their situation; "He distinguishes consistently between those who live parasitically off the slum people, and those whose work [in communities outside the slum] has given them a wider conception and extended standards of comparison," according to *Journal of Commonwealth Literature* contributor David Rabkin. *And a Threefold Cord,* which was completed during one of its author's imprisonments, was published in Berlin and did not achieve the widespread distribution of some of his more recent works.

In *The Stone Country,* which La Guma released in 1967, the author includes perceptions of the South African jail system he had by now become very familiar with. The title refers to the stone-walled world of prison, and the hierarchical social system, racial segregation, and acceptance of brutality toward blacks make the prison a microcosm of South Africa as a whole. Enter new inmate George Adams, who embodies the dignity of the free man, confident in his basic rights. Adams's treatment at the hands of a prison guard named Fatso causes him to slowly realize that, as Abrahams notes, "rights may exist but they are ignored. . . .[in] a world of survival of the fittest." Gradually, Adams is made aware that in prison, as in South Africa, "to exist one must either become a bully or find alternative means of survival that are not any more honorable."

La Guma's 1979 novel *Time of the Butcherbird* would be his last published novel. Written while its author was in self-imposed exile from his native land, the novel's title reflects La Guma's belief that the hour of

South Africa's moral transition would soon be at hand. The butcherbird, common in areas where livestock are housed, preys on disease-carrying ticks and is therefore hailed as a bringer of good luck and renewed health. The history of an Afrikaaner family—a counterpoint to the profiles of impoverished blacks that appear in La Guman's work—is represented through the character of Meulen, a racist landowner participating in a government-sanctioned effort to remove blacks from their homelands and apportion those land among "deserving" whites. Meulen, then, is the parasite that threatens the country, and through his ultimate—and completely justifiable—death at the hand of a black agitator, the country finds itself rid of yet another destructive element threatening its health. Because of the novel's heavy use of symbolism and history, rather than action and current events, "readers have not shown the same enthusiasm for it" as they have other books by La Guma, according to Abrahams.

In the Fog of the Season's End remains La Guma's most highly praised work of fiction, as well as the one that reflects most on the author's own life. The protagonists, Elias and Beukes, are committed members of the resistance movement and are being hunted by the police for their activism against the oppressive white government. During a raid by the secret police, Elias is captured and eventually tortured to death, while Beukes escapes with a gunshot wound. Containing descriptions of acts of graphic violence done to blacks by whites, the novel also reflects La Guma's belief that the fight against apartheid would not be suppressed by such tactics. The power of La Guma's writing leads John Updike, writing for the *New Yorker,* to say of *In the Fog of the Season's End* that it "delivers, through its portrait of a few hunted blacks attempting to subvert the brutal regime of apartheid, a social protest reminiscent, in its closely detailed texture and level indignation, of Dreiser and Zola."

Several of La Guma's books have been translated into Russian and other languages, and portions have been included in numerous anthologies.

BIOGRAPHICAL/CRITICAL SOURCES:

BOOKS

Abrahams, Cecil A., *Alex La Guma,* Twayne, 1985.
Asein, Samuel O., *Alex La Guma: The Man and His Work,* Heinemann, 1987.

Contemporary Literary Criticism, Volume 19, Gale, 1981.
Dictionary of Literary Biography, Volume 117: *Twentieth-Century Caribbean and Black African Writers, First Series,* Gale, 1988.
Duerden, Dennis, and Cosmo Pieterse, editors, *African Writers Talking: A Collection of Interviews,* Heinemann, 1972.
Encyclopedia of World Literature in the Twentieth Century, Volume 3, revised edition, Ungar, 1983.
Gakwandi, Shatto Arthur, *The Novel and Contemporary Experience in Africa,* Africana Publishing, 1977.
Moore, Gerald, *Twelve African Writers,* Indiana University Press, 1980.
Mphahlele, Ezekiel, *African Image,* Praeger, 1962.
Wanjala, C. L., *Standpoints on African Literature,* East African Literature Bureau, Nairobi, Kenya, 1973.
Zell, Hans M., and others, *A New Reader's Guide to African Literature,* 2nd revised and expanded edition, Holmes & Meier, 1983.

PERIODICALS

Black Scholar, July/August, 1986.
Busara, Volume 8, number 1, 1976.
Freedomways, Volume 25, number 3, 1985.
Journal of Commonwealth Literature, June, 1973, pp. 54-61.
Journal of the New African Literature and the Arts, numbers 9-10, 1974, pp. 5-11.
New Statesman, January 29, 1965; November 3, 1972.
New Yorker, January 21, 1974, pp. 84-94.
Phylon, March, 1978, pp. 74-86.
Sechaba (London), February, 1971.
Times (London), November 23, 1985.
Times Literary Supplement, January 21, 1965, p. 52; October 20, 1972.
World Literature Today, winter, 1980.
World Literature Written in English, spring, 1981, pp. 5-16.*

*   *   *

LAMMING, George (William) 1927-

PERSONAL: Born June 8, 1927, in Barbados; emigrated to England, 1950. *Education:* Attended Combermere High School in Barbados.

ADDRESSES: Home—14-A Highbury Place, London N 5, England. *Office*—c/o Allison and Busby, 26 Grand Union Centre, Portobello Rd., London W10 5AH, England.

CAREER: Writer. Worked as schoolmaster in Trinidad, 1946-50; factory worker in England, 1950; broadcaster for British Broadcasting Corp. (BBC) Colonial Service, 1951. Writer-in-residence and lecturer in Creative Arts Centre and Department of Education, University of West Indies, Mona, Jamaica, 1967-68; visiting professor at University of Texas at Austin, 1977, and at University of Pennsylvania. Lecturer in Denmark, Tanzania, and Australia.

AWARDS, HONORS: Kenyon Review fellowship, 1954; Guggenheim Fellowship, 1955; Somerset Maugham Award, 1957; Canada Council fellowship, 1962; Commonwealth Foundation grant, 1976; Association of Commonwealth Literature Writers Award; D.Litt., University of West Indies.

WRITINGS:

NOVELS

In the Castle of My Skin, with introduction by Richard Wright, McGraw, 1953, with a new introduction by the author, Schocken, 1983.
The Emigrants, M. Joseph, 1954, McGraw, 1955, reprinted, Allison & Busby, 1980.
Of Age and Innocence, M. Joseph, 1958, reprinted, Allison & Busby, 1981.
Adventure, M. Joseph, 1960, reprinted, Allison & Busby, 1979.
Water with Berries, Holt, 1972.
Natives of My Person, Holt, 1972.

CONTRIBUTOR OF POETRY TO ANTHOLOGIES

Peter Brent, editor, *Young Commonwealth Poets '65,* Heinemann, 1965.
John Figueroa, editor, *Caribbean Voices,* two volumes, Evans, 1966.
O. R. Dathorne, editor, *Caribbean Verse,* Heinemann, 1968.

CONTRIBUTOR OF SHORT FICTION TO ANTHOLOGIES

Andrew Salkey, editor, *West Indian Stories,* Faber, 1960.
Salkey, editor, *Stories from the Caribbean,* Dufour, 1965, published as *Island Voices,* Liveright, 1970.

O. R. Dathorne, editor, *Caribbean Narrative,* Heinemann, 1966.
Barbara Howes, editor, *From the Green Antilles,* Macmillan, 1966.
Salkey, editor, *Caribbean Prose,* Evans, 1967.
James T. Livingston, editor, *Caribbean Rhythms,* Pocket Books, 1974.

OTHER

The Pleasures of Exile (essays and autobiographical observations), M. Joseph, 1960, reprinted, Allison & Busby, 1984.
(With Henry Bangou and Rene Depestre) *Influencia del Africa en las literaturas antillanas* (title means "The Influence of Africa on the Antillian Literatures"), I. L. A. C. (Montevideo, Uruguay), 1972.
(Editor) *Cannon Shot and Glass Beads: Modern Black Writing,* Pan Books, 1974.
Conversations: Essays, Addresses and Interviews 1953-1990, University of Michigan Press (Ann Arbor, MI), 1998.

Co-editor of Barbados and Guyana independence issues of *New World Quarterly* (Kingston), 1965 and 1967. Contributor to journals, including *Bim* (Barbados), *Savacou, New World Quarterly, Caribbean Quarterly,* and *Casa de las Americas* (Cuba).

SIDELIGHTS: Barbadian writer "George Lamming is not so much a novelist," asserts *New York Times Book Review* contributor Jan Carew, "as a chronicler of secret journeys to the innermost regions of the West Indian psyche." George Davis, however, believes Carew's assessment does not go far enough. Davis notes in his own *New York Times Book Review* critique, "I can think of very few writers who make better use of the fictional moments of their stories to explore the souls of any of us—West Indian or not." In Lamming's essay, "The Negro Writer in His World," the West Indian explains the universality on which Davis comments. In the essay Lamming maintains that black writers are the same as all other writers who use writing as a method of self-discovery. According to Carolyn T. Brown in *World Literature Today,* in Lamming's opinion, "the contemporary human condition . . . involves a 'universal sense of separation and abandonment, frustration and loss, and above all, of man's direct inner experience of something missing.'"

In Lamming's work the "something missing" is a true cultural identity for the West Indian. This lack of identity is, according to Lamming, a direct result of the long history of colonial rule in the region. Caribbean-born writer V. S. Naipaul explains the importance of this idea in his *New Statesman* review of Lamming's novel, *Of Age and Innocence:* "Unless one understands the West Indian's search for identity, [the novel] is almost meaningless. It is not fully realised how completely the West Indian Negro identifies himself with England. . . . For the West Indian intellectual, speaking no language but English, educated in an English way, the experience of England is really traumatic. The foundations of his life are removed." James Ngugi makes a similar observation in his *Pan-Africanist* review of the same novel. "For Lamming," Ngugi writes, "a sense of exile must lead to action and through action to identity. The West Indian's alienation springs . . . from his colonial relationship to England."

Lamming's first four novels explore the West Indian search for identity, a search which often leads to a flight to England followed by, for some, a return to their Caribbean roots. His first novel, *In the Castle of My Skin,* which is nearly universally acclaimed by critics, is a quasi-autobiographical look at childhood and adolescence on Lamming's fictional Caribbean island, San Cristobal. The book "is generally regarded," notes Michael Gilkes in *The West Indian Novel,* "as a 'classic' of West Indian fiction. It is one of the earliest novels of any substance to convey, with real assurance, the life of ordinary village folk within a genuinely realized, native landscape: a 'peasant novel' . . . written with deep insight and considerable technical skill." Several reviewers compare Lamming's prose style in the book to poetry. In *New Statesman and Nation* Pritchett describes Lamming's prose as "something between garrulous realism and popular poetry, and . . . quite delightful"; while in the *San Francisco Chronicle* J. H. Jackson says Lamming "is a poet and a human being who approaches a question vital to him, humanly and poetically." A *Time* contributor finds the book "a curious mixture of autobiography and a poetic evocation of a native life. . . . It is one of the few authentically rich and constantly readable books produced [thus far] by a West Indian." Lamming's next novel, *The Emigrants,* follows a group of West Indians who—like Lamming, himself—leave their native islands for exile in England, while the two novels that follow, *Of Age and Innocence* and *Season of Adventure,* feature a return to San Cristobal. According to Carew, these last two novels also have a bit of autobiography in them because through their action it seems "as though Lamming [is] attempting to rediscover a history of himself by himself."

In Lamming's novels, as critics note, self-discovery is often achieved through an inquiry into his characters' pasts. For example, while *Yale Review* contributor Michael Cook quotes Lamming's *Of Age and Innocence* description of San Cristobal—"an old land inhabiting new forms of men who can never resurrect their roots and do not know their nature," the reviewer comments that "it is obvious" that in "*Season of Adventure* . . . [Lamming] is committed to his characters' at least trying to discover their roots and their natures." Details of the plot seem to verify Cook's assessment for the novel traces Fola Piggott's quest to discover whether her father was European or African. According to Kenneth Ramchand in *The West Indian Novel and Its Background,* "*Season of Adventure* is the most significant of the West Indian novels invoking Africa." In the novel, Ramchand maintains, Lamming invokes "the African heritage not to make statements about Africa but to explore the troubled components of West Indian culture and nationhood." Lamming accomplishes "this without preventing us from seeing that Fola's special circumstances . . . are only a manifestation . . . of every man's need to take the past into account with humility, fearlessness, and receptivity."

After a silence of over a decade Lamming published two new novels almost simultaneously: *Water with Berries* and *Natives of My Person.* Again, his fiction focuses on the effects of history on the present. In both books Lamming uses symbolism to tell his story. In *Water with Berries* Lamming uses a theme previously dealt with in his nonfiction work *The Pleasures of Exile.* A *Times Literary Supplement* reviewer quotes from Lamming's collection of essays: "My subject is the migration of the West Indian writer, as colonial and exile, from his native kingdom, once inhabited by Caliban, to the tempestuous island of Prospero's and his language." Caliban and Prospero are both characters from Shakespeare's *The Tempest,* Caliban being the deformed slave of Prospero, ruler of an enchanted island. According to the *Times Literary Supplement* contributor, Lamming also refers to himself in the same book as an "exiled descendent of Caliban." In *Water with Berries* Lamming uses the plot of *The Tempest* to symbolize the various ills of West Indian society, but critics are divided on the success of the novel. In *World Literature in English* Anthony Boxill notes that Lamming uses *The Tempest* to "help put across his points about disintegration of personality . . . , especially in people who are products of a colonial past. . . . However, the *Tempest* pattern which might have been the strength of this novel proves its undoing. . . . In his unrelenting faithfulness to this . . . pattern Lamming loses touch with the characters he is creating; they cease to be credible." A *Times Literary Supplement* contributor similarly states, "Lamming writes very well, but *Water with Berries* does not entirely convince either as a study of the pains of exile, or as an allegory of colonialism. . . . [And,] as for the melodrama of . . . Lamming's *Tempest* myth, it tells us nothing new."

Other critics praise Lamming's novel and disregard its connections to *The Tempest*. Paul Theroux and George Davis, for instance, find the work a very compelling statement on the effects of colonialism. In *Encounter* Theroux claims, "the poetic prose of the narrative has a perfect dazzle. . . . When expatriation is defined and dramatised . . . *Water with Berries* takes on a life of its own, for . . . Lamming is meticulous in diagnosing the condition of estrangement." *New York Times Book Review* contributor Davis writes: "This is an effectively written fictional work. Lamming brings his characters . . . into the same nightmare of arson, perversity, suicide and murder, which, we are forced to feel, is the legacy of the colonial experience." *Natives of My Person*, according to Gilkes, "is an exceedingly complex work, full of allegorical and historical meanings and echoes. It is an embodiment of all [Lamming's] themes: a kind of *reviewing* process in which he appears to take stock of things." Boxill notes that the novel "provides richly complex insights into human personality and the history of colonialism." It tells the story of the sixteenth-century voyage of the ship *Reconnaissance* from Europe to America by way of Africa. The chief goal of the ship's Commandant is the establishment of a slave-free settlement on the island of San Cristobal, but he is killed by two of the ship's officers before he can accomplish his mission. Some critics find that Lamming's prose detracts from the novel. In *Book World* Theroux calls Lamming "a marvelously skillful writer" but also refers to the novel's "shadowy action and vaguely poetical momentousness."

A *Times Literary Supplement* reviewer complains that Lamming writes "a prose of discovery which is effortful, uncolloquial, and almost always mannered." While Thomas R. Edwards and Carew also regret the complexity of Lamming's prose they are able to find redeeming qualities in the novel. "Lamming's prose is portentous," Edwards notes in the *New York Review of Books*, "hooked on simile, and anxious to suggest more than it says, inviting questions the story never answers. . . . Yet if reading *Natives of My Person* is a voyage into frustration and annoyance, Lamming's story survives and grows in the mind afterward. . . .

This imagined history reveals itself as a version of significances that 'real' history is itself only a version of." Carew similarly comments on the book's difficult prose but calls the work "undoubtedly . . . Lamming's finest novel." In the book, according to Carew's assessment, Lamming expresses better than in any of his other novels his concerns about the effects of colonization on the West Indies and its people. In *Natives of My Person*, Carew maintains, Lamming "succeeds in illuminating new areas of darkness in the colonial past that the colonizer has so far not dealt with; and in this sense it is a profoundly revolutionary and original work."

BIOGRAPHICAL/CRITICAL SOURCES:

BOOKS

Baugh, Edward, editor, *Homecoming: Essays on African and Caribbean Literature, Culture and Politics,* Laurence Hill, 1972.
Black Literature Criticism, Gale, 1992.
Contemporary Literary Criticism, Gale, Volume 2, 1974, Volume 4, 1975, Volume 66, 1991.
Cooke, Michael G., editor, *Modern Black Novelists: A Collection of Critical Essays,* Prentice-Hall, 1971.
Gilkes, Michael, *The West Indian Novel,* Twayne, 1981.
Lamming, George, *In the Castle of My Skin,* McGraw, 1954.
Lamming, George, *Of Age and Innocence,* M. Joseph, 1958.
Lamming, George, *The Pleasures of Exile,* M. Joseph, 1960.
Massa, Daniel, editor, *Individual and Community in Commonwealth Literature,* University Press (Malta), 1979.
Nair, Supriya, *Caliban's Curse: George Lamming and the Revisioning of History,* University of Michigan Press (Ann Arbor), 1996.
Paquet, Sandra Pouchet, *The Novels of George Lamming,* Heinemann, 1982.
Ramchand, Kenneth, *The West Indian Novel and Its Background,* Faber, 1970.

PERIODICALS

Book World, January 23, 1972.
Canadian Literature, winter, 1982.
Caribbean Quarterly, February, 1958.
Encounter, May, 1972.
New Statesman, December 6, 1958; January 28, 1972; December 19, 1980.

New Statesman and Nation, April 18, 1953.

New Yorker, December 5, 1953; May 28, 1955; April 29, 1972.

New York Herald Tribune Book Review, July 17, 1955.

New York Review of Books, March 9, 1972.

New York Times, November 1, 1953; July 24, 1955; January 15, 1972.

New York Times Book Review, February 27, 1972; June 4, 1972; October 15, 1972; December 3, 1972.

Observer, October 8, 1972.

Pan-Africanist, March, 1971.

Punch, August 19, 1981.

San Francisco Chronicle, November 17, 1953; June 24, 1955.

Saturday Review, December 5, 1953; May 28, 1955.

Studies in Black Literature, spring, 1973.

Time, November 9, 1953; April 25, 1955.

Times Literary Supplement, March 27, 1953; February 11, 1972; December 15, 1972; September 4, 1981; October 24, 1986.

World Literature Today, winter, 1983; spring, 1985.

World Literature Written in English, November, 1971; April, 1973; November, 1979.

Yale Review, autumn, 1953; summer, 1973.*

*   *   *

LEE, Andrea 1953-

PERSONAL: Born in 1953, in Philadelphia, PA; married. *Education:* Received M.A. from Harvard University.

ADDRESSES: Office—New Yorker, 25 West 43rd St., New York, NY 10036.

CAREER: Writer. Staff writer for *New Yorker* magazine in New York City.

AWARDS, HONORS: Nomination for American Book Award for general nonfiction, 1981, for *Russian Journal;* Jean Stein Award from American Academy and Institute of Arts and Letters, 1984.

WRITINGS:

Russian Journal (nonfiction), Random House, 1981.
Sarah Phillips (novel), Random House, 1984.

Contributor to periodicals, including *New Yorker, New York Times,* and *Vogue.*

SIDELIGHTS: Andrea Lee has distinguished herself as a noteworthy journalist and novelist. In her nonfiction work, *Russian Journal,* she provides an insightful perspective on contemporary Soviet life, and in her novel, *Sarah Phillips,* she recounts the reckless past of a middle-class black woman. These writings, while embracing different themes, have earned Lee praise as a keen observer and a consummate technician, one whose probing insights are inevitably rendered with concision and grace. As Susan Richards Shreve noted in the *New York Times Book Review,* "Andrea Lee's authority as a writer comes of an unstinting honesty and a style at once simple and yet luminous."

Lee's first book, *Russian Journal,* derives from a diary she kept in 1978 while in the Soviet Union, where her husband was studying for ten months on a fellowship. Relying on public transportation and a rudimentary grasp of the Russian language, Lee visited a wide variety of Soviet places, including public baths, college campuses, farmers' markets, and nightclubs. She met bureaucrats, dissidents, and even contraband sellers; encountered many cynics and youthful materialists; observed a disturbing number of public drunks; and became acquainted with some of the country's more unsettling aspects, notably surveillance. In her journal Lee wrote that, due to their circumstances, she and her husband "got a view of life in Moscow and Leningrad that was very different from that of the diplomats and journalists we knew."

Following the 1981 publication of *Russian Journal,* critics cited the book as a refreshing, if narrow, perspective on Soviet life. Susan Jacoby, writing in the *New York Times Book Review,* called Lee's book "a subtly crafted reflection of both the bleak and golden shadings of Russian life" and added: "The subject matter of this journal is highly idiosyncratic. . . . What Miss Lee offers are the people, places and experiences that touched her most deeply." Like Jacoby, *Washington Post Book World* reviewer Peter Osnos cited the book's worth for "conveying a feeling of place and atmosphere" and declared: "Lee writes very well. There is a warmth and freshness about her style that makes reading [*Russian Journal*] effortless." Osnos was especially impressed with Lee's depiction of the Soviet people, particularly its younger citizens. "What is best about the book—what distinguishes it from other books about the Soviet Union published in recent years—is her accounts of friendships with young people," he contended. Similarly, *Newsweek*'s Walter Clemons praised Lee's "unassuming delicacy and exactness" asserting that "her most winning quality is her capacity for friendship."

Michael Irwin, who discussed *Russian Journal* in the *London Review of Books,* also found Lee an engaging reporter. He praised her "astuteness" and called *Russian Journal* "a considerable exercise in observation, empathy and personal and literary tact." Lee's refusal to write about being a black person in the Soviet Union caused a few reservations among critics reviewing Russian Journal. Susan Jacoby called this omission "regrettable" and contended that Lee's race "must have affected [her Russian friends'] perceptions (and Miss Lee's) in some way." Jacoby added, "Miss Lee's responses would surely have been as interesting as the rest of her observations, and I wish she had included them." Peter Osnos also noted Lee's reluctance to write about race. He described the omission as "slightly awkward" and observed: "Apparently, she feels that her blackness has nothing to do with her time in the Soviet Union. That is her business. But she never even says as much."

As if responding to charges that she avoided racial subjects, Lee followed *Russian Journal* with *Sarah Phillips,* an episodic novel explicitly concerned with a contemporary black woman. The title character is introduced as a woman grown disgusted with her boorish, racist acquaintances—and lovers—in Paris, where she has been living in self-exile. At the end of the first chapter Sarah decides to leave Paris, and in the ensuing sections she recalls events—principally from childhood and adolescence—contributing to her present circumstances. Unlike most black characters in American fiction, Sarah is an assimilated elitist whose background is middle class, and her goal is to scandalize her bourgeois parents. She even accepts tokenism when she becomes the first black student at an exclusive girls' school. Her father is a minister involved in the civil rights movement, an involvement that actually leads to her embarrassment when he is briefly imprisoned for civil disobedience. Bored with America, Sarah leaves the country after her father's death and her graduation from college. She settles in Paris, indulging in various interracial sexual shenanigans, including a *menage-a-quatre.* By novel's end, however, Sarah realizes the emptiness of her assimilation into white society—both European and American—and reaches a greater understanding of herself and her heritage.

With *Sarah Phillips* Lee earned further literary acclaim. In *Saturday Review,* Bruce Van Wyngarden described the novel as a "coming-of-age remembrance in which detail and insight are delightfully, and sometimes poignantly, blended." He also deemed it "an engaging and promising" first novel. Likewise, *Best Sellers* reviewer Francis Goskowski called Sarah

Phillips an "engaging, witty" work and asserted that with it Lee emerged as a "major novelistic talent." Patricia Vigderam was one of several critics who noted the novel's breakthrough perspective on race, particularly the characterization of Sarah as an assimilated black. Critiquing the work for the *Boston Review,* Vigderman conceded that "this novel does not fit easily into the Afro-American tradition, and may even meet with some disapproval," but she nonetheless considered it "a very gracefully written book about black identity." With *Russian Journal* and *Sarah Phillips* Lee has gained recognition as a talented writer of immense promise, and her forthcoming works are greatly anticipated. "Without a doubt," stated Francis Goskowski, "Ms. Lee will be heard from again, and she will command our attention."

BIOGRAPHICAL/CRITICAL SOURCES:

BOOKS

Black Literature Criticism, Gale, 1992.
Contemporary Literary Criticism, Gale, Volume 36, 1986.

PERIODCIALS

African American Review, spring, 1995, p. 164.
Best Sellers, February, 1985.
Boston Review, February, 1985.
Economist, May 29, 1982.
London Review of Books, October 6, 1982.
National Review, September 3, 1982.
New Leader, December 10, 1984.
New Republic, February 24, 1982; November 19, 1984.
Newsweek, October 19, 1981.
New Yorker, April 29, 1996, p. 168.
New York Review of Books, November 5, 1981.
New York Times, December 6, 1984.
New York Times Book Review, October 25, 1981, pp. 11, 22; November 18, 1984.
People, November 23, 1981, pp. 101-02.
Saturday Review, February, 1985, p. 74.
Spectator, June 12, 1982.
Times Literary Supplement, August 13, 1982; April 5, 1985.
Washington Post Book World, October 25, 1981.*

*   *   *

LEE, Don L.
See MADHUBUTI, Haki R.

LEE, Shelton Jackson 1957-
(Spike Lee)

PERSONAL: Born March 20, 1957, in Atlanta, GA; son of William (a musician and composer) and Jacqueline (a teacher; maiden name, Shelton) Lee. *Education:* Morehouse College, B.A., 1979; New York University, M.A., 1983.

ADDRESSES: Home—Brooklyn, NY. *Office*—Forty Acres and a Mule Filmworks, 124 DeKalb Ave., Brooklyn, NY 11217.

CAREER: Screenwriter, actor, and director and producer of motion pictures and music videos. Founder and director, Forty Acres and a Mule Filmworks, Brooklyn, NY, 1986—.

MEMBER: Screen Actors Guild.

AWARDS, HONORS: Student Director's Award, Academy of Motion Picture Arts and Sciences, 1982, for *Joe's Bed-Stuy Barber Shop: We Cut Heads;* Prix de Jeunesse, Cannes Film Festival, and New Generation Award, Los Angeles Film Critics, both 1986, both for *She's Gotta Have It;* Academy Award nomination for best documentary, 1999, for *Four Little Girls.*

WRITINGS:

NONFICTION

Spike Lee's "Gotta Have It": Inside Guerilla Filmmaking (includes interviews and a journal), photographs by brother, David Lee, foreword by Nelson George, Simon & Schuster, 1987.
(With Lisa Jones) *Uplift the Race: The Construction of "School Daze,"* Simon &Schuster, 1988.
(With Jones) *"Do the Right Thing": The New Spike Lee Joint,* Fireside Press, 1989.
(With Jones) *Mo' Better Blues,* Simon & Schuster, 1990.
(With Ralph Wiley) *By Any Means Necessary: The Trials and Tribulations of the Making of "Malcolm X,"* Hyperion, 1992.
Best Seat in the House: A Basketball Memoir, Crown, 1997.

SCREENPLAYS; AND DIRECTOR

She's Gotta Have It, Island, 1986.
School Daze, Columbia, 1988.
Do the Right Thing, Universal, 1989.
Mo' Better Blues, Forty Acres and a Mule, 1991.

Jungle Fever, Forty Acres and a Mule, 1991.
Malcolm X, Forty Acres and a Mule, 1992.
Crooklyn, Forty Acres and a Mule, 1994.
Clockers, Forty Acres and a Mule, 1995.
Girl 6, Fox Searchlight, 1996.
Get on the Bus, Forty Acres and a Mule, 1996.
Four Little Girls (documentary), Direct Cinema, 1997.
He Got Game, Forty Acres and a Mule, 1998.
Summer of Sam, Forty Acres and a Mule, 1999.

Also writer and director of short films, including *The Answer,* 1980, *Sarah,* 1981, and *Joe's Bed-Stuy Barbershop: We Cut Heads,* 1982. Contributor of short films to *Saturday Night Live* and to MTV.

SIDELIGHTS: The son of a musician, Spike Lee has become the equivalent of a composer, conductor, lead cellist,and symphony T-shirt salesman in the industry of filmmaking. Since *She's Gotta Have It* was released in 1986 on a small budget, Lee has proven himself as a screenwriter, director/producer, actor, and merchandiser of films. "I truly believe I was put here to make films, it's as simple as that," Lee wrote in his book *Spike Lee's "Gotta Have It": Inside Guerilla Filmmaking.* "I'm doin' what I'm 'posed to bedoin'. It's not for me to say whether [*She's Gotta Have It*] is a landmark film (I make 'em, that's all) but I do want people to be inspired by it, in particular, black people. Now there is a present example of how we can produce. We can do the things we want to do, there are no mo' excuses. We're tired of that alibi, 'White man this, white man that.' . . . It's on us. So let's all do the work that needs to be done by us all. And to y'all who aren't down for the cause, move out of the way, step aside."

Lee was born in Atlanta, Georgia, where he earned his nickname, Spike. "A lot of people think it's made up—one of those stage names," he explained in *Spike Lee's "Gotta Have It."* "My mother. . . said I was a very tough baby. . . . I was like three or four months old when I got the nickname." Lee's father, jazz musician Bill Lee, soon moved his family to the jazz mecca of Chicago, and from there on to New York City, where the family had settled by the late 1950s. During his youth Lee's leadership ability began to emerge. For neighborhood sports, he said, he "was always the captain of the team, the spark plug. Not the best athlete, though."

A jazz purist, Lee's father placed strains on the family by adhering to his artistic principles. As Lee reported in *Spike Lee's "Gotta Have It"*: "In the early sixties [my father] was the top folk/jazz bassist. If you look on the albums of Peter, Paul and Mary, Bob Dylan, Judy Collins, Odetta, Theodore Bikel, Leon Bibbs and Josh White, you'll see that my father was playing with all of them. He also played with Simon and Garfunkel. He got tired of playing that music, though, and then the electric bass became popular and he refused to play it. To this day, he's never played Fender bass. With that kind of stance, you don't work. . . . I got some of my stubbornness from him, if the word is stubbornness. . . . [It's] nonconformist, to a degree."

Following a long family tradition, Lee attended Morehouse, an all-black college in Atlanta, the third generation in his family to do so. "My father and grandfather went to Morehouse," he explained, adding that "The Lee family has always been like that." Majoring in mass communications, he had decided by his sophomore year to become a filmmaker—though he still did a bit of everything else, including hosting his own radio show on jazz station WCLK and writing for the school newspaper. More importantly, Lee began scripting and shooting short films.

After graduation from Morehouse, Lee enrolled at the New York University (NYU) Film School. "There's no way I could have made the films I made if I lived in [Los Angeles] 'cause I didn't know anybody," he explained in his book. "I couldn't have called people for locations. . . . Plus at USC and UCLA [University of Southern California and University of California, Los Angeles], not everybody makes a film. The teachers assign by committee who gets to make a film."

His senior effort, *Joe's Bed-Stuy Barbershop,* earned Lee a student academy award. Monty Ross starred in the film about a local barber who gets caught up in the numbers racket and organized crime. "That summer before my final year in school I was in Atlanta writing a script," he wrote. "I let Monty read it and he suggested that he act in it. I never thought of Monty . . . coming up to New York, dropping what he was doing, to act in it. But he did. I think Monty gave a very fine performance. What people don't realize is that Monty—a very unselfish person—was not only acting in the film, he was driving the van, he was crewing, he was doing a lot of other things that no doubt affected his performance. But we got the film made."

Winning the student academy award didn't really surprise Lee. "Because I know that NYU is one of the best film schools, and I saw a lot of films that came out of the school. I know that this was as good or better than anything that was in USC or UCLA . . . I never went to NYU expecting teachers to teach me. I just wanted equipment, so I could make films, and learn filmmaking by making films. . . . That's the only way to learn. People call me now wanting to know what the secret to successful filmmaking is. I get so mad. There is no secret formula let's say, for the success of *She's Gotta Have It*. I'm not gonna tell them anything that will help them. We just killed ourselves to get it made. That's how we did it."

After he won the student academy award, some of the larger talent agencies approached Lee and, although they represented him for over a year, nothing much materialized. "I had the first draft of what is now *School Daze,* but then it was called 'Homecoming.' The script was a lot different but I had the third draft of it. It was an all-black film. They said nah. Forget it. Nothing. Not even an 'Afterschool Special.' And there were a lot of my classmates who didn't even win Academy Awards who did get 'Afterschool Specials.'"

Lee's first post-NYU production, *The Messenger,* was a failed venture by a businessman's yardstick. Started in 1984, *The Messenger* was about a Brooklyn bike messenger and his family. After spending forty thousand dollars, Lee decided to terminate the project. "It just never really came together with all the money and stuff," he said in a *Film Comment* article. One of the project's obstacles that Lee was not able to hurdle was the Screen Actors Guild (SAG). Lee had applied for experimental film rates so that he would be able to afford an actor like Laurence Fishburne (later of *What's Love Got to Do with It*), but the Guild refused Lee's application for waiver of the standard rates. "There are too many black actors out of work for them to nix it," he commented in *Spike Lee's "Gotta Have It."* But "they said no. So I had to recast the entire picture in four days with non-SAG people. And it never came together so we were all devastated. I got a list of ten films that had been given a waiver within the [previous] year. All of them were done by white independent filmmakers. All of them worked with a whole lot more money than I had. Yet they said my film was too commercial. . . . That was a definite case of racism."

By 1985 Lee was immersed in his next project, *She's Gotta Have It.* The Lee-penned screenplay explores black female sexuality through its main character, Nola Darling, played by Tracy Camilla Johns. Nola dates three different men: Jamie Overstreet, Greer Childs and Mars Blackmon (played by Lee). One offers stability; another, physical attraction; the third, humor. "Everybody's character was reflected in how they perceived Nola. That's the whole film, how everybody perceives Nola," Lee wrote in *Spike Lee's "Gotta Have It."* Eventually Nola leaves all three of her suitors. "It's about control," she explains in the film. "My body. My mind. Whose gonna own it, them or me?"

With the failure of *The Messenger* the American Film Institute had withdrawn the twenty thousand dollars it previously granted Lee. "There were times when I didn't know where the next nickel was coming from," Lee recalled of this period in his book, "but it would come. Sure enough, the money came whenever we needed it." With eighteen thousand dollars from the New York arts council as his most-sizable funding, Lee assembled a small cast and crew that included family members, and directed *She's Gotta Have It* in only twelve days.

The 1986 release of *She's Gotta Have It* made Lee an international celebrity. The film was a financial success, grossing more than eight million dollars, and critically it was an even bigger success. *Washington Post* reviewer Paul Attanasio deemed it an "impressive first feature" and added that it was "discursive, jazzy, vibrant with sex and funny as heck." Michael Wilmington wrote in the *Los Angeles Times* that Lee's film was "a joyfully idiosyncratic little jazz-burst of a film, full of sensuous melody, witty chops and hot licks." Wilmington was particularly impressed with the film's non-stereotypical perspective and characters, declaring that it "gives you as non-standard a peek at black American life as you'll get: engaging, seductive and happily off-kilter. . . . These characters aren't the radiant winners or sad victims you usually see, and there's not a normal citizen . . . in the bunch." The film's appeal was evident at the Cannes Film Festival. When the power failed during the film's screening, the audience refused to leave until they saw the ending.

That success led to Lee securing approximately six million dollars from Columbia Pictures to film *School Daze,* a musical comedy about rival factions at a black college. Much of the humor in the film derives from the antics of Lee's character. Here he plays Half Pint, a Gamma Phi Gamma hopeful preoccupied with losing his virginity. The factional conflicts at the college are underscored by Half Pint, a Wannabee (as in want-to-be-white), and his relationship with his cousin, Dap, a dark-skinned Jigaboo (a member of the black underclass) and the key figure in a campus campaign to force the university divestiture from South Africa. Dap's rival is Julian, leader of the Gamma Phi Gammas. The characters' conflicts allow Lee to explore bigotry as well as elitism.

The major obstacle placed in Lee's path in filming *School Daze* was reluctance from his alma mater, Morehouse, as well as other Atlanta black colleges (Spelman College, Clark College, Morris Brown College and Atlanta University) to allow the use of their facilities. "There were so many rumors circulating around the [Atlanta University Center] about the movie," he wrote in his second book, *Uplift the Race: The Construction of "School Daze."* "The students were influenced by the propaganda being pushed out by the administrations. When I was at Morehouse the atmosphere was different. The student body was more vocal and certainly more political. We didn't take what the administration told us at face value. I think we would have been really upset if a young Black filmmaker came to our campus to shoot a film and got kicked off by the school. But there wasn't a whimper from any of the students at Morehouse, Spelman, Clark or Morris Brown." As it turned out, after three weeks of shooting, Lee was forced to use just Atlanta University's facilities and reshoot all of the footage shot on other campuses.

School Daze earned commendations from many critics, but it also brought Lee notoriety as a provocateur within the African American community. Prominent blacks complained that Lee had produced an unfavorable depiction of their race, while others, conceding that he offered a valid perspective, nonetheless argued that his perception of black college campus life was one best withheld from a white society.

After the release of *School Daze* Lee shifted his focus from internal prejudice to external racism in *Do the Right Thing.* Occurring on the hottest day of the year, the action of *Do the Right Thing* takes place in Bedford-Stuyvesant, a largely black New York City neighborhood. It evokes real interracial incidents, like one he mentioned in his book *Do the Right Thing:* "I heard a radio newscast that two Black youths had been beaten up by a gang of white youths," Lee wrote. "The two Black kids were hospitalized. They were collecting bottles and cans when they got jumped. This happened on Christmas night. . . . Can you imagine if [this incident] had taken place in the summer, on the hottest day of the year? I'd be a fool not to work the subject of racism into *Do the Right Thing.*

Do the Right Thing centers on a pizzeria owned and run by Sal, ostensibly a non-racist Italian who is comfortable with his black clientele and employees. Trouble begins when Buggin' Out, a black patron, asks Sal to add some black people to his pizzeria's "Wall of Fame," which consists of only Italian-Americans. Sal refuses, tempers rise, and a racial slur ultimately triggers violence. The climax occurs when the police choke a black man to death in front of the whole neighborhood. Sal's delivery boy, Mookie (played by Lee), then incites a riot by throwing a garbage can through the pizzeria window. In a sequence preceding the fight, Lee had stopped the story to have his characters spout racial slurs into the camera. It "was meant to rouse emotions," Lee explained in *Do the Right Thing.* "It's funny the way people react to it. They laugh at every slur except the one directed at their ethnic group." The honesty with which Lee treated his subject earned *Do the Right Thing* substantial praise from some critics and many laughs of self-recognition from audiences. David Chute, reviewing Lee's book about the film in the *Los Angeles Times Book Review,* called *Do the Right Thing* Lee's "most controlled and effective picture" to date and noted that his vision is that of an artist, not a journalist. "A personal frame of reference like this would not seem startling in an Italian-American or WASP director," Chute commented, "but to the great discredit of the American film biz the black version is still a novelty. Not for long."

Lee's next venture, *Mo' Better Blues,* paired him for the first time with Denzel Washington, who would later star in several other Lee films. *Mo' Better Blues* also brought Lee back to his father's work—music— a profession that Spike Lee had avoided. "Being the first born, not becoming a musician was a part of my rebelliousness," he wrote in *Spike Lee's "Gotta Have It."* But jazz was still close to his heart, and when filmmakers such as Clint Eastwood and Woody Allen started making films about it, Lee felt he had to get involved himself. As he said in his book about the making of *Mo' Better Blues:* "I couldn't let Woody Allen do a jazz film before I did. I was on a mission." The film, which shows the conflicts a modern-day trumpeter faces between his music and his love life, was the first motion picture produced by Lee's own company, Forty Acres and a Mule, named for what every black person in America had been promised after the abolition of slavery.

Lee's next release, *Jungle Fever,* was his fifth film in six years. Critics characterized it variously as a film about interracial sex, a cry from the heart about the tragedies of the drug culture, and a collection of vignettes on a wide range of current issues. The film features a married black architect named Flipper and his Italian-American secretary, Angie, who are having an affair. The repercussions from their liaison ripple through their relationships with a host of others, including Flipper's crack-addicted brother and Angie's racist family. Calling *Jungle Fever* Lee's "best movie" in a review for *Newsweek,* Jack Kroll commented that Lee "uses the theme of interracial sex to explore the mythology of race, sex and class in an America where both blacks and whites are reassessing the legacy of integration and the concept of separatism from every point on the political spectrum." Lee's treatment of the issue of skin color, which is sometimes a point of contention even among blacks, was of particular interest to *Times Literary Supplement* contributor Gerald Early, who noted that Lee shows both dark-skinned Flipper and his lighter-complexioned wife as being "obsessed with the insults they endured as children about their colour. What is racial identity if someone can be attacked from outside a group for pretensions of purity, and from inside because of a 'mongrelized' appearance?" Other critics pointed to the powerful drug theme that grows in importance as the film progresses. In his *Time* article on black filmmaking, Richard Corliss summed up *Jungle Fever* as an "assured" film about "the ghetto epidemic of drugs. . . . Who is sleeping with whom matters less here, as it should anywhere, than the people who die and the things that kill them."

The fall of 1992 saw the release of Lee's *Malcolm X.* Nearly three and a half hours long, the film chronicles the life of the controversial and multifaceted black leader who in a single lifetime was a street hustler, black-separatist preacher, and eloquent humanist. Several reviewers acknowledged the challenge of portraying such a complex life on film, and pleasing the various factions in black society that each focused on their favorite aspects of the man. Lee himself felt that many blacks have "a very limited view of Malcolm"; they fail to understand that "the man evolved, was constantly evolving, even at the time of [his] assassination," he noted in a *Time* interview with Janice C. Simpson.

Lee embarked on *Malcolm X* amid a storm of controversy. Black cultural leaders such as poet Amiri Baraka, a vocal critic of Lee's movies, warned the filmmaker not to "trash" Malcolm's legacy. Others worried that Lee would overemphasize certain aspects of Malcolm's life, such as his street years or his split from the militant Black Muslim organization that was rumored to have resulted in Malcolm's assassination. Lee caused a stir of his own before winning the opportunity to make the film by questioning why white director Norman Jewison had been selected to film a black story. He also wrestled with producer Warner Brothers over the movie's length and cost; after he exceeded his budget, financial—but not creative—control of the project was taken from Lee's hands.

Upon its release in 1992, *Malcolm X* met with mixed critical response. Assessing the film in the *New Yorker,* Terrence Rafferty acknowledged the dedication Lee showed in the making of the film but regretted what he saw as its impersonal feel. Still, Rafferty felt that "viewers who know nothing about Malcolm, or who know him only by his formidable reputation as a black-pride firebrand, might find everything in the film fascinating, revelatory." Opining that of all Lee's films it is "the least Spikey," *Time*'s Corliss judged it "the movie equivalent of an authorized biography." Several critics questioned the film's length, a concern Lee addressed in his *Time* interview. "There was so much to tell," he asserted. "This was not going to be an abbreviated, abridged version of *Malcolm X.*" Vincent Canby, writing for the *New York Times,* largely applauded Lee's efforts, calling the movie "an ambitious, tough, seriously considered biographical film that, with honor, eludes easy characterization." He did not find it entirely successful, but as he put it, Lee had "attempted the impossible and almost brought it off." One measure of the film's impact was that soon after its release, Malcolm's autobiography, upon which *Malcolm X* was partly based, reached the top of the *New York Times* nonfiction best-seller list—nearly thirty years after its original 1965 publication. As he had with most of his previous films, Lee released his own print companion to the movie: *By Any Means Necessary: The Trials and Tribulations of the Making of "Malcolm X."*

Lee received a mixed reception with his directoral efforts immediately following *Malcolm X.* 1994's *Crooklyn* takes viewers back to Lee's childhood days growing up in Brooklyn, New York. The film features a black family trying to maintain its cohesiveness and economic well-being during the early 1970s. In particular, it focuses on a struggling jazz musician and his hard-working, sensible wife and on the only daughter out of five children, Troy, whose coming-of-age journey represents the emotional heart of the movie. Critics reacted positively to the film, praising Lee's ability to evoke 1970s Brooklyn and his success in presenting a family drama without a strong central narrative. Discussing the movie in the *Nation,* Stuart

Klawans noted "the unforced honesty and warmth that not only set the picture apart from most others in the theaters today but also establish this movie as a new beginning." Similarly, *Rolling Stone* critic Peter Travers remarked that "*Crooklyn* is rich in funny and touching entertainment" and concluded that "this remarkable movie will haunt you for a good long time."

Clockers and *Girl 6,* released in 1995 and 1996, respectively, were not as well received by critics. Ending his seven-year relationship with Universal Studios, Lee chose to finance his next picture independently. *Get on the Bus,* released in 1996, is a documentary-like portrait of the Million Man March, which drew upwards of a million African American men to Washington, D.C. As *Newsweek* columnist N'Gai Croal commented, "even though his hot streak has cooled, Spike Lee will keep right on shooting."

And continue he did, directing *Four Little Girls* in 1997 and joining again with actor Denzel Washington to release *He Got Game* in 1998. Critical reception to each of these films—the first a documentary about the church bombing that occurred in the city of Birmingham, Alabama, in 1963 and the second a dramatic portrait of a father's attempt to make restitution to his son—showed that Lee's innovation in directing, as well as his ability to cause controversy, had by no means "cooled." Commenting on *Four Little Girls* in *Entertainment Weekly,* contributor Mike D'Angelo praised the Academy Award-nominated work as a "sober, often intensely moving exploration of a community's lingering grief and outrage."

He Got Game depicts the temptations facing a young man from the inner city who has a talent for shooting hoops. Tempted by coaches and agents who want to sign him after his graduation from high school, Jesus Shuttlesworth (who is played by actual N.B.A. player Ray Allen) soon finds that those he trusts—including his girlfriend and his estranged father, a convicted murderer who is released from prison for a week for the purpose of convincing Jesus to sign with the state governor's alma mater—really have their own interests at heart. Critics agreed that the film was an ambitious undertaking; as an *Entertainment Weekly* contributor noted, "Right from the start, Lee invites us to see basketball as a majestic myth of national striving. He's also announcing the grandeur of his ambition, which is to tell an epic tale of sports and celebrity, of fathers and sons, of the physicality of American grace." Remarking on the film's creative contradictions—Lee employs a number of artificial cinematic techniques, employs stereotypical characters,weaves together a tangle of multiple plot lines, and sets the whole film against a sweeping score of traditional Americana by Aaron Copeland punctuated by rap from Public Enemy—in his *New Republic* review, Stanley Kauffmann praised Lee for "working on a subject [basketball] he cares about and . . . doing it with polish." Viewing *He Got Game* as an effective father-son drama, *Maclean's* reviewer Brian D. Johnson noted that "for once, [Lee] refrains from outright preaching. Instead he uses bold storytelling and raw emotion to make a sports movie that sidesteps the usual cliches—one that is not about winning or losing, but about how the players are played."

Continuing to forge his own path as a filmmaker—comparisons to another innovative British director, Alfred Hitchcock (who, like Lee, also appeared in his own films) have been common in reviews of his work—Lee's directoral style has been described by *Entertainment Weekly* contributor Jeff Gordinier as a use of "flashy colors, whirling cameras, [and] political polemic, mixed in with street talk." Well known for his films, his leadership role as a black filmmaker, and his tendency to incite debate within the black community, Lee remarked in *Spike Lee's "Gotta Have It"* that a growing sense of responsibility to his fellow African Americans has accompanied his hard work and ultimate success. "You really carry a burden as a black filmmaker," Lee added. "There are so few black films that when you do one it has to represent every black person in the world. If you're white, you're not going to protest in front of a theater because the film is about this or that because it is one of two hundred white Hollywood films that might have been released that year."

Lee's *Summer of Sam,* released by the Walt Disney Company's Touchstone Pictures, marks a departure for the filmmaker. Lee leaves his familiar subject of the African-American community to examine the problems facing members of an Italian-American neighborhood during the sweltering summer of 1977, when the city was held hostage by the psychopathic killer known as "Son of Sam." Nonetheless, reviewers draw comparisons between this work and Lee's earlier films. "Spike Lee goes into the throbbing heart of the Bronx during an unbelievable summer," writes *Jet* contributor Sylvia P. Flanagan, "to paint a portrait that is rather intimate and panoramic." "Lee has made a movie that is less about Sam than about the summer," a *Newsweek* contributor declares. "The shootings, although graphic, and Son of Sam himself, although frighteningly loony, are mostly just the backdrop against which Lee plays variations on one of his familiar themes, violence and ignorance among working-class white people." "Lee's subject is social breakdown, the descent of order and reason into anger and chaos," says Dave Kehr in *Film Comment.* "As in *Do the Right Thing,* the tension builds to an act of martyrdom—the only question is which of the characters will be sacrificed to the gods of chaos, so that once again order can be restored."

BIOGRAPHICAL/CRITICAL SOURCES:

BOOKS

Authors and Artists for Young Adults, Volume 4, Gale, 1990.

Chapman, Kathleen Ferguson, *Spike Lee,* Creative Education, 1997.

Five for Five: The Films of Spike Lee, Stewart, Tabori, 1991.

Hardy, James Earl, *Spike Lee,* Chelsea House, 1996.

Haskins, Jim, *Spike Lee: By Any Means Necessary,* Walker, 1997.

Jones, Maurice K., *Spike Lee and the African American Filmmakers; A Choice of Colors,* Millbrook Press, 1996.

Lee, Spike, *Spike Lee's "Gotta Have It": Inside Guerilla Filmmaking,* Simon & Schuster, 1987.

Lee, Spike, and Lisa Jones, *Uplift the Race: The Construction of "School Daze,"* Simon & Schuster, 1988.

Lee, Spike, and Lisa Jones, *"Do the Right Thing": The New Spike Lee Joint,* Fireside Press, 1989.

McDaniel, Melissa, *Spike Lee: On His Own Terms,* F. Watts, 1998.

Reid, Mark A., editor, *Spike Lee's Do the Right Thing,* Cambridge University Press, 1997.

PERIODICALS

Advocate, October 31, 1995, p. 49.

African American Review, February, 1998, p. 215; summer, 1998, p. 215.

America, July 1, 1994, p. 18.

American Film, September, 1986; January-February, 1988; July-August, 1989.

American Imago, summer, 1995, p. 155.

Black Scholar, winter, 1993, p. 35.

Chicago Tribune, August 13, 1986; August 20, 1986; October 5, 1986; February 25, 1988; March 3, 1988.

Ebony, January, 1987; September, 1987; May, 1994, p. 28.

Entertainment Weekly, October 14, 1994, p. 70; November 17, 1995, p. 91; March 15,1996, p. 74;

April 5, 1996, p. 55; November/December, 1997, p. 61; May 8, 1998, p. 52; September 4,1998, p. 90.

Essence, September, 1986; February, 1988; July 1988.

Film Comment, October, 1986; July, 1999, p. 75.

Film Quarterly, winter, 1986-87.

Jet, November 10, 1986; February 2, 1988; May 2, 1988; May 16, 1994, p. 56; October 17, 1994, p. 61; October 9, 1995, p. 33; July 19, 1999, p. 38.

London Review of Books, March 25, 1993, p. 24.

Los Angeles Times, August 21, 1986; February 11, 1988; February 12, 1988.

Los Angeles Times Book Review, June 30, 1989, p. 6.

Maclean's, May 4, 1998, p. 68.

Ms., September-October, 1991, p. 78.

Nation, June 20, 1994, p. 882; June 20, 1994, p. 882; April 29, 1996, p. 35; June 1, 1998,p. 35.

National Review, July 26, 1999, p. 46.

New Republic, April 29, 1996, p. 26; June 1, 1998, p. 24.

Newsweek, September 8, 1986, p. 65; February 15, 1988, p. 62; July 3, 1989, pp. 64-66; October 2, 1989, p. 37; August 6, 1990, p. 62; June 10, 1991, pp. 44-47; August 26, 1991, pp. 52-54; November 16, 1992, pp. 66, 71, 74, March 25, 1996, p. 72; April 22, 1996, p. 75; May 4, 1998, p. 80; July 5, 1999, p. 22; July 12, 1999, p. 65.

New Yorker, October 6, 1986, pp. 128-30; July 24, 1989, pp. 78-81; August 13, 1990, pp.82-84; June 17, 1991, p. 99; November 30, 1992, pp. 160-62; May 23, 1994, p. 95.

New York Review of Books, September 28, 1989, p. 37.

New York Times, March 27, 1983; August 8, 1986; April 10, 1986; September 7, 1986; November 14, 1986; August 9, 1987; February 12, 1988; February 20, 1989; October 29, 1992, p. C22; November 15, 1992, p. H1, H23; November 18, 1992, pp. C19, C23; November 19, 1992, p. B4; April 7,1996, p. H13.

New York Times Book Review, December 13, 1987, p. 14; November 29, 1992, p. 3.

New York Times Magazine, August 9, 1987, pp. 26, 29, 39, 41.

People, October 13, 1986, p. 67; July 10, 1989, p. 67; March 5, 1990, pp. 97, 99; May 4,1998, p. 31.

Premiere, August, 1999, p. 28.

Publishers Weekly, November 16, 1992, p. 56.

Rolling Stone, December 1980; April 21, 1988, p. 32; June 30, 1988, p. 21; December 1,1988, p. 31; June 29, 1989, p. 27; July 13, 1989, pp. 104, 107, 109, 174; June 27, 1991, p. 75; July 11,

1991, p. 63; June 2, 1994, p. 75; April, 18, 1996, p. 77.

Time, October 6, 1986, p. 94; July 3, 1989, p. 62; July 17, 1989, p. 92; August 20, 1990,p. 62; June 17, 1991, pp. 64-66, 68; March 16, 1992, p. 71; November 23, 1992, pp. 64-65; November 30,1992; December 19, 1994, p. 29; September 18, 1995; February 26, 1996, p. 71.

Times Literary Supplement, September, 6, 1991, p. 18.

Village Voice, February 16, 1988; March 22, 1988.

Wall Street Journal, November 16, 1992; April 2, 1996, p. A12.

Washington Post, August 22, 1986; August 24, 1986; August 29, 1986; March 20, 1987; February 19, 1988.*

*   *   *

LEE, Spike
See LEE, Shelton Jackson

*   *   *

LEWIS, Padmore
See LEWIS, Sandra Padmore

*   *   *

LEWIS, Sandra Padmore 1957-
(Padmore Lewis)

PERSONAL: Born October 16, 1957, in Barbados; daughter of Desmond (a carpenter) and Etheline (a homemaker; maiden name, Padmore) Spooner; married David A. Lewis (an automotive body repairer), June 16, 1990. *Ethnicity:* "Black." *Education:* Pace University, B.B.A., 1986; Long Island University, M.B.A., 1991. *Avocational interests:* Walking, reading, "making a difference in another person's life."

ADDRESSES: Office—Port Authority of New York and New Jersey, 1 World Trade Center, 69W, New York, NY 10048.

CAREER: Port Authority of New York and New Jersey, New York City, accountant, 1994—. Community volunteer.

MEMBER: Institute of Management Accounting (associate director, 1994—).

WRITINGS:

Some Things I Have Noticed, American Literary Press (Baltimore, MD), 1996.

Some writings appear under the name Padmore Lewis.

WORK IN PROGRESS: Two novels, *For the Love of Friends* and *Time and Years Have Changed Us.*

SIDELIGHTS: Sandra Padmore Lewis commented: "I am an honest and sincere person who always wants to be of some comfort to another person. I want others to know that, no matter what they are going through, somebody else has walked that road before. My work is influenced by the experiences of others. I listen very carefully; then, in the form of poetry, I tell others what I hear them saying or what they should be saying. Then I look within my spirituality to find the most appropriate phrase to suit the occasion. My subjects are issues of an everyday nature: jealousy, loneliness, sickness, dying."

*   *   *

LITTLE, Malcolm   1925-1965
(El-Hajj Malik El-Shabazz, Malcolm X)

PERSONAL: Born May 19, 1925, in Omaha, NE; assassinated February 21, 1965, in New York, NY; son of Earl (a minister and activist) and Louise Little; married wife, Betty (a student nurse), 1958; children: six daughters. *Religion:* Muslim.

CAREER: Activist. Worker in Lost-Found Nation of Islam (Black Muslims) religious sect, 1952-64, began as assistant minister of mosque in Detroit, MI, then organized mosque in Philadelphia, PA, became minister of Mosque Number Seven in Harlem, became national minister, 1963; established Muslim Mosque, Inc., 1964; lecturer and writer. Founded Organization of Afro-American Unity, New York City, 1964.

WRITINGS:

UNDER NAME MALCOLM X

(With Alex Haley) *The Autobiography of Malcolm X,* introduction by M. S. Handler, epilogue by

Haley, Grove, 1965, later edition, Ballantine, 1990.
Malcolm X Speaks: Selected Speeches and Statements, edited and with prefatory notes by George Breitman, Merit Publishers, 1965.
Malcolm X on Afro-American History, Merit Publishers, 1967, expanded edition, Pathfinder Press, 1970.
The Speeches of Malcolm X at Harvard, edited and with an introductory essay by Archie Epps, Morrow, 1968.
Malcolm X Talks to Young People, Young Socialist Alliance, 1969.
Malcolm X and the Negro Revolution: The Speeches of Malcolm X, edited and with an introductory essay by Archie Epps, Owen, 1969.
Two Speeches by Malcolm X, Merit Publishers, 1969.
By Any Means Necessary: Speeches, Interviews, and a Letter by Malcolm X, edited by George Breitman, Pathfinder Press,1970.
The End of White World Supremacy: Four Speeches, edited and with an introduction by Benjamin Goodman, Merlin House, 1971.
Malcolm X: The Last Speeches, Pathfinder Press, 1989.

Work represented in anthologies, including *100 and More Quotes by Garvey, Lumumba, and Malcolm X,* compiled by Shawna Maglangbayan, Third World Press, 1975.

Also speaker, with Bayard Rustin, on recording *A Choice of Two Roads,* Pacifica Archives.

ADAPTATIONS: James Baldwin adapted portions of *The Autobiography of Malcolm X* as *One Day, When I Was Lost: A Scenario,* Dial, 1973; a screenplay based on *The Autobiography of Malcolm X,* directed by Spike Lee, was produced by Forty Acres and a Mule Filmworks, 1992.

SIDELIGHTS: Malcolm Little was a religious and sociopolitical activist who rose to prominence, and notoriety, in the mid-1950s under the name Malcolm X. A staunch, outspoken advocate of black separatism, he inspired many with his efforts on behalf of Elijah Muhammad's Black Muslim religion, which characterizes the black race as superior and the white race as inherently evil. For Malcolm X, the Western black's sole response to racism was total withdrawal from Western culture and society. These radical contentions, while uniting a portion of the American black community, alienated other members, including civil rights activists and pacifists. Eventually Malcolm

X became disillusioned with Elijah Muhammad's controversial religion and left to start his own Muslim organization. This action, in turn, offended Elijah Muhammad and his followers, and in early 1965, while preparing to speak in a Harlem ballroom, Malcolm X was gunned down by men believed sympathetic to the Black Muslims.

As I. F. Stone noted in the *New York Review of Books,* "Malcolm X was born into Black Nationalism." Earl Little, Malcolm's father, was a Baptist minister who strongly supported separatist Marcus Garvey's back-to-Africa movement in the 1920s. For his actions on behalf of Garvey, Earl Little soon found himself the target of hostility while living in Omaha, Nebraska, where members of the racist Ku Klux Klan organization threatened his family because he was sparking dissension among the normally cooperative blacks. The Littles consequently left Omaha, but during the next few years they failed to find a hospitable community and thus moved often. In his autobiography, Malcolm X recalled a particularly harrowing experience in Lansing, Michigan, where his family home was torched by members of the Black Legion, an oddly named band of white supremacists. Shortly afterwards the corpse of Earl Little was found horribly butchered.

Following Earl Little's death, Louise Little and her eight children subsisted on welfare. Eventually, however, the severe strain overwhelmed her and she succumbed to mental illness. Louise Little was then placed in a mental institution and her children were sent separately to various foster homes. Despite this continued adversity and emotional hardship, Malcolm still held aspirations of assimilation in America's predominantly white society. But even those hopes faded after he confided to his high-school English teacher that he hoped to someday become a lawyer, whereupon the teacher urged him towards a vocation instead of a profession and told him to be "realistic about being a nigger."

A distinguished student, Malcolm was shattered by his teacher's racist counseling, and soon afterward he quit high school. Living with a sister in Boston, Malcolm found menial work and began associating with low-lifes and criminals. He became involved with illegal gambling, managed his own prostitution ring, and consorted with drug dealers. Eventually he also sold narcotics, to which he swiftly became addicted, and turned to robbery to sustain his drug habit. He developed a formidable reputation as an enterprising, quick-thinking hustler, becoming notori-

ous in the Boston ghetto as "Detroit Red." With that notoriety, however, came increasing attention from the police, and in early 1946 Malcolm was arrested and charged with robbery. That February—three months before his twenty-first birthday—he was sentenced to ten years imprisonment.

In the penitentiary Malcolm continued his reckless ways, using drugs and presenting such an unsavory demeanor that his fellow inmates referred to him as "Satan." Because of his vicious behavior he was often held in solitary confinement. But he did manage to befriend another convicted burglar, Bimbi, who introduced him to the prison's extensive library. Through the library Malcolm broadened his education and familiarized himself with subjects ranging from philosophy to politics. He also began studying the tenets of the Black Muslims' Lost-Found Nation of Islam, a religion that extolled the superiority of the black race and denounced the white as evil and doomed to destruction. The Black Muslims' founder and leader, Elijah Muhammad, proclaimed himself divine messenger of the Muslim deity, Allah, and—like Marcus Garvey—counseled his followers to abjure white America in favor of an autonomous black society. Elijah Muhammad's doctrine of black pride exerted considerable appeal to Malcolm, who denounced his allegedly enslaving Christian surname and adopted the name Malcolm X.

While still in prison Malcolm X corresponded with Elijah Muhammad, who lived comfortably at Black Muslim headquarters in Chicago, and after obtaining freedom in 1952 he traveled there and commenced a brief tutelage under the Muslim leader. He then served briefly as an assistant minister at a Detroit mosque before becoming minister at Harlem's Mosque Number Seven. It was in Harlem that Malcolm X achieved impressive status as an articulate, mercurial spokesperson for the radical black perspective. From street corners, church pulpits, and college podiums he railed against racism and championed separatism and faith in Allah as the salvation of blacks. He claimed that civil rights, equal opportunity, and integration were all futile within a society that was determinedly racist. Even Christianity was reviled as a method of enslavement and was denounced as a historical distortion—Christ having been, according to Malcolm X, a black. He advised blacks to reject white society and unite under Elijah Muhammad and the Black Muslim faith, which held the true way to dignity for blacks.

Malcolm X proved an impressive representative for Elijah Muhammad, and as he enthusiastically proselytized for the Black Muslims their membership increased significantly. Elijah Muhammad, acknowledging the impressive effectiveness of his acolyte, named him the religion's first national minister. As Malcolm X rose in status, however, he became increasingly critical of Elijah Muhammad's materialism, particularly his many expensive cars and business suits and his lavishly furnished estate in Chicago. In addition, he was dismayed when former secretaries claimed that Elijah Muhammad had seduced them and sired their children, thus violating the sect's prohibitions against sexual promiscuity. Elijah Muhammad, in turn, reportedly grew resentful of Malcolm X's growing prominence across the nation and thus his formidable influence within the Black Muslim organization.

Rivalry between the two men peaked in 1963 when Malcolm X violated Elijah Muhammad's commandment of silence regarding the November 22nd assassination of President Kennedy and termed it a case of "the chicken coming home to roost." Malcolm X, who later explained that his comment was meant to indicate that "the hate in white men. . . finally had struck down the President," was reprimanded by Elijah Muhammad for the potentially incendiary remark. "That was a very bad statement," Elijah Muhammad told him. "The country loved this man." He ordered Malcolm X to refrain from public comment for ninety days, and Malcolm complied.

Within days, however, Malcolm X learned that members of his sect were plotting his demise. His dissatisfaction with the Black Muslims mounted, and he decided to tour Mecca, birthplace of the Muslim prophet Muhammad. Once there, Malcolm X experienced a powerful conversion, one which left him with greater compassion for people of all races and nationalities. He renamed himself El-Hajj Malik El-Shabazz and vowed to promote greater harmony among all blacks, including non-Muslims and civil rights activists he had alienated earlier with his uncompromising positions. Once back in the United States he founded his own Muslim association, the Organization of Afro-American Unity, and began actively working to unite blacks throughout the world.

Once he began operating outside the Black Muslim sect, Malcolm X was apparently perceived as a threat to the organization. "Now I'm out," he stated. "And there's the fear [that] if my image isn't shattered, the Muslims in the movement will leave." He was informed that members within the organization were plotting to end his life, and in mid-February he told the *New York Times* that he was a "marked man."

Around that time his home was fire bombed. But he was undaunted and continued to speak on behalf of black unity and harmony. On February 21, 1965, he stepped to the podium in a Harlem ballroom and greeted the audience of four hundred that had gathered to hear him speak. Within seconds at least three men rose from their seats and began firing at Malcolm X with shotguns and pistols. Seven shots slammed him backwards while spectators scrambled for cover. As gunfire continued—more than thirty shots were reportedly heard—daring witnesses attacked and subdued the assassins. Three men—Talmadge Hayer and Black Muslims Norman 3X Butler and Thomas 15X Johnson—were eventually convicted of the killing, and it is widely believed the assassins intended to intimidate Malcolm X's followers into remaining within the Black Muslim fold.

In the years since his death Malcolm X has come to be recognized as a leading figure in the black struggle for recognition and equality. *The Autobiography of Malcolm X,* published the same year as his death, is highly regarded as a moving account of his own experiences with racism, his criminal past, and his years as an activist for both the Black Muslims and his own Afro-American organization. During the remaining years of the 1960s Malcolm X's speeches and comments were collected and published in volumes such as *Malcolm X Speaks, Malcolm X on Afro-American History,* and *Malcolm X and the Negro Revolution.* Together with the autobiography, these books offer numerous insights into America's social climate from the mid-1950s to the mid-1960s and articulate the concerns of a significant portion of the black community in those years. Additionally, they serve as an imposing indication of Malcolm X's beliefs, his achievements, and his potential, which—like that of President Kennedy, Reverend Martin Luther King, Jr., and Senator Robert Kennedy—were violently rendered unrealized. As I. F. Stone noted in his essay-review for the *New York Review of Books:* "There are few places on earth where whites have not grown rich robbing [blacks]. It was Malcolm's great contribution to help make us aware of this." Stone called Malcolm X's murder "a loss to the country as well as to his race."

BIOGRAPHICAL/CRITICAL SOURCES:

BOOKS

Abbott, Philip, *States of Perfect Freedom: Autobiography and American Political Thought,* University of Massachusetts Press, 1987, pp. 27-57.

Alexander, Rae Pace, *Young and Black in America,* Random House, 1973.

Barr, Roger, *Malcolm X,* Lucent Books, 1994.

Black Literature Criticism, Gale, Volume 2, 1992.

Bloom, Harold, *The Autobiography of Malcolm X,* Chelsea House, 1995.

Breitman, George, *The Last Year of Malcolm X: The Evolution of a Revolutionary,* Merit Publications, 1967.

Breitman, George; Herman Porter; and Baxter Smith, *The Assassination of Malcolm X,* revised edition, Pathfinder,1991.

Brown, Kevin, *Malcolm X: His Life and Legacy,* Millbrook Press, 1995.

Clarke, John Henrik, editor and author of introduction, *Malcolm X: The Man and His Times,* Macmillan, 1969.

Collins, Rodnell P. and A. Peter Bailey, *Seventh Child: A Family Memoir of Malcolm X,* Birch Lane Press, 1998.

Cone, James H., *Martin & Malcolm & America: A Dream or a Nightmare,* Orbis Books, 1991.

Contemporary Literary Criticism, Gale, Volume 82, 1994.

Curtis, Richard, *Life of Malcolm X,* Macrae Smith, 1971.

Darling, Edward, *When Sparks Fly Upward,* Washburn,1970.

Davis, Lenwood G., *Malcolm X: A Selected Bibliography,* Greenwood Press, 1984.

Davis, Lucille, *Malcolm X: A Photo-illustrated Biography,* Bridgestone, 1998.

DeCaro, Louis A., *On the Side of My People: A Religious Life of Malcolm X,* New York University Press, 1996.

Diamond, Arthur, *Malcolm X: A Voice for Black America,* Enslow, 1994.

Dyson, Michael Eric, *Making Malcolm: The Myth and Meaning of Malcolm X,* Oxford University Press, 1995.

Goldman, Peter Louis, *Death and Life of Malcolm X,* University of Illinois Press, 1979.

Gallen, David, *A Malcolm X Reader,* Carroll & Graf,1994.

Haskins, James, *Revolutionaries,* Lippincott, 1971.

Jamal, Hakin A., *From the Dead Level: Malcolm X and Me,* Random House, 1972.

Johnson, Timothy V., *Malcolm X: A Comprehensive Annotated Bibliography,* Garland Publishing, 1986.

Lomax, Louise E., *To Kill a Black Man,* Holloway House,1968.

McKinley, James, *Assassination in America,* Harper, 1977.

Miah, Malik, editor and author of introduction, *Assassination of Malcolm X,* Pathfinder Press, 1976.

Paris, Peter J., *Black Leaders in Conflict: Joseph H. Jackson, Martin Luther King, Jr., Malcolm X, Adam Clayton Powell, Jr.,* Pilgrim Press, 1978.

Parks, Gordon, *Born Black,* Lippincott, 1971.

Perry, Bruce, *Malcolm: The Life of a Man Who Changed Black America,* Station Hill Press, 1991.

Perry, Theresa, *Teaching Malcolm X,* Routledge, 1996.

Playboy Interviews, Playboy Press, 1967.

Sagan, Miriam, *Malcolm X,* Lucent Books, 1997.

Sales, William W., *From Civil Rights to Black Liberation: Malcolm X and the Organization of Afro-American Unity,* SouthEnd Press, 1994.

Shirley, David, *Malcolm X,* Chelsea Juniors (New York),1994.

Stine, Megan, *The Story of Malcolm X,* Civil Rights Leader, Gareth Stevens, 1995.

Strickland, William and Cherll Y. Green, *Malcolm X, Make it Plain,* Viking, 1994.

Wolfenstein, Eugene Victor, *Victims of Democracy: Malcolm X and the Black Revolution,* University of California Press, 1981.

Wood, Joe, *Malcolm X: In Our Own Image,* Anchor Books,1994.

PERIODICALS

American Heritage, February-March, 1995, p. 36.

Catholic World, September, 1967.

Centennial Review, summer, 1972, pp. 221-32.

Christian Century, April 7, 1965, December 23, 1992, p. 1189.

CLA Journal, December, 1979, pp. 125-46.

Commentary, February, 1993, p. 27.

Ebony, October, 1965, June, 1969, February, 1994, p.68, November, 1995, p. 62.

Emerge, February, 1995, p. 59.

Encounter, September, 1973.

Harper's, June, 1964.

Life, March 20, 1964.

Journal of Black Studies, December, 1981.

Nation, March 8, 1965, November 8, 1965.

Negro American Literature Forum, winter, 1970, pp. 107-112.

Negro Education Review, January, 1979.

New Statesman, June 12, 1964.

Newsweek, December 16, 1963, March 8, 1965; November 15, 1965, March 3, 1969, January 8, 1973, May 7, 1979.

New York Review of Books, November 11, 1965.

New York Times, February 22, 1965.

New York Times Book Review, September 11, 1966, April 13, 1969, May 16, 1971.

Quarterly Journal of Speech, February, 1974, pp. 1-13.

Saturday Review, November 20, 1965, July 30, 1966.

Soundings, winter, 1983, pp. 437-49.

Spectator, February 26, 1965.

Time, March 5, 1965; February 23, 1970, June 12, 1972.

Times Literary Supplement, June 9, 1966, May 28, 1971.

Ultimate Reality and Meaning, March, 1990, pp. 33-49.

Washington Post, May 20, 1989.

Yale Review, December, 1966; October, 1983, pp. 1-16.*

*   *   *

LOCKE, Alain (Le Roy) 1886-1954

PERSONAL: Birth-given name, Arthur Locke; born September 13, 1886, in Philadelphia, PA; died following a long illness, June 9 (some sources cite June 10), 1954, in New York, NY; son of Pliny I. (a schoolteacher) and Mary (a schoolteacher; maiden name, Hawkins) Locke. *Education:* Harvard University, B.A. (with honors), 1907, Ph.D., 1918; Oxford University, B.Litt., 1910; graduate study at University of Berlin, 1910-11, and at College de France, Paris. *Religion:* Episcopalian.

CAREER: Howard University, Washington, DC, assistant professor, 1912-17, professor of philosophy, 1917-53, chairperson of philosophy department, 1918-53. Fisk University, exchange professor, 1927-28; Inter-American Exchange Professor in Haiti, 1943; visiting professor at University of Wisconsin—Madison, 1945-46, New School for Social Research, 1947, and City College (now of the City University of New York). Associates in Negro Folk Education, served as secretary and editor.

AWARDS, HONORS: Rhodes Scholar in England, 1907-10; named to 1942 Honor Roll of Race Relations; awarded Haiti's National Order of Honor and Merit.

WRITINGS:

(Editor and contributor) *The New Negro: An Interpretation* (anthology), illustrations by Winold Reiss,

A. and C. Boni (New York City), 1925, reprinted with preface by Robert Hayden, Atheneum (New York City), 1970, and with introduction by Arnold Rampersad, Atheneum, 1992.

(Editor) *Four Negro Poets,* Simon & Schuster (New York City), 1927.

(Editor with Montgomery Gregory) *Plays of Negro Life: A Source-Book of Native American Drama,* illustrations by Aaron Douglas, Harper (New York City), 1927, reprinted, Negro University Press, 1970.

A Decade of Negro Self-Expression (bibliography), [Charlottesville, VA], 1927.

The Negro in America (bibliography), American Library Association (Chicago, IL), 1933.

The Negro and His Music, Associates in Negro Folk Education (Washington, DC), 1936, reprinted, Kennikat (Port Washington, NY), 1968, published with *Negro Art: Past and Present,* Arno Press, 1969.

Negro Art: Past and Present, Associates in Negro Folk Education, 1936, published with *The Negro and His Music,* Arno Press, 1969.

(Editor and annotator) *The Negro in Art: A Pictorial Record of the Negro Artist and of the Negro Theme in Art,* Associates in Negro Folk Education, 1940, reprinted, Hacker (New York City), 1971.

(Editor with Bernhard J. Stern) *When Peoples Meet: A Study in Race and Culture Contacts,* Committee on Workshops, Progressive Education Association (New York City), 1942, revised edition, Hinds, Hayden & Eldredge, 1946.

Le Role du Negre dans la Culture des Ameriques (title means "The Role of the Negro in American Culture"), Impr. de l'Etat, 1943.

The Negro and His Music [and] *Negro Art: Past and Present,* Arno Press, 1969.

Race Contacts and Interracial Relations: Lectures on the Theory and Practice of Race, edited and with an introduction by Jeffrey C. Stewart, foreword by Michael R. Winston, preface by Thomas C. Battle, Howard University Press (Washington, DC), 1992.

Also author of *The Problem of Classification in Theory of Value,* 1918; *The Negro in American Literature,* 1929; *Frederick Douglass: A Biography of Anti-Slavery,* 1935; *Americans All: Immigrants All,* 1939; *World View on Race and Democracy,* 1945; and *The Negro Artist Comes of Age,* 1945. Editor of the "Bronze Booklet" series of studies on Negro cultural achievements. Work represented in anthologies, including *The Black Aesthetic* and *Theatre: Essays on the Arts of the Theatre.* Contributor to periodicals, including *Harlem: A Forum of Negro Life, Phylon, Opportunity, Nation, Annals of the American Academy of Political and Social Science, Modern Quarterly, Theatre Arts, Carolina,* and *Crisis.* Edited a special Harlem issue of *Survey Graphic,* 1925.

SIDELIGHTS: According to some critics, Alain Locke virtually brought about the Harlem Renaissance, a period of great literary and artistic activity originating in New York City during the 1920s, by compiling *The New Negro: An Interpretation,* an anthology of the most outstanding African-American poetry and prose of the early twentieth century. Because of the high literary merit of the works in the anthology, by such authors as Langston Hughes, Countee Cullen, Zora Neale Hurston, James Weldon Johnson, Claude McKay, and Jean Toomer, critics began to take black writing seriously for the first time. *The New Negro* also served as a unifying link for struggling African-American authors who had previously thought that they were alone in their literary endeavors. Exposed to other writers' works and able to study different forms and themes, a generation of African-American authors was inspired by *The New Negro.*

Locke also urged African Americans to seek inspiration and take pride in their rich cultural heritage. In *The Negro in Art: A Pictorial Record of the Negro Artist and of the Negro Theme in Art* Locke stresses that the African-American man should look to the works of his African ancestors for subject matter, methods, and motifs to apply to modern painting and sculpture. The first section of *The Negro in Art* provides examples of seventeenth- to twentieth-century art works by Africans, mostly American. The second section contains illustrations of African subjects in art; and the third part deals with the influence of African art on modern painting and sculpture.

Locke first became aware of the need to promote African culture while touring the American South for six months in 1911. He witnessed prejudice and discrimination, and realized that black *literati* and artists could hold the key to easier race relations. He believed that by setting high standards for themselves and using their talents to gain the respect of white society, African Americans would cast aside their self-doubt, become more confident, and think of themselves as equal to white Americans. Locke's 1916 social study, *Race Contacts and Interracial Relations,* grew out of his experiences in the South.

The author was also interested in interactions between majority and minority groups on a national and international level. On that subject Locke edited, with Bernhard J. Stern, *When Peoples Meet: A Study in Race and Culture Contacts.* While serving as an Inter-American Exchange Professor in Haiti, he wrote *Le Role du Negre dans la Culture des Ameriques* (title means "The Role of the Negro in American Culture").

"Locke began his career . . . as a philosopher," Valerie Sweeney Prince noted in the *Reference Guide to American Literature,* "but his career spans a range that includes philosophy, anthropology, art, music, literature, education, political theory, sociology, and African studies." Out of this eclectic background emerged the aesthetic and cultural theories that motivated his prolific writings. Locke believed that African Americans have an obligation to aspire to the highest possible levels of artistic excellence, partly to compel Caucasian society to take them seriously, but also to increase their self-esteem. He wrote that African Americans need to be perceived and to perceive themselves as Americans, as well as African Americans, but they can best achieve this by looking to their African and ethnic roots, not by imitating European or white standards of experience. He urged that the most talented African-American artists and scholars are the ideal leaders to encourage artistic and intellectual growth among the African-American population at large and to promote the cultural unity that would secure this "renaissance" as a cohesive and enduring movement.

Locke demonstrated his own leadership qualities when he published *The New Negro.* His theories, according to a *Twentieth-Century Literary Criticism* contributor, "were a virtual manifesto for artists involved with the Harlem Renaissance, while his writings on the relationship between culture and aesthetics continue to act as a catalyst in African-American art and literature today." In 1926 the esteemed educator and scholar W. E. B. Du Bois wrote in a *Crisis* review that *The New Negro* "in many ways marks an epoch. . . . It probably expresses better than any book that has been published in the last ten years the present state of thought and culture among American Negroes and it expresses it so well and so adequately . . . that it is a singularly satisfying and inspiring thing."

This was high praise indeed, for Du Bois was an opponent of the theories that Locke espoused. Several critics of the day (and several since) accused Locke of elitism because of his view that a talented few should be the leaders of the ignorant masses. Locke himself was certainly the member of a small, privileged group. The son of schoolteachers grew up in the genteel atmosphere of urban Philadelphia, distinguished himself at Harvard University, where he studied under the prominent philosopher William James, and became the first African American to earn a Rhodes scholarship and a degree from Oxford University. He also pursued philosophical studies in France and Austria before returning to the United States to teach at Howard University for more than thirty years.

Critics praised Locke for his ground-breaking achievements, but they faulted him for placing greater value on the individual than on the community that he or she is called upon to serve. This criticism was based on Locke's implication, according to Ernest D. Mason in the *Dictionary of Literary Biography,* that "little could be expected, politically, from the economically deprived masses alone." Prevailing opinion at the time leaned toward Du Bois's view that it is the community which fosters the freedom of the individual, not the reverse. Other critics supported Locke, Mason wrote, because "the participation of the masses in the movement was considered by Locke to be fundamental" and "the individual [according to Locke] was always submerged in some group or some larger culture and [in fact] received very little positive attention."

This debate did little to slow the progress of the Harlem Renaissance but, in retrospect, some critics declared that the renaissance ultimately failed to fulfill the enormous and lasting promise it offered. Locke himself "expected only one loyalty," commented Mason, "a loyalty to the folk spirit of the larger black community, and [many writers] failed to meet that demand. . . . The rejection of ideology and sociology in black art signaled the decline of the Harlem Renaissance's popularity and Locke's disappointment with it." Mason added: "The New Negro movement had been tumultuous and feverish but had obviously not produced the desired social and economic results. . . . The Harlem Renaissance vision of the New Negro was significantly flawed, weakened by an excessive realism and messianic-rhetorical moralism which tried to recycle ideals of heart, spirit, brotherhood, and the like when crime, poverty, and misery were taking their toll on much of black American life and culture."

Nevertheless, reported *Twentieth-Century Literary Criticism,* "receiving both credit and blame for the success and eventual demise of the Harlem Renaissance, Locke is remembered today as a critic and

philosopher who applied his thinking to a variety of fields and whose works continue to contribute to current issues concerning the nature and function of an African-American aesthetic."

BIOGRAPHICAL/CRITICAL SOURCES:

BOOKS

Butcher, Margaret J., *The Negro in American Culture: Based on Materials Left by Alain Locke,* Knopf (New York City), 1956.

Dictionary of Literary Biography, Volume 51: *Afro-American Writers from the Harlem Renaissance to 1940,* Gale (Detroit, MI), 1987, pp. 313-321.

Harris, Leonard, editor, *The Philosophy of Alain Locke: Harlem Renaissance and Beyond,* Temple University Press (Philadelphia, PA), 1989.

Linnemann, Russell J., editor, *Alain Locke: Reflections on a Modern Renaissance Man,* Louisiana State University Press (Baton Rouge, LA), 1982.

Reference Guide to American Literature, 3rd edition, St. James Press (Detroit), 1994, pp. 528-530.

Stewart, Jeffrey C., *The Critical Temper of Alain Locke: A Selection of His Essays on Art and Culture,* Garland Publishing (New York City), 1983.

Twentieth-Century Literary Criticism, Volume 43, Gale, 1992, pp. 220-249.

Washington, Johnny, *Alain Locke and Philosophy: A Quest for Cultural Pluralism,* Greenwood Press (Westport, CT), 1986.

Washington, Johnny, *A Journey into the Philosophy of Alain Locke,* Greenwood Press, 1994.

PERIODICALS

African American Review, spring, 1995, p. 152.
Journal of American History, September, 1993, p. 724.

OBITUARIES:

PERIODICALS

New York Times, June 10, 1954, p. 31.*

*   *   *

LOCKETT, Reginald (Franklin) 1947-

PERSONAL: Born November 5, 1947, in Berkeley, CA; son of Jewell and Alyce Irene (Matthis) Lockett;

married Faye Arvis West, January 23, 1983 (divorced September 1, 1987); children: Maya Lomasi Lauren Aimee. *Education:* San Francisco State University, B.A., 1971, M.A., 1972.

ADDRESSES: Office—Department of Language Arts, San Jose City College, 2100 Moorpark Ave., San Jose, CA 95128- 2723.

CAREER: North Peralta Community College, Oakland, CA, instructor in English, 1973-75; Laney College, Oakland, instructor in English, 1975-76; San Francisco State University, San Francisco, CA, lecturer in creative writing, 1976-78; City College of San Francisco, San Francisco, reading lab instructor, beginning in 1982; San Jose City College, San Jose, CA, member of department of language arts.

WRITINGS:

Good Times and No Bread (poetry), Jukebox Press, 1978.

Contributor of numerous poems to literary magazines and anthologies; editor, *Folio,* 1977.*

*   *   *

LOCKWOOD, Robert
  See JOHNSON, Robert

*   *   *

LOGAN, Shirley Wilson 1943-

PERSONAL: Born August 1, 1943, in Due West, SC; daughter of John Theodore and Azzie Lee (Ellis) Wilson; married William J. J. Logan (a physician), October 12, 1968; children: Enid Lynette, John Malcolm, Monica Adele. *Ethnicity:* "African American." *Education:* Johnson C. Smith University, B.A. (summa cum laude), 1964; University of North Carolina at Chapel Hill, M.A., 1966; attended Howard University, 1968-70; University of Maryland at College Park, Ph.D., 1988. *Religion:* Protestant.

ADDRESSES: Office—Department of English, University of Maryland at College Park, College Park, MD 20742.

CAREER: Schoolteacher, 1964-67; Howard University, Washington, DC, instructor in English, 1967-70; schoolteacher, 1970-74; Howard University, instructor in English, 1975-77; University of Maryland at College Park, instructor, 1980-92, assistant professor of English, 1992—, coordinator of Professional Writing Program Computer Laboratory, 1986-92, director of Professional Writing Program, 1992—. Middle States Self-Study Task Force on Achieving Excellence in Undergraduate Education, member, 1996.

MEMBER: Coalition of Women Scholars in the History of Rhetoric, National Council of Teachers of English, Conference on College Composition and Communication.

WRITINGS:

(Editor) *With Pen and Voice: A Critical Anthology of Nineteenth-Century African-American Women,* Southern Illinois University Press (Carbondale, IL), 1995.

Contributor to books, including *Nineteenth-Century Women Learn to Write,* edited by Catherine Hobbs, University Press of Virginia (Charlottesville, VA), 1995; *Feminism and Composition,* edited by Susan C. Jarratt and Lynn Worsham, Modern Language Association of America (New York City), 1996; and *Women and the History of Rhetoric: Roses in the Snow,* edited by Molly Meijer Wertheimer, University of South Carolina Press (Columbia, SC), 1996. Contributor to periodicals, including *Microcomputer, Bulletin of Science, Technology, and Society,* and *SAGE: A Scholarly Journal on Black Women.*

SIDELIGHTS: Shirley Wilson Logan told *CA:* "I have a special interest in studying the persuasive writing of nineteenth-century black women, because the work unites my abiding curiosity about the accomplishments of my outspoken and brave foremothers and my longstanding interest in effective communication."

*   *   *

LORDE, Audre (Geraldine) 1934-1992
  (Rey Domini)

PERSONAL: Born February 18, 1934, in New York, NY; died November 17, 1992 of liver cancer, in Christiansted, St. Croix, U.S. Virgin Islands; daughter of Frederic Byron (a real estate broker) and Linda

Gertrude (Belmar) Lorde; married Edwin Ashley Rollins (an attorney), March 31, 1962 (divorced,1970); children: Elizabeth, Jonathan. *Education:* Attended National University of Mexico, 1954; Hunter College (now Hunter College of the City University of New York), B.A., 1959; Columbia University, M.L.S., 1961. *Politics:* Radical. *Religion:* Quaker.

CAREER: Mount Vernon Public Library, Mount Vernon, NY, librarian, 1961-63; Town School Library, New York City, head librarian, 1966-68; City University of New York, New York City, lecturer in creative writing at City College, 1968, lecturer in education department at Herbert H. Lehman College, 1969-70, associate professor of English at John Jay College of Criminal Justice, beginning 1970; professor of English at Hunter College of CUNY, 1980-87, Thomas Hunter Professor, 1987-88. Distinguished visiting professor, Atlanta University, 1968; poet-in-residence, Tougaloo College, 1968. Lecturer throughout the United States. Founder of Kitchen Table, Women of Color Press.

MEMBER: American Association of University Professors, Harlem Writers Guild, Sisterhood in Support of Sisters in South Africa.

AWARDS, HONORS: National Endowment for the Arts grants, 1968 and 1981; Creative Artists Public Service grants, 1972 and 1976; National Book Award nominee for poetry, 1974, for *From a Land Where Other People Live;* Broadside Poets Award, Detroit, 1975; Woman of the Year, Staten Island Community College,1975; Borough of Manhattan President's Award for literary excellence, 1987; Walt Whitman Citation of Merit, poet laureate of New York, 1991.

WRITINGS:

The Cancer Journals (nonfiction), Spinsters Ink, 1980.
Zami: A New Spelling of My Name (fiction), Crossing Press, 1982.
Sister Outsider (nonfiction), Crossing Press, 1984.
Burst of Light, Firebrand Books, 1988.
Need: A Chorale for Black Women Voices, Women of Color Press, 1990.

POETRY

The First Cities, introduction by Diane di Prima, Poets Press, 1968.
Cables to Rage, Broadside Press, 1970.

From a Land Where Other People Live, Broadside Press, 1973.
The New York Head Shop and Museum, Broadside Press, 1974.
Coal, Norton, 1976.
Between Our Selves, Eidolon, 1976.
The Black Unicorn, Norton, 1978.
Chosen Poems Old and New, Norton, 1982.
Our Dead behind Us, Norton, 1986.
Undersong: Chosen Poems Old and New, Norton, 1992.
The Marvelous Arithmetics of Distance, Norton, 1993.
The Collected Poems of Audre Lorde, Norton, 1997.

CONTRIBUTOR OF POETRY TO ANTHOLOGIES

Langston Hughes, editor, *New Negro Poets, USA,* University of Indiana Press, 1962.
P. Breman, editor, *Sixes and Sevens,* Breman Ltd. (London), 1963.
R. Pool, editor, *Beyond the Blues,* Hand & Flower Press (Amsterdam), 1964.
G. Menarini, editor, *I Negri: Poesie e Canti,* Edizioni Academia (Rome), 1969.
C. Major, editor, *New Black Poetry,* International Press, 1969.
T. Wilentz, editor, *Natural Process,* Hill & Wang, 1970.
T. Cade, editor, *The Black Woman,* American Library Publishing, 1970.

Contributor of poetry to other anthologies, including *Soul-Script,* edited by J. Meyer, Simon & Schuster.

OTHER

The Audre Lorde Compendium: Essays, Speeches, and Journals, introduction by Alice Walker, Pandora (London), 1996.

Contributor of poetry to periodicals, including *Iowa Review, Black Scholar, Chrysalis, Black World, Journal of Black Poetry, Transatlantic Review, Massachusetts Review, Pound, Harlem Writers' Quarterly, Freedomways, Seventeen,* and *Women: A Journal of Liberation;* contributor of fiction, under pseudonym Rey Domini, to *Venture* magazine. Editor, *Pound* magazine (Tougaloo, MS), 1968; poetry editor, *Chrysalis* and *Amazon Quarterly.*

SIDELIGHTS: A self-styled "black, lesbian, mother, warrior, poet," writer Audre Lorde dedicated both her life and her creative talent to confronting and addressing the injustices of racism, sexism, and homophobia. Her poetry, and "indeed all of her writing," according to contributor Joan Martin in *Black Women Writers(1950-1980): A Critical Evaluation,* "rings with passion, sincerity, perception, and depth of feeling." Concerned with modern society's tendency to categorize groups of people, Lorde fought the marginalization of such categories as "lesbian" and "black woman," thereby empowering her readers to react to the prejudice in their own lives. While the widespread critical acclaim bestowed upon Lorde for dealing with lesbian topics made her a target of those opposed to her radical agenda, she continued, undaunted, to express her individuality, refusing to be silenced. As she told interviewer Charles H. Rowell in *Callaloo:* "My sexuality is part and parcel of who I am, and my poetry comes from the intersection of me and my worlds. . . . [White, arch-conservative senator] Jesse Helms's objection to my work is not about obscenity . . .or even about sex. It is about revolution and change. . . . Helms represents. . . . white patriarchal power. . . .[and he] knows that my writing is aimed at his destruction, and the destruction of every single thing he stands for." Fighting a battle with cancer that she documented in her highly acclaimed *Cancer Journals,* Lorde died of the illness in 1992.

Born in New York City of West Indian parents, Lorde came to poetry in her early teens, through a need to express herself. Her first poem to be published was accepted by *Seventeen* magazine when she was still in high school. The poem had been rejected by her school paper, Lorde explains in *Black Women Writers,* because her "English teachers . . . said [it] was much too romantic." Her mature poetry, published in volumes including *New York Head Shop and Museum, Coal,* and *The Black Unicorn,* is sometimes romantic also. Often dealing with her lesbian relationships, her love poems have nevertheless been judged accessible to all by many critics. In Martin's words, "one doesn't have to profess heterosexuality, homosexuality, or asexuality to react to her poems. . . . Anyone who has ever been in love can respond to the straightforward passion and pain sometimes one and the same, in Lorde's poems."

While Lorde's love poems composed much of her earliest work, her experiences of civil unrest during the 1960s, along with Lorde's own confusion over her sexuality—a bisexual, she married in 1962 and had two children before divorcing and making a renewed commitment to her female lovers—created a rapid shift to more political statements. As Jerome Brooks

reported in *Black Women Writers (1950-1980): A Critical Evaluation,* "Lorde's poetry of anger is perhaps her best-known work." In her poem "The American Cancer Society, or There Is More Than One Way to Skin a Coon," she protested against white America thrusting its unnatural culture on blacks; in "The Brown Menace or Poem to the Survival of Roaches," she likened blacks to cockroaches, hated, feared, and poisoned by whites. *Poetry* critic Sandra M. Gilbert remarked that "it's not surprising that Lorde occasionally seems to be choking on her own anger . . . [and] when her fury vibrates through taut cables from head to heart to page, Lorde is capable of rare and, paradoxically, loving jeremiads."

Lorde's anger did not confine itself to racial injustice but extended to feminist issues as well, and occasionally she criticized African American men for their role in the perpetuating of sex discrimination: "As Black people, we cannot begin our dialogue by denying the oppressive nature of *male privilege,*" Lorde stated in *Black Women Writers.* "And if Black males choose to assume that privilege, for whatever reason, raping, brutalizing, and killing women, then we cannot ignore Black male oppression. One oppression does not justify another."

Of her poetic beginnings Lorde once commented in *Black Women Writers:* "I used to speak in poetry. I would read poems, and I would memorize them. People would say, well what do you think, Audre. What happened to you yesterday? And I would recite a poem and somewhere in that poem would be a line or a feeling I would be sharing. In other words, I literally communicated through poetry. And when I couldn't find the poems to express the things I was feeling, that's what started me writing poetry, and that was when I was twelve or thirteen." As an adult, her primary poetic goal remained communication. "I have a duty," she stated later in the same publication, "to speak the truth as I see it and to share not just my triumphs, not just the things that felt good, but the pain, the intense, often unmitigating pain." As a mature poet, however, rather than relying solely on poetry as a means of self-expression Lorde often extracted poems from her personal journals. Explaining the genesis of "Power," a poem about the police shooting of a ten-year-old black child, Lorde discussed her feelings when she learned that the officer involved had been acquitted: "A kind of fury rose up in me; the sky turned red. I felt so sick. I felt as if I would drive this car into a wall, into the next person I saw. So I pulled over. I took out my journal just to air some of my fury, to get it out of my fingertips. Those expressed feelings are that poem."

In addition to race problems and love affairs, another important theme that runs through many of Lorde's poems is the parent-child relationship. Brooks saw a deep concern with the images of her deceased father in Lorde's "Father, Son, and Holy Ghost" which carries over to poems dealing with Africa in *The Black Unicorn*. According to Brooks, "the contact with Africa is the contact with the father who is revealed in a wealth of mythological symbols. . . . The fundamental image of the unicorn indicates that the poet is aware that Africa is for her a fatherland, a phallic terrain." Martin, however, took a different view: "Audre Lorde is a rare creature. . . . She is the Black Unicorn: magical and mysterious bearer of fantasy draped in truth and beauty." Further, Martin found the poet's feelings about her mother to be more vital to an understanding of her works. In many of Lorde's poems, the figure of her mother is one of a woman who resents her daughter, tries to repress her child's unique personality so that she conforms with the rest of the world, and withholds the emotional nourishment of parental love. For example, Lorde tells us in *Coal*'s "Story Books on a Kitchen Table": "Out of her womb of pain my mother spat me / into her ill-fitting harness of despair / into her deceits / where anger reconceived me." In *The Black Unicorn*'s "From the House of Yemanja," the mother's efforts to shape the speaker into something she is not do not quench the speaker's desire for the mother's love: "Mother I need / mother I need / . . . I am / the sun and moon and forever hungry." "Balled from Childhood" in *The New York Head Shop and Museum* is Lorde's depiction of the ways in which a child's hopes and dreams are crushed by a restrictive mother. After the mother has made withering replies to her child's queries about planting a tree to give some beauty to their wasteland surroundings, the child gives up in defeat, saying: "Please mommy do not beat me so! /yes I will learn to love the snow! / yes I want neither seed nor tree! / yes ice is quite enough for me! / who knows what trouble- leaves might grow!"

As Martin noted, however, Lorde's ambivalent feelings about her mother "did not make [her] bitter against her own children when circumstances changed her role from that of child to mother." *Coal* includes the poem "Now That I Am Forever with Child," which discusses the birth of Lorde's daughter. "I bore you one morning just before spring," she recounts, "my legs were towers between which / A new world was passing. / Since then / I can only distinguish /

one thread within runnings hours / You, flowing through selves / toward You."

In addition to her poetry, Lorde was noted for eloquent prose, one example of which was her courageous account of her agonizing struggle to overcome breast cancer and mastectomy, *The Cancer Journals*. Her first major prose work, the *Journals* discuss Lorde's feelings about facing the possibility of death. Beyond death, Martin asserted, Lorde feared "she should die without having said the things she as a woman and an artist needed to say in order that her pain and subsequent loss might not have occurred in vain." Recounting this personal transformation was, for Lorde, of primary importance; as AnaLouise Keating noted in *Journal of Homosexuality,* "For Lorde, self-expression and self-discovery are never ends in themselves. Because she sees her desire to comprehend her battle with cancer as 'part of a continuum of women's work, of reclaiming this earth and or power,' she is confident that her self-explorations will empower her readers." Her *Journals* also reveal Lorde's decision not to wear a prosthesis after her breast was removed. As Brooks pointed out, "she does not suggest [her decision] for others, but . . . she uses [it] to expose some of the hypocrisies of the medical profession." Lorde summarized her attitude on the issue thus in the *Journals:* "Prosthesis offers the empty comfort of 'Nobody will know the difference.' But it is that very difference which I wish to affirm, because I have lived it, and survived it, and wish to share that strength with other women. If we are to translate the silence surrounding breast cancer into language and action against this scourge, then the first step is that women with mastectomies must become visible to each other." Martin concluded: "*The Cancer Journals* affords all women who wish to read it the opportunity to look at the life experience of one very brave woman who bared her wounds without shame, in order that we might gain some strength from sharing in her pain."

Lorde's 1982 novel, *Zami: A New Spelling of My Name,* was described by its publishers as a "biomythography, combining elements of history, biography and myth," and Rosemary Daniell, in the *New York Times Book Review,* considered the work "excellent and evocative. . . . Among the elements that make the book so good are its personal honesty and lack of pretentiousness, characteristics that shine through the writing, bespeaking the evolution of a strong and remarkable character." Daniell said that, throughout the book, Lorde's "experiences are painted with exquisite imagery. Indeed, her West Indian heritage shows through most clearly in her use of word pictures that are sensual, steamy, at times near-tropical, evoking the colors, smells—repeatedly, the smells—shapes, textures that are her life."

In the late 1980s Lorde and fellow writer Barbara Smith founded Kitchen Table: Women of Color Press, which was dedicated to furthering the writings of black feminists. Lorde would also become increasingly concerned over the plight of black women in South Africa under apartheid, creating Sisterhood in Support of Sisters in South Africa and remaining an active voice on behalf of these women throughout the remainder of her life. Indeed, Lorde addressed her concerns to not only the United States but the world,encouraging a celebration of the differences that society instead used as tools of isolation. As Allison Kimmich noted in *Feminist Writers,* "Throughout all of Audre Lorde's writing, both nonfiction and fiction, a single theme surfaces repeatedly. The black lesbian feminist poet activist reminds her readers that they ignore differences among people at their peril. . . . Instead, Lorde suggests, differences in race or class must serve as a 'reason for celebration and growth.'"

BIOGRAPHICAL/CRITICAL SOURCES:

BOOKS

Addison, Gayle, editor, *Black Expression,* Weybright & Talley, 1969.
Bigsby, C. W. E., editor, *The Black American Writer,* Penguin, 1969.
Christian, Barbara, editor, *Black Feminist Criticism: Perspectives on Black Women Writers,* Pergamon, 1985.
Contemporary Literary Criticism, Gale, Volume 18, 1981, Volume 71, 1992.
Dictionary of Literary Biography, Volume 41: *Afro-American Poets since 1955,* Gale, 1984.
Draper, James P., editor, *Black Literature Criticism,* Gale, Volume 2, 1992.
Evans, Mari, editor, *Black Women Writers (1950-1980): A Critical Evaluation,* Doubleday, 1984.
Gay and Lesbian Biography, St. James Press, 1997.
Keating, AnaLouise, *Women Reading Women Writing: Self-Invention in Paula Gunn Allen, Gloria Anzaldua, and Audre Lorde,* Temple University Press, 1996.
Kester-Shelton, Pamela, editor, *Feminist Writers,* St. James Press, 1995.
Kosek, Jane Kelly, editor, *Poetry Criticism,* Gale, 1997.
Tate, Claudia, editor, *Black Women Writers at Work,* Continuum, 1984.

PERIODICALS

American Book Review, October-November, 1993, p. 15.
American Poetry Review, March-April, 1980, pp. 18-21.
Callaloo, winter, 1986, pp. 192-208; Volume 9, number 4, 1987, winter, 1991, pp. 83-95.
Colby Library Quarterly, March, 1982, pp. 9-25.
Denver Quarterly, spring, 1981, pp. 10-27.
Essence, January, 1988; March, 1999, p. 68.
Journal of Homosexuality, Volume 26, numbers 2-3, pp. 73-95.
Ms., September, 1974.
Negro Digest, September, 1968.
New York Times Book Review, December 19, 1982.
Poetry, February, 1977.
Signs: Journal of Women in Culture and Society, summer, 1981, pp. 713-36.*

*   *   *

LOVELL, Glenville   1955-

PERSONAL: Born in 1955, in Barbados. *Education:* Studied creative writing in New York City.

ADDRESSES: Home—Brooklyn, NY. *Agent*—c/o Soho Press, 853 Broadway, New York, NY 10003.

CAREER: Novelist, playwright, and actor. Has traveled extensively with theatrical companies.

WRITINGS:

NOVELS

Fire in the Canes, Soho Press (New York City), 1995.
Song of Night, Soho Press, 1998.

Also author of plays.

SIDELIGHTS: Playwright and actor Glenville Lovell made a "notable debut" as a novelist in 1995 with *Fire in the Canes,* according to a *Publishers Weekly* reviewer. The novel, set on an unnamed Caribbean island which apparently shares a number of traits with Lovell's native Barbados, takes place in 1894, some forty years after the emancipation of the slaves living on the island. In the community of Monkey Road, however, living conditions are still impoverished and a sugar-cane plantation economy still dominates.

The structure of the novel is "recursive, akin to one long flashback," reviewer Cyril Dabydeen told readers in *World Literature Today.* It involves possibly supernatural events occurring in a gully near a large plantation, soon after the return to the island of a beautiful light-skinned woman, Peata, and her dark-skinned daughter, Midra, who have been gone for a year. Both have been passionately attracted to the mysterious sailor Prince Johnson, and Midra has borne his child, Hartseed.

The plot also involves Midra's marriage to a local apprentice blacksmith, Brandon Fields, and Hartseed's later meeting with his half-sister Christine, who is also the child of Prince Johnson. Hartseed and Christine, exploring a cave, discover an African-style mask of a monkey, which, when worn, enables them to see scenes of the island's past. The mask also plays a role in stopping the violent destruction of the sugar-cane fields.

In the opinion of *Kirkus Reviews,* these elements added up to "a rambling, discursive novel, heavily laden with folklorish elements." That reviewer praised the neatness of Lovell's ending of the tale, adding that it was perhaps too neat. Some "excessive artfulness" was outbalanced by "sprightly writing . . . and an effective evocation of lush tropical nights," making this, for *Kirkus,* "[a] promising debut, entertaining if somewhat self-conscious in craft."

Another mixed but essentially positive review came from a *Publishers Weekly* critic, who called the narrative "richly descriptive" but complained that secondary characters' stories were not woven smoothly into the main fabric. Despite some "harsh, choppy dialogue," the novel "promises a bright literary future for the author," in the view of the *Publishers Weekly.* Critic Cyril Dabydeen, writing for *World Literature Today,* focused on the character of Prince Johnson as the central figure in the tale, a dominant presence although one that was not frequently onstage. As evidence of Prince Johnson's central importance to the design of *Fire in the Canes,* Dabydeen noted that the flashbacks which composed the book were essentially flashbacks of that character's "life, loves, and death . . . as he propels the other characters." Secure in his pride of Africanness, Prince Johnson was, for Dabydeen, "the positive life-force" whose vital presence affirmed "the primacy of African feelings in the past and present."

As for the more visible female characters, Dabydeen asserted that they were "well carved in the context of unfolding village life," and that Lovell's characters on the whole were handled by their author "unfailingly . . . with a rich appreciation of their feelings . . . through organic use of language combining affection, warmth, and lovemaking." For Dabydeen, first time novelist Lovell is "compelling as he combines the gifts of a natural storyteller with deeper resonances, achieved through a sincere understanding of the possibilities of fiction in recouping lost history."

BIOGRAPHICAL/CRITICAL SOURCES:

PERIODICALS

Choice, March, 1996, p. 1135.
Kirkus Reviews, July 1, 1995, p. 886.
Library Journal, September 15, 1995, p. 93.
New Yorker, December 11, 1995, p. 106.
New York Times Book Review, November 12, 1995, p. 57.
Publishers Weekly, July 24, 1995, p. 46.
World Literature Today, spring, 1996, p. 449.*

*　　*　　*

LYNK, Miles V(andahurst)   1871-1956

PERSONAL: Born June 3, 1871, in Brownsville, TN; died December 29, 1956, in Memphis, TN; son of John Henry (a farmer) and Mary Louise (a farmer) Lynk; married Beebe Steven (a chemist and pharmacist); married second wife, Ola Herin Moore, 1949. *Ethnicity:* African American. *Education:* Self-educated until age of thirteen; apprenticed with a physician, J. C. Hairston; Meharry Medical College, graduated, 1891; Walden University, Nashville, M.S., 1900; University of West Tennessee, Bachelor of Laws degree, 1901.

CAREER: Physician and medical educator. Private practice of medicine, Jackson, TN, 1891-1901; *The Medical and Surgical Observer* (medical journal), publisher, 1892; National Medical Association (NMA), Atlanta, GA, founder (with Robert F. Boyd), 1895; University of West Tennessee, medical college for African Americans, located first in Jackson, then

Memphis, founder (with wife, Beebe Steven), 1900, president, 1900-23.

AWARDS, HONORS: Distinguished Service Medal, National Medical Association, 1952.

WRITINGS:

The Afro-American School Speaker and Gems of Literature for School Commencements, Literary Circles, Debating Clubs, and Rhetoricals Generally, University of West Tennessee Press, 1911.

Sixty Years of Medicine: or, The Life and Times of Miles V. Lynk (autobiography), Twentieth Century Press (Memphis, TN), 1951.

The Black Troopers; or, The Daring Heroism of the Negro Soldiers in the Spanish-American War, AMS Press (New York), 1971.

SIDELIGHTS: In a long and distinguished career, Miles Vandahurst Lynk not only helped to create a medical school that trained hundreds of African Americans, but also founded, edited and published the first black medical journal and served as one of the prime movers in creating the National Medical Association for black physicians. Fine accomplishments for anyone, they seem all the more amazing when it is realized that Lynk was born to former slaves and was self-educated until the age of thirteen.

Lynk was born on June 3, 1871, in Brownsville, Tennessee, the son of John Henry and Mary Louise Lynk. Former slaves, Lynk's parents were farmers leading a basic life close to the land. But Lynk wanted, from an early age, to become a doctor. He was largely self-educated throughout his early years. As he reports in his autobiography, *Sixty Years of Medicine: or, The Life and Times of Miles V. Lynk,* "I cultivated home study [and] literally attended 'Pine Knot College.'" So successful were his independent studies, that at age thirteen he passed his county's teacher's examination, but was too young to use the certificate he earned. He apprenticed for a time with a local Brownsville physician, J. C. Hairston, and then attended Meharry Medical College, graduating second in a class of thirteen in 1891. He practiced medicine in Jackson, Tennessee, until 1901.

In 1892, fresh out of medical school, he began publishing *The Medical and Surgical Observer,* the first black medical journal in the nation. One of the first editions of that journal carried a plea for "an Association of medical men of color, national in character," to parallel the then all-white American Medical Association. In 1895, Lynk, along with Robert F. Boyd, was instrumental in starting the National Medical Association (NMA) in Atlanta, Georgia, an organization with thousands of members today and a well-respected journal.

Private practice, helping to found the NMA, and publishing a medical journal were not enough for Lynk. He pursued his studies even while practicing medicine, earning an M.S. from Walden University in Nashville in 1900, and a Bachelor of Laws degree from the University of West Tennessee in 1901. Around 1900, he and his wife, Beebe Steven (a chemist and pharmacist), mortgaged their house to follow another dream: establishing a medical college for African Americans at the University of West Tennessee, located first in Jackson and then in Memphis, Tennessee. Lynk served as its president and his wife taught pharmacy and chemistry. Always under-funded, the school finally closed in 1923, but not before graduating 266 students, ninety-eight of whom passed the state boards.

Lynk did not confine his activities solely to medical matters. A prolific writer, he also authored a how-to for public speaking and a history of African American soldiers in the Spanish-American War, as well as his own autobiography. Lynk married a second time, in 1949, to Ola Herin Moore, and in 1952 the NMA awarded him its Distinguished Service Medal for a lifetime of work in medicine and the advancement of African Americans. He died on December 29, 1956, in Memphis, Tennessee.

BIOGRAPHICAL/CRITICAL SOURCES:

PERIODICALS

Journal of the National Medical Association, January, 1941, pp. 46-47; November, 1943, pp. 205-06; November, 1952, pp. 475-76; December, 1981, pp. 1219-25.*

M

MAATHAI, Wangari (Muta) 1940-

PERSONAL: Born April 1, 1940, in Kenya; daughter of subsistence farmers; married a Nairobi businessman and politician (marriage ended); children: three. *Education:* Mount St. Scholastica College, B.S. (biology), 1964; University of Pittsburgh, M.S., 1965; University of Nairobi, Ph.D., c. 1971.

*ADDRESSES: Office—*c/o Nairobi University, P.O. Box 30197, Nairobi, Kenya.

CAREER: Environmentalist, educator, political and social activist, and writer. University of Nairobi, Kenya, beginning in 1966 was a faculty member of the department of veterinary medicine, a lecturer, assistant professor, head of the faculty of veterinary medicine, an anatomy professor, and beginning c. 1978 was a professor in Animal Science; Green Belt Movement (an internationally supported environmentalist group), founder, member, and lecturer, beginning c. 1977; Forum for Restoration of Democracy, founder with others, and member, 1991—.

AWARDS, HONORS: Has won numerous awards from various countries, including: Woman of the Year Award, 1983 and 1989; Windstar Award for the Environment, 1989; Goldman Environmental Prize, 1991; Africa Prize for Leadership, 1991; Hunger Project Prize, 1991 (with others); Jane Addams International Women's Leadership Award, 1993; and Edinburgh Medal, 1993.

WRITINGS:

The Green Belt Movement: Sharing the Approach and the Experience, International Environmental Liaison Center (Nairobi, Kenya), 1988.

Contributor to journals and periodicals, including *Ms.* and the *UNESCO Courier.*

SIDELIGHTS: Wangari Maathai has a long string of firsts next to her name: she was the first woman in central or eastern Africa to hold an advanced degree; the first to become an assistant professor at the University of Nairobi; and the first to head a university department in Kenya. But Maathai's real work has been far from the cloistered halls of academia. Since the 1970s Maathai has gained much international support and fame for her grassroots Green Belt Movement, which has planted millions of trees in Africa since 1977. This movement, which has networked with other environmental groups across Africa and the world, has gained Maathai many honors, including the Right Livelihood Foundation's Goldman Environmental Prize. Reporting on the influential, and controversial, protest against the October, 1998, clearing of the first fifty acres—of more than eight hundred acres—of Kenya forest purchased "for a luxury housing project backed by President Daniel arap Moi," *Time* contributor Clive Mutiso described Maathai in these words: "Only a strong person would defy the iron regime of Kenya's President Moi, and Maathai, 58, fits the bill."

Along with the accomplishments already noted, Mutiso told *CA:* "And in 1991 [Maathai's] activism became a political force when she helped start and opposition group called the Forum for the Restoration of Democracy. Once she was teargassed and clubbed unconscious by police. Another time she was arrested and put in a jail cell overnight with no mattress. Always her popularity and idealism have stayed intact." Yet, while Maathai's involvement with environmental as well as human rights issues have earned her worldwide respect, she has been condemned by the Kenyan government as an instigator of protests and political unrest. A courageous, vital, and outspoken woman, Maathai blends the best of science and humanism in her work.

Maathai's respect for the environment, as she has said repeatedly in interviews and public appearances, is part of her birth legacy. Born Wangari Muta Maathai, on April 1, 1940, she was the oldest daughter of subsistence farmers. Raised in Nyeri, Kenya, in the White Highlands, she could easily have been made to assume household responsibilities for her five siblings. Instead, her parents, at the behest of her older brother, sent her to school. A few years later, Maathai's teachers at the Loreto Limuru Girls School became instrumental in obtaining for her a scholarship that enabled her to continue her education in the United States at Mount St. Scholastica College in Kansas. She graduated with a B.S. in biology in 1964, going on to earn an M.S. from the University of Pittsburgh in 1965. According to the *Encyclopedia of World Biography (EWB)*, Maathai "credited her education with giving her the ability to see the difference between right and wrong, and with giving her the impetus to be strong." Maathai's research at Pittsburgh later led to a position at the University of Nairobi in the department of veterinary medicine when she returned to her native Kenya in 1966. Although her male colleagues were slow to recognize her ability, by 1971 she had earned her doctorate from the University of Nairobi, became a lecturer, and later an assistant professor, and finally was promoted to become the head of the faculty of veterinary medicine.

Maathai's professional career was assured by these advances, and it was her husband "who unknowingly provided the basis for her future environmental activities," reported the *EWB* essayist. Following an election promise made by her husband, a Nairobi businessman running for parliament in 1974, Maathai opened an agency that paid poor people to plant trees and shrubs so they could earn a rudimentary living. In the early 1980s, "Maathai's husband abandoned her and their three children later, filing and receiving a divorce on the grounds that she was 'too educated, too strong, too successful, too stubborn and too hard to control,'" according to the *EWB* writer, who added: "Maathai maintained that it was particularly important for African women to know that they could be strong, and to liberate themselves from fear and silence."

While still married, the tree-planting agency Maathai began had evolved into a national organization which later was sponsored by many countries and environmental groups worldwide. Named the Green Belt Movement in 1977, the philosophy of the organization was simple. "The Green Belt Movement is about hope," Maathai told Christopher Boyd in a 1992 *Chicago Tribune* interview. "It tells people they are responsible for their own lives. . . . It raises an awareness that people can take control of their environment, which is the first step toward greater participation in society." Since ninety percent of the African population depends on wood for fuel, the depleting number of trees was leading to a crisis situation. Women had to travel long distances to gather firewood, and even though food was available, the shortage of readily available fuel meant that they could not cook enough food to satisfy their families' needs. Because of this, nutritional deficiencies were developing among the population. Maathai saw a basic solution to this cycle: Plant more trees. The Green Belt movement helped the local population to do this by establishing nurseries that offered free seedlings for communities to plant and tend. The incentive was a small payment for every tree that was planted and preserved for more than three months by the villagers.

Maathai's efforts to fight the deforestation of Kenya have proved incredibly successful over the years, resulting in the planting of over ten million native trees such as acacias, cedars, baobabs, and cotton trees. In addition to conserving the soil and ecology of the land, the Green Belt movement provides employment to eighty thousand workers, and has won worldwide attention for Maathai. She has been richly honored for her efforts, and among her laurels are the Woman of the Year Award for both 1983 and 1989, the Windstar Award for the Environment, 1989, the prestigious Goldman Environmental Prize in 1991, the Africa Prize for Leadership, also in 1991, and the Jane Addams International Women's Leadership Award and the Edinburgh Medal, both in 1993.

Maathai's ideas, many of which oppose Kenyan traditions, have also led her to actively participate in her country's political arena. Her opposition to the one-party government system in Kenya, beginning with her notable and vocal opposition to the construction of a sixty-story office tower in Uhuru Park in Nairobi in 1989, has cost Maathai her freedom many times. For example, although she managed to stop the Uhuru Park construction, her opposition earned her the enmity of Kenya's president, Daniel Arap Moi. And her subsequent increasing involvement with human rights issues has led her to be imprisoned many times. Despite governmental opposition, however, Maathai continues her work for Green Belt and lectures widely. Her message over the years has remained the same, and she firmly believes that one person can make a difference. "In 1997 Maathai responded to pressure from supporters and friends and announced that she was running not only for the Parliament," reported the *EWB* contributor, "but for the presidency under the Liberal Party of Kenya (LPK) in an attempt to defeat President Moi. She got a late start in the process and did not announce her intentions until a month before the election. . . . A few days prior to the December, 1997, election, the LPK leaders withdrew Maathai's candidacy without notifying her. Her bid for a Parliament seat was also defeated in the election; she came in third." The *EWB* essayist concluded, "She [has] continued to be admired worldwide, however, for her visionary work in the environmental arena."

BIOGRAPHICAL/CRITICAL SOURCES:

BOOKS

Encyclopedia of World Biography, 2nd edition supplement, Volume 18, Gale, 1999.
Women's Firsts, Gale, 1997.

PERIODICALS

Africa News Service, October 27, 1997; January 5, 1998.
Africa Report, November-December, 1990, p. 30.
American Biology Teacher, February, 1985, p. 76.
American Forests, September-October, 1990, p. 80.
Chicago Tribune, January 5, 1992, Section VI, p. 1.
E Magazine, January 11, 1997.
Geographical Magazine, April, 1990, p. 51.
Inter Press Service English News Wire, December 10, 1997.
Reader's Digest (Canadian), May, 1996.
Time, April 23, 1990; April 29, 1991; April 27, 1992; December 14, 1998.
Utne Reader, November-December, 1992, pp. 86-87.
Wall Street Journal, May 10, 1991, p. B1.
Women in Action, January 1, 1992.
World Citizen News, February-March, 1997.

OTHER

"Africa Prize Laureates, Professor Wangari Muta Maathai," The Hunger Project, www.thp.org/thp/prize/maathai/maathai.htm, April 13, 1998.

"Awareness Raising; Wangari Maathai Comes from Kenya," BBC World Service, www2.bbc.co.uk./worldservice/BBC_English/women/prog14.htm, April 13, 1998.*

*   *   *

MABRY, Marcus 1967-

PERSONAL: Born in 1967. *Education:* Stanford University, B.A.; attended the Sorbonne, Paris.

ADDRESSES: Agent—c/o Scribner, New York, NY.

CAREER: Journalist. *Newsweek,* correspondent in Washington, DC, and Paris, France.

WRITINGS:

White Bucks and Black-Eyed Peas: Coming of Age Black in White America (memoir), Scribner (New York City), 1995.

SIDELIGHTS: Marcus Mabry's novel, *White Bucks and Black-Eyed Peas: Coming of Age Black in White America,* explores the meaning of African-American identity and success through an account of Mabry's exposure to mainstream white society. Raised by his mother and grandmother, Mabry tells of his family's precarious financial position in *White Bucks;* his mother worked when possible, but the family income was often supplemented with food stamps and welfare payments.

When Mabry won a scholarship to an exclusive preparatory school, he entered a seemingly different world. Upon his arrival, he saw boys playing lacrosse: "Good thing I'd read the [school's] catalog, otherwise I wouldn't have known what they were playing," Mabry wrote in *White Bucks.*

Mabry's education and success caused some dissonance, as he sometimes felt like an outsider in white society and, at the same time, a stranger to those who remained in the neighborhood of his youth. He confesses in *White Bucks,* "I was more comfortable in the White world. It demanded less role-playing of me, so I chose it." Mabry also condemns the racism of white America, however, bemoaning the lack of journalists of color and describing how educated black men are often seen as anomalies.

Reviews of *White Bucks* were generally favorable, although some critics felt the book raised more questions than it answered. A *Publishers Weekly* critic commented on Mabry's relative youth, suggesting that "Mabry might have waited a bit longer to sort it all into perspective." *New York Times Book Review* contributor Constance C. R. White praised the book, however, noting that Mabry's "vigorous account is the white-collar prose equivalent of rap, which at its heart is the expression of some black youths' anger and alienation." Writing in *Booklist,* Mary Carroll called *White Bucks* a "penetrating, gracefully written dissection of life on the racial and generational cusp." *Emerge* contributor Zachary R. Dowdy concluded that Mabry's memoir "is an important and honest contribution to the perennial debate over what it means to be Black."

BIOGRAPHICAL/CRITICAL SOURCES:

PERIODICALS

Booklist, August, 1995, p. 1915.
Emerge, October, 1995, pp. 77-78.
Los Angeles Times Book Review, September 3, 1995, p. 6.
Newsweek, October 2, 1995, p. 89.
New York Times Book Review, October 1, 1995, p. 29.
Publishers Weekly, June 12, 1995, p. 54.*

*   *   *

MADHUBUTI, Haki R.   1942-
(Don L. Lee)

PERSONAL: Born February 23, 1942, Little Rock, AR; original name Donald Luther Lee; name legally changed in 1973; son of Jimmy L. and Maxine (Graves) Lee; married Safisha L.; children: three. *Education:* Attended Wilson Junior College, Roosevelt University, and University of Illinois, Chicago Circle; University of Iowa, M.F.A., 1984.

ADDRESSES: Office—Third World Press, 7524 South Cottage Grove, Chicago, IL 60619; Department of English, Speech, and Theatre, Chicago State University, 95th St. at King Dr., Chicago, IL 60628.

CAREER: DuSable Museum of African American History, Chicago, IL, apprentice curator, 1963-67; Montgomery Ward, Chicago, stock department clerk,

1963-64; post office clerk in Chicago, 1964-65; Spiegels, Chicago, junior executive, 1965-66; Cornell University, Ithaca, NY, writer-in-residence, 1968-69; Northeastern Illinois State College, Chicago, poet-in-residence, 1969-70; University of Illinois, Chicago, lecturer, 1969-71; Howard University, Washington, DC, writer-in-residence, 1970-78; Morgan State College, Baltimore, MD, 1972-73; Chicago State University, Chicago, professor of English, 1984—. Publisher and editor, Third World Press, 1967—. Director of Institute of Positive Education, Chicago, 1969-91. *Military service:* U.S. Army, 1960-63.

MEMBER: African Liberation Day Support Committee (vice-chairperson, 1971-73), Congress of African People (member of executive council, 1970-74), Organization of Black American Culture, Writers Workshop (founding member, 1967-75).

WRITINGS:

UNDER NAME DON L. LEE

Think Black, Broadside Press, 1967, revised edition, 1968, enlarged edition, 1969.
Black Pride, Broadside Press, 1967.
For Black People (and Negroes Too), Third World Press, 1968.
Don't Cry, Scream (poems), Broadside Press, 1969.
We Walk the Way of the New World (poems), Broadside Press, 1970.
(Author of introduction) *To Blackness: A Definition in Thought,* Kansas City Black Writers Workshop, 1970.
Dynamite Voices I: Black Poets of the 1960s (essays), Broadside Press, 1971.
(Editor with P. L. Brown and F. Ward) *To Gwen with Love,* Johnson Publishing, 1971.
Directionscore: Selected and New Poems, Broadside Press, 1971.
(Author of introduction) Marion Nicholas, *Life Styles,* Broadside Press, 1971.
The Need for an African Education (pamphlet), Institute of Positive Education, 1972.

UNDER NAME HAKI R. MADHUBUTI

Book of Life (poems), Broadside Press, 1973.
From Plan to Planet-Life Studies: The Need for Afrikan Minds and Institutions, Broadside Press, 1973.
(With Jawanza Kunjufu) *Black People and the Coming Depression* (pamphlet), Institute of Positive Education, 1975.

(Contributor) *A Capsule Course in Black Poetry Writing,* Broadside Press, 1975.

Enemies: The Clash of Races (essays), Third World Press, 1978.

Earthquakes and Sunrise Missions: Poetry and Essays of Black Renewal, 1973-1983 (poems), Third World Press, 1984.

Killing Memory, Seeking Ancestors (poems), Lotus, 1987.

Say That the River Turns: The Impact of Gwendolyn Brooks (poetry and prose), Third World Press, 1987.

Kwanzaa: A Progressive and Uplifting African American Holiday, Third World Press, 1987.

Black Men: Obsolete, Single, Dangerous?; Afrikan American Families in Transition: Essays in Discovery, Solution, and Hope, Third World Press, 1990.

(Editor) *Confusion by Any Other Name: Essays Exploring the Negative Impact of the Blackman's Guide to Understanding the Blackwoman,* Third World Press, 1992.

(Editor) *Children of Africa,* Third World Press, 1993.

Claiming Earth: Race, Rage, Rape, Redemption, Third World Press, 1994.

GroundWork: Selected Poems of Haki R. Madhubuti, foreword by Gwendolyn Brooks and introduction by Bakari Kitwana, Third World Press, 1996.

(Editor with Karenga) *Million Man March/Day of Absence: A Commemorative Anthology: Speeches, Commentary, Photography, Poetry, Illustrations, Documents,* Third World Press, 1996.

OTHER

Also author of *Back Again, Home,* 1968, and *One Sided Shootout,* 1968; editor of *Why L.A. Happened: Implications of the 1992 Los Angeles Rebellion,* 1993. Contributor to more than one hundred anthologies, including *Black Women Writers (1950-1980): A Critical Evaluation,* edited by Mari Evans, Anchor-Doubleday, 1984, and *Tapping Potential: English and Language Arts for the Black Learner,* edited by Charlotte K. Brooks and others, Black Caucus of National Council of Teachers of English, 1985. Contributor to numerous magazines and literary journals, including *Black World, Negro Digest, Journal of Black Poetry, Essence, Journal of Black History, Chicago Defender,* and *Black American Literature Forum.* Founder and editor of *Black Books Bulletin,* 1972—; contributing editor, *Black Scholar* and *First World.*

SIDELIGHTS: "Poetry in my home was almost as strange as money," Don L. Lee, also known by his Swahili name Haki R. Madhubuti, relates in *Dynamite Voices I: Black Poets of the 1960s.* Abandoned by his father, then bereaved of his mother at the age of sixteen, Madhubuti made his living by maintaining two paper routes and cleaning a nearby bar. Poetry was scarce in his early life, he explains in the same source, because "what wasn't taught, but was consciously learned, in our early educational experience was that writing of any kind was something that Black people just didn't do." Nonetheless, he has become one of the best-known poets of the black arts movement of the 1960s, a respected and influential critic of poetry, and an activist dedicated to the cultural unity of his people. "In many ways," writes Catherine Daniels Hurst in *Dictionary of Literary Biography,* Madhubuti "is one of the most representative voices of his time. Although most significant as a poet, his work as an essayist, critic, publisher, social activist, and educator has enabled him to go beyond the confines of poetry to the establishment of a black press and a school for black children."

The literature of the Harlem Renaissance-a literary movement of the 1920s and 1930s in which the works of many black artists became popular-was not deeply felt by the majority of America's black population, Madhubuti writes. "In the Sixties, however, Black Art in all its various forms began to flourish as never before: music, theater, art (painting, sculpture), films, prose (novel[s], essays), and poetry. The new and powerful voices of the Sixties came to light mainly because of the temper of the times." The writers of this turbulent generation who worked to preserve a cultural heritage distinct from white culture did not look to previous literary traditions-black or white-for inspiration. Says Madhubuti, "The major influences on the new Black poets were/are Black music, Black life style, Black churches, and their own Black contemporaries."

An *Ebony* article on the poet by David Llorens hails him as "a lion of a poet who splits syllables, invents phrases, makes letters work as words, and gives rhythmic quality to verse that is never savage but often vicious and always reflecting a revolutionary black consciousness." As a result, his "lines rumble like a street gang on the page," remarks Liz Gant in a *Black World* review. Though Madhubuti believes, as he declares in *Don't Cry, Scream,* that "most, if not all black poetry will be *political,*" he explains in *Dynamite Voices I* that it must do more than protest, since "mere 'protest' writing is generally a weak reaction to persons or events and often lacks the substance necessary to motivate and move people." Black poetry will be powerful, he says, if it is "a genuine reflection of [the poet] and his people," presenting "the beauty and joy" of the black experience as well as outrage against social and economic oppression.

However, some critics hear only the voice of protest in Madhubuti's work. Paul Breman's piece in C. W. E. Bigsby's *The Black American Writer, Volume 1: Poetry and Drama,* calls him a poet whose "all-out ranting . . . has become outdated more rapidly than one could have hoped." And Jascha Kessler, writing in a *Poetry* review, sees no poetry in Madhubuti's books. "Anger, bombast, raw hatred, strident, aggrieved, perhaps charismatically crude religious and political canting, propaganda and racist nonsense, yes. . . . [Madhubuti] is outside poetry somewhere, exhorting, hectoring, cursing, making a lot of noise." But the same elements that grate against the sensibilities of such critics stem from the poet's cultural objectives and are much better received by the poet's intended audience, say others. "He is not interested in modes of writing that aspire to elegance," writes Gwendolyn Brooks in the introduction of *Don't Cry, Scream.* Madhubuti writes for and to blacks, and "the last thing these people crave is elegance. It is very hard to enchant, with elegant song, the ears of a fellow whose stomach is growling," she notes. Explains Hurst, "often he uses street language and the dialect of the uneducated Black community. . . . He uses unconventional abbreviations and strung-together words . . . in a visually rendered dialect designed to convey the stress, pitch, volume, texture, resonance, and the intensity of the black speaking voice. By these and other means, Madhubuti intends to engage the active participation of a black audience accustomed to the oral tradition of storytelling and song."

Poems in *Don't Cry, Scream* and *We Walk the Way of the New World* show the activist-poet's "increasing concern for incorporating jazz rhythms"; more and more, the poet styled the poems "for performance, the text lapsing into exultant screams and jazz scats," writes Bigsby in *The Second Black Renaissance.* The title poem of *Don't Cry, Scream,* believes Hurst, "should be dedicated to that consummate musician, John Coltrane, whose untimely death left many of his admirers in deep mourning. In this poem (which begs to be read out loud as only the poet himself can do it), Madhubuti strains to duplicate the virtuoso high notes of Coltrane's instrumental sound." Critic Sherley Anne Williams, speaking to interviewer Claudia Tate in *Black Women Writers at Work,* explains why this link to music is significant for the black writer. Whereas white Americans preserve themselves or

their legacy through literature, black Americans have done so in music, in the blues form: "The blues records of each decade explain something about the philosophical basis of historical continuity for black people. It is a ritualized way of talking about ourselves and passing it on. This was true until the late sixties." Madhubuti elaborates in *Dynamite Voices I:* "Black music is our most advanced form of Black art. In spite of the debilitating conditions of slavery and its aftermath, Black music endured and grew as a communicative language, as a sustaining spiritual force, as entertainment, and as a creative extension of our African selves. It was one of the few mediums of expression open to Black people that was virtually free of interferences. . . . To understand . . . art . . . which is uniquely Black, we must start with the art form that has been least distorted, a form that has so far resisted being molded into a *pure* product of European-American culture." Numerous references to black musicians and lines that imitate the sounds of black music connect Madhubuti's poetry to that tradition and extend its life as well.

Madhubuti's poetic voice softened somewhat during the 1970s, during which time he directed his energies to the writing of political essays (*From Plan to Planet-Life Studies: The Need for Afrikan Minds and Institutions* and *Enemies: The Clash of Races*). In addition, he contributed to the establishment of a black aesthetic for new writers through critical essays and reviews. *Dynamite Voices I,* for instance, "has become one of the major contemporary scholarly resources for black poetry," notes Hurst. Fulfilling the role of "cultural stabilizer," he also gave himself to the construction of institutions that promote the cultural independence and education of his people. In a fight against "brain mismanagement" in America, he founded the Third World Press in 1967 to encourage literacy and the Institute of Positive Education in 1969 "to provide educational and communication services to a community struggling to assert its identity amidst powerful, negative forces," he told Donnarae MacCann for an interview published in *Interracial Books for Children Bulletin.*

In the same interview, he defines the publishing goals of the Third World Press: "We look for writers who continue to critically assess the ambivalence of being Black in America. . . . What we are trying to do is to service the great majority of Black people, those who do not have a voice, who have not made it. Black themes over the past years have moved from reaction and rage to contemplative assessments of today's problems to a kind of visionary look at the world," a vision that includes not just blacks, but all people. But the development of the black community remains its main focus, he told David Streitfield for a *Washington Post* article. "There's just so much negative material out there, and so little that helps. That's not to say we don't publish material that is critical, but it has to be constructive." As Streitfield reports, "Third World's greatest success has been with . . . Chancellor Williams' *Destruction of Black Civilization*, which has gone through 16 printings." Other articles also commended the press for breaking even for the first time in nineteen years in 1987.

Summing up Madhubuti's accomplishments as a writer, Williams comments in *Give Birth to Brightness: A Thematic Study in Neo-Black Literature* that as one of "the vocal exponents of Neo-Black literature," he has "come to symbolize most of what is strong and beautiful and vital in Black Experience and Black Art." Hurst's summary states, "His books have sold more than a million copies, without benefit of a national distributor. Perhaps Madhubuti will even succeed in helping to establish some lasting institutions in education and in the publishing world. Whether he does or not, he has already secured a place for himself in American literature. He is among the foremost anthologized contemporary revolutionary poets, and he has played a significant role in stimulating other young black talent. As Stephen Henderson has observed, he is 'more widely imitated than any other Black poet with the exception of Imamu Baraka (LeRoi Jones). . . . His influence is enormous, and is still growing.'"

BIOGRAPHICAL/CRITICAL SOURCES:

BOOKS

Bigsby, C. W. E., *The Black American Writer, Volume 1: Poetry & Drama*, Penguin, 1969.

Bigsby, C. W. E., *The Second Black Renaissance: Essays in Black Literature*, Greenwood Press, 1980.

Contemporary Literary Criticism, Gale (Detroit), Volume 2, 1974; Volume 6, 1976.

Dictionary of Literary Biography, Gale, Volume 5: *American Poets since World War II*, 1980; Volume 41: *Afro-American Poets since 1955*, 1985.

Gibson, Donald B., editor, *Modern Black Poets: A Collection of Critical Essays*, Prentice-Hall, 1973.

Henderson, Stephen, *Understanding the New Black Poetry: Black Speech and Black Music as Poetic References*, Morrow, 1973.

Mosher, Marlene, *New Directions from Don L. Lee*, Exposition, 1975.

Strickland, Michael, *African-American Poetry*, Enslow, 1996.

Tate, Claudia, editor, *Black Women Writers at Work*, Continuum, 1983.

Vendler, Helen, *Part of Nature, Part of Us*, Howard University Press, 1980.

Williams, John A., and Charles F. Harris, editors, *Amistad 2*, Random House, 1971.

Williams, Sherley Anne, *Give Birth to Brightness: A Thematic Study in Neo-Black Literature*, Dial, 1972.

PERIODICALS

Black Collegian, February/March, 1971; September/October, 1974.

Black World, April, 1971; June, 1972; January, 1974.

Chicago Sun Times, December 11, 1987.

Chicago Tribune, December 23, 1987.

Ebony, March, 1969.

Emerge, May, 1995; April, 1996; May, 1996.

Essence, June, 1990, p. 44; July, 1991, pp. 92-4.

Interracial Books for Children Bulletin, Volume 17, number 2, 1986.

Jet, June 27, 1974.

Journal of Negro History, April, 1971.

Los Angeles Times Book Review, March 25, 1990.

National Observer, July 14, 1969.

Negro Digest, December, 1969.

New Lady, July/August, 1971.

New York Times, December 13, 1987.

New York Times Book Review, September 29, 1974.

Poetry, February, 1973.

Publishers Weekly, January 20, 1992, p. 29; December, 1992, pp. 24-5.

Washington Post, June 6, 1971; January 17, 1988.*

*   *   *

MAGONA, Sindiwe 1943-

PERSONAL: Born August 27, 1943, in Tsolo, South Africa; daughter of Sigongo Penrose and Lilian Lili (Mabandla) Magona; children: Thembeka (daughter), Thokozile (daughter), Sandile (son). *Ethnicity:* "Xhosa (African)." *Education:* St. Matthew's Training School, Higher Primary Teachers Certificate, 1961; University of London, General Certificate of Education; University of South Africa, B.A.; Columbia University, M.S., 1983.

ADDRESSES: Home—3030 Johnson Ave., Bronx, NY 10463. *Office*—United Nations, 1 United Nations Plaza, Suite S-805M, New York, NY 10017; fax 212-963-1658. *Agent*—Aaron M. Priest Literary Agency, Inc., 122 East 42nd St., Suite 3902, New York, NY 10168. *E-mail*—magona-gobado@un.org.

CAREER: Domestic worker, 1963-67; primary school-teacher, Cape Town, South Africa, 1967-80; high school teacher of Xhosa language, Cape Town, 1977-81; United Nations, New York City, press officer, 1984—.

MEMBER: International Women's Writing Guild, PEN America, United Nations Society of Writers, Bhala Writers Association.

AWARDS, HONORS: Honorary doctorate from Hartwick College; named among Xhosa heroes of South Africa.

WRITINGS:

To My Children's Children, Interlink Publishing (Brooklyn, NY), 1994.
Living, Loving, and Lying Awake at Night (fiction), Interlink Publishing (Brooklyn, NY), 1994.
Forced to Grow, Interlink Publishing (Brooklyn, NY), 1998.
Mother to Mother (fiction), David Philip, 1998.

Also author of *Push-Push and Other Stories.*

WORK IN PROGRESS: Penrose and Lilian, a memoir of the author's parents; *The Last School Year,* a novel.

SIDELIGHTS: Sindiwe Magona told *CA:* "I come to writing with no great training except my life and the lives of the people of whom I am a part. For so long, others have written about us; I write to change that, instead of moaning about it. We are people of an oral tradition; however, times have changed and our stories must be told in the mode of the time. I write so that African children in my country can see someone like them doing this miraculous thing that for so long has not belonged to us. I write to add to the rising voice of my people, dispersed throughout the world. We need to leave footprints, to show we have lived. And so, I write.

"Although I have read the classics, my inspiration comes from reading works by women, especially African women or writers who are of African de-

scent. The first book by a black woman writer that I ever held in my hand was *I Know Why the Caged Bird Sings* by Maya Angelou. This writer remains my all-time favorite. I regard her as my writing ancestor. I also take delight in Tony Morrison, Ellen Kuzwayo, and Miriam Tlali.

"I write best when I feel very strongly about a subject. At this time, it is South Africa—particularly the lives of African people there—lives that were squandered, wasted, stunted, brutalized, and sacrificed to the ideology of apartheid. We may be in the era of the new South Africa, but the lives being lived out in that country are still very much rooted in the old order. The legacy of that iniquitous system will still play havoc with the lives of many. That is not to say I am pessimistic about my country's future or the future of my people. No; indeed, the opposite is true. To have survived apartheid is no small feat. It is the song of these unsung heroines and heroes I'd like to write about: the millions whose greatness went unnoticed, disguised in acts labeled ordinary or traditional.

"This is linked to my reasons for writing. I want to inspire young black women to make what I call the transition, so that more of us will write our stories instead of telling them. Writing for the African woman is but a transition: old wine in new bottles. She has been telling stories for ages. I myself am in the process of making the transition from telling to writing."

*　　*　　*

MAILLU, David G(ian) 1939-
(Vigad G. Mulila)

PERSONAL: Born October 19, 1939, in Kilugu Location, Kenya; son of Joseph Mulandi and Esther Kavuli; married, wife's name, Hannelore; children: (with another woman) Christine Mwende; (with Hannelore) Elizabeth Kavuli. *Ethnicity:* "Mukamba." *Education:* Received technical school certificate and Doctor of Letters (African literature and African political philosophy). *Politics:* Revolutionarist. *Religion:* Neterism.

ADDRESSES: Home—P.O. Box 20019, Nairobi, Kenya. *Agent*—c/o Jomo Kenyatta Foundation, Enterprise Rd., P.O. Box 30533, Nairobi, Kenya.

CAREER: Writer. Voice of Kenya (radio station), graphic designer, 1964-73; established Comb Books (publishing company), 1972.

AWARDS, HONORS: Jomo Kenyatta Prize for Literature, 1992, for *Broken Drum.*

WRITINGS:

Kisalu and His Fruit Garden and Other Stories, East African Publishing House (Nairobi), 1972.

Ki Kyambonie: Kikamba Nthimo/Muandiki, Comb Books (Nairobi), 1972.

Unfit for Human Consumption, Comb Books (Nairobi), 1973.

My Dear Bottle, Comb Books (Nairobi), 1973.

Troubles, Comb Books (Nairobi), 1974.

After 4:30, Comb Books (Nairobi), 1974.

The Kommon Man, Comb Books (Nairobi), 1975-76.

Kujenga na Kubomoa, Comb Books (Nairobi), 1976.

No! Comb Books (Nairobi), 1976.

Dear Monika, Comb Books (Nairobi), 1976.

Dear Daughter, Comb Books (Nairobi), 1976.

(As Vigad G. Mulila) *English Punctuation,* Comb Books (Nairobi), 1978.

(As Vigad G. Mulila) *English Spelling and Words Frequently Confused,* Comb Books (Nairobi), 1978.

Kadosa, David Maillu Publishers (Nairobi), 1979.

Jese Kristo (produced at Kenya National Theatre, Nairobi, October 19, 1979), National Theatre Company/David Maillu Publishers (Nairobi), 1979.

Hit of Love / Wendo Ndikilo, David Maillu Publishers (Machakos, Kenya), 1980.

For Mbatha and Rabeka, Macmillan (London), 1980.

Benni Kamba 009 in the Equatorial Assignment, Macmillan (London), 1980.

Looking for Mother, Bookwise (Nairobi), 1981.

Kaana Ngy'a, Heinemann Educational Books (Nairobi), 1983.

The Ayah, Heinemann (Nairobi), 1986.

Benni Kamba 009 in Operation DXT, Heinemann Educational Books (Nairobi), 1986.

Untouchable, Maillu (Nairobi), 1987.

The Thorns of Life, Macmillan (London), 1988.

The Poor Child, Heinemann Kenya (Nairobi), 1988.

Our Kind of Polygamy, Heinemann Kenya (Nairobi), 1988.

Pragmatic Leadership: Evaluation of Kenya's Cultural and Political Development, Featuring Daniel arap Moi, President of Republic of Kenya, Maillu (Nairobi), 1988.

The Principles of Nyayo Philosophy, Maillu (Nairobi), 1989.

My Dear Mariana: Kumya Ivu, Maillu (Nairobi), 1989.

Mbengo and the Princess, Maillu (Nairobi), 1989.

How to Look for the Right Boyfriend, Maillu (Nairobi), 1989.

The Black Adam and Eve, Maillu (Nairobi), 1989.

P.O. Box I Love You Via My Heart, Maillu (Nairobi), 1989.

Without Kiinua Mgongo, Maillu (Nairobi), 1989.

Kusoma na Kuandika, Maillu (Nairobi), 1989.

Anayekukeep, Maillu (Nairobi), 1990.

Broken Drum, Jomo Kenyatta Foundation (Nairobi), 1991.

The Last Hunter, Jomo Kenyatta Foundation (Nairobi), 1992.

Journey into Fairyland, Jomo Kenyatta Foundation (Nairobi), 1992.

The Lion and the Hare, Jomo Kenyatta Foundation (Nairobi), 1992.

The Orphan and His Goat Friend, Jomo Kenyatta Foundation (Nairobi), 1993.

Princess Kalala and the Ugly Bird, Jomo Kenyatta Foundation (Nairobi), 1993.

The Priceless Gift, East African Educational Publishers (Nairobi), 1993.

Sasa and Sisi, Jomo Kenyatta Foundation (Nairobi), 1995.

Dancing Zebra, Jomo Kenyatta Foundation (Nairobi), 1995.

The Lost Brother, Jomo Kenyatta Foundation (Nairobi), 1995.

WORK IN PROGRESS: "A number of forthcoming creative and essay works.

SIDELIGHTS: David G. Maillu is Kenya's most prolific writer, and also its most popular author. In the 1970s, the many novels he wrote and published with Comb Books were highly successful, and brought about controversy when some critics suggested that their emphasis on sex and drinking was detrimental to the young people who were reading them.

Maillu was the first of six children born to Joseph Mulandi and Esther Kavuli in Kilungo Location, a poor village in eastern Kenya. His parents were impoverished and illiterate, and did not record his exact birth date, but later Maillu estimated that it was on or around October 19, 1939. His family were members of the Kamba tribe, whose customs forbid naming a child after a living relative. "Maillu" is a tribal name, and later he was baptized "David." "Gian," his middle name, was his own "secret invention," according to Henry Indangasi in *Dictionary of Literary Biography.*

Although Maillu came from a poor and uneducated family, he learned to read from friends before he entered first grade in 1951. Teachers noticed that he was gifted, and he did well in school, eventually undertaking advanced courses through correspondence. Among other subjects, he studied African philosophy, music, and art. According to Indangasi, Maillu told *CA:* "I discovered when I was doing these things that I had creative talents. I wanted to join the University of Nairobi, but they were teaching English literature. I had developed other literary interests." Later, the university began teaching courses based on African culture, but at the time it was heavily influenced by British ideals. Eventually, when he was already widely published, Maillu earned himself a Doctor of Letters in African literature, specializing in African political philosophy.

In 1964 Maillu's early years of basic academics led to a position working for the Voice of Kenya broadcasting department as a graphic designer. He was quickly disillusioned by the job, which he felt was below his skill level and was low-paying, and although he wanted to quit, he stayed there until 1974, when his books were successful enough to allow him to leave. In 1971, he married a German woman, Hannelore, and they had a child, Elizabeth Kavuli. Maillu had another child, Christine Mwendi, with a woman he did not marry.

Maillu's first book, *Kisalu and His Fruit Garden,* was a children's book. He established his own publishing company, Comb Books, which produced many of his books over the next several years. His first novelette, *Unfit for Human Consumption,* was a success: 5,000 copies sold in less than a year. This success was carefully calculated; according to Indangasi, Maillu explained: "Before publishing *Unfit for Human Consumption,* I spent two to three years doing research and interviewing people on what they liked reading. I found that the subjects that interested them were marriage, sex, religion, money, politics, drinking, and human relations in general. I decided that if I was going to be a writer, I had to address those issues and topics."

Unfit for Human Consumption features Jonathan Kinama Ndeti, who lives in Narobi. His wife and children live in the countryside and Kinama uses the situation to drink, meet women, and fight. After being hospitalized with injuries from a fight, he decides to change his life, but before he does, decides he will have one more fling. A series of coincidences, including a prostitute stealing his money, his wife arriving in town, and his loss of his job, lead him to commit

suicide. The story is told in simple language, with little exploration of characters' motives or inner lives. Kinama's bad relationship with his family is never explored or explained, nor is his obsession with sex and drinking. Despite this, or perhaps because of it, the book was extremely popular, and readers seemed to find it a welcome relief from the more serious and political books then being written by African authors. Maillu followed *Unfit for Human Consumption* with several more similar books that emphasized melodramatic relationships, sex, and drinking, as well as two school texts on English grammar and spelling, which Maillu wrote under the pseudonym of Vigad G. Mulila, a transposition of his own name.

After establishing himself as a writer and publisher, Maillu received attention from the publisher Macmillan, and in 1980 published two titles with them: *Benni Kamba 009 in The Equatorial Assignment,* starring a Kenyan spy who fights imperialist interests in Africa; and *For Mbatha and Rabeka,* a love story fraught by the conflict between urban and rural life. These books feature relationships and love, but the lurid and graphic sex of the Comb books is gone; Maillu's voice is more mature, and his scope has broadened.

Although his works were extremely successful with the reading public, they were generally scorned by critics at the University of Nairobi and Kenyatta University College. Other critics, however, suggested that this scorn was motivated by hypocrisy. Elizabeth Mwongera and Richard Arden, declared in their *The Role of Language and Literature in the School Curriculum:* "In the late 1970s when debate on literature was often heated and emotional, most University lecturers of literature were uneasy about racy tales such as *My Dear Bottle* and *After 4:30.* Some of this feeling was based on the fact that his style was weak, and his storyline limited, but might it have not been the case that the stories were too frank and direct?"

Maillu nevertheless took the critics' comments to heart, and in the 1980s began reassessing his work. According to Indangasi, Maillu said: "Some of my readers have said that I write immoral books, and have even gone to the extent of identifying me with the drunks and prostitutes in them. But perhaps you will be surprised to hear that I am a Christian, and that I do not drink. . . . My aim in these books is to show that drinking, prostitution, and loose sex are evil."

In the late 1980s, Maillu turned to writing children's books, most of which were published by a government publisher for Kenyan schoolchildren. In the late

1980s he wrote some novels, notably *The Ayah* and *Untouchable*. *The Ayah* examines the exploitation of female servants in Kenya, and is the first work to treat this problem seriously. In *Untouchable*, Maillu presents a love story between a Kenyan African and a Kenyan Indian, a union that still brings up prejudice and problems and which, Indangasi noted, "is one discussed only in whispers around the country." As in *The Ayah*, Maillu is the first writer to discuss this topic in full-length fiction.

Maillu's best work, which won the Jomo Kenyatta Prize for Literature in 1992, is *Broken Drum,* which covers 200 years of Kenyan history through the marriage of Ngewa and Vikirose. The book shows the encounters between the Kamba people and the Arabs, Portuguese, and British, and their consequences. Indangasi wrote of this epic work: "Maillu, who never stops writing, might produce mightier and more profound works in the future, but *Broken Drum* is certainly at this point in his career his most significant contribution to literature."

BIOGRAPHICAL/CRITICAL SOURCES:

BOOKS

Dictionary of Literary Biography, Volume 157: *Twentieth-Century Caribbean and Black African Writers,* edited by Bernth Lindfors, Gale Research (Detroit, MI), 1996, pp. 150-58.
Mwongera, Elizabeth, and Richard Arden, *The Role of Language and Literature in the School Curriculum,* British Council (Nairobi), 1991.

*   *   *

MAIS, Roger 1905-1955

PERSONAL: Born August 11, 1905, in Kingston, Jamaica; died of cancer, June 21, 1955, in Kingston, Jamaica. *Education:* Attended public schools in the Blue Mountains, Jamaica.

CAREER: Writer. Worked variously as a civil servant, painter, farmer, photographer, and journalist for the *Daily Gleaner* and *Public Opinion.*

WRITINGS:

And Most of All Man (short stories and verse), City Printery (Kingston, Jamaica), 1939.

Face and Other Stories (short stories and verse), Universal Printery, 1942.
The Potter's Field (play), first published in *Public Opinion,* December 23, 1950.
Atlanta at Calydon (play), J. Cape, 1950.
Come Love, Come Death, Hutchinson, 1951.
The Hills Were Joyful Together, J. Cape, 1953, reprinted, with introduction by Daphne Morris, Heinemann, 1981.
(And illustrator) *Brother Man,* J. Cape, 1954, reprinted with introduction by Edward Brathwaite, Heinemann, 1974.
Black Lightning, J. Cape, 1955, reprinted with introduction by Jean D'Costa, Heinemann, 1983.
The Three Novels of Roger Mais (contains *The Hills Were Joyful Together, Brother Man,* and *Black Lightning*), introduction by Norman W. Manley, J. Cape, 1966.
Listen, The Wind, and Other Stories, Longman, c. 1986.

Also author of other plays, such as *Hurricane, Masks and Paper Hats,* and *The First Sacrifice.*

SIDELIGHTS: Roger Mais, "the spokesman of emergent Jamaica," according to Jean D'Costa in her 1978 critique on Mais, is known primarily for his three novels of social protest. Among the first Jamaican novels to realistically examine that country's squalid urban conditions, *The Hills Were Joyful Together, Brother Man,* and *Black Lightning* greatly influenced the development of West Indian literature. Despite his middle-class upbringing in Jamaica's Blue Mountains, Mais empathized with the less fortunate urban slum dwellers and, as a writer, remained "fiercely dedicated to the exposure of social ills in mid-twentieth-century Jamaica," wrote D'Costa.

Of the three novels, *The Hills* provides the most explicit portrait of Caribbean slum life. Set in a ghetto in Kingston, Jamaica, *The Hills* examines the lives of three groups of black lower-class people. "Violence and misery is their common lot," observed reviewer Karina Williamson in the *Journal of Commonwealth Literature.* The Hills's subject matter disturbed many members of Jamaican society, according to Jean Creary, who explained in *The Islands in Between* that Mais's readers were "thrown straight into a world everyone in Jamaica knew existed, and yet which the middle classes were united in a conspiracy of silence to ignore and reject." She found, however, that "within and behind this human underworld lies beauty and pattern." In one particularly acclaimed passage, Williamson wrote, Mais describes the ghetto community's "common capacity for gaiety and goodwill" during a beach celebration. In other instances he depicts sympathy and loyalty between characters despite their misfortunes, indicating that personal integrity can withstand even the most hostile environment. "Mais's attitude . . . is ultimately neither cynical nor defeatist," Williamson explained, asserting that it is the author's balanced perspective that accounts for the novel's literary merit. "The book has its grave weaknesses," Creary admitted, citing wordiness and melodrama, but it succeeds because the author's "weaknesses come from the same source where lies his strength—from his innocent and yet potent awareness of himself and of his environment."

Mais's second novel, *Brother Man,* focuses on Rastafarianism, a Caribbean religious movement in which members seek a return of blacks to Africa. For some of their rituals, which include smoking marijuana—though shunning alcohol—and refusing to cut their hair, Rastafarians were "feared, despised, and rejected" during the 1940s and 1950s, explained Edward Brathwaite in his 1974 introduction to Mais's novel. The protagonist of *Brother Man* is a peaceful Rastafarian leader named John Power or "Bra Man," whose life resembles that of Jesus Christ. "In many ways," wrote Oscar R. Dathorne in *Studies in the Novel,* "the parallel between Christ and Bra Man is followed almost too carefully." Most critics agreed that the novel's credibility weakens whenever Bra Man becomes too Christ-like, healing the sick and teaching in parables, for example. Dathorne added, however, that "in spite of all this, Bra Man is convincing, not only as a messianic Christ-figure but as a person."

Reviewers praised Mais's refinement in *Brother Man* of a complex linguistic technique he had introduced in *The Hills.* Combining the figurative language of the King James Bible with the words and syntax of Jamaican Creole, Mais developed an elaborate writing style that enhanced his allegorical narratives. This style, according to Creary, is especially effective in descriptions of Bra Man, "Mais's vision of the reincarnate Christ. . . . This Gospel Presence fuses with Mais's writing in the rhythmical, Biblical prose." Dathorne agreed, explaining that "the language helps to identify Bra Man, and the rhythm of the Bible is reserved for him."

Black Lightning, Mais's third novel, is a biblical allegory like *Brother Man.* Unlike Mais's first two novels, however, *Black Lightning* skirts social issues, focusing instead on the solitary artist. Set in the Jamaican countryside, the novel follows the progress a sculptor, Jake, makes on a statue he is carving of the biblical hero Samson. "As it takes shape," Creary noted, "the figure of Samson becomes increasingly identified with Jake himself." Initially perceiving himself as strong and independent, the artist begins fashioning his work after his own self-image. After his wife leaves him, Jake becomes more aware of his dependence on her and begins molding his statue into the image of a weaker man. "The finished work Jake contemptuously reveals . . . is not Samson in his prime, but the blinded Samson, a figure of ruined strength leaning on a little boy," related Kenneth Ramchand in *The West Indian Novel and Its Background.* Like Samson, Jake is eventually blinded and, in despair, he kills himself.

Although Mais's first two novels received greater popular and critical acclaim upon their publication, Ramchand believes that the author's third book is his most powerful one. "The work has been virtually disregarded in the West Indies," the critic pointed out, "but I would like to contend that it is in *Black Lightning* that Mais's art and understanding are in greatest harmony, and that it is upon this . . . novel that his reputation must rest." Williamson also lauded *Black Lightning*'s artistic merit and its contribution to Caribbean literature: "*Black Lightning,* more than either of Mais's other novels, seems to me a landmark in the development of the West Indian novel."

A supporter of the Jamaican nationalist movement of the 1930s and 1940s, Mais was imprisoned in 1944 for an essay he wrote, titled "Now We Know," attacking English colonialism. Already the author of two short story collections, *And Most of All Man* and *Face and Other Stories,* Mais began writing his first novel during his six months in prison. Published nine years later, *The Hills Were Joyful Together* was quickly followed by *Brother Man* and *Black Lightning.* The author traveled to Europe in 1951 in search of a more accommodating artistic climate, but he returned to his homeland three years later, suffering from cancer. He died in Kingston in 1955, the year his third novel was published, leaving a fourth novel incomplete.

BIOGRAPHICAL/CRITICAL SOURCES:

BOOKS

D'Costa, Jean, *Roger Mais: "The Hills Were Joyful Together" and "Brother Man,"* Longman, 1978.

Hawthorne, Evelyn J., *The Writer in Transition: Roger Mais and the Decolonization of Caribbean Culture,* P. Lang, 1989.

James, Louis, editor, *The Islands in Between: Essays on West Indian Literature,* Oxford University Press, 1968.

Mais, Roger, *Brother Man,* introduction by Edward Brathwaite, Heinemann, 1974.

Moore, Gerald, *The Chosen Tongue: English Writings in the Tropical World,* Harper, 1969.

Ramchand, Kenneth, *The West Indian Novel and Its Background,* Barnes & Noble, 1970.

Twentieth-Century Literary Criticism, Volume 8, Gale, 1982.

PERIODICALS

Black Images, summer, 1972.
Journal of Commonwealth Literature, December, 1966.
Studies in the Novel, summer, 1972.*

* * *

MAJOR, Clarence 1936-

PERSONAL: Born December 31, 1936, in Atlanta, GA; son of Clarence and Inez (Huff) Major; married Joyce Sparrow, 1958 (divorced, 1964); married Pamela Jane Ritter, May 8, 1980. *Education:* State University of New York at Albany, B.S.; Union for Experimenting Colleges and Universities, Ph.D., 1978.

ADDRESSES: Agent—Susan Bergholz, 17 West 10th St. #5, New York, NY 10011-8769.

CAREER: Writer. Brooklyn College, City University of New York, SEEK program lecturer, 1968-69, lecturer, 1973-75; Sarah Lawrence College, Bronxville, NY, lecturer, 1972-75; Queens College, City University of New York, lecturer, 1972-73, 1975, adjunct lecturer for New York Board of Higher Education, ACE program, 1973; Howard University, Washington, DC, assistant professor, 1974-76; University of Washington, Seattle, assistant professor, 1976-77; University of Colorado, Boulder, associate professor, 1977-81, professor of English, 1981-89; University of California at Davis, professor of English, 1989—, director of creative writing, 1991-93. Visiting professor, University of Nice, France, 1981-82 and 1983; visiting assistant professor, University of Maryland at College Park and State University of New York at Binghamton, 1987. Writer in residence at colleges and universities. Research analyst for Simulmatics Corp., New York City, 1967; newspaper reporter, 1968. Lecturer and guest lecturer at colleges, universities, libraries, and other institutions in the United States, Europe, and Africa. Judge for various literary competitions. Artist; has exhibited and published his photographs and paintings. Member of advisory board, Reading Program, New York Public School District 5, 1970. *Military service:* U.S. Air Force, 1955-57; served as record specialist.

AWARDS, HONORS: Recipient of numerous grants; National Council on the Arts Award, Association of American University Presses, 1970; National Council on the Arts Award, 1970, for *Swallow the Lake;* Pushcart Prize, 1976, for poem "Funeral," from *The Syncopated Cakewalk,* and 1989, for story "My Mother and Mitch"; Fulbright-Hays Inter-University Exchange Award, Franco-American Commission for Education Exchange, Nice, France, 1981-83; Le Prix Maurice Edgar Coindreau nomination, 1982, for French version of *Reflex and Bone Structure;* Western States Book Award for fiction, 1986, for *My Amputations; New York Times Book Review* notable book of the year citation, 1988, for *Painted Turtle: Woman with Guitar; Los Angeles Times* Book Critics Award nomination, 1990, for *Fun & Games.*

WRITINGS:

POETRY

The Fires that Burn in Heaven, [Chicago], 1954.
Love Poems of a Black Man, Coercion (Omaha, NE), 1965.
Human Juices, Coercion, 1966.
Swallow the Lake, Wesleyan University Press (Middletown, CT), 1970.
Symptoms and Madness, Corinth Books (New York City), 1971.
Private Line, Paul Breman (London), 1971.
The Cotton Club, Broadside Press (Detroit, MI), 1972.
The Syncopated Cakewalk, Barlenmir (New York City), 1974.
Inside Diameter: The France Poems, Permanent Press (London and New York City), 1985.
Surfaces and Masks, Coffee House Press (Minneapolis, MN), 1987.
Some Observations of a Stranger at Zuni in the Latter Part of the Century, Sun & Moon (Los Angeles, CA), 1988.

Parking Lots, illustrated by Laura Dronzek, Perishable Press (Mount Horeb, WI), 1992.

Configurations: New and Selected Poems, 1958-1998, Copper Canyon Press (Port Townsend, WA), 1998.

Contributor of poetry to anthologies and to numerous periodicals, including *American Poetry Review, Kenyon Review, Michigan Quarterly Review, Folger Poetry Broadside, Poetry Miscellany, Unmuzzled Ox, Yardbird Reader,* and *Black Orpheus* (Nigeria).

NOVELS

All-Night Visitors, Olympia (New York City), 1969.

No, Emerson Hall (New York City), 1973.

Reflex and Bone Structure, Fiction Collective (New York City), 1975.

Emergency Exit, Fiction Collective, 1979.

My Amputations, Fiction Collective, 1986.

Such Was the Season (Literary Guild alternate selection), Mercury House (San Francisco, CA), 1987.

Painted Turtle: Woman with Guitar, Sun & Moon, 1988.

Dirty Bird Blues: A Novel, Mercury House (San Francisco), 1996.

NONFICTION

The Dark and Feeling: Black American Writers and Their Work (essays), Third Press (New York City), 1974.

Contributor of articles, essays, reviews, and other nonfiction prose to books, anthologies, and numerous periodicals, including *New York Times Book Review, Washington Post Book World, Los Angeles Times Book Review, American Poetry Review, Epoch, American Book Review, John O'Hara Journal, Essence, Negro Digest, Black Scholar, Journal of Black Studies and Research,* and *Black Orpheus* (Nigeria).

EDITOR

Writers Workshop Anthology, Harlem Education Program, 1967.

Man Is Like a Child: An Anthology of Creative Writing by Students, Macomb Junior High School, 1968.

(And author of introduction) *The New Black Poetry,* International Publications, 1969.

Dictionary of Afro-American Slang, International Publications (New York City), 1970, published in England as *Black Slang: A Dictionary of Afro-*

American Talk, Routledge & Kegan Paul (London), 1971, new edition with introduction by Major published as *Juba to Jive: A Dictionary of African-American Slang,* Viking (New York City), 1994.

Jerry Bumpus, *Things in Place* (short stories), Fiction Collective, 1975.

(And author of introduction) *Calling the Wind: Twentieth- Century African-American Short Stories* (Book-of-the-Month-Club selection), Harper Collins/Burlingame (New York City), 1993.

The Garden Thrives: Twentieth-Century African-American Poetry, HarperCollins (New York City), 1995.

SHORT STORIES

Fun & Games, Holy Cow! Press (Duluth, MN), 1990.

Contributor of short fiction to anthologies and to numerous periodicals, including *Massachusetts Review, Essence, Zyzzyva, Witness, Boulevard, Fiction, Chelsea, Baltimore Sun, Black Scholar, Black American Literature Forum, Agni Review, Seattle Review, Hambone,* and *Callaloo.*

Also author of television script, *Africa Speaks to New York,* 1970.

Distinguished contributing editor to *The Pushcart Prize: The Best of the Small Presses,* Pushcart Press (Wainscott, NY), 1977—. Columnist, *American Poetry Review,* 1973-76. Editor, *Coercion Review,* 1958-66; staff writer, *Proof,* 1960-61; associate editor, *Caw,* 1967-70, and *Journal of Black Poetry,* 1967- 70; member of board of directors, *What's Happening* magazine, Columbia University, 1969; contributing editor, *American Poetry Review,* 1976—, and *Dark Waters,* 1977; *American Book Review,* editor, 1977-78, associate editor, 1978—; associate editor, *Bopp,* 1977-78, *Gumbo,* 1978, *Departures,* 1979, and *par rapport,* 1979—; member of editorial board, *Umojo: A Scholarly Journal of Black Studies,* 1979; committee member, *Signes,* 1983—; fiction editor, *High Plains Literary Review,* 1986—.

All-Night Visitors has been translated into Italian and German; *Reflex and Bone Structure* has been translated into French; *Such Was the Season* has been translated into German.

SIDELIGHTS: American writer Clarence Major "has been in the forefront of experimental poetry and prose," Eugene B. Redmond writes in *Parnassus.* "In prose he fits 'loosely' into a category with William Melvin Kelley and Ishmael Reed. But his influences and antecedents are not so easy to identify." Perhaps best known for his novels, Major draws on his experience as a Southern African-American to "[defy] the white-imposed 'traditions' of black literature [and] to develop a brilliant lyricism in new forms of fiction," states Jerome Klinkowitz in *The Life of Fiction*. But Major's art, continues Klinkowitz, "inevitably turns back to the basic social and personal concerns which must remain at the heart of any literary experience." Noting the high incidence of violent scenes in Major's work, *Black Creation* critic Jim Walker comments, "Major has filled [his work] with the violence we expect of Southern life; violence of whites against Blacks, and more unfortunately, violence of Blacks against Blacks. . . . But the point Major is obviously trying to make with these kinds of scenes is that violence is an integral part of life for Southern Blacks and moreover, that it helps shape their lives and attitudes."

Critics praise Major's unique use of language in *My Amputations,* for which he received the Western States Book Award in 1986. *My Amputations* follows well-read parolee Mason Ellis as he impersonates an African-American novelist named Clarence McKay, whom he has taken hostage. McKay's literary agent plays along, and almost no one who meets the imposter on his world-wide lecture tour can tell the difference between Mason and the author whose identity he has usurped. "Major has fashioned a parable of the black writer as the most invisible and misrepresented of us all," notes Greg Tate in a *Washington Post Book World* review. *New York Times Book Review* contributor Richard Perry finds *My Amputations* "a book in which the question of identity throbs like an infected tooth, . . . a picaresque novel that comes wailing out of the blues tradition: it is ironic, irreverent, sexy, on a first-name basis with the human condition, and defined in part by exaggeration and laughter." In a *Nation* review, Stuart Klawans writes: "Mere description cannot convey the wild humor and audacity to be found here, nor the anxiety and cunning. . . . When a writer loads a book with so many references, the reader is entitled to ask whether he knows what he's doing. Believe me, Clarence Major knows. He has fashioned a novel that is simultaneously a deception and one great, roaring self-revelation." Tate comments, "Major feels particular ardor for mixing the rhythms of American slang with those of historical, scientific, mythological and occult texts. . . . The integration of such alchemical language into the mundane human affairs of its subjects

is part of what makes *My Amputations* such a provocative advance in contemporary American writing."

Such Was the Season is "more structured and accessible" than Major's earlier novels, writes David Nicholson in the *Washington Post Book World*. To Nicholson, it "seems rooted in Major's experience, and much of the book's success has to do with the warmth of the central character. . . . Annie Eliza . . . speaks to us for more than 200 pages of things past and present in a voice that is always uniquely hers." In this matriarch of a black middle-class Atlanta family who speaks authentic vernacular, "Major has created a delightfully lifelike, storytelling woman whose candor is matched only by her devotion to truth and her down-to-earth yea-saying to life," Al Young writes in the *New York Times Book Review*. "It is as if Clarence Major, the avid *avant-gardiste,* has himself come home to touch base with the blues and spirituals that continue to nourish and express the lives of those people he writes about so knowingly, and with contagious affection." *Such Was the Season,* Young summarizes, is a "straight-ahead narrative crammed with action, a dramatic storyline and meaty characterization." In the one week described by Annie Eliza, several scandals touching family members erupt in the wake of her daughter-in-law's candidacy for the state senate. Even so, "the book's pleasures have less to do with what happens and more with Annie Eliza and her tale," Nicholson maintains. "Though at first glance Major seems to have abandoned his postmodern explorations, *Such Was the Season* actually has much in common with those earlier works."

In *Fun & Games,* Major's 1990 collection of short "fictions," the author continues to bend and twist social realism around experimental narratives and prose. Writing in the *New York Times Book Review,* Karen Brailsford takes note of Major's "eloquent" prose, but finds that his "plots are frequently pointless, and ultimately disappointing." But while commenting that some of the stories in *Fun & Games* lack "the thematic and technical complexities that are Major's trademark," Maurice Bennett asserts in the *Washington Post Book World* that Major "is still here doing what he has done for the past 25 years: producing some of the very best experimental fiction." He adds, "Major remains at heart the poet he was at the beginning of his career, importing into his fictions a poetic fascination with the 'word' and its power to create realities, whether they be realities of identity, relationship, or phenomena." Merle Rubin, writing in the *Los Angeles Times Book Review,* suggests that

Major uses the "realist mode" to comment on the way we construct reality. "In Major's hands, straightforward realism has a way of wandering off into the labyrinths of literary self-awareness. . . . Major's 'short fictions' remind us that reality is not simply something out there: Ours, as he puts it, is a 'man-made world,' influenced by our ability to reflect, re-imagine, re-interpret and reform it."

Calling the Wind: Twentieth-Century African-American Short Stories, edited and with an introduction by Major, is an anthology of short fiction by African-American writers which "charts both the evolution of the short-story form and the evolution of African American consciousness," comments Howard Junker in the *San Francisco Review of Books. Calling the Wind* includes short fiction from writers such as Charles Chesnutt, Ralph Ellison, Toni Cade Bambara and Terry McMillan. Junker argues that *Calling the Wind* "should be required reading."

Major also edited and authored the introduction to *Juba to Jive: A Dictionary of African-American Slang,* an updated and expanded version of *Dictionary of Afro-American Slang* published originally in 1970. *Juba to Jive,* in the words of Ipeling Kgositsile in the *Village Voice Literary Supplement,* is a "no-nonsense guide to African American verbal expression." Kira Hall in the *Washington Post Book World* finds *Juba to Jive* an "exciting [introduction] to African-American *languaculture,* drawing the reader into an active world of words and phrases which might never appear in the American Heritage Dictionary," despite being spoken daily by many Americans. Applauding Major's ample etymological information on each term, Kgositsile calls *Juba to Jive* a "must buy; read it and learn the roots of a mother tongue." Major's work has "provided a series of systematic searches into different sources of identity—sexual, literary, cultural, visual, socio-economic, familial, regional, national, and personal, as well as ethnic," argues Lisa C. Roney in the *African American Review.* "When he is at his best," Doug Bolling remarks in the *Black American Literature Forum,* "Major helps us to see that fiction created within an aesthetic of fluidity and denial of 'closure' and verbal freedom can generate an excitement and awareness of great value; that the rigidities of plot, characterization, and illusioned depth can be softened and, finally, dropped in favor of new and valid rhythms." Major's achievement, according to Klinkowitz in an *African American Review* overview of Major's career and works, "has been to show just how concretely we live within the imagination—how our lives are shaped by language

and how by a simple act of self-awareness we can seize control of the world and reshape it to our liking and benefit."

BIOGRAPHICAL/CRITICAL SOURCES:

PERIODICALS

African American Review, spring, 1994.
American Anthropologist, June, 1975.
American Book Review, September/October, 1982; September, 1986.
American Heritage, September, 1994, p. 103.
Best Sellers, June 1, 1973.
Black American Literature Forum, number 12, 1978; Volume 12, number 2, 1979; fall, 1983.
Black Creation, summer, 1973.
Black Scholar, January, 1971.
Chicago Sun-Times, April 28, 1974.
Chicago Tribune, October 6, 1986.
Essence, November, 1970.
Greenfield Review, winter, 1971.
Los Angeles Times Book Review, February 18, 1990; April 29, 1990, p. 14.
Ms., July, 1977.
Nation, January 24, 1987.
Negro Digest, December, 1969.
Newsday, November 1, 1987.
New York Times, April 7, 1969.
New York Times Book Review, February 13, 1972; July 1, 1973; November 30, 1975; September 28, 1986; December 13, 1987; May 20, 1990.
Observer (London), May 1, 1994, p. 26.
Obsidian, Volume 4, number 2, 1978.
Parnassus, spring/summer, 1975.
par rapport, Volume 2, number 1, 1979.
Penthouse, February, 1971.
Phylon, winter, 1972.
Plain Dealer (Cleveland), December 3, 1987.
Poetry, August, 1971.
Publishers Weekly, March 24, 1969; March 19, 1973; May 9, 1986; July 4, 1986; July 31, 1987; January 22, 1996, p. 70; May 27, 1996, p. 67.
Quarterly Journal of Speech, April, 1977.
San Francisco Review of Books, Volume 1, number 12, 1976; Volume 7, number 3, 1982; March/April, 1993, p. 14.
Saturday Review, December 5, 1970; April 3, 1971.
Tribune Books (Chicago), October 6, 1986; April 3, 1994, p. 8.
Village Voice Literary Supplement, February, 1987; July 26, 1994, p. 81.
Virginia Quarterly Review, winter, 1971.
Washington Post Book World, September, 13, 1986;

January 10, 1988; February 18, 1990; January 10, 1993, p. 12; July 24, 1994, p. 8.*

*   *   *

MAJOR, Devorah   1952-

PERSONAL: Born 1958, in Berkeley, CA; daughter of Reginald Allman and Helen Gabriel Major; children: Yroko and Iwa. *Ethnicity:* African American.

ADDRESSES: Home—P.O. Box 423634, San Francisco, CA 94102. *E-mail*—dmajor1@ix.netcom.com. *Agent*—Janell Walden Agyeman, 636 NE 72nd Street, Miami, FL 33138.

CAREER: Poet, novelist, performer, editor. Koncepts Cultural Gallery, Oakland, CA, editor of community arts magazine and web site; leader of writing workshops as an artist-in-residence.

AWARDS, HONORS: First Novelist Award, Black Caucus American Library Association, 1996, for *An Open Weave;* Josephine Mills Award for Literary Excellence, Pen Oakland, 1997, for *Street Smarts.*

WRITINGS:

(Editor) *Ascension II,* San Francisco African American Historical & Cultural Society (San Francisco, CA), 1983.
(With Opal Palmer Adisa) *Traveling Women,* Jukebox Press (Oakland, CA), 1989.
An Open Weave (novel), Seal Press (Seattle, WA), 1995.
Street Smarts (poetry), Curbstone Press (Willimantic, CT), 1996.

Short stories featured in anthologies, including *Pushcart XII,* 1987; *I Hear a Symphony,* Penguin, 1995; and *Streetlights: Urban Stories of the Black Experience,* Doubleday, 1996. Essays featured in anthologies, including *California Childhoods,* Creative Arts Books, 1988; *A Single Mother's Companion,* Seal Press, 1995; *Something to Savor,* Womens Press, 1996; and *Father Songs,* Beacon Press, 1997. Poetry featured in anthologies, including,*Practicing Angels; Other Side of That Window,* 1992; *Adam of Ife,* 1993; and *Poetry Like Bread,* 1995. Poetry featured in recordings, including *Fierce/Love; America Fears the Drum;* and *Who Sane/Who Sane.* Contributor to periodicals, including *Zyzzyva, Onthebus, Black Scholar,*

Shooting Star, Caprice, and *Callaloo.*

SIDELIGHTS: Devorah Major is a poet, essayist, performer, and poetry teacher, whose first novel, *An Open Weave,* has a lyrical style. The story revolves around the female members of an extended African American family. While waiting to celebrate a birthday party for teenager Imani, the family and their friends reminisce about their pasts. Grandmother Ernestine, though blind, seems to see deep within the family members and is the one who keeps the family from splintering. Her adopted daughter, Iree, sees into the future during epileptic seizures. The story also relates Imani's determination not to desert a pregnant friend, Amanda, who has been abandoned by her family.

Lisa Nussbaum, in *Library Journal,* observed, "Down-to-earth, gritty, and honest, the story shows how these women weather difficult situations" through love and friendship. A contributor for *Kirkus Reviews* concluded, "Amanda finds at Imani's home a family she has been looking for in all the wrong places—and Imani understands with newfound appreciation the ultimate power of community."

Daniel L. Guillory described major's collection of poetry in *Street Smarts* as "a potpourri of street jive, scat singing, blues, hip-hop, and rap—a decidedly nonliterary style." Dulcy Brainard, in *Publishers Weekly,* judged: "Musical and energetic, major's work calls for a live voice to release its emotional power." Brainard wished that major had delved more deeply into difficult issues, yet called the work "compelling."

BIOGRAPHICAL/CRITICAL SOURCES:

PERIODICALS

Choice, April 1996, p. 1310.
Kirkus Reviews, August 1, 1995, pp. 1050-1051.
Library Journal, September 1, 1995, pp. 208-209; November 1, 1995, p. 80; March 15, 1996, p. 43; May 1, 1996, pp. 97-98.
Publishers Weekly, July 31, 1995, p. 71; March 18, 1996, p. 67.

*   *   *

MALCOLM X
See LITTLE, Malcolm

MANDELA, Nelson R(olihlahla) 1918-

PERSONAL: Born 1918, in Umtata, Transkei, South Africa; son of Henry Mandela (a Tembu tribal chief); married Edith Ntoko (a nurse; divorced); married Nomzamo Winnie Madikileza (a social worker and political activist; divorced), June 14, 1958; children: (first marriage) Makgatho, Thembi (deceased), Makaziwe Phumla Mandela; (second marriage) Zenani (married to Prince Thumbumuzi Dhlamini of Swaziland), Zindziswa. *Education:* Attended University College of Fort Hare and Witwatersrand University; University of South Africa, law degree, 1942.

ADDRESSES: Agent—c/o Carol Publishing.

CAREER: Mandela & Tambo law firm, Johannesburg, South Africa, partner, 1952-c. 1960; political organizer and leader of the African National Congress (ANC), Johannesburg, South Africa, 1944—, held successive posts as secretary and president of the Congress Youth League, deputy national president of the ANC, and commander of the Umkonto we Sizwe ("Spear of the Nation") paramilitary organization; sentenced to five years in prison for inciting Africans to strike and for leaving South Africa without a valid travel document, 1962; sentenced to life imprisonment for sabotage and treason, 1964; incarcerated in various penal institutions, including Robben Island and Pollsmoor prisons, South Africa, 1962-90. President of African National Congress, 1991—; President of South Africa, 1994—.

AWARDS, HONORS: Honorary doctor of law degrees from the National University of Lesotho, 1979, and City College of the City University of New York, 1983; Jawaharlal Nehru Award for International Understanding from the government of India, 1980; Bruno Kreisky Prize for Human Rights from the government of Austria, 1981; named honorary citizen of Glasgow, 1981, and Rome, 1983; Simon Bolivar International Prize from UNESCO, 1983; Litt. D University of Calcutta, 1986; nominated for 1987 Nobel Peace Prize; Human Rights Prize, European Parliament, 1988; Gaddafi International Prize for Human Rights, 1989; L.L.B., University of South Africa, 1989; Human Rights Award, American Jewish Committee, 1993; Nobel Peace Prize, 1993.

WRITINGS:

NONFICTION

No Easy Walk to Freedom, Basic Books, 1965.

Nelson Mandela Speaks, African National Congress Publicity and Information Bureau (London), c. 1970.

The Struggle Is My Life, International Defence and Aid Fund (London), 1978, revised and updated edition, Pathfinder Press, 1986, further revised and updated edition published as *Nelson Mandela: The Struggle Is My Life: His Speeches and Writings Brought Together with Historical Documents and Accounts of Mandela in Prison by Fellow-prisoners,* International Defence and Aid Fund, 1990.

Nelson Mandela, Symbol of Resistance and Hope for a Free South Africa: Selected Speeches since His Release, edited by E. S. Reddy, Sterling, 1990.

Nelson Mandela, Speeches 1990: "Intensify the Struggle to Abolish Apartheid," edited by Greg McCartan, photographs by Margrethe Siem, Pathfinder Press, 1990.

(With Fidel Castro) *How Far We Slaves Have Come! South Africa and Cuba in Today's World,* Pathfinder Press, 1991.

A Better Life for All: Working Together for Jobs, Peace, and Freedom, ANC Department of Information and Publicity, 1994.

Long Walk to Freedom: The Autobiography of Nelson Mandela, Little Brown, 1994.

Nelson Mandela: The Struggle Is My Life: His Speeches and Writings Brought Together with Historical Documents and Accounts of Mandela in Prison by Fellow-Prisoners, Mayibuye Books, 1994.

South and Southern Africa into the Next Century, Institute of Southeast Asian Studies, 1997.

The Essential Nelson Mandela, compiled by Robin Malan, D. Philip Publishers (Cape Town, South Africa), 1997.

In the Words of Nelson Mandela, edited by Jennifer Crwys-Williams, Carol Publishing, 1998.

OTHER

Contributor of articles to the South African political journal *Liberation,* 1953-59; author of introduction to *Oliver Tambo Speaks: Preparing for Power,* Braziller, 1988.

SIDELIGHTS: Nelson Mandela has been called both "the world's most famous political prisoner" and "South Africa's Great Black Hope," by journalist Tom Mathews in *Newsweek.* A leader of the banned African National Congress (ANC) insurgent movement during the 1950s and 60s, Mandela had been jailed by white governments for a quarter of a century for his efforts to enfranchise his fellow blacks. Through his leadership and personal sacrifices, Mandela has come to symbolize the struggle against apartheid, the system of enforced racial inequality that denied political rights to South Africa's black majority. Mandela's release from prison in February, 1990, was followed by a triumphant world tour that included eight major cities in the United States. Strong admiration for the former political prisoner provided a common bond for many Americans who were at odds over how to defeat racial injustice. "No leader since the Reverend Martin Luther King, Jr., has brought together such a diverse coalition in the fight against racial injustice," noted a writer for *Time*. After his release, Mandela engaged in negotiations on behalf of the ANC with then-South African president F. W. de Klerk over a settlement of power that resulted in democratic-styled elections. In these elections, held in 1994, Mandela was elected President of South Africa, completing his astonishing rise to power after decades of imprisonment.

Mandela is descended from Xhosa-speaking tribal chieftains from the Transkei region of South Africa. He left his ancestral home at a young age to avoid an arranged marriage and pursued a professional career in the commercial capital of Johannesburg. Obtaining his law degree from the University of South Africa in 1942, Mandela joined the ANC two years later at the age of twenty-six and helped found the Congress Youth League (CYL) with Walter Sisulu, Oliver Tambo, and others. With Mandela as its secretary, the CYL urged its parent organization, the ANC, to abandon the strictly constitutional approach to reform that it had fruitlessly pursued with successive white minority governments since its founding in 1912 in favor of a more militant and confrontational strategy.

Under strong youth pressure, the ANC adopted a new program of action in 1949 that recognized such non-violent—but sometimes illegal—tactics as electoral boycotts, "stay-at-homes" (general strikes), student demonstrations, and civil disobedience. In June, 1952, Mandela mounted the first major test of the new ANC program by organizing the Defiance Against Unjust Laws campaign, a coordinated civil disobedience of six selected apartheid laws by a multiracial group of some eighty-six hundred volunteers. The government's violent response to the Defiance Campaign generated a backlash of popular support for the ANC that helped thrust Nelson Mandela to national prominence; it also brought him a nine-month suspended jail sentence, a two-year government "banning" order that confined him to Johannesburg and

prohibited him from attending public gatherings, and an order to resign his ANC leadership posts as deputy president of the national organization, president of the Transvaal branch, and president of the CYL. Mandela refused to do so, and as a result he was obliged to conduct most of his political organizing work under the cover of his Johannesburg law partnership with Oliver Tambo and to limit his public profile to writing articles for the pro-ANC journal *Liberation*.

In December, 1956, following a year of ANC-led mass protests against the Nationalists' proposal to create seven tiny tribal "homelands" in which to segregate South Africa's black population, the government brought charges against Mandela and 155 other anti-apartheid leaders under anti-Communist and treason statutes. During most of the four-and-one-half years that the "Treason Trial" lasted, Mandela remained free on bail, continuing to work at his law office during the evenings and discreetly engaging in political activities within the limitations of a new five-year banning order leveled on him in February, 1956.

In March of 1960, an action occurred that marked an historical watershed in the struggle for black rights in South Africa. Responding to a demonstration against "pass laws," which required black South Africans to carry government identification documents, the police in the Johannesburg suburb of Sharpeville turned their weapons on a group of unarmed protesters, killing sixty-nine people. The massacre sparked a wave of angry new protests and public pass-book burnings, to which Pretoria (the seat of the South African government) responded by declaring a state of national emergency. The government banned the ANC and PAC, and detained some eighteen hundred political activists without charges, including Mandela and the other "Treason Trial" defendants. This crackdown prompted the trial lawyers to withdraw from the case, declaring that the emergency restrictions prevented them from mounting an effective defense, and left Mandela, Duma Nokwe, Walter Sisulu, and several others to represent their sizable group of ANC leaders.

As an advocate for his group, Mandela distinguished himself with his legal ability and eloquent statements of the ANC's political and social philosophy. He defended the 1949 Programme of Action and the Defiance Campaign as necessary disruptive tactics when the government was indifferent to legal pressure; he also sought to assuage white fears of a black political takeover by insisting that the ANC's form of nationalism recognized the right of all South African racial groups to enjoy political freedom and nondiscrimination together in the same country. In a unique legal victory for South African black activists, the trial judge acquitted all the defendants for insufficient evidence in March, 1961, finding that the ANC did not have a policy of violence.

Among those anxiously awaiting the verdict was Nomzamo Winnie Madikileza, who had married Mandela during the early stages of the trial. The government's ban of the ANC meant an end to any normal home life for the Mandelas, however. Immediately after his release, Mandela went underground to avoid new government banning orders. He surfaced in late March to deliver the keynote speech at the All-In African Conference held in Pietermaritzburg, which had been organized by the ANC and other opposition political organizations to address the Nationalists' plan to declare a racialist South African republic in May of that year. The All-In Conference opposed this proposal with a demand that the government hold elections for a fully representative national convention empowered to draft a new and democratic constitution for all South Africans. Meeting no response to the assembly's demands from the H. F. Verwoerd government, Mandela helped organize a three-day general strike for the end of May to press for the convention. Verwoerd's security forces mobilized heavily against the strike by suspending civil liberties, making massive preemptive arrests, and deploying heavy military equipment, which succeeded in limiting public support for the action (although hundreds of thousands of Africans nationwide still stayed away from work).

Facing arrest, Mandela once again disappeared underground, this time for seventeen months, assuming numerous disguises in a cat-and-mouse game with the police during which he became popularly known as the "Black Pimpernel." The ANC leader was finally captured disguised as a chauffeur in the province of Natal by police acting on an informer's tip in August, 1962. Brought to trial in October on charges of inciting Africans to strike and leaving the country without a valid travel document, Mandela turned his defense into an indictment of the apartheid system. In an eloquent statement to the presiding judge, the ANC leader rejected the right of the court to hear the case on the grounds that—as a black man—he could not be given a fair trial under a judicial system intended to enforce white domination, and, furthermore, that he considered himself neither legally nor morally bound to obey laws created by a parliament in which he had no representation. Despite his impressive courtroom performance, Mandela was convicted of both charges and sentenced to five years in prison.

Unknown to the authorities at the time of his trial, Mandela and other ANC leaders had reluctantly decided to launch an underground paramilitary movement in 1961 for the first time in the ANC's history. In November of 1961, Mandela helped organize and assumed command of the Umkonto we Sizwe ("Spear of the Nation") guerrilla organization and began planning a sabotage campaign directed against government installations and the economic infrastructure. Umkonto's first military action occurred on December 16, 1961, when the organization simultaneously attacked government buildings in Johannesburg, Port Elizabeth, and Durban. The group went on to engage in many more acts of sabotage over the next year while Mandela traveled surreptitiously to England, Ethiopia, Algeria, and other African countries to meet political leaders, seek arms for the movement, and undergo military training.

Mandela's role in leading Umkonto came to light in June, 1963, when police raided the ANC's underground headquarters in the Johannesburg suburb of Rivonia and discovered documents relating to the armed movement. Nine top ANC leaders were arrested and brought to trial in early 1964 on charges of committing sabotage and conspiring to overthrow the government by revolution with the help of foreign troops. Mandela once again conducted his own defense, using the courtroom as a platform to explain and justify the ANC's turn to armed struggle and to condemn the apartheid regime. Mandela declared at the trial, "It would be unrealistic and wrong for African leaders to continue preaching peace and nonviolence at a time when the Government met our peaceful demands with force." He fully acknowledged helping to found Umkonto and planning acts of sabotage, but he denied the government's contention that the ANC and Umkonto intended to subject the anti-apartheid struggle to revolutionary control, either foreign or domestic.

While he acknowledged being strongly influenced by Marxist thought, Mandela denied ever having been a member of the Communist party, insisting that he held a deep and abiding admiration for Western legal and political institutions and wished to "borrow the best from both East and West" to reshape South African society. As elaborated in the ANC's Freedom Charter (a 1955 manifesto that Mandela helped to draft that remains the basic statement of the group's political purpose), the ANC looked forward to a democratic, pluralist society with certain mildly socialistic reforms—including land redistribution, nationalization of the country's mines, and a progressive tax and incomes policy—intended to dilute the economic power of the white minority and raise the country's black majority out of poverty.

Mandela's trial ended in June, 1964, when he and eight other defendants were convicted of sabotage and treason and sentenced to life imprisonment. Confined to the Robben Island fortress for political prisoners seven miles offshore from Cape Town, the ANC leaders were kept rigidly isolated from the outside world. They were denied access to radio, television, and newspapers, and prohibited from publishing articles, giving public interviews, or even discussing politics with visitors. All Mandela's past speeches and published works were banned, and merely possessing his writings in South Africa was made a criminal offense. Despite these restrictions, two book-length collections of Mandela's best known political statements were published abroad and have since circulated widely among South African anti-apartheid activists.

No Easy Walk to Freedom, published in 1965, includes Mandela's 1953 presidential address to the Transvaal province ANC (in which he discusses the Defiance Campaign), his speech at the 1961 All-In African Conference, and excerpts from his testimony at his three political trials. A second collection, *The Struggle Is My Life,* contains material from 1944 to 1985, including four prison statements from Mandela; and a revised 1986 edition of the title incorporates the memoirs of two of Mandela's fellow prisoners from Robben Island prison who had been released. Six speeches made by Mandela between February and May, 1990, during his first months of freedom, are collected in *Nelson Mandela, Speeches 1990: "Intensify the Struggle to Abolish Apartheid."* Published in 1990, the volume also includes Mandela's 1989 letter to South African president P. W. Botha stressing the need for negotiations between the government and the ANC.

Shortly after her husband's 1962 conviction, Winnie Mandela received her first government banning order restricting her to Johannesburg and preventing her from attending public or private meetings of any kind. In 1965, the government forced her out of her job with the Child Welfare Society by further restricting her to her home township of Orlando West and preventing her from engaging in essential fieldwork elsewhere in the Soweto district. She was then fired from a succession of low-paying jobs in the white commer-

cial district after the security police pressured her employers, and she finally found herself reduced to supporting her two young daughters on the charity of friends and political associates. Despite this hardship, Winnie Mandela continued to work surreptitiously with the ANC during the 1960s by helping produce banned political pamphlets and newsletters in her home. During this period, the suspicious police ransacked the Mandela house repeatedly, but prosecutors could never find enough evidence to bring a court case against her.

In May, 1969, however, Winnie Mandela was arrested with other suspected ANC sympathizers under a new law that allowed the government to detain "terrorist" suspects indefinitely without charges. Taken to Pretoria Prison, she was interrogated virtually non-stop for five days and nights about her supposed links to ANC saboteurs. She was then jailed without charges for seventeen months, spending the first two hundred days of this period incommunicado and in solitary confinement. Finally, under pressure from Nelson Mandela's lawyers, the authorities improved Winnie's confinement conditions and brought her to trial on twenty-one political charges in September, 1970. The trial judge dismissed the case against her and all but one of her co-defendants for insufficient evidence, and Winnie Mandela was released that month.

Though freed from prison, Winnie Mandela was still subjected to close police vigilance in the early 1970s as South Africa's white minority government reacted to new challenges from a growing world anti-apartheid movement and the anti-colonial wars in nearby Mozambique and Angola. Immediately upon her release, she was placed under a new five-year banning order that confined her to her home during the evenings and on weekends. She was subjected to frequent police home searches in ensuing years and was arrested and sentenced to six months in prison for talking to another banned person in 1974. The authorities eventually allowed her banning order to expire in October, 1975, and over the next ten months she was able to enjoy the rights of free association and movement for the first time in many years.

This period of relative freedom for Winnie Mandela coincided with the birth of a militant "Black Consciousness" youth movement led by Stephen Biko and other students in Soweto. The student revolt had as its immediate aim the annulment of the Bantu Education Act, which consigned blacks to inferior education and obliged them to learn Afrikaans, the language of

South African whites of Dutch descent, instead of English. When police shot down a number of unarmed demonstrators in Soweto in June, 1976, however, the township's youth erupted in a fury of uncontrolled rioting and clashes with the security forces that left at least six hundred people dead. Many of the participants in the Soweto uprising who escaped being killed or imprisoned fled the country and made contact with ANC exile headquarters in Lusaka, Zambia. This militant young cadre helped to radicalize the Congress and substantially strengthen its military wing, allowing the ANC to reestablish both a political and military presence inside South Africa by the end of the decade.

The ebb in the popular struggle after the Soweto uprising lasted until 1984, when the townships exploded again over the adoption of a new South African constitution that gave parliamentary representation to "Coloureds" and Indians but not to blacks. The townships remained in a state of near-continuous political turmoil in succeeding years as anti-government youth clashed violently with the security forces and other blacks accused of collaborating with the regime. But, unlike the situation a decade earlier, when the township civilians stood unorganized and alone against the apartheid government, a number of powerful social and political forces joined the fray in the mid-1980s to mount the greatest challenge to white minority rule in South African history. The United Democratic Front (UDF), a coalition of some 680 anti-apartheid organizations that supports the political line of the ANC, organized large street demonstrations and protests by township squatters facing eviction that were harshly repressed by the government in 1985. Meanwhile, the ANC itself stepped up its guerrilla campaign in South Africa and began targeting white residential areas and causing civilian casualties for the first time. The Nationalist government of P. W. Botha also came under mounting attack from abroad as the United States and other Western countries imposed limited trade and investment sanctions on South Africa in a bid to force reform. Finally, in 1987, the one-million-strong black trade union movement began to flex its powerful muscles with strikes by workers in the strategic transport and mining sectors.

A common demand voiced throughout the previous decade by the diverse forces seeking to change the apartheid system was that Nelson Mandela be released immediately. In 1985, Winnie Mandela managed to break her government restrictions and return to Soweto to join the fight for her husband's freedom (this turn of events occurred after her Brandfort house was firebombed and burned to the ground in August of that year while she was in Johannesburg for medical treatment). Accusing the security police of the attack and saying that she feared for her life, Winnie Mandela insisted on moving back to her Soweto house; amid much local and international publicity, the Botha government permitted her to do so. In succeeding months, Winnie Mandela took advantage of the government's weakened position to openly flout her banning orders by giving press interviews and speaking out militantly at public demonstrations and at the funerals of young township victims of government repression.

Speaking at a funeral on a return visit to Brandfort in April, 1986, for example, Winnie Mandela denounced the authorities as "terrorists" and called on blacks to take "direct action" against the government to free the imprisoned nationalist leaders. "The time has come where we must show that we are disciplined and trained warriors," she added in what some observers interpreted as a call to insurrection. In a bid to improve its international image and deflect criticism of a new state of emergency it had imposed the previous month, the Botha regime, in July, 1986, chose not to prosecute Winnie Mandela and instead lifted all banning restrictions on her. Among Winnie Mandela's first public actions once her right to free speech had been restored was to call for international economic sanctions against the apartheid government.

The Botha government met the current crisis with a "divide and rule" strategy combining harsh repression and isolated reforms that did not fundamentally alter the structure of apartheid. While repealing such symbols of apartheid as pass laws and long-standing bans on interracial sex and marriage, the government violently crushed the township uprisings and detained tens of thousands of anti-apartheid protesters without trial under sweeping state-of-emergency powers. Fearing the popular reaction if Mandela were to die in prison, previous South African governments sought to find a way to free him as early as 1973, but the confined ANC leader had always rejected conditions that he accept exile abroad or in the Transkei "homeland" and that he renounce violence by the insurgent organization. In late 1987, the Botha regime began hinting at the possibility that it might finally release Nelson Mandela unconditionally in an attempt to mollify domestic and international public opinion. The advisability of releasing the ANC leader in terms of domestic politics reportedly stimulated a hot debate in the Botha cabinet, with those in favor of the move arguing that Mandela was now more conservative than much of the current ANC leadership and could therefore effect a split in the organization. Detractors contended that freeing South Africa's best-known political prisoner could further alienate hard-line whites and possibly stimulate a black insurrection. Reform-minded South Africans, on the other hand, believed Mandela was the only political leader prestigious enough to win the confidence of both liberal whites and the increasingly alienated black township youth, thereby delivering the country from the specter of race war.

In November, 1987, the authorities unconditionally freed Mandela's long-time comrade-in-arms Govan Mbeki (a top ANC and South African Communist party leader who was convicted at the Rivonia Trial and served twenty-four years on Robben Island), as a way of testing the political waters for Mandela's possible release. In August, 1988, Mandela was diagnosed with tuberculosis, and the announcement prompted a new round of demands from the international community that he should be set free. The next year brought the release of Walter Sisulu— considered by some to be the second most important figure in South Africa's fight against apartheid—along with the rest of the Rivonia prisoners with the exception of Mandela himself. South African president F. W. de Klerk, who succeeded Botha in 1989, came into power on a reform platform; with the Rivonia amnesties, de Klerk initiated the first conciliatory measures which soon included unconditional freedom for Mandela and the lifting of the ban on the ANC (the government had delayed Mandela's pardon with the stipulation that he formally renounce violence, but it finally relented, granting his freedom February 11, 1990). De Klerk was quoted in *Time* as saying, "I came to the conclusion that [Mandela] is committed to a peaceful solution and a peaceful process." Bruce W. Nelan of *Time* suggested that de Klerk intended to demystify Mandela and the anti-apartheid movement by setting its "spiritual leader" free: "By legalizing the ANC, [de Klerk] removes its cloak of underground heroism and turns it into an ordinary political party. Both Mandela and his organization will then be forced by circumstance and expectation to make compromises. And compromises are expected to anger and disillusion segments of the black majority, giving the government opportunities to divide the opposition." Nelan further conjectured that the South African president looked for the end of international sanctions against South Africa by beginning talks with black leaders—and the longer the government dragged

out negotiations, the more likely momentum behind the anti-apartheid movement would falter.

Embarking on a thirteen country tour in June and July, 1990, Mandela was received in the United States as—in the words of Nelan—a "heroic superstar." His mission, however, was political; he wanted both assurances from governments that sanctions would remain in place until South Africa was committed to peaceful change, and donations to revitalize the ANC. In New York City, people jammed the streets to catch a glimpse of Mandela passing by in a ticker tape parade. Speaking at a crossroads in Harlem, Mandela told a crowd nearing 100,000, "I am here to claim you because . . . you have claimed our struggle." Mandela also appeared at rallies in seven other American cities, including Boston, Miami, Detroit, and Los Angeles. In Washington, D.C., President George Bush—who, as vice-president under Ronald Reagan, fought against the Comprehensive Anti-Apartheid Act of 1986—agreed to keep economic sanctions in place, at least for the short term. "I want to find a way to show our appreciation to de Klerk, and yet I don't want to pull the rug out from under Mr. Mandela," Bush was quoted as saying in *Time*.

Upon his return to South Africa, Mandela was faced with serious obstacles which threatened to disrupt any progress he made negotiating with the government. Bloody clashes between the ANC and its backers, and Inkatha, a Zulu organization of about 1.5 million members, had been flaring up since 1987 in Natal Province. Led by Chief Mangosuthu Buthelezi, who "opposes strikes, armed struggle and foreign sanctions against the country's white government," according to Jeffrey Bartholet in *Newsweek,* Inkatha had been targeting the United Democratic Front, an organization comprised of Zulus who support the ANC. While still in prison, Mandela had hoped for a reconciliation with Buthelezi, but his very release sparked two days of violence in Natal that killed fifty people. In March, 1990, Mandela agreed to hold a joint rally with Buthelezi in Durban, but canceled out when the venue appeared too potentially explosive. Two weeks after the ANC announced an end to armed struggle against apartheid in August, 1990, a raid by Inkatha supporters on train passengers at Soweto's Inhlazane Station resulted in a wave of violence that spread to other townships around Johannesburg, leaving more than two hundred people dead. Right-wing politicians exploited the turmoil, attempting to use the ethnic strife as proof of the unviability of a black South African government. "The rivalry plays on white fears that tribalism could rip apart a post-apartheid

South Africa. While de Klerk's National Party ties its future to the ANC, the right-wing Conservative Party has seized on Buthelezi's demands for a role equal to Mandela's," commented Joseph Contreras in *Newsweek*. While de Klerk pressed Mandela to help quell the violence by meeting with Buthelezi, Mandela blamed Pretoria. "Under the noses of the police, Inkatha *impis* go places fully armed and attack and kill people," he reportedly said.

Black-on-black violence continued unabated, with the ANC withdrawing from talks in May, 1991, after the government refused to outlaw tribal weapons carried by Inkatha party members. In the same month, Winnie Mandela was convicted of kidnapping and being an accessory to assault and sentenced to six years in prison. The conviction stemmed from the actions of her bodyguards, who called themselves the Mandela United Football Club although—as John Bierman reported in *Maclean's*—"they never played a single organized game of soccer." In 1988, members of the club kidnapped four black youths from a hostel. According to Bierman, "evidence showed that [Winnie] Mandela's bodyguards took the victims to her Soweto home, where they tied them up and savagely beat them. One of the youths, fourteen year-old James (Stompie) Moeketsi Seipei, was later found dead." Winnie Mandela denied any involvement in the crime, stating in court she was in the Orange Free State—three hundred kilometers away—when it occurred; she has since appealed the decision. Mandela supported his wife throughout her trial. He appeared to observers to be devoted to the woman who supported him through the many years of his imprisonment with her visits and letters, who endured jail and police mistreatment on his behalf. "There have been moments when conscience and a sense of guilt have ravaged every part of my being," Mandela once wrote his wife, agonized by separation from his family.

Mandela insisted that the negative publicity surrounding Winnie's court case had no effect on his negotiations with Pretoria. Although far from fully enfranchising the black population, the government did institute further reforms, including the repeal of the Population Registration Act in June, 1991, which required every South African baby to be documented by race. Although international response was positive, the South African government was far from eradicating apartheid; blacks still didn't have the right to vote. Mandela, whom political experts considered outmaneuvered by de Klerk, had become increasingly cynical of the president, stating, "What he has done is merely to bring about changes which maintain the status quo.

"The ANC addressed their setbacks at a national conference in Durban during July, 1991—the first such gathering in South Africa in thirty years. The party had been splitting between young radicals who favored a more militant approach toward immediate change, and older, conservative leaders who recommended negotiating gradually with the government. The Durban conference reaffirmed the moderate philosophy within the ANC by electing Mandela president, Walter Sisulu deputy president, and Cyril Ramaphosa secretary general. "This is an overwhelming victory for the moderates and a crushing blow to the militants who were outpolled two-to-one," commented South African political expert Donald Simpson in *Maclean's*.

Mandela struggled to balance his group's objectives with assurances to white South Africans that the ANC did not wish to turn the country into a socialist state. "We would nationalize the mines, the banks and other monopolies, but the rest of the economy is based on private enterprise," Mandela informed *Newsweek* in an interview. "Not even the land is nationalized, which is normally the first sector of the economy which socialist [governments] nationalize."

A growing distrust of de Klerk among blacks soured into seething resentment in June, 1992, when about two hundred Inkatha supporters rampaged through the township of Boipatong with guns, machetes and spears, killing at least forty people. Witnesses claimed the Zulu attackers had been assisted by the police. Rejecting calls among militant members to reengage in armed struggle, ANC leaders instead displayed their frustration with the government's inability to control the violence—and the seeming insincerity within de Klerk's National Party in negotiating a new, nonracial constitution—by withdrawing from the talks. A campaign of mass-action (boycotts, strikes and sit-ins) was instituted while the ANC pressed Pretoria with a list of demands, including a full investigation of the Boipatong massacre.

Addressing a Pretoria rally comprised of 70,000 peaceful marchers in August, 1992, Mandela responded to the crowd's calls of "De Klerk must go!" with a statement indicating the true purpose of the march: not to overthrow de Klerk, but to prompt him into faster action towards creating a democratic government. Mandela and de Klerk finally met on September 26, 1992, for the first time since May, agreeing to resume negotiations on the constitution and to accelerate efforts in forging an interim government. Several conditions laid down by the ANC for the resumption of talks were met by de Klerk, namely the erection of fences around single-sex workers' hostels (often the origination point of Inkatha-inspired violence), a ban on carrying tribal weapons in public, and the release of close to five hundred blacks, deemed political prisoners by the ANC. In exchange for the amnesty, the ANC agreed to a general amnesty for white governmental officials accused of crimes during the years of apartheid. One day after Mandela's summit with de Klerk, Buthelezi walked out of negotiations, angered over the deals struck between the two leaders. Buthelezi made it clear that Inkatha would not participate in postapartheid elections, even though political experts suggested de Klerk's Nationalist Party was counting on Buthelezi's (and Inkatha's) support to bolster their showings at the polls against the ANC. De Klerk denied Buthelezi's charges of striking "illegitimate" deals and claimed the real impediment to progress was due to factionalism between the blacks. Addressing this setback on television, de Klerk said, "It appears to me more and more that we won't have peace until Mr. Mandela and Chief Buthelezi make their peace."

Despite his long imprisonment and personal suffering, political setbacks and the unrelenting strife between Inkatha and the ANC, Mandela's efforts to end institutional apartheid were finally realized in June, 1993, when South Africa's first free elections were announced. Scheduled for April 27, 1994, the election was agreed upon by a majority of the country's twenty-six parties as a measure to reassure blacks that change was coming. "And the voters will almost certainly reward Mandela's stoic struggle by conferring on him the leadership of his country," declared Scott MacLeod in *Time*. This prediction proved accurate, as Mandela was elected President, with the ANC capturing sixty-three percent of the popular vote.

Since becoming President, Mandela has worked to heal the racial divisions in South Africa; to achieve South Africa's readmittance to the world community of democratic nations; and to address the crushing poverty of the country's black citizens. Mandela has been successful in luring western private investment into South Africa, but economic progress for South Africa's poor black majority has been slow, prompting some criticism of Mandela's tenure. An increased crime rate is another difficult issue facing Mandela's government. In an interview with *Newsweek,* Mandela declared that "the previous government concentrated not on suppressing crime but on suppressing the liberation movement, and tended to ignore crime. So you could understand why crime in the black areas

rocketed. We inherited that situation." In addition to his political challenges, Mandela went through a messy divorce with Winnie.

In his autobiography *Long Walk to Freedom,* published in 1994, Mandela recounts his remarkable life, including his childhood in the Transkei region; his political beginnings in the 1940s and 1950s with the ANC; his twenty- seven year imprisonment; and the period after his release in 1990. Reviewers greeted the book with praise, commending Mandela's lack of bitterness and thoughtful assessment of his achievements and shortcomings. Terming the book "one of the few political autobiographies that's also a page-turner," *Los Angeles Times Book Review,* contributor Chris Goodrich called *Long Walk to Freedom* "a monumental book, one that well matches its author." Chicago *Tribune Books* reviewer Penelope Mesic concurred, calling the work "a truly wonderful autobiography, sharp, literate, unpretentious and-surprisingly-as emotionally involving as it is informative." For his long struggle on behalf of South Africa's oppressed masses and his efforts toward a peaceful transfer of power from the white minority leadership, Mandela, along with F. W. de Klerk, was awarded the 1993 Nobel Peace Prize.

BIOGRAPHICAL/CRITICAL SOURCES:

BOOKS

Benson, Mary, *Nelson Mandela: The Man and the Movement,* Norton, 1986.

Bray, Rosemary L., *Nelson Mandela,* Greenwillow Books, 1998.

Cooper, Floyd, *Mandela: From the Life of the South African Statesman,* Philomel, 1996.

Harrison, Nancy, *Winnie Mandela* (biography), Braziller, 1986.

Holland, Gini, and Mike White, *Nelson Mandela,* Raintree Steck-Vaughn, 1997.

Juckes, Tim J., *Opposition in South Africa: The Leadership of Z. K. Matthews, Nelson Mandela, and Stephen Biko,* Praeger, 1995.

Mandela, Nelson R., *No Easy Walk to Freedom,* Basic Books, 1965.

Mandela, Nelson R., *The Struggle Is My Life,* Pathfinder Press, 1986.

Mandela, Nelson R., *Long Walk to Freedom: The Autobiography of Nelson Mandela,* Little Brown, 1994.

Mandela, Winnie, *Part of My Soul Went with Him* (autobiography), edited by Anne Benjamin and Mary Benson, Norton, 1985.

Meredith, Martin, *Nelson Mandela: A Biography,* St. Martin's Press, 1998.

Newsmakers: 1990, Gale, 1990.

Roberts, Jack L., *Nelson Mandela: Determined to Be Free,* Millbrook Press, 1995.

Stefoff, Rebecca, *Nelson Mandela: Hero for Democracy,* Fawcett Columbine, 1994.

Strazzabosco, Jeanne, *Learning about Forgiveness from the Life of Nelson Mandela* (juvenile) Rosen, 1996.

PERIODICALS

Christianity Today, July 17, 1995, p. 33.

Crisis, February, 1983.

Detroit News, July 6, 1993, p. 2A.

Ebony, December, 1985; September, 1986; August, 1994, p. 28; January, 1995, p. 78.

Globe and Mail (Toronto), December 14, 1985.

Library Journal, December, 1986, p. 117; September 15, 1990, p. 61.

Los Angeles Times Book Review, January 8, 1995, p. 3.

Maclean's, May 27, 1991, pp. 22-23; July 15, 1991, p. 23.

Ms., November, 1985; January, 1987.

Nation, July 1, 1991, pp. 15-18.

National Review, April 30, 1990, pp. 37-39, January 23, 1995, p. 72.

New Republic, October 19, 1992, pp. 16-19.

New Statesman & Society, June 7, 1985; September 25, 1992, pp. 26-27, January 20, 1995, p. 39.

Newsweek, September 9, 1985; February 24, 1986; February 19, 1990, pp. 44-51; March 5, 1990, p. 31; July 2, 1990, pp. 16-20; August 27, 1990, pp. 41-42; May 27, 1991, p. 33; July 1, 1991, p. 37; March 2, 1992, p. 42; July 6, 1992, p. 47; November 6, 1995, p. 51; April 8, 1996, p. 84.

New York Review of Books, May 8, 1986, February 2, 1995, p. 10.

New York Times, July 19, 1978; July 7, 1985; July 29, 1986; June 21, 1992, sec. 1, pp. 1, 14; October 25, 1992, p. E5; July 7, 1993, p. A3; May 10, 1996, p. A14; May 16, 1996, sec. 4 p. E2.

New York Times Book Review, December 8, 1985; December 18, 1994, p. 1.

People, February 26, 1990, pp. 77-79.

Time, January 5, 1987; August 29, 1988, p. 43; May 29, 1989, p. 77; October 23, 1989, p. 49; December 25, 1989, p. 28; January 29, 1990, p. 49; February 19, 1990, p. 42-44; June 25, 1990, pp. 20-21; December 17, 1990, p. 25; July 1, 1991, pp. 38-39; August 17, 1992, p. 15; June 14,

1993, pp. 34-38; January 3, 1994, p. 34; May 16, 1994, p. 65.

Tribune Books (Chicago), December 18, 1994, p. 1.

U.S. News & World Report, February 27, 1989, p. 13; April 9, 1990, p. 15; May 9, 1994, p. 10; October 17, 1994, p. 92.

*   *   *

MANDRAKE, Ethel Belle
See THURMAN, Wallace (Henry)

*   *   *

MAPANJE, (John Alfred Clement) Jack   1944(?)-

PERSONAL: Born c. March 25, 1944, in Kadango village, Mangochi district (formerly Fort Johnston), Malawi (formerly part of Central African Republic); son of Victoria Mereresi Ziyabu; married Mercy Angela Chandiyama; children: two daughters, one son. *Education:* University of Malawi, received diploma (education; with distinction), c. 1967; Chancellor College, Malawi, B.A. (education; with distinction), 1972; Institute of Education, University of London, M.Phil.; University College, London, Ph.D. (linguistics), c. 1980s. *Religion:* Roman Catholic.

ADDRESSES: Agent—c/o Heinemann, 20 Vauxhall Bridge Rd., London SWIV ZSA, England.

CAREER: Malawi poet, editor, linguist, and educator, writing primarily in English; early poems written in ChiChewa. Mtendere Secondary School, teacher, 1967-69; Bunda College, Malawi, English teacher, c. early 1970s; Chancellor College, University of Malawi, lecturer in English, 1975-c.79; Department of Language and Literature, Chancellor College, professor, 1983-87, became department head; arrested without charge, September 25, 1987; detained without trial in Mikuyu Prison, near Zomba; released from prison, May 10, 1991; received stipend from Society for the Protection of Science and the Humanities; Exeter College, Oxford, research fellow, 1992-93; Greater North International Writer in Residence, 1993; University of Leeds, visiting professor, 1993-94; returned to Malawi, July, 1995, after election of President Muluzi. Conference of Southern African linguists, Zomba, Malawi, co-organizer, 1984; "New Directions in African Writing" conference, London, attendee, 1984; World Poetry Festival, Delhi, India, attendee, 1985; Commonwealth Poetry Prize, African section, judge, 1985, 1986 (chairman of jury, 1986); Second Stockholm Conference for African Writers, Stockholm, Sweden, attendee and speaker, 1986.

AWARDS, HONORS: Malawi Government Scholarship to pursue undergraduate degree; Poetry International Award, 1988; Lillian Hellman and Dashiell Hammett Award, Fund for Free Expression (New York), c. 1988.

WRITINGS:

POETRY

Of Chameleons and Gods, Heinemann Educational Books (London, England and Exeter, NH), 1981.
The Chattering Wagtails of Mikuyu Prison, Heinemann (London and Exeter, NH), 1993.

Contributor of poems to anthologies, including *Mau: 39 Poems from Malawi,* Christian Literature Association in Malawi (Blantyre, Malawi), 1971; and (in the ChiChewa language) *Akoma Akagonera,* edited by Enoch Timpunza-Mvula, Popular Poems (Limbu, Malawi), 1985. Also contributor of poems to periodicals, including *Stand* and *Odi.*

EDITOR

(With Landeg White) *Oral Poetry from Africa: An Anthology,* Longman (New York City and Harlow, England), 1983.
(With Angus Calder and Cosmo Pieterse) *Summer Fires: New Poetry of Africa,* Heinemann (London and Exeter, NH), 1983.

OTHER

(Contributor) *Criticism and Ideology: Second African Writers' Conference, Stockholm 1986,* edited by Kirsten Holst Petersen, Scandinavian Institute of African Studies (Uppsala, Sweden), 1988.

Contributor of articles to periodicals, including *Kalulu* and *Index on Censorship 2* (1995). Author of an unpublished master's thesis, *The Use of Traditional Literary Forms in Modern Malawian Writing in English,* and an unpublished doctoral dissertation in linguistics.

SIDELIGHTS: Malawian poet, professor, and linguist Jack Mapanje neither courted nor shrank from his role

as political prisoner, exile, and ultimately, national hero. Born in approximately 1944 when his nation was still a British colony (the birth date March 25, 1944 is an educated guess, according to James Gibbs in the *Dictionary of Literary Biography*), Mapanje was educated in Catholic mission schools in Malawi, then at Chancellor College of the University of Malawi. Upon gaining a diploma in education, he began his teaching career at a secondary school; returning for a bachelor's degree from 1969 to 1972, he went to the University of London in the latter year to pursue graduate studies under a staff development program.

Returning to Malawi in 1975, Mapanje briefly taught English to agricultural students, then joined Chancellor College as a lecturer in English; he was also active in the Writers' Group at that college, and an advisor to university publications. At the end of the decade, he returned to London to pursue his doctorate in linguistics. In that city, he also co-edited two poetry anthologies, *Oral Poetry from Africa* and *Summer Fires: New Poetry of Africa,* both published in 1983; the latter consisted of entries to the 1991 BBC Poetry Award competition for Africa.

Mapanje, by that time, was gaining recognition as a poet in his own right. His first poetry book manuscript was written in his native ChiChewa, but it was lost, and only a few individual poems from it were subsequently revised by Mapanje from memory and published. From that point, he wrote in English, and his first book, *Of Chameleons and Gods,* was published in 1981. Its several sections give evidence of a poet self-consciously looking for his voice and adopting the persona of the chameleon, a creature known in Malawi culture not only as a changeling but also as a teller of tales and singer of songs. These poems, like the work of other Malawian poets, often disguise political commentary in the forms of traditional oral poetry, ostensibly on more personal subjects. Gibbs, like critic Ursula A. Barnett in *World Literature Today,* cautioned that a knowledge of political events in Malawi was helpful in understanding the poems' references; some critics, lacking this perspective, tended to respond to the work as, in the words of Faith Pullin in *British Books News,* "merely personal and commonplace."

Gibbs praised Mapanje for "playing a cat-and-mouse game with authorities," like "a literary Cheshire cat." Barnett asserted that "Mapanje successfully uses African and contemporary myth and imagery to comment on the state of affairs in Malawi. . . . [His] deep love for his own country is demonstrated not only by his bitterness and despair over shattered dreams . . .

but also by the setting and imagery of the poems. . . . Mapanje's voice is original yet free of artifice. Quietly but strongly it emerges from the turbulent center of Africa." Pullin approved of the "style and wit" of some of the poems; the poems she preferred were those that examined the poet's relationship to his heritage: "Here the reader finds real insight and engagement," Pullin declared.

On his return to Malawi in 1983, Mapanje, as a well-regarded poet, was able to gain a senior appointment at Chancellor College, where he eventually became department head. The repressive national government did allow him to leave the country occasionally to attend conferences; however, the Censorship Board withdrew *Of Chameleons and Gods* from circulation without officially banning it. Mapanje was steadily becoming a more vocal critic of the government, and on September 25, 1987, he was arrested at his club, taken to his office and his home for searches and seizures of his papers, and thrown into the notorious Mikuyu prison without being charged with a crime, and without trial.

The slightly built, bespectacled poet, who walked with a limp owing to a childhood bicycle accident, was well treated by fellow prisoners and viewed with incomprehension by his jailers, who did not understand why international human rights organizations such as Amnesty International were giving them so much trouble. Occasional pieces of mail from outside, and awards such as the 1988 Poetry International Award, were encouraging to the imprisoned poet, as was a visit from his wife and three children in 1989. He was released on May 10, 1991—more than three and a half years after his arrest—as a result, Gibbs surmised, of increased pressure from the donors of the international aid on which Malawi, after two years of poor harvests, was increasingly dependent.

Entering a four-year exile in England, during which he held several distinguished university posts, he was able to return to Malawi in July, 1995, after a democratic government was restored. His second collection of poems, *The Chattering Wagtails of Mikuyu Prison,* had been published in 1993, and Mapanje was literally given red-carpet treatment upon his arrival at the airport in Malawi. The forty-five poems in the book, divided into four sections, were the fruits of the author's experiences in the 1980s and early 1990s, before, during, and after his imprisonment. Wrote Gibbs in the *Dictionary of Literary Biography,* "Every aspect of the collection gains significance from the reader's knowledge of Mapanje's imprisonment."

Also reviewing for *World Literature Today,* Gibbs wrote, "Jack Mapanje's virtues are his clarity of vision, his accessibility, his honesty, and his stubbornness. He has written thoughtful and thought-provoking poems, which are undoubtedly the work of a word artist able to sketch relevant images and of a wordsmith quick to hammer out telling phrases."

Two of the poems singled out by Gibbs (in the *Dictionary of Literary Biography*) for admiring analysis were "The Streak Tease at Mikuyu Prison, 25 September 1987" and "Scrubbing the Furious Walls of Mikuyu," both of which were originally published in Britain's *Stand* magazine. "The Streak Tease at Mikuyu Prison" describes, in harrowing terms, the poet's arrest, detention, and prison experiences, including a strip-search which he ironically compares to a strip-tease he once witnessed in a London club. Gibbs felt that the poem's strength derived from the contrast between the directness and harshness of the experiences and the well-modulated art with which they were described: "He [Mapanje] does not declaim or denounce. . . . Instead he remains a convivial persona, the same companionable Jack, even though he knows how serious matters are, and so creates a poem both profoundly moving and deeply shocking."

"Scrubbing the Furious Walls of Mikuyu" describes the poet's refusal to cooperate with his jailers after being told to erase the wall writings of his fellow inmates. Commenting that "the reader is repeatedly surprised by the energy, even the rage, of Mapanje's adjectives," Gibbs found this poem to be a moving expression of abandonment and defiance. *Stand*'s reviewer for *The Chattering Wagtails of Mikuyu Prison,* Mary Fujimaki, said, "The poems . . . are raw and cold and speak of the unspeakable, the indignities that are endured."

Having at last become a respected man of letters in a democratically governed nation, Mapanje continues to be, in Gibbs' words in *Dictionary of Literary Biography,* "a poet of international stature, with a sure command of the skills required for his profession, acutely sensitive, and courageous in defense of the highest principles."

BIOGRAPHICAL/CRITICAL SOURCES:

BOOKS

Carver, Richard, *Where Silence Rules: The Suppression of Dissent in Malawi,* Human Rights Watch (New York City), 1990.

Contemporary Poets, St. James Press (Chicago), 1996.

Dictionary of Literary Biography, Volume 157: *Twentieth-Century Caribbean and Black African Writers,* Gale (Detroit), 1996, pp. 170-180.

Granqvist, Raoul, and John Stotesbury, *African Voices: Interviews with Thirteen African Writers,* Dangaroo (Mundelstrup, Denmark), 1987.

Smith, Angela, *East African Writing in English,* Macmillan (London and Basingstoke, England), 1989.

Sampietro, Luigi, editor, *Declarations of Cultural Independence in the English-Speaking World,* University of Milan (Milan), 1989.

PERIODICALS

ACLALS Bulletin, December, 1980, pp. 137-143.
Afriscope, vol. 12, no. 3, 1973, pp. 54-59.
British Book News, August, 1981, p. 499; April, 1984, p. 248.
Index on Censorship, vol. 9, no. 5, 1980, pp. 26-29; vol. 17, no. 2, 1988, pp. 18-22.
Journal of Commonwealth Literature, vol. 22, no. 1, 1987, pp. 36-41; vol. 23, no. 1, 1988, pp. 102-115.
Kunapipi, no. 2, 1979, pp. 59-67.
Observer, November 28, 1993, p. 2.
Poetry Review, vol. 80, no. 4, 1990-1991, pp. 49-51.
Review of African Political Economy, autumn, 1990, pp. 26-49.
South African Review of Books, vol. 1, no. 2, 1987-88, pp. 26-27.
Stand, autumn, 1994, p. 84.
Times (London), May 15, 1991, p. 10.
World Literature Today, autumn, 1982, pp. 737-738; spring, 1994, pp. 411-412.

OTHER

African Writers and Their Literature: Central Africa, http://www.ualberta.ca/~omollel/c-afwriters. html (1998).
The File Room, http://www.cd.sc.ehu.es/FileRoom/documents/Cases/322mapanje.html (1998).
Two-Ten Communications, http://www.twoten.press.net/storie...s/TELEVISION_Poet_Persecution.html (1998).*

*   *   *

MARECHERA, Dambudzo 1952-1987

PERSONAL: Born Tambudzai Marechera, June 4, 1952, in Vengere township, Rhodesia (now Zimbabwe); baptized Charles William Marechera, 1965; died of pneumonia and AIDS, August 18, 1987, in Harare, Zimbabwe; son of Isaac (a mortuary attendant) and Masvotwa (a nanny; maiden name Venezia) Marechera. *Education:* Attended the University of Rhodesia, 1972-73, and New College, Oxford University, Oxford, England, 1974-76. *Religion:* Raised in the Anglican Church.

CAREER: Fiction writer, poet, playwright, and man of letters. Contributed poems to literary magazines and participated in student creative writing club, early 1970s.

AWARDS, HONORS: Alfred Beit Scholarship, University of Rhodesia; scholarship to Oxford; co-winner, *Guardian* Fiction Prize, 1979, for *The House of Hunger;* two grants from the Arts Council of Great Britain; special commendation from Noma Award committee, 1991, for *The Black Insider.*

WRITINGS:

FICTION

The House of Hunger (short stories), Heinemann (London), 1978, published as *The House of Hunger: A Novella & Short Stories,* Pantheon (New York City), 1979.
Black Sunlight (novel), Heinemann (London), 1980.
The Black Insider, edited by Flora Veit-Wild, Baobab Books (Harare, Zimbabwe), 1990, Lawrence & Wishart (London), 1992.

POETRY

Cemetery of Mind: Collected Poems of Dambudzo Marechera, edited by Veit-Wild, Baobab Books (Harare, Zimbabwe), 1992.

OTHER

Mindblast; or, The Definitive Buddy (plays, prose narrative, poems, and park diary), College Press (Harare, Zimbabwe), 1984.
Dambudzo Marechera, 4 June 1952-18 August 1987: Pictures, Poems, Prose, Tributes, edited by Flora Veit-Wild and Ernst Schade, Baobab Books (Harare, Zimbabwe), 1988.
Scrapiron Blues (prose narrative, drama, short stories, children's stories, novella, novel fragment, and poem), edited by Flora Veit-Wild, Baobab Books (Harare, Zimbabwe), 1994.

Also the author of lectures: "The African Writer's Experience of European Literature" and "Soyinka, Dostoevsky: The Writer on Trial for His Time," both delivered in Harare, October, 1986, both published in *Dambudzo Marechera: A Source Book on His Life and Work,* edited by Flora Veit-Wild, Hans Zell Publishers (London and New York City), 1992, University of Zimbabwe Publications (Harare, Zimbabwe), 1993. A comprehensive Marechera archive including primary and secondary sources exists in the National Archives of Zimbabwe.

SIDELIGHTS: Although his life and career were cut short prematurely by AIDS, Dambudzo Marechera has exerted a powerful influence on African writing since the 1980s; and although he was sometimes spurned during his lifetime by the Zimbabwean and British literary elite, he has become a favorite of younger Zimbabwean writers and readers.

A troubled and tumultuous personality, Marechera was born in June, 1952, in a township some hundred miles southeast of the capital city of Harare, which was then called Salisbury. He was the third of nine children, and his birth name, Tambudzai (which he altered into its Shona-language form, Dambudzo, as a writer), meant "the one who brings trouble." Trouble came to his family when the youth was thirteen: his father died, and the family was evicted from their township house, moving to a squatters' settlement. His mother felt compelled to turn to prostitution to support her family, and the young future writer, a sensitive, introverted boy, developed a stutter.

The political turmoil of Rhodesia in the 1960's also affected Marechera's childhood, contributing to an atmosphere of violence, poverty, and fear. In a revealing interview in the London Third-World monthly, *South,* in 1984, Marechera looked back upon his environment as a boy as "unbearable." Escaping into reading, he obtained his first book, a Victorian children's encyclopedia, from the local rubbish dump, a process he repeated for numerous other books and comic books.

Marechera had a successful career at a well-regarded Rhodesian secondary school, but according to his editor and biographer Flora Veit-Wild in her article in *Dictionary of Literary Biography,* his unstable personality was already evident during his final year there, when "he started to suffer from hallucinations and developed a persecution complex." Veit-Wild describes Marechera as a person whose psychological problems isolated him from others throughout his life,

and who "expected the world to look after him but invariably offended those who tried to help." He won a scholarship to the University of Rhodesia and participated in the literary life during his attendance there, but was expelled in August, 1973 after campus riots during which one hundred and fifty-five students were arrested, many of them, according to Veit-Wild, future intellectual and political leaders of an independent Zimbabwe. Marechera found a temporary haven at Oxford University's New College, to which he won a scholarship, but despite his avidity for learning, he rebelled against the Oxford educational tradition, alienating many Oxonians through his alcoholism and erratic behavior. An American summer school at New College threatened to leave unless Marechera moved out; and the Junior Common Room cancelled its scholarship program for African students as a result of Marechera's disruptions. He was finally expelled in March, 1976, after setting a fire (which did not cause damage) in the college. Marechera himself claimed that, given a choice between psychiatric treatment or expulsion, he chose the latter.

He then began living as an unemployed fulltime writer. As he told *South* reviewer George Alagiah, he hitchhiked from Oxford to London, then lived in a tent by the River Isis in London while he wrote his first book, containing a novella and short stories, *The House of Hunger.* In despair, in a dwelling which was not roomy enough for him to stand up in, he examined on paper the question, "What happened to my generation?"

His answers made him a literary celebrity almost overnight, as the book won the *Guardian* Prize for first fiction in 1979. In the opinion of Geoff Sadler in *Contemporary Novelists* that book "shows him to be an accomplished stylist whose means of expression has, to a large extent, already been perfected." The tales' relentless vision of violence and squalor put off some people. A *Publishers Weekly* critic called it "so horrific that rather than being effectively disturbing his work grows numbing and deadening." A more typical view, however, resembled that expressed by *Library Journal* reviewer John Mort, who wrote, "There are insights concerning black Zimbabwe here that could be obtained nowhere else." Exceedingly enthusiastic notices came from novelists Doris Lessing in *Books and Bookmen* and Angela Carter in *The Guardian;* the former called Marechera a genius, and Carter proclaimed, "It is rare to find a writer for who imaginative fiction is such a passionate and intimate process of engagement with the world. A terrible beauty is born out of the urgency of his vision."

"But while his work was explosively creative, his life was a gradual process of self-destruction," Veit-Wild commented. At the prize ceremony at which *The House of Hunger* received the *Guardian* Prize, Marechera startled the other participants by appearing in a flamboyant red poncho—and then went over the edge by drunkenly castigating the participants for hypocrisy and throwing china and chairs. He lived in friends' apartments and squatting communities, and depended for income on publishers' advances and arts grants. In 1978 and 1979 he submitted four manuscripts to his publisher, Heinemann, but only one was accepted even though in-house readers' reports showed a keen awareness of the author's gifts. Two of the manuscripts, "A Bowl for Shadows" and "The Black Heretic," have never been found; the remaining one, *The Black Insider,* was published posthumously with some other materials compiled by Veit-Wild.

The title short novel involves a group of characters in a wartorn European city, occupying an abandoned university building as they await destruction. Veit-Wild related that Marechera's main concern in *The Black Insider* was "to undermine the 'African image,' which Marechera viewed as a mask that excused political brutality." Veit-Wild asserted, "While his compatriots were still fighting their nationalist struggle for independence, he had already dismantled the icons and idols of the nationalist era." Marechera, in other words, believed in art for its own sake rather than primarily to advance a political program. He complained in the *South* interview that English-language African literature was stuck in a reformist mode rather than a Dostoevskyan psychological mode. Reviewing *The Black Insider* in *New Statesman & Society,* Adewale Maja-Pearce pointed out some structural and conceptual problems but called it "a more courageous book than almost any other that has come out of the continent in the past thirty years."

Marechera's second published book of fiction, the novel *Black Sunlight,* was not as well-received as his collection of short works. It told the surrealistic story of a Zimbabwean photographer, the narrator, who moves across his nation's violent landscape, and is eventually led to an underground system of caves occupied by a terrorist group. Here, fantasy overtakes reality, culminating in a climax whose chaos is mirrored in its collagist prose: "a final, brilliant invocation of writers as disparate as Horace and Martinelli," stated *New Statesman* reviewer James Lasdun. Hailing Marechera as a writer whose "talents are not modest," Lasdun asserted, however, that *Black Sunlight* was "too flawed to be judged, in literary terms, as

anything but a heroic failure." The novelist, Lasdun believed, had tried to amalgamate too many different elements into one whole.

Marechera returned to Zimbabwe with a British television crew who were filming *The House of Hunger;* he quarreled with the director a few days after arriving, and was banished from the project, which was completed without him. He remained in Zimbabwe, becoming, in Veit-Wild's words, "a familiar figure in the streets of Harare: a homeless wanderer, sleeping in doorways, drinking in hotel bars, sitting on park benches with a typewriter on his lap." His miscellaneous book, *Mindblast; or, The Definitive Buddy,* a formal experiment in which he exposed what he considered the narrowness and corruption of Zimbabwean life, was published in 1984 in that country. Veit-Wild calls it "an important landmark in the literary development of Zimbabwe."

Marechera moved into an apartment in Harare in 1984; he was supported largely by the generosity of friends, in addition to small royalties and fees from readings, book reviews, and lectures. Local publishers rejected two short novels and several volumes of poetry, a circumstance that deepened Marechera's bitterness. Drinking heavily and eating poorly, he succumbed to illness and, in 1987, was diagnosed with AIDS. Upon his death in August, 1987, he was widely mourned as a romantic hero of literature, especially among younger Zimbabweans; in 1988, a special trust was established to promulgate his work and to encourage Zimbabwean authors.

A posthumous collection of his poetry, *Cemetery of Mind,* containing over one hundred and forty poems and a long interview, was published in 1992. Veit-Wild, the book's editor, felt that poetry was perhaps Marechera's greatest strength. Divided into twelve sections that travel through the progressive phases of the poet's life, the book includes a group of love sonnets addressed to an Amelia, which reviewer Tanure Ojaide, in *World Literature Today,* called "some of the most moving and best-crafted in the collection." Most moving in Veit-Wild's view are the AIDS-related poems near the end of the volume, which offer, for that editor, "a painfully intense account of his state of mind in the face of death." Ojaide appreciated the AIDS poems as well for their "highly imaginistic and exhilarating language." He concluded, "To read *Cemetery of Mind* is to be cast under a spell, to be transported from the physical into the realm of the soul. . . . One can only exhale and wonder about the poetic genius of such a young man."

In 1994, Veit-Wild compiled and edited *Scrapiron Blues,* a group of assorted writings on the theme of urban life in Harare. It includes some rather stark stories evidently written for children, and a story sequence, "Tony Fights Tonight," in which the urban setting of middle-class hotel bars is interspersed with postmodern passages in which the narrator argues about the stories with his characters. Veit-Wild stated that these writings lost something in sheer power but gained something in "descriptive distinctiveness and subtlety" over Marechera's earlier work. Calling him "a deconstructionist in the true sense," Veit-Wild applauded Marechera for innovations in style and in perception that shocked readers out of their complacency. "His major quest in life and work was to fight any form of pretence, to unmask all forms of oppression of the individual's freedom and rights."

BIOGRAPHICAL/CRITICAL SOURCES:

BOOKS

Beard, Linda Susan, *Language and Literature in Multicultural Contexts,* edited by Satendra Nandan, University of the South Pacific & the Association for Commonwealth Language and Literature Studies (Suva, Fiji), 1983.

Caute, David, *Culture and Development in Southern Africa,* edited by Preben Kaarsholm, James Currey (London), 1991.

Caute, David, *The Espionage of the Saints: Two Essays on Silence and the State,* Hamish Hamilton (London), 1986.

Imfeld, Al, *African Writers on the Air,* edited by Dieter Brauer and Rudolf Strobinger, Deutsche Welle (Cologne), 1984.

Imfeld, Al, *Portraits of African Writers: 9. Dambudzo Marechera,* Deutsche Welle (Cologne), 1979.

Kirkpatrick, D. L., editor, *Contemporary Novelists,* fourth edition, St. James Press (London), St. Martin's Press (New York), 1986, pp. 573-574.

Dictionary of Literary Biography, Volume 157: Twentieth-Century Caribbean and Black African Writers, third series, Gale (Detroit), 1996, pp. 181-191.

McLoughlin, T. O., *The Writing of East and Central Africa,* edited by G. D. Killam, Heinemann (London), 1984.

Petersen, Kirsten Holst, *An Articulate Anger: Dambudzo Marechera: 1952-87,* Dangaroo Press (Sydney), 1988.

Veit-Wild, Flora, *Patterns of Poetry in Zimbabwe: Interviews and Critical Assessment by Flora Wild with Poems by Chenjerai Hove, Musaemura*

Zimunya, Charles Mungoshi, Hopwell Seyaseya, Kristina Rungano, Albert Chimedza, Dambudzo Marechera, Mambo Press (Gweru), 1988.

Veit-Wild, Flora, *Teachers, Preachers, Non-Believers: A Social History of Zimbabwean Literature,* Hans Zell Publishers (London), 1992, Baobab Books (Harare), 1993.

Zimunya, Musaemura, *Those Years of Drought and Hunger: The Birth of African Fiction in English in Zimbabwe,* Mambo Press (Gweru), 1982.

PERIODICALS

African Literature Association Bulletin, vol. 14, no. 1, 1988, pp. 6-9.

African Literature Today, no. 13, 1983, pp. 201-225.

BBC Arts and Africa, no. 288, 1979, pp. 4-5; no. 659, 1986, pp. 3-4; no. 714, 1987, pp. 2-4.

Current Writing, no. 3, 1991, pp. 147-155.

Daily Times (Nigeria), August 24, 1991, p. 16; August 13, 1991, p. 12.

English in Africa, vol. 18, no. 2, 1991, pp. 36-62.

Journal of Commonwealth Literature, vol. 23, no. 1, 1988, p. 4; vol. 27, no. 1, 1992, pp. 58-70.

Library Journal, October 1, 1979, p. 2120.

Literary Review, no. 35, 1991, pp. 589-600.

London Magazine, December 1987/January 1988, pp. 106-110.

New African, May, 1984, pp. 64-65.

New Statesman, December, 1980, pp. 45-46.

New Statesman & Society, January 31, 1992, p. 39.

Okike, June, 1981, pp. 87-91.

Publishers Weekly, August 6, 1979, p. 87.

Research in African Literatures, vol. 20, no. 3, 1989, pp. 401-411; vol. 21, no. 2, 1990, pp. 79-90.

South, December, 1984, pp. 10-11.

Southern African Review of Books, winter, 1987-88, pp. 9-10.

West Africa, September 14, 1987, pp. 401-411.

World Literature Today, spring, 1994, p. 417; winter, 1996, p. 231.

World Press Review, March, 1985, pp. 58-59.

Zambezia, vol. 14, no. 2, 1987, pp. 113-120.*

*   *   *

MARSHALL, Paule   1929-

PERSONAL: Born April 9, 1929, Brooklyn, NY; daughter of Samuel and Ada (Clement) Burke; married Kenneth E. Marshall, 1950 (divorced, 1963); married Nourry Menard, July 30, 1970; children (first marriage): Evan. *Education:* Brooklyn College (now of the City University of New York), B.A. (cum laude), 1953; attended Hunter College (now of the City University of New York), 1955.

ADDRESSES: Home—407 Central Park West, New York, NY 10025. *Office*—Feminist Press, c/o Gerrie Nuccio, P.O. Box 334, Old Westbury, NY 11568.

CAREER: Freelance writer. Worked as librarian in New York Public Libraries; *Our World* magazine, New York City, staff writer, 1953-56; lecturer on creative writing at Yale University, 1970—; Helen Gould Sheppard Professor in Literature and Culture, New York University, 1997—; lecturer on black literature at colleges and universities including Oxford University, Columbia University, Michigan State University, Lake Forrest College, and Cornell University.

MEMBER: Phi Beta Kappa.

AWARDS, HONORS: Guggenheim fellowship, 1960; Rosenthal Award from the National Institute of Arts and Letters, 1962, for *Soul Clap Hands and Sing;* Ford Foundation grant, 1964-65; National Endowment for the Arts grant, 1967-68; Before Columbus Foundation American Book Award, 1984, for *Praisesong for the Widow; Los Angeles Times* Book Award nomination, 1992, for *Daughters;* MacArthur Foundation fellowship, 1992.

WRITINGS:

Brown Girl, Brownstones (novel), Random House, 1959, reprinted with an afterword by Mary Helen Washington, Feminist Press, 1981.
Soul Clap Hands and Sing (short stories; includes "British Guiana"), Atheneum, 1961.
The Chosen Place, The Timeless People, Harcourt, 1969.
Praisesong for the Widow (novel), Putnam, 1983.
Reena, and Other Stories (includes novella *Merle,* and short stories "The Valley Between," "Brooklyn," "Barbados," and "To Da-duh, in Memoriam"), with commentary by the author, Feminist Press, 1983, reprinted as *Merle: A Novella and Other Stories,* Virago Press, 1985.
Daughters (novel), Athenum, 1991.
Language Is the Only Homeland: Bajan Poets Abroad (nonfiction), Bridgetown (Barbados), 1995.

SIDELIGHTS: "My work asks that you become involved, that you think," writer Paule Marshall once commented in the *Los Angeles Times.* "On the other hand, . . . I'm first trying to tell a story, because I'm always about telling a good story." Marshall received her first training in storytelling from her mother, a native of Barbados, and her mother's West Indian friends, all of whom gathered for daily talks in Marshall's home after a hard day of "scrubbing floor." Marshall pays tribute to these "poets in the kitchen" in a *New York Times Book Review* essay where she describes the women's gatherings as a form of inexpensive therapy and an outlet for their enormous creative energy. She writes: "They taught me my first lessons in the narrative art. They trained my ear. They set a standard of excellence. This is why the best of my work must be attributed to them; it stands as testimony to the rich legacy of language and culture they so freely passed on to me in the wordshop of the kitchen."

The standard of excellence set by these women has served Marshall well in her career as a writer. Her novels and stories have been lauded for their skillful rendering of West Indian-Afro-American dialogue and colorful Barbadian expressions. *Dictionary of Literary Biography* contributor Barbara T. Christian believes that Marshall's works "form a unique contribution to Afro-American literature because they capture in a lyrical, powerful language a culturally distinct and expansive world." This pursuit of excellence makes writing a time-consuming effort, according to Marshall. "One of the reasons it takes me such a long time to get a book done," she explained in the *Los Angeles Times,* "is that I'm not only struggling with my sense of reality, but I'm also struggling to find the style, the language, the tone that is in keeping with the material. It's in the process of writing that things get illuminated."

Marshall indicates, however, that her first novel, *Brown Girl, Brownstones,* was written at a faster pace. "I was so caught up in the need to get down on paper before it was lost the whole sense of a special kind of community, what I call Bajan (Barbadian) Brooklyn, because even as a child I sensed there was something special and powerful about it," she stated in the *Los Angeles Times.* When the novel was published in 1959 it was deemed an impressive literary debut, but because of the novel's frank depiction of a young black girl's search for identity and increasing sexual awareness, *Brown Girl, Brownstones* was largely ignored by readers. The novel was reprinted in 1981, and is now considered a classic in the female bildungsroman genre, along with Zora Neale Hurston's

Their Eyes Were Watching God and Gwendolyn Brooks's *Maud Martha.*

The story has autobiographical overtones, for it concerns a young black Brooklyn girl, Selina, the daughter of Barbadian immigrants Silla and Deighton. Silla, her ambitious mother, desires most of all to save enough money to purchase the family's rented brownstone. Her father Deighton, on the other hand, is a charming spendthrift who'd like nothing better than to return to his homeland. When Deighton unexpectedly inherits some island land, he makes plans to return there and build a home. Silla meanwhile schemes to sell his inheritance and fulfill her own dream.

Selina is deeply affected by this material conflict, but "emerges from it self-assured, in spite of her scars," writes Susan McHenry in *Ms.* Selina eventually leaves Brooklyn to attend college; later, realizing her need to become acquainted with her parents' homeland, she resolves to go to Barbados. McHenry writes: "*Brown Girl, Brownstones* is meticulously crafted and peopled with an array of characters, and the writing combines authority with grace. . . . Paule Marshall . . . should be more widely read and celebrated." Carol Field comments in the *New York Herald Tribune Book Review:* "[*Brown Girl, Brownstones*] is an unforgettable novel written with pride and anger, with rebellion and tears. Rich in content and in cadences of the King's and 'Bajan' English, it is the work of a highly gifted writer."

Marshall's most widely reviewed work to date is *Praisesong for the Widow,* winner of the Before Columbus American Book Award. The novel is thematically similar to *Brown Girl, Brownstones* in that it also involves a black woman's search for identity. This book, though, concerns an affluent widow in her sixties, Avatara (Avey) Johnson, who has lost touch with her West Indian-Afro-American roots. In the process of struggling to make their way in the white-dominated world, Avey and her husband, Jerome (Jay), lost all of the qualities that made them unique. Novelist Anne Tyler remarks in the *New York Times Book Review,* "Secure in her middle class life, her civil service job, her house full of crystal and silver, Avey has become sealed away from her true self."

While on her annual luxury cruise through the West Indies, however, Avey has several disturbing dreams about her father's great aunt, whom she visited every summer on a South Carolina island. She remembers the spot on the island where the Ibo slaves, upon landing in America, supposedly took one look around

at their new life and walked across the water back to Africa. Avey decides to try to escape the uneasiness by flying back to the security of her home. While in her hotel on Grenada awaiting the next flight to New York, Avey reminisces about the early years of her and Jay's marriage, when they used to dance to jazz records in their living room, and on Sundays listen to gospel music and recite poetry. Gradually, though, in their drive for success they lost "the little private rituals and pleasures, the playfulness and wit of those early years, the host of feelings and passions that had defined them in a special way back then, and the music which had been their nourishment," writes Marshall in the novel.

In the morning, Avey becomes acquainted with a shopkeeper who urges her to accompany him and the other islanders on their annual excursion to Carriacou, the island of their ancestors. Still confused from the past day's events, she agrees. During the island celebration, Avey undergoes a spiritual rebirth and resolves to keep in close contact with the island and its people and to tell others about her experience.

Reviewers question if Avey's resolution is truly enough to compensate for all that she and Jay have lost, if "the changes she envisions in the flush of conversion commensurate with the awesome message of the resisting Ibos," to use *Voice Literary Supplement* reviewer Carol Ascher's words. "Her search for roots seems in a way the modern, acceptable equivalent of the straightened hair and white ways she is renouncing," writes *Times Literary Supplement* contributor Mary Kathleen Benet, who adds: "On the other hand there is not much else she can do, just as there was not much else Jerome Johnson could do. Paule Marshall respects herself enough as a writer to keep from overplaying her hand; her strength is that she raises questions that have no answers."

Los Angeles Times Book Review contributor Sharon Dirlam offers this view: "[Avey] has learned to stay her anger and to swallow her grief, making her day of reckoning all the more poignant. She has already missed the chance to apply what she belatedly learns, except for the most important lesson: What matters is today and tomorrow and, oh yes, yesterday-life, at age 30, age 60, the lesson is to live." Jonathan Yardley concludes in the *Washington Post Book World:* "*Praisesong for the Widow* . . . is a work of quiet passion-a book all the more powerful precisely because it is so quiet. It is also a work of exceptional wisdom, maturity and generosity, one in which the palpable humanity of its characters transcends any considerations of race or sex; that Avey Johnson is black and a woman is certainly important, but Paule Marshall understands that what really counts is the universality of her predicament."

Reena, and Other Stories, although a collection of short stories, contains the title story, "Reena" and the novella *Merle,* adapted from the novel *The Chosen Place, The Timeless People.* The title is based on a protagonist of the novel. "Reena" is frequently anthologized, particularly in collections of writings by African American women writers. In her introductory comments to a reissued version of *Black-eyed Susans/ Midnight Birds,* Mary Helen Washington refers to "Reena"'s theme of cultural identity and the role of the African American female. Dr. Washington's commentary and analysis bolster Paule Marshall's accompanying sketch for "Reena." Reena is autobiographical and is a continuation of *Brown Girl, Brownstones.* Marshall describes Reena as "like herself from a West Indian-American background who had attended the free New York City colleges during the forties and fifties. The theme would be our efforts to realize whatever talents we had and to be our own persons in the face of the triple-headed hydra of racism, sexism, and class bias we confronted each day."

Daughters, Marshall's 1991 novel, has been widely acclaimed. According to the author, the novel explores significant personal themes. "Ursa is a young urban woman trying to come to terms with the two worlds that shaped her. . . . Her mother is American, her father West Indian. [I] wanted to write something that was symbolic of the two wings of the black diaspora in this part of the world." Defining the role of the female—upwardly mobile, well-educated—in the black diaspora is the cog around which *Daughters* turns. In the *New York Times Book Review,* Susan Fromberg Schaeffer sees that the key for Ursa is in what she learns from those most important in her life. Ursa learns that "to be human one must be of use. To be of use, men and women must work together—and that the relationship between the sexes is far more complicated than Ursa has ever imagined." Working together involves a struggle—sometimes erupting in conflict between men and women. Ursa discovers by novel's end that she must not evade struggle/conflict toward a common goal. She learns to stop allowing love for another to becloud her judgment, as in the case of ignoring the corruption that her father, Primus, confused with success. Ursa learns that she is "hobbled by love of her father . . . and so complete is his possession of her that she needs to *abort* him." Ursa must break free to define herself, continue to be

"useful," continue to love all humans, yet not be bogged down by that love and get off course. "Marshall shows us how . . . *women* can—and perhaps should—find themselves becoming men's consciences."

BIOGRAPHICAL/CRITICAL SOURCES:

BOOKS

Bruck, Peter, and Wolfgang Karrer, editors, *The Afro-American Novel since 1960,* B. R. Gruener, 1982.

Christian, Barbara, *Black Women Novelists,* Greenwood Press, 1980.

Coser, Stelamaris, *Bridging the Americas: The Literature of Paule Marshall, Toni Morrison, and Gayl Jones,* Temple University Press, 1995.

Denniston, Dorothy Haner, *The Fiction of Paule Marshall: Reconstructions of History, Culture, and Gender,* University of Tennessee Press, 1995.

Dictionary of Literary Biography, Volume 157: *Twentieth-Century Caribbean and Black African Writers, Third Series,* Gale, 1995.

Evans, Mari, editor, *Black Women Writers, 1950-1980,* Anchor Press, 1984.

Morgan, Janice T., and Colette T. Hall and Carol L. Snyder, editors, *Redefining Autobiography in Twentieth-Century Women's Fiction: An Essay Collection,* Garland, 1991, pp. 135-47.

Pettis, Joyce Owens, *Toward Wholeness in Paule Marshall's Fiction,* University Press of Virginia, 1996.

Shaw, Harry B., editor, *Perspectives of Black Popular Culture,* Popular Press, 1990, pp. 93-100.

Sorkin, Adam J., editor, *Politics and the Muse: Studies in the Politics of Recent American Literature,* Popular Press, 1989, pp. 179-205.

Wall, Cheryl A., editor, *Changing Our Own Words: Essays on Criticism, Theory, and Writing by Black Women,* Rutgers University Press, 1989, pp. 196-211.

PERIODICALS

Black American Literature Forum, winter, 1986; spring/summer, 1987.

Callaloo, spring/summer, 1983; winter, 1987, pp. 79-90; winter, 1997, pp. 127-41.

Chicago Tribune Book World, May 15, 1983.

Christian Science Monitor, January 22, 1970; March 23, 1984.

CLA Journal, March, 1961; September, 1972.

College Language Association Journal, September, 1995, pp. 49-61.

Critical Arts, Volume 9, number 1, 1995, pp. 21-29.

Critical Quarterly, summer, 1971.

Essence, May, 1980.

Freedomways, 1970.

Journal of American Culture, winter, 1989, pp. 53-58.

Journal of Black Studies, December, 1970.

Journal of Caribbean Studies, winter, 1989-spring, 1990, pp. 189-99.

London Review of Books, March 7, 1985.

Los Angeles Times, May 18, 1983.

Los Angeles Times Book Review, February 27, 1983.

MELUS, fall, 1995, pp. 99-120.

Ms., November, 1981.

Nation, April 2, 1983.

Negro American Literature Forum, fall, 1975.

Negro Digest, January, 1970.

New Letters, autumn, 1973.

New Yorker, September 19, 1959.

New York Herald Tribune Book Review, August 16, 1959.

New York Review of Books, April 28, 1983.

New York Times, November 8, 1969; February 1, 1983.

New York Times Book Review, November 30, 1969; January 9, 1983; February 20, 1983.

Novel: A Forum on Fiction, winter, 1974.

Obsidian II, winter, 1990, pp. 1-21.

Publishers Weekly, January 20, 1984, pp. 90-91.

Religion and Literature, spring, 1995, pp. 49-61.

Saturday Review, September 16, 1961.

Southern Review, winter, 1992, pp. 1-20.

Times Literary Supplement, September 16, 1983; April 5, 1985.

Village Voice, October 8, 1970; March 22, 1983; May 15, 1984.

Voice Literary Supplement, April, 1982.

Washington Post, February 17, 1984.

Washington Post Book World, January 30, 1983.

World Literature Written in English, autumn, 1985, pp. 285-98.*

*   *   *

MARSON, Una (Maude) 1905-1965

PERSONAL: Born in 1905, in Santa Cruz, St. Elizabeth, Jamaica; died following a heart attack, May 5, 1965, in Jamaica; daughter of Reverend Solomon I. (a justice of the peace and Baptist minister) and Ada (maiden name, Mullings) Marson; married Peter Staples (a dentist) c. 1960 (divorced).

CAREER: Writer. Secretary and then reporter for the *Gleaner,* a newspaper in Kingston, Jamaica; *Cosmopolitan,* owner and editor, beginning 1928; *Jamaican Standard,* London, journalist, beginning 1938; BBC radio, *Caribbean Voices,* master of ceremonies, beginning 1941.

MEMBER: International Alliance of Women (London).

AWARDS, HONORS: Musgrave Medal, Institute of Jamaica, 1930, for *Tropic Reveries.*

WRITINGS:

Tropic Reveries, Gleaner (Kingston, Jamaica), 1930.

Heights and Depths, Gleaner, 1932.

Moth and the Star, privately printed (Kingston, Jamaica), 1937.

Towards the Stars: Poems, University of London Press Ltd. (Bickley, Kent), 1945.

PLAYS

(With Horace Vaz) *At What a Price,* produced in Scala Theatre, London, May, 1933.

London Calling, produced in Ward Theatre, Kingston, Jamaica, 1938.

Pocomania, Ward Theater, Kingston, Jamaica, January 22, 1938.

OTHER

Also contributor of essays to periodicals, including *Keys, Listener, New Cosmopolitan,* and the *Sunday Gleaner.*

SIDELIGHTS: Una Maude Marson was born in Santa Cruz, St. Elizabeth, Jamaica, in 1905. She was the youngest of five children of the Reverend Solomon I. Marson, a justice of the peace and Baptist minister, and Ada Mullings Marson. At the time she lived, very little of the literature of the West Indies was actually written by West Indians, and she was one of the first truly Caribbean writers; Lloyd W. Brown, in *West Indian Poetry,* called her "the earliest female poet of significance to emerge in the West Indies." While Marson was still in secondary school, both her parents died, thus ending her education. She then began working as a secretary and eventually as a reporter for the *Gleaner,* a well-known newspaper in Kingston, Jamaica.

While still in her early twenties, she became the first woman in Jamaica to own and edit a magazine, the *New Cosmopolitan.* The magazine's goals, according to Marson were "to develop literary and artistic talent," and "to encourage talented young people to express themselves freely." The magazine included short stories, poetry, and commentary on world events. Marson used the editorial pages to express her own opinions, which were bold for the time: she encouraged women to play tennis and hockey, and when a white woman was chosen as "Miss Jamaica," she wrote that because most Jamaicans were black, a black Miss Jamaica would have been a better representative.

Marson's first collection of poems, *Tropic Reveries,* was published in 1930, and won the Jamaica Institute's Musgrave Medal. In 1932, her second volume, *Heights and Depths,* was published. Both books explore love and pain, which Marson considered "twin souls," and in almost all of the poems, the narrator is a woman who has been deserted or who has not found love, who wants to die, or who is depressed. Marson moved to London in 1932, and the experience brought her a new awareness of her identity and her poetic voice. Alone, away from her home, and living in an environment of racial prejudice led her to write about her position as a black woman and a West Indian in her third poetry collection, *Moth and the Star.* Marson's pride in her black heritage is especially apparent in these poems.

Marson wrote, directed, produced, and starred in her first play, *At What A Price,* in 1933. She collaborated with writer Horace Vaz, whom she had known in Jamaica. The play tells the story of a young Jamaican girl who moves to Kingston to find work. In the city, away from her parents and loving boyfriend, she is seduced and then abandoned by her boss. Finally she goes back to her home, family, and boyfriend, but as the title notes, "at what a price." The play was the first in London to be produced by black Jamaicans. Its realistic portrayal of Jamaican life was novel, and so was its strong female protagonist. Despite her predicament, Ruth is ambitious, independent, bold, and outspoken, and rationalizes that she is in Kingston looking for work because she is not good-looking enough for an "ornamental" life. She is a feminist, rebelling against the idea that a woman belongs in the home, not at work.

Marson was a member of the International Alliance of Women in London, and in 1935 traveled to the International Congress of Women in Istanbul, Turkey on behalf of the Alliance. Erika J. Waters, in *Dictionary of Literary Biography,* quoted a reporter from the *Manchester Guardian,* who wrote that Marson "astonished the Conference by her intellectual vigor."

In 1936, Marson went back to Jamaica. She worked hard to promote Jamaican literature and the formation of Jamaican publishing companies. Her third collection of poems was published and she wrote and produced two more plays. Marson also founded the Kingston Readers and Writers Club, the Kingston Drama Club, the Jamaica Save the Children Fund, was a member of the Poetry League of Jamaica, and helped to found the Pioneer Press.

Pocomania, Marson's third play, stars an ambitious woman who is bored with her rural life. "I am sick to death of the quietness here," she tells her sister in a letter. When her boyfriend dies, she joins Pocomania, a revivalist religious sect, and is swept up with joy at the drumming at their services. *Pocomania* incorporated Jamaican songs, drumming, and dances, and was innovative for the time, since previously, the rural culture of Jamaica, and the rituals of the cult, were not considered appropriate for the stage.

In 1938, Marson returned to London and became a staff member of the *Jamaican Standard.* In 1941, she became the moderator of a BBC radio show which broadcasted messages from servicemen to their families. She turned this format into *Caribbean Voices,* which presented stories and poems by West Indians. Although others eventually took over the show, it continued to present such well-known writers as V. S. Naipaul, Samuel Selvon, George Lamming, and Derek Walcott. After the war, she went back to Jamaica and worked as organizing secretary of Pioneer Press, a publisher devoted to Jamaican authors. In the early 1950s, Marson moved to Washington, D.C. and about 1960, entered a short-lived marriage with a dentist, Peter Staples, a widower with two grown children. The marriage lasted only a few years, and her time in America was marred by racial prejudice and the experience of segregation. She returned to Jamaica, traveled to England and Israel, and again returned to Jamaica in 1965 where she died of a heart attack. "Marson's accomplishments, then, are both tangible and intangible," wrote Waters. "Her early innovations as a poet and the modern feminist themes present in her plays are significant. She is also remembered for her lifelong advocacy of a strong Jamaican literature and her tireless dedication to that goal."

BIOGRAPHICAL/CRITICAL SOURCES:

BOOKS

Brown, Lloyd W., *West Indian Poetry,* Twayne (Boston), 1978.

Dictionary of Literary Biography, Volume 157: *Twentieth-Century Caribbean and Black African Writers,* Gale Research (Detroit, MI), 1996.*

* * *

MATHABANE, Mark   1960-

PERSONAL: First name originally Johannes; name changed, 1976; born in Alexandra, South Africa; son of Jackson (a laborer) and Magdelene (a washerwoman; maiden name, Mabaso) Mathabane; immigrated to the United States, became U.S. citizen; married Gail Ernsberger (a writer), in 1987; two children. *Education:* Attended Limestone College, 1978, St. Louis University, 1979, and Quincy College, 1981; Dowling College, B.A., 1983; attended Columbia University, 1984. *Religion:* "Believes in God."

ADDRESSES: Home—341 Barrington Park Ln., Kernersville, NC 27284.

CAREER: Lecturer and writer, 1985—.

MEMBER: Authors Guild.

AWARDS, HONORS: Christopher Award, 1986; White House Fellow, 1996-97.

WRITINGS:

Kaffir Boy: The True Story of a Black Youth's Coming of Age in Apartheid South Africa, Macmillan, 1986, published as *Kaffir Boy: Growing out of Apartheid,* Bodley Head, 1987.
Kaffir Boy in America: An Encounter with Apartheid, Scribner, 1989.
(With Gail Mathabane) *Love in Black and White: The Triumph of Love over Prejudice and Taboo,* HarperCollins, 1992.
African Women: Three Generations, HarperCollins, 1994.
Ubuntu (fiction), in press.

SIDELIGHTS: "What television newscasts did to expose the horrors of the Vietnam War in the 1960s, books like *Kaffir Boy* may well do for the horrors of apartheid in the 1980s," Diane Manuel determined in a *Chicago Tribune Book World* review of Mark Matha-bane's first novel. In his 1986 *Kaffir Boy: The True Story of a Black Youth's Coming of Age in Apartheid South Africa,* Mathabane recounts his life in the squalid black township of Alexandra, outside Johannesburg, where he lived in dire poverty and constant fear until he seemingly miraculously received a scholarship to play tennis at an American college. *Washington Post Book World* critic Charles R. Larson called *Kaffir Boy* "violent and hard-hitting," while Peter Dreyer in the *Los Angeles Times Book Review* found Mathabane's autobiography "a book full of a young man's clumsy pride and sorrow, full of rage at the hideousness of circumstances, the unending destruction of human beings, [and] the systematic degradation of an entire society (and not only black South African society) in the name of a fantastic idea."

The Alexandra of *Kaffir Boy* is one of overwhelming poverty and deprivation, of incessant hunger, of horrific crimes committed by the government and citizen gangs, and of fear and humiliation. It is a township where one either spends hours at garbage dumps in search of scraps of food discarded by Johannesburg whites or prostitutes himself for a meal, and where "children grow up accepting violence and death as the norm," reflected Larson. One of Mathabane's childhood memories is of his being startled from sleep, terrified to find police breaking into his family's shanty in search of persons who emigrated illegally, as his parents had, from the "homelands," or tribal reserves. His father was imprisoned following one of these raids, and was repeatedly jailed after that. Mathabane recalls in *Kaffir Boy* that his parents "lived the lives of perpetual fugitives, fleeing by day and fleeing by night, making sure that they were never caught together under the same roof as husband and wife" because they lacked the paperwork that allowed them to live with their lawful spouses. His father was also imprisoned-at one time for more than a year with no contact with his family-for being unemployed, losing jobs as a laborer because he once again lacked the proper documents.

Yet those living in the urban ghettos near Johannesburg are more fortunate than people in the outlying "homelands," where black Africans are sent to resettle. "Nothing is more pathetic in this book than the author's description of a trip he takes with his father to the tribal reserve, ostensibly so that the boy will identify with the homelands," judged Larson. "The son, however, sees the land for what it really is—barren, burned out, empty of any meaning for his generation." In *Kaffir Boy* Mathabane depicts the desolation of the Venda tribal reserve as "mountainous, rugged and bone-dry, like a wasteland. . . . Everywhere I went nothing grew except near lavatories. . . . Occasionally I sighted a handful of scrawny cattle, goats and pigs grazing on the stubbles of dry brush. The scrawny animals, it turned out, were seldom slaughtered for food because they were being held as the people's wealth. Malnutrition was rampant, especially among the children." Larson continued to note that "the episode backfires. The boy is determined to give up his father's tribal ways and acquire the white man's education."

Although Mathabane had the opportunity to get at least a primary education, he still contemplated suicide when he was only ten years old. "I found the burden of living in a ghetto, poverty-stricken and without hope, too heavy to shoulder," he confesses in his memoir. "I was weary of being hungry all the time, weary of being beaten all the time: at school, at home and in the streets. . . . I felt that life could never, would never, change from how it was for me." But his first encounter with apartheid sparked his determination to overcome the adversities.

His grandmother was a gardener for an English-speaking liberal white family, the Smiths, in an affluent suburb of Johannesburg. One day she took her grandson to work, where he met Clyde Smith, an eleven-year-old schoolboy. "My teachers tell us that Kaffirs [blacks] can't read, speak or write English like white people because they have smaller brains, which are already full of tribal things," Smith told Mathabane, the author recalled in his autobiography. "My teachers say you're not people like us, because you belong to a jungle civilization. That's why you can't live or go to school with us, but can only be our servants." He resolved to excel in school, and even taught himself English—blacks were allowed to learn only tribal languages at the time—through the comic books that his grandmother brought home from the Smith household. "I had to believe in myself and not allow apartheid to define my humanity," Mathabane points out.

Mrs. Smith also gave Mathabane an old wooden tennis racket. He taught himself to play, then obtained coaching. As he improved and fared well at tournaments he gained recognition as a promising young athlete. In 1973 Mathabane attended a tennis tournament in South Africa where the American tennis pro

Arthur Ashe publicly condemned apartheid. Ashe became Mathabane's hero, "because he was the first free black man I had ever seen," the author later was cited in the *New York Times*. After watching the pro play, he strove to do as well as Ashe. Mathabane eventually became one of the best players in his country and made contacts with influential white tennis players who did not support apartheid. Stan Smith, another American tennis professional, befriended Mathabane and urged him to apply for tennis scholarships to American schools. Mathabane won one, and *Kaffir Boy* ends with the author boarding a plane headed for South Carolina.

Lillian Thomas in the *New York Times Book Review* asserted that "it is evident that [Mathabane] wrestled with the decision whether to fight or flee the system" in South Africa. The author participated in the 1976 uprisings in Soweto, another black township near Johannesburg, after more than 600 people were killed there when police opened fire on a peaceful student protest. Yet Mathabane continued to be friends with whites whom he had met at his athletic club. He also was the only black in a segregated tournament that was boycotted by the Black Tennis Association, but he participated believing that he would meet people who could help him leave South Africa. Afterward he was attacked by a gang of blacks who resented his association with whites and only escaped because he outran them.

David Papineau in the *Times Literary Supplement* does not find fault with Mathabane for leaving South Africa. The critic contended that Mathabane "does make clear the limited choices facing black youths in South Africa today. One option is political activity, with the attendant risk of detention or being forced underground. . . . Alternatively you can keep your head down and hope for a steady job. With luck and qualifications you might even end up as a white-collar supervisor with a half-way respectable salary."

Mathabane continues his autobiography in *Kaffir Boy in America: An Encounter with Apartheid,* which begins with his studies at Limestone College, South Carolina, in 1978. Armed with copies of the Declaration of Independence and the U.S. Constitution, Mathabane soon learns that the United States is not the promised land after all. *Kaffir Boy in America* recounts Mathabane's determination to get a good education and the beginnings of his career as a journalist and writer. Along the way, Mathabane attempts to understand American popular culture and American attitudes about race. Writing in the *Journal of Modern African Studies*, Mwizenge S. Tembo observes that "*Kaffir Boy in America* shows the extent of the contradictions that exist in the world's leading superpower." A *Library Journal* reviewer finds *Kaffir Boy in America* to be "generally well-written," but notes that "like many sequels, this one lacks the power of the original." Lorna Hahn of the *New York Times Book Review* praises Mathabane's fairness in his discussion of American attitudes toward South Africa and calls *Kaffir Boy in America* "an inspiring account of a young man's self-realization and his commitment to the self-realization of others."

With *In Love in Black and White: The Triumph of Love over Prejudice,* which Mathabane coauthored with his wife, the author responds to those who criticized him for his marriage to Gail Ernsberger, a white American. In chapters divided into each spouse's perspective, the book tackles the hostility that interracial marriages still face from both races. The Mathabanes discuss their initial reactions to each other when they met as graduate students in New York, their rocky courtship and secret marriage, public reaction to their marriage from blacks and whites in both New York and North Carolina, and their experiences in raising biracial children. *Kirkus Reviews* calls *In Love in Black and White* "a personal and candid account of what it means to break an intransigent taboo-and a heartwarming affirmation of love and commitment." Writing in the *New York Times Book Review,* Andrea Cooper finds it "lively" and especially praises Mathabane's "obvious intelligence and quiet passion" and Gail Mathabane's "specific, informal and visual" treatment of the problems of marrying outside one's race.

In 1994, Mathabane published his fourth work of nonfiction, *African Women: Three Generations,* which uses the stories of his mother, grandmother, and sister to tell the larger story of what it means to grow up female and black in South Africa under apartheid and the legacy of colonialism. Under apartheid, the family lives of black women were torn apart as the men were forced to travel far from home seeking employment. The stories each woman tells recount violent beatings and abuse by husbands and lovers, desperate poverty and hunger, deaths of children, and the effects of witchcraft and Christianity on their lives.

African Women breaks down into two parts. The first part, set in South Africa, tells each woman's story from her own first-person perspective, as though she had orally told her tale to Mathabane; the second part involves the reunion of the Mathabane women with their Americanized son on the "Oprah Winfrey" show. Several reviewers found it odd that Mathabane

sent his American wife to South Africa to interview his relatives. Writing in *New Statesman & Society,* Victoria Brittain says that all the women have the same voice and "it is unmistakably the voice of the son, grandson and brother, who escaped from the townships with a tennis scholarship to America, and later graduated from the Columbia School of Journalism." In the *New York Times Book Review,* Veronica Chambers questions Mathabane's decision to tell the women's stories in his voice rather than in their own, and *Booklist* finds the book in need of "tighter editing." Several reviewers were struck by the absence of a larger social and political context for the book, so that the women's problems seem to be "boyfriends and cheating husbands," according to Chambers. Whereas *Booklist* praises the way in which "the political is made personal in scenes of daily confrontation," Chambers writes, "With *African Women: Three Generations,* it feels as though the well is beginning to run dry." *Kirkus Reviews* notes that *African Women* is "a worthy subject, but its treatment is marred by the author's suspect style."

BIOGRAPHICAL/CRITICAL SOURCES:

PERIODICALS

Africa Today, July/September, 1996.
Booklist, February 15, 1994.
Chicago Tribune Book World, April 13, 1986.
Christian Science Monitor, May 2, 1986; April 25, 1994; February 21, 1995.
Journal of Modern African Studies, December, 1990.
Kirkus Reviews, November 15, 1991.
Library Journal, April 1, 1994.
Los Angeles Times Book Review, March 30, 1986.
New Statesman & Society, March 30, 1995, p. 37.
Newsweek, March 9, 1992.
New York Times, March 2, 1987; September 24, 1987; December 14, 1997.
New York Times Book Review, April 27, 1986; August 13, 1989; February 16, 1992; July 31, 1994, p. 25.
People Weekly, July 7, 1986.
Sage, spring, 1995.
Times Literary Supplement, August 21, 1987.
Washington Post Book World, April 20, 1986.*

* * *

MAX
See DIOP, Birago (Ismael)

MBUENDE, Kaire (Munionganda) 1953-

PERSONAL: Born November 28, 1953, in Windhoek, Namibia; son of Gabriel (a schoolteacher) and Lydia Mbuende; married Claudia Karangere Mbuende; children: three. *Ethnicity:* "Namibian." *Education:* Lutheran College, Makumira, Tanzania, B.D., 1978; University of Lund, Sweden, B.A. (with honors), 1980, Ph.D., 1986.

ADDRESSES: Office—Southern African Development Community, Private Bag 0095, Gaborone, Botswana.

CAREER: Statesman and diplomat. Member of South West African People's Organization (SWAPO) Executive Committee, Namibia, 1972-74; SWAPO External Headquarters, Lusaka, Zambia, information officer, 1974-75; University of Aarhus, Denmark, assistant lecturer, 1981; University of Lund, Sweden, assistant lecturer, 1984-86, lecturer, 1986-87; Institute for Future Studies, Stockholm, Sweden, reader, 1987- 89; government of Namibia, member of Constituent Assembly, 1990, member of Parliament, 1990-93, deputy minister of agriculture, water, and rural development, 1990-93; Central Committee, SWAPO, 1991—; Southern African Development Community (SADC), Botswana, executive secretary, 1994—.

WRITINGS:

Namibia the Broken Shield: Anatomy of Imperialism and Revolution, Liber (Malmeo, Sweden), 1986.
(Editor with Peter Katjavivi and Per Frostin) *Church and Liberation in Namibia,* Pluto Press (Winchester MA), 1989.
Social Movements and the Demise of Apartheid Colonialism in Namibia, CODESRIA, in press.

Contributor to periodicals, including *Southern Africa Political, Economic Monthly* and *Namibia Review.* Also author of articles published in numerous other journals and books in Europe and Africa.

SIDELIGHTS: As executive secretary of the Southern African Development Community (SADC) since January, 1994, Kaire Mbuende managed the regional transitions from war to peace, from hostility to cooperation and investment, among nations in Southern Africa. Not so long ago Mbuende played a far different role: until 1989, he helped organize the revolution for independence in Namibia, a South West African country previously a colony of South Africa and the last colony in Africa. In that struggle Mbuende had been imprisoned, tortured, and interrogated by the former South African authorities in Namibia. Now that Namibia is politically free and South Africa has overcome apartheid, the former South African system of segregation and disenfranchisement of people of color, Mbuende has played a leading role in building reconciliation and developing new trade across the region. "My dream is to see a Southern Africa free of conflicts devoting its human and natural resources in pursuit of economic development, social progress, and cultural advancement," Mbuende wrote in an interview with *Contemporary Black Biography (CBB).*

Kaire Munionganda Mbuende was born on November 28, 1953, in the city of Windhoek, Namibia, to Lydia and Gabriel Mbuende, a devoted and nationally known primary school teacher. Mbuende was influenced by the leadership qualities of his grandfather at a young age. "My grandfather's political involvement and his teaching based on a deep religious conviction created a yearning for justice in me at an early age," Mbuende recalled in a faxed interview with *CBB.* Mbuende's grandfather, Gotthard Mbuende, was a member of the Herero Chief Council under the leadership of Chief Hosea Kutako.

Mbuende did not involve himself in politics until he was 18. He participated in a student strike at Augusteun High School in 1970 and subsequently joined the South West African People's Organization (SWAPO), the organization leading the struggle for independence. With other prominent Namibians such as Ndali Kamati, Martin Kapewasha, Jerry Ekandjo, and Festus Naholo, Mbuende founded the SWAPO Youth League in 1971. Mbuende began to help lead democratic protests and civil disobedience against the ruling South African apartheid regime in Namibia.

Throughout the 1970s Mbuende lived the struggle for freedom in Namibia. From 1972 to 1974 he served on the Executive Committee of SWAPO in Namibia and was vice-chairman of the Windhoek Branch, deputizing the late Benjamin Namalambo. During that time Mbuende addressed political rallies and organized and participated in civil disobedience. The South African government in Namibia imprisoned, interrogated, and tortured Mbuende for his political activities.

In July of 1974 Mbuende left Namibia to join the armed revolution against South African apartheid rule in Namibia. After rising to the position of platoon commander in the training program of the People's Liberation Army of Namibia (PLAN), the military wing of SWAPO, Mbuende was appointed to service as an Information Officer with the SWAPO External Headquarters in Lusaka, Zambia. In that post Mbuende produced broadcasts on the political, social, economic, and military situation in Namibia. Soon after Mbuende returned to his studies—first in Tanzania and then in Sweden. While a student Mbuende participated in the campaign to mobilize political, material, and financial support in the Nordic countries for the struggle for independence in Namibia.

Earning a B.D. degree in 1978 from Lutheran College in Makumira, Arusha, Tanzania, and a B.A. in economic history and sociology in 1980 from the University of Lund, Sweden, Mbuende embarked on a career as a social scientist in unofficial exile until free elections were held in Namibia in 1989. Mbuende published numerous articles on sociological theory and development studies and worked as a lecturer, then reader, in universities in Denmark and Sweden until 1989. In 1986 Mbuende attained his Ph.D. in economic sociology from the University of Lund, Sweden. After Mbuende returned to his native country, working after the electoral victory as a minister in the new government, he continued publishing original commentary, then on the practice of economic integration in Southern Africa. When the United Nations-supervised elections provided the opportunity for a new government and political independence, however, Mbuende's focus shifted from the academy back to the struggle for state power.

Mbuende returned to Namibia for the UN-supervised elections in 1989. He rose swiftly with his party, SWAPO. Appointed first the Head of SWAPO Election Directorate in the Gobabis Region (now Omaheke Region), after SWAPO won the historic election Mbuende became a Member of the Constituent Assembly. The Constituent Assembly was charged with the task of writing and adopting the Constitution of the Republic of Namibia in 1989. In 1990, when the Constituent Assembly was transformed into the National Assembly, Mbuende became a Member of Parliament.

Also in 1990 Mbuende began serving his first appointment, as Deputy Minister of Agriculture, Water, and Rural Development for the newly-independent Namibia. This post lasted until 1993, just before Mbuende began his tenure as executive secretary of the Southern African Development Community (SADC), in Botswana. As deputy minister of agriculture, Mbuende faced three challenges. First, he had to change the culture of the civil service from the days of colonialism. Now, priority was to go to "the development of small-scale Africa farmers who constitute the majority of the people of Namibia," he wrote in an interview with *CBB*. Second, Mbuende was charged with boosting crop production that had previously been neglected under colonial rule to render Namibia then "a dumping ground for South African products," Mbuende wrote in the *CBB* interview. Finally, Mbuende had to restructure agricultural production to meet local needs rather than only those of South Africa and international markets.

Mbuende's achievements were numerous. First, he averted a major catastrophe by managing Namibia's food resources effectively during a major drought. Mbuende oversaw the drought relief program in Namibia. Starvation resulted in the Horn of Africa during the drought, but in Namibia not a single life was lost. Mbuende successfully met the routine challenges presented him in his post as well. He made the small-scale African farmer the focus of government programs. He helped move technology into rural areas by establishing Rural Development Centres. He launched a campaign that resulted in a 50 percent increase in maize production and a 75 percent increase in millet production during the 1990-91 growing season. Finally, Mbuende started the slow process of land redistribution with the introduction of affirmative action loans by the Agricultural Bank of Namibia for African farmers in their efforts to acquire commercial farms.

Namibia has also faced the challenge of meeting the rights of minority ethnic peoples. While deputy minister of agriculture, Mbuende contributed to a general improvement in the human rights situation of these minority peoples, particularly for the San in Namibia. Unlike the policy before independence, communal land rights were respected in practice, if not in explicit legislation. President Sam Nujoma set a precedent in Nyae Nyae, formerly Eastern Bushmanland. Nujoma said during a visit to the area that anyone wishing to settle in a communal land must receive the permission of the traditional leaders in the area, in addition to the Ministry of Lands, Resettlement and Rehabilitation. When settlers from the nearby Hereroland attempted to water their cattle from community boreholes without permission in late 1991, the Nyae Nyae Farmer's Cooperative escorted the settlers peacefully back to the Herero border with the promised, although not necessary, backing of the local police and the Regional Commissioner. All this occurred during Mbuende's tenure as Deputy Minister. Mbuende had written in a pre-Independence SWAPO position paper that the San societies were particularly disadvantaged by the violence they were subjected to under apartheid. Now the San's communal land rights were being upheld in practice.

In January of 1994, Mbuende assumed the top position, executive secretary, of the Southern African Development Community (SADC), a leading institution for regional development in Southern Africa. Mbuende brought visionary goals to this historic organization. "My long term goal for SADC is to ensure the political, economic, social, and cultural integration of the countries of Southern Africa," Mbuende wrote in an interview with *CBB*. Politically, integration meant a common commitment to democracy, transparency and open government, accountability, and respect for human rights. In addition, member states would work through SADC to achieve peaceful and diplomatic conflict resolution.

Mbuende hopes that the peaceful political climate will form, in turn, the proper environment for renewed investment in the region. "The promotion of private domestic and foreign investment is high on the agenda," Mbuende wrote in an interview with *CBB*. Mbuende envisions that investment targeted toward the manufacturing and service sectors will transform the region from primary to industry-based economies. His goal is that such investment will take place within a larger economic infrastructure of unity across the region. Eventually, Mbuende hopes that unity will be realized in a Southern African Free Trade Area, to be achieved within the next five years and in turn lead to the establishment of a Customs Union and then a Common Market.

SADC is the successor to SADCC, the Southern African Development Coordination Conference, an organization of regional integration for the states that bordered South Africa while South Africa was still under apartheid rule. The difference between the organizations, after South Africa was freed, was marked. Mbuende explained to Margaret Novicki of *Africa Report* just how the two organizations differed: "Basically what we are talking about in terms of integration is not really market integration—that we are selling or trading more—but political cooperation, cooperation in the field of the military, security, cultural exchange, and information, as well as development cooperation, in infrastructure development and investment. So it is much more comprehensive."

SADC itself was formed by a treaty following two meetings to discuss the role of SADCC in a post-apartheid Southern Africa. SADCC was formed to assist the frontline states in their effort to support the struggle to liberate Namibia and free South Africa. Bordering South Africa to the north and Namibia to the east, these states were economically dependent on South Africa's ports for imports and exports. In order to gain some modicum of economic independence, these states joined together to find alternate ports for their imports and exports. That economic freedom afforded the frontline states more leverage in pressuring South Africa to abandon apartheid. When South Africa was securely on the road to freedom, a new purpose had to be discovered for the economic and political union. The states met in Maputo in 1992, where they decided that there had been too much advantage gained by their mutual cooperation to abandon the organization. Member states decided to deepen their level of cooperation now that South Africa was being freed. In Windhoek, Namibia, in 1992, the member states adopted the treaty founding the Development Community (SADC) out of the Development Coordination Conference (SADCC).

In an interview with *CBB* Mbuende highlighted four areas of achievement since taking the helm of the new SADC in January of 1994. First Mbuende pointed to the implementation of the conflict resolution mechanism between member states. Mbuende cited in particular the use of diplomacy in resolving the conflicts in Lesotho, in the impending crisis in the run up to the elections in Mozambique, and in support of the peace process in Angola. Next Mbuende identified the democratization of South Africa and its subsequent membership in SADC in August of 1994 as a major victory. "It was an honour and privilege to have facilitated the entry of South Africa in SADC," Mbuende wrote.

Third, SADC achieved a high level of cooperation between the public sector and the private sector in developing Southern Africa. The Southern African Economic Summit, held in Johannesburg, South Africa, in May 1995, and jointly organized by SADC and the World Economic Forum testified to that increased cooperation. Mbuende predicted that Summit would become an annual event. Finally, Mbuende cited international relations as an area of achievement. "A qualitatively new relationship was entered into between SADC and European Union through what came to be known as the 'Berlin Initiative' following the convening of a Joint Meeting of Ministers of Foreign Affairs of SADC and the European Union in Berlin in September 1994," Mbuende wrote in an interview with *CBB*. In addition, SADC pursued close relations and an active dialogue with Japan and the United States.

BIOGRAPHICAL/CRITICAL SOURCES:

OTHER

Contemporary Black Biography, written interview, June 2, 1995.

*   *   *

McBRIDE, James C. 1957-

PERSONAL: Born in 1957; son of Andrew McBride (a minister; deceased in 1957) and Ruth McBride Jordan (a homemaker; born, Rachel Shilsky).

ADDRESSES: Office—c/o Riverhead Books, 200 Madison Ave., New York, NY 10016-3903.

CAREER: Worked variously as a jazz saxophonist, composer, and producer; *Washington Post,* journalist; *Boston Globe,* journalist; freelance writer.

WRITINGS:

The Color of Water: A Black Man's Tribute to His White Mother (memoir), Riverhead Books (New York City), 1996.

WORK IN PROGRESS: A novel.

SIDELIGHTS: For Mother's Day in 1981 journalist James C. McBride penned an essay about his mother for the *Boston Globe.* Readers, moved by the piece, wrote to McBride and encouraged him to write a book. More than a decade after McBride first approached his mother about writing her story, Ruth Jordan finally acquiesced. In 1996 *The Color of Water: A Black Man's Tribute to His White Mother* rolled off the presses. The title of the book reflects Jordan's answer to her son's childhood inquiry about the color of God's skin.

The Color of Water is told in chapters that alternate between the mother's recollections and her son's commentary. Jordan explains how she was born in Poland, the daughter of an Orthodox Jewish rabbi-turned-grocer who emigrated to the American South. To escape sexual abuse by her father, Jordan says she fled the South, ending up in New York City. There she met and married minister Andrew McBride,

helped him establish an all-black Baptist church, and gave birth to eight children. James was the youngest and never met his father, who died shortly before his birth. McBride described how Jordan remarried, had four more children, and raised him and his siblings in lower-income neighborhoods in Brooklyn and Queens. To protect her children from stigma, Ruth led her children to believe that she was a light-skinned black, and until late in his childhood, McBride did not question her. When McBride did ask his mother whether he was white or black, her response was: "You're a human being. Educate yourself or you'll be a nobody." The author explains that during his adolescence, he rebelled against his mother and stepfather's authority and was involved in petty crime. Yet he and his siblings overcame many obstacles, earning college degrees and self-respect. McBride gives much credit for the success of their family to his mother's Orthodox background combined with his father's Christianity.

Some reviewers have compared *The Color of Water* with *Divided to the Vein,* by Scott Minerbrook, another African American journalist whose mother was white and father was black. Writing in *Booklist,* Alice Joyce called *The Color of Water* and *Divided to the Vein* "remarkably candid," adding "these memoirs reflect earnestly on issues of self stemming from the interracial marriages of their parents." In the *Chicago Tribune,* John Blades wrote: "Though McBride's disillusionment was not so severe as Minerbrook's, his memoir just as forcefully points out how 'divided to the vein' America remains, not just between black and white but also between black and black." He added: "Similar but very different, the two books are both eye- and mind- opening about the eternal convolutions and paradoxes of race in America, as seen from up-close and microcosmic perspectives."

As he delved into his past, McBride came to take pride in his Jewish heritage and became more empathetic to people of all kinds. "The lingering effects of slavery and color consciousness continue to push us in directions we shouldn't go," according to McBride, as reported by Blades. "What I'd like people to come away with is that we have a lot more in common than we think," he told Norman Oder in *Publishers Weekly.* Blades quoted McBride: "I think America is integrating itself kicking and screaming. But it's absolutely essential that we do. We can't survive any other way." According to a reviewer in *Publishers Weekly:* "This moving and unforgettable memoir needs to be read by people of all colors and faiths."

BIOGRAPHICAL/CRITICAL SOURCES:

PERIODICALS

Booklist, January 1 and 15, 1996, p. 782.
Chicago Tribune, TEMPO section, February 26, 1996, p. 1.
Library Journal, January, 1996, p. 110.
Publishers Weekly, October 30, 1995, pp. 24-25; January 15, 1996, p. 454.
USA Today, January 29, 1996, p. D4.
Wall Street Journal, February 9, 1996, pp. A10, A12.
Washington Post, January 14, 1996, p. 4.*

*   *   *

McCALL, Nathan 1955(?)-

PERSONAL: Born c. 1955; son of a factory worker; divorced twice; children: Monroe, Ian, Maya. *Education:* Norfolk State University, B.A.

ADDRESSES: Office—Washington Post, 1150 15th St. NW, Washington, DC 20017.

CAREER: Reporter, *Virginia Pilot/Ledger Star* and *Atlanta Constitution,* Atlanta, GA; *Washington Post,* Washington, DC, reporter, 1989—.

WRITINGS:

Makes Me Wanna Holler: A Young Black Man in America (autobiography), Random House (New York), 1994.
What's Going On: Personal Essays, Random House, 1997.

ADAPTATIONS: The film rights to *Makes Me Wanna Holler* have been purchased by Columbia Pictures, with John Singleton scheduled to direct.

SIDELIGHTS: When Nathan McCall first applied for work as a journalist, he hid the fact that he had served three years in prison for armed robbery. Eventually, however, he not only told his future employer (the *Washington Post*) about his past, he made it the subject of his first book, *Makes Me Wanna Holler: A Young Black Man in America* (1994). With the publication a few years later of *What's Going On: Personal Essays,* a collection that presents his views on a variety of subjects relating to racism and the lives of African Americans, McCall has been hailed as a writer of clear, unaffected prose that articulates the experiences of troubled young black men across America.

"Sooner or later, every generation must find its voice," Henry Louis Gates, Jr., once wrote in the *New Yorker.* "It may be that ours belongs to Nathan McCall." Gates is one of many reviewers who have praised *Makes Me Wanna Holler.* In his memoir, McCall describes his transformation from an angry and self-destructive criminal to a successful *Washington Post* reporter. He tells of his upbringing in a middle-class section of Portsmouth, Virginia, where he grew up as the son of strict but caring working-class parents. Although he was a good student, McCall was picked on and beaten up by white classmates at his mostly white junior high school. In search of protection, he fell in with a group of tough young blacks. "Alone I was afraid of the world and insecure," he writes in *Makes Me Wanna Holler.* "But I felt cockier and surer of myself when hanging with my boys. . . . There was no fear of standing out, feeling vulnerable, exiled and exposed. That was a comfort even my family couldn't provide."

Throughout high school, McCall and his "boys" regularly engaged in gang fights, burglaries, and "training" girls—that is, gang-raping them. In 1975 he received a sentence of four weekends in jail for the attempted murder of another black youth. While on probation for that crime, however, he held up a fast-food restaurant, an act that earned him twelve years in prison. During a stint as the inmate librarian, McCall came across the story of another angry black man who ends up in jail: Richard Wright's *Native Son.* "I identified strongly with Bigger [Thomas, the novel's protagonist]," he recalled in *Makes Me Wanna Holler.* "The book's portrait of Bigger captured all those conflicting feelings—restless anger, hopelessness, a tough facade among blacks and a deep-seated fear of whites—that I'd sensed in myself but was unable to express."

That an author could describe so clearly the things he himself had been feeling amazed McCall and led him to other books, including *The Autobiography of Malcolm X.* Slowly, he began to see himself not as a "bad nigger" but as "an intelligent-thinking human being." By the time he was released on parole after serving just three years of his sentence, McCall had already decided to pursue a career in journalism. Admitted to the journalism program at Norfolk State University, he eventually graduated with honors.

After graduation, McCall worked first for the *Virginian Pilot/Ledger Star* and then the *Atlanta Journal-Constitution* before being approached by the *Washington Post* about a reporting job. Despite the impressive credentials on his resume, he chose to lie on his application in response to a question about whether he had ever been convicted of a felony. McCall revealed his criminal record during the interview process, however, prompting *Post* officials to reject him. They reconsidered their decision and finally hired him in 1989 to write for the Metro section.

One of the qualities of McCall's writing that initially strikes critics is the power of his narrative voice. As Gates declares, "He is a mesmerizing storyteller whose prose is richly inflected with the vernacular of his time and place. In fact, his colloquial style is so unshowy and unforced that his mastery is easy to overlook." *Washington Post Book World* reviewer Paul Ruffins offers a similar observation, noting that "without indulging in exhibitionism, McCall here strips himself naked in an honest confession. He may have a past he regrets, but *Holler* is a strong downpayment on his redemption."

Many reviewers draw a comparison between McCall and authors such as Malcolm X, Eldridge Cleaver, and Richard Wright—and, more directly, between McCall and the character of Bigger Thomas from Wright's *Native Son*. "In some respects," Gates writes, "I'd venture that the young McCall was closer to Bigger Thomas than Wright was." In fact, contends Ruffins, "McCall's evolution from angry thug to edgy black professional is much more relevant to most people's lives" than the changes described by his predecessors. "Malcolm X, Eldridge Cleaver and George Jackson all discovered religion or revolution, extraordinary truths that transformed their lives. In prison McCall finds his salvation in smaller ideas like, 'Work hard,' and 'Think before you act.'"

Still, some critics find that *Makes Me Wanna Holler* contains its share of flaws. Commenting in the *New York Times Book Review,* Adam Hochschild expresses "mounting exasperation at the way Mr. McCall blames the white world for almost everything he suffers. . . . At the three newspapers Mr. McCall has worked at, in the endless clashes with white colleagues or bosses that he describes, he is always in the right, and the problem is always the other person's racism." But as Hochschild goes on to point out, "Mr. McCall's anger goes far beyond race, for he seldom gives a shred of credence to the point of view of anyone else, white or black." Concludes the re-

viewer: "This fury becomes a substitute for any real analysis of why his early life turned out as it did, and of what can be done to save a generation of young black men from the same fate."

Hochschild is not the only reviewer to note McCall's failure or inability to explain the reasons why he turned to crime. But some critics regard it as one of the book's strengths rather than a weakness. "What sets *[Makes Me Wanna Holler]* apart from similar works by less talented writers is [its] refusal to oversimplify or offer easy prescriptions for the underclass dilemma," asserts Jack E. White in *Time*. Gates, too, finds McCall's ambiguity "a sign of the fierce honesty that infuses the entire book; he's willing to address the question without pretending to have an answer to it."

In the end, McCall maintains he does not feel a part of mainstream society. "At times I feel suspended in a kind of netherworld, belonging fully neither to the streets nor to the establishment," he writes in *Makes Me Wanna Holler*. Such dislocation applies to his position at the *Post* as well, according to *Detroit News* reviewer Ruth Coughlin. "He says it's a place where he doesn't feel comfortable," reports Coughlin, "even though a good thing about being in the mainstream is that it brought him into contact 'with a lot of good whites who made it a lot more complicated for me to just dismiss all white people. I'm there on the rolls, I'm signed up in the personnel office . . . but I don't feel that I belong.'"

The media stir that resulted from the publication of *Makes Me Wanna Holler* prompted McCall to take a leave of absence from the *Post* in order to promote his best-selling book. An excerpt from it appeared in *Newsweek,* and McCall became the subject of numerous print and television interviews.

McCall eventually returned the *Post* and began work on *What's Going On: Personal Essays* (1997). Maintaining the easy, conversational style of his first book, McCall gives his opinions on racism and contemporary black experiences, including his thoughts on the continued influence of Muhammad Ali, the dangers of "gangsta rap," the identity crisis of the black middle class, black men and basketball, and the death of a former "homeboy." McCall takes issue not only with white leaders but also with blacks who can only view themselves as victims.

Booklist's Bonnie Smothers characterizes the topics covered in *What's Going On* as "hot or engaging" and praises McCall as "a very savvy practitioner of personal writing." She rates the description of the dead "homeboy" and his grieving mother as the most affecting essay in the collection and notes that teenagers in particular would value the book for its take on contemporary life.

BIOGRAPHICAL/CRITICAL SOURCES:

BOOKS

McCall, Nathan, *Makes Me Wanna Holler: A Young Black Man in America,* Random House (New York), 1994.

PERIODICALS

At Random, winter, 1994, pp. 45-51.
Booklist, October 1, 1997, p. 292.
Detroit News, February 16, 1994, p. C1.
New Yorker, March 7, 1994, pp. 94-99.
New York Times Book Review, February 27, 1994, p. 11-12.
Publishers Weekly, January 3, 1994, p. 64; September 1, 1997, p. 87.
Time, March 7, 1994, p. 68.
Washington Post Book World, February 6, 1994, p. 2.*

* * *

McDOUGALL, Gay J. 1947-

PERSONAL: Born August 13, 1947, in Atlanta, GA. *Ethnicity:* "African American." *Education:* Attended Agnes Scott College, 1965-67; Bennington College, B.A., 1967-69; Yale Law School, J.D., 1972; London School of Economics, M.A.

ADDRESSES: Office—International Human Rights Law Group, 1601 Connecticut Ave., NW, Ste. 700, Washington, DC 20009.

CAREER: Attorney and civil rights activist. Associated with Debevoise, Plimpton, Lyons & Gates (law firm), New York City; National Conference of Black Lawyers, general counsel; associated with City of New York, Board of Corrections, 1980; Lawyers' Committee for Civil Rights Under Law, Southern Africa Project, director, 1980-94; International Human Rights Law Group, executive director, 1994—.

MEMBER: National Conference of Black Lawyers, Black Forum on Foreign Policy, International Federation of Women Lawyers.

AWARDS, HONORS: Candace Award, National Coalition of 100 Black Women, 1990.

WRITINGS:

Deaths in Detention and South Africa's Security Laws, Lawyers' Committee for Civil Rights Under Law (Washington, DC), 1983.
(With N. Barney Pityana) *Namibia: UN Resolution 435 and the Independence of Namibia,* 1989.
South Africa's Death Squads: A Report, Lawyers' Committee for Civil Rights Under Law, 1990.

SIDELIGHTS: Gay J. McDougall made history in 1994 as the first African American to be appointed to the Washington, D.C.-based International Human Rights Law Group. Such landmark achievements have been typical for McDougall, however. A civil rights activist and international lawyer, she has perhaps been most noted for her role in loosening the grip of apartheid—legally sanctioned racial discrimination—on South Africa. Recently, she has been at work on behalf of the oppressed peoples of other countries as well, including Haiti, Nicaragua, Paraguay, and Bosnia.

McDougall was born in Atlanta in 1947, just as the civil right movement was gaining momentum. Her mother was a teacher active in the church, and Mcdougall had several aunts who were employed as social workers. These female role models sowed the seeds of McDougall's desire to weave social concerns into her professional life. These women were not her only mentors. Growing up in Atlanta during the height of the civil rights era, she saw prominent figures of the movement such as Stokely Carmichael, Julian Bond, and Martin Luther King, Jr. working practically down the street.

McDougall enrolled in Agnes Scott College, a women's school in Decatur, Georgia in 1965. The only black student on campus, she was lonely, and so frustrated by the conservative and highly traditional attitudes and curriculum of the school that, in 1968, she transferred to Bennington College, in Bennington, Vermont. After graduating from Bennington in 1969, she enrolled in Yale Law School and received her law degree in 1972. At both Bennington and Yale, she found a far freer atmosphere that nurtured her growing social conscience. She took an enthusiastic part in voter registration drives and civil rights projects and developed a keen interest in the proliferating African independence movements as well as the United States' march towards true racial equality.

Upon graduation from Yale in 1972, McDougall put her civil rights activities on hold for a short time, while she worked for the New York City-based corporate law firm of Debevoise, Plimpton, Lyons & Gates. "I really was there to learn to be the best professional that I could be, because I thought that the issues that I cared about deserve that," she told the *Washington Post*. The training she wanted took her two years to achieve. After that, having saved a large proportion of her salary, she was able to follow her true wish and work as an unpaid employee for the non-profit National Conference on Black Lawyers (NCBL) in Washington, D.C.

The NCBL was formed in 1968, partly to help minorities and the poor with legal problems, racial issues, and matters concerning voters' rights. The NCBL also addressed international civil rights concerns. Perfectly in tune with the organization's mission, McDougall soon became the NCBL representative to the United Nations (UN), and gained a unique opportunity to fuse her legal training and her civil rights interests by forming a task force to study the increasingly visible African liberation movements. Working for the NCBL was a stimulating experience that she enjoyed.

After two years with the NCBL, McDougall took a job with the New York City Board of Corrections. The Board of Corrections was formed shortly after forty-three inmates were killed in the Attica Prison riot of September 1971. An adjudicating body, the board dealt with the issues that had led to the uprising: inadequate medical attention, poor work wages, unresolved dietary concerns, and insufficient fresh air and exercise. McDougall tackled these issues with zest, then decided to return to the international human rights arena.

McDougall believed that further education would ease her transition into international law so, in 1977, she obtained her master's degree from the London School of Economics. Long favored as an educational institution by international humanitarian and liberation movements, the London School had trained Jomo Kenyatta, future president of Kenya, as well as the contemporary leaders of the struggle for independence in Zimbabwe and South Africa whom she met when she arrived. "It was one of the best moves I've made

in my life, in terms of the people I met, who inspired me and centered me and helped me find exactly what I think in many ways," McDougall explained in the *Washington Post*.

In 1980 McDougall returned to the United States to find a new challenge on her home turf ably provided by the Lawyers' Committee for Civil Rights Under Law. The civil rights group was formed in the early 1960s to provide legal backing for racial equality issues. Using its connections to human rights groups based in other parts of the world, the Lawyers' Committee tried to help counteract the South African government's increasingly sinister record of detentions, tortures, and bannings.

As a result, the Lawyer's Committee formed the Southern Africa Project, charged with the responsibility of making contact with South African lawyers for the purpose of providing them legal assistance to aid South African victims of racism or torture. The Southern Africa Project also provided reports for both the U.S. government and the UN regarding situations in other southern African countries. For example, in 1979, the organization released a seventy-two-page report that played a large part in then-U.S. President Jimmy Carter's decision against unilaterally lifting sanctions against Rhodesia. The sanctions had been set in place because of Rhodesia's white minority government had illegally declared independence from Great Britain, but many felt the penalties were hurting the black citizens as well as the government.

McDougall was asked to direct the Southern Africa Project, a post she kept until 1994. She took part in symposiums and accessed reports that documented a horrifying record of tortures and murders, all aimed at keeping apartheid intact. However, as McDougall noted in a paper called "Proposals for a New United States Policy Towards South Africa," delivered during a 1988 human rights symposium, South Africa was not confining its policies to its own borders. The African country of Namibia, whose "independence" from South Africa had just been announced, was also under pressure by the South African government, which was attempting to influence the upcoming Namibian elections.

McDougall saw to it that the aggression of the South African government towards Namibia was thwarted by the Southern Africa Project. She founded a new group called the Commission on Independence for Namibia, that consisted of 31 distinguished policymakers from the community. She supervised the commission's monitoring of a UN-mandated system instituted to ensure ethical voting in the 1989 Namibian elections. Her efforts at securing a fair election were successful, as 96 percent of the people of Namibia cast their ballots.

The beginning of the 1990s found McDougall with even more challenging duties. Sanctions against South Africa, plus a rising tide of anti-apartheid violence were now making majority rule in that country inevitable. With the release of South African political activist Nelson Mandela from prison, McDougall began to spend long periods in South Africa, unraveling constitutional knots and helping to dismantle the hundreds of laws that had locked apartheid into place. Additionally, she was asked to join fifteen other experts on the Independent Electoral Commission, that was given the task of supervising the country's first multiracial election process. The commission's duties varied widely, dealing with the logistics of setting up more than 150,000 voting booths and other electoral equipment nationwide, plus printing and transporting more than 80 million voting ballots from England. Communications projects were needed to persuade the country's estimated 22 million voters to come to the polls. Also, strategic methods needed to be designed to best ensure fairness in the election.

Not all South Africans were convinced the 1994 election would go smoothly. Primarily Zulu, the Inkatha Political Party, lead by Mangosuthu Gatsha Buthulezi, refused to take part in the elections until a scant five days before the polling began. Reasons for the boycott included a fear that, if the party lost the election to Nelson Mandela's African National Congress (ANC), the Zulu homelands would be abolished as prescribed by the new constitution, and Buthulezi's power would be removed. Despite the threatened boycott, and a wave of violence surrounding the political parties involved, McDougall remained confident. "We are committed to pulling off this election on April 26, 27, and 28," she said in *USA Today*. Her efforts were successful.

After playing such a large role in setting South Africa firmly on its course towards majority rule, McDougall began to focus her attention on other tragic corners of the world. In September of 1994, she accepted a new position as executive director of the International Human Rights Law Group (IHRLG), a Washington-based international advocacy organization devoted to helping frontline advocates protect human rights around the world. Under McDougall's direction, one of the IHRLG's initiatives involved monitoring the repressive military regime of Haiti and its subsequent U.S.-led occupation.

McDougall's IHRLG appointment was just one of the latest in a long list of accomplishments that have positively impacted the international human rights arena. Influenced early in her life by family members, as well as major civil rights activists, she developed quite a consciousness with regard to social issues. This sense of commitment has served her well during her career as advocate for those world citizens that have been forced to live under less than humane conditions.

BIOGRAPHICAL/CRITICAL SOURCES:

BOOKS

Contemporary Black Biography, Volume 11, Gale (Detroit, MI), 1996.

New Pittsburgh Courier, November 5, 1994, p. A2.
New York Amsterdam News, October 29, 1994, p. 22.
USA Today, March 31, 1994, p. 6A.
Washington Informer, November 9, 1994, p. 18.
Washington Post, December 7, 1989, p. B3; April 26, 1994, p. E1.

OTHER

Southern Africa Project *Annual Report,* 1979-80.

*   *   *

McKAY, Claude
See McKAY, Festus Claudius

*   *   *

McKAY, Festus Claudius   1889-1948
(Eli Edwards, Claude McKay)

PERSONAL: Born September 15, 1889 (some sources say 1890), in Sunny Ville, Clarendon Parish, Jamaica, British West Indies (now Jamaica); immigrated to United States, naturalized U.S. citizen, 1940; died of heart failure, May 22, 1948, in Chicago, IL; buried at Calvary Cemetery, Woodside,

NY; son of Thomas Francis (a farmer) and Anne Elizabeth (a farmer; maiden name, Edwards) McKay; married Eulalie Imelda Edwards, July 30, 1914 (marriage ended); children: Ruth Hope. *Education:* Attended Tuskegee Normal & Industrial Institute, 1912, and Kansas State College, 1912-14. *Religion:* Roman Catholic.

CAREER: Writer. Worked as cabinetmaker's apprentice and wheelwright; constable, Jamaican Constabulary, Kingston, Jamaica, 1909; longshoreman, porter, bartender, and waiter, 1910-14; restaurateur, 1914; writer for *Pearsons Magazine,* 1918, and *Workers' Dreadnought* in London, England, 1919; associate editor of *Liberator,* 1921; American Workers representative at Third International in Moscow, U.S.S.R., 1922; artist's model in mid-1920s; worked for Rex Ingram's film studio in France, c. 1926; shipyard worker, c. 1941; worked with the National Catholic Youth Association, 1944-48.

AWARDS, HONORS: Medal from Jamaican Institute of Arts and Sciences, c. 1912; Harmon Foundation Award for distinguished literary achievement from the National Association for the Advancement of Colored People (NAACP), 1929, for *Harlem Shadows: The Poems of Claude McKay* and *Home to Harlem;* award from James Weldon Johnson Literary Guild, 1937; awarded the Order of Jamaica and declared national poet, 1977.

WRITINGS:

UNDER NAME CLAUDE McKAY

Songs of Jamaica (poetry; also see below), introduction by Walter Gardner, Gardner (Kingston, Jamaica), 1912, reprinted Mnemosyne (Miami), 1969.
Constab Ballads (poetry; also see below), Watts (London), 1912.
Spring in New Hampshire, and Other Poems, Richards (London), 1920.
Harlem Shadows: The Poems of Claude McKay, introduction by Max Eastman, Harcourt, Brace (New York), 1922.
Negry v Amerike, translated into Russian by P. Okrimenko, Gosudarstvennoe (Moscow), 1923, published as *The Negroes in America,* re-translated into English from Russian-language version by Robert J. Winter, edited by Alan L. McLeod, Kennikat (Port Washington, NY), 1977.
Sudom Lincha, translated into Russian by A. M. and P. Okrimenko, Ogonek (Moscow), 1925, pub-

lished as *Trial by Lynching: Stories about Negro Life in North America,* re-translated into English from Russian-language version by Robert Winter, edited by Alan L. McLeod, preface by H. H. Anniah Gowda, Centre for Commonwealth Literature and Research, University of Mysore (Mysore), 1977.
Home to Harlem (novel), Harper (New York), 1928.
Banjo: A Story without a Plot (novel), Harper, 1929.
Gingertown (short stories), Harper, 1932.
Banana Bottom (novel), Harper, 1933.
A Long Way from Home (autobiography), Furman (New York), 1937.
Harlem: Negro Metropolis (nonfiction), Dutton (New York), 1940.
Selected Poems, introduction by John Dewey, biographical note by Max Eastman, Bookman (New York), 1953.
The Dialectic Poetry of Claude McKay (contains *Songs of Jamaica* and *Constab Ballads*), edited by Wayne F. Cooper, Books for Libraries Press (Freeport, NY), 1972.
The Passion of Claude McKay: Selected Poetry and Prose, 1912-1948, edited by Wayne F. Cooper, Schocken (New York), 1973.
My Green Hills of Jamaica, and Five Jamaican Short Stories, edited by Mervyn Morris, Howard University Press (Washington, DC), 1975.
Harlem Glory: A Fragment of Aframerican Life, Kerr (Chicago), 1990.

Work represented in anthologies. Contributor to periodicals, including *Workers' Dreadnought, Negro World, Catholic Worker, Ebony, Epistle, Interracial Review, Jewish Frontier, Nation, Seven Arts* (under pseudonym Eli Edwards), *New York Herald Tribune Books,* and *Phylon.*

Collections of McKay's papers are housed in the James Weldon Johnson Collection and in the Papers and Manuscript Collection, both in the Beineke Library, Yale University.

ADAPTATIONS: McKay's poetry has been recorded by Arna Bontemps, *Anthology of Negro Poets in the U.S.A.: 200 Years,* Folkways Records, and *Spectrum in Black: Poems by 20th Century Black Poets,* Scott, Foresman, and Company.

SIDELIGHTS: Festus Claudius McKay, better known as Claude McKay, was a key figure in the Harlem Renaissance, a prominent literary movement of the 1920s. His work ranged from vernacular verse celebrating peasant life in Jamaica to fairly militant poems challenging white authority in America, and from generally straightforward tales of black life in both Jamaica and America to more philosophically ambitious fiction addressing instinctual/intellectual duality, which McKay found central to the black individual's efforts to cope in a racist society. Consistent in his various writings is his disdain for racism and the sense that bigotry's implicit stupidity renders its adherents pitiable as well as loathsome. As Arthur D. Drayton wrote in his essay "Claude McKay's Human Pity" (included by editor Ulli Beier in the volume *Introduction to African Literature*): "McKay does not seek to hide his bitterness. But having preserved his vision as poet and his status as a human being, he can transcend bitterness. In seeing . . . the significance of the Negro for mankind as a whole, he is at once protesting as a Negro and uttering a cry for the race of mankind as a member of that race. His human pity was the foundation that made all this possible."

McKay was born in Sunny Ville, Jamaica, in 1889. The son of peasant farmers, he was infused with racial pride and a great sense of his African heritage. His early literary interests, though, were in English poetry. Under the tutelage of his brother, schoolteacher Uriah Theophilus McKay, and a neighboring Englishman, Walter Jekyll, McKay studied the British masters—including John Milton, Alexander Pope, and the later Romantics—and European philosophers such as eminent pessimist Arthur Schopenhauer, whose works Jekyll was then translating from German into English. It was Jekyll who advised aspiring poet McKay to cease mimicking the English poets and begin producing verse in Jamaican dialect.

At age seventeen McKay departed from Sunny Ville to apprentice as a woodworker in Brown's Town. But he studied there only briefly before leaving to work as a constable in the Jamaican capital, Kingston. In Kingston he experienced and encountered extensive racism, probably for the first time in his life. His native Sunny Ville was predominantly populated by blacks, but in substantially white Kingston blacks were considered inferior and capable of only menial tasks. McKay quickly grew disgusted with the city's bigoted society, and within one year he returned home to Sunny Ville.

During his brief stays in Brown's Town and Kingston McKay continued writing poetry, and once back in Sunny Ville, with Jekyll's encouragement, he published the verse collections *Songs of Jamaica* and *Constab Ballads* in London in 1912. In these two volumes McKay portrays opposing aspects of black life in Jamaica. *Songs of Jamaica* presents an almost celebratory portrait of peasant life, with poems addressing subjects such as the peaceful death of McKay's mother and the black people's ties to the Jamaican land. *Constab Ballads,* however, presents a substantially bleaker perspective on the plight of Jamaican blacks and contains several poems explicitly critical of life in urban Kingston. Writing in *The Negro Novel in America,* Robert Bone noted the differing sentiments of the two collections, but he also contended that the volumes share a sense of directness and refreshing candor. He wrote: "These first two volumes are already marked by a sharpness of vision, an inborn realism, and a freshness which provides a pleasing contrast with the conventionality which, at this time, prevails among the black poets of the United States."

For *Songs of Jamaica* McKay received an award and stipend from the Jamaican Institute of Arts and Sciences. He used the money to finance a trip to America, and in 1912 he arrived in South Carolina. He then traveled to Alabama and enrolled at the Tuskegee Institute, where he studied for approximately two months before transferring to Kansas State College. In 1914 he left school entirely for New York City and worked various menial jobs. As in Kingston, McKay encountered racism in New York City, and that racism compelled him to continue writing poetry.

In 1917, under the pseudonym Eli Edwards, McKay published two poems in the periodical *Seven Arts.* His verses were discovered by critic Frank Hattis, who then included some of McKay's other poems in *Pearson's Magazine.* Among McKay's most famous poems from this period is "To the White Fiends," a vitriolic challenge to white oppressors and bigots. A few years later McKay befriended Max Eastman, communist sympathizer and editor of the magazine *Liberator.* McKay published more poems in Eastman's magazine, notably the inspirational "If We Must Die," which defended black rights and threatened retaliation for prejudice and abuse. "Like men we'll face the murderous, cowardly pack," McKay wrote, "Pressed to the wall, dying, but fighting back!" In *Black Poets of the United States,* Jean Wagner noted that "If We Must Die" transcends specifics of race and is widely prized as an inspiration to persecuted people throughout the world. "Along with the will to resistance of black Americans that it expresses," Wagner wrote, "it voices also the will of oppressed people of every age who, whatever their race and wherever their region, are fighting with their backs against the wall to win their freedom."

Upon publication of "If We Must Die" McKay commenced two years of travel and work abroad. He spent part of 1919 in Holland and Belgium, then moved to London and worked on the periodical *Workers' Dreadnought*. In 1920 he published his third verse collection, *Spring in New Hampshire,* which was notable for containing "Harlem Shadows," a poem about the plight of black prostitutes in the degrading urban environment. McKay used this poem, which symbolically presents the degradation of the entire black race, as the title for a subsequent collection.

McKay returned to the United States in 1921 and involved himself in various social causes. The next year he published *Harlem Shadows,* a collection from previous volumes and periodicals publications. This work contains many of his most acclaimed poems—including "If We Must Die"—and assured his stature as a leading member of the literary movement referred to as the Harlem Renaissance. He capitalized on his acclaim by redoubling his efforts on behalf of blacks and laborers: he became involved in the Universal Negro Improvement Association and produced articles for its publication, *Negro World,* and he traveled to the Soviet Union which he had previously visited with Eastman, and attended the Communist Party's Fourth Congress.

Eventually McKay went to Paris, where he developed a severe respiratory infection and supported himself intermittently by working as an artist's model. His infection eventually necessitated his hospitalization, but after recovering he resumed traveling, and for the next eleven years he toured Europe and portions of northern Africa. During this period he also published three novels and a short story collection. The first novel, *Home to Harlem,* may be his most recognized title. Published in 1928, it concerns a black soldier—Jake—who abruptly abandons his military duties and returns home to Harlem. Jake represents, in rather overt fashion, the instinctual aspect of the individual, and his ability to remain true to his feelings enables him to find happiness with a former prostitute, Felice. Juxtaposed with Jake's behavior is that of Ray, an aspiring writer burdened with despair. His sense of bleakness derives largely from his intellectualized perspective, and it eventually compels him to leave alien, racist America for his homeland of Haiti.

In *The Negro Novel in America,* Robert Bone wrote that the predominantly instinctual Jake and the intellectual Ray "represent different ways of rebelling against Western civilization." Bone added, however, that McKay was not entirely successful in articulating his protagonists' relationships in white society. He

declared that *Home to Harlem* was "unable to develop its primary conflict" and thus "bogs down in the secondary contrast between Jake and Ray." The novel also provides a detailed portrayal of the underside of black urban life, with its prostitutes and gamblers, and McKay was applauded for creating "a work of vivid social realism," according to Alan L. McLeod in the *Dictionary of Literary Biography.* However, McKay himself "stressed that he aimed at emotional realism—he wanted to highlight his characters' feelings rather than their social circumstances," McLeod continued. Nevertheless, it was his glimpse into the "unsavory aspects of New York black life" that was prized by readers—and condemned by such prominent black leaders as W. E. B. Du Bois.

Home to Harlem—with its sordid, occasionally harrowing scenes of ghetto life—proved extremely popular, and it gained recognition as the first commercially successful novel by a black writer. McKay quickly followed it with *Banjo: A Story without a Plot,* a novel about a black vagabond living in the French port of Marseilles. Like Jake from *Home to Harlem,* protagonist Banjo embodies the largely instinctual way of living, though he is considerably more enterprising and quick-witted than the earlier character. Ray, the intellectual from *Home to Harlem,* also appears in *Banjo.* His plight is that of many struggling artists who are compelled by social circumstances to support themselves with conventional employment. Both Banjo and Ray are perpetually dissatisfied and disturbed by their limited roles in white society, and by the end of the novel the men are prepared to depart from Marseilles.

Banjo failed to match the acclaim and commercial success of *Home to Harlem,* but it confirmed McKay's reputation as a serious, provocative artist. "It was apparent to critics that McKay's imagination had been somewhat strained and that the novel was essentially an autobiographical exercise," McLeod remarked. Commentators have found the autobiographical thread in *Home to Harlem* and *Banjo* primarily in the character of Ray, whose peripatetic existence to some extent mirrors the author's own, as does the character's admiration for the beauty of young men's bodies. Patti Cappel Swartz digs for clues to McKay's sexuality in the author's fictional works, and points to a dream sequence in *Home to Harlem* and the fact that "for Ray, the bonds with men will always supersede those with women," as is shown in the conclusion of *Banjo.* "Like McKay, Ray is not the marrying kind, but rather the vagabond who must always travel on," Swartz continued.

In his third novel, *Banana Bottom,* McKay presented a more incisive exploration of his principal theme, the black individual's quest for cultural identity in a white society. *Banana Bottom* recounts the experiences of a Jamaican peasant girl, Bita, who is adopted by white missionaries after suffering a rape. Bita's new providers try to impose their cultural values on her by introducing her to organized Christianity and the British educational system. Their actions culminate in a horribly bungled attempt to arrange Bita's marriage to an aspiring minister. The prospective groom is exposed as a sexual aberrant, whereupon Bita flees white society. She eventually marries a drayman, Jubban, and raises their child in an idealized peasant Jamaican environment. "Bita has pride in blackness, is free of hypocrisy, and is independent and discerning in her values," remarked McLeod. "Praise for *Banana Bottom* has been unanimous."

Critics agree that *Banana Bottom* is McKay's most skillful delineation of the black individual's predicament in white society. Unfortunately, the novel's thematic worth was largely ignored when the book first appeared in 1933. Positive reviews of the time were related to McKay's extraordinary evocation of the Jamaican tropics and his mastery of melodrama. In the ensuing years, though, *Banana Bottom* has gained increasing acknowledgement as McKay's finest fiction and the culmination of his efforts to articulate his own tension and unease through the novel.

McKay's other noteworthy fiction publication during his final years abroad was *Gingertown,* a collection of twelve short stories. Six of the tales are devoted to Harlem life, and they reveal McKay's preoccupation with black exploitation and humiliation. Other tales are set in Jamaica and even in North Africa, McKay's last foreign home before he returned to the United States in the mid-1930s. Once back in Harlem he began an autobiographical work, *A Long Way from Home,* in which he related his own problems as a black individual in a white society. The book is considered unreliable as material for his autobiography because, for example, in it McKay denies his membership in the communist party, as McLeod points out. However, *A Long Way from Home* does state McKay's long-held belief that American blacks should unite in the struggle against colonialism, segregation, and oppression.

By the late 1930s McKay had developed a keen interest in Catholicism. Through Ellen Tarry, who wrote children's books, he became active in Harlem's Friendship House. His newfound religious interest, together with his observations and experiences at the Friendship House, inspired his essay collection, *Harlem: Negro Metropolis,* which offers an account of the black community in Harlem during the 1920s and 1930s. Like *Banjo, Banana Bottom,* and *Gingertown, Harlem: Negro Metropolis* failed to spark much interest from a reading public that was a tiring of literature by and about blacks. Critic McLeod offers a more recent evaluation of the work, the writing of which was based as much on scholarly inquiry as on personal observation, as McKay was absent from the country for a good deal of the period covered: "The book has been superseded by many more-scholarly studies, yet it retains value as a reexamination of Harlem by one who had established a necessary critical distance." With his reputation already waning, McKay moved to Chicago and worked as a teacher for a Catholic organization. By the mid-1940s his health had deteriorated. He endured several illnesses throughout his last years and eventually died of heart failure in May 1948.

In the years immediately following his death McKay's reputation continued to decline as critics found him conventional and somewhat shallow. Recently, however, McKay has gained recognition for his intense commitment to expressing the predicament of his fellow blacks, and he is now admired for devoting his art and life to social protest. As Robert A. Smith wrote in his *Phylon* publication, "Claude McKay: An Essay in Criticism": "Although he was frequently concerned with the race problem, his style is basically lucid. One feels disinclined to believe that the medium which he chose was too small, or too large for his message. He has been heard." McKay continues to be associated with the phenomenon known as the Harlem Renaissance, though he lived outside of the country for much of the period, and has found new audiences among readers of commonwealth literature and gay and lesbian literature. McLeod concluded his essay in *Dictionary of Literary Biography* with the following accolades: "That he was able to capture a universality of sentiment in 'If We Must Die' has been fully demonstrated; that he was able to show new directions for the black novel is now acknowledged; and that he is rightly regarded as one of the harbingers of (if not one of the participants in) the Harlem Renaissance is undisputed."

BIOGRAPHICAL/CRITICAL SOURCES:

BOOKS

African-American Almanac, sixth edition, Gale, 1994.

Bad Object Choices, editors, *How Do I Look,* Bay Press, 1991.

Baker, Houston A., Jr., *Modernism and the Harlem Renaissance,* University of Chicago Press, 1987.

Barton, Rebecca Chalmers, *Witnesses for Freedom: Negro Americans in Autobiography,* Harper, 1948.

Beier, Ulli, editor, *Introduction to African Literature: An Anthology of Critical Writing from "Black Orpheus,"* Longmans, 1967.

Black Literature Criticism, Gale, 1993.

Bone, Robert, *The Negro Novel in America,* rev. ed., Yale University Press, 1965.

Brawley, Benjamin, *The Negro Genius: A New Appraisal of the Achievement of the American Negro in Literature and the Fine Arts,* Dodd, 1937.

Bronze, Stephen, *Roots of Negro Consciousness, the 1920's: Three Harlem Renaissance Authors,* Libra, 1964.

Brown, Lloyd W., *West Indian Poetry,* Twayne, 1978, pp. 39-62.

Contemporary Black Biography, Volume 6, Gale, 1994.

Conroy, Mary James, *Claude McKay: Negro Poet and Novelist,* University Microfilms, 1968.

Cooper, Wayne F., *Claude McKay: Rebel Sojourner in the Harlem Renaissance: A Biography,* Louisiana State University Press, 1987.

Dictionary of Literary Biography, Gale, Volume 4: *American Writers in Paris, 1920-1939,* 1980, Volume 45: *American Poets, 1880-1945, First Series,* 1986, Volume 51: *American Writers from the Harlem Renaissance to 1940,* 1987, Volume 117: *Twentieth-Century Caribbean and Black African Writers, First Series,* 1992.

Duberman, Martin, Martha Vicinus, and George Chauncey, Jr., editors, *Hidden from History: Reclaiming the Gay and Lesbian Past,* Meridian, 1989, pp. 318-31.

Emanuel, James A., and Theodore L. Gross, *Dark Symphony: Negro Literature in America,* Free Press, 1968.

Fullinwider, S. P., *The Mind and Mood of Black America: 20th Century Thought,* Dorsey, 1969.

Gayle, Addison, Jr., *Claude McKay: The Black Poet at War,* Broadside, 1972.

Giles, James R., *Claude McKay,* Twayne, 1976.

Gloster, Hugh M., *Negro Voices in American Fiction,* University of North Carolina Press, 1948.

Huggins, Nathan, *Harlem Renaissance,* Oxford University Press, 1971.

Hughes, Carl Milton, *The Negro Novelist: 1940-1950,* Citadel, 1953.

Kent, George E., *Blackness and the Adventure of Western Culture,* Third World Press, 1972, pp. 36-52.

Lang, Phyllis Martin, *Claude McKay: The Later Years, 1934-48,* University Microfilms, 1973.

LeSeur, Geta J., *The Harlem Renaissance: Revaluations,* Garland, 1989, pp. 219-31.

Lewis, David Levering, *When Harlem Was in Vogue,* Oxford University Press, 1981.

Magill, Frank N., editor, *Masterpieces of African-American Literature,* HarperCollins, 1992.

Massa, Daniel, editor, *Individual and Community in Commonwealth Literature,* University of Malta, 1979, pp. 75-83.

Poetry Criticism, Volume 2, Gale, 1991.

Ramchand, Kenneth, *The West Indian Novel and Its Background,* Barnes & Noble, 1970.

Reference Guide to American Literature, second edition, St. James Press, 1987.

Rothenberg, Paula S., editor, *Race, Class and Gender in the United States,* St. Martins, 1995.

Samuels, Wilfred D., *Five Afro-Caribbean Voices in American Culture, 1917-1929,* Belmont, 1977, pp. 61-82.

Tillery, Tyrone, *Claude McKay: A Black Poet's Struggle for Identity,* University of Massachusetts Press, 1992.

Twentieth-Century Literary Criticism, Gale, Volume 7, 1982, Volume 41, 1991.

Wagner, Jean, *Les Poetes negres des Etats-Unis,* Librairies Istra, 1962, translation by Kenneth Douglas published as *Black Poets of the United States: From Paul Laurence Dunbar to Langston Hughes,* University of Illinois Press, 1973, pp. 197-257.

Wolfe, Susan J., and Julia Penelope, editors, *Sexual Practice, Textual Theory: Lesbian Cultural Criticism,* Blackwell, 1993.

World Literature Criticism, Gale, 1992.

PERIODICALS

African American Review, fall, 1994, p. 447.

America, July 3, 1943.

American Poetry Review, no. 4, 1975, pp. 40-42.

Black Orpheus, June, 1965, pp. 39-48.

Bookman, April, 1928; February, 1930.

Caribbean Quarterly, June, 1983, pp. 22-29.

CLA Journal, March, 1972, pp. 338-44, 345-53; June, 1973; December, 1975; March, 1980, pp. 336-51; September, 1986, pp. 46-58; March, 1989, pp. 296-308.

Crisis, June, 1928.

Extension, September, 1946.

Genders, spring, 1990, pp. 32-46.

Jamaica Journal, May-July, 1986, pp. 46-48.

Journal of American Culture, fall, 1991, pp. 91-96.

Journal of Commonwealth Literature, July, 1970, pp. 33-44.
Journal of Homosexuality, nos. 2-3, 1993, pp. 127-42.
Literary Half-Yearly, July, 1986, pp. 39-45, 65-75.
Negro American Literature Forum, spring, 1971, pp. 15-23.
New York Post, May 22, 1937.
Poetry, February, 1954, pp. 287-90.
Phylon, fall, 1948; fall, 1964, pp. 297-306.
Presence Africaine, first quarter, 1970, pp. 165-69.
Race, July, 1967; November, 1970, pp. 37-51.
Southern Review, no. 1, 1970, pp. 53-66.
Studies in Black Literature, summer, 1972.

*   *   *

McMILLAN, Terry (L.) 1951-

PERSONAL: Born October 18, 1951, in Port Huron, MI; daughter of Edward McMillan and Madeline Washington Tillman; married Jonathan Plummer (a student), September, 1998; children (by an earlier lover, Leonard Welch): Solomon Welch. *Education:* University of California, Berkeley, B.S., 1979; Columbia University, M.F.A., 1979.

ADDRESSES: Agent—Viking Penguin, 375 Hudson St., New York, NY 10014.

CAREER: University of Wyoming, Laramie, instructor, 1987-90; University of Arizona, Tucson, professor, 1990-92; writer.

MEMBER: PEN, Author's League.

AWARDS, HONORS: National Endowment for the Arts fellowship, 1988.

WRITINGS:

NOVELS

Mama, Houghton (Boston), 1987.
Disappearing Acts, Viking (New York City), 1989.
Waiting to Exhale, Viking, 1992.
How Stella Got Her Groove Back, Viking, 1996.
Day Late and a Dollar Short, Viking, in press.

OTHER

(Editor) *Breaking Ice: An Anthology of Contemporary African-American Fiction,* Viking, 1990.

(Author of introduction) Lee, Spike, with Ralph Wiley, *By Any Means Necessary: The Trials and Tribulations of the Making of Malcolm X. . .Including the Screenplay,* Hyperion, 1992.

Contributor to *Five for Five: The Films of Spike Lee,* Stewart, Tabori, 1991.

ADAPTATIONS: Waiting to Exhale was adapted for audio cassette, narrated by Terry McMillan, and as a motion picture starring Whitney Houston and Angela Bassett, Twentieth Century-Fox, 1996; *How Stella Got Her Groove Back* was adapted as a film, starring Angela Bassett, Whoopi Goldberg, Chai Diggs, and Regina King, Twentieth-Century Fox, 1998.

SIDELIGHTS: "Terry McMillan has the power to be an important contemporary novelist," stated Valerie Sayers, reviewing *Disappearing Acts* in the *New York Times Book Review* in 1989. "Watch Terry McMillan. She's going to be a major writer," predicted a book critic in a short but positive review of the same novel in *Cosmopolitan.* McMillan had already garnered attention and critical praise for her first novel, *Mama,* which was published in 1987. Over the next five years, these predictions began to come true. In 1992 McMillan saw the publication of *Waiting to Exhale,* her third novel. Her publisher sent her on a twenty-city, six-week tour, and McMillan appeared on several popular television programs, including the *Oprah Winfrey Show,* the *Arsenio Hall Show,* and *Today.*

"Seriously, I just don't get it; I really don't," the author mused during an interview with Audrey Edwards for *Essence.* But McMillan's honest, unaffected writings have clearly struck a chord with the book-buying public. Paperback rights for *Waiting to Exhale* fetched a hefty 2.64 million dollars, making the deal with Pocket Books the second largest of its kind in publishing history. And in 1992 Twentieth Century-Fox purchased the film rights; *Waiting to Exhale* was released as a major motion picture in 1996.

McMillan grew up in Port Huron, Michigan, a city approximately sixty miles northeast of Detroit. Her working-class parents did not make a point of reading to their five children, but McMillan discovered the pleasure of reading as a teenager shelving books in a local library. Prior to working in the library, she had no exposure to books by black writers. McMillan recalled feeling embarrassed when she saw a book by James Baldwin with his picture on the cover. In a *Washington Post* article, she was quoted as saying, "I . . . did not read his book because I was too afraid.

I couldn't imagine that he'd have anything better or different to say than [German essayist and novelist] Thomas Mann, [U.S. writer] Henry Thoreau, [essayist and poet] Ralph Waldo Emerson. . . . Needless to say, I was not just naive, but had not yet acquired an ounce of black pride."

Later, as a student at a community college in Los Angeles, McMillan immersed herself in most of the classics of African-American literature. After reading Alex Haley's *Autobiography of Malcolm X,* McMillan realized that she had no reason to be ashamed of a people who had such a proud history. At age twenty-five she published her first short story. Eleven years after that, her first novel, *Mama,* was released by Houghton Mifflin.

McMillan was determined not to let her debut novel go unnoticed. Typically, first novels receive little publicity other than the press releases and galleys sent out by the publisher. When McMillan's publisher told her that they could not do more for her, she decided to promote the book on her own. She wrote over 3,000 letters to chain bookstores, independent booksellers, universities, and colleges. Although what she was doing seemed logical in her own mind, the recipients of her letters were not used to such efforts by an author. They found her approach hard to resist, so by the end of the summer of 1987 she had several offers for readings. McMillan then scheduled her own book publicity tour and let her publicist know where she was going instead of it being the other way around.

By the time *Waiting to Exhale* was published, it was the other way around. The scene at a reading from the novel was described in the *Los Angeles Times* this way: "Several hundred fans, mostly black and female, are shoehorned into Marcus Bookstore on a recent Saturday night. Several hundred more form a line down the block and around the corner. The reading . . . hasn't begun because McMillan is greeting those who couldn't squeeze inside. . . . Finally, the writer . . . steps through the throng."

McMillan had come a long way since the publication of her first novel, which started out as a short story. "I really love the short story as a form," stated McMillan in an interview with *Writer's Digest.* "Mama" was just one of several short stories that McMillan had tried with limited success to get into print. Then the Harlem Writer's Guild accepted her into their group and told her that "Mama" really should be a novel and not a short story. After four weeks at the MacDowell artists colony and two weeks

at the Yaddo colony, McMillan had expanded her short story into over 400 pages. When her agent suggested certain revisions to the book, McMillan questioned whether the woman truly understood what the book was about.

Frustrated by this and by certain events taking place in her personal life, McMillan took things into her own hands and sent her collection of short stories to Houghton Mifflin. Hoping that she would at least get some free editorial advice, McMillan was surprised when the publisher contacted her about the novel she had mentioned briefly in her letter to them. She sent them pages from *Mama* and approximately four days later got word from the Houghton Mifflin people that they loved it.

Mama tells the story of the struggle Mildred Peacock has raising her five children after she throws her drunkard husband out of the house. The novel begins: "Mildred hid the ax beneath the mattress of the cot in the dining room." With those words, McMillan's novel becomes "a runaway narrative pulling a crowded cast of funny, earthy characters," stated Sayers in the *New York Times Book Review.* Because of McMillan's promotional efforts, the novel received numerous reviews—the overwhelming majority of which were positive—and McMillan gave thirty-nine readings. Six weeks after *Mama* was published, it went into its third printing.

Disappearing Acts, her second novel, proved to be quite different from *Mama.* For *Disappearing Acts,* McMillan chose to tell the story of star-crossed lovers by alternating the narrative between the main characters. Zora Banks and Franklin Swift fall in love "at first sight" when they meet at Zora's new apartment, where Franklin works as part of the renovating crew. Zora is an educated black woman working as a junior high school music teacher; Franklin is a high-school dropout working in construction. In spite of the differences in their backgrounds, the two become involved, move in together, and try to overcome the fear they both feel because of past failures in love.

Writing in the *Washington Post Book World,* David Nicholson pointed out that although this difference in backgrounds is an old literary device, it is one that is particularly relevant to black Americans: "Professional black women complain of an ever-shrinking pool of eligible men, citing statistics that show the number of black men in prison is increasing, while the number of black men in college is decreasing. Articles on alternatives for women, from celibacy to 'man-sharing' to relationships with blue-collar workers like Franklin have long been a staple of black general interest and women's magazines."

McMillan expressed her thoughts on this issue in an article she wrote titled "Looking for Mr. Right" for the February, 1990, issue of *Essence.* "Maybe it's just me, but I'm finding it harder and harder to meet men. . . . I grew up and became what my mama prayed out loud I'd become: educated, strong, smart, independent and reliable. . . . Now it seems as if carving a place for myself in the world is backfiring. Never in a million years would I have dreamed that I'd be 38 years old and still single."

Throughout the rest of the article, McMillan discusses how she had planned to be married by age twenty-four but found herself attending graduate school instead. She ended up loving and living with men who did not, as she puts it, "take life as seriously as I did." When she was thirty-two years old, she gave birth to her son, Solomon. Shortly after that she ended a three-year relationship with her son's father. Since then McMillan had been involved in what she called "two powerful but short-lived relationships," both of which ended when, without any explanation, the man stopped calling.

McMillan believes that "even though a lot of 'professional' men claim to want a smart, independent woman, they're kidding themselves." She thinks that these men do not feel secure unless they are with passive women or with women who will "back down, back off or just acquiesce" until they appear to be tamed. "I'm not tamable," declared McMillan in *Essence.* In response to a former boyfriend who told her that it is lonely at the top, McMillan replied, "It is lonely 'out here.' But I wouldn't for a minute give up all that I've earned just to have a man. I just wish it were easier to meet men and get to know them."

Reviewers commended McMillan on her ability to give such a true voice to the character of Franklin in *Disappearing Acts.* One reviewer for the *Washington Post Book World* called the novel "one of the few . . . to contain rounded, sympathetic portraits of black men and to depict relationships between black men and black women as something more than the relationship between victimizer and victim, oppressor and oppressed." In the *New York Times Book Review,* another reviewer stated: "The miracle is that Ms. McMillan takes the reader so deep into this man's head—and makes what goes on there so complicated—that [the] story becomes not only comprehensible but

affecting." Not only did McMillan's second novel win critical acclaim, it also was optioned for a film; McMillan eventually wrote the screenplay for Metro-Goldwyn-Mayer.

Leonard Welch, McMillan's former lover and the father of their son, also found that portions of *Disappearing Acts* rung true—so true, in fact, that in August of 1990 he filed a 4.75 million dollar defamation suit against McMillan. Welch claimed that McMillan used him as the model for the novel's main male character, and therefore the book defamed him. The suit also named Penguin USA (parent company of Viking, the publisher of the book) and Simon & Schuster (publisher of the book in paperback) as defendants.

The suit alleged that McMillan had acted maliciously in writing the novel and that she had written it mainly out of vindictiveness and a sense of revenge toward Welch. In addition to believing that the novel realistically portrayed his three-year relationship with McMillan, Welch claimed that he suffered emotional stress. McMillan had dedicated the book to their son, and Welch feared that Solomon would believe the defamatory parts of the novel when he was old enough to read it.

Martin Garbus, the lawyer for Penguin USA, maintained that if McMillan had been an obscure writer who wrote an obscure book, then there would not have been a lawsuit at all. One of McMillan's writing peers was quoted in the *Los Angeles Times* as saying, "I think it's just part of the general nastiness of the time, that people see someone doing well and they want part of it."

The suit raised the issue of the delicate balance fiction writers must maintain. Many novelists draw on their experiences when writing, and most feel that they have an obligation to protect the privacy of an individual. In the *Los Angeles Times,* Garbus explained: "What Terry McMillan has done is no different than what other writers have done. It has to be permissible to draw on your real-life experiences. Otherwise, you can't write fiction." Most people involved in the suit, including Welch's lawyer, agreed that a victory for Welch could set an unfortunate precedent that would inhibit the creativity of fiction writers.

In April of 1991, the New York Supreme Court ruled in McMillan's favor. As reported in the *Wall Street Journal,* the judge in the case wrote that although "the fictional character and the real man share the same occupation and educational background and even like the same breakfast cereal . . . the man in the novel is a lazy, emotionally disturbed alcoholic who uses drugs and sometimes beats his girlfriend." The judge declared that "Leonard Welch is none of these things."

In 1990 Viking published *Breaking Ice: An Anthology of Contemporary African-American Fiction.* Edited by McMillan, the anthology came into being as a result of the anger she experienced after reading a collection of short stories that did not include any black or Third World writers. Her research and book proposal were the first steps in correcting what McMillan felt was the publishing industry's neglect of black writers. She received almost three hundred submissions for the anthology and chose fifty-seven seasoned, emerging, and unpublished writers.

In reviewing *Breaking Ice* for the *Washington Post Book World,* author Joyce Carol Oates characterized the book as "a wonderfully generous and diverse collection of prose fiction by our most gifted African-American writers." Oates credited McMillan's judgment for selecting such "high quality of writing . . . that one could hardly distinguish between the categories [of writers] in terms of originality, depth of vision and command of the language."

McMillan's third novel, *Waiting to Exhale,* tells the stories of four professional black women who have everything except for the love of a good man. The overall theme of the book is men's fear of commitment; a subtheme is the fear of growing old alone. The novel has hit a nerve with its readers—both male and female. Many women seem to identify with McMillan's characters; so do some men. According to the *Los Angeles Times,* one black male from an audience of over two thousand proclaimed: "I think I speak for a lot of brothers. I know I'm all over the book. . . . All I can say is, I'm willing to learn. Being defensive is not the answer." This is precisely the response to the book that McMillan was hoping to get. She wants people to understand that she is not trying to offend or insult black males. She just wants men to be aware of the things they do that make it difficult for women to love them.

One issue that emerged from many reviews of McMillan's earlier books is the amount of profanity she uses. *Waiting to Exhale* met with the same criticism. One critic called her characters male-bashing stand-up comedians who use foul language. For McMillan, reproducing her characters' profane lan-

guage is her way of staying close to them. She believes that basically the language she uses is accurate. She told *Publishers Weekly:* "That's the way we talk. And I want to know why I've never read a review where they complain about the language that male writers use!"

"Fans of McMillan's previous novels . . . will recognize McMillan's authentic, unpretentious voice in every page of *How Stella Got Her Groove Back,* exclaimed Liesl Schillinger in her review of the author's 1996 novel in *Washington Post Book World.* The story of a forty-something business woman whose life has been spent in raising her son and working her way to success and an annual income of 200,000 dollars, *How Stella Got Her Groove Back* finds the resourceful, spunky protagonist off to Jamaica to shake up more than just a boring existence. Stella is determined to fill that empty place in her life where a permanent love interest should be, and a twenty-year-old Jamaican named Winston more than fits the bill. She brings Winston back to the United States with her and, almost unbelievably, he is accepted by her eleven-year-old son, her sisters, and life continues happily ever after. Although noting that McMillan's novel "is not deeper or more searching than the average sitcom, no more dramatically powerful than a backyard barbecue," Richard Bernstein cited *How Stella Got Her Groove Back* as "an irreverent, mischievous, diverting novel that at times will make you laugh out loud" in his *New York Times* review. Maxine Chernoff dubbed the novel "not quite serious enough for summer reading" in her review in the *Chicago Tribune,* but Schillinger added to the praise of the work, hailing McMillan for realizing that "women are ready to read about themselves not only as schemers or sufferers, but as the adventurous heroes of their own lives."

For her portrayal of feisty, tough, black heroines, McMillan has been compared to acclaimed black women writers Alice Walker, Gloria Naylor, and Zora Neale Hurston. McMillan acknowledges the compliment but asserts in the introduction to *Breaking Ice* that her generation of black writers is "a new breed, free to write as we please . . . because of the way life has changed." Life has changed for her generation but it has also stayed the same for many women in one fundamental way: the search for happiness and fulfillment continues. In an article in the *Los Angeles Times,* McMillan maintained: "A house and a car and all the money in the bank won't make you happy. People need people. People crave intimacy."

Ever mindful of the fleeting nature of fame, McMillan views her celebrity status with a clear eye and remains focused on her mission as a writer. "This won't last," she stated in *Essence.* "Today it's me. Tomorrow it will be somebody else. I always remember that."

BIOGRAPHICAL/CRITICAL SOURCES:

BOOKS

Contemporary Literary Criticism, Gale (Detroit), Volume 50, 1988; Volume 61, 1991.

PERIODICALS

Callaloo, summer, 1988.
Cosmopolitan, August, 1989.
Detroit News, September 7, 1992.
Emerge, September, 1992; June, 1996.
English Journal, April, 1996, p. 86.
Esquire, July, 1988.
Essence, February, 1990; October, 1992; May, 1995, p. 52; June, 1996, pp. 50, 54.
Los Angeles Times, February 23, 1987; October 29, 1990; June 19, 1992.
Mademoiselle, July, 1996, p. 77.
Newsweek, January 8, 1996, p. 68; April 29, 1996, pp. 76, 79.
New Yorker, April 29, 1996, p. 102.
New York Review of Books, November 4, 1993, p. 33.
New York Times, May 15, 1996, p. B5, C17.
New York Times Book Review, February 22, 1987; August 6, 1989; May 31, 1992; June 2, 1996, p. 21.
New York Times Magazine, August 9, 1992.
People, July 20, 1992.
Publishers Weekly, May 11, 1992; July 13, 1992; September 21, 1992; May 6, 1996, p. 30.
Time, January 8, 1996, p. 72; May 6, 1996, p. 77.
Tribune Books (Chicago), September 23, 1990; May 31, 1992; May 5, 1996, p. 6.
Village Voice, March 24, 1987.
Wall Street Journal, April 11, 1991.
Washington Post, November 17, 1990.
Washington Post Book World, August 27, 1989; September 16, 1990; May 24, 1992; May 5, 1996, p. 1.
Writer's Digest, October, 1987.*

*   *   *

McPHERSON, James Alan   1943-

PERSONAL: Born September 16, 1943, Savannah, GA;

son of James Allen and Mable (Smalls) McPherson. *Education:* Attended Morgan State University, 1963-64; Morris Brown College, B.A., 1965; Harvard University, LL.B., 1968; University of Iowa, M.F.A., 1969.

ADDRESSES: Office—Department of English, University of Iowa, Iowa City, IA 52242.

CAREER: University of Iowa, Iowa City, instructor in writing at Law School, 1968-69, instructor in Afro-American literature, 1969; University of California, Santa Cruz, faculty member, 1969-70; Morgan State University, Baltimore, MD, faculty member, 1975-76; University of Virginia, Charlottesville, faculty member, 1976-81; University of Iowa, Writers Workshop, Iowa City, professor, 1981—; *Double Take* magazine, editor, 1995—; Stanford University, Palo Alto, CA, behavioral studies fellow, 1997—.

MEMBER: Authors League of America, PEN, American Academy of Arts and Sciences, National Association for the Advancement of Colored People, American Civil Liberties Union.

AWARDS, HONORS: First prize, *Atlantic* short story contest, 1965, for "Gold Coast"; grant from Atlantic Monthly Press and Little, Brown, 1969; National Institute of Arts and Letters award in literature, 1970; Guggenheim fellow, 1972-73; Pulitzer Prize, 1978, for *Elbow Room: Stories;* MacArthur fellowship, 1981; Excellence in Technology award, University of Iowa, 1991; Best American Essays, 1990, 1993, 1994, 1995; Pushcart Prize, 1995.

WRITINGS:

Hue and Cry: Short Stories, Atlantic-Little, Brown (Boston), 1969.
(Editor with Miller Williams) *Railroad: Trains and Train People in American Culture,* Random House (New York City), 1976.
Elbow Room: Stories, Atlantic-Little, Brown, 1977.
(Author of foreword) Breece D'J Pancake, *The Stories of Breece D'J Pancake,* Atlantic-Little, Brown, 1983.
Crabcakes: A Memoir, Simon & Schuster (New York City), 1998.
(Editor with DeWitt Henry) *Fathering Daughters: Reflections by Men,* Beacon Press (Boston), 1998.

CONTRIBUTOR

J. Hicks, editor, *Cutting Edges,* Holt (New York City), 1973.

Nick A. Ford, editor, *Black Insights: Significant Literature by Afro-Americans, 1760 to the Present,* Wiley (New York City), 1976.

Llewellyn Howland and Isabelle Storey, editors, *Book for Boston,* Godine, 1980.

Kimberly W. Benson, editor, *Speaking for You,* Howard University Press, 1987.

Alex Harris, *A World Unsuspected,* [Chapel Hill], 1987.

OTHER

Also contributor to *New Black Voices,* New American Library. Contributor to *Atlantic, Esquire, New York Times Magazine, Playboy, Reader's Digest,* and *Callaloo.* Contributing editor, *Atlantic,* 1969—; editor of special issue, *Iowa Review,* winter, 1984.

SIDELIGHTS: James Alan McPherson's stories of ordinary, working-class people, though often concerning black characters, are noted for their ability to confront universal human problems. "His standpoint," Robie Macauley explains in the *New York Times Book Review,* "[is] that of a writer and a black, but not that of a black writer. [McPherson] refused to let his fiction fall into any color-code or ethnic code." Because of this stance, McPherson's characters are more fully rounded than are those of more racially conscious writers. As Paul Bailey writes in the *Observer Review,* "the Negroes and whites [McPherson] describes always remain individual people-he never allows himself the luxury of turning them into Problems." Explaining his approach to the characters in his stories, McPherson is quoted by Patsy B. Perry of the *Dictionary of Literary Biography* as saying: "Certain of these people [his characters] happen to be black, and certain of them happen to be white; but I have tried to keep the color part of most of them far in the background, where these things should rightly be kept." McPherson has published two collections of short stories, *Hue and Cry: Short Stories* and *Elbow Room: Stories.* In 1978 he was awarded the Pulitzer Prize for fiction.

McPherson was born and raised in Savannah, Georgia, a city in which several cultures—including the French, Spanish, and Indian—have been uniquely blended. He cites this rich cultural heritage as a determining factor in his own ability to transcend racial barriers. The McPherson family also influenced his development of values. His father, at one time the only licensed black master electrician in Georgia, and his mother, a domestic in a white household, had important contacts in both the white and black communities. Through their efforts, McPherson obtained work as a grocery boy in a local supermarket and as a waiter on a train. These experiences formed the basis for several later stories. McPherson's train employment also allowed him to travel across the country. Perry notes that McPherson "affirms the importance of both white and black communities in his development as an individual and as a writer of humanistic ideas."

McPherson's writing career began in the 1960s while he was still attending law school. His story "Gold Coast" won first prize in a contest sponsored by the *Atlantic* magazine and was later published in the magazine as well. The *Atlantic* was to play a pivotal role in McPherson's career. After earning a bachelor's degree, a law degree, and a master's degree in creative writing, McPherson became a contributing editor of the *Atlantic* in 1969. And the magazine, in conjunction with Little, Brown, also published his two collections of short stories.

McPherson's first collection, *Hue and Cry,* deals with characters whose lives are so desperate that they can only rage impotently against their situations. "The fact that these characters . . . ," writes Perry, "know nothing else to do except to sink slowly into madness, scream unintelligibly, or seek refuge . . . provides reason enough for McPherson's hue and cry." The *Times Literary Supplement* critic points to the book's "mostly desperate, mostly black, mostly lost figures in the urban nightmare of violence, rage and bewilderment that is currently America."

Despite the grim nature of his stories, McPherson manages to depict the lives of his characters with sympathy and grace. Bailey allows that McPherson's "powers of observation and character-drawing are remarkable, displaying a mature novelist's understanding of the vagaries and inconsistencies of human affairs." Writing in *Harper's,* Irving Howe maintains that McPherson "possesses an ability some writers take decades to acquire, the ability to keep the right distance from the creatures of his imagination, not to get murkily involved and blot out his figures with vanity and fuss." Granville Hicks of *Saturday Review* notes that McPherson "is acutely aware of the misery and injustice in the world, and he sympathizes deeply with the victims whether they are black or white."

Among the most prominent admirers of *Hue and Cry* is novelist Ralph Ellison. In a statement he contributed to the book's dust jacket, Ellison speaks of the difference between McPherson's writing and that of most other black writers. "McPherson," Ellison claims, "promises to move right past those talented but misguided writers . . . who take being black as a privilege for being obscenely second-rate and who regard their social predicament as Negroes as exempting them from the necessity of mastering the craft and forms of fiction. . . . McPherson will never, as a writer, be an embarrassment to such people of excellence as Willie Mays, Duke Ellington, Leontyne Price-or, for that matter, Stephen Crane or F. Scott Fitzgerald."

Elbow Room, McPherson's second collection, won even more critical praise than its predecessor. Again concerned with characters in desperate situations, the stories of *Elbow Room* are nonetheless more optimistic than McPherson's earlier works, the characters more willing to struggle for some measure of success. They "engage in life's battles with integrity of mind and spirit," as Perry explains. This optimism is noted by several critics. Robert Phillips of *Commonweal,* for example, finds the stories in *Elbow Room* to be "difficult struggles for survival, yet [McPherson's] sense of humor allows him to dwell on moments which otherwise might prove unbearable." Writing in *Newsweek,* Margo Jefferson calls McPherson "an astute realist who knows how to turn the conflicts between individual personalities and the surrounding culture into artful and highly serious comedies of manners."

McPherson's ability to create believable characters, and his focus on the underlying humanity of all his characters, is praised by such critics as Phillips. McPherson's stories, Phillips believes, "ultimately become not so much about the black condition as the human condition. . . . *Elbow Room* is a book of singular achievement." Macauley explains that McPherson has been able "to look beneath skin color and cliches of attitude into the hearts of his characters. . . . This is a fairly rare ability in American fiction." The *New Yorker* reviewer lists several other characteristics of McPherson's stories that are worthy of attention, calling him "one of those rare writers who can tell a story, describe shadings of character, and make sociological observations with equal subtlety."

Speaking of the obstacles and opportunities facing black writers, McPherson writes in the *Atlantic:* "It seems to me much of our writing has been, and continues to be, sociological because black writers have been concerned with protesting black humanity and racial injustice to the larger society in those terms most easily understood by nonblack people. It also

seems to me that we can correct this limitation either by defining and affirming the values and cultural institutions of our people for their education or by employing our own sense of reality and our own conception of what human life should be to explore, and perhaps help define, the cultural realities of contemporary American life."

McPherson broke a silence of nearly twenty years with his 1998 *Crabcakes: A Memoir,* "a profoundly personal tale of displacement and discovery that is poetic and universal," according to a writer for *Kirkus Reviews.* Roy Hoffman in the *New York Times Book Review* reports that the book, "part lilting memoir, part anxious meditation," deals elliptically with McPherson's long struggle with writer's block, his travels in Japan, and his slow recovery of a sense of connection with his past and present. Hoffman faults the author for being "far more elusive than the protagonists in his short fiction. . . . When McPherson writes fiction, he insists that his characters reveal whether they've been abandoned by a lover, frozen out by a child. Why should he, as a memoirist, reveal far less?" Conversely, a reviewer for *Black Studies* deems the book "richly rewarding," and a *Publishers Weekly* reviewer calls the book an "intense mosaic" that "combines James Baldwin's moral compulsion to testify and Ishmael Reed's iconoclastic experimentalism."

BIOGRAPHICAL/CRITICAL SOURCES:

BOOKS

Beavers, Herman, *Wrestling Angels into Song: The Fictions of Ernest J. Faines, and James Alan McPherson,* University of Pennsylvania Press, 1995.
Contemporary Literary Criticism, Volume 19, Gale (Detroit), 1981.
Dictionary of Literary Biography, Volume 38: *Afro-American Writers after 1955: Dramatists and Prose Writers,* Gale, 1985.
Wallace, Jon, *The Politics of Style: Language as Theme in the Fiction of Berger, McGuane, and McPherson,* Hollowbrook, 1992.

PERIODICALS

Antioch Review, winter, 1978.
Atlantic Monthly, December, 1970; February, 1977.
Black Studies, February 1, 1998.
Booklist, June 1, 1998, p. 1682.
Chicago Tribune Book World, May 25, 1969.

Christian Science Monitor, July 31, 1969.

CLA Journal, June, 1979.

Commonweal, September 19, 1969; September 15, 1978.

Critique, summer, 1996, p. 314.

Ebony, December, 1981.

Essence, January, 1998, p. 61.

Guardian Weekly, April 16, 1989.

Harper's, December, 1969.

Kirkus Reviews, November 15, 1997.

Library Journal, January, 1998, p. 100; June 15, 1998, p. 96.

Nation, December 16, 1978.

Negro Digest, October, 1969; November, 1969.

Newsweek, June 16, 1969; October 17, 1977.

New Yorker, November 21, 1977.

New York Review of Books, November 10, 1977.

New York Times Book Review, June 1, 1969; September 25, 1977; September 2, 1979; February 13, 1983; May 13, 1984; February 15, 1998, p. 15.

People, March 30, 1998, p. 39.

Publishers Weekly, November 17, 1997, p. 44; December 15, 1997, p. 36; May 4, 1998, p. 196.

Saturday Review, May 24, 1969.

Spectator, November 22, 1969.

Studies in American Fiction, autumn, 1973.

Times Literary Supplement, December 25, 1969.

Washington Post Book World, October 30, 1977; March 6, 1983.

*   *   *

MEYER, June
  See JORDAN, June

*   *   *

MICHEAUX, Oscar (Devereaux) 1884-1951

PERSONAL: Surname originally spelled Michaux; born January 2, 1884, near Metropolis, IL; died March 26, 1951, in Charlotte, NC; son of Calvin Swan (a farmer) and Belle (a farmer; maiden name, Willingham) Michaux; married first wife (divorced); married Alice B. Russell (an actor), 1929. *Education:* High school graduate.

CAREER: Western Book Supply Company, Sioux City, IA, founder, 1915; director, producer, editor, and marketer of films, including *The Homesteader* (based on his novel *The Homesteader*), Micheaux Film Corporation, 1919; *The Brute,* Micheaux Film Corporation, 1920; (and presenter) *The Symbol of the Unconquered* (also known as *Symbol of the Unconquered: A Story of the Ku Klux Klan*), Micheaux Film Corporation, 1920; (and presenter) *Within Our Gates,* Micheaux Book and Film Company, 1920; *Deceit, or the House behind the Cedars,* Micheaux Film Corporation, 1921; (and presenter) *The Gunsaulus Mystery,* Micheaux Film Corporation, 1921; *The Dungeon,* Micheaux Film Corporation, 1922; *Son of Satan,* Micheaux Film Corporation, 1922; *Uncle Jasper's Will* (also known as *Jasper Landry's Will*), Micheaux Film Corporation, 1922; *The Virgin of the Seminole,* Micheaux Film Corporation, 1922; *The Ghost of Tolston's Manor,* 1923; *Body and Soul,* Micheaux Film Corporation, 1925; *Marcus Garland,* Micheaux Film Corporation, 1925; *Birthright, the Conjure Woman,* Micheaux Film Corporation, 1926; *The Spider's Web,* Micheaux Film Corporation, 1926; *The Broken Violin,* Micheaux Film Corporation, 1927; *The Millionaire,* Micheaux Film Corporation, 1927; *Easy Street,* Micheaux Film Corporation, 1928; *Thirty Years Later,* Micheaux Film Corporation, 1928; *When Men Betray,* Micheaux Film Corporation, 1928; *Wages of Sin,* Micheaux Film Corporation, 1929; *A Daughter of the Congo,* Micheaux Film Corporation, 1930; *Darktown Revue,* Micheaux Film Corporation, 1931; *The Exile,* Empire/Micheaux Film Corporation, 1931; *Black Magic,* Micheaux Film Corporation, 1932; *Veiled Aristocrats,* Micheaux Film Corporation, 1932; *The Girl from Chicago,* Micheaux Film Corporation, 1933; *Ten Minutes to Kill* (also known as *Ten Minutes to Live*), Micheaux Film Corporation, 1933; *Harlem after Midnight,* Micheaux Film Corporation, 1934; *Lem Hawkins' Confession* (also known as *Murder in Harlem*), Micheaux Film Corporation, 1935; *Temptation,* Micheaux Film Corporation, 1936; *Underworld,* Micheaux Film Corporation, 1936; *God's Step Children,* Micheaux Film Corporation, 1938; *Swing* (based on his short story "Mandy"), Micheaux Film Corporation, 1938; *Birthright* (sound version), Micheaux Pictures Corporation, 1939; *Lying Lips,* Micheaux Film Corporation, 1940; *The Notorious Elinor Lee,* Sack Amusement Enterprises, 1940; and *The Betrayal* (based on his novel *The Wind from Nowhere*), Astor Pictures, 1948. Founder of the Micheaux Book and Film Company, the Micheaux Film Corporation, and Micheaux Pictures Corporation, New York City, Chicago, IL, and Sioux City, IA. Worked variously as a lecturer, factory worker, coal miner, Pullman porter, farmer, and at a stockyards and a steel mill.

AWARDS, HONORS: Directors Guild of America Award, lifetime achievement, 1980s; received a star on the Hollywood Walk of Fame. The Black Filmmakers Hall of Fame holds the annual Oscar Micheaux Awards Ceremony to honor black contributions to American film; the Oscar Micheaux Society (Durham, NC) and Oscar Micheaux Festival (Gregory, SD) were founded in Micheaux's honor.

WRITINGS:

NOVELS

The Conquest: The Story of a Negro Pioneer, by the Pioneer, Woodruff Press (Lincoln, NE), 1913.
The Forged Note: A Romance of the Darker Races, Western Book Supply (Lincoln, NE), 1915.
The Homesteader, Western Book Supply (Sioux City, IA), 1917.
The Case of Mrs. Wingate, New York Book Supply, 1944.
The Wind from Nowhere, New York Book Supply (New York City), 1944.
The Story of Dorothy Stanfield, Based on a Great Insurance Swindle, and a Woman, New York Book Supply, 1946.
The Masquerade: An Historical Novel, New York Book Supply, 1947.

Author of short stories, including "Mandy." Contributor to periodicals, including the *Philadelphia Afro-American.*

SCREENPLAYS

The Homesteader (based on his novel *The Homesteader*), Micheaux Film Corporation, 1919.
The Brute, Micheaux Film Corporation, 1920.
The Symbol of the Unconquered (also known as *Symbol of the Unconquered: A Story of the Ku Klux Klan*), Micheaux Film Corporation, 1920.
Within Our Gates, Micheaux Book and Film Company, 1920.
Deceit, or the House behind the Cedars, Micheaux Film Corporation, 1921.
The Gunsaulus Mystery, Micheaux Film Corporation, 1921.
The Dungeon, Micheaux Film Corporation, 1922.
Son of Satan, Micheaux Film Corporation, 1922.
Uncle Jasper's Will (also known as *Jasper Landry's Will*), Micheaux Film Corporation, 1922.
The Virgin of the Seminole, Micheaux Film Corporation, 1922.
The Ghost of Tolston's Manor, 1923.

Body and Soul, Micheaux Film Corporation, 1925.
Marcus Garland, Micheaux Film Corporation, 1925.
Birthright, the Conjure Woman, Micheaux Film Corporation, 1926.
The Spider's Web, Micheaux Film Corporation, 1926.
The Broken Violin, Micheaux Film Corporation, 1927.
The Millionaire, Micheaux Film Corporation, 1927.
Easy Street, Micheaux Film Corporation, 1928.
Thirty Years Later, Micheaux Film Corporation, 1928.
When Men Betray, Micheaux Film Corporation, 1928.
Wages of Sin, Micheaux Film Corporation, 1929.
A Daughter of the Congo, Micheaux Film Corporation, 1930.
Darktown Revue, Micheaux Film Corporation, 1931.
The Exile, Empire/Micheaux Film Corporation, 1931.
Black Magic, Micheaux Film Corporation, 1932.
The Girl from Chicago, Micheaux Film Corporation, 1933.
Ten Minutes to Kill (also known as *Ten Minutes to Live*), Micheaux Film Corporation, 1933.
Harlem after Midnight, Micheaux Film Corporation, 1934.
Lem Hawkins' Confession (also known as *Murder in Harlem*), Micheaux Film Corporation, 1935.
Temptation, Micheaux Film Corporation, 1936.
Underworld, Micheaux Film Corporation, 1936.
God's Step Children, Micheaux Film Corporation, 1938.
Swing (based on his short story "Mandy"), Micheaux Film Corporation, 1938.
(With Thomas Sigismund Stribling) *Birthright* (sound version), Micheaux Pictures Corporation, 1939.
Lying Lips, Micheaux Film Corporation, 1940.
The Notorious Elinor Lee, Sack Amusement Enterprises, 1940.
The Betrayal (based on his novel *The Wind from Nowhere*), Astor Pictures, 1948.

Also wrote other screenplays.

SIDELIGHTS: Using his talent for self-promotion, African American Oscar Micheaux battled prejudice to produce literary and cinematic works during the first half of the twentieth century. In his novels and films, Micheaux created self-reliant black characters who work hard to attain success. Micheaux admired the ideas of civil rights leader and educator Booker T. Washington. According to *Dictionary of Literary Biography* contributor J. Randal Woodland, Washington "urged that blacks better their own condition through diligence and dedication to practical goals." Some critics accused Micheaux of including racist representations of African Americans in his films. Micheaux replied to these charges in a *Philadelphia Afro-American* article, stating: "I am too much imbued with the spirit of Booker T. Washington to engraft false virtues upon ourselves, to make ourselves that which we are not."

In that same 1925 piece in the *Philadelphia Afro-American,* Micheaux admitted that he made films in order "to lay before the race a cross section of its own life, to view the colored heart at close range." Some critics wrote that Micheaux ignored the social constraints that existed for African Americans of the time. These critics did not deter Micheaux from writing, producing, directing, editing, marketing, and raising funds for his films. He made pictures in a wide variety of genres, from melodramas, detective films, Western pictures and romances.

Micheaux's fiction career has two distinct periods. His first three novels, *The Conquest: The Story of a Negro Pioneer, by the Pioneer* (1913), *The Forged Note: A Romance of the Darker Races* (1915), and *The Homesteader* (1917), all contain autobiographical elements, and several critics consider them Micheaux's most important works of fiction. With the commercial success of his novel *The Homesteader,* Micheaux attracted the interest of the film industry.

With the same type of work ethic he had shown during his early literary career, Micheaux became an independent filmmaker, producing a feature film version of *The Homesteader* in 1919. He continued to produce films for the remainder of his lifetime. He wrote four more novels in the 1940s: *The Case of Mrs. Wingate* (1944), *The Wind from Nowhere* (1944), *The Story of Dorothy Stanfield, Based on a Great Insurance Swindle, and a Woman* (1946), and *The Masquerade: An Historical Novel* (1947).

Micheaux's literary and cinematic works incorporate the same themes, and both provide commentary on African American life before the civil rights era.

Most of what is known about Micheaux's early life has been extracted from *The Conquest: The Story of a Negro Pioneer, by the Pioneer,* a work biographers consider an autobiographical novel. Micheaux was born to a farming family on January 2, 1884, in rural Illinois, and was an avid reader as a child. After graduating from high school, Micheaux took a series of jobs in Metropolis and Chicago, Illinois, but was unsatisfied. He left for the frontier, establishing a homestead in rural South Dakota in 1904. After years

of determination and hard work, Micheaux turned his farm into a profitable venture. 1909 proved to be an important year for Micheaux. First, he decided that he wanted to become a writer after attending a minstrel show. In that same year, he fell in love with a white woman, but the relationship failed due to their racial differences. Micheaux's work often features characters' opposition to interracial love affairs. He based *The Conquest* on his experiences in South Dakota, calling the novel "a true story of a negro who was discontented and the circumstances that were the result of that discontent."

After Micheaux completed *The Conquest,* he borrowed money to have it published, and then sold copies to local farmers in South Dakota. Feeling a black audience would be more willing to buy the work, he toured the southern states of the United States, often going door to door. These endeavors were largely successful, and Micheaux wrote *The Forged Note: A Romance of the Darker Races. The Forged Note* and *The Homesteader* were both published by the Western Book Supply, a Sioux City, Iowa company he founded in 1915. Micheaux promoted and marketed *The Forged Note* and *The Homesteader* in the same way he publicized *The Conquest*—with tours and speaking engagements. *The Homesteader* was particularly popular with readers, especially in the South.

The protagonist in *The Conquest* is named Oscar Devereaux, Micheaux's own first and middle names. This similarity seems appropriate in a novel which closely follows Micheaux's own life. Much of the book deals with Devereaux's romance with a white woman. Although the two characters marry, they encounter many problems in the course of the book. Discussing *The Conquest* in the *Dictionary of Literary Biography,* contributor J. Randal Woodland commented: "The tone of the work is often uneven and the writing awkward, but Micheaux's descriptions of the natural beauty of the wilderness can be striking, and the book gains a kind of unity from the sheer force of the narrator's personality." *The Forged Note* also contains autobiographical elements. Its protagonist, Sidney Wyeth, pens an autobiographical novel about his time as a black homesteader in South Dakota. Wyeth travels to the South to sell his book, and Micheaux draws upon his own selling experiences in the South to describe the social problems of African Americans in that region. While Wyeth promotes his book, he grows increasingly concerned about the drinking, gambling, and criminal activity that he witnesses in the black communities. Wyeth blames their economic problems not on white prejudice, but from their own carelessness.

As he began to write *The Homesteader,* Micheaux was determined to present a more positive image of African Americans to his black readers, and wanted to show how self-reliance could lead to success. The book's plot is similar to the storyline of *The Conquest.* *The Homesteader* features an interracial love affair between black farmer Jean Baptiste and Agnes Stewart, the daughter of a local white farmer. Although the characters encounter similar obstacles as the couple in *The Conquest,* the outcome for Jean and Agnes is quite different.

Recognizing his talent, representatives from the Lincoln Motion Picture Company approached Micheaux about turning *The Homesteader* into a film for black audiences. When the two sides could not agree in business negotiations, Micheaux decided that he would make the film himself, despite the fact that he had no knowledge of the industry. Yet Micheaux applied the same determination to filmmaking that he had shown in farming and in writing. Before long, he was producing films at a feverish rate. Beginning with the adaptation of *The Homesteader,* he eventually made over forty feature films. He produced these films for predominantly black audiences, and some critics call these films "race movies" because of their intended audience. Most of his films were shot on a tight budget, and their quality often reflects this fact. Yet critics such as *Contemporary Black Biography* contributor Anne Janette Johnson stated that the pictures are important for other reasons: "Perhaps the most important single figure in the history of race movies, Micheaux is remembered today not so much for the content of his films as for the fact that he made them."

BIOGRAPHICAL/CRITICAL SOURCES:

BOOKS

Contemporary Black Biography, Volume 7, Gale (Detroit, MI), 1994.
Dictionary of Literary Biography, Volume 50: *Afro-American Writers before the Harlem Renaissance,* Gale, 1986.
Twentieth-Century Literary Criticism, Volume 76, Gale, 1998.
Twentieth-Century Western Writers, second edition, St. James Press (Chicago, IL), 1992.
Young, Joseph A., *Black Novelist As White Racist: The Myth of Black Inferiority in the Novels of*

Oscar Micheaux, Greenwood Press (New York City), 1989.

PERIODICALS

American Visions, February/March, 1998, p. 37.
Chronicle of Higher Education, March 3, 1995, pp. A6-A9.
Film Quarterly, spring, 1998, pp. 16-31.*

*   *   *

MILNER, Ron(ald) 1938-

PERSONAL: Born May 29, 1938, in Detroit, MI. *Education:* Attended Columbia University.

ADDRESSES: Office—Crossroads Theatre Co., 320 Memorial Parkway, New Brunswick, NJ 08901. *Agent*—c/o New American Library, 1301 Sixth Ave., New York, NY 10019.

CAREER: Playwright. Writer in residence, Lincoln University, 1966-67; teacher, Michigan State University, 1971-72; founder and director, Spirit of Shango theater company; founder and director, Langston Hughes Theatre; director, *Don't Get God Started,* 1986; led playwriting workshop, Wayne State University.

AWARDS, HONORS: Rockefeller grant; John Hay Whitney fellowship.

WRITINGS:

PLAYS

Who's Got His Own (three-act; also see below), first produced Off-Broadway at American Place Theatre, October 12, 1966.
The Warning—A Theme for Linda (one-act; first produced in New York with other plays as *A Black Quartet* at Chelsea Theatre Center, Brooklyn Academy of Music, April 25, 1969), published in *A Black Quartet: Four New Black Plays,* edited by Ben Caldwell and others, New American Library, 1970.
The Monster (one-act; first produced in Chicago at Louis Theatre Center, October, 1969), published in *Drama Review,* Summer, 1968.
M(ego) and the Green Ball of Freedom (one-act; first produced in Detroit at Shango Theatre, 1971), published in *Black World,* April, 1971.

(Editor, author of introduction with Woodie King, Jr., and contributor) *Black Drama Anthology* (includes *Who's Got His Own*), New American Library, 1971.

What the Wine Sellers Buy (first produced in New York at New Federal Theatre, May 17, 1973), Samuel French, 1974.

These Three, first produced in Detroit at Concept East Theater, 1974.

Season's Reasons, first produced in Detroit at Langston Hughes Theatre, 1976.

Work, first produced for Detroit Public Schools, January, 1978.

Jazz-set, first produced in Los Angeles at Mark Taper Forum, 1980.

Crack Steppin', first produced in Detroit at Music Hall, November, 1981.

Checkmates, produced in Los Angeles at Westwood Playhouse, July, 1987.

Don't Get God Started, first produced on Broadway at Longacre Theatre, October, 1987.

Also author of *Life Agony* (one-act), first produced in Detroit at the Unstable Theatre, and *The Greatest Gift,* produced by Detroit Public Schools.

CONTRIBUTOR

Langston Hughes, editor, *Best Short Stories by Negro Writers,* Little, Brown, 1967.

Ahmed Alhamisi and Harun Kofi Wangara, editors, *Black Arts: An Anthology of Black Creations,* Black Arts, 1969.

Donald B. Gibson, editor, *Five Black Writers,* New York University Press, 1970.

Addison Gayle, Jr., editor, *The Black Aesthetic,* Doubleday, 1971.

William R. Robinson, editor, *Nommo: An Anthology of Modern Black African and Black American Literature,* Macmillan, 1972.

Woodie King, Jr., editor, *Black Short Story Anthology,* Columbia University Press, 1972.

Also contributor to *Black Poets and Prophets,* edited by King and Earl Anthony, New American Library.

OTHER

Contributor to *Negro Digest, Drama Review, Black World,* and other periodicals.

SIDELIGHTS: Ron Milner is "a pioneering force in the contemporary Afro-American theater," writes Beunyce Rayford Cunningham in the *Dictionary of*

Literary Biography. Much of his work has involved growing beyond the theatre of the 1960s, where, as Milner told *Detroit News* reporter Bill Gray, "There used to be a lot of screaming and hate. . . . It was reacting to white racism and the themes were defiant directives at the white community. . . ." He continued, "We're no longer dealing with 'I am somebody' but more of who that 'somebody' really is." While not rejecting the revolutionary movements in black theatre, Milner represents a change in approach: a shift from combative performances to quieter dramas that still make a point. Comments Geneva Smitherman in *Black World,* "Those of us who were patient with our writers—as they lingered for what seems like an eternity in the catharsis/screaming stage—applaud this natural change in the course of theatrical events." Adds Cunningham, "Ron Milner's is essentially a theatre of intense, often lyrical, retrospection devoted primarily to illuminating the past events, personalities, and values which have shaped his struggling people."

Milner grew up in Detroit, on Hastings Street, also known as "'The Valley'—with the Muslims on one corner, hustlers and pimps on another, winos on one, and Aretha Franklin singing from her father's church on the other," reports Smitherman. It "was pretty infamous and supposedly criminal," Milner told David Richards of the *Washington Star-News.* But, he continued, "The more I read in high school, the more I realized that some tremendous, phenomenal things were happening around me. What happened in a Faulkner novel happened four times a day on Hastings Street. I thought why should these crazy people Faulkner writes about seem more important than my mother or my father or the dude down the street. Only because they had someone to write about them. So I became a writer."

Milner's work contains the constant appeal for stronger black families and tighter communities. According to Larry Neal in *The Black American Writer,* "Milner's main thrust is directed toward unifying the family around basic moral principles, toward bridging the 'generation gap.'" This has led some critics to label him a "preacher" and his dramas "morality plays." Not daunted by criticism, Milner told Betty DeRamus in the *Detroit Free Press* that art "has to educate as well as entertain. When people call me a preacher, I consider it a compliment. . .when you get an emotional response it's easier to involve the mind." One of Milner's "morality plays" was very successful, both with the critics and with black audiences.

What the Wine-Sellers Buy centers on the tempting of seventeen-year-old Steve by Rico, a pimp. Rico suggests that turning Steve's girlfriend into a prostitute is the easy way to make money. While Steve resists, future trials lay ahead. According to Cunningham, the play contains "many of the elements of Milner's previous family dramas: a young, innocent person forced to make a conscious decision about the direction of his or her life; a mother who retreats into the church; the figure of a male savior—this time a man of the church who befriends the mother and is determined to save her son. What is new here is the Faustian framework in which the menace to be dealt with is the seductions of street life represented by the pimp." "As in all morality plays, good and the power of love" triumph, DeRamus notes, but adds, "what makes *Wine Sellers* different is that the villain, Rico, is no cardboard figure who is easily knocked down. He is, in fact, so persuasive and logical that he seduces audiences as well as Steve." DeRamus reports that Milner patterned Rico after "the typical American businessman," and quotes Milner's comment that when Rico "talks about everything for profit, trading everything for money, he's talking about society. What he says about society is correct, but he is wrong in what he decides to trade. If you trade life, what do you buy?" In Rico, Milner did not create "simply the stereotypical Black pimp," writes Smitherman. "Rather, Rico is the devious Seducer in our lives, moving to and fro, enticing us to compromise our morality, our politics and even our very souls."

Still, the play leaves critics with a positive impression, as it focuses on young Steve triumphing over Rico's corruption. Edwin Wilson in the *Wall Street Journal* applauds the play's outlook: "the emphasis is not on past grievances and injustices, but on the future—on the problems and perils young people face growing up in broken homes and a hostile environment, and their determination to overcome these forces. . . . The play gives further evidence that black playwrights today . . . are determined to find their own way." Much of Milner's energy in the 1970s was directed to defining and establishing a unique black theatre. "American theater was (and still is) the nut that few blacks are able to crack," Milner and his co-editor, Woodie King, Jr., observe in the introduction to *Black Drama Anthology*. They continue that "Black theater is, in fact, about the destruction of tradition, the traditional role of Negroes in white theater. . . . We say that if this theater is to be, it must—psychically, mentally, aesthetically, and physically,—go home." By "going home," Milner and King mean returning to the experiences that have given blacks

their identity. Added Milner to Smitherman, "'Theater' and 'play' have always meant going to see somebody else's culture and seeing how you could translate it into your own terms. People always felt they were going to a foreign place for some foreign reason. But now there's a theater written to them, of them, for them and about them." Milner believes that a local theatre can also help to unify the community. "Theater lifts a community in more ways than one," he said to Smitherman. "The idea of seeing yourself magnified and dramatized on stage gives you a whole perspective on who you are and where you are. You can isolate your emotions and thoughts and bring them to a place and ritualize them in an audience of people who empathize with you." Milner stresses the need for local theatre to communicate something valuable to its audience; he disapproves of creating art only for aesthetic reasons. "Theater for theater's sake is incest," he told Richards. "It gets thinner and thinner each time and drifts off into abstraction. But when it's directly involved in life, even when its badly done, it can cause people to argue, discuss, grow, or at least clarify where they stand. It's true, the aesthetic side can do something for you spiritually. But you can't let that prevent you from communicating on a basic level."

The play that "could thrust [Milner] into the role of the theater's primary chronicler of the contemporary black middle class," is *Checkmates,* writes Don Shirley for the *Los Angeles Times. Checkmates,* produced in 1987, examines the lives of an upwardly mobile couple in their thirties, who are coping with the stresses of marriage, two careers, and urban life. The pair is complemented by their landlords, an older couple with simpler lives, who remember the days when blacks worked in the fields, not offices. The landlords, despite their lack of sophistication, possess a steadiness that the younger, financially successful couple lack. Milner told Shirley, "It's dangerous to identify with [the younger couple], because you can't tell what they might say or do next. They aren't fixed. They can't say, 'These are the values I stand for.' The point of the older couple's lives was to build for the future. Now here is the future, and there are no rules left for the younger couple." Dan Sullivan, also writing for the *Los Angeles Times* enjoys the play's humor: Milner "knows his people so well that an equally big laugh will come on a quite ordinary remark, revealing more about the speaker than he or she realizes." But he also notes the underlying message. "*Checkmates* gives us a specific sense of today's corporate jungle and its particular risks for blacks, however hip, however educated." While

Milner finds the idea of the middle-class "one-dimensional," he is not hostile to the idea of writing to such an audience. "I was never a writer who said the middle class should be lined up against a wall and shot," he told Shirley. As different as it may seem from his previous work, *Checkmates* still falls in with Milner's basic philosophy toward black theatre, as he told Richards: "For a long time, black writers dwelled on our negative history. They could never see any real victory. For them, the only victory lay in the ability to endure defeat. I was consciously trying to break that. I function a great deal on what I intuitively feel are the needs of the time. And the needs of the time are for the positive."

BIOGRAPHICAL/CRITICAL SOURCES:

BOOKS

Alhamisi, Ahmed and Harun Kofi Wangara, editors, *Black Arts: An Anthology of Black Creations,* Black Arts, 1969.
Authors in the News, Volume 1, Gale, 1976.
Bigsby, C.W.E., editor, *The Black American Writer,* Volume II: *Poetry and Drama,* Penguin Books, 1969.
Black Literature Criticism, Gale, 1992.
Contemporary Literary Criticism, Volume 56, Gale, 1989.
Dictionary of Literary Biography, Volume 38: *Afro-American Writers after 1955: Dramatists and Prose Writers,* Gale, 1985.
Hill, Errol, editor, *The Theater of Black Americans,* Volume 1: *Roots and Rituals: The Search for Identity* [and] *The Image Makers: Plays and Playwrights,* Prentice-Hall, 1980.
King, Woodie, Jr., editor, *Black Short Story Anthology,* Columbia University Press, 1972.
King, Woodie, Jr., and Ron Milner, editors, *Black Drama Anthology,* Columbia University Press, 1972.
Robinson, William R., editor, *Nommo: An Anthology of Black African and Black American Literature,* Macmillan, 1972.

PERIODICALS

Black World, April, 1971; April, 1976.
Crisis, January-February, 1967; October, 1967.
Detroit Free Press, January 5, 1975.
Detroit Free Press Magazine, June 24, 1979.
Detroit News, October 20, 1974.
Drama Review, Summer, 1968.

Los Angeles Times, March 19, 1980; September 3, 1986; July 12, 1987; July 20, 1987.
New Yorker, November 9, 1987.
New York Times, July 21, 1982; October 31, 1987; April 23, 1996, p. B3.
New York Times Book Review, August 28, 1994, p. 9.
Publishers Weekly, June 6, 1994, p. 48.
Wall Street Journal, February 21, 1974.
Washington Star-News, January 5, 1975.*

*   *   *

MISS LOU
    See BENNETT, Louise (Simone)

*   *   *

MORRIS, John
    See HEARNE, John (Edgar Caulwell)

*   *   *

MORRISON, Keith 1942-

PERSONAL: Born May 20, 1942, in Jamaica, West Indies. *Ethnicity:* "Jamaican." *Education:* Art Institute of Chicago, M.F.A., 1965; attended University of Illinois, DePaul University, and Loyola University.

ADDRESSES: Home—87 DeHaro Street, San Francisco, CA.

CAREER: Artist and art educator. Art teacher in public schools, Gary, IN, c. 1964; Hyde Park Art Center, Chicago, IL, teacher of art, 1965-67; Fisk University, Nashville, TN, assistant professor of drawing, 1967-68; DePaul University, Chicago, art department chair, 1969-71; College of Art and Architecture, University of Illinois, Chicago, associate professor of printmaking and department chair, 1971-79; University of Maryland, College Park, art department, professor and chair, 1979-92; San Francisco Art Institute, dean of academic affairs, c. 1992-94; San Francisco State University, dean of creative art, 1994—. Among his art works are *Silhouette, The Ocean Is Green at Port Maria, Prevalence of Ritual, Tombstones,* and *Zombie Jamboree.* Selected exhibitions: Sheraton Hotel, Philadelphia, 1968; Art Institute of

Chicago, 1968, 1971; Smith-Mason Gallery, 1971; University of Iowa, 1971-72; 25th Illinois Invitational, 1972; Illinois Bell Telephone, 1972; Corcoran Gallery of Art, 1983; Brody's Gallery, Washington, DC, 1987, 1991; California Afro-American Museum, Los Angeles, 1989; Bronx Museum, 1990; Alternative Museum, New York City, 1990; Cavin- Morris Gallery, New York City, 1992.

AWARDS, HONORS: Prize, Jamaica Institute, 1959; Bicentennial Award Painting, City of Chicago, 1976; International Painting Award, Organization of African Unity, Liberia, 1979; Danforth Association Award.

WRITINGS:

200 Years of Afro-American Women in Art: A Critic's View, Illinois State University, 1980.
Art in Washington and Its Afro-American Presence: 1940- 1970, Washington Project for the Arts (Washington, DC), 1985.
Keith Morrison: Recent Painting, March 10-April 28, 1990, Alternative Museum, New York City, The Museum (New York), 1990.
(With Louis Cohen and Lawrence Manion) *A Guide to Teaching Practice,* Routledge (New York), 1996.

Contributor of art criticism to periodicals, including *New Art Examiner.*

SIDELIGHTS: Creating works of art that show he "was profoundly influenced by African and Caribbean cultures," according to the *Smithsonian,* Keith Morrison has made his mark in the art world as a painter, printmaker, writer, and educator. He is especially known for his figural paintings that depict a variety of motifs from his home country of Jamaica and the African continent, as well as for his extensive use of metaphors and symbols to illuminate various themes. Morrison has also infused his work with influences from Judeo-Christian religions and his own childhood memories.

In his numerous writings, Morrison has asserted that art by African Americans must be assessed in the total cultural context, and cannot be thought of merely as art by blacks in the United States. As he wrote in *African American Visual Aesthetics: A Postmodernist View,* "The search for a definition of African American art opens into the reality of pan-Africanism, a concept arising from the increasing diversity of people of African descent in the United States."

Morrison was born in Jamaica, and remained there until finishing high school. While growing up he heard many voodoo ceremonies, and his recollections of these rituals served as a wellspring for some of his later artworks. "As a child, Keith Morrison drew and painted constantly and dreamed of becoming an artist," wrote Regenia A. Perry in *Free Within Ourselves: African-American Artists in the Collection of the National Museum of American Art.* Morrison hoped to study art in Italy, but his family wanted him to be schooled in England. Morrison applied to a number of art schools in Great Britain and the United States, and his family finally agreed to let him come to the United States when he was 17 so that he could study at the School of the Art Institute of Chicago.

Morrison studied at the Institute between 1959 and 1965, focusing primarily on abstract expressionism. According to Perry, Morrison "was probably most influenced by the hard- edged abstract paintings of Ellsworth Kelly." (Kelly achieved his artistic fame with paintings that featured wide, flat areas of intense color, and he was also a sculptor.) Morrison's first paintings were vast, black-and-white abstractions that received much critical and popular praise. However, "they did not satisfy his inner longing to create paintings that more specifically reflected the rich and colorful culture of his homeland," noted Perry.

After earning both his B.F.A. and M.F.A. degrees, Morrison began his professional career as an art teacher in the public schools of Gary, Indiana. In 1965 he became an art instructor at the Hyde Park Art Center in Chicago. He began teaching at the college level at Fisk University in Nashville in 1967, as an associate professor of drawing. A year later he joined the faculty at DePaul University as an associate professor of printmaking. Continuing to move up the academic ranks, Morrison eventually became a full professor at the University of Maryland in 1979.

While his early paintings appeared to be standard abstract expressionist efforts, to Morrison they symbolized the efforts of African Americans during the civil rights struggles of the 1960s. These paintings reflected the racial problems of the United States, as well as discrimination experienced by Morrison himself as he tried to build his career as an artist. In his writings about art, Morrison has stressed the importance of black unrest in the 1960s as an influence of today's African American art. "A political agenda, created by some artists during the Civil Rights Movement, informs much of today's art," he wrote in *African American Visual Aesthetics* in 1995.

Morrison's *Banana Republic,* a watercolor painted in 1989, provides an artistic history lesson about racial struggle and domination of the poor by the wealthy. In this painting, boxes, banana peels, and other garbage are strewn about "to symbolize the careless plundering, by First World corporations, of Third World countries," according to Howard Risatti in *Artforum.* His 1990 oil/acrylic painting of the same name continued the theme, but added comic elements to imply childish behavior on the part of adults.

In the mid 1970s, Morrison veered away from abstract painting and focused on figural paintings that revealed his interest in African and Caribbean themes. However, the effects of his training were still having their impact on his work as well. "I wrestle with ideological tensions between African and European values in my work as I do as a person," Morrison said in *Smithsonian.* This duality is clearly displayed in his *Zombie Jamboree.* "The painting, in which three large animals are seated in front of a pond at dusk, was inspired by stories about voodoo ceremonies that Morrison heard as a child," according to *Smithsonian.* "But the figure wearing white is based in part on Ophelia, the tragic heroine in *Hamlet,* while ghosts dancing across the water are a reference to Benjamin Britten's opera *The Turn of the Screw.*" Morrison's interest in the blending of cultures is further demonstrated in his large painting entitled *Night in Tunisia,* in which African sculptures are seen in conjunction with Western musical instruments.

Vanitas, a painting in a show of his work at Brody's Gallery in Washington, D.C., in 1991, provides a clear example of Morrison's Caribbean Afro-American cultural influences. It features a green parrot sitting on a red dressing table that is filled with jewelry and cosmetics. The parrot cavorts on top of an orange hand-mirror as it tries to impress a nearby pigeon.

Many of Morrison's artworks have featured symbols of death and resurrection. This focus is based partly on Morrison's memory of the drowning or possible suicide of a friend of his family, an event that had a major impact on the artist. His heightened awareness of social realism has also inspired much of Morrison's work over the years. This consciousness was in particular evidence in the show at Brody's Gallery. In *Tombstones,* referred to by Risatti as "an allegory of sorts about drug use," Morrison depicts four men gyrating around an evil-looking person who is aiming a gun right at the viewer. Tenements around the fig-

ures are shaped like tombstones, and sneakers are strewn about in the front of the picture. The "tombstones" appear almost like teeth, suggesting "the gaping jaws of a monster," according to Risatti. In his overall review of the show, Risatti noted that Morrison's paintings were "timely because of their socially relevant themes, and instructive because of Morrison's reluctance to sacrifice esthetic or philosophical substance in the service of overt polemics."

In 1988 Morrison became chair of the art department at the University of Maryland. He moved on from there to assume the position of dean of academic affairs at the San Francisco Art Institute, then took a position as dean of creative arts at San Francisco State University. Morrison has organized a number of important exhibitions during his career, including ones for the Washington Project for the Arts, the University of Chicago, and the Brandywine Workshop. He is the author of *Art in Washington and Its Afro-American Presence: 1940-1970,* a well-known exhibition catalogue, and has contributed entries to books of art history and art criticism to periodicals such as the *New Art Examiner.*

BOOKS

Cederholm, Theresa Dickason, editor, *Afro-American Artists,* Boston Public Library, 1973, p. 206.
Contemporary Black Biography, Volume 13, Gale (Detroit, MI), 1996.
Driskell, David C., editor, *African American Visual Aesthetics: A Postmodernist View,* Smithsonian Institution Press, 1995, pp. 17-43.
Perry, Regenia A., *Free within Ourselves: African-American Artists in the Collection of the National Museum of American Art,* Pomengranate, 1992, pp. 146-149.

PERIODICALS

Christian Science Monitor, November 30, 1985.
School Library Journal, February, 1995, p. 51.
Smithsonian, November, 1993, p. 148.
Washington Post, September 21, 1991, p. C2.

OTHER

Additional information for this profile was obtained through a National Museum of American Art video, *African American Artists: Affirmation Today (America Past and Present),* Crystal Productions, 1994.

MORRISON, Toni (Chloe) 1931-

PERSONAL: Born Chloe Anthony Wofford, February 18, 1931, in Lorain, OH; daughter of George and Ramah (Willis) Wofford; married Harold Morrison, 1958 (divorced, 1964); children: Harold Ford, Slade Kevin. *Education:* Howard University, B.A., 1953; Cornell University, M.A., 1955.

ADDRESSES: Office—Random House, 201 East 50th St., New York, NY 10022. *Agent*—Lynn Nesbit, International Creative Management, 40 West 57th St., New York, NY 10019.

CAREER: Texas Southern University, Houston, instructor in English, 1955-57; Howard University, Washington, DC, instructor in English, 1957-64; Random House, New York City, senior editor, 1965-85; State University of New York at Purchase, associate professor of English, 1971-72; State University of New York at Albany, Schweitzer Professor of the Humanities, 1984-89; Princeton University, Princeton, NJ, Robert F. Goheen Professor of the Humanities, 1989—. Visiting lecturer, Yale University, 1976-77, and Bard College, 1986-88; Clark Lecturer at Trinity College, Cambridge, and Massey Lecturer at Harvard University, both 1990.

MEMBER: American Academy and Institute of Arts and Letters, National Council on the Arts, Authors Guild (council), Authors League of America.

AWARDS, HONORS: National Book Award nomination and Ohioana Book Award, both 1975, both for *Sula*; National Book Critics Circle Award and American Academy and Institute of Arts and Letters Award, both 1977, both for *Song of Solomon*; New York State Governor's Art Award, 1986; National Book Award nomination and National Book Critics Circle Award nomination, both 1987, and Pulitzer Prize for fiction and Robert F. Kennedy Award, both 1988, all for *Beloved*; Elizabeth Cady Stanton Award from the National Organization of Women; Nobel Prize in Literature, 1993; National Book Foundation Medal for Distinguished Contribution to American Letters, 1996.

WRITINGS:

The Bluest Eye (novel), Holt (New York City), 1969, reprinted, Plume, 1994.
Sula (novel), Knopf (New York City), 1973.
(Editor) *The Black Book* (anthology), Random House (New York City), 1974.

Song of Solomon (novel; Book-of-the-Month Club selection), Knopf, 1977, Curley Large Print, 1994, reprinted, Knopf, 1995.
Tar Baby (novel), Knopf, 1981.
Dreaming Emmett (play), first produced in Albany, New York, January 4, 1986.
Beloved (novel), Knopf, 1987.
Jazz, Knopf, 1992, text adapted by Celeste Bullock with illustrations by Karen Pica, Research & Education, 1996.
Playing in the Dark: Whiteness and the Literary Imagination, Harvard University Press (Cambridge, MA), 1992.
(Editor) *Race-ing Justice, En-Gendering Power: Essays on Anita Hill, Clarence Thomas, and the Construction of Social Reality,* Pantheon (New York City), 1992.
(Editor) *To Die for the People: The Writings of Huey P. Newton,* Writers and Readers, 1995.
(Contributor) *Arguing Immigration: The Debate Over the Changing Face of America,* edited by Nicolaus Mills, Simon & Schuster (New York City), 1994.
(With Taylor-Guthrie and Danille Kathleen) *Conversations with Toni Morrison,* University Press of Mississippi (Jackson), 1994.
(Editor) Toni Cade Bambara, *Deep Sightings and Rescue Missions: Fiction, Essays, and Conversations,* Pantheon, 1996.
The Dancing Mind, Knopf, 1997.
(Editor with Claudia Brodsky Lacour) *Birth of a Nation'Hood: Gaze, Script, and Spectacle in the O.J. Simpson Case,* Pantheon, 1997.
Paradise, Knopf, 1998.
(Editor) James A. Baldwin, *Collected Essays: Notes of a Native Son, Nobody Knows My Name, The Fire Next Time, No Name in the Street, The Devil Finds Work, and Other Essays,* Library of America, 1998.
(Editor) Baldwin, *James Baldwin: Early Novels and Stories,* Library of America, 1998.
(With son Slade Morrison) *The Big Box* (juvenile), illustrated by Giselle Potter, Hyperion/Jump at the Sun, 1999.

Contributor of essays and reviews to numerous periodicals, including *New York Times Magazine.*

SIDELIGHTS: Nobel laureate Toni Morrison has assumed a central role in the American literary canon. Her award-winning novels chronicle small-town African-American life, employing "an artistic vision that encompasses both a private and a national heritage," to quote *Time* magazine contributor Angela Wigan.

Through works such as *The Bluest Eye, Song of Solomon* and *Beloved,* Morrison has earned a reputation as a gifted storyteller whose troubled characters seek to find themselves and their cultural riches in a society that warps or impedes such essential growth. According to Charles Larson in the *Chicago Tribune Book World,* each of Morrison's novels "is as original as anything that has appeared in our literature in the last 20 years. The contemporaneity that unites them—the troubling persistence of racism in America—is infused with an urgency that only a black writer can have about our society." Morrison's artistry has attracted critical acclaim as well as commercial success; *Dictionary of Literary Biography* contributor Susan L. Blake calls the author "an anomaly in two respects" because "she is a black writer who has achieved national prominence and popularity, and she is a popular writer who is taken seriously." Indeed, Morrison has won several of modern literature's most prestigious citations, including the 1977 National Book Critics Circle Award for *Song of Solomon* and the 1988 Pulitzer Prize for *Beloved. Atlantic* correspondent Wilfrid Sheed notes: "Most black writers are privy, like the rest of us, to bits and pieces of the secret, the dark side of their group experience, but Toni Morrison uniquely seems to have all the keys on her chain, like a house detective. . . . She [uses] the run of the whole place, from ghetto to small town to ramshackle farmhouse, to bring back a panorama of black myth and reality that [dazzles] the senses."

"It seems somehow both constricting and inadequate to describe Toni Morrison as the country's preeminent black novelist, since in both gifts and accomplishments she transcends categorization," writes Jonathan Yardley in the *Washington Post Book World,* "yet the characterization is inescapable not merely because it is true but because the very nature of Morrison's work dictates it. Not merely has black American life been the central preoccupation of her . . . novels . . . but as she has matured she has concentrated on distilling all of black experience into her books; quite purposefully, it seems, she is striving not for the particular but for the universal." In her work Morrison strives to lay bare the injustice inherent in the black condition and blacks' efforts, individually and collectively, to transcend society's unjust boundaries. Blake notes that Morrison's novels explore "the difference between black humanity and white cultural values. This opposition produces the negative theme of the seduction and betrayal of black people by white culture . . . and the positive theme of the quest for cultural identity." *Newsweek* contributor Jean Strouse observes: "Like all the best stories, [Morrison's] are driven by an abiding moral vision. Implicit in all her characters' grapplings with who they are is a large sense of human nature and love—and a reach for understanding of something larger than the moment."

Quest for self is a motivating and organizing device in Morrison's fiction, as is the role of family and community in nurturing or challenging the individual. In the *Times Literary Supplement,* Jennifer Uglow suggests that Morrison's novels "explore in particular the process of growing up black, female and poor. Avoiding generalities, Toni Morrison concentrates on the relation between the pressures of the community, patterns established within families, . . .and the developing sense of self." According to Dorothy H. Lee in *Black Women Writers (1950-1980): A Critical Evaluation,* Morrison is preoccupied "with the effect of the community on the individual's achievement and retention of an integrated, acceptable self. In treating this subject, she draws recurrently on myth and legend for story pattern and characters, returning repeatedly to the theory of *quest.* . . . The goals her characters seek to achieve are similar in their deepest implications, and yet the degree to which they attain them varies radically because each novel is cast in unique human terms." In Morrison's books, blacks must confront the notion that all understanding is accompanied by pain, just as all comprehension of national history must include the humiliations of slavery. She tempers this hard lesson by preserving "the richness of communal life against an outer world that denies its value" and by turning to "a heritage of folklore, not only to disclose patterns of living but also to close wounds," in the words of *Nation* contributor Brina Caplan.

Although Morrison herself told the *Chicago Tribune* that there is "epiphany and triumph" in every book she writes, some critics find her work nihilistic and her vision bleak. "The picture given by . . . Morrison of the plight of the decent, aspiring individual in the black family and community is more painful than the gloomiest impressions encouraged by either stereotype or sociology," observes Diane Johnson in the *New York Review of Books.* Johnson continues, "Undoubtedly white society is the ultimate oppressor, and not just of blacks, but, as Morrison [shows,] . . . the black person must first deal with the oppressor in the next room, or in the same bed, or no farther away than across the street." Morrison is a pioneer in the depiction of the hurt inflicted by blacks on blacks; for instance, her characters rarely achieve harmonious relationships but are instead divided by futurelessness and the anguish of stifled existence. Uglow writes:

"We have become attuned to novels . . . which locate oppression in the conflicts of blacks (usually men) trying to make it in a white world. By concentrating on the sense of violation experienced within black neighborhoods, even within families, Toni Morrison deprives us of stock responses and creates a more demanding and uncomfortable literature." *Village Voice* correspondent Vivian Gornick contends that the world Morrison creates "is thick with an atmosphere through which her characters move slowly, in pain, ignorance, and hunger. And to a very large degree Morrison has the compelling ability to make one believe that all of us (Morrison, the characters, the reader) are penetrating that dark and hurtful terrain—the feel of a human life—simultaneously." Uglow concludes that even the laughter of Morrison's characters "disguises pain, deprivation and violation. It is laughter at a series of bad, cruel jokes. . . . Nothing is what it seems; no appearance, no relationship can be trusted to endure."

Other critics detect a deeper undercurrent to Morrison's work that contains just the sort of epiphany for which she strives. "From book to book, Morrison's larger project grows clear," declares Ann Snitow in the *Voice Literary Supplement.* "First, she insists that every character bear the weight of responsibility for his or her own life. After she's measured out each one's private pain, she adds on to that the shared burden of what the whites did. Then, at last, she tries to find the place where her stories can lighten her readers' load, lift them up from their own and others' guilt, carry them to glory. . . . Her characters suffer—from their own limitations and the world's—but their inner life miraculously expands beyond the narrow law of cause and effect." *Harvard Advocate* essayist Faith Davis writes that despite the mundane boundaries of Morrison's characters' lives, the author "illuminates the complexity of their attitudes toward life. Having reached a quiet and extensive understanding of their situation, they can endure life's calamities. . . . Morrison never allows us to become indifferent to these people. . . . Her citizens . . . jump up from the pages vital and strong because she has made us care about the pain in their lives." In *Ms.,* Margo Jefferson concludes that Morrison's books "are filled with loss—lost friendship, lost love, lost customs, lost possibilities. And yet there is so much life in the smallest acts and gestures . . . that they are as much celebrations as elegies."

Morrison sees language as an expression of black experience, and her novels are characterized by vivid narration and dialogue. *Village Voice* essayist Susan

Lydon observes that the author "works her magic charm above all with a love of language. Her soaring . . . style carries you like a river, sweeping doubt and disbelief away, and it is only gradually that one realizes her deadly serious intent." In the *Spectator,* Caroline Moorehead likewise notes that Morrison "writes energetically and richly, using words in a way very much her own. The effect is one of exoticism, an exciting curiousness in the language, a balanced sense of the possible that stops, always, short of the absurd." Although Morrison does not like to be called a poetic writer, critics often comment on the lyrical quality of her prose. "Morrison's style has always moved fluidly between tough-minded realism and lyric descriptiveness," notes Margo Jefferson in *Newsweek.* "Vivid dialogue, capturing the drama and extravagance of black speech, gives way to an impressionistic evocation of physical pain or an ironic, essay-like analysis of the varieties of religious hypocrisy." Uglow writes: "The word 'elegant' is often applied to Toni Morrison's writing; it employs sophisticated narrative devices, shifting perspectives and resonant images and displays an obvious delight in the potential of language." *Nation* contributor Earl Frederick concludes that Morrison, "with an ear as sharp as glass . . . has listened to the music of black talk and deftly uses it as the palette knife to create black lives and to provide some of the best fictional dialogue around today."

According to Jean Strouse, Morrison "comes from a long line of people who did what they had to do to survive. It is their stories she tells in her novels—tales of the suffering and richness, the eloquence and tragedies of the black American experience." Morrison was born Chloe Anthony Wofford in Lorain, Ohio, a small town near the shores of Lake Erie. *New York Review of Books* correspondent Darryl Pinckney describes her particular community as "close enough to the Ohio River for the people who lived [there] to feel the torpor of the South, the nostalgia for its folkways, to sense the old Underground Railroad underfoot like a hidden stream." While never explicitly autobiographical, Morrison's fictions draw upon her youthful experiences in Ohio. In an essay for *Black Women Writers at Work* she claims: "I am from the Midwest so I have a special affection for it. My beginnings are always there. . . . No matter what I write, I begin there. . . . It's the matrix for me. . . . Ohio also offers an escape from stereotyped black settings. It is neither plantation nor ghetto."

Two important aspects of Chloe Wofford's childhood—community spirit and the supernatural—inform

Toni Morrison's mature writing. In a *Publishers Weekly* interview, Morrison suggests ways in which her community influenced her. "There is this town which is both a support system and a hammer at the same time," she notes. ". . . Approval was not the acquisition of things; approval was given for the maturity and the dignity with which one handled oneself. Most black people in particular were, and still are, very fastidious about manners, very careful about behavior and the rules that operate within the community. The sense of organized activity, what I thought at that time was burdensome, turns out now to have within it a gift—which is, I never had to be taught how to hold a job, how to make it work, how to handle my time." On several levels the pariah—a unique and sometimes eccentric individual—figures in Morrison's fictional reconstruction of black community life. "There is always an elder there," she notes of her work in *Black Women Writers: A Critical Evaluation.* "And these ancestors are not just parents, they are sort of timeless people whose relationships to the characters are benevolent, instructive, and protective, and they provide a certain kind of wisdom." Sometimes this figure imparts his or her wisdom from beyond the grave; from an early age Morrison absorbed the folklore and beliefs of a culture for which the supernatural holds power and portent. Strouse notes that Morrison's world, both within and outside her fiction, is "filled with signs, visitations, ways of knowing that [reach] beyond the five senses."

After graduating from high school in Lorain, Morrison attended Howard University, where she earned a degree in English. Morrison then earned a Master's degree in English literature from Cornell. During this period, Morrison met and married her husband, an architect with whom she had two sons. In 1955, Morrison became an English instructor at Texas Southern University. Two years later, she returned to Howard University, teaching English until 1964. It was during her stint at Howard that Morrison first began to write. When her marriage ended in 1964, Morrison moved to New York, where she supported herself and her sons by working as a book editor at Random House. Morrison held this position until 1985, during which time she influenced several prominent black writers.

In the mid-1960s, Morrison completed her first novel, *The Bluest Eye.* Although she had trouble getting the book into print—the manuscript was rejected for publication several times—it was finally published in 1969. Morrison was thirty-eight. Set in Morrison's hometown of Lorain, Ohio, *The Bluest Eye,* portrays

"in poignant terms the tragic condition of blacks in a racist America," to quote Chikwenye Okonjo Ogunyemi in *Critique: Studies in Modern Fiction.* In *The Bluest Eye,* Morrison depicts the onset of black self-hatred as occasioned by white American ideals such as "Dick and Jane" primers and Shirley Temple movies. The principal character, Pecola Breedlove, is literally maddened by the disparity between her existence and the pictures of beauty and gentility disseminated by the dominant white culture. As Phyllis R. Klotman notes in the *Black American Literature Forum,* Morrison "uses the contrast between Shirley Temple and Pecola . . . to underscore the irony of black experience. Whether one learns acceptability from the formal educational experience or from cultural symbols, the effect is the same: self-hatred." Darwin T. Turner elaborates on the novel's intentions in *Black Women Writers: A Critical Evaluation.* Morrison's fictional milieu, writes Turner, is "a world of grotesques—individuals whose psyches have been deformed by their efforts to assume false identities, their failures to achieve meaningful identities, or simply their inability to retain and communicate love."

Blake characterizes *The Bluest Eye* as a novel of initiation, exploring that common theme in American literature from a minority viewpoint. Ogunyemi likewise contends that, in essence, Morrison presents "old problems in a fresh language and with a fresh perspective. A central force of the work derives from her power to draw vignettes and her ability to portray emotions, seeing the world through the eyes of adolescent girls." Klotman, who calls the book "a novel of growing up, of growing up young and black and female in America," concludes her review with the comment that the "rite of passage, initiating the young into womanhood at first tenuous and uncertain, is sensitively depicted. . . . *The Bluest Eye* is an extraordinarily passionate yet gentle work, the language lyrical yet precise—it is a novel for all seasons."

In *Sula,* Morrison's 1973 novel, the author once again presents a pair of black women who must come to terms with their lives. Set in a Midwestern black community called The Bottom, the story follows two friends, Sula and Nel, from childhood to old age and death. Snitow claims that through Sula, Morrison has discovered "a way to offer her people an insight and sense of recovered self so dignified and glowing that no worldly pain could dull the final light." Indeed, *Sula* is a tale of rebel and conformist in which the conformity is dictated by the solid inhabitants of The

Bottom and even the rebellion gains strength from the community's disapproval. *New York Times Book Review* contributor Sara Blackburn contends, however, that the book is "too vital and rich" to be consigned to the category of allegory. Morrison's "extravagantly beautiful, doomed characters are locked in a world where hope for the future is a foreign commodity, yet they are enormously, achingly alive," writes Blackburn. "And this book about them—and about how their beauty is drained back and frozen—is a howl of love and rage, playful and funny as well as hard and bitter." In the words of *American Literature* essayist Jane S. Bakerman, Morrison "uses the maturation story of Sula and Nel as the core of a host of other stories, but it is the chief unification device for the novel and achieves its own unity, again, through the clever manipulation of the themes of sex, race, and love. Morrison has undertaken a . . . difficult task in *Sula*. Unquestionably, she has succeeded."

Other critics have echoed Bakerman's sentiments about *Sula*. Yardley declares: "What gives this terse, imaginative novel its genuine distinction is the quality of Toni Morrison's prose. *Sula* is admirable enough as a study of its title character, . . . but its real strength lies in Morrison's writing, which at times has the resonance of poetry and is precise, vivid and controlled throughout." Turner also claims that in *Sula* "Morrison evokes her verbal magic occasionally by lyric descriptions that carry the reader deep into the soul of the character. . . . Equally effective, however, is her art of narrating action in a lean prose that uses adjectives cautiously while creating memorable vivid images." In her review, Davis concludes that a "beautiful and haunting atmosphere emerges out of the wreck of these folks' lives, a quality that is absolutely convincing and absolutely precise." *Sula* was nominated for a National Book Award in 1974.

From the insular lives she depicted in her first two novels, Morrison moved in *Song of Solomon* to a national and historical perspective on black American life. "Here the depths of the younger work are still evident," contends Reynolds Price in the *New York Times Book Review,* "but now they thrust outward, into wider fields, for longer intervals, encompassing many more lives. The result is a long prose tale that surveys nearly a century of American history as it impinges upon a single family." With an intermixture of the fantastic and the realistic, *Song of Solomon* relates the journey of a character named Milkman Dead into an understanding of his family heritage and hence, himself. Lee writes: "Figuratively, [Milkman] travels from innocence to awareness, i.e., from igno-

rance of origins, heritage, identity, and communal responsibility to knowledge and acceptance. He moves from selfish and materialistic dilettantism to an understanding of brotherhood. With his release of personal ego, he is able to find a place in the whole. There is, then, a universal—indeed mythic—pattern here. He journeys from spiritual death to rebirth, a direction symbolized by his discovery of the secret power of flight. Mythically, liberation and transcendence follow the discovery of self." Blake suggests that the connection Milkman discovers with his family's past helps him to connect meaningfully with his contemporaries; *Song of Solomon,* Blake notes, "dramatizes dialectical approaches to the challenges of black life." According to Anne Z. Mickelson in *Reaching Out: Sensitivity and Order in Recent American Fiction by Women,* history itself "becomes a choral symphony to Milkman, in which each individual voice has a chance to speak and contribute to his growing sense of well-being."

Mickelson also observes that *Song of Solomon* represents for blacks "a break out of the confining life into the realm of possibility." Charles Larson comments on this theme in a *Washington Post Book World* review. The novel's subject matter, Larson explains, is "the origins of black consciousness in America, and the individual's relationship to that heritage." However, Larson adds, "skilled writer that she is, Morrison has transcended this theme so that the reader rarely feels that this is simply another novel about ethnic identity. So marvelously orchestrated is Morrison's narrative that it not only excels on all of its respective levels, not only works for all of its interlocking components, but also—in the end—says something about life (and death) for all of us. Milkman's epic journey . . . is a profound examination of the individual's understanding of, and, perhaps, even transcendence of the inevitable fate of his life." Gornick concludes: "There are so many individual moments of power and beauty in *Song of Solomon* that, ultimately, one closes the book warmed through by the richness of its sympathy, and by its breathtaking feel for the nature of sexual sorrow."

Song of Solomon won the National Book Critics Circle Award in 1977. It was also the first novel by a black writer to become a Book-of-the-Month Club selection since Richard Wright's *Native Son* was published in 1940. *World Literature Today* reviewer Richard K. Barksdale calls the work "a book that will not only withstand the test of time but endure a second and third reading by those conscientious readers who love a well-wrought piece of fiction." Describing the novel as "a stunningly beautiful book" in her *Washington Post Book World* piece, Anne Tyler adds: "I would call the book poetry, but that would seem to be denying its considerable power as a story. Whatever name you give it, it's full of magnificent people, each of them complex and multilayered, even the narrowest of them narrow in extravagant ways." Price deems *Song of Solomon* "a long story, . . . and better than good. Toni Morrison has earned attention and praise. Few Americans know, and can say, more than she has in this wise and spacious novel."

Morrison's 1981 book *Tar Baby* remained on bestseller lists for four months. A novel of ideas, the work dramatizes the fact that complexion is a far more subtle issue than the simple polarization of black and white. Set on a lush Caribbean Island, *Tar Baby* explores the passionate love affair of Jadine, a Sorbonne-educated black model, and Son, a handsome knockabout with a strong aversion to white culture. According to Caplan, Morrison's concerns "are race, class, culture and the effects of late capitalism—heavy freight for any narrative. . . . She is attempting to stabilize complex visions of society—that is, to examine competitive ideas. . . . Because the primary function of Morrison's characters is to voice representative opinions, they arrive on stage vocal and highly conscious, their histories symbolically indicated or merely sketched. Her brief sketches, however, are clearly the work of an artist who can, when she chooses, model the mind in depth and detail." In a *Dictionary of Literary Biography Yearbook* essay, Elizabeth B. House outlines *Tar Baby*'s major themes; namely, "the difficulty of settling conflicting claims between one's past and present and the destruction which abuse of power can bring. As Morrison examines these problems in *Tar Baby,* she suggests no easy way to understand what one's link to a heritage should be, nor does she offer infallible methods for dealing with power. Rather, with an astonishing insight and grace, she demonstrates the pervasiveness of such dilemmas and the degree to which they affect human beings, both black and white."

Tar Baby uncovers racial and sexual conflicts without offering solutions, but most critics agree that Morrison indicts all of her characters—black and white—for their thoughtless devaluations of others. *New York Times Book Review* correspondent John Irving claims: "What's so powerful, and subtle, about Miss Morrison's presentation of the tension between blacks and whites is that she conveys it almost entirely through the suspicions and prejudices of her black characters. . . . Miss Morrison uncovers all the stereotypical racial fears felt by whites and blacks alike. Like any ambitious writer, she's unafraid to employ these stereotypes—she embraces the representative qualities of her characters without embarrassment, then proceeds to make them individuals too." *New Yorker* essayist Susan Lardner praises Morrison for her "power to be absolutely persuasive against her own preferences, suspicions, and convictions, implied or plainly expressed," and Strouse likewise contends that the author "has produced that rare commodity, a truly public novel about the condition of society, examining the relations between blacks and whites, men and women, civilization and nature. . . . It wraps its messages in a highly potent love story." Irving suggests that Morrison's greatest accomplishment "is that she has raised her novel above the social realism that too many black novels and women's novels are trapped in. She has succeeded in writing about race and women symbolically."

Reviewers have praised *Tar Baby* for its provocative themes and for its evocative narration. *Los Angeles Times* contributor Elaine Kendall calls the book "an intricate and sophisticated novel, moving from a realistic and orderly beginning to a mystical and ambiguous end. Morrison has taken classically simple story elements and realigned them so artfully that we perceive the old pattern in a startlingly different way. Although this territory has been explored by dozens of novelists, Morrison depicts it with such vitality that it seems newly discovered." In the *Washington Post Book World,* Webster Schott claims: "There is so much that is good, sometimes dazzling, about *Tar Baby*—poetic language, . . . arresting images, fierce intelligence—that . . . one becomes entranced by Toni Morrison's story. The settings are so vivid the characters must be alive. The emotions they feel are so intense they must be real people." Maureen Howard states in *New Republic* that the work "is as carefully patterned as a well-written poem. . . . *Tar Baby* is a good American novel in which we can discern a new lightness and brilliance in Toni Morrison's enchantment with language and in her curiously polyphonic stories that echo life." Schott concludes: "One of fiction's pleasures is to have your mind scratched and your intellectual habits challenged. While *Tar Baby* has shortcomings, lack of provocation isn't one of them. Morrison owns a powerful intelligence. It's run by courage. She calls to account conventional wisdom and accepted attitude at nearly every turn."

In addition to her own writing, Morrison during this period was helping to publish the work of other noted black Americans, including Toni Cade Bambara,

Gayle Jones, Angela Davis, and Muhammed Ali. Discussing her aims as an editor in a quotation printed in the *Dictionary of Literary Biography,* Morrison told *CA:* "I look very hard for black fiction because I want to participate in developing a canon of black work. We've had the first rush of black entertainment, where blacks were writing for whites, and whites were encouraging this kind of self-flagellation. Now we can get down to the craft of writing, where black people are talking to black people." One of Morrison's important projects for Random House was *The Black Book,* an anthology of items that illustrate the history of black Americans. *Ms.* magazine correspondent Dorothy Eugenia Robinson describes the work: "*The Black Book* is the pain and pride of rediscovering the collective black experience. It is finding the essence of ourselves and holding on. *The Black Book* is a kind of scrapbook of patiently assembled samplings of black history and culture. What has evolved is a pictorial folk journey of black people, places, events, handcrafts, inventions, songs, and folklore. . . . *The Black Book* informs, disturbs, maybe even shocks. It unsettles complacency and demands confrontation with raw reality. It is by no means an easy book to experience, but it's a necessary one."

While preparing *The Black Book* for publication, Morrison uncovered the true and shocking story of a runaway slave who, at the point of recapture, murdered her infant child so it would not be doomed to a lifetime of slavery. For Morrison the story encapsulated the fierce psychic cruelty of an institutionalized system that sought to destroy the basic emotional bonds between men and women, and worse, between parent and child. "I certainly thought I knew as much about slavery as anybody," Morrison told the *Los Angeles Times.* "But it was the interior life I needed to find out about." It is this "interior life" in the throes of slavery that constitutes the theme of Morrison's Pulitzer Prize-winning novel *Beloved.* Set in Reconstruction-era Cincinnati, the book centers on characters who struggle fruitlessly to keep their painful recollections of the past at bay. They are haunted, both physically and spiritually, by the legacies slavery has bequeathed to them. According to Snitow, *Beloved* "staggers under the terror of its material—as so much holocaust writing does and must."

Many critics consider *Beloved* to be Morrison's masterpiece. In *People* magazine, V. R. Peterson describes the novel as "a brutally powerful, mesmerizing story about the inescapable, excruciating legacy of slavery. Behind each new event and each new charac-

ter lies another event and another story until finally the reader meets a community of proud, daring people, inextricably bound by culture and experience." Through the lives of ex-slaves Sethe and her would-be lover Paul D., readers "experience American slavery as it was lived by those who were its objects of exchange, both at its best—which wasn't very good—and at its worst, which was as bad as can be imagined," writes Margaret Atwood in the *New York Times Book Review.* "Above all, it is seen as one of the most viciously antifamily institutions human beings have ever devised. The slaves are motherless, fatherless, deprived of their mates, their children, their kin. It is a world in which people suddenly vanish and are never seen again, not through accident or covert operation or terrorism, but as a matter of everyday legal policy." *New York Times* columnist Michiko Kakutani contends that *Beloved* "possesses the heightened power and resonance of myth—its characters, like those in opera or Greek drama, seem larger than life and their actions, too, tend to strike us as enactments of ancient rituals and passions. To describe *Beloved* only in these terms, however, is to diminish its immediacy, for the novel also remains precisely grounded in American reality—the reality of Black history as experienced in the wake of the Civil War."

Acclaim for *Beloved* has come from both sides of the Atlantic. In his *Chicago Tribune* piece, Larson claims that the work "is the context out of which all of Morrison's earlier novels were written. In her darkest and most probing novel, Toni Morrison has demonstrated once again the stunning powers that place her in the first ranks of our living novelists." *Los Angeles Times Book Review* contributor John Leonard likewise expresses the opinion that the novel "belongs on the highest shelf of American literature, even if half a dozen canonized white boys have to be elbowed off. . . . Without *Beloved* our imagination of the nation's self has a hole in it big enough to die from." Atwood states: "Ms. Morrison's versatility and technical and emotional range appear to know no bounds. If there were any doubts about her stature as a preeminent American novelist, of her own or any other generation, *Beloved* will put them to rest." London *Times* reviewer Nicholas Shakespeare concludes that *Beloved* "is a novel propelled by the cadences of . . . songs—the first singing of a people hardened by their suffering, people who have been hanged and whipped and mortgaged at the hands of white people—the men without skin. From Toni Morrison's pen it is a sound that breaks the back of words, making *Beloved* a great novel."

Morrison's subsequent novel, *Jazz,* is "a fictive re-creation of two parallel narratives set during major historical events in African-American history-Reconstruction and the Jazz Age," notes *Dictionary of Literary Biography* writer Denise Heinze. Set primarily in New York City during the 1920s, the novel's main narrative involves a love triangle between Violet, a middle-aged woman; Joe, her husband; and Dorcas, Joe's teenage mistress. When Dorcas snubs Joe for a younger lover, Joe shoots and kills Dorcas. Alice seeks to understand the dead girl by befriending Dorcas's aunt, Alice Manfred. Simultaneously, Morrison relates the story of Joe and Violet's parents and grandparents. In telling these stories, Morrison touches on a number of themes: "male/female passion," as Heinze comments; the movement of blacks into large urban areas after Reconstruction; and, as is usually the case with her novels, the effects of racism and history on the African-American community. Morrison also makes use of an unusual storytelling device: an unnamed, intrusive, and unreliable narrator.

"The standard set by the brilliance and intensity of Morrison's previous novel *Beloved* is so high that *Jazz* does not pretend to come close to attaining it," states *Kenyon Review* contributor Peter Erickson. Nevertheless, many reviewers responded enthusiastically to the provocative themes Morrison presents in *Jazz.* "The unrelenting, destructive influence of racism and oppression on the black family is manifested in *Jazz* by the almost-total absence of the black family," declares Heinze. Writing in the *New York Review of Books,* Michael Wood remarks that "black women in *Jazz* are arming themselves, physically and mentally, and in this they have caught a current of the times, a not always visible indignation that says enough is enough." Several reviewers felt that Morrison's use of an unreliable narrator impeded the story's effectiveness. Erickson, for instance, avers that the narrator "is not inventive enough. Because the narrator displays a lack of imagination at crucial moments, she seems to get in the way, to block rather than to enable access to deeper levels." But Heinze states that Morrison's unreliable narrator allows the author to engage the reader in a way that she has not done in her previous novels: "in *Jazz* Morrison questions her ability to answer the very issues she raises, extending the responsibility of her own novel writing to her readers." Heinze concludes: "Morrison thereby sends an invitation to her readers to become a part of that struggle to comprehend totality that will continue to spur her genius."

Morrison's "genius" was recognized a year after the publication of *Jazz* with a momentous award: the Nobel Prize for Literature. The first black and only the eighth woman to win the award, Morrison told Claudia Dreifus of the *New York Times Magazine* that "it was as if the whole category of 'female writer' and 'black writer' had been redeemed. I felt I represented a whole world of women who either were silenced or who had never received the imprimatur of the established literary world." In describing the author after its selection, the Nobel Committee noted, as quoted by Heinze: "She delves into the language itself, a language she wants to liberate from the fetters of race. And she addresses us with the luster of poetry." In 1996 Morrison received another prestigious award, the National Book Foundation Medal for Distinguished Contribution to American Letters. The author's address upon receiving that award was published as *The Dancing Mind.*

In addition to her acclaimed fiction, Morrison has also published nonfiction works. *Playing in the Dark: Whiteness and the Literary Imagination* is a collection of three lectures that Morrison gave at Harvard University in 1990. Focusing on racism as it has manifested itself in American literature, these essays of literary criticism explore the works of authors such as Willa Cather, Mark Twain, and Ernest Hemingway. In 1992 Morrison edited *Race-ing Justice, En-Gendering Power: Essays on Anita Hill, Clarence Thomas, and the Construction of Social Reality,* a collection of eighteen essays about Thomas's controversial nomination to the U.S. Supreme Court.

It is Morrison's fiction, however, that has secured her place among the literary elite. Morrison is an author who labors contentedly under the labels bestowed by pigeonholing critics. She has no objection to being called a black woman writer, because, as she told the *New York Times,* "I really think the range of emotions and perceptions I have had access to as a black person and a female person are greater than those of people who are neither. . . . My world did not shrink because I was a black female writer. It just got bigger." Nor does she strive for that much-vaunted universality that purports to be a hallmark of fine fiction. "I never asked Tolstoy to write for me, a little colored girl in Lorain, Ohio," she told the *New Republic.* "I never asked [James] Joyce not to mention Catholicism or the world of Dublin. Never. And I don't know why I should be asked to explain your life to you. We have splendid writers to do that, but I am not one of them. It is that business of being universal, a word hopelessly stripped of meaning for me. [William] Faulkner wrote what I suppose could be called regional literature and had it published all over the world. That's what I wish to do. If I tried to write a universal novel, it would be water. Behind this question is the suggestion that to write for black people is somehow to diminish the writing. From my perspective there are only black people. When I say 'people,' that's what I mean.''

Black woman writer or simply American novelist, Toni Morrison is a prominent and respected figure in modern letters. In the *Detroit News,* Larson suggests that hers has been "among the most exciting literary careers of the last decade" and that each of her books "has made a quantum jump forward." Ironically, Elizabeth House commends Morrison for the universal nature of her work. "Unquestionably," House writes, "Toni Morrison is an important novelist who continues to develop her talent. Part of her appeal, of course, lies in her extraordinary ability to create beautiful language and striking characters. However, Morrison's most important gift, the one which gives her a major author's universality, is the insight with which she writes of problems all humans face. . . . At the core of all her novels is a penetrating view of the unyielding, heartbreaking dilemmas which torment people of all races." Snitow notes that the author "wants to tend the imagination, search for an expansion of the possible, nurture a spiritual richness in the black tradition even after 300 years in the white desert." Dorothy Lee concludes of Morrison's accomplishments: "Though there are unifying aspects in her novels, there is not a dully repetitive sameness. Each casts the problems in specific, imaginative terms, and the exquisite, poetic language awakens our senses as she communicates an often ironic vision with moving imagery. Each novel reveals the acuity of her perception of psychological motivation of the female especially, of the Black particularly, and of the human generally."

"The problem I face as a writer is to make my stories mean something," Morrison states in *Black Women Writers at Work.* "You can have wonderful, interesting people, a fascinating story, but it's not about anything. It has no real substance. I want my books to always be about something that is important to me, and the subjects that are important in the world are the same ones that have always been important." In *Black Women Writers: A Critical Evaluation,* she elaborates on this idea. Fiction, she writes, "should be beautiful, and powerful, but it should also work. It should have something in it that enlightens; something in it that opens the door and points the way. Something in it that suggests what the conflicts are, what the problems are. But it need not solve those problems because it is not a case study, it is not a recipe." The author who has said that writing "is discovery;

it's talking deep within myself" told the *New York Times Book Review* that the essential theme in her growing body of fiction is "how and why we learn to live this life intensely and well."

In *Paradise,* Morrison's first novel since winning the Nobel Prize for literature in 1993, notes *America* contributor Hermine Pinson, "the writer appears to be reinterpreting some of her most familiar themes: the significance of the 'ancestor' in our lives, the importance of community, the concept of 'home' and the continuing conundrum of race in the United States. The title and intended subject of the text—Paradise—accommodates all of the foregoing themes." "Like *Beloved* . . . *Paradise* centers on a catastrophic act of violence that begs to be understood," *National Catholic Reporter* contributor Judith Bromberg explains. "Morrison meticulously peels away layer upon layer of truth so that what we think we know, we don't until she finally confronts us with raw truth." The conflict, and the violence that results from it, comes out of the dedicated self-righteousness of the leading families of the all-black town of Ruby, Oklahoma. "The story begins in Oklahoma in 1976," Pinson explains, "when nine men from the still all-black town of Ruby invade the local convent on a mission to keep the town safe from the outright evil and depravity that they believe is embodied in the disparate assembly of religious women who live there." "In a show of force a posse of nine descend on the crumbling mansion in the predawn of a summer morning, killing all four of the troubled, flawed women who have sought refuge there," Bromberg states.

Reviewers recognized Morrison's accomplishment in *Paradise.* "*Paradise* is full of challenges and surprises," said *Catholic Century* reviewer Reggie Young. "Though it does not quite come up to the standard of Morrison's masterwork, *Beloved,* this is one of the most important novels of the decade." "This is Morrison's first novel since her 1993 *Jazz,*" wrote Emily J. Jones in *Library Journal,* "and it is well worth the wait." "With *Paradise,*" stated Pinson, "Morrison casts the novel as postmodern Scripture and challenges our most dearly held beliefs and prejudices about ourselves and the world 'out there.'"

BIOGRAPHICAL/CRITICAL SOURCES:

BOOKS

Awkward, Michael, *Inspiriting Influences: Tradition, Revision, and Afro-American Women's Novels,* Columbia University Press, 1989.

Bell, Roseann P., editor, *Sturdy Black Bridges: Visions of Black Women in Literature,* Doubleday, 1979.

Black Literature Criticism, Volume 2, Gale, 1992.

Century, Douglas, *Toni Morrison,* Chelsea House, 1994.

Christian, Barbara, *Black Women Novelists: The Development of a Tradition, 1892-1976,* Greenwood Press, 1980.

Contemporary Literary Criticism, Gale, Volume 4, 1975; Volume 10, 1979; Volume 22, 1982; Volume 55, 1989; Volume 81, 1994, Volume 87, 1995.

Cooey, Paula M., *Religious Imagination and the Body: A Feminist Analysis,* Oxford, 1994.

Cooper-Clark, Diana, *Interviews with Contemporary Novelists,* St. Martin's, 1986.

Coser, Stelamaris, *Bridging the Americas: The Literature of Paule Marshall, Toni Morrison, and Gayl Jones,* Temple University Press, 1995.

Dictionary of Literary Biography, Gale, Volume 6: *American Novelists since World War II,* 1980; Volume 33: *Afro-American Fiction Writers after 1955,* 1984; Volume 143: *American Novelists since World War II, Third Series,* 1994.

Dictionary of Literary Biography Yearbook: 1981, Gale, 1982.

Evans, Mari, editor, *Black Women Writers (1950-1980): A Critical Evaluation,* Doubleday, 1984.

Furman, Jan, *Toni Morrison's Fiction,* University of South Carolina Press, 1996.

Harding, Wendy, and Jacky Martin, *A World of Difference: An Inter-Cultural Study of Toni Morrison's Novels,* Greenwood Press, 1994.

Harris, Trudier, *Fiction and Folklore: The Novels of Toni Morrison,* University of Tennessee Press, 1991.

Heinze, Denise, *The Dilemma of "Double-Consciousness": Toni Morrison's Novels,* University of Georgia Press, 1993.

Holloway, Karla, and Dematrakopoulos, Stephanie, *New Dimensions of Spirituality: A Biracial and Bicultural Reading of the Novels of Toni Morrison,* Greenwood Press, 1987.

Jones, Bessie W. and Vinson, Audrey L., editors, *The World of Toni Morrison: Explorations in Literary Criticism,* Kendall/Hunt, 1985.

Kramer, Barbara, *Toni Morrison, Nobel Prize-Winning Author,* Enslow, 1996.

Ledbetter, Mark, *Victims and the Postmodern Narrative; or, Doing Violence to the Body: An Ethic of Reading and Writing,* St. Martin's, 1996.

McKay, Nellie, editor, *Critical Essays on Toni Morrison,* G.K. Hall, 1988.

Mekkawi, Mod, *Toni Morrison: A Bibliography,* Howard University Library, 1986.

Mickelson, Anne Z., *Reaching Out: Sensitivity and Order in Recent American Fiction by Women,* Scarecrow Press, 1979.

Otten, Terry, *The Crime of Innocence in the Fiction of Toni Morrison,* University of Missouri Press, 1989.

Page, Philip, *Dangerous Freedom: Fusion and Fragmentation in Toni Morrison's Novels,* University Press of Mississippi, 1996.

Peach, Linden, *Toni Morrison,* St. Martin's Press, 1995.

Rainwater, Catherine and Scheick, William J., editors, *Contemporary American Women Writers: Narrative Strategies,* University Press of Kentucky, 1985, pp. 205-07.

Rice, Herbert William, *Toni Morrison and the American Tradition: A Rhetorical Reading,* P. Lang, 1995.

Ruas, Charles, *Conversations with American Writers,* Knopf, 1985.

Smith, Valerie, editor, *New Essays on Song of Solomon,* Cambridge University Press, 1995.

Tate, Claudia, editor, *Black Women Writers at Work,* Continuum, 1986, pp. 117-31.

Taylor-Guthrie, Danille, editor, *Conversations with Toni Morrison,* University Press of Mississippi, 1994.

Weinstein, Philip M., *What Else but Love?: The Ordeal of Race in Faulkner and Morrison,* Columbia University Press, 1996.

Willis, Susan, *Specifying: Black Women Writing the American Experience,* University of Wisconsin Press, 1987.

PERIODICALS

African American Review, summer, 1994, pp. 189, 223; fall, 1994, p. 423; winter, 1994, pp. 571, 659; spring, 1995, p. 55; winter, 1995, pp. 567, 605; spring, 1996, p. 89.

America, August 15, 1998, p. 19.

American Historical Review, February, 1994, p. 327.

American Imago, winter, 1994, p. 421.

American Literature, March, 1980, pp. 87-100; January, 1981; May, 1984; May, 1986.

Atlantic, April, 1981.

Black American Literature Forum, summer, 1978; winter, 1979; winter, 1987.

Black Scholar, March, 1978.

Black World, June, 1974.

Callaloo, October-February, 1981.

Centennial Review, winter, 1988, pp. 50-64.

Chicago Tribune, October 27, 1987.

Chicago Tribune Books, August 30, 1988.

Chicago Tribune Book World, March 8, 1981.

Christian Century, March 18, 1998, p. 322.

CLA Journal, June, 1979, pp. 402-14; June, 1981, pp. 419-40; September, 1989, pp. 81-93.

Commentary, August, 1981.

Contemporary Literature, winter, 1983, pp. 413-29; fall, 1987, pp. 364-77.

Critique, Volume 19, Number 1, 1977, pp. 112-20.

Detroit News, March 29, 1981.

Economist, June 6,1998, p. 83.

Essence, July, 1981; June, 1983; October, 1987; May, 1995, p. 222.

First World, winter, 1977.

Harper's Bazaar, March, 1983.

Harvard Advocate, Volume 107, number 4, 1974.

Hudson Review, spring, 1978.

Jet, February 12, 1996, p. 4.

Kenyon Review, summer, 1993, p. 197.

Library Journal, February 15, 1998, p. 172.

Los Angeles Times, March 31, 1981; October 14, 1987.

Los Angeles Times Book Review, August 30, 1987.

Massachusetts Review, autumn, 1977.

MELUS, fall, 1980, pp. 69-82.

Minority Voices, fall, 1980, pp. 51-63; spring-fall, 1981, pp. 59-68.

Modern Fiction Studies, spring, 1988.

Ms., June, 1974; December, 1974; August, 1987.

Nation, July 6, 1974; November 19, 1977; May 2, 1981; January 17, 1994, p. 59.

National Catholic Reporter, May 22, 1998, p. 35.

New Republic, December 3, 1977; March 21, 1981; March 27, 1995, p. 9.

New Statesman, May 22, 1998, p. 56.

Newsweek, November 30, 1970; January 7, 1974; September 12, 1977; March 30, 1981.

New York, April 13, 1981.

New Yorker, November 7, 1977; June 15, 1981.

New York Post, January 26, 1974.

New York Review of Books, November 10, 1977; April 30, 1981; November 19, 1992, p. 7; February 2, 1995, p. 36.

New York Times, November 13, 1970; September 6, 1977; March 21, 1981; August 26, 1987; September 2, 1987.

New York Times Book Review, November 1, 1970; December 30, 1973; June 2, 1974; September 11, 1977; March 29, 1981; September 13, 1987; October 25, 1992, p. 1.

New York Times Magazine, August 22, 1971; August 11, 1974; July 4, 1976; May 20, 1979; September 11, 1994, p. 73.

Obsidian, spring/summer, 1979; winter, 1986, pp. 151-61.

People, July 29, 1974; November 30, 1987; May 18, 1998, p. 45.

Perspectives on Contemporary Literature, 1982, pp. 10-7.

Philadelphia Inquirer, April 1, 1988.

Publishers Weekly, August 21, 1987; March 2, 1998, p. 29; July 12, 1999, p. 95.

Saturday Review, September 17, 1977.

Southern Review, autumn, 1987.

Spectator, December 9, 1978; February 2, 1980; December 19, 1981.

Studies in American Fiction, spring, 1987; autumn, 1989.

Studies in Black Literature, Volume 6, 1976.

Time, September 12, 1977; March 16, 1981; September 21, 1987; June 17, 1996, p. 73.

Times (London), October 15, 1987.

Times Literary Supplement, October 4, 1974; November 24, 1978; February 8, 1980; December 19, 1980; October 30, 1981; October 16-22, 1987; March 5, 1993.

U.S. News and World Report, October 19, 1987.

Village Voice, August 29, 1977; July 1-7, 1981.

Vogue, April, 1981; January, 1986.

Voice Literary Supplement, September, 1987; December, 1992, p. 15.

Washington Post, February 3, 1974; March 6, 1974; September 30, 1977; April 8, 1981; February 9, 1983; October 5, 1987.

Washington Post Book World, February 3, 1974; September 4, 1977; December 4, 1977; March 22, 1981; September 6, 1987; November 8, 1992, p. 3.

Women's Review of Books, December, 1992, p. 1.

World Literature Today, summer, 1978; spring, 1993, p. 394.

*   *   *

MOSS, Thylias (Rebecca Brasier) 1954-

PERSONAL: Born February 27, 1954, in Cleveland, OH; daughter of a recapper for the Cardinal Tire Company and a maid; married John Lewis Moss (a business manager), July 6, 1973; children: Dennis, Ansted. *Education:* Attended Syracuse University, 1971-73; Oberlin College, B.A., 1981; University of New Hampshire, M.A., 1983.

ADDRESSES: Office—P.O. Box 2686, Ann Arbor, MI 48106. *Agent*—Faith Hamlin, Sanford J. Greenburger Associates, 55 Fifth Ave., New York, NY 10003. *E-mail*—thyliasm@umich.edu.

CAREER: Poet and educator. The May Company, Cleveland, OH, order checker, 1973-74, junior executive auditor, 1975-79, data entry supervisor, 1974-75; Phillips Academy, Andover, MA, instructor, 1984-92; University of Michigan, Ann Arbor, assistant professor, 1993-94, associate professor, 1994-98, professor, 1998—. University of New Hampshire, Durham, visiting professor, 1991-92; Brandeis University, Waltham, MA, Fannie Hurst Poet, 1992.

MEMBER: Academy of American Poets.

AWARDS, HONORS: Cleveland Public Library Poetry Contest, 1978, for "Coming of Age in Sandusky"; four grants, Kenan Charitable Trust, 1984-87; artist's fellowship, Artist's Foundation of Massachusetts, 1987; National Endowment for the Arts grant, 1989; Pushcart Prize, 1990; Dewar's Profiles Performance Artist Award in Poetry, 1991; Witter Bynner Prize, American Academy and Institute of Arts and Letters, 1991; Whiting Writer's award, 1991; Guggenheim fellowship, 1995; MacArthur fellowship, 1996.

WRITINGS:

POETRY

Hosiery Seams on a Bowlegged Woman, Cleveland State University Press (Cleveland, OH), 1983.
Pyramid of Bone, University of Virginia Press (Charlottesville, VA), 1989.
At Redbones, Cleveland State University Press (Cleveland, OH), 1990.
Rainbow Remnants in Rock Bottom Ghetto Sky, Persea (New York City), 1991.
Small Congregations: New and Selected Poems, Ecco Press (Hopewell, NJ), 1993.
Last Chance for the Tarzan Holler: Poems, Persea (New York City), 1997.

OTHER

The Dolls in the Basement (play), produced by New England Theatre Conference, 1984.
Talking to Myself (play), produced in Durham, NH, 1984.
I Want to Be (for children), illustrated by Jerry Pinkney, Dial (New York City), 1993.
Tale of a Sky-Blue Dress (memoir), Avon Books (New York City), 1998.

Larry Levis and Thylias Moss Reading Their Poems (sound recording), 1991.

SIDELIGHTS: Thylias Moss grew up the only child of doting parents in Cleveland, Ohio, met her future husband at age sixteen and has remained married to him ever since, and—though she grew up in working-class surroundings—has spent most of her adult life in the world of college English departments. Her later poetry collections have shown a more relaxed state of mind, but Moss's early work is characterized by almost unremitting portraits of bitterness, anger, and despair.

Moss first won a poetry prize in 1978 for "Coming of Age in Sandusky." Her poems were collected for publication in 1983 as *Hosiery Seams on a Bowlegged Woman,* which was commissioned by Alberta Turner and Leonard Trawick of the Cleveland State University Poetry Center. Six years later came *Pyramid of Bone,* a volume written at the request of the University of Virginia's Charles Rowell. The book was a first runner-up in the National Book Critics Circle Award for 1989, and earned Moss praise from *Publishers Weekly* for her "Rage and unyielding honesty." Reflecting on the difference between the author's life and her work, a critic in *Virginia Quarterly Review* observed "If Thylias Moss's resume is sedate . . . her poetry is anything but." The poems in *Pyramid* are full of disturbing images ("the vinegar she's become cannot sterilize the needle") and agonized statements ("The miracle was not birth but that I lived despite my crimes"), the critic noted.

Moss's third book, *At Redbones,* has a marginally less negative tone, and is also more faithful, in its premise, to the poet's upbringing. That premise is a mythical place call Redbones; part church and part bar, it serves as a refuge of sorts. Describing her own early influences, Moss has cited the "explosions on Sundays" in church, when the preacher "made [the congregation] shout, made them experience glory that perhaps was not actually there. . . . I wanted to make what the preacher called 'text.'" Her other strong influence, she has said, was akin to a bar, though she describes it as more of a schoolroom: the family kitchen on Saturday nights, where her father would sip whiskey and speak "mostly on the dialectics of the soul, asking the forbidden questions, giving words power over any taboo."

With the place called Redbones holding together the poems in her third book, Moss unites two salient influences from her childhood, but the effect is not necessarily—or even usually—comforting. Her images are of racism and brutality, a world in which the Ku Klux Klan is as ever-present as the laundry, and Christian faith offers no refuge: "Bottled Jesus is the / Clorox that whitens old sheets, makes the Klan / a brotherhood of saints." It is a world of sit-ins that took place in the 1960s, when African Americans were denied service at the "whites-only" counters of Southern U.S. eating establishments, and sometimes beaten if they refused to give up their seats: "When knocked from the stool," she writes in "Lunchcounter Freedom," "my body takes its shape from what it falls into." This is a world rife with the old-fashioned racist imagery of Mammy in *Gone with the Wind,* of Buckwheat from *The Little Rascals* movies, of the Aunt Jemima logo on syrup bottles, her smiling face holding "Teeth white as the shock of lynching, thirty-two / tombstones," Moss writes.

Turning from race to religion, Moss describes a physical revulsion in the sacrament of communion. In "Weighing the Sins of the World," receiving the Eucharist—Christ's symbolic blood—becomes a blood transfusion, and it turns out to be the wrong blood type, which is fatal. In "Fullness" she takes on, with similarly strong imagery, the literal substance (Christ's body) for which the bread of communion is a symbol: "One day / the father will place shavings of his own blessed fingers / on your tongue and you will get back in line for / more. You will not find yourself out of line again. / The bread will rise inside you. A loaf of tongue."

The pun on "out of line" in the preceding quote illustrates Moss's facility with language, and *At Redbones* earned her critical praise. Sue Standing of *Boston Review,* for instance, wrote enthusiastically that "If *At Redbones* were a light bulb it would be 300 watt; if it were whiskey, it would be 200 proof; if it were a mule, it would have an awfully big kick." Gloria T. Hull in *Belles Lettres,* also reviewing *At Redbones* along with several other works by African American female poets (one of whom was Maya Angelou) commented that "Thylias Moss is the youngest of this group . . . and the one with whom I was most intrigued. She possesses absolutely stunning poetic skill. . . . [which] she unites with one of the bleakest, most sardonic visions I have ever encountered by an African American woman writer." Marilyn Nelson Waniek in *Kenyon Review* was slightly more limited in her praise, but still found "a fine rage . . . at play in these pages."

With *Rainbow Remnants in Rock Bottom Ghetto Sky* (1991), however, critics were less effusive. *Choice*

reviewer H. Jaskoski referred to "predictable sentiments in unexceptional free verse" in which Moss "brings up the topics young black female poets seem expected to interpret." Moss's use of unusual metaphors, previously described by reviewers in terms such as "arresting," now seemed strained to several reviewers. Rita Signorelli-Pappas in *Belles Lettres,* for instance, cited the lines in "Almost an Ode to the West Indian Manatee": "the hamadryas baboon snubs me, her / nose's uptilt such that the nostrils are mosques / dark with shed sins and the doom that opposes pilgrimage. / She is in love." What, the reviewer asked, was the similarity between mosques and nostrils? The meaning of "the doom that opposes pilgrimage"? Or the explanation of the line "She is in love"?

Mark Jarman in *Hudson Review* referred to poet Charles Simic's praise of Moss as a "visionary story-teller" and pointed out, "but she tells no stories." Jarman, too, assailed Moss's use of strained metaphor: though he confessed to admire the "ambition" of her poems, he wrote that she showed "a kind of complacence in assuming that putting one thing on one side of an equals sign and one on another is imagination." In some cases, critics may have seemed unwilling to allow Moss sufficient freedom as a poet, as for instance when Jarman criticized her use of a colloquialism: "This is the first poet I have encountered who . . . actually has used the word *hopefully* as it is currently employed, which is to say incorrectly."

Though *Rainbow Remnants in Rock Bottom Ghetto Sky* was met by some with negative reviews, many other critics found much to praise in the collection's poems. "Using intricately woven, well-crafted sentences, she writes accessible, sensual, feminist poems about pregnancy, bonding between women, and racial and ethnic identity," wrote Judy Clarence in *Library Journal.* Clarence added that "there's a sense of hopefulness, of the poet's and our individual ability to survive, even to rejoice, in a very imperfect world." A *Publishers Weekly* reviewer also praised the collection, writing "Moss refuses to accept things as they are. . . . [her] writing expertly simulates the processes of her fecund mind, with thoughts overlapping and veering off on tangents that bring us back, with fuller knowledge, to a poem's central concern."

Prairie Schooner reviewer Tim Martin, who also praised *Rainbow Remnants in Rock Bottom Ghetto Sky,* commented, "Readers who delight in originality of image, language, and the striking metaphor might be urged to read Moss. Several poems are tours de force of sheer description." Martin continued, writing that the poet transforms everyday objects and chores into "startling new ways of seeing reality. . . . one gladly accepts as a good trade the occasional excess or lapse in exchange for the times she hits the mark and wakes us up with her use of language." "It is true that such creativity, gone unchecked, can grow into language that might be described as overly difficult or unwieldy. On occasion, Moss spins out long syntactical webs that any number of readings do little to extricate clear meanings from," Martin wrote, adding, however, "The reward is poems that may take backyards for their subjects, but ultimately describe nothing so quotidian for the reader."

Small Congregations (1993) is a collection drawn from the three preceding volumes and arranged into three sections. The collections themes, according to Elizabeth Frost in *Women's Review of Books,* can be identified respectively as religious symbolism, the mythology of African American life, and racist images. The familiar viewpoints on race and religion are combined in "The Adversary," wherein Moss expresses metaphorical sympathy for the devil as a sort of cosmic black man: "Poor Satan. His authority denied him / by a nose, a longer, pointier Caucasian nose. / Where's the gratitude for Satan who is there / for God no matter what; Satan / who is the original Uncle Tom." In her "Interpretation of a Poem by Frost," Moss both pays tribute to and parodies the poet Robert Frost's famous "Stopping by Woods on a Snowy Evening," which in her treatment becomes another instance of white racism confronting "A young black girl stopped by the woods, / so young she knew only one man: Jim Crow." But when Moss turns her vision away from God and whites, and inward toward the African-American home and hearth, the vision often becomes tender, as in "Remembering Kitchens": ". . .and I remove Mama's sweet potato pie, one made—as are her best—in her sleep when she can't interfere, when she's dreaming at the countertop that turns silk beside her elegant leaning, I slice it and put the whipped cream on quick, while the pie is so hot the peaks of cream will froth; these are the Sundays my family suckles grace."

With *I Want to Be* (1993), a book for children illustrated by Jerry Pinkney, Moss took a new and refreshing direction. As a little African-American girl walks home, thinking about the question often asked by adults—"What do you want to be when you grow up?"—she finds in herself some intriguing answers: "I want to be quiet but not so quiet that nobody can hear

me. I also want to be sound, a whole orchestra with two bassoons and an army of cellos. Sometimes I want to be just the triangle, a tinkle that sounds like an itch." Though these metaphors might be a bit challenging to young readers according to reviewers, for adults they are much more comprehensible than those found in Moss's earlier work. The book found praise with critics, suggesting a different and fascinating side of Moss. "The untrammeled exuberance of a free-spirited youngster, eager to explore everything, sings through a poetic story," wrote a critic for *Kirkus Reviews,* later calling the work "exhilarating, verbally and visually: the very essence of youthful energy and summertime freedom."

Moss continued her success as a poet with *Last Chance for the Tarzan Holler* (1998), which reviewer Fred Muratori, in *Library Journal,* called "a massive, acid-edged tribute to mortality in all of its contradictions and wrenching ironies." In this collection, Moss seeks to "finish knowing herself / in time to begin to know something else," touching such topics as sexuality, religion, and motherhood. In his *Library Journal* review, Muratori called the work "Loquacious and impassioned, precise and ragged, willing to risk even boredom in its drive to get at the heart of humanity's conflicted, necessary obsessions." A *Publishers Weekly* reviewer commented, "Moss meditates, starkly and unsentimentally, on death and motherhood, on God, and, beneath them all, on sex and power." Calling the collection's poems "unflinching" and "brilliant," reviewer Donna Seaman, in a piece for *Booklist,* called it "a book of extraordinary range."

Moss's second book to appear in 1998, *Tale of a Sky-Blue Dress,* marked a departure from her previous works. This book, a memoir of the author's childhood, recounts the physical, emotional, and sexual abuse Moss endured as a child at the hands of her babysitter, a teenage girl living in the same apartment building. The book opens with descriptions of a comfortable childhood, adoring parents, and domestic and familial rituals. The warmth of such scenes diminishes, however, when Moss's new babysitter introduces the child to humanity's dark side. The sitter, Lytta Dorsey, frequently wears a blue dress that is several sizes too small and displays an emotionally disturbed mind to her small charge. Moss, who endured the abuse for four years, sought to protect her loving parents from distress and never told them of the tortures she was forced to submit to. She also relates in the book that she was "fascinated with the pull of darkness," according to a reviewer for *Booklist.* Moss writes that Lytta gave her "the gift of darkness" in her life, a life in which her parents had kept her wrapped in a blanket of wonder, protection, and comfort. According to *Detroit Free Press* writer Barbara Holliday, "she thinks perhaps the novelty of cruelty made it exciting." "Is it true," writes Moss in *Tale of a Sky-Blue Dress,* "that I would not be a writer, if not for Lytta?," adding however, "I am not ready to admit to her necessity in my life."

Eventually raped by her tormentor's brother with his sister's encouragement, Moss entered adolescence troubled by the abuses she had suffered. She was drawn into relationships with men that mimicked her abusive relationship with Lytta and undermined her self esteem. Finally, at the age of sixteen, Moss met a young Air Force sergeant whose patient understanding and love helped her move beyond the pain of her childhood.

Tales of a Sky-Blue Dress received positive recognition from reviewers. A *Kirkus Reviews* critic called the book "an elegant, forthright exploration of the effects of evil on a fragile life" and "a stylish, well-wrought memoir that forgoes self-pity for redemption." "This is a story that reads like poetry, even when the memories are the bleakest," declared *Tribune Books* writer Sharman Stein. *New York Times Book Review* critic Paula Friedman commented, "While her analysis of her own surrender is impressive in its depth and unwillingness to settle for the simple role of victim, Moss may finally claim both too much and too little for herself: a 5-year-old is usually at the mercy of her caretakers."

BIOGRAPHICAL/CRITICAL SOURCES:

BOOKS

Bloom, Harold, *The American Religion,* Simon & Schuster (New York City), 1992.
Contemporary Women Poets, St. James Press (Detroit, MI), 1998.
Dictionary of Literary Biography, Volume 120: *American Poets since World War II,* Gale (Detroit, MI), 1992.
Moss, Thylias, *At Redbones,* Cleveland State University Press (Cleveland, OH), 1990.
Moss, Thylias, *Rainbow Remnants in Rock Bottom Ghetto Sky,* Persea (New York City), 1991.
Moss, Thylias, *Small Congregations: New and Selected Poems,* Ecco Press (Hopewell, NJ), 1993.
Moss, Thylias, *I Want to Be,* illustrated by Jerry Pinkney, Dial (New York City), 1993.
Moss, Thylias, *Tale of a Sky-Blue Dress,* Avon Books (New York City), 1998.

PERIODICALS

American Book Review, February, 1992, p. 29.
Belles Lettres, spring, 1991, p. 2; summer, 1992, pp. 62-65.
Bloomsbury Review, fall, 1994, p. 34; January, 1995, p. 19.
Booklist, October 1, 1993, pp. 353-354; January 1, 1998; February 15, 1998.
Boston Review, February, 1991, p. 28.
Callaloo, fall, 1990, p. 912.
Choice, February, 1984, p. 829; February, 1992, p. 896.
Essence, February, 1994, p. 120.
Hudson Review, spring, 1992, pp. 163-164; spring, 1994, pp. 159-160.
Kenyon Review, fall, 1991, pp. 214-226.
Kirkus Reviews, August 1, 1993, p. 1006; March 15, 1998, p. 368; June 1, 1998, p. 799.
Kliatt, July, 1995, p. 19.
Library Journal, May 15, 1991, p. 86; February 15, 1998; April 1, 1998.
Luce, July, 1998.
Michigan Quarterly Review, spring, 1996, p. 399.
Multi Cultural Review, April 1992, p. 73.
Nature, December 30, 1991, p. 861.
New York Times Book Review, September 13, 1998.
Parnassus, January, 1992, p. 65; no. 1, 1996, p. 341.
Poetry Flash, June 29, 1992.
Prairie Schooner, summer, 1994, p. 156.
Publishers Weekly, January 20, 1989, p. 143; April 5, 1991, p. 141; July 5, 1993, p. 7.
School Library Journal, September, 1993, p. 216.
Small Press, summer, 1993, p. 81.
Tribune Books (Chicago), August 2, 1995, p. 11.
Village Voice, February 25, 1992, p. 67.
Virginia Quarterly Review, summer, 1989, p. 100.
Washington Post, April 5, 1998, p. X08.
Women's Review of Books, March, 1994, pp. 11-12.

*   *   *

MPHAHLELE, Es'kia
  See MPHAHLELE, Ezekiel

*   *   *

MPHAHLELE, Ezekiel 1919-
  (Es'kia Mphahlele; Bruno Eseki, a pseudonym)

PERSONAL: Born December 17, 1919, Marabastad

Township, Pretoria, South Africa; son of Moses (a messenger) and Eva (a domestic; maiden name, Mogale) Mphahlele; married Rebecca Mochadibane (a social worker), 1945; children: Anthony, Teresa Kefilwe (deceased), Motswiri, Chabi Robert, Puso. *Education:* Attended Adams Teachers Training College, Natal, 1939-40; University of South Africa, B.A. (with honors), 1949, M.A., 1956; University of Denver, Ph.D., 1968.

ADDRESSES: Office—African Studies Institute, University of the Witwatersrand, Johannesburg 2001, South Africa.

CAREER: Clerk for an institute for the blind, 1941-45; Orlando High School, Johannesburg, South Africa, teacher of English and Afrikaans, 1945-52; *Drum* magazine, Johannesburg, fiction editor, 1955-57; University of Ibadan, Ibadan, Nigeria, lecturer in English literature, 1957-61; International Association for Cultural Freedom, Paris, France, director of African programs, 1961-63; Chemchemi Creative Centre, Nairobi, Kenya, director, 1963-65; University College, Nairobi, lecturer, 1965-66; University of Denver, Denver, CO, visiting lecturer, 1966-68, associate professor of English, 1970-74; University of Zambia, Lusaka, senior lecturer in English, 1968-70; University of Pennsylvania, Philadelphia, professor of English, 1974-77; University of Witwatersrand, Johannesburg, senior resident fellow, 1978—, professor of African literature, 1979—. Inspector of education, Lebowa, Transvaal, 1978-79. University of the Witwatersrand, Johannesburg, senior research fellow at African Studies Institute, 1979-82, professor of African literature, 1983-87, professor emeritus, 1987—. Founding director of Council for Black Education and Research (COBERT), 1980-92.

AWARDS, HONORS: African Arts magazine prize, 1972, for *The Wanderers;* Carnegie Foundation grant, 1980; Claude Harris Leon Foundation Prize, 1985, for outstanding community service; honorary doctorates from University of Pennsylvania, 1982, and University of Natal at Pietermaritzburg, 1983.

WRITINGS:

Man Must Live and Other Stories, African Bookman, 1947.
(Contributor) Prudence Smith, editor, *Africa in Transition,* Reinhardt, 1958.
Down Second Avenue (autobiography), Faber, 1959.
The Living and the Dead and Other Stories, Black Orpheus, 1961.

The African Image (essays), Faber, 1962, Praeger, 1964, revised edition, 1974.
(Editor with Ellis Ayitey Komey) *Modern African Stories,* Faber, 1964.
The Role of Education and Culture in Developing African Countries, Afro-Asian Institute for Labor Studies in Israel, 1965.
A Guide to Creative Writing, East African Literature Bureau, 1966.
In Corner B and Other Stories, Northwestern University Press, 1967.
(Editor and contributor) *African Writing Today,* Penguin, 1967.
The Wanderers (autobiographical novel), Macmillan, 1971.
Voices in the Whirlwind and Other Essays, Hill & Wang, 1972.
Under name Es'kia Mphahlele) *Chirundu* (novel), Lawrence Hill, 1981.
(Under name Es'kia Mphahlele) *The Unbroken Song: Selected Writings of Es'kia Mphahlele,* Ravan Press, 1981.
(Under name Es'kia Mphahlele) *Afrika My Music: An Autobiography, 1957-83,* Ravan Press, 1984, Ohio University Press, 1986.
Father Come Home (juvenile), Ravan Press, 1984.
(Under name Es'kia Mphahlele) *Bury Me at the Marketplace: Selected Letters of Es'kia Mphahlele,* edited by N. Chabani Mangayani, Skotaville, 1984.
Let's Talk Writing: Prose, Skotaville, 1985.
Let's Talk Writing: Poetry, Skotaville, 1985.
Poetry and Humanism, Witwatersrand University Press, 1986.
Echoes of African Art, Skotaville, 1987.
Renewal Time, Readers International, 1988.
(Author of text) Alf Kumalo, *Mandela: Echoes of an Era,* Penguin, 1990.
(Editor with others) *Perspectives on South African English Literature,* Donker, 1992.

CONTRIBUTOR TO ANTHOLOGIES

Langston Hughes, editor, *An African Treasury: Articles, Essays, Stories, Poems by Black Africans,* Crown, 1960.
Jacob Drachler, editor, *African Heritage: An Anthology of Black African Personality and Culture,* Crowell, 1962.
Leonard Sainville, editor, *Anthologie de la litterature negro-africaine: Romaciers et conteurs negro-africains,* Volume II, Presence Africaine, 1963.
Richard Rive, editor, *Modern African Prose,* Heinemann, 1964.

Ulli Beier, editor, *Black Orpheus: An Anthology of New African and Afro-American Stories,* Longmans, 1964, McGraw-Hill, 1965.

W. H. Whiteley, compiler, *A Selection of African Prose,* Volume II, Oxford University Press, 1964.

Anne Tibble, editor, *African-English Literature: A Survey and Anthology,* October House, 1965.

Hughes, editor, *Poems from Black Africa,* Indiana University Press, 1966.

Denny Neville, editor, *Pan African Short Stories,* Humanities, 1966.

Paul Edwards, compiler, *Modern African Narrative: An Anthology,* Humanities, 1966.

Edwards, compiler, *Through African Eyes,* Volume I, Cambridge University Press, 1966.

Lilyan Kesteloot, editor, *Anthologie negro-africaine: Panorama critique des prosateurs, poetes et dramatourges noirs du XXeme siecle,* Gerard, 1967.

Nadine Gordimer and Lionel Abrahams, editors, *South African Writing Today,* Penguin, 1967.

Herbert I. Shore and Megchelina Shore-Bos, editors, *Come Back, Africa: Fourteen Stories from South Africa,* International Publishers, 1968.

Ime Ikiddeh, compiler, *Drum Beats: An Anthology of African Writing,* E. J. Arnold, 1968.

Oscar Ronald Dathorne and Willfried Feuser, editors, *Africa in Prose,* Penguin, 1969.

John P. Berry, editor, *Africa Speaks: A Prose Anthology with Comprehension and Summary Passages,* Evans, 1970.

Joseph O. Okpaku, editor, *New African Literature and the Arts,* Volumes I and II, Crowell, 1970.

Charles Larson, editor, *African Short Stories: A Collection of Contemporary African Writing,* Macmillan, 1970.

Bernth Lindfors, editor, *South African Voices,* African and Afro-American Studies Research Center, 1975.

(Editor with Helen Moffett), *Seasons Come to Pass: A Poetry Anthology for Southern African Students,* Oxford University Press, 1994.

OTHER

Contributor of essays, short stories and poems, sometimes under pseudonym Bruno Eseki, to *Drum, Africa South, Denver Quarterly, Journal of Modern African Studies, Black World, New Statesman,* and other periodicals. Editor, *Black Orpheus,* 1960-66; member of staff, *Presence Africaine,* 1961-63; member of editorial staff, *Journal of New African Literature and the Arts.*

SIDELIGHTS: "A writer who has been regarded as the most balanced literary critic of African literature," Ezekiel Mphahlele can also "be acknowledged as one of its most significant creators," writes Emile Snyder in the *Saturday Review.* Mphahlele's transition from life in the slums of South Africa to life as a professor of English at a large American university was an odyssey of struggle both intellectually and politically. He trained as a teacher in South Africa, but was banned from the classroom in 1952 as a result of his protest of the segregationist Bantu Education Act. Although he later returned to teaching, Mphahlele first turned to journalism, criticism, fiction, and essay writing.

During an exile that took him to France and the United States, Mphahlele was away from Africa for over a decade. Nevertheless, "no other author has ever earned the right to so much of Africa as has Ezekiel Mphahlele," says John Thompson in the *New York Review of Books.* "In the English language, he established the strength of African literature in our time." Some critics, however, feel that Mphahlele's absence from his homeland has harmed his work by separating him from its subject. Ursula Barnett, writing in the conclusion of her 1976 biography *Ezekiel Mphahlele,* asserts that Mphahlele's "creative talent can probably gain its full potential only if he returns to South Africa and resumes his function of teaching his discipline in his own setting, and of encouraging the different elements in South Africa to combine and interchange in producing a modern indigenous literature."

Mphahlele himself has agreed with this assessment, for after being officially silenced by the government of his homeland and living in self-imposed exile for twenty years, Mphahlele returned to South Africa in 1977. "I want to be part of the renaissance that is happening in the thinking of my people," he told *Black Writers.* "I see education as playing a vital role in personal growth and in institutionalizing a way of life that a people chooses as its highest ideal. For the older people, it is a way of reestablishing the values they had to suspend along the way because of the force of political conditions. Another reason for returning, connected with the first, is that this is my ancestral home. An African cares very much where he dies and is buried. But I have not come to die. I want to reconnect with my ancestors while I am still active. I am also a captive of place, of setting. As long as I was abroad I continued to write on the South African scene. There is a force I call the tyranny of place; the kind of unrelenting hold a place has on a person that gives him the motivation to write and a style. The American setting in which I lived for nine years was too fragmented to give me these. I could only identify emotionally and intellectually with the African-American segment, which was not enough. Here I can feel the ancestral Presence. I know now what Vinoba Bhave of India meant when he said: 'Though action rages without, the heart can be tuned to produce unbroken music,' at this very hour when pain is raging and throbbing everywhere in African communities living in this country."

His 1988 publication, *Renewal Time,* contains stories he published previously as well as an autobiographical afterword on his return to South Africa and a section from *Afrika My Music,* his 1984 autobiography. Stories like "Mrs. Plum" and "The Living and the Dead" have received praise by critics reviewing Mphahlele's workd. Charles R. Larson, reviewing the work in the *Washington Post Book World,* says that the stories in the book present "almost ironic images of racial tension under apartheid."

Chirundu, Mphahlele's first novel since his return to South Africa, "tells with quiet assurance this story of a man divided," says Rose Moss in a *World Literature Today* review. The novel "is clearly this writer's major work of fiction and, I suppose, in one sense, an oblique commentary on his own years of exile," observes Charles R. Larson in *World Literature Today.* Moss finds that in his story of a man torn between African tradition and English law, "the timbre of Mphahlele's own vision is not always clear"; nevertheless, the critic admits that "in the main his story presents the confused and wordless heart of his character with unpretentious mastery." "*Chirundu* is that rare breed of fiction—a novel of ideas, and a moving one at that," says Larson. "It has the capacity to involve the reader both intellectually and emotionally." The critic concludes by calling the work "the most satisfying African novel of the past several years."

On the subject of writing, Mphahlele told *CA:* "In Southern Africa, the black writer talks best about the ghetto life he knows; the white writer about his own ghetto life. We see each other, black and white, as it were through a keyhole. Race relations are a major experience and concern for the writer. They are his constant beat. It is unfortunate no one can ever think it is healthy both mentally and physically to keep hacking at the social structure in overcharged language. A language that burns and brands, scorches and scalds. Language that is as a machete with a double edge—the one sharp, the other blunt, the one cutting, the other breaking. And yet there are levels

of specifically black drama in the ghettoes that I cannot afford to ignore. I have got to stay with it. I bleed inside. My people bleed. But I must stay with it."

BIOGRAPHICAL/CRITICAL SOURCES:

BOOKS

Akosu, Tyohdzuah, *The Writing of Ezekeil Mphahlele,* Mellen University Press, 1995.
Barnett, Ursula A., *Ezekiel Mphahlele,* Twayne, 1976.
Contemporary Literary Criticism, Volume 25, Gale, 1983.
Durden, Dennis, editor, *African Writers Talking,* Heinemann, 1972.
Herdeck, Donald E., *African Writers: A Companion to Black African Writing, 1300-1973,* Black Orpheus, 1973.
Manganyi, N. C., *Exiles and Homecomings: A Biography of Es'kia Mphahlele,* Ravan Press, 1983.
Moore, Gerald, *Seven African Writers,* Oxford University Press, 1962.
Moore, *The Chosen Tongue,* Longmans, Green, 1969.
Thuynsma, Peter N., *Footprints Along the Way: A Tribute to Es'kia Mphahlele,* Skotaville, 1989.

PERIODICALS

Modern African Studies, March, 1963.
Nation, March 20, 1972.
New Statesman, April 25, 1959.
New York Review of Books, September 23, 1971.
New York Times Book Review, October 22, 1972.
Saturday Review, June 19, 1971.
Times Literary Supplement, August 11, 1961; March 23, 1967; March 10, 1972.
World Literature Today, summer, 1983; winter, 1983; winter, 1987; winter, 1997, p. 99.*

*   *   *

MULILA, Vigad G.
  See MAILLU, David

*   *   *

MUNGOSHI, Charles L.   1947-

PERSONAL: Born December 2, 1947, in Manyeye Communal Land, (now Zimbabwe); son of Tongayi

Davidson (a farmer) and Phoebe Masoka (a farmer) Mungoshi; married Jesesi Jaboon (a dress designer), June 12, 1976; children: (sons) Farai, Graham, Nyasha, Charles. *Education:* Attended St. Augustine's Mission, Penhalonga, Zimbabwe; Cambridge University, completed O level, 1966. *Religion:* Church of England.

ADDRESSES: Home—47/6156 Uta Crescent, Zengeza 1, Chitungwiza, Zimbabwe.

CAREER: Novelist, short-story writer, poet, editor, and actor. Textbook Sales (booksellers), Harare, Zimbabwe, junior invoicing clerk, 1969-74; Rhodesian Forestry Commission, Forest Research Station, Penhalonga, research assistant, 1967-69; Zimbabwe Publishing House, Harare, literary editor, 1981-85, director/creative writing editor, 1987—; University of Zimbabwe, writer-in-residence, 1985-87; The Literature Bureau, Harare, assistant literary editor, 1981-85. Voluntary creative writing and drama instructor in annual one-week workshop sponsored by Ecumenical Arts Association of Zimbabwe. Actor in radio plays, 1971—, and on Zimbabwe Television's Local Drama Programme, 1985. Founder and chair, Highfield Drama Club, Highfield Community Centre, Harare, 1969-73. Participant in seminars and conferences for various groups, including UNESCO, London and Togo; Zimbabwe International Book Fair; Cultural Workers of Southern Africa, Botswana; British Council, Cambridge; and New Zealand Arts Festival, Wellington.

AWARDS, HONORS: First prize, Literature Bureau Literary Competition, 1969, for *Maunun'unu Maodzamwoyo;* PEN Zimbabwe Book Centre Awards for best novel in English, for *Waiting for the Rain,* and for best novel in Shona, for *Ndiko Kupindana Kwamazuva,* both 1976; PEN-Longman Award for best book of the year in English, 1980, for *The Milkman Doesn't Only Deliver Milk.*

WRITINGS:

IN SHONA

Makunun'unu Maodzamwoyo (novel), College Press (Salisbury, Zimbabwe), 1970.
Ndiko Kupindana Kwamazuva (novel), Mambo Press (Gwelo, Rhodesia), 1975.
Inongova Njakenjake (play; produced on ZTV Local Drama, 1985), Longman (Zimbabwe), 1981.
Kunyarara Hakusi Kutaura? (novel), Zimbabwe Publishing House (Harare), 1983.

IN ENGLISH

Coming of the Dry Season (short stories; includes "Shadows on the Wall," "The Crow," "The Mountain," "The Hero," "The Setting Sun and the Rolling World," "The Lift," "The Ten Shillings," "Coming of the Dry Season," "S.O.S. from the Past," and "The Accident"), Oxford University Press (Nairobi, Kenya), 1972.
Waiting for the Rain (novel), Heinemann African Writers Series (London), 1975; Zimbabwe Publishing House (Harare), 1981.
The Milkman Doesn't Only Deliver Milk: Poems (verse), Poetry Society of Zimbabwe (Avondale, Salisbury, Zimbabwe), 1980.
Some Kinds of Wounds and Other Short Stories (short stories), Mambo Press, 1980.
The Setting Sun and the Rolling World (short stories; includes stories from *Coming of the Dry Season* and *Some Kinds of Wounds*), Heinemann (London), 1987, Beacon Press (Boston), 1989.
Stories from a Shona Childhood, Baobab Books (Harare, Zimbawe), 1989.
One Day, Long Ago: More Stories from a Shona Childhood, Baobab Books, 1991.
Walking Still, Baobab Books, 1997.

OTHER

(Translator) Ngugi wa Thiongo, *Tsanga Yembeu,* published as *A Grain of Wheat,* Zimbabwe Publishing House (Harare), 1988.

Contributor of poetry to anthologies, including *Mambo Book of Zimbabwean Verse,* edited by Colin Style and O-Nan, [Harare], 1986; and *Patterns of Poetry in Zimbabwe,* edited by Flora Wild, [Harare], 1988. Author's work has been translated into Hungarian, German, Bulgarian, Russian, and Dutch.

ADAPTATIONS: Makunun'unu Maodzamwoyo was adapted for television and produced by ZTV Local Drama, 1986.

SIDELIGHTS: Equally fluent in Shona and English, Zimbabwean author Charles Mungoshi has produced award-winning and critically admired work in both languages. Sometimes banned in his native country when it was known as Rhodesia, Mungoshi's writings—which include novels, short stories, plays, and poetry—cast a realistic and unsparing light on the conflicts many Africans feel in making the leap from tribal life to industrial or post-industrial society. This is, as Samuel G. Freedman pointed out in a *New York Times Book Review* piece on Mungoshi's *The Setting Sun and the Rolling World* (1989), a staple theme of African writers; Mungoshi's special achievement in this vein, Freedman felt, was "to evoke the confusion and sorrow of a continent wrenched in two directions with a deceptively minimalistic voice." Freedman specified, moreover, that "Mungoshi proves that spare prose need not equal small ideas."

The Setting Sun and the Rolling World is a compilation from two earlier volumes of Mungoshi's stories, *Coming of the Dry Season* (1972) and *Some Kinds of Wounds* (1980). Among the stories, Freedman singled out "Ten Shillings," about a young, educated man who has spent two years sleeping in drainpipes and gutters, and "The Brother," in which a youth, traveling to the city to stay with his older brother and to receive money for school supplies, is terribly disillusioned after seeing the brother participate in an adulterous orgy that is partly financed with the school-supply funds. These and the other stories in the book, Freedman declared, contain "a broader vision, social and often spiritual;" because of this, "the most intimate encounters resonate with meaning."

Reviewer John Sutherland, writing in the *London Review of Books,* also hailed "The Brother" as perhaps the strongest entry in *The Setting Sun and the Rolling World,* finding its ending "enigmatic" and complex. "Hovering over most of Mungoshi's pieces, as over Southern Africa as a whole, is an impenetrably cloudy future," commented Sutherland. *New Statesman* contributor Alison Fell told readers, "Clear-sighted, passionate and harsh, Mungoshi knows about damage." She called the story "Shadows on the Wall" "perceptive and poetic," and noted that "In Mungoshi's vision the old rule of magic and the new rule of money clash and conjoin, and most of the time it is women and children who come off worst." However, "even when he strips his characters bare, Mungoshi retains a lucid sympathy for the dreams of dignity which have been thwarted." A contributor to *Publishers Weekly* called *The Setting Sun* an "exceptional achievement," objecting only to an occasional tendency to poeticize in prose; Mungoshi's narrative is, most often, marked by "confident simplicity."

Other than *The Setting Sun,* little of Mungoshi's work has appeared in the United States; like most of his work, his 1991 volume of short stories, *One Day, Long Ago: More Stories from a Shona Childhood,* was published by a Zimbabwe house.

BIOGRAPHICAL/CRITICAL SOURCES:

PERIODICALS

Booklist, September 15, 1989, p. 145.
Cresset, February, 1991, p. 26.
Critique, spring, 1995, p. 195.
Economist, April 28, 1990, pp. 97-98.
Kirkus Reviews, July 15, 1989, p. 1025.
Library Journal, September 15, 1989, p. 136.
Listener, November 18, 1982, p. 27.
London Review of Books, April 2, 1987, pp. 19-20.
Los Angeles Times Book Review, October 1, 1989, p. 12.
New Statesman, April 3, 1987, p. 28.
New York Times Book Review, September 24, 1989, p. 23.
Publishers Weekly, August 4, 1989, p. 86.
Times Literary Supplement, April 17, 1987, p. 411.
World Literature Today, summer, 1990, p. 521.

OTHER

Charles Mungoshi Overview, http://www.stg.brown.edu/projects/.../zimbabwe/mungoshi/mungoshiov.html (October 14, 1998).*

*   *   *

MWANGI, Meja 1948-

PERSONAL: Born David Dominic Mwangi, December 27, 1948, in Nyeri, Kenya; son of a domestic worker. *Education:* Attended Kenyatta College; attended University of Iowa, 1975.

ADDRESSES: Agent—c/o Heinemann, Portsmouth, NH.

CAREER: Writer. Assistant director of the films *Out of Africa,* 1985, *Gorillas in the Mist,* 1985, and *White Mischief,* 1988.

AWARDS, HONORS: Jomo Kenyatta Prize, 1974, for *Kill Me Quick;* Commonwealth Writers Prize nomination, 1990, for *Striving for the Wind;* Deutscher Jugendliteratur Preis, 1992, for German-language edition of *Little White Man.*

WRITINGS:

FICTION

Kill Me Quick, Heinemann Educational (London), 1973.

Carcase for Hounds, Heinemann Educational, 1974.
Taste of Death, East African Publishing House (Kenya, Nairobi), 1975.
Going down River Road, Heinemann Educational, 1976.
The Bushtrackers (adapted from a screenplay by Gary Strieker), Longman Drumbeat (Nairobi), 1979.
The Cockroach Dance, Longman Kenya (Nairobi), 1979.
Bread of Sorrow, Longman Kenya, 1987.
The Return of Shaka, Longman Kenya, 1989.
Weapon of Hunger, Longman Kenya, 1989.
Striving for the Wind, Heinemann Kenya, 1990, Heinemann (Portsmouth, NH), 1992.

CHILDREN'S BOOKS

Jimi the Dog, Longman Kenya, 1990.
Little White Man, Longman Kenya, 1990.
The Hunter's Dream, Macmillan (London), 1993.

SIDELIGHTS: Kenyan author Meja Mwangi's novels are usually concerned with the modern social and political situation in Africa, but he has treated this theme in several different ways. His first books touched on the Mau Mau rebellion of the 1950s, in which African guerrilla fighters tried to break the grip of British colonialism. *Taste of Death* and *Carcase for Hounds* belong to this category. The novels *Kill Me Quick, Going down River Road,* and *The Cockroach Dance* focused on the problems brought about by the rapid industrialization Kenya has undergone since achieving independence in 1963. These books have brought Mwangi his greatest critical acclaim. He has, however, been scoffed at by critics for his third class of books, which use Africa and its problems as a backdrop for popular entertainment in the thriller tradition. *Bread of Sorrow, Weapon of Hunger* and *The Return of Shaka* fall into this group.

The son of a maid who worked for white families in the British town of Nyeri, Kenya, Mwangi grew up during the Mau Mau massacres and Kenya's tumultuous independence movement. While violence raged on the outskirts of town, Mwangi spent his childhood absorbing much of the white settlers' culture from both his mother's contact with the settlers in their homes and from his reading of European children's books, which were gifts from his mother's employers. Several members of Mwangi's family were sent to detention camps because they had been active in the revolution. According to Simon Gikandi, writing in the *Dictionary of Literary Biography,* Mwangi recalled being held captive in a detention camp with his mother for a short time. Mwangi was so affected by

what he witnessed and the stories he heard of the Mau Mau uprising that he wrote about it in his first book, *Taste of Death,* when he was seventeen years old (it was not published for several years).

In this novel, the young hero, Kariuki, is swept along by the passion and excitement of the Mau Mau insurrection and Kenya's fight for independence even though he does not understand the basis of the conflict and is not ready to sacrifice his own life for the rebellion. Mwangi glorifies the conflict in the novel, telling of the freedom fighters' futile attempt to avoid death at the hands of colonial forces. Gikandi states that this book "cannot be considered as anything more than juvenilia," yet he allows that it is significant for stating what would become Mwangi's recurrent themes and concerns.

Mwangi's first published novel was the realistic novel *Kill Me Quick* set in the days after Kenya established its independence. The protagonists, two boys who are life-long friends, try to improve their lives by attending school. They move to Nairobi in order to find work, but they discover that their classroom education is worthless in the city. They become stranded in the urban jungle, without hope for improving their situation or the ability to return to their rural homes. Desperate for money, the boys turn to crime and are apprehended, and only after they are incarcerated does the quality of their lives improve. The book gave him immediate literary prominence. A *Choice* contributor calls it "an incisive look at the way crime is created by poverty rather than by innate evil." Gikandi finds that the "poignancy and immediacy" of *Kill Me Quick* "overshadow its limited literary achievement," and states that Mwangi "renders scenes with the hard and sharp ear of a reporter on the beat."

In *Carcase for Hounds,* Mwangi again deals with the themes of pessimism, futility, and hopelessness. A Mau Mau soldier and his mortally wounded revolutionary commander are trapped and surrounded by hostile British forces in a forest, a situation that Mwangi uses as a metaphor for the hopelessness both the revolutionaries and the British colonial forces feel in this stand-off. In *Carcase for Hounds,* "Mwangi has usurped the language of the American thriller, of Raymond Chandler, Mickey Spillane, and Chester Himes," Gikandi writes. The critic find some of the American slang to be "incongruous" with characters' situation, but praises *Carcase for Hounds* as "remarkable for the sheer amount of detail than Mwangi provides about the logistics and organization of the Mau Mau movement."

In *Going down River Road,* which is frequently mentioned as his greatest achievement, Mwangi returns to the horrors of the urban jungle. According to *World Literature Today* contributor Charles R. Larson, Mwangi paints a culture "composed . . . of young bar girls, urban thugs or youths." Gikandi finds it to be a restatement of earlier themes, but calls it "remarkable" for its "stark, detailed images with which Mwangi represents the vital and volatile clandestine culture of the Nairobi underworld. Nobody else has captured this subculture with as much understanding and empathy."

In 1979's *The Cockroach Dance,* Mwangi attempts to realize a balance between entertaining the reader and criticizing society. His main character, a water meter reader, is driven to despair and violence by the hopelessness and injustice he witnesses every day on his job. Mwangi's novelization of Gary Strieker's screenplay *The Bushtrackers* was also published in 1979. *Black Scholar* contributor Roland S. Jefferson called it "the first indigenous novel/film to come out of Africa with an eye toward appealing to the U.S./ westernized culture." The main character reacts to every situation with anger and rage. Jefferson wrote that the novel "highlights a character who views the political and justice system around him as virtually impotent and unable to extract retribution."

In 1987's *Bread of Sorrow,* Mwangi uses the thriller genre to address the problems of apartheid and racial oppression, while his 1989 Americana-packed novel *The Return of Shaka* focuses on an African prince touring the United States on a Greyhound bus, chased across the continent by hired killers. In *Weapon of Hunger,* the worst of Africa's horrors—famine, drought, civil war, the atrocities of revolution—are played against an American pop star's efforts to save the starving. Gikandi was largely critical of these works, charging that they fail to strike a "balance . . . between entertainment and serious ideological narrative." Writing specifically of *Weapon of Hunger* and *The Return of Shaka,* Gikandi accuses Mwangi of having "given in to movie-style values, especially the desire to entertain and thrill the audience; his unabashed celebration of Americana is often embarrassing, not only because his vision of America seems to be drawn from superficial sources but also because it always degenerates into cultural and linguistic cliches." Gikandi further criticizes *The Return of Shaka* as seeming "to have been written for no other reason but to sell copies of it."

Gikandi was more charitable toward the 1990 work *Striving for the Wind,* calling it Mwangi's attempt to "return to his roots as they were so powerfully displayed in *Kill Me Quick* and *Going down River Road.*" In this story, a father and son debate the future of Kenya. "Mwangi rejects the shifting spaces of his thrillers," writes Gikandi, "focusing instead on a static, weary, and worn-out landscape; he rejects the idiom of the movies, seeking instead to capture the language of rural despair and the tyranny of the nouveau riche; the alienated authorial tone of the thrillers gives way to a profound voice that sustains the pessimism and angst of the rural poor." Mwangi's depiction of the depleted Kenyan landscape and the exhausted humans who till it earned the volume a nomination for the Commonwealth Writers Prize, but Gikandi concludes that *Striving for the Wind* is "as dull as the land and people it represents" and advises that ultimately, "Mwangi's real talent is manifested in the novels in which he marries the techniques of the thriller with a profound exposition of the African scene."

Mwangi's disappointment with the negative critical reaction to many of his books led him to begin publishing children's stories in 1990. Perhaps more significantly, he was also spurred in this direction by his feeling that there is far too little literature available for children that shows a Kenyan or African perspective. Set during the 1950s, *Jimi the Dog* and *Little White Man* relate the adventures of Kariuki, a little boy who, like the author, grows up in the shadow of the colonial elite. Although *Jimi the Dog* is, on one level, the story of a little boy and his puppy, it also addresses social issues. *Little White Man* deals more directly with the Mau Mau uprising. It tells of Kariuki's friendship with Nigel, a white planter's son. When Nigel is captured by Mau Maus, Kariuki searches the jungle for him. He finds that his brother Hari is among the rebels. Hari negotiates with government soldiers for Nigel's release, only to be killed by the British.

Mwangi is "a persistent enigma," muses Gikandi. "His career is one no critic has written about without either marked reservations or significant qualifications. He seems to stand, like many of his heroes, as a loner in the literary world."

BIOGRAPHICAL/CRITICAL SOURCES:

BOOKS

Anyidoho, Kofi, and others, editors, *Interdisciplinary Dimensions of African Literature,* Three Continents (Washington, DC), 1985, pp. 11-25.

Chakava, Henry, *Notes on Meja Mwangi's "Kill Me Quick,"* Heinemann Educational (Nairobi), 1976.

Dictionary of Literary Biography, Volume 125: *Twentieth-Century Caribbean and Black African Writers: Second Series,* Gale (Detroit), 1993.

Johansson, Lars, *In the Shadow of Neocolonialism: A Study of Meja Mwangi's Novels, 1973-1990,* Faculty of Arts, University of Umea (Stockholm), 1992.

Killam, G. D., editor, *The Writing of East and Central Africa,* Heinemann (London), 1984, pp. 177-191.

Lindfors, Bernth, editor, *Mazungumzo,* Ohio University Center for International Studies (Athens), 1980, pp. 74-79.

Nichols, Lee, *Conversations with African Writers,* Voice of America (Washington, DC), 1981, pp. 195-204.

Parasuram, A. N., *Guide to Meja Mwangi: Kill Me Quick,* Minerva (Madras, India), 1977.

Wanjala, Chris, *The Season of Harvest: Some Notes on East African Literature,* Kenya Literature Burwau (Nairobi), 1978.

Zell, Hans M., and others, *A New Reader's Guide to African Literature,* Holmes and Meier, 1983.

PERIODICALS

African Literature Today, Number 9, 1978; Number 13, 1983, pp. 146-157.

Afriscope, April, 1976, pp. 25-28.

Association for Commonwealth Literature and Language Studies Bulletin, Volume 7, number 4, 1986, pp. 45-52.

Black Scholar, November/December, 1984, pp. 61-63.

Choice, March, 1976, p. 78; June, 1976, p. 528.

Research in African Literatures, summer, 1985, pp. 179-209.

World Literature Today, autumn, 1977, p. 565; autumn, 1978.*

N

NAYLOR, Gloria 1950-

PERSONAL: Born January 25, 1950, New York, NY; daughter of Roosevelt (a transit worker) and Alberta (a telephone operator; maiden name, McAlpin) Naylor. *Education:* Brooklyn College of the City University of New York, B.A., 1981; Yale University, M.A., 1983.

ADDRESSES: Agent—Sterling Lord Literistic, 65 Bleecker St., New York, NY 10012-2420.

CAREER: Missionary for Jehovah's Witnesses in New York, North Carolina, and Florida, 1968-75; worked for various hotels in New York City, including Sheraton City Squire, as telephone operator, 1975-81; writer, 1981—; One Way Productions, New York City, president, 1990—. Writer in residence, Cummington Community of the Arts, 1983; visiting lecturer, George Washington University, 1983-84, and Princeton University, 1986-87; cultural exchange lecturer, United States Information Agency, India, 1985; scholar in residence, University of Pennsylvania, 1986; visiting professor, New York University, 1986, and Boston University, 1987; Fannie Hurst Visiting Professor, Brandeis University, 1988. Senior fellow, Society for the Humanities, Cornell University, 1988; executive board, Book of the Month Club, 1989-94; producer, One Ways Productions, 1990; visiting scholar, University of Kent, 1992; playwright, Hartford Stage Company, 1994.

AWARDS, HONORS: American Book Award for best first novel, 1983, for *The Women of Brewster Place;* Distinguished Writer Award, Mid-Atlantic Writers Association, 1983; National Endowment for the Arts fellowship, 1985; Candace Award, National Coalition of 100 Black Women, 1986; Guggenheim fellowship, 1988; Lillian Smith Book Award, Southern Regional Council, 1989, for *Mama Day.*

WRITINGS:

FICTION

The Women of Brewster Place, Viking (New York City), 1982.
Linden Hills, Ticknor & Fields (New York City), 1985.
Mama Day, Ticknor & Fields, 1988.
Bailey's Cafe, Harcourt (New York City), 1992.
(Editor) *Children of the Night: The Best Short Stories by Black Writers, 1967 to the Present,* Little, Brown (Boston), 1995.
The Men of Brewster Place, Hyperion (New York City), 1998.

NONFICTION

Centennial, Pindar Press, 1986.
(With Bill Shore) *Revolution of the Heart: A New Strategy for Creating Wealth,* Riverhead Books, 1996.

OTHER

Also author of unproduced screenplay adaptation of *The Women of Brewster Place,* for American Playhouse, 1984, and of an unproduced original screenplay for Public Broadcasting System's "In Our Own Words," 1985. Contributor of essays and articles to periodicals, including *Southern Review, Essence, Ms., Life, Ontario Review,* and *People.* Contributing editor, *Callaloo,* 1984—. "Hers" columnist for *New York Times,* 1986.

ADAPTATIONS: The Women of Brewster Place was adapted as a miniseries, produced by Oprah Winfrey and Carole Isenberg, and broadcast by American Broadcasting Co. (ABC-TV) in 1989; it became a weekly ABC series in 1990, produced by Winfrey, Earl Hamner, and Donald Sipes.

SIDELIGHTS: "I wanted to become a writer because I felt that my presence as a black woman and my perspective as a woman in general had been under-represented in American literature," Gloria Naylor commented. Her first novel, *The Women of Brewster Place,* which features a cast of seven strong-willed black women, won the American Book Award for best first fiction in 1983. Naylor has continued her exploration of the black female experience in two subsequent novels that remain focused on women while also expanding her fictional realm. In *Linden Hills,* for example, Naylor uses the structure of Dante Alighieri's *Inferno* to create a contemporary allegory about the perils of black materialism and the ways in which denying one's heritage can endanger the soul. Naylor's third novel, *Mama Day,* draws on another literary masterpiece—William Shakespeare's play *The Tempest*—and artfully combines Shakespearean elements with black folkloric strains. By drawing on traditional western sources, Naylor places herself firmly in the literary mainstream, broadening her base from ethnic to American writing. Unhappy with what she calls the "historical tendency to look upon the output of black writers as not really American litera-ture," Naylor told *Publishers Weekly* interviewer William Goldstein that her work attempts to "articu-late experiences that want articulating—for those readers who reflect the subject matter, black readers, and for those who don't—basically white middle class readers."

Naylor's first novel grew out of a desire to reflect the diversity of the black experience-a diversity that she feels neither the black nor the white critical establish-ment has recognized. "There has been a tendency on the part of both," she commented, "to assume that a black writer's work should be 'definitive' of black experience. This type of critical stance denies the vast complexity of black existence, even if we were to limit that existence solely to America. While *The Women of Brewster Place* is about the black woman's condition in America, I had to deal with the fact that one composite picture couldn't do justice to the com-plexity of the black female experience. So I tried to

solve this problem by creating a microcosm on a dead-end street and devoting each chapter to a differ-ent woman's life. These women vary in age, personal background, political consciousness, and sexual pref-erence. What they do share is a common oppression and, more importantly, a spiritual strength and sense of female communion that I believe all women have employed historically for their psychic health and survival."

Reviewing *The Women of Brewster Place* in the *Washington Post,* Deirdre Donahue writes: "Naylor is not afraid to grapple with life's big subjects: sex, birth, love, death, grief. Her women feel deeply, and she unflinchingly transcribes their emotions. . . . Naylor's potency wells up from her language. With prose as rich as poetry, a passage will suddenly take off and sing like a spiritual. . . . Vibrating with undisguised emotion, *'The Women of Brewster Place'* springs from the same roots that produced the blues. Like them, her book sings of sorrows proudly borne by black women in America."

To date, Naylor has linked her novels by carrying over characters from one narrative to another. In *The Women of Brewster Place,* one of the young residents is a refugee from Linden Hills, an exclusive black suburb. Naylor's second novel spotlights that affluent community, revealing the material corruption and moral decay that would prompt an idealistic young woman to abandon her home for a derelict urban neighborhood. Though *Linden Hills,* as the book is called, approaches the Afro-American experience from the upper end of the socioeconomic spectrum, it is also a black microcosm. This book "forms the second panel of that picture of contemporary urban black life which Naylor started with in *Women of Brewster Place,"* writes *Times Literary Supplement* contributor Roz Kaveney. "Where that book described the faults, passions, and culture of the good poor, this shows the nullity of black lives that are led in imita-tion of suburban whites."

In addition to shifting her focus, Naylor has also raised her literary sights in her second novel. *Linden Hills,* which has been described as a contemporary allegory with gothic overtones, is an ambitious under-taking structurally modeled after Dante's *Inferno.* Among its many accomplishments, Dante's Italian masterpiece describes the nine circles of hell, Satan's imprisonment in their depths, and the lost souls con-demned to suffer with him. In Naylor's modern ver-sion, "souls are damned not because they have offended God or have violated a religious system but because they have offended themselves. In their single-minded pursuit of upward mobility, the inhabitants of Linden Hill, a black, middle-class suburb, have turned away from their past and from their deepest sense of who they are," writes Catherine C. Ward in *Contemporary Literature.* To correspond to Dante's circles, Naylor uses a series of crescent-shaped drives that ring the suburban development. Her heroes are two young street poets-outsiders from a neighboring community who hire themselves out to do odd jobs so they can earn Christmas money. "As they move down the hill, what they encounter are people who have 'moved up' in American society . . . until eventually they will hit the center of their community and the home of my equivalent of Satan," Naylor told Goldstein. Naylor's Satan is one Luther Nedeed, a combination mortician and real estate tycoon, who preys on the residents' baser ambitions to keep them in his sway.

Naylor's third novel, *Mama Day,* is named for its main character—a wise old woman with magical powers whose name is Miranda Day, but whom everyone refers to as Mama Day. This ninety-year-old conjurer made a walk-on appearance in *Linden Hills* as the illiterate, toothless aunt who hauls about cheap cardboard suitcases and leaky jars of preserves. But it is in *Mama Day* that this "caster of hoodoo spells . . . comes into her own," according to *New York Times Book Review* contributor Bharati Mukherjee. "The portrait of Mama Day is magnificent," she declares.

Mama Day lives on Willow Springs, a wondrous island off the coast of Georgia and South Carolina that has been owned by her family since before the Civil War. The fact that slaves are portrayed as property owners demonstrates one of the ways that Naylor turns the world upside down, according to Rita Mae Brown. Another, continues Brown in the *Los Angeles Times Book Review,* is "that the women possess the real power, and are acknowledged as having it." When Mama Day's grandniece Cocoa brings George, her citified new husband, to Willow Springs, he learns the importance of accepting mystery. "George is the linchpin of *Mama Day,*" Brown says. "His rational mind allows the reader to experience the island as George experiences it. Mama Day and Cocoa are of the island and therefore less immediately accessible to the reader. The turning point comes when George is asked not only to believe in Mama Day's power but to act on it. Cocoa is desperately ill. A hurricane has washed out the bridge so that no mainland doctor can be summoned." Only Mama Day has the power to help George save her life. She gives him a task, which he bungles because he is still limited by purely rational thinking. Ultimately, George is able to save Cocoa, but only by great personal sacrifice.

The plot twists and thematic concerns of *Mama Day* have led several reviewers to compare the work to Shakespeare. "Whereas *Linden Hills* was Dantesque, *Mama Day* is Shakespearean, with allusions, however oblique and tangential, to 'Hamlet,' 'King Lear,' and, especially, 'The Tempest,'" writes Chicago *Tribune Books* critic John Blades. "Like Shakespeare's fantasy, Naylor's book takes place on an enchanted island. . . . Naylor reinforces her Shakespearean connection by naming her heroine Miranda." Mukherjee also believes that *Mama Day* "has its roots in 'The Tempest.' The theme is reconciliation, the title character is Miranda (also the name of Prospero's daughter), and Willow Springs is an isolated island where, as on Prospero's isle, magical and mysterious events come to pass."

Naylor's ambitious attempt to elevate a modern love story to Shakespearean heights "is more bewildering than bewitching," according to Blades. "Naylor has populated her magic kingdom with some appealingly offbeat characters, Mama Day foremost among them. But she's failed to give them anything very original or interesting to do." Mukherjee also acknowledges the shortcomings of Naylor's mythical love story, but asserts, "I'd rather dwell on *Mama Day*'s strengths. Gloria Naylor has written a big, strong, dense, admirable novel; spacious, sometimes a little drafty like all public monuments, designed to last and intended for many levels of use."

BIOGRAPHICAL/CRITICAL SOURCES:

BOOKS

Authors and Artists for Young Adults, Volume 6, Gale (Detroit), 1991.
Black Literature Criticism, Gale, 1992.
Contemporary Literary Criticism, Gale, Volume 28, 1984; Volume 52, 1989.
Fowler, Virginia C., *Gloria Naylor: In Search of Sanctuary,* Prentice Hall, 1996.
Hall, Chekita T., *Gloria Naylor's Feminist Blues Aesthetic,* Garland, 1998.
Harris, Trudier, *The Power of the Porch: The Storyteller's Craft in Zora Neale Hurston, Gloria Naylor, and Randall Kenan,* University of Georgia Press, 1996.

PERIODICALS

Advocate, April 14, 1998, p. 73.
African American Review, summer, 1994, p. 173; spring, 1995, pp. 27, 35.
Booklist, December 1, 1995; January 1, 1996; March 1, 1998, p. 1045.
Chicago Tribune Book World, February 23, 1983.
Christian Science Monitor, March 1, 1985.
Commonweal, May 3, 1985.
Contemporary Literature, Volume 28, number 1, 1987.
Detroit News, March 3, 1985; February 21, 1988.
Ebony, May, 1998, p. 14.
English Journal, January, 1994, p. 81; March, 1994, p. 95.
Essence, June, 1998, p. 70.
Library Journal, June 1, 1998, p. 187.
London Review of Books, August 1, 1985.
Los Angeles Times, December 2, 1982.
Los Angeles Times Book Review, February 24, 1985; March 6, 1988.
Ms., June, 1985.
New Republic, September 6, 1982.
New York Times, February 9, 1985; May 1, 1990.
New York Times Book Review, August 22, 1982; March 3, 1985; February 21, 1988.
People, June 22, 1998, p. 39.
Publishers Weekly, September 9, 1983; February 23, 1998, p. 49.
San Francisco Review of Books, May, 1985.
Times (London), April 21, 1983.
Times Literary Supplement, May 24, 1985.
Tribune Books (Chicago), January 31, 1988.
Washington Post, October 21, 1983; May 1, 1990.
Washington Post Book World, March 24, 1985; February 28, 1988.
Women's Review of Books, August, 1985.
Writer, December, 1994, p. 21.

*   *   *

NJERI, Itabari (Lord)

PERSONAL: Original name Jill Stacey Moreland, name changed to Itabari, 1971, legally changed to Itabari Njeri, 1975, later changed to Itabari Lord Njeri; born in Brooklyn, NY; daughter of Marc Marion Moreland (a historian) and Yvonne Delcinia Lord Moreland Williams (a registered nurse and hospital administrator). *Education:* Studied voice at High School of Music and Art, New York City; received

B.S. from Boston University School of Public Communications, and M.S. from Columbia University Graduate School of Journalism. *Politics:* Independent. *Religion:* "No religious affiliation." *Avocational interests:* Music and community organizing involving education issues and conflict resolution.

ADDRESSES: Office—Los Angeles Times Magazine, Times Mirror Square, Los Angeles, CA 90053. *Agent*—Russell & Volkening, Inc., Literary Agents, 50 West 29th St., New York, NY 10001.

CAREER: Journalist and author. Professional singer and actress, performing in summer stock, in concerts, at nightclubs, and as a studio musician, 1965- 78; Spirit House Movers Theatre Company, actress and singer, 1970-73; affiliated with Blakluv (music and theatre ensemble), 1970-74; National Public Radio (NPR), WBUR-Radio, Boston, MA, reporter, 1972-73, reporter and coproducer of "The Drum" (a weekly program), and rotating host of "Multiversity" (a weekly program), 1973-75; reporter and producer for several radio documentaries, including *The War in Angola,* for NPR and Pacifica Radio; host and producer of the syndicated *Pan African News Report; Greenville News,* Greenville, SC, reporter, feature writer, and arts critic, 1978-81; *Miami Herald,* Miami, FL, feature writer for "Living Today" section, 1981-84, arts writer, essayist, and critic for "Lively Arts" section, 1984-86; *Los Angeles Times,* Los Angeles, CA, staff writer for "View" section, 1986-92; *Los Angeles Times Magazine,* Los Angeles, contributing editor, 1992—. Frequent university lecturer and television and radio talk-show guest on topics including the philosophy of multiculturalism, reporting on inter-ethnic issues, and the art of the memoir and the autobiographical African-American tradition.

MEMBER: Authors Guild, National Association of Black Journalists.

AWARDS, HONORS: Njeri was named "Best New Pop Vocalist" by MGM Records; Hovey Distinguished Lecture Award from University of Michigan; South Carolina Associated Press Award, feature writing, 1980; Lincoln University UNITY Media Award, education reporting, 1982; Penney-University of Missouri Journalism Prize, feature writing, 1983; National Endowment for the Humanities fellowship, 1983-84; Los Angeles Press Club award, excellence in entertainment reporting, 1989; National Association of Black Journalists Award, feature writing, 1990, for year-long *Los Angeles Times* series, "The Challenge of Diversity"; *Every Good-Bye Ain't Gone:*

Family Portraits and Personal Escapades was selected as a notable book of 1990 by the *New York Times Book Review;* American Book Award, Before Columbus Foundation, 1990, for *Every Good-Bye Ain't Gone.*

WRITINGS:

Every Good-Bye Ain't Gone: Family Portraits and Personal Escapades, Times Books (New York City), 1990.
Sushi & Grits: The Challenge of Diversity, Random House (New York City), 1993.
The Last Plantation: Color, Conflict, and Identity; Reflections of a New World Black, Houghton (Boston), 1997.

Work has appeared in anthologies, including *Bearing Witness: Selections from African-American Autobiography in the Twentieth Century,* edited by Henry Louis Gates, Jr., Pantheon, 1991; *Life Studies: A Thematic Reader,* edited by David Cavitch, St. Martin's, 1992; *Voices in Black & White: Writings on Race in America from Harper's Magazine,* edited by Katherine Whittemore and Gerald Marzorati, Franklin Square Press, 1992; and *Lure and Loathing: Race, Identity and the Ambivalence of Assimilation,* edited by Gerald Early, Viking, 1993. Contributor to periodicals, including *Essence, Emerge, Harper's,* and *Boston Globe Magazine.*

WORK IN PROGRESS: A screenplay adaptation of *Every Good-Bye Ain't Gone; The Secret Life of Fred Astaire,* a novel.

SIDELIGHTS: In 1990, Itabari Njeri received the American Book Award for her memoir *Every Good-Bye Ain't Gone: Family Portraits and Personal Escapades.* Njeri—African, East Indian, English, Native American and French—once described herself as "a typical descendant of the African diaspora." Her memoir evokes the life of middle-class African Americans and West Indians in Brooklyn and Harlem during the 1950s, 1960s, and 1970s. Her book, in great part, attempts to challenge racist conceptions of identity in America through an examination of her own family and of her life. "Nobody really knows us," she writes of African Americans. "So institutionalized is the ignorance of our history, our culture, our everyday existence that, often, we do not even know ourselves."

As a child, Njeri lived with her family in New York City and was encouraged to develop a singing talent and pursue a career in opera. Her father, who also had a beautiful voice, admired her when she sang, but had a difficult time showing affection otherwise. He was an alcoholic who often displayed violent behavior, and his problem was compounded because Njeri's mother refused to acknowledge that substance abuse contributed to his strained relations with his family.

Njeri also notes that her father suffered psychologically because his work as a historian, according to Njeri, was overlooked by dominant white culture. Njeri writes: "Since my father at once critiqued the society that denied him and longed for its approbation, he lived with the pain-filled consciousness of one who knows he is a joke. I think, sometimes, he laughed hardest, so often did I stumble upon him alone, chuckling into his balled fist at some silent, invisible, comedian." According to Meg Wolitzer of the *New York Times Book Review,* "the most persuasive piece in the book is Ms. Njeri's portrait of her father, whom she depicts as a brilliant, tormented Marxist historian who would sit for hours in his boxer shorts reading and writing, an applesauce jar of Teacher's Scotch beside him. Despite her father's repeated episodes of violence and neglect, she is charitable toward him—more charitable, even, than a dispassionate author might have been." During her teenage years, Njeri became a member of the Congress of African People (CAP), a Pan-African nationalist group headed by writer Amiri Baraka. While associated with the organization, Njeri was named Itabari by Baraka—she was originally named Jill Moreland—and abandoned a college major in music to study journalism. After a three-year association with the organization, Njeri became dismayed by cultural and sexual chauvinism and anti-Semitic attitudes held by some members of the CAP and left the group. In the early 1970s she began singing and acting with ensembles which included the Spirit House Movers Theatre Company and Blakluv. She eventually abandoned a career in the performing arts, however, for other pursuits. She told *CA:* "I left music not because I couldn't make a living singing modern music (at least if it was jazz or musical theatre) but because I was not willing to endure what one must—sexism, racism, etc.—on the way up."

Though Njeri details many aspects of her professional and personal life in her book, many reviewers found such insights less compelling than the stories that Njeri shares about her family. In addition to commenting on herself and her parents in *Every Good-Bye Ain't Gone* Njeri remarks on members of her extended family, including a cousin who was killed by drug dealers and an aunt who earned a living as a "Moll" during the 1940s and 1950s, involved in activities such as prostitution. Also notable in the memoir, according to several critics, is "Granddaddy," the story of Njeri's trip to Georgia to find out about the death of her grandfather E. A. R. Lord, which occurred in 1960. While growing up, Njeri had been told that white men who had been drag racing while drinking alcohol collided with her grandfather's automobile and then tried to keep the authorities from finding out about the accident. After repeated attempts at unraveling the mystery in a community where people are reluctant to speak about the incident, Njeri eventually discovers that the person driving the other car had not been drag racing and that there had been no attempt to divert local officials. Unbeknownst to the family, Lord's second wife received a court settlement after the accident. In addition to finding out the truth about her grandfather's death, Njeri discovers that the people living in the Georgia community hold racist attitudes that were prevalent in the early 1960s. Njeri writes that shortly after the accident, when Lord's light-skinned wife ran to tell a white officer about the incident, she was told, "Don't worry yourself ma'am. It's just a nigger."

Of Njeri's accomplishment in writing *Every Good-Bye Ain't Gone* Gail Lumet Buckley remarked in the *Los Angeles Times Book Review* that she "is a gifted and generous writer who rarely hides her feelings. These explorations of family myths and revelations of family conflict are a tumble of colliding emotions—love, hate, anger, regret—and are often very funny." And looking toward the future of Njeri's career as an author, Sherley Anne Williams in the *Washington Post* acknowledged that "Njeri's wit and style reveal a complex, independent character that many readers will want to know more about."

In *Bearing Witness: Selections from African-American Autobiography in the Twentieth Century,* Henry Louis Gates, Jr., one of the most influential contemporary scholars of African-American history and culture, placed *Every Good-Bye Ain't Gone* in the following literary and social context: "The African-American literary tradition is distinctive in that an author typically publishes as a first book her or his autobiography." He continued, saying that this is "true for many of the most prominent figures in the African-American tradition, from Frederick Douglass to Itabari Njeri. Through autobiography, these writers could, at once, shape a public 'self' in language, and protest the degradation of their ethnic group by the multiple forms of American racism. Njeri's contribution[s] to

[this] tradition are considerable. [Her text] has played a role for our generation of black intellectuals that Claude Brown's *Manchild in the Promised Land* played at the cusp of the civil rights era."

Njeri told *CA:* "I was not thinking of the great African-American autobiographical tradition when I first started my memoir, but I knew instinctively that by telling key aspects of my family's story, I would be illuminating important aspects of Black life. And I'm always thinking about the larger political picture when I write.

"To impose order on the chaos of memory is a universal impulse fueling the desire to write autobiography. But first and foremost, I hoped to create a work of art out of my experience as a woman of color in the New World at the end of the twentieth century. I wanted to illuminate the beauty, pain and complexity of a particular piece of the African diaspora, a piece central to the American experience. I wanted to tell the truth and make it sing.

"I consider myself a typical New World Black. And I understand that the substance of Black identity is complex. Please note that I consider Black a proper noun, referring not to color, but to culture and history. It is not the narrowly defined notion that obtains in the United States—a notion concocted by slave masters to perpetuate their chattel population, even if many were their own offspring. That notion is commonly known as the one-drop-in-the-bucket theory of descent, or what I think of as the little-dab'll-do-you school of genetics. In other words, one drop of African blood makes you Black in America and erases any other ancestry. Black identity in the New World is composite. I conceive of it no differently than the generally accepted notion of Latino or Hispanic identity, a generic ethnic label for people who are to varying degrees a mixture of Indian, European and African ancestry.

"Americans do not think of Black identity in this way. Therefore, that I acknowledge and embrace the complex substance of Black identity in the New World has led some reviewers to disproportionately emphasize this aspect of my memoir, even to suggest that one of the book's major themes is my attempts to come to terms with my miscegenated background. I've never met a Negro in America who doesn't have a mixed background—they've just been conditioned not to acknowledge it.

"What I write about in *Every Good-Bye* is that some of my relatives, who were phenotypically at the extreme ends of the color spectrum and looked White, suffered because American society has perpetuated by custom and law (and Blacks have accepted) a narrow definition of Black identity, one that exoticizes light-skinned Blacks (and penalizes dark-skinned Blacks). I explore the issue of color oppression thoroughly in several works: 'Sushi & Grits,' an essay published in *Lure and Loathing: Race, Identity and the Ambivalence of Assimilation;* my own collection of essays on diversity, *Sushi & Grits: The Challenge of Diversity;* and *The Last Plantation.*"

While the plantations of the South that dominated the lives of so many of the ancestors of African Americans are gone, "domination . . . breeds insidious offspring," Kanchan Limaye explains in *Reason.* "Oppressed people internalize the values of the oppressor, much like an abused child becoming an abusive parent. Thus their minds become 'the last plantation.'" This mindset is at the core of Njeri's book *The Last Plantation: Color, Conflict, and Identity; Reflections of a New World Black.* In this book, Greg Tate notes in the *Voice Literary Supplement,* "Itabari Njeri plunges into the chaos of American multiculturism. What she comes up with is brave, messy, brilliant, and caustic. A dispatch from the outer limits of the country's internecine race wars, the book reads as an enlightened take on our national obsession." Njeri recognizes that the race issue in the United States in the years ahead cannot be viewed as a black-white issue. Multiculturalism in America is growing on many fronts. New immigrants are shifting the relative size of minorities. Interracial and interethnic marriages continue to create children who carry many heritages within them. And, African Americans are developing a growing awareness of their own multicultural histories. In taking this view, Stanley Crouch comments in the *Los Angeles Times Book Review,* "Going her own way, Njeri brings intellectual sobriety, wit and pathos to the intricacies of her suject, creating a layered combination of memoir, first-class investigative reporting and social meditation."

Njeri's own family history brings together many of these elements, but the journalist also sees important issues highlighted in the events of the day. In particular, Njeri focuses on the 1991 shooting of fifteen-year-old Latasha Harlins by Sun Ja Du, a clerk in a Los Angeles grocery after a dispute over a bottle of orange juice. The tension between the African American and Korean American communities encapsulated in this incident would later explode during the Los Angeles riots. In covering the trial of the shooter, Njeri got to know both the defendant and the victim's

family. And, Patsy Sims, writing in the *New York Times Book Review,* finds "she is evenhanded in her attempts to see both sides: Latasha was no angel, she discovered, nor was Mrs. Du quite the villain she was made out to be." Through this and other examples, "Njeri examines the group strife that makes true coalitions nearly impossible today," Leslie Lockhart observes in *Emerge.* "In the hopes of fostering healing, she picks apart those conflicts." Adds Limaye, "Her book parts the curtain on the problems of those left out of the standard racial debated and helps set the stage for a new dialogue."

As a meditation on personal and social concerns to the author, "*The Last Plantation* lacks the lyricism of Ms. Njeri's highly praised first memoir, *Every Good-Bye Ain't Gone* . . . nevertheless," in the opinion of Patsy Sims, "it offers valuable insights that could help eliminate the narrow black-white categories that have fed this country's racism." *Washington Post Book World* contributor Debra Dickerson is less equivocal in her praise. "*The Last Plantation* is long overdue," she writes. "While there is no shortage of angry and highly verbal black women, Itabari Njeri is one of the few whose anger doesn't bypass her cerebellum before proceeding to her vocal chords. Her discerning, bluntly honest eye cuts through much of the tired, heard-it-all-before analysis usually produced when race is the issue." The result, in the view of Leslie Lockhart is that Njeri "succeeds in a fair and compassionate exploration of touchy topics. With a great sense of urgency, *The Last Plantation* makes a point that should be well-taken: We might all benefit from a reexamination of identity, if it means collective work and progress." Concludes Dickerson, "The combination of Njeri's mellifluous writing, keen powers of observation and journalistic skill marks this work as one that will stand the test of time."

BIOGRAPHICAL/CRITICAL SOURCES:

BOOKS

Gates, Henry Louis, Jr., editor, *Bearing Witness: Selections from African-American Autobiography in the Twentieth Century,* Pantheon (New York City), 1991.

Njeri, Itabari, *Every Good-bye Ain't Gone: Family Portraits and Personal Escapades,* Times Books (New York City), 1990.

PERIODICALS

Black Scholar, spring, 1997, p. 79.

Booklist, February 15, 1997, p. 980.
Emerge, April, 1997, p. 71.
Kirkus Reviews, January 1, 1997, p. 44.
Library Journal, November 1, 1996, p. 80.
Los Angeles Times Book Review, February 25, 1990, p. 1; June 15, 1997, p. 8.
New York Times Book Review, February 4, 1990, p. 9; April 20, 1997, p. 23.
Publishers Weekly, December 16, 1996, p. 48.
Reason, February, 1998, p. 55.
Voice Literary Supplement, summer, 1997, p. 24.
Washington Post, March 2, 1990.
Washington Post Book World, April 6, 1997, p. 4.

*   *   *

NKALA, Nathan 1941-
(Odunke, a joint pseudonym)

PERSONAL: Born October 25, 1941, in Umuawulu, Awka L.G., Nigeria; son of Okonkwo (a farmer and palmwine tapper) and Ndita Udunkwo (a homemaker; maiden name Uzonso Nwobu) Nkala; married Fanny Ebele Ezenwaji (an educator), August 25, 1975; children: Chike, Doris, Kenechi, Obidi. *Education:* University of Ibadan, B.A. (with honors), 1965; University of Nigeria, M.A., 1982. *Religion:* Christian. *Avocational interests:* Reading and writing, scrabble, lawn tennis.

ADDRESSES: Home—P.O. Box 1093, Enugu, Nigeria. *Agent*—c/o Fouth Dimension Publishing Co. Ltd., House 16, Fifth Ave., City Layout, PMB 01164, Enugu, Nigeria.

CAREER: Civil service of Eastern Nigeria, began in administrative class, 1965, became Director General/ Administrative Secretary, beginning 1992; freelance writer, c. 1988—.

MEMBER: Nigerian Institute of Management (MNIM), Institute of Personnel Management of Nigeria (AIPM), ODUNKE Community of Artists (executive member).

AWARDS, HONORS: Short story prize, Radio Netherlands, 1971; Macmillan Nigeria Prize, 1981.

WRITINGS:

(With others) *The Insider, Stories of War & Peace from Nigeria,* Nwamife (Enugu, Nigeria), 1971.

(With others, under joint pseudonym Odunke) *OJADILE* (play), OUP, 1977.
Mezie, the Ogbanje Boy (novel), Macmillan (Nigeria), 1981.
Bridal Kidnap, Leadway Books (Onitsha, Nigeria), 1988.
(With others, under joint pseudonym Odunke) *ONUKWUBE* (play), UPL, 1988.
Drums and the Voice of Death (novel), Fourth Dimension Publications (Enugu, Nigeria), 1996.
(With Patricia Davison) *Lobedu* (nonfiction), Heritage Library of African Peoples, 1997.

Also contributor of chapters to books, including "Towards an Inspired Policy for the Management of Urban Development in Anambra State," *The Nigeria Manager: Challenges, Development and Effectiveness,* Longman UK, 1982; "Inter-Cadre Career Paths and Over-Establishment," *Management Study of Anambra State Civil Service,* UNN, 1982; "Traditional Channels of Communication and Rural Development Policy Implementation: The Neglected Symbiotic Relationship," *Mass Communication and National Development,* edited by Ikechukwu Nwosu, Frontier Publishers, 1990; and "The Role of Top Management in Government-owned Companies," *Managing Government-owned Companies,* edited by Pita Ejiofor, Fourth Dimension.

WORK IN PROGRESS: Before the Bar-beach Show, a novel, for Fourth Dimension (Enugu, Nigeria); (with others, under joint pseudonym Odunke) *DI-JI-MUTA OFEKE,* a play, for UPL; *Biographical Notes on African Writers,* a nonfiction book; research on oral literature among the Igbo people, the "human anchorage" to modern African literature.

SIDELIGHTS: Nathan Nkala is a Nigerian writer who has authored several books. His book *Drums and the Voice of Death* is a novel about the Nigerian Civil War and is divided into four main sections and a prologue. The novel's prologue introduces readers to protagonist Kanayo, who is facing a death sentence for committing "robbery with violence." As the novel progresses, Kanayo flashes back to his participation in the Nigerian Civil War. The first two sections deal with events before that conflict, as the Igbo people of eastern Nigeria get ready to declare themselves as the nation of Biafra. The third section describes the war itself, ending in the defeat of the Igbo people. The fourth portrays the war's aftermath, in which Kanayo and his fellows deal with their ensuing feelings of powerlessness by planning a robbery.

In addition to Kanayo, *Drums and the Voice of Death* is peopled by characters such as Ichere Aku, an evil lawyer who, as Chimalum Nwankwo put it in his review of the novel for *World Literature Today,* "repeatedly and amazingly manages to pull away from a deserved death." Another character, Colonel Onyeanatugwu, is based upon a real-life colonel in the Biafran Army. Nwankwo cited "the novel's admixture of elegant prose with lyric poetry" in praising it, and went on to conclude that *Drums and the Voice of Death* "will find a good place in the treasury of works from the Nigerian civil war."

BIOGRAPHICAL/CRITICAL SOURCES:

BOOKS

Nkala, Nathan, *Drums and the Voice of Death,* Fourth Dimension, 1996.

PERIODICALS

OKIKE, October, 1996, p. 121.
World Literature Today, spring, 1997, p. 441.

*   *   *

NKOSI, Lewis   1936-

PERSONAL: Born December 5, 1936, in Natal, South Africa; son of Samson and Christine Margaret (Makathini) Nkosi; married Bronwyn Ollernshaw; children: Louise, Joy (twins). *Education:* Attended M. L. Sultan Technical College, 1954-55, and Harvard University, 1961-62; University of London, diploma in English literature, 1974; attended University of Sussex, 1977.

*ADDRESSES: Home—*Flat 4, Burgess Park Mansions, Fortune Green Rd., London NW6, England. *Office—*Department of English, University of Zambia, PO Box 31338, Lusaka, Zambia. *Agent—*Deborah Rogers Ltd., 29 Goodge St., London WC1, England.

CAREER: Ilanga lase Natal (title means "Natal Sun," Zulu-English weekly newspaper), staff member, 1955; *Drum* (magazine), chief reporter, Johannesburg, South Africa, 1956-60, *Golden City Post* (*Drum* Sunday newspaper), chief reporter, 1956-60; *South African Information Bulletin,* staff member, 1962-68; *The New African,* London, England, literary editor, 1965-68. Editor of journal in Dar es Salaam, Tanzania,

during 1960s. Correspondent in southern United States, *Observer* (London). Producer of British Broadcasting Company (BBC) radio series "Africa Abroad," 1962-65, interviewer of leading African writers for National Education Television (NET) series "African Writers of Today," 1963. Visiting Regents Professor of African Literature, University of California, Irvine, 1970; Professor of English, University of Zambia, Lusada.

AWARDS, HONORS: Nieman fellowship in journalism, Harvard University, 1961-62; Dakar World Festival of Negro Arts prize, 1966, for *Home and Exile and Other Selections.*

WRITINGS:

The Rhythm of Violence (also see below; play; first produced in London, 1963), Oxford University Press, 1964.
Home and Exile and Other Selections (essays), Longmans, Green, 1965, expanded edition, Longman, 1983.
(Contributor) *African Writing Today,* edited by Ezekiel Mphalele, Penguin, 1967.
(Contributor) *Plays from Black Africa* (includes *The Rhythm of Violence*), edited by Frederic N. Litto, Hill & Wang, 1968.
We Can't All Be Martin Luther King (radio play), BBC, 1971.
The Chameleon and the Lizard (libretto), first produced in London at Queen Elizabeth Hall, 1971.
Malcolm (play), first produced in London, 1972.
The Transplanted Heart: Essays on South Africa, Ethiope Publishing, 1975.
Tasks and Masks: Themes and Styles of African Literature, Longman (London), 1981, published as *Tasks and Masks: An Introduction to African Literature,* Longman, 1982.
Mating Birds, East African Publishing House, 1983, Harper, 1987.

Also author of screenplay, *Come Back Africa,* 1959. Author of television play, *Malcolm,* produced in England and Sweden in 1967. Author of radio play, *The Trial,* 1969. Contributor to periodicals and journals, including *Guardian, New Statesman, Observer, Transition, Black Orpheus, Spectator, West Africa, African Report, African Today,* and *New Yorker.*

SIDELIGHTS: Exiled after leaving South Africa to study at Harvard University, Lewis Nkosi has written short stories, plays, and criticism from his adopted home in England. Much of his work, however, deals with African literature and social concerns. "As a playwright and short-story writer, he is also the most subtly experimental of the black South African writers, many of whom are caught in the immediacy of the struggle against apartheid," comments Henry Louis Gates, Jr. in the *New York Times Book Review*.

According to Alistair Niven in *British Book News* Nkosi is "one of the architects of the contemporary black consciousness in South Africa." *Mating Birds,* Nkosi's first novel, brought him wide critical attention. The book focuses on South Africa's response to miscegenation through the story of a young man, Ndi Sibiya, a rural chief's son, who "meets" a white stripper named Veronica, on a segregated beach. Although the rules of apartheid keeps them from speaking to each other, a wordless flirtation commences. Sibiya becomes pulled into an obsessive relationship with Veronica and ends up following her everywhere. Eventually, Veronica seems to invite her suitor back to her bungalow, where Sibiya believes he is seduced. Veronica, however, calls the police and accuses Sibiya of rape, for which he is arrested. According to South African law, if he is found guilty, he can be executed. Many critics see the novel as a comment on apartheid. According to *Nation* contributor George Packer, "*Mating Birds* feels like the work of a superb critic. Heavy with symbolism, analytical rather than dramatic, it attempts nothing less than an allegory of colonialism and apartheid, one that dares to linger in complexity." Gates writes that *Mating Birds* "confronts boldly and imaginatively the strange interplay of bondage, desire and torture inherent in interracial sexual relationships within the South African prison house of apartheid." Critics have also praised Nkosi's portrayal of Sibiya's feelings for Veronica. Margaret Walters claims in the *Observer,* "the most remarkable thing in this short novel is the account of the obsession that grips Sibiya." Gates says that summarizing the plot "does not capture the book's lyrical intensity or its compelling narrative power. Mr. Nkosi has managed to re-create for his readers all the tortures of an illicit obsession, especially the ambiguities and interdeterminacy of motivation and responsibility." And *Washington Post Book World* contributor Alan Ryan writes, "*Mating Birds* is very possibly the finest novel by a South African, black or white, about the terrible distortion of love in South Africa since Alan Paton's *Too Late the Phalarope*."

But some readers dislike even the possibility of rape to convey Sibiya's response to white society. "Nkosi's handling of the sexual themes complicates the distribution of our sympathies, which he means to be un-

equivocally with the accused man," points out Rob Nixon in the *Village Voice*. "For in rebutting the prevalent white South African fantasy of the black male as a sex-crazed rapist, Nkosi edges unnecessarily close to reinforcing the myth of the raped woman as someone who deep down was asking for it." For Gates, however, the question of whether Sibiya rapes Veronica remains unclear. This causes problems for the reader, as "we are never certain who did what to whom or why." He quotes Sibiya's reflections on his trial: "But how could I make the judges or anyone else believe me when I no longer knew what to believe myself?. . . Had I raped the girl or not?" Gates continues, "We cannot say. Accordingly, this novel's great literary achievement—its vivid depiction of obsession—leads inevitably to its great flaw." Sara Maitland in the *New Statesman* objects to Nkosi's portrayal of Veronica: "Surely there must be another way for Nkosi's commitment, passion and beautiful writing to describe the violence and injustice of how things are than this stock image of the pale evil seductress, the eternally corrupting female?" Despite the novel's shortcomings, says Michiko Kakutani in the *New York Times, Mating Birds* "nonetheless attests to the emergence of . . . a writer whose vision of South Africa remains fiercely his own."

West Coast Review of Books contributor Sherman W. Smith believes that "Lewis Nkosi certainly must be one of the best writers out of Africa in our time." And Ryan suggests that "Nkosi's quiet voice is likely to linger in the ear long after the shouts and cries have faded away."

BIOGRAPHICAL/CRITICAL SOURCES:

BOOKS

Contemporary Literary Criticism, Volume 45, Gale, 1987.

PERIODICALS

Best Sellers, July, 1986.
Books and Bookmen, October, 1986.
British Book News, March, 1987.
Choice, June, 1982.
Listener, August 28, 1986.
London Review of Books, August 7, 1986.
Nation, November 22, 1986, pp. 570-574.
New Statesman & Society, August 29, 1986, pp. 25-26; January 22, 1988, p. 32.
New Yorker, May 26, 1986.
New York Times, March 22, 1986.

New York Times Book Review, May 18, 1986, p. 3.
Observer, July 27, 1986.
Southern Review, January, 1987, pp. 106-118.
Spectator, August 16, 1986.
Times Literary Supplement, August 13, 1964, p. 723; February 3, 1966, p. 85; August 27, 1982, p. 928; August 8, 1986, p.863.
Village Voice, July 29, 1986, p. 46.
West Coast Review of Books, September, 1986.
World Literature Today, spring, 1983, pp. 335-337; summer, 1984, p. 462.*

* * *

NYAMFUKUDZA, S(tanley) 1951-
(Stanley Nyamfukudza)

PERSONAL: Born in 1951.

ADDRESSES: Home—Zimbabwe. *Agent*—c/o College Press Publishers, 15 Douglas Rd., P.O. Box 3041, Workington, Harare, Zimbabwe.

CAREER: Novelist, short-story writer, poet, and editor.

WRITINGS:

The Non-Believer's Journey (novel), Heinemann (London), 1980, Heinemann (Exeter, NH), 1981.
Aftermaths, College Press (Harare, Zimbabwe), 1983.
(As Stanley Nyamfukudza) *If God Was a Woman* (short stories), College Press (Harare, Zimbabwe), 1991.
(Editor) *New Accents One: An Anthology of New Poetry,* College Press (Harare, Zimbabwe), 1993.

SIDELIGHTS: Zimbabwean writer S. Nyamfukudza came to the attention to the Western literary world with his 1980 novel *The Non-Believer's Journey.* This novel is set during the long war of liberation of Zimbabwe from the European colonial regime that had renamed it Rhodesia. That war made for "fertile material for fiction which explores the relationship between individual commitment and a violent national situation," in the opinion of African novelist Ben Okri, writing in *New Statesman;* and it was that relationship between individual commitment (or lack of it) and national strife that Nyamfukudza explores. As *Times Educational Supplement* critic Edward Blishen presented it, *The Non-Believer's Journey* expresses its author's commitment to freedom from external rule, but at the same time the novel is "marked by a quite

extraordinary detachment" on the intra-Zimbabwean conflict between two ethnic groups, the Ndebele and the Shona.

The Non-Believer's Journey depicts the reluctant trip that an urbanized schoolteacher, Sam, makes to his rural village in order to attend the funeral of his uncle, who has been murdered as an informer. The novel's opening scene, in which Sam vomits out the window after a night's drunkenness, sets a tone for the novel and represents, for *World Literature Today* reviewer Robert Cancel, "a promising beginning suggesting all sorts of possibilities for humor, irony or bawdiness." Sam's cynicism, his feeling of being lost within his troubled environment, is first shown here. As he travels from the city of Salisbury to his native village, he engages in a series of dialogues with people he meets, often judging them hypocrites or fools. The bus is delayed by a roadblock; there is an unpleasant encounter with an ill-educated white soldier. In the village, tension arises as Sam re-encounters a woman he has not seen in seven years; when local guerrillas try to trap him into helping them his refusal leads to a fatal fight with one of their comrades.

For reviewer Blishen, this material added up to a novel that was to be recommended "for its rawness" and for the "remarkably subtle" rendition of a character who is destroyed by his own impossible wish for detachment. Reviewer Cancel was less enthusiastic, writing that Sam's "self-obsessed cynicism" was a result of thin characterization rather than of deeply explored ideas or feelings; the dialogue too, Cancel declared, was problematic, so that Sam did not achieve "the status of a roguish anti-hero, a Tom Jones." Cancel did find "some interesting moments and descriptions" in the novel, however, pointing out that Nyamfukudza's "portrayal of urban and township attitudes and environments often rings true." For Cancel, the bus ride from city to countryside was "probably the novel's most affecting scene." Novelist-critic Okri praised Nyamfukudza's work highly, recognizing Sam as "something of an anti-hero." Wrote Okri, "*The Non-Believer's Journey* is well written, its scenes drawn with ironic confidence, the failure of intellectual individualism vividly presented. Its subject is important and, as a picture of a place and of the lostness of a city people, its realism is admirable and sometimes disturbing." Although Okri felt that the novel's "purposeful pointlessness" sometimes verged into the missing of its own point, he concluded that "Nyamfukudza writes tight, energetic prose and, when all is said, *The Non-Believer's Journey* is a worthwhile book indeed."

A decade later Nyamfukudza produced another book-length work of fiction, this time the short-story collection *If God Was a Woman*. As the title suggests, the volume's ten tales explore the relationships between men and women, and the title story overtly elaborates on the idea of a ruling goddess. *World Literature Today* reviewer Pamela J. Olubunmi Smith felt that the first two stories in the collection were its weakest, bogging down in a style marred by "seemingly overpolished college-English" and Americanisms. She was quick to add, however, that "the technique accelerates after the first two stories." She singled out three stories for their "convincing narration": the title story, "Eaten Promises," and "Days without Hope," in which a man lists excuses for not taking responsibility after he makes a woman pregnant.

BIOGRAPHICAL/CRITICAL SOURCES:

PERIODICALS

British Book News, January, 1981, p. 57.
New Statesman, January 30, 1981, p. 20.
Times Educational Supplement, January 23, 1981, p. 21.
World Literature Today, winter, 1983, pp. 163-164; autumn, 1992, p. 765.

*   *   *

NYAMFUKUDZA, Stanley
   See NYAMFUKUDZA, S(tanley)

O

ODUNKE
See NKALA, Nathan

* * *

OGUNDIPE-LESLIE, 'Molara

PERSONAL: Born in Lagos, Nigeria; married; children: two daughters. *Education:* Graduated from University of Ibadan, Nigeria (first-class honors).

CAREER: Writer and educator. University of Ibadan, former faculty member; Ogun State University, Nigeria, Department of English, former chair; lecturer in English and African literature at universities in Africa, Canada, and the United States, including Columbia University, Harvard University, University of California—Berkeley, and Northwestern University. Contributing essayist and member of editorial board, *The Guardian* (newspaper), Nigeria. National director of Social Mobilization, Federal Government of Nigeria, 1987-89.

MEMBER: Women in Nigeria (founding member), Association of African Women for Research and Development (founding member).

WRITINGS:

(Contributor) *Sisterhood Is Global: The International Women's Movement Anthology,* edited by Robin Morgan, Doubleday (Garden City, NY), 1984.
Sew the Old Days and Other Poems, Evans Bros. (Nigeria), 1985.

(Contributor) *Theorizing Black Feminisms,* edited by Stanlie James and Abena Busia, Routledge (New York City), 1993.
Re-Creating Ourselves: African Women and Critical Transformations, Africa World Press (Trenton, NJ), 1994.
(Editor, with Carole Boyce Davis, and contributor) *Moving Beyond Boundaries,* New York University Press (New York City), Volume 1: *International Dimensions of Women's Writing,* 1995, Volume 2: *Black Women's Diasporas,* 1995.

Also author of *Towards a Double-Gendered Cosmos: Essays on African Literature.*

SIDELIGHTS: An educator, poet, and activist for social change within her native Nigeria, 'Molara Ogundipe-Leslie is the author of numerous essays that analyze the way social and economic class differences prohibit women from uniting to form a global feminist consciousness. A contributor to Robin Morgan's groundbreaking *Sisterhood Is Global: The International Women's Movement Anthology,* and the author of the 1994 essay collection *Re-Creating Ourselves: African Women and Critical Transformations,* Ogundipe-Leslie remains an outspoken critic of the patriarchal traditions that are still revered throughout the African continent.

In an essay entitled "The Female Writer and Her Commitment," originally published in *The Guardian* in 1983 and reprinted in *Re-Creating Ourselves,* Ogundipe-Leslie asserts that, in her view, "female writers cannot usefully claim to be concerned with various social predicaments in their countries or in Africa without situating their awareness and solutions within the larger global context of imperialism and neo-colonialism." Indeed, the colonization of many African nations by the British put an end to women's economic power and, thus, their autonomy. Similar to Marxist feminists, Ogundipe-Leslie contends that women's true liberation is conditional upon the breakdown of both patriarchy and capitalism.

Re-Creating Ourselves includes other essays that address such wide-ranging topics as little-studied works of literature, the masculine dialogue of revolutionary politics, and the implications of modern capitalism's inequitable economic practices. The diversity of these issues reflects their author's broad area of social concern as well as the philosophical basis of her feminism. "[M]en are not the enemy," Ogundipe-Leslie writes in the essay "Not Spinning on the Axis of Maleness," published in *Sisterhood Is Global* in 1984. "The enemy is the total societal system. . . . But," she adds of the social transformation necessary in order to attain an equitable global society, "men do become enemies when they seek to retard or even block these necessary historical changes."

BIOGRAPHICAL/CRITICAL SOURCES:

BOOKS

Morgan, Robin, editor, *Sisterhood Is Global: The International Women's Movement Anthology,* Doubleday (Garden City, NY), 1984.

Ogundipe-Leslie, 'Molara, interview in *In Their Own Voices: African Women Writers Talk,* James Currey (London), 1990.

Ogundipe-Leslie, 'Molara, *Re-Creating Ourselves: African Women and Critical Transformations,* Africa World Press (Trenton, NJ), 1994.

Otukunefor, Henrietta, and Obiagele Nwodo, editors, *Nigerian Female Writers: A Critical Perspective,* Malthouse (Lagos, Nigeria), 1989.

*   *   *

OGUNYEMI, Chikwenye Okonjo 1939-

PERSONAL: Born October 30, 1939, in Lagos, Nigeria; daughter of Joseph Adigwe and Dora Mgbolie (Okocha) Okonjo; married E. Olanrewaju Ogunyemi, October 24, 1964 (deceased); children: Omolola Ijeoma, Enuma Olanrewaju. *Education:* University College, Ibadan, Nigeria, B.A. (with honors), 1964; University of London, B.A.; Columbia University,

New York City, M.A., 1968, Ed.M., 1972; University of Ibadan, Ph.D., 1978.

ADDRESSES: Office—Sarah Lawrence College, Bronxville, NY 10708. *Agent*—c/o University of Chicago Press, 5801 Ellis Ave., Chicago, IL 60637. *E-mail*—ogunyemi@mail.slc.edu.

CAREER: Literary critic, writer, and educator specializing in fiction by Nigerian women and the African diaspora. Queen's College, City University of New York, instructor, 1971-72; University of Ibadan, Ibadan, Nigeria, instructor in literature, beginning 1972; moved to United States as political exile; Sarah Lawrence College, Bronxville, NY, educator, 1989—.

MEMBER: Modern Language Association, College Language Association, African Literature Association.

AWARDS, HONORS: American Association of University Women fellow, 1970-1971; Copeland Fellow; recipient of Hewlett-Mellon grant.

WRITINGS:

Africa Wo/Man Palava: The Nigerian Novel by Women, University of Chicago Press (Chicago, IL), 1996.

Contributor to anthologies, including *Revising the Word and the World: Essays in Feminist Literary Criticism,* edited by VeVe A. Clark, Ruth-Ellen B. Joeres, and Madeon Sprengnether, University of Chicago Press (Chicago, IL), 1993. Co-editor of two special issues of *Research in African Literatures* on women writers. Author of scholarly articles and book chapters on African literature, African American literature, and black women's literature contributed to academic journals and books.

SIDELIGHTS: Nigerian literary critic Chikwenye Okonjo Ogunyemi, living in exile in the United States in response to the political problems of her homeland, has become known as an important theorist of the fiction written in English by Nigerian women. In an article originally published in the journal *Signs* in 1985, she elaborated a concept she dubbed "womanism" as an alternative to Western feminism. (The term "womanism" was also used, independently, by the African American novelist Alice Walker to make a similar distinction; Ogunyemi expressed pleasure at seeing this independent convergence, according to critic Judith Kent Green in *National Women's Studies*

Association (NWSA) Journal.) Womanism, as Green explained it, embodies a racial as well as a gender consciousness and was aimed not so much at redressing women's universal grievances against men, but at allowing Nigerian women and men to reconcile with each other in a joint effort to overcome that nation's recent history of turmoil. Green saw womanism as less confrontational than feminism; for another critic, Aderemi Raji-Oyelade in the Canadian journal *Ariel,* Ogunyemi's womanism was a "deconstructive exercise" that aimed "vital questions at the pretentious universalism and covert provincialism of Western feminist theorizing."

Ogunyemi's womanism saw book-length expression in her 1996 volume, *Africa Wo/Man Palava: The Nigerian Novel by Women.* The volume was, Raji-Oyelade reported, "the first sustained book-length study of the tradition of the Nigerian novel by women spanning 28 years (1966-1994)" and also "perhaps the most significant theory of narrative by a Nigerian female critic on the novel genre to date." The study is organized into two major parts. In Part One, Ogunyemi surveys and analyzes the history and tradition of female literature, both written and oral, in Africa, emphasizing the mother/goddess figure who, for Ogunyemi, is a central motif in womanism. Part Two studies eight specific female Nigerian novelists. Three important older novelists, Flora Nwapa, Adaora Lily Ulasi, and Buchi Emecheta, are given a chapter apiece; the last chapter gives "brief but insightful" treatment (in Raji-Oyelade's phrase) to five young novelists: Funilayo Fakunle, Zaynab Alkah, Eno Obong, Ifeoma Okoye, and Simi Bedford, all of whom, in the view of *Choice*'s P. W. Stine, "deserve to be better known." In the main, Raji-Oyelade observed, Ogunyemi interpreted these novelists as "constructive activists in nation-building," their fiction serving as "narratives of nationhood."

Ogunyemi uses certain Nigerian terms as names for some of her central theoretical concepts. She makes much of the Portuguese-derived word *palaver,* meaning a kind of lengthy, diplomatic discourse, and its homophone *palava,* meaning trouble or quarrel. For Ogunyemi, women and men must come together in talking about a healing process in the Nigerian community; thus, the title phrase, "Wo/Man Palava," which includes both sexes in its discourse. Critic Green saw this approach as somewhat "ambivalent about feminism"; for example, Green reported, Ogunyemi did not condemn the widespread African practice of female circumcision, although she did express hope that it would diminish as education pro-

gressed. Green felt that Ogunyemi's book was repetitious at times and could have used editorial input to correct this as well as the "unsettling shifts in tone." She concluded, however, that, "Reading these critical discussions, . . . professors will find valuable insights into how to approach African writing in English in a responsible and enlightened manner."

Raji-Oyelade hailed Ogunyemi for challenging "the chauvinist strategies of reading the African novel." That critic wrote, "Without doubt, Chikwenye O. Ogunyemi has succeeded in achieving a deliberate, methodical construction of a woman-centered vernacular theory." *Africa Wo/Man Palava,* the critic continued, "has drawn on a series of textual stitches to create a common quilt of a womanist ideology in Nigerian women's literature." *Choice* reviewer Stine concluded, "This book skillfully combines literary criticism, content analysis, and African 'womanist' ideology. It should be in any library that seeks geographical and gender breadth."

BIOGRAPHICAL/CRITICAL SOURCES:

PERIODICALS

Ariel, July, 1997, pp. 182-86.
Choice, September, 1996, p. 120.
NWSA Journal, Summer, 1997, pp. 180-83.

OTHER

Chikwenye Okonjo Ogunyemi's home page, http://www.cis.upenn.edu/~ogunyemi/momhome.html (October 6, 1998).
Sarah Lawrence College, http://www.slc.edu/about/faculty/literature.html (October 6, 1998).
Womanist Theory and Research, http://www.uga.edu/~womanist/1995/mezu.html (October 6, 1998).*

*   *   *

OJAIDE, Tanure 1948-

PERSONAL: Born April 24, 1948, in Okpara Inland, Nigeria; son of Dafetanure (a farmer) and Avwerhoke (a trader; maiden name Odjegba) Ojaide; married Anne Numuoja (a school teacher and administrator), 1976; children: Obaro, Dafe, Eloho, Amreghe, Kowho. *Education:* University of Ibadan, B.A. (English), 1971; Syracuse University, M.A. (creative writing), 1979; Ph.D. (English), 1981. *Ethnicity:*

"African." *Politics:* "Left of center." *Religion:* "Fallen Catholic/free thinker." *Avocational interests:* Traveling, observing nature.

ADDRESSES: Home—7629 Dayberry Ln., Charlotte, NC 28227. *Office*—African-American and African Studies Department, University of North Carolina-Charlotte, Charlotte, NC, 28223. *E-mail*—tojaide@ email.uncc.edu.

CAREER: Poet and educator. St. Kevin's College, Kokori, Nigeria, teacher, 1971-73; Federal Government College, Warri, Nigeria, English teacher, 1973-75; Petroleum Training Institute, Effurun, lecturer in English and communication, 1975-77; University of Maiduguri, Nigeria, lecturer in English/communications, 1977-85, senior lecturer, 1985-87, reader, 1987-89; Whitman College, Walla Walla, WA, Visiting Johnston Professor of Third World Literatures, 1989-90; University of North Carolina at Charlotte, assistant professor, 1990-93, associate professor, 1993-98, professor of African-American and African studies, 1998—, also became chair of African Studies Academy; National Endowment for the Humanities fellow, 1990-2000; Albright College, Reading, PA, National Endowment for the Humanities Professor, 1996-97.

MEMBER: International Black Writers, African Studies Association, African Literature Association, Associated Writing Programs, Modern Language Association, North Carolina Writers Network, Association of Nigerian Authors.

AWARDS, HONORS: Fellow in writing, University of Iowa, 1985; Africa Regional Winner, Commonwealth Poetry Prize, 1987, for *Labyrinths of the Delta;* BBC Arts and Africa Poetry Award, 1988, for "The Fate of Vultures"; Association of Nigerian Authors' Poetry Prize, 1988, for *The Fate of Vultures and Other Poems,* and 1994, for *Invoking the Warrior Spirit;* All-Africa Okigbo Poetry Prize, 1988, for *The Eagle's Vision,* and 1997, for *The Daydream of Ants;* Roll of Honor Award, Ahmadu Bello University Creative Writers Association, 1989; National Merit Award nomination, Nigeria, 1989; honorable mention, Noma Award Committee, 1990; Southern Regional Education Board grants, 1992 and 1994; research grants, University of North Carolina, Charlotte, 1992-93, 1993-94, 1995-96; curriculum/instructional development grant, University of North Carolina, Charlotte, 1993-94; fellow, Headlands Center for the Arts (Sausalito, CA), 1994; faculty research support grants, University of North Carolina, Charlotte, 1996-97 and 1998-99; summer research grants, University of North Carolina, Charlotte, 1997 and 1999; National Endowment for the Humanities Professorship, 1996-97; National Endowment for the Humanities Fellowship, 1999-2000.

WRITINGS:

POETRY

Children of Iroko and Other Poems, Greenfield Press (New York City), 1973.
(With S. S. Ugheteni) *Yono Urhobo: Obe Rerha,* Macmillan (Lagos, Nigeria), 1981.
Labyrinths of the Delta, Greenfield Review Press (New York City), 1986.
The Eagle's Vision, Lotus Press (Detroit), 1987.
Poems, Poetry International (Rotterdam), 1988.
The Endless Song, Malthouse Press (Lagos), 1989.
The Fate of Vultures and Other Poems, Malthouse Press (Lagos), 1990.
The Blood of Peace, Heinemann (Oxford), 1991.
The Daydream of Ants, Malthouse Press (Lagos), 1997.
Cannons for the Brave, Malthouse (Oxford), 1998.
Delta Blues and Home Songs, Kraft Books (Ibadan, Nigeria), 1998.
Invoking the Warrior Spirit, Heinemann (Ibadan, Nigeria), 1998.

Also contributor of poems to periodicals, including *Nimrod, New Letters, Okike, Madison Review, Europe, Syracuse Review, West Africa, Chelsea, Poetry Europe, London Magazine, Poetry Review, Obsidian II, Pale Fire Review, Washington Review, Blue Moon, Soho Square, Hayden's Ferry Review, Agon, Paintbrush, Wasafiri,* and *Illuminations.* Contributor of poems to anthologies, including *For Neruda/Chile,* edited by Walter Lowenfels Beacon Press (Boston), 1974; *Aftermath: African, Caribbean & Asian Poetry,* Greenfield (New York City), 1977; *The Fate of Vultures: New Poetry of Africa,* Heinemann (Oxford), 1989; *The Heinemann Book of African Poetry in English,* edited by Adewale Maja-Pearce, Heinemann (Oxford), 1990; *Border Lines: Contemporary Poems in English,* edited by Andy Wainwright, Copp Clark Longman (Toronto), 1995; *Poesie d'Afrique au Sud du Sahara (1945-95),* edited by Bernard Magnier, Editions UNESCO (Paris), 1995; *New Poets of West Africa,* edited by Tijan Sallah, Malthouse Press (Lagos), 1995; *Rainbow Voices: An Anthology of Poetry,* selected by J. O. Hendry, Hodder & Stoughton (Johannesburg/London), 1996; *Poetry 2000: An Anthology of Poems,* selected by Thomas Olver and

Frances Olver, Hodder & Stoughton (Johannesburg/London), 1996; *Emergency Kit: Poems for Strange Times,* edited by Jo Shpcott and Matthew Sweeney, Faber and Faber (London), 1996; and *Ogoni's Agonies,* Africa World Press (Trenton, NJ), 1998.

OTHER

The Poetry of Wole Soyinka (criticism), Malthouse (Oxford), 1994.

Poetic Imagination in Black Africa: Essays on African Poetry (criticism), Carolina Academic Press (Durham, NC), 1996.

Great Boys: An African Childhood (autobiography), Africa World Press (Trenton, NJ), 1998.

Contributor to books on African studies and African poets, including *Contemporary Literary Criticism,* edited by Daniel G. Marowski and Roger Metuz, Gale, Volume 36, 1986, and Volume 43, 1987; *Research on Wole Soyinka,* edited by Bernth Lindfors and James Gibbs, Africa World Press (Trenton, NJ), 1993; *Africana Studies: A Survey of Africa and the African Diaspora,* edited by Mario Azevedo, Carolina Academic Press (Durham, NC), 1993; *Of Dreams Deferred, Dead or Alive: African Perspectives on African-American Literature,* edited by Femi Ojo-Ade, Greenwood Press (Westport, CT), 1996; *Ken Saro-Wiwa, Writer and Environmental Activist: Essays in Assessment,* edited by Craig W. McLuckie and Aubrey McPhail, Lynne Rienner Publishers, 1998; and *Black Literature Criticism,* Gale. Contributor of articles and reviews to periodicals, including *Greenfield Review, BA SHIRU, UMOJA, Syracuse Scholar, Research in African Literatures, Liwuram: Journal of the Humanities, Callaloo, Chelsea, Literary Half-Yearly, Annals of Borno, Black Literature Forum, Geneve-Afrique, Literary Endeavour, The Jos Journal of Language and Literature, African Studies Review, College Literature, Middle Atlantic Writers Association Review, Mother Earth Journal, CLA Journal, Women's Studies Quarterly, African Book Publishing Record,* and *World Literature Today.*

WORK IN PROGRESS: Writing poems, short stories, and a novel; also *Invoking the Warrior Spirit: Selected and New Poems,* for Africa World Press (Trenton, NJ), expected in 1999.

SIDELIGHTS: Poet Tanure Ojaide was born in Okpara Inland, Nigeria, and, though he now writes and teaches in North Carolina, his work is deeply rooted in his home. Ojaide grew up in the Delta region of Nigeria, an area of forest and river, mostly

under the care of his maternal grandmother, whom he pays tribute to in his poem "A Verdict of Stone": "In your flitting twilight, you called / my name with your last breath, / and I held you; but you were already / irrevocably possessed for the endless journey."

In an article in *Research in African Literatures,* Tijan M. Sallah described Ojaide as one of the finest of the new crop of Nigerian poets and remarked, "Of the new generation of African poets and their poetry, there are only a few that one would read and return to. . . . Tanure Ojaide belongs to those few." Ojaide and his contemporaries have been working to develop what Ode S. Ogedo referred to in another *Research in African Literatures* article as "a new, Africanized voice that would free them of the old constraints" of poetic forms derived from European cultures.

A unifying theme of Ojaide's poetry is his hatred of tyrants and his commitment to social change. He views the poet as a warrior who throws *assegais* (spears) at despotic leaders. With poems that serve as both art form and weapon, Ojaide takes aim at African dictators; as Sallah noted in *Research in African Literatures,* he sums them up as "greedy, ruthless, and lacking in any coherent social vision and who, far from being benevolent, exploit the coercive authority of the state for often pernicious ends." In his poem "The Fate of Vultures," for example, Ojaide compares ruthless Nigerian politicians with these carrion-eating, scavenging birds, always on the lookout for a quick profit from another's death.

Ojaide deplores the economic and social crisis that has developed in some parts of Africa, where the old values of respect for age, hard work, food production, and artisan's skills have fallen away and been replaced by a dangerous hunger for worthless, showy consumer goods. As Ojaide writes, "In Agbarha / Nobody wakes to work; / everybody washes his mouth with gin / and sits at home / on a floor-mat of a throne. / Are you surprised / at kwashiorkor princes and princesses, / prostitute queens and beggar kings?"

Ojaide often draws on his own cultural metaphors, and his poems are full of such African animals as hyenas and vultures as well as references to common aspects of Nigerian culture: blacksmiths, hunters, oil-palms, rubber trees, gods, and chiefs. "His ability to integrate technical virtuosity with cultural authenticity makes him admirable," Sallah remarked, but Ojaide's work is not only relevant to Africa: the Nazi Holocaust, racism in America, and problems in Bangladesh also appear in his work.

Ojaide believes that poets are special people, gifted with greater perception of society, people, and truth. As Ojaide told *CA,* "I write because I love writing. I also feel that others may like to share my experiences. I write about what I feel, what I experience, and what I imagine."

BIOGRAPHICAL/CRITICAL SOURCES:

PERIODICALS

Research in African Literatures, winter, 1986; spring, 1995, p. 20; summer, 1998, p. 230.

*   *   *

OKIGBO, Christopher (Ifenayichukwu) 1932-1967

PERSONAL: Born in 1932, in Ojoto, Nigeria; died August, 1967; son of James (a school teacher) Okigbo; married wife, Sefi, in 1963; children: Ibrahimat (daughter). *Education:* University of Ibadan, B.A., 1956.

CAREER: Nigerian Department of Research and Information, Lagos, Nigeria, private secretary to the Minister, 1955-56; affiliated with Nigerian Tobacco Company and United Africa Company; Fiditi Grammar School, Fiditi, Nigeria, Latin teacher, 1959-60; University of Nigeria, Nsukka, assistant librarian, 1960-62; Cambridge University Press, Ibadan, Nigeria, Nigerian representative, 1962-66; founder of small publishing company with Chinua Achebe in Enugu, 1967. Member of editorial staff of Mbari Press. *Military service:* Biafran Defense Forces, 1967; became major; killed in action.

AWARDS, HONORS: Dakar Festival of Arts first prize for *Limits,* 1966 (refused); posthumously awarded Biafran National Order of Merit.

WRITINGS:

POETRY

Heavensgate, Mbari Press, 1962.
Limits, Mbari Press, 1964, originally published in periodical *Transition,* 1962.
Poems: Four Canzones (contains "Song of the Forest," "Debtor's Lane," "Lament of the Flutes," and "Lament of the Lavender Mist"), published in periodical *Black Orpheus,* 1968.

Labyrinths, with Path of Thunder, Africana, 1971.
Collected Poems, Heinemann, 1986.

Works represented in anthology "African Writers Series," number 62, Heinemann, 1971. Contributor of poetry to periodicals, including *Transition* and *Black Orpheus.* Coeditor of *Transition.*

SIDELIGHTS: "There wasn't a stage when I decided that I definitely wished to be a poet," Christopher Okigbo once commented, "there was a stage when I found that I couldn't be anything else."

Paul Theroux calls Okigbo "an obscure poet, possibly the most difficult poet in Africa." He suggests two approaches to Okigbo's work. One is to examine the words he used, many springing from his wide knowledge of other writers, and all having a special meaning in the context of his own work. The other is to "listen to his music." According to Theroux, one can hear three separate melodies in it: "the music of youth, the clamour of passage (that is, growing up) and lastly, the sounds of thunder."

Part of the difficulty, according to Sunday Anozie, lies in the fact that "Okigbo's poetry is constantly exploring two irregular dimensions of myth . . . myth as a privileged religious mode of cognition" and myth, with totem, as "affective and even evaluative in a given cultural context." Anozie also notes the derivative nature of the poet's work, the "wide range of references to and echoes of other poets," which further obscure his poetry.

In Theroux's opinion, *Heavensgate* and *Limits* express the "music of growth," a music which also suggests the danger inherent in growing up. The bird imagery running through both poems is related to the speaker, the poet who appears in all of Okigbo's work and would seem to represent Okigbo himself. *Silences* and *Distances* speak of the disillusionments which can follow maturation and the loss of innocence. "It is safe to say that very few poems achieve the music and harmony that *Silences* does," Theroux commented. *Distances,* however, is characterized by pain, shocking images such as that of the "horizontal stone" which represents a morgue slab holding a corpse, and the repetition of the line, "I was the sole witness to my homecoming," indicating solitude at the attainment of maturity.

Okigbo felt none of the conflict between old and new that often seems to pose a problem for educated Africans. He often went back to his village for festivals and major religious ceremonies, and his own religion combined Christian and pagan elements. In an interview with Marjory Whitelaw, he described the family shrine which housed their ancestral gods, the male Ikenga and the female Udo, whom he considered different aspects of the same force represented by the Christian god. Unlike others in his family, he never made sacrifices to these deities, but he declared: "My creative activity is in fact one way of performing these functions in a different manner. Every time I write a poem, I am in fact offering a sacrifice." Okigbo's maternal grandfather, of whom he was believed to be a reincarnation, was the priest of a shrine to Idoto, the river goddess, and the poet's idea of his own priesthood is apparent in much of his writing.

In spite of this oneness with his background and the local themes and images which abound in his work, Okigbo did not adhere to the literary concept of negritude, which, he felt, emphasized racial differences. He told Marjory Whitelaw: "I think I am just a poet. A poet writes poetry and once a work is published it becomes public property. It's left to whoever reads it to decide whether it's African poetry or English. There isn't any such thing as a poet trying to express African-ness. Such a thing doesn't exist. A poet expresses himself."

His interest in social and political change in his own country, however, formed an inseparable part of his work. Okigbo told Whitelaw of his conviction that the poet in any society could not examine his own identity in isolation, but that "any writer who attempts a type of inward exploration will in fact be exploring his own society indirectly." Okigbo's concern for humanity was perhaps best expressed in his commitment to the Biafran secession. He lost his life in August, 1967, fighting as a volunteer for the Biafran forces.

Anozie wrote: "Nothing can be more tragic to the world of African poetry in English than the death of Christopher Okigbo, especially at a time when he was beginning to show maturity and coherence in his vision of art, life and society, and greater sophistication in poetic form and phraseology. Nevertheless his output, so rich and severe within so short a life, is sure to place him among the best and the greatest of our time."

BIOGRAPHICAL/CRITICAL SOURCES:

BOOKS

Anozie, Sunday O., *Christopher Okigbo: Creative Rhetoric,* Evans Brothers Limited, 1972, 203 p.

Black Literature Criticism, Volume 3, Gale (Detroit), 1992.
Contemporary Literary Criticism, Gale, Volume 25, 1983, Volume 84, 1995.
Dictionary of Literary Biography, Volume 125: *Twentieth-Century Caribbean and Black African Writers, Second Series,* Gale, 1993.
Egudu, Romanus, *Four Modern West African Poets,* NOK (New York City), 1977.
Knipp, Thomas R., *African Literature in Its Social and Political Dimensions,* edited by Eileen Julien, Mildred Mortimer, and Curtis Schade, Three Continents Press, 1984, pp. 41-50.
Lindfors, Bernth, *When the Drumbeat Changes,* edited by Carolyn A. Parker and Stephen H. Arnold, African Literature Association and Three Continents Press, 1981, pp. 199-214.
Mazrui, Ali A., *The Trial of Christopher Okigbo,* Third Press (New York City), 1971.
Moore, Gerald, *The Chosen Tongue: English Writing in the Tropical World,* Harper & Row, 1969, pp. 163-76.
Ngate, Jonathan, *Explorations: Essays in Comparative Literature,* edited by Makota Ueda, University Press of America, pp. 253-77.
Nwoga, Donatus Ibe, editor, *Critical Perspectives on Christopher Okigbo,* Three Continents Press, 1984, 367 p.
Okafor, Dubem, *The Dance of Death: Nigerian History and Christopher Okigbo's Poetry,* Africa World Press (Trenton, NJ), 1997.
Poetry Criticism, Volume 7, Gale, 1994.
Theroux, Paul, *Introduction to Nigerian Literature,* edited by Bruce King, Africana Publishing Corporation, pp. 135-51.

PERIODICALS

African Arts, 1968, pp. 68-70.
African Literature Today, 1968, pp. 14-25.
Books Abroad, spring, 1971.
Journal of Commonwealth Literature, July, 1968, pp. 79-91; July, 1970.
Journal of the New African Literature and the Arts, fall, 1967, pp. 1-13.
Nigeria Magazine, April-June, 1985, pp. 6-13.
Poetry, 1964, p. 400.
Presence Africaine, 1967, pp. 158-66.
Research in African Literatures, spring, 1978, pp. 65-78.
Studies in Black Literature, summer, 1973, pp. 1-8.
World Literature Written in English, autumn, 1990, pp. 131-44.*

OKRI, Ben 1959-

PERSONAL: Born in March 15, 1959, in Minna, Nigeria. *Education:* Attended Urhobo College, Warri, Nigeria, and the University of Essex, England.

ADDRESSES: Agent—c/o Jonathan Cape, 20 Vauxhall Bridge Rd., London SW1V 25A, England.

CAREER: Writer. Poetry editor, *West Africa* magazine, 1981-87; broadcaster, "Network Africa," BBC World Service, 1984-85. Visiting Fellow at Trinity College, Cambridge, England. Has also worked as a writer and reviewer for the *Guardian, Observer,* and the *New Statesman.*

AWARDS, HONORS: Commonwealth Writers' Prize for Africa; *Paris Review* Aga Khan prize for fiction; Booker Prize for fiction, 1991, for *The Famished Road.*

WRITINGS:

Flowers and Shadows (novel), Longman (London), 1980.
The Landscapes Within (novel), Longman, 1981.
Incidents at the Shrine (short stories), Heinemann (London), 1986.
Stars of the New Curfew (short stories), Secker & Warburg (London), 1988, Viking (New York City), 1989.
The Famished Road (novel), Cape (London), 1991.
An African Elegy, (poetry), Cape, 1992.
Songs of Enchantment, (novel), Doubleday (New York City), 1993.
Astonishing the Gods, (novel), Phoenix House (London), 1995.
Dangerous Love, (novel), Phoenix House, 1996.

SIDELIGHTS: Novelist, poet, and short story writer Ben Okri continually seeks in his writings to capture the post-independent Nigerian worldview, including the civil war and the ensuing violence and transformation, no matter how troubling or painful these events may be. In an essay written in 1991, Okri stated that "if the poet begins to speak only . . . of things he can effortlessly digest and recognise, of things that do not disturb, frighten, stir, or annoy us . . . in restricted terms and exclusively with restricted language, then what hope is there for us." Indeed Harry Garuba asserted in the *Dictionary of Literary Biography* that "even though the manner in which [Okri] explores these issues has sometimes become a matter of contention among his peers, there is, nonetheless, little

doubt about the importance of his contribution to the development of the contemporary Nigerian novel." With publication of *The Famished Road,* Okri won praise of the highest form from Henry Louis Gates, Jr., who wrote in the *New York Times Book Review*: "[Okri] has ushered the African novel into its own post-modern era through a compelling extension of traditional oral forms that uncover the future in the past. But while *The Famished Road* may signal a new achievement for the African novel in English, it would be a dazzling achievement for any writer in any language."

Okri uses nightmarish imagery and surrealist contortions of reality to portray the bizarre social and political conditions inside Nigeria. "Dreams are the currency of Okri's writing," said Giles Foden in the *Times Literary Supplement,* dreams "made on the stuff of Africa's colossal economic and political problems." *The Economist* noted of Okri's collective oeuvre, "It has often been hard to tell whether he was describing dream or reality—and it did not seem to matter much anyway." Critics have associated Okri's techniques with those practiced by magic realists, a school of writers who incorporate supernatural elements into otherwise realistic settings. Michiko Kakutani, reviewing *Stars of the New Curfew* for the *New York Times,* commented that Okri's Africa "seems like a continent dreamed up, in tandem, by Hieronymus Bosch and Jorge Luis Borges—a land where history has quite literally become a nightmare." However, Okri insists that the supernatural elements in his works are realistic representations of the Nigerian experience, demonstrating the continuity between the realistic and mystical realms of experience that exists for Nigerians.

Beginning with his first novel, *Flowers and Shadows,* published when Okri was only twenty-one, Okri devoted much of his work to describing the political and social chaos inside Nigeria, a country that has not had a stable government for nearly thirty years. The pictures he creates are dark and often violent. In his review of *Incidents at the Shrine* for the London *Observer,* Anthony Thwaite called Okri "an obsessive cataloguer of sweat, phlegm, ordure and vomit," and Kakutani noted that the author's characters "live in a state of suspended animation, their private lives overshadowed by political atrocities, whatever ideals they might have had eroded by the demands of day-to-day survival." The narrator of the title story of *Stars of the New Curfew* is a vagabond medicine salesman whose cures often backfire, sending people to violent, grisly deaths. He is constantly on the run from his victims, but cannot outrun his visions. An unnamed character in the story "Worlds That Flourish," also in *Stars of the New Curfew,* flees a hellish city only to find himself in a more literal hell, where some people have wings but can not fly, others have feet that face backward, and an old neighbor appears with three eyes. Susan Cronje, who called the book "an important comment on Nigerian society" in her review for *New Statesman & Society,* said that "Okri's writing is suffused with helpless anger at the alienation of Nigerian society, the corruption not only of the rulers but also of the ruled who seem to connive at their own oppression."

Okri's 1991 novel, *The Famished Road,* which received England's prestigious Booker Prize, further explores the Nigerian dilemma. Charles R. Larson, writing in *World & I,* remarked that "the power of Ben Okri's magnificent novel is that it encapsulates a critical stage in the history of a nation . . . by chronicling one character's quest for freedom and individuation." *The Famished Road*'s main character is Azaro, an *abiku* child torn between the spirit and natural world. His struggle to free himself from the spirit realm is paralleled by his father's immersion into politics to fight the oppression of the poor. The novel introduces a host of people all of whom "blend together . . . to show us a world which may look to the naked eye like an unattractive ghetto, but which is as spiritually gleaming and beautiful as all the palaces in Heaven— thanks to the everyday, continuing miracle of human love," wrote Carolyn See in the *Los Angeles Times.*

By novel's end, Azaro recognizes the similarities between the nation and the *abiku;* each is forced to make sacrifices to reach maturity and a new state of being. This affirming ending also "allows rare access to the profuse magic that survives best in the dim forests of their spirit," according to Rob Nixon of the *Village Voice.* Similarly, in her appraisal for the London *Observer,* Linda Grant commented, "Okri's gift is to present a world view from inside a belief system." *Detroit Free Press* contributor John Gallagher deemed the work "a majestically difficult novel that may join the ranks of greatness."

In *Songs of Enchantment,* Okri continues to explore the story and themes raised in *The Famished Road.* However, while the focus in the first book was on the efforts of Azaro's parents to keep him among the living, the focus in the second book is, wrote Charles R. Larson in the *Chicago Tribune,* "an equally difficult battle to restore the greater community to its earlier harmony and cohesiveness." As Azaro further

chronicles the oppression that has hold of his village and his family, the landscape increasingly becomes intermingled with the political and social chaos. At one point, Azaro leaves the village with his father: "It was impossible to determine how long we had been running, or how far we had travelled. But after awhile, it seemed as if Dad had been running in a straight line which paradoxically curved into an enchanted circle. We couldn't break out of the forest." This sequence functions metaphorically, as Azaro comes to realize that the entire nation of Nigeria is undergoing a similarly debilitating series of changes. Because of this, *Songs of Enchantment* more clearly explicates Okri's concerns with the problems visited upon Africa after decolonization. Wrote Larson, "The wonder of *Songs of Enchantment* . . is that it carries on so richly the saga of nation building implying that countries that have broken the colonial yoke may face an even more difficult struggle."

Okri further makes use of the dreamlike world he is so adept at creating, as well as the world of suspended disbelief inherent to the folk tale. For *The Songs of Enchantment* is closer to a collection of folk tales than to the novel, and this form further emphasizes Okri's theme of redemption as well as the confusion that is visited upon Azaro and his countrymen. As Judy Cooke pointed out in *New Statesman & Society,* "Many folk tales are working towards a creation myth, examining causation and identity . . . Okri's work is perhaps best enjoyed in this context."

Like *The Songs of Enchantment,* Okri's next novel also revisited the landscape of one of his earlier works. *Dangerous Love* is a reworking of Okri's second novel, *The Landscapes Within,* published 15 years earlier. *Dangerous Love* tells the story of Omovo, a young clerk in a chemicals firm who in his spare time paints canvases that depict his bleak ghetto surroundings. Although the "dangerous love" of the title refers to Omovo's love affair with a married woman, the spiritual evil that has consumed Nigeria makes Omovo's art—the belief that he can redream his world—just as dangerous.

Like *The Landscape Within, Dangerous Love* is essentially a *kuenstlerroman*—a novel that traces the evolution of an artist, for Omovo uses his art as a way of finding a spiritual place for himself. Alan Riach wrote in *Contemporary Novelists* of *The Landscapes Within:* "Social and political corruption are the condition and context of Omovo's artistic effort." Indeed, throughout the novel, Omovo debates with himself and his friends the role of the Nigerian artist and the art they produce. "I think because our lives are so hard our art needs to soothe, to massage, more than it needs to pry open our wounds," argues Omovo at one point in the novel. However, the uncompromising reality of the Nigeria presented by Okri—the slums, the poverty, the corruption—make it clear that Okri does not hold to this view. As Ruth Pavey wrote in *New Statesman & Society*, "Okri conveys a poignant sense of a generation caught between languages and identities, . . . More poignant still is the hindsight we now have: that their fears for the future were better founded than their hopes."

Michael Kerrigan of the *Times Literary Supplement* wrote of *Dangerous Love,* "The painter-protagonist, Omovo, is as lost as the reader is in a disturbing slumscape which, though all too oppressively real, seems to clamor for allegorical interpretation." However, it is in *Astonishing the Gods* that Okri truly creates such a landscape; Alev Adil wrote in the *Times Literary Supplement* that the novel "has jettisoned reality altogether, preferring to inhabit an allegorical space that bears no scars or traces of modernity whatsoever." Okri creates a nameless hero, who, upon learning to read and thus discovering that he and his people are invisible because they are not included in any history books, sets out on a quest to become visible. However, the quest turns into a spiritual journey of understanding for the hero, who achieves perfect invisibility after a series of tests that culminates in his naming of the Invisibles' dream: "creativity and grace." The message of the hero's embracing of his natural state is dual. Wrote Amit Chauduri in *The Spectator,* "One can read this book . . . as an affirmation and celebration of the creativity and contributions of those communities which are, to all purposes, 'invisible' to the greater world, and also as an autobiography of an African writer who has 'arrived,' in every sense of that word, in the West."

New Statesman & Society reviewer Guy Mannes-Abbott, who saw *Astonishing the Gods* as a work "about language and change," compared Okri's belief in the ability of language to create possibilities, as demonstrated in the novel, to Okri's own language, which he finds "properly worked and exact, [fulfilling] Calvino's prescription for lightness—being like a bird, rather than a feather." He asserted that *Astonishing the Gods* is "an impressive, brave and often beautiful little book that is not for the literal-minded." Similarly, Charles R. Larson of the *Nation* called *Astonishing the Gods* "the most remarkable novel of [Okri's] career" and welcomed it as "a dazzling and unabashedly spiritual narrative at a time when most

writers are afraid to articulate matters of the soul in public."

Okri explores the tensions between hope and despair in graceful, controlled, and spare language. "His fiction is full of the thresholds of (im)possibility, of mutability and self-renewal, and is rendered in correspondingly unrestricted language: rich, opaque, sometimes rapturous," wrote Mannes-Abbott in *New Statesman & Society*. Of his writing in *Incidents at the Shrine,* Sara Maitland said in *New Statesman & Society* that "sentence by sentence he turns in beautiful, strong prose, dense with lyricism and metaphor, skipping elegantly along the edge of surrealism and never collapsing into it." Okri's descriptions of Nigeria are so finely etched that locale takes on a life of its own. As Pavey wrote of the ghetto backdrop in *Dangerous Love,* "Smelly, noisy, colourful, overcrowded and hot, the character of the place assumes a central role."

All of these fine aspects of Okri's work led Maureen Freely, who reviewed *Stars of the New Curfew* for the London *Observer,* to comment: "There are many novelists who write as well as Okri, many who share his gift for recreating the texture of everyday life, many who can cut through the surface to expose, as he does, the myths our elders and betters use to keep us in our place. There are very few novelists who can do all three. The fact that Ben Okri has done so in short stories, without ever losing his balance, his humour, or his edge, makes his accomplishment all the more exceptional."

BIOGRAPHICAL/CRITICAL SOURCES:

BOOKS

Contemporary Literary Criticism, Volume 87, Gale (Detroit), 1995.
Contemporary Novelists, sixth edition, St. James Press (Detroit), 1996.
Dictionary of Literary Biography, Volume 157: *Twentieth-Century Caribbean and Black African Writers,* Gale (Detroit), 1996.

PERIODICALS

Christian Science Monitor, November 23, 1987; July 10, 1992.
Detroit Free Press, August 30, 1992, p. 9P.
Economist, June 15, 1996, p. 3.
London Times, July 24, 1986.

Los Angeles Times Book Review, September 24, 1989, pp. 3, 13; June 8, 1992, p. 6.

Nation, May 27, 1996, p. 31.

New Statesman & Society, May 9, 1986, p. 35; July 13, 1986, p. 27; July 25, 1986, p. 30; October 17, 1986, p. 36; July 29, 1988, pp. 43-44; March 22, 1991, p. 44; March 26, 1993, p. 41; March 24, 1995, p. 25; April 12, 1996, p. 37.

New York Times, July 28, 1989.

New York Times Book Review, August 13, 1989, p. 12; June 28, 1992, pp. 3, 20; October 10, 1993.

Observer (London), July 10, 1988, p. 42; October 27, 1991, p. 61.

Spectator, April 1, 1995, p. 33.

Time, June 19, 1989.

Times (London), April 7, 1996.

Times Literary Supplement, August 8, 1986, p. 863; August 5-11, 1988, p. 857; April 19, 1991, p. 22; April 17, 1992, p 8; March 10, 1995; April 5, 1996, p. 26.

Tribune Books (Chicago), July 16, 1989, p. 6; June 14, 1992; October 10, 1993, p. 1.

Village Voice, August 25, 1992, p. 87.

Washington Post, August 7, 1989.

Washington Post Book World, May 24, 1992; October 3, 1993.

World & I, March, 1992, pp. 383-387.

World Literature Today, spring, 1990, p. 349.*

*   *   *

OMOTOSO, Kole 1943-

PERSONAL: Born Bankole Ajibabi Omotoso, April 21, 1943, in Akure, Nigeria; son of Gabriel Omotoso Falibuyan and Ajibabi Daramola Osukoti; married; children: one daughter and two sons. *Education:* Attended King's College, Lagos; University of Ibadan, B.A., 1968; University of Edinburgh, Ph.D., 1972.

ADDRESSES: Agent—c/o Hans Zell, Northvale, NJ.

CAREER: Ibadan University, Ibadan, Oye, Nigeria, lecturer, 1972-76; University of Ife, Ife, Nigeria, professor, beginning c. 1976; University of Western Cape, Cape Town, South Africa, professor of English, 1992—.

MEMBER: African Writers' Association, Association of Nigerian Authors (founder; national secretary, 1981-84; president, 1986-87).

WRITINGS:

Notes, Q & A on Peter Edwards' West African Narrative, Onibonoje (Ibandan, Nigeria), 1968.

Pitched against the Gods (stage play), first produced at Deen Playhouse, Ikare, Nigeria, 1969.

The Edifice, Heinemann (London), 1971.

The Combat, Heinemann, 1972.

Miracles and Other Stories, Onibonoje, 1973, revised, 1978.

Fella's Choice, Ethiope (Benin City, Nigeria), 1974.

Sacrifice, Onibonoje, 1974, revised, 1978.

The Curse (play), New Horn (Ibadan), 1976.

The Scales, Onibonoje, 1976.

(Coeditor) *The Indigenous for National Development: Essays on Social, Political, Education, Economic & Cultural Issues,* Onibonoje, 1976.

Shadows in the Horizon: A Play about the Combustibility of Private Property, Omotoso/Sketch, 1977.

Kole Omotoso of Nigeria (recording), Voice of America (Washington, DC), 1978.

To Borrow a Wandering Leaf, Olaiya Fagbamigbe (Akure), 1979.

The Form of the African Novel, Olaiya Fagbamigbe, 1979, revised edition, McQuick, 1986.

Memories of Our Recent Boom, Longman (Harlow, United Kingdom), 1982.

The Theatrical into Theatre: A Study of the Drama and Theatre of the English-Speaking Caribbean, New Beacon (London), 1982.

Kingdom of Chance and Other Stories, Onibonoje, 1982.

Discovering African Literature, Ikenga (Oxford, England), 1982.

A Feast in the Time of Plague, Dramatic Arts/Unife, 1983.

The Girl Sunshine, Dramatic Arts/Unife, 1983.

The Last Competition (stage play), first produced at National Theatre, Lagos, 1983.

All This Must Be Seen (travel articles), Progress (Moscow), 1986.

Just before Dawn, Spectrum (Ibadan), 1988.

(Editor) *Fellow Nigerians: Famous First Words of Nigerian Coup-makers, 1966-1985,* House of Books (Ile-Ife), 1989.

Season of Migration to the South: Africa's Crises Reconsidered, Tafelberg (Cape Town), 1994.

(Editor with Yvette Hutchison) *Open Space: Six Contemporary Plays from Africa,* Kagiso (Groote Schuur, South Africa), 1995.

Achebe or Soyinka?: A Study in Contrasts, Hans Zell (Northvale, NJ), 1996.

Contributor to periodicals and newspapers, including Lagos *Sunday Times, Top Life,* Lagos *Sunday Concord Okike,* and *Index on Censorship.*

SIDELIGHTS: Kole Omotoso is a prominent Nigerian writer who writes both to offer answers to Nigeria's problems as well as to entertain. Although he grew up believing in the nationalist dreams of peace and prosperity for independent Africa, as an adult he was forced to confront the reality of civil war and numerous coups d'etat—events that have caused a steady decline in the quality of life for many Nigerians.

His writings reflect anxiety over Africa's future, but never despair. It is his belief that the artist must help lead the way to a better life for the common people, and this is reflected in his writing. "Art for art's sake is intellectual crap," Omotoso tells J. B. Alston in *Yoruba Drama in English.* "Whereas if you are committed to communicating with everyone who reads your works, that's a very basic and responsible kind of commitment."

Omotoso, the nephew of Yoruba author Olaiya Fagbamigbe, began writing in primary school. His first influences were family folktales, and his first audience his schoolmates. By the time he was in secondary school, Omotoso began to be published, but in English, rather than his native Yoruba. Later, when he went to Great Britain to study Arabic, the racism he experienced there provided the inspiration for his first novel. With the publication of *The Edifice,* Omotoso's career blossomed. He wrote essays, plays, short stories, and novels. Among them was *Miracles and Other Stories,* a collection that focused on the plight of poor children in Nigeria. During his career, the author's work has become increasingly politicized. The content of his novels reflects Omotoso's concern with the future of his homeland. He was strongly influenced by the shaky political climate of Nigeria, a country where military rule predominates. Omotoso struggled against the limitations of that situation.

In 1977, the author released his play *Shadows in the Horizon* privately, after publishers deemed it too controversial. The piece was successful; ultimately, it was translated into Russian. Like other authors, including the well-known playwright Wole Soyinka, whom Omotoso calls his major influence, African themes are important in his work. Even in a book such as *Fella's Choice,* which is modelled on the James Bond series, Omotoso had serious intent. His objective in writing that thriller, according to *Dictionary of Literary Biography* contributor F. Odun Balogun, "was to win Nigerian youths away from Western detective fiction and the ideology it propagates. In *Fella's Choice* Omotoso tempers the heroic individualism characteristic of the Western detective novel with an emphasis on communal ethics. . . . The novel's theme, which concerns neutralizing the anti-African designs of the secret agents of apartheid South Africa, has political importance." *The Scales* is another thriller that holds serious African themes at its core.

Omotoso followed *Fella's Choice* with another novel, *Sacrifice,* which concerns a doctor's quandary when he practices medicine in the same town where his mother plies her trade as a prostitute. It was this profession that allowed her to send her son to medical school. Balogun comments: "Africa, the novel suggests, has first to understand and come to terms with its past, however sordid, before it can move forward."

In 1992, Omotoso and his family left Nigeria, where the social commentary of the author's work put them in danger of retribution by the military elite of that country. The first book Omotoso published after moving to post-apartheid South Africa, *Season of Migration to the South,* was suppressed in his native land.

Omotoso's fiction nearly always reflects a preoccupation with the future of the common folk of his country. In *Yoruba Drama in English,* he is quoted as saying that "the conscious artist can contribute towards building a new mode of life. Anything he does—the way he presents his characters, the way he lives his own life—is likely to influence what other people are going to do." Assessing the author's body of work, Balogun concludes that throughout his career, Omotoso "has steadily been acquiring what it takes to become a great African writer."

BIOGRAPHICAL/CRITICAL SOURCES:

BOOKS

Agetua, John, *Interviews with Six Nigerian Writers,* Bendel Newspapers Corporation (Benin City), 1974, pp. 9-16.

Alston, J. B., *Yoruba Drama in English,* Edwin Mellen, 1989, pp. 107-115.

Dictionary of Literary Biography: Volume 125: *Twentieth-Century Caribbean and Black-African Writers, Second Series,* Gale (Detroit), 1993.

Lindfors, Bernth, editor, *Dem-Say: Interviews with Eight Nigerian Writers,* African and Afro-American Studies and Research Center, University of Texas (Austin), 1974.

Nazareth, Peter, *The Third World Writer,* Kenya Literature Bureau (Nairobi), 1978, pp. 71-86.

Nichols, Lee, *Conversations with African Writers,* Voice of America, 1981, pp. 218-229.

PERIODICALS

African Book Publishing Record, no. 2, 1976, pp. 12-14.

African Literature Today, 13, 1983, pp. 98-121.

BBC Arts and Africa, Number 74, 1975; Number 433, 1982; Number 610, 1985.

Commonwealth Essays and Studies, autumn, 1984, pp. 36-50.

Cultural Events in Africa, Number 103, 1973, pp. 2-12.

Daily Times (Lagos), March 12, 1974, p. 12.

Guardian (Lagos), June 9, 1986, p. 10; November 22, 1986.

Indigo (Lagos), Volume 2, number 3, 1975.

Journal of Commonwealth Literature, Volume 25, number 1, 1990, pp. 98-108.

Newswatch (Lagos), April 15, 1985.

Notre Librairie, July-September, 1989, pp. 68-70.

Spear (Lagos), July, 1976; September, 1976.

Theatre Research International, autumn, 1982, pp. 235-244.

Transition (Kampala, Uganda), Number 44, 1974.

Vanguard (Lagos), August 8, 1985.

World Literature Written in English, April, 1977, pp. 39-53.*

*   *   *

OSUNDARE, Niyi 1947-

PERSONAL: Born March 12, 1947, in Ikerri, Nigeria. *Education:* University of Ibadan, B.A. (English; honors), 1972; University of Leeds, M.A. (English), 1974; York University, Toronto, Canada, Ph.D. (English), 1979.

ADDRESSES: Agent—Heinemann Educational Books, Ighodaro Road Jericho, PMB 5205, Ibadan, Oyo State, Nigeria

CAREER: Writer and freelance journalist. Lecturer, University of Ibadan, 1982—; also taught at the Uni-

versity of Wisconsin and the University of New Orleans, 1990-92.

AWARDS, HONORS: Commonwealth Poetry Prize, 1986, for *The Eye of the Earth;* Association of Nigerian Authors Poetry Prize 1986, for *The Eye of the Earth;* Cadbury Poetry Prize, 1989; Fulbright scholarship, 1990, 1991; Noma Prize, 1991, for *Waiting Laughters: A Long Song in Many Voices.*

WRITINGS:

Songs of the Marketplace, New Horn Press (Ibadan), 1983.

Village Voices, Evans Brothers (Ibadan), 1984.

A Nib in the Pond, Department of Literature in English, University of Ife (Ife-Ife), 1986.

The Eye of the Earth, Heinemann Educational Books (Ibadan), 1986.

The Writer as Righter: The African Literary Artist and His Social Obligations (Ife Monograph Series on Literature and Criticism, 4th Series, No. 5), Department of Literature in English, University of Ife, 1986.

Moonsongs, Spectrum Books (Ibadan), 1988.

Songs of the Season, Heinemann Educational Books, 1990.

Waiting Laughters: A Long Song in Many Voices, Malthouse Press (Ikeja, Lagos), 1990.

Selected Poems, Heinemann International Literature and Textbooks (Oxford), 1992.

African Literature and the Crisis of Post-Structuralist Theorising (Dialogue in African Philosophy Monograph Series, No. 2), Options Book and Information Service (Ibadan), 1993.

Midlife, Heinemann Educational Books, 1993.

Also contributor of numerous poems and essays to anthologies and literary periodicals, including *African Concord, African Literature Today, Journal of African and Comparative Literature, Okike, Newswatch, Topical Issues in Communication Arts,* and *West Africa.*

SIDELIGHTS: Oluwaniyi Osundare was born in 1947 in Ikerri, a Yoruba village in western Nigeria. His father's father was a healer, diviner, and herbalist, and Osundare often went to the forest with him to gather roots and herbs for cures. In addition to the powers of plants, the healer also had to know incantations to make them work, and so when he was a young boy, Osundare was taught that language is magical and powerful. Osundare's father was a noted speaker, singer, drummer, and composer, and once when Osundare's mother told him he was too old to drum, he told her he was not too old to stop living. Osundare's father, in addition to imparting his love of words and music, also told him that education would give him wings. He took his father's advice, and ultimately earned a Ph.D. in English.

Osundare is the first English-speaking poet to be awarded the most prestigious book award in Africa, the Noma Prize. He is considered one of a group of poets of what Don Burness, in *Dictionary of Literary Biography*, called an "alter-native" tradition: Africans who write in English. Drawing on diverse inspirations including the oral traditions of his home village, Walt Whitman, and William Wordsworth, he celebrates the earth and human life, but also criticizes social and political forces that value money and technology over nature and humanity.

Osundare is devoted to making his poetry accessible. He does not believe that writers need extensive education in order to become writers. Rather, what they need is dedication. He told Elizabeth Rosen in *Writer's Digest,* "I have this feeling that one hasn't become a writer until one has distilled writing into a habit, and that habit has been forced into an obsession. . . . It has to be something as organic, physiological and psychological as speaking or sleeping or eating." In his works Osundare also champions the poor and dispossessed. Burness wrote, "Osundare has been praised for his combination of lyrical grace and passionate solidarity with the wretched of the earth, and [his collection] *Village Voices* gives ample evidence that such an evaluation is valid." The book describes the widening dichotomy between Nigeria's poor and the corrupt rich, who profited off the Nigerian oil boom in the late 1970s and early 1980s.

Osundare's collection *The Eye of the Earth* is notable for its elegant style, musical voice, rich metaphors, and social commentary, as well as its plea for people to live lives more balanced with the harmony of nature. Burness remarked that "Rooted in reality, he soars to a vision of man and the earth as brothers and narrates his own initiation into the society of singers of the world's natural landscapes. *The Eye of the Earth* may be Osundare's outstanding achievement to date." *Midlife,* Osundare's most recent collection, is autobiographical and deeply rooted in his life and in his African home. Like African singing, it involves the audience; the audience asks questions and participates in the poems. Phrases in Yoruba, Osundare's native language, occur frequently and are not always translated.

Burness summed up Osundare's life and work by writing that Osundare's readiness "to explore new poetic territory . . . sets him apart. . . . Wherever he travels, poetry is his companion. Osundare is the opposite of the recluse in his tower, for he prefers a peripatetic existence, bringing the music of his poetry to students and lovers of poetry wherever he finds them."

BIOGRAPHICAL/CRITICAL SOURCES:

BOOKS

Dictionary of Literary Biography, Volume 157: *Twentieth-Century Caribbean and Black African Writers,* Gale (Detroit, MI), 1996.

PERIODICALS

Writer's Digest, April, 1995, p. 6.*

*   *   *

OUSMANE, Sembene   1923-

PERSONAL: Name cited in some sources as Ousmane Sembene; born January 8, 1923, in Ziguinchor, Casamance,Senegal. *Education:* Attended technical school; studied at Gorki Film Studios in early 1960s.

ADDRESSES: Home—c/o P.O. Box 8087, Yoff, Dakar, Senegal.

CAREER: Worked as fisherman in Casamance, Senegal, and as plumber, mechanic's aid, and bricklayer in Dakar, Senegal, before World War II; worked as docker and stevedore in Marseilles, France, in late 1940s; became union leader. Writer and filmmaker; founder, editor, *1st Wolof Language Monthly.* Military service: Served in French Army during World War II.

AWARDS, HONORS: Literature prize from Dakar Festival of Negro Arts, 1966, for *Vehi-Ciosane ou Blanche-genese, suivi du Mandat;* prize from Cannes Film Festival, 1967, for "Le Noire de. . ."; special prize from Venice Film Festival, 1968, and award for best foreign film from Atlanta Film Festival, 1970, both for "Mandabi;" Gold Metal from the Venice Film Festival, 1992, for "Guelwaar."

WRITINGS:

Le Docker noir (novel; title means "The Black Docker"), Nouvelles Editions Debresse, 1956.

Oh Pays, mon beau peuple! (novel; title means "Oh My Country, My Beautiful People"), Le Livre Contemporain, 1957.

Les Bouts de bois de Dieu (novel), Amiot-Dumont, 1960, translation by Francis Price published as *God's Bits of Wood,* Doubleday, 1962.

Voltaieque (short stories), Presence Africaine, 1962, translation by Len Ortzen published as *Tribal Scars, and Other Stories,* INSCAPE, 1974.

Vehi-Ciosane; ou, Blanche-genese, suivi du Mandat (two novellas), Presence Africaine, 1965, translation by Clive Wake published as *The Money Order, With White Genesis,* Heinemann, 1971.

Xala (novel; title means "Impotence"), Presence Africaine, 1973, translation by Clive Wake published as *Xala,* Lawrence Hill, 1976.

Dernier de l'empire (novel), Harmattan, 1981, translation by Adrian Adams published as *The Last of the Empire,* Heinemann, 1983.

Niiwam; suivi de Taaw: nouvelles (novel), Presence Africaine (Paris), 1987, translated as *Niiwam; and Taaw,* Heinemann, 1992.

Also author of the novel *Fat Ndiay Diop,* 1976.

OTHER PUBLISHED FICTION

"Le Noire de. . ." (short story), published in *Presence africaine* in 1961, translation by Ellen Conroy Kennedy published as "Black Girl" in *African Short Stories,* edited by Charles R. Larson, Macmillan, 1970.

Referendum (novel; first novel in *L'Harmattan* trilogy), published in *Presence africaine* in 1964.

SCREENPLAYS; AND DIRECTOR

Le Noire de. . . (adapted from Ousmane's story; also see above), Actualities Francais/Films Domirev of Dakar, 1966 (released in the United States as *Black Girl,* New Yorker Films, 1969).

Mandabi (adapted from Ousmane's novella *The Money Order;* also see above), Jean Maumy, 1968 (released in the United States by Grove Press, 1969).

Emitai, Paulin Soumanou Vieya, 1971 (released in the United States by New Yorker Films, 1973).

Xala (title means *Impotence*), Societe Nationale Cinematographique/Films Domirev, 1974 (released in the United States by New Yorker Films, 1975).

Ceddo, released in the United States by New Yorker Films, 1978 (first released in 1977).

Also screenwriter and director of *Borom Sarret,* 1964; *Niaye,* 1964; *Tauw,* 1970; the unreleased film *Songhays,* 1963; and *Guelwaar.*

OTHER

Ousmane Sembene: Dialogues with Critics and Writers, edited by Samba Gadjigo, Massachusetts Press, 1993.

Contributor to periodicals, including *Presence africaine.* Founding editor of periodical *Kaddu.*

SIDELIGHTS: Sembene Ousmane is a respected Senegalese artist who has distinguished himself in both literature and film. He was born in 1923 in the Casamance region and attended school only briefly before working as a fisherman. After moving to Senegal's capital, Dakar, Ousmane found various jobs in manual labor. He worked in Dakar during the late 1930s, but when World War II began he was drafted by the colonial French into their armed forces, and he eventually participated in the Allied invasion of Italy. When the war ended Ousmane returned home to the Casamance area and resumed his early life as a fisherman. After a short period, however, he traveled back to France, where he found work as a stevedore on the Marseilles docks.

Ousmane's experiences as a dockworker provided background for his first novel, *Le Docker noir* ("The Black Docker"). In this work Ousmane wrote of a black stevedore who writes a novel but is robbed of the manuscript by a white woman. Much of the novel delineates the ensuing consequences of that incident. Although *Le Docker noir* proved somewhat flawed, it nonetheless represented an alternative career for Ousmane after a back injury rendered him unfit for dock work. With *Le Docker noir* Ousmane sought to express the plight of many minorities including Spaniards and Arabs as well as blacks exploited and abused at the French dockyards. But while he specified afterwards that his perspective was that of the minority, and thus contrary to that of whites, Ousmane was quick to add that he was not advocating negritude, a black-pride movement that he dismissed as sentimental and narrow-minded in its emphasis. He remained, however, a champion of black rights in Africa.

Ousmane's concern over conflicting philosophies within Africa's black community is evident in his second novel, *Oh Pays, mon beau peuple!* ("Oh My Country, My Beautiful People"), which concerns the failings of an ambitious Senegalese farmer returning home after a long absence. Accompanied by his white wife, the farmer alienates himself from both whites and blacks, for both groups resent his interracial marriage and his efforts to modernize the community's farming system. Eventually the farmer's behavior becomes intolerable to the villagers, and he is killed. Like *Le Docker noir, Oh Pays, mon beau peuple!* was written in French, but unlike the earlier novel, Ousmane's second work fared well throughout much of Europe and was even published in Japan. After completing *Oh Pays, mon beau peuple!* Ousmane spent a few years traveling in many of the countries where the novel was earning acclaim. He eventually left Europe, however, and visited Cuba, China, and even the Soviet Union, where he studied filmmaking at a leading studio.

In 1960 Ousmane published his third novel, *Les Bouts de bois de Dieu* (*God's Bits of Wood*), which became his first work to gain significant attention from English readers. *God's Bits of Wood* is a fictionalized account of a railroad workers' strike that stalled transportation from Dakar to Niger in late 1947 and early 1948. Much more ambitious than Ousmane's previous works, the third novel is a sweeping, epic-style account featuring several characters and spanning Senegal's political and social extremes. In 1970, when the novel appeared in English translation, *Times Literary Supplement*'s reviewer T. M. Aluko wrote that Ousmane's work "was a vivid rendering of the strike and the strikers." Aluko also cited Ousmane's particular skills as a novelist, declaring that he possessed "the ability to control a wide social panorama, without once losing sight of, or compassion for, the complexity and suffering of individuals."

Ousmane followed *God's Bits of Wood* with a short story collection, *Voltaieque* (*Tribal Scars*), and *Referendum,* the first part of a trilogy entitled *L'Harmattan* ("The Storm"). He then completed *Vehi-Ciosane; ou, Blanche-genese, suivi du Mandat* (*The Money Order, With White Genesis*), a volume comprised of two novellas. The book was an immense critical success, earning Ousmane the literature prize from the 1966 Dakar Festival of Negro Arts. By the mid-1960s Ousmane was also working in film. In 1964 he completed his first notable work in that medium, the sociological study *Borom Sarret,* and three years later he wrote and directed *Le Noire de. . .* (*Black Girl*), which detailed the degrading circumstances endured by an African servant in a French household. These

films were shown together in New York City in 1969, and A. H. Weiler writing in the *New York Times* called both works insightful and provocative. Weiler also wrote that Ousmane's films derived from "the quiet distinctions of simplicity, sincerity and subdued anger toward the freed black man's new burdens." In addition, Weiler contended that the works "put a sharp, bright focus on an emerging, once dark African area."

Ousmane enjoyed even greater acclaim as a filmmaker with *Mandabi,* his adaptation of his own novella *The Money Order. Mandabi* is a comedy about a middle-aged fool, Dieng, who receives a considerable financial sum from a nephew in Paris. Much of the humor in *Mandabi* derives from Dieng's vain, foolhardy efforts to secure identification papers necessary for cashing the money order. In the course of his efforts Dieng is swindled, robbed, thrashed, and publicly humiliated by his greedy family and fellow citizens. Adding further to the humor is the actual behavior of Dieng, an arrogant dimwit who smugly parades about his village oblivious of the animosity he provokes. In the *New York Times,* Roger Greenspun noted as much when he wrote that because Dieng "is such a pompous fool, so blithely superior to his two wives, so gluttonous with his food and confident in his walk, his troubles seem deserved and funny." Greenspun described Ousmane's directorial style as "spare, laconic, slightly ironic" and added that he "displays a reticence towards his characters that grants him freedom from explicit moral judgment."

Humor did not figure in Ousmane's next film, *Emitai,* which he completed in 1971. In this work he chronicles a conflict between Senegalese natives and French colonialists at the beginning of World War II. The conflict centers on the natives' opposition to French troops sent into the Senegalese village to commandeer several tons of rice. Neither faction particularly cherishes the rice: For the villagers it is intended for use in religious ceremonies; for the French, it is rendered unnecessary by a change in military tactics. Nonetheless, neither side concedes to the other, and the conflict is resolved with futile violence. In his *New York Times* review, Roger Greenspun found *Emitai* a refreshing, if sobering, counterpoint to the Hollywood adventure films of the 1930s and 1940s, observing that "the absolute ineffectiveness of massed spears against a few well-placed rifles should lay to rest the memories of a good many delicious terrors during Saturday afternoons at the movies." Greenspun also commended Ousmane's directorial reserve and subtlety and declared that the filmmaker's relatively detached style resulted in a film "that keeps surprising you with its ironic sophistication."

Ousmane's next filmmaking venture, *Xala,* marked his return to comedy. In *Xala* he lampoons the increasing Westernization of African politics and business. The protagonist of *Xala* is El Hadji, a corrupt bureaucrat who also serves his community as an importer of fairly exotic goods, including whiskey, yogurt, and perfume. Like his Western counterparts, El Hadji wears costly European business suits, totes a briefcase, and continually confers with advisers and fellow bureaucrats. His corrupt ways, while causing no good to his community, have contributed greatly to his considerable prosperity. That prosperity, however, is undermined when El Hadji takes a third wife and discovers that he is suddenly impotent. Apparently the victim of a curse, El Hadji consults witch doctors, including one fellow who sports an expensive business suit while squatting in his hut. That witch doctor fails to cure El Hadji, but for a substantial sum another doctor is able to restore the bureaucrat's sexuality. Unfortunately, troubles continue to plague El Hadji when he is implicated in a corrupt business action and is dismissed, by equally corrupt fellow bureaucrats, from the community's chamber of commerce. More marital problems then ensue, for El Hadji fails to pay his witch doctor and is thus once again impotent. Another cure is then attempted, one in which El Hadji must remove his clothing and allow several cripples to spit on him. He complies, but a much greater catastrophe awaits him. *Xala* was released in 1974, only months after Ousmane had published his novel of the same title. When the film was shown in the United States in 1975, it was commended in the *New York Times* as "an instructive delight" and as "cutting, radiant and hilarious." *Time*'s reviewer, Richard Eder, added that Ousmane's film was George Orwell's novel *Animal Farm* "applied to African independence."

Similarly, Ousmane's novel *Xala* was cited by *Nation* reviewer Eve Ottenberg as a witty portrait of "the destruction of tribal values." She wrote that the themes of *Xala* allowed Ousmane "to show people at their most flawed, eccentric, energetic and comic."

Ousmane continued to probe cultural discontinuity in *Ceddo,* his 1977 film about religious conflict in an unspecified African kingdom. This conflict is triggered when a Catholic king converts to Islam and brings a Moslem teacher into his band of advisers. The king's associates then convert to Islam, too, leaving only the common villagers outside the Islamic faith. Resentful of the king's changing policies, the villagers kidnap the king's daughter and thus force him to negotiate. During meetings between factions, the opportunistic Islamic teacher intercedes and precipitates the slaughter of all the non-Moslems. Vincent Canby, in his review for the *New York Times,* noted that the manner of *Ceddo* was "reserved, cool, almost stately." He confirmed that the obviously anti-Moslem film had been banned in Senegal, but Canby observed that the banning was prompted by a seemingly trivial aspect: Ousmane refused to render the spelling of the film's title to be consistent with his government's own spelling. Ousmane's stature as an African artist has risen steadily since he published his first work in 1956. In the ensuing years he has used his art to protest injustice against blacks and to decry the increasing disintegration of black Africa's heritages. He has also established himself as a formidable filmmaker in a medium where commercial considerations are usually dominant over the artistic, and the critical acclaim accorded his films in the United States testifies to his wide appeal and considerable achievements. Ousmane's works thus transcend cultural specifics and assure him recognition as a leading artist of his time.

BIOGRAPHICAL/CRITICAL SOURCES:

BOOKS

Brench, A. C., *The Novelists' Inheritance in French Africa: Writing From Senegal to Cameroon,* Oxford University Press, 1967.

Dathorne, O. R., *African Literature in the Twentieth Century,* Heinemann Educational, 1976.

Petty, Sheila, *A Call to Action: The Films of Ousmane Sembene,* Praeger (Westport, CT), 1996.

Silver, Helene and Hans M. Zell, editors, *A Reader's Guide to African Literature,* Africana Publishing, 1971.

PERIODICALS

Africa Report, February, 1963.

American Cinematographer, November, 1972.

Black Orpheus, November, 1959.

Cineaste, Volume 6, number 1, 1973.

Cinema Quebec, March/April, 1973.

Courier, January, 1990, p. 4.

Film Quarterly, spring, 1973.

Nation, April 9, 1977.

New Yorker, May 16, 1977.

New York Times, January 13, 1969; September 30, 1969; November 9, 1969; February 10, 1973; October 1, 1975; January 27, 1978.
New York Times Book Review, November 28, 1976.
Quarterly Review of Film Studies, spring, 1979.
Times Literary Supplement, October 16, 1970.
World Literature Today, winter, 1978.*

P

PARKS, Gordon (Alexander Buchanan) 1912-

PERSONAL: Born November 30, 1912, in Fort Scott, KS; son of Andrew Jackson and Sarah (Ross) Parks; married Sally Alvis, 1933 (divorced, 1961); married Elizabeth Campbell, December, 1962 (divorced, 1973); married Genevieve Young (a book editor), August 26, 1973; children: (first marriage) Gordon, Jr. (deceased), Toni (Mrs. Jean-Luc Brouillaud), David; (second marriage) Leslie. *Education:* Attended high school in St. Paul, Minnesota. *Politics:* Democrat. *Religion:* Methodist.

ADDRESSES: Home—860 United Nations Plaza, New York, NY 10017. *Agent*—(Film) Ben Benjamin, Creative Management Associates, 9255 Sunset Blvd., Los Angeles, CA 90069.

CAREER: Photographer, writer, film director, and composer. Worked at various jobs prior to 1937; free-lance fashion photographer in Minneapolis, 1937-42; photographer with Farm Security Administration, 1942-43, with Office of War Information, 1944, and with Standard Oil Company of New Jersey, 1945-48; *Life,* New York City, photo-journalist, 1948-72; *Essence* (magazine), New York City, editorial director, 1970-73. President of Winger Corp. Film director, 1968—, directing motion pictures for Warner Brothers-Seven Arts, Metro-Goldwyn-Mayer (M.G.M.), and Paramount Pictures, including *"The Learning Tree,* Warner Brothers, 1968, *Shaft,* M.G.M., 1971, *Shaft's Big Score,* M.G.M., 1972, *The Super Cops,* M.G.M., 1974, and *Leadbelly,* Paramount, 1975, as well as several documentaries. Composer of concertos and sonatas performed by symphony orchestras in the United States and Europe.

MEMBER: Authors Guild (member of council, 1973-74), Authors League of America, Black Academy of Arts and Letters (fellow), Directors Guild of America (member of national council, 1973-76), Newspaper Guild, American Society of Magazine Photographers, Association of Composers, and Directors, American Society of Composers, Authors, and Publishers, American Federation of Television and Radio Artists, National Association for the Advancement of Colored People, Directors Guild of New York (member of council), Urban League, Players Club (New York City), Kappa Alpha Mu.

AWARDS, HONORS: Rosenwald Foundation fellow, 1942; once chosen Photographer of the Year, Association of Magazine Photographers; Frederic W. Brehm award, 1962; Mass Media Award, National Conference of Christians and Jews, for outstanding contributions to better human relations, 1964; Carr Van Adna Journalism Award, University of Miami, 1964, Ohio University, 1970; named photographer-writer who had done the most to promote understanding among nations of the world in an international vote conducted by the makers of Nikon photographic equipment, 1967; A.F.D., Maryland Institute of Fine Arts, 1968; Litt.D., University of Connecticut, 1969, and Kansas State University, 1970; Spingarn Medal from National Association for the Advancement of Colored People, 1972; H.H.D., St. Olaf College, 1973, Rutgers University, 1980, and Pratt Institute, 1981; Christopher Award, 1980, for *Flavio;* President's Fellow award, Rhode Island School of Design, 1984; named Kansan of the Year, Native Sons and Daughters of Kansas, 1986; World Press Photo award, 1988; Artist of Merit, Josef Sudek Medal, 1989; additional awards include honorary degrees from Fairfield University, 1969, Boston University, 1969, Macalaster

College, 1974, Colby College, 1974, Lincoln University, 1975, Columbia College, 1977, Suffolk University, 1982, Kansas City Art Institute, 1984, Art Center and College of Design, 1986, Hamline University, 1987, American International College, 1988, Savannah College of Art and Design, 1988, University of Bradford (England), 1989, Rocheseter Institute of Technology, 1989, Parsons School of Design, 1991, Manhattanville College, 1992, College of New Rochele, 1992, Skidmore College, 1993, Montclair State University, 1994, and awards from Syracuse University School of Journalism, 1963, University of Miami, 1964, Philadelphia Museum of Art, 1964, Art Directors Club, 1964, 1968, and International Center of Photography, 1990.

WRITINGS:

Flash Photography, [New York], 1947.
Camera Portraits: The Techniques and Principles of Documentary Portraiture, F. Watts (New York City), 1948.
The Learning Tree (novel; also see below), Harper (New York City), 1963.
A Choice of Weapons (autobiography), Harper, 1966, reprinted, Minnesota Historical Society, 1986.
A Poet and His Camera (poems), self-illustrated with photographs, Viking (New York City), 1968.
(And composer of musical score) *The Learning Tree* (screenplay; based on novel of same title), produced by Warner Brothers-Seven Arts, 1968.
Gordon Parks: Whispers of Intimate Things (poems), self-illustrated with photographs, Viking, 1971.
Born Black (essays), self-illustrated with photographs, Lippincott (Philadelphia), 1971.
In Love (poems), self-illustrated with photographs, Lippincott, 1971.
Shaft (screenplay), Metro-Goldwyn-Mayer, 1971.
Shaft's Big Score (screenplay), Metro-Goldwyn-Mayer, 1972.
(Contributor of photographs) Jane Wagner, *J.T.,* Dell (New York CIty), 1972.
The Super Cops (screenplay), Metro-Goldwyn-Mayer, 1974.
Moments without Proper Names (poems), self-illustrated with photographs, Viking, 1975.
Leadbelly (screenplay), Metro-Goldwyn-Mayer, 1976.
Flavio, Norton (New York City), 1978.
To Smile in Autumn: A Memoir, Norton, 1979.
Shannon (novel), Little, Brown (Boston), 1981.
Voices in the Mirror: An Autobiography, Doubleday (New York City), 1990.
(Author of foreword) Ann Banks, editor, *Harlem: Photographs by Aaron Siskind, 1932-1940,* Smithsonian Institution Press, 1991.

(Author of introduction) Mandy Vahabzadeh, *Soul Unsold,* Graystone Books, 1992.
(Author of introduction) Ming Smith, *A Ming Breakfast: Grits and Scrambled Moments,* De Ming Dynasty, 1992.
Arias in Silence, Bulfinch Press, 1994.
Glimpses Toward Infinity, Little, Brown, 1996.
(With Eli Reed) *Black in America,* Norton, 1997.
Half Past Autumn: A Retrospective, Bulfinch, 1997.
(Author of introduction) Archie Givens, editor, *Spirited Minds: African American Books for Our Sons and Our Brothers,* Norton, 1997.

Also author of *Martin,* a ballet, 1990, and of several television documentaries produced by National Educational Television, including *Flavio* and *Mean Streets.* Contributor to *Show, Vogue, Venture,* and other periodicals.

SIDELIGHTS: Gordon Parks's "life constitutes an American success story of almost mythic proportions," Andy Grundberg once commented in the *New York Times.* A high school dropout who had to fend for himself at the age of sixteen, Parks overcame the difficulties of being black, uneducated, and poor to become a *Life* magazine photographer; a writer of fiction, nonfiction, and poetry; a composer; and a film director and producer. The wide scope of Parks's expertise is all the more impressive when viewed in its historical context, for many of the fields he succeeded in formerly had been closed to blacks. Parks was the first black to work at *Life* magazine, *Vogue,* the Office of War Information, and the Federal Security Administration. He was also the first black to write, direct, produce, and score a film, *The Learning Tree,* based on his 1963 novel. Parks maintains that his drive to succeed in such a variety of professions was motivated by fear. "I was so frightened I might fail that I figured if one thing didn't work out I could fall back on another," Parks stated in the *Detroit News.*

Born and raised in Fort Scott, Kansas, Parks endured pain at an early age when his mother died when he was fifteen. Sent to live with a sister and her husband in Minneapolis, Parks was evicted from the household and had to earn a living. His first professional endeavor was photography, a craft he practiced as a free-lance fashion photographer in Minneapolis and later as a Rosenwald Foundation fellow in 1942. In 1948 he was hired as a *Life* magazine photographer, and throughout his over twenty-year affiliation with that publication photographed world events, celebrities, musicians, artists, and politicians. In addition to his work for *Life,* Parks has exhibited his photography and illustrated his books with photos. In a *New York Times* review of one of Parks's photography exhibitions, Hilton Kramer notes that while Parks is a versatile photographer, "it is in the pictures where his 'black childhood of confusion and poverty' still makes itself felt that he moves us most deeply." Grundberg similarly notes that Parks's "most memorable pictures, and the most vividly felt sections of the exhibition, deal specifically with the conditions and social fabric of black Americans."

Parks found, however, that despite his love of and expertise in photography, he needed to express in words the intense feelings about his childhood. This need resulted in his first novel, *The Learning Tree,* which in some ways parallels Parks's youth. The novel concerns the Wingers, a black family living in a small town in Kansas during the 1920s, and focuses in particular on Newt, the Wingers' adolescent son. A *Time* reviewer comments: "[Parks's] unabashed nostalgia for what was good there, blended with sharp recollections of staggering violence and fear, makes an immensely readable, sometimes unsettling book."

Parks explores his life further in several autobiographical volumes. *A Choice of Weapons* begins when Parks is sixteen and describes how, after his mother's death and an unsuccessful stint living with relatives in Minneapolis, Parks found himself out on the street. For a decade, Parks struggled to feed and clothe himself, all the while cultivating his ambition to be a photographer. The book's theme, according to *Washington Post* contributor Christopher Schemering, is that "one's choice of weapons must be dignity and hard work over the self-destructive, if perhaps understandable, emotions of hate and violence." Alluding to the unfortunate circumstances of his youth, Parks expressed a similar view in the *Detroit News*. "I have a right to be bitter, but I would not let bitterness destroy me. As I tell young black people, you can fight back, but do it in a way to help yourself and not destroy yourself."

Observing that "what [Parks] has refused to accept is the popular definition of what being black is and the limitations that the definition automatically imposes," Saunders Redding concludes in the *New York Times Book Review*: "*A Choice of Weapons* is . . . a perceptive narrative of one man's struggle to realize the values (defined as democratic and especially American) he has been taught to respect."

To Smile in Autumn, Parks's second autobiographical volume, covers the years from 1943 to 1979. Here

Parks celebrates "the triumph of achievement, the abundance and glamour of a productive life," writes *New York Times Book Review* contributor Mel Watkins. Parks also acknowledges, however, that his success was not without a price. Ralph Tyler comments in the *Chicago Tribune Book World*: "Although this third memoir doesn't have the drama inherent in a fight for survival, it has a drama of its own: the conflict confronting a black American who succeeds in the white world." As Parks writes in *To Smile in Autumn*: "In escaping the mire, I had lost friends along the way. . . . In one world I was a social oddity. In the other world I was almost a stranger."

Schemering notes that the book contains material "recast" from Parks's earlier work, *Born Black,* and is in this respect somewhat disappointing. He writes: "It's unfortunate to see a major talent and cultural force coast on former successes. Yet, even at half-mast, Parks manages a sporadic eloquence, as in the last few pages when he pays tribute to his son Gordon Parks, Jr., who died in a plane crash." Watkins offers this view: "Gordon Parks emerges here as a Renaissance man who has resolutely pursued success in several fields. His memoir is sustained and enlivened by his urbanity and generosity."

In *Voices in the Mirror: An Autobiography* Parks again recounts his amazing life, from the pain of his mother's death when he was fifteen to his later career success as a photographer and filmmaker. Writing in the *Washington Post Book World,* Hettie Jones avers that "the book grabs your attention at once and keeps it through the century and across three continents." *New York Times Book Review* contributor Michael Eric Dyson remarks that *Voices* is Parks's "most poignant self-portrait" to date and calls the volume "an eloquent missive from the front line of poetry and pain."

BIOGRAPHICAL/CRITICAL SOURCES:

BOOKS

Authors in the News, Volume 2, Gale (Detroit), 1976.
Black Literature Criticism, Gale, 1992.
Contemporary Literary Criticism, Gale, Volume 1, 1973, Volume 16, 1981.
Dictionary of Literary Biography, Volume 33: *Afro-American Fiction Writers after 1955,* Gale, 1984.
Harnan, Terry, *Gordon Parks: Black Photographer and Film Maker,* Garrard, 1972.
Monaco, James, *American Film Now: The People, the Power, the Money, the Movies,* New American Library, 1979.

Parks, Gordon, *A Choice of Weapons,* Harper, 1966, reprinted, Minnesota Historical Society, 1986.

Parks, Gordon, *The Learning Tree,* Fawcett, 1987.

Parks, Gordon, *To Smile in Autumn: A Memoir,* Norton, 1979.

Parks, Gordon, *Voices in the Mirror: An Autobiography,* Doubleday, 1990.

Rolansky, John D., editor, *Creativity,* North-Holland Publishing, 1970.

Turk, Midge, *Gordon Parks,* Crowell, 1971.

PERIODICALS

America, July 24, 1971.

American Photo, September-October, 1991.

American Visions, December, 1989; February, 1991; February-March, 1993, p. 14.

Best Sellers, April 1, 1971.

Black Enterprise, January, 1992.

Black World, August, 1973.

Chicago Tribune Book World, December 30, 1979.

Commonweal, September 5, 1969.

Cue, August 9, 1969.

Detroit Free Press, January 9, 1966.

Detroit News, February 1, 1976.

Ebony, July, 1946.

Entertainment Weekly, March 27, 1992.

Films and Filming, April, 1972; October, 1972.

Films in Review, October, 1972.

Focus on Film, October, 1971.

Horn Book, April, 1971; August, 1971.

Jet, August 29, 1988; April 30, 1990; July 31, 1995, p. 21.

Journal of American History, December, 1987.

Library Journal, January, 1992.

Life, October, 1994, p. 26; February, 1996, p. 6.

Modern Maturity, June-July, 1989; October-November, 1990.

Newsweek, April 29, 1968; August 11, 1969; July 17, 1972; April 19, 1976.

New York, June 14, 1976.

New Yorker, November 2, 1963; February 13, 1966.

New York Herald Tribune, August 25, 1963.

New York Times, October 4, 1975; December 3, 1975; March 1, 1986.

New York Times Book Review, September 15, 1963; February 13, 1966; December 23, 1979; December 9, 1990, p. 19; March 1, 1996, p. 16.

PSA (Photographic Society of America) Journal, November, 1992.

Publishers Weekly, October 12, 1990.

Saturday Review, February 12, 1966; August 9, 1969.

School Library Journal, February, 1991.

Show Business, August 2, 1969.

Smithsonian, April, 1989.

Time, September 6, 1963; September 29, 1969; May 24, 1976.

Variety, November 6, 1968; June 25, 1969.

Vogue, October 1, 1968; January, 1976.

Washington Post, October 20, 1978; January 24, 1980.

Washington Post Book World, November 18, 1990, p. 4.*

*　　*　　*

PATTERSON, Frederick D(ouglass) 1901-1988

PERSONAL: Born October 10, 1901, in Washington, DC; died April 26, 1988, in New Rochelle, NY; son of William Ross (a school principal and lawyer) and Mamie Brooks (a music teacher and homemaker) Patterson; married Catherine Elizabeth Moton, June, 1935; children: Frederick Douglass, Jr. *Ethnicity:* "African American." *Education:* Attended Prairie View State College, 1915-19; Iowa State University, degree in veterinary medicine, 1923, M.Sc., 1927; Cornell University, Ph.D. (bacteriology), 1932.

CAREER: Association founder. Virginia State University, Petersburg, VA, instructor in veterinary medicine and chemistry, 1923-27, director of School of Agriculture, 1927-28; Tuskegee Institute (now Tuskegee University), director of veterinary medicine and instructor in bacteriology, 1928-31, 1933-34, director of Department of Agriculture, 1934-35, president, 1935-53. George Washington Carver Foundation, founder, 1940; United Negro College Fund (UNCF), founder, 1944, president, 1964-66; Phelps-Stokes Fund, president, 1953-70; Robert R. Moton Institute, head officer, beginning 1970.

AWARDS, HONORS: Honorary Doctorates from Lincoln University, Virginia State University, and Wilberforce University; Presidential Medal of Freedom, 1987; Spingarn Medal, National Association for the Advancement of Colored People (NAACP), 1988; United Negro College Fund (UNCF) founded the Frederick D. Patterson Research Institute in his honor, 1996.

WRITINGS:

Robert Russa Moton of Tuskegee and Hampton, University of North Carolina Press, 1956.

The College Endowment Funding Plan, American Council on Education (Washington, DC), 1976.

Chronicles of Faith: The Autobiography of Frederick Douglass Patterson, University of Alabama Press (Tuscaloosa), 1991.

SIDELIGHTS: Frederick D. Patterson has been instrumental in furthering the cause of higher education among people of African American descent since the 1920s. While president of Tuskegee Institute (now Tuskegee University), his innovative ideas brought the college to the educational forefront. Under his leadership, the school flourished. His ability to raise money for education also lead to his work with the United Negro College Fund (UNCF). As one of the founders of the UNCF, and later its president, he helped raise millions of dollars for college educations across the United States.

Patterson was born October 10, 1901, in the Anacostia section of Washington, DC, to Mamie and William Patterson. The couple had moved to the nation's capital from Texas two or three years previously with their other five children. Patterson's father thought he would be able to find better work in Washington due to the lesser amount of racial problems there than in Texas. He named his youngest son after educator and abolitionist Frederick Douglass, whose onetime home was a couple of blocks away from where they lived.

Patterson's mother was a music teacher and his father was a school principal. They had both received their college degrees from Prairie View College in Texas. Once they arrived in Washington, his father returned to school at Howard University to study law. Patterson's father passed the Washington, DC, bar shortly after Patterson was born. Despite all the hard work his parents did to improve the life of the family, nothing could stop them both from dying of tuberculosis before Patterson was two years old. The same illness would also claim one of Patterson's brothers a few years later.

Patterson initially went to live with a friend of the family, "Aunt" Julia Dorsey. His siblings all went to live with different family friends except his oldest sister, Wilhelmina Bessie, who was old enough to support herself and attend the Washington Conservatory of Music. In his book, *Chronicles of Faith: The Autobiography of Frederick Douglass Patterson,* Patterson wrote, "I called Aunt Julia my Civil War aunt, because she was born during slavery." They continued living in his parents' house while Patterson was still young, and, in time, he also started school locally.

When Patterson was about seven years old his sister, Bessie, assumed his guardianship. She had finished school and was looking for work. She knew some of the family relatives and decided to move to Texas where she thought she would have the most assistance in finding employment. Over the next few years Patterson and Bessie lived in several different cities. She was often unable to find work teaching where Patterson could live with her. So Patterson lived with different members of the family while attending school. From the fourth through the eighth grades Patterson attended Sam Houston College. Although called a college, Sam Houston also had primary and high school divisions, too. "I didn't object to school, but I didn't do much with [it]," Patterson commented in *Chronicles of Faith.* "At the time I didn't take my studies seriously. I finished the eighth grade many whippings later." His classmates that year voted Patterson least likely to succeed.

From the eighth grade through the end of high school Patterson attended another boarding school at a college. This one was at Prairie View College, where his parents had attended. Bessie had secured a job teaching and directing the choir at the school, so the two of them lived together there in Prairie View, Texas. During the summers, he took odd jobs to earn money. One of these was as a driver for a wealthy family. Although Patterson had never driven before applying for the position, he got the job and taught himself to drive. He also taught himself how to play tennis, which became a lifelong hobby. Patterson says he became interested in school when he had to do his work study in the agriculture department. In his last couple years of high school, he worked for two veterinarians; it motivated him so much, spending time with the animals, that he decided he would go to college to become a veterinarian.

Because the veterinarians he worked with at Prairie View had attended Iowa State University in Ames, Iowa, Patterson decided that he, too, would go to Iowa for schooling. Since being an out-of-state student is more expensive than being a commuter, he moved to Ames and lived there awhile before registering for school. Patterson worked many different jobs while putting himself through veterinary school. He worked at a hotel, washing and ironing clothes, cooking, being a janitor, and running a rug cleaning business to make ends meet. He lived with six other people on the second floor of a business. He was one of very few black students at Iowa State at that time, and for a while, the only black student in the veterinary program. Patterson said in *Chronicles of Faith* that the only time he had problems with discrimination was when he had to go to military camp one summer in college. Part of his schooling was paid for by the Student Army Corps. He spent the summer training with the Army and, in exchange for the financial subsidy, he was a reservist when he finished school. At this camp, students were segregated by race for dinner. He and one other black student ate at a table separated from all the other white students. Patterson noted that after he returned to Iowa State the other students that had also been at the military camp treated him differently than they had before, "they treated me as a pariah," commented Patterson. "I learned a lesson with regard to race that I never forgot: how people feel about you reflects the way you permit yourself to be treated. If you permit yourself to be treated differently, you are condemned to an unequal relationship."

Patterson graduated with a degree in veterinary medicine in 1923. At that time, he moved to Columbus, Ohio, to live with his brother John. He only stayed briefly in Ohio, but did manage to pass the licensing examination for veterinarians in that state. It was shortly after that Patterson was offered a job as professor of veterinary medicine and chemistry at Virginia State University in Petersburg, Virginia. Patterson worked for three years teaching at Virginia State and decided he would return to Iowa State for his master's degree. Once he completed his master's, he was promoted to director of the agriculture program at Virginia State. After being on the job for only a year, Patterson accepted a job with Tuskegee Institute in Tuskegee, Alabama. It was a more important place to research and teach, as Patterson explained in his book.

Patterson taught bacteriology and was head of the Veterinary Department at Tuskegee. In 1932 he took a leave from his job to earn his doctoral degree from Cornell University in Ithaca, New York. After being back a year at Tuskegee, Dr. Patterson was made head of the Agriculture Department there. He only remained on that job for a year before he was named President of Tuskegee. That same year he married Catherine Moton, daughter of Robert Russa Moton, the former President of Tuskegee. Many people at first were not happy with Patterson as President. They thought he had gotten the job because he married Mr. Moton's daughter. Dr. Patterson, however, managed to quell the talk when he took the school from the brink of bankruptcy and stabilized Tuskegee's money flow within a few years of becoming President.

Among changes at Tuskegee brought about by Patterson was the new division of domestic service, with a four year program in nutrition and personal services. He also began a program which changed how sharecroppers and poor farmers lived. Wood for houses had become expensive, so with the help of the School of Mechanical Industries, Patterson designed a house of concrete block. The materials for this house could be found on most farms as the building blocks were made with the local clay soil and a little cement. Soon such houses were appearing all over the South. Patterson also started the George Washington Carver Foundation in 1940. This fund was used to encourage and fund scientific research by African Americans.

One of the more well-known feats of Patterson's administration was the start of the black Army Air Corps at Tuskegee. The school initially used a former cow pasture as the runway. Several pilots were recruited and instruction began. This program led to the group of pilots known as the Tuskegee Airmen, well-known for their bravery in World War II. Although Dr. Patterson drew criticism for the program because of the discriminatory policies of the military, the program was a commercial success with extensive training for black pilots in military and commercial fields.

According to the *New York Times,* "Dr. Patterson soon learned that the school's continuing leadership role brought letters from other schools asking for advice on how to raise money. In 1943 he wrote a column in *The Pittsburgh Courier* proposing the creation of a consortium of black colleges that would raise money for their mutual benefit." About one year later in 1944, twenty-seven schools came together to form the United Negro College Fund (UNCF). The first year the UNCF raised over 750,000 dollars for its member colleges. These days a yearly telethon hosted by entertainer Lou Rawls raises millions for the organization and is its most prominent fundraiser. This act by Dr. Patterson is viewed by many as his most important act during his life. He served as President of the UNCF from 1964-66.

In 1953 Patterson retired from Tuskegee. He became president of the Phelps-Stokes Fund. Phelps-Stokes was started in 1901 and funds the education of African students as well as African American and Native American students in the United States. Dr. Patterson was president of the fund from 1953-70. It was during this work that he organized the Cooperative College Development Program to assign federal money to pay for the improvement and maintenance of the physical plants of black colleges.

In 1970 Dr. Patterson left Phelps-Stokes to head up the Robert R. Moton Institute. This institute was established to boost the endowments of black colleges. It has served as a stabilizing influence for several schools during periods of cutbacks in federal funding. In 1987 Patterson was awarded the Presidential Medal of Freedom by Ronald Reagan. In 1988 he was awarded the National Association for the Advancement of Colored People (NAACP) Spingarn Medal for "his belief that human productivity and well-being in a free society are the end products of determination and self-preparation."

On April 26, 1988, Patterson died in New Rochelle, New York. Donald Stewart, former president of the College Board of the National Association of Schools and Colleges, called Dr. Patterson "a visionary and pioneer in American higher education and in Black American higher education," in the *New York Times.* "He broke new ground for minority students and was always looking ahead into the next decade for new ways to finance education." In memory of his many years of service and dedication to his job the UNCF in 1996 announced the founding of the Frederick D. Patterson Research Institute. It is the first major research center devoted to black educational data and policy.

BIOGRAPHICAL/CRITICAL SOURCES:

BOOKS

Contemporary Black Biography, Volume 12, Gale, 1996.
Patterson, Frederick D., *Chronicles of Faith: The Autobiography of Frederick Douglass Patterson,* University of Alabama Press, 1991.
Salzman, Jack, David Lionel Smith and Cornel West, editors, *Encyclopedia of African-American Culture and History,* Simon & Schuster (New York City), 1996.

PERIODICALS

Current Biography Yearbook, 1947.
Jet, July 27, 1987, p. 22; May 16, 1988, p. 8.
Newsday (Long Island, NY), April 28, 1988, p. 49.
New York Times, April 27, 1988, p. B8

OTHER

Frederick D. Patterson Research Institute, Press Release, February 22, 1996.*

P'BITEK, Okot 1931-1982

PERSONAL: Born in 1931, in Gulu, Uganda; died July 19, 1982; son of a schoolteacher; married twice. *Education:* Attended King's College, Budo; Government Training College, Mbarara, teaching certificate; Bristol University, certificate of education; University College of Wales, LL.B.; Institute of Social Anthropology, Oxford, B.Litt, 1963.

CAREER: Taught school in the area of Gulu, Uganda, and played on the Ugandan national soccer team in the mid-1950s; Makerere University, Kampala, Uganda, lecturer in sociology, 1964; Uganda National Theater and Uganda National Cultural Center, Kampala, director, 1966-68; University of Iowa, Iowa City, fellow of international writing program, 1969-70, writer in residence, 1971; University of Nairobi, Nairobi, Kenya, senior research fellow at Institute of African Studies and lecturer in sociology and literature, 1971-78; University of Ife, Ife, Nigeria, professor, 1978-82; Makerere University, Kampala, Uganda, professor of creative writing, 1982; writer. Visiting lecturer at University of Texas, 1969. Founder of the Gulu Arts Festival, 1966, and the Kisumu Arts Festival, 1968.

AWARDS, HONORS: Jomo Kenyatta Prize for Literature from the Kenya Publishers Association, for *Two Songs,* 1972.

WRITINGS:

POETIC NOVELS

Song of Lawino: A Lament, East African Publishing, 1966, Meridian Books, 1969 (also see below).
Song of Ocol, East African Publishing, 1970 (also see below).
Song of a Prisoner, introduction by Edward Blishen, illustrations by E. Okechukwu Odita, Third Press, 1971 (also see below).
Two Songs: Song of Prisoner [and] Song of Malaya, illustrations by Trixi Lerbs, East African Publishing, 1971.
Song of Lawino and Song of Ocol, introduction by G.A. Heron, illustrations by Frank Horley, East African Publishing, 1972.

OTHER

Lak tar miyo kinyero wi lobo? (novel; title means "Are Your Teeth White? Then Laugh!"), Eagle

Press, 1953; published in English as *White Teeth,* Heinemann Kenya, 1989.

African Religions in Western Scholarship, East African Literature Bureau, 1970.

Religion of the Central Luo, East African Literature, 1971.

Africa's Cultural Revolution (essays), introduction by Ngugi wa Thiong'o, Macmillan Books for Africa, 1973.

(Compiler and translator) *The Horn of My Love* (folk songs), Heinemann Educational Books, 1974.

(Compiler and translator) *Hare and Hornbill* (folktales), Heinemann Educational Books, 1978.

(Compiler and translator) *Acholi Proverbs,* Heinemann Kenya, 1985.

Contributor to periodicals, including *Transition.*

SIDELIGHTS: Often referred to as "Uganda's best known poet," Okot p'Bitek had a distinguished career in the fields of sport, education, and the arts. While serving as a teacher in his native Uganda during the 1950s he played on the country's national soccer team, going to the 1956 Summer Olympic Games in London, England. P'Bitek stayed in Great Britain to obtain degrees from several universities before returning to Uganda to teach at the college level.

He published his first book, *Lak tar miyo kinyero wi lobo?* (title means "Are Your Teeth White? Then Laugh!"), in 1953 but it was the 1966 publication of his *Song of Lawino* that brought p'Bitek his first real acclaim. In the same year, p'Bitek was named director of the Uganda National Theater and Cultural Center. In this post he founded the successful Gulu Arts Festival, a celebration of the traditional oral history, dance, and other arts of his ancestral Acholi people. Due to political pressures, however, p'Bitek was forced from his directorship after two years. He moved to Kenya, where, with the exception of visits to universities in the United States, he remained throughout the reign of Ugandan dictator Idi Amin. After founding the Kisumu Arts Festival in Kenya and later serving as a professor in Nigeria, p'Bitek eventually returned to Makerere University in Kampala, Uganda. He was a professor of creative writing there when he died in 1982.

P'Bitek sought, in his role as cultural director and author, to prevent native African culture from being swallowed up by the influences of Western ideas and arts. He was particularly interested in preserving the customs of his native Acholi. While serving as director for the Uganda National Theater and Cultural

Center, p'Bitek proclaimed in an interview with Robert Serumaga which appeared in *African Writers Talking*: "The major challenge I think is to find what might be Uganda's contribution to world culture. . . . [W]e should, I think, look into the village and see what the Ugandans—the proper Ugandans—not the people who have been to school, have read—and see what they do in the village, and see if we cannot find some root there, and build on this." He further explained to Serumago his feelings about the influence of Western culture on his own: "I am not against having plays from England, from other parts of the world, we should have this, but I'm very concerned that whatever we do should have a basic starting point, and this should be Uganda, and then, of course, Africa, and then we can expand afterwards."

Song of Lawino, p'Bitek's most famous work, takes as its central issue the defense of Acholi tradition against the encroachment of Western cultural influences. P'Bitek originally composed *Song of Lawino* in the Acholi language (sometimes known as Lwo or Luo), then translated it into English before its publication. He put the English words to traditional Acholi verse patterns, however, and the result was pleasing to many critics. A reviewer in the *Times Literary Supplement* lauded p'Bitek's creation thus: "In rewriting his poem in English he has chosen a strong, simple idiom which preserves the sharpness and frankness of [its] imagery, a structure of short, free verses which flow swiftly and easily, and an unconde-scending offer of all that is local and specific in the original." Categorized as a poetic novel, *Song of Lawino* is narrated by an Acholi woman named Lawino who tells an audience her life story in the form of an Acholi song. Her main complaint is against her husband, Ocol, who neglects her because of her adherence to Acholi ways. Ocol, in contrast, tries to become as westernized as possible, rejecting his culture as backward and crude. His negative feelings toward his background are further symbolized by his preferring his mistress, Clementine (Tina), over Lawino. Clementine is thoroughly westernized, from her name to her high-heeled shoes. Lawino tells us that her rival straightens her hair, uses lipstick, and "dusts powder on her face / And it looks so pale; / She resembles the wizard / Getting ready for the midnight dance." Lawino speaks disdainfully of what she perceives as unnatural behavior on the part of her husband and his mistress; in favorable opposition to this she praises the life of her village. Most critics agree that Lawino's loving descriptions of the simple Acholi rural activities and rituals leave the reader with no doubt as to whose side the author takes. As reported in the *Times Literary Supplement,* "It is

Lawino's voice that we need to hear, reminding us of the human reality behind glib rejections of the backward, the primitive, the 'bush people.'"

P'Bitek later wrote *Song of Ocol,* which purports to offer Lawino's husband's defense, but most reviewers concurred that Ocol's words merely confirm Lawino's condemnation of him. Another *Times Literary Supplement* critic judged that *Song of Ocol* "savo[rs] too much of a conscientious attempt to give a voice to an essentially dull, pompous, and vindictive husband." P'Bitek's next poetic novels, published as *Two Songs: Song of Prisoner [and] Song of Malaya,* together won him the Kenya Publishers Association's Jomo Kenyatta Prize in 1972. *Song of Prisoner* relates the thoughts, both hopeful and despairing, of a political prisoner, and, according to the *Times Literary Supplement,* "its imagery has much of the freshness and inventive energy of Okot's best work." The narrator describes his cell as a cold, imprisoning woman and relates his feelings of betrayal, his fears of his lover's unfaithfulness, and his daydreams of merrymaking. *Song of Malaya* is written in the persona of a prostitute and tells of the abuses she suffers. Judged slightly sentimental by some critics, the prose poem discusses, among other things, the irony in the fact that prostitutes are often rounded up and jailed by men who were their patrons the previous evening.

In his later years, p'Bitek's literary efforts turned primarily to translation. He published *The Horn of My Love,* a collection of Acholi folksongs both in Acholi and in English translation, in 1974, and *Hare and Hornbill,* a collection of African folktales, in 1978. In *The Horn of My Love,* declared reviewer Gerald Moore in the *Times Literary Supplement,* "p'Bitek argues the case for African poetry as poetry, as an art to be enjoyed, rather than as ethnographic material to be eviscerated." The book contains ceremonial songs about death, ancient Acholi chiefs, and love and courtship. *Hare and Hornbill,* according to Robert L. Berner in *World Literature Today,* is divided roughly in half between tales of humans and tales of animals, including one about a hare seducing his mother-in-law. "P'Bitek is particularly qualified to deal with these tales," Berner proclaimed, and "reveals a thorough understanding of African folk materials."

BIOGRAPHICAL/CRITICAL SOURCES:

BOOKS

Heron, George A., *The Poetry of Okok p'Bitek,* Heinemann, 1976.

P'Bitek, Okot, *Song of Lawino: A Lament,* East African Publishing, 1966.
Pieterse, Cosmo, and Dennis Duerden, editors, *African Writers Talking,* Africana Publishing, 1972.

PERIODICALS

Research in African Literatures, 1985.
Times Literary Supplement, February 16, 1967; November 5, 1971; February 21, 1975.
World Literature Today, summer, 1979.
World Literature Written in English, November, 1977.*

* * *

PETRY, Ann (Lane) 1908-1997

PERSONAL: Born October 12, 1908, in Old Saybrook, CT; died April 28, 1997, near Old Saybrook, CT; daughter of Peter Clarke (a pharmacist) and Bertha (a chiropodist, hairdresser, and businesswoman; maiden name, James) Lane; married George D. Petry, February 28, 1938; children: Elisabeth Ann. *Education:* University of Connecticut, Ph.G., 1931; attended Columbia University, 1943-44. Gardening, sewing, cooking, writing poetry.

CAREER: Writer. James' Pharmacy, Old Saybrook and Old Lyme, CT, pharmacist, 1931-38; *Amsterdam News* (Harlem weekly newspaper), New York City, writer and advertising saleswoman, 1938-41; *People's Voice,* New York City, reporter and editor of woman's page, 1941-44. Visiting professor of English, University of Hawaii, Honolulu, 1974-75. Also worked as a teacher and as an actress with the American Negro Theatre, all in New York City.

MEMBER: PEN, Authors Guild, Authors League of America (secretary, 1960).

AWARDS, HONORS: Houghton Mifflin literary fellowship, 1946; Litt.D., Suffolk University, 1983; special citation from the City of Philadelphia, 1985; D.L., University of Connecticut, 1988; D.H.L., Mount Holyoke College, 1989.

WRITINGS:

FICTION; FOR ADULTS

The Street, Houghton (Boston), 1946.

Country Place, Houghton, 1947.
The Narrows, Houghton, 1953.
Miss Muriel and Other Stories, Houghton, 1971.

JUVENILE

The Drugstore Cat, Crowell (New York City), 1949.
*Harriet Tubman: Conductor on the Underground Rail-
    road,* Harper (New York City), 1955, published
    in England as *A Girl Called Moses: The Story of
    Harriet Tubman,* Methuen (London), 1960.
The Common Ground, Crowell, 1964.
Tituba of Salem Village, Crowell, 1964.
Legends of the Saints, Crowell, 1970.

OTHER

Contributor to books, including *The Writer's Book,*
edited by Helen Hull, Harper, 1950; *A View from the
Top of the Mountain: Poems after Sixty,* edited by Tom
Koontz and Thom Tammaro, Barnwood (Daleville,
IN), 1981; and *Rediscoveries II,* edited by David
Madden and Peggy Bach, Carroll & Graf (New
York), 1988; contributor of short stories to antholo-
gies. Contributor to periodicals, including *New Yorker,
Opportunity, Holiday, Negro Digest, Redbook,* and
Horn Book.

A large collection of Petry's papers is housed at
Boston University's Mugar Memorial Library.

SIDELIGHTS: With the publication of *The Street* in
1946, Ann Petry became the first black female author
to address many of the problems faced by scores of
disadvantaged black women. Following in what
Arthur P. Davis described in his book *From the Dark
Tower: Afro-American Writers from 1900 to 1960* as
"the tradition of hard-hitting social commentary
which characterized the Richard Wright school of
naturalistic protest writing," *The Street* tells the story
of Lutie Johnson's attempts to shield herself and her
young son from the world outside their tiny Harlem
apartment. Despite what he terms "a bad sag in the
last third of the book which is almost fatal," the *New
Republic*'s Bucklin Moon was moved enough by the
author's unflinching portrayal of violence and degradation to remark, "Mrs. Petry knows what it is to live
as a Negro in New York City and she also knows how
to put it down on paper so that it is as scathing an
indictment of our society as has ever appeared. . . .
To this reviewer Mrs. Petry is the most exciting new
Negro writer of the last decade." In the *New York
Times,* Alfred Butterfield noted that "Ann Petry has
chosen to tell a story about one aspect of Negro life

in America, and she has created as vivid, as spiritually and emotionally effective a novel as that rich and
important theme has yet produced. . . . It deals with
its Negro characters without condescension, without
special pleading, without distortion of any kind. . . .
It overflows with the classic pity and terror of good
imaginative writing."

After *The Street,* Petry wrote two more novels for
adults: *Country Place* in 1947 and *The Narrows* in
1953. Both take place not in the tenements of New
York City but in small, middle-class New England
towns, a change in locale that critic Carl Milton
Hughes defined in *The Negro Novelist: 1940-1950* as
the author's "assertion of freedom as a creative artist
with the whole of humanity in the American scene as
her province." In short, declared Hughes, "Petry's
departure from racial themes and the specialized Negro problem add to her maturity."

Although she changed the setting, Petry did not alter
her premises and plots. As she did in *The Street,*
Petry continued to build her stories around the same
basic themes of adultery, cruelty, violence, and evil.
Country Place, for example, examines the disillusionment of a returned soldier, Johnnie Roane, who discovers in the midst of a terrible storm that the town
gossip about his wife's infidelity is true; though shattered by the realization, Roane resists the impulse to
kill her and her lover and decides instead to make a
new life for himself in New York.

In a similar challenge to socially accepted behavior,
The Narrows deals with the tragic affair between a
young, well-educated black man and a rich white
girl—an affair that is doomed as soon as the townspeople, both black and white, find out about it. Some
reviewers, such as the *New York Herald Tribune
Weekly Book Review*'s Rose Feld and Richard
Sullivan of the *New York Times,* criticized *Country
Place*'s occasional plot improbabilities as well as
Petry's technique of switching the identity of her
narrator in mid-story, but most regard it as a worthy
follow-up to *The Street.* Claimed J. C. Smith of the
Atlantic: "Most of the characters are well done, but,
curiously enough, Johnny Roane, the hero, is not. . . .
Taken as a whole, though, *Country Place* is a good
story. . . . It preaches no sermons, waves no flags.
It tells a plausible narrative of . . . some very human
people." Feld cited "the feel of a small town, the
integrity of dialogue, and the portrayal of Johnnie, of
Glory, and of Mrs. Gramby" as being among the
"exceedingly good" parts of *Country Place,* while
Sullivan noted that "despite the violence of its events,

it is a rather quiet book, carefully and economically phrased" and "full of fresh, effective writing." Bradford Smith of the *Saturday Review of Literature,* however, suggested that Petry never really developed her basic theory, declaring, "The book seems to say (though not for the first time) that humanity is as degraded in a small town as in Studs Lonigan's Chicago. The trouble is that, while the reader is made to understand the social forces which produced Studs Lonigan, there is no comparable explanation for Mrs. Petry's characters. Her 'good' people . . . are shadowy, while her 'bad' people lack motivation or background."

About Petry's third novel, *The Narrows,* Arna Bontemps commented in the *Saturday Review:* "A novel about Negroes by a Negro novelist and concerned, in the last analysis, with racial conflict, *The Narrows* somehow resists classification as a 'Negro novel,' as contradictory as that may sound. In this respect Ann Petry has achieved something as rare as it is commendable. Her book reads like a New England novel, and an unusually gripping one." Admitting that in less skilled hands the theme "might have been merely sensational," Mary Ross concluded in the *New York Herald Tribune Book Review* that Petry "builds a novel that has depth and dignity. There is power and insight and reach of imagination in her writing." In the *New York Times,* Wright Morris commented that in *The Narrows* Petry's "canvas has depth and complexity, but the surface drama central to the tragedy is like a tissue of tabloid daydreams, projected by the characters."

In his book *Black on White: A Critical Survey of Writing by American Negroes,* David Littlejohn also observed that Petry has always had "an uncomfortable tendency to contrive sordid plots (as opposed to merely writing of sordid events). She seems to require a 'shocking' chain of scandalous doings . . . on which to cast her creative imagination." Nevertheless, he stated, "so wise is her writing, . . . so real are her characters, so total is her sympathy, that one can often accept the faintly cheap horrors and contrivances. . . . And if one allows himself to be overexcited by these intrigues . . . he misses, I think, the real treasures of Ann Petry's fiction." Among these treasures, Littlejohn noted, can be found a "solid, earned, tested intelligence," "a prose that is rich and crisp," and "characters of shape and dimension, people made out of love, with whole histories evoked in a page. . . . This, to me, the intelligence, the style, and above all the creative sympathy, is what sets Ann Petry . . . into a place almost as prominent and prom-

ising as that of Richard Wright, James Baldwin, and Ralph Ellison. She is not, of course, writing 'about' the race war. . . . But if an American Negro can, despite all, develop such an understanding of other people as Ann Petry's—and more prodigious still, convey that understanding—then let her write what Peyton Place-plots she will, she is working toward a genuine truce in the war."

Critique: Studies in Modern Fiction reviewer Thelma J. Shinn also praised Petry's ability to understand and depict people—not just black people, but all people who are weakened and disillusioned by poverty and by racial and sexual stereotypes. Maintained Shinn: "Petry has penetrated the bias of black and white, even of male and female, to reveal a world in which the individual with the most integrity is not only destroyed but is often forced to become an expression of the very society against which he is rebelling. . . . Ann Petry does not ignore the particular problems of blacks; her portrayals . . . display potentiality enough for admiration and oppression enough for anger to satisfy any black militant. Her first concern, however, is for acceptance and realization of individual possibilities—black and white, male and female. Her novels protest against the entire society which would contrive to make any individual less than human, or even less than he can be." Petry's work also included a number of books for young people.

About *Harriet Tubman: Conductor on the Underground Railroad,* which tells the story of the courageous escaped slave and abolitionist who transported more than three hundred slaves to freedom, Elizabeth Yates noted in the *Christian Science Monitor,* "Ann Petry, writing with sympathy and fidelity, has made Harriet Tubman live for present-day readers of any age, who pick up this biography and come under its power."

In their book *For Reading Out Loud! A Guide to Sharing Books with Children,* Mary Margaret Kimmel and Elizabeth Segel described the biography as "first-rate," adding that the author's "eloquent prose creates a vivid picture" of the life and times of Harriet Tubman. *Tituba of Salem Village* inspired Alice Dalgliesh to assert in the *Saturday Review* that it is "one of the strongest books of the year, and the best one about witchcraft that has yet been written for young people." Based on the 1692 Salem witch trials, the book explores the experiences of a slave girl from Barbados who finds herself accused of witchcraft and unable to defend herself against the superstition and paranoia which characterized religious belief in late seventeenth-century New England. Jane Manthorne commented in *Horn Book Magazine* that Tituba's story "becomes a masterful construction of innocence betrayed by mounting malevolence." Madeleine L'Engle commended Petry's "artistry" in the *New York Times Book Review,* observing, "at the end of the book we are left with a feeling of hope, and of the ultimate triumph of good over evil."

Petry told an audience in a speech published in *Horn Book Magazine* that she felt affected by numerous books as a child, to the extent of acting out scenes from some of her favorite books, a childhood trait which she indicated transcends generations when books and stories inspire children's imaginations. She added that her historical books for juveniles have several messages for young readers, including the simple reminder that black men and women have formed an integral part of American history: "Over and over again I have said: These characters are people. Look at them, listen to them; watch Harriet Tubman in the nineteenth century, a heroic woman, a rescuer of other slaves. Look at Tituba in the seventeenth century, a slave involved in the witchcraft trials in Salem Village. Look at them and remember them. Remember for what a long, long time black people have been in this country, have been a part of America: a sturdy, indestructible, wonderful part of America, woven into its heart and into its soul." She continued, "These women were slaves. I hoped that I had made them come alive, turned them into real people. I tried to make history speak across the centuries in the voices of people—young, old, good, evil, beautiful, ugly."

BIOGRAPHICAL/CRITICAL SOURCES:

BOOKS

Bone, Robert A., *The Negro Novel in America,* revised edition, Yale University Press (New Haven, CT), 1965, pp. 157, 180-85.

Children's Literature Review, Volume 12, Gale (Detroit), 1987.

Contemporary Authors Autobiography Series, Volume 6, Gale, 1988, pp. 253-69.

Contemporary Literary Criticism, Gale, Volume 1, 1973, Volume 7, 1977, Volume 18, 1981.

Davis, Arthur P., *From the Dark Tower: Afro-American Writers from 1900 to 1960,* Howard University Press (Washington, DC), 1974.

De Montreville, Doris, and Donna Hill, editors, *Third Book of Junior Authors,* H. W. Wilson (Bronx, New York), 1972.

Dictionary of Literary Biography, Volume 76: *Afro-American Writers, 1940-1955,* Gale, 1988, pp. 140-47.

Gillespie, John, and Diana Lembo, *Juniorplots: A Book Talk Manual for Teachers and Librarians,* Bowker (Ann Arbor, MI), 1967, pp. 23-26.

Holladay, Hilary, *Ann Petry,* Twayne, 1996.

Hughes, Carl Milton, *The Negro Novelist: 1940-1950,* Citadel Press (New York), 1953, pp. 160-63.

Kimmel, Margaret Mary, and Elizabeth Segel, *For Reading Out Loud! A Guide to Sharing Books with Children,* Dell (New York City), 1983, pp. 101-02.

Littlejohn, David, *Black on White: A Critical Survey of Writing by American Negroes,* Viking (New York City), 1966.

O'Brien, John, editor, *Interviews with Black Writers,* Liveright (New York City), 1973.

Twentieth-Century Children's Writers, St. Martin's (New York City), 1978, pp. 993-94.

Warfel, Harry R., *American Novelists of Today,* American Book Co. (New York), 1951.

PERIODICALS

Atlantic, November, 1947.

Black American Literature Forum, winter, 1980, pp. 135-41.

Christian Science Monitor, February 8, 1946; August 25, 1955, p. 13; August 19, 1971.

Commonweal, February 22, 1946.

Crisis, January, 1946, pp. 48-49.

Critique: Studies in Modern Fiction, Volume 16, number 1, 1974.

Horn Book Magazine, February, 1965, p. 65; April, 1965, pp. 147-51.

Nation, August 29, 1953.

Negro American Literature Forum, summer, 1972, pp. 54-57, 60.

Negro Digest, June, 1946, pp. 63-64.

New Republic, February 11, 1946.

New Yorker, February 9, 1946; October 11, 1947; August 29, 1953.

New York Herald Tribune Book Review, November 13, 1949, p. 16; August 16, 1953.

New York Herald Tribune Weekly Book Review, October 5, 1947.

New York Times, February 10, 1946; September 28, 1947; August 16, 1953.

New York Times Book Review, November 6, 1949, p. 24; November 1, 1964, p. 8.

Opportunity, April-June, 1946, pp. 78-79.

Pharmacy in History, Volume 28, number 1, 1986.

San Francisco Chronicle, August 26, 1953.

Saturday Review, August 22, 1953; November 7, 1964, p. 55; October 2, 1971.

Saturday Review of Literature, March 2, 1946; October 18, 1947.

Studies in American Fiction, spring, 1987, pp. 81-93.

Times Literary Supplement, May 2, 1986.*

*   *   *

PHILIP, M(arlene) Nourbese   1947-

PERSONAL: Middle name is pronounced "noor-BEH-seh"; Born in 1947, in Moriah, Tobago, West Indies; immigrated to Canada, 1968; became Canadian citizen; daughter of Parkinson Philip-Yeates (an elementary school principal) and Undine (a homemaker; maiden name, Bowles) Philip; married Delf Omar King (an engineer), February 3, 1969 (divorced, 1974); married (by common law) Paul Chandless Chamberlain (an education administrator), October, 1975; children: (first marriage) Bruce Omar; (second marriage) Hardie Osei, Hesper Salmon Zahra. *Education:* University of the West Indies (Kingston, Jamaica), B.Sc. (economics), 1968; University of Western Ontario (London, Ontario, Canada), M.A. (political science), 1970, LL.B., 1973; Bar Admission Course (Osgoode Hall, Toronto, Ontario), 1974-75. *Religion:* Orisha. *Avocational interests:* Walking, needlework, short-wave radio.

ADDRESSES: Office—c/o Mercury Press, 2569 Dundas Street West, Toronto, Ontario M6P 1X7, Canada.

CAREER: Writer and poet, 1968—. Parkdale Community Legal Services, Toronto, Ontario, Canada, articling student, 1973-75; lawyer in private practice, Toronto, 1975-82; Carswell Publishing, Toronto, on staff, 1981-88; Ontario Legal Aid, Toronto, interviewing lawyer, 1983-86; Workers' Compensation Appeals Tribunal, Toronto, vice chair, 1986-88; Canada Council, nonfiction jury member, 1989; York University, North York, Ontario, creative fiction lecturer, 1989-91; Ontario College of Art, Toronto, lecturer/course director; Banff Centre of the Arts, Banff, Alberta, resident, 1990, 1993-94; University of Toronto, Toronto, lecturer, 1992—.

MEMBER: Vision 21: Canadian Culture in the Twenty-First Century (founding member).

AWARDS, HONORS: Book of the Year for Children Medal finalist, Canadian Association of Children's Librarians, 1988, for *Harriet's Daughter;* Casa de las Americas Literary Prize (anglophone Caribbean poetry), 1988, for *She Tries Her Tongue, Her Silence Softly Breaks;* Tradewinds Journal Prize, 1988, for poetry and short-story writing; Max and Greta Ebel Memorial Award for Children's Writing finalist, Canadian Society of Authors, Illustrators and Performers, 1989, for *Harriet's Daughter;* Our Choice selection, Canadian Children's Book Centre, 1989/1990, for *Harriet's Daughter;* City of Toronto Book Awards finalist, Toronto City Council, 1990, for *Harriet's Daughter;* Canadian Learning Materials of the Year Award, Ontario School Library Association, 1990, for *Harriet's Daughter;* Guggenheim Fellow, John Simon Guggenheim Memorial Foundation, 1990-91, for poetry; National Magazine Award for Poetry finalist, National Magazine Awards Foundation, 1992, for "The Question of Language is the Answer to Power"; Lawrence Foundation Award, 1995, for the short story, "Stop Frame."

WRITINGS:

YOUNG ADULT FICTION

Harriet's Daughter (Caribbean Writers), Heinemann International, 1988, Women's Press, 1988.

ADULT FICTION

Looking for Livingstone: An Odyssey of Silence, Mercury Press, 1991.

POETRY

Thorns, Williams Wallace, 1980.
Salmon Courage, Williams Wallace, 1983.
She Tries Her Tongue, Her Silence Softly Breaks, Ragweed Press, 1989.

ESSAY COLLECTIONS

Frontiers: Essays and Writings in Racism and Culture, 1894-1992, Mercury Press, 1992.
Showing Grit: Showboating North of the 44th Parallel, Poui Publications, 1993.

PLAYS

Coups and Calypsos (drama), first reading, Cahoots Theatre Projects play reading series, Toronto, 1994.

OTHER

Also author of the short stories "Bad Words," "Burn Sugar," "Just a Name," "Whose Idea Was It Anyway?," and "The Tall Rains." Contributor of short stories, poetry, reviews and essays to numerous anthologies, magazines, journals, and newspapers.

WORK IN PROGRESS: Two novels, poetry, essays.

SIDELIGHTS: M. Nourbese Philip is a poet, novelist, essayist, playwright, lecturer, and lawyer. Her contribution to Canadian literature for young people is a single novel but one important for its view and voice. Writing in *Books in Canada,* Phil Hall described Philip as "one of a small group of writers who are creating the first modern Black women's written culture in Canada."

Born in Tobago in 1947, Philip was the third of five children strictly raised in a family that placed a very high value on education. When Philip was eight, her family moved to Trinidad. She attended elementary and secondary school there constantly encouraged by her parents to set her sights on a professional career. At the time, Trinidad and Tobago were under British colonial rule and the curriculum Philip studied and the staff who taught it were British. In a *Books in Canada* interview with Barbara Carey, Philip commented, "European knowledge, the way we were taught it, almost drowned out any sense of my own culture. We learned about King Arthur and daffodils and nightingales, while surrounded by hummingbirds, hibiscus, and a silenced tradition of insurrection."

Philip remembers how thrilled her parents were about the potential for their children's futures when Trinidad and Tobago became an independent member of the British Commonwealth in 1962. "I still have a vivid image in my mind of my parents having long discussions about politics on the front porch," she told Elspeth Cameron of *Chatelaine.* "They were so excited about their children having a chance to get an education."

After graduating from Bishop Anstey High School, an Anglican girls' school, Philip left family and home to attend the University of the West Indies in Kingston, Jamaica. In 1968, with an economics degree in hand, she immigrated to Canada. She married and had her first child in 1969. London, Ontario, and the University of Western Ontario were "home" for the next several years as she earned degrees in political science and law.

The next stop on Philip's itinerary was Toronto where she articled at the Parkdale Legal Clinic. After being called to the Bar in 1975, she practiced law for five years in a partnership and then ran a private practice for two years out of her home.

While she was growing up in colonial Trinidad, there was nothing to cause Philip to think that she might ever become a writer. "Writing was just beyond the pale as a way of being or as a way of living," she told Barbara Carey of *Books in Canada.* "Becoming a spy seemed much more real than becoming a writer, because at least you could work for the Empire. There is, however, another way in which spying and writing are connected for me. They require similar qualities and activities: keen observation and discipline, eavesdropping and looking into other people's lives; and even the requirements of secrecy and silence, and working in codes."

When her marriage started to break up, Philip began to write. "Writing was what saved me, mentally and emotionally," she told Barbara Carey. As she kept journals and wrote poems, Philip became increasingly aware that she was more interested in writing than in practicing law.

Thorns, Philip's first book of poetry, was published in 1980. Shortly after the publication in 1983 of *Salmon Courage,* a second collection, she had a strong sense of needing more time for her writing. In the introduction to *She Tries Her Tongue, Her Silence Softly Breaks,* her award-winning third collection of poems, she states, "The last thing I expected to end up doing was writing, and when I upsed and left a safe and decent profession, I was the most surprised person."

When her first child was in his early teens, Philip became aware of how few good books there were for young black people. She told Janice Williamson in an interview for *Sounding Differences,* "I thought, well, why don't I try and write something!" The "something" turned out to be *Harriet's Daughter,* a story about a Caribbean-Canadian girl set in the Toronto neighborhood where Philip's son went to junior high school.

Writing the story was one thing. Philip soon discovered that getting it published was another. Even with the efforts of her agent, Philip couldn't interest Canadian publishers. Some publishing houses declined to even read the manuscript because it was a story about black kids. Those who did read it admitted enjoying the story but felt there wouldn't be a market for it.

Philip was devastated. Recalling how easily she, as a black child, had enjoyed and identified with *Anne of Green Gables,* she was convinced that people read across cultures. Why wouldn't Canadians enjoy *Harriet's Daughter*? She told Janice Williamson that the experience "really put me in a tailspin. I went to see a therapist, because I thought, if they tell me the writing's not good enough, I can work on it. But this response was like telling me that I had to go and change myself."

Philip resorted to sending *Harriet's Daughter* to two publishers in England. When both indicated interest in the book, she chose Heinemann thinking that its educational arm might help *Harriet's Daughter* find its way onto the Caribbean exam curriculum. Women's Press in Toronto bought Canadian rights shortly after Philip made her Heinemann decision. Both publishers released *Harriet's Daughter* in 1988.

The story of fourteen-year-old Margaret who considers Harriet Tubman her role model, resents her Dad's lectures about "Good West Indian Discipline," and determines to help a recently-arrived schoolmate return to her Gran in Tobago made its mark. Writing in the *Toronto Star,* Michele Landsberg said, "Lively, funny, and toughly realistic about the pains of adolescence, *Harriet's Daughter* is also a celebration of bright, resilient kids discovering their own strength." Elizabeth Montgomery of *CCL: Canadian Children's Literature* described Margaret as "feisty, intelligent, brave and kind." Nominated for the Book of the Year for Children Medal, the Max and Greta Ebel Memorial Award for Children's Writing and the City of Toronto Book Awards, *Harriet's Daughter* was also an Our Choice selection and the winner of the 1990 Canadian Learning Materials of the Year Award.

Philip writes primarily for an adult audience and poetry is her particular passion. "The obsession that has chosen me is language," Philip told H. J. Kirchhoff of the *Globe and Mail.* Raised in an educator's home, she learned to speak "proper" English. But she also loved to hear the language of the street, the everyday language of the people. There is a rhythmic quality to what she calls the Caribbean "demotic" that captivates her. Throughout her writing, Philip moves between the formal and informal languages, using the demotic to full advantage. There are examples in *Harriet's Daughter.* Much of the dialogue is in dialect and the new girl at school talks "Tobago talk."

The issue of language is important "in terms of young black kids who come up from the Caribbean," Philip told H. J. Kirchhoff. "They feel there's something wrong with their language. They do need something to tell them it's not appropriate for a job interview, but reading it in a book gives validity to something that for so long they have been told is not good enough."

Philip, the writer, is also social critic and activist. As a woman and writer of color, Philip has been critical of the Canadian publishing industry for not seeking out more minority writers. She has also challenged institutions such as the Writers' Union of Canada and PEN Canada to become more inclusive and play a more active role in developing writers from ethnic communities. She is a founding member of Vision 21: Canadian Culture in the Twenty-First Century, a group of artists and others committed to heightening awareness of racism in the arts.

As a thought-provoking and passionate voice in contemporary Canadian literature, Philip does not hesitate to acknowledge the influence Canada has had on her body of work. She told Janice Williamson in *Sounding Differences,* "Canada is unique when compared to the States or England. Both of these places have strong traditions of black writing and black literature. Canada doesn't. As a black writer. it has been very painful to survive here. There is a danger of falling into the void and just giving up. But if you come through that, the work becomes stronger. In a sense I could be more daring here in Canada."

Since the publication of *Harriet's Daughter* in 1988, Philip has been a prolific author of poetry, essays, plays and fiction for adults.

BIOGRAPHICAL/CRITICAL SOURCES:

BOOKS

Nourbese Philip, Marlene, *She Tries Her Tongue, Her Silence Softly Breaks,* Ragweed Press, 1989.
Williamson, Janice, *Sounding Differences: Conversations with Seventeen Canadian Women Writers,* University of Toronto Press, 1993, pp. 221-244, 361-362.

PERIODICALS

Books in Canada, January-February, 1989, pp. 1-2; September, 1991, pp. 17-21.
CCL: Canadian Children's Literature, no. 54, 1989, p. 83; no. 84, 1996, pp. 91-93.

Chatelaine, November 1990, pp. 86-87, 123, 125, 127-128.
Globe and Mail, January 4, 1990, p. C5.
Quill & Quire, August, 1989, pp. 15-16.
Toronto Star, January 29, 1991, p. D1.

* * *

PINCKNEY, Darryl 1953-

PERSONAL: Born in 1953, in Indianapolis, IN. *Education:* Attended Columbia University and Princeton University.

ADDRESSES: Home—New York, NY. *Office*—c/o Penguin Books, 375 Hudson St., New York, NY 10014-3657.

CAREER: Columbia University, New York City, teacher, 1992—; critic; essayist; novelist.

AWARDS, HONORS: Hodder Fellow at Princeton University; received grants from Ingram Merrill Foundation and Guggenheim Foundation; Whiting Writers' Award, Mrs. Giles Whiting Foundation, 1986; Art Seidenbaum Award for first fiction, *Los Angeles Times,* 1992, for *High Cotton.*

WRITINGS:

High Cotton, Farrar, Straus (New York City), 1992.
(Author of introduction) Harriet Beecher Stowe, *Uncle Tom's Cabin: Or, Life among the Lowly,* Dutton, 1997.

Contributor of reviews and articles to periodicals, including *New York Review of Books, Vanity Fair, Vogue, Granta,* and *New York Times.*

WORK IN PROGRESS: A critical book on African American literature.

SIDELIGHTS: The relationship between the narrator of Darryl Pinckney's picaresque novel, *High Cotton,* and its author has caused reviewers to speculate that the narrative is more of a memoir than a work of fiction. *Newsday*'s Jonathan Mandell describes the work as "a semi-autobiographical novel of growing up as a member of what W. E. B. DuBois called the 'talented tenth'—the African-American elite, the black middle class." Writing in *New York Review of*

Books, Michael Wood lauds Pinckney's book as "delicately, intelligently tracing pieces of an uninvented life. The art is in the selection of the traces and in the angle of vision."

In the course of the novel, the narrator moves from the sheltered world of his extended family into the white world, and eventually into the realm of large historical movements—the civil rights struggle and the politics of black cultural nationalism. "Pinckney brilliantly combines empathy and acid as he details the attractions of black nationalism and its rhetoricians—revealed to be every bit as bourgeois and status-obsessed as an earlier generation of would-be assimilationists," writes Henry Louis Gates, Jr. in *Washington Post Book World.* Because of the deft handling of the complexities of the narrator's skeptical voice, a diverse historical and cultural span, and racial ambiguity, Pinckney's first novel has been widely praised, and received the 1992 *Los Angeles Times*'s Art Seidenbaum Award for first fiction. In the *New York Review of Books,* Wood comments on the author's style, pointing out that "it can't let go, but it learns to relax, and at its best Pinckney's prose—funny, observant, lyrical, self-deprecating—is as good as any now being written in English."

Pinckney is a member of the fourth generation in his family to be college educated. One of the most vivid characters in his book is that of Grandfather Eustace, a Harvard-educated minister who loses his congregation because of his haughty, superior attitude. The narrator confesses that he spends a great deal of his life running from the specter of this snobbish, intelligent, eloquent old man, only to realize after the grandfather's death that he shares many traits with him. *Los Angeles Times Book Review* critic Richard Eder calls the narrator's encounters with his grandfather "the richest and most suggestive parts of the book." Gates characterizes Grandfather Eustace as "a figure both admired and despised, determining his grandson's actions precisely to the degree that he seeks to flee the pattern of his grandfather's life, to outwit his logic, to escape the net of the fate that closes in upon him. Rarely has history found a more suggestive embodiment. This rendering of the past-in-the-present is a major achievement."

Though Pinckney's *High Cotton* is heavily grounded in sociology, Gail Lumet Buckley points out in the *Los Angeles Times Book Review* that the novel also possesses a religious aspect, for it "questions the meaning of human suffering." Edmund White in the *New York Times Book Review* asserts that Pinckney explores dimensions of the American race problem with "excruciating honesty and the total freedom from restraint that [German poet and playwright Johann] Schiller said we find nowhere else but in authentic works of art." Gates comments that "Pinckney's relation to black America's literary past is distinguished by an intense, and self-conscious, ambivalence—and he has turned that ambivalence into an advantage both intellectual and literary."

Negative comment on *High Cotton* focused mostly on Pinckney's detached, cool tone. Adam Mars-Jones, a *Times Literary Supplement* reviewer, characterizes it as "a little bit of experience, remembered or invented, and a lot of analysis, overlaid on it, as if the registers didn't clash; that is the dismaying pattern. . . . A vivid spark every few pages, smothered before it can catch by a fire-blanket of nervous, insistent literary effect." Yet numerous other critics saw the author's tone as perfectly suited to his story. "Since *High Cotton*'s narrator was born into a position of relative privilege, he must speak of oppression from the fringes," defends *Nation* reviewer Hilton Als. "Throughout the book, he is pulled between inclusion in one faction of his society . . . and exclusion from most others because of it. . . . Pinckney's wit—distanced, learned—saves him, time and again, from first-novel sentimentality and self-absorption. Such nonwriting supported by nonthinking never appears. . . . Pinckney elevates despair to the lyrical."

BIOGRAPHICAL/CRITICAL SOURCES:

BOOKS

Contemporary Literary Criticism, Volume 76, Gale (Detroit), 1993, pp. 98-113.

PERIODICALS

Chicago Tribune, March 3, 1992, p. 3.
Christian Science Monitor, February 28, 1992, p. 13.
Los Angeles Times Book Review, February 23, 1992, pp. 3, 8; November 8, 1992.
Nation, May 18, 1992, pp. 667-670.
Newsday, March 8, 1992.
New York Review of Books, March 26, 1992, pp. 13-14.
New York Times, March 5, 1992, p. C21; April 4, 1992; April 9, 1992, pp. C17, C26.
New York Times Book Review, February 2, 1992.
Partisan Review, no. 2, 1992, pp. 288-291.
Times (London), August 13, 1992.

Times Literary Supplement, August 14, 1992, p. 17.
Wall Street Journal, February 5, 1992, p. A9.
Washington Post Book World, February 23, 1992, pp. 1, 9.*

* * *

PLAATJE, Sol(omon) T(shekisho) 1876-1932

PERSONAL: Born October 9, 1876, in South Africa; died June 19, 1932, in South Africa; son of Johannes and Martha Plaatje; married Elizabeth (Lilith) M'belle. *Education:* Attended Lutheran Berlin Missionary School.

CAREER: Worked as a messenger in Kimberley, Cape Province, South Africa, 1894-99; court interpreter in Mafeking, Cape Province, beginning in 1898; clerk in Cape civil service, 1899-1902; *Koranta ea Becoana* (Tswana-English newspaper), editor, 1902-10; *Tsala ea Becoana* (title means "Friend of the Tswana"), editor, 1910-13; *Tsala ea Batho* (title means "Friend of the People"), editor, 1913-15. Founder and general secretary of the South African Native National Congress (became African National Congress), beginning in 1912; government lobbyist in the United Kingdom and the United States, rallying against South African racial policies; political activist; writer.

WRITINGS:

Native Life in South Africa: Before and since the European War and the Boer Rebellion, King, 1916, Ohio University Press (Athens), 1991.
(With Daniel Jones) *A Sechuana Reader, in International Phonetic Orthography,* University of London Press, 1916, Farnborough, 1970.
(With Silas T. Molema) *The Silas T. Molema and Solomon T. Plaatje Papers,* compiled by Marcelle Jacobson, Library, University of the Witwatersrand (Johannesburg), 1978.
Mhudi: An Epic of Native Life a Hundred Years Ago, Lovedale, 1930, Heinemann, 1978.
The Boer War Diary of Sol T. Plaatje, edited by John L. Comaroff, Macmillan (New York City), 1973, published as *Mafeking Diary,* Ohio University Press, 1990.
Sol Plaatje: Selected Writings, edited by Brian Willan, Ohio University Press, 1997.

Contributor to numerous South African newspapers.

TRANSLATOR

Sechuana Proverbs, with Literal Translations and Their European Equivalents, Kegan Paul, 1916.

William Shakespeare, *Diphosho-phosho* (*A Comedy of Errors*), Morija, 1930.

Shakcspcarc, *Dintshontsho tsa bo-Juliuse Kesara* (*Julius Caesar*), Witwatersrand University Press, 1937.

SIDELIGHTS: Decades before the political reality of apartheid, Sol Plaatje was helping to lead the struggle for reform in South Africa. He served as the first secretary to the South African Native National Congress, which would later be renamed the African National Congress, and authored the first novel in English by a black South African, *Mhudi: An Epic of Native Life a Hundred Years Ago.* Plaatje was also one of the first historians of his own people, the Barolong of south-central Africa, and worked as a translator, newspaper editor, and diarist.

Brian Willan, in his biography *Sol Plaatje: South African Nationalist, 1876-1932,* stated that in his writing, "Plaatje was concerned to offer something of a corrective to the predominant view in the literature and the stereotypes of white South Africans (and others) that his people were murderous savages, saved only by the coming of the white man. He also has a fresh perspective to offer upon the Boers themselves. In *Mhudi* they are viewed not as the embodiment of the advance of civilisation, but as a strange and far from heroic group of travellers."

Plaatje—the surname came from a nickname for his father—grew up in a large family near Kimberley, a center of South Africa's diamond industry, which was only beginning to develop at the time of his birth. His family, whose ancestors were among Christianity's earliest converts in southern Africa, sent Plaatje to a missionary school. While Plaatje did not receive much formal education—he was to leave the school at the age of seventeen to begin working for the Kimberley post office—he demonstrated special intelligence by learning eight languages. His native language was Tswana, but the youth soon learned English as well as six other European and African languages. He became one of the elite of his region, marrying into the family of a court interpreter.

Plaatje's first break came when he took a court interpreter job himself in Mafeking in 1898, a year before the city came under siege during the Second Anglo-Boer War. The five-month resistance by British and native forces in Mafeking was one of England's few victories in the war's early stages and consequently received much attention. Plaatje emulated others trapped in the city by keeping and later publishing a personal diary of his experiences during the siege. Many such diaries were printed and given wide distribution, but Plaatje's remained unpublished until 1973. However, the siege changed Plaatje's outlook. In 1902 he left the civil service and became a newspaper editor. Over the next decade he worked on numerous newspapers and joined the group that would become the African National Congress, becoming its secretary.

In 1913, the recently formed Union of South Africa passed the Native Lands Act, which helped lay the foundation for apartheid. Plaatje was one of the strongest opponents of the law, which threatened the property rights of all South African non-whites. Plaatje wrote editorials against the act and joined a deputation of leaders who traveled to Britain to lobby the Empire to repeal the act. The group was unsuccessful, but Plaatje remained in England after World War I broke out. He remained abroad for several years.

Plaatje used his time in England to write three books. *Native Life in South Africa,* considered his most important work, attacked the Native Lands Act. Willan, in a *Dictionary of Literary Biography* essay, called the work "a wide-ranging defense of African political rights and an often-emotive account of the steps taken over the years by South Africa's rulers to exclude Africans from political power." Willan remarked on the book's "personal, often nostalgic tone." Plaatje's contemporaries, though, especially whites, were most struck by the fact that the work marked the first time a black South African had written a book expounding the claims of Africans.

Plaatje also produced two works on his native language, Tswana, or Sechuana. One, *A Sechuana Reader,* was a linguistic description of the language, written to guard the integrity of the language in the face of a changing world. The other, *Sechuana Proverbs,* which Plaatje translated, was a collection of proverbs in Tswana with English translations and European equivalents where they existed. Soon after the books appeared, Plaatje returned to South Africa briefly, but then left, first for a second deputation to Great Britain and then to the United States, where he met political leader Marcus Garvey and educator and writer W. E. B. Du Bois, among others.

From 1920 until he died in 1932, Plaatje continued his newspaper work, with more success at writing for other papers than in editing his own. He devoted himself more to the Tswana language, producing a new dictionary and translations of six Shakespeare plays, of which only two were published. They were the first translations of Shakespeare into an African language. In 1930, *Mhudi* came out. The work failed to truly make its mark until reissued in 1978, long after Plaatje's death. In fact, Plaatje's impact has only really begun to be assessed in the 1980s.

Willan remarked: "*Mhudi* was the outcome of a quite conscious and deliberate attempt on Plaatje's part to marry together two different cultural traditions: African oral forms and traditions, particularly those of the Barolong, on the one hand; and the written traditions and forms of the English language and literature on the other. The full extent to which these African oral traditions have found their way into *Mhudi* may never be fully known, although if Plaatje's own collection of Tswana folktales had survived we would probably have been in a much better position to make some sort of assessment."

J. M. Phelps, assessing *Mhudi* in *English Studies in Africa*, found that Plaatje "successfully portrays how the pride of power works in destructive combination with the common human weakness of ascribing the cause of hostilities to the other side. Shown as particularly vulnerable to capture in the tangle of war's cause and effect are the young, eager to fight before they think. . . . The narrative effectively dramatizes the countervailing resources in the various communities which can unite the generations, and which do prevail when they are fostered by tradition, democratic process, and respect for the freedom of speech."

Plaatje is generally considered more a man of letters than an author. He produced a wide variety of work, from diaries to polemical essays and translations to a novel. "A man of deeply conservative instinct," Willan writes in his biography, "he drew inspiration from both African and European traditions, and was sustained throughout a life of ceaseless endeavour by a vision of what South Africa could be, given only the freedom to draw upon what he saw as the best of those traditions, created from South Africa's unique historical experience." A newspaper obituary for the former newspaperman in *Umteteli wa Bantu*, quoted by Willan in the biography, described the writer more succinctly: "For Plaatje, scholar and patriot, the most fitting epitaph would be: 'He loved his people.'"

BIOGRAPHICAL/CRITICAL SOURCES:

BOOKS

Black Literature Criticism Supplement, Gale (Detroit), 1996.
Dictionary of Literary Biography, Volume 125: *Twentieth Century Caribbean and Black African Writers, Second Series,* Gale, 1993.
Mphahlelele, Ezekiel, *The African Image,* Faber (London), 1962.
Twentieth-Century Literary Criticism, Volume 73, Gale, 1998.
Pampallis, John, *Sol Plaatje,* Maskew Miller Longman (Cape Town, South Africa), 1992.
Willan, Brian, *Sol Plaatje: South African Nationalist, 1876-1932,* University of California Press (Berkeley), 1984, published as *Sol Plaatje: A Biography,* Ravan (Johannesburg, South Africa), 1984.

PERIODICALS

Communique, volume 9, number 1, 1984, pp. 3-13.
English in Africa, March, 1977, pp. 1-6, 14; May, 1987, pp. 41-65.
English Studies in Africa, number 1, 1993, pp. 47-56.
International Journal of African Historical Studies, No. 4, 1990, pp. 733-735.
Journal of Commonwealth Literature, June, 1973, pp. 1-19.
Times Educational Supplement, August 21, 1987.
Times Literary Supplement, November 30, 1973, p. 1472.
University of Witwatersrand Historical and Literary Papers: Inventories of Collections, number 7, 1978.
Washington Post Book World, November 24, 1985.
Yearbook of English Studies, 13, 1983, pp. 181-195.*

*　　*　　*

PLOWDEN, Martha Ward 1948-

PERSONAL: Born February 24, 1948, in Atlanta, GA; daughter of Isiah Paul, Sr. (a minister) and Annie Mae (a nurse's aide; maiden name, Haley) Ward; married Nathaniel Plowden (a United Parcel Service supervisor), December 31, 1972; children: Natalie Ward. *Education:* Clark College, B.S., 1969; Atlanta University, M.S.L.S., 1975, Specialist Degree, 1977; further graduate study at Georgia State University and Walden University, 1980, 1995. *Politics:* Democrat. *Religion:* Baptist.

ADDRESSES: Home—3104 Topaz Lane S.W., Atlanta, GA 30331. *E-mail*—nplowden@compuserv. com.

CAREER: Southern Bell Telephone Co., Atlanta, GA, operator; Taliaferro County Elementary and High School, Crawfordville, GA, librarian; Grady Memorial Hospital, Atlanta, food service supervisor; Clark College, Atlanta, librarian; Atlanta Public Schools, Atlanta, media specialist; Metro Atlanta Skills Center, Atlanta, mathematics instructor. Clark Atlanta University, adjunct professor; Young Men's Christian Association, member of board of directors, 1975-79; volunteer for American Red Cross, Oakhill Homes, United Negro College Fund, and Martin Luther King's Center for Nonviolent Social Change.

MEMBER: National Association of Educators, National Association of Black School Educators, American Library Association, National Association for the Advancement of Colored People (member of Atlanta board of directors; chairperson of ACT-SO Program), National Council of Negro Women, Georgia Association of Educators, Georgia Library Media Association, Georgia Nutrition Association, Atlanta Association of Educators, Atlanta Urban League Guild (past president), Greater Atlanta Panhellenic Council (vice-president), Phi Delta Kappa, Delta Sigma Theta, Kappa Delta Epsilon, Eta Phi Beta, Atlanta Epicureans, Continental Colony Community Association.

AWARDS, HONORS: Academic Incentive Award Area II in Media; fellowship for study of Library Science, Atlanta University; Million Dollar Club Medallion, NAACP, 1982 and 1984.

WRITINGS:

Famous Firsts of Black Women, illustrated by Ronald Jones, Pelican Publishing (Gretna, LA), 1993.
Olympic Black Women, illustrated by Ronald Jones, Pelican Publishing, 1996.

Regional editor, *Library Scene.*

WORK IN PROGRESS: Updating *Famous Firsts of Black Women;* another book on the Olympics.

BIOGRAPHICAL/CRITICAL SOURCES:

PERIODICALS

Horn Book Guide, fall, 1996, p. 362.
School Library Journal, March, 1994, p. 244.

Skipping Stones, winter, 1995, p. 31; February-March, 1996, p. 31.

*   *   *

PORTER, Connie (Rose)   1959-

PERSONAL: Born 1959, in NY. *Education:* Attended Louisiana State University.

CAREER: Writer.

WRITINGS:

All-Bright Court (novel), Houghton, 1991.
Imani All Mine (novel) Houghton, 1998.

"AMERICAN GIRLS" SERIES; PUBLISHED BY PLEASANT CO. (MIDDLETON, WI)

Meet Addy: An American Girl, illustrated by Melodye Rosales, 1993.
Addy Learns a Lesson: A School Story, illustrated by Melodye Rosales, 1993.
Addy's Surprise, illustrated by Melodye Rosales, 1993.
Happy Birthday, Addy!: A Springtime Story, illustrated by Bradford Brown, 1993.
Changes for Addy: A Winter Story, illustrated by Bradford Brown, 1994.
Addy Saves the Day: A Summer Story, illustrated by Bradford Brown, 1994.

SIDELIGHTS: Connie Porter is the author of two novels for adults as well as several books for children about the character Addy in the popular "American Girls" historical series. Her 1991 novel *All-Bright Court* garnered much positive critical response and was repeatedly praised as an exceptional debut novel. Following the publication of a half-dozen "Addy" titles, Porter released her second novel, *Imani All Mine,* in 1998. Both adult novels have in common central characters who are young, poor, and black. While the first book is set during the 1960s and 1970s, the second takes place during the 1990s.

All-Bright Court tells the story of a group of Southern blacks who move to a Northern steel town in search of higher-paying jobs, better living conditions, and a more egalitarian society. Faced with frequent layoffs and cruel and dangerous conditions in the mill in which they work, however, they find they have only traded one set of hardships for another. Yet a strong sense of community pervades the low-rent apartment complex where the novel is set, and, through vignettes centering on the Taylor family and their friends and neighbors, Porter depicts the many facets of poverty in an American ghetto. Adrian Oktenberg of *Women's Review of Books* calls Porter's work "a novel of vision and integrity, wherein a community is seen whole, embedded in its economics and history, sparing nothing, and whose stories are told with great compassion."

After posting a high score on an intelligence test, one of the Taylors' sons, Mikey, is offered a scholarship to a private school and a possible way out of the cycle of poverty and degradation in which his family is trapped. His new friends expose him to a wealthy white world, and Mikey eventually takes on the speech and values of that other world and becomes ashamed of his family and the way they live. Jonathan Yardley comments in the *Washington Post Book World* that "Porter is sensitive to every nuance of the cultural encounter Mikey undergoes, and portrays each step of his journey with as much clarity as sympathy."

Porter earns praise for her depiction of both the desperation of the lives of her characters as well as the dignity inherent in their manner of coping. Gary Krist remarks in the *Hudson Review* that she "writes simply but powerfully, and with a command of detail that lends authority to the world she depicts." Commenting in the *New York Times,* Michiko Kakutani asserts: "Though her prose is often lyrical, even poetic, [Porter] does not shirk from showing the reader the harsh reality of her characters' daily lives. . . . Indeed, the emotional power of *All-Bright Court* resides in her finely rendered characters, people who come alive for the reader as individuals one has known first hand."

All-Bright Court is based on a short story that Porter wrote as a student at Louisiana State University. The original piece was only twelve pages long and included descriptions of the place, family, and some of the events she later used in her novel. The expanded version fulfilled the author's hopes of writing about the steel industry and about the area in which she grew up.

In 1993, Porter released *Meet Addy: An American Girl,* the first book in a historical series that features a young black slave named Addy who escapes to freedom with her mother during the American Civil War.

In *Addy Learns a Lesson,* the title character faces the challenges of living in the urban North and finding friends at her school. Addy possesses "affability and pluck," notes *Publishers Weekly* contributor Diane Roback, who finds the series of novels "bright" and "poignant."

After producing five more books in the "American Girls" series, Porter addressed a more mature audience with her next publication, the 1998 novel *Imani All Mine.* While Tasha, her protagonist, is only 15 years old, she has not experienced an average childhood. An honors student, Tasha plans to go to college and thereby escape the hardships of life in a poor inner-city neighborhood. But she becomes pregnant after being raped by a schoolmate and decides to keep her baby, whom she names Imani, meaning "faith." Tasha loves her child very deeply and tries to nurture her in a dangerous environment filled with drugs, gangs, poverty, and bigotry. She struggles to be a good mother while she deals with more common teen issues, including her emerging sexuality and her mother's new, white boyfriend.

Tasha serves as an effective narrator, speaking in the language of the street. Critic Karen Anderson applauds the author's creation in a *Library Journal* review, saying "Porter . . . gives Tasha great wisdom, grace, charm, and a moving poetic voice." *Booklist*'s Vanessa Bush calls *Imani All Mine* a "deceptively simple novel" and, like Anderson, notes that "through Tasha's stark voice, Porter offers well-drawn characters." A reviewer for *Publishers Weekly* finds that sometimes the book has a "[young adult] simplicity" but nonetheless enjoys the way "Porter spins the tale in a series of flashbacks, telling Tasha's story in a nonlinear fashion and with a bold dialect, mirroring the survival strategies of indirection that Tasha employs."

In an interview furnished by her publisher, Porter names many authors as being influential on her writing. As a child, she loved Lois Lenski and Beverly Cleary; later, she read Langston Hughes, Nella Larsen, Nikki Giovanni, Richard Wright, Louise Meriwether, Rosa Guy, and Maya Angelou, among others. When asked to describe herself as a writer, she said, "I would describe myself as a black female writer. I surely have been black and female all my life and now, because I'm a writer, I do not want to stop describing myself in that way. I do no fear that because there is some descriptive tag before the word 'writer' that I will be pigeonholed. Racism and sexism are what can pigeonhole you. They can limit, even stop you. Not describing myself as a black woman will not prevent that from happening."

BIOGRAPHICAL/CRITICAL SOURCES:

BOOKS

Contemporary Literary Criticism, Volume 70, Gale, 1992, pp. 96-101.

PERIODICALS

American Libraries, February, 1992, p. 192.
Belles Lettres, winter, 1991, p. 7.
Booklist, August, 1993, p. 2063; January 1, 1999, p. 834.
Chicago Tribune, August 25, 1991, p. 4.
Detroit Free Press, September 8, 1991, p. 8P.
Essence, September, 1991, p. 50.
Hudson Review, spring, 1992, p. 141-42.
Library Journal, February 1, 1999, p. 122.
Los Angeles Times Book Review, October 13, 1991, p. 9; September 6, 1992, p. 11.
New Yorker, September 9, 1991, p. 96.
New York Times, September 10, 1991, p. C14.
New York Times Book Review, October 27, 1991, p. 12; August 16, 1992, p. 32.
Publishers Weekly, July 5, 1993, p. 73; November 23, 1998, p. 58.
Tribune Books (Chicago), August 25, 1991, p. 4.
Washington Post Book World, August 11, 1991, p. 3; December 1, 1991, p. 3; July 26, 1992, p. 12.
Women's Review of Books, April, 1992, pp. 16-17.*

*   *   *

PORTER, James A(mos)   1905-1970

PERSONAL: Born December 22, 1905, in Baltimore, MD; died of cancer, February 28, 1970; son of Reverend John Porter; married Dorothy Burnett (a research librarian), 1929; children: Constance. *Ethnicity:* "African American." *Education:* Howard University, B.S., 1927; studied with Dimitri Romanovsky at the Art Students League; New York University, M.A., 1947; additional studies in Paris, Belgium, West Africa, Egypt, Cuba, and Haiti.

CAREER: Painter, educator, and art historian. Howard University, Washington, DC, professor, 1927-70, art department chair and director of the Howard University Gallery of Art, 1953-70. Paintings

and drawings in collections at Howard University, Lincoln University (MO), Harmon Foundation, IBM, Hampton Institute (VA), and National Archives; numerous exhibitions and one-person shows, 1928-70.

MEMBER: International Congress on African Art and Culture, American Federation of Arts, Arts Council of Washington, DC, Symposium on Art and Public Education.

AWARDS, HONORS: Harmon Foundation, honorable mention, 1929; Schomburg Portrait Prize, 1933; National Gallery of Art medal for distinguished service to art, 1966; Pyramid Club, Philadelphia, recognition for Achievement in Art; Association for the Study of Negro Life and History, awards for book reviews published in the *Journal of Negro History.*

WRITINGS:

Modern Negro Art, Dryden, 1943, reprinted with new introduction by David C. Driskell, Howard University Press (Washington, DC), 1992.
Robert S. Duncanson, Midwestern Romantic-Realist, [Springfield, MA], 1951.
Ten Afro-American Artists of the Nineteenth Century, Howard University Gallery of Art (Washington, DC), 1967.

Contributor of book reviews to periodicals, including *Journal of Negro History.* Illustrator for *Playsongs of the Deep South* and *Talking Animals,* both published by Associated Publishers.

SIDELIGHTS: Just as many art historians prefer the dust of library stacks to the colorful mess of the studio, many artists choose to remain ignorant of the artistic past that has, without their knowledge, shaped their work. James A. Porter, however, relished the challenges and pleasures of both pursuits. As an instructor at Howard University for over 40 years, Porter's pioneering research into the work of early African American artists rescued a great deal of important art from obscurity. At the same time he worked with and inspired some of the twentieth century's most successful black artists. Additionally, Porter was an acclaimed painter in his own right, remaining active as an artist throughout his distinguished academic career.

Porter was born on December 22, 1905 in Baltimore, Maryland. His father, the Reverend John Porter, was a leader in the African Methodist Episcopal church, and religion played a major role in Porter family life.

The Reverend Porter wanted James, one of eight children, to become a minister. Instead, James fell in love with drawing and painting, and from an early age he knew he wanted to be an artist.

The Porter family moved to Washington, DC, when James was in high school. Once settled in Washington, the Reverend introduced his son to James V. Herring, the head of Howard University's art department, in the hope that Herring would talk James out of pursuing his artistic dreams. The ploy backfired, and Herring, recognizing the young Porter's talent, not only encouraged him to continue making art, but urged him to do it at Howard when he was done with high school.

Porter graduated from high school at the top of his class and was offered a scholarship to Yale. Since the scholarship covered only tuition, and he could not afford living expenses, Porter had to decline the offer. Howard University, on the other hand, was close enough to allow Porter to live at home, so he accepted a scholarship, arranged by Herring, to attend that school.

Porter entered Howard in 1923. He performed so well as a student that, upon graduating in 1927, he was offered a teaching position. In preparation for his career as an art instructor, he spent the summer studying art education at Columbia University in New York. Porter continued to hone his painting skills at the same time, studying at the Art Students League with the well-known painting tutor Dimitri Romanovsky.

In the course of his studies, Porter became acutely aware of how poorly the art community in the United States had kept track of African American artists. He began to take an interest in unearthing information about gifted but forgotten black artists of the past. While conducting research in this area at the Harlem branch library, he met Dorothy Burnett, a research librarian whose specialty was black American writing before 1835. Porter and Burnett found that their areas of interest overlapped quite a bit. The two fell in love, and were married in 1929.

As his drawing and painting skills developed further, Porter began to gain recognition as an artist. In 1929 he won an honorable mention from the Harmon Foundation, an organization committed to honoring "distinguished achievements among Negroes." The Harmon Foundation honored Porter again in 1933, awarding him its Schomburg portrait prize for his painting *Woman Holding Jug*. By this time, Porter had brought Dorothy back with him to Howard where she joined the staff of the university's library. She eventually became director of the library, and earned a national reputation of her own for her work on early African American writers.

Porter's technical excellence at drawing was apparent from the start of his career. More than any other form, Porter's portraits and figural compositions most frequently gained attention. His early paintings, such as "Sarah"—for which he was first noticed by the Harmon Foundation—showed a great deal of emotion. Many of his best works were portraits of family, friends, and Howard University luminaries.

During the 1930s, Porter traveled widely and broadened his knowledge of artistic styles around the world and throughout history. In 1935 he received a fellowship from the Institute of International Education, which he used to study medieval archaeology at the Sorbonne in Paris. When his work in Paris was completed, Porter traveled throughout Europe studying European and African art with the aid of a grant from the Rockefeller Foundation. Returning to the United States, Porter earned his master's degree in art history from New York University in 1937. He then returned to Howard University to resume his teaching career.

Porter continued his research on African American artists. The next several years of work in this area resulted in the 1943 publication of *Modern Negro Art,* a pioneering effort that has remained an important source of information on the topic ever since. *Modern Negro Art* was essentially a critical survey of African American artists through the time of its publication. The book brought many of the profiled artists back into the public eye after decades—sometimes more than a century—of obscurity.

Porter continued to travel in search of artistic insight over the next several years. During the 1945-46 academic year, he studied art in Cuba and Haiti, again with financial assistance from the Rockefeller Foundation. Much of the material he collected on this trip was used to develop a Latin-American art curriculum at Howard. Porter also spent a great deal of time during the 1940s studying the life and work of Robert S. Duncanson, a Civil War-era black artist from Cincinnati, Ohio. His research on Duncanson resulted in the 1951 publication of a monograph on the subject, as well as a major article in the journal *Art in America.*

After his trip to the Caribbean, Porter's paintings began to take on a more decorative quality. *On a Cuban Bus* and *Lydia,* for example, showed a warm, realistic style that attempted to interpret the lively side of the African American spirit. In the 1950s and early 1960s, Porter also dabbled in more modern approaches, such as cubism—for example, *Girl in a Shattered Mirror* (1955)—and fauvism—*Toromaquia* (1962).

When Herring retired from Howard in 1953, Porter inherited the positions of art department chair and director of the Howard University Gallery of Art. Although the administrative tasks associated with these jobs ate into his time for painting and research, Porter adjusted by regularly working well into the night. Dorothy Porter's expertise in locating research references was also of great assistance. Porter made another trip to Europe in 1955, this time as a fellow of the Belgium-American Art Seminar. In Belgium, he followed up on his earlier research into Flemish and Dutch art of the sixteenth, seventeenth, and eighteenth centuries.

In 1963 the Washington, D.C., *Evening Star* newspaper awarded Porter a grant to travel to West Africa and Egypt, where he was to research the art and architecture of those regions for his next book. He was so inspired by what he saw that he set up a studio in Lagos, Nigeria, and quickly created at least twenty-five new paintings. "You can't help painting when you're in Africa—the skies, the red earth, the verdure and the dress of the people—all of them reinforce one's feeling for color," Porter was quoted in *Free within Ourselves: African-American Artists in the Collection of the National Museum of American Art.*

In addition to being quite conscious of color, Porter's new paintings were in a style far more expressionistic than anything he had done before. Africa also had a profound effect on his thinking about art. He began to feel that African themes had been developing unconsciously in his painting for years, and he reexamined much of his past work with regard to that notion. Although he continued to work over the next several years on a book about the influence of African art in the West, it was never finished.

In 1966 Porter was one of twenty-five artists honored for outstanding achievement in the arts by President Lyndon B. Johnson as part of the National Gallery of Art's twenty-fifth anniversary celebration. The following year, Porter organized an exhibition as part of Howard's centennial festivities. Entitled "Ten Afro-American Artists of the Nineteenth Century," the exhibition included works by Edmonia Lewis, Henry Ossawa Tanner, Duncanson, and others whose artistic gifts had been ignored largely because of their race.

Toward the end of the 1960s, Porter was diagnosed as having cancer, and he became seriously ill. His illness did not stop him from traveling to Africa once more, this time to chair a conference in Rhodesia on Zimbabwean culture. His health continued to deteriorate, however, and he died on February 28, 1970, just a week after chairing a conference in the United States on African American artists.

In 1992 the Howard University Gallery of Art mounted an exhibition of Porter's work. The retrospective, "James A. Porter, Artist and Art Historian: The Memory of the Legacy," emphasized Porter's unique ability to carry out the dual roles of artist and scholar, each with commitment and excellence. Porter's third role, that of teacher, has had perhaps the most lasting effect of all. Starmanda Bullock Featherstone, a Howard art professor and guest curator of the 1992 retrospective, was quoted as saying in a *Washington Post* review of the exhibition, that "all his students say that they studied under the master, James A. Porter."

BIOGRAPHICAL/CRITICAL SOURCES:

PERIODICALS

American Visions, December, 1992/January, 1993, pp. 26-30.
Negro History Bulletin, October, 1954, pp. 5-6; April, 1970, p. 99.
Washington Post, November 27, 1992, p. B2.*

*   *   *

POWELL, Adam Clayton, Jr. 1908-1972

PERSONAL: Born November 29, 1908, in New Haven, CT; died of cancer, April 4, 1972, in Miami, FL; son of Adam Clayton (a minister) and Mattie (Fletcher) Powell; married Isabel Washington (a dancer), March 8, 1933 (divorced, 1943); married Hazel Scott (a pianist and singer), 1945 (divorced, 1960); married Yvette Marjorie Flores Diago, 1960 (separated, 1965); children: Preston (adopted); (second marriage) Adam Clayton III; (third marriage) Adam Diago. *Education:* Colgate University, B.A.,

1930; Columbia University, M.A., 1932; D.D., Shaw University, 1938.

CAREER: Abyssinian Baptist Church, New York City, manager and assistant pastor, 1930-36, pastor, 1936-71; New York City Council, New York City, member, 1941-45; United States House of Representatives, Washington, DC, member, 1945-67 and 1969-70, chairman of House Committee on Education and Labor, 1960-67.

AWARDS, HONORS: LL.D., Virginia Union University; golden medallion from Ethiopia for relief work.

WRITINGS:

Marching Blacks: An Interpretive History of the Rise of the Black Common Man, Dial, 1945, revised edition, 1973.
The New Image in Education: A Prospectus for the Future by the Chairman of the Committee on Education and Labor, U.S. Government Printing Office, 1962.
Keep the Faith, Baby!, Trident, 1967.
Adam by Adam, Dial 1971.

Author of weekly column, "The Soap Box," Amsterdam News, c. late 1930s. Editor, People's Voice, c. 1940.

SIDELIGHTS: "Before black power, before black pride, before the civil rights movement took its first steps in the dusty streets of Montgomery, Alabama, before any of it, there was Adam," declared Newsweek writer David M. Alpern in an article on Adam Clayton Powell, Jr. "For 30 years, [he] did more than any other man to dramatize the quest of Negro Americans and, by an outrageous larger-than-life style, give his people a vicarious piece of the white man's action. He was New York's first black city councilman, Harlem's first black congressman—and the most celebrated black politician in the nation."

Powell's legacy is decidedly mixed, however. Writing in the New York Times, Thomas A. Johnson once described him as a man who played many roles throughout his often colorful lifetime: "He was at once the leader of the largest church congregation in the nation, a political demagogue, a Congressional rebel, a civil rights leader three decades before the Montgomery bus boycott, a wheeler-dealer, a rabble-rouser, a grandstander, a fugitive, a playboy and a most effective chairman of the House Committee on Education and Labor." As such, Powell's many politi-

cal and social achievements are in danger of being forgotten or at the very least overshadowed by the scandals he was involved in and his oversized ego. In a review of Wil Haygood's 1992 biography King of the Cats: The Life and Times of Adam Clayton Powell, Jr., critic Thomas Kessner said of Powell, "Today little more than a memory remains." He then went on to note, "If there is a weakness in this lively biography, it is one of degree: Mr. Haygood fails to convey the epic quality of Powell's tragic squandering of his extraordinary gifts."

Powell was born in Connecticut but grew up in the Harlem district of New York City. There his father served as pastor of the venerable Abyssinian Baptist Church, the oldest black congregation in the North and one of the largest Protestant churches in the entire country. As a youngster, Powell was exposed to the ideas of black nationalist leader Marcus Garvey and also attended meetings of the African Nationalist Pioneer Movement. "Marcus Garvey was one of the greatest mass leaders of all time," Powell later wrote. "He was misunderstood and maligned, but he brought to the Negro people for the first time a sense of pride in being black."

During the Depression, Powell became a leader in his own right. He spearheaded a series of demonstrations against department stores, bus lines, hospitals, the telephone company, and other big businesses in Harlem, forcing them to hire blacks. He subsequently became chairman of the Coordinating Committee on Employment and organized picket lines outside the executive offices of the 1939-40 World's Fair (which was held in New York City), thereby gaining jobs at the event for hundreds of black workers.

Powell also organized the social and welfare programs at the Abyssinian Baptist Church, including a vocational guidance clinic as well as a soup kitchen and relief operation that supplied food, clothing, and fuel for thousands of local residents. He served as the leader of the militant Harlem People's Committee and quickly earned a reputation, noted Ebony's Simeon Booker, "for scrap, for agitation and for stinging rebuke." So outspoken was "Fighting Adam" (one of his nicknames) that Booker credited him with single-handedly changing the course of national Negro affairs.

In 1941 Powell was elected to the New York City Council, becoming the first African American ever to serve in that capacity. He remained in office for four years, turning a voteless community into a "ballot kingdom," as Booker observed. Powell then built on his political success in Harlem and won election to the U.S. House of Representatives. Arriving in Washington in 1945, the new legislator continued his fight against racial discrimination. Although unwritten rules excluded him from public places such as dining rooms, steam baths, and barber shops, Powell defiantly made use of these facilities, often with his entire staff in tow. On the House floor he debated furiously with Southern segregationists. According to Booker, Powell "upset tradition on Capitol Hill—against the wishes and combined efforts of many of his colleagues. Like no other Negro, except possibly the late Malcolm X, Adam knew how to anger, to irritate and to cajole his white counterparts."

Powell tackled a variety of causes. He fought for the admission of black journalists to the Senate and House press galleries. He introduced legislation to ban racist transportation, and he brought to the attention of Congress the discriminatory practices of groups such as the Daughters of the American Revolution (DAR). In addition, he challenged racial bias in the armed forces and authored the Powell Amendment, which attempted to deny federal funds to projects that tolerated discrimination.

As chairman of the House Committee on Education and Labor, a position that made him perhaps the most powerful black in America, Powell compiled an extraordinary record. Under his direction the committee passed 48 major pieces of social legislation, including the 1961 Minimum Wage Bill, the Manpower Development and Training Act, the Anti-Poverty Bill, the Juvenile Delinquency Act, the Vocational Educational Act, and the National Defense Educational Act.

But as Powell "became influential, powerful and dominating. . .he frequently clashed with Democrats, government officials, labor and educational leaders, and even the President on segregation and discrimination policies," explained Booker. "While Southern chairmen blocked civil rights legislation at will, Adam tried to bottle major legislation whenever he felt it needed some anti-bias safeguards. This tactic brought him into open conflict with the 'white power structure.'" The resulting tension, coupled with Powell's high rate of absenteeism, prompted his fellow legislators to censure him. The situation was further exacerbated by his reputation as a playboy who liked to surround himself with a bevy of beautiful women and accusations involving tax evasion and misuse of public funds. Powell's response was characteristically blunt. "The things other Congressmen

try to hide, I do right out in the open," he declared. "I'm not a hypocrite."

Powell's penchant for attracting the public's attention also brought him into conflict with other black leaders. "He credited himself with being more powerful than the leaders and probably he was," noted Booker, "but the shortcoming was that the black teamwork he stressed, he never carried out." It was not until March 1960, that his flamboyant and outspoken public image finally began to jeopardize his political effectiveness. During a television interview, Powell referred to a 63-year-old Harlem widow named Ester James as a "bag woman," a slang term for someone who collects payoff money for corrupt police. A libel suit ensued, but Powell ignored the charge against him and refused to apologize or come to a settlement. After Mrs. James won the case and was awarded damages, the congressman still would not comply with the court ruling. Eventually, Powell was found guilty of civil contempt but avoided arrest by appearing in New York City only on Sundays when officials could not serve him with a summons. Following his conviction on a criminal contempt charge in 1966, he took up residence on the Bahamian island of Bimini.

In response to this conviction and other alleged misbehavior, a select committee of Powell's fellow representatives launched an investigation, and on March 1, 1967, the House voted 307 to 116 to expel him from the ninetieth Congress. Powell thus became the first committee chairman to be removed from the House in 160 years. Nevertheless, in a special election held two months later to fill his vacant seat, Powell's constituents overwhelmingly voted him back into office. Ultimately, he paid the damages he owed to Mrs. James and was readmitted to Congress in January 1969. His colleagues then fined him for misuse of funds and stripped him of his seniority.

During this tumultuous period, white liberals with whom Powell had worked abandoned him, while black leaders rallied to his defense. The resulting breach in the civil rights movement sent a questionable message to activists, in the view of Francis E. Kearns. As he noted in *Commonweal:* "The chief significance of Adam Clayton Powell's recent difficulties with Congress lies not in the state of the Congressman's personal fortunes or even in the constitutional question of whether the House may deny a district representation by its duly elected Congressman. . . . Clearly Powell's censurable behavior hardly approaches in gravity the misconduct of some other Congressmen who have escaped punitive action. . . . The unseating of one of the most powerful Negro politicians in American history at the very time when a battery of editorialists are urging the Negro to temper his militancy is hardly likely to demonstrate that legislative action offers a viable alternative to mob action in the streets."

Six months after Powell's return to Congress, the United States Supreme Court ruled that the 1967 House decision to expel him had been unconstitutional. "From now on, America will know the Supreme Court is the place where you can get justice," Powell told reporters. But his political career was already coming to an end. In 1969 he was defeated by Charles B. Rangel in the Democratic primary after having been hospitalized for cancer. He died in Miami in 1972 following prostate surgery.

Powell's writings were as controversial as his lifestyle. Beginning in 1936, he published a weekly column in the *Amsterdam News* entitled "The Soap Box." He used this forum to attack President Franklin Roosevelt's New Deal, to criticize New York Mayor Fiorello La Guardia as a politician who was only interested in the city's black residents at election time, and to promote an alliance of all poor people in order to advance the interests of blacks. According to Charles V. Hamilton in *Adam Clayton Powell, Jr.: The Political Biography of an American Dilemma,* Powell's columns helped him become "one of the identifiable young leaders in a community seething with social controversy and suffering from no lack of self-appointed and organized groups claiming to point the way for the residents to alleviate their problems."

Powell's first book, published not long after he was elected to Congress, captured the attention of the mainstream press. *Marching Blacks* presented his views on race relations in the United States and advocated the mass migration of African Americans from the South to the North and West. Critical response was mixed. In the *New York Times Book Review,* Frank Adams remarked on the author's "intemperance" and "intransigence," describing the book as "the battle cry of an embittered man who avows the hope that his cause will triumph without bloodshed, but warns that only the conscience of white America can prevent another civil war from being fought with all the fury of the war that freed the slaves." However, H. A. Overstreet, writing in the *Saturday Review,* appraised the volume as "a non-violent fighting book" and the "story of Negro unification. . . . In few books is the ugliness of racial injustice so vividly and succinctly described; in few is the case so clearly stated for the fact that race prejudice is poison that

kills dignity and decency in the souls of race haters." Mainstream civil rights activist Roy Wilkins saw *Marching Blacks* as a work of blatant self-promotion, declaring in the *New York Herald Tribune Weekly Book Review,* "[the book's purpose] is—never subtly—to urge [readers] to follow Mr. Powell. . . . The author in two remarkable chapters . . . sets forth how the people chose him, and how he, as the Joshua of a race, led them around the Jericho of proscription, frustration and hate, until the walls came tumbling down."

Keep the Faith, Baby! is a collection of Powell's sermons and speeches. Again, the book received praise on some fronts and criticism on others. *Saturday Review*'s David Poling maintained that Powell "has to be considered above average in ability to relate scripture to the needs and problems of everyday life. There is a directness, an economy of words that eludes too many preachers." However, Poling also drew repeated line-by-line comparisons of Powell's writings with earlier pieces by other writers, noting that "one of Pastor Powell's difficulties is giving credit to original sources. Quotation marks are about as rare as his appearances in Harlem." In a review for *Negro History Bulletin,* Clifford W. Edwards dismissed the book as "a rather colorless, conservative and ordinary sampling of sermons."

Powell's autobiography met with mixed reviews as well. A *New Yorker* critic described *Adam by Adam* as an "impenitent apologia," while Martin Kilsen of the *New York Times Book Review* found the book "deficient in serious self-analysis." At the same time, he praised the author as "a discerning observer of American politics, both at the city and national levels, as well as of the pattern of cruel defeats and illustrations that surround the life of the ghetto Negro." Writing for the *New Leader,* David M. Oshinsky declared that "perhaps the greatest tragedy of all is Powell's failure to understand the reasons for his final political defeat. He devotes less than two paragraphs to it, concluding only that the election was rigged." Oshinsky also displayed a bit of prescience in his review. "If taken seriously," he observed, *"Adam by Adam* may well insure Powell's future anonymity—a fate he neither wants nor deserves."

BIOGRAPHICAL/CRITICAL SOURCES:

BOOKS

Hamilton, Charles V., *Adam Clayton Powell, Jr.: The Political Biography of an American Dilemma,* Atheneum, 1991.

Powell, Adam Clayton, Jr., *Adam by Adam,* Dial 1971.

PERIODICALS

Commonweal, January 27, 1967.
Ebony, March, 1967; January, 1971; June, 1972.
Life, March 24, 1967.
Nation, February 16, 1946, pp. 201-02.
Negro History Bulletin, October, 1967, p. 22-23.
New Leader, February 7, 1972, pp. 20-21.
Newsweek, April 1, 1968; December 2, 1968; January 13, 1969; June 30, 1969.
New Yorker, November 13, 1971, pp. 202-03.
New York Herald Tribune Weekly Book Review, February 17, 1946.
New York Times Book Review, February 3, 1946; November 7, 1971, pp. 4, 16, 18; February 21, 1993.
Saturday Review, February 9, 1946, pp. 34, 36; April 22, 1967, pp. 86, 89-90.

Time, January 12, 1942; June 15, 1942; January 10, 1969; June 27, 1969.

OBITUARIES:

PERIODICALS

L'Express, April 10, 1972.
Newsweek, April 17, 1972.
New York Times, April 5, 1972.
Time, April 17, 1972.
Washington Post, April 6, 1972.*

*   *   *

PROVIST, d'Alain
  See DIOP, Birago (Ismael)

R

RAMPERSAD, Arnold 1941-

PERSONAL: Born November 13, 1941, in Trinidad, West Indies; married in 1985; children: one. *Education:* Bowling Green State University, B.A. and M.A.; Harvard University, M.A. and Ph.D.

ADDRESSES: Home—Princeton, NJ. *Office*—Department of English, Princeton University, Princeton, NJ 08544.

CAREER: Stanford University, Stanford, CA, professor of English, 1974-83; Rutgers University, New Brunswick, NJ, professor of English, 1983-88; Columbia University, New York City, Zora Neale Hurston Professor of English, 1988-90; Princeton University, Princeton, NJ, Woodrow Wilson Professor of Literature, 1990—.

MEMBER: American Studies Association, Modern Language Association.

AWARDS, HONORS: National Book Critics Circle Award nomination for biography, 1986, Anisfield-Wolf Book Award in Race Relations, Cleveland Foundation, 1987, and Clarence L. Holte Prize, Phelps Stokes Fund, 1988, all for *The Life of Langston Hughes, Volume 1: 1902-1941: I, Too, Sing America;* Pulitzer Prize finalist in biography, 1989, and American Book Award, Before Columbus Foundation, 1990, both for *The Life of Langston Hughes,* Volume 2: *1941-1967: I Dream a World.*

WRITINGS:

Melville's Israel Potter: A Pilgrimage and Progress (essay), Bowling Green University Popular Press, 1969.

The Art and Imagination of W. E. B. Du Bois, Harvard University Press, 1976.
The Life of Langston Hughes, Oxford University Press, Volume 1: *1902-1941: I, Too, Sing America,* 1986, Volume 2: *1941-1967: I Dream a World, 1988.*
(Editor with Deborah E. McDowell) *Slavery and the Literary Imagination,* Johns Hopkins University Press, 1989.
(Editor) Richard Wright, *Works,* two volumes, Library of America Series, 1991.
(With Arthur Ashe) *Days of Grace: A Memoir,* Knopf, 1993.
(Editor) *Richard Wright: A Collection of Critical Essays,* assistant editors, Bruce Simon and Jeffrey Tucker, Prentice Hall (NJ), 1995.
(Editor) *The Collected Poems of Langston Hughes,* associate editor David Roessel, Vintage Books (New York), 1995.
Jackie Robinson: A Biography, Knopf (New York), 1997.

Contributor to books, including *Artist and Influence 1986: The Challenges of Writing Black Biography,* Billops, 1987; *Voices and Visions: The Poet in America,* edited by Helen Vendler, Random House, 1987; *Afro-American Literary Study in the 1990s,* edited by Houston A. Baker, Jr., and Patricia Redmond, University of Chicago Press, 1989; *The Harlem Renaissance: Revaluations,* edited by Amritjit Singh, William S. Shriver, and Shantley Brodwin, Garland, 1989; and *African American Writers,* edited by Valerie Smith, Scribners, 1991. Contributor to periodicals, including *American Literature, Yale Review, Southern Review, Steppingstones, Langston Hughes Review, American Literature Forum, Kennesaw Review,* and *Menckeniana: A Quarterly Review.*

SIDELIGHTS: American educator, literary critic, and writer Arnold Rampersad is best known for his two-volume biography *The Life of Langston Hughes,* a critically acclaimed study of the leading black poet to emerge from the Harlem Renaissance in the 1920s. The first of the volumes, *I, Too, Sing America,* earned Rampersad the 1988 Clarence L. Holte Prize and the second, *I Dream a World,* received an American Book Award.

Rampersad began his literary career in the late 1960s with the publication of a lengthy essay titled *Melville's Israel Potter: A Pilgrimage and Progress,* an examination of American writer Herman Melville's *Israel Potter: His Fifty Years of Exile.* Among Melville's lesser known works, this short fictionalized narrative concerns a forgotten soldier's struggle for existence in the years following the American Revolution. Though Melville's book received little critical attention at the time of its publication in the 1850s, Rampersad maintains that it is a carefully crafted and effective piece of literature. Critics generally credit Rampersad with presenting in *Melville's Israel Potter* an absorbing and penetrating study of both Melville's character and writing style.

Rampersad's 1976 publication *The Art and Imagination of W. E. B. Du Bois* explores the motivations and views of prominent civil rights activist W. E. B. Du Bois. The author presents Du Bois as a sensitive, imaginative, and passionate thinker who wrote persuasively about the oppression of black Americans. Commenting in the *New Republic* on the impact of *The Art and Imagination of W. E. B. Du Bois* in the realm of black studies, Michael Cooke noted, "Rampersad's is an important and necessary book. Clearly it is the product of wide, patient reading, and the expression of a firm and yet mobile intelligence."

More than half a dozen years of research went into Rampersad's next project, the completion of volume one of *The Life of Langston Hughes.* Subtitled *1902-1941: I, Too, Sing America,* the book spans the first four decades of the controversial black American poet's life. Rampersad combed through six thousand folders of papers and correspondence housed at Yale University and traveled across the United States, the Soviet Union, and southwestern Europe to prepare the volume. He begins by tracing Hughes's formative years: the son of an absentee mother and a cold and self-hating father, Hughes spent most of his early years with his maternal grandmother. Rampersad writes in the first volume: "[Hughes's] first day out he took his dinner, then returned to his seat to stare out of the train window and brood on what he had left behind and the life that awaited him now in Mexico. Cheerlessly he thought of his angry mother and his forbidding father. In particular, he brooded on his father's hatred of blacks." Rampersad theorizes that Hughes's dysfunctional childhood fueled in him a life-long desire to attain the love and respect of the entire black race. Christopher Hitchens commented in *The Observer:* "Arnold Rampersad's finely written and carefully researched book does not say so explicitly, but makes it clear that Hughes had no talent for politics. He was in effect compelled to take stands."

Rampersad closes the first volume of *The Life of Langston Hughes* at the beginning of 1941, a time when Hughes was depressed, in ill health, and facing financial hardship and public scorn because of the radical poetry—such as "Goodbye, Christ"—he had written in the early 1930s. It ends in with Hughes "broke and ruint," writes Rampersad. Hughes is in a California hospital bed, suffering from an illness he described as arthritis or sciatica but what others said was a venereal disease. The second volume, subtitled *1941-1967: I Dream a World,* follows Hughes through the height of the civil rights movement in the United States and the growth in popularity of a younger generation of black writers. Focusing on Hughes's use of dialect and lyrical simplicity in his prosaic and poetic portraits of blacks, Rampersad maintains that Hughes's efforts to celebrate the true beauty and voice of black American men and women in his writing actually alienated black intellectuals and critics. Though often praised by white critics as an insightful and sensitive writer of the black experience in the United States, Hughes was scorned by some black intellectuals for allegedly depicting black life in a negative way. Such misunderstanding, implies Rampersad, characterized the writer's entire life.

Rampersad, too, does not shy away from some of the ambiguities and ironies that helped to foster misunderstanding and sometimes scorn toward Hughes. Rampersad addresses the questions of Hughes's sexuality; he deals with Hughes's refusal to admit that there were tremendous social injustices in the Soviet Union even though he came face-to-face with many during a trip to Russia; and he indicates that at the same time Hughes was carrying the banner of socialism he was accepting money from capitalist patrons. According to *Kirkus Reviews,* Rampersad refuses to "beautify" his subject.

Widely regarded as the definitive biography of Hughes, Rampersad's striking two-volume study *The*

Life of Langston Hughes earned critical praise for its comprehensiveness and readability. "This may be the best biography of a black writer we have had," lauded David Nicholson in the *Washington Post Book World.* And John A. Williams, writing in the *Los Angeles Times Book Review,* commented: "No other biography of Hughes can match the grace and richness of Rampersad's writing, or his investigative and interpretive abilities. . . . Writing solidly, with an ear for nuance and an eye that measures out Hughes' place in American literature, Rampersad establishes some important points, often ignored, about the importance of the poet."

New York Times Book Review contributor Rita Dove offered unequivocal praise for *The Life of Langston Hughes,* stating, "In his superlative study of . . . the most prominent Afro-American poet of our century, Arnold Rampersad has performed that most difficult of feats: illuminating a man who, despite all his public visibility, was quite elusive." In her review of the second volume of the life of Hughes, Dove commended the biographer for candidly representing America's tumultuous racial and political past while deftly portraying the life of a gifted figure in the country's literature: "Mr. Rampersad offers a compelling interpretation of a significant chunk of American cultural history, which makes this biography not only entertaining but essential reading."

Rampersad commented that he sees himself "as a literary historian, someone concerned with the combination of history and literature." Although he does not consider himself primarily a biographer, Rampersad said that a good biography should be readable and have some degree of narrative power while "[adhering] to basic standards of accuracy and documentation, of substantiation by multiple sources in the pivotal areas in a subject's life."

BIOGRAPHICAL/CRITICAL SOURCES:

BOOKS

Contemporary Literary Criticism, Volume 44, Gale, 1987.

PERIODICALS

Kirkus Reviews, July 1, 1986.
Los Angeles Times Book Review, September 4, 1988.
Nation, January 20, 1932.
New Republic, April 6, 1932.
New York Review of Books, February 16, 1989.

New York Times, September 30, 1986.
New York Times Book Review, March 29, 1959; October 12, 1986; October 9, 1988.
Observer (London), January 18, 1987.
Publishers Weekly, January 15, 1988.
Washington Post Book World, January 4, 1987.
Voice Literary Supplement, July, 1988.
Yale Review, autumn, 1988.

*   *   *

RANDALL, Dudley (Felker) 1914-

PERSONAL: Born January 14, 1914, in Washington, DC; son of Arthur George Clyde (a Congregational minister) and Ada Viola (a teacher; maiden name, Bradley) Randall; married Ruby Hands, May 27, 1935 (marriage dissolved); married Mildred Pinckney, December 20, 1942 (marriage dissolved); married Vivian Spencer (a psychiatric social worker), May 4, 1957; children: (first marriage) Phyllis Ada (Mrs. William Sherron III). *Education:* Wayne University (now Wayne State University), B.A., 1949; University of Michigan, M.A.L.S., 1951; graduate study, University of Ghana, 1970. *Politics:* Independent. *Religion:* Congregational.

ADDRESSES: Home—12651 Old Mill Place, Detroit, MI 48238. *Office*—Broadside Press, P.O. Box 04257, Northwestern Station, Detroit, MI 48204.

CAREER: Ford Motor Co., River Rouge, MI, foundry worker, 1932-37; U.S. Post Office, Detroit, MI, carrier and clerk, 1938-51; Lincoln University, Jefferson City, MO, librarian, 1951-54; Morgan State College, Baltimore, MD, associate librarian, 1954-56; Wayne County Federated Library System, Wayne, MI, 1956-69, began as assistant branch librarian, became branch librarian, 1956-63, head, reference-interloan department, 1963-69; University of Detroit, Detroit, reference librarian and poet-in-residence, 1969-75. Visiting lecturer, University of Michigan, 1969. Founder and general editor, Broadside Press, Detroit, 1965-1977, consultant, 1977—. Founder, Broadside Poets Theater and Broadside Poetry Workshop, 1980. Member, Advisory Panel on Literature, Michigan Council for the Arts, and New Detroit, Inc., both since 1970. Has participated in several poetry seminars and festivals, including the East-West Culture Learning Institute's Seminar on socio-literature at the University of Hawaii. *Military service:* U.S. Army, signal corps, 1942-46.

MEMBER: International Afro-American Museum, National Association for the Advancement of Colored People, American Library Association, Michigan Library Association, Michigan Poetry Society, Detroit Society for the Advancement of Culture and Education.

AWARDS, HONORS: Tompkins Award, Wayne State University, 1962, 1966; Kuumba Liberation Award, 1973; Arts Award in Literature, Michigan Foundation for the Arts, 1975; D.Litt., University of Detroit, 1978; Creative Artist Award in Literature, Michigan Council for the Arts, 1981; National Endowment for the Arts fellowship, 1981, senior fellowship, 1986; appointed First Poet Laureate of the City of Detroit by Mayor Coleman A. Young, 1981.

WRITINGS:

(Contributor) Rosey E. Pool, editor and author of introduction, *Beyond the Blues,* Hand and Flower Press, 1962.
(With Margaret Danner) *Poem Counterpoem,* Broadside Press, 1966.
(Editor and contributor with Margaret G. Burroughs) *For Malcolm: Poems on the Life and Death of Malcolm X,* Broadside Press, 1967, 2nd edition, 1969.
Cities Burning, Broadside Press, 1968.
(Editor) *Black Poetry: A Supplement to Anthologies Which Exclude Black Poets,* Broadside Press, 1969.
(Author of introduction) Sonia Sanchez, *We a BaddDDD People,* Broadside Press, 1970.
Love You, Paul Breman, 1970.
More to Remember: Poems of Four Decades, Third World Press, 1971.
(Editor and author of introduction) *The Black Poets,* Bantam, 1971.
(Contributor) Addison Gayle, Jr., editor, *The Black Aesthetic,* Doubleday, 1971.
After the Killing, Third World Press, 1973.
(With Gwendolyn Brooks, Keorapetse Kgositsile, and Haki R. Madhubuti) *A Capsule Course in Black Poetry Writing,* Broadside Press, 1975.
Broadside Memories: Poets I Have Known, Broadside Press, 1975.
A Litany of Friends: New and Selected Poems, Lotus Press, 1981, 2nd edition, 1983.
Homage to Hoyt Fuller, Broadside Press, 1984.
(Editor with Louis J. Cantoni) *Golden Song: The Fiftieth Anniversary Anthology of the Poetry Society of Michigan, 1935-1985,* Harlo, 1985.

Contributor of poems to anthologies, including *American Negro Poetry, New Negro Poets: USA, Ik Ben de Nieuwe Neger, La Poesie Negro-Americaine,* and *Kaleidoscope.* Also contributor of poems, short stories, articles, and reviews to *Midwest Journal, Free Lance, Black World, Black Academy Review, Umbra, Negro Digest, Journal of Black Poetry, Beloit Review, Wayne Review,* and *New World Review.*

SIDELIGHTS: The influence of Dudley Randall, founder of Broadside Press and Detroit's first poet laureate, "has been one of the strongest—some say the strongest—in the black poetry movement of the last 15 years," writes Suzanne Dolezal. The 1982 article in *Detroit* magazine, a *Detroit Free Press* supplement, continues, "As publisher of Detroit's Broadside Press between 1965 and 1977, Randall provided a forum for just about every major black poet to come along during those years. And dozens of anthologies include his own rapid, emotional lyrics about Detroit's bag ladies, lonely old drunks, strapping foundry workers and young women with glistening, corn- rowed hair." R. Baxter Miller explains Randall's importance in the *Dictionary of Literary Biography: Afro-American Poets since 1955*: "Beyond Randall's contributions as a poet, his roles as editor and publisher have proven invaluable to the Afro-American community." Randall's interest in poetry has been lifelong.

Born in Washington, D.C., the son of a minister and a teacher, he wrote his first poem when he was four years old, moved to Detroit when he was nine, and saw his poems first published in the *Detroit Free Press* when he was thirteen. A bright student, Randall graduated early. After working in Ford's River Rouge foundry for five years and serving in the army, he extended his reputation for scholarship by earning a master's degree in library science from the University of Michigan and by studying the humanities. Randall, who became the reference librarian for Wayne County, also became fluent in Russian, visited Europe, Africa, and Russia, and later translated many Russian poems into English.

Randall's first books, however, did not display his range, Miller indicates. *Poem Counterpoem,* a unique volume in which "ten poems each by [Margaret] Danner and Randall. . . . are alternated to form a kind of double commentary on the subjects they address in common," contains "only the verses appropriately matched with Danner's," the essayist relates; and while *Cities Burning,* Randall's second opus, presents the spirit of the poet's urban environment and the politics of his times, it gathers only those poems that treat "the theme of a disintegrating era."

But the third and more inclusive collection *More to Remember: Poems of Four Decades* "displays [Randall's] artistic breadth" in poems that address universal themes and explore "contradictions in human psychology and the black arts movement," observes Miller. Miller also sees "Randall's aesthetic theory" in poems that depict "the artist as a modifier of both literary tradition and classical form." Randall defines this aesthetic himself in *Negro Digest*: "Precision and accuracy are necessary for both white and black writers. . . . 'A black aesthetic' should not be an excuse for sloppy writing." He believes that for writers who adhere to the "black aesthetic" there is a future, "as long as their rejection of 'white standards' rejects only what is false. . . . How else can a black writer write than out of his black experience? Yet what we tend to overlook is that our common humanity makes it possible to write a love poem, for instance, without a word of race, or to write a nationalistic poem that will be valid for all humanity."

Later collections of Randall's poems also show his careful craftsmanship. Reviewing *After the Killing* (1973), Frank Marshall Davis declares, "Dudley Randall again offers visual proof of why he should be ranked in the front echelon of Black poets." When the poet evades "cliches and hackneyed rhymes, he excels at his craft," says Miller, who also believes that verses in *A Litany of Friends: New and Selected Poems* (1981) "demonstrate Randall's technical skill." Brief notices about Randall's books in library trade journals are generally complimentary, in keeping with Davis's comment in *Black World* magazine and Miller's assessment.

Reviewers recognize Randall's work as a bridge between earlier black writers and the generation that raised its voice of affirmation in the 1960s. "Exploring racial and historical themes, introspective and self-critical, his work combines ideas and forms from Western traditional poetry as well as from the Harlem Renaissance movement," Miller notes. Writing in the *Negro Digest* in 1969, Ron Welburn concurs: "[Randall's] is a keen functional awareness of what black poetry has been and remains, and there is no hint of an alienation from the ethos being developed by the new stylists." Welburn's review foresaw that younger poets would be somewhat influenced by Randall's voice and perhaps more potently by his example: "he is contributing something to black lit-

erature that has a lasting value." Broadside Press—Randall's other contribution to black poetry in America—began in 1963.

Randall had composed the poem "Ballad of Birmingham" after a bomb exploded in an Alabama church, killing four children. "Folk singer Jerry Moore of New York had it set to music, and I wanted to protect the rights to the poem by getting it copyrighted," the publisher recalls in *Broadside Memories: Poets I Have Known*. Leaflets, he learned, could be copyrighted, so he published the poem as a broadside, a single sheet of paper that could be printed and sold for a minimal price. Randall's "Dressed All in Pink," composed after John F. Kennedy's assassination, also recorded by Moore, became number two of the Broadside series, which was to include close to 100 titles by 1982.

Randall became a book publisher when poets at a Fisk University conference nominated him to collect and publish "the many poems being written about the slain black leader" Malcolm X, reports Dolezal. The printing was delayed so that *For Malcolm: Poems on the Life and Death of Malcolm X* was not the first Broadside book published, but when it came out in 1967, it was a success. By that time aware that major publishers were seldom accepting works by young black poets, Randall "became dedicated to giving the emerging black poetry the forum it needed," Dolezal notes. Indeed, Randall's encouragement was essential to the writing careers of several black poets. Etheridge Knight, for example, was in prison when he contributed three poems to the Broadside anthology *For Malcolm,* and Randall's visits "convinced a hesitant Knight of his talent," Dolezal reports. Randall published first books for Knight and for Haki R. Madhubuti (formerly Don L. Lee), two poets who now enjoy international acclaim. Altogether, the press produced nearly sixty volumes of poetry and criticism under Randall's tenure, all showcasing black writers, who rewarded his dedication by remaining loyal to Broadside even when larger publishing houses with generous promotion budgets beckoned. Gwendolyn Brooks insisted that Randall, not Harper & Row, would publish her autobiography; Sonia Sanchez preferred Broadside to the Third World Press, the small press founded by Madhubuti. Poet Nikki Giovanni explained to Dolezal, "Broadside was neither mother nor father of the poetry movement, but it was certainly midwife. Dudley understood the thrust of the movement, which was essentially vernacular. He . . . allowed his poets to find their own voices. That was the charm of Broadside."

By 1977, Randall's determination to supply low-priced books even to stores already in debt to him brought the small press, also deeply in debt, to the crisis point. The Alexander Crummell Memorial Center, a church in Highland Park, Michigan, bought the press, retaining Randall as its consultant. Though the poets he once published have found other publishers since the sale, Randall continues to be concerned for new poets, and anticipates the publication of more new works when the press revives. But Dolezal concludes that whether or not that hope materializes, "Randall's achievement remains intact." Furthermore, as the poet laureate of a sprawling midwestern metropolis told *New York Times* contributor Harold Blum, there is always plenty to do: "[A poet] can change the way people look and feel about things. And that's what I want to do in Detroit."

BIOGRAPHICAL/CRITICAL SOURCES:

BOOKS

Barksdale, Richard K. and Keneth Kinnamon, editors, *Black Writers in America: A Comprehensive Anthology,* Macmillan, 1972.
Black Poets: The New Heroic Genre, Broadside Press, 1983.
Contemporary Literary Criticism, Volume 1, Gale, 1973.
Dictionary of Literary Biography, Volume 41: *Afro-American Poets since 1955,* Gale, 1985.
Gayle, Addison, editor, *The Black Aesthetic,* Doubleday, 1971.
King, Woodie, Jr., editor, *The Forerunners: Black Poets in America,* Howard University Press, 1981.
Randall, Dudley, *Broadside Memories: Poets I Have Known,* Broadside Press, 1975.
Randall, Dudley, *A Litany of Friends: New and Selected Poems,* Lotus Press, 1981, new edition, 1983.

PERIODICALS

Black American Literature Forum, volume 17, number 3, 1983; February, 1984.
Black World, September, 1974.
Callaloo, Volume 6, number 1, 1983.
Detroit Free Press, April 11, 1982.
Library Journal, February 15, 1971; March 15, 1972.
Negro Digest, February, 1965; September, 1965; January, 1968; December, 1969.
New York Times, January 30, 1984.
New York Times Book Review, part 2, February 13, 1972.

Obsidian, volume 2, number 1, 1976.*

*   *   *

REED, Ishmael 1938-
(Emmett Coleman)

PERSONAL: Born February 22, 1938, Chattanooga, TN; son of Henry Lenoir (a fundraiser for YMCA) and Thelma Coleman (a homemaker and salesperson); stepfather, Bennie Stephen Reed (an auto worker); married Priscilla Rose, September, 1960 (divorced, 1970); married Carla Blank (a modern dancer); children: (first marriage) Timothy, Brett (daughter); (second marriage) Tennessee Maria (daughter). *Education:* Attended State University of New York at Buffalo, 1956-60. *Politics:* Independent.

ADDRESSES: Office—c/o Avon Books, Div. Hearst Corp., 1790 Broadway, New York, NY 10019.

CAREER: Writer. Yardbird Publishing Co., Inc., Berkeley, CA, cofounder, 1971, editorial director, 1971-75; Reed, Cannon & Johnson Communications Co. (a publisher and producer of videocassettes), Berkeley, cofounder, 1973—; Before Columbus Foundation (a producer and distributor of work of unknown ethnic writers), Berkeley, cofounder, 1976—; Ishmael Reed and Al Young's *Quilt* (magazine), Berkeley, cofounder, 1980—. Teacher at St. Mark's in the Bowery prose workshop, 1966; guest lecturer, University of California, Berkeley, 1968—, University of Washington, 1969-70, State University of New York at Buffalo, summer, 1975, and fall, 1979, Yale University, fall, 1979, Dartmouth College, summers, 1980-81, Sitka Community Association, summer, 1982, University of Arkansas at Fayetteville, 1982, Columbia University, 1983, Harvard University, 1987, and Regents lecturer, University of California, Santa Barbara, 1988. Judge of National Poetry Competition, 1980, King's County Literary Award, 1980, University of Michigan Hopwood Award, 1981. Chair of Berkeley Arts Commission, 1980 and 1981. Coordinating Council of Literary Magazines, chair of board of directors, 1975-79, advisory board chair, 1977-79.

MEMBER: Authors Guild of America, PEN, Celtic Foundation.

AWARDS, HONORS: Certificate of Merit, California Association of English Teachers, 1972, for *19 Necro-*

mancers from Now; nominations for National Book Award in fiction and poetry, 1973, for *Mumbo Jumbo* and *Conjure: Selected Poems, 1963-1970;* nomination for Pulitzer Prize in poetry, 1973, for *Conjure;* Richard and Hinda Rosenthal Foundation Award, National Institute of Arts and Letters, 1975, for *The Last Days of Louisiana Red;* John Simon Guggenheim Memorial Foundation award for fiction, 1974; Poetry in Public Places winner (New York City), 1976, for poem "From the Files of Agent 22," and for a bicentennial mystery play, *The Lost State of Franklin,* written in collaboration with Carla Blank and Suzushi Hanayagi; Lewis Michaux Award, 1978; American Civil Liberties Award, 1978; Pushcart Prize for essay "American Poetry: Is There a Center?," 1979; Wisconsin Arts Board fellowship, 1982; associate fellow of Calhoun College, Yale University, 1982; A.C.L.U. publishing fellowship; three New York State publishing grants for merit; three National Endowment for the Arts publishing grants for merit; California Arts Council grant; associate fellow, Harvard Signet Society, 1987—.

WRITINGS:

FICTION

The Free-Lance Pallbearers, Doubleday (New York City), 1967.
Yellow Back Radio Broke-Down, Doubleday, 1969.
Mumbo Jumbo, Doubleday, 1972.
The Last Days of Louisiana Red, Random House (New York City), 1974.
Flight to Canada, Random House, 1976.
The Terrible Twos, St. Martin's/Marek (New York City), 1982.
Reckless Eyeballing, St. Martin's, 1986.
The Terrible Threes, Atheneum (New York City), 1989.
Japanese by Spring, Atheneum, 1993.

NONFICTION

Shrovetide in Old New Orleans (essays; original manuscript entitled *This One's on Me*), Doubleday, 1978.
God Made Alaska for the Indians: Selected Essays, Garland (New York City), 1982.
Writin'Is Fightin': Thirty-Seven Years of Boxing on Paper, Atheneum, 1988, revised and expanded edition published as *Writing Is Fighting: Forty-Three Years of Boxing on Paper,* Addison-Wesley (Reading, MA), 1998.
Airing Dirty Laundry, Addison-Wesley, 1993.

Contributor to numerous volumes, including *Amistad I: Writings on Black History and Culture,* Vintage Books, 1970; *The Black Aesthetic,* Doubleday, 1971; *Nommo: An Anthology of Modern Black African and Black American Literature,* Macmillan, 1972; *Cutting Edges: Young American Fiction for the 70s,* Holt, 1973; *Superfiction; or, The American Story Transformed: An Anthology,* Vintage Books, 1975; and *American Poets in 1976,* Bobbs-Merrill (New York), 1976.

EDITOR

(Under pseudonym Emmett Coleman) *The Rise, Fall, and . . . ? of Adam Clayton Powell,* Beeline (Albany, NY), 1967.
(Also author of introduction, and contributor) *19 Necromancers from Now,* Doubleday, 1970.
(With Al Young) *Yardbird Lives!,* Grove (New York City), 1978.
(And contributor) *Calafia: The California Poetry,* Y-Bird Books, 1979.
(With Kathryn Trueblood and Shawn Wong) *The Before Columbus Foundation Fiction Anthology: Selections from the American Book Awards, 1980-1990,* Norton (New York City), 1992.
MultiAmerica: Essays on Cultural Wars and Cultural Peace, Viking, 1996.

POETRY

catechism of d neoamerican hoodoo church, Paul Breman (London), 1970, Broadside Press (Highland Park, MI), 1971.
Conjure: Selected Poems, 1963-1970, University of Massachusetts Press (Amherst, MA), 1972.
Chattanooga: Poems, Random House, 1973.
A Secretary to the Spirits, illustrations by Betye Saar, NOK Publishers (New York City), 1977.
New and Collected Poems, Atheneum, 1988.

Poetry also represented in anthologies, including *Where Is Vietnam? American Poets Respond: An Anthology of Contemporary Poems,* Doubleday, 1967; *The New Black Poetry,* International Publishers (New York City), 1969; *The Norton Anthology of Poetry,* Norton, 1970; *The Poetry of the Negro, 1746-1970,* Doubleday, 1970; *Afro-American Literature: An Introduction,* Harcourt, 1971; *The Writing on the Wall: 108 American Poems of Protest,* Doubleday, 1971; *Major Black Writers,* Scholastic (New York City), 1971; *The Black Poets,* Bantam (New York City), 1971; *The Poetry of Black America: Anthology of the 20th Century,* Harper, 1972; and *Giant Talk: An*

Anthology of Third World Writings, Random House, 1975.

OTHER

Ishmael Reed Reading His Poetry (cassette), Temple of Zeus, Cornell University Press (Ithaca, NY), 1976.
Ishmael Reed and Michael Harper Reading in the UCSD New Poetry Series (reel), University of California, San Diego, 1977.
(Author of introduction) Elizabeth A. Settle and Thomas A. Settle, *Ishmael Reed: A Primary and Secondary Bibliography,* G. K. Hall (Boston, MA), 1982.
Cab Calloway Stands In for the Moon, Bamberger, 1986.
(With Richard Nagler) *Oakland Rhapsody: The Secret Soul of an American Downtown,* North Atlantic Books, 1995.
Conversations with Ishamel Reed, edited by Bruce Dick and Amritjit Singh, University Press of Mississippi, 1995.
The Poet and the Poem from the Library of Congress, Ishmael Reed (cassette), Library of Congress, 1996.
Ishmael Reed and Garrett Hongo Reading Their Poems in the Mumfoud Room (cassette), Library of Congress, 1996.

Also author, with wife, Carla Blank, and Suzushi Hanayagi, of a bicentennial mystery play, *The Lost State of Franklin.* Executive producer of pilot episode of soap opera *Personal Problems* and copublisher of *The Steve Cannon Show: A Quarterly Audio-Cassette Radio Show Magazine.*

Author of foreword, *Dark Eros,* edited by Reginald Martin, St. Martin's, 1997. Contributor of fiction to such periodicals as *Fiction, Iowa Review, Nimrod, Players, Ramparts, Seattle Review,* and *Spokane Natural;* contributor of articles and reviews to numerous periodicals, including *Black World, Confrontation: Journal of Third World Literature, Essence, Le Monde, Los Angeles Times, New York Times, Playgirl, Rolling Stone, Village Voice, Washington Post,* and *Yale Review;* and contributor of poetry to periodicals, including *American Poetry Review, Black Scholar, Black World, Essence, Liberator, Negro Digest, Noose, San Francisco Examiner, Oakland Tribune, Life, Connoisseur,* and *Umbra.* Cofounder of periodicals *East Village Other* and *Advance* (Newark community newspaper), both 1965. Editor of *Yardbird*

Reader, 1972-76; editor-in-chief, *Y'Bird* magazine, 1978-80; and coeditor of *Quilt* magazine, 1981.

ADAPTATIONS: Some of Reed's poetry has been scored and recorded on *New Jazz Poets;* a dramatic episode from *The Last Days of Louisiana Red* appears on *The Steve Cannon Show: A Quarterly Audio-Cassette Radio Show Magazine,* produced by Reed, Cannon & Johnson Communications.

SIDELIGHTS: The novels of contemporary black American writer Ishmael Reed "are meant to provoke," writes *New York Times* contributor Darryl Pinckney. "Though variously described as a writer in whose work the black picaresque tradition has been extended, as a misogynist or an heir to both [Zora Neale] Hurston's folk lyricism and [Ralph] Ellison's irony, he is, perhaps because of this, one of the most underrated writers in America. Certainly no other contemporary black writer, male or female, has used the language and beliefs of folk culture so imaginatively, and few have been so stinging about the absurdity of American racism." Yet this novelist, poet, and essayist is not simply a voice of black protest against racial and social injustices but instead a confronter of even more universal evils, a purveyor of even more universal truths.

Reed's first novel, *The Free-Lance Pallbearers,* introduces several thematic and stylistic devices that reappear throughout his canon. In this novel, as in his later works, Reed's first satirical jab is at the oppressive, stress-filled, Western/European/Christian tradition. But in *The Free-Lance Pallbearers,* the oppressor/oppressed, evil/good dichotomy does not absolve blacks. While Reed blames whites, called HARRY SAM in the novel, for present world conditions, he also attacks culpable individuals from different strata in the black community and satirizes various kinds of black leaders in the twentieth century. Reed implies that many such leaders argue against white control by saying they want to improve conditions, to "help the people," but that in reality they are only waiting for the chance to betray and exploit poor blacks and to appropriate power.

Among the black characters whom Reed puts into a negative light in *The Free-Lance Pallbearers* are Elijah Raven, the Muslim/Black Nationalist whose ideas of cultural and racial separation in the United States are exposed as lies; Eclair Pockchop, the minister fronting as an advocate of the people's causes, later discovered performing an unspeakable sex act on

SAM; the black cop who protects white people from the blacks in the projects and who idiotically allows a cow-bell to be put around his neck for "meritorious service"; Doopeyduk's neighbors in the projects who, too stupid to remember their own names, answer to "M/Neighbor" and "F/Neighbor"; and finally Doopeyduk himself, whose pretensions of being a black intellectual render all his statements and actions absurd. Yet Reed reserves his most scathing satire for the black leaders who cater to SAM in his palace: "who mounted the circuitous steps leading to SAM'S, assuring the boss dat: 'Wasn't us boss. 'Twas Stokely and Malcolm. Not us, boss. No indeed. We put dat ad in da *Times* repudiating dem, boss? Look, boss. We can prove it to you, dat we loves you. Would you like for us to cook up some strange recipes for ya, boss? Or tell some jokes? Did you hear the one about da nigger in the woodpile? Well, seems dere was this nigger, boss. . . .'"

The rhetoric of popular black literature in the 1960s is also satirized in *The Free-Lance Pallbearers.* The polemics of the time, characterized by colloquial diction, emotionalism, direct threats, automatic writing, and blueprints for a better society, are portrayed by Reed as representing the negative kind of literature required of blacks by the reading public. Reed suggests that while literature by blacks might have been saying that blacks would no longer subscribe to white dictates, in fact the converse was true, manifested in the very literature that the publishing houses generally were printing at the time.

In his second novel, *Yellow Back Radio Broke-Down,* Reed begins to use at length Hoodoo (or Voodoo) methods and folklore as a basis for his work. Underlying all of the components of Hoodoo, according to scholars, are two precepts: 1) the Hoodoo idea of syncretism, or the combination of beliefs and practices with divergent cultural origins, and 2) the Hoodoo concept of time. Even before the exportation of slaves to the Caribbean, Hoodoo was a syncretic religion, absorbing all that it considered useful from other West African religious practices. As a religion formed to combat degrading social conditions by dignifying and connecting man with helpful supernatural forces, Hoodoo is said to thrive because of its syncretic flexibility, its ability to take even ostensibly negative influences and transfigure them into that which helps the "horse," or the one possessed by the attributes of a Hoodoo god. Hoodoo is bound by certain dogma or rites, but such rules are easily changed when they become oppressive, myopic, or no longer useful.

Reed turns this concept of syncretism into a literary method that combines aspects of "standard" English, including dialect, slang, argot, neologisms, or rhyme, with less "standard" language, whose principal rules of discourse are taken from the streets, popular music, and television. By mixing language from different sources in popular culture, Reed employs expressions that can both evoke interest and humor through seeming incongruities and create the illusion of real speech. In *Black American Literature Forum,* Michel Fabre draws a connection between Reed's use of language and his vision of the world, suggesting that "his so-called nonsense words raise disturbing questions . . . about the very nature of language." Often, "the semantic implications are disturbing because opposite meanings coexist." Thus Reed emphasizes "the dangerous interchangeability of words and of the questionable identity of things and people" and "poses anguishing questions about self-identity, about the mechanism of meaning and about the nature of language and communication."

Syncretism and synchronicity, along with other facets of Hoodoo as literary method, are central to *Yellow Back Radio Broke-Down.* The title is street-talk for the elucidation of a problem, in this case the racial and oligarchical difficulties of an Old West town, Yellow Back Radio; these difficulties are explained, or "broke down," for the reader. The novel opens with a description of the Hoodoo fetish, or mythical cult figure, Loop Garoo, whose name means "change into." Loop embodies diverse ethnic backgrounds and a history and power derived from several religions.

The year 1972 saw the publication of Reed's first major volume of poetry, *Conjure: Selected Poems, 1963-1970,* followed in 1973 by *Chattanooga: Poems,* and in 1977 by *A Secretary to the Spirits.* Although the poem in *Conjure* beginning "I am a cowboy in the boat of Ra" continues an earlier Reed interest in Egyptian symbolism, after this work he lyrically draws his symbols from Afro-American and Anglo-American historical and popular traditions-two distinct but intertwined sources for the Afro-American aesthetic. "Black Power Poem" succinctly states the Hoodoo stance in the West: "may the best church win. / shake hands now and come out conjuring"; a longer poem, "Neo-Hoodoo Manifesto," defines all that Hoodoo is and thus sheds light on the ways Reed uses its principles in writing, primarily through his absorption of material from every available source and his expansive originality in treating that material.

The theme of *Mumbo Jumbo,* Reed's 1972 novel, is the origin and composition of the "true Afro-American aesthetic." Testifying to the novel's success in fulfilling this theme, Houston Baker in *Black World* calls *Mumbo Jumbo* "the first black American novel of the last ten years that gives one a sense of the broader vision and the careful, painful, and laborious 'fundamental brainwork' that are needed if we are to define the eternal dilemma of the Black Arts and work fruitfully toward its melioration. . . . [The novel's] overall effect is that of amazing talent and flourishing genius." *Mumbo Jumbo*'s first chapter is crucial in that it presents the details of the highly complex plot in synopsis or news-flash form. Reed has a Hoodoo detective named Papa LaBas (representing the Hoodoo god Legba) search out and reconstruct a black aesthetic from remnants of literary and cultural history. Lending the narrative authenticity, Reed inserts various scholarly devices: facts from nonfictional, published works; photographs and historical drawings; and a bibliography.

At the opening of *Mumbo Jumbo,* set in New Orleans in the 1920s, white municipal officials are trying to respond to "Jes Grew," an outbreak of behavior outside of socially conditioned roles; white people are "acting black" by dancing half-dressed in the streets to an intoxicating new loa (the spiritual essence of a fetish) called jazz. Speaking in tongues, people also abandon racist and other oppressive endeavors because it is more fun to "shake that thing." One of the doctors assigned to treat the pandemic of Jes Grew comments, "There are no isolated cases in this thing. It knows no class no race no consciousness. It is self-propagating and you can never tell when it will hit." No one knows where the germ has come from; it "jes grew." In the synoptic first chapter, the omniscient narrator says Jes Grew is actually "an anti-plague. Some plagues caused the body to waste away. Jes Grew enlivened the host. Other plagues were accompanied by bad air (malaria). Jes Grew victims said the air was as clear as they had ever seen it and that there was the aroma of roses and perfumes which had never before enticed their nostrils. Some plagues arise from decomposing animals, but Jes Grew is electric as life and is characterized by ebullience and ecstasy. Terrible plagues were due to the wrath of God; But Jes Grew is the delight of the gods."

Hoodoo time resurfaces in *Mumbo Jumbo.* Certain chapters which have detailed past events in the past tense are immediately followed by chapters that begin with present-tense verbs and present-day situations, mirroring Hoodoo/oral culture. The juxtaposition links all of the actions within a single narrative time frame. Commenting on his use both of time and of fiction-filled news-flashes, Reed says in *Shrovetide in Old New Orleans* that in writing *Mumbo Jumbo,* he "wanted to write about a time like the present or to use the past to prophesy about the future—a process our ancestors called necromancy. I chose the twenties because they are very similar to what's happening right now. This is a valid method and has been used by writers from time immemorial. Nobody ever accused James Joyce of making up things. Using a past event of one's country or culture to comment on the present."

The close of *Mumbo Jumbo* finds Jes Grew withering with the burning of its text, the Book of Thoth, which lists the sacred spells and dances of the Egyptian god Osiris. LaBas says Jes Grew will reappear some day to make its own text: "A future generation of young artists will accomplish this," says LaBas, referring to the writers, painters, politicians, and musicians of the 1960s, "the decade that screamed," as Reed termed it in *Chattanooga*.

In the course of the narrative, Reed constructs his history of the true Afro-American aesthetic and parallels the uniting of Afro-American oral tradition, folklore, art, and history with a written code, a text, a literate recapitulation of history and practice. By calling for a unification of text and tradition, Reed equates the Text (the Afro-American aesthetic) with the Vedas, the Pentateuch, the Koran, the Latin Vulgate, the Book of Mormon, and all "Holy" codifications of faith. *Mumbo Jumbo,* which itself becomes the Text, appears as a direct, written response to the assertion that there is no "black" aesthetic, that black contributions to the world culture have been insignificant at best.

The Last Days of Louisiana Red consists of three major story lines that coalesce toward the close of the novel to form its theme. The first and main plot is the tale of Ed Yellings, an industrious, middle-class black involved in "The Business," an insider's term for the propagation of Hoodoo. Through experimentation in his business, Solid Gumbo Works, Yellings discovers a cure for cancer and is hard at work to refine and market this remedy and other remedies for the various aspects of Louisiana Red, the Hoodoo name for all evil. When he is mysteriously murdered, Hoodoo detective Papa LaBas appears, and the stage is set for the major part of the action. This action involves participants in the novel's second and third story lines, the tale of the Chorus and the recounting of the mythical Antigone's decision to oppose the dictates of the state. The Chorus symbolizes black Americans who will not disappear. Even though they are relegated by more powerful forces to minor roles, they work for the right to succeed or fail depending upon their merits. Therein lies Reed's theme in *The Last Days of Louisiana Red.*

In *The Terrible Twos,* Reed maintains the implicit notions of Hoodoo while using his main story line to resurrect another apocryphal tale: the legend of Santa Claus and his assistant/boss, Black Peter. The time frame of the novel is roughly Christmas 1980 to Christmases of the 1990s, covering the years during and after Ronald Reagan's presidency. The evil of *The Terrible Twos* is selfishness fed by an exclusive monetary system, such as capitalism. Yet Reed does not endorse any other sort of government now in existence but criticizes any person or system that ignores what is humanly right in favor of what is economically profitable. Santa Claus (actually an out-of-work television personality) exemplifies the way Hoodoo fights this selfish evil: by bringing those who were prosperous to the level of those who have nothing and are abandoned. Santa characterizes American capitalists, those with material advantages, as infantile, selfish and exclusionary because their class station does not allow them to empathize with those who are different: "'Two years old, that's what we are, emotionally—Americans, always wanting someone to hand us some ice cream, always complaining, Santa didn't bring me this and why didn't Santa bring me that.' People in the crowd chuckle. 'Nobody can reason with us. Nobody can tell us anything. Millions of people staggering about passing out in the snow and we say that's tough. We say too bad to the children who don't have milk. I weep as I read these letters the poor children send me at my temporary home in Alaska.'" The story continues in *The Terrible Threes,* set in the late 1990s and featuring many of the characters who populate *The Terrible Twos.* In the sequel, John O'Brien reveals in *Washington Post Book World,* "the country is in a state of chaos, having chased its president into a sanatorium after he revealed on national television a White House conspiracy to purge America of its poor and homeless, as well as to destroy Nigeria." "Reed's eerie, weird, implausible world has a way of sounding all too real, too much like what we hear on the evening news," O'Brien concludes. "And Reed has an unnerving sense of what will show up next on our televisions. He is without doubt our finest satirist since Twain."

In *The Terrible Twos* Reed leaves overt Hoodoo references as a subtext and focuses on the Rasta and Nicolaite myths, two conflicting quasi-religious cults revitalized by Black Power. He also concentrates on the myths of power and privilege created by "the vital people," those who are white and wealthy. However, the racist policies of the Nicolaites are eventually thwarted by inexplicable circumstances that stem from the supernatural powers of Hoodoo and from the Hoodoo notion that time is circular and that therefore the mighty will possibly—even probably—fall.

Several critics warn that readers will find *Threes* near-incomprehensible without first reading *Twos.* Further, *New York Times Book Review* critic Gerald Early observes, "The major problem with *The Terrible Threes* is that it seems to vaporize even as you read it; the very telling artifices that held together Mr. Reed's novelistic art in previous works, that cunning combination of boundless energy and shrewdly husbanded ingenuity, are missing here. . . . I like *The Terrible Threes,* but it seems more a work for Reed fans among whom I count myself." *Los Angeles Times Book Review* contributor Jacob Epstein finds that "Reed's vision of the future (and our present and past) is original and subversive. Subversion is out of style these days, but unfashionable or not, Reed is an always interesting writer and this book deserves to be read."

Reckless Eyeballing is a satiric allegory. Ian Ball, a black male writer, responds to the poor reception of his earlier play, *Suzanna,* by writing *Reckless Eyeballing,* a play sure to please those in power with its vicious attacks against black men. ("Reckless eyeballing" was one of the accusations against Emmett Till, the young Chicago black who was murdered in Mississippi in 1953 for "looking and whistling at a white woman.") Tremonisha Smarts, a black female writer whose first name is drawn from a Scott Joplin opera of that title, is alternately popular and unpopular with the white women who are promoting her books. The battle for whose vision will dominate in the literary market and popular culture is fierce.

In Joplin's opera, the character Tremonisha represents the powers of assimilation into American culture in opposition to the "powers of the Hoodoo men." Thus, not only does Reed's version of the Tremonisha character allude to the original Tremonisha's disagreement with early African American currents, but she also becomes one of the critical forces that Reed has long opposed. While this allusive connection suggests that Reed is covering the same, familiar Hoodoo ground covered before, he moves in this novel toward unearthing the universal structures of Hoodoo, which are rooted in the apocryphal rites of other religions. For example, Reed found connections between the shared traditions of Judaism and Hoodoo in *The Legends of Genesis* by Hermann Gunkel, in David Meltzer's magazine *TREE,* and in Mike Gold's *Jews without Money,* the last of which includes a description of a Jewish woman similar to the Mambos and Conjure Women of Hoodoo origin. Reed thus reminds readers that Hoodoo is ever-changing by constantly absorbing materials from diverse cultures. He also warns his readers that he, too, is ever-changing and that a sure way to be misled is to believe that one has Hoodoo's concepts (and Reed's) pinned down as to their "one true" meaning.

In addition to his novels and poetry, Reed has also written numerous essays and nonfiction pieces about contemporary American society and politics. Thirty-five of these essays, written between 1978 and 1993, were collected and published as *Airing Dirty Laundry.* Among Reed's subjects are the chronic misrepresentation of blacks by the white-owned, conservative mass media, which he says ignores the truth about welfare and drug abuse to paint an inaccurate portrait of black Americans; the misguided attacks on multicultural education in schools; and contemporary black intellectuals—among them Toni Cade Bambara and Langston Hughes—who have had a significant impact on white America, even though most whites have not heard of them. Chicago *Tribune Books* contributor George Packer remarks that Reed's charges grow "dreary over the course of a whole book of mainly first drafts." Jill Nelson, however, writing in the *New York Times Book Review,* observes: "Always provocative, sometimes infuriating, this collection reminds us that the purpose of art is not to confirm and coddle but to provoke and confront."

BIOGRAPHICAL/CRITICAL SOURCES:

BOOKS

Boyer, Jay, *Ishmael Reed,* Boise State University Press, 1993.
Contemporary Literary Criticism, Gale (Detroit), Volume 2, 1974; Volume 3, 1975; Volume 5, 1976; Volume 6, 1976; Volume 8, 1980; Volume 32, 1985.
Dictionary of Literary Biography, Gale, Volume 2: *American Novelists since World War II,* 1978; Volume 5: *American Poets since World War II,* 1980; Volume 33: *Afro-American Fiction Writers after 1955,* 1984.
Joyce, Joyce Ann, *Warriors, Conjurers and Priests: Defining African-Centered Literary Criticism,* Third World Press, 1994.

Klinkowitz, Jerome, *Literary Subversions: New American Fiction and the Practice of Criticism,* Southern Illinois University Press (Carbondale, IL), 1985.
Ludwig, Sami, *Concrete Language: Intercultural Communication in Maxine Hong Kingston's "The Woman Warrior" and Ishmael Reed's "Mumbo Jumbo,"* [New York], 1996.
Martin, Reginald, *Ishmael Reed and the New Black Aesthetic Critics,* Macmillan (London), 1987.
O'Donnell, Patrick, and Robert Con Davis, editors, *Intertextuality and Contemporary American Fiction,* Johns Hopkins University Press (Baltimore, MD), 1989.
Ostendorf, Berndt, *Black Literature in White America,* Noble, 1982.
Settle, Elizabeth A., and Thomas A. Settle, *Ishmael Reed: A Primary and Secondary Bibliography,* G. K. Hall (Boston, MA), 1982.

PERIODICALS

American Book Review, May/June, 1983; October/November, 1994, p. 17.
American Poetry Review, May/June, 1976; January/February, 1978.
Arizona Quarterly, autumn, 1979.
Black American Literature Forum, Volume 12, 1978; spring, 1979; spring, 1980; fall, 1984.
Black Enterprise, January, 1973; December, 1982; April, 1983; October, 1994, p. 169.
Black World, October, 1971; December, 1972; January, 1974; June, 1974; June, 1975; July, 1975.
Chicago Review, fall, 1976.
Chicago Tribune Book World, April 27, 1986.
Critical Inquiry, June, 1983.
Essence, July, 1986; July, 1994, p. 38.
Harper's, December, 1969.
Iowa Review, spring, 1982, pp. 117-31.
Los Angeles Times, April 29, 1975.
Los Angeles Times Book Review, April 20, 1986; June 4, 1989; April 14, 1991, p. 10.
MELUS, spring, 1984.
Mississippi Quarterly, winter, 1984-85, pp. 21-32.
Mississippi Review, Volume 20, numbers 1-2, 1991.
Modern Fiction Studies, summer, 1976; spring, 1988, pp. 97-123.
Modern Poetry Studies, autumn, 1973; autumn, 1974.
Nation, September 18, 1976; May 22, 1982.
Negro American Literature Forum, winter, 1967; winter, 1972.
Negro Digest, February, 1969; December, 1969.
New Republic, November 23, 1974.
New Yorker, October 11, 1969.

New York Review of Books, October 5, 1972; December 12, 1974; August 12, 1982; January 29, 1987; October 12, 1989, p. 20.

New York Times, August 1, 1969; August 9, 1972; June 17, 1982; April 5, 1986; September 28, 1995, p. A1; February 7, 1996, p. C12; May 13, 1997, p. C14.

New York Times Book Review, August 6, 1972; November 10, 1974; September 19, 1976; July 18, 1982; March 23, 1986; May 7, 1989; April 7, 1991, p. 32; February 13, 1994, p. 28.

Obsidian: Black Literature in Review, spring/summer, 1979; spring/summer, 1986, pp. 113-27.

Partisan Review, spring, 1975.

People Weekly, December 16, 1974.

PHYLON: The Atlanta University Review of Race and Culture, December, 1968; June, 1975.

Review of Contemporary Fiction, summer, 1984; spring, 1987; summer, 1994, p. 227.

San Francisco Review of Books, November, 1975; January/February, 1983.

Saturday Review, October 14, 1972; November 11, 1978.

Times Literary Supplement, May 18, 1990, p. 534; July 15, 1994, p. 22.

Tribune Books (Chicago), April 11, 1993, p. 3; December 12, 1993, p. 4.

Twentieth Century Literature, April, 1974.

Village Voice, January 22, 1979.

Virginia Quarterly Review, winter, 1973.

Washington Post Book World, March 16, 1986; June 25, 1989, pp. 4, 6; November 12, 1989, p. 16; April 14, 1991, p. 12; January 26, 1992, p. 12; March 21, 1993, p. 6.

World Literature Today, autumn, 1978.*

*   *   *

REGULUS, Evelyn Judy
   See BUEHLER, Evelyn Judy

*   *   *

RIDENHOUR, Carlton 1960-
   (Chuck D)

PERSONAL: Born in 1960, in Long Island, NY. *Education:* Attended Adelphi College.

ADDRESSES: Home—Atlanta, GA. *Office*—c/o Def Jam, CBS Records, 51 West 52nd St., New York, NY 10019.

CAREER: Musician, known as Chuck D, 1987—. Member of rap group Public Enemy. Recordings with Public Enemy, all on the Def Jam label, include: *Yo! Bum Rush the Show,* 1987; *It Takes a Nation of Millions to Hold Us Back,* 1988; *Fear of a Black Planet,* 1990; *Apocalypse '91: The Enemy Strikes Back,* 1991; *Muse Sick N Hour Mess Age,* 1994. Music with Public Enemy represented on other recordings, including *Do the Right Thing* (movie soundtrack), Motown, 1989. Other recordings include the singles "Check Out the Radio" and "Lies," Vanguard, 1984; (with Flavor Flav) *Greatest Misses,* Def Jam, 1992; and *Autobiography of Mistachuck,* 1996.

Host, as Chuck D, of radio program *The Super Spectrum Mix Show,* WBAU, 1983-84. Lecturer at educational institutions, including School of the Art Institute of Chicago, Emory University, Harvard University and Yale University. Spokesperson for Music Television's "Enough is Enough" and "Rock the Vote" campaigns. Appeared as a reporter/commentator for *Fox News,* 1996—.

AWARDS, HONORS: Platinum record, and best album award, *Village Voice* Critics' Poll, both 1988, for *It Takes a Nation of Millions to Hold Us Back;* best rap group award, *Rolling Stone* Reader's Picks, 1991; platinum record, 1990, for *Fear of a Black Planet.*

WRITINGS:

UNDER NAME CHUCK D

(With Yusaf Jah) *Fight the Power: Rap, Race, and Reality,* foreword by Spike Lee, Delacorte (New York City), 1997.

SIDELIGHTS: Carl Ridenhour, known to his fans as Chuck D, is a founding member of the prominent rap group Public Enemy, ranking among the most important figures in rap music. He became involved in music while a student at Adelphi University, where he served as host of campus station WBAU's *Super Spectrum Mix Show* in the early 1980s. Around this time Chuck D completed his first recording, but he found music writing so difficult that he did not intend to pursue a music career. He did, however, collaborate with Hank Shocklee on the recording "Public Enemy Number 1." Chuck D's vocals on that recording so impressed rap performer-entrepreneur Rick

Rubin that he determined to obtain Chuck D for the new record company Def Jam. Chuck D thereupon engaged fellow rapper Flavor Flav and other friends, including Shocklee's brother, Keith, and turntable whiz Terminator X, and announced the formation of Public Enemy. The group was represented by a logo, designed by Chuck D, that featured a person caught in the cross hairs of a rifle scope.

Yo! Bum Rush the Show, Public Enemy's first recording, quickly established the band among the most distinctive acts in rap music, one capable of augmenting their vocals with aggressive rhythms and jarring sounds. Havelock Nelson and Michael Gonzales, in their book *Bring the Noise: A Guide to Rap Music and Hip-Hop Culture,* ranked the 1987 record, which featured a revised version of "Public Enemy Number 1," among "the most relevant, ambitious projects ever committed to vinyl" and noted its "bristling, active soundscapes" and "post-apocalypse visions."

Public Enemy next released *It Takes a Nation of Millions to Hold Us Back,* which further established the band at the vanguard of rap music. In this recording, which many critics rank as the band's masterpiece, Chuck D's militant vocals merge with Flavor Flav's offbeat commentaries and a host of instrumentations—courtesy of collaborators referred to as the Bomb Squad—to form what Simon Glickman and Lorna M. Mabunda, writing in *Contemporary Black Biography,* described as "an assaultive, effects-strewn sonic landscape." According to Glickman and Mabunda, with their second recording Public Enemy had "brought about a revolution in rap." Public Enemy won further acclaim in 1989 when their compelling song "Fight the Power" was featured in filmmaker Spike Lee's *Do the Right Thing.* The song also appears on the group's third recording, *Fear of a Black Planet,* which includes the provocative "Welcome to the Terrordome."

By the time that *Fear of a Black Planet* appeared, Public Enemy had gained some unwanted publicity. Professor Griff, known as the group's "minister of information," found himself accused of anti-Semitism, and Flavor Flav fell under arrest for abusing a girlfriend. Terminator X, meanwhile, departed to pursue a solo career, and Hank Shocklee also withdrew from the group. Chuck D, though, remained active with a range of projects, including a fourth Public Enemy recording, *Apocalypse '91: The Enemy Strikes Back.* He also found himself in demand as a public speaker, in which capacity he served at Emory University and at the School of the Art Institute of

Chicago. In addition, he appeared on MTV's "Enough Is Enough" special, where he spoke against drug use and violence.

Chuck D, still within Public Enemy, endeavored a stylistic change with the relatively soulful *Muse Sick N Hour Mess Age,* a 1994 recording that replaced the Bomb Squad's aggressive sounds with samples from soul music recordings. The work did not win widespread acclaim, but it found favor with some critics, who welcomed it as an appealing alternative to the violent, gangster-oriented themes of other rap recordings.

In 1997 Chuck D teamed with Yusaf Jah to write *Fight the Power: Rap, Race, and Reality,* a volume appraising rap music as a viable art form. A *Booklist* reviewer reported that the work provides "valuable insights," while a *Publishers Weekly* critic declared that Chuck D expresses himself with such sincerity that "even familiar ideas are granted new power."

BIOGRAPHICAL/CRITICAL SOURCES:

BOOKS

Contemporary Black Biography, Volume 9, Gale Research (Detroit, MI), 1995.
Nelson, Havelock, and Michael Gonzales, *Bring the Noise: A Guide to Rap Music and Hip-Hop Culture,* Harmony, 1991.

PERIODICALS

Booklist, October 15, 1997, p. 375.
Entertainment Weekly, May 12, 1995, p. 62; October 25, 1996, p. 116.
People, June 30, 1997, p. 16.
Publishers Weekly, September 29, 1997, p. 76; October 6, 1997, p. 64.
Time, May 26, 1997, p. 124.
Variety, October 6, 1997.*

*   *   *

RIVE, Richard (Moore)   1931-1989

PERSONAL: Surname rhymes with "leave"; born March 1, 1931, in Cape Town, South Africa; died June 4, 1989, in Elfindale, South Africa; son of Nancy (Ward) Rive. *Education:* Hewat Training College (now Hewat College of Education), Cape Town,

South Africa, teacher's diploma, 1951; University of Cape Town, B.A., 1962, B.Ed., 1968; Columbia University, M.A., 1966; Oxford University, D.Phil., 1974. *Avocational interests:* Mountain climbing, coaching track athletes.

CAREER: Former teacher of English and Latin at South Peninsula High School, Cape Town, South Africa; affiliated with Harvard University, Cambridge, MA, 1987; Hewat College of Education, Cape Town, lecturer in English, became head of department of English, 1988-89.

AWARDS, HONORS: Farfield Foundation fellowship to travel and study contemporary African literature in English and French, 1963; Fulbright scholar, 1965-66, and Heft scholar, 1965-66; named Writer of the Year for South Africa, 1970, for "The Visits"; African Theatre Competition Prize, British Broadcasting Corp. (BBC), 1972, for *Make Like Slaves.*

WRITINGS:

(Editor and contributor) *Quartet: New Voices from South Africa,* Crown (New York City), 1963.
African Songs (short stories), Seven Seas (Berlin), 1963.
(Compiler) *Modern African Prose,* Heinemann (London), 1964, revised edition, 1967.
Emergency (novel), introduction by Ezekiel Mphahlele, Faber (London), 1964, Collier Books (New York City), 1970.
Selected Writings: Stories, Essays, and Plays, Ad Donker (Johannesburg), 1977.
Writing Black (autobiography), D. Philip (Cape Town), 1982.
Advance, Retreat: Selected Short Stories, D. Philip, 1983, St. Martin's (New York City), 1989.
"Buckingham Palace," District Six (novel; also see below), D. Philip, 1986, Ballantine (New York City), 1987.
"Buckingham Palace," District Six (play; based on his novel), produced in Cape Town, 1989. *Emergency Continued* (novel), D. Philip, 1990.
(With Tim Couzens) *Seme: The Founder of the ANC,* Africa World Press (Lawrenceville, NJ) 1992.

Also author of the stage play *Make Like Slaves,* 1972. Contributor to anthologies, including *Darkness and Light: An Anthology of African Writing,* edited by Peggy Rutherford, Drum Publications (Johannesburg), 1958, published as *African Voices,* Grosset, 1959; *An African Treasury: Articles, Essays, Stories, Poems by Black Africans,* edited by Langston Hughes, Crown,

1960; *Poems from Black Africa,* edited by Langston Hughes, Indiana University Press, 1963; *Modern African Stories,* edited by Ellis Ayitey and Ezekiel Mphahlele, Faber & Faber, 1964; *Pan African Short Stories,* edited by Neville Denny, Thomas Nelson, 1965; *African Writing Today,* edited by Ezekiel Mphahlele, Penguin, 1967; *Anthologie de la litterature negro-africaine: Romanciers et conteurs negro-africains,* Volume 2, edited by Leonard Sainville, Presence Africaine, 1968; and *The African Assertion: A Critical Anthology of African Literature,* edited by Austin J. Shelton, Jr., Odyssey Press, 1968. Contributor to periodicals in Africa, Europe, Asia, New Zealand, and the United States. Assistant editor, *Contrast* (literary quarterly). Rive's work has been translated into twelve languages, including Russian.

SIDELIGHTS: Richard Rive, a native of Cape Town, South Africa, and the son of a black American father and a South African mother of mixed heritage, often wrote of the injustices of apartheid with "delightful humor where one would expect bitterness and anger," noted Kofi Anyidoho in *World Literature Today.* Rive's specialty lay in presenting "the ironies inherent in racial relationships," acknowledged Robert L. Berner in a *World Literature Today* review of *Selected Writings: Stories, Essays, and Plays.* Rive also used multiple images and themes to unify his fiction writing. In the *Journal of the New African Literature and the Arts,* Bernth Lindfors described Rive's style as "characterized by strong rhythms, daring images, brisk dialogue, and leitmotifs (recurring words, phrases, images) which function as unifying devices."

In 1964 Rive published *Emergency,* which focuses on the declaration of a state of emergency in Cape Town following the Sharpeville massacre in which black protesters were gunned down by police in 1960. In the introduction to the novel, Ezekiel Mphahlele commented that "the novelist in the South African setting has to handle material that has become by now a huge cliche, violence, its aftermath, and the response it elicits. In this he travels a path that has many pitfalls." By focusing on the humanity of his characters—primarily teachers and students—so they are neither "tiny" nor "poetic," Mphahlele felt that Rive "has avoided these pitfalls." *Dictionary of Literary Biography* contributor Martin Trump noted that the book was informed by a "spirit of courage and almost reckless defiance of authority."

In 1982, Rive published *Writing Black,* an autobiographical series of sketches and essays that is supplemented by information on other African and African-

American writers. Anyidoho said of the work, "Rive's design rarely abandons us to the singular beauty or horror of the individual episode or sketch." Instead of focusing on the meaning of each separate instance, in *Writing Black* Rive demonstrated the "larger patterns of converging significance." Trump observed that this work "makes it clear that Rive is little persuaded by the calls for an African or black aesthetic. For him African literature takes its place among other world literatures and must be assessed along with them and by means of the same standards and critical techniques." Rive emphasized in his autobiography that he aimed to be a voice for all oppressed people, although "a stressing of racial differences comes out strongly in his stories," remarked Stephen M. Finn in the *Reference Guide to Short Fiction.* "His characters are aware, often grossly conscious, of them because of their suffering."

Along those lines, *"Buckingham Palace," District Six* dramatizes the oppressive actions of the apartheid government in Cape Town. In relating the story of the inhabitants of District Six, a "colored" slum slated for demolition by the government, Rive "brilliantly intensifies their tragedy by homing in on their humorous humanity rather than on their eventual dispersal," commented a *Publishers Weekly* reviewer. Rive's talent, according to William Walsh in the *Times Educational Supplement,* allowed him to "keep in productive balance irony bordering on despair" and characters that demonstrate the humor and strangeness of the human condition. William Finnegan, writing in the *New York Times Book Review,* criticized some of these characters and situations, remarking that those based on "worn-smooth issues . . . sink nearly to the level of a television sitcom." Nevertheless, Finnegan found that the novel "gains sudden, almost headlong momentum and a genuine power" when describing the "war" of the government against District Six. Trump deemed this novel, which the author eventually adapted into a play, "arguably Rive's best individual work. In it he manages, by means of chapters that focus closely on individual characters, to utilize one of his greatest talents: his ability as a short-story writer."

That ability was on display in *Advance, Retreat: Selected Short Stories.* In this volume, according to Tony Eprile in the *New York Times Book Review,* Rive presents some of his "finest stories and provides a loose chronology of the mixed-race population's evolving consciousness." Returning in the early stories to his District Six roots, Rive depicts the street life in this once multiracial section of Cape Town.

But Eprile believed that "Rive's real strengths come through in the stories that focus on the pain of racial awareness." In the story "Resurrection," Rive describes the funeral of a dark-skinned woman of mixed race, all but one of whose children turned out white. Mavis, the black daughter, recalls how she refused to comfort her mother when she complained of being ignored by her white children: "Don't you understand that you are black and your bloody children are white! Jim and Rosie and Sonny are white! And you made me black. You made me black!. . . Ma, why did you make me black?" With these works, Eprile commented, "Richard Rive's historical place in the development of South African literature is assured. This human, sharply observant collection of stories shows his is a voice to be discovered by each new reader, a voice that lingers long after one has read the stories."

Rive's final novel, *Emergency Continued,* is a sequel to *Emergency.* In this book, Rive has devised a novel within a novel to tell the story of a part-time writer and schoolteacher, Andrew Dreyer. Maya Jaggi described Dreyer in the *Times Literary Supplement* as "a political activist during an earlier state of emergency twenty-five years before [who] lives quietly in a prosperous 'Coloured' suburb [of Cape Town], having opted for a life of 'cultivated withdrawal' into a career and family concerns." Dreyer's political consciousness is reawakened when he must search for his son who is on the run from the security police. The story is told through letters to a former colleague and chapters of a novel Dreyer is writing. At one point in the book Rive writes, "I am going to quote the words of a banned man, which are illegal in this country only for those who dare not to listen to them. . . . 'It is not I who am here in the dock, but the illegal South African government. It is not I who am being sentenced to imprisonment, but the members of the apartheid regime. It is not I who will languish in jail, but the perpetrators of racialism who are . . . jailing themselves. I go willingly to serve my sentence because I know that I represent the future of this country. And one thing you cannot do, you cannot jail the future.'"

On June 4, 1989, just two weeks after completing *Emergency Continued,* Rive was found beaten and stabbed to death at his home near Cape Town. "Rive's untimely death occurred when he was at the peak of his literary powers," Trump lamented, noting that "Rive's works of the 1980s indicate that there was little falling off in his powers as a writer. . . . His death deprives South Africa of one of its most urbane writers."

BIOGRAPHICAL/CRITICAL SOURCES:

BOOKS

Dictionary of Literary Biography, Volume 125: *Twen-tieth-Century Caribbean and Black African Writ-ers,* Gale, 1993.
Reference Guide to Short Fiction, St. James, 1994.
Rive, Richard, *Emergency,* Collier Books, 1970.
Rive, Richard, *Writing Black,* D. Philip, 1982.

PERIODICALS

Ariel, April, 1985.
Canadian Literature, winter, 1990.
Chicago Tribune, June 6, 1989.
Choice, December, 1991.
Current Writing in Southern Africa, October, 1989.
Index on Censorship, December, 1984.
Journal of the New African Literature and the Arts, fall, 1966.
New Statesman, April 15, 1988.
New York Times, June 5, 1989.
New York Times Book Review, October 4, 1987; January 17, 1988; January 7, 1990; January 27, 1991; August 25, 1991.
Publishers Weekly, June 12, 1987; October 20, 1989.
South African Literary Journal, December, 1980; December, 1981; July, 1983; December, 1983; September, 1985.
Times Educational Supplement, August 21, 1987.
Times Literary Supplement, April 1, 1965; August 2, 1991.
Transition, February, 1966.
World Literature Today, spring, 1978; summer, 1982; summer, 1990; winter, 1992.*

*   *   *

RODGERS, Carolyn M(arie) 1945-

PERSONAL: Born December 14, 1945, in Chicago, IL; daughter of Clarence and Bazella (Colding) Rodgers. *Education:* Attended University of Illinois, 1960-61; Roosevelt University, B.A., 1981; University of Chicago, M.A. (English), 1984. *Religion:* African Methodist Episcopal.

ADDRESSES: Home—12750 South Sangamon, Chicago, IL 60643.

CAREER: Young Mens Christian Association, Chicago, IL, social worker, 1963- 68; Columbia College,

lecturer in Afro-American literature, 1968-69; University of Washington, Seattle, instructor in Afro-American literature, summer, 1970; Albany State College, Albany, GA, writer-in-residence, 1972; Malcolm X College, Chicago, writer-in-residence, 1972; Indiana University, Bloomington, instructor in Afro-American literature, summer, 1973; Chicago State University, Chicago, English remediation tutor, 1981; Columbia College, instructor, 1989-91; Harold Washington College, faculty advisor to student newspaper and instructor in English, 1998—.

MEMBER: Organization of Black American Culture Writers Workshop, Gwendolyn Brooks Writers Workshop, Delta Sigma Theta.

AWARDS, HONORS: First Conrad Kent Rivers Memorial Fund Award, 1968; National Endowment for the Arts grant, 1970; Poet Laureate Award, Society of Midland Authors, 1970; National Book Award nomination, 1976, for *how i got ovah: New and Selected Poems*; Carnegie Award, 1979; PEN awards; Gwendolyn Brooks fellowship.

WRITINGS:

POETRY

Paper Soul, Third World Press (Chicago), 1968.
Songs of a Blackbird, Third World Press, 1969.
Two Love Raps, Third World Press, 1969.
Now Ain't That Love, Broadside Press (Detroit), 1970.
For H. W. Fuller, Broadside Press, 1970.
For Flip Wilson, Broadside Press, 1971.
Long Rap/Commonly Known as a Poetic Essay, Broadside Press, 1971.
how i got ovah: New and Selected Poems, Doubleday (New York City), 1975.
The Heart as Ever Green: Poems, Doubleday, 1978.
Translation: Poems, Eden Press (Chicago), 1980.
Finite Forms: Poems, Eden Press, 1985.
Morning Glory, Eden Press, 1989.
We're Only Human, Eden Press, 1994.
A Train Called Judah, Eden Press, 1996.
The Girl with Blue Hair, Eden Press, 1996.
Salt, Eden Press, 1998.

OTHER

(Editor) *Roots* (anthology), Indiana University Press (Bloomington), 1973.
A Little Lower than Angels (novel), Eden Press, 1984.

Contributor to anthologies, including *Black Arts,* edited by Ahmed Alhamsi and Harun K. Wangara, Broadside Press, 1969; *Brothers and Sisters,* edited by Arnold Adoff, Macmillan, 1970; *We Speak as Liberators,* edited by Orde Coombs, Dodd, 1970; *Natural Process,* edited by Ted Wilentz and Tom Weatherley, Hill & Wang, 1970; *Jump Bad,* edited by Gwendolyn Brooks, Broadside Press, 1971; *The Black Poets,* edited by Dudley Randall, Bantam, 1971; *Blackspirits,* edited by Woodie King, Random House, 1972; *Afro-American Writing,* edited by Richard A. Long and Eugenia W. Collier, New York University Press, 1972; *Nommo,* edited by William R. Robinson, Macmillan, 1972; *The Poetry of Black America,* edited by Adoff, Harper, 1973; *Understanding the New Black Poetry,* edited by Stephen Henderson, Morrow, 1973; *Black Sister,* Indiana University Press, 1983; *Confirmation Anthology,* edited by Amiri Baraka, Morrow, 1984; *Masterpieces of African-American Literature,* edited by Frank N. Magill, HarperCollins, 1992; *Father Songs,* edited by Gloria Wade-Gayles, Beacon Press, 1997; and *Honey, Hush,* edited by Daryl Cumber Dance, Norton, 1998.

Former reviewer for Chicago *Daily News* and columnist for Milwaukee *Courier.*

SIDELIGHTS: Carolyn M. Rodgers is known primarily for her association with the Chicago Organization of Black American Culture of the 1960s. Calling her "one of the most sensitive and complex poets to emerge from this movement and struggle with its contradictions," essayist Bettye J. Parker-Smith suggests in *Black Women Writers (1950-1980): A Critical Evaluation* that Rodgers has been "instrumental in helping create, and give a new definition or receptive power to, poetry as a Black art form." Among Rodgers' published poetry are the collections *Songs of a Blackbird, how i got ovah: New and Selected Poems,* and *The Heart as Ever Green.*

Although Rodgers' poetry has always concerned the search for self, it has evolved over several decades from a militant, sociological perspective to a more introspective one. Jean Davis indicates in a *Dictionary of Literary Biography* essay that while Rodgers has spent most of her career as a poet in her native Chicago, she has since gone on to gain national recognition for "her thematic concerns with feminist issues," in particular those issues that directly affect African American women in a transitional society. Angelene Jamison asserts in her essay for *Black Women Writers (1950-1980),* that like "most of the Black women poets . . . casually referred to only as

by-products of the New Black Arts Movement," Rodgers still awaits the attention her work deserves, as well as her "appropriate place in literature."

Rodgers began writing "quasi seriously" as a response to the frustrations she experienced during her first year at college, going on to participate in the Organization of Black American Culture's Writers Workshop and becoming closely associated with the prolific black arts movement of the 1960s. The poet's spiritual and philosophical take on the problems of African Americans, and her effort to communicate with blacks on a unique level, suggest to Parker-Smith that Rodgers is "an exemplar of the 'revolutionary poet.'" Rodgers, who considers her work both art as well as polemic, has professed no distinctly defined political stance; rather, as she told Evans, she feels literature "functions as a type of catharsis or amen arena" in the lives of people. "I think it speaks not only to the political sensibility but to the heart, the mind, the spirit, and the soul of every man, woman, and child," the poet explained. Noting that Rodgers' poetry voices varied concerns, including "revolution, love, Black male-female relationships, religion, and the complexities of Black womanhood," Jamison declares that "through a skillfully uncluttered use of several literary devices, she convincingly reinterprets the love, pain, longings, struggles, victories, the day-to-day routines of Black people from the point of view of the Black woman. Gracefully courageous enough to explore long-hidden truths, about Black women particularly, her poetry shows honesty, warmth, and love for Black people."

Rodgers' first volume of poetry, 1968's *Paper Soul,* "reflects the duality of an individual struggling to reconcile complex realities, dilemmas, and contradictions," in the opinion of Davis, who recognizes a thematic shift in the poet's second volume of poetry, *Songs of a Blackbird.* Davis suggests that the former addresses "identity, religion, revolution, and love, or more accurately a woman's need for love," whereas the latter deals with "survival, street life, mother-daughter conflict, and love." Indicating that these poems are increasingly concerned with "the black woman poet as a major theme," Davis states that "questions of identity for the poet remain connected with relationships between black men and women but become more centrally located in the woman's ability to express herself."

While Rodgers' poetry of the late-1960s is characterized by Davis as "vivid and forceful," her early volumes were not unanimously praised. Rodgers' "po-ems, especially the early works, are efforts to break the silences, to break down the walls," according to *Contemporary Women Poets* essayist Janis Butler Holm, citing such works as "U Name This One," which describes life on Chicago's streets, "where pee wee cut lonnell fuh fuckin wid/ his sistuh and blood baptized the street/ at least twice ev'ry week and judy got/ kicked outa grammar school fuh bein pregnant/ and died tryin to ungrow the seed." Davis credits the poet's "use of speech patterns and of lengthened prose-like lines" with sparking trepidation on the part of contemporary critics. Such stylistic measures were "an attempt at breaking away from the restrictions of conventional forms and modes, and most especially from those considered appropriate for women poets," according to Davis Inasmuch as language structure and theme were the general hallmarks of the black art movement during this period, Parker-Smith cites Rodgers' incorporation of obscenities and the pattern of black speech as especially courageous for a woman poet. Although acknowledging a certain inconsistency in the language of her early poetry, Davis believes that "Rodgers nonetheless had an eye for the contra-dictions of black experience, particularly the revolu-tionary or militant experience of the 1960s."

Parker-Smith describes what she perceives as two stages of Rodgers' work, what she refers to as the poet's "two distinct and clear baptisms." The poet's early work is "rough-hewn, folk-spirited, and held 'down at the river' amid water moccasins in the face of a glaring midday sun." Rodgers' poems in *Paper Soul, Two Love Raps,* and *Songs of a Blackbird* reveal "her impudence, through the use of her wit, obsceni-ties, the argumentation in her love and revolution poems, and the pain and presence of her mother," according to Parker-Smith, who suggests that "the ribald outcry, the incongruity and cynicism that char-acterize the first period are links in Rodgers' chain of personal judgments—her attempts to come to grips with 'self'—and with the Black Arts Movement as a whole."

The poet's second phase finds her more mature, more sophisticated, her judgements more modulated. Dur-ing this time, Rodgers moved from Chicago-based Third World Press to a larger commercial publishing house, as well as breaking from the Organization of Black American Culture. Considering *how i got ovah* and *The Heart as Ever Green: Poems* within the scope of this second phase, Parker-Smith finds that Rodgers closely examines "the revolution, its contradictions, and her relationship to it."

In Rodgers's *how i got ovah: New and Selected Po-ems,* written in the mid-1970s, the poet exhibits a heightened "clarity of expression and a respect for well-crafted language," according to Davis, who per-ceives "humor, sincerity, and love" in the autobio-graphical poems about "black revolution, feminism, religion, God, the black church, and the black family, especially the mother." Similarly, Hilda Njoki McElroy writes in *Black World:* "It is obvious that Carolyn Rodgers loves her craft and her people. *how i got ovah* is a result of this love match. It is an important literary contribution containing many aspects of hu-man frailty/achievement, love/hate, positive/negative, funny/sad, beautiful/ugly which makes it deeeeep, very deeeeep." Suggesting that these poems "reveal Rodgers' transformation from a . . . militant Black woman to a woman intensely concerned with God, traditional values, and her private self," Davis adds that "although her messages often explore social con-flict, they usually conclude with a sense of peace, hope, and a desire to search for life's real treasure— inner beauty."

Identity and potentiality continue to be central themes throughout Rodgers' work that have solidified in what Davis terms an "evolving feminism." "I see myself as becoming," Rodgers told Evans. Davis suggests that "determination to grow and to be is the most preva-lent idea" in Rodgers's *The Heart as Ever Green,* where "the themes of human dignity, feminism, love, black consciousness, and Christianity are repeated throughout." Suggesting that the "level of honesty" in Rodgers' work correlates with the poet's own level of freedom, Jamison believes that "in a variety of idioms ranging from the street to the church, she writes about Black women with a kind of sensitivity and warmth that brings them out of the poems and into our own lives." Jamison adds that "clearly, her art-istry brings these women to life, but it is her love for them that gives them their rightful place in literature. The love, the skill, indeed the vision, which she brings to her poetry must certainly help Black women rediscover and better understand themselves."

Although survival represents a dominant theme in her stories and poetry, Davis believes that Rodgers "in-terweaves the idea of adaptability and conveys the concomitant message of life's ever-changing avenues for black people whom she sees as her special audi-ence." She quotes Rodgers' regarding her writing being "for whoever wants to read it. . . one poem doesn't do that. But I try to put as many as I can in a book. A poem for somebody young, religious people, the church people. Just people. Specifically, Black people. I would like for them to like me."

BIOGRAPHICAL/CRITICAL SOURCES:

BOOKS

Contemporary Women Poets, St. James Press (Detroit), 1997.
Dictionary of Literary Biography, Volume 41: *Afro-American Poets since 1955,* Gale (Detroit), 1985.
Evans, Mari, editor, *Black Women Writers (1950-1980): A Critical Evaluation,* Doubleday, 1984.

PERIODICALS

Black Scholar, March, 1981, p. 90.
Black World, August, 1970: February, 1976.
Booklist, September 1, 1978, p. 20.
Chicago Tribune, November 19, 1978.
Kirkus Reviews, April 15, 1978, p. 490.
Library Journal, August, 1978, p. 1516.
Negro Digest, September, 1968.
Publishers Weekly, April 24, 1978, p. 75.
Washington Post Book World, May 18, 1975.

*   *   *

RUGANDA, John 1941-

PERSONAL: Born May 30, 1941, in Kabavole, Uganda; married Flavia Murumba; children: four sons, three daughters. *Education:* Attended St. Leo's College; Makerere University, B.A. (with honors), 1967; University of New Brunswick, M.A., 1984, Ph.D., 1989.

ADDRESSES: Agent—c/o Heinemann Kenya, P.O. Box 45314, Nairobi, Kenya, Africa.

CAREER: Writer. Oxford University Press of Eastern Africa, editorial and sales representative in Uganda, 1968-72, staff member in Nairobi, Kenya, office, c. 1973; University of Nairobi, Nairobi, Kenya, lecturer, 1973-82, co-founder of Nairobi University Free Travelling Theatre company, c. 1973. Founding member of Makerere Free Traveling Theatre, elected chief organizer, 1966; co-founder of Makonde Group theater company, 1971. Director of stage productions.

AWARDS, HONORS: Creative Writing Senior Fellowship, Makerere University, 1972-73.

WRITINGS:

STAGE PLAYS

The Burdens (produced in Kampala, Uganda, 1970), Oxford University Press (New York City), 1972.
Black Mamba [and] *Covenant with Death* (*Black Mamba* produced in Kampala, 1972), East African Publishing House (Nairobi, Kenya), 1973.
(Translator) Bertolt Brecht, *The Good Woman of Setzuan,* produced in Nairobi, 1978.
The Floods (produced in Nairobi, 1979), East African Publishing House (Nairobi), 1980.
(And director) *Music without Tears* (produced in Nairobi, 1981), Bookwise (Nairobi), 1982.
(And director) *Echoes of Silence* (produced in Nairobi, 1985), Heinemann Kenya (Nairobi), 1986.

TELEVISION PLAYS

The Secret of the Season, Voice of Kenya, 1973.
The Floods (adapted from Ruganda's play), Voice of Kenya, 1973 (also see above).
The Illegitimate, Voice of Kenya, 1982.

RADIO PLAYS

My Father the Glutton, Radio Uganda, 1971.
Covenant with Death (adapted from Ruganda's play), BBC African Theatre Programme, 1974 (also see above).
Black Mamba (adapted from Ruganda's play), BBC African Theatre Programme, 1977 (also see above).

OTHER

(With Kivu Tha Kibwana and Oluoch Obura) *Majira Ya Ukame,* East African Literature Bureau (Nairobi), 1976.
Telling the Truth Laughingly: The Politics of Francis Imbuga's Drama, East African Educational Publishers (Nairobi), 1992.

Work represented in anthologies, including *Drum Beat: East African Poems,* edited by Lennard Okola, East African Publishing House (Nairobi), 1967; *New Voices of the Commonwealth,* edited by H. Sergeant, Evans (London), 1968; *Poems from East Africa,* edited by David Cook and David Rubardiri, Heinemann (London), 1971; *Tradition, Challenge and Change,* Fomas (Halifax), 1987; and *Stella Awinja Muka,* edited by Stanley Muka, Uzima Press (Nairobi), 1987. Author of foreword, *Otongolia,* Alakie-Akinyi Mboya, Oxford University Press (Nairobi), 1986. Contributor of poetry, fiction, and nonfiction to periodicals, including *Canadian Theater Review, Penpoint, Umma,* and *Zuka.*

SIDELIGHTS: John Ruganda is a prominent African playwright. He was born in 1941 in Kabavole, Uganda, and he studied at nearby St. Leo's College before earning an undergraduate degree from Makerere University in 1967. He then became a representative for Oxford University Press in Africa, where he worked in editorial and sales from 1968 to 1972. Ruganda left his increasingly turbulent homeland of Uganda in 1973 and joined the faculty of the University of Nairobi in Kenya. He taught there for nearly ten years, then traveled to Canada, where he earned a master's degree and a doctorate from the University of New Brunswick in the 1980s.

Ruganda saw production of his first play in 1970, and in the ensuing years he established himself as a talented playwright with particular interest in the articulation and examination of various aspects of African culture, including the exploitation of fellow Africans by capitalists and conniving politicians. Fellow playwright Francis Imbuga, calling Ruganda "Uganda's best-known playwright and one of East and Central Africa's leading dramatists," wrote in the *Dictionary of Literary Biography* that Ruganda "dramatizes the African man's plight and struggle for survival in a hostile social, economic, and political environment in which he is reduced to the position of passive observer by a small class of cutthroat businessmen and political opportunists." Imbuga also affirmed that Ruganda's plays "tend to revolve around a few central themes that are of immediate relevance not only to the East African region . . . but also to the rest of Africa and indeed to other nations that have undergone similar historical experiences."

The Burdens, Ruganda's first play, details the predicament of Wamala, an arrogant, elitist cabinet minister who has participated in a failed bid to overthrow the very administration that counts him among its members. In the wake of his disgrace, Wamala and his family are forced to live in poverty among the citizenry that so disgusts them. Wamala eventually succumbs to alcoholism while his wife supports the family through black-market sales. The couple begins to grow apart and to argue violently. During one such altercation, Wamala is killed by his wife. Esiaba Irobi, writing in *Contemporary Dramatists,* acknowledged *The Burdens* as "a well-knit play" and "a competent satirical study of postindependence disillusionment in African politics."

Ruganda's next play, *Black Mamba,* concerns a lascivious white professor who regularly procures—through the aid of a houseboy—native women for sexual exploitation. Upon exposure, the professor faces the loss of his job and his home, but not before the abetting houseboy has schemed to engage his own wife for the professor's pleasure. Imbuga wrote in the *Dictionary of Literary Biography* that the houseboy's action reflects "the postindependence African personality: he will sell his country and destroy its image for capital gain."

Covenant with Death, another of Ruganda's plays from the early 1970s, serves as a consideration of an African folktale. In this legend, the goddess of fruition grants a couple's plea for a child but imposes the stipulation that the offspring must never experience the sex act. When the child, a girl, becomes fully grown and learns of her restriction, she flees from home and eventually begins living with a white man. *Covenant with Death* relates the return journey of the heroine, Matama, who longs to rejoin her parents after years of city life. Before she can see her parents again, however, the diseased Matama dies. Imbuga speculated: "The fact that Matama only turns her back on her enjoyable life in the city when she is dying might be Ruganda's subtle way of castigating Africa's over-glorification of the past, which tends to get in the way of possibilities for development."

In *The Floods,* which realized production in 1979, Ruganda addresses an abusive military dictatorship and details its grim effect on both perpetrators and victims. Here, a former bureau chief, who enacted grim measures during Ugandan dictator Idi Amin's bloodthirsty reign, becomes concerned that he might be betrayed by his girlfriend, an ambitious intellectual. To thwart what he perceives to be her likely treachery, he conspires to fabricate flood warnings and lure her aboard a rescue ship, whereupon she will be massacred along with the other passengers. The scheme only partially succeeds, for the flood announcement is made and the passengers are executed, but the girlfriend is not aboard.

Music without Tears examines what Esiaba Irobi, writing in *Contemporary Dramatists,* called "the collective hysteria that engulfed Uganda in the post-Idi Amin period of the country's turbulent history." In this play, instability follows the military overthrow of Amin. Wak, who had fled Uganda during Amin's horrific reign, returns home only to find himself resented by the brother and sister whom he had left behind. Wak eventually learns that he had been betrayed by the very brother who had come to resent his escape. Irobi described *Music without Tears* as "a study in tyranny, even within the family."

In another key play, *Echoes of Silence,* Ruganda explores ethnic tensions and domestic dissatisfaction. The play's central characters are Okoth-Okach, who is visiting the home of a friend from another tribe, and Njoroge Njunguna, the friend's wife. With the friend absent, Okoth-Okach and Njoroge enter into conversation and discover that each of them is unhappily married. In realizing a greater understanding, and sympathy, for each other, the two characters manage to break through ethnic stereotypes and suspicions of each other's tribe. Imbuga noted as much in the *Dictionary of Literary Biography,* writing that "the main conflict in *Echoes of Silence* is the result of deeply rooted tensions caused by an undercurrent of general ethnic biases and suspicions between . . . communities of Kenya."

Aside from his stage plays, Ruganda has written television and radio productions, some of which are ad-aptations of his stage works. In addition, he has translated Bertolt Brecht's play *The Good Woman of Setzuan.* Among Ruganda's other publications is *Telling the Truth Laughingly: The Politics of Francis Imbuga's Drama.*

BIOGRAPHICAL/CRITICAL SOURCES:

BOOKS

Contemporary Dramatists, sixth edition, St. James Press (Detroit, MI), 1999.
Dictionary of Literary Biography, Volume 157: *Twentieth-Century Caribbean and Black African Writers,* Third Series, Gale (Detroit, MI), 1995.

PERIODICALS

African Perspectives, September-October, 1977, pp. 30, 38.
New African, December, 1980, pp. 51-53.*

S

SALKEY, (Felix) Andrew (Alexander) 1928-1995

PERSONAL: Born January 30, 1928, in Colon, Panama; died from congestive heart failure, April 28, 1995, in Massachusetts; son of Andrew Alexander and Linda (Marshall) Salkey; married Patricia Verden, February 22, 1957; children: Eliot Andrew, Jason Alexander. *Education:* Attended St. George's College, Kingston, Jamaica, and Munro College, St. Elizabeth, Jamaica; University of London, B.A., 1955. *Avocational interests:* Collecting contemporary paintings by unestablished painters and classical and contemporary editions of novels, books of poetry, and literary criticism.

CAREER: Writer and broadcast journalist. British Broadcasting Corp. (BBC-Radio), London, England, interviewer, scriptwriter, and editor of literary program, 1952-56; Comprehensive School, London, assistant master of English literature and language, 1957-59; freelance writer and general reviewer of books and plays, 1956-76; Hampshire College, Amherst, MA, professor of writing, 1976-95. Narrator in film *Reggae,* 1978.

AWARDS, HONORS: Thomas Helmore poetry prize, 1955, for long poem, "Jamaica Symphony"; Guggenheim fellowship, 1960, for novel *A Quality of Violence,* and for folklore project; Sri Chinmoy Poetry Award, 1977; Casa de las Americas Poetry Prize, 1979, for *In the Hills Where Her Dreams Live: Poems for Chile, 1973-1978;* D.Litt., Franklin Pierce College, 1981.

WRITINGS:

A Quality of Violence (novel), Hutchinson (London), 1959.

Escape to an Autumn Pavement, Hutchinson, 1960.
The Late Emancipation of Jerry Stover, Hutchinson, 1968.
The Adventures of Catullus Kelly, Hutchinson, 1969.
Havana Journal, Penguin, 1971.
Georgetown Journal: A Caribbean Writer's Journey from London via Port of Spain to Georgetown, Guayana, 1970, New Beacon Books (London), 1972.
Anancy's Score (short stories), Bogle-L'Ouverture, 1973.
Caribbean Essays: An Anthology, Evans Brothers, 1973.
Come Home, Malcolm Heartland, Hutchinson, 1976.
Anancy, Traveller (short stories), Bogle-L'Ouverture, 1988.
In the Border Country and Other Stories, Bogle-L'Ouverture, 1994.

EDITOR

West Indian Stories, Faber (London), 1960.
(Editor of Caribbean section) *Young Commonwealth Poets '65,* Heinemann (London), 1965.
(And author of introduction) *Stories from the Caribbean,* Elek (London), 1965, published as *Island Voices: Stories from the West Indies,* Liveright (New York City), 1970.
(And author of introduction) *Breaklight: An Anthology of Caribbean Poetry,* Hamish Hamilton, 1971, published as *Breaklight: The Poetry of the Caribbean,* Doubleday, 1972.
(With others) *Savacou 3-4,* two volumes, Caribbean Artists Movement (Kingston, Jamaica), 1972.
Caribbean Essays, Evans (London), 1973.
(And author of introduction) *Writing in Cuba since the Revolution: An Anthology of Poems, Short Stories, and Essays,* Bogle-L'Ouverture, 1977.

Caribbean Folk Tales and Legends, Bogle-L'Ouverture, 1983.

JUVENILES

Hurricane, illustrated by William Papas, Oxford University Press (London), 1964, Oxford University Press (New York City), 1979.
Earthquake, illustrated by William Papas, Oxford University Press, 1965, Roy (New York City), 1969.
The Shark Hunters (reader), illustrated by Peter Kesteven, Nelson (London), 1966.
Drought, illustrated by William Papas, Oxford University Press (London), 1966.
Riot, illustrated by William Papas, Oxford University Press (London), 1967.
(Editor) *Caribbean Prose: An Anthology for Secondary Schools,* Evans, 1967.
Jonah Simpson, illustrated by Gerry Craig, Oxford University Press (London), 1969, Roy, 1970.
Joey Tyson, Bogle-L'Ouverture (London), 1974.
The River that Disappeared, Bogle-L'Ouverture, 1979.
Danny Jones, Bogle-L'Ouverture, 1983.
The One: The Story of How the People of Guyana Avenge the Murder of Their Pasero with Help from Anancy and Sister Buxton (novel), Bogle-L'Ouverture, 1985.
Brother Anancy and Other Stories, Longman, 1994.

POETRY

Jamaica, Hutchinson, 1973, 2nd edition, 1983.
Land, Readers and Writers (London), 1976.
In the Hills Where Her Dreams Live: Poems for Chile, 1973-1978, Casa de las Americas (Havana), 1979, enlarged edition published as *In the Hills Where Her Dreams Live: Poems for Chile, 1973-1980,* Black Scholar Press (Sausalito, CA), 1981.
Away, Allison & Busby (London), 1980.

OTHER

(Author of introduction) Linton Kwesi Johnson, *Dread Beat and Blood,* Bogle-L'Ouverture, 1975.
(Author of introduction) *Walter Rodney: Poetic Tributes,* Bogle-L'Ouverture, 1985.

Contributor of over thirty radio plays and features to British Broadcasting Corp., over twelve radio plays and features to radio stations in Belgium, Germany, and Switzerland, and many short stories, essays, fea-

tures, and articles to newspapers and magazines in England, Europe, and Africa.

SIDELIGHTS: Andrew Salkey was best known for his novels, poetry, and other works inspired by Jamaica and the Caribbean. Although he wrote a collection of short stories, several volumes of poetry, and edited a number of anthologies, he is perhaps better known for his adult novels and books for young people. Described by Peter Nazareth in *World Literature Today* as a "Third World storyteller extraordinaire in the Afro-Caribbean mold," Salkey wrote books that contain significant themes, vivid imagery, lively dialogue, and spirited characterization. A reviewer for the *Times Literary Supplement* noted that a reader can recognize Salkey's fiction "by the importance of the themes he treats and sometimes by the sheer exhilaration and inventiveness of his dialogue and the exuberance of his characterization."

Writing in the *Dictionary of Literary Biography,* Anthony Boxill called Salkey "one of the most prolific and versatile of West Indian writers. He has written over twenty books, including novels for adults, novels for children, collections of short stories, books of poems, and travel-cum-political journals. Furthermore, as an editor he has done much to promote and make available West Indian writing both to adults and young people."

Salkey's novels deal, according to Jeremy Poynting in *Contemporary Novelists,* "with the situation of the brown-skinned Jamaican, a man whose social origins lie between the black masses and the white elite, whose tongue is divided between standard and dialect, who is driven towards exile and then caught by 'a double lock-out,' who has missed his role in history and is caught between attraction to women and flight from the 'tender snare.' There is a yet bigger ambivalence in the novels which subsumes all these, between the hope that the Salkey hero can hold these divisions in complementary creative tension, and the fear that they will destroy him."

One of Salkey's best known novels is *A Quality of Violence,* which is set in rural Jamaica during a prolonged drought. The drought tears away at the social fabric of the farming community as the residents begin to lose confidence in themselves and faith in their religion. "Thinking that their Christian faith is inadequate to cope with their problems," explained Boxill, "the people turn to Pocomania, a cult combining Christian and African rituals. The collision of these two sources of faith divides the people, and it results ultimately in violence and death." The conflict between the two faiths is mirrored in the conflict between the lighter-skinned Christians, who seek a rational solution to their problems, and the darker-skinned pagans, who turn to ritual sacrifice. *A Quality of Violence,* noted Boxill, "is considered by many critics to be [Salkey's] best because of its suggestiveness and the austerity of its language, which embodies the aridity of the people and the landscape."

Salkey once expressed his thoughts on writing fiction in this manner: "I tend to write in a fairly straight line, from beginning to middle to end, although in fits and starts, and I don't mind going back over certain parts of the composition, rewriting and re-casting them, again and again, until they fit together with the other parts and help the whole story to shape up nicely. I like my writing to entertain me, if I can manage it; I like it to turn me on to write more and more, and to write well. Finally, I suppose the most important feature of my work as a writer is the matter of the central place I always give to persons and personal relationships in my storytelling. I simply couldn't make a narrative move without them."

BIOGRAPHICAL/CRITICAL SOURCES:

BOOKS

Contemporary Novelists, 6th edition, St. James, 1996.
Dictionary of Literary Biography, Volume 125: *Twentieth-Century Caribbean and Black African Writers, Second Series,* Gale, 1993.
James, Louis, editor, *The Islands in Between: Essays on West Indian Literature,* Oxford University Press (London), 1968, pp. 100-108.
Salkcy, Andrew, *Caribbean Folk Tales and Legends,* Bogle-L'Ouverture, 1983.
Twentieth-Century Children's Writers, 4th edition, St. James Press, 1995.

PERIODICALS

Choice, March, 1995, p. 1059.
Contemporary Literature, summer, 1998, p. 212.
Jamaica Journal, June, 1968, pp. 46-54; November, 1986-January, 1987, pp. 39-43.
Library Journal, March 15, 1970.
Los Angeles Times, January 9, 1981.
Presence Africaine, fall, 1970, pp. 146-49.
Times Literary Supplement, February 20, 1969; October 16, 1969; July 20, 1973; January 9, 1981.
World Literature Today, summer, 1979; autumn, 1980; spring, 1981; summer, 1981; summer, 1983.

World Literature Written in English, November, 1972, pp. 67-80; autumn, 1988, pp. 341-56.

OBITUARIES:

PERIODICALS

Times (London), May 1, 1995, p. 19.*

*   *   *

SANCHEZ, Sonia 1934-

PERSONAL: Born Wilsonia Benita Driver, September 9, 1934, Birmingham, AL; daughter of Wilson L. and Lena (Jones) Driver; married Albert Sanchez (divorced); children: Anita, Morani Neusi, Mungu Neusi. *Education:* Hunter College (now Hunter College of the City University of New York), B.A., 1955; post-graduate study, New York University. *Politics:* "Peace, freedom, and justice."

ADDRESSES: Home—407 West Chelten Ave., Philadelphia, PA 19144. *Office*—Department of English, Temple University, Philadelphia, PA 19122.

CAREER: Staff member, Downtown Community School, New York City, 1965-67; San Francisco State College (now University), San Francisco, instructor, 1966-68; University of Pittsburgh, Pittsburgh, PA, assistant professor, 1969-70; Rutgers University, New Brunswick, NJ, assistant professor, 1970-71; Manhattan Community College of the City University of New York, New York City, assistant professor of Black literature and creative writing, 1971-73; City College of the City University of New York, New York City, teacher of creative writing, 1972; Amherst College, Amherst, MA, associate professor, 1972-75; University of Pennsylvania, Philadelphia, PA, 1976-77; Temple University, Philadelphia, associate professor, 1977, Laura H. Carnell Professor of English, 1979—, faculty fellow in provost's office, 1986-87, presidential fellow, 1987-90. Adjunct professor, Haverford College, Haverford, PA, 1984-86; Distinguished Minority Faculty Fellow, University of Delaware, Newark, DE, 1987; Distinguished Poet-in-Residence, Spelman College, Atlanta, GA, 1989; Zale Writer in Residence, Newcomb College, Tulane University, New Orleans, LA, 1992. Member, Literature Panel of the Pennsylvania Council on the Arts, Literary Arts Task Force of the National African American Museum Project, and Poetry in the Schools Project.

MEMBER: Poetry Society of America, American Studies Association, Academy of American Poets, PEN, National Association for the Advancement of Colored People.

AWARDS, HONORS: PEN Writing Award, 1969; National Institute of the Arts and Letters grant, 1970; honorary Ph.D., Wilberforce University, 1972; National Endowment for the Arts Award, 1978-79; Honorary Citizen of Atlanta, 1982; Tribute to Black Women Award, Black Students of Smith College, 1982; Lucretia Mott Award, 1984; American Book Award from Before Columbus Foundation, 1985, for *Homegirls & Handgrenades;* International Womens Award from Mayor's Commission for Women, Philadelphia, 1987; Welcome Award from Museum of Afro American History, Boston, 1990; Women Pioneers Hall of Fame citation from Young Women's Christian Association, 1992; Oni Award from International Black Women's Congress, 1992; Roots Award from PAN-African Studies Community Education Program, 1993; PEN fellowship in the arts, 1993-94; Legacy Award from Jomandi Productions, 1994.

WRITINGS:

Homecoming (poetry), Broadside Press (Highland Park, MI), 1969.
We a BaddDDD People (poetry), with foreword by Dudley Randall, Broadside Press, 1970.
It's a New Day: Poems for Young Brothas and Sistuhs (juvenile), Broadside Press, 1971.
(Editor) *Three Hundred and Sixty Degrees of Blackness Comin' at You* (poetry), 5X Publishing Co. (New York City), 1971.
A Sun Lady for All Seasons Reads Her Poetry (record album), Folkways, 1971.
Ima Talken bout the Nation of Islam, TruthDel, 1972.
Love Poems, Third Press (New York City), 1973.
A Blues Book for Blue Black Magical Women (poetry), Broadside Press, 1973.
The Adventures of Fat Head, Small Head, and Square Head (juvenile), Third Press, 1973.
(Editor and contributor) *We Be Word Sorcerers: 25 Stories by Black Americans,* Bantam (New York City), 1973.
I've Been a Woman: New and Selected Poems, Black Scholar Press (San Francisco), 1978.
A Sound Investment and Other Stories (juvenile), Third World Press (Chicago), 1979.
Crisis in Culture—Two Speeches by Sonia Sanchez, Black Liberation Press (New York City), 1983.
Homegirls & Handgrenades (poems), Thunder's Mouth Press (New York City), 1984.

Under a Soprano Sky (poems), Africa World Press (Trenton, NJ), 1987.
Wounded in the House of a Friend, Beacon Press (Boston, MA), 1995.
Does Your House Have Lions?, Beacon Press, 1995.
Like the Singing Coming Off the Drums: Love Poems, Beacon Press, 1998.

PLAYS

The Bronx Is Next, first produced in New York at Theatre Black, October 3, 1970 (included in *Cavalcade: Negro American Writing from 1760 to the Present,* edited by Arthur Davis and Saunders Redding, Houghton, 1971).
Sister Son/ji, first produced with *Cop and Blow* and *Players Inn* by Neil Harris and *Gettin'It Together* by Richard Wesley as *Black Visions,* Off-Broadway at New York Shakespeare Festival Public Theatre, 1972 (included in *New Plays from the Black Theatre,* edited by Ed Bullins, Bantam, 1969).
Dirty Hearts, published in *Breakout: In Search of New Theatrical Environments,* Swallow Press (Chicago), 1973.
Uh Huh; But How Do It Free Us?, first produced in Chicago at Northwestern University Theater, 1975 (included in *The New Lafayette Theatre Presents: Plays with Aesthetic Comments by Six Black Playwrights, Ed Bullins, J. E. Gaines, Clay Gross, Oyamo, Sonia Sanchez, Richard Wesley,* edited by Bullins, Anchor Press, 1974).
Malcolm Man/Don't Live Here No More, first produced in Philadelphia at ASCOM Community Center, 1979.
I'm Black When I'm Singing, I'm Blue When I Ain't, first produced in Atlanta, GA, at OIC Theatre, April 23, 1982.
Black Cats Back and Uneasy Landings, first produced in Philadelphia at Freedom Theatre, 1995.

OTHER

(Editor and author of introduction) *Living at the Epicenter: The 1995 Morse Poetry Prize Selected and Introduced by Sonia Sanchez,* Northeastern University Press, 1995.

Contributor to anthologies, including *Black Fire: An Anthology of Afro-American Writing,* edited by Le Roi Jones and Ray Neal, Morrow (New York City), 1968; *We Speak as Liberators: Young Black Poets,* edited by Orde Coombs, Dodd (New York City), 1971; *Understanding the New Black Poetry: Black Speech and*

Black Music as Poetic References, edited by Stephen Henderson, Morrow, 1973; *Giant Talk: An Anthology of Third World Writings,* edited by Quincy Troupe and Rainer Schulte, Random House (New York City), 1975; *Understanding Poetry,* edited by Brooks and Warren, Holt (New York City), 1976; *Confirmation: An Anthology of African-American Women,* edited by Amiri and Amina Baraka, Morrow, 1983; *Every Shut Eye Ain't Asleep: An Anthology of Poetry by African Americans since 1945,* edited by Michael S. Harper and Anthony Walton, Little, Brown, 1994; and *Celebrating America: A Collection of Poems and Images of the American Spirit,* edited by Laura Whipple, Philomel Books (New York City), 1994.

SIDELIGHTS: Sonia Sanchez is often named among the strongest voices in black nationalism, the cultural revolution of the 1960s in which many black Americans sought a new identity distinct from the values of the white establishment. C. W. E. Bigsby comments in *The Second Black Renaissance: Essays in Black Literature* that "the distinguishing characteristic of her work is a language which catches the nuance of the spoken word, the rhythms of the street, and of a music which is partly jazz and partly a lyricism which underlies ordinary conversation." Her emphasis on poetry as a spoken art, or performance, connects Sanchez to the traditions of her African ancestors, an oral tradition preserved in earlier slave narratives and forms of music indigenous to the black experience in America. In addition to her poetry, for which she has won many prizes, Sanchez has contributed equally well-known plays, short stories, and children's books to the body of black American literature. *Belles Lettres* contributor Kamili Anderson cites the poet's work for its "precision and insightfulness" and commends Sanchez for her "substantial and finely honed literary talents."

In *Southern Women Writers: The New Generation,* Joanne Veal Gabbin notes that much of Sanchez's work reveals her Southern roots, even though she lived in New York City from late childhood onward. "Throughout her poetry . . . Sanchez demonstrates the complexity of her Southern imagination," the critic writes. "Though she spent a relatively short period of her life in the South, her way of looking at the world is generously soaked in the values she learned during her childhood in Birmingham, Alabama. The importance of the family and love relationships, her fascination with the past and her ancestry, her search for identity amid the chaos and deracination of the North, her communion with nature, her exploration of the folk culture, her response to an evangeli-

cal religious experience, and her embracing of a militancy nurtured in fear and rage are Southern attitudes that inform her poetry. . . . Her early Southern experience watered her sensibility—the greening of her mind—and nourished her purpose as a poet: to create positive values for her community."

Born Wilsonia Benita Driver in Birmingham, Sanchez faced many difficulties as a youngster. Her mother died when she was only a year old, and for a time Sanchez and her sister were cared for by their paternal grandmother, Elizabeth "Mama" Driver. This beloved grandparent is the "Dear Mama" of Sanchez's poem by the same name in *Under a Soprano Sky.* Mama Driver died when Sanchez was five, and the frail youngster endured a period of family instability, including abuse and neglect by a stepmother and frequent moves from one relative's house to another's. When Sanchez was nine her father married a third time and took his family north to New York City. Gabbin writes: "In the small apartment she shared with her sister, her father, and his third wife, [Sanchez] felt hemmed in. Her tiny bedroom, whose window faced a redbrick wall, further mocked her sense of loss, now far from the greener open space of the South."

Sanchez reached adulthood in Harlem, which only thirty years before had been the cradle of the first literary renaissance in the United States to celebrate the works of black writers. Political science and poetry were the subjects of her studies at Hunter College and New York University during the 1950s. In the next decade Sanchez began to combine these interests into one activity, "the creat[ion] of social ideals," as she wrote for a section about her writings in *Black Women Writers (1950-1980): A Critical Evaluation,* edited by Mari Evans. For Sanchez, writing and performing poetry is a means of constructive political activism to the extent that it draws her people together to affirm pride in their heritage and build the confidence needed to accomplish political goals. Yet the terms of "black rhetoric," or words by themselves, are not enough, she says often in poems and interviews. Biographers cite her record of service as an educator, activist, and supporter of black institutions as proof of her commitment to this belief. Writing in the *Dictionary of Literary Biography,* Kalamu ya Salaam introduces Sanchez as "one of the few creative artists who have significantly influenced the course of black American literature and culture."

Before Sanchez became recognized as a part of the growing black arts movement of the 1960s, she worked in the Civil Rights movement in New York City. At that time, she, like many educated black people who enjoyed economic stability, held integrationist ideals. But after hearing Malcolm X say that blacks would never be fully accepted as part of mainstream America despite their professional or economic achievements, she chose to base her identity on her racial heritage. David Williams reports that the title of her first book, *Homecoming,* announces this return to a sense of self grounded in the realities of her urban neighborhood after having viewed it for a time from the outside through the lens of white cultural values. In the title poem, "Sanchez presents the act of returning home as a rejection of fantasy and an acceptance of involvement," notes Williams in *Black Women Writers (1950-1980).* For the same reasons, Sanchez did not seek a major publisher for the book. She preferred Dudley Randall's Broadside Press, a publisher dedicated to the works of black authors, that was to see many of her books into print.

Reacting to the poems in *Homecoming,* Johari Amini's review in *Black World* warns that they "hurt (but doesn't anything that cleans good) and [the] lines are blowgun dartsharp with a wisdom ancient as Kilimanjaro." Haki Madhubuti's essay in *Black Women Writers (1950-1980)* comments on this same effect, first remarking that Sanchez "is forever questioning Black people's commitment to struggle," saying again later that she is "forever disturbing the dust in our acculturated lives."

One aspect of her stand against acculturation is a poetic language that does not conform to the dictates of standard English. Madhubuti writes, "More than any other poet, [Sanchez] has been responsible for legitimizing the use of urban Black English in written form. . . . She has taken Black speech and put it in the context of world literature." Salaam elaborates, "In her work from the 1960s she restructured traditional English grammar to suit her interest in black speech patterns"—a technique most apparent, he feels, in *We a BaddDDD People.* In one poem cited by Madhubuti which he says is "concerned with Black-on-Black damage," Sanchez predicts that genuine "RE VO LU TION" might come about "if mothas programmed / sistuhs to / good feelings bout they blk / men / and i / mean if blk / fathas proved / they man / hood by fighten the enemy. . . ." These reviewers explain that by inserting extra letters in some words and extra space between lines, words, and syllables within a poem, Sanchez provides dramatic accents and other clues that indicate how the poem is to be said aloud.

Sanchez is also known as an innovator in the field of education. During the 1960s, she taught in San Francisco's Downtown Community School and became a crusader and curriculum developer for black studies programs in American colleges and universities. Materials on black literature and history had been absent from the schools she had attended, and she has worked to see that other young people are not similarly disenfranchised. Sanchez was, in fact, the first college professor ever to offer a full-fledged seminar on literature by black American women—she accomplished this while teaching at Amherst College in Massachusetts. Since then Sanchez has remained in the academic arena, striving to shape and encourage the next generation. She wrote two books for her children (*The Adventures of Fat Head, Small Head, and Square Head,* and *A Sound Investment and Other Stories*) for reasons she expressed to interviewer Claudia Tate in *Black Women Writers at Work:* "I do think that it's important to leave a legacy of my books for my children to read and understand; to leave a legacy of the history of black people who have moved toward revolution and freedom; to leave a legacy of not being afraid to tell the truth. . . . We must pass this on to our children, rather than a legacy of fear and victimization."

Because she takes action against oppression wherever she sees it, she has had to contend with not only college administrators, but also the FBI, and sometimes fellow members of political organizations. Reviewers note that while her early books speak more directly to widespread social oppression, the plays she wrote during the 1970s give more attention to the poet's interpersonal battles. For example, *Uh Huh; But How Do It Free Us?* portrays a black woman involved in the movement against white oppression who also resists subjection to her abusive husband. This kind of resistance, writes Salaam, was not welcomed by the leaders of the black power movement at that time.

Sanchez became a voice in what Stephen E. Henderson calls "a revolution within the Revolution" that grew as black women in general began to reassess their position as "the victims not only of racial injustice but of a sexual arrogance tantamount to dual colonialism—one from without, the other from within, the Black community," he writes in his introduction to Evans's book. This consciousness surfaces in works that treat politics in the context of personal relationships. Sanchez told Tate, "If we're not careful, the animosity between black men and women will destroy us." To avoid this fate, she believes, women must refuse to adopt the posture of victims and "move on" out of damaging relationships with men, since, in her words recorded in the interview, "If you cannot remove yourself from the oppression of a man, how in the hell are you going to remove yourself from the oppression of a country?"

Consequently, *A Blues Book for Blue Black Magical Women,* written during her membership in the Nation of Islam, examines the experience of being female in a society that "does not prepare young black women, or women period, to be women," as she told Tate. One section tells about her political involvements before and after she committed herself to the establishment of ethnic pride. In this book, as in her plays and stories, "Sanchez uses many of the particulars of her own life as illustrations of a general condition," writes Salaam. He offers that Sanchez "remains the fiery, poetic advocate of revolutionary change, but she also gives full voice to the individual human being struggling to survive sanely and to find joy and love in life." *Love Poems* contains many of the haiku Sanchez wrote during a particularly stressful period of her life in which she was beset by the problems of relocation, illness and poverty. The poems in these two books are no less political for their being more personal, according to reviewers. "The haiku in her hands is the ultimate in activist poetry, as abrupt and as final as a fist," comments Williams. In Salaam's opinion, "No other poet of the 1960s and 1970s managed so masterfully to chronicle both their public and personal development with poetry of such thoroughgoing honesty and relevant and revelatory depth."

Speaking in *Black Women Writers (1950-1980)* of the creative tension between protest and affirmation in her writing, Sanchez declared: "I still believe that the age for which we write is the age evolving out of the dregs of the twentieth century into a more humane age. Therefore I recognize that my writing must serve a dual purpose. It must be a clarion call to the values of change while it also speaks to the beauty of a nonexploitative age." Throughout her poems, Sanchez emphasizes the importance of strong family relationships, and exposes the dangers of substance abuse among people who hope to be the vital agents of change, relates Richard K. Barksdale in *Modern Black Poets: A Collection of Critical Essays.* Her message, as he notes, is that the desired revolution will not come about through "violence, anger, or rage"; rather, "political astuteness and moral power" among black people are needed to build the new world. Commenting on the content of the poems as it has broadened over the years, Madhubuti observes

that Sanchez "remains an intense and meticulous poet who has not compromised craft or skill for message."

Sanchez has continued to develop a more private, introspective womanist poetry in works such as *Under a Soprano Sky,* a book that contains moving love poems to those people who inspired her and those family members who nurtured her. Gabbin states that in Sanchez's poems, "one senses a power that is feminine, and consciously so. It comes from her understanding of her connections with the universe, her connections with her ancestors, and her strong matrilineal ties with a universe that has given to its kind not only the responsibility but, indeed, the power to bear the children and nurture seed. Her power comes from a faith in continuity; seeds grow into flowers and produce their own seeds. Sanchez clearly presents the life cycle and cherishes it."

Constant evolution has characterized Sanchez's career. With each successive book, she has driven her craft to a new level. In *Does Your House Have Lions?,* her most formally structured work, she carries on her characteristic musical style, enriched by what *Hungry Mind* reviewer Jabari Asim describes as "the swift changes, rhythm breaks, and solo flights associated with jazz." The book has a complex, jazzlike structure, and is divided into four sections, each focusing on a different voice that is based on a specific rhyme tonal pattern. The voices combined present the painful chronology of the life and death of Sanchez's brother: his alienation from the family, his struggle with HIV, and the family's reactions, including those of recent ancestors and distant African forebears. June Jordan of *Poetry Editor* says that Sanchez's blend of compassion and outrage "shines through this very personal account of a family's tragedy. The narrative takes on the elevated tones of Greek tragedy, or maybe the more solemn works of Wole Soyinka, and gives some sense of how overwhelming, painful, and powerful family bonds can be."

BIOGRAPHICAL/CRITICAL SOURCES:

BOOKS

Bankier, Joanna, and Deirdre Lashgari, editors, *Women Poets of the World,* Macmillan (New York City), 1983.

Bell, Bernard W., *The Folk Roots of Contemporary Afro-American Poetry,* Broadside Press, 1974.

Bigsby, C. W. E., editor, *The Second Black Renaissance: Essays in Black Literature,* Greenwood Press (Westport, CT), 1980.

Black Literature Criticism, Gale (Detroit), 1992, pp. 1647-70.

Contemporary Literary Criticism, Volume 5, Gale, 1976.

Dictionary of Literary Biography, Volume 41: *Afro-American Poets since 1955,* Gale, 1985.

Dictionary of Literary Biography Documentary Series, Volume 8, Gale, 1991, pp. 226-53.

Evans, Mari, editor, *Black Women Writers (1950-1980): A Critical Evaluation,* with introduction by Stephen E. Henderson, Doubleday-Anchor (New York City), 1984.

Gibson, Donald B., editor, *Modern Black Poets: A Collection of Critical Essays,* Prentice-Hall (New York City), 1973.

Hartigan, Karelisa V., editor, *The Many Forms of Drama,* University Press of America (Lanham, MD), 1985.

Inge, Tonette Bond, editor, *Southern Women Writers: The New Generation,* University of Alabama Press, 1990, pp. 180-203.

Joyce, Joyce A., *Ijala: Sonia Sanchez and the African Poetic Tradition,* Third World Press (Chicago, IL), 1996.

Poetry Criticism, Volume 9, Gale, 1994, pp. 202-46.

Randall, Dudley, *Broadside Memories: Poets I Have Known,* Broadside Press, 1975.

Redmond, Eugene B., *Drumvoices: The Mission of Afro-American Poetry, A Critical History,* Anchor, 1976.

Tate, Claudia, editor, *Black Women Writers At Work,* Continuum, 1983.

PERIODICALS

Belles Lettres, winter, 1989, p. 14.

Black Scholar, May, 1979; January, 1980; March, 1981.

Black World, August, 1970; April, 1971; September, 1971; April, 1972; March, 1975.

Booklist, February 15, 1997, p. 996.

Book World, January 27, 1974.

CLA Journal, September, 1971.

Ebony, March, 1974.

Emerge, May, 1995, p. 61.

Essence, July, 1979.

Library Journal, April 15, 1997, p. 85.

New Republic, February 22, 1975.

Newsweek, April 17, 1972.

Phylon, June, 1975.

Poetry, October, 1973.

Poetry Editor, 1996.

Poetry Review, April, 1985.

Publishers Weekly, October 1, 1973; July 15, 1974; February 27, 1995; February 24, 1997, p. 84.

Time, May 1, 1972.*

SAX, Robert
See JOHNSON, Robert

*   *   *

SAXTON, Robert
See JOHNSON, Robert

*   *   *

SCOTT, Daryl Michael 1958-

PERSONAL: Born April 14, 1958, in Chicago, IL; son of Melvin and Mary (Brown) Scott; married, wife's name Lelia, November 2, 1992; children: Brent Lattisaw, Joy Savannah. *Ethnicity:* "Black/African American." *Education:* Attended Marquette University, 1984, and Stanford University, 1994.

ADDRESSES: E-mail—dms35@columbia.edu.

CAREER: Columbia University, New York City, associate professor of history, 1993—. *Military service:* U.S. Army, 1977-81.

AWARDS, HONORS: James Rawley Prize, Organization of American Historians, 1998, for *Contempt and Pity.*

WRITINGS:

Contempt and Pity, University of North Carolina Press (Chapel Hill, NC), 1997.

WORK IN PROGRESS: After Cotton: Race, the State, and the Making of Sunbelt Georgia.

*   *   *

SENIOR, Olive (Marjorie) 1941-

PERSONAL: Born December 23, 1941, in Jamaica; immigrated to Canada, 1991. *Education:* Carleton University, B.S., 1967.

ADDRESSES: Agent—Nicole Aragi, Watkins/Loomis Agency, 133 East 35th St., Suite 1, New York, NY 10016.

CAREER: Daily Gleaner (newspaper), Jamaica, reporter and sub-editor; Jamaica Information Service, information officer, 1967-69; Jamaica Chamber of Commerce, public relations officer, 1969-71; *JCC Journal,* editor, 1969-71; Institute of Social and Economic Research, University of the West Indies, Jamaica, publications editor, 1972-77; *Social and Economic Studies,* editor, 1972-77; freelance writer and researcher, part-time teacher in communications, publishing consultant, and speech writer, Jamaica, 1977-82; Institute of Jamaica Publications, managing editor, 1982-89; *Jamaica Journal,* editor, 1982-89; freelance teacher, writer, lecturer, internationally, 1989-94; University of the West Indies, Cave Hill, Barbados, visiting lecturer/writer-in-residence, 1990; Caribbean Writers Summer Institute, University of Miami, Florida, director of fiction workshop, 1994, 1995; St. Lawrence University, Canton, NY, Dana Visiting Professor of creative writing, 1994-95.

AWARDS, HONORS: Commonwealth Writers' prize, 1967; Gold, Silver, and Bronze medals for poetry and fiction, Jamaica Festival Literary Competitions, 1968-70; winner in two categories, Longman International Year of the Child Short Story Competition, 1978; Institute of Jamaica Centenary medal for creative writing, 1979; UNESCO award for study in the Philippines, 1987; Jamaica Press Association award for editorial excellence, 1987; United States Information Service, International Visitor award, 1988; Institute of Jamaica, Silver Musgrave medal for literature, 1989; Hawthornden fellow, Scotland, 1990; International Writer-in-Residence, Arts Council of England, 1991; F.G. Bressani Literary prize for poetry, 1994, for *Gardening in the Tropics.*

WRITINGS:

POETRY

Talking of Trees, Calabash (Kingston, Jamaica), 1986.
Gardening in the Tropics, McClelland & Stewart (Toronto), 1994.

SHORT STORIES

Summer Lightning and Other Stories, Longman (London), 1986.
Arrival of the Snake-Woman, Longman, 1989.
(With others) *Quartet,* Longman, 1994.
Discerner of Hearts, McClelland & Stewart, 1995.

OTHER

The Message Is Change: A Perspective on the 1972 General Elections, Kingston Publishers (Kingston), 1972.
Pop Story Gi Mi (four booklets on Jamaican heritage for schools), Ministry of Education (Kingston), 1973.
A-Z of Jamaican Heritage, Heinemann and Gleaner Company Ltd. (Kingston), 1984.
Working Miracles: Women's Lives in the English-Speaking Caribbean, Indiana University Press (Bloomington), 1991.

SIDELIGHTS: Olive Senior is one of the most significant contemporary Caribbean writers. A journalist who has won acclaim for her poetry and short stories, she has also written several important nonfiction books about Caribbean culture, such as *A-Z of Jamaican Heritage.* Her fiction and poetry frequently focus on social and racial issues in Jamaica. Senior "has also played a vital role in putting women's issues on the literary agenda of her region," commented Denise deCaires Narain in the *Dictionary of Literary Biography.*

Senior was raised in a rural district of Jamaica, and in Narain's opinion, a sense of "rural isolation" pervades her work. At Montego Bay High School, she excelled at writing, and even began a magazine to showcase her own and her peers' work. After school and during vacations, she worked at Jamaica's most distinguished newspaper, the *Daily Gleaner.* In 1967, she earned a bachelor of journalism degree at Carleton University in Toronto.

Her first published book was the poetry collection *Talking of Trees.* In it, Senior presents "serious and noisy poems about the natural world while little ignoring the horrors of Jamaica's colonial history," wrote Susan M. Schultz in *Contemporary Women Poets.* The book's first section focuses on personal themes, while the second half is more political in nature. "Taken as a whole, the volume offers a series of lovingly detailed portraits of Jamaica, testifying to the toughness of the landscape and cityscape and to the resilience of its people," declared Narain.

Summer Lightning and Other Stories confirmed Senior's standing in the literary world by winning the 1987 Commonwealth Writer's Prize. Many reviewers praised *Summer Lightning* for its sensitive, many-layered evocation of Jamaican culture. "The total effect is of a particular world illuminated from every angle, and by the time we turn the final page, intimately known," Evelyn O'Callaghan wrote in *Journal of West Indian Literature*. "There is much the reader can learn from Olive Senior's short fiction—about the rich resources of Jamaican speech varieties, about superstitions and folk beliefs and the details of daily life in rural society. . . . *Summer Lightning* is a slim, well-crafted and beautifully packaged offering of treats to be savoured and enjoyed."

Senior's second story collection, *Arrival of the Snake-Woman and Other Stories,* is "more somber" than *Summer Lightning,* according to Narain. It "evokes a complex composite picture of rural and urban Jamaica. Although as in her first collection Senior often uses binary oppositions to structure her stories, she problematizes these to point to the inadequacy of the binary paradigm for interrogating the complex . . . reality of Caribbean culture." In *Discerner of Hearts,* another story collection, Senior provides "a juxtaposition of lively voices, rigid class lines and competing societies," noted Maggie Garb in the *New York Times Book Review*. "Spotlighting the multiple marks of class and racial difference on the tiny Caribbean island, Ms. Senior offers a luminous portrait of people struggling to find their own place in a changing world."

"Senior's short stories and poetry are the work of a creative talent of great sensitivity which expresses tremendous understanding of the human condition, particularly that of poor people both rural and urban," affirmed Velma Pollard in *Callaloo*. "The work is knit together by a common landscape and a recurring concern for humanity." Senior commented to Charles H. Rowell in an interview for *Callaloo*: "For me, writing, literature, is inextricably fused with magic. Though most of my writing is in a realistic vein, I am conscious at all times of other possibilities lurking just beyond consciousness, of the great ineffable mystery that lies at the core of each life, at the heart of every story."

BIOGRAPHICAL/CRITICAL SOURCES:

BOOKS

Bardolph, Jacqueline, editor, *Short Fiction in the New Literatures in English,* Facultie des Lettres & Sciences Humaines, 1989, pp. 89-94.
Chamberlin, J. E., *Come Back to Me My Language: Poetry and the West Indies,* University of Illinois Press, 1993.
Contemporary Women Poets, St. James, 1998.

Cudje, Selwyn, editor, *Caribbean Women Writers,* Calaloux, 1990.
Davies, Carole Boyce, and Elaine Savory Fido, *Out of the Kumbla: Caribbean Women and Literature,* Africa World Press, 1990.
Dictionary of Literary Biography, Volume 157: *Twentieth-Century Caribbean and Black African Writers, Third Series,* Gale, 1995.
Kinnery, Malcolm, and Michael Rose, *Critical Strategies,* Bedford Books, 1989.
Nasta, Susheila, editor, *Motherlands: Black Women's Writing from Africa, the Caribbean and South Asia,* Women's Press, 1991.
O'Callaghan, Evelyn, *Woman Version: Theoretical Approaches to West Indian Fiction,* Macmillan, 1993.

PERIODICALS

Ariel, A Review of International English Literature, January, 1993, pp. 13-33.
Callaloo, summer, 1988, pp. 480-90, 540-51; winter, 1993, pp. 34-43.
Commonwealth Essays and Studies, spring, 1991, pp. 42-48.
Everywoman, June, 1991, pp. 19-22.
Journal of Caribbean Studies, spring, 1988, pp. 143-62.
Journal of West Indian Literature, October, 1986, pp. 92-94.
Kunapipi, Number 2, 1986, pp. 11-20.
Ms., November-December, 1995, p. 88.
New Voices, September, 1986, pp. 31-34.
New York Times Book Review, April 17, 1988, p. 42; October 1, 1995, p. 32.
Third World Quarterly, April, 1988, pp. 995-98.
Times Literary Supplement, April 1, 1988, p. 364.
Women's Review of Books, November, 1987, p. 13.
World Literature Today, summer, 1990, p. 514.

*   *   *

SEPAMLA, (Sydney) Sipho 1932-

PERSONAL: Born 1932, in Johannesburg, South Africa; father a teacher and miner; mother a domestic worker; married Marilyn Rekgethile; children: one daughter and four sons. *Education:* Attended Kilnerton Training College and Pretoria Normal College.

ADDRESSES: Office—c/o Fuba Academy, P.O. Box 4202, Johannesburg 2000, South Africa.

CAREER: Writer. Teacher in secondary school; personnel officer for company in East Rand; editor, *New Classic* and *S'ketsh!* magazines. Director of the Fuba Academy.

AWARDS, HONORS: Co-recipient, Thomas Pringle award, English Academy of Southern Africa, for "The Odyssey" and "I Remember Sharpeville"; Order of Arts and Literature from the French government, 1985, for services to publishing; award from Woza Afrika Foundation, 1986, for *Third Generation*.

WRITINGS:

POETRY

Hurry Up to It!, Donker (Johannesburg), 1975.
The Blues Is You in Me, Donker, 1976.
The Soweto I Love, Three Continents Press (Washington, DC), 1977.
Children of the Earth, Donker, 1983.
Selected Poems, edited by Mbulelo Vizikhungo Mzamane, Donker, 1984.
From Gore to Soweto, Skotaville (Johannesburg), 1988.
Rainbow Journey, Vivlia Publishers (Florida Hills, South Africa), 1996.

NOVELS

The Root Is One, Rex Collings (London), 1979.
A Ride on the Whirlwind, Donker, 1981, Heinemann (London), 1984.
Third Generation, Skotaville, 1986.
Scattered Survival, Skotaville, 1988.

SIDELIGHTS: Sipho Sepamla is one of the most important modern poets in South Africa. He and poet Mongane Serote are credited with sparking the black poetry revival in South Africa during the 1970s. Together with Oswald Mtshali and Mafika Gwala, they became known as the "Soweto Poets"—not because they lived in Soweto, but in reference to the so-called Soweto uprising against apartheid that began in the city on June 16, 1976, and then spread across South Africa. *Dictionary of Literary Biography* contributor Stephen Gray commented that of all the Soweto group "Sepamla's career . . . has been the most sustained and productive and includes four novels as well as six slim volumes of poetry. . . . He is also the only one who stayed behind in South Africa, and his work has the added interest of bearing witness to daily events of the toughest years of apartheid rule."

Sepamla was pushed to learn English well by a blind uncle, who had his nephew purchase the English-language newspaper *The Star* and read the whole thing to him each day. Booker T. Washington's *Up from Slavery,* read during the sixth grade, made a lasting impression on Sepamla, as did numerous English writers, local preachers, and the movies. He did not, however, begin seriously writing until he was well into his thirties. He studied at Kilnerton Training College and applied to the University of the Witwatersrand, hoping to study medicine; but he did not gain entry. Instead, he attended Pretoria Normal College and became a schoolteacher.

During the 1950s, Sepamla moonlighted as a manager and talent scout for the area's lively jazz scene. But black art, and all kinds of black culture, were increasingly repressed throughout the 1950s. The 1960 Sharpesville Massacre, in which sixty-nine black protesters were killed by the police, while another 180 were wounded, marked the beginning of a "cultural blackout," in the words of Gray. During this time, Sepamla experimented with theater work and journalism, particularly journalism about show business. He was also beginning to work on poetry.

His first significant poems, "To Whom It May Concern" and "I Remember Sharpesville," took him some five years to write. "To Whom It May Concern" is probably still his most famous work—a worker's "ironic plea to his overlord," as Gray described it, a work of "cheeky and entertaining protest." Gray further noted that "in a sense Sepamla had revived a tradition by striking out for the future with a new gesture of wit on the one hand, defiance on the other." In his first collection, *Hurry Up to It!,* "he uses humor and irony as weapons of protest, which give the poetry an essentially private dimension despite the public nature of the subject of apartheid," observed Kirsten Holst Petersen in *Contemporary Poets. The Blues Is You in Me,* published the following year, is a more direct political protest.

Sepamla's short stories and novels are full of "gritty realism" and provide "substantial, detailed vignettes of township life, focusing on the domestic values and internal realities of typical communities," stated Gray. His first novel, *The Root is One,* chronicles the week preceding a "township removal," in which free blacks are forced to dismantle their village and leave for government housing. It is "a melancholy, sparse work," in Gray's view, one "without clear heroes or heroines. Juda, the main character, finally betrays his best friend, Spiwo, organizer of the antiremoval demonstrations, to the location superintendent. As the bulldozers move in unimpeded, Juda then hangs himself in the rubble."

Sepamla's second novel, *A Ride on the Whirlwind*, was banned by the South African Publications Control Board. It told of a liberation fighter's mission to assassinate a member of the apartheid establishment. Gray called this book "a happy combination of interesting and relevant material—the intriguing battle for power waged in Soweto—dealt with in a striking and accessible form." Although he used the formula for popular political thrillers, Sepamla "never allows the story to become incredible or maudlin," and he serves as an able "tour guide of the seething zones of combat of urban South Africa, panoramic in its scope and fascinating in its detail."

Petersen remarked that "Sepamla is a case of a peace-loving man, imbued with a generous love for humankind and natural inclination towards gradualism, persuasion rather than violence, antiracism, and belief in the values of education and art, who is pushed into bitterness, hatred, and an increasingly radical form of protest." By the time *The Soweto I Love* was written, Petersen declared, "the last illusions about peaceful solutions and the good intentions of the system have been broken, naked violence has erupted, and a new order of consciousness has been born, carrying the poet along with it."

BIOGRAPHICAL/CRITICAL SOURCES:

BOOKS

Alvarez-Pereyre, Jacques, *The Poetry of Commitment in South Africa,* Heinemann, 1984.
Barnett, Ursula A., *A Vision of Order: A Study of Black South African Literature in English (1914-1980),* University of Massachusetts Press, 1983.
Chapman, Michael, *South African English Poetry: A Modern Perspective,* Donker, 1984.
Chapman, Michael, editor, *Soweto Poetry,* McGraw-Hill (Johannesburg), 1982.
Contemporary Poets, St. James, 1996.
Davis, Geoffrey V., editor, *Crisis and Conflict: Essays on Southern African Literature,* Die Blaue Eule (Essen), 1980, pp. 133-42.
Dictionary of Literary Biography, Volume 157: *Twentieth-Century Caribbean and Black African Writers, Third Series,* Gale, 1995.

Granqvist, Raoul, and John Stotesbury, editors, *African Voices: Interviews with Thirteen African Writers,* Dangaroo Press (Mundelstrup, Denmark), 1989, pp. 59-61.
Harlow, Barbara, *Resistance Literature,* Methuen, 1987.
Herber, Avril, editor, *Conversations: Some People, Some Place, Some Time South Africa,* Bateleur (Johannesburg), 1979.
Ngara, Emmanuel, and Andrew Morrison, editors, *Literature, Language and the Nation,* Association of University Teachers of Literature and Language (Harare), 1989, pp. 64-82.
Petersen, Kirsten Holst, editor, *Criticism and Ideology: Second African Writers' Conference, Stockholm 1986,* Scandinavian Institute of African Studies (Uppsala), 1988, pp. 205-16.
Watts, Jane, *Black Writers from South Africa: Towards a Discourse of Liberation,* Macmillan (London), 1989.
Welch, Robert, and Suheil Badi Bushrui, editors, *Literature and the Art of Creation,* Barnes & Noble (Totowa, NJ), 1988, pp. 124-39.
Williams, S., and others, *A Bibliography on Sidney Sipho Sepamla (1932-),* Subject Reference Department, University of South African Sanlam Library (Pretoria), 1980.

PERIODICALS

ADA, number 4, 1987, pp. 18-19.
Crux, volume 22, number 3, 1988, pp. 5-16.
Deutsche Welle Transkription, November 22, 1980, pp. 1-10; December 29, 1980, pp. 1-10; January 10, 1981, p. 11.
Drum, March 8, 1973, pp. 52-53.
Index on Censorship, January-February, 1978, pp. 3-8; volume 11, number 4, 1982, pp. 15-16; volume 12, number 3, 1983, p. 12.
Geneve-Afrique, volume 18, number 2, 1980, pp. 79-93.
Liberator, volume 6, number 3, 1985, pp. 15-24.
New Classic, volume 3, 1976, pp. 48-63.
Playboy, May, 1972, pp. 166-69.
Presence Africaine, number 140, 1986, pp. 10-24.
Pretoria News, March 3, 1987, p. 8.
Rand Daily Mail, November 23, 1979, p. 12.
Research in African Literatures, volume 19, number 1, 1988, pp. 65-88.
South, May, 1985, p. 97.
Staffrider, volume 7, numbers 3-4, 1988, pp. 303-309.
Wasafiri, spring, 1986, pp. 11-14.

SEROTE, Mongane Wally 1944-

PERSONAL: Born May 8, 1944, in Sophiatown, South Africa; married Pethu Serote. *Education:* Columbia University, M.F.A., 1979.

ADDRESSES: Home—28 Penton St., P.O. Box 38, London N1 9PR, England. *Agent*—Jane Gregory Agency, Riverside Studios, Crisp Rd., Hammersmith, London W6 9RL, England.

CAREER: Poet, novelist, short story writer, and playwright. African National Congress, London, England, cultural attache in Department of Arts and Culture, 1986—. Copywriter for advertising agency, Johannesburg, South Africa; Medu Arts Ensemble, Gaborone, Botswana, staff member.

AWARDS, HONORS: Ingrid Jonker prize, 1973; Fulbright scholarship.

WRITINGS:

POETRY

Yakhal'inkomo, Renoster (Johannesburg), 1972.
No Baby Must Weep, Donker (Johannesburg), 1975.
Tsetlo, Donker, 1975.
Behold Mama, Flowers, Donker, 1978.
The Night Keeps Winking, Medu Art Ensemble (Gaborone, Botswana), 1982.
Selected Poems, edited by Mbulelo Vizikhungo Mzamane, Donker, 1982.
A Tough Tale, Kliptown Books (London), 1987.
Third World Express, D. Philip (Cape Town), 1992.
Come and Hope with Me, D. Philip, 1994.

Contributor of poetry to periodicals, including *Classic* and *Bolt.*

OTHER

To Every Birth Its Blood (novel), Raven Press (Johannesburg), 1981, Thunder's Mouth Press (New York), 1989.
On the Horizon, foreword by Raymond Suttner, Congress of South African Writers (Fordsburg, South Africa), 1990.

Author of preface to *Mapantsula: The Book,* Congress of South African Writers, 1991, and of afterword to *Culture and Empowerment: Debates, Workshops, Art and Photography from the Zabalaza Festival,* COSAW Pub. (Johannesburg), 1993.

SIDELIGHTS: Mongane Wally Serote is best known as a poet, and he is considered one of the foremost black South African poets of his generation. His poetry is strongly political in its subject and in its form; Serote's reliance on the repetitive structure of song makes his poetry ideal for recitation, an important factor in South Africa where it is estimated that half the adult black population is illiterate. Serote writes in English, a language associated with his country's oppressors but distinguished from the Afrikaans of the former South African regime. His novel *To Every Birth Its Blood* extends the themes of his poetry in its depiction of the variety of responses to political and cultural oppression.

Serote grew up in Alexandra, a poor, black township in Johannesburg. His hometown has remained "a distinctive signature for him," wrote David Attwell in the *Dictionary of Literary Biography,* "a specific urban geography transformed by experience into an ambivalent symbol of both mothering and oppression." Serote's education was disrupted by the passage of the segregationist Bantu Education Act, but he did attend college. In 1969, he was detained under the Terrorism Act and held for nine months, though no charges were ever brought against him. In 1974, he left South Africa to study at Columbia University in New York City. When he returned to Africa in 1979, he chose to live in Botswana rather than return to his segregated homeland. In February, 1990, he finally returned to South Africa. Serote, along with Sipho Sepamla, Oswald Mbuyiseni Mtshali, and Mafika Gwala, is identified as one of the "Soweto Poets," whose verses reflect a new spirit of expression and rebellion bursting forth during the 1970s after decades of cultural repression.

Serote's poetry documents the struggles, hopes, and despair of people suffering under apartheid. His first two collections, *Yakhal'inkomo* and *Tsetlo,* contain mostly lyric poems and dramatic monologues. "The early poems, written in free verse, present a reflective persona who witnesses and evaluates his world in a language that is sharply metaphoric and whose tones are sometimes bitter, sometimes ironic, but invariably passionate and authoritative," said Attwell.

His poems gain much of their emotional intensity through striking imagery, evocative metaphors, and repetition. Reviewers have noted that what has sometimes been taken for stylistic innovation in Serote's poetry is often a hybrid of African oral traditions, the language of the urban black townships of South Africa, and Western poetic conventions such as the pan-egyric and the elegy. It is this aspect of Serote's skill as a poet that allows him to address his white oppressors as well as his own community and to write self-reflexive poems concerning the role of the poet in South African society as a cultural freedom fighter.

Serote has especially been commended for his sensitivity to the complex role of women in a traditionally male-dominated society. Children, too, play a pivotal role in Serote's poetry, being the most innocent of the victims of apartheid and the focal point of hope for change for the black people of South Africa. As Serote's poetry has evolved, it has moved away from the despair of his earlier works toward hope for the future.

In the novel *To Every Birth Its Blood,* Serote surveys several generations of black South Africans who offer responses to life under apartheid. The first half of the novel centers on Tsietsi Molope, a black journalist who is imprisoned, beaten, and tortured by police, then released back to his life in Alexandra. William Finnegan, writing in the *New York Times Book Review,* described Molope as "alienated, humane, inept and chronically depressed; he seeks his solace in booze and jazz." The interior monologue that dominates this half of the work documents the chaotic, despairing nature of Molope's humiliation and defeat, which is exacerbated by his arbitrary arrest and equally unexplained release.

As the novel progresses, Serote introduces other characters who become radicalized as the apartheid government increases its pressures on the black population of the country: Molope's parents are slowly politicized by their visits to his brother, a political prisoner; Molope's nephew belongs to the generation whose uprising in 1976 ushers in a new era in black South African response to apartheid. The second half of the novel focuses on these young revolutionaries, and Serote portrays their violent protests and the equally violent response by the authorities with intense dramatic effect. L. Tremaine, reviewing *To Every Birth Its Blood* for *Choice,* commented: "No other South African novelist articulates the interactions between the collective and the personal dramas of oppression and revolution more searchingly or with a more nearly equal mix of commitment and compassion."

In more recent work, Serote has addressed the still-troubled, confusing social conditions that followed the ban of apartheid. Discussing *Third World Express,* Attwell commented: "Characteristically Serote is sensitive to the moment and deals with the situation in terms of a dialectic of frustration and hope. But Serote's poem also embodies a larger, utopian vision that extends beyond the present to a time when peace and democracy will be shared by all."

Serote wrote in *Southern African Review of Books:* "Writing, which is a segment of culture which is life itself, cannot be divorced from economics or politics. It is how societies are organized that says how they will eradicate ignorance. It is for all these issues . . . that I can say that the first commitment of any writer is to politics; the second, which makes the writer, is in writing."

BIOGRAPHICAL/CRITICAL SOURCES:

BOOKS

Alvarez-Pereyre, Jacques, *The Poetry of Commitment in South Africa,* Heinemann (London), 1984.

Barnett, Ursula, *A Vision of Order: A Study of Black South African Literature in English (1914-1980),* University of Massachusetts Press, 1983.

Bramsback, Birgit, and Martin Croghan, *Anglo-Irish and Irish Literature: Aspects of Language and Culture,* Uppsala University, 1988, pp. 219-27.

Campscreur, Willem, and Joost Divendal, editors, *Culture in Another South Africa,* Olive Branch, 1989.

Chapman, Michael, *South African English Poetry: A Modern Perspective,* Donker, 1984.

Chapman, Michael, editor, *Soweto Poetry,* McGraw-Hill, 1982.

Contemporary Poets, St. James Press, 1996.

Daymond, M. J., and others, editors, *Momentum: On Recent South African Writing,* University of Natal Press, 1984, pp. 171-81.

Dictionary of Literary Biography, Volume 125: *Twentieth-Century Caribbean and Black African Writers, Second Series,* Gale, 1993.

Gordimer, Nadine, *The Black Interpreters,* Spro-Cas/Ravan, 1973.

Wilhelm, P., and J. Polley, editors, *Poetry South Africa,* Donker, 1976, pp. 35-46.

Wilkinson, Jane, *Orpheus in Africa: Fragmentation and Renewal in the Work of Four African Writers,* Bulzoni Editore, 1990.

Williams, S., and others, compilers, *A Bibliography on Mongane Wally Serote (1944-),* University of South Africa Sanlam Library, 1980.

PERIODICALS

Bloody Horse, volume 4, 1981, pp. 73-79; volume 5, 1981, pp. 38-45.
Choice, March, 1990, p. 1155.
Contrast, volume 11, number 4, 1977, pp. 51-62.
English Academy Review, volume 3, 1985, pp. 25-49, 65-79, 81-88; January, 1987, pp. 67-76.
English in Africa, number 1, 1977, pp. 47-54; number 1, 1979, pp. 72-81; number 1, 1982, pp. 45-54.
Geneve-Afrique, volume 18, 1980, pp. 79-83.
Index on Censorship, number 4, 1973, pp. 85-88.
Literary Criterion, volume 12, number 4, 1977, pp. 33-52.
Matatu, numbers 3-4, 1988, pp. 32-43.
New Classic, volume 3, 1976, pp. 48-63.
New Nation, volume 3, number 7, 1970, pp. 10-11, 13, 20-21.
New York Times Book Review, May 7, 1989, p. 38.
Playboy, May, 1972, pp. 166-69.
Rand Daily Mail, July 29, 1982.
Research in African Literatures, volume 16, 1985, pp. 5-19; volume 19, 1988, pp. 65-88.
Saiwa, A Journal of Communication, February, 1984, pp. 56-62.
Southern African Review of Books, February-May, 1990.
Span, volume 24, 1987, pp. 81-95.
Staffrider, volume 4, number 1, 1981, pp. 30-32.
Theoria, volume 45, 1975, pp. 1-11.
UNISA English Studies, number 1, 1988, pp. 26-32.

*   *   *

SHELBY, Uncle
  See SILVERSTEIN, Shel(by)

*   *   *

SILVERSTEIN, Shel(by) 1932-1999
  (Uncle Shelby)

PERSONAL: Born in 1932, in Chicago, IL; died of a heart attack, May 8, 1999, in Key West, FL; divorced; children: Matthew.

ADDRESSES: Office—c/o Grapefruit Productions, 106 Montague St., Brooklyn, NY 11201.

CAREER: Cartoonist, composer, lyricist, folksinger, writer, and director. *Playboy,* Chicago, IL, writer and cartoonist, 1956-99. Appeared in film, *Who Is Harry Kellerman and Why Is He Saying Those Terrible Things about Me?,* 1971. *Military service:* Served with U.S. forces in Japan and Korea during 1950s; cartoonist for Pacific *Stars and Stripes.*

AWARDS, HONORS: New York Times Outstanding Book Award, 1974, Michigan Young Readers'Award, 1981, and George G. Stone Award, 1984, all for *Where the Sidewalk Ends: The Poems & Drawings of Shel Silverstein; School Library Journal* Best Books Award, 1981, Buckeye Award, 1983 and 1985, George G. Stone Award, 1984, and William Allen White Award, 1984, all for *A Light In the Attic;* International Reading Association's Children's Choice Award, 1982, for *The Missing Piece Meets the Big O.*

WRITINGS:

SELF-ILLUSTRATED

Now Here's My Plan: A Book of Futilities, foreword by Jean Shepherd, Simon & Schuster (New York City), 1960.
Uncle Shelby's ABZ Book: A Primer for Tender Young Minds (humor), Simon & Schuster, 1961.
Playboy's Teevee Jeebies (drawings), Playboy Press (Chicago), 1963.
Uncle Shelby's Story of Lafcadio, the Lion Who Shot Back (juvenile), Harper (New York City), 1963.
The Giving Tree (juvenile), Harper, 1964.
Uncle Shelby's Giraffe and a Half (verse; juvenile), Harper, 1964, published in England as *A Giraffe and a Half,* J. Cape (London), 1988.
Uncle Shelby's Zoo: Don't Bump the Glump! (verse; juvenile), Simon & Schuster, 1964.
(Under pseudonym Uncle Shelby) *Who Wants a Cheap Rhinoceros!* Macmillan (New York City), 1964.
More Playboy's Teevee Jeebies: Do-It-Yourself Dialog for the Late Late Show (drawings), Playboy Press, 1965.
Where the Sidewalk Ends: The Poems & Drawings of Shel Silverstein (poems), Harper, 1974.
The Missing Piece (juvenile), Harper, 1976.
Different Dances (drawings), Harper, 1979.
A Light in the Attic (poems), Harper, 1981.
The Missing Piece Meets the Big O (juvenile), Harper, 1981.
(With Cherry Potts) *Poetry Galore and More,* Upstart Library, 1993.
Falling Up: Poems and Drawings, HarperCollins, 1996.

PLAYS

The Lady or the Tiger Show (one-act; from the short story by Frank Stockton), first produced in New York City at Ensemble Studio Theatre, May, 1981.

(And director) *Gorilla,* first produced in Chicago, 1983.

Wild Life (contains *I'm Good to My Doggies, Nonstop, Chicken Suit Optional,* and *The Lady or the Tiger Show*), first produced in New York City, 1983.

Remember Crazy Zelda? first produced in New York City, 1984.

The Crate, first produced in New York City, 1985.

The Happy Hour, first produced in New York City, 1985.

One Tennis Shoe, first produced in New York City, 1985.

Little Feet, first produced in New York City, 1986.

Wash and Dry, first produced in New York City, 1986.

The Devil and Billy Markham (drama; produced in New York City at Lincoln Center, December, 1989, with David Mamet's *Bobby Gould in Hell* under the collective title *Oh, Hell*) published in *Oh, Hell!: Two One-Act Plays,* Samuel French (New York City), 1991.

(Contributor) Billy Aronson, editor, *The Best American Short Plays 1992-1993: The Theatre Annual since 1937,* Applause (Diamond Bar, CA), 1993.

OTHER

(Contributor) Myra Cohn Livingston, editor, *I Like You, If You Like Me: Poems of Friendship,* Margaret McElderry Books (New York City), 1987.

(With David Mamet) *Things Change* (screenplay), Grove Press (New York City), 1988.

Also composer and lyricist of songs, including "A Boy Named Sue," "One's on the Way," "The Unicorn," "Boa Constrictor," "So Good to So Bad," "The Great Conch Train Robbery," and "Yes, Mr. Rogers." Albums of Silverstein's songs recorded by others include *Freakin' at the Freakers Ball,* Columbia, 1972; *Sloppy Seconds,* Columbia, 1972; *Dr. Hook,* Columbia, 1972; and *Bobby Bare Sings Lullabys, Legends, and Lies: The Songs of Shel Silverstein,* RCA Victor, 1973. Albums of original motion picture scores include *Ned Kelly,* United Artists, 1970, and *Who Is Harry Kellerman and Why Is He Saying Those Terrible Things about Me?* Columbia, 1971. Other recordings include *Drain My Brain,* Cadet; *Dirty*

Feet, Hollis Music, 1968; *Shel Silverstein: Songs and Stories,* Casablanca, 1978; *The Great Conch Train Robbery,* 1980; and *Where the Sidewalk Ends,* Columbia, 1984. *The Giving Tree* has been translated into French.

SIDELIGHTS: Shel Silverstein was best known for his collections of children's poetry *Where the Sidewalk Ends: The Poems & Drawings of Shel Silverstein* and *A Light in the Attic,* both of which enjoyed extended stays on the *New York Times* Bestseller List. Silverstein was also the author of the children's classic *The Giving Tree.* In addition to his writings for children, Silverstein served as a longtime *Playboy* cartoonist, wrote several plays for adults, and penned and recorded such country and novelty songs as Johnny Cash's "A Boy Named Sue."

Silverstein's talents were well-developed when he joined the U.S. armed forces in the 1950s. Stationed in Japan and Korea, he worked as a cartoonist for the Pacific edition of the military newspaper *Stars and Stripes.* After leaving the military, Silverstein became a cartoonist for *Playboy* in 1956, and his work for that magazine resulted in such collections as *Playboy's Teevee Jeebies* and *More Playboy's Teevee Jeebies: Do-It-Yourself Dialog for the Late Late Show.*

Silverstein's career as a children's author began with the 1963 publication of *Uncle Shelby's Story of Lafcadio, the Lion Who Shot Back.* In a *Publishers Weekly* interview, he confided to Jean F. Mercier: "I never planned to write or draw for kids. It was Tomi Ungerer, a friend of mine, who insisted . . . practically dragged me, kicking and screaming, into (editor) Ursula Nordstrom's office. And she convinced me that Tomi was right, I could do children's books." *Lafcadio* concerns a lion who obtains a hunter's gun and practices until he becomes a good enough marksman to join a circus. A *Publishers Weekly* reviewer called the book "a wild, free-wheeling, slangy tale that most children and many parents will enjoy immensely."

Although *Lafcadio* and *Uncle Shelby's Giraffe and a Half* met with moderate success, it was not until *The Giving Tree* that Silverstein first achieved widespread fame as a children's writer. The story of a tree that sacrifices its shade, fruit, branches, and finally its trunk to a little boy in order to make him happy, *The Giving Tree* had slow sales initially, but its audience steadily grew. As Richard R. Lingeman reported in the *New York Times Book Review,* "Many readers saw a religious symbolism in the altruistic tree; ministers preached sermons on *The Giving Tree;* it was discussed in Sunday schools." Despite its popularity as a moral or fable, the book was on occasion attacked by feminist critics for what they perceived as its inherent sexism; Barbara A. Schram noted in *Interracial Books for Children:* "By choosing the female pronoun for the all-giving tree and the male pronoun for the all-taking boy, it is clear that the author did indeed have a prototypical master/slave relationship in mind . . . How frightening that little boys and girls who read *The Giving Tree* will encounter this glorification of female selflessness and male selfishness."

In 1974 Silverstein published the collection of poems titled *Where the Sidewalk Ends.* Earning Silverstein favorable comparisons to Dr. Seuss and Edward Lear, *Where the Sidewalk Ends* contained such humorous pieces as "Sarah Cynthia Sylvia Stout / Would Not Take the Garbage Out," "Dreadful," and "Band-Aids." The collection and its 1981 successor, *A Light in the Attic,* continue to be popular with both children and adults; *Publishers Weekly* called the latter book "a big, fat treasure for Silverstein devotees, with trenchant verses expressing high-flown, exhilarating nonsense as well as thoughts unexpectedly sober and even sad."

Silverstein's 1976 *The Missing Piece,* like *The Giving Tree,* has been subject to varying interpretations. The volume chronicles the adventures of a circle who, lacking a piece of itself, goes along singing and searching for its missing part. But after the circle finds the wedge, he decides he was happier on the search—without the missing wedge—than he is with it. As Anne Roiphe explained in the *New York Times Book Review, The Missing Piece* can be read in the same way as "the fellow at the singles bar explaining why life is better if you don't commit yourself to anyone for too long—the line goes that too much to-getherness turns people into bores—that creativity is preserved by freedom to explore from one relationship to another. . . . This fable can also be interpreted to mean that no one should try to find all the answers, no one should hope to fill all the holes in themselves, achieve total transcendental harmony or psychic order because a person without a search, loose ends, internal conflicts and external goals becomes too smooth to enjoy or know what's going on. Too much satisfaction blocks exchange with the outside." Silverstein published a sequel, *The Missing Piece Meets the Big O,* in 1981. This work is told from the missing piece's perspective, and as in the original, the book's protagonist discovers the value of self-sufficiency.

Beginning in 1981, Silverstein concentrated on writing plays for adults. One of his best known, *The Lady or the Tiger Show,* has been performed on its own and with other one-act works collectively entitled *Wild Life.* Updating a short story by American novelist and fiction writer Frank Stockton, *The Lady or the Tiger Show* concerns a game show producer willing to go to extreme lengths to achieve high ratings. Placed in a life-or-death situation, the contestant of the show is forced to choose between two doors; behind one door lies a ferocious tiger, while the girl of his dreams is concealed behind the other. The play was characterized in *Variety* as "a hilarious harpooning of media hype and show biz amorality."

With *Falling Up,* Silverstein returned to poetry for children (and adults) after a fifteen-year absence. This collection of 140 poems with drawings ranges in subject matter "from tattoos to sun hats to God to—no kidding—a garden of noses," wrote Susan Stark in the *Detroit News. Publishers Weekly* called the poems "vintage Silverstein," a work "cheeky and clever and often darkly subversive," focusing on the unexpected. Judy Zuckerman reported in the *New York Times Book Review,* "Mr. Silverstein's expressive line drawings are perfectly suited to his texts, extending the humor, and sometimes the strangeness of his ideas."

Silverstein also collaborated with American playwright, scriptwriter, director, and novelist David Mamet on several projects. The two cowrote the screenplay for Mamet's 1988 film *Things Change,* which starred Joe Mantegna and Don Ameche. Silverstein's play *The Devil and Billy Markham* and Mamet's *Bobby Gould in Hell* have also been published and produced together under the collective title *Oh, Hell.* Performed as a monologue, *The Devil and Billy Markham* relates a series of bets made between Satan and a Nashville songwriter and singer. Although the work received mixed reviews, William A. Henry III noted in *Time* that "Silverstein's script, told in verse with occasional bursts of music, is rowdy and rousing and raunchily uproarious, especially in a song about a gala party where saints and sinners mingle."

Silverstein died of a heart attack in May, 1999. According to an obituary in *Publishers Weekly,* Robert Warren, the editorial director of HarperCollins Children's Books and Silverstein's editor, commented that "He had a genius that transcended age and gender, and his work probably touched the lives of more people than any writer in the second half of the 20th century." An obituary in the *Media Industry Newsletter* related that *Playboy* founder Hugh Hefner, the man credited with giving Silverstein his break, called him "a Renaissance man. He was a giant as a talent, a giant as a human being."

BIOGRAPHICAL/CRITICAL SOURCES:

BOOKS

Children's Literature Review, volume 5, Gale (Detroit), 1983, pp. 208-13.
Something about the Author, Gale, volume 27, 1982, volume 33, 1983, Volume 92, 1997.
Twentieth-Century Children's Writers, 3rd edition, St. James Press (Detroit), 1989, pp. 886-87.

PERIODICALS

Back Stage, May 21, 1999, p. 58.
Billboard, May 22, 1999, p. 93.
Book Week, March 21, 1965.
Detroit News, November 4, 1979; May 1, 1996.
Entertainment Weekly, May 21, 1999, p. 14.
Hollywood Reporter, May 12, 1999, p. 13.
Independent, May 25, 1999, p. S7.
Interracial Books for Children, volume 5, number 5, 1974.
Maclean's, May 24, 1999, p. 9.
Media Industry Newsletter, May 17, 1999.
Nation, January 29, 1990, pp. 141-44.
New Republic, January 29, 1990, pp. 27-28.
Newsweek, December 7, 1981.
New York, May 30, 1983, p. 75; December 18, 1989, pp. 105-7.
New Yorker, November 14, 1988, p. 89; December 25, 1989, p. 77.
New York Times, May 29, 1981; October 11, 1981.
New York Times Book Review, September 24, 1961; September 9, 1973; November 3, 1974; May 2, 1976; April 30, 1978; November 25, 1979; November 8, 1981; March 9, 1986, pp. 36-37; May 19, 1996, p. 29.
People Weekly, August 18, 1980; May 24, 1999, p. 64.
Publishers Weekly, October 28, 1963; February 24, 1975; September 18, 1981; April 29, 1996; May 17, 1999, p. 32.
Rolling Stone, June 24, 1999, p. 26.
Saturday Review, November 30, 1974; May 15, 1976.
Time, December 18, 1989, p. 78; May 24, 1999, p. 35.
United Press International, May 11, 1999.
Variety, May 11, 1983, p. 112; December 13, 1989, p. 89.

Washington Post Book World, April 12, 1981.
Wilson Library Bulletin, November, 1987, p. 65.*

*   *   *

SINGLETON, John   1968-

PERSONAL: Born January 6, 1968, in Los Angeles, CA; son of Danny Singleton (a mortgage broker) and Sheila Ward (a sales executive). *Education:* University of Southern California, B.A., 1990.

ADDRESSES: Home—Baldwin Hills, CA. *Office*—New Deal Productions, 10202 West Washington Blvd., Metro Bldg., Room 203, Culver City, CA 90232-3119. *Agent*—Bradford W. Smith, Creative Artists Agency, 9830 Wilshire Blvd., Beverly Hills, CA 90212-1804.

CAREER: Screenwriter and film director. Director of *The Champ,* Home Box Office (HBO), and music video *Remember the Time.*

MEMBER: Academy of Motion Picture Arts and Sciences.

AWARDS, HONORS: Three awards from University of Southern California School of Cinema-Television, including Jack Nicholson Award (twice); Academy Award ("Oscar") nominations for best director and best original screenplay, Academy of Motion Picture Arts and Sciences, 1991, both for *Boyz N the Hood.*

WRITINGS:

SCREENPLAYS; AND DIRECTOR

Boyz N the Hood, Columbia, 1991.
(And coproducer) *Poetic Justice,* Columbia, 1993.
(And producer) *Higher Learning,* Columbia, 1994.

OTHER

(With Veronica Chambers) *Poetic Justice: Film-Making South Central Style,* Delta, 1993.

SIDELIGHTS: John Singleton was nominated for an Academy Award for his role as writer and director of the 1991 film *Boyz N the Hood,* which chronicles the struggles of three black friends growing up in South Central, a neighborhood of Los Angeles. While Singleton addresses issues and themes of specific relevance to blacks in *Boys N the Hood,* the motion picture proved commercially successful with diverse audiences. With this venture, Singleton became one of a number of young black filmmakers who redefined mainstream cinema beginning in the mid-1980s. Shunning the traditional Hollywood formula which resolves the conflict happily, artists such as Spike Lee, Matty Rich, and Singleton strive to tell authentic black urban stories in which the problems defy simple solutions. Intrigued by this new cinematic trend, critics as well as audiences have responded favorably to Singleton's work. "No first film in the new wave of films by and about black Americans states the case for the movement's longevity more forcefully than *Boyz N the Hood,*" declared *Detroit News* film critic Susan Stark.

In *Boyz N the Hood,* the main characters—Tre Styles and his friends Ricky and Doughboy—attempt to live through adolescence despite the constant threat of violence and the temptation to profit from the illegal drug business. Opening with the statistic that one out of every twenty-two black males will be murdered—most by other black males—the film emphasizes the difficulty of survival in the "hood" (slang for neighborhood). Singleton believes that the proliferation of black-on-black crime is partially due to the absence of adult male role models in black communities. The author argues in *Boyz* that the chain of violence can only be halted by concerned fathers who set an example for their sons.

Singleton advocates this solution because he is evidence of its success. Although he lived with his mother, Singleton considers the weekends he spent with his father paramount to his development and success as a filmmaker. He believes that having a dream—and a father to encourage it—kept him out of trouble. "A young boy needs a man to show him how to be a man," Singleton stated in *Elle.* "Black men need to be responsible fathers for their sons." The author notes that it was his father who took him to see movies—such as George Lucas's *Star Wars*—leaving him determined at the age of nine to become a filmmaker. In high school Singleton discovered that the film business revolved around screenplays and began working on his writing skills. He enrolled in film school at the University of Southern California, and by the time he graduated he had made a few eight-millimeter films, won several writing awards, and signed a contract with the influential talent company, Creative Artists Agency. Soon after graduation, his screenplay for *Boyz N the Hood* won him a three-year contract with Columbia Pictures.

Singleton accepted the contract, but, fearing that another director would distort his point of view, insisted that he direct *Boyz N the Hood* himself. "It's my story, I lived it," he explained in *New York Times Magazine.* "What sense would it have made to have some white boy impose his interpretation on my experience?" In *Elle,* he added, "Having a black man directing raw street-life narratives gives them a certain credibility." It was important to Singleton that every aspect of the production be marked by authenticity. After securing the position of director, Singleton hired a nearly all-black crew and solicited three black Los Angeles gang members to help him fine-tune the dialogue and select the wardrobe. Singleton wanted to deliver his message in language that the average black audience member could understand, because, as he expressed in *Interview,* "I made my film for the regular brother off the street." *Time* contributor Richard Corliss noted the success of this venture, calling the film "a harrowing document true to the director's south-central Los Angeles milieu; he paints it black."

Boyz N the Hood portrays "a tragic way of life," according to *New York* contributor David Denby. The hood is an inner-city world in which constant gunshots, sirens, and police helicopter searchlights serve as reminders that danger is never far away. Tre Styles adopts this environment as his new home when, as a troubled ten-year-old, he is sent by his divorced mother to live with his father, Furious. As Tre grows up, Furious teaches him responsibility and dignity, making him strong enough to resist the lure of the street and stay in school. Tre counts as his friends athletic, college-bound Ricky and street-smart Doughboy, half-brothers who live with their mother. Transferring her feelings about their respective fathers on her sons, the mother favors Ricky but has little hope for Doughboy. Tre's friendships draw him into a violent confrontation from which he narrowly escapes. At film's end, Tre, guided by his father's example, manages to survive and go to college, while Ricky and Doughboy—who lack a male role model—are killed.

Though Singleton acted as both writer and director for *Boyz N the Hood,* he considers himself primarily a screenwriter. As he related in *New York Times Magazine,* "In this business, you get hired for your vision, and your vision begins with your script. I'm a writer first, and I direct in order to protect my vision." Although *Detroit Free Press* contributor Kathy Huffhines appreciated the fact that "he puts his anger into words, not just camera angles," Singleton considers the visual aspect of his screenplay more important than the spoken element. He remarked in *New York Times Magazine,* "I strive toward saying things visually—that verbal stuff is for T.V." Critics responded positively to Singleton's first writing and directing effort, which they found authentic and effective. *New York Times* contributor Janet Maslin commented, "Singleton's terrifically confident first feature places [him] on a footing with Spike Lee as a chronicler of the frustration faced by young black men growing up in urban settings." Responding to its style, subject matter, and direction, Stark called *Boyz N the Hood* "a smart, smooth, astonishingly authoritative debut piece."

Yet several reviewers, noting the many speeches which Furious Styles imparts to Tre, found the script verbose. Referring to "the ideological burden" of Singleton's script, Stark maintained that the film "is over-stuffed with ideas." *People* contributor Ralph Novak, calling the film "pedantic," expressed, "Every issue is accompanied by a preachy piece of dialogue." Stark, however, believed Singleton was aware of this problem. She asserted that by adding a line in which Furious is compared to a preacher, Singleton "both anticipates and diffuses negative reaction" to Furious's speeches. Some critics also expressed concern about the attitudes toward women in Singleton's film. "In *Boyz N the Hood,*" stated Corliss, "most of the women are shown as doped-up, career-obsessed or irrelevant to the man's work of raising a son in an American war zone." Huffhines observed that Singleton's "diamond-hard belief in the importance of fatherhood shortchanges motherhood," noting, "he's clearly down on Tre's mother for being cooly ambitious." She added, however, that Singleton's obvious respect for his main characters outweighs the problems with the minor characters, and named Singleton "the most impressive" of the year's young black filmmakers.

Singleton followed *Boyz N the Hood* with *Poetic Justice* in 1993. A love story, the movie featured singer Janet Jackson and rap artist Tupac Shakur. In 1994 Singleton offered *Higher Learning,* a film set on a fictional college campus and dealing with issues of race, violence, and sex. The movie's characters include Malik Williams, a black track star who is convinced the university only wants him for his athletic abilities; Deja, Malik's confident and ambitious girlfriend; Kristen, a white freshman coping with date rape; Remy, a white student from Idaho who joins a Neo-Nazi group; and Professor Phipps, trying to educate his students and forestall violence. The film re-

ceived mixed reactions from critics. Writing in *Commonweal,* Richard Aleva remarked that the film is "a work of good intentions, and these intentions seem to have leached every last ounce of originality out of Singleton and much of his intelligence [as] well." Similarly, commenting on the film's roles, *Time* reviewer Richard Schickel declared that "These aren't really characters; they are points on a rigidly conceived political spectrum." However, while conceding that the film is "seriously flawed," a *Rolling Stone* critic averred that "Compelling questions of identity are being addressed" in *Higher Learning.*

BIOGRAPHICAL/CRITICAL SOURCES:

PERIODICALS

Advertising Age, January 27, 1992, p. 42.
Advocate, July 27, 1993, p. 77.
Commonweal, February 24, 1995, p. 55.
Detroit Free Press, July 12, 1991, pp. 1C, 4C.
Detroit News, July 12, 1991, pp. 1D, 3D; July 20, 1991, pp. 1C, 3C-4C.
Detroit News and Free Press, July 14, 1991, pp. 1A, 8A.
Ebony, April, 1995, p. 122.
Elle, June, 1991, pp. 52-61.
Emerge, March, 1996, p. 38.
Entertainment Weekly, July 23, 1993, pp. 28, 43; August 13, 1993, p. 12; January 13, 1995, p. 32; July 28, 1995, p. 68.
Esquire, August, 1993, pp. 59-65, 108.
Essence, September, 1991, p. 43; November, 1991, pp. 64, 112; August, 1993, p. 48.
Insight on the News, August 12, 1991, p. 44.
Interview, July, 1991, p. 20; July, 1993, p. 36.
Jet, July 15, 1991, p. 56; September 2, 1991, p. 11; June 1, 1992, p. 56; July 19, 1993, p. 54; January 23, 1995, p. 14.
Los Angeles Magazine, February, 1991, p. 18.
Los Angeles Times Book Review, August 8, 1993, p. 11.
Maclean's, July 29, 1991, p. 47.
National Review, September 23, 1991, pp. 54-56.
New Republic, September 2, 1991, pp. 26-27; August 23 and August 30, 1993, pp. 30-31.
New Statesman & Society, October 25, 1991, pp. 30-31.
Newsweek, July 29, 1991, pp. 48-49.
New York, July 22, 1991, pp. 40-41; July 29, 1991, p. 49.
New Yorker, August 2, 1993, pp. 76-78.
New York Times, July 12, 1991, pp. C1, C15; July 14, 1991, p. 10.

New York Times Magazine, July 14, 1991, pp. 15-19, 38-40, 44.

People, July 22, 1991, pp. 14-15; January 23, 1995, p. 83.

Premiere, November, 1991, p. 128; August, 1993, p. 70.

Rolling Stone, August 19, 1993, pp. 81-83; January 26, 1995, p. 66.

Time, June 17, 1991, pp. 64-68; December 7, 1992, p. 21; January 23, 1995, p. 57.

Variety, July 26, 1993, pp. 28-29; January 9, 1995, p. 71.

Wilson Library Bulletin, October, 1991, pp. 70-71.*

*   *   *

SOYINKA, Wole 1934-

PERSONAL: Name is pronounced "*Woh*-leh Shaw-*yin*-ka"; given name, Akinwande Oluwole; born July 13, 1934, in Isara, Nigeria; son of Ayo (a headmaster) and Eniola Soyinka; married; four children. *Education:* Attended University of Ibadan; University of Leeds, B.A. (with honors), 1959. *Religion:* "Human liberty."

ADDRESSES: Office—P.O. Box 935, Abeokuta, Ogun, Nigeria. *Agent*—Greenbaum, Wolff & Ernst, 437 Madison Ave., New York, NY 10022.

CAREER: Playwright, poet, and novelist. University of Ibadan, Nigeria, research fellow in drama, 1960-61, chairman of department of theatre arts, 1967-71; University of Ife, professor of drama, 1972; Cambridge University, Cambridge, England, fellow of Churchill College, 1973-74; University of Ife, chairman of department of dramatic arts, 1975-85. Director of own theatre groups, Orisun Players and 1960 Masks, in Lagos and Ibadan, Nigeria, and Unife Guerilla theatre, Ife-Ife, 1978. Visiting professor at University of Sheffield, 1974, University of Ghana, 1975, Cornell University, 1986, and Yale University, 1979-80. Goldwin Smith professor for African Studies and Theatre Arts, Cornell University, 1988-91. Robert W. Woodruff Professor of the Arts, Emory University. Director of plays and actor on stage, film and radio.

MEMBER: International Theatre Institute (president), Union of Writers of the African Peoples (secretary-general), AAAL, African Academy of Sciences.

AWARDS, HONORS: Rockefeller Foundation grant, 1960; John Whiting Drama Prize, 1966; Dakar Negro Arts Festival award, 1966; *New Statesman* Jock Campbell Award, *New Statesman,* 1968, for *The Interpreters;* Nobel Prize in Literature, 1986; Leopold Sedan Senghor Award, 1986; Enrico Mattei Award for Humanities, 1986; named Commander of the Federal Republic of Nigeria by General Ibrahim Babangida, 1986; named Commander of the French Legion of Honor, 1989; named Commander of Order of the Italian Republic, 1990; D.Litt., Yale University, University of Leeds, 1973, University of Montpellier, France, and University of Lagos; Prisoner of Conscience Prize, Amnesty International.

WRITINGS:

POETRY

Idanre and Other Poems, Methuen, 1967, Hill & Wang, 1969.

Poems from Prison, Rex Collings, 1969, expanded edition published as *A Shuttle in the Crypt,* Hill & Wang, 1972.

(Editor and author of introduction) *Poems of Black Africa,* Hill & Wang, 1975.

Ogun Abibiman, Rex Collings, 1976.

Mandela's Earth and Other Poems, Methuen, 1990.

Early Poems, Oxford University Press, 1997.

PLAYS

The Invention, first produced in London at Royal Court Theatre, 1955.

A Dance of the Forests (also see below; first produced in London, 1960), Oxford University Press, 1962.

The Lion and the Jewel (also see below; first produced at Royal Court Theatre, 1966), Oxford University Press, 1962.

Three Plays (includes *The Trials of Brother Jero* [also see below], one-act, produced Off-Broadway at Greenwich Mews Playhouse, November 9, 1967; *The Strong Breed* [also see below], one-act, produced at Greenwich Mews Playhouse, November 9, 1967; and *The Swamp Dwellers* [also see below]), Mbari Publications, 1962, Northwestern University Press, 1963.

Five Plays: A Dance of the Forests, The Lion and the Jewel, The Swamp Dwellers, The Trials of Brother Jero, The Strong Breed, Oxford University Press, 1964.

The Road (produced in Stratford, England, at Theatre Royal, 1965), Oxford University Press, 1965.

Kongi's Harvest (also see below; produced Off-Broadway at St. Mark's Playhouse, April 14, 1968), Oxford University Press, 1966.

Rites of the Harmattan Solstice, produced in Lagos, 1966.

Three Short Plays, Oxford University Press, 1969.

The Trials of Brother Jero, Oxford University Press, 1969, published with "The Strong Breed" as *The Trials of Brother Jero and The Strong Breed: Two Plays,* Dramatists Play Service, 1969.

Kongi's Harvest (screenplay), produced by Calpenny-Nigerian Films, 1970.

Madmen and Specialists (two-act; produced in Waterford, CT, at Eugene O'Neill Memorial Theatre, August 1, 1970), Methuen, 1971, Hill & Wang, 1972.

(Contributor) *Palaver: Three Dramatic Discussion Starters* (includes *The Lion and the Jewel*), Friendship Press, 1971.

Before the Blackout (revue sketches; also see below), Orisun Acting Editions, 1971.

(Editor) *Plays from the Third World: An Anthology,* Doubleday, 1971.

The Jero Plays: The Trials of Brother Jero, and *Jero's Metamorphosis,* Methuen, 1973.

(Contributor) *African Theatre: Eight Prize Winning Plays for Radio,* Heinemann, 1973.

Camwood on the Leaves, Methuen, 1973, published with "Before the Blackout" as *Camwood on the Leaves and Before the Blackout: Two Short Plays,* Third Press, 1974.

(Adapter) *The Bacchae of Euripides: A Communion Rite* (first produced in London at Old Vic Theatre, August 2, 1973), Methuen, 1973, Norton, 1974.

Collected Plays, Oxford University Press, Volume 1: *A Dance of the Forests, The Swamp Dwellers, The Strong Breed, The Road, The Bacchae,* 1973, Volume 2: *The Lion and the Jewel, Kongi's Harvest, The Trials of Brother Jero, Jero's Metamorphosis, Madmen and Specialists,* 1974.

Death and the King's Horseman (produced at University of Ife, 1976; produced in Chicago at Goodman Theatre, 1979; produced in New York at Vivian Beaumont Theatre, March, 1987), Norton, 1975.

Opera Wonyosi (light opera; produced in Ife-Ife, 1977), Indiana University Press, 1981.

Priority Projects, revue; produced on Nigeria tour, 1982.

A Play of Giants (produced in New Haven, CT, 1984), Methuen, 1984.

Six Plays, Methuen, 1984.

Requiem for a Futurologist (produced in Ife-Ife, 1983), Rex Collings, 1985.

The Beatification of Area Boy, first produced in Leeds, England, 1996.

Also author of television script, "Culture in Transition."

OTHER

The Interpreters (novel), Deutsch, 1965.

(Translator) D. O. Fagunwa, *The Forest of a Thousand Daemons: A Hunter's Saga* (novel), Nelson, 1967, Humanities, 1969.

(Contributor) D. W. Jefferson, editor, *The Morality of Art,* Routledge & Kegan Paul, 1969.

(Contributor) O. R. Dathorne and Wilfried Feuser, editors, *Africa in Prose,* Penguin, 1969. *The Man Died: Prison Notes of Wole Soyinka,* Harper, 1972, 2nd edition, Rex Collings, 1973.

Season of Anomy (novel), Rex Collings, 1973.

Myth, Literature and the African World (essays), Cambridge University Press, 1976.

Ake: The Years of Childhood (autobiography), Random House, 1981.

Art, Dialogue, and Outrage (essays), New Horn, 1988.

Isara: A Voyage around "Essay," (biography of the author's father), Random House, 1989.

Ibadan: The Penkelemes Years: A Memoir, Spectrum Books (Ibadan), 1994.

The Open Sore of a Continent: A Personal Narrative of the Nigerian Crisis, Oxford University Press, 1996.

The Burden of Memory, the Muse of Forgiveness (nonfiction), Oxford University Press (New York City), 1998.

Co-editor, *Black Orpheus,* 1961-64; editor, *Transition* (now *Ch'Indaba*), 1974-76.

SIDELIGHTS: Many critics consider Wole Soyinka Africa's finest writer. The Nigerian playwright's unique style blends traditional Yoruban folk-drama with European dramatic form to provide both spectacle and penetrating satire. Soyinka told *New York Times Magazine* writer Jason Berry that in the African cultural tradition, the artist "has always functioned as the record of the mores and experience of his society." His plays, novels, and poetry all reflect that philosophy, serving as a record of twentieth-century Africa's political turmoil and its struggle to reconcile tradition with modernization. Eldred Jones states in his book *Wole Soyinka* that the author's work touches on universal themes as well as addressing specifically African concerns: "The essential ideas which emerge from a reading of Soyinka's work are not specially African ideas, although his characters and their mannerisms are African. His concern is with man on earth. Man is dressed for the nonce in African dress and lives in the sun and tropical forest, but he represents the whole race." As a young child, Soyinka was comfortable with the conflicting cultures in his world, but as he grew older he became increasingly aware of the pull between African tradition and Western modernization.

Ake, his village, was mainly populated with people from the Yoruba tribe, and was presided over by the *ogboni,* or tribal elders. Soyinka's grandfather introduced him to the pantheon of Yoruba gods and to other tribal folklore. His parents were key representatives of colonial influences, however: his mother was a devout Christian convert and his father acted as headmaster for the village school established by the British. When Soyinka's father began urging Wole to leave Ake to attend the government school in Ibadan, the boy was spirited away by his grandfather, who administered a scarification rite of manhood. Soyinka was also consecrated to the god Ogun, ruler of metal, roads, and both the creative and destructive essence. Ogun is a recurring figure in Soyinka's work and has been named by the author as his muse.

Ake: The Years of Childhood, Soyinka's account of his first ten years, stands as "a classic of childhood memoirs wherever and whenever produced," states *New York Times Book Review* contributor James Olney. Numerous critics have singled out Soyinka's ability to recapture the changing perspective of a child as the book's outstanding feature; it begins in a light tone but grows increasingly serious as the boy matures and becomes aware of the problems faced by the adults around him. The book concludes with an account of a tax revolt organized by Soyinka's mother and the beginnings of Nigerian independence. "Most of 'Ake' charms; that was Mr. Soyinka's intention," writes John Leonard of the *New York Times.* "The last 50 pages, however, inspire and confound; they are transcendent." Olney agrees that "the lyricism, grace, humor and charm of 'Ake' . . . are in the service of a profoundly serious viewpoint that attempts to show us how things should be in the community of men and how they should not be. Mr. Soyinka, however, does this dramatically, not discursively. Through recollection, restoration and re-creation, he conveys a personal vision that was formed by the childhood world that he now returns to evoke and exalt in his autobiography. This is the ideal circle of autobiography at its best. It is what makes 'Ake,'

in addition to its other great virtues, the best introduction available to the work of one of the liveliest, most exciting writers in the world today."

Soyinka published some poems and short stories in *Black Orpheus,* a highly regarded Nigerian literary magazine, before leaving Africa to attend the University of Leeds in England. There his first play was produced. "The Invention" is a comic satire based on a sudden loss of pigment by South Africa's black population. Unable to distinguish blacks from whites and thus enforce its apartheid policies, the government is thrown into chaos. "The play is Soyinka's sole direct treatment of the political situation in Africa," notes Thomas Hayes in the *Dictionary of Literary Biography Yearbook: 1986.*

Soyinka returned to Nigeria in 1960, shortly after independence from colonial rule had been declared. He began to research Yoruba folklore and drama in depth and incorporated elements of both into his play "A Dance of the Forests." "A Dance of the Forests" was commissioned as part of Nigeria's independence celebrations. In his play, Soyinka warned the newly independent Nigerians that the end of colonial rule did not mean an end to their country's problems. It shows a bickering group of mortals who summon up the *egungun* (spirits of the dead, revered by the Yoruba people) for a festival. They have presumed the *egungun* to be noble and wise, but they discover that their ancestors are as petty and spiteful as any living people. "The whole concept ridicules the African viewpoint that glorifies the past at the expense of the present," suggests John F. Povey in *Tri- Quarterly.* "The sentimentalized glamour of the past is exposed so that the same absurdities may not be reenacted in the future. This constitutes a bold assertion to an audience awaiting an easy appeal to racial heroics." Povey also praises Soyinka's skill in using dancing, drumming, and singing to reinforce his theme: "The dramatic power of the surging forest dance [in the play] carries its own visual conviction. It is this that shows Soyinka to be a man of the theatre, not simply a writer."

After warning against living in nostalgia for Africa's past in "A Dance of the Forests," Soyinka lampooned the indiscriminate embrace of Western modernization in "The Lion and the Jewel." A *Times Literary Supplement* reviewer calls this play a "richly ribald comedy," which combines poetry and prose "with a marvellous lightness in the treatment of both." The plot revolves around Sidi, the village beauty, and the rivalry between her two suitors. Baroka is the village chief, an old man with many wives; Lakunle is the enthusiastically Westernized schoolteacher who dreams of molding Sidi into a "civilized" woman.

In *Introduction to Nigerian Literature,* Eldred Jones comments that "The Lion and the Jewel" is "a play which is so easily (and erroneously) interpreted as a clash between progress and reaction, with the play coming down surprisingly in favour of reaction. The real clash is not between old and new or between real progress and reaction. It is a clash between the genuine and the false; between the well-done and the half-baked. Lakunle the school teacher would have been a poor symbol of any desirable kind of progress. . . . He is a man of totally confused values. [Baroka's worth lies in] the traditional values of which he is so confident and in which he so completely outmaneouvres Lakunle who really has no values at all." Bruce King, editor of *Introduction to Nigerian Literature,* names "The Lion and the Jewel" "the best literary work to come out of Africa."

Soyinka was well established as Nigeria's premier playwright when in 1965 he published his first novel, *The Interpreters.* The novel allowed him to expand on themes already expressed in his stage dramas and to present a sweeping view of Nigerian life in the years immediately following independence. Essentially plotless, *The Interpreters* is loosely structured around the informal discussions among five young Nigerian intellectuals. Each has been educated in a foreign country and returned hoping to shape Nigeria's destiny. They are hampered by their own confused values, however, as well as the corruption they encounter everywhere. Some reviewers liken Soyinka's writing style in *The Interpreters* to that of James Joyce and William Faulkner. Others take exception to the formless quality of the novel, but Eustace Palmer asserts in *The Growth of the African Novel:* "If there are reservations about the novel's structure, there can be none about the thoroughness of the satire at society's expense. Soyinka's wide-ranging wit takes in all sections of a corrupt society—the brutal masses, the aimless intellectuals, the affected and hypocritical university dons, the vulgar and corrupt businessmen, the mediocre civil servants, the illiterate politicians and the incompetent journalists. [The five main characters are all] talented intellectuals who have retained their African consciousness although they were largely educated in the western world. Yet their western education enables them to look at their changing society with a certain amount of detachment. They are therefore uniquely qualified to be interpreters of this society. The reader is impressed by their honesty, sincerity, moral idealism, concern for truth and justice and aversion to corruption, snobbery and hypocrisy; but anyone who assumes that Soyinka presents all the interpreters as models of behaviour will be completely misreading the novel. He is careful to expose their selfishness, egoism, cynicism and aimlessness. Indeed the conduct of the intellectuals both in and out of the university is a major preoccupation of Soyinka's in this novel. The aimlessness and superficiality of the lives of most of the interpreters is patent."

Neil McEwan points out in *Africa and the Novel* that for all its seriousness, *The Interpreters* is also "among the liveliest of recent novels in English. It is bright satire full of good sense and good humour which are African and contemporary: the highest spirits of its author's early work. . . . Behind the jokes of his novel is a theme that he has developed angrily elsewhere: that whatever progress may mean for Africa it is not a lesson to be learned from outside, however much of 'modernity' Africans may share with others." McEwan further observes that although *The Interpreters* does not have a rigidly structured plot, "there is unity in the warmth and sharpness of its comic vision. There are moments which sadden or anger; but they do not diminish the fun." Palmer notes that *The Interpreters* notably influenced the African fiction that followed it, shifting the focus "from historical, cultural and sociological analysis to penetrating social comment and social satire."

The year *The Interpreters* was published, 1965, also marked Soyinka's first arrest by the Nigerian police. He was accused of using a gun to force a radio announcer to broadcast incorrect election results. No evidence was ever produced, however, and the PEN writers' organization launched a protest campaign, headed by William Styron and Norman Mailer. Soyinka was released after three months. He was next arrested two years later, during Nigeria's civil war. Soyinka was completely opposed to the conflict, and especially to the Nigerian Government's brutal policies toward the Ibo people who were attempting to form their own country, Biafra. He traveled to Biafra to establish a peace commission composed of leading intellectuals from both sides; when he returned, the Nigerian police accused him of helping the Biafrans to buy jet fighters. Once again he was imprisoned. This time Soyinka was held for more than two years, although he was never formally charged with any crime. Most of that time he was kept in solitary confinement. When all of his fellow prisoners were vaccinated against meningitis, Soyinka was passed by;

when he developed serious vision problems, they were ignored by his jailers. He was denied reading and writing materials, but he manufactured his own ink and began to keep a prison diary, written on toilet paper, cigarette packages and in between the lines of the few books he secretly obtained. Each poem or fragment of journal he managed to smuggle to the outside world became a literary event and a reassurance to his supporters that Soyinka still lived, despite rumors to the contrary. He was released in 1969 and left Nigeria soon after, not returning until a change of power took place in 1975.

Published as *The Man Died: Prison Notes of Wole Soyinka,* the author's diary constitutes "the most important work that has been written about the Biafran war," believes Charles R. Larson, contributor to *Nation.* "'The Man Died' is not so much the story of Wole Soyinka's own temporary death during the Nigerian Civil War but a personified account of Nigeria's fall from sanity, documented by one of the country's leading intellectuals." Gerald Weales's *New York Times Book Review* article suggests that the political content of *The Man Died* is less fascinating than "the notes that deal with prison life, the observation of everything from a warder's catarrh to the predatory life of insects after a rain. Of course, these are not simply reportorial. They are vehicles to carry the author's shifting states of mind, to convey the real subject matter of the book; the author's attempt to survive as a man, and as a mind. The notes are both a means to that survival and a record to it." Larson underlines the book's political impact, however, noting that ironically, "while other Nigerian writers were emotionally castrated by the war, Soyinka, who was placed in solitary confinement so that he wouldn't embarrass the government, was writing work after work, books that will no doubt embarrass the Nigerian Government more than anything the Ibo writers may ever publish." A *Times Literary Supplement* reviewer concurs, characterizing *The Man Died* as "a damning indictment of what Mr. Soyinka sees as the iniquities of wartime Nigeria and the criminal tyranny of its administration in peacetime." Many literary commentators feel that Soyinka's work changed profoundly after his prison term, darkening in tone and focusing on the war and its aftermath.

In the *Dictionary of Literary Biography Yearbook: 1986,* Hayes quotes Soyinka on his concerns after the war: "I have one abiding religion—human liberty. . . . conditioned to the truth that life is meaningless, insulting, without this fullest liberty, and in spite of the despairing knowledge that words alone seem unable to

guarantee its possession, my writing grows more and more preoccupied with the theme of the oppressive boot, the irrelevance of the color of the foot that wears it and the struggle for individuality." In spite of its satire, most critics had found *The Interpreters* to be ultimately an optimistic book.

In contrast, Soyinka's second novel expresses almost no hope for Africa's future, says John Mellors in *London Magazine:* "Wole Soyinka appears to have written much of *Season of Anomy* in a blazing fury, angry beyond complete control of words at the abuses of power and the outbreaks of both considered and spontaneous violence. . . . The plot charges along, dragging the reader (not because he doesn't want to go, but because he finds it hard to keep up) through forest, mortuary and prison camp in nightmare visions of tyranny, torture, slaughter and putrefaction. The book reeks of pain. . . . Soyinka hammers at the point that the liberal has to deal with violence in the world however much he would wish he could ignore it; the scenes of murder and mutilation, while sickeningly explicit, are justified by . . . the author's anger and compassion and insistence that bad will not become better by our refusal to examine it."

Like *Season of Anomy,* Soyinka's postwar plays are considered more brooding than his earlier work. "Madmen and Specialists" is called "grim" by Martin Banham and Clive Wake in *African Theatre Today.* In the play, a doctor returns from the war trained as a specialist in torture and uses his new skills on his father. The play's major themes are "the loss of faith and rituals" and "the break-up of the family unit which traditionally in Africa has been the foundation of society," according to Charles Larson in the *New York Times Book Review.* Names and events in the play are fictionalized to avoid censorship, but Soyinka has clearly "leveled a wholesale criticism of life in Nigeria since the Civil War: a police state in which only madmen and spies can survive, in which the losers are mad and the winners are paranoid about the possibility of another rebellion. The prewar corruption and crime have returned, supported by the more sophisticated acts of terrorism and espionage introduced during the war." Larson summarizes: "In large part 'Madmen and Specialists' is a product of those months Soyinka spent in prison, in solitary confinement, as a political prisoner. It is, not surprisingly, the most brutal piece of social criticism he has published."

In a similar tone, "A Play of Giants" presents four African leaders—thinly disguised versions of Jean

Bedel Bokassa, Sese Seko Mobutu, Macias Ngeuma, and Idi Amin—meeting at the United Nations building, where "their conversation reflects the corruption and cruelty of their regimes and the casual, brutal flavor of their rule," discloses Hayes. In Hayes's opinion, "A Play of Giants" demonstrates that "as Soyinka has matured he has hardened his criticism of all that restricts the individual's ability to choose, think, and act free from external oppression. . . . [It is] his harshest attack against modern Africa, a blunt, venomous assault on . . . African leaders and the powers who support them."

In *Isara: A Voyage around "Essay,"* Soyinka provides a portrait of his father, Akinyode Soditan, as well as "vivid sketches of characters and culturally intriguing events that cover a period of 15 years," Charles Johnson relates in the *Washington Post*. The narrative follows S. A., or "Essay," and his classmates through his years at St. Simeon's Teacher Training Seminary in Ilesa. Aided by documents left to him in a tin box, Soyinka dramatizes the changes that profoundly affected his father's life. The Great Depression that brought the Western world to its knees during the early 1930s was a time of economic opportunity for Africans. The quest for financial gain transformed African culture, as did Mussolini's invasion of Ethiopia and the onset of World War II. More threatening was the violent civil war for the throne following the death of their king. An aged peacemaker named Agunrin resolved the conflict by an appeal to the people's common past.

"As each side presents its case, Agunrin, half listening, sinks into memories that unfold his people's collective history, and finally he speaks, finding his voice in a scene so masterfully rendered it alone is worth the price of the book," Johnson claims. The book is neither a strict biography nor a straight historical account. However, "in his effort to expose Western readers to a unique, African perspective on the war years, Soyinka succeeds brilliantly," Johnson comments. *New York Times* reviewer Michiko Kakutani writes that, in addition, "Essay emerges as a high-minded teacher, a mentor and companion, blessed with dignity and strong ideals, a father who inspired his son to achievement."

In his 1996 work, *The Open Sore of a Continent: A Personal Narrative of the Nigerian Crisis,* Soyinka takes an expansive and unrestrained look at Nigeria's dictatorship. A collection of essays originally delivered as lectures at Harvard, *The Open Sore* questions the corrupt government, the ideas of nationalism, and international intervention. The book begins with the execution of Ken Saro-Wiwa. For Soyinka, his death, along with the annulment of the recent elections, signals the disintegration of the state. According to Robert Kaplan in the *New York Times Book Review,* Soyinka "uses these harsh facts to dissect, then reinvent not just Nigeria but the concept of nationhood itself."

In 1998, Soyinka ended a four-year self-imposed exile from Nigeria. His exile can be traced back to 1993, when a democratically elected government was to have assumed power. Instead, General Ibrahim Babangida, who had ruled the nation for eight years, prohibited the publication of the voting results and installed his deputy, General Sani Abacha, as head of the Nigerian state. Soyinka, along with other pro-democracy activists, was charged with treason for his criticism of the military regime. Faced with a death sentence, Soyinka went into exile in 1994, during which time he traveled and lectured in Europe and the United States. Following the death of Abacha, who held control for five years, the new government, led by General Abdulsalem Abubakar, released numerous political prisoners and promised to hold civilian elections. Soyinka's return to his homeland renewed hope for a democratic Nigerian state.

Soyinka's work is frequently described as demanding but rewarding reading. Although his plays are widely praised, they are seldom performed, especially outside of Africa. The dancing and choric speech often found in them are unfamiliar and difficult for non-African actors to master, a problem Holly Hill notes in her London *Times* review of the Lincoln Center Theatre production of "Death and the King's Horseman." She awards high praise to the play, however, saying it "has the stateliness and mystery of Greek tragedy." When the Swedish Academy awarded Soyinka the Nobel Prize in Literature in 1986, its members singled out "Death and the King's Horseman" and "A Dance of the Forests" as "evidence that Soyinka is 'one of the finest poetical playwrights that have written in English,'" reports Stanley Meisler of the *Los Angeles Times*. Hayes summarizes Wole Soyinka's importance: "His drama and fiction have challenged the West to broaden its aesthetic and accept African standards of art and literature. His personal and political life have challenged Africa to embrace the truly democratic values of the African tribe and reject the tyranny of power practiced on the continent by its colonizers and by many of its modern rulers."

BIOGRAPHICAL/CRITICAL SOURCES:

BOOKS

Adelugba, Dapo, *Wole Soyinka: A Birthday Letter, and Other Essays,* University of Ibadan, 1984.

Adelugba, Dapo, editor, *Before Out Very Eyes: Tribute to Wole Soyinka,* Spectrum, 1987.

Agetua, John, *When the Man Died: Views, Reviews and Interview on Wole Soyinka's Controversial Book,* Agetua, 1972.

Bamikunle, Aderemi, *Introduction to Soyinka's Poetry: Analysis of A Shuttle in the Crypt,* Ahmadu Bello University Press, 1991.

Banham, Martin and Clive Wake, *African Theatre Today,* Pitman Publishing, 1976.

Banham, *Wole Soyinka's "The Lion and the Jewel,"* Rex Collings, 1981.

Black Literature Criticism, Gale, 1992.

Chinweizu, Onwuchekwa Jemie, and others, *Toward the Decolonization of African Literature,* Routledge, 1985, pp. 163-238.

Coger, Greta M. K., *Index of Subjects, Proverbs, and Themes in the Writings of Wole Soyinka,* Greenwood, 1988.

Contemporary Literary Criticism, Gale, Volume 3, 1975, Volume 5, 1976, Volume 14, 1980, Volume 36, 1986, Volume 44, 1987.

Dictionary of Literary Biography, Volume 125: *Twentieth-Century Caribbean and Black African Writers, Second Series,* Gale, 1993.

Dictionary of Literary Biography Yearbook: 1986, Gale, 1987, pp. 3-18.

Drama Criticism, Volume 2, Gale, 1992.

Duerden, Dennis, and Cosmo Pieterse, editors, *African Writiers Talking: A Collection of Radio Interviews,* Heinemann, 1972.

Dunton, C. P., *Notes on "Three Short Plays,"* Longman, 1982.

Egudu, Romanus N., *Modern African Poetry and the African Predicament,* Barnes & Noble, 1978, pp. 104-24.

Etherton, Michael, *The Development of African Drama,* Hutchinson, 1982, pp. 242-84.

Fraser, Robert, *West African Poetry: A Critical History,* Cambridge University Press, 1986, pp. 231-50, 265-70, 295-300.

Gakwandi, Shatto Arthur, *The Novel and Contemporary Experience in America,* Heinemann, 1977, pp. 66-86.

Gibbs, James, editor, *Study Aid to "Kongi's Harvest,"* Rex Collings, 1973.

Gibbs, editor, *Critical Perspectives on Wole Soyinka,* Three Continents, 1980.

Gibbs, editor, *Notes on "The Lion and the Jewel,"* Longman, 1982.

Gibbs, *Wole Soyinka,* Macmillan, 1986.

Gibbs, Ketu Katrak and Henry Gates, Jr., editors, *Wole Soyinka: A Bibliography of Primary and Secondary Sources,* Greenwood Press, 1986.

Goodwin, K. L., *Understanding African Poetry: A Study of Ten African Poets,* Heinemann, 1982.

Graham-White, Anthony, *The Drama of Black Africa,* French, 1974.

Herdeck, Donald E., *Three Dynamite Authors: Derek Walcott (Nobel 1992), Naguib Mahfouz (Nobel 1988), Wole Soyinka (Nobel 1986): Ten Bio-Critical Essays from Their Works as Published by Three Continents Press,* Three Continents Press (Colorado Springs), 1995.

Irele, Abiola, *The African Experience in Literature and Ideology,* Heinemann, 1981.

Jeyifo, Biodun, *The Truthful Lie: Essays in the Sociology of African Literature,* New Beacon, 1985, pp. 11-45.

Jones, Eldred, editor, *African Literature Today, Number 5: The Novel in Africa,* Heinemann, 1971.

Jones, editor, *African Literature Today, Number 6: Poetry in Africa,* Heinemann, 1973.

Jones, *Wole Soyinka,* Twayne, 1973 (published in England as *The Writings of Wole Soyinka,* Heinemann, 1973), revised, Currey, 1988.

Katrak, Ketu, *Wole Soyinka and Modern Tragedy: A Study of Dramatic Theory and Practice,* Greenwood Press, 1986.

King, Bruce, editor, *Introduction to Nigerian Literature,* Africana Publishing, 1972.

Larson, Charles R., *The Emergence of African Fiction,* revised edition, Indiana University Press, 1972.

Laurence, Margaret, *Long Drums and Cannons: Nigerian Dramatists and Novelists,* Praeger, 1968.

Lindfors, Bernth, and James Gibbs, editors, *Research on Wole Soyinka,* Africa World, 1992.

Maduakor, Obi, *Wole Soyinka: An Introduction to His Writing,* Garland, 1986.

McEwan, Neil, *Africa and the Novel,* Humanities Press, 1983.

Moore, Gerald, *Wole Soyinka,* Africana Publishing, 1971.

Morell, Karen L., editor, *In Person—Achebe, Awoonor, and Soyinka at the University of Washington,* African Studies Program, Institute for Comparative and Foreign Area Studies, University of Washington, 1975.

Ogunba, Oyin, *The Movement of Transition: A Study of the Plays of Wole Soyinka,* Ibadan University Press, 1975.

Ogunba and others, editors, *Theatre in Africa,* Ibadan University Press, 1978.

Okpu, B., *Wole Soyinka: A Bibliography,* Libriservice, 1984.

Olaniyan, Tejumola, *Scars of Conquest / Masks of Resistance: The Invention of Cultural Identities in African, African-American, and Carribbean Drama,* Oxford University Press (New York City), 1995.

Omotoso, Kole, *Achebe Or Soyinka: A Study in Contrasts,* Zell (London, UK), 1996.

Page, Malcolm, *Wole Soyinka: Bibliography, Biography, Playography,* 1979.

Palmer, Eustace, *The Growth of the African Novel,* Heinemann, 1979.

Parsons, E. M., editor, *Notes on Wole Soyinka's "The Jero Plays,"* Methuen, 1982.

Pieterse, Cosmo, and Dennis Duerden, editors, *African Writers Talking: A Collection of Radio Interviews,* Africana Publishing, 1972.

Probyn, editor, *Notes on "The Road,"* Longman, 1981.

Quayson, Ato, *Strategic Transformations in Nigerian Writing: Orality and History in the Work of Rev. Samuel Johnson, Amos Tutuola, Wole Soyinka, and Ben Okri,* Indiana University Press, 1997.

Ricard, Alain, *Theatre et Nationalisme: Wole Soyinka et LeRoi Jones,* Presence Africaine, 1972.

Roscoe, Adrian A., *Mother Is Gold: A Study in West African Literature,* Cambridge University Press, 1971, pp. 48-63, 219-52.

Soyinka, Wole, *The Man Died: Prison Notes of Wole Soyinka,* Harper, 1972.

Soyinka, *Myth, Literature and the African World,* Cambridge University Press, 1976.

Soyinka, *Ake: The Years of Childhood,* Random House, 1981.

Tucker, Martin, *Africa in Modern Literature: A Survey of Contemporary Writing in English,* Ungar, 1967.

Wilkinson, Jane, *Talking with African Writers,* Currey, 1992, pp. 90-108.

World Literature Criticism, Gale, 1992.

Wright, Derek, *Wole Soyinka Revisited,* Twayne, 1993.

PERIODICALS

African American Review, spring, 1996, p. 99.
America, February 12, 1983.
American Theatre, January, 1997, p. 26.
Ariel, July, 1981.
Black Orpheus, March, 1966.
Black World, August, 1975, pp. 20-48.
Book Forum, Volume 3, number 1, 1977.

Books Abroad, summer, 1972; spring, 1973.
British Book News, December, 1984; April, 1986.
Chicago Tribune Book World, October 7, 1979.
Christian Science Monitor, July 31, 1970; August 15, 1970.
Commonweal, February 8, 1985.
Commonwealth Essays and Studies, (special on Wole Soyinka) spring, 1991.
Contemporary Review, April, 1997, p. 211.
Detroit Free Press, March 20, 1983; October 17, 1986.
Detroit News, November 21, 1982.
Free Inquiry, fall, 1997, p. 48.
Globe and Mail (Toronto), June 7, 1986; January 6, 1990.
Jet, July 18, 1994, p. 27.
London Magazine, April/May, 1974.
Los Angeles Times, October 17, 1986.
Los Angeles Times Book Review, October 15, 1989.
Nation, October 11, 1965; April 29, 1968; September 15, 1969; November 10, 1969; October 2, 1972; November 5, 1973; May 27, 1996, p. 31.
New Perspectives, summer, 1994, p. 61.
New Republic, October 12, 1974; May 9, 1983; December 18, 1995, p. 12; June 16, 1997, p. 33.
New Statesman, December 20, 1968.
Newsweek, November 1, 1982.
New Yorker, May 16, 1977.
New York Review of Books, July 31, 1969; October 21, 1982.
New York Times, November 11, 1965; April 19, 1970; August 11, 1972; September 23, 1982; May 29, 1986; May 31, 1986; June 15, 1986; October 17, 1986; November 9, 1986; March 1, 1987; March 2, 1987; November 3, 1989; August 26, 1996, p. 26.
New York Times Book Review, July 29, 1973; December 24, 1973; October 10, 1982; January 15, 1984; November 12, 1989; May 15, 1994, p. 24; August 11, 1996.
New York Times Magazine, September 18, 1983.
Progressive, August, 1997, p. 36.
Publishers Weekly, June 3, 1996.
Research in African Literatures, spring, 1983.
Saturday Review/World, October 19, 1974.
Spectator, November 6, 1959; December 15, 1973; November 24, 1981.
Time, October 27, 1986; December 5, 1994, p. 29.
Times (London), October 17, 1986; April 6, 1987; March 15, 1990.
Times Literary Supplement, April 1, 1965; June 10, 1965; January 18, 1968; December 31, 1971; March 2, 1973; December 14, 1973; February 8, 1974; March 1, 1974; October 17, 1975; August

5, 1977; February 26, 1982; September 23, 1988; March 22-29, 1990; February 24, 1995; June 13, 1997, p. 27.
Tribune Books (Chicago), November 19, 1989; July 31, 1994.
Tri-Quarterly, fall, 1966.
Village Voice, August 31, 1982.
Washington Post, October 30, 1979; October 17, 1986; November 10, 1989.
Washington Post Book World, November 10, 1996, p. 4.
World, February 13, 1973.
World Literature Today, winter, 1977; autumn, 1981; summer, 1982.*

* * *

STEINER, K. Leslie
See DELANY, Samuel R(ay, Jr.)

* * *

STEWART, Jeffrey C. 1950-

PERSONAL: Born March 18, 1950, in Chicago, IL; son of Henry C. (a manufacturer) and Melva J. (a beautician) Stewart; married Marta Reid. Ethnicity: "African American." *Education:* Attended University of California, Los Angeles, 1967-69; University of California, Santa Cruz, B.A., 1971; Yale University, M.A., M.Phil., Ph.D., 1979. *Religion:* Episcopalian. *Avocational interests:* Dog breeding.

ADDRESSES: Office—Department of History, George Mason University, 4400 University Dr., Fairfax, VA 22030. *Agent*—Marie Brown Associates, 625 Broadway, New York, NY 10012.

CAREER: George Mason University, Fairfax, VA, associate professor of history, 1986—. Staff member of Museo, Inc. (museum studies consulting firm).

MEMBER: American Association of Museums, Organization of American Historians.

AWARDS, HONORS: Fellow at National Humanities Center, 1990-91, and Woodrow Wilson Center for International Scholars, 1992-93.

WRITINGS:

(Editor) *The Critical Temper of Alain Locke: A Selection of His Essays on Art and Culture,* Garland Publishing (New York City), 1983.
To Color America: Portraits by Winold Reiss, Smithsonian Institution Press (Washington, DC), 1989.
Winold Reiss: An Illustrated Checklist of His Portraits, Smithsonian Institution Press (Washington, DC), 1990.
(Author of introduction) *Narrative of Sojourner Truth, a Bondswoman of Olden Time: With a History of Her Labors and Correspondence Drawn from Her "Book of Life,"* Oxford University Press (New York City), 1991.
(Editor and author of introduction) *Race Contacts and Inter-Racial Relations,* foreword by Michael R. Winston, preface by Thomas C. Battle, Howard University Press (Washington, DC), 1992.
1001 Things Everyone Should Know about African American History, Doubleday (New York City), 1996.
(Editor, author of introduction, and contributor) *Paul Robeson: Artist and Citizen,* Rutgers University Press (New Brunswick, NJ), 1998.

WORK IN PROGRESS: Enter the New Negro: A Biography of Alain Locke, for Oxford University Press.

SIDELIGHTS: As the editor of 1998's *Paul Robeson: Artist and Citizen,* Jeffrey C. Stewart helped highlight the hundredth anniversary of the birth of political activist, athlete, actor, and singer Paul Robeson. The multifaceted figure, who loved Communism, is sympathetically portrayed by various contributors who collectively address "virtually every aspect of Robeson," according to Ray Olson in *Booklist.*

Among the volume's sixteen essays is Stewart's discussion of "Robeson as an icon of physical beauty," remarked Olson, who called Stewart's essay "one of the best in the book."

BIOGRAPHICAL/CRITICAL SOURCES:

PERIODICALS

Booklist, February 15, 1998, p. 965.
Library Journal, July, 1996.
School Library Journal, February, 1999.
U.S. News & World Report, February 2, 1998, p. 7.*

SULLIVAN, Otha Richard 1941-

PERSONAL: Born December 28, 1941, in Hatties-burg, MS; son of Benjamin Franklin (in business) and Iola Estella (a homemaker; maiden name, Booth) Sullivan. *Education:* University of Kansas, B.S., 1965; Wayne State University, M.S., 1969, Ed.D., 1973.

ADDRESSES: Home—14187 Archdale Rd., Detroit, MI 48227. *Office*—Detroit Public Schools, 10025 Third St., Detroit, MI 48203. *Agent*—Clausen, Mays & Tahan, 249 West 34th St., New York, NY 10001.

CAREER: Classroom teacher at public schools in Detroit, MI, 1965-69; high school counselor, High-land Park, MI, 1969-70; University of Detroit, De-troit, administrator, 1970-73; director of special edu-cation for public schools, Highland Park, 1970-73; Howard University, Washington, DC, associate pro-fessor, 1977-79; ombudsman for public schools, Washington, DC, 1979-83; District of Columbia De-partment of Corrections, Washington, administrator, 1983-87; Highland Park Community College, High-land Park, executive vice-president, 1990-91; Alcorn State University, Lorman, MS, associate professor, 1987-90; Detroit Public Schools, counselor, 1990—.

MEMBER: Council for Exceptional Children, Urban League, National Association for the Advancement of Colored People, Kappa Alpha Psi.

AWARDS, HONORS: Booker T. Washington Educator's Achievement Award, 1998.

WRITINGS:

African American Inventors and Discoverers, Wiley (New York City), 1997.

Contributor to magazines and newspapers, including *Freedomways Journal, Black Collegian, Dollars and Sense, Journal of the International Association of Pupil Personnel Workers, Natchez Democrat,* and *About Time Journal.*

WORK IN PROGRESS: A book on affirmations; a book chronicling the life of a young man growing up in Mississippi, completion expected in 2000.

SIDELIGHTS: Otha Richard Sullivan told *CA:* "My primary motivation for writing is to inform. As a teacher, I recognize that students are more involved in the educational process when they can look at in-dividuals and their struggles and identify how these people were able to overcome adversities. Students are able to develop skills to overcome formidable challenges, and this helps them to approach and over-come other obstacles. Starting out as a teacher of social science, I immediately realized that many youths do not know their history. This lack of knowl-edge often leads to difficulties and wasted time before the young people come to an epiphany about how they will plan and direct their lives.

"My work is greatly influenced by my heroes, my mother and father, who taught me that education is the key that opens doors to opportunities. As a student in elementary school, I was influenced by my teach-ers, who introduced me to the brilliance and achieve-ments of black Americans who were systematically missing from the pages of history, the textbooks we used, and the audiovisual materials. My favorite teacher, Mrs. M. W. Chambers, infused black history in her classes on a daily basis, and this served to motivate students to greater achievement. Conse-quently, I developed a mission to write books and articles on the achievements of black Americans.

"The seeds for *African American Inventors* were sown at a middle school in Detroit, where I taught science. One day I asked students to name two black inven-tors. Most of them were stumped, unable to name two. I realized then that I had a responsibility to teach them about the myriad contributions of black Ameri-cans. At the same time, I began to unearth research completed some years ago at the Howard University library. I made a vow that, at the end of the year, students would identify, discuss, share, and apply the ingredients of success of many black Americans."

T-V

TARRY, Ellen 1906-

PERSONAL: Born in 1906, in Birmingham, AL; children: Elizabeth. *Education:* Attended Alabama State College for Negroes Bank Street College Writers' Laboratory.

ADDRESSES: Home—New York, NY.

CAREER: Worked as a newspaperwoman, teacher, and social worker; served as deputy assistant to the Regional Administrator for Equal Opportunity, Department of Housing and Urban Development; writer. Co-founder, Friendship House (Chicago); worked for Archdiocese of New York.

WRITINGS:

Janie Belle, illustrations by Myrtle Sheldon, Garden City Publishing (New York City), 1940.

Hezekiah Horton, illustrations by Oliver Harrington, Viking (New York City), 1942.

(With Marie Hall Ets) *My Dog Rinty,* illustrations by Alexander Alland and Alexandra Alland, Viking, 1946, new edition, 1964.

The Runaway Elephant, illustrations by Harrington, Viking, 1950.

The Third Door: The Autobiography of an American Negro Woman, McKay (New York City), 1955, reprinted, Negro Universities Press (Westport, CT), 1971, new edition with introduction by Nellie Y. McKay, University of Alabama Press (University), 1992.

Katharine Drexel: Friend of the Neglected, illustrations by Donald Bolognese, Farrar, Straus (New York City), 1958.

Martin de Porres: Saint of the New World, illustrations by James Fox, Vision Books (Coos Bay, OR), 1963.

Young Jim: The Early Years of James Weldon Johnson, Dodd (New York City), 1967.

The Other Toussaint: A Modern Biography of Pierre Toussaint, a Post-Revolutionary Black, St. Paul Editions (Boston), 1981.

Pierre Toussaint: Apostle of Old New York, Pauline Books (Boston), 1998.

Author of weekly column, "Negroes of Note," in the *Birmingham Truth*; contributor to many Catholic periodicals.

SIDELIGHTS: Ellen Tarry's writings have been heavily influenced by her involvement in the civil rights movement. As a result, she became one of the first authors to use African-Americans as main characters in books for children. She began her writing career at the *Birmingham Truth* newspaper, for which she eventually became a reporter, columnist, and editorialist. After some years at the paper, she left the South for New York City. There she was accepted into a group of journalists and creative writers that included Claude McKay, James Weldon Johnson, Countee Cullen, and Langston Hughes. She also worked at Friendship House, an interracial justice center in Harlem. It was there that she began a story hour for the children in the neighborhood, and using her young audiences to test out the stories she was writing. Her first published book, *Janie Belle,* was soon followed by *Hezekiah Horton*—both notable for showing African-American children as the main characters. The character of Hezekiah Horton was also featured in *The Runaway Elephant.*

My Dog Rinty, published in 1946, told in words and photos the story of a little boy whose troublesome dog became a valuable rat-hunter. Contemporary reviewers praised it first as a story of a boy and his dog, but many also noted with approval the way in which the author presented life in Harlem in a realistic, matter-of-fact style. "Showing the social range in a community, any community, from hardship to decency to comfort to luxury . . . indicating that the poor in old buildings live poorly; suggesting a concrete solution, that the buildings be replaced: all this was novel in a picturebook in 1946," noted Barbara Bader in *American Picturebooks from Noah's Ark to the Beast Within.*

Tarry, who converted to Roman Catholicism as a young woman, also wrote biographies of two notable black Catholics: St. Martin de Porres, who lived in South America in the seventeenth century; and Pierre Toussaint, a Haitian slave who was brought to New York City by his owner around 1787. Toussaint eventually won his freedom, became wealthy, and bought the freedom of many other slaves. Known for his good works and piety, he became a leading citizen of Old New York. Tarry's research and writing on Toussaint were encouraged by a letter of Pontifical Blessing from Pope Paul VI. "Students and scholars from all over the United States have expressed interest in the life of this Haitian slave who became a respected citizen," wrote Tarry in a *Something about the Author Autobiography Series (SAAS)* essay. "This book transformed me from being a writer to that of a resource person on the life and times of this man."

Perhaps Tarry's most significant book is her autobiography, *The Third Door: The Autobiography of an American Negro Woman.* The book, written in 1955, struck a determined and hopeful tone on the subject of civil rights. Reviewing a new edition of the book published in 1995, William L. Andrews allowed that "to some readers today this faith, rooted in the dauntlessness of Tarry's middle-class Southern family, in her commitment to moral and educational self-improvement, and in her socially conscious Catholicism, may elicit little more than an ironic reminder of a time when terms like integration and freedom now possessed an unquestioned moral authority and bespoke what seemed then a social inevitability." Still, Andrews noted, "we can still find much of use in reading *The Third Door*" if doing so "contributes to a re-evaluation of the kind of faith that Tarry took for granted in her vision of a color-blind multiethnic America."

"Tarry is at pains to show what an African American woman can do in alliance with fair-minded whites to bring about racial harmony and justice," observed Andrews. "For every recollection of discrimination and humiliation she suffered at the hands of bigots south and north, she gives her reader instances of successful interracial cooperation." The reviewer found Tarry's acceptance of patriarchal authority, especially in the form of the Catholic church, to be "problematic"; yet he concluded that *The Third Door* is "absorbing and provocative. . . . For students of the tradition of the African American women's autobiography, [it] will undoubtedly prove a challenging and instructive text."

BIOGRAPHICAL/CRITICAL SOURCES:

BOOKS

Bader, Barbara, *American Picturebooks from Noah's Ark to the Beast Within,* Macmillan (New York City), 1976.
Children's Literature Review, Volume 26, Gale (Detroit), 1992.
Something about the Author Autobiography Series, Volume 16, Gale, 1993.
Tarry, Ellen, *The Third Door: The Autobiography of an American Negro Woman,* McKay, 1955, reprinted, Negro Universities Press, 1971.

PERIODICALS

African American Review, spring, 1995, p. 147.
Bulletin of the Center for Children's Books, November, 1967, p. 50.
Chicago Sunday Tribune Magazine of Books, October 22, 1950, p. 15; May 22, 1955, p. 3.
Kirkus Service, June 1, 1967, p. 651.
Library Journal, September 15, 1942, p. 797.
New York Herald Tribune, September 13, 1942, p. 9.
New York Herald Tribune Book Review, October 8, 1950, p. 28.
New York Herald Tribune Weekly Book Review, May 19, 1946, p. 12.
New York Times, January 21, 1968.
New York Times Book Review, June 16, 1946, p. 33; January 21, 1968, p. 28.
Saturday Review of Literature, November 14, 1942; August 10, 1946, p. 31.
Virginia Kirkus' Bookshop Service, June 1, 1946, p. 252; August 15, 1950, p. 465.
Virginia Kirkus' Service, February 15, 1963, pp. 189-90.
Washington Post Book World, October 29, 1967, p. 20.*

TATE, Eleanora E(laine) 1948-

PERSONAL: Born April 16, 1948, in Canton, MO; daughter of Clifford and Lillie (Douglas) Tate (raised by her grandmother, Corinne E. Johnson); married Zack E. Hamlett III (a photographer), August 19, 1972; children: Gretchen R. *Education:* Drake University, B.A., 1973. *Avocational interests:* Freshwater and saltwater fishing, hiking, gardening, eating chocolate cake, listening to stories, attending festivals.

ADDRESSES: Home—P.O. Box 3581, Morehead City, NC 28557. *Office*—Tate & Associates, P.O. Box 3581, Morehead City, NC 28557. *Agent*—Charlotte Sheedy, Charlotte Sheedy Literary Agency, 145 West 86th St., New York, NY 10024.

CAREER: Iowa Bystander, West Des Moines, news editor, 1966-68; *Des Moines Register* and *Des Moines Tribune,* Des Moines, IA, staff writer, 1968-76; *Jackson Sun,* Jackson, TN, staff writer, 1976-77; Kreative Koncepts, Inc., Myrtle Beach, SC, writer and researcher, 1979-81; Positive Images, Inc., Myrtle Beach, SC, president and co-owner (with husband, Zack E. Hamlett III), 1983-93; Tate & Associates, Morehead City, NC, media consultant, 1993—. Contributor to black history and culture workshops in Des Moines, IA, 1968-76; giver of poetry presentations, including Iowa Arts Council Writers in the Schools program, 1969-76, Rust College, 1973, and Grinnell College, 1975; free-lance writer for *Memphis Tri-State Defender,* 1977; guest author of South Carolina School Librarians Association Conference, 1981 and 1982; writer-in-residence, Elgin, SC, Chester, SC, and the Amana colonies, Middle, IA, all 1986.

MEMBER: National Association of Black Storytellers, Inc. (member of the board, 1988-92, president, 1991-92, life member, 1992—), Arts in Basic Curriculum Steering Committee, South Carolina Academy of Authors (vice-president of the board of directors, 1988-90; member of the board, 1987—), North Carolina Writers Network (member of the board, 1996-97), South Carolina Arts Commission Artists in Education, Concerned Citizens Operation Reach-Out of Horry County (South Carolina), Horry Cultural Arts Council (president of the board of directors, 1990-92), Twin Rivers Reading Council of IRA.

AWARDS, HONORS: Finalist, fifth annual Third World Writing Contest, 1973; Unity Award, Lincoln University, 1974, for educational reporting; Community Lifestyles award, Tennessee Press Association,

1977; Bread Loaf Writer's Conference fellowship, 1981; *Just an Overnight Guest* (film) listed among the "Selected Films for Young Adults 1985" by the Young Adult Committee of the American Library Association; Parents' Choice Award, 1987, for *The Secret of Gumbo Grove;* Presidential Award, National Association of Negro Business and Professional Women's Clubs, Georgetown chapter, 1988; Grand Strand Press Association Award, Second Place, for Social Responsibilities and Minority Affairs, 1988; Addy Award, Coastal Advertising Federation, 1988; Notable Children's Book, National Council for the Social Studies/Children's Book Council (NCSS/CBC), 1990, for *Thank You, Dr. Martin Luther King, Jr.!;* Children's Book of the Year selection, Child Study Children's Book Committee, 1990, for *Thank You, Dr. Martin Luther King, Jr.!;* Excellent Communicator Award, Department of Pupil Services, Horry County School District, 1990; recognition from the South Carolina House of Representatives, June 9, 1990, for her literary and community efforts in South Carolina; Grace Brooks Memorial Humanitarian Award, South Carolina Action Council for Cross-Cultural Mental Health and Human Services, 1991; Board of Directors Award, Horry Cultural Arts Council, 1991; "Pick of the Lists," American Booksellers Association (ABA), 1992, for *Front Porch Stories at the One-Room School,* and 1996, for *A Blessing in Disguise;* Distinguished Woman of the Year in the Arts, Carteret County Council for Women, 1993; *Front Porch Stories at the One-Room School* was on the List of Recommended Books for Summer Reading, *This Morning* (CBS-TV), 1994; named North Carolina Kidfest Festival Author, 1998; recipient of numerous other awards for journalism and community service.

WRITINGS:

(Editor with husband, Zack E. Hamlett III, and contributor) *Eclipsed* (poetry), privately printed, 1975.

(Editor and contributor) *Wanjiru: A Collection of Blackwomanworth,* privately printed, 1976.

Just an Overnight Guest, Dial (New York), 1980.

The Secret of Gumbo Grove, F. Watts (New York), 1987.

Thank You, Dr. Martin Luther King, Jr.!, F. Watts, 1990.

Retold African Myths (short stories), illustrated by Don Tate II, Perfection Learning Corporation, 1992.

Front Porch Stories at the One-Room School, Bantam/Skylark (New York), 1992.

A Blessing in Disguise, Delacorte Press (New York), 1995.

Don't Split the Pole: Tales of Down Home Folk Wisdom, Delacorte Press, 1997.

OTHER

Also contributor to books, including *Children of Longing,* edited by Rosa Guy, Bantam, 1970; *Impossible?* (juvenile), Houghton (Boston), 1972; *Broadside Annual 1972,* Broadside Press (Highland Park, MI), 1972; *Communications* (juvenile), Heath (Lexington, MA), 1973; *Off-Beat* (juvenile), Macmillan (New York), 1974; *Sprays of Rubies* (anthology of poetic prose), Ragnarok, 1975; *Valhalla Four,* Ragnarok, 1977; and *In Praise of Our Fathers and Our Mothers,* Just Us Books (East Orange, NJ), 1997.

Contributor of poetry and fiction to periodicals, including *Journal of Black Poetry* and *Des Moines Register Picture Magazine.*

ADAPTATIONS: Just an Overnight Guest was adapted as a film starring Fran Robinson, Tiffany Hill, Rosalind Cash, and Richard Roundtree, Phoenix/B.F.A. Films & Video, 1983, broadcast on Wonderworks (PBS) and Nickelodeon; *The Secret of Gumbo Grove* was adapted for audiotape, Recorded Books, Inc., 1997.

WORK IN PROGRESS: African American Musicians, a title in the "Black Stars" biography series, for Wiley.

SIDELIGHTS: Eleanora E. Tate was born in 1948 in Canton, a small town in northeastern Missouri, where, during her early childhood, legal segregation was still enforced. She attended first grade in 1954 at the town's one-room grade school for African-Americans. The following year her class was integrated into Canton's white school system. Tate's novels, each focusing on a young African-American girl, are set in the places from her life that she knows well. Her first novel, *Just an Overnight Guest,* takes place in Nutbrush, Missouri, a small town modeled after Canton. In the story nine-year-old Margie becomes angry when her mother invites Ethel Hardisen, a half-black, half-white four-year-old, to stay with the family for a night. Ethel, Margie says, "broke stuff, stole candy, threw rocks at people. Once she hit me in the back with a piece of concrete." Ethel's visit is mysteriously extended, despite her bad behavior, and Margie begins to see Ethel as competition for her parents' affection. Only at the end of the book does Margie

learn that Ethel had been an abused, neglected child, whose father is Margie's irresponsible Uncle Jake.

Tate once explained that she wrote *Just an Overnight Guest* "to add my voice . . . to the thought that children's childhoods can be happy if they can learn that they can do anything they set their minds to." The book, moreover, drew praise from critics. Merri Rosenberg of the *New York Times Book Review* writes, "Eleanora Tate does a fine job presenting the emotional complexities of Margie's initiation into adult life's moral ambiguities. . . . If she drives home her point with a slightly heavy hand . . . [she] has imbued the situation with enough realism to make it plausible." In *Horn Book Magazine* Celia Morris praises Tate for capturing "the nuances of small-town life, the warmth of a Black family struggling with a problem, and the volatile emotions of a young child."

In her second novel, *The Secret of Gumbo Grove* (1987), the setting is similar to Myrtle Beach, South Carolina. The story, explains Tate, is about an eleven-year-old girl, Raisin Stackhouse, who "loves history, but she can't seem to find any positive Black history in her hometown of Gumbo Grove, South Carolina's most famous ocean-side resort, until she stumbles on to an old cemetery owned by her church. . . . The townspeople aren't too happy with her discovery [of the area's history of racial segregation] . . . because they are ashamed with their own families' past." Linda Classen, writing in the *Voice of Youth Advocates,* considers the book important, for it gives "a feeling for life in a black community before blacks had rights, which . . . not many young people today can comprehend." In the *Bulletin of the Center for Children's Books,* Betsy Hearne calls the ending, when Raisin is given a surprise community service award, "a bit tidy," although she goes on to say that the book "will be satisfying for young readers, who can enjoy this as a leisurely, expansive reading experience."

Also set in Gumbo Grove is Tate's third novel, *Thank You, Dr. Martin Luther King, Jr.!,* a story narrated by nine-year-old Mary Elouise, who is embarrassed about being black and who spends much of her energy trying to please a conceited, blond-haired classmate. She finds it especially embarrassing when her patronizing, uninformed white teacher effusively praises Martin Luther King, Jr. It eventually falls upon the grandmother to help Mary appreciate her black heritage.

Tate approaches this sensitive story with great care. In the *Bulletin of the Center for Children's Books,* Zena Sutherland, though critical of the book's "repetitive and slow paced" style, praises Tate for not falling prey to racial stereotyping. "One of the strong points of her story," Sutherland says, "is that there is bias in both races, just as there is understanding in both." *Booklist*'s Denise Wilms echoes this view: "Tate tackles a sensitive issue, taking pains to keep characters multidimensional and human."

A Blessing in Disguise also takes place in the setting introduced in *The Secret of Gumbo Grove*. According to *Publishers Weekly* critics Elizabeth Devereaux and Diane Roback, its narrator, Zambia Brown, has a "witty and sassy voice" that "instantly grabs readers' attention." Zambia is a twelve-year-old girl who lives with her aunt and uncle in Deacon's Neck. Her alcoholic, drug-addicted mother has been hospitalized for years, and her father, a nightclub owner and drug dealer, lives with a second wife and two teenaged daughters in Gumbo Grove. Zambia longs to live with her father, whom she views as sophisticated and glamorous. But when he opens a new club on her street in Deacon's Neck, he brings crime along with him. Zambia is almost killed in a shooting that does take the life of one of her half-sisters. Becky Kornman observes in *Voice of Youth Advocates* that the story shows "it is possible [for Zambia] to love her father, but hate the things he does." While Roger Sutton of *Bulletin of the Center for Children's Books* writes that the novel presents a much "bleaker theme and atmosphere" than those found in Tate's other stories of Gumbo Grove, he also states that it frankly shows how an "African-American community can be threatened from within."

Tate returns to Nutbrush, Missouri, for her next book, *Front Porch Stories at the One-Room School,* the sequel to *Just an Overnight Guest.* At the beginning Margie and Ethel, now three years older, are lying around on a hot summer night, so bored that their "life is duller than dirt." This problem, however, is solved when the father takes them on a walk to an old, one-room building, formerly the grade school for the town's African-American children. The father then begins to tell a number of stories about his childhood, which not only entertain the children but also teach them something important about their heritage. In an afterward to the book, Tate reveals that "most of the stories that [the father] tells . . . are based on my own actual experiences, or on stories I heard and greatly embellished." Although a *Publishers Weekly* reviewer finds the book "somewhat heavy-handed," with a "stilted dialogue that at times borders on the saccharine," the critic also praises Tate's "evocative language," which "conjures up rural

southern life." The book, moreover, points out Tate's special concern for father-daughter relationships. Tate once remarked, "It has been said little black boys need fathers. I believe little black girls need fathers. I emphasize that. It's something that hasn't been played up in recent years. I see it every day with my husband and my daughter."

While living in Myrtle Beach, South Carolina, Tate and her husband Zack founded Positive Images, a public relations agency dedicated to highlighting positive stories and images of black people, in an attempt to help people of all ethnic backgrounds to become more aware of black history, and more proud of the black community's contemporary identity. Tate considers their efforts a success. "We did a lot of work, poked a lot of information about African Americans into a lot of northeastern South Carolina minds," she once declared. "We wrote stories in a positive light about the local African American community that didn't get into white papers on a regular basis." Tate found it significant that "one could actually 'see' Black people in Zack's photos because he knew how to correctly use a camera. Black people weren't just dark dots in the pictures. So that was another way that people could 'see' themselves, visually, literally, in a positive light."

In 1992, Tate and her husband moved to Morehead City and ended their work with Positive Images, in part so that the author could have more time to concentrate on her writing. She reflected: "I want to get closer to God. . . . God has been my refuge and my everything now that I have recognized who God is. God has made it possible to write, and I really look for that spiritual guidance when I write."

BIOGRAPHICAL/CRITICAL SOURCES:

BOOKS

Children's Literature Review, Volume 37, Gale, 1996.

PERIODICALS

About . . . Time, November-December, 1997, p. 24.
African American Review, spring, 1998, p. 85.
Booklist, November 1, 1980, p. 408; May 15, 1987, pp. 1450-51; April 15, 1990, p. 1636; August, 1992, p. 2014; August, 1998, p. 2029.
Bulletin of the Center for Children's Books, October, 1980, p. 42; June, 1987, p. 199; June, 1990, p. 254; February, 1995, p. 216.

Christian Science Monitor, May 1, 1987, pp. B3-B4.
Des Moines Register, March 1, 1981.
Essence, December, 1992, p. 108.
Horn Book, December, 1980, pp. 643-44; fall, 1995, p. 305.
Interracial Books for Children Bulletin, Number 2, 1981, pp. 21-22.
Kirkus Reviews, February 15, 1981, p. 215; March 1, 1987, p. 380; February 1, 1990, p. 186; July 15, 1992, p. 926; February 15, 1995, p. 233; October 15, 1997, p. 1589.
Kliatt, April, 1989, p. 18.
Myrtle Beach Sun News, November 23, 1980.
New York Times Book Review, February 8, 1981, p. 20.
Publishers Weekly, August 10, 1992, p. 71; December 5, 1994, p. 77; June 3, 1996, p. 85; October 6, 1997, p. 84; February 15, 1999, p. 109.
Reading Teacher, February, 1994, pp. 404-405.
School Library Journal, October, 1980, p. 42; March, 1990, pp. 220-21; March, 1992, pp. 163-67; February, 1995, p. 115.
Voice of Youth Advocates, August-September, 1987, p. 123; April, 1995, p. 28.
Washington Post Book World, May 10, 1981.

*   *   *

TERVALON, Jervey 1958-

PERSONAL: Born November 23, 1958, in New Orleans, LA; son of Hillary (a postal worker) and Lolita (a retired key-punch operator) Tervalon; married Gina Harris (a retired personal analyst); children: Giselle. *Education:* University of California, Santa Barbara, B.A., 1980; University of California, Irvine, M.F.A. (creative writing).

ADDRESSES: Home—Pasadena, CA. *Office*—142 Lincoln Ave., Pasadena, CA 91103. *Agent*—Roy Harris, Lance & Harris, Inc., 156 5th Ave., New York, NY 10001.

CAREER: Taught in the Los Angeles public schools during the 1980s; University of California, Santa Barbara, instructor in literature, c. 1992-96; freelance writer, c. 1994—; St. Mary's College, Moraga, CA, instructor, c. 1996—.

AWARDS, HONORS: New Voices Award, Quality Paperback Book Club, 1994; Disney Screenwriters Fellowship; fellowships from University of California, Irvine and Pasadena Arts Commission.

WRITINGS:

Understand This (novel), Morrow (New York, NY), 1994.
(Contributor) *Absolute Disaster: Fiction from Los Angeles,* edited by Lee Montgomery, Santa Monica Review, 1996.
Living for the City, Incommunicado Press, 1998.

Contributor of short stories to periodicals, including *Spectrum Magazine, Details,* and *Statement.* Contributor of a nonfiction essay for the *L.A. Weekly.*

WORK IN PROGRESS: Not Sentimental, a fictional history of black Los Angeles; a third novel.

SIDELIGHTS: Novelist Jervey Tervalon was born in New Orleans, Louisiana, but moved to Los Angeles, California with his family when he was a young boy. Both parents encouraged him to read and to enter college when the time came. After he obtained his bachelor's degree, he went to teach English at a disadvantaged high school in Los Angeles. The things he saw there touched him deeply, and he was especially affected by the murder of a good student who was in the wrong place at the wrong time. Tervalon left high school teaching to return to college in pursuit of a degree in creative writing. While there he began writing a novel inspired by his experiences and observations as a teacher. The book served as his master's thesis and was published to much acclaim in 1994 under the title *Understand This.*

Understand This begins with a murder. Though the novel is narrated by eight different characters, one of the most important is Francois, a young African-American in his last year of high school. Shortly after he finishes playing football with his friend Doug, Doug is shot and killed by his own drug addict girlfriend, who is pregnant by him. *Understand This* then goes on to present the effects of this killing on Francois, Doug's brother and sister, the killer, and others. Narrators of the story also include Margot, Francois' girlfriend, whose grades and determination will enable her to leave the Los Angeles ghetto through college; Francois' mother, a nurse who is determined to move her family to relative safety in Georgia; and Michaels, a caring high school teacher who is quickly reaching the point of burn-out and leaving the students who desperately need him.

Understand This has met with a great deal of praise from critics. Bob Sipchen in the *Los Angeles Times Book Review* applauded the novel's differences from more typical stories of African-American, urban poor affected by violence. "Shrugging off the *de rigueur* overlay of rage and recrimination, resisting the peer pressure to posture macho, [Tervalon] is freer to flex his wit, work out his fine observational skills, and inject his warmth into the yarn," Sipchen affirmed. He went on to laud the author as "daring," and explained that *Understand This* "explores more difficult landscape—geographic and interior—than many of its angrier and grittier brethren." This comment fits with what Tervalon himself emphasized about his novel to Dennis McLellan in the *Los Angeles Times.* "We rarely talk about the internal psychology of these kids. We kind of ignore it and think only of the external. Sometimes there's fear and depression," he added, "but you don't see it. You just see the veneer of a kid that's unscarred, but inside they're suffering." McLellan approved *Understand This* as "a gritty tale." Alison Baker, discussing the novel in the *Washington Post* commended it as well, judging that "Tervalon succeeds in his larger mission, which is to show us this particular way of American life." She went on to observe that "good literature has no agenda; it's not propaganda. Tervalon offers no 'solutions.' He's given us a portrait of people who live in a certain world at a certain time and do the best they can." Baker concluded: "*Understand This* is perhaps less an order than a plea."

BIOGRAPHICAL/CRITICAL SOURCES:

PERIODICALS

Los Angeles Times, April 4, 1994, sec. "View."
Los Angeles Times Book Review, March 20, 1994, pp. 2, 7.
Washington Post, April 7, 1994, p. C2.

*   *   *

THOMAS, Clarence 1948-

PERSONAL: Born June 23, 1948, in Savannah, GA; married Virginia Lamp (a Congressional aide), May 30, 1987; children: Jamal Adeen. *Education:* Attended Conception Seminary, 1967-68; Holy Cross College. A.B. (cum laude), 1971; Yale University, J.D., 1974.

ADDRESSES: Office—United States Supreme Court, Supreme Court Building, 1 First St. N.E., Washington, DC 20543.

CAREER: Admitted to the Bar of Missouri, 1974; State of Missouri, Jefferson City, Assistant Attorney General, 1974-77; Monsanto Company, St. Louis, MO, attorney, 1977-79; legislative assistant to Senator John Danforth, Washington, DC, 1979-81; U.S. Department of Education, Assistant Secretary for Civil Rights, 1981-82; U.S. Equal Employment Opportunity Commission, chair, 1982-90; U.S. Court of Appeals, Washington, DC, judge, 1990-91; U.S. Supreme Court, associate justice, 1991—.

WRITINGS:

Clarence Thomas—Confronting the Future: Selections from the Senate Confirmation Hearings and Prior Speeches, introduction by Gordon Crovitz, Regnery Gateway (Washington, DC), c. 1992.

SIDELIGHTS: The nomination of Clarence Thomas to the United States Supreme Court in 1991 sparked some of the most intense controversy over race and gender in America since the Civil Rights Movement. Following the resignation of the first African-American to sit on the Supreme Court bench, Thurgood Marshall, President George Bush chose the politically conservative Thomas, another African-American, to fill the vacancy. But Thomas was suddenly accused of sexual harassment by Anita Hill, a law school professor and former employee of Thomas at the Department of Education and the Equal Employment Opportunity Commission (EEOC). This allegation dominated Thomas's Senate confirmation hearing and made headlines for weeks. Though Thomas's nomination was approved by the Senate Judiciary Committee, the prurient nature of the allegations against him continued to fuel bitter national arguments across race and gender lines. The events surrounding this controversial period are depicted with the collection of some of Thomas's speeches leading up to the controversy and his remarks during the Senate Confirmation hearings in *Clarence Thomas—Confronting the Future.*

Thomas grew up in the Jim Crow-era South, and his childhood experience of segregation and poverty influenced his firm conservative views. Born in 1948 in Savannah, Georgia, he was raised in a single-parent home in the rural community of Pinpoint, Georgia. He had little contact with his father though he was close to his grandfather, who ran a small ice-and-oil delivery business in Savannah. Thomas admired the strong work ethic he saw around him in the African-American community and embraced the model of Booker T. Washington, who advocated self-help for African-Americans instead of dependence on government assistance. Thomas was to develop a philosophy that rejected any kind of racial discrimination, including affirmative action policies or other types of preferential treatment, for minorities.

Thomas attended Holy Cross College, from which he received a B.A. in 1971, and Yale University, where he earned a J.D in 1974. He was admitted to the Bar in the state of Missouri that year, taking a position as assistant attorney general in Jefferson City and then moving on to private practice as an attorney for Monsanto Company in St. Louis from 1977 to 1979.

In 1979, Thomas moved to Washington, D.C., to work as a legal assistant to Senator John Danforth of Missouri. Danforth had met Thomas while Thomas was a law student at Yale and was to become one of his strongest supporters through the contested confirmation hearing. Danforth praised Thomas highly for his serious commitment to his job and has noted that Thomas was "clearly the most popular person in the office." After leaving Senator Danforth's staff, Thomas was appointed to posts at the Department of Education (1981-82) and the Equal Employment Opportunity Commission (1982-90). According to Senator Paul Simon of Illinois, Thomas's performance in these posts was not distinguished. Simon pointed out that, though Thomas was capable, his position at EEOC was difficult because the Reagan Administration had no interest in enforcing anti-discrimination laws. In 1990 Thomas was appointed a judge in the U.S. Court of Appeals and was nominated to the Supreme Court in early October, 1991.

In the Court of Appeals, Thomas heard more than one hundred fifty cases but wrote only twenty-five opinions. His decisions were consistently conservative: in criminal cases, he tended to reject such defenses of entrapment, inadmissible evidence, or incompetent legal counsel. One of the controversial decisions in which Thomas participated was the denial of the special prosecutor's request for a rehearing after Lieutenant Colonel Oliver North's conviction for lying to Congress about the Iran-Contra affair had been overturned. Thomas voted with the majority and publicly praised North's actions in defying Congress, which Thomas had said was "out of control." Critics of the Bush Administration protested Thomas's nomination to the Supreme Court, claiming that he lacked experience and did not possess a distinguished judicial record. They also argued that Thomas's conservative views would interfere with his ability to judge constitutional matters. Despite this criticism, however, most observers believed Thomas's nomination would be affirmed without much difficulty.

When Thomas's nomination was announced, Anita Hill, a law professor who had worked under him at the Department of Education and at EEOC from 1981 to 1983, informed the Senate Judiciary Committee that Thomas had engaged in sexually harassing behavior, which included inappropriate comments about her physical appearance, conversations about sexual or pornographic matters, and pressure to date him. Hill's accusations were leaked to the press and became the focus of Thomas's highly publicized confirmation hearing. Thomas vigorously denied any wrongdoing and criticized the media for its handling of the matter, contending that he had been made the victim of a "high-tech lynching." African-Americans were torn by the proceedings. According to media sources, some felt betrayed by Hill, who is African-American, and worried that her allegations would reinforce negative stereotypes of African-Americans. Many who had not initially supported Thomas came to his defense, while feminists rallied to Hill's cause. Conservative whites were also incensed by the allegations, which they saw as a leftist plot to keep control of the Supreme Court.

On October 16, 1991, the Senate Judiciary Committee, all male and all white, approved Thomas's nomination by a vote of fifty-two to fifty-eight. This was the narrowest margin by which any Supreme Court justice had ever been confirmed. The confirmation was protested by women's groups, in particular African-American Women in Defense of Ourselves, who took out a full-page advertisement in the *New York Times* denouncing Thomas.

With the publication of *Clarence Thomas—Confronting the Future,* the public was able to witness a new side to the controversy surrounding Thomas's confirmation. According to Mark Cunningham, who reviewed the volume for the *National Review,* the collection "allows us to rediscover the true Mr. Thomas and to examine the Judiciary Committee's dog-and-pony show at our leisure." Cunningham remarked that the "greatest injustice" of the controversy was that it forced him to play a passive role in the proceedings and hid the real nature of Thomas's character from the public as "a man who had won against poverty and segregation." Cunningham interpreted the book as depicting the attempts of the Left to maintain control of the Supreme Court "by violating every civil liberty and procedural nicety a liberal court is said to protect." Cunningham also commented on the personal toll the hearings had on Thomas and his family and acknowledged that the book is "unabashedly pro-Thomas."

Since assuming his responsibilities on the Supreme Court, Thomas has kept a low profile. He asks few questions from the bench, observers say, and has written few opinions. But he has become what the liberals who had initially opposed him had feared: a judicial activist. Though Thomas has asserted his belief in judicial restraint—impartial consideration of constitutional matters—he has consistently substituted his personal views in cases regarding race. Jeffrey Rosen, in a *New Yorker* article, argued that new scholarship shows that "Thomas is wrong to insist that the Fourteenth Amendment to the Constitution was intended to forbid racial discrimination in all circumstances" and concludes that "Thomas is trapped . . . between his moral commitment to a color-blind Constitution and an interpretative methodology that compels him to reject it." In his first three years on the Court, claim reporters Jane Mayer and Jill Abramson, Thomas "has proved himself the most political of justices," whose decisions have caused "a blurring of the distinction between politics and law that has bothered some judicial ethics experts, including some of Thomas's fellow justices."

Only four months after his appointment to the Court, Thomas drew criticism for his dissent from the seven to two majority in Hudson versus McMillan, a case involving two guards who severely beat a shackled prisoner. Thomas's opinion that the beating was not "cruel and unusual" was criticized by the Court for ignoring "the concepts of dignity, civilized standards, humanity and decency that animate the Eighth Amendment." Thomas has also consistently upheld capital punishment, insisting that a convict's background should not be considered in sentencing because it might lead to arbitrary leniency that might discriminate against African-American defendants.

According to media sources, though some African-Americans have been pleased with Thomas's Supreme Court decisions, others have been surprised and angered by his refusal to rule sympathetically for minority and civil rights litigants. Thomas's position in a series of voting rights cases in 1994 and 1995 provoked particular outrage in the black community. But Thomas is unswayed by such reactions. He continues to engage in fervid discussions of race with black conservative academics such as Thomas Sowell, Shelby Steele, Walter Williams, and Glenn Loury, who have said that Thomas is more compassionate than his critics realize. Thomas also speaks frequently on college campuses, where he proves to be an inspirational speaker, especially among African-American audiences. Though rumors spread at the beginning of Thomas's tenure that he would retire from the bench early, Thomas has vowed to remain in his position as associate justice on the Supreme Court for many decades.

BIOGRAPHICAL/CRITICAL SOURCES:

BOOKS

The African American Almanac, sixth edition, Gale (Detroit, MI), 1994.

Danforth, John C., *Resurrection: The Confirmation of Clarence Thomas,* Viking (New York), 1994.

Dictionary of Twentieth-Century Culture, Volume 5: *African American Culture,* Gale (Detroit, MI), 1996.

Hall, Kermit L., editor, *The Oxford Companion to the Supreme Court of the United States,* Oxford University Press (New York City), 1992.

Mayer, Jane, and Jill Ambramson, *Strange Justice: The Selling of Clarence Thomas,* Houghton Mifflin (Boston), 1994.

Morrison, Toni, editor, *Race-ing, Justice, Engendering Power: Essays on Anita Hill, Clarence Thomas and the Social Construction of Reality,* Pantheon (New York City), 1992.

Newsmakers, Gale (Detroit, MI), 1992.

Simon, Paul, *Advice and Consent: Clarence Thomas, Robert Bork and the Intriguing History of the Supreme Court's Nomination Battles,* National Press Books (Washington, DC), c. 1992.

Smitherman, Geneva, editor, *African-American Women Speak Out On Anita Hill-Clarence Thomas,* Wayne State University Press (Detroit, MI), 1995.

Spradling, Mary Mace, editor, *In Black and White,* Gale (Detroit, MI), 1985.

Who's Who among Black Americans, ninth edition, Gale (Detroit, MI), 1997.

PERIODICALS

Advertising Age, July 8, 1991, p. 4; August 5, 1991, p. 3; October 14, 1991, p. 8; November 4, 1991, p. 35; May 20, 1996, p. 57.

Advocate, August 13, 1991, p. 15; November 19, 1991, pp. 8-9.

America, October 5, 1991, p. 1; October 26, 1991, p. 283; November 2, 1991, p. 321; November 9, 1991, p. 342.

American City & Country, July, 1985, p. 62.

American Spectator, September, 1991, p. 8; October, 1991, p. 31; November, 1991, p. 37; December, 1991, pp. 8, 31-32; March, 1992, pp. 18-31; May, 1992, pp. 62-63; May, 1993, pp. 34-41; September, 1994, pp. 55-56; January, 1995, pp. 30-52.

Atlantic, February, 1987, p. 70.

Barron's, August 26, 1991, p. 10.

Black Enterprise, May, 1982, p. 26; October, 1991, p. 13; January, 1992, p. 14.

Business Week, July 15, 1991, p. 27; July 22, 1991, p. 37; August 5, 1991, p. 64B; August 12, 1991, p. 12; September 16, 1991, p. 32; September 30, 1991, p. 28; October 21, 1991, p. 32; October 28, 1991, pp. 30-36, 150; July 1, 1996, pp. 34.

Christian Century, July 24, 1991, p. 707; September 4, 1991, p. 798; October 2, 1991, p. 869; October 23, 1991, p. 955; March 11, 1992, pp. 267-268.

Christianity Today, August 19, 1991, p. 42; October 28, 1991, pp. 34-35, 72; November 25, 1991, pp. 72.

Chronicle of Higher Education, July 10, 1991, p. A17; October 23, 1991, p. A1; November 6, 1991, p. A60; November 13, 1991, p. B1; January 8, 1992, p. B2; November 8, 1996, p. A12.

Commentary, January, 1992, pp. 26-36; February, 1992, pp. 26-35.

Commonweal, August 9, 1991, p. 451; October 25, 1991, pp. 595-599; November 8, 1991, pp. 632-633, 627-628; March 27, 1992, pp. 5-6.

Congressional Quarterly Weekly Report, December 9, 1995, pp. 317-320.

Economist, July 6, 1991, pp. A32, 15; September 7, 1991, p. A26; October 12, 1991, p. A25; October 19, 1991, pp. 14, A32; June 15, 1996, pp. 27-28.

Emerge, November, 1994, p. 22; November, 1996, pp. 7, 38-46, 108.

Essence, December, 1991, p. 134; January, 1992, pp. 58-62; March, 1992, pp. 54-59.

Film Comment, January-February, 1992, pp. 7-13.

Forbes, August 5, 1991, p. 33; October 28, 1991, p. 90; November 11, 1991, pp. 23, 56; June 2, 1997, p. 28.

Fortune, April 19, 1982, p. 143; September 16, 1985, p. 26; November 18, 1991, pp. 227-228.

Glamour, January, 1992, p. 34; February, 1996, p. 38.

Good Housekeeping, September, 1997, p. 216.

Governing, March, 1992, p. 53.

Harper's, September, 1991, p. 8; December, 1991, pp. 10-16.

Hispanic, September, 1991, p. 60.

Humanist, November-December, 1991, p. 23; January-February, 1992, p. 39; May-June, 1992, pp. 47-50.

Insight on the News, July 15, 1991, p. 32; October 28, 1991, p. 48; November 11, 1991, pp. 17-18, 21-22, 40; November 18, 1991, pp. 17-18, 40; March 30, 1992, pp. 23-24; May 11, 1992, p. 40; May 17, 1993, p. 40; March 7, 1994, pp. 20-26; September 4, 1995, pp. 8-11.

Interview, January, 1992, p. 55.

Jet, March 1, 1982, p. 6; April 19, 1982, p. 6; May 24, 1982, p. 40; July 5, 1982, p. 8; September 13, 1982, p. 8; April 2, 1984, p. 1; July 23, 1984, p. 17; November 26, 1984, p. 4; September 16, 1985, p. 16; April 14, 1986, p. 8; July 21, 1986, p. 24; August 11, 1986, p. 6; October 12, 1987, p. 38; March 5, 1990, p. 12; July 22, 1991, p. 5; August 5, 1991, p. 6; August 19, 1991, pp. 4, 8; August 26, 1991, p. 4; September 2, 1991, p. 4; September 23, 1991, p. 4; September 30, 1991, p. 6; November 4, 1991, pp. 4-9; November 25, 1991, p. 4; February 3, 1992, p. 9; March 9, 1992, p. 6; March 16, 1992, p. 5; June 8, 1992, p. 32; November 14, 1994, pp. 4-5; November 28, 1994, p. 22; July 3, 1995, p. 9; September 4, 1995, p. 36; September 11, 1995, p. 8; October 2, 1995, pp. 34-35; June 17, 1996, p. 7; July 1, 1996, pp. 4-7; March 3, 1997, pp. 6-7.

Life, January, 1992, pp. 62-73.

Maclean's, July 15, 1991, p. 43; September 23, 1991, p. 4; October 21, 1991, p. 78; October 28, 1991, pp. 24-27.

Meet the Press, July 21, 1991, p. 1; September 8, 1991, p. 1.

Ms., January-February, 1992, pp. 34-46.

Nation, March 26, 1990, p. 405; July 29, 1991, p. 148; August 12, 1991, p. 180; September 23, 1991, p. 336; September 30, 1991, pp. 357, 364; October 14, 1991, p. 434; October 28, 1991, pp. 501-504; November 4, 1991, pp. 537, 542; November 11, 1991, p. 573-574, 577; November 25, 1991, pp. 679-680; November 2, 1992, p. 492.

National Catholic Reporter, February 26, 1982, p. 5; July 19, 1991, p. 32; July 19, 1991, p. 26; August 2, 1991, p. 7; December 27, 1991, p. 11; April 24, 1992, p. 17.

National Review, March 30, 1992, p.50, 53; August 12, 1991, p. 36; September 9, 1991, pp. 16, 21;

October 7, 1991, pp. 10, 35; October 21, 1991, p. 18; November 4, 1991, pp. 12-15, 22; November 18, 1991, p. 40; December 2, 1991, p. 64; November 2, 1992, pp. 14-16; May 10, 1993, pp. 23-27; May 24, 1993, p. 16; June 21, 1993, pp. 55-58; October 18, 1993, p. 20; January 24, 1994, pp. 48-53; April 3, 1995, pp. 51-54.

Nation's Cities Weekly, July 5, 1982, p. 3; July 8, 1991, p. 16.

NEA Today, October, 1991, p. 6.

New Leader, October 7, 1991, p. 3; November 4, 1991, pp. 5-8.

New Republic, July 29, 1991, pp. 6, 12; August 5, 1991, pp. 4, 7; August 19, 1991, p. 4; September 9, 1991, p. 18; September 30, 1991, pp. 16, 18, 23; October 7, 1991, p. 20; October 14, 1991, p. 14; October 28, 1991, pp. 7-9; November 4, 1991, pp. 8, 42; November 11, 1991, pp. 4, 13-15, 46; November 18, 1991, pp. 34-35; January 6, 1992, pp. 16-19; September 21, 1992, pp. 18-22; February 22, 1993, pp. 29-36; May 30, 1994, p. 6; December 19, 1994, pp. 27-34; June 12, 1995, pp. 12-13; July 31, 1995, pp. 19-25.

New Statesman & Society, October 18, 1991, p. 13; November 1, 1991, p. 16.

Newsweek, March 9, 1981, p. 29; February 22, 1982, p. 26; July 15, 1991, pp. 16, 64; July 22, 1991, p. 18; July 29, 1991, p. 27; August 12, 1991, p. 26; August 19, 1991, p. 10; September 16, 1991, pp. 18, 23; September 23, 1991, p. 18; October 21, 1991, pp. 24-33, 41-45; October 28, 1991, pp. 24-26, 28, 30-33, 82; October 5, 1992, pp. 58-59; April 19, 1993, p. 74; November 14, 1994, pp. 52-56.

New York, July 29, 1991, p. 12; October 28, 1991, pp. 28-32; December 16, 1991, pp. 30-37.

New Yorker, July 15, 1991, p. 21; April 29 and May 6, 1996, pp. 66-73; October 28, 1991, p. 29; November 4, 1991, pp. 106-113; September 27, 1993, pp. 38-52; December 12, 1994, pp. 9-10.

New York Review of Books, October 10, 1991, p. 52; November 7, 1991, p. 41.

New York Times, October 1, 1997, p. A19.

New York Times Book Review, October 25, 1992.

New York Times Magazine, October 27, 1991, p. 20; November 3, 1991, p. 18; November 17, 1991, p. 56.

Nuestro, May, 1986, p. 47.

People Weekly, July 22, 1991, p. 40; October 28, 1991, pp. 10, 40; November 11, 1991, pp. 108-115; November 14, 1994, pp. 145-146; October 6, 1997, pp. 127-128.

Playboy, January, 1993, p. 45; January, 1995, pp. 140-146.

Progressive, September, 1991, pp. 8, 17; November, 1991, p. 11; April, 1992, pp. 9-10; November, 1993, pp. 37-43; October, 1997, pp. 18-21.

Public Opinion Quarterly, winter, 1993, pp. 575-593.

Publishers Weekly, May 4, 1992, pp. 20-22; August 29, 1994, p. 24.

Reason, October, 1991, p. 6; January, 1992, p. 58; February, 1992, pp. 22-33.

Reference and Research Book News, March, 1993, p. 24.

Regardie's, December-January, 1991, pp. 68-74.

Scholastic Update, November 1, 1991, pp. 2-9, 20.

Society, March-April, 1996, pp. 11-25.

Texas Monthly, January, 1995, pp. 106-118.

Tikkun, September/October, 1991, pp. 7, 23; January-February, 1992, pp. 17-33.

Time, January 20, 1986, p. 25; July 15, 1991, p. 18; August 12, 1991, p. 6; September 16, 1991, p. 24; September 23, 1991, p. 20; October 14, 1991, p. 17; October 21, 1991, pp. 34-48, 104; October 28, 1991, pp. 23, 74, 104; March 9, 1992, p. 31; July 13, 1992, pp. 30-31; December 19, 1994, p. 83; June 26, 1995, p. 36; July 31, 1995, pp. 8-9.

U.S. News and World Report, March 14, 1983, p. 67; July 15, 1991, pp. 17, 22, 84; July 22, 1991, p. 50; August 12, 1991, p. 8; August 19, 1991, p. 13; September 16, 1991, pp. 24, 33; September 23, 1991, p. 18; September 30, 1991, p. 19; October 7, 1991, p. 12; October 14, 1991, pp. 8, 12; October 21, 1991, pp. 16, 32; October 28, 1991, pp. 16, 20, 25, 34, 38-40; March 2, 1992, p. 12; June 8, 1992, p. 10; October 12, 1992, pp. 28, 37, 39; August 22, 1994, p. 19; November 7, 1994, p. 63; June 24, 1996, p. 22.

Utne Reader, January-February, 1993, pp. 56-57.

Vanity Fair, January, 1992, pp. 46-51.

Variety, July 8, 1991, pp. 3, 22.

Vital Speeches, June 15, 1994, pp. 514-518.

World Press Review, October, 1991, p. 40.

OTHER

Reason, http://www.reasonmag.com/cthomasint.html (1998).*

*   *   *

THOMAS, Joyce Carol 1938-

PERSONAL: Born May 25, 1938, in Ponca City, OK; daughter of Floyd David (a bricklayer) and Leona (a housekeeper and hair stylist; maiden name, Thompson) Haynes; married Gettis L. Withers (a chemist), May 31, 1959 (divorced, 1968); married Roy T. Thomas, Jr. (a professor), September 7, 1968 (divorced, 1979); children: Monica Pecot, Gregory Withers, Michael Withers, Roy T. Thomas III. *Education:* Attended San Francisco City College, 1957-58, and University of San Francisco, 1957-58; College of San Mateo, A.A., 1964; San Jose State College (now University), B.A., 1966; Stanford University, M.A., 1967.

ADDRESSES: Home—Berkeley, CA. *Agent*—c/o Mitch Douglas, International Creative Management, 40 West 57th St., New York, NY 10019.

CAREER: Worked as a telephone operator in San Francisco, CA, 1957-58; Ravenwood School District, East Palo Alto, CA, teacher of French and Spanish, 1968-70; San Jose State College (now University), San Jose, CA, assistant professor of black studies, 1969-72, reading program director, 1979-82, professor of English, 1982-83; Contra Costa College, San Pablo, CA, teacher of drama and English, 1973-75; St. Mary's College, Moranga, CA, professor of English, 1975-77; full-time writer, 1981-84; visiting associate professor of English at Purdue University, spring, 1983; full professor of creative writing, University of Tennessee, 1989—.

MEMBER: Dramatists Guild, Authors Guild, Authors League of America.

AWARDS, HONORS: Danforth Graduate Fellow, University of California at Berkeley, 1973-75; Stanford University scholar, 1979-80, and Djerassi Fellow, 1982 and 1983; *New York Times* outstanding book of the year citation, American Library Association (ALA) best book citation, *Booklist* Children's Reviewers' Choice Award, and Before Columbus American Book Award, Before Columbus Foundation (Berkeley, CA), all 1982, and National Book Award for children's fiction, 1983, all for *Marked by Fire;* Coretta Scott King Honor Book Award, ALA, 1984, for *Bright Shadow;* named Outstanding Woman of the Twentieth Century, Sigma Gamma Rho, 1986; *A Gathering of Flowers: Stories about Being Young in America* was a National Conference of Christians and Jews recommended title for children and young adults, 1991; Coretta Scott King Honor Book Award, ALA, and Notable Children's Trade Book in the field of social studies, National Council for Social Studies and Children's Book Council, both 1994, for *Brown Honey in Broomwheat Tea.*

WRITINGS:

YOUNG ADULT NOVELS

Marked by Fire, Avon (New York City), 1982.
Bright Shadow (sequel to *Marked by Fire*), Avon, 1983.
Water Girl, Avon, 1986.
The Golden Pasture, Scholastic (New York City), 1986.
Journey, Scholastic, 1990.
When the Nightingale Sings, HarperCollins (New York City), 1992.

POETRY

Bittersweet, Firesign Press, 1973.
Crystal Breezes, Firesign Press, 1974.
Blessing, Jocato Press, 1975.
Black Child, illustrated by Tom Feelings, Zamani Productions, 1981.
Inside the Rainbow, Zikawana Press, 1982.
Brown Honey in Broomwheat Tea, illustrated by Floyd Cooper, HarperCollins, 1993.
Gingerbread Days, illustrated by Cooper, Harper Collins, 1995.
The Blacker the Berry: Poems, HarperCollins (New York City), 1997.
Crowning Glory: Poems, HarperCollins, 1997.

PLAYS

(And producer) *A Song in the Sky* (two-act), produced in San Francisco at Montgomery Theater, 1976.
Look! What a Wonder! (two-act), produced in Berkeley at Berkeley Community Theatre, 1976.
(And producer) *Magnolia* (two-act), produced in San Francisco at Old San Francisco Opera House, 1977.
(And producer) *Ambrosia* (two-act), produced in San Francisco at Little Fox Theatre, 1978.
Gospel Roots (two-act), produced in Carson, CA, at California State University, 1981.
I Have Heard of a Land, produced in Oklahoma City, OK, at Claussen Theatre, 1989, published by HarperCollins, 1997.
When the Nightingale Sings (musical; based on Thomas's novel of the same title), produced in Knoxville, TN, at Clarence Brown Theatre, 1991.

OTHER

(Editor) *A Gathering of Flowers: Stories about Being Young in America,* HarperCollins, 1990.

Contributor to periodicals, including *American Poetry Review, Black Scholar, Calafia, Drum Voices, Giant Talk,* and *Yardbird Reader.* Editor of *Ambrosia* (women's newsletter), 1980.

ADAPTATIONS: Marked by Fire was adapted by James Racheff and Ted Kociolek for the stage musical *Abyssinia,* first produced in New York City at the C.S.C. Repertory Theatre in 1987.

SIDELIGHTS: Joyce Carol Thomas's background as a migrant farm worker in rural Oklahoma and California supplies her with the prolific stock of characters and situations that fill her novels. The author admittedly fell in love with words and with the songs she heard in church, and has spent much of her time as a writer trying to recreate the sounds of singing with her written language. She is well known for her book of poems *Brown Honey in Broomwheat Tea;* her ground-breaking anthology, *A Gathering of Flowers: Stories about Being Young in America;* and her young adult novels *Marked by Fire* and *Bright Shadow,* which are set in Thomas's hometown and focus on the indomitable spirit of Abyssinia Jackson and her people.

Thomas grew up in Ponca City, Oklahoma, a small, dusty town where she lived across from the school. "Although now I live half a continent away from my hometown," Thomas related in *Something about the Author Autobiography Series (SAAS),* "when it comes to my writing I find that I am still there." She has set three of her novels in her hometown: *Marked by Fire, Bright Shadow,* and *The Golden Pasture.* Thomas loved school as a child and became anxious whenever it appeared she might be late because she did not want to miss anything. However, she usually missed the first month of school in order to finish up her farm work. Times were lean for Thomas's family, but they always made do. This she attributes partly to her mother's genius at making healthy foods that were not expensive; she has memories of huge spreads being laid out for Sunday dinners. These scenes of food have stuck with Thomas, for she finds food is one of the focuses in her novels. "Because in such a home food was another language for love, my books are redolent of sugar and spice, kale and collards," Thomas commented in *SAAS.*

When Thomas was ten years old, the family moved to rural Tracy, California. There Thomas learned to milk cows, fish for minnows, and harvest tomatoes and grapes. She also became intimately acquainted

with black widow spiders—there was a nest of them under her bed. She was later to use this experience in her novel *Journey.* Likewise, she had a similar experience with wasps when her brother locked her in a closet containing a wasp nest; *Marked by Fire* contains some scary scenes with these insects. In Tracy, California, Thomas continued her long summers harvesting crops. She worked beside many Mexicans and began a love affair with their language. "When the Spanish speakers talked they seemed to sing," Thomas remarked in *SAAS.*

When she went to college—which she managed to do by working full-time as a telephone operator as well as raising her children—she majored in Spanish and French. "From this base of languages I taught myself all I know about writing," she related in *SAAS.* She went on to earn a master's degree from Stanford University, and then taught foreign languages in public school. From 1973 to 1978, Thomas wrote poetry and plays for adults and became a celebrated author. She traveled to conferences and festivals all over the world, including Lagos, Nigeria.

In 1982, Thomas's career took a turn when she published *Marked by Fire,* a novel for a young adult audience. Steeped in the setting and traditions of her hometown, the novel focuses on Abyssinia Jackson, a girl who was born in a cotton field during harvest time. The title refers to the fact that she received a burn on her face from a brush fire during her birth. This leaves her "marked for unbearable pain and unspeakable joy," according to the local healer. The pain begins when Abyssinia is raped by an elder in the church when she is ten. Abby becomes mute after the violent act and is nursed back to health through the strength of the local women and her family. Abby's mother is named Patience in honor of Thomas's mother, who was a very patient parent. Strong, the father, has left the family in their time of need, but returns to them later—ironically—because he is not strong enough to face a crisis in his life. When Abby eventually regains her voice, she is able to tell her friend Lily Norene that after the rape she "felt dirty. Dirtier than playing in mud. The kind of dirt you can't ever wash off. . . . But the worst part was I felt like I was being spit on by God." It is the seeming abandonment by God that strikes Abby to the core—she must work through the horror before she can recover completely. Mother Barker, the town's midwife and healer, has a special role in the rehabilitation of Abby. In a more macabre way, so does Trembling Sally, a frightening, crazy woman who assaults the young girl with strange trials of fire, water, and insects. Eventually, Abby recovers with Mother Barker's help.

Marked by Fire has been well received by critics. Wendell Wray wrote in *Best Sellers* that Thomas "captures the flavor of black folk life in Oklahoma. . . . She has set for herself a very challenging task. . . . But Thomas' book works." Critic Dorothy Randall-Tsuruta commented in *Black Scholar* that Thomas's "poetic tone gives this work what scents give the roses already so pleasing in color. In fact often as not the lyrical here carries the reader beyond concerns for fast action. There too Thomas's short lived interest in writing plays figures in her fine regard and control of dialog." Hazel Rochman, writing in *School Library Journal,* admitted that "the lack of a fast-paced narrative line and the mythical overtones may present obstacles to some readers," but said that "many will be moved" by Abby's story. The book was placed on required reading lists at many high schools and universities. Commenting on her stormy novel, Thomas once stated that "as a writer I work to create books filled with conflict. . . . I address this quest in part by matching the pitiful absurdities and heady contradictions of life itself, in part by leading the heroine to twin fountains of magic and the macabre, and evoking the holy and the horrible in the same breath. Nor is it ever enough to match these. Through the character of Abyssinia, I strive for what is beyond these, seeking, as do many writers, to find newer worlds."

Bright Shadow, a sequel to *Marked by Fire,* was published in 1983. In this work, Abyssinia goes to college and ends up falling in love with Carl Lee Jefferson. Abby is a young woman now, searching for what she wants as she completes her pre-medical studies. For reasons she can't figure out, Abby's father disapproves of Carl Lee. She suspects, however, that it is because of Carl Lee's alcoholic father. At the same time, the psychically sensitive Abby begins to have forebodings about her aunt's new husband. These feelings are validated when Aunt Serena is found brutally murdered. Carl Lee begins to show his true colors when he is there to support Abby through her grief. Soon he has a revelation of his own when he finds out that the mysterious Cherokee woman that has been lurking around town is actually his mother. Despite these difficult hurdles, nothing is able to disrupt the young couple's love and support for one another. It is because of Carl Lee that Abby finds the light when all she can see are the dark shadows of her aunt's death. *Bright Shadow* concludes when Abby has a dream in which her aunt revisits her and gives her a lesson: "We are all taken from the same source:

pain and beauty. One is the chrysalis that gives to the other some gift that even in death creates a new dimension in life."

Critical reaction to *Bright Shadow* was generally more mixed than for *Marked by Fire. School Library Journal* contributor Carolyn Caywood found the plot of *Bright Shadow* touched with melodrama and lacking in credibility, but admitted that Thomas's "story is readable and her sensuously descriptive passages celebrating the physical beauty of the black characters are a nice touch." In the *Bulletin of the Center for Children's Books,* Zena Sutherland said that *Bright Shadow* as "a love story . . . is appealing, and the characterization is strong." However, she felt that "the often-ornate phraseology" sometimes weakens the story. Several of Thomas's later books also feature the popular characters she created in *Marked by Fire* and *Bright Shadow,* including *The Golden Pasture,* which journeys back to Carl Lee's earlier life on his grandfather's ranch, and *Water Girl,* which tells the story of Abyssinia's teenage daughter Amber.

In 1990 Thomas edited the well-received anthology, *A Gathering of Flowers: Stories about Being Young in America.* The characters in these pieces represent various ethnic groups, including Native Americans, Asians, Hispanics, African Americans, and Anglos, and the authors include Gerald Vizenor, Jeanne Wakatsuki Houston, and Gary Soto. A critic noted in the *Bulletin of the Center for Children's Books* that "The collection is indeed rich and colorful, containing strong individual voices." *Voice of Youth Advocates* reviewer Judith A. Sheriff declared, "These stories will provide young adults with authentic glimpses of ethnic worlds they may seldom encounter personally."

In 1992 Thomas published *When the Nightingale Sings,* a young adult novel about the orphaned Marigold. The fourteen-year-old girl—a talented gospel singer—is living with a foster mother whose verbal abuse and bad temper make her less than an ideal parent. Although she is forced to spend her time cleaning and giving singing lessons to Ruby's unlikable children, Marigold resists believing in her foster mother's insults and instead concentrates on her singing. When the members of the Rose of Sharon Baptist Church hear her voice in the distance, their search for a new lead gospel singer just might be over. Although *Bulletin of the Center for Children's Books* contributor Betsy Hearne found the book's realistic plot to be at odds with its "fairy tale tone," Hazel S. Moore commented in *Voice of Youth Advocates,* "The element of suspension carries the story back to its roots—the African American family deeply involved with the African American Church."

Thomas's award-winning 1993 work, *Brown Honey in Broomwheat Tea,* is a collection of poetry illustrated by Floyd Cooper. *School Library Journal* reviewer Lyn Miller-Lachmann described it as "twelve short, interrelated poems about family, love, and African-American identity" which "are accessible, lyrical, and moving, with thought-provoking phrases and images." In the course of the book a family battles poverty and growing pains with love and pride. Cathy Collison, writing in the *Detroit Free Press,* commented on the recurring imagery that links the pieces: "The poems return often to tea, brewing the words into a blend as rich and seasoned as the warm Cooper portrait of a grandmother."

In 1995 Thomas and Cooper produced a companion volume to *Brown Honey in Broomwheat Tea* titled *Gingerbread Days.* Like its predecessor, *Gingerbread Days* contains twelve poems dealing with love and family in an African-American setting, but in this case the poems all relate to a month of the year. The narrator of the poems is a young boy, and as each month passes he learns valuable lessons about the love of his parents and grandparents, the independence of his sister, and the bonds of family. Critics praised Thomas for her restrained, inspirational verse and remarked that *Gingerbread Days* is a worthy successor to *Brown Honey in Broomwheat.* With her imagination and ability to bring authenticity to her novels, Thomas has been highly praised and often compared to other successful African-American women authors, like Maya Angelou, Toni Morrison, and Alice Walker. Thomas takes scenes and characters from her youth and crafts them into powerful fiction. "If I had to give advice to young people," Thomas commented in her *SAAS* essay, "it would be that whatever your career choice, prepare yourself to do it well. Quality takes talent and time. Believe in your dreams. Have faith in yourself. Keep working and enjoying today even as you reach for tomorrow. If you choose to write, value your experiences. And color them in the indelible ink of your own background."

BIOGRAPHICAL/CRITICAL SOURCES:

BOOKS

Authors and Artists for Young Adults, Volume 12, Gale (Detroit, MI), 1994.
Children's Literature Review, Volume 19, Gale, 1990.
Contemporary Literary Criticism, Volume 35, Gale, 1985.
Dictionary of Literary Biography, Volume 33: *Afro-American Fiction Writers after 1955,* Gale, 1984.
Pearlman, Mickey, and Katherine U. Henderson, editors, *Inter/view: Talks with America's Writing Women,* University Press of Kentucky, 1990.
Something about the Author Autobiography Series, Volume 7, Gale, 1989, pp. 299-311.
Thomas, Joyce Carol, *Bright Shadow,* Avon, 1983.
Thomas, Joyce Carol, *Marked by Fire,* Avon, 1982.
Yalom, Margaret, editor, *Women Writers of the West,* Capra Press, 1982.

PERIODICALS

Bakersfield Californian, February 9, 1983.
Berkeley Gazette, July 21, 1983.
Best Sellers, June, 1982, pp. 123-124.
Black Scholar, summer, 1982, p. 48.
Booklist, September 15, 1995, p. 176.
Bulletin of the Center for Children's Books, February, 1984, p. 119; January, 1991; February, 1993, p. 194.
Detroit Free Press, December 22, 1993.
Horn Book Magazine, March-April, 1996, p. 219.
New Directions, January/February, 1984.
Publishers Weekly, October 11, 1993, p. 87; September 25, 1995, p. 57.
San Francisco Chronicle, April 12, 1982.
School Library Journal, March, 1982, p. 162; January, 1984, pp. 89-90; November, 1993; January, 1996, p. 107.
Voice of Youth Advocates, December, 1990; June, 1993, p. 96.
Wilson Library Bulletin, June, 1994, p. 136.*

*   *   *

THOMAS, June Manning 1950-

PERSONAL: Born June 20, 1950, in Orangeburg, SC; daughter of Hubert Vernon (a college president) and Ethel (a college professor; maiden name, Braynon) Manning; married Richard W. Thomas (a college professor), April 11, 1971; children: Kemba Thomas Mazloomian, Ali Manning. "African-American." *Education:* Attended Furman University, 1967-68; Michigan State University, B.A. (magna cum laude), 1970; University of Michigan, Ph.D., 1977. *Religion:* Baha'i.

ADDRESSES: Home—2828 Southwood Dr., East Lansing, MI 48823. *Office*—Urban and Regional Planning Program, 201 Urban Planning and Landscape Architecture Bldg., Michigan State University, East Lansing, MI 48824-1121; fax 517-355-7697. *E-mail*—thomasj@pilot.msu.edu.

CAREER: Coordinator of a voters' education project in Orangeburg, SC, 1968; Michigan State University, East Lansing, codirector of Office of Black Affairs, 1970; Michigan Department of Social Services, policy planner, 1974; Michigan State University, instructor, 1976-77, assistant professor of urban and metropolitan studies and urban planning, 1977-81; Cleveland State University, Cleveland, OH, associate professor of urban studies, 1981-82; Michigan State University, associate professor, 1982-95, professor of urban and regional planning and urban affairs, 1995—, director of Urban and Regional Planning Program, 1996—. University of Michigan, King-Chavez-Parks Visiting Scholar, 1990. Michigan Department of Commerce, special assistant and program evaluator for Manufacturing Services Bureau, 1985-86. National Properties Committee of the Baha'i Faith, member, 1984-86; Planning Commission of Meridian Township, MI, member, 1984-87; Lansing Fair Housing Center, founding member of board of directors, 1984-89; consultant to City of Detroit and Community Development Services, Inc.

MEMBER: American Planning Association (charter member), American Institute of Certified Planners, Association for Collegiate Schools of Planning (chairperson of Standing Committee on Diversity in Planning Education, 1994-96), Society for American City and Regional Planning History (charter member; member of governing board, 1990-94, 1995-99), Planners Network, Association for Baha'i Studies, Danforth Associates, Michigan State University Black Faculty and Administrators' Association, Phi Beta Kappa.

AWARDS, HONORS: Woodrow Wilson fellow, 1971; Theodora Kimball Hubbard Prize, National Conference on American Planning History, 1991; Gold Award, Society of National Association Publications, 1995, for the feature article "Planning History"; grants from U.S. Department of Housing and Urban Development, 1994-96, and Aspen Institute, 1996-97.

WRITINGS:

(With Robert L. Green and others) *Discrimination and the Welfare of Urban Minorities,* C.C Thomas (Springfield, IL), 1981.

(Contributor) Paul R. Porter and David C. Sweet, editors, *Rebuilding America's Cities: Roads to Recovery,* Center for Urban Policy Research (New Jersey), 1984.

(With Joe Darden, Richard C. Hill, and Richard W. Thomas) *Detroit: Race and Uneven Development,* Temple University Press (Philadelphia, PA), 1987.

(Contributor) Gregory D. Squires, editor, *Unequal Partnerships,* Rutgers University Press (New Brunswick, NJ), 1989.

(Contributor) W. Dennis Keating, Norman Krumholz, and Philip Star, editors, *Revitalizing Urban Neighborhoods,* University Press of Kansas (Lawrence, KS), 1996.

Redevelopment and Race: Planning a Finer City in Postwar Detroit, Johns Hopkins University Press (Baltimore, MD), 1997.

(Editor with Marsha Ritzdorf, and contributor) *Urban Planning and the African American Community: In the Shadows,* Sage Publications (Thousand Oaks, CA), 1997.

(Contributor) Thomas Boston and Catherine Ross, editors, *The Inner City: Urban Poverty and Economic Development in the Next Century,* Transaction Books (New Brunswick), 1997.

(Contributor) Leonie Sandercock, editor, *Making the Invisible Visible: A Multicultural Planning History,* University of California Press (Berkeley, CA), 1998.

Contributor of articles and reviews to academic journals, including *Journal of Baha'i Studies, Review of Black Political Economy, Economic Development Quarterly, American Quarterly,* and *Community Development Journal.* Member of editorial board, *Journal of the American Planning Association,* 1985—, and *Journal of Planning Education and Research,* 1988-92.

*   *   *

**THURMAN, Wallace (Henry) 1902-1934
(Patrick Casey, Ethel Belle Mandrake)**

PERSONAL: Born August 16, 1902, in Salt Lake City, UT; died of tuberculosis, December 22 (some sources say December 21), 1934, in New York, NY; buried in Silver Mount Cemetery, New York, NY; son of Oscar and Beulah Thurman; married Louise Thompson (a schoolteacher), August 22, 1928 (separated). *Education:* Attended University of Utah, 1919-20, and University of Southern California, 1922-23.

CAREER: Reporter and editor for *The Looking Glass,* New York City, 1925; member of the editorial staff of *Messenger,* New York City, 1925-26; circulation manager of *World Tomorrow,* New York City, 1926; member of editorial staff of McFadden Publications, New York City, c. 1929; began as reader, became editor-in-chief of Macaulay Publishing Co., New York City, c. 1930. Founder and editor of *Outlet, Harlem: A Forum of Negro Life,* and *Fire!!*

WRITINGS:

(With William Jourdan Rapp) *Harlem: A Melodrama of Negro Life in Harlem* (three-act play), first produced on Broadway at the Apollo Theater, February 20, 1929.
The Blacker the Berry: A Novel of Negro Life, Macaulay (New York), 1929, reprinted with an introduction by Shirlee Taylor Haizlip, Scribner (New York), 1996.
Infants of the Spring, Macaulay, 1932, reprinted, with afterword by John A. Williams, Southern Illinois University Press (Carbondale), 1979, with a new foreword by Amritjit Singh, Northeastern University Press (Boston), 1992.
(With A. L. Furman) *The Interne,* Macaulay, 1932, University Microfilms (Ann Arbor, MI), 1973.
Tomorrow's Children (screenplay), Bryan Foy Productions, 1934.
High School Girl (screenplay), Bryan Foy Productions, 1935.

Also author of unpublished plays, including *Jeremiah, the Magnificent,* 1930, *Savage Rhythm,* 1931, and *Singing the Blues,* 1932. Worked as a ghostwriter, sometimes under the pseudonyms Patrick Casey or Ethel Belle Mandrake, for books and periodicals, including *True Story.*

Works represented in anthologies, including *The Negro Caravan, Anthology of American Negro Literature, The Black Writer of America,* and *Black American Literature: Fiction.* Contributor to periodicals, including *New Republic, Independent, New York Times, Negro World, Opportunity,* and *Dance Magazine.* Author of column, "Inking."

The largest collection of Wallace Thurman's papers is in the James Weldon Johnson Collection at the Beinecke Library, Yale University. Some of his let-ters are in the Moorland-Springarn Research Center at Howard University; others are in the William Jourdan Rapp Collection at the University of Oregon Library.

SIDELIGHTS: Wallace Thurman settled in New York City at the beginning of the Harlem Renaissance, a period of heightened black literary activity during the mid-1920s. Because of his unconventional lifestyle and penchant for parties and alcohol, he became popular in Harlem social circles, but he was only considered a minor literary figure. His fame lay with his influence on and support of younger and talented writers of the era and with his realistic—although sensationalized—portrayals of the lower classes of black American society. Thurman was lauded as a satirist and often used satire to accuse blacks of prejudice against darker-skinned member of their race. He also rejected the belief that the Harlem Renaissance was a substantial literary movement, claiming that the 1920s produced no outstanding writers and that those who were famous exploited and allowed themselves to be patronized by whites. He claimed, as did a number of authors of the decade, that white critics judged black works by lower standards than they judged white efforts. Thurman maintained that black writers were held back from making any great contribution to the canon of Negro literature by their race-consciousness and decadent lifestyles.

Thurman was born and raised in the American West, spending his early youth in Salt Lake City, Utah. His father left the family to move to California when Wallace was very young, and the author saw him only once after that. He was raised by his mother and a grandmother, "Ma Jack," to whom he dedicated his first novel. A nervous, sickly child, Thurman thought of himself as a writer from a very young age, and wrote his first novel when he was ten years old. He was a voracious reader with strong preferences. According to *Dictionary of Literary Biography* essayist Phyllis R. Klotman, "His appetite for reading was never sated, but teachers were unable to influence his eclectic taste. He read the comedies and tragedies of Shakespeare as well as the sonnets; he did not care for George Berkeley, David Hume, or Immanuel Kant, but he did care for Friedrich Nietzsche; he read and reread Gustave Flaubert (*Madame Bovary*), Charles Baudelaire, Charles Saint-Beuve, and Stendahl; he led himself through Herbert Spencer, Henrik Ibsen, Thomas Hardy, Fyodor Dostoyevski, Havelock Ellis, and Sigmund Freud." Thurman's great capacity for reading lasted into adulthood. Poet Langston Hughes, sketching Thurman's portrait in *The Big Sea: An*

Autobiography, called him "strangely brilliant," and commented, "Thurman had read so many books because he could read eleven lines at a time. He would get from the library a great pile of volumes that would have taken me a year to read. But he would go through them in less than a week, and be able to discuss each one at great length with anybody."

While in Los Angeles Thurman wrote a column, "Inklings," for a black-oriented newspaper. He then founded a magazine, *Outlet,* hoping to initiate on the West Coast a literary renaissance like the one happening in Harlem. *Outlet* lasted only six months, and in 1925 Thurman went east. In New York City he took a job as a reporter and editor at *The Looking Glass,* then became managing editor of the *Messenger,* where his editorial expertise earned him notoriety. He published short works by the poet and author Langston Hughes—not because Thurman thought them especially good, but because they were the best available—and pieces by the writer Zora Neale Hurston. He left in the autumn of 1926 to join the staff of a white-owned periodical, *World Tomorrow.*

In the summer of 1926 Hughes asked Thurman to edit *Fire!!,* a magazine that Hughes and artist and writer Bruce Nugent were planning. Hurston, the author Gwendolyn Bennett, and another artist, Aaron Douglas, were members of the editorial board. The board intended *Fire!!* to "satisfy pagan thirst for beauty unadorned," as was stated in the foreword to the first issue. *Fire!!* would offer a forum for younger black writers who wanted to stand apart from the older, venerated black literati, and it would be strictly literary, with no focus on contemporary social issues. Thurman agreed to edit the magazine and advanced a good deal of the publication money. The first issue featured short stories by Thurman, Hurston, and Bennett, poetry by Hughes, Countee Cullen, and Arna Bontemps, a play by Hurston, illustrations by Douglas, and the first part of a novel by Nugent. But *Fire!!* folded after one issue; it was plagued by financial and distribution problems and received mediocre reviews. It was also ignored by a number of white critics and harshly criticized by some blacks who thought it irreverent.

Two years later Thurman published *Harlem: A Forum of Negro Life,* a more moderate, broadly focused magazine, also devoted to displaying works by younger writers. The new effort, unlike the avant-garde *Fire!!,* would appeal to all age groups and was "to be a general magazine . . . on current events and debates on racial and non racial issues," Thurman

wrote to the critic Alain Locke. The first volume contained an essay by Locke, a book review by Thurman, poetry by Alice Dunbar Nelson and Hughes, fiction by Hughes and George Schuyler, a theater review by the editor Theophilus Lewis, and a directory of New York City churches and nightclubs. But *Harlem,* too, failed after its premier issue.

Thurman's first play was entitled *Harlem: A Melodrama of Negro Life in Harlem.* It opened on Broadway February 20, 1929, at the Apollo Theater, bringing Thurman immediate success. He collaborated on the drama with William Jourdan Rapp, a white man who later became the editor of *True Story* and would remain Thurman's lifelong friend. *Harlem* centers on the members of the Williams family who relocate to New York City to escape economic difficulties at the time of the "great migration" of Southerners to the North during the first two decades of the twentieth century. But instead of finding the city a promised land, they encounter many of the problems that often plagued the families of the migration: unemployment and tensions between generations heightened by difficulties in adjusting to city life.

Harlem received mixed reviews—ranging from "exciting" to "vulgar"—but was generally considered interesting. It was criticized by blacks who did not care for its focus on the seedier elements of life, such as illicit sex, liquor, wild parties thrown to collect rent money, and gambling. R. Dana Skinner stated in a 1929 *Commonweal* review of *Harlem* that he was especially upset by "the particular way in which this melodrama exploits the worst features of the Negro and depends for its effects solely on the explosions of lust and sensuality." Nevertheless, Skinner felt it "captured the feel of life" and was "constantly entertaining." *Harlem* played for an impressive ninety-three performances in what was considered a poor theater season, and it was taken on tour to the West Coast, the Midwest, and Canada.

In 1930 Thurman again collaborated with Rapp on a three-act play, *Jeremiah, the Magnificent,* based on black nationalist Marcus Garvey's "back to Africa" movement of the early 1900s. Garvey had called for an exodus of blacks to Africa so that there they could create their own country and attain personal freedoms in a society where they would be in the majority. Although Thurman portrayed Garvey as a vain and unwise man, the playwright thought Garvey did much to promote the black ideal in the hope of fostering Negro unity worldwide. The play remained unpublished and was only performed once, after Thurman had died. Thurman's other unproduced and unpublished plays include *Singing the Blues,* written in 1931, and *Savage Rhythm,* written the following year.

Thurman's first novel, *The Blacker the Berry,* was published in 1929. Taken from the folk-saying "the blacker the berry, the sweeter the juice," its title was ironic, for the novel was an attack on prejudice within the race. Emma Lou, the protagonist, is a dark-skinned girl from Boise who is looked down upon by her fairer family members and friends. When she attends school at the University of Southern California in Los Angeles she again is scorned, so she travels to Harlem, where she believes that she won't be snubbed because of her dark coloring. But like the Williamses in *Harlem* and Thurman in his own life, Emma Lou is disillusioned with the city. She becomes unhappy with her work, her love affairs, and the pronounced discrimination in the nightclubs, where lighter skinned females starred in extravagant productions while darker skinned performers were forced to sing off stage. She uses hair straighteners and skin bleachers, and takes on the appearance and attitudes of the fairer-skinned people who degrade her. She in turn snubs darker men, whom she thinks inferior, and takes up with Alva, a man who is light-skinned but cruel. After viewing Alva in a lovers' embrace with another man, Emma Lou realizes how hypocritical she's become. Critics praised Thurman for devoting a novel to the plight of the dark-skinned black girl, but they faulted him for being too objective: he recounted Emma Lou's tale without handing down any judgment on the world in which she lived. They also criticized Thurman for trying to do too much with *The Blacker the Berry,* accusing him of crafting a choppy, and occasionally incoherent, narrative by touching on too many themes.

Thurman's next novel, *Infants of the Spring,* also is set in 1920s Harlem. The story revolves around Raymond Taylor, a young black author who is trying to write a weighty novel in a decadent, race-oriented atmosphere. Taylor resides in a boardinghouse, nicknamed "Niggeratti Manor," with a number of young blacks who pretend to be aspiring authors. Thurman makes these pretenders the major victims of his satire, suggesting that they have destroyed their creativity by leading such decadent lives. Critics contend that Thurman based his characters on well-known figures of the Harlem Renaissance, including Hughes, Locke, Hurston, Cullen, Nugent, and Douglas.

In *Infants of the Spring* Thurman suggests that all American artists and writers—black and white—are overrated. He vigorously attacks black writers patronized by whites, who praise everything black authors produce, regardless of quality, as novel and ingenious. *Infants* received criticism similar to that of *The Blacker the Berry.* Reviewers objected to Thurman's examining too many issues and not presenting them clearly, and his not making a universal statement about the lifestyles presented. But unlike Thurman's first novel, which was considered too objective, *Infants* was thought to be overly subjective and Thurman overly argumentative. Yet critics praised him for his frank discussion of black society. Assessed Martha Gruening in the *Saturday Review:* "No other Negro writer has so unflinchingly told the truth about color snobbery within the color line, the ins and outs of 'passing' and other vagaries of prejudice. . . . [*Infants of the Spring*'s] quota of truth is just that which Negro writers, under the stress of propaganda and counterpropaganda, have generally and quite understandably omitted from their picture." In addition, critics considered *Infants of the Spring* one of the first books written expressly for black audiences and not white critics.

Thurman's third and final novel, *The Interne,* was a collaboration with Abraham L. Furman, a white man Thurman met while working at Macaulay's Publishing Company. The novel portrays medical life at an urban hospital as seen through the eyes of a young white doctor, Carl Armstrong. In his first three months at the hospital, Armstrong's ideals are shattered, during which time he witnesses staff members' corrupt behavior and comes in contact with bureaucratic red tape. Armstrong himself participates in the vice but soon realizes his own loss of ethics and saves himself by taking up doctoring in the country. Critics could not agree whether Thurman's accounts of medical wrongdoing were based on fact; many claimed that the novel had no semblance of reality while others stressed that incidents were actual, if unusual.

In 1934 Thurman returned to the West Coast to write screenplays. While in California he continued to lead a decadent lifestyle, drank excessively, and wrote two screenplays for Bryan Foy Productions, *Tomorrow's Children,* released in 1934, and *High School Girl,* released the following year. *Tomorrow's Children* was a production about the Masons, a poor white family supported by their seventeen-year-old daughter. She takes care of her younger brothers and sisters, who are either mentally or physically impaired, her drunken father, and her constantly pregnant mother. Two social workers, sent by a compassionate doctor, declare that if they wish to receive welfare

money, the mother, father, and daughter must be ster-
ilized. *Tomorrow's Children* was based on circumstances rarely explored in Hollywood at that time, and
was considered groundbreaking because it used the
medical term "vasectomy" to explain the procedure of
male sterilization. Because of its revolutionary subject
matter, *Tomorrow's Children* was banned in New
York when it was released.

In ill health, Thurman returned to New York City in
May, 1934, and went on one last drinking binge with
his Harlem friends. He collapsed in the middle of the
reunion party and was taken, ironically, to City Hospital, on Welfare Island, New York, the institution he
condemned in *The Interne*. After spending half a year
in the ward for incurables diagnosed with tuberculosis, he died there on December 22, 1934. His funeral
services were held in New York City on Christmas
Eve.

BIOGRAPHICAL/CRITICAL SOURCES:

BOOKS

Abramson, Doris E., *Negro Playwrights in the Ameri-
can Theatre, 1929-1959,* Columbia University
Press, 1969.
Anderson, Jervis, *This Was Harlem: A Cultural Por-
trait 1900-1950,* Farrar, Straus, 1982.
Black Literature Criticism, Gale, Volume 3, 1992.
Bone, Robert, *The Negro Novel in America,* revised
edition, Yale University Press, 1965, pp. 65-94.
Bontemps, Arna, editor, *The Harlem Renaissance
Remembered,* Dodd, 1972.
Brown, Sterling, *The Negro in American Fiction,*
Kenikat Press, 1968, pp. 131-50.
Contemporary Black Biography, Volume 16, Gale,
1987.
Dictionary of Literary Biography, Volume 51: *Afro-
American Writers from the Harlem Renaissance to
1940,* Gale, 1987.
Gay and Lesbian Literature 2, St. James, 1998.
Gloster, Hugh, *Negro Voices in American Fiction,*
University of North Carolina Press, 1948, pp.
157-73.
Huggins, Nathan Irvin, *Harlem Renaissance,* Oxford
University Press, 1971.
Hughes, Langston, *The Big Sea: An Autobiography,*
Hill & Wang, 1963, pp. 233-41.
Huggins, Nathan, *Harlem Renaissance,* Oxford Uni-
versity Press, 1971.
Johnson, James Weldon, *Black Metropolis,* Da Capo
Press, 1930.
Kornweibel, Theodore, Jr., *No Crystal Stair: Black
Life and the Messenger, 1917-1928,* Greenwood
Press, 1975.
Kramer, Victor, A., *The Harlem Renaissance Re-ex-
amined,* AMS Press, 1987, pp. 201-11.
Lewis, David Levering, *When Harlem Was in Vogue,*
Knopf, 1981.
Singh, Amritjit, *The Novels of the Harlem Renais-
sance: Twelve Black Writers 1923-1933,* Pennsyl-
vania State University Press, 1976, pp. 2-36.
Twentieth-Century Literary Criticism, Volume 6,
Gale, 1982.
van Notten-Krepel, E. M. B. F., *Wallace Thurman's
Harlem Renaissance,* Rijksuniversiteit te Leiden,
1994.

PERIODICALS

African American Review, winter, 1993, p. 693.
Black World, November, 1970, pp. 77-85; February,
1976, pp. 29-35.
Commonweal, March 6, 1929.
Crisis, July, 1929, pp. 249-50.
Nation, February 10, 1932.
New Yorker, March 2, 1929.
New York Times, February 21, 1929; March 3, 1929;
April 7, 1929; February 28, 1932; June 5, 1932.
Opportunity, April, 1929; October, 1930; January,
1935.
Saturday Review, March 12, 1932, p. 585; June 22,
1940.
Western American Literature, spring, 1971, pp. 53-9.

OTHER

McIver, Dorothy Jean Palmer McIver, *Stepchild in
Harlem: The Literary Career of Wallace Thurman*
(Ph.D. dissertation), University of Alabama,
1983.
Wright, Shirley Haynes, *A Study of the Fiction of
Wallace Thurman* (dissertation), East Texas State
University, 1983.*

*   *   *

TLALI, Miriam 1933-

PERSONAL: Born in 1933, in Doornfontein, Johannesburg, South Africa; daughter of a newspaper publisher; married Stephen Lehutso. *Education:* Attended
Witwatersrand University, and Roma University,
Lesotho, South Africa.

ADDRESSES: Agent—c/o Ravan Press Ltd., P.O. Box 145, Randburg, 2125, South Africa.

CAREER: Novelist, short story writer, and journalist. Electronics shop clerk, Johannesburg, South Africa; cofounder, *Staffrider,* (African Writers Association); cofounder and board member, Skotaville, (first black publishing house under South African apartheid rule).

MEMBER: African Writers Association (cofounder).

WRITINGS:

NOVELS

Muriel at Metropolitan, Ravan Press (Johannesburg), 1975, Three Continents Press (Washington, DC), 1979.
Amandla, Ravan Press, 1980.

SHORT STORIES

Mihloti (includes interviews, plays, and essays), Skotaville (Johannesburg), 1984.
Soweto Stories, Pandora (London), 1989, published as *Footprints in the Quag: Stories and Dialogues from Soweto,* David Philip (Johannesburg), 1989.

SIDELIGHTS: Miriam Tlali, an author of novels and short stories, was born to African parents in Doornfontein, a suburb of Johannesburg, South Africa. Doornfontein was declared exclusively African under the now-defunct South African rule of apartheid, and Tlali has lived most of her life as an oppressed African woman in her own homeland. However, she has not shied away from memorializing on paper apartheid's devastating effects on the human lives and the human psyche and has published such works as *Muriel at Metropolitan* and *Amandla.*

Tlali is the daughter of industrious, well-read parents who were among the first persons in Lesotho to own a printing press. Her father's company, Tlali & Company, had published a newspaper for many years prior to Tlali's birth. Her father died when she was young, but Tlali absorbed the books and literature that he left behind and acquired a voracious appetite for learning. Education, however, was difficult for Tlali to obtain. She won a place at Witwatersrand University, but after two years there the South African government passed laws that prevented white universities from accepting African students. Tlali was forced to leave the school, and she turned to Roma University in

Lesotho. However, Tlali's finances quickly dried up and she was forced to drop out of school and take a job as a clerk in a Johannesburg electrical and radio shop. This employment experience would become the subject of her first novel, *Muriel at Metropolitan.*

Muriel at Metropolitan describes Tlali's horrific experiences at an electrical store called Metropolitan Radio through an African character called "Muriel." Muriel is forced to work in an isolated area, obscured from the other employees behind stacks of file cabinets and trapped inside a chicken wire screen. Her boss, Mr. Block, is appreciative of Muriel's skills, but he is demanding: when Muriel asks to leave the office to care for her ill son, Mr. Block denies the request. Although Muriel performs important functions in the office, she receives lower pay than her white coworkers, and she is required to address her peers as "Mrs.," while they may address Muriel by her first name.

The very nature of Muriel's job is as cruel as the treatment of her co-workers. Metropolitan's business involves the sale of radios and other electronic equipment to a largely African population, and Muriel is required to screen customers, to write letters notifying customers of impending repossessions, and to translate conversations between collectors and debtors. In carrying out these duties, she suffers pangs of guilt for committing what she feels is a betrayal of her people.

Tlali unveils the many layers of pain experienced by Muriel with little emotion critics commented. Reviewer Peggy Crane, writing in *Books and Bookmen,* said that the simplicity of this approach is one of the book's strengths and helps to reveal "an inner serenity and self-confidence in Muriel's character." The straightforward writing style, according to *Dictionary of Literary Biography* essayist Lauretta Ngcobo, allows Tlali to reveal "the poverty of the human spirit under apartheid. Instead of striving to convince the reader," explained Ngcobo, Tlali "simply uncovers the inhumanity where black meets white."

Tlali had to arrange for her husband to sign her book contract, and parts of *Muriel at Metropolitan* were banned by the South African government. Tlali's second full-length fiction effort, *Amandla,* was likewise banned by South African officials. *Amandla,* which translates as "Power is ours," is a departure from the neutral tone of *Muriel at Metropolitan.* The book describes the Soweto student uprising of 1976 by skipping from episode to episode. Violence provides a cohesive theme, as buses and schools and municipal buildings and beer halls are set ablaze. The 1976 uprising was led by children, and Tlali puts the characters through harrowing encounters with police, military troops, and other Africans. "She captures the immediacy of the turmoil, enabling readers to share what it must have been like for those who were there," wrote Ngcobo. "Tlali attempts not only to provide information about the struggle but also to inject into the oppressed community a new kind of morality, one associated with creating a more disciplined combative force out of the society as a whole."

Tlali's third book, *Mihloti,* is a collection of various prose pieces that Tlali wrote over a number of years as a writer for *Staffrider,* the magazine co-founded by Tlali. The title translates as "tears," a physiological phenomenon that informs much of the work in *Mihloti.* Tlali writes in the introduction to *Mihloti,* "Now that I am a mother, I shed tears for my children . . . I have often shed tears for the fate of all black children. . . . For our denigrated humanity which *we* must retrieve."

Soweto Stories, also published as *Footprints in the Quag: Stories and Dialogues from Soweto,* is a collection of short stories and is Tlali's fourth book. This effort finds Tlali exploring the familiar themes of racial and sexual oppression. The thread that runs through *Soweto Stories* is the proposition that the condition of Africans is tied to their flight from the countryside and into the cities. This relocation has caused many Africans to lose touch with traditions that keep the human spirit alive. The extended family is an antidote to the rootlessness of city life because, Tlali writes, "you know who to 'run to.' It is important that you know that you are not alone, that you are never an 'orphan.'"

BIOGRAPHICAL/CRITICAL SOURCES:

BOOKS

Blain, Virginia, Patricia Clements, and Isobel Grundy, *Feminist Companion to Literature in English,* Yale University Press (New York City), 1990.

Chapman, Michael, *Soweto Poetry,* McGraw-Hill (Johannesburg), 1979.

Clayton, Cherry, editor, *Women and Writing in South Africa: A Critical Anthology,* Heinemann (Marshalltown, South Africa), 1989.

Contemporary Novelists, sixth edition, St. James Press, 1995.

Dictionary of Literary Biography, Volume 157: *Twentieth-Century Caribbean and Black African Writers,* Third Series, Gale (Detroit), 1995.

MacKenzie, Craig, and Cherry Clayton, editors, *Between the Lines: Interviews with Bessie Head, Sheila Roberts, Ellen Kuzwayo, Miriam Tlali,* National English Literary Museum (Grahamstown, South Africa), 1989.

Ndebele, Njabulo S., *Rediscovery of the Ordinary: Essays on South African Literature and Culture,* Congress of South African Writers (Johannesburg), 1991.

Ramelb, Carol, editor, *Biography: East and West,* University of Hawaii Press (Honolulu, HI), 1989, pp. 122-126.

Schipper, Mineke, editor, *Unheard Words: Women and Literature in Africa, the Arab World, Asia, the Caribbean, and Latin America,* Allison & Busby (London), 1985.

Watts, Jane, *Black Writers from South Africa: Towards a Discourse of Liberation,* St. Martin's Press (New York City), 1989.

Wylie, Hal, Dennis Brutus, and Juris Silenieks, editors, *African Literature—1988: New Masks,* Three Continents Press and the African Literature Association (Washington, DC), 1990.

PERIODICALS

African Literature Association Bulletin, vol. 17, no. 3, 1991, pp. 40-42.

Awa-Finnaba, March, 1987, pp. 43-52.

BBC Arts and Africa, no. 267, 1979, pp. 3-6; no. 549, 1984, pp. 1-5; no. 640, 1986, pp. 3-5.

Books & Bookmen, March, 1976, p. 22; July, 1979, p. 63.

Choice, February. 1980, p. 1590.

Current Writing, vol. 2, no. 1, 1990, pp. 35-44.

English in Africa, vol. 17, no. 2, 1990, pp. 25-36.

English Journal, March, 1995, p. 55.

Essence, October, 1987, p. 28.

Isivivane, June, 1990, pp. 37-38.

Matatu, vol. 3-4, 1988, pp. 111-124.

Research in African Literatures, spring, 1988, pp. 65-88.

Staffrider, vol. 7, no. 3-4, 1988, pp. 303-309.

Times Literary Supplement, April 1, 1994, p. 10.*

*   *   *

TOLSON, M. B.
See TOLSON, Melvin B(eaunorus)

TOLSON, Melvin B(eaunorus) 1898(?)-1966
(M. B. Tolson)

PERSONAL: Born February 6, 1898 (some sources say 1900), in Moberly, MO; died of cancer, August 29 (one source says August 28), 1966; buried in Guthrie, OK; son of Alonzo A. (a minister and teacher) and Lera (one source says Leah; maiden name, Hurt) Tolson; married Ruth Southall, January 29, 1922; children: Melvin B. Jr., Arthur, Wiley Wilson, Ruth Marie. *Education:* Attended Fisk University, Nashville, TN, c. 1918-19; Lincoln University, Oxford, PA, B.A. (with honors), 1923; Columbia University, M.A., 1940.

CAREER: Worked at a meat-packing plant; Wiley College, Marshall, TX, teacher of English and speech, 1924-47, as well as tennis, football, and boxing coach, director of Log Cabin Theatre, and organizer of Wiley Forensic Society; Langston University, Langston, OK, professor of creative literature and director of Dust Bowl Theatre, 1947-65; Tuskegee Institute, Tuskegee, AL, Avalon Professor of the Humanities, 1965-66. Mayor of Langston, OK, 1952-58.

AWARDS, HONORS: First place in American Negro Exposition National Poetry Contest, 1939, for "Dark Symphony"; Omega Psi Phi Award for creative writing, 1945; Poet Laureate of Liberia, 1947; Bess Hokin Prize, Poetry magazine, 1951, for "E. & O. E."; Knight of the Order of the Star of Africa, Liberia, 1954; appointed permanent Bread Loaf Fellow in Poetry and Drama, 1954; District of Columbia Citation and Award for Cultural Achievement in Fine Arts, 1965; National Institute and American Academy of Arts and Letters Award in Literature, 1966; Lincoln University, D.L., 1954, D.H.L., 1965; fellowships from Rockefeller Foundation and Omega Psi Phi.

WRITINGS:

Rendezvous with America (poetry; includes "Rendezvous with America," "Dark Symphony," "Of Men and Cities," "The Idols of the Tribe," "Ballad of the Rattlesnake," and "Tapestries of Time"), Dodd (New York), 1944.

(And director) *The Fire in the Flint* (play; adapted from Walter White's novel of the same title), first produced in Oklahoma City, OK, at National Convention of the National Association for the Advancement of Colored People, June 28, 1952.

(Under name M. B. Tolson) *Libretto for the Republic of Liberia* (poetry), preface by Allen Tate, Twayne (New York), 1953.

(Under name M. B. Tolson) Harlem Gallery: *Book One, The Curator* (poetry), introduction by Karl Shapiro, Twayne, 1965.

A Gallery of Harlem Portraits (poetry; includes "Harlem," "Hilmar Enick," and "Harold Lincoln"), edited with afterword by Robert M. Farnsworth, University of Missouri Press (Columbia), 1979.

Caviar and Cabbage: Selected Columns by Melvin B. Tolson from the Washington Tribune, 1937-1944 (articles), edited with introduction by Robert M. Farnsworth, University of Missouri Press, 1982.

Also author of novel *Beyond the Zaretto;* author of plays, including *Black No More* (adapted from George Schuyler's novel of the same title), 1952, *Black Boy,* 1963, *The Moses of Beale Street,* and *Southern Front.* Work represented in numerous anthologies, including *Golden Slippers,* 4th edition, edited by Arna Bontemps, Harper (New York), 1941; *The Poetry of the Negro, 1746-1949,* edited by Langston Hughes and Arna Bontemps, Doubleday (New York), 1949; *Black Voices,* edited by Abraham Chapman, New American Library (New York), 1968; *The Writing on the Wall,* edited by Walter Lowenfels, Doubleday, 1969; *The Black Experience,* edited by Francis E. Kearns, Viking (New York), 1970; *The Poetry of Black America,* edited by Arnold Adoff, Harper, 1973; and *Understanding the New Black Poetry,* edited by Stephen Henderson, Morrow (New York), 1973. Author of weekly column "Caviar and Cabbage" in *Washington Tribune,* 1937-44. Contributor to periodicals, including *American Poet, Arts Quarterly, Atlantic Monthly, Midwest Journal, Modern Monthly, Modern Quarterly, Negro Digest,* and *Pittsburgh Courier.*

The principal collection of Tolson's papers are kept in the manuscript division of the Library of Congress.

SIDELIGHTS: Known for his complex, challenging poetry, Melvin B. Tolson earned little critical attention throughout most of his life, but he eventually won a place among America's leading black poets. He was, in the opinion of Allen Tate, author of the preface to *Tolson's Libretto for the Republic of Liberia,* the first black poet to assimilate "completely the full poetic language of his time and, by implication, the language of the Anglo-American tradition." Even more, according to Karl Shapiro in his introduction to *Tolson's Harlem Gallery: Book One, The Curator,* Tolson wrote and thought "in Negro," thus adding to the quality of his best work. His sonnets, free verse, and epic poems, which employ both standard English and black idiom, illuminate the lives of black Americans and consider the role of black artists in white society. Noted James R. Payne in *World Literature Today,* Tolson's work is "a rich body of American poetry . . . that will give a great deal of satisfaction to readers."

Publication of Tolson's first collection of poetry, *Rendezvous with America,* came five years after his poem "Dark Symphony" won first place in the American Negro Exposition National Poetry Contest in 1939. Donald B. Gibson, an essayist for the *Reference Guide to American Literature,* remarked that "on the basis of his first volume of poetry . . . it would hardly have been possible to predict the kind of poet Melvin Tolson was to be a decade later. A poet who writes 'I gaze upon her silken loveliness / She is a passionflower of joy and pain / On the golden bed I came back to possess' does not show particular promise. Likewise the lines 'America is the Black Man's country / The Red Man's, the Yellow Man's / The Brown Man's, the White Man's' are not suggestive of the great lines yet to come." And yet, Gibson assured, some of Tolson's early poetry does foreshadow his future verses. The essayist singled out the poem "An Ex-Judge at the Bar" as being "in style and content very much like a good deal of the later poetry and untypical of the rather commonplace character of much of the first volume." It is "in tone typically Tolsonian. The juxtaposition of the formal and the informal, the classical and the contemporary, the familiar and the unusual accounts in large measure for the unique character of Tolson's best poetry."

Other critics also had praise for *Rendezvous with America.* The award-winning "Dark Symphony," included in the collection, "celebrates . . . the historic contribution of black Americans and their struggle to gain recognition for their achievements, ending with a proud and defiant prediction of black accomplishment and cultural realization," asserted Robert M. Farnsworth in the *Dictionary of Literary Biography.* Other poems in the volume, written during World War II, address the war's destruction, human aspirations and corruption, and the possibility of achieving "a new democracy of nations," according to Farnsworth. Poet and journalist Frank Marshall Davis, quoted by Farnsworth, characterized Tolson's writing in the volume as mature and masterful but "yet too complex for the masses"; many critics attribute the neglect of much of Tolson's writing to his complexity and erudition.

Appointed poet laureate of Liberia in 1947, Tolson attracted increased attention with his *Libretto for the Republic of Liberia,* an epic poem commemorating the African nation's centennial. Observed poet and critic John Ciardi in *Nation,* Tolson creates "a vision of Africa past, present, and future" with abundant imagery and "prodigious eclecticism." Portraying Liberia as an offshoot of America, newer and smaller with hopes of achieving more, Tolson continues the allusiveness and vision displayed in his earlier work. Ciardi commended the poet's "force of language and . . . rhythm," concluding that Tolson "has established a new dimension for American Negro poetry." Gibson described the *Libretto* as "pyrotechnic," and credited Tolson with creating "a system of tensions not unlike the dynamic forces holding an atom or a galaxy together. Each element threatens to go off on its own; yet as long as the balance of forces remains constant, the system functions."

Published in 1965, *Tolson's Harlem Gallery: Book One, The Curator* was the product of years of work and is widely considered a poetic masterpiece. Robert Donald Spector, reviewing the poem for *Saturday Review* the year it appeared, judged that it "marks [Tolson] as one of America's great poets." Originally a sonnet, in the early 1930s it became the book length *Gallery of Harlem Portraits,* which remained unpublished during Tolson's life; in the 1950s Tolson conceived it as part of a five-book epic about Harlem and black America and revised it as *Harlem Gallery: Book One, The Curator.* A fictional gallery curator "provides the central point of view" in the poem's discussions of black art and life, remarked Farnsworth, "but three major characters, all practicing artists, dramatically amplify the reader's view of the black artist's dilemma and achievement." Stanzas in the style of blues music punctuate the portraits, reinforcing Tolson's points or offering ironic commentary. Payne found such stanzas "very effective, among the most effective elements of the book." Still, while Tolson used black elements such as the blues, focusing on black characters and a black setting, he did not espouse separatism. According to Blyden Jackson's *New Republic* critique, "The brotherhood of man and the universality of serious art . . . catalyze [the poem's] perceptions."

Tolson's skillful delineation of character, his ability to turn discussions of aesthetics into social commentary, his breadth of vision, and his deftness with language garnered critical acclaim. Reviewers compared *Harlem Gallery* to works by Walt Whitman, Edgar Lee Masters, Hart Crane, and T. S. Eliot and praised with Spector "the richness and variety of [Tolson's] characters" and the "allusiveness that absorbs classical, Biblical, oriental, and African references." Admitting that *Harlem Gallery* presents the same complexity and involved syntax that rendered Tolson's earlier works somewhat inaccessible, Jackson asserted that "nevertheless [it] is a fine product of the imagination. . . . [Tolson] achieved a memorable presentation of the human comedy and of human values." Responding to other critics' neglect of Tolson's work, Spector declared, "Here is a poet whose language, comprehensiveness, and values demand a critical sensitivity rarely found in any establishment. . . . Whatever his reputation in the present critical climate, Tolson stands firmly as a great American poet." And Gibson summarized: "Tolson, by virtue of an extraordinary mind and intelligence, keeps a vast array of disparate elements in constant relationship. His poetry is, therefore, coherent, and its primary effect is of the containment and control of vast reserves of energy."

BIOGRAPHICAL/CRITICAL SOURCES:

BOOKS

Berube, Michael, *Marginal Forces/Cultural Centers: Tolson, Pynchon, and the Politics of the Canon,* Cornell University Press, 1992.
Contemporary Literary Criticism, Gale, Volume 36, 1986, Volume 105, 1986.
Dictionary of Literary Biography, Gale, Volume 48: *American Poets, 1880-1945, Second Series,* 1986, Volume 76: *Afro-American Writers, 1940-1955,* 1988.
Farnsworth, Robert M., Melvin B. Tolson, *1898-1966: Plain Talk and Poetic Prophecy,* University of Missouri Press, 1984.
Flasch, Joy, *Melvin B. Tolson,* Twayne, 1972.
Gibson, Donald B., editor, *Modern Black Poets: A Collection of Critical Essays,* Prentice-Hall, 1973.
Reference Guide to American Literature, 3rd edition, St. James, 1994.
Russell, Mariann, *Melvin B. Tolson's Harlem Gallery: A Literary Analysis,* University of Missouri Press, 1980.
Tolson, M. B., *Harlem Gallery: Book One, The Curator,* introduction by Karl Shapiro, Twayne, 1965.

PERIODICALS

African-American Review, summer, 1972.
Black American Literature Forum, fall, 1990, pp. 453-72.
Black World, December, 1972, pp. 4-29.
Callaloo, winter, 1989, pp. 192-215.

CLA Journal, March, 1986, pp. 261-75.
Nation, February 27, 1954.
New Letters, spring, 1980, pp. 125-27.
New Republic, December 4, 1976.
New York Times Book Review, December 10, 1944, p. 29.
Obsidian II: Black Literature in Review, winter, 1987, pp. 69-87.
Phylon, Number 1, 1954, pp. 96-97; Number 4, 1965, pp. 408-10.
Saturday Review, August 7, 1965.
World Literature Today, winter, 1983; summer, 1990.*

*   *   *

TRICE, Dawn Turner

PERSONAL: Married David; children: Hannah.

ADDRESSES: Home—Chicago, IL. *Agent*—c/o Crown Publishing Group, 2015 50th St., New York, NY 10022.

CAREER: Novelist and journalist; editor at *Chicago Tribune.* Panelist on books by African American writers, Public Library Association, Kansas City, MO, 1998.

AWARDS, HONORS: Alex Award, Margaret Alexander Edwards Trust, Top Ten Adult Book for Young Adults published in 1997, for *Only Twice I've Wished for Heaven;* Honor book, BCALA Literary Awards, Black Caucus of the American Library Association, 1998, for *Only Twice I've Wished for Heaven.*

WRITINGS:

NOVELS

Only Twice I've Wished for Heaven, Crown (New York City), 1997.

WORK IN PROGRESS: A novel.

SIDELIGHTS: The citation naming *Chicago Tribune* editor Dawn Turner Trice's first novel, *Only Twice I've Wished for Heaven,* as a 1998 Black Caucus of the American Library Association honor book called it "an enchanting and absorbing story of possibilities and entanglements, half-truths and lies interwoven into a fascinating tale." Many book reviewers and readers agreed. *Only Twice I've Wished for Heaven* is the story of Tempestt "Temmy" Saville's coming-of-age as an eleven-year-old black girl in Chicago in 1975, as remembered by Temmy as an adult.

Temmy lives in a fence enclave, a planned community of African American professionals on Chicago's lake shore; finding it emotionally sterile, she escapes frequently through a hole in the fence and spends her time on rundown 35th Street, specifically at a liquor store called O'Cala Food and Drug. The proprietress, Jonetta Goode, is a former prostitute and a generous soul; she befriends Temmy and teaches her much about life on a street where unlicensed stores and street preachers abound.

Temmy, meanwhile, is worried about her best friend Valerie, who spends half her time with her father in the planned community and half with her mother in the projects. Dispatching a couple of 35th Street characters to check on Valerie's doings, Temmy discovers that her friend has been forced into prostitution to support her mother's drug habit. Alarmed, she sets out to intervene, but is too late: Valerie is killed, with Temmy the only eyewitness. Later, a street preacher is convicted of the crime.

These events are narrated alternately by the adult Temmy and by Miss Jonetta, who provide two very different viewpoints on reality. Indeed, the interplay between Temmy's middle-class consciousness and the more streetwise observations of Jonetta provide one of the novel's more fascinating sources of social commentary, for each character is knowledgeable about the side of life that the other is relatively ignorant. For *Publishers Weekly* reviewer, Sybil S. Steinberg, 35th Street itself was "hellishly fascinating" as a setting for fiction. Steinberg praised the "powerful" novel for its "vibrant characters" and noted that the author "obliquely provides insight into the crucial social issues that help shape the lives of African Americans."

Booklist contributor Joanne Wilkinson called the novel an "amazingly accomplished debut . . . filled with memorable characters and images. . . . striking and inventive" and praised Trice as "a writer to watch." However, Wilkinson noted that the novel's ending might have been drawn out a bit too long. *Library Journal* reviewer Amy A. Begg considered *Only Twice I've Wished for Heaven* "poignant and melodic," and concluded, "this novel will stay with the reader long after the final chapter has been finished."

BIOGRAPHICAL/CRITICAL SOURCES:

PERIODICALS

Booklist, November 15, 1996, p. 573.
Library Journal, September 15, 1996, p. 98.
Publishers Weekly, November 4, 1996, p. 62.

OTHER

Barnes & Noble, http://www.barnesandnoble.com (1998).
Black Caucus of the American Library Association, http://www.bcala.org (1998).*

                              *   *   *

TURNEY, Denise
  See CAMPBELL, Rhonda

                              *   *   *

TUTU, Desmond M(pilo) 1931-

PERSONAL: Born October 7, 1931, in Klerksdorp, Transvaal, South Africa; son of Zachariah (a school teacher), and Aletta (a domestic servant) Tutu; married Leah Nomalizo Shenxane, July 2, 1955; children: Trevor Thamsanqa, Theresa Thandeka, Naomi Nontombi, Mpho Andrea. *Education:* Bantu Normal College, Pretoria, South Africa, teacher's diploma, 1953; University of South Africa, Johannesburg, B.A., 1954; St. Peter's Theological College, Johannesburg, L.Th., 1960; King's College, London, B.D., 1965, M.Th., 1966. *Avocational interests:* Music, reading, jogging.

ADDRESSES: Home—Bishopscourt, Claremont, Cape Province 7700, South Africa. *Office*—c/o Diocesan Office, P.O. Box 1131, Johannesburg 2000, South Africa.

CAREER: Teacher at high schools in Johannesburg, South Africa, 1954-55, and in Krugersdorp, South Africa, 1955-58; ordained as deacon, 1960, and Anglican priest, 1961; St. Alban's Church, Benoni, Johannesburg, curate, 1960-61; St. Mary's Cathedral, Johannesburg, priest, 1961; St. Philip's Church, Alberton, Transvaal, South Africa, curate, 1961-62;

St. Alban's Church, Golders Green, London, England, part-time curate, 1962-65; St. Mary's Church, Bletchingley, Surrey, England, part-time curate, 1965-66; lecturer at Federal Theological Seminary, Alice, Cape Province, South Africa, 1967-69; lecturer in theology at University of Botswana, Lesotho, and Swaziland, 1970-72; World Council of Churches' Theological Education Fund, Bromley, Kent, England, associate director, 1972-75; St. Augustine's Church, Grove Park, Kent, England, curate, 1972-75; dean of Johannesburg, Johannesburg, 1975-76; bishop of Lesotho, South Africa, 1976-78; general secretary of South African Council of Churches, 1978-85; assistant Anglican bishop of Johannesburg, 1978-85, bishop, 1984-86; St. Augustine's Parish, Soweto, South Africa, rector, 1981-85; archbishop of Cape Town and Anglican primate of southern Africa, 1986—; social reformer and political activist.

Chaplain at University of Fort Hare, 1967-69, and University of Western Cape, Cape Town, 1988—; visiting professor at General Theological Seminary, New York City, 1984; Richard Feetham Academic Freedom Lecture, University of the Witwatersrand, Johannesburg, 1985; President, All Africa Conference of Churches, 1987—; Chancellor, University of Western Cape, 1988—. Participant at several international conferences, including the "Salvation Today" conference, Bangkok, Thailand, Anglican Consultative Council, Port of Spain, Trinidad, and the World Council of Churches' 6th Assembly, Vancouver, Canada, 1983. Trustee of Phelps Stoke Fund.

MEMBER: National Association for the Advancement of Colored People (NAACP).

AWARDS, HONORS: Fellow of King's College, London, 1978; Prix d'Athene from Onassis Foundation, 1980; designated member of International Social Prospects Academy, 1983; Family of Man Gold Medal Award, 1983; Martin Luther King, Jr., Humanitarian Award, 1984; Nobel Peace Prize from Norwegian Nobel Committee, 1984, for "role as unifying leader . . . in the campaign to resolve the problem of apartheid in South Africa"; Sam Ervin Free Speech Award, 1985; Order of Southern Cross, Brazil, 1987; Order of Merit of Brasilia, Brazil, 1987; Albert Schweitzer Humanitarian Award, Emmanuel College, 1988; Freedom of the Borough of Lewisham, U.K., 1990, Freedom of the City of Kinshasa, 1990. Recipient of over thirty honorary doctoral degrees, including LL.D. from Harvard University, 1979, D.Th. from Ruhr University, and D.D. from Aberdeen University, 1984 and Oxford University, 1990.

WRITINGS:

Crying in the Wilderness, Eerdmans, 1982.
Hope and Suffering: Sermons and Speeches, [Johannesburg], 1983, revised edition, edited by William B. Eerdmans, Eerdmans, 1984.
(Author of foreword) Omar Badsha, editor, *South Africa: The Cordoned Heart,* Gallery Press, 1986.
(Author of foreword) *The War against Children: South Africa's Youngest Victims,* Lawyers Committee for Human Rights, 1986.
(Contributor) Buti Tlhagale and Itumeleng Mosala, editors, *Hammering Swords Into Ploughshares: Essays in Honor of Archbishop Mpilo Desmond Tutu,* Eerdmans, 1987.
(Author of foreword) Frank England, editor, *Bounty in Bondage: The Anglican Church in Southern Africa, Essays in Honor of Edward Iing, Dean of Cape Town,* Ohio University Press, 1989.
(With Naomi Tutu) *The Words of Desmond Tutu,* Newmarket Press, 1989.
(Author of foreword) Martin Prozesky, editor, *Christianity Amidst Apartheid: Selected Perspectives on the Church in South Africa,* Saint Martin's Press, 1990.
(Contributor) Jim Cole, editor *Filtering People: Understanding and Confronting Our Prejudices,* New Society Publishers, 1990.
(Author of foreword) Sue Williamson, *Resistance Art in South Africa,* St. Martin's, 1990.
The Rainbow People of God: The Making of a Peaceful Revolution, Doubleday, 1994.
(Editor and author of introduction) *An African Prayer Book,* Doubleday, 1995.
(With Michael Jesse Battle) *Reconciliation: The Ubuntu Theology of Desmond Tutu,* Pilgrim Press, 1997.
(With Godfrey W. Ashby) *Go out and Meet God: A Commentary on the Book of Exodus,* Eerdmans, 1998.
(With Lawrence Boadt) *The Hebrew Prophets: Visionaries of the Ancient World,* Griffin Trade, 1999.
No Future without Forgiveness, Doubleday, 1999.

Also author of several articles and reviews.

SIDELIGHTS: As archbishop of Capetown, leader of the Anglican Church in southern Africa, and one of the world's foremost black critics of South Africa's history of apartheid, Desmond M. Tutu has been "nothing if not impassioned," wrote Joshua Hammer in *People* magazine. "Like all great preachers, his every speech and press conference is a blaze of emotion, his every gesture a drop of oil fueling the oratorical fire. Waving his arms, punching the air like a boxer, the elfin . . . figure draws in his followers with a stream of whispers, shouts and sobs, punctuated with roars of laughter." Yet until he received the Nobel Peace Prize in 1984, Tutu was little known outside his native South Africa.

During the 1970s and into the 1980s, first as general secretary of the South African Council of Churches, then as bishop of Johannesburg, and later as archbishop of Capetown, Tutu campaigned vigorously for the abolition of apartheid, South Africa's long-standing system of government that defined and allocated political power and privileges to different groups of people on the basis of skin color and ethnic background. He became internationally famous as the face of opposition to apartheid within South Africa. When apartheid was finally abolished in the early 1990s, Tutu stepped out of the limelight somewhat to let colleagues such as President Nelson Mandela take center stage in reintegrating South Africa into the world community. Nonetheless, his profile as a consistently thoughtful, humane critic of his country's social injustices remains high.

Tutu's first recollections of the apartheid system in operation came when he was growing up in the western Transvaal mining town of Klerksdorp. He told Marc Cooper and Greg Goldin of *Rolling Stone* that the constant racial taunts of the white boys were not "thought to be out of the ordinary," but as he got older he "began finding things eating away at [him]." Recalling one incident in which he heard his father referred to as "boy," Tutu remarked, "I knew there wasn't a great deal I could do, but it just left me churned. . . . What he must have been feeling . . . being humiliated in the presence of his son. Apartheid has always been the same systematic racial discrimination: it takes away your human dignity and rubs it in the dust and tramples it underfoot." Young Tutu also witnessed the harsh economic realities of the government's discriminatory policies while attending the local school. The white children, for whom the government had arranged free school meals, disliked the institutional food and threw it away, preferring to eat what their mothers packed for them. Many black school children of poor families, recalled Tutu, were reduced to scavenging in the cafeteria's rubbish bins for food during lunch periods.

In 1943 the Tutu family moved to Johannesburg where Desmond's father continued to teach and his mother worked as a cook at a missionary school for the blind. The new surroundings greatly affected

young Tutu. Not only was he deeply moved by the dedication and service shown by staff members to the children in the school where his mother worked, but it was here that he first met Father Trevor Huddleston, who became his most influential mentor and friend. A leading British critic of South Africa's apartheid system, Huddleston served as the parish priest in Sophiatown, a black slum district of Johannesburg. In an interview with the *Observer,* Tutu recalled his first meeting with the priest: "I was standing with my mother one day, when this white man in a cassock walked past and doffed his big black hat to her. I couldn't believe it—a white man raising his hat to a simple black labouring woman." Huddleston, who was beginning to build an international reputation as an outspoken opponent of apartheid and whom the South African authorities recognized as one of their most controversial critics, became a close friend of Tutu. When the young African contracted tuberculosis as a teenager and was hospitalized for almost twenty months, Huddleston visited him nearly every day. "Like many people, I came under the spell of Trevor Huddleston. I will never forget his compassion, caring, love and deep spirituality," Tutu told *People* reporters Peter Hawthorne and Dawn Clayton. The impact of Huddleston's friendship on Tutu's later life was immense.

Following full recovery from tuberculosis, Tutu resumed his education, and entered the School of Medicine at Witwatersrand University with the intention of becoming a doctor. When his family could no longer afford the tuition fees, however, he was forced to drop out of medical school and begin training as a teacher instead. Tutu received his B.A. from the University of Johannesburg in 1954 and taught high school in Johannesburg and Krugersdorp until 1957. It was then that Tutu's previous experiences with apartheid and the compassion he felt for his fellow man combined to change and redirect what might otherwise have been an uneventful career. While teaching at Munsieville High School in Krugersdorp, the South African government announced plans to introduce a state-run system of education especially intended for students in black districts. Limiting both the quality and extent of education, the system was considered by many to be deliberately second-rate. Tutu, along with several of his colleagues, found the plan ubiquitous and resigned. As a young man newly married, without a job, and sensing a growing urge to serve his community and country, Tutu, in retrospect, said he felt as if God had grabbed him by the scruff of his neck and, whether it was convenient or not, had sent him off to spread God's word. That same year, inspired by the ideals of his mentor Trevor Huddleston, he began theological studies with the priests of the Community of the Resurrection, the Anglican order to which Huddleston belonged.

Following ordainment as a priest in 1961, Tutu began to establish his career in the Anglican church, working in small parishes in England and South Africa. Concurrently he continued his education and in 1966 received a master's degree in theology from King's College, London. In 1972 he accepted a position in England as associate director of the Theological Education Fund. Thoroughly enjoying his role, he traveled extensively throughout Asia and Africa and presided over the allocation of World Council of Churches scholarships. Thoughts of South Africa and the discrimination faced by his black countrymen seemed to surface continually, however, demanding his consideration. Throughout the early 1970s, tensions increased between an angry black community and a white-dominated government determined to maintain its political powers. Finally, in 1975, Tutu decided to return to his homeland and "contribute what I could to the liberation struggle," he explained to Hawthorne and Clayton. Upon returning, his presence and commitment to the cause of black Africans was felt almost immediately.

As Tutu ascended the ecclesiastical ranks of the Anglican church—in 1976 he was consecrated bishop of Lesotho, one of the government-designated black homelands—his involvement in the antiapartheid cause assumed an importance concomitant with his position. Choosing always to live in his parish, he closely monitored the feelings of his congregation and the local community; during the 1970s, in an atmosphere of mounting racial tensions, Tutu attempted to pacify angry black youths, encouraging them to seek change through peaceful means. In 1976, he met with black activist Nhato Motlana in an effort to curb the potential violence of youths in the black township of Soweto on the outskirts of Johannesburg. He also wrote to the incumbent South African Prime Minister Balthazar J. Vorster, warning him of the dangerous situation in Soweto. Tutu later claimed that Vorster dismissed his letter as a ploy engineered by political opponents. On June 16, 1976, however, racial tensions exploded into racial violence as black demonstrators met untempered reprisal from white security forces. Six hundred blacks were shot to death in the confrontation.

The tragic consequences of the Soweto riots seemed to mark a watershed in the attention given to the antiapartheid struggle in South Africa. Thereafter the situation received more extensive coverage from the world's press, which supplied the West with explanations of the escalating racial conflict and attempted to expose the possible reasons for it. For Tutu the increasing number of violent confrontations between blacks and security forces marked a change in his perception of his own involvement. Until the Soweto riots, he made himself generally available to discuss the situation with any representative from any side; following the riots he began to use his growing influence and openly initiated peaceful negotiation. This was not done in deference to the government; Tutu had become a highly visible and vocal critic.

By 1978 Tutu had been appointed the first black secretary general of the South African Council of Churches, and his personal attitude toward apartheid had hardened. He felt he could no longer condone the system on either political or moral grounds, and he determinedly set out to promote peaceful change toward a truly democratic system of government in South Africa. As head of the Council Tutu became spokesman for its thirteen million members, thus gaining increased political strength; due to its racial composition—eighty percent black—the Council was an ideal vehicle for voicing political opposition to the apartheid system. Under Tutu's direction the Council not only became openly critical of the South African government, but it also supported a network of anti-government protest. Responsible for paying the legal fees of arrested black protesters, for supporting the families of imprisoned activists, and for financing anti-government demonstrations, the Council did not endear itself to the South African authorities. The South African government began to single out Council leaders—Tutu prominent among them—for criticism, with the help of press agencies that supported government views. In addition Tutu and his colleagues were constantly harassed with accusations of minor misdemeanors and, through government legislation, were deprived of certain rights of free movement. But in 1979, on two occasions, Tutu openly challenged the government, seriously confronting its credibility in the eyes of the rest of the world.

The first challenge came after the passing of the Group Areas Act, a policy that gave the government the power to forcibly remove blacks from their homes in urban South Africa and relocate them in government designated tribal homelands. The act made it virtually impossible for blacks to continue working at the better-paying city jobs without enduring lengthy and uncomfortable journeys every day or paying to live in one of the government's single-sexed hostels located in the city suburbs. And for those blacks who stayed in the homelands to work, their only hope was to eke out a meager living from very poor farmland. Appalled by the situation and by conditions in the homelands, Tutu compared the South African government with that of Nazi Germany, denouncing the forced relocation of blacks as South Africa's "final solution" to the black "problem." Although he later retracted the wording of his outburst, he continued to protest the policy and chided the government in Pretoria for deliberately starving people in South Africa while it boasted about its grain exports to nearby Zambia.

Tutu voiced his second major condemnation of the South African government before an international audience in autumn of 1979, which probably marks the beginning of his visibility in the world's media. In an interview for a Danish television program, Tutu called on the government of Denmark to cease buying South African coal as a sign of support for the anti-apartheid cause. The appeal moved people in Western countries to consider economic sanction as the ultimate weapon in the battle against apartheid. Concerned citizens, particularly in Europe, had voiced disapproval of South Africa's white minority government for years, but they had never found an effective means of critical expression that would force the white government to reconsider its policies. Tutu's proposal offered a method that later became a principal part of the strategy in the worldwide fight against apartheid. It also successfully focused attention upon the real possibility of positive change in South Africa.

Tutu's actions brought him very close to serious government reprisals. Returning from Denmark in 1979, authorities seized his passport, a move generally seen as a warning of possible imprisonment—the fate of two previous government critics, Nelson R. Mandela and Victor Tambo—or expulsion from the country. Tutu ignored the signal, however, and continued his antiapartheid campaign. The South African government eventually returned his passport in January, 1981, but confiscated it again in April. Thereafter Tutu was allowed to travel outside South Africa only with the government's permission and special travel documents that listed his nationality as "undetermined." In August, 1982, the South African government denied Tutu permission to go to New York to receive an honorary doctorate from Columbia University. Since the university does not grant degrees in absentia, Columbia's president traveled to South Af-

rica and personally presented Tutu his degree in a ceremony held in Johannesburg.

It was during a permitted stay in the United States, on October 16, 1984, that Desmond Tutu received word that he was the 1984 Nobel peace laureate. Part of the Nobel citation read: "It is the committee's wish that the Peace Prize now awarded to Desmond Tutu should be regarded not only as a gesture of support to him and to the South African Council of Churches of which he is leader, but also to all individuals and groups in South Africa who, with their concern for human dignity, fraternity and democracy, incite the admiration of the world." According to *Time,* "much of white South Africa reacted grumpily or indifferently to the news." Said Tutu, in response: "You feel humble, you feel proud, elated and you feel sad. One of my greatest sadnesses is that there are many in this country who are not joining in celebrating something that is an honor for this country." Less than a month later, on November 3, 1984, Tutu was elected as the first Anglican bishop of Johannesburg; he subsequently resigned as secretary general of the South African Council of Churches.

Tutu immediately expanded his efforts to abolish apartheid. He called upon the international community to use diplomatic, political, and economic pressures to convince the South African government in Pretoria to rid itself of apartheid. Maintaining a strong belief in nonviolence, Tutu was positive such actions offered the only viable means of avoiding massive bloodshed. His request caused considerable reaction in the United States. In December, 1984, Tutu traveled to Washington, DC, to meet with President Ronald Reagan. He tried to persuade the president to impose economic sanctions against South Africa, arguing that such a measure would help put an end to police violence and lead to the release of political prisoners. But Reagan preferred, instead, to remain on friendly terms with Pretoria, believing only diplomacy would produce positive change in South Africa, a policy he called "constructive engagement." The president's stance provoked a nationwide response as hundreds of antiapartheid demonstrators picketed South African consulates and embassies throughout the country. In a well-received speech before a bipartisan congressional committee, Tutu called on the United States to make a stand against racism. In response to the bishop's appeal, increasing numbers of state and local government, educational institutions, and labor unions began plans to withdraw investments from companies doing business with South Africa. Pretoria viewed the American developments with growing concern.

Over the next several months civil unrest in South Africa escalated from boycotts, strikes, and stone-throwing clashes between township blacks and police to bloody riots symptomatic of civil war. By July, 1985, more than 500 people had been killed, including four leaders of the largely black nationalist United Democratic Front (UDF) party. Many of the victims were black government employees and town councilors attacked by blacks loyal to UDF, some were blacks who had patronized white businesses, others were killed when police opened fire on rioters. The deteriorating situation prompted President Botha to declare a state of emergency in more than thirty districts throughout the country, including Johannesburg and most of the Transvaal provinces. Invoking the emergency powers of South Africa's 1953 Public Security Act, the government was allowed to impose curfews, arrest and detain suspects for fourteen days without a warrant, interrogate prisoners without the presence of lawyers, and tighten censorship on the press. International response to Botha's move was guarded, but antiapartheid leaders in South Africa were incensed. Asked in a *Newsweek* interview if the state of emergency changed South Africa's situation, Bishop Tutu replied: "Declaring a state of emergency is a typical reaction. It doesn't really change much: it just removes the last vestiges of our rights, and it means that whatever they do to us now, they can do with more impunity."

The government outlawed funeral marches, for example, sensing that the traditionally communal affairs represented subversion and civil disorder. Funeral services, however, were permitted. During one instance in the black township of Daveyton, reported *Time,* police and military units surrounded the tent where family, friends, and community members gathered for the burial service of a young black woman shot and killed during a demonstration. Army troops held guns ready, police dogs were positioned atop armored cars, and helicopters surveyed the area from above. It was the largest display of government force since Botha's declaration of emergency began. The tension mounted as the government forces waited to see if the crowd would, in defiance, march to the cemetery located several blocks away. Just when violence seemed likely to erupt, Bishop Tutu arrived and the atmosphere relaxed immediately. The coffin of the slain girl was brought into the tent and set before the clergyman, who calmly performed the religious service. According to *Time,* "Tutu told the gathering that he had asked the government, 'Please allow us to mourn, to bury our dead with dignity, to share the burden of our sorrow. Do not rub salt in our wounds

. . . I appeal to you because we are already hurt, already down. We are humans, not animals. When we have a death, we cry.'" In warning to the authorities, reported *Time,* "the bishop declared, 'I have been a minister for 24 years, and I am not going to start now being told what to preach. I do not want to defy the government. But Scripture says that when there is a conflict between the law of God and the law of man, we must obey the law of God. I will continue to preach as instructed.'" After the completion of the religious service, the police ordered the crowd to disperse, allowing people in vehicles only to go to the cemetery. Tutu pleaded with the police commandant to provide buses, warning that violence could otherwise erupt. After an hour of tense waiting, buses finally arrived and transported the mourners to the cemetery. A potentially bloody confrontation was avoided, order had been maintained, and peace prevailed. Recalling for a *Time* reporter the confrontation with the police commandant, Tutu chuckled and said, "He saluted me. Twice."

During the weeks following the Daveyton incident, international condemnation of Pretoria's declared state of emergency increased. Canada prepared to toughen its limited economic sanctions, the U.S. House of Representatives approved the first imposition of broad economic sanctions against South Africa, and more than a dozen European nations recalled their diplomats in a gesture of disapproval. By the end of 1985, the rand (South Africa's monetary unit) lost fifty percent of its value. President Botha, however, was determined not to succumb to external pressure and his declaration of emergency held firm. Tutu also held firm to his own declaration to rid South Africa of apartheid, and he continued his outspoken appeal for international support of the antiapartheid cause. "We face a catastrophe in this land," warned Tutu, according to *Newsweek.* "Only the action of the international community, by applying pressure, can save us." Speaking in Wales some time later, reported *New Statesman,* Tutu declared, "It is still possible for us to move back from the edge of a precipice if the international community is prepared to intervene decisively." But international action was slow to develop, especially in the United States where President Reagan insisted on maintaining his current policy of deploring the apartheid system while opposing punitive sanctions. Angry with the Reagan administration's attitude, Tutu, according to *Newsweek,* observed: "President Reagan has [imposed sanctions on] Poland, Nicaragua and Libya. He is not opposed to sanctions per se. He is opposed to them when blacks are involved." Tutu also asserted, "In my view, the Reagan administration's support and collaboration with [the South African government] is immoral, evil and totally unchristian. You are either for or against apartheid, and not by rhetoric. You are either on the side of the oppressed or on the side of the oppressor. You can't be neutral."

Over the next several months antiapartheid forces did gain support in the United States when the House of Representatives approved a bill that would impose a trade embargo on South Africa. President Reagan still refused to approve sanctions, however, and promised to veto such a bill. In a speech made in July, 1986, Reagan stated that current U.S. policy toward South Africa would remain unchanged. Tutu's reaction, as disclosed in *Newsweek,* was unusually blunt: "[Tutu] called the speech 'nauseating,' likened Reagan to the 'great white chief of old' and said, 'The West, for my part, can go to hell.'" Pretoria seemed pleased with Reagan's message. Meanwhile the situation in South Africa worsened and Tutu's speeches began to take on fatalistic undertones. Speaking with *Time,* Tutu said: "I think the white ruling class is quite ready to do a Samson on us. That is, they will pull down the pillars, even if it means they perish in the process. They are really scared that we are going to treat them as they treated us."

In early September, 1986, Tutu was elected archbishop of Capetown and the primate of the Anglican Church for all of southern Africa. Conducting his final service in Johannesburg before his enthronement as archbishop, according to *Time,* Tutu assured his congregation: "Despite all that the powers of the world may do, we are going to be free." But in a British Broadcasting Corporation interview reported by *Time* in April, 1987, President Botha declared, "I am not prepared to sacrifice my rights so that the other man can dominate me with his greater numbers. . . . I never read in the Bible that to be good means I must commit suicide to please the other man." Shortly thereafter, Pretoria toughened its policies against antiapartheid demonstrators even more. According to *Time* the South African government "announced a new emergency regulation banning South Africans from doing or saying anything to bring about the release of people who have been detained without trial"—an estimated eight thousand, including two thousand minors. The government also declared it "illegal to participate in 'any campaign, project or action aimed at accomplishing the release' of detainees. Among the forbidden acts . . . are the signing of petitions, the sending of telegrams and even the wearing of political stickers or shirts bearing antidetention slogans."

Time reported that Tutu and other critics in South Africa "said they would ignore the restrictions and continue to speak their minds." Holding a prayer service to protest Pretoria's action, the archbishop warned: "Beware when you take on the Church of God. Others have tried and have come a cropper." He then added, "The government has gone crazy. I want to tell them that I am not going to stop calling for the release of detainees in or out of church." Governments worldwide, including the United States, also expressed official disapproval. Faced with such widespread opposition, Pretoria retreated somewhat, but they had once again fueled the fires of civil unrest and the antiapartheid cause. Tutu, adhering to his conviction that democracy and freedom could exist in South Africa, continued his campaign for the peaceful liberation of his countrymen. In the early 1990s, increasing pressure within and outside of South Africa finally led the government of F. W. DeKlerk to abolish apartheid and institute majority rule. Nelson Mandela, long imprisoned, was released from prison and was elected president of the new South Africa. Tutu's conviction that his countrymen would eventually be free became reality.

Many of Tutu's orations have been collected in *Hope and Suffering: Sermons and Speeches,* described as "vintage Tutu" by Huston Horn in the *Los Angeles Times Book Review.* "Tutu's gaze rarely wanders from a benign, visionary South Africa ruled together by blacks and whites," explained Horn, and "the bishop's preachments [still] have contemporary relevance and ring." Colman McCarthy of *Washington Post Book World* called the book "stunning" and concluded that Bishop Tutu, even without his Nobel, "would still have been a force that no regime could stop or silence."

In 1994, after the fall of apartheid, Tutu published *The Rainbow People of God: The Making of a Peaceful Revolution.* A collection of sermons, speeches, and letters, the book charts Tutu's long struggle against apartheid. Michael Novak, reviewing the book in *Washington Post Book World,* remarked that "these documents show [Tutu] to have been from the first a thinker with a clear, consistent and humane strategic concept, which required constant bravery on his part . . . between 1976 and 1994." According to Chicago *Tribune Books* contributor George Packer, "one has a powerful sense of Tutu's fundamentally sound moral judgment. He never appears to be acting out an idea of himself, and his reactions to crises almost always proved wise, as if no amount of weariness or confusion or rage could poison the core of his character."

BIOGRAPHICAL/CRITICAL SOURCES:

BOOKS

Black Literature Criticism, Gale, Volume 3, 1992.
Cheney, Patricia, *Archbishop Desmond Tutu: Man of Peace,* Millbrook Press, 1995.
Contemporary Literary Criticism, Gale, Volume 80, 1994.
Kunnie, Julian, *Models of Black Theology: Issues in Class, Culture, and Gender,* Trinity Press International, 1994.
Tlhagale, Buti and Itumeleng Mosala, editors, *Hammering Swords into Ploughshares: Essays in Honor of Archbishop Mpilo Desmond Tutu,* Eerdmans, 1987.

PERIODICALS

Chicago Tribune, July 7, 1980.
Christian Century, November 3, 1993, p. 1086; March 20, 1996, p. 324.
Christianity Today, October 5, 1992, p. 39.
Christian Science Monitor, April 26, 1979; March 28, 1984.
Economist, March 28, 1987; April 18, 1987; August 19, 1995, p. 38.
Emerge, June, 1995, p. 22.
Jet, April 24, 1995, p. 35; November 27, 1995, p. 23.
Library Journal, December, 1994, p. 99.
Maclean's, August 12, 1985; April 14, 1986; March 13, 1989, p. 22; June 17, 1996, p. 25.
Manchester Guardian Weekly, October 28, 1984.
Newsday, October 17, 1984.
New Statesman, May 30, 1986; March 18, 1988, p. 18.
Newsweek, October 29, 1984; December 17, 1984; July 29, 1985; August 4, 1986.
New York Times, October 17, 1984; April 11, 1996, p. A4.
New York Times Magazine, March 14, 1982.
Observer (London), August 8, 1982; May 8, 1983.
People, December 17, 1984.
Rolling Stone, November 21, 1985.
Time, October 29, 1984, January 14, 1985; August 19, 1985; August 4, 1986; September 15, 1986; April 13, 1987; April 27, 1987.
Tribune Books (Chicago), December 18, 1994, p. 3.

Washington Post, October 17, 1984; October 19, 1984.
Washington Post Book World, October 2, 1994, p. 1.
World Press Review, January, 1995, p. 10.*

*   *   *

TUTUOLA, Amos   1920-1997

PERSONAL: Born 1920, in Abeokuta, Nigeria; died from hypertension and diabetes, June 8, 1997, in Ibadan, Nigeria; son of Charles (a cocoa farmer) and Esther (Aina) Tutuola; married Alake Victoria, 1947; children: Olubunmi, Oluyinka, Erinola, five others. *Education:* Attended schools in Nigeria. *Religion:* Christian.

CAREER: Worked on father's farm; trained as a coppersmith; employed by Nigerian Government Labor Department, Lagos, and by Nigerian Broadcasting Corp., Ibadan, Nigeria. Freelance writer. Visiting research fellow, University of Ife, 1979; associate, international writing program at University of Iowa, 1983. *Military service:* Royal Air Force, 1943-45; served as metal worker in Nigeria.

MEMBER: Modern Language Association of America, Mbari Club (Nigerian authors; founder).

AWARDS, HONORS: Named honorary citizen of New Orleans, 1983; *The Palm-Wine Drinkard and His Dead Palm-Wine Tapster in the Dead's Town* and *My Life in the Bush of Ghosts* received second place awards in a contest held in Turin, Italy, 1985; Noble Patron of Arts, Pan African Writers Association, 1992.

WRITINGS:

The Palm-Wine Drinkard and His Dead Palm-Wine Tapster in the Dead's Town, Faber, 1952, Grove, 1953.
My Life in the Bush of Ghosts, Grove, 1954, reprinted, Faber, 1978.
Simbi and the Satyr of the Dark Jungle, Faber, 1955.
The Brave African Huntress, illustrated by Ben Enwonwu, Grove, 1958.
The Feather Woman of the Jungle, Faber, 1962.
Ajaiyi and His Inherited Poverty, Faber, 1967.
(Contributor) *Winds of Change: Modern Short Stories from Black Africa,* Longman, 1977.

The Witch-Herbalist of the Remote Town, Faber, 1981.

The Wild Hunter in the Bush of the Ghosts (facsimile of manuscript), edited with an introduction and a postscript by Bernth Lindfors, Three Continents Press, 1982, 2nd edition, 1989.

Pauper, Brawler, and Slanderer, Faber, 1987.

The Village Witch Doctor and Other Stories, Faber, 1990.

The Palm-Wine Drinkard [and] *My Life in the Bush of Ghosts,* Grove Press, 1994.

WORK REPRESENTED IN ANTHOLOGIES

Rutherford, Peggy, editor, *Darkness and Light: An Anthology of African Writing,* Drum Publications, 1958.

Hughes, Langston, editor, *An African Treasury: Articles, Essays, Stories, Poems by Black Africans,* Crown, 1960.

Hughes, Langston, and Christiane Reynault, editors, *Anthologie africaine et malgache,* Seghers, 1962.

Ademola, Frances, editor, *Reflections,* African Universities Press, 1962, new edition, 1965.

Sainville, Leonard, editor, *Anthologie de la litterature negroafricaine: Romanciers et conteurs negro africains,* two volumes, Presence Africaine, 1963.

Whiteley, W. H., compiler, *A Selection of African Prose,* two volumes, Oxford University Press, 1964.

Rive, Richard, editor, *Modern African Prose,* Heinemann Educational, 1964.

Komey, Ellis Ayitey and Ezekiel Mphahlele, editors, *Modern African Stories,* Faber, 1964.

Tibble, Anne, editor, *African-English Literature: A Survey and Anthology,* Peter Owen, 1965.

Edwards, Paul, compiler, *Through African Eyes,* two volumes, Cambridge University Press, 1966.

Mphahlele, Ezekiel, editor, *African Writing Today,* Penguin, 1967.

Beier, Ulli, editor, *Political Spider: An Anthology of Stories from "Black Orpheus,"* Heinemann Educational, 1969.

Larson, Charles, editor, *African Short Stories: A Collection of Contemporary African Writing,* Macmillan, 1970.

ADAPTATIONS: Kola Ogunmola has written a play in Yoruba entitled *Omuti,* based on *The Palm-Wine Drinkard,* published by West African Book Publishers.

SIDELIGHTS: With the publication of his novel *The Palm-Wine Drinkard and His Dead Palm-Wine Tapster in the Dead's Town* in 1952, Amos Tutuola became the first internationally recognized Nigerian writer. Since that time, Tutuola's works, in particular *The Palm-Wine Drinkard,* have been the subject of much critical debate. *The Palm-Wine Drinkard* was praised by critics outside of Nigeria for its unconventional use of the English language, its adherence to the oral tradition, and its unique, fantastical characters and plot. Nigerian critics, on the other hand, described the work as ungrammatical and unoriginal. Discussing the first criticism in his book *The Growth of the African Novel,* Eustace Palmer writes: "Tutuola's English is demonstrably poor; this is due partly to his ignorance of the more complicated rules of English syntax and partly to interference from Yoruba." The second criticism, concerning Tutuola's lack of originality, is based on similarities between Tutuola's works and those of his predecessor, O. B. Fagunwa, who writes in the Yoruba language.

The influence of Fagunwa's writings on Tutuola's work has been noted by several critics, including Abiola Irele, who writes in *The African Experience in Literature and Ideology:* "It is clear that much of the praise and acclaim that have been lavished upon Tutuola belong more properly to Fagunwa who provided not only the original inspiration but indeed a good measure of material for Tutuola's novels. The echoes of Fagunwa in Tutuola's works are numerous enough to indicate that the latter was consciously creating from a model provided by the former." Irele adds, however, "that despite its derivation from the work of Fagunwa, Tutuola's work achieves an independent status that it owes essentially to the force of his individual genius."

Tutuola's genius is described by reviewers as an ability to refashion the traditional Yoruba myths and folktales that are the foundation of his work. Eustace Palmer notes, for instance, in *The Growth of the African Novel:* "Taking his stories direct from his people's traditional lore, he uses his inexhaustible imagination and inventive power to embellish them, to add to them or alter them, and generally transform them into his own stories conveying his own message." O. R. Dathorne comments in an essay published in *Introduction to Nigerian Literature:* "Tutuola is a literary paradox; he is completely part of the folklore traditions of the Yorubas and yet he is able to modernize these traditions in an imaginative way. It is on this level that his books can best be approached. . . . Tutuola deserves to be considered seriously because his work represents an intentional attempt to fuse folklore with modern life."

In *The Palm-Wine Drinkard,* for example, the Drinkard's quest for his tapster leads him into many perilous situations, including an encounter with the Red Fish, a monster Tutuola describes as having thirty horns "spread out as an umbrella," and numerous eyes that "were closing and opening at the same time as if a man was pressing a switch on and off." Tutuola also amends a traditional tale concerning a Skull who borrows appendages belonging to other persons in order to look like a "complete gentleman" to include references to modern warfare. Tutuola writes: "If this gentleman went to the battle field, surely, enemy would not kill him or capture him and if bombers saw him in a town which was to be bombed, they would not throw bombs on his presence, and if they did throw it, the bomb itself would not explode until this gentleman would leave that town, because of his beauty." Gerald Moore observes in *Seven African Writers* that these descriptions are evidence "of Tutuola's easy use of the paraphernalia of modern life to give sharpness and immediacy to his imagery."

The Palm-Wine Drinkard was hailed by critics such as V. S. Pritchett and Dylan Thomas, the latter of whom describes the work in the *Observer* as a "brief, thronged, grisly and bewitching story." Thomas concludes: "The writing is nearly always terse and direct, strong, wry, flat and savoury. . . . Nothing is too prodigious or too trivial put down in this tall, devilish story." The work also has been favorably compared to such classics as *The Odyssey, Pilgrim's Progress,* and *Gulliver's Travels.* Some critics, however, expressed reservations about Tutuola's ability to repeat his success. According to Charles R. Larson's *The Emergence of African Fiction,* critic Anthony West stated, "*The Palm-Wine Drinkard* must be valued for its own freakish sake, and as an unrepeatable happy hit."

Despite the reservations of critics like West, Tutuola went on to publish several additional works, and while critics are, as Larson observes in *The Emergence of African Fiction,* "a little less awed now than they were in the early 1950's," Tutuola's works continue to merit critical attention. Among the more widely reviewed of these books is *The Witch-Herbalist of the Remote Town.* Published thirty years after *The Palm-Wine Drinkard,* this book involves a quest initiated by the protagonist, a hunter, to find a cure for his wife's barrenness. The journey to the Remote Town takes six years; along the way the hunter encounters bizarre and sometimes frightening places and people, including the Town of the Born-and-Die Baby

and the Abnormal Squatting Man of the Jungle, who can paralyze opponents with a gust of frigid air by piercing his abdomen. The hunter eventually reaches the Remote Town, and the witch-herbalist gives him a broth guaranteed to make his wife fertile. The plot is complicated though, when the hunter, weak from hunger, sips some of the broth.

As with *The Palm-Wine Drinkard,* critical commentary of *The Witch-Herbalist of the Remote Town* focuses in particular on Tutuola's use of the English language. Edward Blishen, for instance, comments in the *Times Educational Supplement:* "The language is wonderfully stirring and odd: a mixture of straight translation from Yoruba, and everyday modern Nigerian idiom, and grand epical English. The imagination at work is always astonishing. . . . And this, not the bargain, is folklore not resurrected, but being created fresh and true in the white heat of a tradition still undestroyed." *Voice Literary Supplement* critic Jon Parales writes: "His direct, apparently simple language creates an anything-can-happen universe, more whacky and amoral than the most determinedly modern lit." *Washington Post Book World* contributor Judith Chettle offers this view: "Tutuola writes with an appealing vigor and his idiosyncratic use of the English idiom gives the story a fresh and African perspective, though at times the clumsiness of some phrasing does detract from the thrust of the narrative. No eye-dabbing sentimentalist, Tutuola's commentary is clear-eyed if not acerbic, but underlying the tale is a quiet and persistent lament for the simpler, unsophisticated and happier past of his people."

An *Africa Today* contributor, Nancy J. Schmidt, observes that Tutuola's language has become increasingly more like that of standard English over the years. She cites other differences between this work and earlier ones as well. "Tutuola's presence is very evident in *Witch-Herbalist,* but the strength of his presence and his imagination are not as strong as they once were," writes Schmidt, who adds that "neither Tutuola nor his hero seem to be able to take a consistent moral stand, a characteristic that is distinctly different from Tutuola's other narratives." Commenting on the reasons for these differences, Schmidt writes: "They may reflect contemporary Yoruba culture, Tutuola's changing attitude toward Yoruba and Nigerian cultures as well as his changing position in Yoruba and Nigerian cultures, the difficulties of writing an oral narrative for an audience to whom oral narratives are becoming less familiar and less related to daily behavior, and the editorial policies for publishing African fictional narratives in the 1980s."

In the *New York Times Book Review* Charles Larson likewise notes Tutuola's use of standard English, but maintains that "the outstanding quality of Mr. Tutuola's work—the brilliance of the oral tradition—still remains." Larson concludes: "*The Witch-Herbalist of the Remote Town* is Mr. Tutuola at his imaginative best. Every incident in the narrative breathes with the life of the oral tradition; every episode in the journey startles with a kind of indigenous surrealism. Amos Tutuola is still his continent's most fantastic storyteller."

Tutuola's 1990 story collection, *The Village Witch Doctor and Other Stories,* contains eighteen stories based on traditional Yoruba fables. Like most of his previous work, the stories in this collection deal with greed, betrayal, and tricksterism. In the title story, for instance, a village witch doctor tricks others again and again before getting a dose of his own medicine. *Dictionary of Literary Biography* reviewer Bernth Lindfors remarks that "the same buoyant imagination [found in his earlier work] is in evidence, the same fascination with comically grotesque fantasy worlds. Tutuola, after more than forty years of writing, remains a very resourceful raconteur."

BIOGRAPHICAL/CRITICAL SOURCES:

BOOKS

Black Literature Criticism, Gale, 1992.
Collins, Harold R., *Amos Tutuola,* Twayne, 1969.
Contemporary Literary Criticism, Gale, Volume 5, 1976, Volume 14, 1980, Volume 29, 1984.
Dictionary of Literary Biography, Volume 125: *Twentieth-Century Caribbean and Black African Writers,* second series, Gale, 1993.
Herskovits, Melville J. and Francis S. Herskovits, *Dahomean Narrative: A Cross-Cultural Analysis,* Northwestern University Press, 1958.
Irele, Abiola, *The African Experience in Literature and Ideology,* Heinemann, 1981.
King, Bruce, editor, *Introduction to Nigerian Literature,* Evans Brothers, 1971.
Larson, Charles R., *The Emergence of African Fiction,* revised edition, Indiana University Press, 1972.
Laurence, Margaret, *Long Drums and Cannons: Nigerian Dramatists,* Praeger, 1969.
Lindfors, Bernth, editor, *Critical Perspectives on Amos Tutuola,* Three Continents Press, 1975.
Lindfors, *Early Nigerian Literature,* Africana Publishing, 1982.
Moore, Gerald, *Seven African Writers,* Oxford University Press, 1962.
Palmer, Eustace, *The Growth of the African Novel,* Heinemann, 1979.
Tucker, Martin, *Africa in Modern Literature: A Survey of Contemporary Writing in English,* Ungar, 1967.
Tutuola, Amos, *The Palm-Wine Drinkard and His Dead Palm-Wine Tapster in the Dead's Town,* Faber, 1952, Grove, 1953.

PERIODICALS

Africa Today, volume 29, number 3, 1982.
Ariel, April, 1977.
Books Abroad, summer, 1968.
Critique, fall/winter, 1960-61; fall/winter, 1967-68.
Journal of Canadian Fiction, vol. 3, no. 4, 1975.
Journal of Commonwealth Literature, August, 1974; August, 1981; volume 17, number 1, 1982.
Listener, December 14, 1967.
London Review of Books, April 2, 1987.
Los Angeles Times Book Review, August 15, 1982.
Nation, September 25, 1954.
New Statesman, December 8, 1967.
New Yorker, April 23, 1984.
New York Times Book Review, July 4, 1982.
Observer, July 6, 1952; November 22, 1981.
Okikie, September, 1978.
Presence Africaine, third trimester, 1967.
Spectator, October 24, 1981.
Times Educational Supplement, February 26, 1982.
Times Literary Supplement, January 18, 1968; February 26, 1982; August 28, 1987; May 18, 1990, p. 534.
Voice Literary Supplement, June, 1982.
Washington Post, July 13, 1987.
Washington Post Book World, August 15, 1982.
World Literature Today, summer, 1991, p. 539.

OBITUARIES:

PERIODICALS

New York Times, June 15, 1997.
Washington Post, June 22, 1997.*

*   *   *

ULASI, Adaora Lily 1932-

PERSONAL: Born 1932, in Aba, Nigeria; daughter of an Igbo chief who served as a district court judge and his wife; married (divorced, 1972). *Education:* Attended several girls' schools in Nigeria; attended Pepperdine College; University of Southern California, B.A. (journalism), 1954.

ADDRESSES: Home—England. *Agent*—c/o Onibonoje Press & Book Industries, Felele Layout, Molete, P.O. Box 3109, Ibadon, Nigeria.

CAREER: Nigerian novelist and editor. Nigerian *Daily Times* and *Sunday Times,* women's page editor; *Woman's World* magazine, editor.

WRITINGS:

NOVELS

Many Thing You No Understand, Michael Joseph (London), 1970, Fontana (London), 1973.
Many Thing Begin for Change, Michael Joseph (London), 1971, Fontana (London), 1975.
The Night Harry Died, 1974.
The Man from Sagama, Fontana (London), 1978.
Who Is Jonah?, Onibonoje Publishers (Idaban, Nigeria), 1978.

Also the author of poetry, articles, and book reviews.

SIDELIGHTS: Adaora Lily Ulasi published five novels during the 1970s, and was, according to a writer for the *Bloomsbury Guide to Women's Literature,* not only the first Nigerian woman to write detective novels in English, but also, in her previous career, one of her nation's first female journalists. The daughter of a chief descended from the Royal House of Nnewi of the Igbo people, Ulasi grew up listening to her father's tales of his years of service as a district court judge. From this she became, even as a child, sensitive to the ironic contradictions in the British system of colonial law imposed upon an African culture.

After being educated in Nigerian girls' schools, she traveled to California to receive her professional training in journalism, first at Pepperdine College and then at the University of Southern California. Armed with a degree in journalism, she returned to Nigeria and worked for several years as a women's page editor on a major daily and Sunday newspaper. When she was married, she traveled to England with her husband and had three children. In 1972, the couple divorced, and Ulasi, already a critically acclaimed novelist, returned to Nigeria for four years to work as editor of the magazine *Woman's World.* She returned to England in 1976 and remained there, turning her

hand to writing poetry, articles, and book reviews as well as fiction.

The predominant pattern in her novels, according to a writer in the *Feminist Companion to Literature in English,* has been a contrast between native Africans and British colonial officials as they become involved in solving crimes. She often uses pidgin dialect for her black African characters, a practice that some critics have frowned upon but others have praised. A *Bloomsbury Guide* writer called her pidgin dialect "badly realized" and complained that it turned some characters into "comic stereotypes," but critic Barry Cole, reviewing Ulasi's first novel, *Many Thing You No Understand,* for the *Spectator* found that the pidgin added "delight and humour to an intelligent and often hilarious picture of an already dying empire." Her works have also been praised for their satirical criticism of not only colonial power but male power— what a *Times Literary Supplement* reviewer of *Many Things You No Understand* termed "the vanities of the ruling sex, the bawdy boasting, the attempt to conceal feminine traits."

Many Thing You No Understand, set in 1935, features an Englishman named Mason and his Scottish junior colleague, MacIntosh, as they attempt to deal with the ritual beheading of a victim by two Igbo villagers. Mason, older and wiser and more acculturated to the African culture, wishes to leave native customs alone; newcomer McKenzie wants to bring British justice to bear on the killers. Meanwhile, surprises are revealed about the relationships between the white men and their black servants, and about the role of the tribal chief, who stays in the background, "as if he were a Shakespearian Duke," a *Times Literary Supplement* critic observed. The same reviewer commended Ulasi for her "shrewd multi-racial comedy, laced with very tall tales which may be readily swallowed." Commenting upon Ulasi's ambitiousness in writing dialogue for her British characters, the reviewer called that element of the novel "about as 'realistic' as the average English thriller or television drama script," and had high praise for Ulasi's gifts as a craftsman of suspense. The reviewer asserted that Ulasi possessed "the cunning of a whodunit writer, offering surprising denouements for which she has carefully laid clues."

Spectator critic Barry Cole opined that an appendix describing the degree of reality of this dramatized custom would have been helpful for the Western reader. He praised Ulasi's characterizations and her portrayal of the historical moment at which old African ways—and old British ways as well—were succumbing to new times. "Flawed but original" was Cole's summary of a book which came close, he declared, to proving that novelists are the best historians.

BIOGRAPHICAL/CRITICAL SOURCES:

BOOKS

Blain, Virginia, Patricia Clements, and Isabel Grundy, *The Feminist Companion to Literature in English,* Yale University Press (New Haven, CT), 1990.
Buck, Claire, editor, *Bloomsbury Guide to Women's Literature,* Prentice Hall (New York City), 1992.

PERIODICALS

Spectator, June 20, 1970, pp. 822-823.
Times Literary Supplement, June 18, 1970, p. 653.*

*   *   *

Van PEEBLES, Melvin 1932-

PERSONAL: Born August 21, 1932, in Chicago, IL; children: Mario, Meggan, Melvin. *Education:* Graduated from Ohio Wesleyan University, also attended University of Amsterdam.

ADDRESSES: Office—c/o Simon and Schuster, 1230 Avenue of the Americas, New York, NY 10020-1586.

CAREER: Writer, actor, producer of plays, director, and composer. Worked as operator of cable cars in San Francisco, California, and as a floor trader for the American Stock Exchange. Director of motion pictures, including *Watermelon Man,* 1970. *Military service:* U.S. Air Force; served as navigator-bombardier.

MEMBER: Directors Guild of America, French Directors Guild.

AWARDS, HONORS: First Prize from Belgian Festival for *Don't Play Us Cheap.*

WRITINGS:

Un ours pour le F.B.I. (novel), Buchet-Chastel, 1964, translation published as *A Bear for the F.B.I.,* Trident, 1968.

Un American en enfer (novel), Editions Denoel, 1965, translation published as *The True American: A Folk Fable,* Doubleday, 1976.
Le Chinois du XIV (short stories), Le Gadenet, 1966.
La Fete a Harlem [and] *La Permission* (two novels; former adapted from the play by Van Peebles, *Harlem Party;* also see below), J. Martineau, 1967, translation of *La Fete a Harlem* published as *Don't Play Us Cheap: A Harlem Party,* Bantam, 1973.
Sweet Sweetback's Baadasssss Song (adapted from the screenplay by Van Peebles; also see below), Lancer Books, 1971.
The Making of Sweet Sweetback's Baadasssss Song (nonfiction), Lancer Books, 1972, collector edition, Neo Press (Ann Arbor, MI), 1994.
Aint Supposed to Die a Natural Death (play; directed by the author and produced in New York City at the Ethel Barrymore Theatre, 1971; adapted from the recordings by Van Peebles, *Brer Soul* and *Aint Supposed to Die a Natural Death*), Bantam, 1973.
Just an Old Sweet Song, Ballantine, 1976.
(With Kenneth Vose, Leon Capetanos, and Lawrence Du Kose) *Greased Lightning* (screenplay; produced by Warner Bros., 1977), Yeah, 1976.
Bold Money: A New Way to Play the Options Market, Warner Books, 1986.
Bold Money: How to Get Rich in the Options Market, Warner Books, 1987.
(With Mario Van Peebles) *No Identity Crisis: A Father and Son's Own Story of Working Together,* Block and Chip, 1989.
Panther (novel), Thunder's Mouth Press (New York City), 1995.
(Author of introduction) Chester B. Himes, *Yesterday Will Make You Cry,* Norton, 1998.

Also author of screenplay of his novel *Panther,* which was made into a movie directed by his son, Mario Van Peebles.

OTHER

Harlem Party (play), produced in Belgium, 1964, produced as *Don't Play Us Cheap,* directed by the author and produced in New York City at the Ethel Barrymore Theatre, 1972.
(And director) *The Story of a Three Day Pass* (screenplay), Sigma III, 1968.
Watermelon Man, Columbia Pictures, 1970.
(And director) *Sweet Sweetback's Baadasssss Song* (screenplay), Cinemation Industries, 1971.

Sophisticated Gents (television screenplay; adapted from *The Junior Bachelor Society* by John A. Williams), produced as a four hour miniseries and broadcast on NBC-TV, September, 1981.

Waltz of the Stork (play), directed by author and produced in New York City at the Century Theatre, 1982.

Champeeen! (play), directed by author and produced in New York City at the New Federal Theatre, 1983.

Also author and director of *Don't Play Us Cheap* (adapted from the play by Van Peebles). Also creator of short films, including *Sunlight, Cinema 16,* and *Three Pick Up Men for Herrick,* Cinema 16.

Composer for recordings, including *Brer Soul, Aint Supposed to Die a Natural Death, Watermelon Man* (soundtrack for the motion picture), *Serious as a Heart Attack, Sweet Sweetback's Song* (soundtrack for the motion picture), and *Don't Play Us Cheap* (soundtrack for the motion picture).

SIDELIGHTS: Melvin Van Peebles began his career as an artist by creating short films. He had hoped that his first film efforts would lead to a filmmaking opportunity in Hollywood but moguls there were unimpressed. Instead of obtaining a position as a director or even assistant director, he was offered a job as an elevator operator. Seemingly at a dead end, Van Peebles suddenly received word from Henri Langlois, an associate of the French Cinematheque film depository who'd been impressed with Van Peebles's films. Langlois invited Van Peebles to come to Paris. There, Van Peebles enjoyed brief celebrity as an avant-garde filmmaker. But he had no opportunities to pursue filmmaking.

Van Peebles worked for some time as an entertainer in cafes until he discovered a means by which he could once again take up filmmaking. In France, one could gain entry into the Directors Guild if he wished to adapt his own French writings. So Van Peebles, in self-taught French, began writing novels. His first work, *A Bear for the F.B.I.,* concerned events in the life of an American middle-class black. Critical response was favorable, with Martin Levin remarking in the *New York Times Book Review* that "Van Peebles crystallizes the racial problem with rare subtlety." However, Van Peebles noted that the subtlety of the novel hindered his chances of being published in the United States. "I wrote the first work and my 'calling card,' to establish my reputation so I

could get my 'black' novels published," Van Peebles claimed. "But the publishers aren't interested unless you either lacerate whites or apologize to them."

American publishers displayed a similar lack of interest toward Van Peebles's next novel, *The True American,* which was written in 1965 but not published in the United States until 1976. It is the story of George Abraham Carver, a black prisoner who is accidentally killed by falling rocks. Carver arrives in Hell and learns that blacks are treated well there. This is because the majority of Hell's residents are white and, supposedly, the preferential attention the blacks receive causes the white residents more grief. Despite the "promising" premise, the novel was reviewed unfavorably in *New Yorker.* "Unfortunately" wrote the critic, "the book never really lives up to its promise, largely because of its pasteboard characters, its meandering plot, and its author's tendency to use a two-ton sledgehammer to drive home every point he makes about racist America."

Van Peebles continued to write, though, and produced in rapid succession a collection of short stories, *Le Chinois du XIV,* and two short novels, *La Fete a Harlem* and *La Permission.* At the same time, he was also arranging another film project. With the financial assistance of the French Ministry of Cultural Affairs and a private citizen, Van Peebles made *The Story of a Three Day Pass,* a film about a black soldier's encounter with a French woman. *The Story of a Three Day Pass* attracted substantial audiences in France and, upon its release in the United States, Van Peebles was in demand in Hollywood.

In 1969, after returning to the United States, Van Peebles agreed to direct a film written by Herman Raucher entitled *Watermelon Man.* This film deals with a white insurance agent who awakens one morning to discover that he's turned into a black man. "It's authentic stuff," related Van Peebles, "that laughs *with,* not at people." Later, he insisted, "I thought I had to make *Watermelon Man* in order to do the films I really wanted to do.

Van Peebles's next film, *Sweet Sweetback's Baadasssss Song,* is probably his best known work to date. He made the film in three weeks, using nonunion crews while keeping union officials disinterested by spreading rumors that he was making a pornographic film, something unworthy of their attention. Hollywood had refused to finance the film after a reading of the screenplay failed to impress studio officials. Fortunately, Van Peebles received a sizeable loan from Bill Cosby, which enabled him to complete the film. There was also difficulty promoting the film. Distributors declined to present it, theatres refused to book it, and talk shows refused to host Van Peebles. Eventually, he resorted to promoting it himself by passing out leaflets on street corners. Such determination ultimately paid off for Van Peebles. As a writer for *Time* noted, Van Peebles's "fast talk, plus audience word of mouth, made it a limited success. But that was enough." After the initial success of the film, it was mass-released to more than one hundred theatres and enjoyed brief status as the top money-making film in *Variety.*

The film elicited a variety of critical responses. The story of a black sex-show performer who avenges a youth's beating at the hands of two policemen by murdering them and eventually escapes to Mexico enraged some reviewers. Robert Hatch accused him in *Nation* of relying "on rather irresponsible con-temporary emotionalism to revitalize stock films he must have seen in his childhood." In the *New York Times* Vincent Canby claimed, "instead of dramatizing injustice, Van Peebles merchandizes it." He also declared that "the militancy of *Sweet Sweetback* is of a dull order, seemingly designed only to reinforce the prejudices of black audiences without in any way disturbing those prejudices." Clayton Riley conceded in the *New York Times,* "The film is an outrage," but then observed that it was "designed to blow minds." He wrote, "Through the lens of the Van Peebles camera comes a very basic Black America, unadorned by faith, and seething with an eternal violence." In the same review, Riley contended, "It is a terrifying vision, the Blood's nightmare journey through Watts, and it is a vision Black people alone will really understand in all of its profane and abrasive substance." In his study of black filmmakers published in the 1979 book, *American Film Now: The People, the Power, the Money, the Movies,* James Monaco takes a new look at Van Peebles's 1971 screenplay. "[*Sweet Sweetback's Baadasssss Song*] situates itself squarely in a long and important tradition in Black American narrative art," Monaco writes. "The Sweetback character has been mimicked and repeated a number of times since, but never with such purity of purpose and such elan. Van Peebles bent the medium of film to his will. No one else has bent it so far or so well since."

Van Peebles told a *Time* reporter that the film was not just for black audiences. "If films are good," he expressed, "the universality of the human experience will transcend the race and creed and crap frontiers." But he also noted that the film does have some specific messages for blacks. "Of all the ways we've been exploited by the Man, the most damaging is the way he destroyed our self-image," he asserted. "The message of *Sweetback* is that if you can get it together and stand up to the Man, you can win." In a *New York Times* interview, Van Peebles asked a writer, "When's the last time you saw a film in which the black man won in the end?" He then declared, "In my film, the black audience finally gets a chance to see some of their own fantasies acted out—about rising out of the mud and kicking ass."

After the success of *Sweet Sweetback,* Van Peebles was inundated with filmmaking offers from Hollywood studios. However, he insisted that he maintain his independence. "I'll only work with them on my terms," he stated. "I've whipped the man's ass on his own turf. I'm number one at the box office—which is the way America measures things—and I did it on my own. Now they want me, but I'm in no hurry."

Much of Van Peebles's more recent work has been as a playwright. *Aint Supposed to Die a Natural Death,* his first play to be produced in the United States, proved to be a popular one with Broadway audiences. In *Cue* Marilyn Stasio called it a "tremendously vital musical with a dynamic new form all its own." She also wrote, "The show is an electrifying piece of theatre without having songs, a book, a story line, choreography, or even standard production numbers—and yet all these elements are on the stage, skillfully integrated into a jolting new experience." And Peter Bailey commented in *Black World* that *Aint Supposed to Die a Natural Death* "presented us with an effective and meaningful evening in the theater. Broadway has never seen anything like it. Van Peebles' characters come alive and make us deal with them on their own terms."

A writer for *Variety* was impressed with the U.S. production of another Van Peebles play, "Don't Play Us Cheap." The reviewer noted that "this new show does not seem to be infused with hate, and it offers what appears to [be] a racial attitude without foul language, deliberate squalor or snarling ugliness." The same critic observed that "points are made with humor rather than rage and are probably more palatable for general audiences." "*Don't Play Us Cheap* is a somewhat special show," concluded the writer for *Variety,* "probably with greater meaning and appeal for black audiences than for whites." Van Peebles later adapted the play for film.

In 1986, Van Peebles published *Bold Money: A New Way to Play the Options Market* adding another twist to his variety of writing talents. As a result of losing an interesting wager with a friend, Van Peebles was obliged to take the examination to become an options trader. After failing the exam, Van Peebles became a clerk on the floor of the American Stock Exchange in order to learn enough to pass the exam. As Van Peebles told Laurie Cohen and Fred Marc Biddle in the *Chicago Tribune,* "If I had to find one characteristic that is most symbolic of me, I think I am tenacious."

After trading options for three years and passing the examination, Van Peebles was asked by Warner Books to write a how-to-book on making money in the options market. A critic for *Kirkus Reviews* writes of *Bold Money: A New Way to Play the Options Market* that Van Peebles's "often impudent but prudent text is an excellent choice for rookies seeking a like-it-is introduction to a fast game." A year after his first money book was published he wrote *Bold Money: How to Get Rich in the Option Market.*

In his 1995 novel, *Panther,* Peebles offers the story of Judge Taylor, a Vietnam veteran who is recruited by the militant Black Panthers to be their spy against the government. Set in 1967 and 1968—the early days of the Black Panther movement—the novel mixes fictional characters such as Judge with actual figures such as Huey Newton and Bobby Seale. Judge performs his duties as a double agent well but is eventually suspected by both sides of being an enemy. A *Publishers Weekly* reviewer called the novel "engrossing." Van Peebles adapted his novel into a screenplay, which was then made into a move directed by his son, Mario Van Peebles.

BIOGRAPHICAL/CRITICAL SOURCES:

BOOKS

Contemporary Literary Criticism, Gale, Volume 2, 1974, Volume 20, 1982.
Monaco, James, *American Films Now: The People, the Power, the Money, the Movies,* Oxford University Press, 1979.

PERIODICALS

American Visions, April-May, 1995, p. 1.
Best Sellers, October 15, 1968.
Black World, April, 1972.
Booklist, February 15, 1986, p. 839; May 15, 1995, p. 1633.
Chicago Tribune, March 24, 1986.
Cue, October 30, 1971; May 27, 1972.
Film Quarterly, summer, 1991, pp. 30-1; fall, 1995, p. 65.
Films in Review, November/December, 1990, p. 567.
Kirkus Reviews, December 1, 1985; May 1, 1995, p. 587.
Library Journal, July, 1995, p. 124.
Los Angeles Magazine, June, 1995, p. 107.
Nation, May 24, 1971.
Newsweek, June 6, 1969, June 21, 1971.
New Yorker, March 1, 1976, p. 100.
New York Times, May 18, 1969; April 24, 1971; May 9, 1971; September 29, 1981; January 6, 1982.
New York Times Book Review, October 6, 1968.
People Weekly, March 7, 1994, p. 212.
Publishers Weekly, May 15, 1995, p. 69.
Saturday Review, August 3, 1968.
Time, August 16, 1971.
Variety, May 24, 1971; February 8-14, 1989, p. 11; August 22, 1994, p. 5.*

W-Z

WALKER, Alice (Malsenior) 1944-

PERSONAL: Born February 9, 1944, in Eatonton, GA; daughter of Willie Lee and Minnie Tallulah (Grant) Walker; married Melvyn Rosenman Leventhal (a civil rights lawyer), March 17, 1967 (divorced, 1976); children: Rebecca. *Education:* Attended Spelman College, 1961-63; Sarah Lawrence College, B.A., 1965.

ADDRESSES: Home—San Francisco, CA. *Office*—Harcourt Brace Jovanovich, 111 5th Ave., New York, NY 10003-1005.

CAREER: Writer. Wild Trees Press, Navarro, CA, co-founder and publisher, 1984-88. Has been a voter registration worker in Georgia, a worker in Head Start program in Mississippi, and on staff of New York City welfare department. Writer in residence and teacher of black studies at Jackson State College, 1968-69, and Tougaloo College, 1970-71; lecturer in literature, Wellesley College and University of Massachusetts—Boston, both 1972-73; distinguished writer in Afro-American studies department, University of California, Berkeley, spring, 1982; Fannie Hurst Professor of Literature, Brandeis University, Waltham, MA, fall, 1982. Lecturer and reader of own poetry at universities and conferences. Member of board of trustees of Sarah Lawrence College. Consultant on black history to Friends of the Children of Mississippi, 1967. Co-producer of film documentary, *Warrior Marks,* directed by Pratibha Parmar with script and narration by Walker, 1993.

AWARDS, HONORS: Bread Loaf Writer's Conference scholar, 1966; first prize, *American Scholar* essay contest, 1967; Merrill writing fellowship, 1967; McDowell Colony fellowship, 1967, 1977-78; National Endowment for the Arts grant, 1969, 1977; Radcliffe Institute fellowship, 1971-73; Ph.D., Russell Sage College, 1972; National Book Award nomination and Lillian Smith Award from the Southern Regional Council, both 1973, both for *Revolutionary Petunias and Other Poems;* Richard and Hinda Rosenthal Foundation Award, American Academy and Institute of Arts and Letters, 1974, for *In Love and Trouble: Stories of Black Women;* Guggenheim fellowship, 1977-78; National Book Critics Circle Award nomination, 1982, and Pulitzer Prize and American Book Award, both 1983, all for *The Color Purple;* Best Books for Young Adults citation, American Library Association, 1984, for *In Search of Our Mother's Gardens: Womanist Prose;* D.H.L., University of Massachusetts, 1983; O. Henry Award, 1986, for "Kindred Spirits"; Langston Hughes Award, New York City College, 1989; Nora Astorga Leadership award, 1989; Fred Cody award for lifetime achievement, Bay Area Book Reviewers Association, 1990; Freedom to Write award, PEN West, 1990; California Governor's Arts Award, 1994; Literary Ambassador Award, University of Oklahoma Center for Poets and Writers, 1998.

WRITINGS:

POETRY

Once: Poems (also see below), Harcourt (New York City), 1968.
Five Poems, Broadside Press (Highland Park, MI), 1972.
Revolutionary Petunias and Other Poems (also see below), Harcourt, 1973.

Goodnight, Willie Lee, I'll See You in the Morning (also see below), Dial (New York City), 1979.

Horses Make a Landscape Look More Beautiful, Harcourt, 1984.

Alice Walker Boxed Set—Poetry: Good Night, Willie Lee, I'll See You in the Morning; Revolutionary Petunias and Other Poems; Once, Poems, Harcourt, 1985.

Her Blue Body Everything We Know: Earthling Poems, 1965-1990 Complete, Harcourt, 1991.

FICTION; NOVELS EXCEPT AS INDICATED

The Third Life of Grange Copeland, Harcourt, 1970.

In Love and Trouble: Stories of Black Women, Harcourt, 1973.

Meridian, Harcourt, 1976.

You Can't Keep a Good Woman Down (short stories), Harcourt, 1981.

The Color Purple, Harcourt, 1982.

Alice Walker Boxed Set—Fiction: The Third Life of Grange Copeland, You Can't Keep a Good Woman Down, and In Love and Trouble, Harcourt, 1985.

The Temple of My Familiar, Harcourt, 1989.

Possessing the Secret of Joy, Harcourt, 1992.

Everyday Use, edited by Barbara Christian, Rutgers University Press (New Brunswick, NJ), 1994.

FOR CHILDREN

Langston Hughes: American Poet (biography), Crowell (New York City), 1973, revised edition, Harper Collins, in press.

To Hell with Dying, illustrations by Catherine Deeter, Harcourt, 1988.

Finding the Green Stone, Harcourt, 1991.

NONFICTION

In Search of Our Mothers' Gardens: Womanist Prose, Harcourt, 1983.

Living by the Word: Selected Writings, 1973-1987, Harcourt, 1988.

(With Pratibha Parmar) *Warrior Marks: Female Genital Mutilation and the Sexual Blinding of Women,* Harcourt, 1993, reprinted, 1996.

Alice Walker Banned, with introduction by Patricia Holt, Aunt Lute Books (San Francisco), 1996.

Anything We Love Can Be Saved: A Writer's Activism, Random House (New York City), 1997.

OTHER

(Editor) *I Love Myself When I'm Laughing . . . and Then Again When I Am Looking Mean and Impressive: A Zora Neale Hurston Reader,* introduction by Mary Helen Washington, Feminist Press, 1979.

The Same River Twice: Honoring the Difficult: A Meditation of Life, Spirit, Art, and the Making of the film "The Color Purple," Ten Years Later, Scribner, 1996.

Contributor to anthologies, including *Voices of the Revolution,* edited by Helen Haynes, E. & J. Kaplan (Philadelphia), 1967; *The Best Short Stories by Negro Writers from 1899 to the Present: An Anthology,* edited by Langston Hughes, Little, Brown (Boston), 1967; *Afro-American Literature: An Introduction,* Harcourt, 1971; *Tales and Stories for Black Folks,* compiled by Toni Cade Bambara, Zenith Books (New York City), 1971; *Black Short Story Anthology,* compiled by Woodie King, New American Library (New York City), 1972; *The Poetry of Black America: An Anthology of the Twentieth Century,* compiled by Arnold Adoff, Harper (New York City), 1973; *A Rock against the Wind: Black Love Poems,* edited by Lindsay Patterson, Dodd (New York City), 1973; *We Be Word Sorcerers: Twenty-five Stories by Black Americans,* edited by Sonia Sanchez, Bantam (New York City), 1973; *Images of Women in Literature,* compiled by Mary Anne Ferguson, Houghton (Boston), 1973; *Best American Short Stories: 1973,* edited by Margaret Foley, Hart-Davis, 1973; *Best American Short Stories, 1974,* edited by M. Foley, Houghton, 1974; *Chants of Saints: A Gathering of Afro-American Literature, Art and Scholarship,* edited by Michael S. Harper and Robert B. Stepto, University of Illinois Press (Chicago), 1980; *Midnight Birds: Stories of Contemporary Black Women Authors,* edited by Mary Helen Washington, Anchor Press (New York City), 1980; and *Double Stitch: Black Women Write about Mothers and Daughters,* edited by Maya Angelou, HarperCollins (New York City), 1993.

Contributor to numerous periodicals, including *Negro Digest, Denver Quarterly, Harper's, Black World, Essence, Canadian Dimension,* and the *New York Times.* Contributing editor, *Southern Voices, Freedomways,* and *Ms.*

ADAPTATIONS: The Color Purple was made into a feature film directed by Steven Spielberg, Warner Bros., 1985.

SIDELIGHTS: Alice Walker has earned critical and popular acclaim as a major American novelist and intellectual. Her literary repuatation was secured with her Pulitzer-Prize-winning third novel, *The Color Purple,* which was transformed into a popular film by Steven Spielberg. Upon the release of the novel in 1982, critics sensed that Walker had created something special. "*The Color Purple* . . . could be the kind of popular and literary event that transforms an intense reputation into a national one," according to Gloria Steinem of *Ms.* Judging from the critical enthusiasm for *The Color Purple,* Steinem's words have proved prophetic. Walker "has succeeded," as Andrea Ford notes in the *Detroit Free Press,* "in creating a jewel of a novel." Peter S. Prescott presents a similar opinion in a *Newsweek* review. "I want to say," he comments, "that *The Color Purple* is an American novel of permanent importance, that rare sort of book which (in Norman Mailer's felicitous phrase) amounts to 'a diversion in the fields of dread.'"

Jeanne Fox-Alston and Mel Watkins both feel that the appeal of *The Color Purple* is that the novel, as a synthesis of characters and themes found in Walker's earlier works, brings together the best of the author's literary production in one volume. Fox-Alston, in the *Chicago Tribune Book World,* remarks: "Celie, the main character in Walker's third . . . novel, *The Color Purple,* is an amalgam of all those women [characters in Walker's previous books]; she embodies both their desperation and, later, their faith." Watkins states in the *New York Times Book Review:* "Her previous books . . . have elicited praise for Miss Walker as a lavishly gifted writer. *The Color Purple,* while easily satisfying that claim, brings into sharper focus many of the diverse themes that threaded their way through her past work."

Walker was born in Eatonton, Georgia, a southern town where most African-American people toiled at the difficult job of tenant farming. Her writing reflects these roots, where black vernacular was prominent and the stamp of slavery and oppression were still present. When she was eight, Walker was accidentally shot in the eye by a brother playing with his BB gun. Her parents, who were too poor to afford a car, could not take her to a doctor for several days. By that time, her wound was so bad that she had lost the use of her right eye. This handicap eventually aided her writer's voice, because she withdrew from others and became a meticulous observer of human relationships and interaction.

An excellent student, Walker was awarded a scholarship to Spelman College in 1961. The civil rights movement attracted her, and she became an activist.

In 1963, she decided to continue her education at Sarah Lawrence College in New York, where she began to work seriously on writing poems, publishing several in a college journal. After graduation, she moved to Mississippi to teach and continue her social activism, and she met and married Melvyn Leventhal, a Jewish civil rights lawyer. The two became the only legally married interracial couple living in Jackson, Mississippi. After their divorce in 1976, Walker's literary output increased.

Walker coined the term "Womanist," to describe her philosophical stance on the issue of gender. As a Womanist, which is different from a feminist, she sees herself as someone who appreciates women's culture, emotions, and character. Her work often reflects this stance, and, paradoxically, the universality of human experience. Walker's central characters are almost always black women; Walker, according to Steinem, "comes at universality through the path of an American black woman's experience. . . . She speaks the female experience more powerfully for being able to pursue it across boundaries of race and class." This universality is also noted by Fox-Alston, who remarks that Walker has a "reputation as a provocative writer who writes about blacks in particular, but all humanity in general."

However, many critics recognize a particularly black and female focus in Walker's writings. For example, in her review of *The Color Purple,* Ford suggests that the novel transcends "culture and gender" lines but also refers to Walker's "unabashedly feminist viewpoint" and the novel's "black . . . texture." Walker does not deny this dual bias; the task of revealing the condition of the black woman is particularly important to her. Thadious M. Davis, in his *Dictionary of Literary Biography* essay, comments: "Walker writes best of the social and personal drama in the lives of familiar people who struggle for survival of self in hostile environments. She has expressed a special concern with 'exploring the oppressions, the insanities, the loyalties and the triumph of black women.'" Walker explains in a *Publishers Weekly* interview: "The black woman is one of America's greatest heroes. . . . Not enough credit has been given to the black woman who has been oppressed beyond recognition."

Walker's earlier books—novels, volumes of short stories, and poems—have not received the same degree of attention, but neither have they been ignored. Gloria Steinem points out that *Meridian,* Walker's second novel, "is often cited as the best novel of the civil rights movement, and is taught as part of some American history as well as literature courses." In *Everyday Use,* Barbara Christian finds the story "Everyday Use," first published in Walker's collection *In Love and Trouble: Stories of Black Women,* to be "pivotal" to all of Walker's work in its evocation of black sisterhood and black women's heritage of quilting. William Peden, writing in *The American Short Story: Continuity and Change, 1940-1975,* calls this same collection "a remarkable book," and Barbara Smith observes in *Ms.* that "this collection would be an extraordinary literary work, if its only virtue were the fact that the author sets out consciously to explore with honesty the texture and terror of black women's lives . . . the fact that Walker's perceptions, style, and artistry are also consistently high makes her work a treasure." Similarly, Mary Helen Washington remarks in a *Black World* review that "the stories in *In Love and Trouble* . . . constitute a painfully honest, searching examination of the experiences of thirteen black women."

Walker bases her description of black women on what Washington refers to as her "unique vision and philosophy of the Black woman." According to Barbara A. Bannon of *Publishers Weekly,* this philosophy stems from the "theme of the poor black man's oppression of his family and the unconscious reasons for it." Walker, in her interview with the same magazine, asserts: "The cruelty of the black man to his wife and family is one of the greatest [American] tragedies. It has mutilated the spirit and body of the black family and of most black mothers." Through her fiction, Walker describes this tragedy. For instance, Smith notes: "Even as a black woman, I found the cumulative impact of these stories [contained *In Love and Trouble*] devastating. . . . Women love their men, but are neither loved nor understood in return. The affective relationships are [only] between mother and child or between black woman and black woman." David Guy's commentary on *The Color Purple* in the *Washington Post Book World* includes this evaluation: "Accepting themselves for what they are, the women [in the novel] are able to extricate themselves from oppression; they leave their men, find useful work to support themselves." Watkins further explains: "In *The Color Purple* the role of male domination in the frustration of black women's struggle for independence is clearly the focus."

Some reviewers criticize Walker's fiction for portraying an overly negative view of black men. Katha Pollitt, for example, in the *New York Times Book Review,* calls the stories in *You Can't Keep a Good Woman Down* "too partisan." The critic adds: "The black woman is always the most sympathetic character." Guy notes: "Some readers . . . will object to her overall perspective. Men in [*The Color Purple*] are generally pathetic, weak and stupid, when they are not heartlessly cruel, and the white race is universally bumbling and inept." Charles Larson, in his *Detroit News* review of *The Color Purple,* points out: "I wouldn't go as far as to say that all the male characters [in the novel] are villains, but the truth is fairly close to that." However, neither Guy nor Larson feel that this emphasis on women is a major fault in the novel. Guy, for example, while conceding that "white men . . . are invisible in Celie's world," observes: "This really is Celie's perspective, however—it is psychologically accurate to her—and Alice Walker might argue that it is only a neat inversion of the view that has prevailed in western culture for centuries." Larson also notes that by the end of the novel, "several of [Walker's] masculine characters have reformed."

This idea of reformation, this sense of hope even in despair, is at the core of Walker's vision, even though, as John F. Callahan states in *New Republic,* "There is often nothing but pain, violence, and death for black women [in her fiction]." In spite of the brutal effects of sexism and racism suffered by the characters of her short stories and novels, critics note what Art Seidenbaum of the *Los Angeles Times* calls Walker's sense of "affirmation . . . [that] overcomes her anger." This is particularly evident in *The Color Purple,* according to several reviewers. Ford, for example, asserts that the author's "polemics on . . . political and economic issues finally give way to what can only be described as a joyful celebration of human spirit—exulting, uplifting and eminently universal." Prescott discovers a similar progression in the novel. He writes: "[Walker's] story begins at about the point that most Greek tragedies reserve for the climax, then . . . by immeasurable small steps . . . works its way toward acceptance, serenity and joy." Walker, according to Ray Anello, who quotes the author in *Newsweek,* agrees with this evaluation. Questioned about the novel's importance, Walker explains: "Let's hope people can hear Celie's voice. There are so many people like Celie who make it, who come out of nothing. People who triumph."

Davis refers to this idea as Walker's "vision of survival" and offers a summary of its significance in Walker's work. "At whatever cost, human beings have the capacity to live in spiritual health and beauty; they may be poor, black, and uneducated, but their inner selves can blossom." This vision, extended to all humanity, is evident in Walker's collection *Living by the Word: Selected Writings 1973-1987*. Although "her original interests centered on black women, and especially on the ways they were abused or underrated," *New York Times Book Review* contributor Noel Perrin believes that "now those interests encompass all creation." Judith Paterson similarly observes in *Tribune Books* that in *Living by the Word*, "Walker casts her abiding obsession with the oneness of the universe in a question: Do creativity, love and spiritual wholeness still have a chance of winning the human heart amid political forces bent on destroying the universe with poisonous chemicals and nuclear weapons?" Walker explores this question through journal entries and essays that deal with Native Americans, racism in China, a lonely horse, smoking, and response to the criticism leveled against both the novel and film version of *The Color Purple*. Many of these treatments are personal in approach, and Jill Nelson finds many of them trivial. Writing in the *Washington Post Book World*, Nelson comments that "*Living by the Word* is fraught with . . . reaches for commonality, analogy and universality. Most of the time all Walker achieves is banality." But Derrick Bell differs, noting in his *Los Angeles Times Book Review* critique that Walker "uses carefully crafted images that provide a universality to unique events." The critic further asserts that *Living by the Word* "is not only vintage Alice Walker: passionate, political, personal, and poetic, it also provides a panoramic view of a fine human being saving her soul through good deeds and extraordinary writing."

Harsh criticisms of Walker's work crested with the 1989 publication of her fourth novel, *The Temple of My Familiar*. The novel, featuring several of the characters of *The Color Purple*, reflects concerns hinted at in that novel and confronted directly in *Living by the Word*: racism, a reverence for nature, a search for spiritual truths, and the universality referred to by reviewers Nelson and Bell. But according to David Gates in his *Newsweek* review, the novel "is fatally ambitious. It encompasses 500,000 years, rewrites Genesis and the Beatitudes and weighs in with mini-lectures on everything from Elvis (for) to nuclear waste (against)." David Nicholson of the *Washington Post Book World* feels that *The Temple of My Familiar* "is not a novel so much as it is an ill-fitting collection of speeches . . . a manifesto for the Fascism of the New Age. . . . There are no characters, only types representative of the world Walker lives in or wishes could be." In a similar vein, *Time*'s Paul Grey notes that "Walker's relentless adherence

to her own sociopolitical agenda makes for frequently striking propaganda," but not for good fiction. Though generally disliked even by sympathetic critics, the novel has its defenders. Novelist J. M. Coetzee, writing in the *New York Times Book Review*, implores the reader to look upon the novel as a "fable of recovered origins, as an exploration of the inner lives of contemporary black Americans as these are penetrated by fabulous stories," and Bernard W. Bell, writing in the *Chicago Tribune*, feels that the novel is a "colorful quilt of many patches," and that its "stylized lovers, remembrances of things past, bold flights of fantasy and vision of a brave new world of cultural diversity and cosmic harmony challenge the reader's willingness to suspend disbelief."

A *Publishers Weekly* reviewer of Walker's 1991 children's story *Finding the Green Stone* says that "the tone is ethereal and removed . . . while the writing style, especially the dialogue, is stiff and didactic." But for Walker's collected poems, *Her Blue Body Everything We Know: Earthling Poems, 1965-1990 Complete*, a *Publishers Weekly* reviewer has high praise, characterizing Walker as "composed, wry, unshaken by adversity," and suggesting that her "strong, beautiful voice" beckons us "to heal ourselves and the planet."

Critics are nearly unanimous in their praise of Walker's controversial fifth novel, *Possessing the Secret of Joy*, about the practice of female genital mutilation in certain African, Asian and Middle Eastern cultures. Writing in the *Los Angeles Times Book Review*, Tina McElroy Ansa says that taking on such a taboo subject shows Walker's depth and range and feels that her portrait of the suffering of Tashi—a character from *The Color Purple*—is "stunning." "The description of the excision itself and its after effect is graphic enough to make one gag," but is the work of a thoughtful, impassioned artist, rather than a sensationalist, notes Charles R. Larson in the *Washington Post Book World*. And Donna Haisty Winchell writes in her *Dictionary of Literary Biography* essay that *Possessing the Secret of Joy* is "much more concise, more controlled, and more successful as art" than *The Temple of My Familiar* and demonstrates an effective blend of "art and activism."

Walker's concerns about the international issue of female genital mutilation prompted her to further explore the issue, both on film and in the book *Warrior Marks: Female Genital Mutilation and the Sexual Blinding of Women*, co-authored with documentary film director Pratibha Parmar. According to *Publish-

ers Weekly, Warrior Marks is a "forceful account" of how the two filmed a documentary on the ritual circumcision of African women.

In 1995, Walker produced *The Same River Twice: Honoring the Difficult.* The book focuses mainly on Walker's feelings about, and struggles with, the filming of her novel *The Color Purple.* While having the book transformed into a film by Steven Spielberg was a high point in her life, it was also riddled with difficulties. First, Spielberg rejected Walker's screenplay of the book and implemented one with which Walker was not happy. In addition, the film itself was met with controversy and attacks on Walker's ideas—some people thought she had attacked the character of black people in general and black men specifically. Also at the time, Walker's mother was critically ill, while Walker herself was suffering from a debilitating illness that turned out to be Lyme Disease. Included in the book are fan letters, reviews, and Walker's original version of the script. Francine Prose in *Chicago Tribune Book World* finds fault with the book, feeling that Walker's protests about how things did not go her way ring of artistic posturing: "Walker seems to have so lost touch with the lives and sensibilities of ordinary humans that she apparently cannot hear how her complaints . . . might sound to the less fortunate, who have been less generously favored by greatness."

Regardless of such criticism, however, Walker's literary reputation is secure. Among her recent works, which are mostly nonfiction, is 1997's *Anything We Love Can Be Saved: A Writer's Activism.*

BIOGRAPHICAL/CRITICAL SOURCES:

BOOKS

Allan, Tuzyline Jita, *Womanist and Feminist Aesthetics: A Comparative Review,* Ohio University Press, 1995.

Bestsellers '89, Issue 4, Gale (Detroit), 1989.

Black Literature Criticism, Volume 1, Gale, 1992, pp. 1808-1829.

Christian, Barbara, editor, *Everyday Use,* Rutgers University Press (New Brunswick, NJ), 1994.

Contemporary Literary Criticism, Gale, Volume 5, 1976, Volume 6, 1976, Volume 9, 1978, Volume 19, 1981, Volume 27, 1984, Volume 46, 1988, Volume 58, 1990, Volume 103, 1998.

Dictionary of Literary Biography, Gale, Volume 6: *American Novelists since World War II,* second series, 1980, Volume 33: *Afro-American Fiction Writers after 1955,* 1984, Volume 143: *American Novelists since World War II,* third series, 1994, pp. 277-93.

Evans, Mari, editor, *Black Women Writers (1950-1980): A Critical Evaluation,* Anchor (New York City), 1984.

Johnson, Yvonne, *The Voices of African American Women: The Use of Narrative and Authorial Voice in the Works of Harriet Jacobs, Zora Neale Hurston, and Alice Walker,* P. Lang, 1995.

Kaplan, Carla, *The Erotics of Talk: Women's Writing and Feminist Paradigms,* Oxford University Press, 1996.

Kramer, Barbara, *Alice Walker: Author of "The Color Purple,"* Enslow, 1995.

O'Brien, John, *Interviews with Black Writers,* Liveright (New York City), 1973.

Peden, William, *The American Short Story: Continuity and Change, 1940-1975,* 2nd revised and enlarged edition, Houghton, 1975.

Prenshaw, Peggy W., editor, *Women Writers of the Contemporary South,* University Press of Mississippi (Jackson), 1984.

Short Story Criticism, Volume 5, Gale, 1990, pp. 400-24.

Walker, Alice, *The Same River Twice: Honoring the Difficult: A Meditation of Life, Spirit, Art, and the Making of the film "The Color Purple," Ten Years Later,* Scribner, 1996.

PERIODICALS

African American Review, spring, 1995, p. 67.

American Scholar, winter, 1970-71; summer, 1973.

Ann Arbor News, October 3, 1982.

Atlantic, June, 1976.

Black Scholar, April, 1976.

Black World, September, 1973; October, 1974.

Booklist, November 15, 1995, p. 514.

Chicago Tribune, December 20, 1985; April 23, 1989.

Chicago Tribune Book World, August 1, 1982; September 15, 1985.

Commonweal, April 29, 1977.

Critique, summer, 1994.

Detroit Free Press, August 8, 1982; July 10, 1988; January 4, 1989.

Detroit News, September 15, 1982; October 23, 1983; March 31, 1985.

Entertainment Weekly, December 30, 1994, p. 64.

Essence, February, 1996, p. 84.

Freedomways, winter, 1973.

Globe and Mail (Toronto), December 21, 1985.

Jet, February 10, 1986.

Library Journal, November 15, 1994, p. 103; December, 1995, p. 110.

Los Angeles Times, April 29, 1981; June 8, 1983.

Los Angeles Times Book Review, August 8, 1982; May 29, 1988; May 21, 1989, p. 1; July 5, 1992, p. 4.

Ms., February, 1974; July, 1977; July, 1978; June, 1982; September, 1986.

Nation, November 12, 1973; December 17, 1983.

Negro Digest, September/October, 1968.

New Leader, January 25, 1971.

New Republic, September 14, 1974; December 21, 1974; May 29, 1989, pp. 28-29.

Newsweek, May 31, 1976; June 21, 1982; April 24, 1989, p. 74; June 8, 1992, pp. 56-57.

New Yorker, February 27, 1971; June 7, 1976.

New York Review of Books, January 29, 1987.

New York Times, December 18, 1985; January 5, 1986.

New York Times Book Review, March 17, 1974; May 23, 1976; May 29, 1977; December 30, 1979; May 24, 1981; July 25, 1982; April 7, 1985; June 5, 1988; April 30, 1989, p. 7; June 28, 1992, p. 11; January 14, 1996, p. 18.

New York Times Magazine, January 8, 1984.

Oakland Tribune, November 11, 1984.

Observer (London), October 11, 1992, p. 61.

Parnassus: Poetry in Review, spring/summer, 1976.

People Weekly, April 29, 1996, p. 36.

Poetry, February, 1971; March, 1980.

Publishers Weekly, August 31, 1970; February 26, 1988; March 1, 1991, p. 64; October 25, 1991, p. 66; October 25, 1993, p. 49; February 24, 1997, p. 77.

Saturday Review, August 22, 1970.

Southern Review, spring, 1973.

Time, May 1, 1989, p. 69.

Times Literary Supplement, August 19, 1977; June 18, 1982; July 20, 1984; September 27, 1985; April 15, 1988; September 22, 1989, p. 1023; October 9, 1992, p. 22.

Tribune Books (Chicago), July 17, 1988; April 23, 1989, p. 5; June 21, 1992, p. 3; January 21, 1996, p. 5.

Tulsa World, March 29, 1998.

Washington Post, October 15, 1982; April 15, 1983; October 17, 1983.

Washington Post Book World, November 18, 1973; October 30, 1979; December 30, 1979; May 31, 1981; July 25, 1982; December 30, 1984; May 29, 1988; May 7, 1989, p. 3; July 5, 1992, p. 1; January 16, 1994, pp. 4-5.

World Literature Today, winter, 1985; winter, 1986.

Yale Review, autumn, 1976.*

WALKER, Joseph A. 1935-

PERSONAL: Born February 23, 1935, in Washington, DC; son of Joseph (a house painter) and Florine Walker; married Barbara Brown (divorced, 1965); married Dorothy A. Dinroe, 1970. *Education:* Howard University, B.A., 1956; Catholic University of America, M.F.A., 1970; New York University, Ph.D.

ADDRESSES: Home—New York, NY. *Office*—Department of Drama, Howard University, 2400 6th St., NW, Washington, DC 20059.

CAREER: Educator, actor, director, playwright, choreographer, producer. Worked as taxi driver, shoe and cosmetics salesman, and postal clerk; English teacher at junior high and high schools in Washington, DC, and New York City; actor, set designer, and playwright, in New York City, beginning 1967; Negro Ensemble Company, New York City, playwright, director and choreographer, beginning 1969; Yale University, New Haven, Connecticut, playwright-in-residence, 1970-71; City College of the City University of New York, New York City, instructor; Howard University, Washington, DC, instructor of advanced acting and playwrighting. Actor in stage productions, including *The Believers,* 1967, *Cities of Beziques,* 1969, *Once in a Lifetime, A Raisin in the Sun,* and *Purlie Victorious;* in motion pictures, including *April Fools,* 1969, and *Bananas,* 1971; and in television program *N.Y.P.D.* (ABC-TV); narrator of *In Black America* (CBS-TV). Co-founder and artistic director of The Demi-Gods (dance-music theatre repertory company). *Military service:* U.S. Air Force; became second lieutenant.

AWARDS, HONORS: Obie Award, 1971, Antoinette Perry (Tony) Award, 1973, Elizabeth Hull-Kate Award from Dramatist Guild, First Annual Audelco Award, John Gassner Award from Outer Circle, Drama Desk Award, Black Rose, all for *The River Niger;* Guggenheim fellowship, 1973; Rockefeller Foundation grant, 1979.

WRITINGS:

PLAYS

(With Josephine Jackson) *The Believers* (first produced Off-Broadway at the Garrick Theatre, May 9, 1968), published in *The Best Plays of 1967-1968,* edited by Otis L. Guernsey, Dodd, 1968.

The Harangues (two one-act plays), first produced Off-Broadway at St. Mark's Playhouse, December 30, 1969.

Ododo (title means "The Truth"; first produced Off-Broadway at St. Mark's Playhouse, November 24, 1970), published in *Black Drama Anthology,* edited by Woodie King and Ron Milner, Columbia University Press, 1972.

Yin Yang, first produced Off-Off-Broadway at the Afro-American Studio, June 30, 1972, produced Off-Broadway at St. Mark's Playhouse, May 30, 1973.

The River Niger (three-act; first produced Off-Broadway at St. Mark's Playhouse, December 5, 1972; also see below), Hill & Wang, 1973.

Antigone Africanus, first produced in New York, 1975.

The Lion Is a Soul Brother, first produced in New York, 1976.

District Line, first produced Off-Broadway at Theatre Four, December, 1984.

Also author of *Themes of the Black Struggle* and *The Hiss.*

OTHER

The River Niger (screenplay; based on play of the same title), Cine Artists, 1976.

Contributor to periodicals, including the *New York Times.*

ADAPTATIONS: *The River Niger* was made into a film starring Cicely Tyson and James Earl Jones.

SIDELIGHTS: The dramas of Joseph A. Walker explore various aspects of black life such as male-female relationships, interracial strife, and family and community bonds. However, the focus of most of his works is on the psyche of black American males. Cut off from their ancestral home and exploited by whites, these disoriented men are portrayed as lacking a sense of identity, purpose, and self-worth. Efforts by some of these men to obtain power and wealth are most often thwarted by white America's black sycophants.

Whether or not one agrees with this simplistic ideology, frequently exhorted in the 1960's and 1970's, Walker's plays are still relevant because of their compelling depictions of those black males stagnated by feelings of impotence, frustration, and hopelessness. While the black male characters are deftly drawn and complex, Walker's portraits of black women and whites rarely escape the limitations of stereotypes. Black women seldom have any personal goals, but instead function as either supporters or "castrators" of their men. White women serve as sexual playmates and status symbols for their black lovers. White men exploit blacks and destroy those who pose a threat to their way of life. Lacking depth and plausible motivations for their actions, some critics feel these characters weaken the credibility of Walker's plays.

As its title suggests, *The Harangues* is used as a vehicle for the playwright to vent his opinions. Composed of two episodes and two one-act plays, the work portrays a despairing view of black life. In the first episode, a 15th-century West African man chooses to kill his son rather than subject him to life as a slave in the New World. The second episode mirrors the first by showing a contemporary black American revolutionary who kills his child rather than allow him to grow up in a despondent society. Black women plead for their children's lives in the episodes, but are conspicuously absent in the one-acts. The first one-act, set in Washington, DC, concerns a black male and his pregnant white fiancee. Incredibly, with little hesitation, the white woman agrees to assist her lover in the murder of her father who will disinherit her if she marries. However, the plan backfires and results in the death of the scheming black man due to the actions of a traitorous black "friend." In the second one-act, unless they can convince him of their worthiness to live, a deranged black man threatens to kill his three captives: a white liberal and an assimilationist black man and his white lover. After exposing their perverted lives, only the white woman who endures several sexual indignities is deemed to be virtuous. However, as the death penalty is being carried out, the woman takes a bullet meant for her contemptible black lover. In an ensuing struggle, the assimilationist gains control of his captor's gun and kills him. As in the first one-act, a desperate black man dies at the hands of a black minion of the white race.

In sharp contrast to the pessimistic outlook which envelopes *The Harangues, The River Niger* celebrates the enduring qualities of the black man and offers a hopeful vision of the future. Johnny Williams, a middle-aged house painter and poet living in Harlem, uses liquor to escape the bleak reality of a life stagnated by unrealized dreams. Johnny places his hopes for the future in his son Jeff's career in the air force. But his son's homecoming brings another disappointment to Johnny's life. Jeff admits that he was dismissed from the military which he abhorred. He contends his ouster was due to his refusal to be a "supernigger"—a black man who tries to prove he has capabilities comparable to whites. He further announces he will no longer be bound by familial and societal expectations but will instead seek only to fulfill his own needs and desires. Despite his intentions, Jeff soon finds himself involved in the self-destructive affairs of his former gang. When prison terms appear imminent for Jeff and the gang after they are betrayed by one of their members, Johnny has a shoot-out with the traitor which results in both of their deaths. But before Johnny dies, he demands to take the rap for the shooting and the gang's alleged offense. Johnny's wife Mattie admonishes her family and the gang not to fail to cooperate and carry out her husband's wishes. Johnny's heroic gesture provides Jeff and other gang members with a new lease on life and a powerful example of the unconditional selfless love that a father can have for his son. The portraits of the men are well crafted and realistic. The characters function as representatives of differing moral values, abilities, aspirations, and perspectives within the black community. Johnny emerges as the most eloquent and convincing spokesman who, through his poem "The River Niger," speaks of the need to be cognizant of one's unbreakable link to all people of African descent.

Although the play's black women represent various age groups and cultures, they share similar attitudes toward their men. The women serve their men's needs with little concern for their own desires or ambitions. Mattie even accepts the fact that her husband chooses to confide in his West Indian friend instead of her. Incredibly, during a conversation between Mattie and Jeff's South African lover, Johnny's wife agrees with the younger woman that women are incapable of having a similar type of relationship because "women don't trust one another." Despite this and several other questionable remarks made by the women, their behavior as selfless and loyal supporters of their men foreshadows the concluding message of the play. As Johnny's final actions and his demand for cooperation demonstrate, survival of the race requires a communal effort with little thought of self-interest.

A Washington, D.C., taxi-stand serves as the setting for *District Line*. The play depicts a day in the lives of six cab drivers: two white and three black males and one black female. The drivers reveal their past experiences, present concerns, and aspirations as they interact with each other and their passengers. Black males continue to be Walker's most poignant characterizations. Of greatest interest are the scenes concerning two drivers—Doc, a moonlighting Howard

University professor and Zilikazi, an exiled South African revolutionary. Women characters, whether black or white, appear to be gratuitous in the drama and remain stereotypes. However, the playwright does portray white men in roles other than the liberal or oppressor of blacks. Still, the work suffers in comparison to Walker's other plays because of a few fundamental flaws. Dramatic action is not adequately developed and sustained throughout the play and the work lacks a central theme to tie all the scenes together. Consequently, the drama fails to create the intense emotional impact characteristic of Walker's other plays.

BIOGRAPHICAL/CRITICAL SOURCES:

BOOKS

Contemporary Literary Criticism, Volume 19, Gale, 1981.
Dictionary of Literary Biography, Volume 38: *Afro-American Writers after 1955: Dramatists and Prose Writers,* Gale, 1985.

PERIODICALS

Black World, April, 1971.
Christian Science Monitor, January 23, 1970.
Cue, December 5, 1970.
Modern Drama, December, 1976.
Nation, February 2, 1970; December 25, 1972.
New Republic, September 29, 1973.
New York, December 14, 1970.
New Yorker, January 24, 1970; December 16, 1972.
New York Times, May 10, 1968; January 14, 1970; January 25, 1970; November 25, 1970; December 6, 1970; December 14, 1970; December 6, 1972; December 17, 1972; March 28, 1973; May 31, 1973; December 5, 1984.
Saturday Review, February 14, 1970.
Show Business, November 28, 1970.
Time, January 1, 1973.
Variety, December 9, 1970.
Village Voice, January 22, 1970.
Washington Post, April 13, 1973.*

*   *   *

WALKER, Margaret (Abigail) 1915-1998

PERSONAL: Born July 7, 1915, in Birmingham, Alabama; died December, 1998, in Chicago, Illinois;

daughter of Sigismund C. (a Methodist minister) and Marion (Dozier) Walker (a music teacher); married Firnist James Alexander, June 13, 1943 (deceased); children: Marion Elizabeth, Firnist James, Sigismund Walker, Margaret Elvira. *Education:* Northwestern University, B.A., 1935; University of Iowa, M.A., 1940, Ph.D., 1965. *Religion:* Methodist.

CAREER: Worked as a social worker, newspaper reporter, and magazine editor; Livingstone College, Salisbury, NC, member of faculty, 1941-42; West Virginia State College, Institute, West Virginia, instructor in English, 1942-43; Livingstone College, professor of English, 1945-46; Jackson State College, Jackson, Mississippi, professor emeritus of English (professor beginning in 1949), director of Institute for the Study of the History, Life, and Culture of Black Peoples, 1968-98. Lecturer, National Concert and Artists Corp. Lecture Bureau, 1943-48. Visiting professor in creative writing, Northwestern University, Spring, 1969. Staff member, Cape Cod Writers Conference, Craigville, Massachusetts, 1967 and 1969. Participant, Library of Congress Conference on the Teaching of Creative Writing, 1973.

MEMBER: National Council of Teachers of English, Modern Language Association, Poetry Society of America, American Association of University Professors, National Education Association, Alpha Kappa Alpha.

AWARDS, HONORS: Yale Series of Younger Poets Award, 1942, for *For My People* ; named to Honor Roll of Race Relations, a national poll conducted by the New York Public Library, 1942; Rosenthal fellowship, 1944; Ford fellowship for study at Yale University, 1954; Houghton Mifflin Literary fellowship, 1966; Fulbright fellowship, 1971; National Endowment for the Humanities, 1972; Doctor of Literature, Northwestern University, 1974; Doctor of Letters, Rust College, 1974; Doctor of Fine Arts, Dennison University, 1974; Doctor of Humane Letters, Morgan State University, 1976.

WRITINGS:

POETRY

For My People (contains "For My People"), Yale University Press, 1942, reprinted, Ayer Co., 1969.
Ballad of the Free, Broadside Press, 1966.
Prophets for a New Day, Broadside Press, 1970.
October Journey, Broadside Press, 1973.

This Is My Century, University of Georgia Press, 1989.

PROSE

Jubilee (novel), Houghton, 1965, Bantam, 1981.
How I Wrote "Jubilee", Third World Press, 1972.
(With Nikki Giovanni) *A Poetic Equation: Conversations between Nikki Giovanni and Margaret Walker,* Howard University Press, 1974, reprinted with new postscript, 1983.
Richard Wright: Daemonic Genius, Dodd, 1987.
On Being Female, Black, and Free: Essays by Margaret Walker, 1932-1992, University of Tennessee Press (Knoxville, TN), 1997.

CONTRIBUTOR

Addison Gayle, editor, *Black Expression,* Weybright & Tally, 1969.
Stanton L. Wormley and Lewis H. Fenderson, editors, *Many Shades of Black,* Morrow, 1969.
Henderson, Stephen, *Understanding the New Black Poetry: Black Speech and Black Music as Poetic References,* Morrow, 1973.

Also contributor to numerous anthologies, including Adoff's *Black Out Loud,* Weisman and Wright's *Black Poetry for All Americans,* and Williams's *Beyond the Angry Black.*

OTHER

Contributor to *Yale Review, Negro Digest, Poetry, Opportunity, Phylon, Saturday Review,* and *Virginia Quarterly.*

SIDELIGHTS: When *For My People* by Margaret Walker won the Yale Younger Poets Series Award in 1942, "she became one of the youngest Black writers ever to have published a volume of poetry in this century," as well as "the first Black woman in American literary history to be so honored in a prestigious national competition," notes Richard K. Barksdale in *Black American Poets between Worlds, 1940-1960.* Walker's first novel, *Jubilee,* is notable for being "the first truly historical black American novel," according to University of Maryland professor Joyce Anne Joyce, reports Washington Post contributor Crispin Y. Campbell. It was also the first work by a black writer to speak out for the liberation of the black woman. The cornerstones of a literature that affirms the African folk roots of black American life, these two books have also been called visionary for looking toward a new cultural unity for black Americans that will be built on that foundation.

The title of Walker's first book, *For My People,* denotes the subject matter of "poems in which the body and spirit of a great group of people are revealed with vigor and undeviating integrity," says Louis Untermeyer in the *Yale Review.* Here, in long ballads, Walker draws sympathetic portraits of characters such as the New Orleans sorceress Molly Means; Kissie Lee, a tough young woman who dies "with her boots on switching blades;" and Poppa Chicken, an urban drug dealer and pimp. Other ballads give a new dignity to John Henry, killed by a ten-pound hammer, and Stagolee, who kills a white officer but eludes a lynch mob. In an essay for *Black Women Writers (1950-1980): A Critical Evaluation,* Eugenia Collier notes, "Using . . . the language of the grass-roots people, Walker spins yarns of folk heroes and heroines: those who, faced with the terrible obstacles which haunt Black people's very existence, not only survive but prevail—with style." Soon after it appeared, the book of ballads, sonnets and free verse found a surprisingly large number of readers, requiring publishers to authorize three printings to satisfy popular demand.

Some critics found fault with the sonnets in the book, but others deemed it generally impressive, R. Baxter Miller summarizes in Black American Poets between Worlds. "The title poem is itself a singular and unique literary achievement," Barksdale claims. In *Black American Literature: A Critical History,* Roger Whitlow elaborates, "The poem, written in free verse, rhythmically catalogues the progress of black American experience, from the rural folkways, religious practices, and exhausting labor of the South, through the cramped and confusing conditions of the northern urban centers, to what she hopes will be a racial awakening, blacks militantly rising up to take control of their own destinies." Collier relates, "The final stanza is a reverberating cry for redress. It demands a new beginning. Our music then will be martial music; our peace will be hard-won, but it will be 'written in the sky.' And after the agony, the people whose misery spawned strength will control our world. This poem is the hallmark of Margaret Walker's works. It echoes in her subsequent poetry and even in her monumental novel *Jubilee.* It speaks to us, in our words and rhythms, of our history, and it radiates the promise of our future. It is the quintessential example of myth and ritual shaped by artistic genius."

Reviewers especially praise Walker's control of poetic technique in the poem. Dudley Randall writes in Addison Gayle's *The Black Aesthetic,* "The poem gains its force . . . by the sheer overpowering accumulation of a mass of details delivered in rhythmical parallel phrases." To cite Barksdale, "it is magnificently wrought oral poetry. . . . In reading it aloud, one must be able to breathe and pause, pause and breathe preacher-style. One must be able to sense the ebb and flow of the intonations. . . . This is the kind of verbal music found in a well-delivered down-home folk sermon." By giving the poem a musical rhythm, Walker underscores the poem's message, observes Barksdale: "The poet here is writing about the source of the Black peoples' blues, for out of their troubled past and turbulent present came the Black peoples' song." In this case, Walker steps forward to remind her people of the strength to be found in their cultural tradition as she calls for a new, hopeful literature that can inspire social action.

"If the test of a great poem is the universality of statement, then 'For My People' is a great poem," remarks Barksdale. The critic explains in Donald B. Gibson's *Modern Black Poets: A Collection of Critical Essays* that the poem was written when "world-wide pain, sorrow, and affliction were tangibly evident, and few could isolate the Black man's dilemma from humanity's dilemma during the depression years or during the war years." Thus, the power of resilience presented in the poem is a hope Walker holds out not only to black people, but to all people, to "all the adams and eves." As she once remarked, "Writers should not write exclusively for black or white audiences, but most inclusively. After all, it is the business of all writers to write about the human condition, and all humanity must be involved in both the writing and in the reading."

Jubilee, a historical novel, is the second book on which Walker's literary reputation rests. It is the story of a slave family during and after the civil war, and took her thirty years to write. During these years, she married a disabled veteran, raised four children, taught full time at Jackson State College in Mississippi, and earned a Ph.D. from the University of Iowa. The lengthy gestation, she believed, partly accounted for the book's quality. As she told Claudia Tate in *Black Women Writers at Work,* "Living with the book over a long period of time was agonizing. Despite all of that, *Jubilee* is the product of a mature person," one whose own difficult pregnancies and economic struggles could lend authenticity to the lives of her characters. "There's a difference between writing about something and living through it," she said in the interview; "I did both."

The story of *Jubilee*'s main characters Vyry and Randall Ware was an important part of Walker's life even before she began to write it down. As she explained in *How I Wrote "Jubilee,"* she first heard about the "slavery time" in bedtime stories told by her maternal grandmother. When old enough to recognize the value of her family history, Walker took initiative, "prodding" her grandmother for more details, and promising to set down on paper the story that had taken shape in her mind. Later on, she completed extensive research on every aspect of the black experience touching the Civil War, from obscure birth records to information on the history of tin cans. "Most of my life I have been involved with writing this story about my great-grandmother, and even if *Jubilee* were never considered an artistic or commercial success I would still be happy just to have finished it," she claimed.

Soon after *Jubilee* was published in 1966, Walker was given a Fellowship award from Houghton-Mifflin, and a mixed reception from critics. Granting that the novel is "ambitious," *New York Times Book Review* contributor Wilma Dykeman deemed it "uneven." Arthur P. Davis, writing in *From the Dark Tower: Afro-American Writers, 1900-1960,* suggests that the author "has crowded too much into her novel." Even so, say reviewers, the novel merits praise. Abraham Chapman of the *Saturday Review* appreciates the author's "fidelity to fact and detail" as she "presents the little-known everyday life of the slaves," their music, and their folkways. In the *Christian Science Monitor,* Henrietta Buckmaster comments, "In Vyry, Miss Walker has found a remarkable woman who suffered one outrage after the other and yet emerged with a humility and a mortal fortitude that reflected a spiritual wholeness." Dykeman concurs, "In its best episodes, and in Vyry, 'Jubilee' chronicles the triumph of a free spirit over many kinds of bondages." Later critical studies of the book emphasize the importance of its themes and its position as the prototype for novels that present black history from a black perspective. Claims Whitlow, "It serves especially well as a response to white 'nostalgia' fiction about the antebellum and Reconstruction South."

Walker's next book to be highly acclaimed was *Prophets for a New Day,* a slim volume of poems. Unlike the poems in *For My People,* which, in a Marxist fashion, names religion an enemy of revolution, says Collier, *Prophets for a New Day* "reflects

a profound religious faith. The heroes of the sixties are named for the prophets of the Bible: Martin Luther King is Amos, Medgar Evars is Micah, and so on. The people and events of the sixties are paralleled with Biblical characters and occurrences. . . . The religious references are important. Whether one espouses the Christianity in which they are couched is not the issue. For the fact is that Black people from ancient Africa to now have always been a spiritual people, believing in an existence beyond the flesh." One poem in *Prophets* that harks back to African spiritism is "Ballad of Hoppy Toad" with its hexes that turn a murderous conjurer into a toad. Though Collier feels that Walker's "vision of the African past is fairly dim and romantic," the critic goes on to say that this poetry "emanates from a deeper area of the psyche, one which touches the mythic area of a collective being and reenacts the rituals which define a Black collective self." Perhaps more importantly, in all the poems, says Collier, Walker depicts "a people striking back at oppression and emerging triumphant."

Walker disclosed in *A Poetic Equation: Conversations between Nikki Giovanni and Margaret Walker* that the poem "Ballad of the Free" in *Prophets* articulates "better than even 'For My People' so much of what I [feel] about black people and the whole movement toward freedom." Davis calls the book "the best poetical comment to come from the civil rights movement—the movement which came to a climax with the march on Washington and which began thereafter to change into a more militant type of liberation effort." Barksdale shares this view; as he comments in *Black American Poets between Worlds,* "Because of her experience, background, and training—her familial gift of word power, her intensive apprenticeship in Chicago's literary workshop in the 1930s, and her mastery of Black orature—her *Prophets* . . . stands out as the premier poetic statement of the death-riddled decade of the 1960s. The poems of this small volume reflect the full range of the Black protest during the time—the sit-ins, the jailings, the snarling dogs, the . . . lynching of the three Civil Rights workers in Mississippi. All of the poems in the volume touch the sensitive nerve of racial memory and bring back, in sharply etched detail, the trauma and tension and triumphs of that period."

In the same essay, Barksdale relates that Walker's books owed little to her academic life and much to a rich cultural sensibility gained in her youth. "There was . . . New Orleans with its . . . folk mythology, its music, . . . and its assortment of racial experiences to be remembered and recalled." And there was the shaping influence of Walker's parents. Born in Jamaica but educated at Atlanta's Gammon Theological Institute, her father Sigismond was a Methodist preacher. Her mother, Marion (nee Dozier), was a musician. "So [the poet] grew up in a household ruled by the power of the word, for undoubtedly few have a greater gift for articulate word power than an educated Jamaican trained to preach the doctrine of salvation in the Black South," Barksdale remarks. In such a home, survival "without mastery of words and language was impossible," he adds, citing Walker's comment. And, given her family background, Walker felt destined for an academic career.

That career was characterized by opposition and difficulty. In the interview with Tate, Walker reflected, "I'm a third-generation college graduate. Society doesn't want to recognize that there's this kind of black writer. I'm the Ph.D. black woman. That's horrible. That is to be despised. I didn't know how bad it was until I went back to school [to teaching] and found out." With her older children nearing college age, Walker had taken leave from her position at Jackson State University to earn an advanced degree in hope that afterward she would be given more pay. She returned only to be slighted by the administration. Eventually, she developed the school's black studies program, attaining personal fulfillment only during the last years of her career as an educator.

Walker died of breast cancer in Chicago in 1998, however her legacy is important in the world of letters. Discouragements of many kinds did not prevent Walker from producing works that have encouraged many. *For My People, Jubilee,* and *Prophets for a New Day* are valued for their relation to social movements of twentieth century America. In 1937, the poem "For My People" called for a new generation to gather strength from a militant literature, and the black literature of the 1960s—including the autobiographies of Malcolm X, Eldridge Cleaver, Huey Newton, and Angela Davis, to name just a few—answered that challenge, suggests C. W. E. Bigsby in *The Second Black Renaissance: Essays in Black Literature.* Her example over the years also proved to be instructive. This summary of Walker's achievement closes the epilogue of *How I Wrote "Jubilee":* "She has revealed the creative ways in which methods and materials of the social science scholar may be joined with the craft and viewpoint of the poet/novelist to create authentic black literature. She has reaffirmed for us the critical importance of oral tradition in the creation of our history. . . . Finally, she has made awesomely clear to us the tremendous costs which must be paid in stubborn, persistent work and commitment if we are indeed to write our own history and create our own literature."

BIOGRAPHICAL/CRITICAL SOURCES:

BOOKS

Bankier, Joanna, and Dierdre Lashgari, editors, *Women Poets of the World,* Macmillan, 1983.

Baraka, Amiri, *The Black Nation,* Getting Together Publications, 1982.

Bigsby, C. W. E., editor, *The Second Black Renaissance: Essays in Black Literature,* Greenwood Press, 1980.

Carmichael, Jacqueline Miller, *Trumpeting a Fiery Sound: History and Folklore in Margaret Walker's Jubilee,* University of Georgia Press, 1998.

Contemporary Literary Criticism, Gale, Volume 1, 1973, Volume 2, 1976.

Davis, Arthur P., *From the Dark Tower: Afro-American Writers, 1900 to 1960,* Howard University Press, 1974.

Emanuel, James A., and Theodore L. Gross, editors, *Dark Symphony: Negro Literature in America,* Free Press, 1968.

Evans, Mari, editor, *Black Women Writers (1950-1980): A Critical Evaluation,* Anchor/Doubleday, 1982.

Gayle, Addison, editor, *The Black Aesthetic,* Doubleday, 1971.

Gibson, Donald B., editor, *Modern Black Poets: A Collection of Critical Essays,* Prentice-Hall, 1983.

Jackson, Blyden, and Louis D. Rubin, Jr., *Black Poetry in America: Two Essays in Historical Interpretation,* Louisiana State University Press, 1974.

Jones, John Griffith, in *Mississippi Writers Talking,* Volume II, University of Mississippi Press, 1983.

Kent, George E., *Blackness and the Adventure of Western Culture,* Third World Press, 1972.

Lee, Don L., *Dynamite Voices I: Black Poets of the 1960s,* Broadside Press, 1971.

Miller, R. Baxter, editor, *Black American Poets between Worlds, 1940-1960,* University of Tennessee Press, 1986.

Pryse, Marjorie, and Hortense J. Spillers, editors, *Conjuring: Black Women, Fiction, and Literary Tradition,* Indiana University Press, 1985.

Redmond, Eugene B., *Drumvoices: The Mission of Afro-American Poetry—A Critical Evaluation,* Doubleday, 1976.

Tate, Claudia, editor, *Black Women Writers at Work,*
　　Continuum, 1983.
Whitlow, Roger, *Black American Literature: A Criti-*
　　cal History, Nelson Hall, 1973.

PERIODICALS

Atlantic, December, 1942.
Best Sellers, October 1, 1966.
Black World, December, 1971; December, 1975.
Books, January 3, 1973.
Book Week, October 2, 1966.
Callaloo, May, 1979; fall, 1987.
Christian Science Monitor, November 14, 1942; Sep-
　　tember 29, 1966; June 19, 1974.
CLA Journal, December 1977.
Common Ground, autumn, 1943.
Ebony, February, 1949.
Freedomways, summer, 1967.
Mississippi Quarterly, fall, 1988; fall, 1989.
National Review, October 4, 1966.
Negro Digest, February, 1967; January, 1968.
New Republic, November 23, 1942.
New York Times, November 4, 1942.
New York Times Book Review, August 2, 1942; Sep-
　　tember 25, 1966.
Opportunity, December, 1942.
Publishers Weekly, April 15, 1944; March 24, 1945.
Saturday Review, September 24, 1966.
Times Literary Supplement, June 29, 1967.
Washington Post, February 9, 1983.
Yale Review, winter, 1943.*

*　　*　　*

WARUK, Kona
　　See HARRIS, (Theodore) Wilson

*　　*　　*

WASHINGTON, Mary Helen 1941-

PERSONAL: Born January 21, 1941, in Cleveland,
OH; daughter of David C. and Mary Catherine
(Dalton) Washington. *Education:* Notre Dame Col-
lege, B.A., 1962; University of Detroit, M.A., 1966,
Ph.D., 1976.

ADDRESSES: Office—Department of English, University of Maryland, College Park, MD 20742.

CAREER: High school teacher of English in the public
schools of Cleveland, OH, 1962-64; St. John College,
Cleveland, instructor in English, 1966-68; University
of Detroit, Detroit, MI, assistant professor of English, 1972-75, director of Center for Black Studies,
beginning 1975; Boston Harbor College, University
of Massachusetts, Boston, associate professor of English, 1980-89; University of Maryland, College
Park, MD, professor of English, 1989—.

MEMBER: National Council of Teachers of English,
College Language Association, Michigan Black Studies Association.

AWARDS, HONORS: Richard Wright Award for Literary Criticism from *Black World,* 1974.

WRITINGS:

(Editor and author of introduction) *Black-Eyed Susans:*
　　Classic Stories by and about Black Women,
　　Doubleday (New York City), 1975.
(Editor and author of introduction and critical notes)
　　Midnight Birds: Stories by Contemporary Black
　　Women Writers, Doubleday, 1980, published in
　　England as *Any Woman's Blues: Stories by Black*
　　Women Writers, Virago Press (London), 1980.
(Editor and author of introduction and critical notes)
　　Invented Lives: Narratives of Black Women,
　　1860-1960, Doubleday, 1987.
(Editor and author of introduction and critical notes)
　　Memory of Kin: Stories of Family by Black Writ-
　　ers, Doubleday, 1991.

Contributor of articles and reviews to *Negro Digest*
and *Black World.*

SIDELIGHTS: Mary Helen Washington is the editor
and author of introductions and critical notes of three
valued anthologies containing the work of some of the
best black women writers. In reviews of all three
books, *Black-Eyed Susans: Classic Stories by and*
about Black Women, Midnight Birds: Stories by Con-
temporary Black Women Writers, and *Invented Lives:*
Narratives of Black Women, 1860-1960, reviewers
have praised Washington for expertly assembling
unique and sensitive stories describing the life and
plight of black women.

Black-Eyed Susans, Washington's first anthology,
presents the writing of such authors as Toni Cade

Bambara, Gwendolyn Brooks, Louise Meriwether, Toni Morrison, Jean Wheeler Smith, and Alice Walker. Joyce Carol Oates writes in *Ms.* that *Black-Eyed Susans* "constitutes an indictment of stereotyped thinking." Oates goes on to state that "no one has been so misunderstood, perhaps, as the black woman: she has been defined by others, whether white writers or black men writers, always seen from the outside, ringed in by convenient stereotypes. . . . What strikes the reader who comes to most of these stories for the first time is the wide range of their humanity. All the protagonists are black women: they are *black* women, black *women,* and fiercely individualistic *persons.* And the fiction that presents them is of a high order, the product of painstaking craftsmanship. There is much anger, and no little despair and heartbreak, but emotion has been kept under control; each of the stories is a work of art, moving and convincing."

Marlene Veach writes in *Best Sellers* that Washington's second book, *Midnight Birds,* "is a collection of stories that revolts against ideologies and attitudes that impress women into servitude. It deals with the real lives and actual experiences of black women, in the hope of demolishing racial and sexual stereotypes." Margaret Atwood writes in a *Harvard Review* of *Midnight Birds* that "this is American writing at its finest, by turns earthy, sinuous, thoughtful, and full of power." Atwood continues to explain that the writers included in this collection, Toni Cade Bambara, Alexis De Veaux, Gayl Jones, Toni Morrison, Ntozake Shange, Alice Walker, and others, "know exactly whom they are writing for. They are writing for other black American women, and they believe in the power of their words. They see themselves as giving a voice to the voiceless. They perceive writing as the forging of saving myths, the naming of forgotten pasts, the telling of truths."

In *Invented Lives* Washington chose to highlight the work of ten women, including Harriet Jacobs, Frances E. W. Harper, Zora Neale Hurston, and Dorothy West, who wrote between the years of 1860 and 1960. Washington states in a *New York Times Book Review* interview conducted by Rosemary L. Bray that "a lot of people think the tradition of black women writing began in the last 20 years. In fact, black women have been writing about their experiences in America for more than 200 years. . . . I found black women working as domestics, writers, migrant farmers, artists, secretaries—and having economic and personal problems centering around these jobs."

Henry Louis Gates, Jr., comments in the *New York Times Book Review* that in each author's selection "we hear a black woman *testifying* about what the twin scourges of sexism and racism, merged into one oppressive entity, actually *do* to a human being, how the combination confines the imagination, puzzles the will and delimits free choice. What unites these essays, short stories and novel excerpts is their common themes: 'Their literature is about black women; it takes the trouble to record the thoughts, words, feelings, and deeds of black women, experiences that make the realities of being black in America look very different from what men have written.'"

Although the contributors to Washington's anthologies are all of black heritage, their tales can be understood and felt by all women. For example, calling *Midnight Birds* "a book that is difficult to fault," Buchi Emecheta remarks in the *Washington Post* that this collection "speaks through its admirable selection of stories to black women in particular and to all women in general. The message is clear: it is about time we women start talking to each other, the white to the black, the black American to her African sister, ironing out our differences. For as Toni Morrison said, 'Because when you don't have a woman to really talk to, whether it be an aunt or a sister or a friend, that is the real loneliness.'"

BIOGRAPHICAL/CRITICAL SOURCES:

PERIODICALS

America, January 31, 1981.
Belles Lettres, May, 1988, p. 11.
Best Sellers, August, 1980.
Essence, July, 1988, p. 28.
Harvard Review, February, 1981.
Kliatt Young Adult Paperback Book Guide, April, 1990, p. 30.
Library Journal, January 15, 1980.
Modern Fiction Studies, spring, 1988, p. 134; fall, 1993, p. 828.
Ms., March, 1976; July, 1980; January, 1988, p. 76.
Nation, April 30, 1988, p. 615.
New Directions for Women, March, 1988, p. 16.
New York Times Book Review, October 4, 1987.
Publishers Weekly, December 3, 1979.
Times Literary Supplement, October 30, 1981.
Village Voice Literary Supplement, April, 1988, p. 20.
Washington Post, June 3, 1980.
Washington Post Book World, January 7, 1990, p. 12.
Women's Review of Books, February, 1988, p. 15.

WATKINS, Frances Ellen
See HARPER, Frances Ellen Watkins

*   *   *

WESLEY, Patricia Jabbeh

PERSONAL: Born in Liberia; daughter of Moses Chee Jabbeh (a property supervisor) and Hneh Datedor (a nurse assistant; also known as Mary Hneh and Mary Williams); married Mlen-Too Wesley (a minister and business consultant), December 19, 1980; children: Besie-Nyesuah (daughter), Mlen-Too II (son), Gee (son), Ade-Juah (daughter). *Education:* University of Liberia, B.A. (cum laude), 1980; Indiana University—Bloomington, M.Sc., 1985. *Religion:* Christian.

ADDRESSES: Home—3504 Croyden Ave., Kalamazoo, MI 49006. *Office*—Department of English, Western Michigan University, Kalamazoo, MI 49008.

CAREER: University of Liberia, Monrovia, instructor in English and writing, 1980-90; Grand Valley State University, Allendale, MI, instructor in writing, 1992-94; Aquinas College, Grand Rapids, MI, instructor in literature and writing, 1993-96; Western Michigan University, Kalamazoo, research associate, 1998—. Davenport College of Business, instructor, 1992-97. Kalamazoo Institute of Arts, storyteller and Africa outreach researcher, 1995—; Arts Council of Greater Kalamazoo, member.

MEMBER: Friends of Poetry, Black Arts and Culture.

AWARDS, HONORS: World Bank grant for the United States, 1983-85; Arts Council of Greater Kalamazoo, individual artist grants, 1997, 1998, and Irving S. Gilmore grant, 1998.

WRITINGS:

(Contributor) Abby Bogomolny, editor, *New to North America,* Burning Bush (Jeffersonville, PA), 1997.
Before the Palm Could Bloom: Poems of Africa, Western Michigan University (Kalamazoo, MI), 1998.

Contributor of poems to periodicals, including *Michigan College English Association Annual Journal.*

WORK IN PROGRESS: More Than Conquerors: A Family's Story, a memoir of the Liberian civil war, 1989-96; *African Alphabet Name Book for Children; Iyeeh's Praise Songs: Collected Poems.*

SIDELIGHTS: Patricia Jabbeh Wesley told *CA:* "When I began writing during my elementary school days, I knew that this was something I enjoyed, something which no one could ever take away from me. It was my way of coming into myself—my little closet of protection from the confusing world of a stepchild who was too smart to be loved. I took every advantage of poetry since, and today, more than thirty years later, I have discovered that what I love to do can earn me a living.

"I am originally from Liberia, West Africa, a little country that has produced almost no significant writers, even though West Africa as a whole has such celebrated writers as Chinua Achebe and Nobel Prize winner Wole Soyinka. When I began to take writing seriously, this factor weighed heavily upon me. I would use my talent to usher my country into the world's literary scene—to enable African artists to see themselves as belonging to the community.

"The circumstances of my life in Africa and America have been my motivation. I see the world differently than an American who was brought up in this country. I see the tears, the pain, the suffering, and the injustice that plague the world family; however, I see the laughter in the tears, the peace that comes with poverty, the simplicity of the villager, the rural ruggedness of life and its immense beauty. I often take the two into question in my poetry or prose. I compare the beauty and peacefulness of the village where I spent part of my childhood to the city with its wars, disease, and uncaring, cold, and materialistic people. I often write about the beauty of waters—the Atlantic of my past, rough, troubled, yet beautiful.

"For me, literature can only be beautiful if the words it uses have feelings for where they exist. Therefore, many of my poems written in America speak of being an African in America, of losing home to my new home. I write about the loneliness of the aged, the fear of being consumed by the city, the loneliness of the crowd. My motivation comes from my surroundings. As a mother, I can look at my children and write a poem about the life I am giving them here and now.

"I dislike poetry or prose that is ordinary yet never writes about ordinary people. I believe that the literature of the ordinary is powerful because it has eyes for its surroundings. When nature appears in my poems, I make nature succumb to the people I write about. It is our nature; therefore, if the trees are green, they must be green for the people whose houses are knocked down when the tornado strikes.

"My first book of poems, *Before the Palm Could Bloom: Poems of Africa,* is a book that brings out all of these. The reader will see a cross-section of life in its reality: the village and its ruggedness as well as the city, the beauty as well as the ugliness of family, of tradition, of celebrations. I have poems that cry out against the pain caused by the Liberian civil war that destroyed so much and so many children. What I seek to do in my writing is to explore the beauty of everything around me, whether that beauty is in itself an ugliness or not. For me, whether literature writes about the ugliness of pain, of the nature of people, or about the beauty of all of these, literature will always be very beautiful if it uses language profoundly."

*   *   *

WESLEY, Valerie Wilson 1947-

PERSONAL: Born November 22, 1947; married Richard Wesley (a screenwriter and playwright); children: two daughters. *Education:* Howard University, received undergraduate degree; Graduate School of Journalism, Columbia University, M.A.; Bank Street College of Education, M.A.

ADDRESSES: Agent—c/o Putnam Berkley Publishing Group, 200 Madison Ave., New York, NY 10016. *E-mail*—Valwilwes@aol.com.

CAREER: Scholastic News, former associate editor; *Essence,* New York City, began as senior editor, became executive editor, then contributing editor.

AWARDS, HONORS: Griot Award, New York chapter of National Association of Black Journalists; Best Book for Reluctant Readers citation, American Library Association, c. 1993, for *Where Do I Go from Here?;* Shamus Award nomination, c. 1994, for *When Death Comes Stealing;* named author of the year, Go Go, Girls book club.

WRITINGS:

BIOGRAPHIES

(With Wade Hudson) *Afro-Bets Book of Black Heroes from A to Z: An Introduction to Important Black*

Achievers for Young Readers, Just Us Books (East Orange, NJ), 1988.

JUVENILE FICTION

Where Do I Go from Here? (young adult novel), Scholastic (New York City), 1993.
Freedom's Gifts: A Juneteenth Mystery, illustrated by Sharon Wilson, Simon & Schuster (New York City), 1997.

"TAMARA HAYLE" MYSTERY NOVELS

When Death Comes Stealing, Putnam (New York City), 1994.
Devil's Gonna Get Him, Putnam (New York City), 1995.
Where Evil Sleeps, Putnam (New York City), 1996.
No Hiding Place, Putnam (New York City), 1997.
Easier to Kill, Putnam (New York City), 1998.

Contributor of fiction to periodicals, including *Essence, New York Times, Ms., Family Circle, Creative Classroom,* and *TV Guide.*

SIDELIGHTS: Valerie Wilson Wesley's contribution to literature includes books for children and young adults, as well as adult mysteries. Wesley, an editor for *Essence,* published her first book with Wade Hudson. *Afro-Bets Book of Black Heros from A to Z: An Introduction to Important Black Heroes* was reviewed by Sylvia Meisner of *School Library Journal* who noted that the book satisfied an increasing demand for new information on African American leaders and celebrities.

Wesley's work continued to fill a niche for literature that focuses on the cultural and discriminatory issues that blacks face in America. An African American herself, Wesley's next work, *Where Do I Go from Here?,* tells the story of Nia, a young black female who receives a scholarship to a prestigious white boarding school and tries to find her place there. When a racially based fight causes Nia and a wealthy white peer to be suspended from the school, Wesley creates a situation which reviewer Kim Carter, in a review for *Voice of Youth Advocates,* called a success in "portraying the human similarities that cross racial and economic distinctions."

Wesley's next books established an ongoing series and a new niche for her literary work, this time as a mystery novelist. According to an article in *American Visions,* mystery writing such as Wesley's has contributed to a rising trend that features black authors publishing mysteries with black characters. As a result, the article noted, "the American fictional detective is changing." Wesley's mysteries feature an female African American private investigator who is a single mother and ex-cop from Newark, NJ. Throughout the series, Wesley places Tamara Hayle, her feisty heroine, in a number of life-threatening situations. In the first mystery of the series, *When Death Comes Stealing,* Hayle investigates the murders of several sons of her ex-husband, fearing that her own son is next. A *Publishers Weekly* critic noted that while Wesley's adult fiction debut revealed little of Hayle's character, the author had created "a broad, interesting cast." The reviewer added that the book's strength lay in "its portrayal of black family life in dangerous times." A critic for *Kirkus Reviews* commented that Hayle's "descriptions of other characters are quick and often funny, even in grim situations. . . . Her colorful personality and cultural insight spice up a serviceable plot."

Wesley's second book in the series, *Devil's Gonna Get Him,* places protagonist Hayle in a situation where she is hired to follow boyfriend of the daughter of a wealthy and powerful African American Newark man, Lincoln Storey. Hayle is reluctant to trail the boyfriend, who is a former lover, but through a number of events and twists, ends up delving into Storey's dirty past and becoming the target of danger herself. Stuart Miller, in a review for *Booklist,* declared, "Wesley has crafted an intriguing plot showcasing the appealing Tamara." A *Publishers Weekly* critic was less enthusiastic about the plot, but commented that the author's "characterization is powerful; the down-to earth observations of single-mother Tamara . . . amply fill out the thin spots." A *Kirkus Reviews* commentator also praised Wesley's characterization of Hayle, and commented that "her unapologetically plainspoken voice . . . makes this tale as memorable as her debut."

Where Evil Sleeps features Hayle solving mysteries and putting herself in dangerous situations in Jamaica. On vacation in Kingston, Hayle is convinced to accompany a friend and her husband to a seedy bar for drinks. While there, a power outage allows someone to steal Hayle's purse and murder her friend's husband and another man. Though an old friend surfaces to remove Hayle from the events surrounding the crime, she eventually finds herself again embroiled in sleuthing.

A fourth book in the series, *No Hiding Place,* is driven, according to a *Publishers Weekly* reviewer,

more by "Wesley's compassion for the people of inner-city Newark than by her plotting." Nonetheless, the story—which features murder, suicide, old flames, and troubled teenagers—takes a look at the impact of the rise of a new African American middle class and how it relates to the poorer inner-city. A critic for *Kirkus Reviews* also faulted the plot and commented that the novel's strength lay its "sharp, subtle portrait of two families whose tangle relationship packs a world of insight into a single painful case." The *Publishers Weekly* reviewer praised Hayle's "consistently sharp, honest voice" for its ability to drive the novel as it explores "complex social issues." *Booklist*'s Stuart Miller wrote that Wesley's depiction of urban ghetto life had the "ring of authenticity," adding "there is not a shred of sentimentality in this story's grim but ultimately satisfying resolution."

A fifth Tamara Hayle mystery, *Easier to Kill,* features Mandy Magic, a popular and successful radio personality. After finding herself the victim of tire slashings, graffiti, and anonymous notes, Mandy hires Hayle to investigate. As Hayle investigates these seemingly small crimes, she realizes that Mandy's past holds damaging secrets, including time she spent working as a prostitute. "Wilson keeps peeling back layers from Mandy's carefully constructed life with . . . skill and determination."

Wesley is also the author of *Freedom's Gifts: A Juneteenth Story,* which departs from her previous mystery focus. The story, illustrated by Sharon Wilson and written for a juvenile audience, addresses racial issues and the African American fight for freedom in a context that can be appreciated by young and older readers alike. The story, set in 1943 Texas, refers to the celebration of "Juneteenth": June 19th, the annual anniversary of Texas black slaves' freedom in 1865. Two young protagonists from New York visit their great-great-aunt in Texas, who moves them with her tale of slavery and subsequent freedom. Ironically, segregation is still a reality in the 1943 setting, prompting the aunt to remind the children that there is still more freedom to fight for. A *Publishers Weekly* critic called the story "sophisticated and distinctive" and praised Wesley's treatment of a "sensitive and important subject."

BIOGRAPHICAL/CRITICAL SOURCES:

BOOKS

Heising, Willetta L, *Detecting Women 2,* Purple Moon Press (Dearborn, MI), 1996-97.

Who's Who among African Americans, Gale (Detroit, MI), 1996.

PERIODICALS

American Visions, April/May, 1997, pp. 18-21.
Armchair Detective, fall, 1994, p. 495; fall, 1995, p. 463; fall, 1996, p. 499.
Black Enterprise, August, 1982, pp. 39-44.
Booklist, December 15, 1993, p. 748; March 15, 1994, p. 1361; June 1, 1994, pp. 1775, 1787; July, 1995, pp. 1862-1863, 1869; May 1, 1997, p. 1468; August, 1997, p. 1884.
Book Report, January, 1994, p. 50.
Center for Children's Books Bulletin, June, 1997, p. 378.
Children's Book Review Service, February, 1994, p. 121; spring, 1997, p. 145.
Essence, February, 1994, p. 121.
Horn Book Guide, spring, 1994, p. 92.
Kirkus Reviews, December 1, 1993, p. 1531; May 15, 1994, p. 670; June 1, 1995, p. 744; July 15, 1996, p. 1010; August 1, 1997, p. 1164.
Kliatt, May, 1995, p. 53; July, 1996, p. 16.
Los Angeles Times Book Review, August 14, 1994, p. 7.
Library Journal, July, 1994, p. 132.
Ms., July, 1995, p. 75.
New York Times Book Review, June 22, 1997, pp. 102-103.
Publishers Weekly, November 8, 1993, p. 79; May 23, 1994, p. 80; May 22, 1995, p. 50; April 15, 1996, p. 63; July 15, 1996, p. 59; March 31, 1997, p. 75; July 7, 1997, p. 53.
Rapport, June, 1996, p. 24.
School Library Journal, December, 1988, p. 117; November, 1993, pp. 126-127; June, 1997, p. 102-103.
Voice of Youth Advocates, February, 1994, p. 375.
Washington Post Book World, August 21, 1994, p. 6; August 18, 1996, p. 8.

OTHER

Amazon.com, http://www.amazon.com, 1998.
Barnes & Noble, http://shop.barnesandnoble.com, 1998.
Tamara Hayle Mysteries, http://www.TamaraHayle.com, 1998.

*   *   *

WHITMAN, Albery Allson 1851-1901

PERSONAL: Born May 30, 1851, near Munfordville, KY; died of pneumonia, June 29, 1901, in Atlanta, GA; son of slaves; married; wife's name, Caddie; children: two daughters. *Ethnicity:* "African American." *Education:* Attended school for one year. *Religion:* African Methodist Episcopal.

CAREER: Poet, 1871-1901. Worked as an itinerant preacher, and founded and preached at several churches throughout the South; also worked as a schoolteacher, in a plough factory, and as a laborer in railroad construction.

WRITINGS:

Essays on the Ten Plagues and Miscellaneous Poems, c. 1871.
Leelah Misled, Richard LaRue (Elizabethtown, KY), 1873.
Not a Man, and Yet a Man, Republic Printing Company (Springfield, OH), 1877, Mnemosyne Publishing Co. (Miami, FL), 1969.
The Rape of Florida, Nixon-Jones Printing Co. (St. Louis, MO), 1884, revised edition published as *Twasinta's Seminoles,* Nixon-Jones Printing Co. (St. Louis, MO), 1885, reprinted as *The Rape of Florida,* Literature House (Upper Saddle River, NJ), 1970.
Twastina's Seminoles/Not a Man and Yet a Man/ Drifted Leaves: A Collection of Poems, Nixon-Jones Printing, 1890. *The World's Fair Poem,* Holsey Job Print (Atlanta, GA), 1893.
An Idyl of the South: An Epic Poem in Two Parts, Metaphysical Publishing Company (New York City), 1901.
The Octoroon, n.p., 1901.

SIDELIGHTS: Considered "The Poet Laureate of the Negro Race," Albery Allson Whitman was born to slave parents on a small family farm near Munfordville in Hart County, Kentucky. Whitman began working as a young child and was himself a slave for twelve years. He went to school for only one year, but he was a prolific writer and author of several volumes of poetry that have been called the most ambitious poetry written by an African American in the nineteenth century; he is considered "one of the most important black poets between Phillis Wheatley and Paul Laurence Dunbar," explained *Dictionary of Literary Biography* contributor Blyden Jackson.

He became an orphan after his mother died in 1862 and his father died in 1863. He never spoke harshly of his youth in slavery or of owners of the farm where he grew up, and seemed to feel a great attachment to the area. After the Civil War ended Whitman began traveling. From 1864 to 1870, he worked in Ohio and Kentucky in a plough shop and as a laborer on a railroad construction crew. He also attended school for about seven months, and on the basis of this experience he taught school in Carysville, Ohio, and in Kentucky near the farm where he had been born. In 1870 he studied under Bishop Daniel A. Payne at Wilberforce University, and was later general financial agent of Wilberforce.

Whitman was never formally ordained as a minister, but he was pastor of an African Methodist Episcopal church in Springfield, Ohio, in 1877. From 1878 through 1883, he founded churches and was a pastor in Ohio, Kansas, Texas, and Georgia. Whitman traveled to various churches for his preaching duties, and in 1901 he went to Anniston, Alabama, where he contracted pneumonia. He was taken home to Atlanta, but died a week later from the illness.

The poetry Whitman wrote during these years was highly praised by critics as well as by other poets. Whitman's poetry celebrated the idea of art for art's sake, and it was deeply optimistic. He was influenced by poets, such as Spenser, Longfellow, Whittier, and William Cullen Bryant, and echoes of their work can be heard in his. However, his poetry also reveals his own interests, talents, and originality. *Leelah Misled,* for instance, is about a young white girl who loses her virginity to McLambert, a wealthy philanderer who betrays her. *In Not a Man and Yet a Man,* the hero, Rodney, is considered to be black although he is "eighty-five per cent Anglo-Saxon." For 5,000 lines, the epic poem describes his youth and adulthood. It is a melodramatic tale of slavery, whites warring against Native Americans, murder, kidnapping, and love, ending with Rodney's sale into deeper and more appalling slavery in the deep South. Eventually he escapes with his love, Leeona, a light-skinned Creole woman; they flee to Canada, but return to the United States to fight for the North in the Civil War.

The Rape of Florida tells the story of two Seminole chiefs and the white deception of the Seminole people despite their innate nobility. Unlike most of Whitman's other works, *The World's Fair Poem* is a collection of two social-protest poems, defending African Americans against white stereotypes and promoting them as important citizens of America. In *An Idyl of the South,* Whitman presents a story about the love of a white man, Sheldon Maury, and a beautiful slave woman, Lena. "Whitman," explained Jackson, "was a writer for whom self-expression was a supreme condition of his existence. His verse was often too long, too digressive, and shallowly facile. Yet his poetry should be read for the many lines that display his original genius."

BIOGRAPHICAL/CRITICAL SOURCES:

BOOKS

Dictionary of Literary Biography, Volume 50: *Afro-American Writers Before the Harlem Renaissance,* Gale (Detroit, MI), 1986.*

*   *   *

WIDEMAN, John Edgar 1941-

PERSONAL: Born June 14, 1941, in Washington, DC; son of Edgar and Betty (French) Wideman; married Judith Ann Goldman, 1965; children: Daniel Jerome, Jacob Edgar, Jamila Ann. *Education:* University of Pennsylvania, B.A., 1963; New College, Oxford, B.Phil., 1966.

ADDRESSES: Office—Department of English, University of Massachusetts—Amherst, Amherst, MA 01003.

CAREER: Howard University, Washington, DC, teacher of American literature, summer, 1965; University of Pennsylvania, Philadelphia, 1966-74, began as instructor, professor of English, 1974, director of Afro-American studies program, 1971-73; University of Wyoming, Laramie, professor of English, 1974-1985; University of Massachusetts—Amherst, professor of English, 1986—. Made U.S. Department of State lecture tour of Europe and the Near East, 1976; Phi Beta Kappa lecturer, 1976; visiting writer and lecturer at numerous colleges and universities; has also served as administrator/teacher in a curriculum planning, teacher-training institute sponsored by National Defense Education Act. Assistant basketball coach, University of Pennsylvania, 1968-72. National Humanities Faculty consultant in numerous states; consultant to secondary schools across the country, 1968—.

MEMBER: Association of American Rhodes Scholars (member of board of directors and of state and national selection committees), American Studies Association (council, 1980-81), Modern Language Association, American Academy of Arts and Sciences, Phi Beta Kappa.

AWARDS, HONORS: Received creative writing prize, University of Pennsylvania; Rhodes Scholar, Oxford University, 1963; Thouron fellow, Oxford University, 1963-66; Kent fellow, University of Iowa, 1966, to attend creative writing workshop; named member of Philadelphia Big Five Basketball Hall of Fame, 1974; Young Humanist fellow, 1975—; PEN/Faulkner Award for fiction, 1984, for *Sent for You Yesterday*; National Book Award nomination, 1984, for *Brothers and Keepers*; John Dos Passos Prize for Literature from Longwood College, 1986; Lannan award, 1991; MacArthur fellow, 1993; honorary doctorate, University of Pennsylvania.

WRITINGS:

A Glance Away (novel), Harcourt, 1967.
Hurry Home (novel), Harcourt, 1970.
The Lynchers (novel), Harcourt, 1973.
Damballah (short stories), Avon, 1981.
Hiding Place (novel), Avon, 1981.
Sent for You Yesterday (novel), Avon, 1983.
Brothers and Keepers (memoirs), H. Holt, 1984, reprinted, Vintage, 1995.
The Homewood Trilogy (includes *Damballah, Hiding Place,* and *Sent For You Yesterday*), Avon, 1985.
Reuben (novel), H. Holt, 1987.
Fever (short stories), H. Holt, 1989.
Philadelphia Fire (novel), H. Holt, 1990.
All Stories Are True, Vintage Books, 1992.
The Stories of John Edgar Wideman, Pantheon Books, 1992.
A Glance Away, Hurry Home, and *The Lynchers: Three Early Novels by John Edgar Wideman,* Holt, Henry, and Co., 1994.
Fatheralong, Pantheon, 1994.
The Cattle Killing, Houghton Mifflin, 1996.
(With Bonnie Tusmith) *Conversations with John Edgar Wideman,* University Press of Mississippi, 1998.

Contributor of articles, short stories, book reviews, and poetry to periodicals, including *American Poetry Review, Negro Digest, Black American Literature Forum, Black World, American Scholar, Gentleman's Quarterly, New York Times Book Review, North American Review,* and *Washington Post Book World.*

SIDELIGHTS: John Edgar Wideman has been hailed by Don Strachen in the *Los Angeles Times Book Review* as "the black Faulkner, the softcover Shakespeare." Such praise is not uncommon for this author, whose novel *Sent for You Yesterday* was selected as the 1984 PEN/Faulkner Award winner over works by

Bernard Malamud, Cynthia Ozick, and William Kennedy. Wideman attended Oxford University in 1963 on a Rhodes scholarship, earned a degree in eighteenth-century literature, and later accepted a fellowship at the prestigious University of Iowa Writers' Workshop. Yet this "artist with whom any reader who admires ambitious fiction must sooner or later reckon," as the *New York Times* called him, began his college career not as a writer, but as a basketball star. "I always wanted to play pro basketball—ever since I saw a ball and learned you could make money at it," he told Curt Suplee in the *Washington Post.* Recruited by the University of Pennsylvania, Wideman first studied psychology, attracted by the "mystical insight" he told Suplee that he thought this major would yield. When his subjects of study instead "turned out to be rats" and clinical experiments, Wideman changed his major to English, while continuing to be mainly concerned with basketball. He played well enough to earn a place in the Philadelphia Big Five Basketball Hall of Fame, but, he told Suplee, as his time at the university drew to a close, "I knew I wasn't going to be able to get into the NBA [National Basketball Association]. What was left?" The Rhodes scholarship answered that question. Wideman began to concentrate on his writing rather than sports and did so with such success that his first novel, *A Glance Away,* was published just a year after he earned his degree from Oxford.

The story of a day in the life of a drug addict, *A Glance Away* reflects the harsh realities that Wideman saw and experienced during his youth in Pittsburgh's ghetto, Homewood. And, though the author later resided in other locales, including Wyoming, his novels continued to describe black urban experiences. He explained to Suplee, "My particular imagination has always worked well in a kind of exile. It fits the insider-outside view I've always had. It helps to write away from the center of the action."

Wideman's highly literate style is in sharp contrast to his gritty subject matter, and while reviews of his books have been generally favorable from the start of his writing career, some critics initially expressed the opinion that such a formal style was not appropriate for his stories of street life. For example, Anatole Broyard praised *The Lynchers* in his *New York Times* review, stating: "Though we have heard the themes and variations of violence before in black writing, *The Lynchers* touches us in a more personal way, for John Edgar Wideman has a weapon more powerful than any knife or gun. His weapon is art. Eloquence is his arsenal, his arms cache. His prose, at its best, is a black panther, coiled to spring." But Broyard went on to say that the book is not flawless: "Far from it. Mr. Wideman ripples too many muscles in his writing, often cannot seem to decide whether to show or snow us. . . . [He] is wordy, and *The Lynchers* is as shaky in its structure as some of the buildings his characters inhabit. But he can *write,* and you come away from his book with the feeling that he is, as they say, very close to getting it all together." In the *New York Times,* John Leonard commented on the extensive use of literary devices in *The Lynchers:* "Flashback, flashforward, first person, third person, journals, identity exchange, interior monologue, dreams (historical and personal), puns, epiphanies. At times the devices seem a thicket through which one must hack one's weary way toward meanings arbitrarily obscure, a vegetable indulgence. But John Edgar Wideman is up to much more than storytelling. . . . He is capable of moving from ghetto language to [Irish writer James] Joyce with a flip of the page."

Saturday Review critic David Littlejohn agreed that Wideman's novels are very complex, and in his review of *Hurry Home* he criticized those who would judge this author as a storyteller: "Reviewers . . . are probably more responsible than anyone else for the common delusion that a novel is somehow contained in its discernible, realistic plot. . . . *Hurry Home* is primarily an experience, not a plot: an experience of words, dense, private, exploratory, and non-progressive." Littlejohn described *Hurry Home* as a retelling of an American myth, that of "the lonely search through the Old World" for a sense of cultural heritage, which "has been the pattern of a hundred thousand young Americans' lives and novels." According to Littlejohn, Wideman's version is "spare and eccentric, highly stylized, circling, allusive, antichronological, far more consciously symbolic than most versions, than the usual self-indulgent and romantic works of this genre—and hence both more rewarding and more difficult of access." Reviewing the same book in the *New York Times Book Review,* Joseph Goodman stated: "Many of its pages are packed with psychological insight, and nearly all reveal Mr. Wideman's formidable command of the techniques of fiction. Moreover, the theme is a profound one—the quest for a substantive sense of self. . . .The prose, paratactic and rich with puns, flows as freely as thought itself, giving us . . . Joycean echoes. . . . It is a dazzling display. . . . We can have nothing but admiration for Mr. Wideman's talent."

Enthusiastic reviews such as these established Wideman's reputation in the literary world as a major tal-

ent. When his fourth and fifth books—*Damballah,* a collection of short stories, and *Hiding Place,* a novel—were issued originally as paperbacks, some critics, such as John Leonard and Mel Watkins, reacted with indignation. Leonard's *New York Times* review used extensive quotes from the books to demonstrate Wideman's virtuosity, and stated, "That [these] two new books will fall apart after a second reading is a scandal." Watkins's *New York Times Book Review* article on the two books, which were published simultaneously, had special praise for the short-story volume, and ended with a sentiment much like Leonard's on the books' binding. "In freeing his voice from the confines of the novel form," Watkins wrote, "[Wideman] has written what is possibly his most impressive work. . . . Each story moves far beyond the primary event on which it is focused. . . . Like [Jean] Toomer, Mr. Wideman has used a narrative laced with myth, superstition and dream sequences to create an elaborate poetic portrait of the lives of ordinary black people. . . . These books once again demonstrate that John Wideman is one of America's premier writers of fiction. That they were published originally in paperback perhaps suggests that he is also one of our most underrated writers." Actually, it was the author himself who had decided to bring the books out as original paperbacks. His reasons were philosophical and pragmatic. "I spend an enormous amount of time and energy writing and I want to write good books, but I also want people to read them," he explained to Edwin McDowell in the *New York Times.* Wideman's first three novels had been slow sellers "in spite of enormously positive reviews," he told Suplee, and it was his hope that the affordability of paperbacks would help give him a wider readership, particularly among "the people and the world I was writing about. A $15.95 novel had nothing to do with that world."

Damballah and *Hiding Place* had both been set in Homewood, Wideman's early home, and in 1983 he published a third book with the same setting, *Sent for You Yesterday.* Critics were enthusiastic. "In this hypnotic and deeply lyrical novel, Mr. Wideman again returns to the ghetto where he was raised and transforms it into a magical location infused with poetry and pathos," wrote Alan Cheuse in the *New York Times Book Review.* "The narration here makes it clear that both as a molder of language and a builder of plots, Mr. Wideman has come into his full powers. He has the gift of making 'ordinary' folks memorable." Stated Garett Epps in the *Washington Post Book World,* "Wideman has a fluent command of the American language, written and spoken, and a fierce, loving vision of the people he writes about. Like the writing of William Faulkner, Wideman's prose fiction is vivid and demanding—shuttling unpredictably between places, narrators and times, dwelling for a paragraph on the surface of things, then sneaking a key event into a clause that springs on the reader like a booby trap. . . . *Sent for You Yesterday* is a book to be savored, read slowly again and again."

When he ventured into nonfiction for the first time with his book *Brothers and Keepers,* Wideman continued to draw inspiration from the same source, Homewood. In this book, Wideman comes to terms with his brother Robby, younger by ten years, whose life was influenced by the street, its drugs, and its crime. The author writes, "Even as I manufactured fiction from the events of my brother's life, from the history of the family that had nurtured us both, I knew something of a different order remained to be extricated. The fiction writer was a man with a real brother behind real bars [serving a life sentence in a Pennsylvania penitentiary]." In his review in the *Washington Post Book World,* Jonathan Yardley called *Brothers and Keepers* "the elder Wideman's effort to understand what happened, to confess and examine his own sense of guilt about his brother's fate (and his own)." The result, according to the reviewer, is "a depiction of the inexorably widening chasm that divides middle-class black Americans from the black underclass." Wideman's personal experience, added Yardley, also reveals that for the black person "moving out of the ghetto into the white world is a process that requires excruciating compromises, sacrifices and denials, that leaves the person who makes the journey truly at home in neither the world he has entered nor the world he has left."

Wideman has, however, made a home for himself in literary circles, and at the same time has learned from his experience how to handle his success. When *Sent for You Yesterday* won the PEN/Faulkner Award—the only major literary award in the United States to be judged, administered, and largely funded by writers—Wideman told Suplee he felt "warmth. That's what I felt. Starting at the toes and filling up. A gradual recognition that it could be real." Still, the author maintained that if such an honor "doesn't happen again for a long time—or never happens again—it really doesn't matter," because he "learned more and more that the process itself was important, learned to take my satisfaction from the writing" during the years of comparative obscurity. "I'm an old jock," he explained. "So I've kind of trained myself to be low-key. Sometimes the crowd screams, sometimes the crowd doesn't scream."

The narrator of Wideman's 1987 novel, *Reuben,* provides inexpensive legal aid to residents of Homewood. One of his clients is Kwansa, a young black prostitute whose husband, a recovering drug addict, kidnaps and seeks legal custody of their illegitimate child as revenge against her. Another customer is Wally, an assistant basketball coach at a local white university who seeks Reuben's counsel for two reasons, one being the killing of a white man in Chicago and the other being his fear that he will be blamed for the illegal recruiting practices of his department. Reviewing the book in *Washington Post Book World,* Noel Perrin characterized Wideman's novels as myths. "In the end," Perrin wrote, "one sees that all the shocks—the murders, the fantasies, burnings, strong words—all of them amount to a kind of metaphor for the psychic damage that human beings do to each other and that is no less hurtful than spread-eagled beating, just less visible to the outer eye."

In *Philadelphia Fire,* Wideman brings together two stories, combining fact in fiction. In the first, he describes the events in Philadelphia when the police, under the direction of black mayor Wilson Goode, bombed the headquarters of an organization known as Move, a group that had defied city eviction notices and was armed with weapons. The police bombing killed six adults and five children, destroyed fifty three homes, and left 262 people homeless. Wideman's novel begins with a quote by William Penn, the founder of Pennsylvania, stating his dream that the town would "never be burnt, and always be wholesome." As Chicago *Tribune Books* reviewer Paul Skenazy pointed out, *Philadelphia Fire* tries to make sense of the changes that have occurred since Penn's statement, changes that include poverty and racism and that result in the burning of the Philadelphia neighborhood. The other story being told in the book is that of Wideman's relationship with his son who has received a life sentence for murder. "Few pages of prose," Skenazy said, "carry as much pain as do Wideman's thoughts on his son, his words to him in prison, his feelings of confusion as a father." Skenazy concluded that *Philadelphia Fire* is "about a person, and a nation, losing its grip, destroying the very differences and dissonance that provide spirit, beauty, life." Rosemary L. Bray in the *New York Times Book Review* concurred; "the author takes his readers on a tour of urban America perched on the precipice of hell," Bray wrote, "a tour in which even his own personal tragedy is part of the view."

In 1992, Wideman published *The Stories of John Edgar Wideman,* a volume that combined several earlier story collections, including *Damballah,* originally published in 1981, 1989's *Fever,* and *All Stories Are True* from 1992. Michael Harris wrote in the *Los Angeles Times Book Review* that a comparison between Wideman and Faulkner makes sense "because of the scope of Wideman's project, his ear for voices, . . . and the way he shows the present as perpetually haunted by the past." *New York Times Book Review* contributor Michael Gorra also believed the Faulkner comparison is apt. "It is appropriate," Gorra wrote, "because both are concerned with the life of a community over time. It is appropriate because they both have a feel for the anecdotal folklore through which a community defines itself, because they both often choose to present their characters in the act of telling stories, and because in drawing on oral tradition they both write as their characters speak, in a language whose pith and vigor has not yet been worn into cliche." It is Gorra's conclusion that "the more you read John Edgar Wideman, the more impressive he seems."

Wideman's 1994 book, *Fatheralong,* like *Philadelphia Fire* and the Homewood stories, juxtaposes Wideman's personal life with larger issues. Mel Watkins in the *New York Times Book Review* referred to it as a hybrid of memoir and "a meditation on fatherhood, race, metaphysics, time and the afterlife." Wideman explores his strained relationship with his father and his troubles with his own son, and then frames them in the context of all father-son relationships as well as America's racist legacy. A *Village Voice* critic found the sections on Wideman's son, Jacob, to be his "most artful work. The Jacob sections overshadow simply because they're so much better written, their subject more emotionally grasped than any other." Mitchell Duneier in the *Los Angeles Times Book Review* called *Fatheralong* "a masterpiece of sociological speculation, constructed with such an abundance of wisdom as to compensate for its lack of evidence regarding questions to which there are no easy answers." In the Chicago *Tribune Books,* Michael Boynton, calling the work "part memoir, part manifesto," concluded "*Fatheralong* is an odd, sad book. Filled with flashes of insight told in Wideman's distinctive prose-poetry, it is at once personal and essentially opaque. . . . It leaves the reader wanting to know more, hoping that its author will one day find the key he has been looking for."

Wideman returned to fiction with his 1996 novel, *The Cattle Killing.* In it, he weaves together memories from his narrator's childhood in Philadelphia with the plight of blacks in the city in the late-eighteenth century and the story of the South African Xhosa tribe,

pulling threads of history, religion, and race to form his story. The complex story was met with mostly positive reviews, with critics finding flaws in the novel's coherence but praising Wideman's imaginative storytelling powers.

BIOGRAPHICAL/CRITICAL SOURCES:

BOOKS

Black Literature Criticism, Gale, 1992.
Contemporary Literary Criticism, Gale, Volume 5, 1976, Volume 34, 1985, Volume 36, 1986, Volume 67, 1992.
Dictionary of Literary Biography, Volume 33: *Afro-American Fiction Writers after 1955,* Gale, 1984, Volume 143: *American Novelists since World War II,* third series, Gale, 1994.
Mbalia, Doreatha D., *John Edgar Wideman: Reclaiming the African Personality,* Associated University Presses (London), 1995.
O'Brien, John, editor, *Interviews with Black Writers,* Liveright, 1973.
Wideman, John Edgar, *Brothers and Keepers,* H. Holt, 1984, reprinted, Vintage, 1995.
Wideman, John Edgar, *Philadelphia Fire,* H. Holt, 1990.

PERIODICALS

American Scholar, autumn, 1967.
Booklist, August, 1994, p. 1987; September 15, 1994, p. 153.
Christian Science Monitor, July 10, 1992.
Journal of Negro History, January, 1963.
Kirkus Reviews, August 1, 1996, p. 1092.
Library Journal, March 1, 1994, p. 134; September 15, 1994, p. 85; July, 1996, p. 164.
Los Angeles Times, November 11, 1987.
Los Angeles Times Book Review, April 17, 1983; December 23, 1984; December 29, 1985; September 30, 1990; September 13, 1992; December 25, 1994, p. 2.
Michigan Quarterly Review, winter, 1975.
Negro Digest, May, 1963.
New Republic, July 13, 1992.
New Statesman, September 1, 1995, p. 34.
Newsweek, May 7, 1970.
New York Magazine, October 1, 1990.
New York Review of Books, May 11, 1995, p. 27.
New York Times, April 2, 1970; May 15, 1973; November 27, 1981; May 16, 1984; October 29, 1984; September 4, 1986; July 21, 1992.

New York Times Book Review, September 10, 1967; April 19, 1970; April 29, 1973; April 11, 1982; May 15, 1983; November 4, 1984; January 13, 1985; December 15, 1985; May 11, 1986; November 30, 1986; November 8, 1987; October 16, 1988; December 10, 1989; September 30, 1990; October 14, 1990; November 17, 1991; June 14, 1992; November 13, 1994, p. 11.

Publishers Weekly, August 12, 1996, p. 63.

Saturday Review, October 21, 1967; May 2, 1970.

Shenandoah, winter, 1974.

Tikkun, March-April, 1995, p. 80.

Time, October 1, 1990.

Times (London), December 6, 1984.

Times Literary Supplement, December 21, 1984; January 16, 1987; August 5, 1988; August 23, 1991.

Tribune Books (Chicago), December 23, 1984; November 29, 1987; October 28, 1990; November 24, 1991; October 23, 1994, p. 8.

Village Voice, October 25, 1994.

Washington Post, May 10, 1984; May 12, 1984.

Washington Post Book World, July 3, 1983; October 21, 1984; November 15, 1987; October 16, 1988; October 21, 1990.

Whole Earth Review, summer, 1995, p. 78.

*   *   *

WILLIAMS, Denis (Joseph Ivan) 1923-

PERSONAL: Born February 1, 1923, in Georgetown, Guyana; son of Joseph Alexander (a merchant) and Isabel (Adonis) Williams; married Catherine Hughes, 1949 (divorced, 1974); married Toni Dixon (a poultry farmer), August 21, 1975 (separated, 1982); children: (first marriage) Janice, Evelyn, Isabel, Charlotte; (second marriage) Miles, Morag, Everard, Rachael, Denis, Kibileri Wishart Williams. *Education:* Attended Camberwell School of Art, 1946-48; University of Guyana, M.A., 1979. *Politics:* None. *Religion:* Christian.

ADDRESSES: Home—13, Thorne's Dr., D'Urban Backlands, Botanic Gardens, Georgetown, Guyana. *Office*—Department of Culture, Ministry of Education, 15 Carifesta Ave., Georgetown, Guyana; and Walter Roth Museum of Anthropology, 65 Main St., P.O. Box 10187, Georgetown, Guyana. *Agent*—John Wolfers, 42 Russel Sq., London WC1, England.

CAREER: Central School of Art, London, England, lecturer in art, 1950-57; Khartoum School of Art, Khartoum, Sudan, lecturer in art, 1957-62; University of Ife, Ife, Nigeria, lecturer in African studies, 1962-66; University of Lagos, Lagos, Nigeria, lecturer in African studies, 1966-68; National History and Arts Council, Georgetown, Guyana, art consultant, 1968-74; Ministry of Education, Georgetown, director of art and department of culture, 1974—. Founder and director of Walter Roth Museum. Artist, exhibiting work at numerous art shows and in many one-man exhibitions. Visiting tutor at Slade School of Fine Art, University of London, 1950-52; visiting professor at Makerere University, 1966; visiting research scholar, Smithsonian Institution, 1980. Chairman of National Trust, Georgetown, 1978-88. Member of International Visitor Program, United States Information Agency, 1985.

MEMBER: National Commissions for the Acquisition, Preservation, Republication of Research Materials on Guyana.

AWARDS, HONORS: Second prize from *London Daily Express* "Artists under Thirty-five" competition, 1955; Golden Arrow of Achievement, government of Guyana, 1973; first prize in National Theatre's mural competition, 1976; awarded Cacique's Crown of Honour, 1989; D.Litt., University of West Indies, 1989; received numerous grants from University of Ife, International African Institute, University of Lagos, Smithsonian Institution, and UNESCO.

WRITINGS:

Other Leopards (novel), New Authors (London), 1963.

The Third Temptation (novel), Calder & Boyars (London), 1968.

Giglioli in Guyana, 1922-1972 (biography), National History and Arts Council (Georgetown, Guyana), 1970.

Image and Idea in the Arts of the Caribbean, National History and Arts Council, 1970.

Icon and Image: A Study of Sacred and Secular Forms of African Classical Art, New York University Press (New York), 1974.

(With others) *Contemporary Art in Guyana,* Bovell's Printery (Georgetown, Guyana), 1976.

The Amerindian Heritage, Walter Roth Museum of Anthropology (Georgetown, Guyana), 1984.

Habitat and Culture in Ancient Guyana, Edgar Mittelholzer Memorial Lectures, 1984.

Ancient Guyana, Guyana Department of Culture (Georgetown), 1985.

Pages in Guyanese Prehistory, Walter Roth Museum of Anthropology, 1988.

The Archaic of North-Western Guyana, History Society, University of Guyana (Turkeyen, Guyana), 1989.

Contributor to several books, including *Africa in the Nineteenth and Twentieth Centuries,* edited by Joseph C. Anene and Godfrey N. Brown, Thomas Nelson, 1966; *Sources of Yoruba History,* edited by S. O. Biobaku, Clarendon Press, 1973; and *Advances in World Archaeology,* Volume 4, Academic Press, 1985. Contributor to *The Dictionary of World Art,* Macmillan; contributor of numerous articles to African studies and anthropology journals, including *Africa: Journal of the International African Institute London, Lagos Notes and Records, Carifesta Forum, Archaeology and Anthropology,* and *Odu: University of Ife Journal of African Studies.* Editor of *Odu,* 1964, *Lagos Notes and Records,* 1967, and *Archaeology and Anthropology,* 1978—.

WORK IN PROGRESS: A novel, *The Sperm of God.*

SIDELIGHTS: Denis Williams is best known for his paintings and his work in archaeology and social anthropology. He has taught painting at several English schools and mounted exhibitions of his art in Paris and London. In the field of archaeology, he has devoted many years to the study of Amerindian remains and culture. His nonfiction titles include *Ancient Guyana, The Archaic of North-Western Guyana,* and *Image and Idea in the Arts of Guyana.* He is also the author of two novels, *Other Leopards* and *The Third Temptation.*

Other Leopards, published in 1963, is rated "a major contribution to the Caribbean literature of the 1960s" by Louis James, a contributor to the *Dictionary of Literary Biography.* The story is set in Sudan, a country in the transitional region between the African Sahara and the equatorial forests. At the time of the novel, Sudan is torn by political and religious tensions between Muslim and Christian groups. The protagonist, Lobo Lionel Froad, is a man of mixed African and European lineage. He searches for the key to his own identity, but without success. A "massa/slave relationship is intimated in his relationship with Hughie King, the English archaeologist for whom he works," said James. "He is in love with two women, the black Eve and the English Catherine. His personal relationships are as disastrous as his intellectual ones, and he is only able to express himself in violence. . . . At every point Froad finds himself an alien." At last,

Froad murderously attacks Hughie King, and flees naked to hide in a tree, "uncertain whether the approaching light is a pursuer or just the dawn."

James offered this assessment of the novel's significance: "In the years of widening political independence for the region, West Indian writers were seeking an identity, trapped, as many saw it, between the intellectual hegemony of Europe and the ancestral culture of Africa. Williams, writing out of his own experience, created in his protagonist Froad an archetype of this dilemma. Yet, at the same time, Williams's highly individual imagination created a work that undermined the very stereotype it invoked and that remains as immediate today as when it was first written."

Williams once told *CA:* "A Colonial artist or writer who has received his professional education in Britain and made his first home there is not likely easily to forget that experience. I find that in my own case the experience has proven not only formative, but to a degree even determinative. It seems to have shaped the entire course of my subsequent development. Thus, to me, it is impossible to imagine a career built other than upon the solid foundation of early recognition and acceptance which was accorded to me during the first half of the fifties in London. Paradoxically, however, as Fanon has so perceptively shown, given the circumstances and the day, acceptance on this level was in fact far the most unacceptable, indeed probably the most humiliating, of choices open to the Colonial artist.

"This may explain the rapid and apparently permanent darkness which followed the explosion of Caribbean writing in Britain during the time I was there. Colonial territories were all becoming independent, which was quickly to render the Colonial artist or writer obsolete; for just as national independence seems to have pulled the rug from under the feet of the Colonial writer, new national writers were arising in English- and French-speaking West Africa and in the Caribbean.

"By this time I was myself in Africa writing Other Leopards, or trying to resolve some of the problems of identity which provided the theme for that novel. By the time of its completion it was becoming evident that even though the new African literature was being written all around me, and by familiar hands, Africa did not represent the uttermost swing of the pendulum in my reaction from an unwilling acceptance in Europe. Indeed, the African experience tended to reveal to me deeply ingrained attitudes to various aspects of European art, life, and literature that had remained so far undetected. Odd as it may seem, it was very easy to write *The Third Temptation* (in an experimental French idiom) simultaneously with my study of African classical art, which in itself represented an intellectual search for African roots.

"I have since returned to Guyana, and see clearly that such a thing could never take place against my rediscovered background. However, if this means that the pendulum has at last reached its ultimate distance of travel, it is no comfort to realize that my first true Caribbean novel, *The Sperm of God,* has remained unfinished now for over thirteen years."

BIOGRAPHICAL/CRITICAL SOURCES:

BOOKS

Cartey, Wilfred, *Whispers from the Caribbean: I Going Away, I Going Home,* University of California, Los Angeles, 1991.

Dathorne, O. R., *The Black Mind: A History of African Literature,* University of Minnesota Press, 1974.

Dictionary of Literary Biography, Volume 117: Twentieth-Century Caribbean and Black African Writers, First Series, Gale, 1992.

Fox, C. J., and Walter Michel, *Wyndham Lewis on Art: Collected Writings, 1913-1956,* Thames & Hudson, 1969.

Gilkes, Michael, *The West Indian Novel,* Twayne, 1981, pp. 142-44.

James, Louis, editor, *The Islands in Between,* Oxford University Press (London), 1968, pp. 7-10.

Moore, Gerald, *The Chosen Tongue,* Longman, 1969.

Ramchand, Kenneth, *The West Indian Novel and Its Background,* Faber, 1974.

PERIODICALS

African Literature Today, Volume 14, 1984, pp. 118-26.

Daily Express, April 28, 1955.

Geo, May, 1981.

New World: Guyana Independence Issue, 1966, pp. 94-104.

Science Digest, November, 1981.

Science News, January 24, 1981.

Transition, Volume 3, number 10, 1963, pp. 57-58.

Twentieth Century Studies, Volume 10, 1973, pp. 37-59.

WILLIAMS, Greg(ory) Alan

PERSONAL: Grew up in Des Moines, IA.

ADDRESSES: Agent—c/o Doubleday, 1540 Broadway, New York, NY, 10036-4094.

CAREER: Actor and author. Actor in films, including *Above the Law,* Warner Bros., 1988; *Major League,* Mirage/Morgan Creek Productions, 1989; *The Package,* Orion, 1989; *In the Line of Fire,* Columbia, 1993; *Stag,* Lions Gate Films Inc./Rampage Entertainment, 1997.

Actor in TV movies: *Howard Beach: Making a Case for Murder,* World International Network/Brittcadia Productions, 1989; *No One Would Tell,* Frank & Bob Films II, 1996; *Project: ALF,* UFA/Alien Productions, 1996; *Dying to Belong,* 1997. Actor in TV series: *Baywatch,* 1989, and *Baywatch Nights,* All American Television Productions, 1995.

WRITINGS:

A Gathering of Heroes: Reflections on Rage and Responsibility: A Memoir of the Los Angeles Riots, Academy Chicago Publishers (Chicago), 1994.

Boys to Men: Maps for the Journey (essays), Doubleday (New York City), 1996.

SIDELIGHTS: Greg Alan Williams is an actor who has been featured on the television shows *Baywatch,* a popular drama about California lifeguards, and *Baywatch Nights,* a mystery show wherein two of the *Baywatch* lifeguards work as private detectives. In addition to being an actor, Williams is a published writer.

Books by Williams include *A Gathering of Heroes,* which recalls the Los Angeles riots, and *Boys to Men: Maps for the Journey,* which features essays concerning the realization of self-fulfillment. A *Publishers Weekly* reviewer said of *Boys to Men*: "Williams offers a special message to black youths concerned that there may be only one way to be authentically black."

BIOGRAPHICAL/CRITICAL SOURCES:

PERIODICALS

Entertainment Weekly, November 24, 1995, pp. 85-86.

Publishers Weekly, December 30, 1996, p. 50.*

WILLIAMS, John A(lfred) 1925-
(J. Dennis Gregory, a pseudonym)

PERSONAL: Born December 5, 1925, in Jackson, MS; son of John Henry (a laborer) and Ola Mae Williams; married Carolyn Clopton, 1947 (divorced); married Lorrain Isaac, October 5, 1965; children: (first marriage) Gregory D., Dennis A.; (second marriage) Adam J. *Education:* Syracuse University, A.B., 1950, graduate study, 1950-51. *Avocational interests:* Travel (has visited Belgium, Cameroon, the Caribbean, Congo, Cyprus, Denmark, Egypt, Ethiopia, France, Germany, Ghana, Great Britain, Greece, Israel, Italy, Mexico, the Netherlands, Nigeria, Portugal, Senegal, Spain, the Sudan, and Sweden), tennis.

*ADDRESSES: Home—*693 Forest Ave., Teaneck, NJ 07666.

CAREER: Writer. Case worker for county welfare department, Syracuse, NY; public relations department, Doug Johnson Associates, Syracuse, NY, 1952-54, and later with Arthur P. Jacobs Co.; Columbia Broadcasting System (CBS), Hollywood, CA, and New York City, staff member for radio and television special events programs, 1954-55; Comet Press Books, New York City, publicity director, 1955-56; *Negro Market Newsletter,* New York City, publisher and editor, 1956-57; Abelard-Schuman Ltd., New York City, assistant to the publisher, 1957-58; American Committee on Africa, New York City, director of information, 1958; European correspondent for *Ebony* and *Jet* (magazines), New York City, 1958-59; Station WOV, New York, special events announcer, 1959; *Newsweek,* New York City, correspondent in Africa, 1964-65. Lecturer in writing, City College of the City University of New York, 1968; lecturer in Afro-American literature, College of the Virgin Islands, summer, 1968; guest writer at Sarah Lawrence College, Bronxville, NY, 1972; regents lecturer, University of California, Santa Barbara, 1972; distinguished professor of English, La Guardia Community College, 1973-74, 1974-75; visiting professor, University of Hawaii, summer, 1974, and Boston University, 1978-79; Rutgers University, professor of English, 1979-90, Paul Robeson Professor of English, 1990—; Exxon Professor of English, New York University, 1986-87; Band Center Fellow, Bard College, 1994-95. National Education Television, narrator and co-producer of programs, 1965-66, interviewer on *Newsfront* program, 1968. *Military service:* U.S. Naval Reserve, pharmacist's mate, active duty, 1943-46; served in the Pacific.

MEMBER: Authors Guild, Authors League of America, PEN, Rabinowitz Foundation (member of board of directors), Coordinating Council of Literary Magazines (chair, 1984), New York State Council on the Arts (member of board of directors).

AWARDS, HONORS: Award from National Institute of Arts and Letters, 1962; centennial medal for outstanding achievement from Syracuse University, 1970; Lindback Award, Rutgers University, 1982, for distinguished teaching; American Book Award, Before Columbus Foundation, 1983, for *!Click Song;* LL.D. from Southeastern Massachusetts University, 1978, and from Syracuse University, 1995.

WRITINGS:

NOVELS

The Angry Ones, Ace Books (New York City), 1960, published as *One for New York,* Chatham Bookseller (Madison, NJ), 1975.
Night Song, Farrar, Straus (New York City), 1961.
Sissie, Farrar, Straus, 1963, published in England as *Journey out of Anger,* Eyre & Spottiswoode (London), 1965.
The Man Who Cried I Am, Little, Brown (Boston), 1967.
Sons of Darkness, Sons of Light: A Novel of Some Probability, Little, Brown, 1969.
Captain Blackman, Doubleday (New York City), 1972.
Mothersill and the Foxes, Doubleday, 1975.
The Junior Bachelor Society, Doubleday, 1976.
!Click Song, Houghton (Boston), 1982.
The Berhama Account, New Horizons Press (Chico, CA), 1985.
Jacob's Ladder, Thunder's Mouth (New York City), 1987.
Clifford's Blues, Coffee House, 1999.

NONFICTION

Africa: Her History, Lands, and People, Cooper Square (Totowa, NJ), 1962, 3rd edition, 1969.
(Under pseudonym J. Dennis Gregory, with Harry J. Anslinger) *The Protectors: The Heroic Story of the Narcotics Agents, Citizens and Officials in Their Unending, Unsung Battles against Organized Crime in America and Abroad,* Farrar, Straus, 1964.
This Is My Country Too, New American Library (New York City), 1965.

The Most Native of Sons: A Biography of Richard Wright, Doubleday, 1970.

The King God Didn't Save: Reflections on the Life and Death of Martin Luther King, Jr., Coward (New York City), 1970.

Flashbacks: A Twenty-Year Diary of Article Writing, Doubleday, 1973.

(Author of introduction) *Romare Bearden,* Abrams (New York City), 1973.

Minorities in the City, Harper (New York City), 1975.

(With son, Dennis A. Williams) *If I Stop I'll Die: The Comedy and Tragedy of Richard Pryor,* Thunder's Mouth, 1991.

EDITOR

The Angry Black (anthology), Lancer Books, 1962, 2nd edition published as *Beyond the Angry Black,* Cooper Square, 1966.

(With Charles F. Harris) *Amistad I,* Knopf (New York City), 1970.

(With Harris) *Amistad II,* Knopf, 1971.

Yardbird No. 1, Ishmael Reed (Berkeley, CA), 1979.

The McGraw-Hill Introduction to Literature, McGraw (New York City), 1985, 2nd edition, 1994.

Bridges: Literature across Cultures, McGraw, 1994.

Approaches to Literature, McGraw, 1994.

OTHER

The History of the Negro People: Omowale—The Child Returns Home (television script; filmed in Nigeria), National Education Television, 1965.

The Creative Person: Henry Roth (television script; filmed in Spain), National Education Television, 1966.

Sweet Love, Bitter (screenplay), Film 2 Associates, 1967.

Last Flight from Ambo Ber (play; first produced in Boston, 1981), American Association of Ethiopian Jews, 1984.

Contributor to numerous anthologies and of numerous stories and articles to newspapers and magazines, including *Negro Digest, Yardbird, Holiday, Saturday Review, Ebony, Essence, Emerge, Nation,* and *New York.* Member of editorial board, *Audience,* 1970-72; contributing editor, *American Journal,* 1972— .

ADAPTATIONS: The Junior Bachelor Society was adapted for television by National Broadcasting Corp. (NBC) as *Sophisticated Gents* in 1981.

SIDELIGHTS: John A. Williams, says *Dictionary of Literary Biography* contributor James L. de Jongh, is "arguably the finest Afro-American novelist of his generation," although he "has been denied the full degree of support and acceptance some critics think his work deserves." Part of the reason for this, Williams believes, may be because of racial discrimination. In 1961, for instance, he was awarded a grant to the American Academy in Rome based on the quality of his novel *Night Song,* but the grant was rescinded by the awarding panel. Williams felt that this happened because he was black and because of rumors that he was about to marry a white woman, which he later did. However, Alan Dugan, "the poet who eventually was awarded the prize, courageously made public the issue at the presentation ceremony," explains Jeffrey Helterman, another *Dictionary of Literary Biography* commentator, and the resulting scandal caused the American Academy to discontinue its prize for literature for a time.

Williams's first three novels trace the problems facing blacks in a white society. The books *The Angry Ones, Night Song,* and *Sissie* relate attempts by black men and women to come to terms with a nation that discriminates against them. In *The Angry Ones,* for instance, the protagonist Steve Hill "struggles with various kinds of racial prejudice in housing and employment, but the focus [of the novel] is on his growing realization of the way his employers at Rocket Press destroy the dreams of would-be authors," explains Helterman. Like Williams himself, Hill perceives that he is being exploited by a white-dominated industry in which a black artist has no place. Williams has said that "the plain, unspoken fact is that the Negro is superfluous in American society as it is now constructed. Society must undergo a restructuring to make a place for him, or it will be called upon to get rid of him."

The Man Who Cried I Am, a novel that brought Williams international recognition, further explores the exploitation of blacks by a white society. The protagonist, Max Reddick, is a black writer living in Europe, as did Williams for a time. Max is married to a Dutch woman, and he is dying of colon cancer. His chief literary rival and mentor is one Harry Ames, a fellow black author, but one who "packages racial anger and sells it in his books," according to Helterman. While in Paris to attend Harry's funeral Max learns that Harry has in fact been murdered because he had uncovered a plot by the Western nations to prevent the unification of black Africa. Max himself unearths another conspiracy: America's genocidal solution to the race problem—code-named "King Alfred"—which closely resembles Hitler's "Final Solution." Finally Max, and a Malcolm X-like figure called Minister Q, are captured by the opposing forces and put to death. *The Man Who Cried I Am* escapes the protest novel format of most black literature by putting the situation on an epic scale. Jerry H. Bryant describes the book in *Critique: Studies in Modern Fiction* as "Williams's adaptation of the rhetoric of black power to his own needs as a novelist," calling it "in a sense Williams's *Huckleberry Finn.* It reflects his deep skepticism over the capacity of America to live up to its professed ideals, and a development of deep pessimism about whites in particular and man in general." "What purpose does the King Alfred portion of the novel serve?" asks Robert E. Fleming in *Contemporary Literature.* "In one sense, black people have been systematically killed off in the United States since their first introduction to its shores. Malnutrition, disease, poverty, psychological conditioning, and spiritual starvation have been the tools, rather than military operations and gas chambers, but the result has often been the same. King Alfred is not only a prophetic warning of what might happen here but a fictional metaphor for what has been happening and is happening still," he concludes.

The Man Who Cried I Am includes a character named Paul Durrell, who is obviously based on civil rights leader Martin Luther King. Durrell is presented in a negative light, and Williams's unfavorable opinion of Durrell's real-life counterpart became all the more evident in his 1970 nonfiction book, *The King God Didn't Save: Reflections on the Life and Death of Martin Luther King, Jr.* In this unflattering biography, Williams portrays Dr. King as a man who allowed himself to be manipulated by high-ranking federal agents and as a leader who was badly out of touch with the community he influenced so strongly.

In addition to *The King God Didn't Save,* Williams published another biography in 1970. Intended for reading by a young adult audience, *The Most Native of Sons: A Biography of Richard Wright* relates the life of the radical black author whose work profoundly influenced Williams. Williams states in his *Contemporary Authors Autobiography Series* entry that he considers *!Click Song* to be his "very best novel." Like *The Man Who Cried I Am,* the book details the careers of two writers, in this case Paul Cummings and Cato Caldwell Douglass, friends who attended school on the GI Bill after World War II. Cummings is Jewish; it is his reaffirmation of his

Jewishness that provides the theme for his novels, and his suicide opens the book. Douglass, on the other hand, is black; his problem, as Jervis Anderson indicates in the *New York Times Book Review,* is to overcome racism in the publishing industry. *Chicago Tribune Book World* contributor Seymour Krim compares the two characters: Cummings "was a more successful competitor, a novelist who had won a National Book Award and all the attention that goes with it, while Cato was forced to lecture for peanuts before Black Studies groups. A further irony is the fact that Cummings was a 'passed' Jew who had only recently declared his real name, Kaminsky, in an effort to purge himself. Purge or not, his writing has gone downhill since his born-again declaration, while his earnings have gone up." Roy Hoffman, writing for the *Washington Post Book World* points out, however, that "as Paul's career skyrockets, his private life goes to shambles. As Cato's career runs into brick walls, his personal life grows ever more fulfilled, ever more radiant."

"*!Click Song* is at least the equal of Williams's other masterpiece, *The Man Who Cried I Am,*" states de Jongh. "The emotional power, the fluid structuring of time, the resonant synthesis of fiction and history are similar. But the novelist's mastery is greater, for Williams's technique here is seamless and invisible," the reviewer concludes. Other critics also celebrate Williams's work; says Krim, "Unlike a James Baldwin or an Amiri Baraka, Williams is primarily a storyteller, which is what makes the reality of Black Rage become something other than a polemic in his hands. . . . Before [Cato Douglass's] odyssey is ended, we know in our bones what it is like to be a gifted black survivor in America today; we change skins as we read, so to speak, and the journey of living inside another is so intense that no white reader will ever again be able to plead ignorance." Although Williams's writing explores racial themes, he has stated that he dislikes being categorized as a black author. In his view, that label only facilitates the segregation of black writers and their work from the rest of American literature.

In an interview with Shirley Horner, published in the *New York Times,* he confessed that he was "pessimistic" about the possibility that racial tensions in modern American society could ever be resolved. He added, however, that "it's the kind of pessimism that would be delighted to be proved wrong, absolutely wrong." Commenting specifically on relations between blacks and Jews, he stated: "I don't think those days of black-Jewish cooperation were ever that glorious; it's nice to think that they were. . . . Blacks and Jews in 1993 are even less willing to learn from each other, so few people try." He explained that he and his wife, who is Jewish, had moved to Teaneck, New Jersey, because they thought that "the town would not be inhospitable to a mixed marriage." Asked if they had suffered many slights because of their marriage, Williams acknowledged: "We've had our share, as we expected we would. I'm sure that there are lots of things that go on because of our marriage that I'm totally unaware of. . . . In such a marriage, you both have to be strong in ways that are sometimes not very visible. A sense of humor helps."

BIOGRAPHICAL/CRITICAL SOURCES:

BOOKS

Cash, Earl A., *Evolution of a Black Writer,* Third Press, 1975.
Contemporary Authors Autobiography Series, Volume 3, Gale (Detroit), 1986.
Contemporary Literary Criticism, Gale, Volume 5, 1976, Volume 13, 1980.
Dictionary of Literary Biography, Gale, Volume 2: *American Novelists since World War II,* 1978, Volume 33: *Afro-American Fiction Writers after 1955,* 1984.
Gayle, Addison, Jr., editor, *Black Expression: Essays by and about Black Americans in the Creative Arts,* Weybright and Talley, 1969, pp. 365-72.
Muller, Gilbert H., *John A. Williams,* Twayne (New York City), 1984.
O'Brien, John, editor, *Interviews with Black Writers,* Liveright (New York City), 1973, pp. 225-43.

PERIODICALS

Black Literature Forum, spring/summer, 1987, pp. 25-42.
Black World, June, 1975.
Bloomsbury Review, January/February, 1988, p. 10; October/November, 1991, p. 13.
Chicago Tribune Book World, April 18, 1982; November 17, 1985.
Contemporary Literature, spring, 1973.
Critic, April, 1963.
Critique: Studies in Modern Fiction, Volume 16, number 3, 1975.
Detroit News, June 6, 1982.
Library Journal, November 1, 1961; September 15, 1967.
Los Angeles Times Book Review, May 9, 1982; November 29, 1987.

Nation, September 18, 1976.
New Yorker, August 16, 1976.
New York Times, June 13, 1993.
New York Times Book Review, May 6, 1973, pp. 34-35; July 11, 1976; April 4, 1982; October 18, 1987; November 15, 1987.
Prairie Schooner, spring, 1976.
Publishers Weekly, November 11, 1974; February 1, 1999, p. 77.
Studies in Black Literature, spring, 1972, pp. 24-32.
Time, April 12, 1982.
Washington Post Book World, March 23, 1982; October 4, 1987.*

*　　*　　*

WILLIAMS, Sherley Anne 1944-

PERSONAL: Born August 25, 1944, in Bakersfield, CA; daughter of Jessee Winson (a laborer) and Lelia Marie (maiden name, Siler) Williams; children: John Malcolm. *Education:* Fresno State College (now California State University, Fresno), B.A., 1966; Howard University, graduate study, 1966-1967; Brown University, M.A., 1972.

ADDRESSES: Office—Department of Literature, University of California, San Diego, La Jolla, CA 92093.

CAREER: Fresno State College (now California State University, Fresno), Fresno, CA, co-director of tutorial program, 1965-66, lecturer in ethnic studies, 1969-70; Miles College, Atlanta, GA, administrative internal assistant to president, 1967-68; affiliated with Systems Development Corporation, Santa Monica, CA, 1968-69; Federal City College, Washington, DC, consultant in curriculum development and community educator, 1970-72; California State University, Fresno, associate professor of English, 1972-73; University of California, San Diego, La Jolla, assistant professor, 1973-76, associate professor, 1976-1982, professor of Afro-American literature, 1982—, department chairman, 1976-1982.

MEMBER: Poetry Society of America, Modern Language Association.

AWARDS, HONORS: National Book Award nomination, 1976, for *The Peacock Poems;* Fulbright lecturer, University of Ghana, 1984; *Dessa Rose* was named a notable book in 1986 by the *New York Times; Working Cotton* was named a Ralph Caldecott Medal honor book by the American Library Association, 1993.

WRITINGS:

Give Birth to Brightness: A Thematic Study in Neo-Black Literature, Dial, 1972.
The Peacock Poems, Wesleyan University Press, 1975.
Some One Sweet Angel Chile (poems), Morrow, 1982.
Dessa Rose: A Riveting Story of the South During Slavery, Morrow, 1986.
Working Cotton, illustrated by Carole Byard, Harcourt, 1992.
Girls Together, illustrated by Varnette P. Honeywood, Harcourt, 1997.

Also author of *Letters from a New England Negro,* a full-length drama produced in 1982; *Ours to Make,* 1973, and *The Sherley Williams Special,* 1977, both for television; and *Traveling Sunshine Good Time Show and Celebration,* 1973, a stageshow. Author of introduction to *Their Eyes Were Watching God,* University of Illinois, 1991.

SIDELIGHTS: American critic, poet, novelist, and educator Sherley Anne Williams during her early years may have seemed an unlikely candidate for fame. As a girl, she lived in a Fresno, California, housing project and worked with her parents in fruit and cotton fields. Her father died of tuberculosis before her eighth birthday, and her mother, a practical woman from rural Texas who had tried to discourage Williams's early interest in reading, died when Williams was just sixteen. "My friends were what you would call juvenile delinquents. Most of them didn't finish school," and her future, she told Mona Gable in a *Los Angeles Times Magazine* interview, amounted to having children. But a series of events—including guidance from a science teacher and the discovery of Richard Wright's *Black Boy,* Ertha Kitt's *Thursday's Child,* and other books by black authors about their lives—stimulated her desire to write. "It was largely through these autobiographies I was able to take heart in my life," she told Gable.

Williams studied at Fresno State, Fisk, Howard, and Brown Universities before deciding to become a writer and to support herself by teaching. Now a professor of Afro-American literature at the University of California, San Diego, Williams has become well-known for her books of criticism, poetry, and fiction, and is "living an extraordinary life," remarks

poet Philip Levine, her mentor at Fresno State. The publication of *Give Birth to Brightness: A Thematic Study in Neo-Black Literature* in 1975 encouraged Williams to pursue a writing career. The essays are, she says in the book's dedication, "a public statement of how I feel about the treasure one small aspect of Blackness in America," and the collection is dedicated to her son Malcolm. *Give Birth to Brightness* claims that "a shared racial memory and a common future" are the foundations of the new black literature, reports Lillie P. Howard in the *Dictionary of Literary Biography: Afro-American Poets since 1955.* Howard relates that the author's aim is to create "a new tradition built on a synthesis of black oral traditions [such as the blues] and Western literate forms."

Different from both the Harlem Renaissance (in which black writers spoke to white audiences) and from the literary protests of the 1960's, the new writers "speak directly *to* Black people *about themselves*" in order to move them toward self-knowledge and collective freedom"; Williams states this is achieved in art that presents a "liberating vision" of black life, past and future, one that goes beyond protest. Reviewers found some fault with *Give Birth to Brightness,* but it was generally well received. Writing in the *New York Times,* Mel Watkins notes, "Miss Williams persuasively demonstrates the commonality of viewpoint that she asserts characterizes neo-black fiction. Moreover, she evokes a real sense of what the street life is about." He takes issue with her portrayal of the street rebel as a symbolic hero, calling it a 'dangerous and highly romantic idea' which may not be shared by all blacks, since they, too, may be victimized by streetmen. "Criticisms such as this notwithstanding," he adds, "Miss Williams has written a readable and informative survey of black literature. In using both her knowledge of Western literature and her understanding of black life, she provides insight into the sadly neglected area of reversed values that plays such a significant role in much black literature." Howard comments, "As a first major publication, *Give Birth to Brightness* is impressive."

The Peacock Poems, her second published book, was also critically acclaimed. The volume of autobiographical poems, some about her early family life and the balance about her feelings as a single mother, drew a National Book Award nomination for poetry in 1976. Expressing herself in blues poetry, "Williams fingers the 'jagged' edges of pain that is both hers and ours," Howard observes. She says the poems also assert and demonstrate "the therapeutic regenerative powers" of traditional black music.

Blues shapes the poems in *Some One Sweet Angel Chile,* as well. One of its sections looks at the life of blues singer Bessie Smith. "Singing the blues gave Smith a temporary lifeline which sustained her through all her sufferings," Howard relates. Other sections depict experiences of black women after the Civil War and in more recent times. Williams explains the focus of her early work in an interview with Claudia Tate, published in *Black Women Writers at Work:* "I wanted specifically to write about lower-income black women. . . . We were missing these stories of black women's struggles and their real triumphs. . . . I wanted to write about them because they had in a very real sense educated me and given me what it was going to take to get me through the world."

Two economically disadvantaged women tell their stories in Williams's first novel, *Dessa Rose.* The book begins with the memories of its title character, a whip-scarred, pregnant slave woman in jail for violent crimes against white men. Dessa recalls her life on the plantation with her love, a life that ended when he was killed by their master. In turn, Dessa had killed the master, was arrested and chained to other slaves in a coffle, from which she escaped, again by violence to her white captors. Tracked down and sentenced to die after the birth of her child, who would be valuable property to the whites, Dessa is interviewed by Adam Nehemiah, a white author who expects to become famous when he publishes the analysis of her crimes. When asked why she kills white men, Dessa replies evenly, "Cause I can." After Dessa escapes again, Rufel Sutton, a white woman in economic distress, provides refuge for her and other runaway slaves simply because she can. Marcia Gillespie, contributing editor to *Ms.* magazine, notes that Rufel breastfeeds Dessa's newborn infant for the same reason, and because the alternative is too severe for her to consider. "As a result of this extraordinary bond, the two women achieve one of the most intricate and ambivalent relationships in contemporary fiction," Elaine Kendall remarks in the *Los Angeles Times.* In a scam designed by the runaways, Rufel earns money for a new life, selling them as slaves, waiting for them to escape, and selling them again. All goes well until the end, when Dessa is arrested by the enraged Nehemiah, but the two women elude his grasp with the aid of a female officer who is sent to verify Dessa's identity by examining her scars. When the group disbands, Rufel goes off to prosperity in the East; the blacks go west to the hardships of prejudice on the frontier. "Thus has Sherley Anne Williams breathed wonderful life into the bare bones of the

past," believes *New York Times* reviewer Christopher Lehmann-Haupt. "And thus does she resolve more issues than are dreamed of in most history textbooks."

Dessa Rose, Gable writes, "was an instant critical success. There were favorable reviews in the *Washington Post,* the *Boston Globe,Ms.* and a number of other publications. Writing in the *New York Times,* David Bradley called it 'artistically brilliant, emotionally affecting and totally unforgettable.'" As "one of the biggest hits of the literary season," the book commanded a third printing only months after its debut, as well as six figure amounts for paperback and film rights—all unusual for a first novel, Gable reports. "What makes *Dessa Rose* such an unlikely commercial hit and what prompted the *New York Times* to give it two glowing reviews and place it for two weeks on its influential recommended reading list is the book's unflinchingly realistic portrayal of American slavery," Gable suggests. For instance, the sexual exploitation of black men and women that was common to the condition of slavery is fully drawn here, say reviewers, in "a plot dealing with all the [sadism and lust] that Harriet Beecher Stowe [author of *Uncle Tom's Cabin*] did not dare to mention," as London *Times* reviewer Andrew Sinclair phrases it. Furthermore, notes Jane Perliz in the *New York Times Book Review,* Williams intends Dessa's rebellion, based on an actual uprising led by a pregnant slave in 1829, to refute the myth that black women were the passive collaborators of abusive masters under the system.

These realities, not apparent in *Gone with the Wind,* were also absent from William Styron's *Confessions of Nat Turner,* a novel about a slave revolt leader that enraged Williams because it suggested that Turner's rebellion was motivated by his lust for a white woman. With *Dessa Rose,* "Williams not only wanted to challenge Styron's . . . view of slavery, which she believes dismissed the brutal social and political conditions that led to Turners's revolt, but to show up the 'hypocrisy of the literary tradition' by detailing the strengths of black culture," Gable relates. That resilience, Williams told her, was the ability to build strong family relations despite slavery's attack on the black family. Williams told Gable she also hoped the novel would "heal some wounds" made by racism left in the wake of slavery. In her view, she explained, fiction is one way to conceive of "the impossible, . . . and putting these women together, I could come to understand something not only about their experience of slavery but about them as women, and imagine the basis for some kind of honest rapprochement between black and white women."

Michele Wallace, writing in the *Women's Review of Books,* notes, for example, the change in Dessa's feelings for Rufel when she realizes that white women, too, are raped by white men. Wallace adds, "*Dessa Rose* reveals both the uniformities and the idiosyncracies of 'woman's place,' while making imaginative and unprecedented use of its male characters as well. Sherley Anne Williams's accomplishment is that she take the reader someplace we're not accustomed to going, some place historical scholarship may never take us, into the world that black and white women shared in the antebellum South. But what excites me the most, finally, about this novel is its definition of friendship as the collective struggle that ultimately transcends the stumbling-blocks of race and class.

In 1992, Williams published her first children's book, *Working Cotton.* Based on the text of two verses from the 1975 collection *Peacock Poems,* this poignant picture book tells the story of Shelan, a child laborer isolated by the endless job of picking cotton with her family in the California fields. The story, which was inspired by the author's own childhood experiences, presents "a way of life concentrated in a single day," comments Hazel Rochman in *Booklist.* Skillfully illustrated with impressionist acrylics by Carole Byard, *Working Cotton* garnered rave reviews for portraying a girl robbed of her youth—of the usual girlhood play and friendships—but rich in dignity as she lives out this early chapter of her unusually hard life.

BIOGRAPHICAL/CRITICAL SOURCES:

BOOKS

Contemporary Literary Criticism, Volume 89, Gale, 1995.
Dictionary of Literary Biography, Volume 41: *Afro-American Poets since 1955,* Gale, 1985.
Fisher, Dexter and Robert B. Stepto, editors, *Afro-American Literature: The Reconstruction of Instruction,* Modern Language Association of America, 1979.
Henderson, Stephen, *Understanding the New Black Poetry,* Morrow, 1973.
Tate, Claudia, editor, *Black Woman Writers at Work,* Continuum, 1983.
Williams, Sherley Anne, *Give Birth to Brightness: A Thematic Study in Neo-Black Literature,* Dial, 1972.

PERIODICALS

African American Review, fall, 1993, p. 365; summer, 1994, p. 223.

Black American Literature Forum, fall, 1986.
Black Scholar, March, 1981.
Black World, June, 1976.
Booklist, September 1, 1992, p. 55.
Commonweal, December 3, 1982.
Essence, August, 1986; December, 1986.
Los Angeles Times, July 23, 1986; August 8, 1986.
Los Angeles Times Book Review, July 4, 1982.
Los Angeles Times Magazine, December 7, 1986.
Ms., September, 1986.
National Catholic Reporter, December 23, 1994, p. 9.
New Statesman, September 16, 1994, p. 24.
New Yorker, September 8, 1986.
New York Times, July 8, 1982; July 12, 1986.
Publishers Weekly, February 19, 1982; May 30, 1986; October 3, 1986; July 6, 1992, p. 55.
Times (London), March 19, 1987.
Virginia Quarterly Review, spring, 1976.
Washington Post Book World, August 3, 1986.
Women's Review of Books, Volume 4 number 1, October, 1986.*

*   *   *

WILSON, August 1945-

PERSONAL: Born Frederick August Kittel, in 1945, in Pittsburgh, PA; son of Frederick August (a baker) and Daisy (a cleaning woman; maiden name, Wilson) Kittel, and stepfather, David Bedford; married second wife, Judy Oliver (a social worker), 1981 (marriage ended); married Constanza Romero (a costume designer); children: (first marriage) Sakina Ansari.

ADDRESSES: Office—c/o John Breglio, Paul Weiss Rifkind Wharton & Garrison, 1285 Avenue of the Americas, New York, NY 10019.

CAREER: Writer. Cofounder (with Rob Penny), scriptwriter, and director of Black Horizons on the Hill (theatre company) Pittsburgh, PA, 1968-78; scriptwriter for Science Museum of Minnesota, St. Paul, 1979.

AWARDS, HONORS: Award for best play of 1984-85 from New York Drama Critics Circle, 1985, Antoinette Perry ("Tony") Award nomination from League of New York Theatres and Producers, 1985, and Whiting Writers' Award from the Whiting Foundation, 1986, all for *Ma Rainey's Black Bottom;* Outstanding Play Award from American Theatre Critics, 1986, Drama Desk Outstanding New Play Award, 1986,

New York Drama Critics Circle Best Play Award, 1986, Pulitzer Prize for drama, Antoinette Perry Award for best play, and award for best Broadway play from Outer Critics Circle, all 1987, all for *Fences;* John Gassner Award for best American playwright from Outer Critics Circle, 1987; named Artist of the Year by *Chicago Tribune,* 1987; Literary Lion Award from New York Public Library, 1988; New York Drama Critics Circle Best Play award, and Antoinette Perry Award nomination for best play, both 1988, both for *Joe Turner's Come and Gone;* Drama Desk Outstanding New Play Award, New York Drama Critics Circle Best Play Award, Antoinette Perry Award for Best Play, American Theatre Critics Outstanding Play Award, and Pulitzer Prize for drama, all 1990, all for *The Piano Lesson;* Black Filmmakers Hall of Fame Award, 1991; Antoinette Perry Award nomination for best play, and American Theatre Critics' Association Award, both 1992, both for *Two Trains Running;* Clarence Muse Award, 1992; recipient of Bush and Guggenheim Foundation fellowships.

WRITINGS:

Jitney (two-act play), first produced in Pittsburgh, PA, at the Allegheny Repertory Theatre, 1982.

Ma Rainey's Black Bottom (play; first produced in New Haven, CT, at the Yale Repertory Theatre, 1984; produced on Broadway at the Cort Theatre, October, 1984; also see below), New American Library (New York City), 1985.

Fences (play; first produced at Yale Repertory Theatre, 1985; produced on Broadway at 46th Street Theatre, March, 1987; also see below), New American Library, 1986.

Joe Turner's Come and Gone (play; first produced at Yale Repertory Theatre, 1986; produced on Broadway at Barrymore Theatre, March, 1988; also see below), New American Library, 1988.

The Piano Lesson (play; first produced in New Haven at the Yale Repertory Theatre, 1987; produced on Broadway at Walter Kerr Theatre, 1990; also see below), New American Library, 1990.

(And author of preface) *August Wilson: Three Plays* (contains *Ma Rainey's Black Bottom, Fences,* and *Joe Turner's Come and Gone*), afterword by Paul C. Harrison, University of Pittsburgh Press (Pittsburgh), 1991.

Two Trains Running (first produced at Yale Repertory Theatre, 1990, produced at Walter Kerr Theatre, 1992), New American Library/Dutton, 1993.

Seven Guitars (first produced in Chicago at Goodman Theatre, 1995), Dutton, 1996.

The Piano Lesson (teleplay; adapted from his play), "Hallmark Hall of Fame," CBS-TV, 1995.

Also author of the plays *The Homecoming,* 1979, *The Coldest Day of the Year,* 1979, *Fullerton Street,* 1980, *Black Bart and the Sacred Hills,* 1981, and *The Mill Hand's Lunch Bucket,* 1983. Author of the book for a stage musical about jazz musician Jelly Roll Morton. Work represented in *A Game of Passion: The NFL Literary Companion,* Turner, 1994, *Selected from Contemporary American Plays,* 1990, and *The Poetry of Blackamerica,* Adoff. Contributor to periodicals, including *Black Lines* and *Connection.*

WORK IN PROGRESS: A screenplay adaptation of *Fences.*

SIDELIGHTS: August Wilson has been hailed since the mid-1980s as an important talent in the American theatre. He spent his childhood in poverty in Pittsburgh, Pennsylvania, where he lived with his parents and five siblings. Though he grew up in a poor family, Wilson felt that his parents withheld knowledge of even greater hardships they had endured. "My generation of blacks knew very little about the past of our parents," he told the *New York Times* in 1984. "They shielded us from the indignities they suffered." Wilson's goal is to illuminate that shadowy past with a series of plays, each set in a different decade, that focus on black issues. *Ma Rainey's Black Bottom, Fences, Joe Turner's Come and Gone, The Piano Lesson, Two Trains Running,* and *Seven Guitars* are part of this ambitious project.

Wilson has noted that his real education began when he was sixteen years old. Disgusted by the racist treatment he endured in the various schools he had attended until that time, he dropped out and began educating himself in the local library. Working at menial jobs, he also pursued a literary career and successfully submitted poems to black publications at the University of Pittsburgh. In 1968 he became active in the theatre by founding—despite lacking prior experience— Black Horizons on the Hill, a theatre company in Pittsburgh. Recalling his early theatre involvement, Wilson described himself to the *New York Times* as "a cultural nationalist . . . trying to raise consciousness through theater."

According to several observers, however, Wilson found his artistic voice—and began to appreciate the black voices of Pittsburgh—after he moved to St. Paul, Minnesota, in 1978. In St. Paul Wilson wrote his first play, *Jitney,* a realistic drama set in a Pittsburgh taxi station. *Jitney,* noted for the fidelity with which it portrayed black urban speech and life, had a successful engagement at a small theater in Pittsburgh. Wilson followed *Jitney* with another play, *Fullerton Street,* but this work failed to strengthen his reputation.

Wilson then resumed work on an earlier unfinished project, *Ma Rainey's Black Bottom,* a play about a black blues singer's exploitation of her fellow musicians. This work, whose title role is named after an actual blues singer from the 1920s, is set in a recording studio in 1927. In the studio, temperamental Ma Rainey verbally abuses the other musicians and presents herself—without justification—as an important musical figure. But much of the play is also set in a rehearsal room, where Ma Rainey's musicians discuss their abusive employer and the hardships of life in racist America.

Eventually, the musicians are all revealed to have experienced, in varying degrees, racist treatment. The most resigned member is the group's leader, a trombonist who has learned to accept racial discrimination and merely negotiates around it. The bassist's response is to wallow in hedonism and ignore his nation's treatment of blacks, while the pianist takes an intellectual approach to solving racial problems. The group's trumpeter, however, is bitter and cynical. He is haunted by the memory of his mother's rape by four white men. Tensions mount in the play when the sullen trumpeter clashes with Ma Rainey and is fired. The manager of the recording studio then swindles him in a recording rights agreement, and a subsequent and seemingly insignificant incident precipitates a violent act from the trumpeter, who has simply endured too much abuse. The London *Times*'s Holly Hill called the play's climactic moment "a melodramatically violent act."

Ma Rainey's Black Bottom earned Wilson a trip to the O'Neill Theatre Center's National Playwrights Conference. There Wilson's play impressed director Lloyd Richards from the Yale Repertory Theatre. Richards worked with Wilson to refine the play, and when it was presented at Yale in 1984 it was hailed as the work of an important new playwright. Frank Rich, who reviewed the Yale production in the *New York Times,* acclaimed Wilson as "a major find for the American theater" and cited Wilson's ability to write "with compassion, raucous humor and penetrating wisdom."

Wilson enjoyed further success with *Ma Rainey's Black Bottom* after the play came to Broadway later in

1984. The *Chicago Tribune*'s Richard Christiansen reviewed the Broadway production as "a work of intermittent but immense power" and commended the "striking beauty" of the play's "literary and theatrical poetry." Christiansen added that "Wilson's power of language is sensational" and that *Ma Rainey's Black Bottom* was "the work of an impressive writer." The London *Times*'s Hill agreed, calling Wilson "a promising new playwright" and hailing his work as "a remarkable first play."

Wilson's subsequent plays include the Pulitzer Prize-winning *Fences,* which is about a former athlete who forbids his son to accept an athletic scholarship, and *Joe Turner's Come and Gone,* which concerns an ex-convict's efforts to find his wife. Like *Ma Rainey's Black Bottom,* these plays underwent extensive rewriting. Guiding Wilson in this process was Lloyd Richards, dean of Yale's drama school and director of the school's productions of Wilson's plays. "August is a wonderful poet," Richards told the *New York Times* in 1986. "A wonderful poet turning into a playwright." Richards added that his work with Wilson involved "clarifying" each work's main theme and "arranging the material in a dynamic way."

Both *Fences* and *Joe Turner's Come and Gone* were praised when they played on American stages. The *New York Times*'s Frank Rich, in his review of *Fences,* wrote that the play "leaves no doubt that Mr. Wilson is a major writer, combining a poet's ear for vernacular with a robust sense of humor (political and sexual), a sure instinct for cracking dramatic incident and passionate commitment to a great subject." And in his critique of *Joe Turner's Come and Gone,* Rich speculated that the play "will give a lasting voice to a generation of uprooted black Americans." Rich contended that the work was "potentially its author's finest achievement yet" and described it as "a teeming canvas of black America . . . and a spiritual allegory."

In 1990, Wilson claimed his second Pulitzer Prize, this time for *The Piano Lesson.* Set during the Great Depression of the 1930s, this drama pits brother against sister in a contest to decide the future of a treasured heirloom—a piano, carved with African-style portraits by their grandfather, an enslaved plantation carpenter. The brother wants to sell it to buy land, while the sister adamantly insists that the instrument carries too much family history to part with. Acclaim for the play was widespread, although some commentators were put off by the supernatural elements that came to play in the climax of this otherwise realistic piece. "When ghosts begin resolving realistic plays, you can be sure the playwright has failed to master his material," wrote Robert Brustein in the *New Republic*. Brustein also found the play overlong and repetitious, and asserted that Wilson's focus on the effects of racism was limiting him artistically. Others praised the work unreservedly, however, including Clive Barnes of the *New York Post*. He declared: "This is a play in which to lose yourself—to give yourself up . . . to August Wilson's thoughts, humors and thrills, all caught in a microcosm largely remote for many of us from our own little worlds, yet always talking the same language of humanity." Frank Rich of the *New York Times* wrote that Wilson has given "miraculous voice" to the black experience, and William A. Henry III of *Time* dubbed the play's piano "the most potent symbol in American drama since Laura Wingfield's glass menagerie" in the Tennessee Williams classic. Barnes concluded: "This is a wonderful play that lights up man. See it, wonder at it, and recognize it." Wilson later adapted *The Piano Lesson* for a "Hallmark Hall of Fame" television production. It was judged a success by John J. O'Connor, who wrote in the *New York Times:* "If anything, *The Piano Lesson* is even more effective in this shortened version."

Two Trains Running continued Wilson's projected ten-play cycle about black American history. The play, which came to Broadway in 1992, is set in a run-down diner on the verge of being sold. Reactions by the diner's regular patrons to the pending sale make up the body of the drama. Some critics, such as the *New Yorker*'s Mimi Kramer, found the play less subtle and dramatic than its predecessors, but *Newsweek*'s David Ansen praised the "musical eloquence" of Wilson's language, which he felt enhanced a "thematically rich" work. And Henry wrote in *Time* that *Two Trains Running* is a "delicate and mature" play that shows Wilson "at his lyrical best."

Two Trains Running was followed in 1995 by *Seven Guitars*. Set in the 1940s, it recounts the tragic story of blues guitarist Floyd Barton, whose funeral opens the play. Action then flashes back to recreate the events of Floyd's last week of life. *Seven Guitars* was the first major production of a Wilson play without the direction of Richards, who was forced to abandon the project due to illness. The task of directing fell to Walter Dallas, whose staging at the Goodman Theatre in Chicago William Tynan characterized as "skillful" in a *Time* review. Yet the critic's overall assessment was mixed. "Part bawdy comedy, part dark elegy, part mystery," he wrote, "August Wilson's rich new

play, *Seven Guitars,* nicely eludes categorization. . . . But though full and strong in its buildup, the play loses its potency as it reaches its climax. . . . Though Floyd is as charming and sympathetic a protagonist as we could want, the surprising truth is that his death has little effect on us. We leave the theater entertained and admiring but not truly moved." Vincent Canby differed markedly in his judgment, writing in the *New York Times:* "Though the frame of 'Seven Guitars' is limited and employs only seven characters, Mr. Wilson writes so vividly that the play seems to have the narrative scope and depth of a novel. When the curtain comes down, it's difficult to remember which characters you've actually seen and which you have come to know only through stories recollected on stage. . . . 'Seven Guitars' plays with such speed that you begin the journey one minute, and the next thing you know, you're leaving the theater on a high."

Further praise came from *Newsweek* reviewer Jack Kroll, who called *Seven Guitars* "a kind of jazz cantata for actors," with "a gritty, lyrical polyphony of voices that evokes the character and destiny of these men and women who can't help singing the blues even when they're just talking." The play, he continued, "bristles with symbolism" and with "anguished eloquence." Kroll found the protagonist's death "shocking, unexpected, yet inevitable" and the characters overall "not victims, wallowing in voluptuous resentment," but "tragic figures, bursting with the balked music of life."

Discussing Wilson's body of work, Lawrence Bommer stated in the *Chicago Tribune*, "August Wilson has created the most complete cultural chronicle since Balzac wrote his vast 'Human Comedy,' an artistic whole that has grown even greater than its prize-winning parts." As for the playwright, he has repeatedly stressed that his first objective is simply getting his work produced. "All I want is for the most people to get to see this play," he told the *New York Times* while discussing *Joe Turner's Come and Gone.* Wilson added, however, that he was not opposed to having his works performed on Broadway. He told the *New York Times* that Broadway "still has the connotation of Mecca" and asked, "Who doesn't want to go to Mecca?"

BIOGRAPHICAL/CRITICAL SOURCES:

BOOKS

Bogumil, Mary L., *Understanding August Wilson,* University of South Carolina Press, 1998.

Herrington, Joan, *I Ain't Sorry for Nothin' I Done: August Wilson's Process of Playwriting,* Limelight Editions, 1998.

McDonough, Carla J., *Staging Masculinity: Male Identity in Contemporary American Drama,* McFarland & Co., 1997.

Shafer, Yvonne, *August Wilson: A Research and Production Sourcebook,* Greenwood Press, 1998.

PERIODICALS

African American Review, spring, 1996, p. 99.
Boston Globe, February 3, 1995, section 3, p. 47.
Chicago Tribune, October 15, 1984; June 8, 1987; December 17, 1987; December 27, 1987, pp. 4-5; January 20, 1993, p. section 1, p. 20; January 24, 1993, section 13, pp. 8- 9; January 26, 1993, section 1, p. 16; January 15, 1995, section 13, pp. 16-17, 21.
Chicago Tribune Book World, February 9, 1986, pp. 12- 13.
Christian Science Monitor, October 16, 1984, pp. 29-30; March 27, 1987, pp. 1, 8; March 30, 1988, p. 21.
Ebony, January, 1985; November, 1987, pp. 68, 70, 72, 74.
Esquire, April, 1989, pp. 116, 118, 120, 122-27.
Essence, August, 1987, pp. 51, 111, 113.
Journal and Constitution (Atlanta), October 17, 1993, p. N1; October 13, 1994, p. D11; January 9, 1995, p. D5.
Los Angeles Times, November 24, 1984; November 7, 1986; April 17, 1987; June 7, 1987; June 8, 1987; June 9, 1987; February 6, 1988.
Maclean's, May 28, 1990, p. 62; May 18, 1992, pp. 56- 57.
Massachusetts Review, spring, 1988, pp. 87-97.
Nation, April 18, 1987, p. 518; June 1, 1990, pp. 832-33; June 8, 1992, pp. 799-800.
New Republic, May 21, 1990, pp. 28-30.
Newsweek, April 6, 1987; April 11, 1988, p. 82; April 27, 1992, p. 70; February 6, 1995, p. 60.
New York, April 6, 1987, pp. 92-94; May 7, 1990, pp. 82-83.
New Yorker, April 6, 1987, p. 81; April 11, 1988, p. 107; April 30, 1990, p. 85; April 27, 1992, p. 85.
New York Newsday, April 20, 1987, p. 47.
New York Post, March 28, 1988; April 17, 1990.
New York Times, April 11, 1984; April 13, 1984; October 12, 1984; October 22, 1984, p. C15; May 5, 1985, p. 80; May 6, 1986; May 14, 1986; May 19, 1986, p. C11; June 20, 1986; March 27, 1987, p. C3; April 5, 1987, II, pp. 1, 39; April 9, 1987; April 17, 1987; May 7, 1987; December 10, 1987; December 11, 1987; March 27, 1988, pp. 1, 34; March 28, 1988, p. C15; January 30, 1989, p. 69; April 17, 1990, p. C13; March 10, 1991, section 2, pp. 5, 17; January 25, 1995, pp. C13-C14; February 3, 1995, p. D26; February 5, 1995, section 2, pp. 1, 5.
New York Times Book Review, March 3, 1996, p. 22.
New York Times Magazine, June 10, 1987, pp. 36, 40, 49, 70.
People, May 13, 1996, p. 63.
Saturday Review, January-February, 1985, pp. 83, 90.
Theater, fall-winter, 1984, pp. 50-55; summer-fall, 1986, pp. 64; summer-fall, 1988, pp. 69-71.
Theatre Journal, December, 1994, pp. 468-76.
Time, April 6, 1987, p. 81; April 27, 1987; April 11, 1988, pp. 77-78; January 30, 1989, p. 69; April 27, 1992, pp. 65-66; February 6, 1995, p. 71.
Times (London), November 6, 1984; April 18, 1987; April 24, 1987.
Variety, February 26, 1996, p. 175.
Vogue, August, 1988, pp. 200, 204.
Washington Post, May 20, 1986; April 15, 1987; June 9, 1987; October 4, 1987; October 9, 1987.*

* * *

WRIGHT, Jay 1935-

PERSONAL: Born May 25, 1935, in Albuquerque, NM. *Education:* Attended University of New Mexico; earned B.A. from University of California, Berkeley; earned M.A. from Rutgers University; further study at Union Theological Seminary.

ADDRESSES: Home—Piermont, NH.

CAREER: Poet and playwright. Has worked as poet-in-residence at several universities, including Talledega University, Tougaloo University, Texas Southern University, and Dundee University. *Military service:* Served in the U.S. Army.

AWARDS, HONORS: National Council on the Arts grant, 1967; Hodder fellow in playwriting, Princeton University, 1970-71; Ingram Merrill Foundation award, 1974; Guggenheim Fellowships, 1974, 1975; 5-year MacArthur Fellowship, 1986.

WRITINGS:

(Contributor) Langston Hughes, editor, *New Negro Poets: U.S.A.,* Indiana University Press, 1964.

Death as History (chapbook), Kriya Press, 1967.

(Contributor) Dudley Randall and Margaret Burroughs, editors, *For Malcolm: Poems on the Life and Death of Malcolm X,* edited by Broadside Press, 1967.

Balloons: A Comedy in One Act (drama), Baker's Plays (Boston), 1968.

(Contributor) LeRoi Jones and Larry Neal, editors, *Black Fire,* Morrow, 1968.

(Author of introduction) Henry Dumas, *Poetry for My People,* edited by Hale Chaffield and Eugene Redmond, Southern Illinois University Press (Carbondale), 1970.

The Homecoming Singer (poetry; contains the poems "Collection Time," "A Non-Birthday Poem for My Father," "The Fisherman's Fiesta," "Wednesday Night Prayer Meeting," "The Baptism," "Billie's Blues," "Jason's One Command," "Preparing to Leave Home," "The Hunting Trip Cook," "The Homecoming Singer," "An Invitation to Madison County," "Reflections Before the Charity Hospital," "Variations on a Theme by Leroi Jones," "First Principles," and "Beginning Again"), Corinth, 1971.

(Contributor) Arnold Adoff, editor, *The Poetry of Black America,* Harper, 1972.

(Contributor) Abraham Chapman, editor, *New Black Voices,* New American Library, 1972.

Soothsayers and Omens (poetry; contains the poems "The Death of an Unfamiliar Sister," "The Charge," "Sources," "Benjamin Banneker Helps to Build a City," "Benjamin Banneker Sends His 'Almanac' to Thomas Jefferson," "Binu," "Altars and Sacrifice," "Dead," and "Second Conversations with Ogotemmeli"), Seven Woods Press (New York City), 1976.

Dimensions of History (poetry; contains the poems "The Second Eye of the World: The Dimensions of Rites and Acts," "Modulations: The Aesthetic Dimension," "Rhythm, Charts, and Changes," "The Body Adorned and Bare," "Retablose," "d," "The Log Book of Judgements," "Landscapes: The Physical Dimension," "W. E. B. DuBois at Harvard," "Crispus Attucks," and "What Is True"), Kayak (Santa Cruz, CA), 1976.

The Double Invention of Komo (poetry; contains the poems "The third phase of the coming out of Komo," "Afterword," "Opening of the Cycle of Redemption," "The Abstract of Knowledge/The First Test," "The Opening of the Ceremony/The Coming Out of Komo," and "The Initiate Takes His First Six Signs, the Design of His Name"), University of Texas Press (Austin), 1980.

Explications/Interpretations (contains the poem "Twenty-Two Tremblings of the Postulant"), in the *Callaloo* Poetry Series, Books on Demand, 1984.

Selected Poems of Jay Wright, edited by Robert B. Stepto, afterword by Harold Bloom, Books on Demand, 1987.

Elaine's Book, Books on Demand, 1988.

Boleros, Princeton University Press, 1991.

Work represented in numerous anthologies. Contributor to *Black World, Callaloo, Journal of Negro Poetry, Negro American Literature Forum, Negro Digest, Evergreen Review, Hiram Poetry Review, Nation,* and other periodicals.

SIDELIGHTS: Jay Wright is a contemporary black American poet whose work is acknowledged for its evocative language, introspective tone, and mythological imagery. He is the author of plays, essays, and books of poetry which focus on a rediscovery of the African American heritage through historical study and personal experience. His poetry, often autobiographical and allegorical in nature, has been compared by some critics to the works of T. S. Eliot, Walt Whitman, and Hart Crane, and shows the various artistic influences of Dante, Nicholas Guillen, Alejo Carpenter, St. Augustine, and the West African griots—entertainers whose recitals include tribal histories and genealogies. A recurring theme in Wright's poetry is the attempt to overcome a sense of exclusion, whether from society or from one's cultural identity, and to find growth and unity through a connection between American society (the experience of the present) and African traditions (the heritage of the past). Ultimately, as a *Choice* reviewer expressed it, Wright searches for "a new point of origin" for a wider African American cultural identity. Weaving together the mythology and culture of many lands, Wright's poetry heavily reflects the influence of his birthplace in the American Southwest, as well as the heritage of his African ancestry. His poems explore history from this multicultural standpoint and often take the form of allegorical journeys and spiritual quests wherein the persona finally achieves growth.

Wright was born in 1935 in New Mexico, and spent his childhood in Albuquerque and his teen years in San Pedro, California. The early exposure to Mexican, Spanish, and Navajo cultures provided by his upbringing in the Southwest has proved to have a lasting effect on his poetry, as geography and culture have become major themes in his work. For a short time after high school, Wright played baseball in the Arizona/Texas and California State Leagues, and he briefly studied chemistry at the University of New Mexico. Before the term was over, however, Wright joined the United States Army, serving for three years in the Medical Corps. After his discharge, he attended the University of California, earned his bachelor's degree in 1961, won a Rockefeller Brothers theological fellowship, and studied for one semester at Union Theological Seminary. Wright went on to Rutgers University to complete his masters degree in comparative literature in 1967, and a year later was awarded a Woodrow Wilson/National Endowment for the Arts Poets-in-Concert fellowship which enabled him to tour the South. In that same year, 1967, he published his first chapbook of poems, titled *Death as History*. Around this time Wright published a play, *Balloons: A Comedy in One Act,* and in 1970 he was granted a Hodder fellowship in playwriting from Princeton University in 1970. One of his previous plays, *Welcome Back, Black Boy,* had been produced in California.

Wright's first major published collection, 1971's *The Homecoming Singer,* established his reputation as a gifted poet. The theme of bridging past and present, settings that enhance discovery, and meditations on feelings of exclusion from society or personal identity are all evident in these early poems. Geographical settings become backdrops for the autobiographical persona's spiritual, emotional, and intellectual growth. "The individual poems . . . are firmly grounded in well- defined geographical settings" that function not simply as atmosphere, explained Phillip M. Richard in the *Dictionary of Literary Biography,* but "as symbolic renderings of the persona's inner state." Themes are further explored through experience in such poems as "The Hunting Trip Cook," where a young boy struggles with anger mixed with affection toward his father, who serves as cook on a white man's hunting trip; "Wednesday Night Prayer Meeting," in which a young man questions the relevance of traditional religion; and "Beginning Again," the final poem of the book, which ends with a homecoming and a promise for the future.

Reviewers of *The Homecoming Singer* were largely enthusiastic, and Wright was christened "a major poet of this era" by Eugene B. Redmond in *Drumvoices: The Mission of Afro-American Poetry, A Critical History,* as quoted by Richard. Critics especially admired Wright's use of syntax and rhythm: "His verse re-

sembles prose," wrote David Kalstone in the *New York Times Book Review,* "yet the lines pause at points where he branches out with participles and oddities of syntax to discover what energies are available in worlds he can't belong to. The rhythms—there are few full stops—deceive us into sharing others' dreams." The reviewer concluded, "It is hard to know where Wright will go from here—and important to find out." Robert B. Shaw in *Poetry* admired Wright's Mexican scenes, his "seeking, questioning" meditations and, especially, the final dream vision of the poem, which he described as "one of the more eloquent evocations of an American muse that I have read."

Wright published *Homecoming Singer* while living in Mexico, where he remained from 1968 until 1971. He then moved to Scotland, where he resided from 1971 until 1973, before publishing two volumes of poetry in 1976: *Soothsayers and Omens* and *Dimensions of History*. Wright's interest in the importance of African mythology to the continuity of black awareness (spanning all the way back to Africa) is developed in these works, and is connected to the theme of individual growth achieved through spiritual quest. In *Soothsayers and Omens,* for example, the persona is a seeker on a personal, spiritual quest in a Mexican setting, while in *Dimensions of History* the speaker of the poem is an African dyeli, the tribal historical archivist who explores the collective values of the tribe. "Haunting and evocative, *Soothsayers and Omens* powerfully reveals the Afro-American sense of participation in a tradition and world view other than that in which blacks live in America," declared Richard, "and most successfully of all Wright's books, it assimilates a mythological world view to personal experience." Similarly, Richard noted, Wright incorporates experience in the use of collages in *Dimensions of History* to "dramatize the musical, artistic, or ritualistic acts which the persona wishes to present as the embodiments of spiritual tradition."

The underlying mythology in both *Soothsayers and Omens* and *Dimensions of History* is based on African religions. *Soothsayers and Omens* focuses on the cosmology of the Dogon, which relies heavily on numerology, the process of creation, and symbols, some of which are associated with such material elements as earth, air, fire and water. The doctrine is usually taught by a "Nani," a spiritual instructor in Dogon mythology. Since unity is a crucial concept in Wright's poetry, there is a definite correlation between the spiritual and the physical world in his work. "For Wright," Richard pointed out, "ideas reside primarily in things; thus his poetry frequently focuses on the ritual objects and acts of the native American and African cultures which he finds to be the wellsprings of those spiritual traditions." Wright's researches into West African mythology include the religions of the Dogon and Bambara of Mali, the Komo (an all-male community of the Bambara), and the tribes of Akan and Nuer. Wright acknowledges that he is the "beneficiary" of, among others, French anthropologist Marcel Griaule, whose expeditions to Dakar, Mali, Chad, and Cameroon have provided insight into the African mythology which is the dominant motif of much of Wright's work.

Many reviewers praised the clarity of Wright's poetic vision in *Soothsayers and Omens* and *Dimensions of History.* E. Ethelbert Miller in *Library Journal* proclaimed that "Wright's explorations into African philosophy and the poems that result must be considered bridges healing the wounds that exist within the souls of black Americans." Others pointed to Wright as a "learned" and "mythological" poet, one who is, in Richard's words, "conversant in anthropology, the philosophy of science, and the European literatures of the Renaissance and the Middle Ages." Richard concluded that "Wright's poetry is, in large measure, the fruit of this extensive scholarly enterprise." John Hollander in *Times Literary Supplement* called the works "allegorical at many levels," and Harold Bloom in the *New Republic* asserted that *Dimensions of History* is "the year's best book of poems from a small press."

In 1980 Wright published *The Double Invention of Komo.* This work is, according to many critics, his "most ambitious book," a complex succession of poems following the Komo initiation rites of the African Bambara people. The ritual is a series of instructions into the "central intellectual, spiritual, and social values of Komo culture," wrote Richard. The first section of the book deals with the preparation of the initiate for the ceremony, including a dance in which the creation of the world is dramatized; the second section details the actual ceremony, a ritual involving four signs delineating the values of the tribe. According to Komo beliefs, the initiate ultimately realizes that everything in creation is interlinked. The autobiographical element in this work is distinctive because Wright's own literary history is allegorized into the story. *The Double Invention of Komo* is Wright's "intellectual biography," asserted Richard. He "uses the dialogue between ritual celebrant and initiate as a means of situating speeches by or addresses to writers and thinkers central to the poet's development." The

persona's dialogue in the poem, then, serves as a synopsis of Wright's own literary quests for knowledge, and includes debates with, among others, Dante and St. Augustine, and spiritual journeys to Italy, Germany, Mexico, the United States, and France. Isidore Okpewho added in *Callaloo* that *The Double Invention of Komo* "closes one phase of Wright's poetic output . . . that is, to establish the sources of his black consciousness by a careful and steady archaeology of knowledge."

Typical of critical reactions to *The Double Invention of Komo* was that of John Hollander in the *Times Literary Supplement,* who declared the work a "considerable achievement of a major imagination." Judith McPheron in *Library Journal* described the poetry as "chant-like" and "oracular," but puzzled over the tone, and remarked that "while the poems seem to cling to some large, ritual pattern, it doesn't become quite clear to the reader." Okpewho, however, asserted that "there is no doubt that Wright has continued to address himself . . . to concerns that are peculiarly American in the broadest sense. . . . He has endeavored to inscribe the African sources of his people into the American cultural soul." And Richard judged the work "an important book in terms of its artistic and cultural ambition."

In 1984 Wright found a publisher for *Explications/ Interpretations,* a book of poetry he had written prior to 1980's *The Double Invention of Komo.* As is the case here, Wright often wrote his poetry some years before it was actually published. *Explications/Interpretations* is somewhat easier to understand than some of Wright's previously published poetry, but, according to some reviewers, is just as "spellbinding" as his other works. *Explications/Interpretations* is evidence of Wright's increasing maturity as a poet, said J. N. Igo, Jr. in *Choice.* Calling him "an astonishing poet," Igo asserted that Wright's poetry is "vital, genuine, fresh, and haunting, to be reread and reread."

Two of Wright's recent works, *Elaine's Book* and *Boleros,* experiment with the use of speech, dialect, and setting. *Elaine's Book,* Wright's 1988 publication, was written as a birthday gift for his wife's sister. The language of the poems varies from standard English, to black vernacular, to Spanish. "This volume is Jay Wright at his best," wrote R. G. O'Meally in *Choice.* The poems are "far-reaching in mythic and historic reference yet dramatically in the here and now." A *Virginia Quarterly Review* critic concluded "Wright's language . . . is sinuous, beautiful. This is a book worth puzzling over for a long time." Like *Elaine's Book,* Wright's *Boleros,* published in 1991, is multicultural in voice and location. Unlike his previous works, however, there is a tendency in *Boleros* to create words in a "sensual" exploration of the volume's central question: "What is love's habitation. . . ?" M. Waters in *Choice* recommended the book for its "resplendent and evocative language."

Selected Poems of Jay Wright, produced in 1987, is an anthology of Wright's previously published works, with an introduction by Robert B. Stepto and an afterword by poetry critic Harold Bloom. The collection is "superb," wrote R. G. O'Meally in *Choice,* "for it brings together the strongest poems of one of America's strongest poets." Numerous reviewers, however, cautioned that Wright is a complex poet. Shaw confessed in *Poetry* that "I have found in this book some poems I was moved by, a great many more I was intrigued by, but not many that I am certain I understand." Critic John Hollander in *Times Literary Supplement* designated Wright "the most intellectual and the most imaginatively serious and ambitious black American poet I know of. . . . He is also the most difficult." Another commentator, Jack Shreve in *Library Journal,* insisted: "Wright is an intellectual poet, a poet's poet. . . . Tackling Wright's poetry is no mean task," but may be rewarding. Many reviewers, such as Richard, advised careful rereading, so that the reader might be "assimilated into the world of the poem." Further, Hollander specified that understanding Wright's poems "will take . . . the imaginative and moral work that poetry, rather than merely eloquent verse, requires of its readers." This often involves paying careful attention to the author-provided notes, and familiarizing oneself with the references or sources cited in the glossaries to help interpret the work. Finally, the works as a whole are comprehensive in nature, with each volume of poetry building upon the themes presented in the previous one. In a 1983 interview with Charles H. Rowell in *Jay Wright: A Special Issue, Callaloo,* the poet suggested a reading of his major works in the following planned sequence and as chronologically written: *The Homecoming Singer, Soothsayers and Omens, Explications/Interpretations, Dimensions of History,* and *The Double Invention of Komo.*

BIOGRAPHICAL/CRITICAL SOURCES:

BOOKS

Harper, Michael S., and Robert B. Stepto, editors, *Chant of Saints: A Gathering of Afro-American Literature, Arts and Scholarship,* University of Illinois Press, 1979.

Negro Almanac, Gale, 1989, p. 1021.

PERIODICALS

Black American Literature Forum, fall, 1990, pp. 473-489.

Black World, September, 1973.

Callaloo, fall, 1983, pp. 85-102; summer, 1991, pp. 692-726.

English Studies: A Journal of English Language and Literature, Volume 51, 1970, pp. 112-137.

Explicator, Volume 32, 1974.

Georgia Review, Volume 27, 1973, pp. 71-81; Volume 28, 1974, pp. 257-268.

Library Journal, May 1, 1987, p. 69; May 15, 1991, p. 86.

Minnesota Review, Volume 2, 1972, pp. 13-32.

Modern Poetry Studies, Volume 2, 1972, pp. 252-259.

Mosaic: A Journal for the Interdisciplinary Study of Literature, Volume 7, number 3, 1974, pp. 163-170.

New Republic, November 20, 1976, pp. 20-23, 26; November 26, 1977, pp. 24-26.

Newsweek, March 3, 1969.

New York Times Book Review, July 30, 1972, pp. 4, 15.

Parnassus: Poetry in Review, spring/summer, 1981, pp. 306-314.

Poetry, April, 1988, pp. 45-47.

Salmagundi, Volume 22-23, 1973, pp. 222-233.

Southern Humanities Review, Volume 6, 1972, pp. 134-153.

Virginia Quarterly Review, summer, 1989, pp. 98-99.

Yale Review, March, 1988, pp. 293-294.*

*   *   *

YERBY, Frank G(arvin) 1916-1991

PERSONAL: Born September 5, 1916, in Augusta, GA; died of heart failure, November 29, 1991, in Madrid, Spain; buried in Almudena Cemetery, Madrid, Spain; son of Rufus Garvin (a postal clerk) and Wilhelmina (Smythe) Yerby; married Flora Helen Claire Williams, March 1, 1941 (divorced); married Blanca Calle-Perez (Yerby's secretary, translator, researcher, and "general manager"), July 27, 1956; children: (first marriage) Jacques Loring, Nikki Ethlyn, Faune Ellena, Jan Keith. *Education:* Paine

College, A.B., 1937; Fisk University, M.A., 1938; graduate study, University of Chicago, 1939. *Politics:* Independent. *Religion:* Agnostic.

CAREER: Novelist. Florida Agricultural and Mechanical College (now University), Tallahassee, instructor in English, 1939-40; Southern University and Agricultural and Mechanical College, Baton Rouge, LA, instructor in English, 1940-41; Ford Motor Co., Dearborn, MI, laboratory technician, 1941-44; Ranger (Fairchild) Aircraft, Jamaica, NY, chief inspector, Magnaflux, 1944-45; resident of Madrid, Spain, beginning 1955; also lived in France for an extended period in the 1950s.

MEMBER: Authors Guild, Authors League of America, Real Sociedad Hipica Espanola (Madrid), Madrid Country Club.

AWARDS, HONORS: O. Henry Memorial Award, 1944, for best first short story, "Health Card"; Doctor of Letters, Fisk University, 1976, and Doctor of Humane Letters, Paine College, 1977; named honorary citizen of State of Tennessee by Governor's Proclamation, 1977.

WRITINGS:

NOVELS; ORIGINALLY PUBLISHED BY DIAL (NEW YORK CITY)

The Foxes of Harrow, 1946, reprinted, Buccaneer Books (Cutchogue, NY), 1976.
The Vixens, 1947, reprinted, Dell (New York City), 1976.
The Golden Hawk, 1948.
Pride's Castle, 1949.
Floodtide, 1950.
A Woman Called Fancy, 1951.
The Saracen Blade, 1952.
The Devil's Laughter, 1953.
Benton's Row, 1954.
The Treasure of Pleasant Valley, 1955.
Captain Rebel, 1956.
Fairoaks, 1957.
The Serpent and the Staff, 1958.
Jarrett's Jade, 1959.
Gillian, 1960.
The Garfield Honor, 1961.
Griffin's Way, 1962.
The Old Gods Laugh: A Modern Romance, 1964.
An Odor of Sanctity: A Novel of Medieval Moorish Spain, 1965.
Goat Song: A Novel of Ancient Greece, 1968.

Judas My Brother: The Story of the Thirteenth Disciple, 1968.
Speak Now: A Modern Novel, 1969.
The Dahomean: An Historical Novel, 1971 (published in England as *The Man from Dahomey,* Heinemann (London), 1972).
The Girl from Storyville: A Victorian Novel, 1972.
The Voyage Unplanned, 1974.
Tobias and the Angel, 1975.
A Rose for Ana Maria, 1976.
Hail the Conquering Hero, 1977.
A Darkness at Ingraham's Crest: A Tale of the Slaveholding South, 1979.
Western: A Saga of the Great Plains, 1982.

NOVELS; PUBLISHED BY DOUBLEDAY (NEW YORK CITY)

Bride of Liberty, 1954.
Devilseed, 1984.
McKenzie's Hundred, 1985.

Work represented in numerous anthologies, including *The Best Short Stories by Negro Writers: An Anthology from 1899 to the Present,* edited by Langston Hughes, Little, Brown (Boston), 1967; *The Poetry of the Negro, 1746-1970,* edited by Hughes and Arna Bontemps, Doubleday, 1970; and *Blacklash,* edited by Stewart H. Benedict, Popular Library, 1970. Also contributor to *Harper's, Liberty, Colliers, France Soir, Le Meuse, La Laterne, Berlin Zeitung,* and numerous other periodicals.

ADAPTATIONS: The Foxes of Harrow was filmed by Twentieth Century-Fox in 1951; *The Golden Hawk* and *The Saracen Blade* were filmed by Columbia in 1952 and 1954, respectively; *Pride's Castle* was filmed for television.

SIDELIGHTS: A prolific novelist who published thirty-three tales of adventure, Frank G. Yerby sold over fifty-five million hardback and paperback books during the course of his lifetime. While many of these novels were best-sellers, their popularity had little effect on Yerby's critical stature. Since the appearance of his first novel, *The Foxes of Harrow,* in 1946, the author was routinely—and some say unfairly—slighted by critics. Early in his career, for instance, when Yerby was producing mainstream fiction, black reviewers attacked him for abandoning his race. Those who knew his work, but not his color, accused him of squandering his writing talent on cardboard characters and hackneyed plots. Still others objected to his "over-blown" prose and the way he sensationalized his material. Writing in *The Negro Novel in*

America, Robert A. Bone dubbed him "the prince of the pulpsters." In the face of such criticism, Yerby steadfastly maintained his integrity: "The only excuse for writing is that you love it beyond measure and beyond reason," he once told *CA,* adding that "to make any compromise whatsoever for the sake of sales or popularity is to join the world's oldest profession. I believe that a writer should have the guts to starve; and that if he doesn't come close to it most of the time, he'd better take a long, hard look at what he's doing. . . . I write only because I have to. What I get out of it financially doesn't come under consideration at all. I write exactly what I feel and think . . . , but within that framework I try to give pleasure to the reading public."

Yerby's novels are characterized by colorful language, complex plot lines, and a multiplicity of characters. Hugh M. Gloster called Yerby's formula "the recipe of Southern historical romance," listing the following ingredients in *Crisis* magazine: "a bold, handsome, rakish, but withal somewhat honorable hero; a frigid, respectable wife; a torrid unrespectable mistress; and usually a crafty, fiendish villain." According to the *Washington Post Book World,* "a typical Yerby plot seems to involve a strong man who has to choose between two women and . . . more-than-generous helpings of revenge, madness, suffering and violence." *Time* summed up his writing as "a crude, shrewd combination of sex, violence, sadism, costuming and cliche."

A common criticism of Yerby's fiction is that he habitually solved apparently insoluble problems through a *deus ex machina,* or stroke of fate. "Despite his skillful tangling and untangling of exciting narratives which mesmerize even many sophisticated readers, Yerby too often depends on contrived endings," wrote Darwin T. Turner in *The Black Novelist.* Nick Aaron Ford echoed this sentiment in *Phylon,* writing that in all Yerby's books "there are scenes of great literary power, followed by episodes of incredible adventure, with too little preparation for the miraculous results. . . . This is not to say that Yerby is an inferior writer. He has rich imagination, a talent for vivid expression, ability to create pity and terror, and an understanding of the suffering of the poor and the oppressed. In short, he possesses the qualifications that could make of him a great novelist. But it appears that Yerby is satisfied with popularity without greatness. He says emphatically, 'I think the novelist has a professional obligation to please his reading public.'" A more sensitive arena is Yerby's treatment of racial issues.

The second of four children of a racially mixed couple, Yerby encountered his share of discrimination as a boy. "When I was young," he told *People* magazine, "a bunch of us black kids would get in a fight with white kids and then I'd have to fight with a black kid who got on me for being so light." Though he was an excellent student, and, after graduation, secured teaching positions at a number of black universities, Yerby became dissatisfied with what he regarded as the "stifling" atmosphere of these "Uncle Tom factories" and abandoned academia for a wartime factory job in Detroit. His first published fiction, which earned him an O. Henry Memorial Award in 1944, was a bitter story of racial injustice called "Health Card." He published five other short stories during the early 1940s, each of them concerned with blacks and their living conditions. He discovered, however, that most American readers were uninterested in reading about bigotry and race problems. *Dictionary of Literary Biography* contributor Jeffrey D. Parker uoted Yerby as saying in a *Harper's* magazine article: "The idea dawned on me that to continue to follow the route I had mapped out for myself was roughly analogous to shouting one's head off in Mammoth Cave." Accordingly, he abandoned the direct treatment of black themes in his fiction for almost thirty years. Instead, he set out to write a historical novel that would have broad appeal. Employed during the day at a defense plant, he worked on his book at night.

Yerby described his philosophy at that time in a 1982 interview with the *New York Times Book Review,* quoted by Parker: "Nobody ever went broke underestimating the taste of the American public, so I set out to write the worst possible novel it was humanly possible to write and still get published." He admitted, however, that despite his cynical approach, the book "sort of got hold of me, and about half way through, I started revising and improving it." The result was *The Foxes of Harrow,* a lush southern romance which traces the fortunes of the dashing young Stephen Fox in his rise from poverty to great wealth. It is "a good, old-fashioned obese historical novel of the Old South that seems, more than once, to be haunted by the affluent ghost of Scarlett O'Hara," according to the *New York Times.* While acknowledging Yerby's ability to hold the reader captive with his fast-paced plotting and vivid prose, many critics dismissed the book as socially insignificant melodrama. *New Yorker* contributor, Edmund Wilson, for instance, noted that Yerby "has packed everything in— passion, politics, creole society, sex, the clash of races, and war—but he never captures the faintest flutter of the breath of life." In N. L. Rothman's view, "the book rings throughout with colorful passions and the words to match. It is not a historical novel—for that must have some reality in it—," he continued in the *Saturday Review of Literature,* "but it is a good example of the technicolored fantasies that have been passing as such of late."

In later years, Yerby himself belittled the work, telling *People* magazine that *The Foxes of Harrow* comprised "every romantic cliche in history." The novel's literary shortcomings had no effect on its enormous popularity, however. With sales of over 2 million copies, *The Foxes of Harrow* became one of the hottest titles of the decade. It was translated into at least twelve languages, reprinted in several national magazines, and made into a lucrative movie starring Rex Harrison and Maureen O'Hara. Though Yerby despised the film adaptation, he was pleased with his novel's popular acceptance. He went on to publish a string of historical novels with Anglo-Saxon protagonists, leading Hugh M. Gloster to surmise that Yerby "gained his laurels by focusing upon white rather than Negro characters. Performance—and not pigmentation—has been the basis of his success."

Yerby staunchly defended his focus, explaining to *CA* that "the novelist hasn't any right to inflict on the public his private ideas on politics, religion or race. If he wants to preach he should go on the pulpit." Later he stated: "My mother was Scotch-Irish, a grandparent was an Indian; I've far more Irish blood than Negro. I simply insist on remaining a member of the human race. I don't think a writer's output should be dictated by a biological accident. It happens there are many things I know far better than the race problem." Yerby's personal solution to problems of discrimination was to leave the country. He moved from the United States to Spain in 1955 and remained there until his death in 1991.

Despite his contempt for didactic fiction, Yerby did address racial issues indirectly in several novels, some critics have said. "In his earliest novels, the racial problems are employed peripherally, almost perfunctorily, and occupy little space or overt interest in the novel," wrote Jack B. Moore in the *Journal of Popular Culture.* "None the less Yerby's racial attitudes pervade these early novels of the South, sometimes in obvious and sometimes in disguised fashion." Darwin T. Turner saw Yerby's position manifested in "the theme of the outcast who, as in existentialist literature, pits his will against a hostile universe. By intelligence and courage, he proves himself superior to a society which rejects him because of his alien, inferior, or illegitimate birth."

His second novel, *The Vixens,* utilized research material on the south he hadn't been able to incorporate into his first book. He followed *The Vixens* with a string of other southern romances, set for the most part in the nineteenth century. Commenting on Yerby's southern tales, Parker noted that although *A Darkness at Ingraham's Crest* is an unmistakable "indictment against the South and slavery," in other books the author had "done much to perpetuate the myths surrounding the 'Old South.'" With *The Golden Hawk,* in 1948, Yerby turned to picaresque adventure in other lands and earlier centuries. And his research, which had been admittedly careless in his first novels, became meticulous.

One of his most ambitious projects was *Judas, My Brother: The Story of the Thirteenth Disciple,* published in 1969. Based on thirty years of research, it was the author's attempt to present a demythologized account of the origin of Christianity. Parker quoted Yerby as saying that this book examines the question of "whether any man truly has the right to impose, by almost imperial fiat, belief in things that simply are not so. To me, irrationality is dangerous; perhaps the most dangerous force stalking through the world today. This novel . . . is one man's plea for an ecumenicism broad enough to include reasonable men; and his effort to defend his modest intellect from intolerable insult." Still, Parker concludes that "for all the polemics, *Judas, My Brother* [is a] costume novel," best read as entertainment. But while Yerby's novels of the 1950s and 1960s qualified as popular fiction, some critics were willing to admit that they also reflected serious concerns. In addition to escapism, they "exhibit another dimension, disregarded by the readers who lament Yerby's failure to write an historical novel and by the others who condemn his refusal to write an overtly polemical treatise on the plight of the American Negro," according to Darwin T. Turner in *The Black Novelist.* "Ideas—bitter ironies, caustic debunkings, painful gropings for meaning—writhe behind the soap-opera facade of his fiction."

In 1971, after protesting his indifference to racial issues for many years, Yerby addressed the matter directly in *The Dahomean: An Historical Novel,* his novel of Black Africa. Set in the nineteenth century, *The Dahomean* traces the life of Nyasanu/Hwesu as he advances in position from a chief's son to governor of an entire province, only to be sold into American slavery by two jealous relatives. "At the same time, his rise and fall illustrates the customs and folkways of his country: the rites of manhood and marriage; the feudal system; war," according to a critic for the *New York Times Book Review.* "Virtues of the book," said Turner, writing in *Black World,* "are the presentation of an exciting and illuminating history of Black people and a determined focus of the story on a single lack hero. But there is more. In *The Dahomean,* Yerby's strength reveals itself to best advantage and even his former weaknesses become strengths. . . . Yerby is at his best when he envelops his plot with a history he has unearthed painstakingly and with a serious or satirical but always devastating debunking of historical legends and myths. That achievement is superior in *The Dahomean,* not so much in the presentation of historical facts as in the presentation of a people and a culture." In a prefatory note to the novel, Yerby explained that part of his reason for writing the book was "to correct, so far as possible, the Anglo-Saxon reader's historical perspective" on black history. By portraying the Dahomean culture in all its rich complexity, Yerby dispelled the myth of a totally primitive Africa, even hinting at times that the tribal cultures "sometimes surpassed in their subtlety, their complexity, their dignity the ones to which the slaves were brought," in the *Best Sellers* critic's words. But in depicting the cruelties that certain tribesmen perpetrated on their black brothers, including selling them into slavery, Yerby also shattered the illusion that blacks are inherently superior morally. What Yerby seemed to be suggesting, Turner maintained, is that "the differences between people do not stem from a difference of blood, but a difference of opportunity and power."

Hailed by several reviewers as Yerby's masterpiece, *The Dahomean* also settled an old score for the author, as he explained in a letter to *CA:* "I am much more relaxed about racial matters, that increased tranquility being due in part to the fact that *The Dahomean* received (with one lone exception) rave notices from the critics. Thereafter, reviewers seemed to have waked up to what I was actually writing as distinct from and opposed to 1) what I used to write; and 2) what they thought I was writing. In short, I seem to have succeeded in changing many critics' minds. Pleasantly surprising was the high praise bestowed upon this novel by the critics of the South African papers. Needless to say, black critics immediately removed me from the list of 'non-conductors' and welcomed me back into the fold like a sinner redeemed by faith." Later, in that same letter, Yerby postulated that critical reaction to his books reflected

the reviewers' biases: "Those who confuse literature with sexual morality damn them; those wise enough, emotionally mature enough to realize that the two things have practically nothing to do with each other, generally like them very much indeed." Since the publication of *The Dahomean,* Yerby admitted, "two things have been of considerable comfort to me. First is the fact that I am no longer accused of colorful, purplish over writing. And the second is the dawning realization that fifty-five million readers in eighty-two countries and twenty-three languages (who have bought and paid for my novels) are not necessarily all idiots. Strangely enough (or perhaps not so strangely after all) the degree of appreciation for a novel of mine is directly increased by the degree of knowledge the reader has of the subject. In other words, people who know the themes I've written about either by reason of having lived through them, or deeply and professionally studied them, find no fault with my novels. I am praised by experts, attacked by—well, let's be kind and call them amateurs." Ultimately, however, critical reaction is incidental. Yerby, who in his later years turned increasingly to subjects he found personally—rather than commercially—appealing, worked from compulsion. As he told *People* magazine, "I won't stop writing as long as there's a breath in me." Some of Yerby's manuscripts are held at the Mugar Memorial Library, Boston University.

BIOGRAPHICAL/CRITICAL SOURCES:

PERIODICALS

Best Sellers, February 15, 1968; January 1, 1969; September 1, 1971; November, 1982.
Black World, February, 1972.
Book Week, February 10, 1946; April 27, 1947.
Crisis, January, 1948.
Journal of Popular Culture, spring, 1975.
Los Angeles Times Book Review, November 7, 1982.
Negro Digest, July, 1968; April, 1969.
Newsweek, November 30, 1959.
New Yorker, February 9, 1946; April 24, 1948.
New York Herald Tribune Book Review, May 4, 1947; June 12, 1949; October 22, 1950; July 15, 1951; September 21, 1952; October 4, 1953; November 14, 1954; December 19, 1954; October 14, 1956; September 22, 1957.
New York Times, February 10, 1946; May 2, 1948; May 15, 1949; September 10, 1950; May 6, 1951; April 6, 1952; November 15, 1953; December 5, 1954; September 23, 1956; September 8, 1957; October 12, 1958.

New York Times Book Review, November 10, 1968;
    October 17, 1971; September 17, 1972.
People, March 30, 1981.
*Phylon: The Atlanta University Review of Race and
    Culture,* Volume 25, number 1, 1954.
Publishers Weekly, May 10, 1971; June 4, 1982.
Saturday Review, May 10, 1952; October 27, 1956;
    August 24, 1957.
Saturday Review of Literature, February 23, 1946;
    May 8, 1948; June 18, 1949; September 30,
    1950; June 23, 1951.
Time, May 5, 1947; September 4, 1950; April 7,
    1952; November 23, 1953; November 29, 1954.
Times Literary Supplement, March 27, 1959.
Washington Post Book World, August 15, 1982.

OBITUARIES:

PERIODICALS

Chicago Tribune, January 12, 1992, p. 7.
Los Angeles Times, January 1, 1992, p. A22.
New York Times, January 8, 1992, p. D19.*

* * *

YOUNG, Al(bert James) 1939-

PERSONAL: Born May 31, 1939, in Ocean Springs,
MS; son of Ernest Albert James (a professional musician and auto worker) and Mary (Campbell) Young;
married Arlin June Belch (a freelance artist), October
8, 1963; children: Michael James. *Education:* Attended University of Michigan, 1957-61; University
of California, Berkeley, B.A., 1969. *Politics:* Independent. *Religion:* "Free Thinker."

ADDRESSES: Office—514 Bryant St., Palo Alto, CA
94301. *Agent*—Lynn Nesbit, International Creative
Management, 40 West 57th St., New York, NY
10019.

CAREER: Freelance musician playing guitar and
flute, and singing professionally throughout the
United States, 1957-64; KJAZ-FM, Alameda, CA,
disc jockey, 1961-65; San Francisco Museum of Art,
San Francisco, CA, writing instructor, 1967-69; Berkeley Neighborhood Youth Corps, Berkeley, CA,
writing instructor and language consultant, 1968-69;
Stanford University, Stanford, CA, Edward H. Jones
lecturer in creative writing, 1969-74; screenwriter for

Laser Films, New York City, 1972, Stigwood Corpo-
ration, London, and New York City, 1972, Verdon
Productions, Hollywood, CA, 1976, First Artists
Ltd., Burbank, CA, 1976-77, and Universal Studios,
Hollywood, CA, 1979; director, Associated Writing
Programs, 1979—.

Writer in residence, University of Washington, Seattle, 1981-82. Vice-president, Yardbird Publishing
Cooperative. Lecturer and speaker at numerous universities throughout the country.

MEMBER: American Association of University Professors, Authors League of America, Authors Guild,
Writers Guild of America, Committee of Small Magazine Editors and Publishers, East Bay Negro Historical Society, San Francisco Press Club, Sigma Delta
Pi.

AWARDS, HONORS: Wallace E. Stegner fellowship
in creative writing, Stanford University, 1966-67;
National Endowment for the Arts grants, 1968, 1969,
1975; Joseph Henry Jackson Award, San Francisco
Foundation, 1969, for *Dancing: Poems;* National Arts
Council awards for poetry and editing, 1968-70; California Association of Teachers of English special
award, 1973; Guggenheim fellowship, 1974; Outstanding Book of the Year citation, *New York Times,*
1980, for *Ask Me Now;* Pushcart Prize, Pushcart
Press, 1980; Before Columbus Foundation award,
1982; Fulbright fellowship Council for International
Exchange of Scholars, 1984.

WRITINGS:

NOVELS

Snakes: A Novel, Holt, 1970.
Who Is Angelina?, Holt, 1975.
Sitting Pretty, Holt, 1976.
Ask Me Now, McGraw-Hill, 1980.
Seduction By Light, Dell, 1988.

POETRY

Dancing: Poems, Corinth Books, 1969.
The Song Turning Back into Itself, Holt, 1971.
Some Recent Fiction, San Francisco Book Company,
    1974.
Geography of the Near Past, Holt, 1976.
The Blues Don't Change: New and Selected Poems,
    Louisiana State University Press, 1982.
Heaven: Collected Poems, 1956-90, Creative Arts
    Book Co., 1992.

EDITOR

James P. Girard, *Changing All Those Changes,* Yardbird Wing, 1976.

William Lawson, *Zeppelin Coming Down,* Yardbird Wing, 1976.

(With Ishmael Reed) *Yardbird Lives!,* Grove Press, 1978.

(And contributor) Ishmael Reed, editor, *Calafia: The California Poetry,* Y'Bird Books, 1979.

Believers, Ploughshares Books, 1993.

African American Literature: A Brief Introduction and Anthology, HarperCollins, 1995.

CONTRIBUTOR

Wallace Stegner and Richard Scowcroft, editors, *Stanford Short Stories 1968,* Stanford University Press, 1968.

The Heath Introduction to Poetry, Heath, 1975.

John Ciardi and Miller Williams, editors, *How Does a Poem Mean?,* Houghton, 1976.

OTHER

Bodies and Soul: Musical Memoirs, Creative Arts Book Co., 1981.

Kinds of Blue: Musical Memoirs, Creative Arts Book Co., 1984.

Things Ain't What They Used to Be: Musical Memoirs, Creative Arts Book Co., 1987.

(With Janet Coleman) *Mingus—Mingus: Two Memoirs,* Limelight Editions, 1991.

Drowning in the Sea of Love: Musical Memoirs, Ecco Press, 1995.

Also author of screenplays, *Nigger,* and *Sparkle,* both 1972; co-writer of screenplays, *A Piece of the Action,* 1977, *Bustin' Loose,* 1981, and *The Stars and Their Courses,* 1984. Contributor of articles, short stories, and reviews to *Audience, California Living, New Times, Rolling Stone, Evergreen Review, Encore, Journal of Black Poetry,* and others. Founding editor, *Loveletter,* 1966-68; co-editor, *Yardbird Reader,* 1972-76; contributing editor, *Changes,* 1972—, and *Umoja,* 1973—; co-editor and co-publisher, *Quilt,* 1981—.

SIDELIGHTS: American poet and novelist Al Young's art destroys "glib stereotypes of black Americans," states William J. Harris in the *Dictionary of Literary Biography,* presenting an image of the black person in "the American tradition of the singular individual."

"Not surprisingly," the contributor continues, "his work illustrates the complexity and richness of contemporary Afro-American life through a cast of highly individualized black characters. Since he is a gifted stylist and a keen observer of the human comedy, he manages to be both a serious and an entertaining author." In his oeuvre, says Harris, Young explores themes of "the beauty of black music and speech, the importance of family love, the dignity and romance of vocation, the quest for identity and the need to come to terms with one's life."

Snakes, Young's first novel, is the story of MC, a young musician whose successful jazz single, called "Snakes," meets with a modest success in Detroit, his home town. Eventually, he leaves home for New York in order to start a career as a jazz musician. Like many of Young's characters MC is black, but the author's interest in him lies not only in his blackness, but also in his humanity; as Harris declares, "although it is important that MC . . . is undeniably black, it is equally important that he is young and trying to come to terms with who he is." MC faces, among other problems, the bleakness of his Detroit environment, but, as L. E. Sissman points out in the *New Yorker, Snakes* "offers some alternative to hopelessness." Sissman suggests that MC's pursuit of jazz as a vocation "gives his life purpose; it palliates the terrors and disjunctures of the ghetto; it restores his adolescence to a semblance of normal adolescent joy and hope." And Douglass Bolling of *Negro American Literature Forum* concludes that "*Snakes* is clearly a work which seeks to reach out for the universals of human experience rather than to restrict itself to Black protest or Black aesthetic considerations."

Similar statements are made about the main characters of *Who Is Angelina?* and *Sitting Pretty;* according to Jacqueline Adams in the *Christian Science Monitor,* Angelina "represents that classical Everyman figure struggling against conformity, commercialized sentiments, crime, life's insanities and riddles to find peace, happiness, security, honesty, love, beauty, soul." Sidney J. Prettymon, the philosophical janitor and protagonist of *Sitting Pretty,* is, in the opinion of Mel Watkins in the *New York Times Book Review,* "the natural man, with no pretenses, just trying to live with as little chaos as possible and to enjoy the simple pleasures of growing old." Even Durwood Knight, the ex-basketball player hero of *Ask Me Now,* says James A. Steck in the *San Francisco Review of Books,* discovers "how 'you learn everything there is to know about life no matter what line of endeavor you take up.'"

Young's novel *Seduction By Light,* published in 1988, was his first novel in eight years. It is the story of Mamie Franklin, a middle-aged former actress who now works as a maid in Los Angeles. Several reviewers have commented on Mamie's voice. Calvin Forbes writes in *Washington Post Book World,* "Mamie Franklin speaks her mind in a voice rich in the rhythms of Afro-American speech. Young has a poet's ear and a feeling for jazz, qualities that show in his grasp of the idioms of his characters; several passages in the novel are verbal jazz riffs and a pure joy to read." Robert Ward in the *New York Times Book Review* declares, "Frankly, I felt myself *wanting* to resist Al Young's jazzy, baggy novel. . . . But Mamie Franklin is so charming, her voice so human, that I was quickly won over." He concludes, "Al Young is a poet, a gentle philosopher and a man of real sensibility. *Seduction By Light* is brilliant, funny and sweet."

Young writes about the impact of music on his life in *Drowning in the Sea of Love: Musical Memoirs,* one in a series of his essay collections on this topic. He uses his favorite jazz, blues, pop, and classical pieces as entries into his own memories. A reviewer for the *Los Angeles Times Book Review* writes that the experience of reading Young's stories "[feels] like an after-midnight gig."

According to a contributor in *Black Literature Criticism,* "Young's work shows his ability to capture the language of the ghetto as well as his metaphysical attachment to the details of everyday life." His poetry is a clear example of this. In *Heaven: Collected Poems 1956-1990,* Young's voice fills nearly 300 pages. A reviewer in *Publishers Weekly* says the work "is devised with broad brushstrokes and unrestricted affection for the ordinary world." Among his influences, according to the collection's introduction, are LeRoi Jones, Mayakovsky, and Federico Garcia Lorca.

In his early career Young performed as a jazz musician, and his fascination with these musical rhythms permeates his writing. Harris states that "dancing and music figure as central metaphors in [Young's] poetry," and his novels, which are also "rich in black language." Not only is music the subject of *Snakes,* notes *Paunch*'s Neil Schmitz, but "the music heard in [the novel] is the music of voices speaking." "It is this elusive sound," he continues, "which hangs Grail-like before MC's imagination throughout *Snakes,* which figures finally as the novel's unifying theme." He concludes, "MC's quest for the right language in his

music is a reflection of Young's discovery of the music in his language." Dean Flower remarks in the *Hudson Review,* "I don't know of any other black novel where the vernacular is used so well [as in *Sitting Pretty*], unless it be in Young's own *Snakes* and *Who Is Angelina?*" He is persuaded that "the beauty of Young's vernacular method is that it brings alive a thoroughly engaging human being"; and Sheldon Frank of the *National Observer* notices that *Sitting Pretty* "talks music all the time." "In sum," concludes Harris, "Al Young has captured much of the beauty and complexity of black life and black speech in his impressive and extensive oeuvre."

BIOGRAPHICAL/CRITICAL SOURCES:

BOOKS

Black Literature Criticism, Gale, Volume 3, 1992.

Chapman, Abraham, editor, *New Black Voices,* New American Library, 1972.

Contemporary Literary Criticism, Volume 19, Gale, 1981.

Dictionary of Literary Biography, Volume 33: Afro-American Fiction Writers After 1955, Gale, 1984.

O'Brien, John, editor, *Interviews with Black Writers,* Live-right, 1973, pp. 259-69.

Rush, Theresa Gunnels, Carol Fairbanks Myers, and Esther Spring Arata, *Black American Writers Past and Present: A Biographical and Bibliographical Dictionary,* Scarecrow Press, 1975.

PERIODICALS

American Book Review, January, 1982, p. 16; April-May, 1991, p. 10-11.

Booklist, January 15, 1995, p. 887.

California Living (Sunday Supplement of *San Francisco Chronicle/Examiner*), May 3, 1970.

Choice, June, 1986, p. 1509; October, 1992, p. 303.

Christian Science Monitor, March 6, 1975; December 7, 1984.

Greenfield Review, summer/fall, 1982.

Hudson Review, summer, 1976, pp. 270-82.

Kite, June 9, 1976.

Kliatt, September, 1990, p. 29.

Library Journal, September 15, 1980, p. 1865; November 15, 1988, p. 87; August, 1992, p. 106.

Los Angeles Times Book Review, April 12, 1992, p. 10; April 23, 1995, p. 6.

MELUS, winter, 1978.

National Observer, July 24, 1976.

Negro American Literature Forum, summer, 1974, pp. 223-25.

New Yorker, July 11, 1970, pp. 77-9; August 4, 1980.

New York Times, January 23, 1975.

New York Times Book Review, May 17, 1970; February 9, 1975; May 23, 1976; July 6, 1980; January 24, 1987; February 5, 1989, p. 11.

Paunch, February, 1972.

Peninsula Magazine, June, 1976.

Poetry, May, 1977; March, 1993, pp. 339-55.

Publishers Weekly, August 3, 1992, p. 65; December 19, 1994, p. 43.

San Francisco Review of Books, August, 1979; September, 1980; summer, 1989, p. 21.

Saturday Review, August 22, 1970; March 20, 1976.

Southwest Review, autumn, 1981, pp. 427-33.

Stanford Observer, March, 1970.

Time, June 29, 1970.

Times Literary Supplement, July 30, 1971.

Washington Post Book World, May 17, 1970; December 11, 1988, p. 3.

Western American Literature, summer, 1980, pp. 93-102.

World Literature Today, summer, 1981, p. 515.

Yale Review, June, 1970, pp. 551-69.*

*   *   *

ZU-BOLTON, Ahmos II 1935-

PERSONAL: Born October 21, 1935, in Poplarville, MS; son of Ahmos (a soldier) and Annie Lou (maiden name, McGee) Zu-Bolton; married; wife's name, Kathy (divorced, 1977); children: Bojavai, Sonoma, Amber Easter. *Education:* Attended Louisiana State University, 1965-67, and Los Angeles City College; California State Polytechnic University, B.A. (English literature), 1971.

*ADDRESSES: Office—*Copastetic Community Book Center, 1616 Marigny, New Orleans, LA 70117.

CAREER: Writer. Shortstop for Shreveport Twins, American Negro Baseball League, 1954-57; *Energy West Poetry Journal,* editor, 1970-72; *Hoo-Doo* (magazine), Galveston, TX, founder and editor, 1971-78; Howard University, Washington, DC, associate director of Afro-American Resource Center, 1973-76; writer-in-residence, Georgia State Arts Commission, 1975; poet-in-residence, Texas Commission on the Arts, 1977-82; folklorist-in-residence, Galveston Arts Center, Galveston, TX, 1979; writer-in-residence, Northlake Arts Camp, 1984-85; Xavier University, New Orleans, LA, professor of English

and writer-in-residence, 1987-89; Tulane University, New Orleans, professor of English and writer-in-residence, 1992—; director of Copastetic Community Book Center, New Orleans, LA. Organizer of HooDoo festivals in New Orleans, Galveston, Austin and Houston, beginning in 1977; producer and director of plays and musicals. *Military service:* U.S. Army, served as medic, 1967-69.

MEMBER: Association of Black Storytellers (member of board of directors, 1989—.

AWARDS, HONORS: Creative Writing Fellowship, National Endowment for the Arts, 1979; Critic's Fellowship, Texas Commission on the Arts and Humanities, 1980; Editor's Fellowship, Coordinating Council of Literary Magazines, 1981; Creative Writing Fellowship, Louisiana Division of the Arts, 1987; Folklore Fellowship, Ford Foundation, 1989.

WRITINGS:

A Niggered Amen (poetry), Solo Press (San Luis Obispo, CA), 1975.

(Editor with E. Ethelbert Miller, and author of introduction) *Synergy: An Anthology of Washington, D.C., Blackpoetry,* Energy BlackSouth Press (Houston, TX), 1975.

Work represented in anthologies, including *Poems by Blacks,* edited by Pinkie Gordon Lane, South & West (Fort Smith, AR), 1975; *Giant Talk: An Anthology of Third World Writings,* edited by Quincy Troupe and Rainer Schulte, Random (New York City), 1975; and *Yardbird Lives!,* edited by Ishmael Reed and Al Young, Grove Press (New York City), 1978. With Kwa Tamani, Zu-Bolton is also the editor of *Griots' Works* (anthology), 1971; and has written *Stumbling Thru: Earth(ing) Poems,* 1980; *Ain't No Spring Chicken,* 1990; and *All My Lies Are True,* 1990. He has also written plays, including *The Widow Paris: A Folklore of Marie Laveau; The Funeral Family Reunion: A One-Woman Drama; The Break-In; Louisiana Souvenir: A Choreo-Folkpoem.* Contributor to periodicals, including *Alternative, First World, Ideas, Open Places,* and *The Spirit That Moves Us.* Co-editor of *Last Cookie,* 1972, and *Blackbox,* 1974-77.

SIDELIGHTS: Ahmos Zu-Bolton II is a poet and playwright who is also known for his editing and publishing endeavors on behalf of African-American culture. Lorenzo Thomas, writing in the *Dictionary of Literary Biography,* described Zu-Bolton as "one of the most dynamic poets and energetic literary organizers of the 1970s and 1980s [and] an artist who applies much of his talent to the community."

Zu-Bolton was born in 1935 in Poplarville, Mississippi. In 1965 he was among those students selected to integrate Louisiana State University. He was drafted into the army in 1967 and sent to Vietnam. Afterwards, he resumed his education, graduating from California State Polytechnic University in 1971. Shortly afterward, he founded *Hoo-Doo,* a magazine devoted to African-American activism and arts. Thomas wrote that *HooDoo* "served to carry the message of black arts poetry to a grassroots audience the [black arts] movement may not have previously reached." Towards the end of the 1970s Zu-Bolton organized a series of HooDoo Festivals in which African-American artists read and performed at churches, colleges, and restaurants in Louisiana and Texas. During this decade he also served as associate director of Howard University's Afro-American Resource Center and presided as writer-in-residence at the Georgia State Arts Commission. In the 1980s he continued to appear as writer-in-residence at such institutions as the Texas Commission on the Arts and Xavier University. In 1992 he joined the faculty of Tulane University, where he served as both professor of English and writer-in-residence.

During his career, Zu-Bolton has tirelessly promoted African-American arts. As well as editing *HooDoo* and organizing HooDoo Festivals, he has edited such periodicals as *Energy West Poetry Journal* and *Blackbox.* In addition, he collaborated with E. Ethelbert Miller in editing *Synergy: An Anthology of Washington, D.C., Blackpoetry.*

Zu-Bolton's own poetry—including work in his notable debut collection, *A Niggered Amen*—is distinguished by his sympathetic, but scarcely sentimental, portraits of African Americans and by his deft handling of poetic techniques. It also shows his wide range of influences, which include his father; a mathematician who instructed him in math and discussed literature with him when he was in high school; and works such as Ayn Rand's *The Fountainhead* and Richard Wright's *Native Son.* In the *Dictionary of Literary Biography,* Lorenzo Thomas reported that "Zu-Bolton's poetry draws on the early influences of his mentors and depends upon his ability to recognize important aspects of human character."

Among Zu-Bolton's notable poems are "The Crown," which concerns an African-American Vietnam veteran who is killed in a holdup, and "Homeless," which Lorenzo Thomas described as a "'sorrow song' from one who has experienced the lopsided benefits of racial integration." Thomas called the poem "a fine lyric" and "a spiritual from a liberated generation." Still other key poems in Zu-Bolton's canon are "Taxicab Blues," which contrasts European and African-American cultures, and "A Galveston Rock of Ages," which concerns a baseball player. Thomas wrote that in "A Galveston Rock of Ages" "Zu-Bolton's wonderfully evocative economy . . . captures the reader's attention and illumines both the meaning and the moment of a character's life."

In addition to his poetry, Zu-Bolton has written several plays, including *The Widow Paris: A Folklore of Marie Laveau, The Funeral, Family Reunion,* and *The Break-In.*

BIOGRAPHICAL/CRITICAL SOURCES:

BOOKS

Dictionary of Literary Biography, Volume 41: *Afro-American Poets Since 1955,* Gale, 1985.*

Black Writers
Cumulative Author Index
(Numeral appearing below refers to edition in which
the author's most recent entry appears.)

Black Writers
Cumulative Nationality Index

(Authors are listed alphabetically under country of origin
and/or their country of citizenship. Numeral refers to edition
in which the author's most recent entry appears.)

ANTIGUA
Kincaid, Jamaica **3**

ARUBA
Bishop, Maurice **1**

BARBADOS
Brathwaite, Edward (Kamau) **3**
Clarke, Austin C(hesterfield) **1**
Foster, Cecil (A.) **3**
Kennedy, Adrienne (Lita) **3**
Lamming, George (William) **3**
Lewis, Sandra Padmore **3**
Lovell, Glenville **3**

BOTSWANA
Head, Bessie **3**

BRITISH VIRGIN ISLANDS
Anderson, Jervis (B.) **2**

CAMEROON
Bebey, Francis **1**
Biyidi, Alexandre **3**
Dipoko, Mbella Sonne **2**

CANADA
Clarke, Austin C(hesterfield) **1**
Hearne, John (Edgar Caulwell) **3**
Philip, M(arlene) Nourbese **3**

CHILE
Godoy Alcayaga, Lucila **2**

CUBA
Guillen, Nicolas (Cristobal) **2**

EGYPT
Boutros-Ghali, Boutros **3**

ENGLAND
Appiah, (K.) Anthony **2**
Dabydeen, David **1**
Guthrie, Thomas Anstey **3**
Harris, (Theodore) Wilson **3**
James, C(yril) L(ionel) R(obert) **2**
Phillips, Caryl **2**

ETHIOPIA
Gabre-Medhin, Tsegaye (Kawessa) **2**

FRANCE
Diop, David Mandessi **2**
Schwarz-Bart, Simone **2**

FRENCH GUINEA
Damas, Leon-Gontran **1**

GAMBIA
Peters, Lenrie (Wilfred Leopold) **1**

GERMANY
Ayim, May **2**

GHANA
Aidoo, (Christina) Ama Ata **1**
Anyidoho, Kofi **3**
Armah, Ayi Kwei **1**
Awoonor, Kofi (Nyidevu) **3**
Ayittey, George B. N. **3**
Brew, (Osborne Henry) Kwesi **2**
Busia, Kofi Abrefa **2**
Casely-Hayford, J(oseph) E(phraim) **2**
de Graft, John Coleman **2**
Djoleto, (Solomon Alexander) Amu **3**
Konadu, S(amuel) A(sare) **2**
Nkrumah, Kwame **2**
Quaye, Cofie **2**
Selormey, Francis **1**
Sutherland, Efua (Theodora Morgue) **1**

GUADELOUPE
Boucolon, Maryse **3**
Conde, Maryse **2**
Schwarz-Bart, Simone **2**

GUINEA
Laye, Camara **1**

GUYANA
Allsopp, (Stanley Reginald) Richard **3**
Braithwaite, (Eustace) E(dward) R(icardo) **1**
Carew, Jan (Rynveld) **2**
Dabydeen, David **1**
Dathorne, O(scar) R(onald) **3**
Harris, (Theodore) Wilson **3**
Heath, Roy A(ubrey) K(elvin) **3**
Mittelholzer, Edgar Austin **1**
Seymour, A(rthur) J(ames) **2**
Van Sertima, Ivan **2**
Walrond, Eric (Derwent) **1**
Williams, Denis (Joseph Ivan) **3**

HAITI
Price-Mars, Jean **2**
Roumain, Jacques (Jean Baptiste) **1**
Thoby-Marcelin, (Emile) Philippe **1**

JAMAICA
Adisa, Opal Palmer **3**
Barrett, (Eseoghene) Lindsay **2**
Bennett, Louise (Simone) **3**
Brodber, Erna (May) **2**
Ciee, Grace **2**
Cliff, Michelle **2**
Collins, Merle **3**

De Lisser, H(erbert) G(eorge) **2**
Figueroa, John J(oseph Maria) **2**
Garvey, Marcus (Moziah Jr.) **1**
Gordon, Lewis Ricardo **3**
Johnson, Linton Kwesi **3**
Mais, Roger **3**
Marson, Una **3**
McKay, Festus Claudius **3**
McNeill, Anthony **2**
Morrison, Keith **3**
Patterson, (Horace) Orlando (Lloyd) **1**
Reid, Vic(tor Stafford) **1**
Scott, Dennis (Courtney) **2**
Senior, Olive (Marjorie) **3**
Thelwell, Michael Miles **2**

KENYA
Kenyatta, Jomo **3**
Maathai, Wangari (Muta) **3**
Maillu, David G. **3**
Mazrui, Ali A(l'Amin) **2**
Mbiti, John S(amuel) **1**
Mwangi, Meja **3**
Ngugi wa Thiong'o **2**
Njau, Rebeka **2**
Odaga, Asenath (Bole) **2**
Ogot, Grace **2**

LIBERIA
Wesley, Patricia Jabbeh **3**

MALAWI
Kayira, Legson Didimu **1**
Mapanje, (John Alfred Clement) Jack **3**

MARTINIQUE
Cesaire, Aime (Fernand) **3**
Fanon, Frantz **1**

NAMIBIA
Mbuende, Kaire (Munionganda) **3**

NIGERIA
Achebe, (Albert) Chinua(lumogu) **3**
Alagoa, Ebiegberi Joe **3**
Aluko, T(imothy) M(ofolorunso) **1**
Amadi, Elechi (Emmanuel) **1**
Anozie, Sunday O(gbonna) **2**
Awolowo, Obafemi Awo **2**
Bandele, Biyi **3**
Chinweizu **3**
Clark, John Pepper **1**
Echeruo, Michael J(oseph) C(hukwudalu) **2**
Egudu, Romanus N(nagbo) **2**
Ekwensi, Cyprian (Odiatu Duaka) **3**
Emecheta, (Florence Onye) Buchi **3**
Euba, Femi **2**
Ike, Vincent Chukwuemeka **3**

727

Cruz, Ricardo Cortez **3**
Cullen, Countee **1**
Cummings, Pat (Marie) **2**
Cuney, William Waring **1**
Curtis, Christopher Paul **3**
Dance, Daryl Cumber **2**
Dandridge, Rita B(ernice) **2**
Danner, Margaret (Essie) **1**
Darden, Christopher **3**
Davis, Angela (Yvonne) **3**
Davis, Arthur P(aul) **2**
Davis, Benjamin O(liver) Jr. **2**
Davis, Charles T(witchell) **1**
Davis, Frank Marshall **3**
Davis, George **1**
Davis, Michael D. **2**
Davis, Nolan **1**
Davis, Ossie **3**
Davis, Thulani **3**
Davis, (William) Allison **1**
Deal, Borden **2**
DeCosta-Willis, Miriam **2**
Delany, A(nnie) Elizabeth **3**
Delany, Samuel R(ay Jr.) **3**
Demby, William **3**
Dent, Thomas C(ovington) **1**
Derricotte, Toi **2**
De Veaux, Alexis **3**
Dixon, Melvin (W.) **2**
Dodson, Owen (Vincent) **1**
Dove, Rita (Frances) **2**
Driver, David E. **3**
Drummond, William Joe **1**
Du Bois, David G(raham) **1**
Du Bois, Shirley Graham **1**
Du Bois, W(illiam) E(dward) B(urghardt) **3**
Dumas, Henry L. **1**
Dunbar, Paul Laurence **3**
Dunham, Katherine **1**
Dunnigan, Alice Allison **1**
Duplechan, Larry **3**
Dyson, Michael Eric **3**
Edelman, Marian Wright **3**
Edmonds, (Sheppard) Randolph **1**
Edwards, Deborah R. **3**
Edwards, Junius **2**
Elder, Lonne III **3**
Ellison, Ralph (Waldo) **3**
El Muhajir **1**
Emanuel, James A. **1**
Eskridge, Ann E. **3**
Evans, Mari **1**
Everett, Percival L. **2**
Fabio, Sarah Webster **1**
Fair, Ronald L. **1**
Fauset, Jessie Redmon **1**
Fax, Elton Clay **2**
Feelings, Muriel (Grey) **1**
Feelings, Thomas **1**
Fields, Julia **1**
Fisher, Rudolph **3**
Fleming, Ray(mond) **1**
Flournoy, Valerie (Rose) **3**
Floyd, Samuel A(lexander) Jr. **2**
Forbes, Calvin **1**
Ford, Nick Aaron **1**
Forrest, Leon (Richard) **2**
Franklin, J(ennie) E(lizabeth) **1**
Franklin, John Hope **2**
French, Albert **3**
Frye, Charles A(nthony) **3**
Fulani, Lenora (Branch) **3**
Fuller, Charles (H. Jr.) **2**

Fuller, Hoyt (William) **1**
Gaines, Ernest J(ames) **3**
Gates, Henry Louis Jr. **3**
Gayle, Addison Jr. **1**
Gibson, Donald B. **1**
Gibson, P(atricia) J(oann) **2**
Gibson, Richard (Thomas) **2**
Gilbert, Christopher **2**
Gilbert, Herman Cromwell **2**
Gilroy, Beryl **2**
Giovanni, Nikki **3**
Goines, Donald **3**
Golden, Marita **3**
Gomez, Jewelle **2**
Gordon, Vivian V(erdell) **2**
Gordone, Charles **3**
Goss, Clay(ton E.) **3**
Graham, Lorenz (Bell) **1**
Greaves, William **1**
Green, Daryl D. **3**
Greenfield, Eloise **2**
Greenlee, Sam **1**
Gregory, Dick **1**
Grimke, Angelina (Emily) Weld **1**
Grimke, Charlotte L(ottie) Forten **1**
Grosvenor, Verta Mae **3**
Gunn, William Harrison **3**
Guy, Rosa (Cuthbert) **2**
Guy-Sheftall, Beverly **2**
Hairston, William (Russell Jr.) **2**
Haley, Alex(ander Murray Palmer) **3**
Halliburton, Warren J. **2**
Hamilton, Charles V(ernon) **2**
Hamilton, Virginia **3**
Hampton, Henry (Eugene), Jr. Jr.) **2**
Handy, W(illiam) C(hristopher) **3**
Hansberry, Lorraine (Vivian) **3**
Hansberry, William Leo **3**
Hansen, Joyce (Viola) **2**
Hare, Nathan **2**
Harper, Frances Ellen Watkins **3**
Harper, Michael S(teven) **1**
Harris, Thomas Walter **2**
Harrison, Paul Carter **2**
Haskins, James S. **3**
Hawkins, Walter Everette **3**
Hawkins, W(alter) Lincoln **3**
Hayden, Robert C(arter) Jr. **1**
Hayden, Robert E(arl) **3**
Haygood, Johnnie **3**
Haygood, Wil **2**
Haywood, Gar Anthony **3**
Heard, Nathan C(liff) **1**
Hemphill, Essex **2**
Henderson, David **1**
Henderson, George Wylie **1**
Henderson, Stephen E. **1**
Henries, A. Doris Banks **1**
Henshaw, James Ene **2**
Hernton, Calvin C(oolidge) **1**
Herron, Carolivia **2**
Hill, Leslie Pinckney **1**
Hilliard, David **2**
Himes, Chester (Bomar) **2**
Hoagland, Everett (III) **1**
Hobson, Julius W(ilson) **1**
Hollins, Etta R(uth) **1**
Holly, Ellen (Virginia) **3**
Hopkins, Pauline Elizabeth **3**
Hord, Frederick (Lee) **2**
Horne, Aaron **2**
Horne, Frank (Smith) **1**
House, Gloria **2**

Howard, Elizabeth Fitzgerald **2**
Howard, Vanessa **3**
Hubbard, Dolan **3**
Hudson, Wade **3**
Huggins, Nathan Irvin **1**
Hughes, (James) Langston **3**
Hull, Gloria T(heresa Thompson) **2**
Hunt, Marsha **3**
Hunter, Kristin (Eggleston) **1**
Hunter-Gault, Charlayne **2**
Hurston, Zora Neale **3**
Hutchinson, Earl Ofari **2**
Ione, Carole **2**
Jackson, Angela **3**
Jackson, George (Lester) **1**
Jackson, Jesse **1**
Jackson, Sheneska **3**
Jeffers, Lance **1**
Jefferson, Roland S. **2**
Joans, Ted **1**
Johnson, Charles (Richard) **3**
Johnson, Charles S(purgeon) **3**
Johnson, Fenton **1**
Johnson, Georgia Douglas (Camp) **1**
Johnson, James Weldon **3**
Johnson, Robert **3**
Johnson, Whittington B. **3**
Jones, Edward P. **3**
Jones, Gayl **3**
Jones, Jacqueline **1**
Jones, Nettie (Pearl) **2**
Jordan, Barbara (Charline) **1**
Jordan, Emma Coleman **3**
Jordan, June **3**
Josey, E(lonnie) J(unius) **2**
Joyce, Donald Franklin **2**
Kaufman, Bob (Garnell) **1**
Kearse, Amalya (Lyle) **3**
Kelley, William Melvin **1**
Kenan, Randall (G.) **3**
Kennedy, Adrienne (Lita) **3**
Kennedy, Florynce (Rae) **3**
Kersey, Tanya-Monique **2**
Killens, John Oliver **2**
Kincaid, Jamaica **3**
King, Coretta Scott **1**
King, Martin Luther Sr. **1**
King, Martin Luther Jr. **3**
King, Woodie Jr. **2**
Knight, Etheridge **3**
Kunjufu, Johari M. Amini **1**
Ladner, Joyce A(nn) **2**
Lane, Pinkie Gordon **2**
Larsen, Nella **1**
Lee, Andrea **3**
Lee, George W(ashington) **1**
Lee, Shelton Jackson **3**
Lester, Julius (Bernard) **2**
Lewis, Theophilus **1**
Lightfoot, Claude M. **1**
Lightfoot, Sara Lawrence **2**
Lincoln, C(harles) Eric **2**
Little, Malcolm **3**
Locke, Alain (Le Roy) **3**
Lockett, Reginald (Franklin) **3**
Logan, Rayford W(hittingham) **1**
Logan, Shirley Wilson **3**
Lomax, Louis E(manuel) **1**
Long, Richard A(lexander) **2**
Lorde, Audre (Geraldine) **3**
Lucas, W(ilmer) F(rancis Jr.) **1**
Lynk, Miles V(andahurst) **3**
Mabry, Marcus **3**

Mackey, William Wellington 1
Madgett, Naomi Long 2
Madhubuti, Haki R. 3
Major, Clarence 3
major, devorah 3
Marshall, Paule 3
Martin, Herbert Woodward 1
Martin, Reginald 2
Matheus, John F(rederick) 1
Mathis, Sharon Bell 2
Mayfield, Julian (Hudson) 1
Mays, Benjamin E(lijah) 1
Mays, James A(rthur) 1
McCall, Nathan 3
McClellan, George Marion 1
McCluskey, John (A.) Jr. 1
McDougall, Gay J. 3
McElroy, Colleen J(ohnson) 2
McKissack, Patricia (L'Ann) C(arwell) 2
McMillan, Terry (L.) 3
McPherson, James Alan 3
Micheaux, Oscar 3
Miller, E(ugene) Ethelbert 2
Miller, May 2
Miller, Warren 2
Millican, Arthenia Jackson Bates 2
Milner, Ron(ald) 1
Mitchell, Loften 1
Molette, Barbara Jean 1
Molette, Carlton W(oodard) II 1
Moody, Anne 1
Morrison, Toni 3
Morrow, E(verett) Frederic 1
Mosley, Walter 2
Moss, Thylias (Rebecca Brasier) 3
Motley, Willard (Francis) 1
Murphy, Beatrice M. 2
Murray, Albert L. 2
Murray, (Anna) Pauli(ne) 2
Myers, Walter Dean 2
Naylor, Gloria 3
Neal, Lawrence (P.) 1
Nelson, Alice Ruth Moore Dunbar 3
Nichols, Charles H(arold) 1
Njeri, Itabari (Lord) 3
Nugent, Richard Bruce 1
Occomy, Marita (Odette) Bonner 2
O'Daniel, Therman B(enjamin) 1
Offord, Carl Ruthven 2
Ottley, Roi (Vincent) 2
Painter, Nell Irvin 1
Palmer, C(yril) Everard 1
Parker, Pat 2
Parker, Percy Spurlark 2
Parks, Gordon (Alexander Buchanan) 3
Patterson, Frederick D(ouglass) 3
Patterson, Lindsay 1
Pemberton, Gayle Renee 2
Perkins, (Useni) Eugene 2
Perry, Margaret 1
Perry, Richard 1
Petry, Ann (Lane) 3
Pharr, Robert Deane 1
Pinckney, Darryl 3
Plowden, Martha Ward 3
Plumpp, Sterling D(ominic) 1
Poitier, Sidney 1
Polite, Carlene Hatcher 1
Porter, Connie (Rose) 3
Porter, James A(mos) 3
Poston, Theodore Roosevelt Augustus Major
    1
Powell, Adam Clayton Jr. 3

Quarles, Benjamin (Arthur) 1
Rampersad, Arnold 3
Randall, Dudley (Felker) 3
Randolph, A(sa) Philip 2
Rashad, Johari M(ahasin) 2
Raspberry, William J(ames) 2
Redding, (Jay) Saunders 1
Redmond, Eugene B. 2
Reed, Ishmael 3
Rhone, Trevor (Dave) 1
Rice, Mitchell F. 2
Richardson, Nola 1
Richardson, Willis 1
Ridenhour, Carl 3
Rivers, Conrad Kent 1
Robeson, Paul (Leroy Bustill) 1
Robinet, Harriette Gillem 2
Robinson, Max (C.) 1
Robinson, William H(enry) 1
Rodgers, Carolyn M(arie) 3
Rollins, Charlemae Hill 1
Rowan, Carl T(homas) 2
Rustin, Bayard 1
Salaam, Kalamu ya 2
Sampson, Henry T(homas) 2
Sanchez, Sonia 3
Schuyler, George Samuel 2
Schuyler, Philippa Duke 1
Scott, Daryl Michael 3
Scott, Nathan A(lexander) Jr. 2
Scott-Heron, Gil 1
Seale, Robert George 1
Sengstacke, John H(erman Henry) 1
Shange, Ntozake 3
Sharp, Saundra 1
Shaw, Bernard 1
Sherman, Charlotte Watson 2
Shine, Ted 1
Shockley, Ann Allen 1
Silverstein, Shel(by) 3
Simmons, Herbert A(lfred) 1
Singleton, John 3
Smith, Barbara 2
Smith, Jessie Carney 2
Smith, William Gardner 1
Southerland, Ellease 1
Sowell, Thomas 2
Spellman, Alfred B. 1
Stepto, Robert B(urns) 1
Steptoe, John (Lewis) 1
Stewart, Jeffrey C. 3
St. John, Primus 1
Stone, Charles Sumner Jr. 2
Sullivan, Otha Richard 3
Tarry, Ellen 3
Tate, Eleanora E(laine) 3
Taulbert, Clifton L(emoure) 2
Taylor, Mildred D. 1
Teague, Robert 2
Teish, Luisah 2
Tervalon, Jervey 3
Thomas, Clarence 3
Thomas, Joyce Carol 3
Thomas, June Manning 3
Thompson, Era Bell 2
Thurman, Howard 1
Thurman, Wallace (Henry) 3
Tolson, Melvin B(eaunorus) 3
Toomer, Jean 1
Toure, Askia Muhammad Abu Bakr el 2
Trice, Dawn Turner 3
Troupe, Quincy (Thomas Jr.) 2
Turner, Darwin T(heodore Troy) 1

Turpin, Waters Edward 1
Van Deburg, William L. 2
Van Dyke, Henry 1
Van Peebles, Melvin 3
Vanzant, Iyanla (Rhonda) 2
Vertreace, Martha M. 2
Vroman, Mary Elizabeth (Gibson) 1
Wade-Gayles, Gloria Jean 2
Walker, Alice (Malsenior) 3
Walker, Joseph A. 3
Walker, Margaret (Abigail) 3
Wallace, Ruby Ann 1
Walter, Mildred Pitts 2
Ward, Douglas Turner 1
Ward, Theodore (James) 1
Washington, Booker T(aliaferro) 1
Washington, Mary Helen 3
Wayans, Keenan Ivory 2
Weatherly, Tom 1
Welburn, Ron(ald Garfield) 1
Welsing, Frances Cress 2
Wesley, Richard (Errol) 1
Wesley, Valerie Wilson 3
West, Dorothy 2
White, Edgar (B.) 1
White, Walter F(rancis) 1
Whitman, Albery Allson 3
Wideman, John Edgar 3
Wilkins, Roger (Wood) 1
Wilkins, Roy 1
Wilkinson, Brenda 2
Williams, Chancellor 2
Williams, Eric (Eustace) 2
Williams, Greg(ory) Alan 3
Williams, John A(lfred) 3
Williams, Samuel Arthur 1
Williams, Sherley Anne 3
Wilson, August 3
Wilson, Carletta 2
Woodson, Carter G(odwin) 2
Wright, Charles Stevenson 1
Wright, Jay 3
Wright, Richard (Nathaniel) 1
Wright, Sarah E(lizabeth) 2
Wright, Stephen Caldwell 2
Yarbrough, Camille 2
Yerby, Frank G(arvin) 3
Young, Al(bert James) 3
Young, Whitney M(oore) Jr. 1
Zu-Bolton, Ahmos II 3

ZAIRE
Lopes, Henri (Marie-Joseph) 2
Mudimbe, V. Y. 2

ZIMBABWE
Dangarembga, Tsitsi 3
Marechera, Dambudzo 3
Mungoshi, Charles L. 3
Nyamfukudza, S(tanley) 3
Samkange, Stanlake (John Thompson) 2